PISA 2009 Results: What Makes a School Successful?

RESOURCES, POLICIES AND PRACTICES

(VOLUME IV)

Please cite this publication as:
OECD (2010), *PISA 2009 Results: What Makes a School Successful? – Resources, Policies and Practices (Volume IV)*
http://dx.doi.org/10.1787/9789264091559-en

ISBN 978-92-64-09148-1 (print)
ISBN 978-92-64-09155-9 (PDF)

Photo credits:
Getty Images © Ariel Skelley
Getty Images © Geostock
Getty Images © Jack Hollingsworth
Stocklib Image Bank © Yuri Arcurs

Foreword

One of the ultimate goals of policy makers is to enable citizens to take advantage of a globalised world economy. This is leading them to focus on the improvement of education policies, ensuring the quality of service provision, a more equitable distribution of learning opportunities and stronger incentives for greater efficiency in schooling.

Such policies hinge on reliable information on how well education systems prepare students for life. Most countries monitor students' learning and the performance of schools. But in a global economy, the yardstick for success is no longer improvement by national standards alone, but how education systems perform internationally. The OECD has taken up that challenge by developing PISA, the Programme for International Student Assessment, which evaluates the quality, equity and efficiency of school systems in some 70 countries that, together, make up nine-tenths of the world economy. PISA represents a commitment by governments to monitor the outcomes of education systems regularly within an internationally agreed framework and it provides a basis for international collaboration in defining and implementing educational policies.

The results from the PISA 2009 assessment reveal wide differences in educational outcomes, both within and across countries. The education systems that have been able to secure strong and equitable learning outcomes, and to mobilise rapid improvements, show others what is possible to achieve. Naturally, GDP per capita influences educational success, but this only explains 6% of the differences in average student performance. The other 94% reflect the potential for public policy to make a difference. The stunning success of Shanghai-China, which tops every league table in this assessment by a clear margin, shows what can be achieved with moderate economic resources and in a diverse social context. In mathematics, more than a quarter of Shanghai-China's 15-year-olds can conceptualise, generalise, and creatively use information based on their own investigations and modelling of complex problem situations. They can apply insight and understanding and develop new approaches and strategies when addressing novel situations. In the OECD area, just 3% of students reach that level of performance.

While better educational outcomes are a strong predictor of economic growth, wealth and spending on education alone are no guarantee for better educational outcomes. Overall, PISA shows that an image of a world divided neatly into rich and well-educated countries and poor and badly-educated countries is out of date.

This finding represents both a warning and an opportunity. It is a warning to advanced economies that they cannot take for granted that they will forever have "human capital" superior to that in other parts of the world. At a time of intensified global competition, they will need to work hard to maintain a knowledge and skill base that keeps up with changing demands.

PISA underlines, in particular, the need for many advanced countries to tackle educational underperformance so that as many members of their future workforces as possible are equipped with at least the baseline competencies that enable them to participate in social and economic development. Otherwise, the high social and economic cost of poor educational performance in advanced economies risks becoming a significant drag on economic development. At the same time, the findings show that poor skills are not an inevitable consequence of low national income – an important outcome for countries that need to achieve more with less.

But PISA also shows that there is no reason for despair. Countries from a variety of starting points have shown the potential to raise the quality of educational outcomes substantially. Korea's average performance was already high in 2000, but Korean policy makers were concerned that only a narrow elite achieved levels of excellence in PISA. Within less than a decade, Korea was able to double the share of students demonstrating excellence in reading literacy. A major overhaul of Poland's school system helped to dramatically reduce performance variability among

schools, reduce the share of poorly performing students and raise overall performance by the equivalent of more than half a school year. Germany was jolted into action when PISA 2000 revealed a below-average performance and large social disparities in results, and has been able to make progress on both fronts. Israel, Italy and Portugal have moved closer to the OECD average and Brazil, Chile, Mexico and Turkey are among the countries with impressive gains from very low levels of performance.

But the greatest value of PISA lies in inspiring national efforts to help students to learn better, teachers to teach better, and school systems to become more effective.

A closer look at high-performing and rapidly improving education systems shows that these systems have many commonalities that transcend differences in their history, culture and economic evolution.

First, while most nations declare their commitment to education, the test comes when these commitments are weighed against others. How do they pay teachers compared to the way they pay other highly-skilled workers? How are education credentials weighed against other qualifications when people are being considered for jobs? Would you want your child to be a teacher? How much attention do the media pay to schools and schooling? Which matters more, a community's standing in the sports leagues or its standing in the student academic achievement league tables? Are parents more likely to encourage their children to study longer and harder or to spend more time with their friends or in sports activities?

In the most successful education systems, the political and social leaders have persuaded their citizens to make the choices needed to show that they value education more than other things. But placing a high value on education will get a country only so far if the teachers, parents and citizens of that country believe that only some subset of the nation's children can or need to achieve world class standards. This report shows clearly that education systems built around the belief that students have different pre-ordained professional destinies to be met with different expectations in different school types tend to be fraught with large social disparities. In contrast, the best-performing education systems embrace the diversity in students' capacities, interests and social background with individualised approaches to learning.

Second, high-performing education systems stand out with clear and ambitious standards that are shared across the system, focus on the acquisition of complex, higher-order thinking skills, and are aligned with high stakes gateways and instructional systems. In these education systems, everyone knows what is required to get a given qualification, in terms both of the content studied and the level of performance that has to be demonstrated to earn it. Students cannot go on to the next stage of their life – be it work or further education – unless they show that they are qualified to do so. They know what they have to do to realise their dream and they put in the work that is needed to achieve it.

Third, the quality of an education system cannot exceed the quality of its teachers and principals, since student learning is ultimately the product of what goes on in classrooms. Corporations, professional partnerships and national governments all know that they have to pay attention to how the pool from which they recruit is established; how they recruit; the kind of initial training their recruits receive before they present themselves for employment; how they mentor new recruits and induct them into their service; what kind of continuing training they get; how their compensation is structured; how they reward their best performers and how they improve the performance of those who are struggling; and how they provide opportunities for the best performers to acquire more status and responsibility. Many of the world's best-performing education systems have moved from bureaucratic "command and control" environments towards school systems in which the people at the frontline have much more control of the way resources are used, people are deployed, the work is organised and the way in which the work gets done. They provide considerable discretion to school heads and school faculties in determining how resources are allocated, a factor which the report shows to be closely related to school performance when combined with effective accountability systems. And they provide an environment in which teachers work together to frame what they believe to be good practice, conduct field-based research to confirm or disprove the approaches they develop, and then assess their colleagues by the degree to which they use practices proven effective in their classrooms.

Last but not least, the most impressive outcome of world-class education systems is perhaps that they deliver high-quality learning consistently across the entire education system, such that every student benefits from excellent learning opportunities. To achieve this, they invest educational resources where they can make the greatest difference, they attract the most talented teachers into the most challenging classrooms, and they establish effective spending choices that prioritise the quality of teachers.

These are, of course, not independently conceived and executed policies. They need to be aligned across all aspects of the system, they need to be coherent over sustained periods of time, and they need to be consistently implemented. The path of reform can be fraught with political and practical obstacles. Moving away from administrative and bureaucratic control toward professional norms of control can be counterproductive if a nation does not yet have teachers and schools with the capacity to implement these policies and practices. Pushing authority down to lower levels can be as problematic if there is not agreement on what the students need to know and should be able to do. Recruiting high-quality teachers is not of much use if those who are recruited are so frustrated by what they perceive to be a mindless system of initial teacher education that they will not participate in it and turn to another profession. Thus a country's success in making these transitions depends greatly on the degree to which it is successful in creating and executing plans that, at any given time, produce the maximum coherence in the system.

These are daunting challenges and thus devising effective education policies will become ever more difficult as schools need to prepare students to deal with more rapid change than ever before, for jobs that have not yet been created, to use technologies that have not yet been invented and to solve economic and social challenges that we do not yet know will arise. But those school systems that do well today, as well as those that have shown rapid improvement, demonstrate that it can be done. The world is indifferent to tradition and past reputations, unforgiving of frailty and complacency and ignorant of custom or practice. Success will go to those individuals and countries that are swift to adapt, slow to complain and open to change. The task of governments will be to ensure that countries rise to this challenge. The OECD will continue to support their efforts.

***

This report is the product of a collaborative effort between the countries participating in PISA, the experts and institutions working within the framework of the PISA Consortium, and the OECD Secretariat. The report was drafted by Andreas Schleicher, Francesca Borgonovi, Michael Davidson, Miyako Ikeda, Maciej Jakubowski, Guillermo Montt, Sophie Vayssettes and Pablo Zoido of the OECD Directorate for Education, with advice as well as analytical and editorial support from Marilyn Achiron, Simone Bloem, Marika Boiron, Henry Braun, Nihad Bunar, Niccolina Clements, Jude Cosgrove, John Cresswell, Aletta Grisay, Donald Hirsch, David Kaplan, Henry Levin, Juliette Mendelovitz, Christian Monseur, Soojin Park, Pasi Reinikainen, Mebrak Tareke, Elisabeth Villoutreix and Allan Wigfield. Volume II also draws on the analytic work undertaken by Jaap Scheerens and Douglas Willms in the context of PISA 2000. Administrative support was provided by Juliet Evans and Diana Morales.

The PISA assessment instruments and the data underlying the report were prepared by the PISA Consortium, under the direction of Raymond Adams at the Australian Council for Educational Research (ACER) and Henk Moelands from the Dutch National Institute for Educational Measurement (CITO). The expert group that guided the preparation of the reading assessment framework and instruments was chaired by Irwin Kirsch.

The development of the report was steered by the PISA Governing Board, which is chaired by Lorna Bertrand (United Kingdom), with Beno Csapo (Hungary), Daniel McGrath (United States) and Ryo Watanabe (Japan) as vice chairs. Annex C of the volumes lists the members of the various PISA bodies, as well as the individual experts and consultants who have contributed to this report and to PISA in general.

Angel Gurría
OECD Secretary-General

Table of Contents

BOXES

FIGURES

TABLES

Executive Summary

Since school is where most learning happens, what happens in school has a direct impact on learning. In turn, what happens in school is influenced by the resources, policies and practices approved at higher administrative levels in a country's education system.

Successful school systems – those that perform above average and show below-average socio-economic inequalities – provide all students, regardless of their socio-economic backgrounds, with similar opportunities to learn.

Systems that show high performance and an equitable distribution of learning outcomes tend to be comprehensive, requiring teachers and schools to embrace diverse student populations through personalised educational pathways. In contrast, school systems that assume that students have different destinations with different expectations and differentiation in terms of how they are placed in schools, classes and grades often show less equitable outcomes without an overall performance advantage.

Earlier PISA assessments showed these expectations to be mirrored in how students perceived their own educational future. The results of these differences can also be seen in the distribution of student performance within countries and in the impact that socio-economic background has on learning outcomes:

- In countries, and in schools within countries, where more students repeat grades, overall results tend to be worse.
- In countries where more students repeat grades, socio-economic differences in performance tend to be wider, suggesting that people from lower socio-economic groups are more likely to be negatively affected by grade repetition.
- In countries where 15-year-olds are divided into more tracks based on their abilities, overall performance is not enhanced, and the younger the age at which selection for such tracks first occurs, the greater the differences in student performance, by socio-economic background, by age 15, without improved overall performance.
- In school systems where it is more common to transfer weak or disruptive students out of a school, performance and equity both tend to be lower. Individual schools that make more use of transfers also perform worse in some countries.

These associations account for a substantial amount of the differences in the outcomes of schooling systems. For example, the frequency with which students are transferred across schools is associated with a third of the variation in country performance. This does not necessarily mean that if transfer policies were changed, a third of country differences in reading performance would disappear, since PISA does not measure cause and effect. The transfer of pupils who do badly may be partly a symptom, rather than a cause, of schools and school systems that are not producing satisfactory results, especially for lower-achieving students. It is worth noting that the schools with lower transfer rates tend to have greater autonomy and other means of addressing these challenges. The cluster of results listed above suggests that, in general, school systems that seek to cater to different students' needs through a high level of differentiation in the institutions, grade levels and classes have not succeeded in producing superior overall results, and in some respects they have lower-than-average and more socially unequal performance.

Most successful school systems grant greater autonomy to individual schools to design curricula and establish assessment policies, but these school systems do not necessarily allow schools to compete for enrolment.

The incentive to deliver good results for all students is not just a matter of how a school's student body is defined. It also depends on the ways in which schools are held accountable for their results and what forms of autonomy they are allowed to have – and how that could help influence their performance. PISA has looked at accountability both in terms of the information that is made available about performance and in terms of the use made of that information – whether by administrative authorities through rewards or control systems, or by the parents, for example through their choice of school. Thus the issues of autonomy, evaluation, governance and choice interact in providing a framework in which schools are given the incentives and the capacity to improve. PISA 2009 finds that:

- In countries where schools have greater autonomy over what is taught and how students are assessed, students tend to perform better.
- Within countries where schools are held to account for their results through posting achievement data publicly, schools that enjoy greater autonomy in resource allocation tend to do better than those with less autonomy. However, in countries where there are no such accountability arrangements, the reverse is true.
- Countries that create a more competitive environment in which many schools compete for students do not systematically produce better results.
- Within many countries, schools that compete more for students tend to have higher performance, but this is often accounted for by the higher socio-economic status of students in these schools. Parents with a higher socio-economic status are more likely to take academic performance into consideration when choosing schools.
- In countries that use standards-based external examinations, students tend to do better overall, but there is no clear relationship between performance and the use of standardised tests or the public posting of results at the school level. However, performance differences between schools with students of different social backgrounds are, on average, lower in countries that use standardised tests.

After accounting for the socio-economic and demographic profiles of students and schools, students in OECD countries who attend private schools show performance that is similar to that of students enrolled in public schools.

On average, socio-economically disadvantaged parents are over 13 percentage points more likely than socio-economically advantaged parents to report that they consider "low expenses" and "financial aid" as very important determinants in choosing a school. If children from socio-economically disadvantaged backgrounds cannot attend high-performing schools because of financial constraints, then school systems that offer parents more choice of schools for their children will necessarily be less effective in improving the performance of all students.

School systems considered successful spend large amounts of money on education, and tend to prioritise teachers' pay over smaller classes.

School systems differ in the amount of time, human, material and financial resources they invest in education. Equally important, school systems also vary in how these resources are spent:

- At the level of the school system and net of the level of national income, PISA shows that higher teachers' salaries, but not smaller class sizes, are associated with better student performance. Teachers' salaries are related to class size in that if spending levels are similar, school systems often make trade-offs between smaller classes and higher salaries for teachers. The findings from PISA suggest that systems prioritising higher teachers' salaries over smaller classes tend to perform better, which corresponds with research showing that raising teacher quality is a more effective route to improved student outcomes than creating smaller classes.
- Within countries, schools with better resources tend to do better only to the extent that they also tend to have more socio-economically advantaged students. Some countries show a strong relationship between schools' resources and their socio-economic and demographic background, which indicates that resources are inequitably distributed according to schools' socio-economic and demographic profiles.
- In other respects, the overall lack of a relationship between resources and outcomes does not show that resources are not important, but that their level does not have a systematic impact within the prevailing range. If most or all schools have the minimum resource requirements to allow effective teaching, additional material resources may make little difference to outcomes.

In more than half of all OECD countries, over 94% of 15-year-old students reported that they had attended pre-primary schools for at least some time.

Students who had attended pre-primary school tend to perform better than students who have not. This advantage is greater in school systems where pre-primary education lasts longer, where there are smaller pupil-to-teacher ratios at the pre-primary level and where there is higher public expenditure per pupil at that level of education. Across all participating countries, school systems with a higher proportion of students who had attended pre-primary education tend to perform better.

Schools with better disciplinary climates, more positive behaviours among teachers and better teacher-student relations tend to achieve higher scores in reading.

Across OECD countries, 81% of students report that they feel they can work well in class most of the time, 71% report that they never, or only in some classes, feel that other students don't listen, and 72% say that their teacher never, or only in some lessons, has to wait a long time before students settle down to learn.

Meanwhile, 28% of students in OECD countries are enrolled in schools whose principals report that their teaching staff's resistance to change negatively affects students or that students' needs are not met; 23% attends schools whose principals report that students are not encouraged by teachers in the school; 22% attend schools whose principals believe that learning is hindered by low teacher expectations; and 17% of students attend schools whose principals say that teacher absenteeism hampers learning.

Introduction to PISA

THE PISA SURVEYS

Are students well prepared to meet the challenges of the future? Can they analyse, reason and communicate their ideas effectively? Have they found the kinds of interests they can pursue throughout their lives as productive members of the economy and society? The OECD Programme for International Student Assessment (PISA) seeks to answer these questions through its triennial surveys of key competencies of 15-year-old students in OECD member countries and partner countries/economies. Together, the group of countries participating in PISA represents nearly 90% of the world economy.[1]

PISA assesses the extent to which students near the end of compulsory education have acquired some of the knowledge and skills that are essential for full participation in modern societies, with a focus on reading, mathematics and science.

PISA has now completed its fourth round of surveys. Following the detailed assessment of each of PISA's three main subjects – reading, mathematics and science – in 2000, 2003 and 2006, the 2009 survey marks the beginning of a new round with a return to a focus on reading, but in ways that reflect the extent to which reading has changed since 2000, including the prevalence of digital texts.

PISA 2009 offers the most comprehensive and rigorous international measurement of student reading skills to date. It assesses not only reading knowledge and skills, but also students' attitudes and their learning strategies in reading. PISA 2009 updates the assessment of student performance in mathematics and science as well.

The assessment focuses on young people's ability to use their knowledge and skills to meet real-life challenges. This orientation reflects a change in the goals and objectives of curricula themselves, which are increasingly concerned with what students can do with what they learn at school and not merely with whether they have mastered specific curricular content. PISA's unique features include its:

- Policy orientation, which connects data on student learning outcomes with data on students' characteristics and on key factors shaping their learning in and out of school in order to draw attention to differences in performance patterns and identify the characteristics of students, schools and education systems that have high performance standards.
- Innovative concept of "literacy", which refers to the capacity of students to apply knowledge and skills in key subject areas and to analyse, reason and communicate effectively as they pose, interpret and solve problems in a variety of situations.
- Relevance to lifelong learning, which does not limit PISA to assessing students' competencies in school subjects, but also asks them to report on their own motivations to learn, their beliefs about themselves and their learning strategies.
- Regularity, which enables countries to monitor their progress in meeting key learning objectives.
- Breadth of geographical coverage and collaborative nature, which, in PISA 2009, encompasses the 34 OECD member countries and 41 partner countries and economies.[2]

The relevance of the knowledge and skills measured by PISA is confirmed by studies tracking young people in the years after they have been assessed by PISA. Longitudinal studies in Australia, Canada and Switzerland display a strong relationship between performance in reading on the PISA assessment at age 15 and future educational attainment and success in the labour-market (see Volume I, Chapter 2).[3]

The frameworks for assessing reading, mathematics and science in 2009 are described in detail in *PISA 2009 Assessment Framework: Key Competencies in Reading, Mathematics and Science* (OECD, 2009a).

Decisions about the scope and nature of the PISA assessments and the background information to be collected are made by leading experts in participating countries. Governments guide these decisions based on shared, policy-driven interests. Considerable efforts and resources are devoted to achieving cultural and linguistic breadth and balance in the assessment materials. Stringent quality-assurance mechanisms are applied in designing the test, in translation, sampling and data collection. As a result, PISA findings are valid and highly reliable.

Policy makers around the world use PISA findings to gauge the knowledge and skills of students in their own country in comparison with those in other countries. PISA reveals what is possible in education by showing what students in the highest performing countries can do in reading, mathematics and science. PISA is also used to gauge the pace of educational progress, by allowing policy makers to assess to what extent performance changes observed nationally are in line with performance changes observed elsewhere. In a growing number of countries, PISA is also used to set policy targets against measurable goals achieved by other systems, to initiate research and peer-learning designed to identify policy levers and to reform trajectories for improving education. While PISA cannot identify cause-and-effect relationships between inputs, processes and educational outcomes, it can highlight key features in which education systems are similar and different, sharing those findings with educators, policy makers and the general public.

THE FIRST REPORT FROM THE 2009 ASSESSMENT

This volume is the fourth of six volumes that provide the first international report on results from the PISA 2009 assessment. It explores the relationships between student-, school- and system-level characteristics, and educational quality and equity. It explores what schools and school policies can do to raise overall student performance and, at the same time, moderate the impact of socio-economic background on student performance, with the aim of promoting a more equitable distribution of learning opportunities.

The other volumes cover the following issues:

- Volume I, *What Students Know and can Do: Student Performance in Reading, Mathematics and Science,* summarises the performance of students in PISA 2009. It provides the results for reading in the context of how performance is defined, measured and reported, and then examines what students are able to do in reading. After a summary of reading performance, it examines the ways in which this performance varies on subscales representing three aspects of reading. It then breaks down results by different formats of reading texts and considers gender differences in reading, both generally and for different reading aspects and text formats. Any comparison of the outcomes of education systems needs to take into consideration countries' social and economic circumstances and the resources they devote to education. To address this, the volume also interprets the results within countries' economic and social contexts. The volume concludes with a description of student results in mathematics and science.
- Volume II, *Overcoming Social Background: Equity in Learning Opportunities and Outcomes,* starts by closely examining the performance variation shown in Volume I, particularly the extent to which the overall variation in student performance relates to differences in results achieved by different schools. The volume then looks at how factors such as socio-economic background and immigrant status affect student and school performance, and the role that education policy can play in moderating the impact of these factors.
- Volume III, *Learning to Learn: Student Engagement, Strategies and Practices,* explores information gathered on students' levels of engagement in reading activities and attitudes towards reading and learning. It describes 15-year-olds' motivations, engagement and strategies to learn.
- Volume V, *Learning Trends: Changes in Student Performance Since 2000,* provides an overview of trends in student performance in reading, mathematics and science from PISA 2000 to PISA 2009. It shows educational outcomes over time and tracks changes in factors related to student and school performance, such as student background and school characteristics and practices.
- Volume VI, *Students On Line: Reading and Using Digital Information,* explains how PISA measures and reports student performance in digital reading, and analyses what students in the 20 countries participating in this assessment are able to do.

Box IV.A **Key features of PISA 2009**

Content

- The main focus of PISA 2009 was reading. The survey also updated performance assessments in mathematics and science. PISA considers students' knowledge in these areas not in isolation, but in relation to their ability to reflect on their knowledge and experience and to apply them to real-world issues. The emphasis is on mastering processes, understanding concepts and functioning in various contexts within each assessment area.
- For the first time, the PISA 2009 survey also assessed 15-year-old students' ability to read, understand and apply digital texts.

Methods

- Around 470 000 students completed the assessment in 2009, representing about 26 million 15-year-olds in the schools of the 65 participating countries and economies. Some 50 000 students took part in a second round of this assessment in 2010, representing about 2 million 15-year-olds from 10 additional partner countries and economies.
- Each participating student spent two hours carrying out pencil-and-paper tasks in reading, mathematics and science. In 20 countries, students were given additional questions via computer to assess their capacity to read digital texts.
- The assessment included tasks requiring students to construct their own answers as well as multiple-choice questions. The latter were typically organised in units based on a written passage or graphic, much like the kind of texts or figures that students might encounter in real life.
- Students also answered a questionnaire that took about 30 minutes to complete. This questionnaire focused on their background, learning habits, attitudes towards reading, and their involvement and motivation.
- School principals completed a questionnaire about their school that included demographic characteristics and an assessment of the quality of the learning environment at school.

Outcomes

PISA 2009 results provide:

- a profile of knowledge and skills among 15-year-olds in 2009, consisting of a detailed profile for reading and an update for mathematics and science;
- contextual indicators relating performance results to student and school characteristics;
- an assessment of students' engagement in reading activities, and their knowledge and use of different learning strategies;
- a knowledge base for policy research and analysis; and
- trend data on changes in student knowledge and skills in reading, mathematics, science, changes in student attitudes and socio-economic indicators, and in the impact of some indicators on performance results.

Future assessments

- The PISA 2012 survey will return to mathematics as the major assessment area, PISA 2015 will focus on science. Thereafter, PISA will turn to another cycle beginning with reading again.
- Future tests will place greater emphasis on assessing students' capacity to read and understand digital texts and solve problems presented in a digital format, reflecting the importance of information and computer technologies in modern societies.

All data tables referred to in the analysis are included at the end of the respective volume. A Reader's Guide is also provided in each volume to aid in interpreting the tables and figures accompanying the report.

Technical annexes that describe the construction of the questionnaire indices, sampling issues, quality-assurance procedures, the process followed for developing the assessment instruments, and information about reliability of coding are posted on the OECD PISA website (*www.pisa.oecd.org*). Many of the issues covered in the technical annexes are elaborated in greater detail in the *PISA 2009 Technical Report* (OECD, forthcoming).

THE PISA STUDENT POPULATION

In order to ensure the comparability of results across countries, PISA devoted a great deal of attention to assessing comparable target populations. Differences between countries in the nature and extent of pre-primary education and care, in the age of entry to formal schooling, and in the structure of the education system do not allow school grade levels to be defined so that they are internationally comparable. Valid international comparisons of educational performance, therefore, need to define their populations with reference to a target age. PISA covers students who are aged between 15 years 3 months and 16 years 2 months at the time of the assessment and who have completed at least 6 years of formal schooling, regardless of the type of institution in which they are enrolled, whether they are in full-time or part-time education, whether they attend academic or vocational programmes, and whether they attend public or private schools or foreign schools within the country. (For an operational definition of this target population, see the *PISA 2009 Technical Report* [OECD, forthcoming].) The use of this age in PISA, across countries and over time, allows the performance of students to be compared in a consistent manner before they complete compulsory education.

As a result, this report can make statements about the knowledge and skills of individuals born in the same year who are still at school at 15 years of age, despite having had different educational experiences, both in and outside school.

Stringent technical standards were established to define the national target populations and to identify permissible exclusions from this definition (for more information, see the PISA website *www.pisa.oecd.org*). The overall exclusion rate within a country was required to be below 5% to ensure that, under reasonable assumptions, any distortions in national mean scores would remain within plus or minus 5 score points, *i.e.* typically within the order of magnitude of two standard errors of sampling (see Annex A2). Exclusion could take place either through schools that participated or students who participated within schools. There are several reasons why a school or a student could be excluded from PISA.

■ Figure IV.A ■

A map of PISA countries and economies

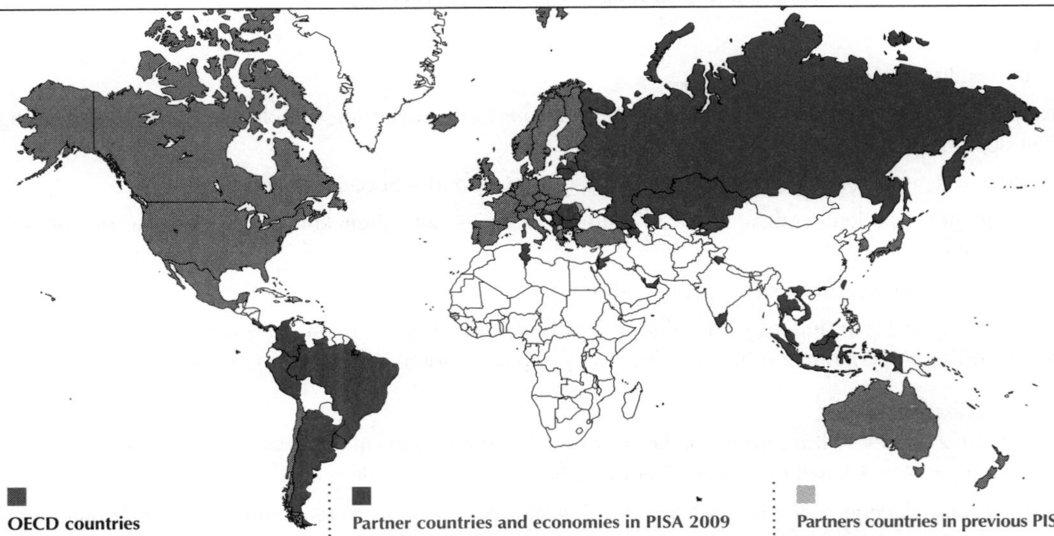

OECD countries

Australia
Austria
Belgium
Canada
Chile
Czech Republic
Denmark
Estonia
Finland
France
Germany
Greece
Hungary
Iceland
Ireland
Israel
Italy
Japan
Korea
Luxembourg
Mexico
Netherlands
New Zealand
Norway
Poland
Portugal
Slovak Republic
Slovenia
Spain
Sweden
Switzerland
Turkey
United Kingdom
United States

Partner countries and economies in PISA 2009

Albania
Argentina
Azerbaijan
Brazil
Bulgaria
Colombia
Costa Rica*
Croatia
Georgia*
Himachal Pradesh-India*
Hong Kong-China
Indonesia
Jordan
Kazakhstan
Kyrgyzstan
Latvia
Liechtenstein
Lithuania
Macao-China
Malaysia*
Malta*
Mauritius
Miranda-Venezuela*
Montenegro
Netherlands-Antilles*
Panama
Peru
Qatar
Romania
Russian Federation
Serbia
Shanghai-China
Singapore
Tamil Nadu-India*
Chinese Taipei
Thailand
Trinidad and Tobago
Tunisia
Uruguay
United Arab Emirates*
Viet Nam*

Partners countries in previous PISA surveys

Dominican Republic
Macedonia
Moldova

* These partner countries and economies carried out the assessment in 2010 instead of 2009.

Schools might be excluded because they are situated in remote regions and are inaccessible or because they are very small, or because of organisational or operational factors that precluded participation. Students might be excluded because of intellectual disability or limited proficiency in the language of the test.

In 29 out of 65 countries participating in PISA 2009, the percentage of school-level exclusions amounted to less than 1%; it was less than 5% in all countries. When the exclusion of students who met internationally established exclusion criteria is also taken into account, the exclusion rates increase slightly. However, the overall exclusion rate remains below 2% in 32 participating countries, below 5% in 60 participating countries, and below 7% in all countries except Luxembourg (7.2%) and Denmark (8.6%). In 15 out of 34 OECD countries, the percentage of school-level exclusions amounted to less than 1% and was less than 5% in all countries. When student exclusions within schools are also taken into account, there were 9 OECD countries below 2% and 25 countries below 5%. Restrictions on the level of exclusions in PISA 2009 are described in Annex A2.

The specific sample design and size for each country aimed to maximise sampling efficiency for student-level estimates. In OECD countries, sample sizes ranged from 4 410 students in Iceland to 38 250 students in Mexico. Countries with large samples have often implemented PISA both at national and regional/state levels (e.g. Australia, Belgium, Canada, Italy, Mexico, Spain, Switzerland and the United Kingdom). This selection of samples was monitored internationally and adhered to rigorous standards for the participation rate, both among schools selected by the international contractor and among students within these schools, to ensure that PISA results reflect the skills of 15-year-old students in participating countries. Countries were also required to administer the test to students in identical ways to ensure that students receive the same information prior to and during the test (for details, see Annex A4).

Notes

1. The GDP of countries that participated in PISA 2009 represents 87% of the 2007 world GDP. Some of the entities represented in this report are referred to as partner economies. This is because they are not strictly national entities.

2. Thirty-one partner countries and economies originally participated in the PISA 2009 assessment and ten additional partner countries and economies took part in a second round of the assessment.

3. Marks, G.N (2007); Bertschy, K., M.A Cattaneo and S.C. Wolter (2009); OECD (2010a).

Reader's Guide

Data underlying the figures

The data referred to in this volume are presented in Annex B and, in greater detail, on the PISA website (*www.pisa.oecd.org*).

Five symbols are used to denote missing data:

a The category does not apply in the country concerned. Data are therefore missing.

c There are too few observations or no observation to provide reliable estimates (*i.e.* there are fewer than 30 students or less than five schools with valid data).

m Data are not available. These data were not submitted by the country or were collected but subsequently removed from the publication for technical reasons.

w Data have been withdrawn or have not been collected at the request of the country concerned.

x Data are included in another category or column of the table.

Country coverage

This publication features data on 65 countries and economies, including all 34 OECD countries and 31 partner countries and economies (see Figure IV.A). The data from another ten partner countries were collected one year later and will be published in 2011.

The statistical data for Israel are supplied by and under the responsibility of the relevant Israeli authorities. The use of such data by the OECD is without prejudice to the status of the Golan Heights, East Jerusalem and Israeli settlements in the West Bank under the terms of international law.

Calculating international averages

An OECD average was calculated for most indicators presented in this report. The OECD average corresponds to the arithmetic mean of the respective country estimates.

Readers should, therefore, keep in mind that the term "OECD average" refers to the OECD countries included in the respective comparisons.

Rounding figures

Because of rounding, some figures in tables may not exactly add up to the totals. Totals, differences and averages are always calculated on the basis of exact numbers and are rounded only after calculation.

All standard errors in this publication have been rounded to one or two decimal places. Where the value 0.00 is shown, this does not imply that the standard error is zero, but that it is smaller than 0.005.

Reporting student data

The report uses "15-year-olds" as shorthand for the PISA target population. PISA covers students who are aged between 15 years 3 months and 16 years 2 months at the time of assessment and who have completed at least 6 years of formal schooling, regardless of the type of institution in which they are enrolled and of whether they are in full-time or part-time education, of whether they attend academic or vocational programmes, and of whether they attend public or private schools or foreign schools within the country.

Reporting school data

The principals of the schools in which students were assessed provided information on their schools' characteristics by completing a school questionnaire. Where responses from school principals are presented in this publication, they are weighted so that they are proportionate to the number of 15-year-olds enrolled in the school.

Focusing on statistically significant differences

This volume discusses only statistically significant differences or changes. These are denoted in darker colours in figures and in bold font in tables. See Annex A3 for further information.

Abbreviations used in this report

ESCS	PISA index of economic, social and cultural status
GDP	Gross domestic product
ISCED	International Standard Classification of Education
PPP	Purchasing power parity
S.D.	Standard deviation
S.E.	Standard error

Further documentation

For further information on the PISA assessment instruments and the methods used in PISA, see the *PISA 2009 Technical Report* (OECD, forthcoming) and the PISA website (*www.pisa.oecd.org*).

This report uses the OECD's StatLinks service. Below each table and chart is a url leading to a corresponding Excel workbook containing the underlying data. These urls are stable and will remain unchanged over time. In addition, readers of the e-books will be able to click directly on these links and the workbook will open in a separate window, if their Internet browser is open and running.

1

Some Features Shared by High-Performing School Systems

How do resources for education, and education policies and practices relate to reading performance? And what is their relationship with the socio-economic background of countries, schools and students? This chapter presents a summary of selected features shared by "successful" school systems, defined by relatively high-achieving students and greater equity in learning outcomes, because socio-economic background has only a moderate impact on performance.

Since school is where most learning takes place, what happens in school has a direct impact on learning. In turn, what happens in school is influenced by the resources, policies and practices at higher administrative levels within a country's education system.

Volume I, *What Students Know and Can Do,* shows that student performance in PISA varies widely in every subject assessed by PISA. In searching for effective policies to improve learning outcomes, policy makers and educators need to understand to what extent variation lies between countries, stems from performance differences among schools within countries, and results from variations in performance among individual students within schools.

This in turn leads to the question of how resources, policies and practices relate to those performance differences at the level of the education system, at the school level and among individual students; and how those resources, policies and practices affect the relationship between student performance and the economic and social background of countries, schools and students. This volume addresses these questions.

This chapter begins with a summary of selected features shared by those education systems that show relatively high performance levels among their students and a moderate impact of socio-economic background on learning outcomes. The impact of socio-economic background on performance is used throughout this volume as a measure of equity in the distribution of learning opportunities within a school system: the less learning outcomes depend on students' family context and socio-economic background, the greater the equity.[1] Chapter 2 examines in greater detail how resources, policies and practices relate to student performance and to what extent positive relationships observed at the school level translate into positive relationships at the level of the education system. Chapter 3 discusses how PISA describes and measures education resources, policies and practices, and shows where countries stand on these issues. Chapter 4 then describes the learning environment in schools.

PERFORMANCE DIFFERENCES AMONG COUNTRIES, SCHOOLS AND STUDENTS

In the PISA 2009 assessment of reading literacy, 25% of the performance variation observed among students in the participating countries results from performance differences among countries (see Chapter 2 of Volume I, *What Students Know and Can Do*). Among OECD countries, the corresponding proportion is 11%. Countries with higher national incomes tend to perform better: some 6% of the performance differences among OECD countries can be predicted on the basis of the countries' national income (see Figure I.2.1 in Volume I); this rises to 30% when the partner countries and economies that participated in PISA are included. The analysis of the policies and practices at the level of education systems seeks to explain the performance variation among countries.[2]

■ Figure IV.1.1 ■

How much of the variation in reading performance lies between countries, schools and students

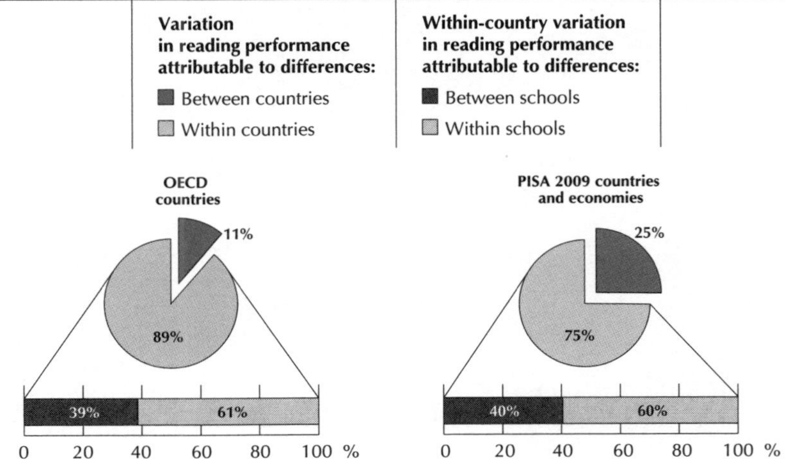

Source: OECD, *PISA 2009 Database.*

StatLink http://dx.doi.org/10.1787/888932343361

On average across all participating countries, 40% of the performance variation observed within countries lies between schools,[3] of which 23 percentage points are attributable to differences in schools' socio-economic intake (Table II.5.1 in Volume II). Among OECD countries, the corresponding proportions are 39% and 24 percentage points. Differences in the policies and practices applied by schools contribute to this portion of the overall variation in student performance.

The remaining 60% of the performance variation in the participating countries, and 61% among OECD countries, results from differences in the performance of individual students within schools (Figure IV.1.1).

COMMON CHARACTERISTICS OF SUCCESSFUL SCHOOL SYSTEMS

Among the features of schools and school systems that were measured by PISA, some are common to successful school systems. "Successful school systems" are defined here as those that perform above the OECD average in reading (493 points) and in which students' socio-economic background has a smaller impact on reading performance than is the case in a typical OECD country (on average across OECD countries, 14% of the variation in reading scores is explained by socio-economic background). As shown in Volume II, *Overcoming Social Background*, Korea, Finland, Canada, Japan, Norway, Estonia, Iceland and the partner economy Hong Kong-China performed at higher levels than the OECD average and also showed a weaker relationship between socio-economic background and performance.

This volume shows that three of the four features of school systems examined by PISA 2009 relate to student performance and equity in education: first, how students are selected for entry into schools and classrooms; second, the extent to which individual schools are granted autonomy to make decisions on curricula and assessments, and whether schools are allowed to compete for student enrolment; and third, where spending on education is directed. The existence of standards-based external examinations also relates positively to student performance, but regarding the use of student assessments, which is the fourth feature examined by PISA, high-performing school systems tend to use the data resulting from these assessments differently.

As shown in subsequent chapters of this volume, school systems with low levels of vertical and horizontal differentiation – that is, school systems in which: all students, regardless of their background, are offered similar opportunities to learn; socio-economically advantaged and disadvantaged students attend the same schools; and students rarely repeat grades or are transferred out of schools because of behavioural problems, low academic achievement or special learning needs – are more likely to perform above the OECD average and show below-average socio-economic inequalities. Of the 13 OECD countries that have low levels of student differentiation (Figure IV.3.2), Canada, Estonia, Finland, Iceland and Norway perform above the OECD average and show only a moderate impact of socio-economic background on student performance. Among the school systems with above-average performance and below-average socio-economic inequalities, none show high levels of student differentiation. However, among the school systems with high average performance but comparatively large socio-economic inequalities, Belgium, the Netherlands and Switzerland routinely select and sort students into schools, programmes or grades. This suggests that the level of differentiation is not closely related to average performance, but does relate to socio-economic inequalities in education (see Chapter 2).

The results from PISA 2009 also show that those school systems that grant individual schools authority to make decisions about curricula and assessments while limiting school competition are more likely to be performing above the OECD average and show below-average socio-economic inequalities. Many school systems with high average performance but comparatively large socio-economic inequalities tend to allow higher levels of school competition. Results from PISA also suggest that giving parents and students a choice of schools (as indicated by whether schools compete for students) does not relate positively to equity in education if their choice is constrained by financial or logistical considerations, such as additional tuition fees or transportation to and from schools. For example, on average, across the 14 countries that administered the PISA parent questionnaire, socio-economically disadvantaged parents are over 13 percentage points more likely than advantaged parents to report that they consider "low expenses" and "financial aid" to be very important determining factors in choosing a school (see Chapter 2). Of the 38 school systems that offer schools greater autonomy in determining their curricula, but offer limited school choice to parents and students, Canada, Estonia, Finland, Iceland, Japan and Norway show above-average performance and below-average socio-economic inequalities (Figure IV.3.5).

Two school systems show comparatively high levels of spending by educational institutions that prioritise teachers' salaries over class size (Figure IV.3.7). Both Japan and Korea show above-average performance and below-average socio-economic inequalities. This is consistent with the finding that high levels of investment in higher teachers' salaries tend to concur with higher performance in education systems (see Chapter 2).

■ Figure IV.1.2 ■

Selected characteristics of school systems with reading performance above the OECD average

Four areas		
1. Selecting and grouping students (Figure IV.3.2)	V	High vertical differentiation
	v	Low vertical differentiation
	H	High horizontal differentiation at the system level
	h	Medium horizontal differentiation at the system level
	h	Low horizontal differentiation at the system level
	Hsc	High horizontal differentiation at the school level
	hsc	Low horizontal differentiation at the school level
2. Governance of schools (Figure IV.3.5)	A	More school autonomy for curriculum and assessment
	a	Less school autonomy for curriculum and assessment
	C	More school competition
	c	Less school competition
3. Assessment and accountability policies (Figure IV.3.6)	B	Frequent use of assessment or achievement data for benchmarking and information purposes
	b	Infrequent use of assessment or achievement data for benchmarking and information purposes
	D	Frequent use of assessment or achievement data for decision making
	d	Infrequent use of assessment or achievement data for decision making
4. Resources invested in education (Figure IV.3.7)	E	High cumulative expenditure by educational institutions per student aged 6 to 15
	e	Low cumulative expenditure by educational institutions per student aged 6 to 15
	S	Large class size and high teachers' salaries
	s	Small class size and/or low teachers' salaries

	Reading performance (score points)	Strength of relationship between students' socio-economic background and reading performance (% variance explained)		Four areas: 1. Selecting and grouping students (Figure IV.3.2)	2. Governance of schools (Figure IV.3.5)	3. Assessment and accountability policies (Figure IV.3.6)	4. Resources invested in education (Figure IV.3.7)	Countries with similar system characteristics in the four areas
Hong Kong-China	533	Below-average impact of socio-economic background on reading performance	4.5	v + ***h*** + hsc	A + C	B + D	e + S	—
Iceland	500		6.2	v + h + hsc	A + c	B + D	E + s	Australia, Canada, Sweden, United Kingdom, United States
Estonia	501		7.6	v + h + hsc	A + c	B + D	e + s	New Zealand, Poland, Latvia, Lithuania, Russian Federation
Finland	536		7.8	v + h + hsc	A + c	b + d	E + s	—
Japan	520		8.6	v + ***h*** + hsc	A + c	b + D	E + S	—
Canada	524		8.6	v + h + hsc	A + c	B + D	E + s	Australia, Iceland, Sweden, United Kingdom, United States
Norway	503		8.6	v + h + hsc	A + c	B + d	E + s	—
Korea	539		11.0	v + ***h*** + hsc	A + C	B + D	E + S	—
Shanghai-China	556	Average impact of socio-economic background on reading performance	12.3	v + ***h*** + hsc	A + c	B + D	e + S	Thailand
Australia	515		12.7	v + h + hsc	A + C	B + D	E + s	—
Netherlands	508		12.8	V + H + Hsc	A + C	b + d	E + s	—
Switzerland	501		14.1	V + H + Hsc	A + c	b + d	E + s	—
Poland	500		14.8	v + h + hsc	A + c	B + D	e + s	Estonia, New Zealand, Latvia, Lithuania, Russian Federation
Singapore	526		15.3	v + H + hsc	A + c	B + D	e + S	—
New Zealand	521	Above-average impact of socio-economic background on reading performance	16.6	v + h + hsc	A + c	B + D	e + s	Estonia, Poland, Latvia, Lithuania, Russian Federation
Belgium	506		19.3	V + H + hsc	A + C	b + d	E + s	—

Note: Cells shaded in grey are the most prevailing patterns among school systems with above-average reading performance and below-average impact of socio-economic background on reading performance within each of the four areas. For other countries and economies, see Tables IV.1.1a and IV.1.1b.
StatLink http://dx.doi.org/10.1787/888932343361

Among systems with comparatively high levels of spending on education that prioritise small class size, performance patterns are mixed. There are also a number of lower-performing systems with similar spending choices.

In short, many successful school systems share some common features: low levels of student differentiation; high levels of school autonomy in formulating curricula and using assessments with low levels of school competition; and spending in education that prioritises teachers' salaries over smaller classes. However, the fact that such characteristics are more likely to be found among successful school systems does not mean that they are necessary or sufficient for success. Not all successful school systems share the same organisational characteristics, and not all school systems that are organised in this way achieve high levels of performance and a moderate impact of socio-economic background on student performance.

THE LEARNING ENVIRONMENT INSIDE SCHOOLS AND CLASSROOMS

Research on what makes schools effective finds that learning requires an orderly and co-operative environment, both in and outside the classroom (Jennings and Greenberg, 2009). Effective schools are characterised by amiable and supportive teacher-student relations that extend beyond the walls of the classroom. In such schools, academic activities and high student performance are valued by both students and teachers (Scheerens and Bosker, 1997; Sammons, 1999; Taylor, Pressley and Pearson, 2002).

Because of difficulties in comparing such data across countries (see Box IV.1.1 below), the discussion on learning environments in this volume focuses on how certain features of these environments relate to reading performance *within* each country. Results from PISA 2009 show that, in general, students perform better in schools with more disciplined classrooms, partly because such schools tend to have more students from advantaged socio-economic backgrounds, who generally perform better, partly because the favourable socio-economic background of students relates to a climate that is conducive to learning, and partly for reasons unrelated to socio-economic factors. Results from PISA 2009 also show that even though the learning environment in schools and classrooms is partially shaped by the resources, policies and practices of the systems and schools, disciplined classrooms themselves tend to go hand in hand with higher performance. Chapters 2 and 4 provide more detailed definitions and analyses of the individual indicators that describe the learning environment.

THE PISA 2009 EVIDENCE BASE

The resources, policies and practices of schools and school systems discussed in this volume are mainly based on students' and school principals' responses to the PISA background questionnaires. Responses from parents are used for the countries that administered the optional PISA questionnaire to parents. However, caution is required when interpreting the data collected from students, parents and school principals (see Box IV.1.1 below).

For some of the system-level features, PISA results are complemented by data about school systems from OECD's Education Database (OECD, 2010a).[4]

Box IV.1.1 **Interpreting the data from students, parents and schools**

PISA 2009 asked students and school principals (and parents, for some countries) to answer questions about the learning environment and organisation of schools, and social and economic contexts in which learning takes place. These are self-reports rather than external observations and may be influenced by cross-cultural differences in how individuals respond. For example, students' self-perceptions of classroom situations may reflect the actual classroom situation imperfectly, or students may choose to respond in a way that does not accurately reflect their observations because certain responses may be more socially desirable than others.

Several of the indices presented in this volume summarise the responses of students, parents or school principals to a series of related questions. The questions were selected from larger constructs on the basis of theoretical considerations and previous research. Structural equation modelling was used to confirm the theoretically expected dimensions of the indices and validate their comparability across countries. For this purpose, a model was estimated separately for each country and collectively for all OECD countries. For detailed information on the construction of these indices, see Annex A1.

...

In addition to the general limitation of self-reported data, there are other limitations, particularly those concerning the information collected from principals, that should be taken into account when interpreting the data:

- An average of only 264 principals were surveyed in each OECD country, and in 6 countries and economies, fewer than 150 principals were surveyed. In 5 of these 6 countries, this was because fewer than 150 schools were attended by 15-year-old students.
- Although principals can provide information about their schools, generalising from a single source of information for each school and then matching that information with students' reports is not straightforward. Students' opinions and performance in each subject depend on many factors, including all the education that they have acquired in earlier years and their experiences outside the school setting, rather than just the period in which they have interacted with their current teachers.
- Principals may not be the most appropriate sources of some information related to teachers, such as teachers' morale and commitment (see Box IV.1.2).
- The learning environment examined by PISA may only partially reflect the learning environment that shaped students' educational experiences earlier in their school careers, particularly in education systems where students progress through different types of educational institutions at the pre-primary, primary, lower secondary and upper secondary levels. To the extent that students' current learning environment differs from that of their earlier school years, the contextual data collected by PISA are an imperfect proxy for students' cumulative learning environments, and the effects of those environments on learning outcomes is likely to be underestimated.
- In most cases, 15-year-old students have been in the present school for only two to three years. This means that much of their reading development took place earlier, in other schools, which may have little or no connection with the present school.
- In some countries, the definition of the school in which students are taught is not straightforward because schools vary in the level and purpose of education. For example, in some countries, sub-units within schools (*e.g.* study programmes, shifts and campuses) were sampled instead of schools as administrative units. Despite these caveats, information from the school questionnaire provides unique insights into the ways in which national and sub-national authorities seek to realise their educational objectives.

In using results from non-experimental data on school performance, such as the PISA Database, it is also important to bear in mind the distinction between school effects and the effects of schooling, particularly when interpreting the modest association between factors such as school resources, policies and institutional characteristics and student performance. The effect of schooling is the influence on performance of not being schooled *versus* being schooled. As a set of well-controlled studies has shown, this can have significant impact not only on knowledge but also on fundamental cognitive skills (*e.g.* Ceci, 1991; Blair *et al.,* 2005). School effects are education researchers' shorthand way of referring to the effect on academic performance of attending one school or another, usually schools that differ in resources or policies and institutional characteristics. Where schools and school systems do not vary in fundamental ways, the school effect can be modest. Nevertheless, modest school effects should not be confused with a lack of an effect by schooling.

The analyses that relate the performance and equity levels of school systems to educational policies and practices are carried out through a correlation analysis. A correlation is a simple statistic that measures the degree to which two variables are associated with each other. Given the nested nature of the PISA sample (students nested in schools that, in turn, are nested in countries), other statistical techniques, such as Hierarchical Linear Models, Structural Equation Modeling or Meta-Analytical Techniques, may seem more appropriate. Yet, even these sophisticated statistical techniques cannot adequately take into account the nature of the PISA sample because participating countries are not a random sample of countries. The system-level correlations presented here are consistent with results from PISA 2006, which use more sophisticated statistical techniques. Given that the limitations of a correlation analysis using PISA data are not completely overcome by using more sophisticated statistical tools, the simplest method was used. The robustness and sensitivity of the findings are checked against other specifications (see Annex A6). Cautionary notes are provided to help the reader interpret the results presented in this volume correctly.

In contrast, the within-country analyses are based on mixed-effects models appropriate for the random sampling of schools and the random sampling of students within these schools.

Information based on reports from school principals or parents has been weighted so that it reflects the number of 15-year-olds enrolled in each school.

Unless otherwise noted, comparisons of student performance refer to the performance of students on the reading scale.

PISA did not collect data from teachers, so inferences about teaching and learning are made indirectly, from the perspective of students and school principals. Since students learn from a variety of teachers throughout their school careers, it is difficult to establish direct links between teachers' characteristics and students' performance in PISA. It has not yet been possible to formulate a reliable methodology to link students and teachers in large-scale, cross-sectional surveys like PISA so that meaningful inferences can be made regarding the influence of teachers' characteristics and behaviour on learning outcomes. Although teachers' reports on their attitudes and experiences are missing in PISA, the OECD's Teacher and Learning International Survey (TALIS) provides a useful overview of lower secondary school teachers' professional development, their beliefs, attitudes and practices, teacher appraisal and feedback, and school leadership (see Box IV.1.2 below).

Box IV.1.2 **TALIS: Teacher and Learning International Survey**

PISA measures students' knowledge and skills in reading, mathematics and science and relates these to students' background and school experiences. But PISA does not cover the experiences and attitudes of teachers – those who have the most direct impact on student learning at school (Greenwald, Hedges and Laine, 1996; Nye, Konstantopoulos and Hedges, 2004; Rivkin, Hanushek and Kain, 2005).

The OECD's Teacher and Learning International Survey (TALIS) examines aspects of lower secondary school teachers' professional development, their beliefs, attitudes and practices, teacher appraisal and feedback, and school leadership. Its robust international indicators and analysis on teachers and teaching help countries review and develop policies to create the conditions for effective schooling. Its cross-country analyses allow countries facing similar challenges to learn about different policy approaches and their impact on the school environment.

Having surveyed over 90 000 teachers and principals in 23 OECD and partner countries,[5] TALIS results indicate that:

- A large proportion of teachers in most surveyed countries are satisfied with their jobs and feel they make an educational difference for their students.
- Teachers are often thwarted in their efforts because of a lack of qualified staff, suitable equipment and instructional support, disruptive student behaviour and/or bureaucratic procedures.
- Better and more targeted professional development can help improve teacher effectiveness. Many teachers believe that certification programmes and individual and collaborative research can help improve their work, yet these are the least common forms of professional development in which teachers engage.
- Teachers generally believe that appraisal and feedback make a big difference in their work by improving teachers' instructional and classroom management practices and teachers' self-confidence.
- On average, three-quarters of teachers in all countries report that they would receive no recognition for improving the quality of their work or for being more innovative in their teaching. Three-quarters of teachers also say that the most effective teachers in their school do not receive the most recognition, and that monetary rewards are not altered for persistently underperforming teachers.
- School leadership plays a crucial role in shaping teachers' working lives and development. Schools with strong instructional leadership are those where teachers engage in professional development to address the weaknesses identified in appraisals, where there are better student-teacher relations, where there is greater collaboration among teachers, and where greater recognition is given to innovative teachers.
- Public policy can improve conditions for effective teaching if it addresses such factors as school climate, teaching beliefs, co-operation among teachers, teacher job satisfaction, professional development and teaching techniques (OECD, 2009b).

Given that much of the variation in teaching effectiveness lies among individual teachers rather than among schools or countries, policies and individualised professional development programmes should target teachers, not just schools or school systems.

Notes

1. Volume II, *Overcoming Social Background,* considers two dimensions of equity to identify successful school systems: the strength and the slope of the socio-economic gradient (see Volume II, Chapter 3). In order to provide a simpler description of successful school systems, this volume uses only the proportion of variation in performance explained by socio-economic status (*i.e.* the strength of the socio-economic gradient) as a measure of equity.

2. In mathematics, 31% of the performance variation among participating countries is attributable to differences among countries; among OECD countries, that percentage is 14%. In science, 28% of the performance variation among participating countries is attributable to differences among countries; among OECD countries, the percentage is 13%.

3. In both mathematics and science, and across OECD countries as well as across all partner countries and economies, approximately 40% of the performance variation lies between countries and the remaining 60% lies between students within schools.

4. For the countries that do not participate in the OECD's annual data collection, these data have been collected separately.

5. Countries participating in TALIS are: Australia, Austria, Belgium (Flemish Community), Estonia, Denmark, Hungary, Iceland, Ireland, Italy, Korea, Mexico, Norway, Poland, Portugal, the Slovak Republic, Slovenia, Spain, Turkey, and partner countries Brazil, Bulgaria, Lithuania, Malaysia and Malta.

2

How Resources, Policies and Practices are Related to Student Performance

By focusing on selected organisational features of schools and school systems, this chapter details how resources, policies and practices relate to student performance, and how far positive relationships at the school level translate into positive relationships at the level of the education system. The chapter also discusses how the environment within schools affects learning outcomes.

Chapter 1 shows to what extent the performance variation among students stems from performance differences among countries, between schools within countries, or among students within schools. This chapter takes these analyses further by examining in greater detail how resources, policies and practices relate to student performance, and to what extent positive relationships observed at the school level translate into positive relationships at the level of the education system. Since reading was the focus of the PISA 2009 assessment, the analyses focus on reading. However, the patterns observed for mathematics and science are similar. Chapter 3 discusses how PISA describes and measures education resources, policies and practices, and shows where countries stand on these issues. Chapter 4 describes the learning environment in schools.

HOW PISA EXAMINES RESOURCES, POLICIES, PRACTICES AND LEARNING OUTCOMES

When examining the relationship between student performance and resources, policies and practices, this volume takes into account the socio-economic differences among students and schools. The advantage of doing this lies in comparing similar entities, namely education systems and schools with similar socio-economic backgrounds. At the same time, there is a risk that such adjusted comparisons underestimate the strength of the relationship between student performance and resources, policies and practices, since most of the differences in performance are often attributable both to policies and to socio-economic background. For example, it may be that in better-performing schools, parents have high expectations for the school and exert pressure on the school to fulfil those expectations. After accounting for socio-economic factors, an existing relationship between parents' expectations of the school and student performance may no longer be apparent as an independent relationship because these schools often have an advantaged socio-economic intake. Even though the relationship between parental expectations and student performance may exist, it is no longer observed, simply because it has been accounted for along with the socio-economic differences.

Conversely, analyses that do not take socio-economic background into account can overstate the relationship between student performance and resources, policies and practices, as the level of resources and the kinds of policies adopted may also relate to the socio-economic background of students, schools and countries. At the same time, analyses without adjustments may paint a more realistic picture of the schools that parents choose for their children. They may also provide more information for other stakeholders who are interested in the overall performance of students, schools and systems, including any effects that may be related to the socio-economic intake of schools and systems. For example, parents may be primarily interested in a school's absolute performance standards, even if a school's higher achievement record stems partially from the fact that the school has a larger proportion of socio-economically advantaged students.

The analyses in this volume present relationships both before and after accounting for socio-economic differences, and focus on differences among countries and among schools within countries.

Relationships between the organisational characteristics of a school system and the school system's performance in PISA, as well as the impact of socio-economic background on performance, are established through correlational analysis.[1] The analyses are undertaken first on the basis of the OECD countries and then extended to all countries and economies that participated in PISA (Table IV.2.1).

Within school systems, these relationships are established through multilevel regression analysis. In each of the following sections, a set of interrelated resources, policies and practices are considered jointly to establish their relationship with student performance.[2] For the reasons explained above, two approaches are used: an unadjusted one that examines the relationships as they present themselves to students, families and teachers in the schools irrespective of the socio-economic context, and a "like-with-like" approach that examines the relationships after accounting for the socio-economic and demographic background of students and schools. The methodology of both approaches is presented in Annex A5.

How selecting and grouping students are related to student performance

Volume II, *Overcoming Social Background,* highlights the challenges school systems face in addressing the needs of diverse student populations. To meet these challenges, some countries have adopted non-selective and comprehensive school systems that seek to provide all students with similar opportunities, leaving it to each teacher and school to provide for the full range of student abilities, interests and backgrounds. Other countries respond to diversity by grouping students, whether between schools or between classes within schools, with the aim of serving students according to their academic potential and/or interests in specific programmes. The underlying assumption in differentiation is often that students' talents will develop best when students can stimulate each other's interest in learning, and create an environment that is more conducive to effective teaching.

The analysis presented in this chapter covers not only curricular differentiation (*i.e.* tracking or streaming) and school selectivity, but also other forms of horizontal differentiation and vertical differentiation. Vertical differentiation refers to the ways in which students progress through the education systems as they become older. Even though the student population is differentiated into grade levels in practically all schools in PISA, in some countries, all 15-year-old students attend the same grade level, while in other countries they are dispersed throughout various grade levels as a result of policies governing the age of entrance into the school system and/or grade repetition.

Horizontal differentiation refers to differences in instruction within a grade or education level. Horizontal differentiation, which can be applied by the education system or by individual schools, groups students according to their interests and/or performance. At the system level, horizontal differentiation can be applied by schools that select students on the basis of their academic records, by offering specific programmes (vocational or academic, for example), and by setting the age at which students are admitted into these programmes. Individual schools can apply horizontal differentiation by grouping students according to ability or transferring students out of the school because of low performance, behavioural problems or special needs.[3]

Chapter 3 complements this analysis with a detailed description of how different education systems implement these policies and practices and how various forms of differentiation are interrelated.

Vertical differentiation and performance

PISA shows that the prevalence of grade repetition is negatively related to the learning outcomes of education systems, even after accounting for countries' national income. In other words, school systems with high rates of grade repetition are also school systems that show lower student performance, whatever the causal nature of this relationship. Some 15% of the variation in performance across OECD countries after per capita GDP has been accounted for can be explained by differences in the rates of grade repetition (Figure IV.2.1a and Table IV.2.1).

This negative relationship between grade repetition and student performance is mirrored at the school level. In 24 OECD countries and 27 partner countries and economies, schools with more students who repeat grades tend to achieve lower scores than schools with fewer students who repeat grades. After accounting for the socio-economic and demographic background of students and schools, the relationship between student performance and grade repetition is observed in 22 OECD countries and 21 partner countries and economies (Figure IV.2.1b).

Grade repetition is not just negatively related to average performance, but also to the impact of students' socio-economic background on their performance. School systems that differentiate students vertically through grade repetition show a stronger relationship between socio-economic background and learning outcomes, even after accounting for the country's national income (Figure IV.2.1a). In other words, and consistent with the literature on grade repetition, students from socio-economically disadvantaged backgrounds appear to be hurt most by grade repetition (Hauser, 2004; Alexander, Entwisle and Dauber, 2003). Although the objective of grade repetition is for these students to have more opportunities to learn, underperforming students do not seem to benefit from repeating a grade. One hypothesis to explain this negative relationship is that having the option to have low-performing students repeat a grade places fewer demands on teachers and schools to help struggling and disadvantaged students improve their performance.[4]

Horizontal differentiation at the system level and performance

Horizontal differentiation at the system level, as measured by the number of programmes available to 15-year-olds, the age of first selection into these programmes and the percentage of selective schools in a system, appears to be unrelated to the average performance of education systems (Figure IV.2.1a). While highly selective schools, whose principals report that they use students' academic records or recommendations from feeder schools to decide who will be admitted, tend to perform better than non-selective schools in many countries (Figure IV.2.1b), the prevalence of selectivity in the education system does not relate to the system's overall performance level. Instead, education systems that contain a large proportion of selective schools tend to have greater variation in performance between schools (Table IV.2.1).

School systems that track students early into different educational programmes show lower levels of equity, but do not achieve higher levels of average performance than systems that track students later in their school careers. This finding is consistent with prior research showing that inequality is greater in more differentiated school systems (Causa and Cahpuis, 2009; Schütz, West and Woessmann, 2007). Inequalities are particularly large in education systems in which horizontal differentiation occurs at early ages. Education systems in the OECD countries range from essentially undivided secondary education until the age of 15 (14 OECD countries and 7 partner countries and economies)

to systems with 4 or more school types or distinct educational programmes (the Netherlands, the Slovak Republic, the Czech Republic, Ireland, Austria, Luxembourg, Belgium, Switzerland and Germany, and the partner countries and economies Croatia, Trinidad and Tobago, Shanghai-China, Qatar, Kyrgyzstan and Singapore; see Table IV.3.2a). For example, education systems in which the first age of selection occurs one year earlier tend to show a stronger relationship between a school's performance and its socio-economic profile (*i.e.* a 10.8 score point difference corresponding to 1 unit on the *PISA index of economic, social and cultural status* of the school) (Table IV.2.3). Even if the corresponding relationship within schools is somewhat weaker in these education systems, this advantage is much smaller than the larger socio-economic disparities among schools. Thus, on balance, early selection into different institutional tracks is associated with larger socio-economic inequalities in learning opportunities without being associated with better overall performance.

The reason why the age at which differentiation begins is closely associated with socio-economic selectivity may be because students are more dependent upon their parents and their parents' resources when they are younger. In systems with a high degree of institutional differentiation, parents from higher socio-economic backgrounds may be in a better position to promote their children's chances than in a system in which such decisions are taken at a later age, when students themselves play a bigger role.

Horizontal differentiation at the school level and performance

Two forms of horizontal differentiation at the school level appear negatively related to student performance: the more frequently schools transfer students to another school because of students' low academic achievement, behavioural problems or special learning needs, and the more schools group students by ability in all subjects, the lower the school system's performance in PISA (Figure IV.2.1a). In fact, over one-third of the variation in student performance across countries can be explained by the rate at which schools transfer students.

■ Figure IV.2.1a ■

How school systems' policies for selecting and grouping students are related to educational outcomes

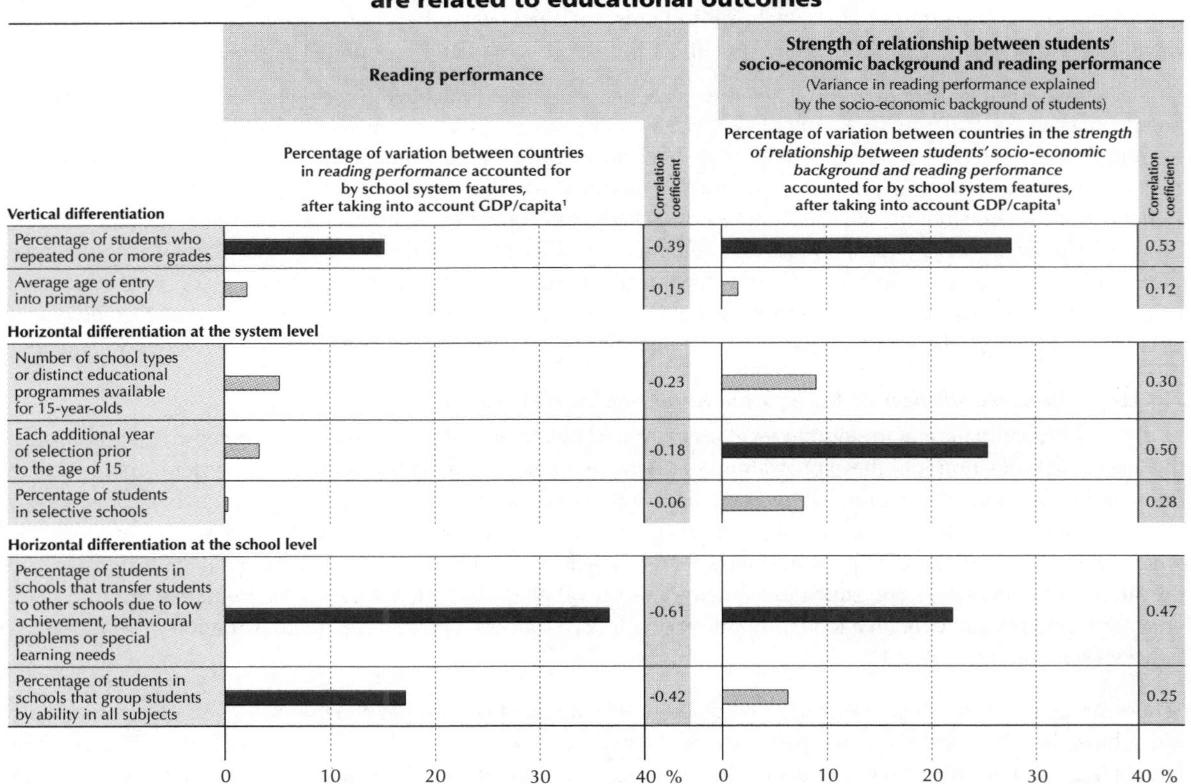

Note: Correlations that are statistically significant at the 5% level ($p<0.05$) are marked in a darker tone.
1. The percentage is obtained by squaring the correlation coefficient and then multiplying it by 100.
Source: OECD, *PISA 2009 Database*, Table IV.2.1.
StatLink http://dx.doi.org/10.1787/888932343380

One hypothesis is that school transfers may hurt student achievement because transferring out of a school is usually difficult for students (see Chapter 3). Another hypothesis is that in systems where transferring students is a common policy or practice, teachers and the school community have less of an incentive to commit themselves to helping lower-achieving students improve.[5]

In a few countries, there is also a negative relationship between transferring students and performance at the school level (Figure IV.2.1b). As is true at the level of the school system, individual schools from which students are likely to be transferred to another school because of low academic achievement, behavioural problems or special learning needs tend to achieve lower scores than schools that do not transfer students. The relationship between ability grouping for all subjects and performance is negative in a few countries, while this relationship is positive in other countries (Figure IV.2.1b). However, whether schools group students based on their ability for all subjects seems to be closely related to schools' socio-economic profile, since in almost all countries, there is no independent relationship between grouping students by ability and performance, after accounting for the socio-economic background of students and schools.

■ Figure IV.2.1b ■

Countries in which school policies for selecting and grouping students are related to reading performance

Schools' policies on selecting and grouping students (the model includes all these policies)		Without accounting for the socio-economic and demographic background of students and schools		With accounting for the socio-economic and demographic background of students and schools	
		Negative relationship	Positive relationship	Negative relationship	Positive relationship
Percentage of students who repeated one or more grades	***OECD***	Austria, Belgium, Canada, Chile, Czech Republic, Denmark, Estonia, Finland, Germany, Hungary, Ireland, Israel, Italy, Luxembourg, Mexico, New Zealand, Poland, Portugal, Slovak Republic, Spain, Switzerland, Turkey, United Kingdom, United States		Austria, Canada, Chile, Czech Republic, Denmark, Estonia, Finland, Hungary, Ireland, Israel, Italy, Luxembourg, Mexico, Netherlands, Poland, Portugal, Slovak Republic, Spain, Switzerland, Turkey, United Kingdom, United States	
		OECD average change in score: **-2.3**		OECD average change in score: -0.1	
	Partner	Albania, Argentina, Azerbaijan, Bulgaria, Brazil, Colombia, Croatia, Dubai (UAE), Hong Kong-China, Indonesia, Jordan, Kyrgyzstan, Latvia, Lithuania, Macao-China, Montenegro, Panama, Peru, Qatar, Romania, Russian Federation, Serbia, Singapore, Thailand, Trinidad and Tobago, Tunisia, Uruguay		Albania, Argentina, Azerbaijan, Brazil, Colombia, Croatia, Dubai (UAE), Hong Kong-China, Indonesia, Jordan, Kyrgyzstan, Latvia, Macao-China, Panama, Peru, Qatar, Romania, Serbia, Trinidad and Tobago, Tunisia, Uruguay	
School with high academic selectivity for school admittance	***OECD***	Ireland	Austria, Canada, Switzerland, Chile, Czech Republic, Finland, Hungary, Netherlands, Poland, Slovak Republic, Slovenia, Turkey, United Kingdom, United States		Austria, Czech Republic, Denmark, Hungary, Korea, Netherlands, Slovenia, Sweden, Switzerland, Turkey
		OECD average change in score: 17.3		OECD average change in score: **7.6**	
	Partner		Bulgaria, Hong Kong-China, Croatia, Latvia, Peru, Dubai (UAE), Qatar, Shanghai-China, Russian Federation, Singapore, Chinese Taipei	Montenegro	Bulgaria, Croatia, Shanghai-China
School is very likely to transfer students with low achievement, behavioural problems or special learning needs	***OECD***	Australia, Japan, Netherlands, United States	Austria, Italy, Spain, Switzerland	Israel	Denmark, Switzerland
		OECD average change in score: **-4.9**		OECD average change in score: -1.5	
	Partner	Dubai (UAE), Chinese Taipei	Brazil, Colombia, Indonesia	Dubai (UAE)	Indonesia
School with ability grouping for all subjects	***OECD***	Czech Republic, Denmark, Portugal, Slovak Republic	Australia, Greece, Japan		United States
		OECD average change in score: -3.0		OECD average change in score: -1.5	
	Partner		Kyrgyzstan		Panama

Note: Only those school systems where there is a statistically significant relationship between school policies for selecting and grouping students and reading performance are listed. OECD averages in bold denote that the estimate is statistically significant at the 5% level (p<0.05).
Source: OECD, *PISA 2009 Database*. Tables IV.2.2b and IV.2.2c.
StatLink http://dx.doi.org/10.1787/888932343380

School systems that transfer students to other schools more frequently also tend to show a stronger relationship between students' socio-economic background and performance, even after accounting for countries' national income (Figure IV.2.1a). This suggests that transferring students tends to be associated with socio-economic segregation in school systems, where students from socio-economically advantaged backgrounds end up in higher-performing schools while students from disadvantaged backgrounds end up in lower-performing schools. Within schools, however, transferring students leads to more homogeneous student populations, and the effect of students' socio-economic background on performance is mitigated. Not surprisingly, therefore, in these types of systems, PISA shows levels of socio-economic inequity *between* schools to be relatively larger than levels of inequity *within* schools. Within a system, when the proportion of schools that transfer students is 10 percentage points higher, the score point difference associated with 1 unit difference in the socio-economic background of schools is +5.1 points, while the score point difference associated with 1 unit increase in students' socio-economic background is -2.5 points[6] (Table IV.2.3). In other words, within schools, the positive effect of transfers is outweighed by the negative effect on inequalities between schools.

Figure IV.2.2 shows that in school systems with low rates of student transfers, school principals tend to report that schools have more responsibility for establishing student assessment policies, deciding which courses are offered, determining course content and choosing textbooks. Across OECD countries, 20% of the variation in rates of student transfers is related to the differences in the *index of school responsibility for curriculum and assessment.* One hypothesis to explain this relationship is that school systems with fewer options to transfer students use other instruments to work with struggling students and that they have the autonomy to do so.

■ Figure IV.2.2 ■

School systems with low transfer rates tend to give more autonomy to schools to determine curricula and assessments

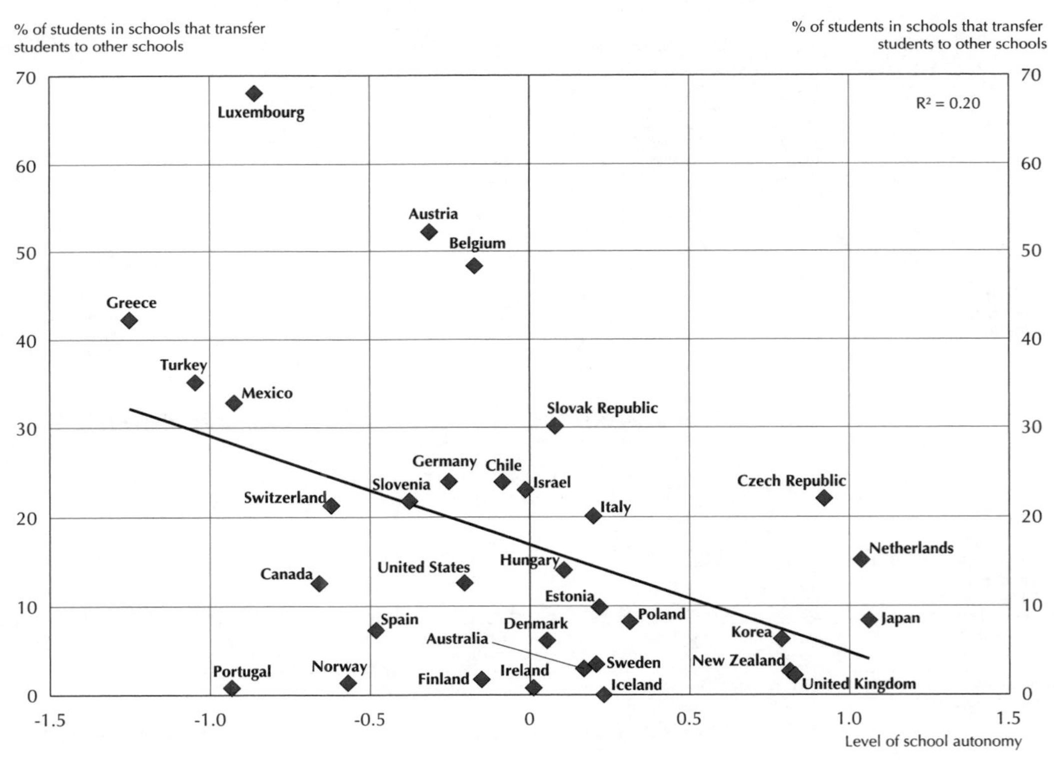

Note: The level of school autonomy is measured by the index of school responsibility for curriculum and assessment. Positive values indicate greater autonomy.
Source: OECD, *PISA 2009 Database*, Tables IV.3.3a and IV.3.6.
StatLink http://dx.doi.org/10.1787/888932343380

On average across OECD countries, school policies and practices for selecting and grouping students solely account for 2.6% of the performance variation among schools. This percentage is especially high in Israel and the partner countries Argentina, Panama, Trinidad and Tobago, and Tunisia (Figure IV.2.3 and Table IV.2.2a). Much of the relationship between how schools select and group students and performance is also related to the socio-economic and demographic backgrounds of students and schools. On average across OECD countries, 9.6% of the variation in student performance is jointly related to both schools' policies on selecting and grouping students and on socio-economic and demographic background. This joint portion is particularly large in Luxembourg, Turkey, Chile, Hungary and Italy, and the partner countries Trinidad and Tobago, Argentina, Uruguay and Peru. In these countries, policies on selecting and grouping students are closely related to socio-economic disparities in the school system.

Box IV.2.1 **How to interpret the figures**

Figures IV.2.3, IV.2.5, IV.2.7, IV.2.9, IV.2.11 and IV.2.13 in this chapter analyse the extent to which variation in student performance is related to a particular school characteristic. Their values are extracted from Tables IV.2.2a, IV.2.4a, IV.2.9a, IV.2.12a, IV.2.13a and IV.2.14a, respectively.

Figure IV.2.3, for example, examines different aspects of schools' policies and practices on selecting and grouping students (see Table IV.2.2b for the different aspects included). The total length of the bar to the right of the vertical line represents between-school variation in student performance for each country. The longer the bar, the greater the differences in student performance among schools.

For example, Figure IV.2.3 considers the extent to which between-school variation can be explained by differences in schools' policies and practices on selecting and grouping students, either independently of students' and schools' socio-economic and demographic background (light blue) or jointly with those factors (dark blue). This means that the total length of the two sections (light blue and dark blue combined) present the overall variation attributable to schools' policies and practices on selecting and grouping students.

The variation jointly accounted for by both schools' policies, practices and resources, and students' and schools' socio-economic and demographic background (dark blue) provides an indication of the extent to which school policies, practices and resources are inequitably distributed according to students' and schools' socio-economic and demographic profiles.

The figure also shows the amount of variation attributable to socio-economic and demographic background independent of schools' policies and practices on selecting and grouping students (dark grey), and the amount of variation that is not attributable either to socio-economic and demographic background or to schools' policies and practices on selecting and grouping students (light grey) (see Table IV.2.2c for the socio-economic and demographic aspects included).

The variation in performance is presented as a percentage of the average variation in student performance across OECD countries, so that performance differences can be compared across all participating countries and economies. The OECD average variation in student performance is set to 100%.

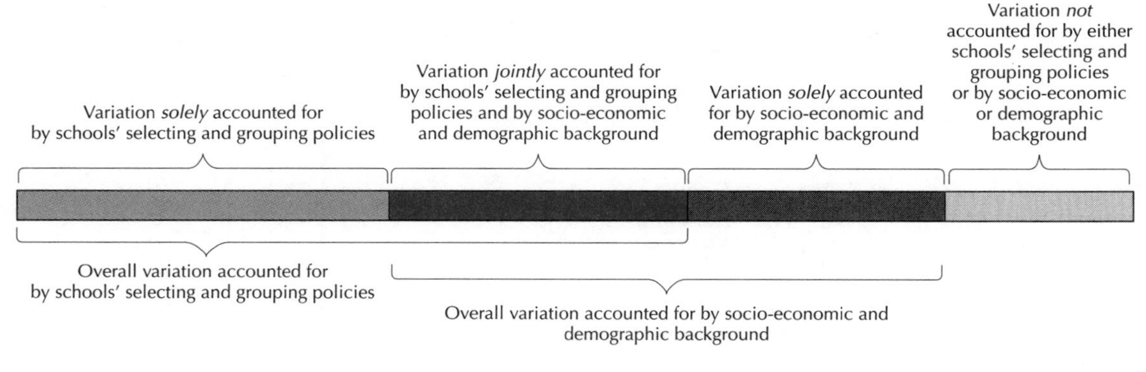

■ Figure IV.2.3 ■

How school policies for selecting and grouping students are related to reading performance

Expressed as a percentage of the average variance in reading performance in OECD countries (100% is the average total variance in reading performance across OECD countries)

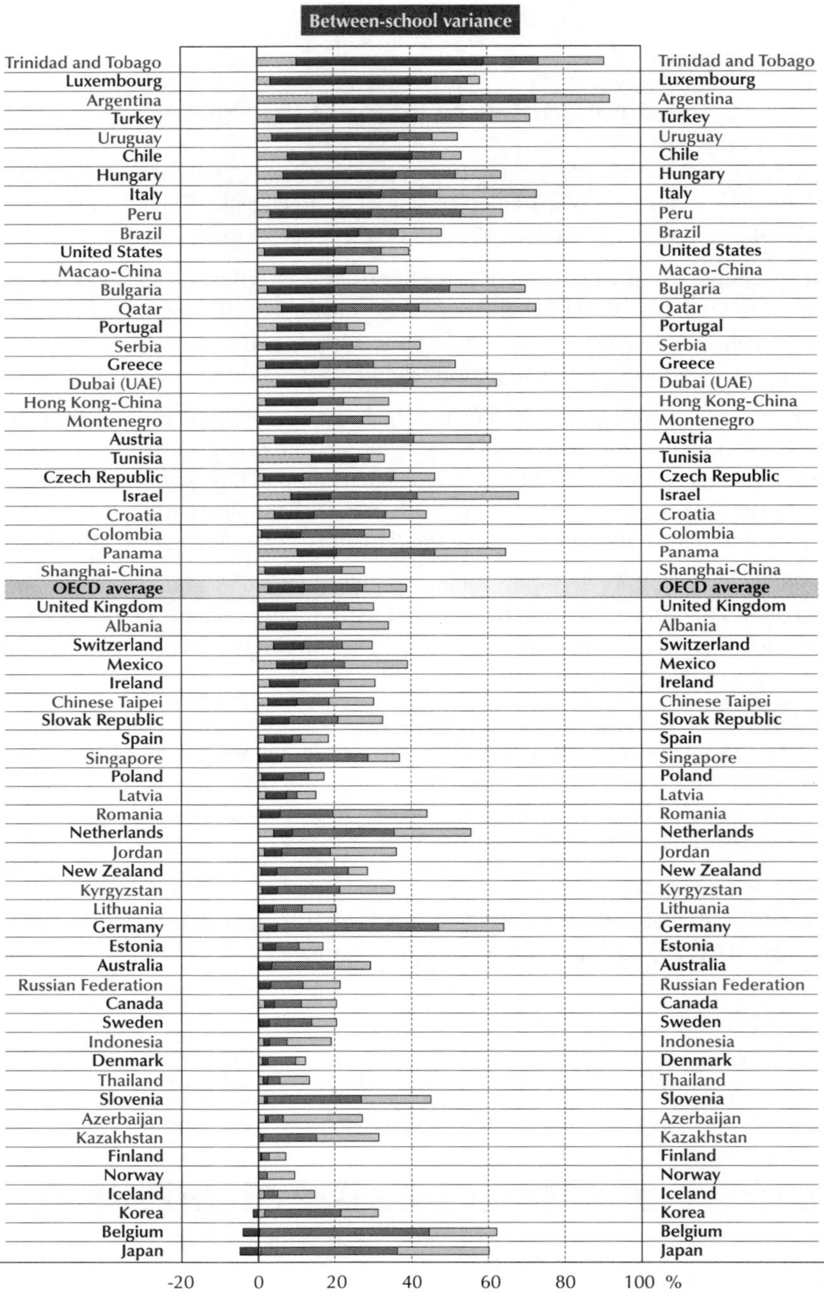

Countries are ranked in descending order of the variance jointly accounted for.

Source: OECD, *PISA 2009 Database*, Table IV.2.2a.

StatLink http://dx.doi.org/10.1787/888932343380

How the governance of school systems is related to student performance

Another important organisational feature of school systems is the extent to which parents and students can choose the school they attend and the degree to which schools are considered autonomous entities that make organisational decisions independently of district, regional or national entities. "Exit", "voice" and "loyalty" are three options available to consumers when they face insufficient or deteriorating quality of goods or services. These options are also commonly used to explain or justify school choice. As applied to school choice, "exit" offers parents the possibility to select or choose a school other than the one assigned to their child; "voice" refers to parents' opportunities to influence or change their child's school; and "loyalty" indicates that parents either might not have "exit" or "voice" options, or choose not to exercise them. School choice and parent voice are, of course, inextricably linked. When school choice is limited, there is likely to be more parent voice. Similarly, when there are ample opportunities for "voice", fewer parents are likely to "exit" and choose another school for their children.

Since the early 1980s, educational reforms in many countries have intended to improve the quality of instruction in schools by offering a greater diversity of courses, greater autonomy for schools to respond to local needs, and more choice for parents. Yet some of the assumptions underlying such reforms have been called into question (Schneider, Teske and Marschall, 2002; Hess and Loveless, 2005; Berends and Zottola, 2009). It is unclear, for example, whether parents have the necessary information to choose the best schools for their children. It is also unclear whether parents always give sufficient priority to the quality of the school when making these choices. Also school choice may lead to the unintended racial/ethnic or socio-economic segregation of schools (Gewirtz, 1995; Whitty and Halpin, 1998; Karsten, 1999; Viteritti, 1999; Plank and Sykes, 2003; Hsieh and Urquiola, 2006; Heyneman, 2009; Bunar, 2010a; Bunar, 2010b).

This section explores related areas of the governance of school systems and school performance. Chapter 3 provides a more detailed discussion of how school autonomy and school choice is arranged across school systems.

School autonomy and performance

Cross-country analysis of PISA suggests that the prevalence of schools' autonomy to define and elaborate their curricula and assessments relates positively to the performance of school systems, even after accounting for national income (Figure IV.2.4a). School systems that provide schools with greater discretion in deciding student-assessment policies, the courses offered, the course content and the textbooks used are also school systems that perform at higher levels in reading.[7] In contrast, greater responsibility in managing resources appears to be unrelated to a school system's overall student performance.

The positive relationship between schools' autonomy in defining and elaborating its curricula and assessment policies and student performance that is observed at the level of the education system can play out differently within countries (Figure IV.2.4b). For example, after accounting for the socio-economic background of students and schools, and for other factors related to school autonomy and school competition, schools in the Netherlands, Switzerland and Belgium that have more autonomy in defining their curricula and assessment practices also show higher performance. In contrast, schools in Luxembourg and Italy that have higher levels of autonomy regarding curricular decisions show lower reading scores when compared with schools with lower autonomy in this area. Among the partner countries and economies, Dubai (UAE) and Lithuania show a positive relationship between schools that have higher levels of curricular autonomy and higher performance. In Bulgaria, Argentina, Chinese Taipei, Peru and Shanghai-China, schools with greater autonomy show poorer student performance. Local responsibility for designing curricula, therefore, seems to be positively related to the performance of the school systems, but not always to the performance of individual schools. There are various explanations for these different patterns within countries. For example, more autonomous schools may perform better because countries may deliberately provide better-performing schools with more discretion, while imposing more constraints and regulation on lower-performing schools. Conversely, more autonomous schools may perform worse where these schools cater to lower-performing students who did not obtain access to more prestigious public programmes.

While there is a clear relationship between the degree of curricular autonomy a school system offers its schools and the system's performance, this relationship is less clear when the degree of autonomy in allocating resources is analysed through measures such as: selecting teachers for hire, dismissing teachers, establishing teachers' starting salaries, determining teachers' salary increases, formulating the school budget, and deciding on budget allocations within the school. The absence of a clear relationship could result from autonomy in allocating resources changing the ways in which resources are distributed, which, in turn, may benefit some schools but not necessarily improve the system's

overall performance. The relationship between a school's performance and its autonomy in allocating resources also differs by country. In Greece, Korea and Chile, schools that have greater autonomy in allocating resources also achieve higher scores in reading, even after students' and schools' socio-economic backgrounds are taken into account. In contrast, in Switzerland, schools that have greater autonomy in allocating resources show lower scores. Among the partner countries and economies, schools with greater autonomy in allocating resources show higher levels of student performance in Peru, but lower levels in Croatia, Kyrgyzstan, Colombia and Thailand (Figure IV.2.4b).

Within countries, the relationship between the autonomy of schools in allocating resources and learning outcomes is related to systems' accountability arrangements in important ways. For example, information on the results of external examinations and assessments often provides an important framework for the autonomy of schools by providing a basis for schools and parents to make appropriate decisions for students (Fuchs and Woessmann, 2007). Data from PISA show that in school systems where most schools post achievement data publicly, there is a positive relationship between school autonomy in resource allocation and student performance. In particular, in school systems in the OECD that have no schools posting achievement data publicly, after students' and schools' socio-economic background are taken into account, a student who attends a school with greater autonomy in allocating resources than the average OECD school[8] tends to perform 3.2 points lower in reading than a student attending a school with an average level of autonomy. In contrast, in a school system where all schools post achievement data publicly, a student who attends a school with above-average autonomy scores 2.6 points higher in reading than a student attending a school with an average level of autonomy (Table IV.2.5).

School choice and performance

The degree of competition among schools is one way to measure school choice. Competition among schools is intended to provide incentives for schools to innovate and create more effective learning environments. However, cross-country correlations of PISA do not show a relationship between the degree of competition and student performance. Among school systems in the OECD countries, the proportion of schools that compete with other schools for student enrolment seems unrelated to the school system's overall student performance, with or without accounting for socio-economic background (Figure IV.2.4a).

Within countries, a positive relationship is often evident between the degree of school competition and schools' performance when the backgrounds of students and schools are not taken into account. In these cases, schools that compete for enrolment perform 15 points higher, on average across the OECD, than schools that do not compete for enrolment. In Canada, the Czech Republic, Germany, Italy, Mexico, Poland, Portugal, the Slovak Republic, Spain, Turkey and the partner countries and economies Bulgaria, Hong Kong-China, Kyrgyzstan, Peru and Trinidad and Tobago, schools that compete for enrolment perform better when the backgrounds of students and schools are not taken into account. However, in all of these countries and economies except Germany and Turkey, the positive relationship between school competition and student performance is no longer statistically significant when the socio-economic background of students and schools is accounted for (Figure IV.2.4b and Table IV.2.4c).

The fact that the positive relationship between school competition and performance is no longer apparent[9] after accounting for the socio-economic background of students and schools may reflect the fact that socio-economically advantaged students, who tend to achieve higher scores (see Volume II, *Overcoming Social Background*), are also more likely to attend schools that compete for enrolment, even after accounting for location and attendance in private schools (Table IV.2.6). Also, privileged schools may tend to compete more in order to attract high-performing students, who tend to be socio-economically advantaged.

Why are socio-economically advantaged students more likely to attend schools that compete for enrolment? To understand differences in how parents choose schools for their children, PISA asked parents a series of questions regarding school choice in the questionnaire, which was distributed in eight OECD countries. On average, socio-economically disadvantaged parents are over 13 percentage points more likely than advantaged parents to report that they considered "low expenses" and "financial aid" to be very important determining factors in choosing a school (Table IV.2.7). While parents from all backgrounds cite academic achievement as an important consideration when choosing a school for their children, socio-economically advantaged parents are, on average, 10 percentage points more likely than disadvantaged parents to cite that consideration as "very important". These differences suggest that socio-economically disadvantaged parents consider that they have more limited choices of schools for their children because of financial constraints. If children from socio-economically disadvantaged backgrounds cannot attend high-performing schools because of financial constraints, then school systems that offer parents more school choices for their children will necessarily be less effective in improving the performance of all students.

The extent to which schools compete with each other for enrolment can be related to equity. Research has shown that school choice – and, by extension, school competition – is related to greater levels of segregation in the school system and, consequently, lower levels of equity (Gewirtz, 1995; Whitty and Halpin, 1998; Karsten, 1999; Viteritti, 1999; Plank and Sykes, 2003; Hsieh and Urquiola, 2006; Heyneman, 2009; Bunar, 2010a; Bunar, 2010b). Table IV.2.1 shows the cross-country correlation between the percentage of schools that compete with each other and the between- and within-school gradients of the *PISA index of economic, social and cultural status*. The between-school gradient shows the strength of the relationship between the school's average socio-economic background and school performance, while the within-school gradient depicts the average strength of the same relationship within schools. If, as suggested by the literature, school competition produces socio-economic segregation among schools, the correlation between school competition and the between-school gradient should be positive and the correlation with the within-school gradient should be non-existent or negative. This is also what the results from PISA show: a greater prevalence of school competition is related to a stronger relationship between a school's average socio-economic background and the school's average student performance. For example, education systems that have an additional 10 percentage points of schools competing for students in the same area tend to show a stronger relationship between a school's performance and its socio-economic profile (*i.e.* a 2.8 score point difference corresponding to 1 unit on the *PISA index of the economic, social and cultural status* of the school) (Table IV.2.8).

Does the existence of private schools in a system make a difference in overall performance? In PISA, private schools are those that are independently managed and operated, irrespective of whether they are publicly or privately funded.[10] The results from PISA suggest that the proportion of private schools in a school system is unrelated to the system's overall performance (Figure IV.2.4a).

Within OECD countries, on average, students who attend private schools perform 25 score points higher in reading than students who attend public schools (Figure IV.2.4b and Table IV.2.4b). This relationship holds in 15 OECD countries. However, students who attend private schools are also from more advantaged socio-economic backgrounds, so part of the positive relationship between private schools and performance is due to the socio-economic characteristics of the school and students, rather than to an advantage intrinsic in private schools. After accounting for the socio-economic and demographic characteristics of students and schools, the OECD average is reduced to 3.4 score points and is no longer statistically significant (Table IV.2.4c). In fact, of the 15 OECD countries that show a positive relationship between attendance in private schools and performance, only 3 show a clear advantage in attending private school: in Slovenia, Canada and Ireland, students of similar backgrounds who attend private schools score at least 24 points higher in the reading assessment than students who attend public schools. In contrast, in Japan and the United Kingdom, students from similar backgrounds who attend private schools score at least 31 points lower than students who attend public schools. In Japan, a common explanation for this outcome is that some students who cannot attend public schools known for their high performance may opt for private schools as a second choice.

All this said, even though there may be no performance advantage for private schools after accounting for socio-economic background, private schools may still be an attractive alternative for parents who want to capitalise on the socio-economic advantages that these schools offer, including student peers from advantaged backgrounds, additional resources or the better policies and practices that are often found in more socio-economically advantaged schools.

The proportion of private schools in a school system is also unrelated to the system's level of equity in education (Figure IV.2.4a). On average across OECD countries, a very low proportion of the variation in performance is explained by differences in how schools are governed. Only 1% of the performance variation is attributable solely to differences in how schools are governed and 5% is attributable to both the governance of schools and socio-economic background (Figure IV.2.5 and Table IV.2.4a). Thus, most of the weak relationship between performance differences and differences in the governance of schools is related to differences in socio-economic background among schools. This suggests that socio-economically advantaged schools tend to compete with other schools in the same area for students or they are managed privately.

The proportion of performance variation between schools that is attributable both to how schools are governed and to socio-economic backgrounds is 15 percentage points or higher in Turkey, Luxembourg, Chile, the United States and the partner countries Peru, Uruguay, Argentina, Panama and Brazil. In these school systems, positive relationships between school governance and performance are closely related to the socio-economic disparities in the school system (Table IV.2.4a).

■ Figure IV.2.4a ■

How the governance of school systems is related to educational outcomes

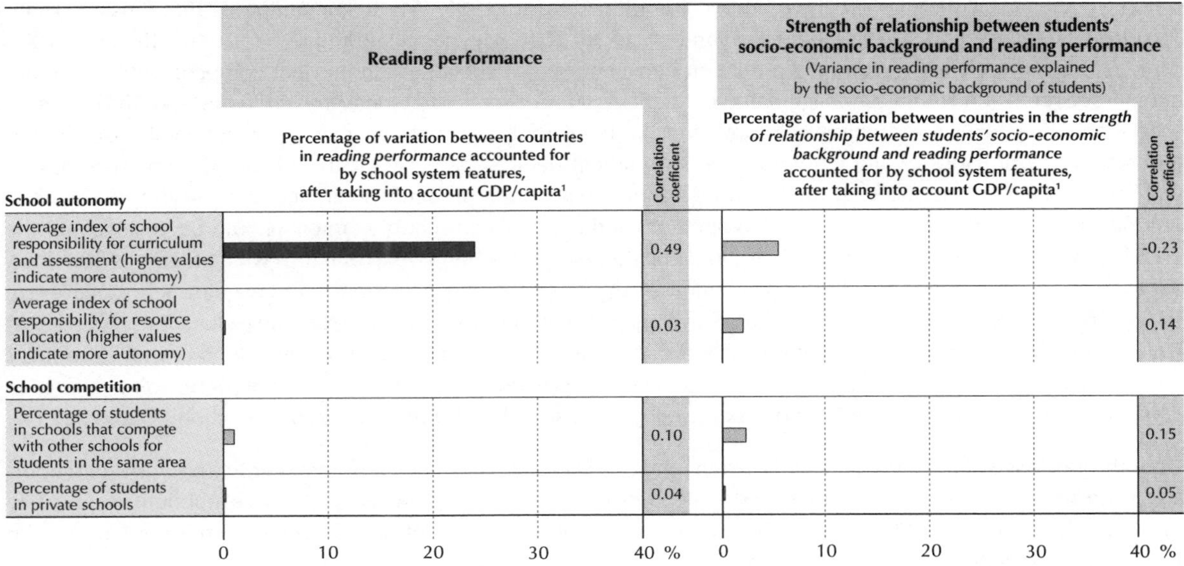

Note: Correlations that are statistically significant at the 5% level (p<0.05) are marked in a darker tone.
1. The percentage is obtained by squaring the correlation coefficient and then multiplying it by 100.
Source: OECD, *PISA 2009 Database*, Table IV.2.1.
StatLink http://dx.doi.org/10.1787/888932343380

■ Figure IV.2.4b ■

Countries in which school governance is related to reading performance

School governance (the model includes all of these features of school governance)		Without accounting for the socio-economic and demographic background of students and schools: Negative relationship	Without accounting: Positive relationship	With accounting for the socio-economic and demographic background of students and schools: Negative relationship	With accounting: Positive relationship
Index of school responsibility for curriculum and assessment (higher values indicate more autonomy)	*OECD*	Austria, Germany	Luxembourg, Portugal, Switzerland	Italy, Luxembourg	Belgium, Netherlands, Switzerland
		OECD average change in score: 1.6		OECD average change in score: -1.0	
	Partner	Argentina, Bulgaria, Kazakhstan, Panama, Peru, Serbia, Shanghai-China	Dubai (UAE)	Argentina, Bulgaria, Peru, Shanghai-China, Chinese Taipei	Dubai (UAE), Lithuania
Index of school responsibility for resource allocation (higher values indicate more autonomy)	*OECD*	Estonia, Switzerland	Chile, Germany, Greece, Korea, Luxembourg, Spain	Switzerland	Chile, Greece, Korea
		OECD average change in score: 10.8		**OECD average change in score: 5.8**	
	Partner	Albania, Azerbaijan, Croatia	Argentina, Peru, Singapore	Colombia, Croatia, Kyrgyzstan, Thailand	Peru
School competes with other schools for students in the same area	*OECD*	United Kingdom	Canada, Czech Republic, Germany, Italy, Mexico, Poland, Portugal, Slovak Republic, Spain, Turkey	Australia, Denmark, Korea	Germany, Turkey
		OECD average change in score: 14.9		OECD average change in score: 0.9	
	Partner		Bulgaria, Hong Kong-China, Kyrgyzstan, Peru, Trinidad and Tobago	Argentina, Brazil, Colombia, Macao-China, Chinese Taipei	
Private school	*OECD*	Luxembourg	Australia, Austria, Canada, Chile, Czech Republic, Estonia, Hungary, Ireland, Mexico, New Zealand, Poland, Slovenia, Spain, Sweden, United Kingdom, United States	Japan, United Kingdom	Canada, Ireland, Slovenia
		OECD average change in score: 26.6		OECD average change in score: 3.4	
	Partner	Indonesia, Trinidad and Tobago, Tunisia	Albania, Argentina, Brazil, Colombia, Jordan, Kyrgyzstan, Panama, Peru, Qatar, Uruguay	Hong Kong-China, Kazakhstan, Chinese Taipei, Tunisia	Argentina, Colombia, Kyrgyzstan, Qatar

Note: Only those school systems where there is a statistically significant relationship between school governance and reading performance are listed. OECD averages in bold denote that the estimate is statistically significant at the 5% level (p<0.05).
Source: OECD, *PISA 2009 Database.*, Tables IV.2.4b and IV.2.4c.
StatLink http://dx.doi.org/10.1787/888932343380

■ Figure IV.2.5 ■

How the governance of schools is related to reading performance

Expressed as a percentage of the average variance in reading performance in OECD countries (100% is the average total variance in reading performance across OECD countries)

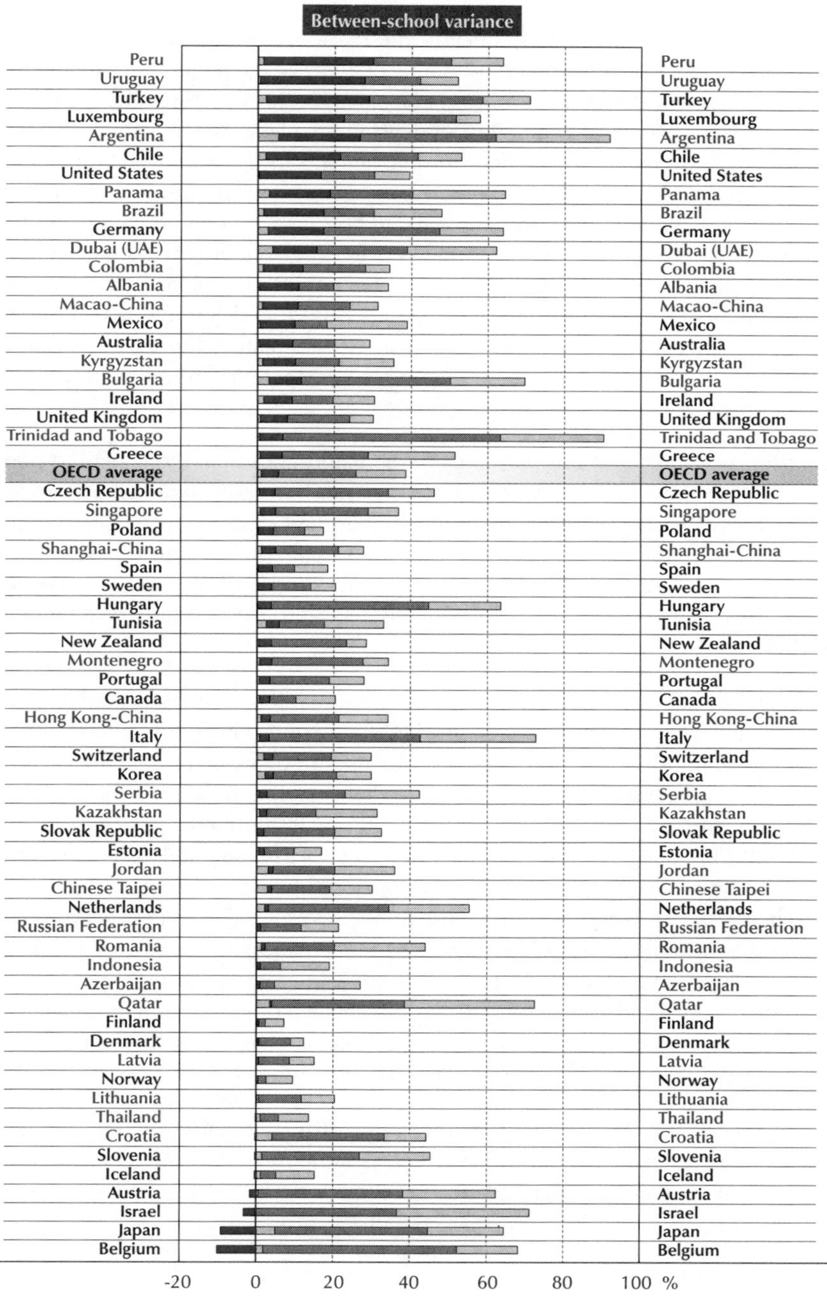

Countries are ranked in descending order of the variance jointly accounted for.

Source: OECD, *PISA 2009 Database*, Table IV.2.4a.

StatLink http://dx.doi.org/10.1787/888932343380

How assessment and accountability policies are related to student performance

The shift in public and government thinking from mere control over the resources and content of education towards a focus on outcomes has, in many countries, resulted in the development of standards to measure the quality of educational institutions. Countries' approaches to standard-setting range from defining broad educational goals to formulating concise performance expectations in well-defined subject areas. Setting these standards has, in turn, often led to the establishment of accountability systems. Over the last decade, assessments of student performance have become common in many OECD countries, and the results are often widely reported and used to inform both specialised and public debate. However, the rationale for assessments and the nature of the instruments used vary greatly within and across countries. OECD countries, for example, use different forms of external assessments, external evaluations or inspections, as well as individual schools' self-evaluations.

One aspect relating to accountability systems concerns the existence of standards-based external examinations. These are examinations that focus on a specific school subject and assess a major portion of what students studying this subject are expected to know or be able to do (Bishop, 1998, 2001).[11] Essentially, they define performance relative to an external standard, not relative to other students in the classroom or school. Perhaps more important, such examinations usually have real consequences for the students' progression or certification in the education systems. PISA asked school principals whether they use standardised tests to measure student learning. These standardised tests, which may be voluntary and implemented by schools, often only have indirect consequences for students. For teachers, standardised assessments may provide valuable information on students' learning needs and may be used to tailor their instruction accordingly. In some countries, such as Brazil, Hungary, Italy, Malaysia, Mexico, Poland and the Slovak Republic, such tests are also used to determine teachers' salaries or to guide professional development (OECD, 2009b). At the school level, information from standardised tests can be used to determine the allocation of additional resources, and what interventions are required to establish performance targets and to monitor progress.

Across OECD countries, countries that use standards-based external examinations tend to perform higher, even when accounting for national income:[12] students in school systems that use standards-based external examinations perform, on average across OECD countries, 16 points higher than students in school systems that do not use these examinations (Figure IV.2.6a).[13] In contrast, there is no measurable relationship between the prevalence of standardised tests and the performance of school systems, and that also holds for most countries at the school level (Figure IV.2.6b). This may be because, in part, the content and use of standardised tests vary considerably across schools and systems.

PISA also examined whether student achievement data is posted publicly, communicated to parents, used to make decisions regarding the allocation of resources, or tracked by administrative authorities. Across school systems, there is no measurable relationship between these various uses of assessment data for accountability purposes and the performance of school systems (Figure IV.2.6a). When looking at this relationship within countries, the pattern is mixed, but on average across OECD countries, the within-country relationship is positive for some measures (Figure IV.2.6b). This may be because policies on the use of assessment data differ greatly across countries. A somewhat consistent pattern emerges, however, in the relationship between schools that post achievement data publicly and those schools' performance. Schools whose principals report that student achievement data are posted publicly perform better than schools whose achievement data is not made publicly available in seven OECD countries and in nine partner countries and economies. However, since in most of these countries the schools that post achievement data publicly tend to be socio-economically advantaged schools, this performance advantage remains visible only in Turkey and the partner countries and economies Romania, Chinese Taipei, Colombia, Kyrgyzstan and Hong Kong-China, once socio-economic background is accounted for (Figure IV.2.6b).

On average across OECD countries, 2% of the performance variation is attributable solely to various aspects of schools' assessment and accountability practices, but a further 4% is attributable to both assessment and accountability practices, and the socio-economic and demographic background of students and schools (Figure IV.2.7 and Table IV.2.9a).

Although the use of standardised tests tends to be unrelated to school performance, it does relate to levels of equity within school systems. School systems that have high proportions of students in schools that use standardised tests tend to show a lower impact of socio-economic background on learning outcomes between schools and a higher impact of socio-economic background on learning outcomes within schools (Table IV.2.1).[14]

■ Figure IV.2.6a ■

How school systems' assessment and accountability policies are related to educational outcomes

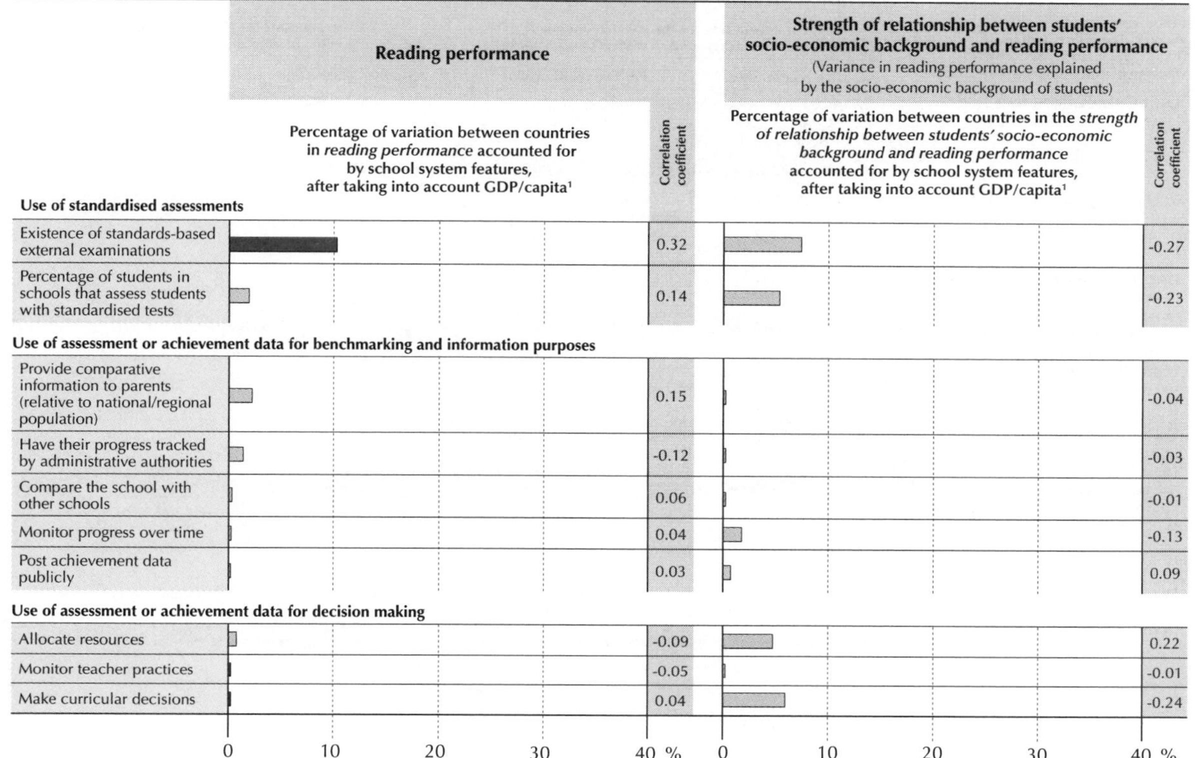

Note: Correlations that are statistically significant at the 10% level (p<0.10) are marked in a darker tone.
1. The percentage is obtained by squaring the correlation coefficient and then multiplying it by 100.
Source: OECD, *PISA 2009 Database*, Table IV.2.1.
StatLink http://dx.doi.org/10.1787/888932343380

Critics of the use of standardised tests that are based on student performance levels rather than on individual student progress argue that these may reinforce the advantages of schools that serve students from socio-economically advantaged backgrounds (Ladd and Walsh, 2002; Downey, Von Hippel and Hughes, 2008). In addition, teachers may respond strategically to accountability measures by sorting out or retaining disadvantaged students (Jacob, 2005; Jennings, 2005). However, while the results from PISA support the notion that the prevalence of testing is related to socio-economic inequities *within* schools, the higher level of socio-economic equalities *between* schools in school systems that use standardised tests is much greater than socio-economic inequities within schools (Table IV.2.10). One explanation for the positive association between the prevalence of standardised tests and improved equity in school systems is that such tests provide schools with instruments to compare themselves with other schools. This, in turn, allows schools to observe the inequities among schools, which could be considered the first step towards redressing them. The results from PISA also show higher levels of socio-economic equity in school systems that use achievement data to make decisions about the curriculum and track achievement data over time.

How resources invested in education are related to student performance

Effective schools require the right combination of trained and talented personnel, appropriate curricula, adequate facilities and motivated students who are ready to learn. At the same time, demands for investments in education need to be balanced against other demands on public expenditure and the overall burden of taxation. As discussed in Chapter 3, school systems differ in the amount of time, human, material and financial resources they invest in education. Equally important, school systems also vary in how these resources are spent.

■ Figure IV.2.6b ■

Countries in which school assessment and accountability policies are related to reading performance

School assessment and accountability policies (the model includes all of these assessment and accountability policies)		Without accounting for the socio-economic and demographic background of students and schools		With accounting for the socio-economic and demographic background of students and schools	
		Negative relationship	**Positive relationship**	**Negative relationship**	**Positive relationship**
Use of standardised tests	*OECD*	Austria, Belgium, Chile, Germany, Italy, United Kingdom, United States	Hungary, Portugal, Slovak Republic	Austria, Belgium	
		OECD average change in score: -3.0		OECD average change in score: -1.2	
	Partner	Bulgaria, Jordan, Singapore	Azerbaijan, Colombia, Hong Kong-China, Lithuania, Shanghai-China, Uruguay		Azerbaijan, Hong Kong-China, Shanghai-China
Use of assessment or achievement data: Provide information to parents (benchmark students to national or regional populations)	*OECD*	Slovak Republic, Switzerland	Turkey	Hungary, Slovak Republic, Switzerland	
		OECD average change in score: 0.7		OECD average change in score: -1.4	
	Partner	Brazil, Dubai (UAE), Jordan, Kazakhstan, Qatar, Chinese Taipei	Montenegro, Trinidad and Tobago	Jordan, Latvia, Qatar	Hong Kong-China, Montenegro
Use of assessment or achievement data: Have their progress tracked by administrative authorities	*OECD*	Denmark, Ireland, Slovenia, United Kingdom, United States	Austria, Norway, Switzerland	Luxembourg	Germany, Japan, Norway, Switzerland, United Kingdom
		OECD average change in score: -1.4		OECD average change in score: 2.7	
	Partner		Brazil, Lithuania, Russian Federation	Singapore	Panama, Peru, Romania, Russian Federation, Chinese Taipei
Use of assessment or achievement data: Compare to other schools	*OECD*	Chile	Austria, Denmark, Germany, Greece, Japan, Spain, Turkey	Australia, Chile	Austria, Greece, Switzerland
		OECD average change in score: **5.5**		OECD average change in score: 1.8	
	Partner	Albania, Brazil, Colombia, Indonesia, Kyrgyzstan, Russian Federation, Chinese Taipei, Uruguay	Jordan, Trinidad and Tobago, Tunisia	Indonesia, Kyrgyzstan, Panama, Chinese Taipei	Azerbaijan, Tunisia
Use of assessment or achievement data: Monitor school's progress	*OECD*	Australia, Switzerland, Turkey	Chile, Czech Republic, Mexico, United States	Austria, Finland, Korea, United Kingdom	Sweden, United States
		OECD average change in score: 0.1		OECD average change in score: -2.1	
	Partner	Hong Kong-China, Lithuania	Albania, Kazakhstan, Peru	Lithuania, Serbia	Albania, Bulgaria, Kazakhstan, Montenegro
Use of assessment or achievement data: Post achievement data publicly	*OECD*		Australia, Germany, Greece, Italy, Slovak Republic, Slovenia, Turkey	Switzerland	Turkey
		OECD average change in score: **13.7**		OECD Average change in score: **4.0**	
	Partner	Argentina, Azerbaijan, Kazakhstan, Montenegro, Qatar	Albania, Colombia, Croatia, Hong Kong-China, Kyrgyzstan, Lithuania, Peru, Romania, Chinese Taipei	Azerbaijan, Kazakhstan, Qatar	Colombia, Hong Kong-China, Kyrgyzstan, Romania, Chinese Taipei
Use of assessment or achievement data: Allocate resources	*OECD*	Canada, Italy, Japan			
		OECD average change in score: **-6.6**		OECD average change in score: -5.2	
	Partner	Albania		Colombia, Macao-China, Chinese Taipei	Hong Kong-China
Use of assessment or achievement data: Monitor teacher practices	*OECD*	Belgium, Hungary	Netherlands		Australia, Netherlands
		OECD average change in score: -2.5		OECD average change in score: -3.0	
	Partner	Azerbaijan, Dubai (UAE), Hong Kong-China, Lithuania, Tunisia	Peru, Chinese Taipei	Azerbaijan, Hong Kong-China, Tunisia	Chinese Taipei
Use of assessment or achievement data: Make curricular decisions	*OECD*	Italy	Denmark		
		OECD average change in score: 0.9		OECD average change in score: 1.0	
	Partner	Bulgaria, Colombia, Hong Kong-China, Qatar, Shanghai-China	Chinese Taipei	Serbia, Shanghai-China	

Note: Only those school systems where there is a statistically significant relationship between school assessment and accountability policies and reading performance are listed. OECD averages in bold denote that the estimate is statistically significant at the 5% level (p<0.05).
Source: OECD, *PISA 2009 Database*. Tables IV.2.9b and IV.2.9c.
StatLink http://dx.doi.org/10.1787/888932343380

■ Figure IV.2.7 ■

How schools' assessment and accountability policies are related to reading performance

Expressed as a percentage of the average variance in reading performance in OECD countries (100% is the average total variance in reading performance across OECD countries)

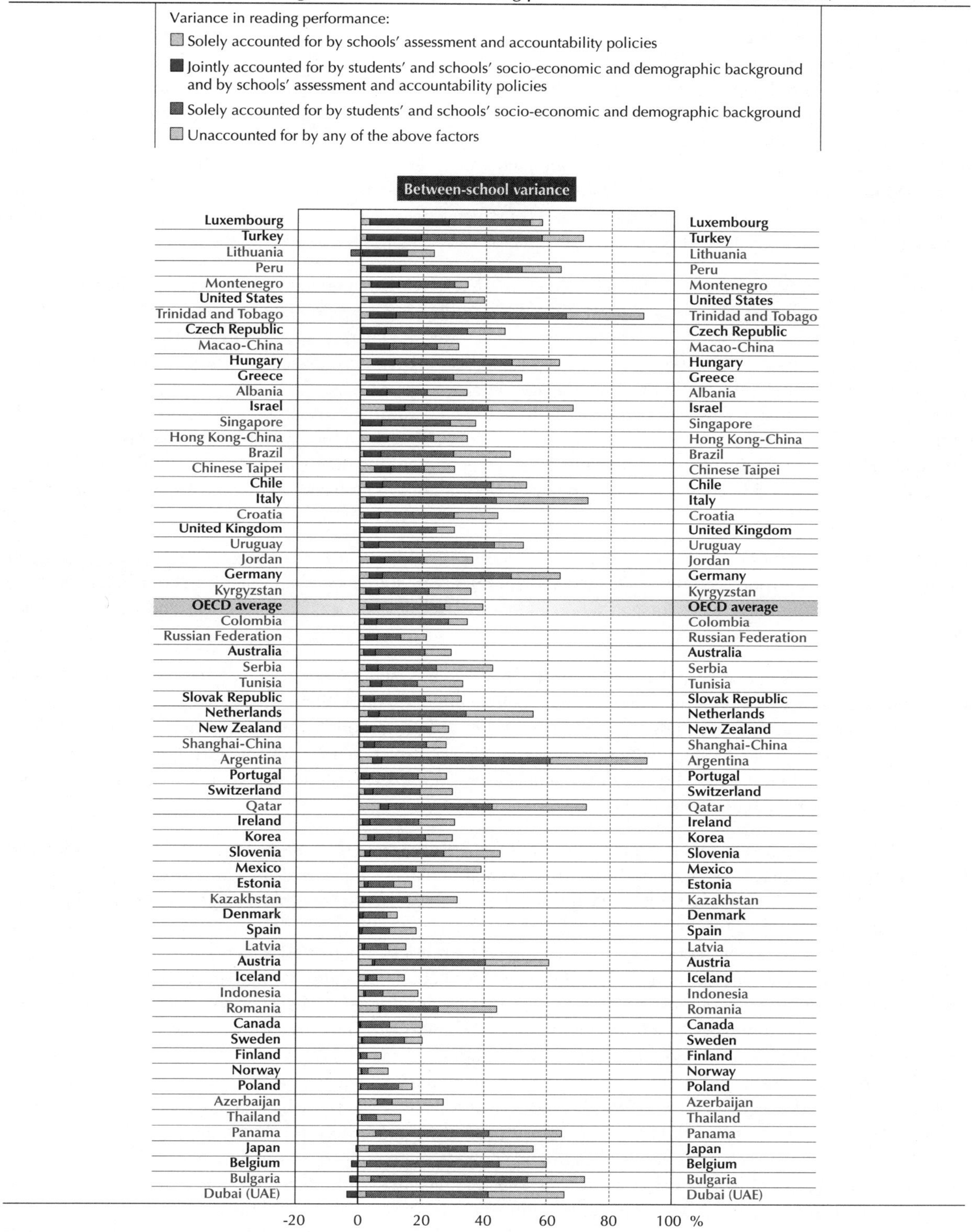

Countries are ranked in descending order of the variance jointly accounted for.
Source: OECD, *PISA 2009 Database*, Table IV.2.9a.
StatLink http://dx.doi.org/10.1787/888932343380

Yet, research usually shows a weak relationship between educational resources and student performance, with more variation explained by the quality of human resources (*i.e.* teachers and school principals) than by material and financial resources, particularly among industrialised nations (Fuller, 1987; Greenwald, Hedges and Laine, 1996; Buchmann and Hannum, 2001; Rivkin, Hanushek and Kain, 2005).

The generally weak relationship between resources and performance observed in past research is also seen in PISA. At the level of the education system, accounting for the level of national income, the only type of resource that PISA shows to be correlated with student performance is the level of teachers' salaries relative to national income (Figure IV.2.8).[15] As shown in Chapter 3, teachers' salaries are related to class size in that if spending levels are similar, school systems often make trade-offs between smaller classes and higher salaries for teachers. The findings from PISA suggest that teachers' salaries are correlated with overall performance, such that school systems that choose to invest in higher salaries for teachers show higher-than-average student performance. This is consistent with school-effects research that underscores the cost-effectiveness of investing in teacher quality rather than in reducing class size (Greenwald, Hedges and Laine, 1996; Rivkin, Hanushek and Kain, 2005).

Within school systems, where relationships between resources invested in education and reading performance are observed, they are typically closely associated with corresponding socio-economic differences: socio-economically advantaged schools also tend to be schools with better educational resources. Across OECD countries, and considering aspects that relate to class size, instruction time, participation in after-school lessons, availability of extra-curricular activities, and the school principal's perception of teacher shortages and a lack of material resources that adversely affects instruction, only 5% of the variation in student performance is attributable solely to the differences in the educational resources available to the schools. In contrast, 18% of the variation in student performance is attributable jointly to spending on education and the socio-economic and demographic background of students and schools (Figure IV.2.9 and Table IV.2.12a). Improving equity will thus require considering the disparities in resources among schools.

In Turkey, Italy, Luxembourg, Chile and the partner countries Trinidad and Tobago, Argentina, Peru, Uruguay and Panama, 30 percentage points or more of the variation in student performance is attributable to both factors. In these countries, socio-economically advantaged schools tend to have more educational resources and tend to perform better.

In other words, while much of the variation in student performance cannot be predicted solely by the levels of resources, resources are closely related to the socio-economic composition of individual schools, such that socio-economically advantaged students attend schools with better resources. Which resources are most likely to be oriented towards socio-economically advantaged students? Which school systems distribute resources more equitably? A correlational analysis between each school's resource level and its average socio-economic background sheds light on how resources are distributed.

Across OECD countries, it is more common for schools that serve students from socio-economically advantaged backgrounds to have larger class sizes and offer more extracurricular activities (Table IV.2.11). In 22 OECD countries, PISA shows a moderate or strong positive relationship between the socio-economic background of the school and the average class size. In 12 OECD countries, there is a moderate or strong positive relationship between the socio-economic background of the school and the *index of extra-curricular activities,* which measures the amount of extra-curricular activities offered at the school. In three OECD countries, there is a moderate relationship between the school's average socio-economic background and the *index of quality of educational resources.* This index, constructed from school principals' reports, measures the extent to which the lack of certain resources hinders the school's ability to provide instruction. High levels in the index indicate more resources. In three OECD countries, schools with more advantaged socio-economic backgrounds are less likely to suffer from teacher shortages, as indicated by the *index of teacher shortage.* This index measures the extent to which the lack of qualified teachers hinders a school's ability to provide instruction, as reported by the school principal. In two OECD countries, schools with advantaged socio-economic backgrounds provide more hours of instruction than socio-economically disadvantaged schools. In two OECD countries, socio-economically disadvantaged schools provide more hours of instruction than advantaged schools. When considering the relationships between schools' socio-economic profile and class size, learning time, extracurricular activities, teacher shortages and material resources, Japan, Luxembourg and Mexico show the strongest relationship between the availability of resources at school and the school's socio-economic intake, since three out of those five features are related to the schools' average socio-economic status.

The lack of correlation between the level of resources and performance or equity among school systems does not mean that resource levels do not affect performance at all. Rather, it implies that, given the variation in resources observed in PISA, they are unrelated to performance or equity. A school system that lacks teachers, infrastructure and textbooks will almost certainly perform at lower levels; but given that most school systems in PISA appear to satisfy the minimum resource requirements for teaching and learning, the lack of a relationship between many of the resource aspects and both equity and performance may result simply from a lack of sufficient variation among OECD countries. Within each school system, most of the relationship between school resources and reading performance is also closely associated with schools' socio-economic and demographic profile. This suggests the need for more consideration on how to distribute resources for schools more equitably.

■ Figure IV.2.8 ■

How school systems' resources are related to educational outcomes

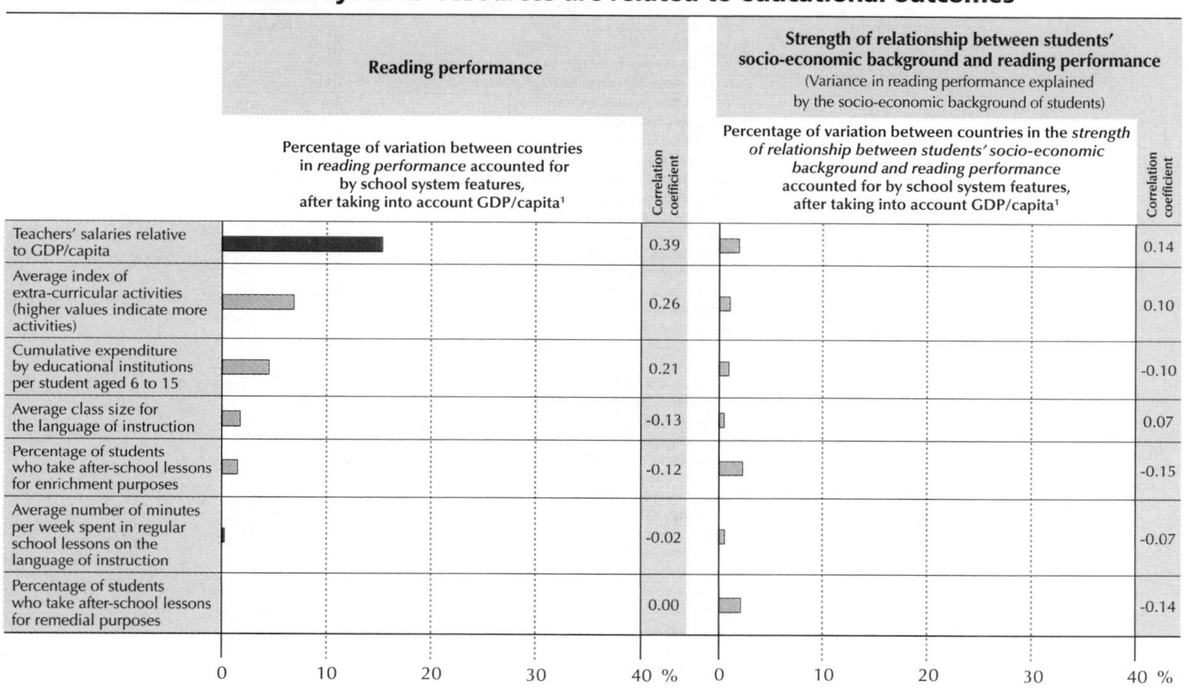

Note: Correlations that are statistically significant at the 5% level ($p<0.05$) are marked in a darker tone.
1. The percentage is obtained by squaring the correlation coefficient and then multiplying it by 100.
Source: OECD, *PISA 2009 Database*, Table IV.2.1.
StatLink http://dx.doi.org/10.1787/888932343380

Resources invested in education include more than human and material resources; they also include students' learning time, which involves how learning time is distributed across subjects and over a student's career, including the incidence and intensity of pre-primary education, and the age at which primary schooling starts. Volume II, *Overcoming Social Background*, suggests that students who attended pre-primary education perform better in PISA than students who did not. This relationship holds even after taking into account students' socio-economic background, signalling that the relationship between pre-school attendance and performance at age 15 is not mainly a reflection of socio-economically advantaged students attending pre-primary education. When examining who benefits more by attending pre-primary education, socio-economically disadvantaged and advantaged students benefit equally from pre-school attendance in most countries, while in some countries the impact of pre-school attendance on performance is greater for students with an immigrant background than for native students. In countries that spend more on pre-school education per student, the advantage of attending pre-school for students from immigrant backgrounds tends to be greater.

■ Figure IV.2.9 ■

How school resources are related to reading performance

Expressed as a percentage of the average variance in reading performance in OECD countries (100% is the average total variance in reading performance across OECD countries)

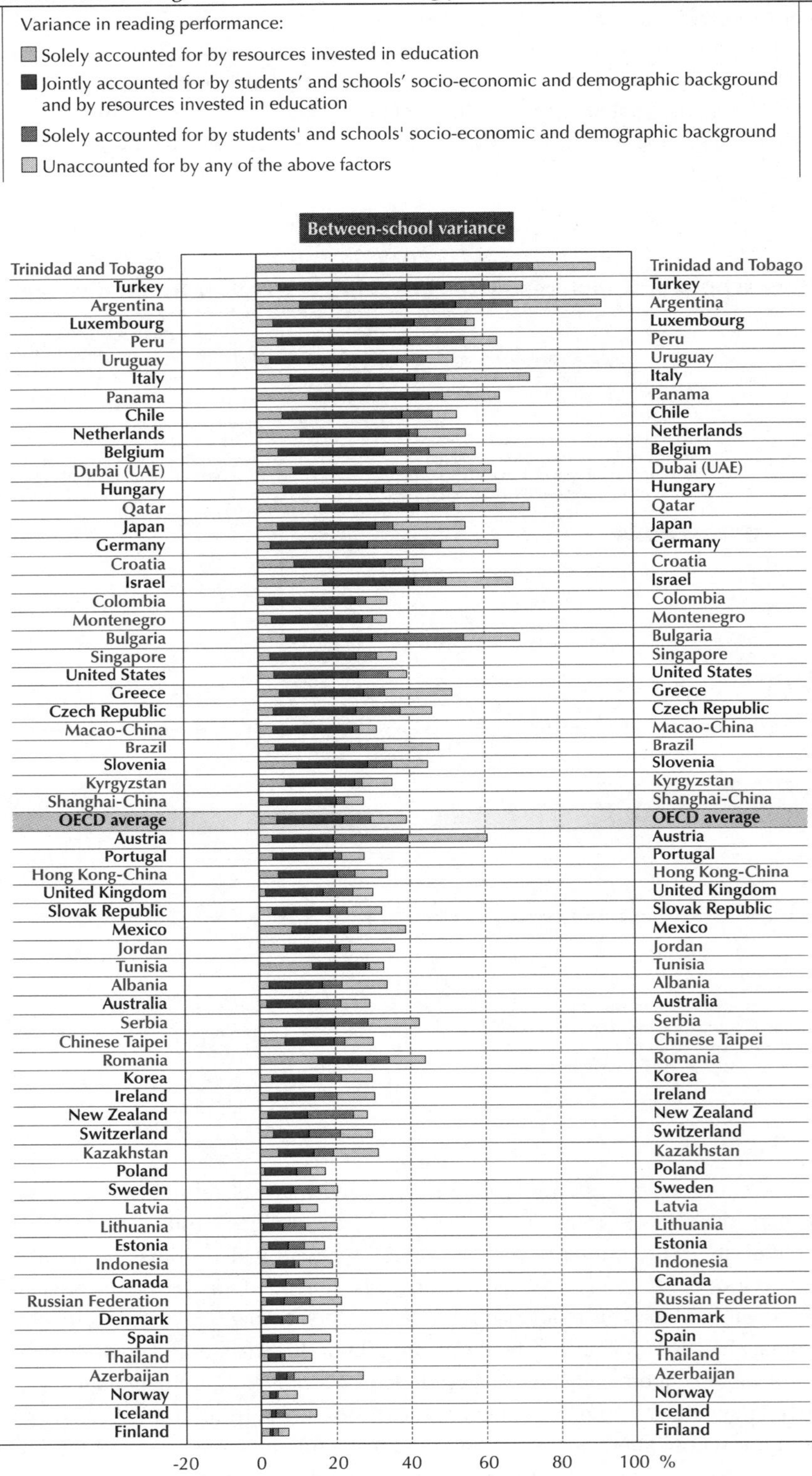

Countries are ranked in descending order of the variance jointly accounted for.

Source: OECD, *PISA 2009 Database*, Table IV.2.12a.

StatLink http://dx.doi.org/10.1787/888932343380

The analyses in Volume II also show that the benefit of attending pre-primary education varies by country, and that this variability is largely explained by the PISA indicators related to the quality of pre-school education. The performance advantage among students who had attended pre-primary education is larger in countries where pre-primary education lasts longer, where there are smaller pupil-to-teacher ratios at the pre-primary level and where there is higher public expenditure per pupil at the pre-primary level of education.

Do the individual benefits of attending pre-primary education add up to better overall performance among school systems in which more students attend pre-school? The results from PISA show no relationship between the average performance of OECD countries and the proportion of students in these countries who had attended pre-primary school. However, when considering all countries and economies participating in PISA, they show a positive relationship between the proportion of students who attended pre-primary education and the average performance of the school system, even after taking into account the country's national income. School systems that show a 10 percentage point advantage in the proportion of students who attended pre-primary education are school systems that also score, on average, 12.3 points higher in reading performance.[16] This may reflect the fact that the majority of students in most OECD countries have access to pre-primary education, and of these students, a large proportion attend for more than one year. In fact, in more than half of all OECD countries, more than 92% of 15-year-old students reported that they attended pre-primary schools for at least some time (see Table IV.3.18).

How resources, policies and practices are related to each other

Many of the aspects related to the organisation of school systems are closely interrelated (Figure IV.2.10). For example, school systems that offer a greater number of programmes to 15-year-old students also tend to select students earlier. School systems with a greater number of programmes are also school systems with higher transfer rates and school systems with higher transfer rates also tend to be systems with higher rates of grade repetition.

■ Figure IV.2.10 ■

How selected organisational features are inter-related

Values in the cells present partial correlation coefficients between two relevant measures after accounting for GDP/capita
Correlation coefficients range from -1.00 (*i.e.* a perfect negative linear association) to +1.00 (*i.e.* a perfect positive linear association). When a correlation coefficients is 0, there is no linear relationship between two measures.

Upper triangle is across OECD countries

Lower triangle is across participating countries and economies

	Percentage of students who repeated one or more grades	Each additional year of selection prior to the age of 15	Number of school types or distinct educational programmes available for 15-year-olds	Percentage of students in selective schools	Percentage of students in schools that group students by ability in all subjects	Percentage of students in schools that transfer students to other schools due to low achievement, behavioural problems or special learning needs	Average index of school responsibility for curriculum and assessment (higher values indicate more autonomy)	Average index of school responsibility for resource allocation (higher values indicate more autonomy)	Existence of standards-based external examinations	Teachers' salaries relative to GDP/capita
Percentage of students who repeated one or more grades		0.23	**0.36**	0.08	**0.55**	**0.41**	**-0.40**	-0.14	**-0.56**	*0.33*
Each additional year of selection prior to the age of 15	0.10		**0.75**	**0.63**	0.29	**0.56**	-0.02	0.12	-0.02	0.17
Number of school types or distinct educational programmes available for 15-year-olds	-0.01	**0.64**		**0.63**	**0.45**	**0.48**	0.07	0.17	0.03	0.30
Percentage of students in selective schools	-0.14	**0.41**	**0.55**		**0.44**	*0.32*	*0.31*	0.25	0.19	0.24
Percentage of students in schools that group students by ability in all subjects	*0.22*	0.09	**0.30**	*0.24*		**0.45**	-0.11	0.13	-0.08	0.20
Percentage of students in schools that transfer students to other schools due to low achievement, behavioural problems or special learning needs	**0.31**	**0.27**	*0.26*	**0.27**	**0.37**		**-0.44**	-0.23	-0.29	0.05
Average index of school responsibility for curriculum and assessment (higher values indicate more autonomy)	*-0.25*	-0.07	0.01	*0.23*	*-0.23*	**-0.27**		**0.59**	**0.52**	0.06
Average index of school responsibility for resource allocation (higher values indicate more autonomy)	-0.07	0.06	0.08	**0.27**	0.01	-0.04	**0.53**		0.19	-0.25
Existence of standards-based external examinations	**-0.60**	-0.03	0.03	0.13	-0.03	-0.18	**0.47**	0.12		-0.28
Teachers' salaries relative to GDP/capita	0.13	0.03	0.05	0.24	0.00	-0.10	**0.33**	-0.04	0.03	

Note: Correlation coefficients that are statistically significant at the 5% level ($p < 0.05$) are indicated in bold and at the 10% level ($p < 0.10$) are in italic.
StatLink http://dx.doi.org/10.1787/888932343380

School systems with higher transfer rates or higher grade repetition rates also tend to offer less autonomy to schools in formulating curricula and assessments and are also somewhat less likely to use standardised tests to measure their students' achievement. School systems that provide schools with more responsibility to set their own curricula and assessment policies are also school systems in which schools have more responsibility for allocating resources.

In summary, when characteristics related to a school system's overall performance (*i.e.* grade repetition, transfer rates, ability grouping, curricular autonomy, the existence of standards-based external examinations and teachers' salaries) and national income are considered together, 58% of the variation in performance across OECD countries is accounted for. Examining the variation in performance across all participating countries and economies, these 6 system characteristics together with national income account for 62% of the variation across systems.[17]

HOW THE LEARNING ENVIRONMENT IS RELATED TO STUDENT PERFORMANCE

How schools are organised and governed tends to influence learning in schools and classrooms indirectly. PISA has also looked at aspects of the learning environment that affect learning more directly. This section examines how teacher-student relations, disciplinary climate, student- and teacher-related factors affecting school climate, teachers' stimulation of students, school principals' leadership and their perceptions of parents' pressure to raise academic standards and achievement relate to student performance. Most of the measures of the learning environment are based on the perceptions and opinions of students and school principals (see Chapter 4). Since it is difficult to compare perceptions and options across countries (see Box IV.1.1), this section examines relationships between these aspects and student performance within each country.

PISA shows that, across OECD countries, 3% of the variation in student performance is attributable solely to the differences in learning environment, while 9% is attributable to both socio-economic background and the learning environment (Figure IV.2.11 and Table IV.2.13a).

Students' backgrounds are closely related to the learning environment, and these two factors are, in turn, strongly linked to performance – perhaps because students from socio-economically advantaged backgrounds bring with them a higher level of discipline and more positive perceptions of school values, or perhaps because parents' expectations of classroom discipline and teacher commitment are higher in schools whose student populations are from socio-economically advantaged backgrounds. Conversely, schools whose student populations come from disadvantaged backgrounds may not be put under the same kind of parental pressure to improve classroom discipline or to ensure that absent or unmotivated teachers are replaced. Thus, policy makers need to consider the joint influence of socio-economic background and learning environment if they want to ensure that all schools, regardless of the profile of their student populations, have committed teachers and orderly classrooms.

In some countries, the joint influence of the socio-economic background and the learning environment on performance is particularly large. For example, 15 percentage points or more is attributable jointly to the learning environment and socio-economic background in Luxembourg, Germany, Japan, Turkey, Italy, the Czech Republic, Chile and the partner countries and economies Trinidad and Tobago, Argentina, Croatia, Uruguay, Singapore, Montenegro and Macao-China (Figure IV.2.11 and Table IV.2.13a). In most countries and economies, only a small proportion – five percentage points or less – in performance variation is attributable solely to the learning environment, except in Israel, Japan and Italy, where more than seven percentage points is attributable solely to that factor.

Among the various characteristics related to the learning environment, which of those examined are positively related to student performance? Results show that in many countries, schools with better disciplinary climates, more positive behaviour among teachers and better teacher-student relations tend to achieve higher scores in reading, even after socio-economic background is accounted for (Figure IV.2.12 and Table IV.2.13c).

For example, even after accounting for the socio-economic and demographic background of students and schools, the performance of schools is positively related to higher values on the *index of teacher-student relations* in 10 OECD countries and 7 partner countries and economies; it is related to higher values on the *index of disciplinary climate* in 16 OECD countries and 22 partner countries and economies; and is positively related to higher values on the *index of teacher-related factors affecting school climate* in 14 OECD countries and 6 partner countries and economies. School principals' perceptions of parents' pressure to raise academic standards and achievement is related to higher student performance in 19 OECD countries and 10 partner countries and economies; but after the socio-economic background of students and schools is taken into account, that positive relationship is found in only four OECD countries and five partner countries and economies.

■ Figure IV.2.11 ■

How the learning environment at school is related to reading performance

Expressed as a percentage of the average variance in reading performance in OECD countries (100% is the average total variance in reading performance across OECD countries)

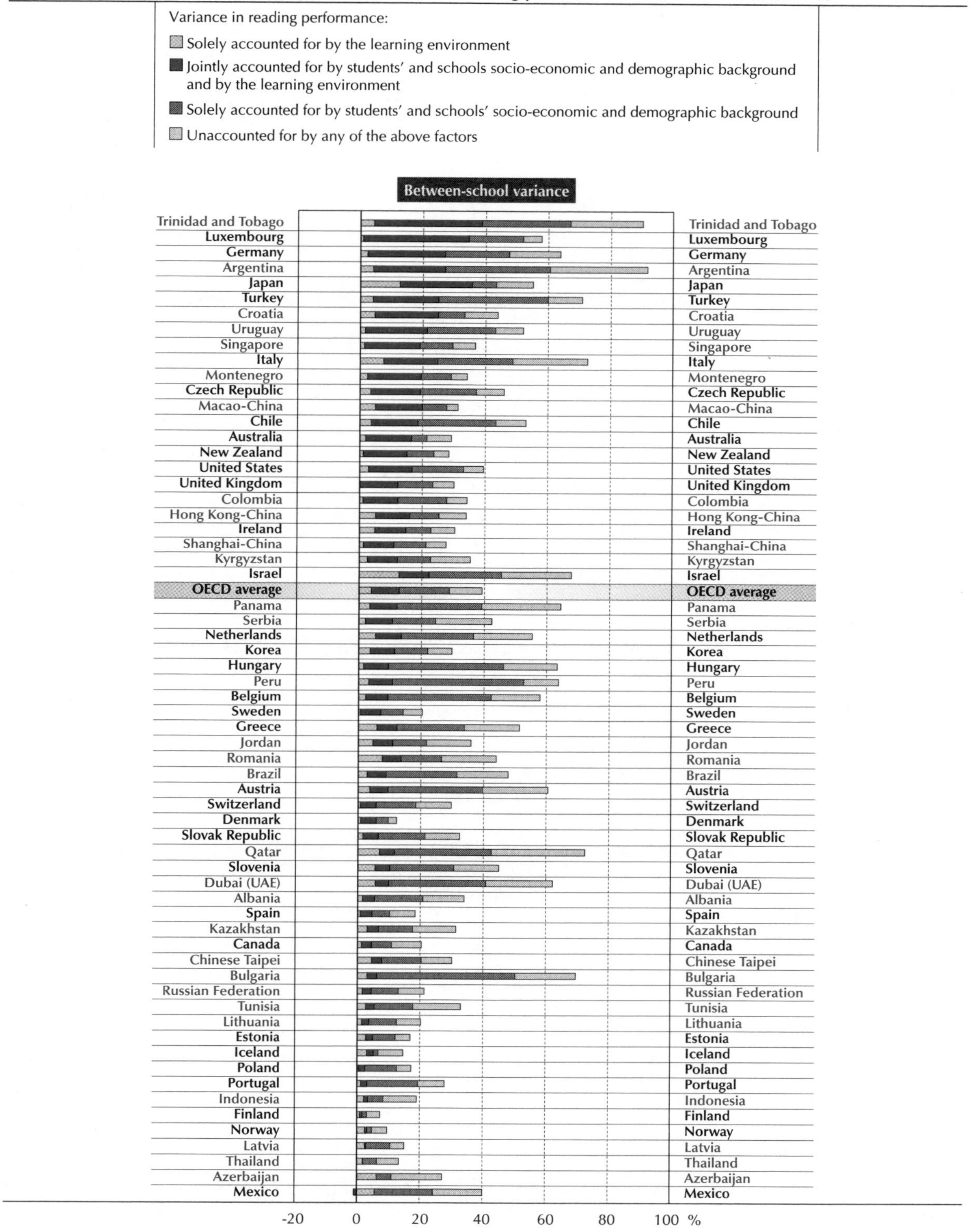

Countries are ranked in descending order of the variance jointly accounted for.
Source: OECD, *PISA 2009 Database*, Table IV.2.13a.
StatLink http://dx.doi.org/10.1787/888932343380

■ Figure IV.2.12 ■

Countries in which the learning environment at school is related to reading performance

Learning environment (the model includes all of these features of learning environment)		Without accounting for the socio-economic and demographic background of students and schools		With accounting for the socio-economic and demographic background of students and schools	
		Negative relationship	Positive relationship	Negative relationship	Positive relationship
Index of teacher-student relations (higher values indicate better relationships) (school average)	*OECD*	Austria, Germany, Spain, Switzerland	Australia, Denmark, Finland, Iceland, Ireland, Israel, Japan, Mexico	Austria	Australia, Czech Republic, Estonia, Greece, Iceland, Ireland, Israel, Japan, Mexico, Portugal
		OECD average change in score: 10.1		**OECD average change in score: 16.7**	
	Partner	Argentina, Colombia, Croatia, Kazakhstan, Kyrgyzstan, Montenegro, Panama, Serbia, Uruguay	Hong Kong-China, Jordan, Qatar, Shanghai-China, Tunisia	Kazakhstan, Kyrgyzstan	Bulgaria, Brazil, Hong Kong-China, Jordan, Peru, Qatar, Tunisia
Index of disciplinary climate (higher values indicate better climate) (school average)	*OECD*		Australia, Austria, Belgium, Czech Republic, Denmark, France, Iceland, Ireland, Italy, Japan, Netherlands, New Zealand, Slovak Republic, Slovenia, Spain, Sweden, Switzerland, Turkey		Australia, Austria, Czech Republic, Denmark, Greece, Israel, Italy, Japan, Mexico, Netherlands, New Zealand, Norway, Poland, Slovak Republic, Slovenia, Spain
		OECD average change in score: 28.6		**OECD average change in score: 17.8**	
	Partner		Azerbaijan, Croatia, Dubai (UAE), Hong Kong-China, Kazakhstan, Kyrgyzstan, Lithuania, Macao-China, Montenegro, Panama, Qatar, Romania, Russian Federation, Singapore, Serbia, Shanghai-China, Trinidad and Tobago, Uruguay		Azerbaijan, Brazil, Colombia, Croatia, Dubai (UAE), Hong Kong-China, Jordan, Kazakhstan, Kyrgyzstan, Latvia, Lithuania, Macao-China, Panama, Peru, Qatar, Romania, Russian Federation, Shanghai-China, Singapore, Chinese Taipei, Trinidad and Tobago, Uruguay
Index of teachers' stimulation of reading engagement (higher values indicates more stimulation) (school average)	*OECD*	Denmark, Greece, Israel, Slovak Republic	Austria, France, Germany	Israel, New Zealand	
		OECD average change in score: 0.1		**OECD average change in score: -5.4**	
	Partner	Brazil, Hong Kong-China, Indonesia, Singapore, Tunisia		Brazil, Hong Kong-China, Indonesia, Latvia, Singapore	Montenegro
Index of student-related factors affecting school climate (higher values indicate a positive student behaviour)	*OECD*	Czech Republic, Estonia, Germany, Italy, Japan, Luxembourg, Netherlands, Slovak Republic		Israel	Slovenia
		OECD average change in score: -7.7		**OECD average change in score: -2.2**	
	Partner	Croatia, Trinidad and Tobago, Uruguay		Brazil, Croatia, Macao-China, Shanghai-China, Uruguay	Chinese Taipei
Index of teacher-related factors affecting school climate (higher values indicate a positive teacher behaviour)	*OECD*		Australia, Austria, Belgium, Canada, Chile, Czech Republic, Denmark, Estonia, Germany, Greece, Hungary, Ireland, Italy, Japan, Korea, Luxembourg, Netherlands, New Zealand, Slovak Republic, Spain, Switzerland, United Kingdom, United States		Austria, Belgium, Chile, Czech Republic, Estonia, Germany, Greece, Israel, Italy, Japan, Korea, Mexico, Netherlands, Spain
		OECD average change in score: 19.0		**OECD average change in score: 7.9**	
	Partner		Argentina, Bulgaria, Brazil, Croatia, Dubai (UAE), Hong Kong-China, Indonesia, Singapore, Trinidad and Tobago, Uruguay	Chinese Taipei	Argentina, Brazil, Croatia, Romania, Thailand, Uruguay
Parents expect the school to set high academic standards and pressure for students to achieve them	*OECD*		Belgium, Canada, Chile, Czech Republic, Denmark, Greece, Ireland, Israel, Italy, Japan, Korea, New Zealand, Norway, Poland, Portugal, Slovenia, Sweden, Turkey, United Kingdom		Canada, Italy, New Zealand, Norway
		OECD average change in score: 26.9		OECD average change in score: 2.9	
	Partner	Azerbaijan	Albania, Brazil, Croatia, Kazakhstan, Latvia, Lithuania, Russian Federation, Singapore, Trinidad and Tobago, Uruguay	Azerbaijan	Bulgaria, Kazakhstan, Latvia, Lithuania, Trinidad and Tobago
Index of school principal's leadership (higher values indicate more leadership roles taken)	*OECD*	Finland, Israel, Italy, Slovak Republic	Mexico, Spain	Israel, Italy	
		OECD average change in score: -3.0		**OECD average change in score: -2.4**	
	Partner	Hong Kong-China	Jordan, Panama, Peru	Chinese Taipei	

Note: Only those school systems where there is a statistically significant relationship between the learning environment and performance are listed. OECD averages in bold denote that the estimate is statistically significant at the 5% level ($p<0.05$).
Source: OECD, *PISA 2009 Database*, Tables IV.2.13b and IV.2.13c.
StatLink http://dx.doi.org/10.1787/888932343380

■ Figure IV.2.13 ■

How student and school characteristics are related to reading performance

Expressed as a percentage of the average variance in reading performance in OECD countries (100% is the average total variance in reading performance across OECD countries)

Countries are ranked in descending order of the between-school variance jointly accounted for.

Source: OECD, *PISA 2009 Database*, Table IV.2.14a.

StatLink http://dx.doi.org/10.1787/888932343380

In summary, students perform better in schools that have better class discipline, more positive behaviour among teachers and better teacher-student relations, partly because such schools tend to have more students from advantaged backgrounds, who generally perform well, partly because the favourable socio-economic background of students reinforces a climate that is conducive to learning, and partly for reasons unrelated to socio-economic aspects. This relationship, which is not linked to socio-economic background, signals that a positive learning environment has, in itself, an independent relationship with performance, regardless of a school's socio-economic intake. In contrast, parental expectations of both their children and their children's schools are related to performance mainly because parents with high expectations tend to be those from more advantaged socio-economic backgrounds.

HOW THE FEATURES OF SCHOOLS AND SCHOOL SYSTEMS ARE INTERRELATED

Previous sections have described how organisational configurations of schools systems and the learning environment in individual schools interrelate with socio-economic factors to influence student performance. These relationships can also be examined in association with the findings discussed in Volume III, *Learning to Learn*, which focus on the association between students' reading habits, their approaches to learning and student performance.

After considering the socio-economic and demographic characteristics of students, their reading habits and approaches to learning, the learning environment and school organisation, across OECD countries, almost one-third of the student-level variation and almost nine-tenths of the between-school variation in performance can be explained by aspects measured by PISA (Figure IV.2.13 and Table IV.2.14a).

The learning environment shows an independent relationship with performance (Table IV.2.14c). However, the learning environment seems to be closely related to a school's organisational configuration, (this is evident when comparing the relationships between organisational variables in Tables IV.2.2c, IV.2.4c, IV.2.9c and IV.2.12c with the comparable estimates in Table IV.2.14c). School systems may thus shape the conditions for better learning outcomes, by providing organisational arrangements that promote better teacher-student relations, better disciplinary climates and better working environments for teachers.

Notes

1. The correlation is a measure of the association between two variables but does not necessarily establish a causal relationship between these variables. Two variables can be associated (*e.g.* as one variable increases, so does the other) because of a causal relationship or because a common factor influences the variation in both variables simultaneously. Both raw correlations and partial correlations are presented. Raw correlations display the overall level of association between two variables; partial correlations account for national income, as measured by the per capita GDP of each country.

2. Since the characteristics of students and schools within each section are interrelated, it is important to estimate their overall relationship with student and school performance. Each section uses multilevel regression models with individual students' performance scores as the dependent variable, and includes student-level variables in the level-1 model and school-level variables in the level-2 model for the intercept.

3. For details on the rationale for analysing this particular set of characteristics and for measuring each feature, see Chapter 3.

4. Similar results are obtained through alternative statistical models with different specifications (*i.e.* 3-level hierarchical linear models). See further information in Annex A6. Given that there is a strong relationship between standards-based external examinations and repetition rates at the system level (Figure IV.2.10), the relationship between repetition rates and performance is not statistically significant when accounting for standards-based external examinations.

5. Similar results are obtained through alternative statistical models with different specifications (*i.e.* 3-level hierarchical linear models). See further information in Annex A6.

6. One unit in a students' socio-economic background is equivalent to one standard deviation in the *PISA index of economic, social and cultural status* across OECD.

7. Curricular autonomy, by comparison, also shows a positive relationship with individual schools' performance in a larger number of countries than for which a negative relationship is observed. The extent to which schools have autonomy is correlated with the rate at which schools transfer students because of low performance, special needs or behavioural problems (Figure IV.2.2). After taking student transfer rates into account, curricular autonomy at the system level is moderately related to student performance (correlation of 0.31, p-value of 0.10).

8. One unit on the index is equivalent to one standard deviation above the OECD average on the *index of school responsibility for curricula and assessments.*

9. This refers to the independent, or net, relationship between school competition and performance.

10. Private schools in this analysis include private schools that are dependent on and independent of the government. Private schools are classified as government-dependent private schools if they receive more than 50% of their funding from local, regional, state and/or national government sources. Schools are classified as government-independent private schools if they receive less than 50% of their funding from public sources.

11. Standards-based external examinations are defined according to John Bishop's definition of "curriculum-based external examination system" (CBEES). CBEES offers signals of student accomplishments that have real consequences for the student and defines achievement relative to an external standard, not relative to other students in the classroom or the school. To enable fair comparisons of achievement across schools and across students at different schools, CBEES: is organised by discipline and keyed to the content of specific course sequences, which allocates the responsibility of preparing the student for particular examinations to one or a small group of teachers; signals multiple levels of achievement in the subject rather than indicating merely a pass-fail signal; and covers almost all secondary school students (Bishop, 1998; Bishop, 2001).

12. It is statistically significant at the 7% level when national income is taken into account.

13. This is based on the bivariate regression model with the existence of standards-based external examinations regressed on reading performance. Taking into account per capita GDP, the performance advantage for systems with standards-based external examinations is also 16 points. Across all countries and economies that participated in PISA 2009, the performance advantage for systems with standards-based external examinations is 17 points when not accounting for per capita GDP and 15 points when accounting for per capita GDP.

14. One may argue that this positive relationship between a greater use of standardised tests and equity is spurious because standardised tests are less frequently used in school systems that stratify their student populations early (Figure IV.2.10). This is because these school systems may have less of an incentive to implement standardised tests, since selection has already taken place (*i.e.* standardised tests are administered before the age of 15 or takes place through repetition/transfers). The correlation between the proportion of schools that use standardised tests and the equity measure, which is the impact of students' and schools' socio-economic impact on performance, is examined after accounting for the first age of selection and national income. The result shows that the relationship between a greater use of standardised tests and equity is still significant (-0.35).

15. Similar results are obtained through alternative models with different specifications (*i.e.* three-level hierarchical linear models). See further information in Annex A6.

16. These estimates result from an OLS regression model that regresses system-level reading scores on the percentage of students who attended pre-primary education (ISCED 0) and per capita GDP. Model fit for the model with all countries yields an R^2 of 0.52; model fit for the model restricted to OECD countries yields an R^2 of 0.17. The estimate for a 10 percentage point increase in pre-primary school attendance rates on reading performance is 4.5 (not statistically significant) in the sample restricted to OECD countries. Models for all countries are run with a sample size of 61 and models for OECD countries are run with a sample size of 33.

17. Caution is required as these results are based on only a limited number of cases. Due to a large amount of missing data regarding standards-based external examinations and teachers' salaries, the result for OECD countries is based on 26 OECD countries and the result for all participating countries is based on 35 countries and economies. Without including standards-based external examinations and teachers' salaries, four system characteristics and national income account for 50% of the variation in performance across 33 OECD countries and 60% of the variation in performance across 60 participating countries and economies.

3

How Schooling is Organised

This chapter provides detailed descriptions and in-depth analyses of selected organisational features of schools and systems that affect student performance. These include how students are sorted into grades, schools and programmes, school autonomy, school competition, how schools and school systems use student assessments, and resources devoted to education.

Digging deeper into the findings of Chapters 1 and 2, this chapter describes how PISA defines various aspects of school organisation that are related to student performance and shows where countries stand on these policies and practices.

SELECTING AND GROUPING STUDENTS

As explained in Chapter 2, school systems use vertical and horizontal differentiation to cater to students with different abilities, needs and interests.

Chapter 2 finds that school systems that track students at an early age tend to show a stronger impact of socio-economic background on learning outcomes, signalling larger socio-economic inequalities. School systems with higher grade-repetition and student-transfer rates tend to show lower student performance and a stronger impact of socio-economic background on learning outcomes. Ability grouping within schools tends to be related to lower performance levels at the system level. Selective schools perform at higher levels than non-selective schools, but a system as a whole does not benefit from having more selective schools.

Vertical differentiation

One-room schools, where all students, regardless of age, shared the same classroom and were taught by the same teacher, were commonplace in many countries in the early 19th century. As student populations grew in size and diversity, schooling was increasingly differentiated vertically: younger students would concentrate on basic studies, and as they progressed, they would enter more complex and differentiated study programmes. This vertical differentiation resulted in the creation of different grades and education levels (Sorensen, 1970; Tyack, 1974). This section describes two major aspects of variability in the grades that 15-year-olds students attend: their age of entry into the school system and grade repetition. It then examines how school systems differ in the way 15-year-old students are distributed across grades and education levels (Figure IV.3.1).

Age of entry into the school system

Many school systems establish a statutory age of entry into school, typically age five or six. Nevertheless, children of the same age often follow different developmental trajectories. Some parents believe that their children could benefit from waiting another year before they start school, and education systems may allow them to postpone enrolment for a year (Graue and DiPerna, 2000). Vertical differentiation in such school systems is thus less age-based than in other school systems.

As a result of different age-of-entry policies and practices as well as differences in grade-retention rates, the 15-year-olds assessed by PISA may be in different grades. In PISA 2009, students were asked at what age they entered primary school. Most students are at most one year younger or older than the statutory age of entry; but in countries where parents have more freedom to choose when their children enter school, students are often two or more years above or below the usual age of entry. In Ireland and the United Kingdom, the average age of entry into primary schools is at or below five years, while in eight countries the age of entry is higher than six-and-a-half years (Figure IV.3.1). The age of entry does not vary greatly in Japan, Poland, Korea, the Slovak Republic and Finland, with more than 98% of students entering primary schools within a two-year window.[1] In Canada, the United States, the United Kingdom and Australia, the proportion of PISA students who first attended school outside the usual two years of school entry exceeds 15%. Among the partner countries and economies, no education system has an average starting age for primary schools below five years. In 16 of the 31 partner countries and economies, the average starting age for PISA students exceeds six-and-a-half years. Only in Montenegro do almost all students (more than 98%) enter primary school within the two-year window. In 13 partner countries and economies, the rate at which PISA students entered primary schools outside the two years exceeds 15%; and in Brazil, Qatar, Trinidad and Tobago, Colombia, Macao-China and Dubai (UAE), at least one in five 15-year-old students entered primary school outside the usual two years of entry.

Grade repetition

Grade repetition is also a form of vertical differentiation as it seeks to adapt the curriculum to student performance and create homogeneous learning environments by distributing students across grades. Although some research suggests that repeating a grade generally does not yield improvements in learning outcomes and is associated with high economic and social costs (Alexander, Entwisle and Dauber, 2003; Hauser, 2004), grade repetition is still commonly used in many countries to create more homogeneous learning environments. In most countries, the requirement to repeat a year typically follows a formal or informal assessment of the student by the teacher or school towards the end of the school year.

■ Figure IV.3.1 ■

Age at which students enter school and how they progress

	Country	Age of entry into primary school: Average age (years old)	Grade repetition: Percentage of students who repeated one or more grades	Percentage of students in: Lower secondary education (%)	Percentage of students in: Upper secondary education (%)
OECD	Australia	5.2	8.4	81	19
	Austria	6.2	12.6	7	93
	Belgium	5.9	34.9	9	91
	Canada	5.2	8.4	15	85
	Chile	6.0	23.4	5	95
	Czech Republic	6.4	4.0	54	46
	Denmark	6.6	4.4	99	1
	Estonia	6.9	5.6	98	2
	Finland	6.7	2.8	100	0
	France	5.9	36.9	37	63
	Germany	6.3	21.4	97	3
	Greece	6.3	5.7	7	93
	Hungary	6.8	11.1	10	90
	Iceland	5.8	0.9	98	2
	Ireland	4.5	12.0	62	38
	Israel	6.3	7.5	14	86
	Italy	5.9	16.0	1	99
	Japan	6.0	0.0	0	100
	Korea	6.0	0.0	4	96
	Luxembourg	6.2	36.5	62	38
	Mexico	6.2	21.5	44	56
	Netherlands	6.0	26.7	74	26
	New Zealand	5.1	5.1	6	94
	Norway	5.8	0.0	100	0
	Poland	7.0	5.3	99	1
	Portugal	6.0	35.0	44	56
	Slovak Republic	6.3	3.8	39	61
	Slovenia	6.7	1.5	3	97
	Spain	5.9	35.3	100	0
	Sweden	6.6	4.6	98	2
	Switzerland	6.5	22.8	79	21
	Turkey	6.9	13.0	4	96
	United Kingdom	5.0	2.2	0	100
	United States	5.9	14.2	11	89
	OECD average	6.1	13.0	46	54
Partners	Albania	6.6	4.7	53	47
	Argentina	6.0	33.8	39	61
	Azerbaijan	6.6	1.7	55	45
	Brazil	7.4	40.1	25	75
	Bulgaria	6.9	5.6	7	93
	Chinese Taipei	6.9	1.6	35	65
	Colombia	6.0	33.9	37	63
	Croatia	6.7	2.8	0	100
	Dubai (UAE)	5.8	12.6	19	81
	Hong Kong-China	6.1	15.6	34	66
	Indonesia	6.3	18.0	54	46
	Jordan	6.1	6.6	100	0
	Kazakhstan	6.6	1.7	80	20
	Kyrgyzstan	6.8	4.3	79	21
	Latvia	6.8	11.1	97	3
	Liechtenstein	6.5	21.5	94	6
	Lithuania	6.8	3.9	100	0
	Macao-China	6.1	43.7	61	39
	Montenegro	6.7	1.8	2	98
	Panama	5.7	31.8	44	56
	Peru	6.0	28.1	30	70
	Qatar	6.2	14.8	19	81
	Romania	6.9	4.2	100	0
	Russian Federation	6.7	3.2	71	29
	Serbia	6.9	2.0	2	98
	Shanghai-China	6.8	7.5	42	58
	Singapore	6.7	5.4	4	96
	Thailand	6.4	3.5	24	76
	Trinidad and Tobago	5.2	28.8	36	64
	Tunisia	5.9	43.2	44	56
	Uruguay	5.9	38.0	39	61

Source: OECD, *PISA 2009 Database*, Table IV.3.1.
StatLink http://dx.doi.org/10.1787/888932343399

In PISA, 15-year-old students were asked whether they had repeated a grade in primary, lower secondary or upper secondary school. Across OECD countries, on average, 13% of students reported that they had repeated a grade at least once: 7% of students had repeated a grade in primary school, 6% of students had repeated a lower secondary grade and 2% of students had repeated an upper secondary grade (Figure IV.3.1 and Table IV.3.1). Grade repetition is non-existent in Korea, Japan and Norway. Over 95% of students in 8 other OECD countries and 12 partner countries and economies reported they had never repeated a grade. In contrast, over 25% of students in France, Luxembourg, Spain, Portugal, Belgium and the Netherlands, as well as in the partner countries and economies Macao-China, Tunisia, Brazil, Uruguay, Colombia, Argentina, Panama, Trinidad and Tobago and Peru reported they had repeated a grade.

Differentiation in grade and education levels

The modal grade level and the proportion of students in lower and upper secondary schools differ across the countries participating in PISA, depending on the different age-of-entry policies, policies on cut-off dates for enrolment[2] and grade-retention policies.

In OECD countries, the majority of 15-year-old students attend the modal grade level. On average across OECD countries, 26% of 15-year-olds attend grade levels that are above or below the modal grade level in their country, but this varies across OECD countries (Table IV.3.1). While in some school systems almost all 15-year-olds share the same grade (*i.e.* Japan, Norway, Iceland and the United Kingdom), in other countries, 15-year-olds are spread out across different grades. In the Czech Republic, the Netherlands, Austria, Luxembourg and Germany and the partner countries and economies Brazil, Macao-China, Colombia, Peru, Indonesia, Azerbaijan, Panama, Albania and Tunisia, almost half of all students attend a different grade than the modal grade.

On average across OECD countries, 54% of 15-year-old students attend upper secondary programmes, and in 19 of the 34 OECD countries, the majority of students do so. In 15 of these countries, over 80% of 15-year-olds attend upper secondary programmes and practically all students in Japan and the United Kingdom attend these programmes. In contrast, in 10 OECD countries, less than 20% of 15-year-olds attend upper secondary programmes. Practically no 15-year-olds in Spain, Norway, Finland, Poland and Denmark are enrolled at the upper secondary level of education. In the Czech Republic, Portugal and Mexico, almost half of all students are enrolled in lower secondary programmes while the other half attend upper secondary programmes. In 6 partner countries and economies, less than 20% of 15-year-olds attend upper secondary programmes, while in 7 other partner countries and economies, over 80% of 15-year-olds attend upper secondary programmes (Figure IV.3.1).

Horizontal differentiation at the system level

Programmes of study and age of selection

School systems often tailor their curricula to better meet their students' needs. In comprehensive school systems, all 15-year-old students follow the same programme, while in stratified school systems, students are streamed into different programmes. Some of these programmes may be strictly academic, others contain strong vocational components, and yet others may offer combinations of academic and vocational programmes (Kerckhoff, 2000; LeTendre, Hofer and Shimizu, 2003).

Among the 34 OECD countries, 14 countries' school systems are comprehensive in that they offer a single programme of study to all 15-year-olds. Yet, even within comprehensive programmes, students are often able to enrol in different programmes and courses that reflect their various interests and academic goals (see the section on horizontal differentiation at the school level below). In the remaining 19 OECD countries with stratified school systems, 15-year-olds are streamed into at least two different study programmes. Such streaming takes place at an average age of 14 but occurs as early as at the age of 10 in Germany and Austria and at age 11 in the Czech Republic, Hungary, the Slovak Republic and Turkey (Table IV.3.2a).

Among the partner countries and economies, seven offer a single programme of study to 15-year-olds, while in 19 countries and economies, students are streamed into different study programmes. Liechtenstein and Trinidad and Tobago select students for streaming before the age of 12, but most other partner countries and economies with stratified systems delay selection until students are 15 years old (Table IV.3.2a).

These organisational policies must also be taken into account when comparing other characteristics of school systems, such as performance, equity and school climate, as they signal different educational experiences and trajectories for students. As shown in Chapter 2, the degree of streaming and the age at which such streaming takes place are closely related to the impact of socio-economic background on learning outcomes.

School admission policies

Admission and placement policies establish frameworks for selecting students for academic programmes and streaming. In countries with large performance differences between programmes and schools, or where socio-economic segregation is firmly entrenched in residential segregation, admission and grouping policies can have a major impact on parents and students. Some schools may be better able to attract motivated students and retain good teachers, while in other schools, a "brain drain" of students and staff risks reinforcing low school performance. As shown in Volume II, *Overcoming Social Background*, the socio-economic context of the school in which students are enrolled tends to be much more strongly related to student learning outcomes than students' individual socio-economic background.

To assess the selectivity of education systems, school principals were asked how frequently they considered the following factors when admitting students to their schools: students' residences students' academic records (including placement tests); recommendations from feeder schools; parents' endorsements of the instructional or religious philosophy of the school; students' needs or desires for a specific programme; and the past or present attendance of other family members at the school. School systems that are composed of highly selective schools are more likely to have homogeneous student populations within the schools since students with similar academic aptitudes and/or backgrounds are selected into the same schools. While schools may perform at a higher level when their student populations are homogeneous, low-performing students will be less likely to benefit from their high-achieving peers.

On average across OECD countries, 36% of students are enrolled in schools whose principals reported that their schools are highly selective (Table IV.3.2b).[3] In 10 of the 34 OECD countries, more than half of all students attend schools that always consider recommendations from feeder schools or academic transcripts when making admission decisions. Of these countries, in the Netherlands, Japan and Hungary, more than 85% of students are selected for schools on the basis of academic records or recommendations. In contrast, more students attend non-selective schools – that is, schools that select on the basis of residence or agreement with the schools' educational philosophy, or have an open-door policy – in Portugal, Spain, Iceland, Sweden, Finland, Denmark, Norway and Greece, where less than 10% of all students attend schools that are academically selective.

In no partner country or economy do less than 10% of all students attend selective schools and, with the exception of Uruguay, Brazil and Lithuania, in no partner country or economy do less than 20% of all students attend such schools. In contrast, more than 80% of the students in Croatia, Serbia, Singapore, Hong Kong-China and Liechtenstein attend schools whose principals reported that they always consider academic records or recommendations from feeder schools when making admissions decisions.

Horizontal differentiation at the school level

In some education systems, individual schools can choose to differentiate students horizontally within the school or choose to transfer students out of the school because of low achievement, special learning needs or behavioural problems. These school-level policies are less relevant in systems with high levels of vertical and/or horizontal differentiation at the level of the school system, as these systems have already differentiated students to a large degree.

Student transferring policies

Transferring students to other schools because of low academic achievement, behavioural problems or special learning needs is a way for schools to reduce the heterogeneity of the learning environment and to facilitate instruction. Students may move to other schools for several reasons but, whatever the reason, transfers generally pose difficulties for students. Transferring schools can imply a loss of social capital since students transfer out of social networks. When school transfers are motivated by behavioural problems, low academic achievement and special learning needs, students who are transferred out are also more likely to be received by schools with a higher prevalence of these types of students. Students who are transferred for these reasons not only pay the price in terms of social capital, but are also less likely to benefit from higher-achieving peers and orderly environments. In addition, transferred students might be perceived negatively in new schools, and that could affect students' motivation and attitudes towards learning.

PISA 2009 asked school principals about policies governing student transfers, namely about the likelihood of transferring a student to another school because of low academic achievement, high academic achievement, behavioural problems, special learning needs, parents' or guardians' request, or other reasons (Table IV.3.3a).

On average across OECD countries, 18% of students attend a school in which school principals reported that the school would likely transfer students with low achievement, behavioural problems or special learning needs. Yet transfer policies vary across countries: in Iceland, Ireland, Portugal, Norway, Finland, the United Kingdom, New Zealand, Australia and Sweden less than 5% of students attend schools whose school principals reported that the school would likely transfer students for these reasons. In contrast, in Luxembourg, Austria, Belgium, Greece and Turkey, around one-third or more of students attend a school whose principal reported that students with low achievement, behavioural problems or special learning needs will "very likely" be transferred out of the school.

Among the partner countries and economies, it is rare for students in Liechtenstein and Singapore to attend schools in which school principals reported that students will be transferred out of the school for low achievement, behavioural problems or special learning needs. In contrast, the practice is common in schools in Macao-China, Jordan, Qatar, Colombia, Indonesia, Romania, Kyrgyzstan, Chinese Taipei and Bulgaria, where around one-third or more of students attend schools that will very likely transfer a student with low achievement, behavioural problems or special learning needs to another school.

Ability grouping within schools

In some school systems, students are also grouped within the schools they attend based on their abilities. The intent behind this practice is much the same as for other types of differentiation, namely to better meet students' needs by creating a more homogeneous learning environment and making it easier for teachers to teach. Because individual schools are nested in a broader organisation, the practice of grouping students according to their ability within schools is partly determined by whether or not there are other forms of differentiation between and within schools, including the number of programmes available to students, grade repetition or transfer policies.

PISA asked school principals to report whether students were grouped by ability into different classes or within a class, and whether these groupings were made in all or only selected subjects. If ability grouping extends to all subjects, it creates a very different learning environment than if it is done for just a few subjects since there is little interaction between students in different groups, and lower-achieving students are unlikely to benefit the way they might if they share a class with their higher-achieving peers (Table IV.3.4).

On average across OECD countries, 13% of students are in schools whose principals reported that students are grouped by ability in all subjects. In Luxembourg, the Netherlands and Switzerland, over one-third of students attend schools that stream students in all subjects by ability, while in 19 other OECD countries, less than 10% of students attend such schools.

Among the partner countries and economies, ability grouping is more common than across OECD countries. In only four partner countries and economies do less than 10% of students attend schools that group students in all subjects. Ability grouping in all subjects is particularly common in Jordan, the Russian Federation, Qatar, Dubai (UAE) and Kazakhstan, where around one-third or more of students attend such schools.

Country profiles in selecting and grouping students

The organisational arrangements that govern selecting and assigning students to classes and schools are often closely interrelated. Some school systems are highly differentiated, combining various possibilities of selection, including vertical differentiation and horizontal differentiation, at both system and school levels. Other school systems are characterised by low levels of differentiation and seek to address heterogeneity within the classroom through instructional practices, such as individualised attention from teachers during class or remedial instruction, either during the school day or after school, in an attempt to keep all students at a similar academic level. Using the information on the kinds of differentiation adopted by each school system, a latent profile analysis identifies categories of school systems according to the types of vertical and horizontal differentiation they adopt (see Annex A5 for technical details). The analysis is based on three dimensions of selecting students into schools, and identifies several categories: two categories (*i.e.* low or high level of differentiation) on vertical differentiation, three categories (*i.e.* low, medium or high level of differentiation) on horizontal differentiation at the level of the education system, and two categories (*i.e.* low or high level of differentiation) on horizontal differentiation at the school level. Countries and economies are grouped such that all school systems in each category share similar differentiation policies and practices (Figure IV.3.2).

Among all OECD countries, Australia, Canada, Denmark, Estonia, Finland, Greece, Iceland, New Zealand, Norway, Poland, Sweden, the United Kingdom and the United States are characterised by low levels of differentiation in selecting and grouping students. In these school systems, students are not systematically streamed, schools are not selective in their admissions processes, and students usually do not repeat grades and are not transferred to other schools. As a result, classrooms tend to be heterogeneous. Four partner countries, Kazakhstan, Latvia, Lithuania and the Russian Federation, also fit into this category.

School systems in six OECD countries, Ireland, Israel, Italy, Japan, Korea and Slovenia, stratify students into different programmes based on the students' academic performance, usually before they are 15 years old (*i.e.* horizontal differentiation at the level of the school system). Grade repetition is not common in these school systems, nor is horizontal differentiation at the school level. Seven partner countries and economies, Albania, Azerbaijan, Dubai (UAE), Hong Kong-China, Montenegro, Shanghai-China and Thailand, also belong to this category.

In four OECD countries, Austria, the Czech Republic, Hungary and the Slovak Republic, school systems also apply horizontal differentiation at the level of the school system. These school systems are characterised by their use of streaming and early selection into these programmes based on students' academic performance, but generally, they do not use grade repetition or school-level differentiation. Three partner countries, Croatia, Liechtenstein and Singapore, also belong to this category.

Turkey and the partner countries Bulgaria and Serbia are characterised by high levels of horizontal differentiation at the school and system levels. These systems do not use vertical differentiation, but often create homogeneous classrooms by grouping students according to ability, transferring students or streaming students, through early tracking or selective admission.

■ Figure IV.3.2 ■

How school systems select and group students for schools, grades and programmes

		Low vertical differentiation		**High vertical differentiation**	
		Students who repeated one or more grades: 7% Students out of modal starting ages: 7%		Students who repeated one or more grades: 29% Students out of modal starting ages: 11%	
		Low horizontal differentiation at the school level	**High horizontal differentiation at the school level**	**Low horizontal differentiation at the school level**	**High horizontal differentiation at the school level**
		Schools that transfer students to other schools due to low achievement, behavioural problems or special learning needs: 15%	Schools that transfer students to other schools due to low achievement, behavioural problems or special learning needs: 33%	Schools that transfer students to other schools due to low achievement, behavioural problems or special learning needs: 15%	Schools that transfer students to other schools due to low achievement, behavioural problems or special learning needs: 33%
		Schools that group students by ability in all subjects: 8%	Schools that group students by ability in all subjects: 38%	Schools that group students by ability in all subjects: 8%	Schools that group students by ability in all subjects: 38%
Low horizontal differentiation at the system level	Number of school types or distinct educational programmes: 1.1 First age of selection: 15.8 Selective schools: 17%	Australia,[1] Canada,[2] Denmark, Estonia,[2] Finland,[2] Greece, Iceland,[2] New Zealand,[1] Norway,[2] Poland,[1] Sweden, United States, United Kingdom, Kazakhstan, Latvia, Lithuania, Russian Federation	Jordan	Spain, Argentina, Brazil, Tunisia, Uruguay	Chile, Colombia, Peru
Medium horizontal differentiation at the system level	Number of school types or distinct educational programmes: 3.0 First age of selection: 14.5 Selective schools: 42%	Ireland, Israel, Italy, Japan,[2] Korea,[2] Slovenia, Albania, Azerbaijan, Dubai (UAE), Hong Kong-China,[2] Montenegro, Shanghai-China,[1] Thailand	Indonesia, Kyrgyzstan, Qatar, Romania, Chinese Taipei	Mexico, Portugal	Luxembourg, Macao-China, Panama
High horizontal differentiation at the system level	Number of school types or distinct educational programmes: 4.3 First age of selection: 11.2 Selective schools: 61%	Austria, Czech Republic, Hungary, Slovak Republic, Croatia, Liechtenstein, Singapore[1]	Turkey, Bulgaria, Serbia	Belgium,[1] Germany, Trinidad and Tobago	Netherlands,[1] Switzerland[1]

Note: The estimates in the grey cells indicate the average values of the variables used in latent profile analysis in each group. See Annex A5 for technical details.
1. Perform higher than the OECD average in reading.
2. Perform higher than the OECD average in reading and where the relationship between students' socio-economic background and reading performance is weaker than the OECD average.
Source: OECD, *PISA 2009 Database*.
StatLink http://dx.doi.org/10.1787/888932343399

Among the countries whose school systems use vertical differentiation to create homogeneous learning environments, the Netherlands and Switzerland also apply high levels of horizontal differentiation at the school level and at the level of the school system. In contrast, Spain and four partner countries, Argentina, Brazil, Tunisia and Uruguay, use vertical differentiation as the primary and almost only form of selecting and distributing students. The OECD countries Belgium, Chile, Mexico, Portugal, Luxembourg, Germany and the partner countries and economies Peru, Colombia, Macao-China, Panama and Trinidad and Tobago, use vertical differentiation and either horizontal differentiation at the school level or at the level of the school system.

To examine how these policies and practices are reflected in students' academic performance, the between-school variation in students' performance can be compared among the OECD countries in the different categories with high, medium and low levels of differentiation. For example, the Netherlands and Switzerland have high levels of vertical and horizontal differentiation at the level of the school system and high levels of horizontal differentiation at the school level. Chile, Turkey and Luxembourg have high levels of differentiation in two of three dimensions. Not surprisingly, therefore, on average across these 5 OECD countries, 53% of the variation in student performance is attributable to the differences among schools.[4] In contrast, on average in the 13 OECD countries that have been categorised as having school systems with low levels of differentiation in all three dimensions, only 23% of the variation in student performance is attributable to the differences among schools.

As discussed in Chapters 1 and 2, these organisational features are also related to the average performance of school systems and to the impact of socio-economic background on learning outcomes. School systems with above-average student performance and a below-average impact of socio-economic background on learning outcomes are more likely to be those with low levels of all three types of differentiation. The 13 OECD countries that have low levels of vertical differentiation, horizontal differentiation at the level of the school system and horizontal differentiation at the school level have an average student performance of 505 score points with 12% of the variation in achievement explained by students' socio-economic background; across OECD countries, the average student performance is at 403 score points, with 14% of variation explained by students' socio-economic background. School systems that differentiate either vertically or horizontally have either lower levels of equity or lower levels of performance (Tables IV.1.1a, IV.1.1b and IV.1.1c).

GOVERNANCE OF SCHOOL SYSTEMS

Another important organisational feature of school systems is how they are governed. This idea of governance includes two elements: the degree to which schools are considered autonomous entities that make decisions independently of district, regional or national entities; and whether schools are allowed to compete for enrolment and the degree to which students and parents can choose schools. Chapter 2 shows that the relationship between school governance and performance and equity is complex. Autonomy in designing curricula and assessments seems to benefit the entire school system. It mainly relates to performance through its interaction with the school's socio-economic profile.

School autonomy

Since the early 1980s, school reforms have focused on giving schools greater autonomy over a wide range of institutional operations in an effort to raise performance levels (Whitty, 1997; Carnoy, 2000). More decision-making responsibility and accountability has devolved to school principals and, in some cases, management responsibilities have devolved to teachers or department heads. In order to gauge the extent to which school staff have a say in decisions relating to school policy and management, PISA 2009 asked school principals to report whether the teachers, the principal, the school's governing board, the regional or local education authorities or the national education authority had considerable responsibility for allocating resources to schools (appointing and dismissing teachers, establishing teachers' starting salaries and salary raises, formulating school budgets and allocating them within the school) and responsibility for the curriculum and instructional assessment within the school (establishing student-assessment policies, choosing textbooks, determining which courses are offered and the content of those courses). This information was combined to create two composite indices: an *index of school responsibility for resource allocation,* and an *index of school responsibility for curriculum and assessment,* such that both indices have an average of zero and a standard deviation of one for OECD countries. Higher values indicate more autonomy for school principals and teachers.

In most countries, few schools have a major influence on teachers' salaries. Across OECD countries, around three-quarters of students are in schools whose principals reported that only national and/or regional education authorities have considerable responsibility for establishing teachers' starting salaries and determining teachers' salary increases (Figure IV.3.3a). Some 95% or more of students in Austria, Belgium, Greece, Italy, Ireland, Spain,

Turkey and the partner countries Albania, Argentina, Croatia, Jordan, Romania, Tunisia and Uruguay are in schools whose principals reported that only regional and/or national education authorities have considerable responsibility for these two tasks. In contrast, school principals and/or teachers have more responsibility for tasks related to resources, such as selecting and hiring teachers, dismissing teachers, formulating the school budget and deciding on budget allocations within the school. Around 80% or more of students in Denmark, Estonia, Hungary, the Netherlands, New Zealand and the partner countries and economies Bulgaria, Hong Kong-China, Latvia, Macao-China and Shanghai-China are in schools whose principals reported that principals and/or schools have considerable responsibility for at least three of these four tasks.

School autonomy, as measured by the *index of school responsibility for resource allocation*, is greatest in the Netherlands, the Czech Republic and the partner countries and economies Macao-China and Bulgaria, as reported by school principals in these countries. In all of these countries, most schools are responsible for hiring and dismissing teachers and formulating and allocating budgets. In contrast, responsibility for resource allocation is lowest among schools in Greece, Turkey, Italy and the partner countries Romania and Tunisia.

Schools within a country show varying degrees of autonomy in allocating resources. School principals in Greece, Turkey, Ireland and the partner country Romania reported similar levels of autonomy in allocating resources, while in Chile, Hungary, the Czech Republic and the partner countries and economies Peru, Dubai (UAE) and Qatar, some schools are entitled to allocate resources while in other schools these decisions are made by national or regional educational authorities (Table IV.3.5). In some countries, upper secondary schools tend to have more autonomy in allocating resources than lower secondary schools, while in a few countries the reverse is true. Private schools tend to have higher degrees of autonomy in almost all countries.

In general, schools that are given responsibility for resource allocation are not necessarily entitled to make curricular decisions. Greece, Turkey and the partner countries Tunisia, Jordan and Serbia are among those countries that grant the least responsibility to schools in making decisions about curricula and assessments, as measured by the *index of responsibility for curriculum and assessment* (Figure IV.3.3b). Relatively higher levels of school autonomy in setting curricula and assessment practices are observed in Japan, the Netherlands, the Czech Republic, the United Kingdom, New Zealand and the partner economies Hong Kong-China and Macao-China, where the index scores are at least four-fifths of a standard deviation higher than the OECD average.

Examining in detail school principals' responses to individual questionnaire items composing the index, around 80% or more of students are in schools whose principals reported that only school principals and/or teachers have a considerable responsibility for establishing student assessment policies, choosing which textbooks are used, determining course content, and deciding which courses are offered in the Czech Republic, Japan, Korea, the Netherlands, New Zealand, the United Kingdom and the partner countries and economies Hong Kong-China, Macao-China and Thailand. Meanwhile, these are mainly only under the responsibility of regional and/or national education authority in Greece and the partner countries Jordan and Tunisia.

Not all schools within the same system have the same level of discretion over their curricula and assessments. For example, in the Slovak Republic, Chile, Israel, Sweden and the partner countries/economies Dubai (UAE), Lichtenstein, Shanghai-China, Peru, Kyrgyzstan and Indonesia, some schools can formulate their own curricula and assessments while other schools must abide by decisions taken by the school governing board or national/regional authorities (Table IV.3.6). The opposite is true in Greece, Portugal, Turkey and the partner countries Tunisia, Serbia, Croatia and Bulgaria, where all schools have somewhat similar levels of autonomy in designing their curricula. In some countries, there is a difference in the degree of schools' autonomy in deciding curricula and assessments between upper- and lower secondary schools, but the pattern is not consistent: upper secondary schools tend to have more autonomy in this area than lower secondary schools in some countries, while the reverse is observed in other countries. In most countries, private schools tend to have higher degrees of autonomy in making decisions about curricula and assessments.

Some caution is warranted when interpreting the degree of responsibility schools have in allocating resources, formulating curricula and using student assessments. Decision-making arrangements vary widely across countries, so the questions posed to school principals were general; thus, responses may depend on how school principals interpreted the questions. For example, when school principals were asked who has considerable responsibility for formulating the school budget, some school principals might have related this question to the regular budget of the school, while others may not have had any involvement in the regular budget and may therefore have related the question to supplementary budgets, *i.e.* contributions from parents or the community.

■ Figure IV.3.3a ■

How much autonomy individual schools have over resource allocation

Percentage of students in schools whose principals reported that only "principals and/or teachers", only "regional and/or national education authority" or both "principals and/or teachers" and "regional and/or national education authority" have a considerable responsibility for the following tasks

- A Selecting teachers for hire
- B Dismissing teachers
- C Establishing teachers' starting salaries
- D Determining teachers' salaries increases
- E Formulating the school budget
- F Deciding on budget allocations within the school

- 1 Only "principals and/or teachers"
- 2 Both "principals and/or teachers" and "regional and/or national education authority"
- 3 Only "regional and/or national education authority"

		A			B			C			D			E			F			Variability in the index (S.D.)
		1	2	3	1	2	3	1	2	3	1	2	3	1	2	3	1	2	3	
OECD	Australia	61	20	19	43	12	45	12	5	84	13	6	81	68	16	16	93	6	0	0.9
	Austria	13	35	52	5	26	68	1	0	99	1	0	99	11	9	80	84	12	4	0.3
	Belgium	75	13	12	63	21	17	0	1	99	0	1	99	56	18	26	63	19	17	0.3
	Canada	54	39	7	17	35	48	3	5	92	4	6	91	25	30	45	76	19	5	0.5
	Chile	69	8	23	59	3	38	37	1	62	37	1	62	55	9	36	71	9	20	1.2
	Czech Republic	100	0	0	99	1	0	77	15	8	65	25	11	55	36	9	75	24	1	1.2
	Denmark	97	2	0	69	15	16	20	10	70	16	14	70	80	13	8	98	2	0	0.9
	Estonia	98	2	0	95	5	0	7	20	73	12	33	55	37	54	9	85	15	1	0.6
	Finland	32	43	25	18	19	63	8	7	84	5	15	80	36	41	23	92	6	1	0.5
	France	w	w	w	w	w	w	w	w	w	w	w	w	w	w	w	w	w	w	w
	Germany	29	36	34	7	14	79	3	0	97	4	15	81	29	4	67	97	2	2	0.5
	Greece	0	1	99	0	2	98	0	0	100	0	0	100	34	7	59	59	7	34	0.1
	Hungary	99	1	0	97	2	1	49	7	44	56	7	37	73	15	12	92	5	2	1.2
	Iceland	94	6	0	93	7	0	7	13	80	4	16	80	57	30	13	77	22	0	0.5
	Ireland	61	25	14	36	14	50	0	2	98	1	0	99	60	13	27	89	5	6	0.2
	Israel	67	30	3	49	38	13	9	4	87	13	6	80	15	26	59	66	24	11	0.8
	Italy	9	10	82	9	6	84	3	0	97	3	0	96	7	7	86	69	11	21	0.5
	Japan	25	2	73	22	1	77	13	0	87	16	3	80	28	4	69	89	3	8	1.0
	Korea	32	6	62	23	4	74	8	0	92	6	0	94	29	12	58	86	6	8	0.7
	Luxembourg	21	41	38	19	36	45	6	0	94	6	0	94	31	57	12	78	14	8	0.8
	Mexico	34	5	61	22	4	73	8	0	92	6	0	94	46	6	48	71	7	22	0.8
	Netherlands	100	0	0	99	1	0	72	8	20	55	12	33	99	1	0	100	0	0	1.0
	New Zealand	100	0	0	89	7	4	9	3	88	15	21	64	95	4	1	99	1	0	0.7
	Norway	72	21	6	44	22	34	8	4	88	6	13	81	55	28	17	88	12	1	0.6
	Poland	87	12	1	90	10	0	9	20	71	4	20	77	7	42	51	26	43	31	0.4
	Portugal	13	57	30	14	0	86	5	0	94	5	0	94	63	10	27	89	3	8	0.7
	Slovak Republic	98	2	0	98	2	0	39	27	34	32	33	35	45	40	15	70	27	3	1.1
	Slovenia	96	4	1	88	10	1	7	11	82	13	31	56	26	49	26	78	21	1	0.6
	Spain	31	3	66	32	1	67	3	2	95	3	2	95	63	4	33	93	4	3	0.6
	Sweden	96	4	0	63	17	20	57	16	27	69	22	9	64	20	16	93	5	2	1.1
	Switzerland	82	15	3	60	26	15	8	8	84	8	13	79	35	30	35	83	13	4	0.7
	Turkey	1	1	99	2	2	96	1	0	99	1	0	99	34	19	47	56	16	28	0.2
	United Kingdom	90	9	0	70	22	8	52	23	25	67	17	15	57	29	14	95	5	1	1.1
	United States	88	12	0	75	19	6	17	5	78	18	6	75	54	29	16	83	13	4	0.9
	OECD average	61	14	25	51	13	37	17	7	77	17	10	73	46	22	32	81	12	8	0.7
Partners	Albania	8	14	78	7	14	79	3	0	97	3	1	96	33	12	55	61	8	31	0.5
	Argentina	44	5	51	27	3	70	2	1	97	1	4	96	22	5	73	64	12	24	0.4
	Azerbaijan	40	22	38	61	17	22	35	6	59	13	3	84	5	6	89	20	4	76	0.3
	Brazil	17	7	76	14	8	78	8	1	91	7	1	92	14	5	80	21	6	73	0.8
	Bulgaria	93	5	2	97	2	1	66	20	14	84	12	4	73	22	5	92	7	1	1.1
	Colombia	21	5	75	21	1	78	14	0	86	13	1	86	58	5	36	87	5	8	1.0
	Croatia	90	10	0	84	11	5	1	1	98	2	1	97	26	34	40	68	23	9	0.4
	Dubai (UAE)	65	12	23	67	9	24	62	3	34	68	1	31	75	2	22	92	3	5	1.2
	Hong Kong-China	83	15	2	79	17	4	18	24	58	15	12	74	84	15	2	91	9	0	0.9
	Indonesia	29	12	59	26	11	63	20	9	70	23	11	66	83	11	5	78	14	8	1.0
	Jordan	6	1	93	4	1	95	1	1	98	2	0	98	83	1	17	70	2	28	0.4
	Kazakhstan	88	10	2	95	4	2	17	10	73	8	10	82	8	13	79	17	19	64	0.7
	Kyrgyzstan	74	14	11	68	13	19	18	4	77	13	3	84	12	7	81	19	7	74	0.6
	Latvia	94	4	2	96	4	0	10	15	75	18	25	57	62	25	12	81	16	3	0.7
	Liechtenstein	41	0	59	37	0	63	6	0	94	39	17	45	37	0	63	100	0	0	1.0
	Lithuania	96	4	0	99	1	0	11	7	81	6	8	86	25	27	48	42	29	28	0.5
	Macao-China	92	4	4	91	5	4	91	4	5	90	4	5	95	5	0	84	16	0	1.0
	Montenegro	89	11	0	82	18	0	0	5	95	10	11	78	12	21	68	65	22	13	0.3
	Panama	22	3	76	20	8	72	14	5	81	14	8	79	70	15	15	43	10	47	0.9
	Peru	38	15	47	30	9	61	22	2	76	22	2	77	60	9	31	79	6	15	1.3
	Qatar	52	3	44	54	5	41	47	3	50	47	4	50	43	4	53	52	4	44	1.2
	Romania	1	9	91	4	11	86	0	2	97	1	4	95	7	25	68	40	13	47	0.1
	Russian Federation	95	4	1	95	5	0	35	15	50	29	20	51	8	30	63	46	28	27	0.7
	Serbia	72	28	1	64	30	7	1	8	90	16	19	65	9	27	64	74	16	10	0.3
	Shanghai-China	98	2	0	99	1	0	36	5	59	43	6	51	91	2	6	98	1	1	1.1
	Singapore	14	38	48	14	24	62	4	3	93	7	17	75	49	22	29	91	8	1	0.6
	Chinese Taipei	73	13	14	74	14	12	18	7	75	23	7	70	50	13	37	78	8	14	1.0
	Thailand	30	20	50	59	12	28	29	14	56	72	24	5	70	20	10	90	7	2	1.1
	Trinidad and Tobago	17	14	69	6	4	90	2	1	96	6	5	89	46	28	26	75	12	12	0.6
	Tunisia	2	0	98	1	0	99	1	1	99	1	0	99	10	18	72	78	13	9	0.3
	Uruguay	17	5	78	13	1	86	3	1	96	2	1	96	13	12	75	49	16	35	0.6

Source: OECD, *PISA 2009 Database*, Table IV.3.5.

StatLink http://dx.doi.org/10.1787/888932343399

■ Figure IV.3.3b ■

How much autonomy individual schools have over curricula and assessments

Percentage of students in schools whose principals reported that only "principals and/or teachers", only "regional and/or national education authority" or both "principals and/or teachers" and "regional and/or national education authority" have a considerable responsibility for the following tasks

- A Establishing student assessment policies
- B Choosing which textbooks are used
- C Determining course content
- D Deciding which courses are offered

- 1 Only "principals and/or teachers"
- 2 Both "principals and/or teachers" and "regional and/or national education authority"
- 3 Only "regional and/or national education authority"

		A			B			C			D			Variability in the index (S.D.)
		1	2	3	1	2	3	1	2	3	1	2	3	
OECD	Australia	65	33	2	92	8	0	46	40	14	75	24	1	0.9
	Austria	57	27	15	94	5	1	37	40	23	32	40	29	0.8
	Belgium	78	19	4	94	4	1	32	42	26	40	46	13	0.8
	Canada	28	62	10	40	49	11	12	51	38	44	54	3	0.6
	Chile	72	21	6	73	20	7	43	22	35	64	20	16	1.0
	Czech Republic	95	5	0	89	11	1	83	16	1	88	11	1	0.8
	Denmark	61	28	11	100	0	0	56	32	12	47	39	14	0.9
	Estonia	63	33	3	66	32	2	66	30	4	79	20	2	0.9
	Finland	50	43	7	98	2	0	32	52	16	55	39	6	0.8
	France	w	w	w	w	w	w	w	w	w	w	w	w	w
	Germany	71	21	9	84	13	3	21	47	32	80	18	2	0.7
	Greece	20	12	68	7	8	85	1	3	96	6	5	88	0.3
	Hungary	94	6	0	98	2	0	49	36	15	43	28	29	0.9
	Iceland	92	8	1	93	4	3	61	26	13	48	42	10	0.9
	Ireland	87	13	0	97	3	0	29	37	34	78	21	1	0.7
	Israel	80	20	0	53	43	4	52	44	5	44	50	6	1.0
	Italy	91	8	1	99	1	0	59	27	14	49	25	27	0.9
	Japan	98	2	0	89	8	3	93	6	1	94	5	2	0.7
	Korea	92	6	2	96	4	0	89	8	2	79	17	4	0.8
	Luxembourg	9	33	58	13	80	7	9	72	20	18	61	21	0.6
	Mexico	56	15	29	63	11	26	14	7	79	5	5	91	0.5
	Netherlands	99	1	0	100	0	0	87	12	1	89	10	1	0.6
	New Zealand	81	17	2	99	1	0	79	20	1	92	8	0	0.8
	Norway	38	36	27	97	2	1	30	40	30	23	33	44	0.7
	Poland	92	8	0	92	8	0	93	7	0	40	31	29	0.8
	Portugal	35	37	28	98	2	0	5	3	92	10	5	86	0.4
	Slovak Republic	76	21	3	56	39	5	48	47	5	52	48	1	1.0
	Slovenia	46	48	5	72	27	1	34	59	6	28	52	20	0.8
	Spain	44	34	23	95	5	0	32	31	37	30	31	39	0.8
	Sweden	66	30	3	99	1	0	66	26	8	53	25	22	1.0
	Switzerland	57	27	16	40	40	20	21	41	38	24	50	27	0.7
	Turkey	42	29	30	14	18	68	9	15	76	14	21	65	0.4
	United Kingdom	88	12	0	98	2	0	77	20	2	86	14	0	0.8
	United States	46	40	13	62	28	10	36	46	18	58	37	4	0.9
	OECD average	66	23	11	78	15	8	45	31	24	50	28	21	0.8
Partners	Albania	51	16	33	91	8	1	35	7	57	35	12	53	0.8
	Argentina	74	20	6	81	16	3	28	43	29	8	30	61	0.6
	Azerbaijan	54	8	38	50	6	43	27	9	64	37	5	58	0.8
	Brazil	47	27	26	88	9	2	35	25	40	18	17	65	0.8
	Bulgaria	25	37	38	88	12	1	10	26	65	10	15	75	0.4
	Colombia	39	21	39	92	3	4	69	23	8	64	14	23	0.8
	Croatia	26	36	38	63	34	3	11	50	39	2	25	72	0.4
	Dubai (UAE)	77	10	13	55	17	27	62	13	26	59	16	25	1.1
	Hong Kong-China	93	7	0	93	7	0	81	17	2	87	13	0	0.8
	Indonesia	67	28	6	80	13	7	75	18	7	49	23	28	0.9
	Jordan	27	4	70	4	1	95	7	1	93	7	1	92	0.5
	Kazakhstan	31	22	47	16	14	70	11	18	71	40	22	37	0.5
	Kyrgyzstan	65	8	26	68	8	23	59	10	31	44	7	49	1.0
	Latvia	56	40	4	71	27	2	19	46	36	30	42	28	0.6
	Liechtenstein	69	25	6	54	5	40	41	0	59	53	9	38	1.1
	Lithuania	75	20	5	89	11	1	50	35	15	75	20	5	0.9
	Macao-China	95	0	5	100	0	0	94	6	0	81	14	4	0.8
	Montenegro	40	32	28	5	30	65	5	34	61	20	36	44	0.6
	Panama	41	25	34	52	26	22	41	23	36	26	23	51	0.8
	Peru	75	15	10	52	12	37	53	23	24	45	18	37	1.0
	Qatar	45	18	37	37	16	47	31	9	60	35	17	48	0.9
	Romania	42	36	22	86	13	1	46	33	20	31	41	29	0.7
	Russian Federation	63	25	12	65	27	8	21	40	39	71	22	7	0.8
	Serbia	49	44	7	19	59	23	2	41	57	0	12	87	0.2
	Shanghai-China	86	9	5	49	17	34	45	22	33	52	28	20	1.0
	Singapore	57	41	2	72	24	3	44	38	18	66	31	4	0.9
	Chinese Taipei	74	17	8	92	8	0	81	16	3	68	25	7	0.9
	Thailand	79	18	2	89	10	1	89	11	0	91	8	1	0.8
	Trinidad and Tobago	50	45	5	29	62	10	21	40	39	34	51	15	0.7
	Tunisia	11	11	78	0	1	99	3	14	83	4	9	87	0.1
	Uruguay	23	30	47	31	36	33	3	26	71	21	19	59	0.4

Source: OECD, *PISA 2009 Database*, Table IV.3.6.
StatLink http://dx.doi.org/10.1787/888932343399

Since the degree of autonomy of each stakeholder was not identified, the responses were given equal weight, regardless of the actual influence stakeholders had on different aspects of decision making. However, a comparison of the responses from school principals with data provided by national authorities indicates a fairly close correspondence,[5] suggesting that the responses from school principals are not distorted by cultural and contextual bias (OECD, 2010b). It is worth noting that variation within countries can be explained, in part, by regional differences, particularly in federal education systems (see Table S.IV.d).

School choice

Students in some school systems are encouraged or even obliged to attend their neighbourhood school. However, reforms over the past decades have tended to give more authority to parents and students to choose schools that meet their educational needs or preferences best (Heyneman, 2009). Across OECD countries, more than half of the countries reported a reduction in restrictions on school choice among schools that are publicly managed and publicly funded. Twelve OECD countries reported the creation of new autonomous public schools and ten reported that new funding mechanisms had been put in place to promote school choice (OECD, 2010a).

When students and parents can choose schools based on academic criteria, schools then compete for students, which, in turn, may prompt schools to organise programmes and teaching to better respond to diverse student requirements and interests, and so reduce the costs of failure and mismatches (Berends, 2009). In some school systems, schools not only compete for student enrolment, but also for funding. Direct public funding of independently managed institutions, based on student enrolments or student credit-hours, is one model. Another method is giving money to students and their families through scholarships or vouchers for them to spend in public or private educational institutions of their choice.

According to responses from school principals, across OECD countries, an average of 76% of the students assessed by PISA attend schools that compete with at least one other school for enrolment. Only in Switzerland, Norway and Slovenia do less than 50% of the students attend schools that compete with other schools in this way. In contrast, in the Netherlands, Australia, Belgium, the Slovak Republic and Japan, over 90% of students attend schools that compete with other schools for enrolment (Table IV3.8a). In some countries, school competition is more common at the upper secondary level than at the lower secondary level, while in other countries the reverse is true (Table IV.3.8b).

Some 13 OECD countries and 5 partner countries and economies allow parents and students to choose public schools and also incorporate vouchers or tax credits in their school-choice arrangements.[6] Eleven OECD countries and seven partner countries and economies offer a choice of public schools, but do not offer vouchers or tax credits; two OECD countries and four partner countries and economies restrict parents and students in the choice of public schools, but offer tax or voucher credits to attend other schools; and in four OECD countries and one partner country, parents and students must attend the public school nearest to where they live and they are not offered any kind of subsidy to attend other schools (Figure IV.3.4).

Judging by the reports of school principals, competition among schools is consistent with these school-choice arrangements at the level of the school system, and is greatest in school systems that grant parents and students the freedom to choose public schools and offer subsidies in the form of vouchers or tax credits to attend other schools. In countries with these characteristics, 85% of students attend schools whose principals reported that they compete with at least one other school for enrolment. The lowest levels of school competition are found in countries that restrict attendance to public schools and do not offer subsidies to attend other schools. In the average country in this category, 52% of students attend schools whose principals reported that they compete for student enrolment with at least one other school (Figure IV.3.4). Levels of school competition are similar in countries that restrict attendance to public schools and offer subsidies, and in countries that do not restrict attendance to public schools but offer no subsidies. In these countries, around 75% of students attend schools whose principals reported that they compete with other schools for enrolment. However, competition among schools is less frequent in remote and rural areas, where public schools are usually located at greater distances from each other, making it more difficult for parents and students to choose a school other than the one that is closest to their home (Table IV.2.6).

The partner countries and economies show similar levels of school competition as among OECD countries. School competition is greatest in Macao-China, Hong Kong-China, Indonesia, Singapore and Chinese Taipei, where over 95% of students are in schools whose principals reported that they compete with at least one other school for student enrolment. In contrast, in Montenegro, only 37% of students are enrolled in such schools and in Liechtenstein and Uruguay less than 60% of students are enrolled in such schools (Table IV.3.8a).

■ Figure IV.3.4 ■

Countries in which parents can choose schools for their children

Prevalence of school competition by school choice arrangements

More freedom to choose public schools: At most one restriction on choosing public schools (region, district or other restrictions)		Less freedom to choose public schools: At least two restrictions on choosing public schools (region, district or other restrictions)	
Vouchers or Tax Credits to attend other schools: Vouchers or tax credits offered to attend public, government-dependent or private-independent schools	**No Vouchers or Tax Credits to attend other schools:** No vouchers or tax credits offered to attend public, government-dependent or private-independent schools	**Vouchers or Tax Credits to attend other schools:** Vouchers or tax credits offered to attend public, government-dependent or private-independent schools	**No Vouchers or Tax Credits to attend other schools:** No vouchers or tax credits offered to attend public, government-dependent or private-independent schools
Belgium, Chile, Estonia, France, Germany, Italy, Korea, Luxembourg, New Zealand, Portugal, Slovak Republic, Spain, United Kingdom, Lithuania, Macao-China, Montenegro, Qatar, Singapore	Austria, Czech Republic, Denmark, Finland, Japan, Hungary, Ireland, Mexico, Netherlands, Slovenia, Sweden, Bulgaria, Colombia, Hong Kong-China, Kyrgyzstan, Latvia, Peru, Shanghai-China	Poland, United States, Argentina, Thailand, Brazil, Chinese Taipei	Iceland, Israel, Norway, Switzerland, Croatia

Note: Bars represent the average percentages of school competition in OECD countries, by four categories of school choice arrangements.
Source: OECD, *PISA 2009 Database*, Tables IV.3.7 and IV.3.8a.
StatLink http://dx.doi.org/10.1787/888932343399

Public and private stakeholders

School education takes place mainly in public schools, defined by PISA as schools managed directly or indirectly by a public education authority, government agency, or governing board appointed by government or elected by public franchise. Nevertheless, with an increasing variety of educational opportunities, programmes and providers, governments are forging new partnerships to mobilise resources for education and to design new policies that allow all stakeholders to participate more fully and share the costs and benefits more equitably. Private education is not only a way of mobilising resources from a wider range of funding sources, but it is sometimes also considered a way of making education more cost-effective. Publicly financed schools are not necessarily also managed publicly. Governments can transfer funds to public and private educational institutions according to various allocation mechanisms (see section on school choice) (OECD, 2007).

Across OECD countries, 15% of students are enrolled in schools that are privately managed, that is, managed directly or indirectly by a non-governmental organisation, *e.g.* a church, trade union, business or other private institution (Table IV.3.9). More than 50% of students in the Netherlands, Ireland and Chile are enrolled in privately managed schools. In contrast, in Turkey, Iceland and Norway, more than 98% of students attend schools that are managed publicly.

Schools that are managed publicly are most common among the partner countries and economies. In particular, in the Russian Federation, Azerbaijan, Lithuania, Romania, Montenegro, Latvia, Serbia, Singapore, Tunisia, Croatia and Bulgaria, less than 2% of students attend schools that are managed privately. In contrast, in Macao-China and Hong Kong-China, more than 90% of students attend privately managed schools, and in Dubai (UAE), Indonesia, Argentina and Chinese Taipei, over one-third of students attend privately managed schools.

Country profiles in the governance of school systems

The preceding comparisons can be summarised in a latent profile analysis. This analysis categorises school systems into groups that share similar profiles in the way they allow schools and parents to make decisions that affect their children's education. The groupings are based on school autonomy and school competition. Two categories

are identified for each feature and the interplay between these features results in four groups: school systems that offer high levels of autonomy to schools in designing and using curricula and assessments[7] and encourage more competition between schools; school systems that offer low levels of autonomy to schools and limit competition between schools; school systems that offer high levels of autonomy to schools, but limit competition between schools; and school systems that offer low levels of autonomy to schools, yet encourage more competition between schools (Figure IV.3.5).

Across OECD countries, the most common configuration is the one that gives schools discretion over curricular and assessment decisions, and restricts competition for enrolment among schools. These school systems have relatively little competition for enrolment among schools, and private schools are not widely available in these countries. Twenty-three OECD countries and fifteen partner countries and economies share this configuration.

The configuration that offers relatively low levels of autonomy to schools and low levels of school competition is found in 4 OECD countries and 11 partner countries.

Six OECD countries and five partner countries and economies reported configurations that offer high levels of autonomy and competition, either in the form of a high prevalence of private schools or greater competition among schools for enrolment. In these school systems, schools have the authority to design curricula, and parents and students can choose from a variety of schools for their children.

When examining these results, it is important to keep in mind that 15-year-olds may be at different education levels in different countries. However, the results from PISA show that the policies and practices concerning school autonomy and school competition tend to be closely related between these levels.[8]

Chapter 1 shows that the school systems with above-average performance and a below-average impact of socio-economic background on student performance tend to grant higher levels of autonomy to schools in formulating and using curricula and assessments and lower levels of school competition. However, not all OECD countries that share this configuration show above-average performance (Table IV.1.1). This suggests that although high levels of school autonomy in decisions affecting curricula and assessments and low levels of school competition could be pathways to successful school systems, other conditions must be in place for this configuration to be effective in improving performance and equity.

■ Figure IV.3.5 ■

How school systems are governed

		Less school competition Schools that complete with other schools for students in the same area: 73% Private schools: 8%	**More school competition** Schools that complete with other schools for students in the same area: 89% Private schools: 52%
Less school autonomy for curriculum and assessment	Establish student assessment policies: 61% Choose which textbooks are used: 55% Determine course content: 14% Decide which courses are offered: 18%	Greece, Mexico, Portugal, Turkey, Albania, Azerbaijan, Bulgaria, Croatia, Kazakhstan, Jordan, Montenegro, Qatar, Serbia, Tunisia, Uruguay,	–
More school autonomy for curriculum and assessment	Establish student assessment policies: 92% Choose which textbooks are used: 97% Determine course content: 85% Decide which courses are offered: 87%	Austria, Canada,[2] Czech Republic, Denmark, Estonia,[2] Finland,[2] Germany, Hungary, Iceland,[2] Israel, Italy, Japan,[2] Luxembourg, New Zealand,[1] Norway,[2] Poland,[1] Slovak Republic, Slovenia, Spain, Sweden, Switzerland,[1] United Kingdom, United States, Panama, Argentina, Brazil, Colombia, Kyrgyzstan, Latvia, Liechtenstein, Lithuania, Peru, Romania, Russian Federation, Shanghai-China,[1] Singapore,[1] Thailand, Trinidad and Tobago	Australia,[1] Belgium,[1] Chile, Ireland, Korea,[2] Netherlands,[1] Dubai (UAE), Hong Kong-China,[2] Indonesia, Macao-China, Chinese Taipei

Note: The estimates in the grey cells indicate the average values of the variables used in latent profile analysis in each group. See Annex A5 for technical details.
1. Perform higher than the OECD average in reading.
2. Perform higher than the OECD average in reading and where the relationship between students' socio-economic background and reading performance is weaker than the OECD average.
Source: OECD, *PISA 2009 Database*.
StatLink http://dx.doi.org/10.1787/888932343399

ASSESSMENT AND ACCOUNTABILITY POLICIES

To ensure that instruction is effective, most schools evaluate student learning, usually through teachers' assessments, required assignments or tests. Standardised tests are often used to compare students and schools at the national or regional level. Evaluation of student learning outcomes can also be used to hold schools and other actors in education accountable for what is one of the principal functions of schooling.

The cross-country analysis in Chapter 2 shows that the use of standards-based external examinations tends to be positively related to a system's overall performance, while the use of standardised tests or assessment data for benchmarking or decision making is not consistently related to learning outcomes. However, in some countries, schools that post achievement data publicly tend to perform better; and the use of standardised tests tends to be associated with a lower impact of socio-economic background on student performance.

Assessment practices and purposes

Among OECD countries, the Czech Republic, Denmark, Estonia, Finland, Hungary, Iceland, Ireland, Israel, Italy, Japan, Korea, Luxembourg, the Netherlands, New Zealand, Norway, Poland, the Slovak Republic, Slovenia, Turkey and the United Kingdom all use standards-based external examinations throughout the system for students at the secondary education level. While in some countries the standards-based external examinations during or at the end of secondary education are the same for all students, in other countries, *e.g.* the United Kingdom, students have a choice between different examination levels for a given subject. Among the partner countries and economies, Azerbaijan, Bulgaria, Colombia, Croatia, Dubai (UAE), Hong Kong-China, Indonesia, Jordan, Kyrgyzstan, Latvia, Liechtenstein, Lithuania, Montenegro, the Russian Federation, Shanghai-China, Singapore, Chinese Taipei and Trinidad and Tobago all have system-wide examinations as well (Table IV.3.11).

Beyond national examinations, schools can independently choose to use standardised tests in order to assess their students in a metric that allows for comparisons with national or regional norms. In PISA 2009, school principals were asked to report the types and frequency of assessments used: standardised tests, teacher-developed tests, teachers' judgmental ratings, student portfolios, or student assignments. They were also asked to report on the purposes of the assessments. These include informing parents about their children's progress, making decisions about grade promotion or retention, grouping students for instructional purposes, monitoring and comparing school performance, judging teachers' effectiveness, and/or identifying areas for improvement in the curriculum or teaching methods.

An average of 76% of students in OECD countries are enrolled in schools whose principals reported that they use standardised tests for 15-year-old students. However, standardised tests are relatively uncommon in Slovenia, Belgium, Spain, Austria and Germany, where less than half of students attend schools that assess students through standardised tests. In contrast, the use of standardised tests is practically universal, according to school principals' reports, in Luxembourg, Finland, Korea, the United States, Poland, Denmark, Sweden and Norway, where over 95% of students attend schools that use this form of assessment at least once a year. In the partner countries and economies Qatar, Singapore, Hong Kong-China, Azerbaijan, Kyrgyzstan, Latvia, Indonesia and Tunisia, the use of standardised tests is also almost universal according to school principals' reports, whereas in Uruguay and Serbia, less than half the students attend schools that use such tests (Table IV.3.10).

The purpose of assessments, whether standardised tests or other forms, vary. At the school level, these assessments can be used by schools to compare themselves to other schools, to monitor progress, or to make decisions about instruction. Some 59% of students across OECD countries are in schools whose principals reported that they use achievement data to compare their students' achievement levels either with those in other schools or to national or regional performance measures. This practice is most common in the United States, New Zealand and the United Kingdom, where over 90% of students attend schools that use achievement data for comparative purposes. In Belgium, Japan, Austria, Spain and Greece, less than one-third of students attend schools that use achievement information this way (the last column in Table IV.3.12).

It is more common for schools to use achievement information to monitor school progress from year to year; on average some 77% of students in OECD countries attend schools that do so. In 21 OECD countries, more than 80% of students attend schools that use achievement data this way. Only in Denmark, Luxembourg, Switzerland and Austria do less than 50% of students attend schools that use achievement data to monitor progress.

Data on student achievement can also be used to identify aspects of instruction or the curriculum that could be improved. Across OECD countries, 77% of students are in schools that reported doing so, and in New Zealand, the United States, the United Kingdom, Iceland, Poland, Mexico, Chile, Spain and Israel, more than 90% of students attend schools that use achievement data to identify areas of instruction or the curriculum that need improvement. Using achievement data for these purposes is less common in Greece and Switzerland, where less than 50% of students attend schools that use achievement data this way.

Among the partner countries and economies, the use of such achievement data also varies: over 90% of students in the Russian Federation, Kazakhstan, Singapore, Kyrgyzstan, Azerbaijan, Latvia, Romania, Indonesia and Tunisia attend schools that use achievement data to compare themselves to other schools or with national/regional performance; yet in Uruguay and Macao-China, less than 25% of students attend schools that use achievement data in this way. As across OECD countries, the use of achievement data to monitor school progress is common among the partner countries and economies: in 26 of the 31 partner countries and economies, over 80% of students attend schools that use achievement data for monitoring purposes. It is also common for schools in the partner countries and economies to use achievement data to identify aspects of the curriculum that could be improved: in 19 partner countries and economies, over 90% of students attend schools that use achievement data in this manner.

Accountability arrangements

The shift in public and government concern away from mere control over the resources for and content of education towards a focus on outcomes has resulted in the establishment of standards of quality for educational institutions. Standard-setting among countries ranges from defining broad educational goals to formulating explicit performance expectations in well-defined subject areas.

Performance standards are typically associated with accountability systems. Over the past decade, accountability systems based on student performance have become more common in many OECD countries, and results are often widely reported and used in public debate to inform parents about school choice and to prompt improvements in schools. The rationale for and nature of these accountability systems, however, vary greatly within and across countries. The OECD countries use different forms of external assessment, external evaluation or inspection, and schools' own quality-assurance and self-evaluation efforts.

Given the importance of accountability systems in the policy and public debate, and given the diversity of accountability systems across OECD countries (OECD, 2007), PISA 2009 collected data on the nature of accountability systems and the ways in which the resulting information was used and made available to various stakeholders and the public at large.

Some school systems make achievement data publicly available to inform stakeholders of the comparative performance of schools and, where school-choice programmes are available, to make parents aware of the choices available to them. Across OECD countries, an average of 37% of students attend schools whose principals reported that they make achievement data available to the public, while in Belgium, Finland, Switzerland, Japan, Austria and Spain, less than 10% of students attend schools that make their data publicly available. In contrast, in the United States and the United Kingdom, more than 80% of students attend schools that make student achievement data publicly available (Table IV.3.13).

School-level achievement data can also be tracked over time by administrative authorities: across OECD countries, an average of 66% of students attend schools whose principals reported that achievement data are tracked over time by administrative authorities. In 25 OECD countries, more than 50% of students attend schools in which the schools' achievement is tracked over time. In the United States, the United Kingdom and New Zealand, over 90% of students attend schools that are tracked over time in this manner.

Achievement data can also be used to determine how resources are distributed. Across OECD countries, an average of 33% of students attend schools whose principals reported that they use achievement data in this way. In Israel, Chile and the United States, more than 70% of students attend schools in which the principal reported that instructional resources are allocated according to the school's achievement data. This practice is rare in Iceland, Greece, Japan, the Czech Republic and Finland, where less than 10% of students attend schools that use achievement data in this way.

Similar accountability arrangements exist within the partner countries and economies. It is common for student achievement data to be made public in Azerbaijan and Kazakhstan. In these countries, more than 80% of students attend schools where principals reported that student achievement data is publicly posted. It is not common for achievement data to be made public in Shanghai-China, Argentina, Panama, Tunisia and Uruguay, where less than 10% of students attend schools that make their achievement data public (Table IV.3.13). Achievement data is tracked by administrative authorities in practically all schools in the Russian Federation, Kazakhstan, Montenegro, Kyrgyzstan and Singapore. Less than half of the students in Chinese Taipei, Liechtenstein and Macao-China attend schools where achievement data is tracked by administrative authorities. Achievement data is widely used in Indonesia, Singapore, Kyrgyzstan and Kazakhstan to allocate instructional resources. This is not the case in the majority of schools in Croatia, Lithuania and Serbia, where less than 20% of students attend schools that use achievement data in this way.

Most school systems make students' achievement data, relative to other students in the same school, available to parents. This can take the form of report cards or teacher-formulated assessments that are sent home. Other schools also provide information on the students' academic standing compared with other students in the country or region or within the school (Table IV.3.14). Across OECD countries, an average of 52% of students attend schools whose principals reported that they provide parents with information on their students' academic standing, either compared to a national/regional population or compared with other students in the school. But in Austria, Italy and the Netherlands, and the partner countries and economies Macao-China, Hong Kong-China, Uruguay and Lithuania, over 80% of students attend schools that do not provide any information regarding the academic standing of the students, either compared to a national/regional population or compared with other students in the school (the last column in Table IV.3.14). In contrast, in Sweden, the United States, Korea, Chile, Norway and Turkey, and the partner countries and economies Azerbaijan, Kyrgyzstan, Colombia, Kazakhstan, the Russian Federation, Qatar and Romania, more than 80% of students attend schools that provide parents with this kind of information.

Students' achievement data can also be used to monitor teacher practices, and an average of 59% of students across OECD countries attend schools whose principals reported doing so. Over 80% of students in Poland, Israel, the United Kingdom, Turkey, Mexico, Austria and the United States attend schools that use achievement data to monitor teacher practices. Many schools across OECD countries complement this information with qualitative assessments, such as teacher peer reviews, assessments for school principals or senior staff, or observations by inspectors or other persons external to the school. School principals in Finland, however, rarely use student achievement data, reviews or observations to monitor teacher practices. Some 18% of students in Finland attend schools that use student assessments to monitor teachers; around 20% of students attend schools that use more qualitative and direct methods to monitor teacher practices; and only 2% of students attend schools that monitor teacher practices using observations of classes by inspectors or other persons external to the school (Table IV.3.15). Among the partner countries and economies, most schools in Singapore, the Russian Federation, Azerbaijan, Kazakhstan, Kyrgyzstan and Albania use student achievement data to monitor teacher practices.

Country profiles in assessment and accountability policies

To summarise the results and patterns of evaluation and accountability arrangements across countries, this section presents the results of a latent profile analysis. This analysis divides the OECD countries into four groups that share similar profiles based on two features (Figure IV.3.6). The first is whether achievement data are used for various benchmarking and information purposes. The second is whether achievement data are used to make decisions that affect the school. The assumption is that school systems that use achievement data for benchmarking and information purposes are more likely to use this data to compare themselves with other schools, monitor progress across time, have their progress tracked by administrative authorities, make their achievement data public and provide parents with their child's achievement benchmarked to national or regional populations. School systems that use achievement data for decision-making are more likely to use achievement data to determine the allocation of resources, make curricular decisions, and evaluate teachers' instruction.

The cross-classification of these two categories for each feature renders four groups. Most OECD countries (16) and partner countries and economies (24) are classified into groups that use achievement data for benchmarking and information purposes and for making decisions that affect the school. Three OECD countries and three partner countries use achievement data for benchmarking and information purposes, but not for making decisions affecting the school. A third group, comprising three OECD countries and five partner countries and economies, uses achievement data for making decisions affecting the school, but not for benchmarking and information purposes. The fourth group, composed of nine OECD countries and one partner country, is less likely to have schools that use achievement data either for benchmarking and information purposes or decision making.

Chapter 2 shows that the existence of standards-based external examinations is associated with higher levels of performance, while there is no clear relationship between performance and various uses of assessment for accountability purposes. However, the use of achievement data to make decisions about the curriculum and track achievement data over time is related to higher levels of socio-economic equity in school systems (Table IV.2.1a). When the countries are grouped according to the various aspects of assessment and accountability arrangements, no clear relationship with performance is discerned (Table IV.1.1).

■ Figure IV.3.6 ■

How school systems use student assessments

		Infrequent use of assessment or achievement data for benchmarking and information purposes	Frequent use of assessment or achievement data for benchmarking and information purposes
		Provide comparative information to parents: 32%	Provide comparative information to parents: 64%
		Compare the school with other schools: 38%	Compare the school with other schools: 73%
		Monitor progress over time: 57%	Monitor progress over time: 89%
		Post achievement data publicly: 20%	Post achievement data publicly: 47%
		Have their progress tracked by administrative authorities: 46%	Have their progress tracked by administrative authorities: 79%
Infrequent use of assessment or achievement data for decision making	Make curricular decisions: 60% Allocate resources: 21% Monitor teacher practices: 50%	Austria, Belgium,[1] Finland,[2] Germany, Greece, Ireland, Luxembourg, Netherlands,[1] Switzerland,[1] Liechtenstein	Hungary, Norway,[2] Turkey, Montenegro, Tunisia, Slovenia
Frequent use of assessment or achievement data for decision making	Making curricular decisions: 88% Allocating resources: 40% Monitor teacher practices: 65%	Denmark, Italy, Japan,[2] Spain, Argentina, Macao-China, Chinese Taipei, Uruguay	Australia,[1] Canada,[2] Chile, Czech Republic, Estonia,[2] Iceland,[2] Israel, Korea,[2] Mexico, New Zealand,[1] Poland,[1] Portugal, Slovak Republic, Sweden, United Kingdom, United States, Albania, Azerbaijan, Brazil, Bulgaria, Colombia, Croatia, Dubai (UAE), Hong Kong-China,[2] Indonesia, Jordan, Kazakhstan, Kyrgyzstan, Latvia, Lithuania, Panama, Peru, Qatar, Romania, Russian Federation, Shanghai-China,[1] Singapore,[1] Thailand, Trinidad and Tobago, Serbia

Note: The estimates in the grey cells indicate the average values of the variables used in latent profile analysis in each group. See Annex A5 for technical details.
1. Perform higher than the OECD average in reading.
2. Perform higher than the OECD average in reading and where the relationship between students' socio-economic background and reading performance is weaker than the OECD average.
Source: OECD, *PISA 2009 Database*.
StatLink http://dx.doi.org/10.1787/888932343399

RESOURCES INVESTED IN EDUCATION

Effective school systems require the right combination of trained and talented personnel, adequate educational resources and facilities and motivated students ready to learn. In the public debate, factors such as class and school size, the quality of teaching materials, perceived staff shortages and teacher quality are frequently associated with performance.

Chapter 2 shows that some high-performing school systems tend to prioritise higher salaries for teachers over smaller classes. At the level of individual schools, higher student scores tend to be related to more learning time in mathematics and science, a higher percentage of students who attended pre-primary schools for more than one year, and better educational resources. Chapter 2 also shows that most of the relationship between school resources and schools' performance is also related to schools' socio-economic intake. In other words, school resources are the most important set of mediators through which the socio-economic background of students and schools affects performance.

Time resources

Learning time

Because the PISA population is composed of 15-year-olds, students in many countries are drawn from various grade levels and from both lower and upper secondary schools. It is important to keep this in mind when comparing the amount of time students invest in classes on the language of instruction, because these lessons may be compulsory at one level but not at another.

On average across OECD countries, students reported spending approximately 3 hours and 40 minutes per week in classes on the language of instruction. Students spend over five hours per week in classes on the language of instruction in Canada, Chile and Denmark, but less than three hours per week in Austria, Finland, the Netherlands, Hungary, Slovenia, the Slovak Republic and Ireland. Although there is widespread variation in the amount of time students spend in classes on the language of instruction across OECD countries, there are also noteworthy variations within countries. Whereas in Norway, Poland, Ireland, Slovenia and Finland all students are exposed to a similar amount of learning time on the language of instruction across the school system, in Chile, Israel and Canada, there is a wide variation in the amount of learning time on the language of instruction (Table IV.3.16a).

Box IV.3.1 **Interpreting data on student learning time**

The data on students' learning time used in this report are based on 15-year-old students' self-reports on their "typical" use of time per week at the time of the PISA data collection. The time students spend learning each subject might vary according to the week. The number of instruction weeks per year may also vary across education systems, depending on the length of the school year and vacation time. The scatter plot below presents the relationship between the numbers of hours per week and the number of hours per year students spend in regular school lessons on the language of instruction. The system-level data on the number of weeks of instruction time, as part of the teachers' working time (OECD, 2009c), is used as a proxy for the number of instruction weeks per year in each education system. This is then multiplied by the number of school lessons per week, taken from the students' reports. This linear relationship between two indicators, as seen in the scatter plot, confirms that the numbers of hours per week spent in regular school lessons is a good proxy for the number of hours per year spent in regular school lessons.

■ Figures IV.3.a ■

Relationship between learning hours per week and learning hours per year in the language of instruction

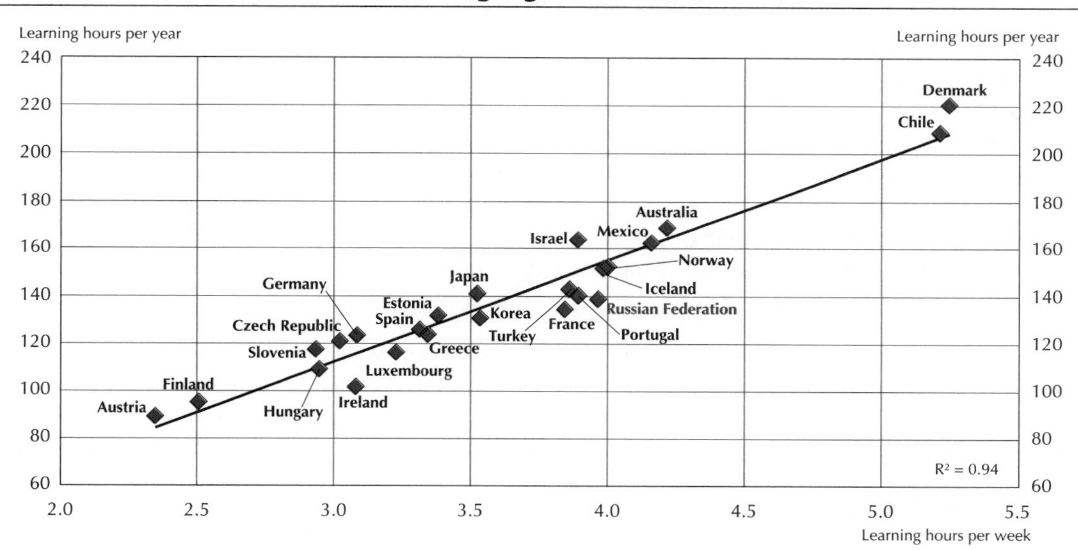

Source: OECD, *PISA 2009 Database;* OECD, 2009c, Table D4.2.
StatLink http://dx.doi.org/10.1787/888932343399

There are several reasons to be careful when interpreting the data. The learning time in regular school lessons that students reported in PISA may be only partially indicative of the learning time that shapes students' educational experiences. Earlier schooling experiences should be considered in order to develop a complete picture of a student's learning time. Students might also spend more time in after-school lessons or individual study during a year when they have an entrance or exit examination.

Variation in the amount of time that is invested in learning the language of instruction is observed both among and within schools. High levels of between-school variation indicate that certain schools offer more time for learning the language of instruction than other schools, such that students attending different schools may be exposed to very different amounts of time learning the language of instruction. High levels of within-school variation indicate that students attending the same school may receive different amounts of time learning the language of instruction. Between-school variation in the language of instruction learning time is greatest in Korea, the Slovak Republic, Poland and Japan, while within-school variations in the amount of time spent learning the language of instruction are greatest in Hungary, France and Portugal. Again, such between-school variation can reflect the fact that 15-year-olds attend different levels of education in the school system.

Among the partner countries and economies, average learning time on the language of instruction does not exceed five hours per week. It is less than three hours per week in Bulgaria, Serbia, Thailand, Montenegro, Latvia, Croatia and Azerbaijan. Variation in learning time on the language of instruction is lowest in Tunisia, Montenegro, Serbia and Macao-China, indicating that 15-year-olds across those school systems receive similar amounts of class time on the language of instruction. Variation is greatest in Argentina, Peru, Indonesia and Singapore.

Although reading was the focus of the 2009 PISA assessment, it is worth considering the time spent learning mathematics and science as well, since learning time in different subjects is related to performance in those subjects in different ways (OECD, 2010b). Learning time in mathematics and science differs among OECD countries, with the OECD average for both subjects combined at 6 hours and 40 minutes per week. The learning time for both subjects is around 10 hours or more per week in Canada and Chile, but is less than 6 hours per week in Norway, Hungary, Ireland, Turkey, the Netherlands, Austria and Slovenia. Similar levels of variation are seen in instruction in mathematics and science across the partner countries and economies. The average amount of learning time devoted to mathematics and science is highest in Singapore, where the average student is exposed to more than 11 hours of mathematics and science instruction per week. In contrast, in Romania, Montenegro and Croatia, the average student is exposed to less than five hours of mathematics and science classes per week. In general, across OECD countries, students in lower secondary schools tend to spend more time in classes in the language of instruction than students in upper secondary schools, while students in upper secondary schools tend to spend more time in science classes than students in lower secondary schools (Table IV.3.16b).

Formal instruction can occur both in and outside of school. Students can take part in after-school lessons in the form of enrichment or remedial courses with individual tutors or in group lessons provided by school teachers, or other independent courses, and may spend different amounts of time in them (Table IV.3.17b). These lessons can be financed publicly and offered as a free resource for students in need, or can be paid for by students and their families. On average across OECD countries, 28% of students attend at least one enrichment course and 26% attend at least one remedial course. In ten OECD countries, more than one-third of students attend at least one enrichment course; in Greece, Israel and Poland more than half the students do. Remedial courses are most common in Korea, Greece, the United Kingdom and Japan. In contrast, remedial and enrichment courses are generally uncommon in Denmark and Norway (Table IV.3.17a).

Among the partner countries and economies, enrichment courses are very common in Kazakhstan, Indonesia, Azerbaijan and Trinidad and Tobago, where over two-thirds of students reported taking part in enrichment courses. Over two-thirds of the students in Kazakhstan and the Russian Federation take part in some kind of remedial course. Remedial after-school classes are relatively uncommon in Latvia, Uruguay, Liechtenstein, Brazil and Montenegro.

Early childhood education

Whether and how long students are enrolled in pre-primary education also figures into the amount of time invested in education. Many of the inequalities that exist within school systems are already present when students enter formal schooling and persist as students progress through the school system (Entwisle, Alexander and Olson, 1997; Downey, Von Hippel and Broh, 2004). Because inequalities tend to grow when school is out-of-session, earlier entrance into the school system may reduce educational inequalities. In addition, with earlier entrance into pre-primary school, students are better prepared to enter and succeed in formal schooling (Hart and Risely, 1995; Heckman, 2000).

As discussed in Chapter 2, in most countries, students who have attended pre-primary schools tend to perform better than those who have not, even after accounting for students' socio-economic background.

On average across OECD countries, 72% of students reported that they had attended more than one year of pre-primary education. Attendance in pre-primary education is practically universal in Japan, the Netherlands, Hungary, Belgium, Iceland, France, where over 90% of 15-year-olds reported that they had attended pre-primary school for more than one year. More than 90% of students in 27 OECD countries attended pre-primary school for at least some time, and 98% of students in Japan, Hungary, France and the United States reported having done so. Pre-primary education is rare in Turkey, where less than 30% of 15-year-olds went to pre-primary school for at least a year. More than one year of pre-primary education is uncommon in Chile, Ireland, Canada and Poland, where less than 50% of students attended pre-primary school for that length of time (Table IV.3.18).

Among the partner countries and economies, in Liechtenstein, Hong Kong-China and Singapore, more than 90% of students attended more than one year of pre-primary schooling. In 10 of the 34 partner countries and economies, more than 90% of students attended pre-primary education for some time. Only in Liechtenstein and Chinese Taipei did more than 98% of students reported that they attended pre-primary school for some time. In contrast, in Azerbaijan, Kyrgyzstan and Kazakhstan, less than 50% of students attended pre-primary education; and in Azerbaijan, Kyrgyzstan, Tunisia, Qatar and Indonesia, less than 25% of students attended pre-primary education for more than one year.

Extra-curricular activities

Extra-curricular activities take many forms, including sports activities, academic activities, and courses in the arts and culture, and they can also improve students' non-cognitive skills. Skills such as task persistence, independence, following instructions, working well within groups, dealing with authority figures and fitting in with peers are, in turn, related to students' success in school - and beyond (Farkas, 2003; Carneiro and Heckman, 2005; Covay and Carbonaro, 2009).

In PISA 2009, school principals were asked to report whether the following extra-curricular activities are offered by the school: a band, an orchestra or choir; school plays or school musicals; a school yearbook, a newspaper or magazine; volunteering or service activities; a book club; a debating club or debating activities; a school club or competition for foreign language, math or science; an academic club; an art club or art activities; a sport team or sports activities; lectures and/or seminars; collaboration with local libraries; and collaboration with local newspapers. An *index of extra-curricular activities* captures the array of extra-curricular activities offered by the school. Higher levels of this index indicate greater availability of extra-curricular activities (Table IV.3.19).

The availability of extra-curricular activities is greatest in New Zealand, the United States, Korea and the United Kingdom. In these countries, the average student attends a school in which the availability of extra-curricular activities is over one standard deviation above that of the OECD. In contrast, Denmark, Norway and Switzerland score lowest on the index of extra-curricular activities, so that the average student attends a school in which the availability of extra-curricular activities is less than one half of a standard deviation of that in the OECD. Within countries, schools vary in how many extra-curricular activities they offer. This variation is greatest in Greece, Mexico, Austria and Chile, but relatively modest in Japan, Estonia, the Czech Republic, Switzerland and the Netherlands.

Among the partner countries and economies Kazakhstan, Hong Kong-China, Qatar, Singapore, Romania and Thailand show high levels of extra-curricular offerings: in these six countries and economies, the average student attends a school that is over one standard deviation above the OECD average on the measure of extra-curricular offerings. In contrast, Argentina, Uruguay, Brazil and Indonesia show the lowest levels of extra-curricular activities. The variation among schools is greatest in Tunisia, Shanghai-China, Brazil, Albania, Jordan, Montenegro, Azerbaijan, Indonesia and Thailand, while Liechtenstein, Lithuania, Latvia and Serbia offer all of their students similar levels of extra-curricular activities.

Human resources

Teacher shortages and salaries

Teachers are widely believed to be the most essential resource for learning (Greenwald, Hedges and Laine, 1996; Gamoran, Secada, and Marrett, 2000; Rivkin, Hanushek and Kain, 2005). A shortage of teachers implies that teachers are often overloaded with instructional and administrative work, unable to meet the variety of student needs, and often designated to teach subjects outside their expertise. Sometimes, less qualified teachers are hired, undermining students' opportunities to learn or certain courses may be dropped from the curriculum.

School principals surveyed by PISA reported on the extent to which they think instruction in their school is hindered by a lack of qualified teachers and staff in key areas. This information was combined to create a composite *index of teacher shortage*, such that the index has an average of 0 and a standard deviation of 1 for the OECD countries. Higher values on the index indicate the perception of more problems with instruction due to teacher shortages. Caution is required in interpreting these results: school principals across countries and economies, or even within countries and economies, may have different expectations and benchmarks to determine whether there is a lack of qualified teachers. Nonetheless, these school principals' reports provide valuable information that can be used to assess whether school leaders can provide their students with adequate human resources (Table IV.3.20).

School principals in Turkey and Luxembourg are more likely to have reported that instruction in their schools is hindered by a lack of adequate human resources. This was less likely to be reported in Portugal, Spain, Poland and Slovenia. Although school systems vary in the extent to which a lack of human resources is seen to hinder instruction, countries vary, too, in how they interpret a lack of human resources. School principals in Portugal, Poland, Slovenia and Spain share similar opinions concerning how human resources hinder instruction within their schools. In contrast, the reports of school principals in Turkey and Chile varied widely: some school principals considered the lack of qualified human resources a hindrance in their schools, while others did not share this view.

Lower secondary teachers' salaries in the average OECD country are 118% of the per capita GDP, corrected for differences in purchasing power parities. Relative to their country's national income, lower secondary teachers in Korea, Mexico, Germany, Portugal and Switzerland earn the most. Annual earnings for Korean lower secondary teachers, for example, are almost twice the level of national income, while those of Mexico, Germany, Portugal and Switzerland still exceed 150% of the per capita GDP. In contrast, teachers in Estonia, Norway, Iceland, Hungary, Israel, the Czech Republic, Sweden, the United States and Poland earn less than the national per capita income. Salaries relative to national income provide a rough indicator of the competitiveness of teaching positions. In absolute terms with adjusting for differences in purchasing power parities, lower secondary teachers with 15 years of experience earn more than USD 50 000 per year in Luxembourg, Switzerland, Germany, Ireland and Korea and less than USD 30 000 per year in Estonia, Hungary, Poland, Israel, the Czech Republic, Mexico and Iceland. The distribution of teachers' salaries for upper secondary teachers is similar to that of lower secondary teachers (Tables IV.3.21a and IV.3.21c).

Among the partner countries and economies, school principals in Kyrgyzstan, Thailand and Jordan were more likely to have reported that a lack of adequate human resources hinders instruction in their schools. This notion is less common in Romania, Bulgaria and Serbia. Yet within countries, schools vary in the extent to which school principals reported that a lack of human resources hinder instruction in their schools. This variation is greatest in Shanghai-China, Jordan, Macao-China, Chinese Taipei, Kazakhstan, Colombia, and relatively modest in Romania, Bulgaria, Tunisia, Montenegro and Serbia.

Class size

Class size can affect how much time and attention a teacher can give to individual students, as well as the social dynamics among students. However, research on class size has generally found a weak relationship between class size and student performance (Ehrenberg *et al.*, 2001; Piketty, 2006). Class size also seems to be more important in the earlier years of schooling than it is for 15-year-olds (Finn, 1998).

Among OECD countries, students reported an average of 24.6 students in their class on the language of instruction. Country averages range from fewer than 20 students per classroom in Belgium, Switzerland, Iceland, Finland and Denmark, to more than 30 students per classroom in Japan, Chile, Korea and Mexico. Class sizes also differ within countries. Most students in Finland, Denmark, Switzerland, Poland and Greece, for example, attend classes of similar size, while there is more variation in class size in Mexico, Turkey, Israel and the United States. In many countries, the size of classes varies more across than within schools. In Korea, Japan, Greece and Slovenia, over 80% of the variation in class size occurs between schools, with little variation occurring within school. In Turkey, Ireland and the United States, over 65% of the variation in class size occurs within schools, indicating that students attending the same school may attend classes of different sizes (Table IV.3.22).

The distribution of class size in partner countries and economies follows a similar pattern to that of OECD countries. There are fewer than 20 students per class in Liechtenstein, Azerbaijan and Latvia, and more than 30 students per class in 10 partner countries and economies. In Chinese Taipei, Shanghai-China, Macao-China, Thailand, Hong Kong-China and Colombia, the average class size is more than 35 students. Variations in class size within each country tend to be greater in partner countries and economies than in OECD countries.

Material resources

While an adequate physical infrastructure and up-to-date textbooks do not guarantee good learning outcomes, the absence of such resources is likely to have an adverse effect on learning. School principals were asked to report on the extent to which the school's capacity to provide instruction was hindered by the shortage or inadequacy of several types of resources, including: science laboratory equipment, instruction materials, such as textbooks, computers for instruction, Internet connectivity, computer software for instruction, library materials and audio-visual resources.

Box IV.3.2 **Availability and use of resources: School libraries**

Research on the effects of school resources has generally found a weak independent relationship to student learning, particularly in industrialised countries (Coleman, 1966; Heyneman and Loxley, 1983; Fuller, 1987; Buchmann and Hannum, 2001). One explanation of these weak effects is the "black box assumption of educational production". This assumption treats school resources as educational inputs for producing student learning and measures the relationship between student learning and the availability of various resources at the school or in the students' households. Yet what matters for student achievement and other educational outcomes is not necessarily the availability of resources. What matters is the quality of the resources, the availability and use of those resources, and the quality of their use (Gamoran, Secada and Marrett, 2000).

To understand the interplay between the availability of educational resources, their quality and the quality of their use and the eventual educational impact of this use, PISA asked students and school principals about the availability of a school library, the quality of the school library and how students use libraries, including the school library or another type of library, such as a public library (Table IV.3.24).

In general, most students in the OECD reported having access to a school library: an average of 90% of students in OECD countries reported having access to a school library. But over a quarter of all students do not have access to a quality library: 29% of students attend schools in which the school principal reported that instruction is hindered "to some extent" or "a lot" by a lack of sufficient library materials. Even the availability of a good library does not guarantee that it is used: only 64% of students borrow books for school-related activities a few times or more a year, and only 52% borrow books for pleasure a few times a year.

The availability of a school library does not seem to influence students' use of a library much: students reported using libraries at similar rates, regardless of whether the school offers a library or not. Compared to 66% of students who have access to a good-quality school library and reported borrowing books for school-related activities a few times or more per year, 56% of students who do not have access to a school library reported borrowing books for school-related activities a few or more times per year; a nine percentage-point difference. Compared to 54% of students who have good-quality school libraries and borrow books for pleasure, 47% borrow books for pleasure even though they do not have access to a school library - a difference of only slightly more than six percentage points.

Also, the quality of the resource does not seem to affect its use: whether the library is of good or poor quality does not seem to affect the frequency with which students borrow books for pleasure or school-related activities. Compared to the 54% borrowing rate for books for pleasure when students have a good library available to them, 52% of students borrow books for school-related activities when only an insufficient library is available. Compared to 66% of students who borrow books for school-related activities when they have a good library available to them, 62% of students who have a poor school library borrow books for school-related activities.

In sum, the availability of school resources seems at most weakly related to students' use of libraries. Students who borrow books for pleasure or school-related activities will use whatever library they can find to borrow books, while students who do not wish to borrow books are minimally more likely to borrow books if they have a school library available to them.

	School with no library	School with library		Total
		Principals reported a lack of sufficient library materials hinders instruction "to some extent" or "a lot"	Principals reported a lack of sufficient library materials hinders instruction "very little" or "not at all"	
Students borrow books for pleasure	47%	52%	54%	**52%**
Students borrow books for school-related activities	56%	62%	66%	**64%**

Note: The OECD averages are shown. For the results by country, see Table IV.3.24.

This information was combined to create a composite *index of material resources* such that the index has an average of zero and a standard deviation of one for the OECD countries. Higher values indicate less hindrance of instruction due to a lack of resources. It is best to be cautious when analysing these results: school principals within and across countries might have different benchmarks to judge the lack of instructional resources within their schools. Nonetheless, these responses provide valuable information on the school leaders' ability to provide what they consider to be necessary for quality instruction.

School principals in Switzerland, the United States, Japan, Slovenia, the United Kingdom, Australia and Iceland were less likely to have reported that instruction in school is hindered by a lack of adequate material resources, while school principals in Turkey and Mexico were more likely to have reported this. Although school systems vary in the extent to which a lack of material resources may hinder instruction, countries differ in the extent to which they perceive this as a problem. School principals across the school system in Norway, the Czech Republic, Estonia, Turkey and Denmark have relatively similar opinions concerning how a lack of material resources hinders instruction within their schools. In contrast, these opinions vary widely in Mexico, Chile, Australia, Ireland and Israel (Table IV.3.23).

Among the partner countries and economies, school principals in Singapore, Liechtenstein, Dubai (UAE) and Hong Kong-China were less likely to have reported that a lack of adequate material resources hinders instruction in their schools. This view was more commonly reported in Kyrgyzstan, Indonesia, Colombia and Peru. Yet schools vary in the extent to which school principals reported this problem. The variation is greatest in Panama, Argentina and Peru, and relatively modest in Montenegro, Lithuania, Latvia and Bulgaria.

Spending on education

Spending on educational resources as discussed above can be summarised in overall spending per student. Depending on the way resources are allocated, this financial investment can take the form of buildings and infrastructure, salaries paid to teachers, administrators and support staff, and transportation and meals for students. For a student, these resources are allocated throughout his or her educational career, and countries spend different amounts per student. Total expenditure by educational institutions per student from age 6 to 15 exceeds USD 100 000 (PPP-corrected dollars) in Luxembourg, the Unites States, Switzerland and Norway. In Luxembourg, cumulative expenditure per students exceeds USD 150 000. In contrast, in Turkey, Mexico, Chile, the Slovak Republic and Poland, cumulative expenditure per student over this period is less than USD 40 000. In Mexico and Chile, cumulative expenditure is less than USD 25 000 per student; and in Turkey, cumulative expenditure is less than USD 13 000 dollars per student (Table IV.3.21b).

Country profiles in resources invested in education

To summarise the results and patterns of spending on education across countries, this section presents the results of a latent profile analysis. This analysis groups countries according to the amount of resources they invest in education as measured by cumulative expenditure. Countries are also grouped according to how these resources are invested: whether priority is given to teachers' salaries or to providing smaller classes and better infrastructure. While other resources for education, such as time and extra-curricular activities, are considered important in understanding schooling, OECD data indicate that most spending is directed either towards increases in teachers' salaries or smaller class size (OECD, 2010a).

OECD countries can be grouped into four categories, depending on the amount of resources they invest and the spending choices they make (Figure IV.3.7). Countries may invest relatively small or large amounts of resources in education, and each of these countries may choose to focus this investment on factors such as teachers' salaries or smaller class size. Most OECD countries prioritise smaller class sizes: the Czech Republic, Estonia, Greece, Hungary, Israel, New Zealand, Poland, Portugal, the Slovak Republic and Turkey spend less on education and focus limited resources on smaller class sizes; Australia, Austria, Belgium, Canada, Denmark, Finland, France, Germany, Iceland, Ireland, Italy, Luxembourg, the Netherlands, Norway, Slovenia, Spain, Sweden, Switzerland, the United Kingdom and the United States spend more on education and also focus resources on smaller classes. Only four OECD countries prioritise teachers' salaries: two of these countries, Mexico and Chile, spend relatively small amounts on education and two, Japan and Korea, invest relatively large amounts in education.

All partner countries and economies are classified in the groups that spend relatively less on education. The partner countries and economies vary more with respect to how they invest their resources: 21 partner countries and economies focus their investment on smaller class sizes while 10 partner countries and economies focus their investment on higher salaries for teachers.

The average student performance between two OECD countries that invest heavily in education and privilege spending on teachers' salaries is 530 points, and only 10% of the variation in performance is explained by students' socio-economic background (Table IV.1.1a, Table IV.1.1b and Table IV.1.1c).

■ Figure IV.3.7 ■

How school systems allocate resources for education

		Small class size and/or low teachers' salaries	**Large class size and high teachers' salaries**
		Class size for the language of instruction: 23	**Class size for the language of instruction: 36**
		Teachers' salaries relative to GDP/capita[1]: 118	**Teachers' salaries relative to GDP/capita[1]: 172**
Low cumulative expenditure on education	**Cumulative expenditure by educational institutions per student aged 6 to 15: USD 39 463**	Czech Republic, Estonia,[3] Hungary, Greece, Israel, New Zealand,[2] Poland,[2] Portugal, Slovak Republic, Turkey, Albania, Argentina, Azerbaijan, Bulgaria, Croatia, Dubai (UAE), Kazakhstan, Kyrgyzstan, Latvia, Liechtenstein, Lithuania, Montenegro, Panama, Peru, Qatar, Romania, Russian Federation, Serbia, Tunisia, Trinidad and Tobago, Uruguay	Chile, Mexico, Brazil, Colombia, Hong Kong-China,[3] Jordan, Indonesia, Macao-China, Shanghai-China,[2] Singapore,[2] Chinese Taipei, Thailand
High cumulative expenditure on education	**Cumulative expenditure by educational institutions per student aged 6 to 15: USD 81 238**	Australia,[2] Austria, Belgium,[2] Canada,[3] Denmark, Finland,[3] France, Germany, Iceland,[3] Ireland, Italy, Luxembourg, Norway,[3] Netherlands,[2] Slovenia, Spain, Sweden, Switzerland,[2] United Kingdom, United States	Japan,[3] Korea[3]

Note: The estimates in the grey cells indicate the average values of the variables used in latent profile analysis in each group. See Annex A5 for technical details.
1.This is the weighted average of upper and lower secondary teachers. The average is computed with weighting teachers' salaries for upper and lower secondary education according to the respective 15-year-old students enrolment (for countries with valid information on both if 15-year-old students are both at the upper and lower secondary schools).
2. Perform higher than the OECD average in reading.
3. Perform higher than the OECD average in reading and where the relationship between students' socio-economic background and reading performance is weaker than the OECD average.
Source: OECD, *PISA 2009 Database.*
StatLink http://dx.doi.org/10.1787/888932343399

Notes

1. The two-year window refers to the two ages at which students most frequently started primary school in each country.

2. In some countries, 15-year-old students attend two different grade levels simply because of the relationship between the cut-off date for enrolling in schools and the date on which the PISA assessment began. PISA's target population is defined as all students aged from 15 years and 3 (completed) months to 16 years and 2 (completed) months at the beginning of the assessment period.

3. Highly selective schools are defined as schools where principals reported at least one of the following factors to be "always" considered for student admittance: "students' records of academic performance" or "recommendations of feeder schools".

4. This is measured by the between-school variation in performance, which is expressed as a percentage based on the average variance in student performance in reading across OECD countries (Table IV.2.2a).

5. In order to validate the responses of school principals, those responses are compared with the system-level data submitted by the national authorities in each participating country/economy regarding the level of schools' influence in determining the curriculum, assessment policy and allocation of resources. Although the questions are not identical to those asked of school principals in the PISA questionnaire, the responsibility in the resource-allocation index derived from the school principals' reports correlates at 0.730 with responses from national authorities regarding schools' influence in managing personnel across the 35 countries with comparable data, and at 0.674 with responses from national authorities regarding schools' influence in planning and structures.

6. This does not mean that vouchers or tax credits are universally available in these countries. In some countries, vouchers or tax credits are available in education systems, but only a limited proportion of students practice these. For further information, see *Education at a Glance* (OECD, 2010a) Annex 3, available on line: *www.oecd.org/edu/eag2010.*

7. Only schools' autonomy in curricula and assessments is considered in this analysis, as school autonomy in resource allocation is not necessarily related to their autonomy in curricula and assessments. In addition, school autonomy in resource allocation is not related to performance at the system level (Table IV.2.1).

8. At the country level, the correlation between autonomy in resource allocation as measured for all students and those attending lower secondary schools only and upper secondary schools only is 0.891 and 0.800, respectively. The correlation between curricular autonomy as measured for all students and those attending only lower secondary and only upper secondary schools is 0.916 and 0.872, respectively. The correlation between school competition calculated for all students and that calculated for students who attend only lower secondary and only upper secondary schools is 0.576 and 0.326, respectively. The correlation between the proportion of private schools as calculated for all students and that calculated for students who attend only lower secondary and only upper secondary schools is 0.713 and 0.625, respectively.

4
The Learning Environment

Students perform better in orderly classrooms and with the support of engaged teachers and parents. Using reports from students, school principals and, for some countries, parents, this chapter describes and analyses six key aspects of the learning environment: teacher and student behaviours that affect learning, the disciplinary climate, teacher-student relations, how teachers stimulate students' engagement in reading, parents' involvement in and expectation of schooling, and school principals' leadership.

Research into what makes schools effective finds that learning requires an orderly and co-operative environment, both in and outside the classroom (Jennings and Greenberg, 2009). In effective schools, academic activities and student academic performance are valued by both students and teachers (Scheerens and Bosker, 1997; Sammons, 1999; Taylor, Pressley and Pearson, 2002).

The learning environment is also shaped by parents and school principals. Parents who are engaged in their children's education are more likely to support their school's efforts and participate in school activities, thus adding to available resources (Epstein, 2001). Because they want their children to receive the best education possible, parents often put pressure on schools to raise their academic standards. School principals, in turn, can define their schools' educational objectives and guide their schools towards achieving them.

The results from PISA 2000 and PISA 2003 suggested that students and schools perform better when parental expectations are high, classrooms are well-disciplined and relations between students and teachers are amiable and supportive. Results from PISA 2009 confirm these findings. In general, students perform better in schools with more disciplined classrooms, partly because such schools tend to have more students from advantaged socio-economic backgrounds, who generally perform better, and partly for reasons unrelated to socio-economic background. Parental expectations of both their children and their children's schools are also closely related to socio-economic background and affect the learning environment.

This chapter describes the learning environment in the participating countries in detail, using reports from students and principals and reports from parents in the countries that administered the optional questionnaire for parents. More specifically, this chapter examines the quality of teacher-student relations and the disciplinary climate inside classrooms. It also analyses the degree to which student and/or teacher behaviour hinders the quality of instruction, how parents can encourage school administrators to raise standards and improve instruction, and how much school principals are involved in school matters.

Data presented in this chapter should be interpreted with caution (see Box IV.1.1). Students and principals in different countries, or even in different schools within the same country, may not apply the same criteria when assessing the school climate. For example, principals in countries with generally low absenteeism may consider a modest level of absenteeism in their school to be a major disciplinary problem. Meanwhile, students are likely to consider the disciplinary climate from the perspective of their experiences in other classes or schools, rather than measured against some objective standard or national average. In addition, respondents may adjust their responses in the belief that their genuine perceptions may be considered unacceptable within their society. Despite these problems of interpretation, many of the patterns revealed by PISA 2009 are strikingly similar across countries.

TEACHER-STUDENT RELATIONS

Positive teacher-student relations are crucial in establishing an environment that is conducive to learning. Research finds that students, particularly disadvantaged students, learn more and have fewer disciplinary problems when they feel that their teachers are devoted to their academic success (Gamoran, 1993) and when they have good working relations with their teachers (Crosnoe, Johnson and Elder, 2004). One explanation is that positive teacher-student relations help transmit social capital, create communal learning environments and promote and strengthen adherence to norms conducive to learning (Birch and Ladd, 1998).

PISA 2009 asked students to indicate the extent of their agreement with several statements regarding their relationships with teachers in school. These statements include whether they get along with the teachers, whether teachers are interested in their personal well-being, whether teachers take the student seriously, whether teachers are a source of support if the student needs extra help, and whether teachers treat the student fairly. This information was combined to create a composite *index of teacher-student relations* such that the index has an average of zero and a standard deviation of one for the OECD countries. Higher values indicate better teacher-student relations.

Results from PISA 2009 suggest that students in the OECD are generally satisfied with the quality of teacher-student relations. For example, on average across OECD countries, 85% of students reported to agree or strongly agree that they get along with their teachers, 79% reported that teachers treat them fairly, 79% reported that teachers are available if students need extra help, 67% reported that teachers really listen, and 66% reported that their teachers are interested in their well-being (Figure IV.4.1).

■ Figure IV.4.1 ■

Students' views of teacher-student relations

Index of teacher-student relations based on students' reports

- A — I get along well with most of my teachers.
- B — Most of my teachers are interested in my well-being.
- C — Most of my teachers really listen to what I have to say.
- D — If I need extra help, I will receive it from my teachers.
- E — Most of my teachers treat me fairly.

		Percentage of students agreeing or strongly agreeing with the following statements					Variability in the index (S.D.)	School variability in the distribution of the index (Proportion of the index variance between schools)
		A	B	C	D	E		
OECD	Australia	85	78	71	84	85	1.0	0.04
	Austria	87	59	61	67	77	1.1	0.07
	Belgium	83	63	67	84	86	0.9	0.04
	Canada	89	80	74	89	88	1.0	0.07
	Chile	85	74	72	77	71	1.0	0.06
	Czech Republic	80	67	57	78	72	0.9	0.06
	Denmark	89	79	71	79	85	1.0	0.06
	Estonia	86	76	60	85	75	0.8	0.04
	Finland	87	49	63	84	80	0.9	0.03
	France	78	53	62	80	88	0.9	0.05
	Germany	85	58	69	71	77	1.1	0.05
	Greece	87	66	62	63	65	1.0	0.06
	Hungary	86	68	79	77	74	0.9	0.05
	Iceland	88	73	74	82	80	1.1	0.09
	Ireland	82	76	63	77	81	1.0	0.03
	Israel	83	61	68	70	80	1.1	0.10
	Italy	82	72	62	77	79	1.0	0.08
	Japan	73	28	63	64	74	1.0	0.05
	Korea	79	60	57	83	75	0.8	0.06
	Luxembourg	82	59	63	72	78	1.1	0.04
	Mexico	86	77	77	78	75	1.0	0.05
	Netherlands	87	61	66	85	85	0.8	0.02
	New Zealand	88	77	73	87	86	1.0	0.04
	Norway	84	57	55	74	74	1.0	0.06
	Poland	81	35	60	73	71	0.9	0.04
	Portugal	94	89	82	90	82	0.9	0.03
	Slovak Republic	85	71	66	79	75	0.8	0.08
	Slovenia	80	30	56	74	74	0.9	0.08
	Spain	82	70	67	68	79	1.0	0.09
	Sweden	89	75	71	82	82	1.0	0.07
	Switzerland	85	69	70	82	83	1.1	0.07
	Turkey	86	88	78	87	69	1.2	0.04
	United Kingdom	86	78	69	88	83	0.9	0.04
	United States	90	81	74	88	89	1.1	0.08
	OECD average	85	66	67	79	79	1.0	0.06
Partners	Albania	89	86	89	92	94	1.0	0.06
	Argentina	83	75	73	68	80	1.0	0.08
	Azerbaijan	90	77	86	91	89	1.1	0.06
	Brazil	86	81	74	78	83	1.0	0.05
	Bulgaria	85	53	71	80	73	1.1	0.07
	Colombia	86	82	75	79	91	1.0	0.06
	Croatia	87	65	60	69	70	0.9	0.05
	Dubai (UAE)	89	83	75	87	79	1.1	0.04
	Hong Kong-China	89	71	67	89	82	0.9	0.03
	Indonesia	93	82	63	85	91	0.8	0.04
	Jordan	83	81	77	80	71	1.2	0.04
	Kazakhstan	93	83	80	93	89	0.9	0.14
	Kyrgyzstan	90	69	75	89	87	0.9	0.06
	Latvia	86	65	69	85	82	0.9	0.06
	Liechtenstein	82	66	66	78	75	1.2	0.11
	Lithuania	85	56	66	78	80	1.1	0.06
	Macao-China	83	64	53	78	71	0.9	0.03
	Montenegro	89	69	75	76	79	1.0	0.10
	Panama	90	83	77	79	89	1.1	0.04
	Peru	88	81	82	85	83	1.0	0.08
	Qatar	78	77	71	80	74	1.2	0.05
	Romania	89	62	77	74	84	0.9	0.04
	Russian Federation	88	76	73	82	80	0.9	0.07
	Serbia	89	86	69	72	80	1.0	0.03
	Shanghai-China	89	81	79	90	85	0.9	0.03
	Singapore	91	81	74	88	87	0.9	0.04
	Chinese Taipei	88	72	64	89	83	0.9	0.03
	Thailand	87	77	82	83	87	0.8	0.14
	Trinidad and Tobago	84	80	67	82	78	1.1	0.03
	Tunisia	83	51	72	77	81	1.0	0.06
	Uruguay	88	71	81	67	73	1.0	0.04

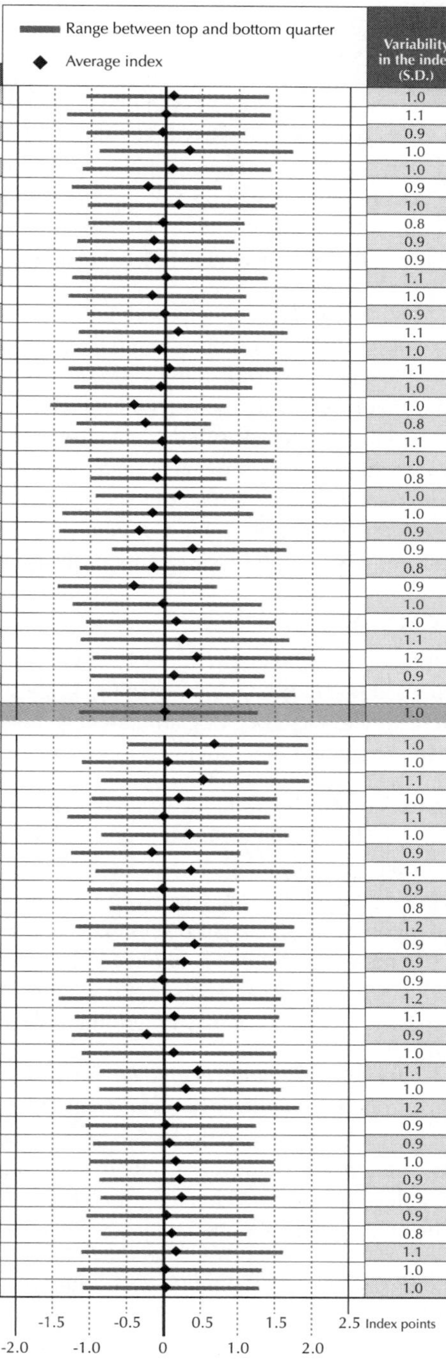

Note: Higher values on the index indicate positive teacher-student relations.
Source: OECD, *PISA 2009 Database*, Table IV.4.1.
StatLink http://dx.doi.org/10.1787/888932343418

Although a large majority of students in OECD countries reported good teacher-student relations, there is large variation in the *index of teacher-student relations* across OECD countries. On average, the *index of teacher-student relations* is highest in Turkey, Portugal, Canada and the United States, and lowest in Japan, Slovenia, Poland and Korea. For example, over 80% of students in the United States agree or strongly agree that their teachers are interested in their well-being, but only 28% of students in Japan and 30% of students in Slovenia reported teachers' interest in their well-being. Differences in student-reported teacher interest in their well-being may reflect either different student expectations of their teachers' level of involvement or different roles that teachers assume with respect to their students. In either case, a low percentage of agreement with these statements indicates a mismatch between student expectations and what teachers are actually doing. That discrepancy may influence the quality of the learning environment within schools.

Although students reported positive relationships between students and teachers across OECD countries, not all students within each country experience the same type of relationship with their teachers. Teacher-student relations often vary widely within countries, as measured by the standard deviation of the *index of teacher-student relations*. Within-country variation (*i.e.* the standard deviation at the student level) is the lowest in the Netherlands, Korea, the Slovak Republic and Estonia, signalling that teacher-student relations are relatively similar across students and schools in those countries. In Turkey, Israel, Iceland, Switzerland, Luxembourg, Austria, the United States and Germany, there is more variation in teacher-student relations.

Students in partner countries and economies also generally reported good relationships with their teachers. As is the case in OECD countries, most students reported that they get along with their teachers (87%), that teachers treat them fairly (82%), that teachers are available if extra help is needed (81%), that teachers are interested in students' well-being (74%) and that teachers really listen (73%). The *index of teacher-student relations* is highest in Albania, Azerbaijan, Panama and Kazakhstan. This index is lowest in Macao-China and Croatia among the partner countries and economies, but their index scores are higher than those for the four lowest OECD countries discussed above. The variation in the *index of teacher-student relations* is lowest in Indonesia and Thailand, signalling that teacher-student relations are relatively similar across students and schools in those countries, and highest in Qatar, Liechtenstein and Jordan, where there is more variation in the quality of relations that students have with their teachers.

DISCIPLINARY CLIMATE

The disciplinary climate in the classroom and school can also affect learning. Classrooms and schools with more disciplinary problems are less conducive to learning, since teachers have to spend more time creating an orderly environment before instruction can begin (Gamoran and Nystrand, 1992). More interruptions within the classroom disrupt students' engagement and their ability to follow lessons.

Students were asked to describe the frequency with which interruptions occur in reading lessons. This included how often – never, in some, in most or in all lessons on the language of instruction – students don't listen to what the teacher says, there is noise and disorder, the teacher has to wait a long time for students to quieten down, students cannot work well and students don't start working for a long time after the lesson begins. These responses were combined to create a composite *index of disciplinary climate* such that the index has an average of zero and a standard deviation of one for the OECD countries. Higher values indicate a better disciplinary climate within the classroom. When comparing estimates across school systems, it is important to keep in mind that several factors beyond students' experiences in school may determine the patterns of these responses (see Box IV.1.1).

The majority of students in OECD countries enjoy orderly classrooms in their lessons on the language of instruction. Some 75% of students reported that they never or only in some lessons feel that students don't start working for a long time after the lesson begins, 71% of students reported that they never or only in some lessons feel that students don't listen, 68% reported that noise never or only in some lessons affects learning, 72% reported that their teacher never or only in some lessons has to wait a long time before students settle down, and 81% of the students attend classrooms where they feel they can work well practically most of the time (Figure IV.4.2).

Across OECD, the *index of disciplinary climate* is highest in Japan and Korea. The *index of disciplinary climate* in Korea is one-third of a standard deviation higher than that of the OECD average, and Japan has a disciplinary climate that is three-quarters of a standard deviation higher than the OECD average level. In contrast, the student-reported *index of disciplinary climate* in Greece, Finland, the Netherlands, Norway, Luxembourg and France is, on average, more than 20% of a standard deviation below the OECD average.

■ Figure IV.4.2 ■

Students' views of how conducive classrooms are to learning

Index of disciplinary climate based on students' reports

- **A** Students don't listen to what the teacher says.
- **B** There is noise and disorder.
- **C** The teacher has to wait a long time for the students to quieten down.
- **D** Students cannot work well.
- **E** Students don't start working for a long time after the lesson begins.

Percentage of students reporting that the following phenomena happen "never or hardly ever" or "in some lessons"

Chart legend: Range between top and bottom quarter; ◆ Average index

		A	B	C	D	E	Variability in the index (S.D.)	School variability in the distribution of the index (Proportion of the index variance between schools)
OECD	Australia	68	61	71	82	76	1.0	0.12
	Austria	73	74	71	77	70	1.2	0.17
	Belgium	72	63	68	85	71	1.0	0.10
	Canada	71	61	72	82	73	1.0	0.14
	Chile	74	63	65	82	70	0.9	0.13
	Czech Republic	63	66	68	75	70	1.1	0.22
	Denmark	72	65	78	88	82	0.8	0.16
	Estonia	70	69	73	80	78	1.0	0.24
	Finland	60	52	63	80	68	0.9	0.14
	France	64	56	64	76	63	1.1	0.15
	Germany	85	84	78	82	81	1.0	0.13
	Greece	55	58	62	56	65	0.9	0.15
	Hungary	71	71	69	80	78	1.0	0.16
	Iceland	74	67	73	84	81	0.9	0.12
	Ireland	64	65	70	81	75	1.1	0.10
	Israel	78	75	73	77	74	1.0	0.19
	Italy	66	68	70	81	74	1.1	0.23
	Japan	92	90	93	87	91	0.9	0.27
	Korea	90	77	88	90	87	0.8	0.08
	Luxembourg	60	65	64	71	64	1.2	0.05
	Mexico	79	73	79	83	77	0.9	0.12
	Netherlands	68	59	63	81	55	0.9	0.08
	New Zealand	68	61	68	82	74	1.0	0.09
	Norway	67	61	66	77	67	0.9	0.17
	Poland	67	74	74	79	80	1.0	0.17
	Portugal	78	76	80	86	79	1.0	0.10
	Slovak Republic	67	74	73	81	75	0.9	0.16
	Slovenia	59	66	68	78	70	1.1	0.23
	Spain	73	74	73	83	73	1.0	0.14
	Sweden	75	67	71	83	76	0.9	0.18
	Switzerland	72	74	74	81	76	1.0	0.10
	Turkey	86	77	74	77	78	0.9	0.08
	United Kingdom	73	68	74	86	81	1.0	0.14
	United States	76	72	79	87	82	1.0	0.14
	OECD average	71	68	72	81	75	1.0	0.15
Partners	Albania	89	88	86	87	88	0.8	0.13
	Argentina	67	57	62	74	66	1.0	0.17
	Azerbaijan	90	90	88	87	86	1.0	0.12
	Brazil	75	60	67	76	63	0.9	0.12
	Bulgaria	69	72	73	75	77	1.0	0.09
	Colombia	82	78	81	88	77	0.8	0.11
	Croatia	59	68	69	75	73	1.0	0.14
	Dubai (UAE)	77	72	73	83	77	1.0	0.17
	Hong Kong-China	87	88	89	88	86	0.9	0.08
	Indonesia	84	75	79	84	84	0.9	0.12
	Jordan	81	75	74	76	74	1.0	0.14
	Kazakhstan	88	93	91	88	92	0.9	0.17
	Kyrgyzstan	86	88	84	82	86	0.9	0.05
	Latvia	78	78	79	86	86	0.9	0.21
	Liechtenstein	71	81	76	79	80	0.9	0.14
	Lithuania	78	82	84	84	84	0.9	0.13
	Macao-China	80	86	84	85	80	0.8	0.12
	Montenegro	72	82	80	82	81	0.9	0.08
	Panama	77	73	75	81	76	0.9	0.07
	Peru	83	77	85	85	82	0.8	0.06
	Qatar	72	68	66	73	70	1.1	0.09
	Romania	89	89	89	89	87	0.8	0.13
	Russian Federation	81	86	85	85	89	1.0	0.14
	Serbia	63	74	74	79	75	0.9	0.14
	Shanghai-China	85	88	90	87	89	0.9	0.18
	Singapore	78	70	77	87	83	0.9	0.07
	Chinese Taipei	78	81	80	84	78	0.9	0.08
	Thailand	91	85	86	91	91	0.7	0.07
	Trinidad and Tobago	71	69	66	81	75	1.0	0.09
	Tunisia	76	62	66	69	65	0.9	0.06
	Uruguay	74	67	69	80	74	1.0	0.13

Chart axis (Index points): -1.5, -0.5, 0.5, 1.5, 2.5; -2.0, -1.0, 0, 1.0, 2.0

Note: Higher values on the index indicate a better disciplinary climate.
Source: OECD, *PISA 2009 Database*, Table IV.4.2.
StatLink http://dx.doi.org/10.1787/888932343418

The *index of disciplinary climate* also varies within OECD countries. It varies the most in Luxembourg and Austria, and least in Korea and Denmark. In the latter group of countries, students across the school system experience relatively similar levels of classroom disruptions. In contrast, students in the former group of countries experience varying levels of classroom disruptions, and the teaching conditions in classrooms vary greatly, depending on the classroom or school. The variation in disciplinary climate can occur between or within schools. Higher levels of between-school variation mean that students and teachers within the same school share similar levels in the *index of disciplinary climate*. Such is the case in Japan, Estonia, Italy, Slovenia and the Czech Republic, where more than 20% of the variation in the *index of disciplinary climate* occurs between schools. In other school systems, most of the variation in the *index of disciplinary climate* occurs within schools, meaning that students and teachers experience different levels of classroom disruption, depending on their classmates, teachers or a combination of the two.

The disciplinary climate also varies between and within schools among partner countries and economies. Among these countries and economies, the *index of disciplinary climate* is at least one-third of a standard deviation above the OECD average level in Kazakhstan, Azerbaijan, Albania, Shanghai-China, the Russian Federation, Romania, Hong Kong-China, Kyrgyzstan and Thailand; but it is more than 10% of a standard deviation below the OECD average in Argentina, Tunisia, Brazil and Croatia. The *index of disciplinary climate* varies the most in Qatar, Jordan and Croatia and is most homogeneous in Thailand, Macao-China and Peru. In Latvia, it is more a school-level attribute, where more than 20% of the variance in the *index of disciplinary climate* occurs between schools.

HOW TEACHERS STIMULATE STUDENTS' ENGAGEMENT WITH READING

Volume III, *Learning to Learn,* highlights the positive and strong relationship between students' level of engagement with reading and how well they learn. Research suggests that students who are substantively engaged, that is, who are interested in what is being taught, learn much more than students who are only procedurally engaged, that is, who follow the rules and do assignments as required, or who have no interest in what is being taught. Research also suggests that more interaction between teachers and students in the classroom promotes substantive engagement. This occurs when teachers ask questions that require more than a simple recitation of received knowledge, and when teachers incorporate previous answers into subsequent questions and/or further discussion (Nystrand and Gamoran, 1991).

PISA 2009 asked students to evaluate their interactions with their teachers to measure the extent to which teachers stimulate students' engagement with reading. Students were asked to describe the frequency with which teachers ask students to explain the meaning of a text, ask questions that challenge students, give enough time for students to think about their answers, recommend a book or author to students, encourage students to express their opinions about a text, help students relate the stories they read to their lives, and show students how the information in the texts builds on what they already know. Students were asked to report whether each of these behaviours occurs "never or hardly ever", "in some lessons", "in most lessons", or "in all lessons". These answers were combined to create a composite *index of teachers' stimulation of students' reading engagement* such that the index has an average of zero and a standard deviation of one for the OECD countries. Higher values indicate greater involvement among teachers in stimulating students' engagement with reading according to students' reports. When comparing estimates across school systems, it is important to keep in mind that several factors beyond students' experiences in school may determine the patterns of these responses (see Box IV.1.1).

A large percentage of students in OECD countries reported that teachers actively stimulate their engagement with reading. For example, 60% of students reported that teachers give them enough time to think about their answers in most or all lessons. In Hungary, the United States and Turkey, more than 70% of students reported this to be the case in most or all lessons, while in Mexico, Greece, Korea and Norway, less than 50% of students reported that teachers give them enough time to think about their answers in most or all lessons. On average across OECD countries, 59% of students reported that teachers ask challenging questions in most or all lessons. In Denmark, Turkey and Greece, three-quarters or more of students reported that teachers ask challenging questions. In Finland, Sweden, Austria and Iceland, less than 45% of students reported that teachers ask such questions. Teachers can also stimulate reading engagement by encouraging students to express their opinions about a text. On average, among OECD countries, 55% of students reported that teachers encourage students in this way in most or all lessons. In Turkey, Poland and the United States, over two-thirds of students reported such encouragement, while in Korea, the Netherlands and Iceland, less than 40% of students reported that teachers encourage them to express their opinions about a text.

Student engagement with reading can also be stimulated by teachers asking students to explain the meaning of a text. On average among OECD countries, 52% of students reported that teachers do this in most or all of their lessons. Some 70% of students in Turkey and Denmark reported this, while less than 35% of students in Iceland, Sweden, Finland and the Netherlands reported that teachers ask them to explain the meaning of a text.

■ Figure IV.4.3 ■

Students' views of how well teachers motivate them to read

Index of teachers' stimulation of students' reading engagement based on students' reports

- A: The teacher asks students to explain the meaning of a text.
- B: The teacher asks questions that challenge students to get a better understanding of a text.
- C: The teacher gives students enough time to think about their answers.
- D: The teacher recommends a book or author to read.
- E: The teacher encourages students to express their opinion about a text.
- F: The teacher helps students relate the stories they read to their lives.
- G: The teacher shows students how the information in texts builds on what they already know.

		Percentage of students reporting that the following phenomena occur "never or hardly ever" or "in some lessons"							Variability in the index (S.D.)	School variability in the distribution of the index (Proportion of the index variance between schools)
		A	B	C	D	E	F	G		
OECD	Australia	63	67	68	30	63	32	50	1.0	0.07
	Austria	39	42	55	30	54	26	38	1.0	0.07
	Belgium	43	56	65	24	51	27	34	0.9	0.05
	Canada	61	65	68	37	65	44	53	1.0	0.10
	Chile	48	59	59	49	57	43	57	1.0	0.09
	Czech Republic	46	54	58	43	49	23	33	0.9	0.07
	Denmark	76	80	60	30	58	45	50	0.9	0.07
	Estonia	49	67	63	45	59	29	40	0.8	0.08
	Finland	35	35	63	38	47	17	24	0.8	0.07
	France	62	60	69	43	58	27	47	0.9	0.06
	Germany	50	53	61	19	58	26	44	0.9	0.04
	Greece	65	75	45	26	60	33	40	0.9	0.07
	Hungary	56	64	71	38	63	45	52	0.9	0.10
	Iceland	30	44	53	25	38	32	36	1.0	0.09
	Ireland	59	67	63	30	63	29	46	1.0	0.04
	Israel	41	46	55	26	45	31	36	1.2	0.15
	Italy	48	61	63	47	60	32	35	0.9	0.10
	Japan	55	66	61	25	42	30	29	1.1	0.08
	Korea	38	45	46	19	26	32	33	1.0	0.05
	Luxembourg	58	60	56	36	55	28	42	1.0	0.01
	Mexico	42	60	44	54	58	37	45	1.0	0.07
	Netherlands	35	49	61	29	36	18	35	0.9	0.05
	New Zealand	62	65	65	34	61	33	50	1.0	0.04
	Norway	45	53	47	28	41	20	28	0.9	0.08
	Poland	66	73	60	48	67	45	55	1.0	0.06
	Portugal	64	49	68	46	63	37	51	0.9	0.03
	Slovak Republic	44	60	57	35	52	38	39	0.9	0.09
	Slovenia	63	68	62	41	65	46	48	1.0	0.07
	Spain	41	49	53	48	53	27	40	1.0	0.09
	Sweden	34	41	58	44	56	30	35	0.9	0.07
	Switzerland	45	45	61	27	56	32	41	0.9	0.05
	Turkey	71	75	70	59	67	51	53	1.1	0.06
	United Kingdom	67	63	68	26	65	30	55	1.0	0.07
	United States	69	73	70	43	66	51	59	1.2	0.07
	OECD average	52	59	60	36	55	33	43	1.0	0.07
Partners	Albania	59	80	68	51	73	60	61	0.9	0.06
	Argentina	45	61	64	49	58	34	43	1.0	0.08
	Azerbaijan	52	80	66	64	75	56	64	1.2	0.10
	Brazil	38	44	61	55	61	41	51	1.0	0.04
	Bulgaria	52	70	67	52	61	43	55	1.1	0.04
	Colombia	48	62	53	57	62	51	51	0.9	0.09
	Croatia	64	69	61	43	68	50	47	1.0	0.05
	Dubai (UAE)	63	72	68	41	67	49	57	1.1	0.06
	Hong Kong-China	55	64	60	22	44	35	38	0.9	0.09
	Indonesia	44	69	72	44	56	46	49	1.0	0.07
	Jordan	61	62	65	49	66	54	58	1.2	0.08
	Kazakhstan	80	87	81	78	82	75	74	1.1	0.11
	Kyrgyzstan	70	84	74	68	72	70	68	1.1	0.09
	Latvia	52	72	62	43	71	40	51	0.9	0.10
	Liechtenstein	36	38	55	31	48	29	39	0.9	0.18
	Lithuania	61	72	64	55	68	38	51	0.9	0.04
	Macao-China	49	54	43	17	37	30	31	0.8	0.06
	Montenegro	71	73	67	54	68	65	66	1.1	0.07
	Panama	40	58	60	50	62	49	53	1.0	0.04
	Peru	63	66	56	63	71	55	58	1.0	0.06
	Qatar	53	64	60	45	60	49	56	1.3	0.06
	Romania	50	49	56	63	66	43	47	0.9	0.05
	Russian Federation	83	86	80	79	84	74	75	1.2	0.08
	Serbia	68	74	61	47	67	45	51	1.0	0.05
	Shanghai-China	63	47	68	29	59	46	50	0.9	0.04
	Singapore	51	57	68	22	49	36	45	0.9	0.05
	Chinese Taipei	37	48	44	39	41	48	48	1.0	0.03
	Thailand	39	51	54	47	64	58	60	1.0	0.07
	Trinidad and Tobago	60	70	67	40	63	47	59	1.2	0.05
	Tunisia	62	58	65	65	69	47	55	1.0	0.06
	Uruguay	56	57	55	43	55	31	45	1.0	0.04

Note: Higher values on the index indicate higher teacher stimulation of reading engagement.
Source: OECD, *PISA 2009 Database*, Table IV.4.3.
StatLink http://dx.doi.org/10.1787/888932343418

On average across OECD countries, 43% of students reported that, in most or all of their lessons, their teachers show how the texts they read build on what they already know. While more than 55% of students in the United States, Chile, Poland and the United Kingdom reported this kind of stimulation, less than 30% of students in Finland, Norway and Japan reported similar class activities.

On average among OECD countries, 36% of students reported that teachers recommend books or authors to students in most or all lessons. While in Mexico and Turkey more than half of all students reported that teachers recommend books to them, less than a quarter of students in Korea, Germany and Belgium reported this. Meanwhile, some 33% of all students, on average across OECD countries, reported that their teacher helps students relate the contents of a text to their lives in most or all lessons. More than half of all students in Turkey and the United States reported this, while less than 20% of student in Finland and the Netherlands did (Figure IV.4.3).

Taking all these responses together, according to students' reports, teachers prompt student interest in reading the most in Turkey, the United States and Poland. In these three countries, the average level of the *index of teacher stimulation of students' reading engagement* is at least one-quarter of a standard deviation above the OECD average. In contrast, in Korea, Iceland, the Netherlands, Norway and Finland, this level falls to one-third of a standard deviation or lower below the OECD average. In most school systems, this variation occurs within schools, signalling that different students within the same schools have different perceptions about the extent to which teachers stimulate their reading engagement. The variation is greatest in the United States, Israel, Turkey and Japan, while the *index of teacher stimulation of students' reading engagement* is relatively more homogeneous in Finland and Estonia.

Among partner countries and economies, teachers' role in stimulating interest in reading follows a similar pattern to that of OECD countries. The highest levels of the *index of teacher stimulation of students' reading engagement* are observed in Kazakhstan, the Russian Federation, Kyrgyzstan, Azerbaijan, Montenegro and Albania. In most countries, the greatest part of the variation occurs within schools. The variation between schools is largest in Liechtenstein and Kazakhstan, while there is relatively little variation between schools in Chinese Taipei and Panama.

STUDENT-RELATED FACTORS AFFECTING SCHOOL CLIMATE

The learning atmosphere in schools is also influenced by student and teacher behaviour (OECD, 2009b). PISA 2009 asked school principals to indicate the extent to which learning is hindered by behaviours such as student absenteeism, the use of alcohol or illegal drugs, bullying, disruption of classes by students, and students' lack of respect for teachers. These questions were combined to create a composite *index of student-related factors affecting school climate* that has a mean of zero and a standard deviation of one in the OECD countries. Positive values reflect principals' perceptions that student-related behaviours hinder learning to a lesser extent, and negative values indicate that school principals believe students' behaviour hinders learning to a greater extent compared to the OECD average. When comparing estimates across school systems, it is important to keep in mind that several factors beyond principals' experiences in school may be determining the patterns in these responses (see Box IV.1.1).

Most students attend schools in which principals reported that student-related factors affect instruction "very little" or "not at all". Nonetheless, a substantial number of students attend schools whose principal reported that student-related factors hinder learning to "some extent" or "a lot". Across OECD countries, 48% of students attend schools whose principals reported student absenteeism as a problem; 33% whose school principals reported that students skipping lessons is a problem; 40% whose school principals reported that student disruptions in class is a problem; 24% whose principals reported a lack of student respect for teachers; 9% where student drug use hinders learning; and 14% of students in the OECD countries attend schools where the principal reported that bullying hinders student learning to "some extent" or "a lot" (Figure IV.4.4).

The responses of school principals indicate that learning is disrupted by student behaviour the most in Turkey, where the average student attends a school in which the *index of student-related factors affecting school climate* is more than one and a half standard deviations below the OECD average. School principals in Finland, Canada, Slovenia, the Slovak Republic, Ireland and Austria also reported high levels of student behaviours that hinder student learning. In these six countries, the *index of student-related factors affecting school climate* is more than one-fifth of a standard deviation below that of the OECD average. In contrast, student behaviour is less of a concern in Japan, Korea, Denmark, Belgium and Mexico, where the average student attends a school that is more than one-fifth of a standard deviation above the OECD average. Within countries, the level of student disruption of classes is relatively homogeneous in Norway, the United Kingdom, Finland and the Slovak Republic and heterogeneous in Turkey, Chile, Hungary and Greece.

■ Figure IV.4.4 ■

School principals' views of how student behaviour affects students' learning

Index of student-related factors affecting school climate based on school principals' reports

- A Student absenteeism
- B Disruption of classes by students
- C Students skipping classes
- D Students lacking respect for teachers
- E Student use of alcohol or illegal drugs
- F Students intimidating or bullying other students

Percentage of students in schools whose principals reported that the following phenomena hindered the learning of students "not at all" or "very little"

Range between top and bottom quarter
◆ Average index

		A	B	C	D	E	F	Variability in the index (S.D.)
OECD	Australia	52	69	77	77	96	81	1.0
	Austria	44	55	60	70	97	71	0.9
	Belgium	69	72	79	83	95	89	1.0
	Canada	31	71	42	82	70	85	0.8
	Chile	43	68	53	87	86	86	1.1
	Czech Republic	37	43	75	62	95	93	0.8
	Denmark	62	58	83	86	100	93	0.8
	Estonia	50	62	37	77	96	89	0.8
	Finland	27	38	57	67	96	71	0.7
	France	w	w	w	w	w	w	w
	Germany	77	55	84	82	93	82	0.9
	Greece	61	54	72	74	92	87	1.0
	Hungary	48	63	73	82	96	91	1.0
	Iceland	74	53	80	77	90	92	0.8
	Ireland	39	56	79	71	89	80	0.8
	Israel	46	57	58	81	97	93	0.9
	Italy	51	56	51	81	95	92	0.9
	Japan	67	91	89	76	98	93	0.9
	Korea	79	76	93	71	92	87	0.9
	Luxembourg	60	52	84	77	95	93	0.8
	Mexico	60	74	74	90	90	88	0.9
	Netherlands	66	64	77	78	87	75	0.7
	New Zealand	46	68	67	80	90	90	0.9
	Norway	63	41	78	65	98	88	0.7
	Poland	39	69	62	83	97	91	0.8
	Portugal	56	54	59	76	97	93	1.0
	Slovak Republic	32	46	25	79	97	95	0.7
	Slovenia	29	50	36	74	88	91	1.0
	Spain	67	57	73	72	95	92	1.0
	Sweden	49	58	61	78	99	82	0.7
	Switzerland	73	63	82	83	91	89	0.8
	Turkey	14	23	22	29	31	35	1.4
	United Kingdom	62	85	89	88	97	97	0.7
	United States	44	84	70	79	79	91	0.8
	OECD average	52	60	67	76	91	86	0.9
Partners	Albania	75	92	85	94	98	98	0.9
	Argentina	57	82	56	88	91	90	1.1
	Azerbaijan	60	73	95	83	96	93	1.0
	Brazil	50	36	57	63	89	81	1.0
	Bulgaria	43	59	62	70	84	82	1.3
	Colombia	53	49	64	80	86	81	1.0
	Croatia	19	48	29	56	94	88	0.9
	Dubai (UAE)	73	81	84	85	95	91	1.2
	Hong Kong-China	83	83	90	84	98	92	0.9
	Indonesia	67	92	83	85	98	94	0.8
	Jordan	42	56	70	62	87	85	1.2
	Kazakhstan	28	62	42	54	63	60	1.6
	Kyrgyzstan	49	64	60	62	66	69	1.4
	Latvia	32	74	68	82	94	91	0.8
	Liechtenstein	70	46	94	82	93	72	0.9
	Lithuania	74	90	86	91	97	89	0.7
	Macao-China	69	68	68	66	75	69	1.8
	Montenegro	30	80	44	87	100	100	0.8
	Panama	61	84	69	88	95	89	0.9
	Peru	62	80	70	89	93	87	1.0
	Qatar	50	77	76	76	93	90	1.2
	Romania	49	86	61	78	99	89	0.9
	Russian Federation	20	86	32	68	82	82	1.2
	Serbia	16	60	37	81	91	94	0.8
	Shanghai-China	61	64	64	64	69	74	1.7
	Singapore	64	75	83	86	100	94	0.9
	Chinese Taipei	54	56	61	60	71	69	1.7
	Thailand	39	72	62	87	88	92	0.8
	Trinidad and Tobago	32	46	51	58	88	70	0.9
	Tunisia	31	61	70	85	98	87	0.8
	Uruguay	44	84	49	84	97	88	1.1

-3.5 -2.5 -1.5 -0.5 0 0.5 1.5 2.5 Index points

Note: Higher values on the index indicate a positive student behaviour.
Source: OECD, *PISA 2009 Database*, Table IV.4.4.
StatLink http://dx.doi.org/10.1787/888932343418

In 6 of the 31 partner countries and economies, the average student attends a school in which the *index of student-related factors affecting school climate* is more than one-fifth of a standard deviation below the OECD average. In Trinidad and Tobago, Croatia and Kazakhstan, the average student attends a school that is more than half a standard deviation below the OECD average, while in Dubai (UAE), Albania, Azerbaijan and Indonesia, students disrupt learning to a lesser extent, on average. In these countries, the average student attends a school that is half a standard deviation above the OECD average in the *index of student-related factors affecting school climate*. Within countries, the level of student behaviour that hinders learning is relatively homogeneous in Lithuania, Thailand, Tunisia and Indonesia and relatively heterogeneous in Macao-China, Shanghai-China, Chinese Taipei and Kazakhstan.

TEACHER-RELATED FACTORS AFFECTING SCHOOL CLIMATE

As described in Chapter 2, students in more favourable learning environments tend to perform better in reading. This is corroborated by the literature on effective schools and learning environments, which suggests that learning is best accomplished when students have good relations with their teachers (Jennings and Greenberg, 2009), and when teachers have high expectations for their students, especially when those students are from disadvantaged backgrounds (Gamoran, 1993; Gamoran *et al.,* 1997; Jussim and Harber, 2005).

To determine the extent to which these and other teacher-related behaviours influence student learning across schools and within school systems, school principals were asked to report the extent to which they perceived learning in their schools to be hindered by such factors as teachers' low expectations of students, poor student-teacher relations, absenteeism among teachers, staff resistance to change, teachers not meeting individual students' needs, teachers being too strict with students and students not being encouraged to achieve their full potential. The responses were combined to create an *index of teacher-related factors affecting school climate* that has a mean of zero and a standard deviation of one in the OECD countries. Positive values reflect principals' perceptions that teacher-related behaviours hinder learning to a lesser extent, and negative values indicate that school principals believe teachers' behaviour hinders learning to a greater extent compared to the OECD average. When comparing estimates across school systems, it is important to keep in mind that several factors beyond principals' experiences in schools may be determining the patterns in these responses, as described in Box IV.1.1.

The majority of students across OECD countries attend schools whose principals agree that teacher-related factors in their schools affect learning either "not at all" or only "very little". However, a substantial number of students are enrolled in schools whose principals reported that teacher-related behaviour affects student learning "a lot" or "to some extent": 28% of students are enrolled in schools whose principals reported that staff's resistance to change negatively affects students; 28% are enrolled in schools whose principals reported that students' needs are not met; 22% attend schools whose principals believe that learning is hindered by low teacher expectations; 23% attend schools whose principals reported that students are not encouraged by teachers to achieve their full potential in the school; 17% attend schools whose principals reported that teacher absenteeism hinders learning; and 12% attend schools whose principals reported that the quality of student-teacher relations is poor (Figure IV.4.5).

In particular, less than 10% of students in Denmark and Hungary attend schools whose principals believe that the staff's resistance to change negatively affects students, while more than 50% of students in Turkey and Italy attend schools whose principals believe this is the case in their schools. Less than 10% of students in Hungary and the Czech Republic attend schools whose principals reported that individual students' needs are not met by teachers, but more than 50% of students in Turkey and the Netherlands attend such schools. Less than 5% of students in Denmark and Luxembourg attend schools whose principals believe that student learning is affected by teachers' low expectations for students, while 72% of students in Turkey and 49% of students in Chile attend such schools. According to school principals' reports, the incidence of teachers not sufficiently encouraging their students is highest in Turkey and the Netherlands and lowest in Denmark, the United Kingdom, Iceland and Poland. In Korea, Portugal, Japan, the Czech Republic, Switzerland, New Zealand, Hungary, Spain, Italy and the United States, less than 10% of students attend schools whose principals believe that teacher absenteeism is not a problem. In contrast, over 70% of students in Turkey attend schools whose principals believe that teacher absenteeism adversely affects student learning. Less than 5% of students in Poland, Denmark, the United Kingdom, Belgium, Hungary and Portugal attend schools whose principals reported that poor student-teacher relations hinder learning, while three-quarters of all students in Turkey attend such schools.

■ Figure IV.4.5 ■

School principals' views of how teacher behaviour affects students' learning

Index of teacher-related factors affecting school climate based on school principals' reports

- **A** Teachers' low expectations of students
- **B** Poor student-teacher relations
- **C** Teachers not meeting individual students' needs
- **D** Teacher absenteeism
- **E** Staff resisting change
- **F** Teachers being too strict with students
- **G** Students not being encouraged to achieve their full potential

Percentage of students in schools whose principals reported that the following phenomena hindered learning "not at all" or "very little"

		A	B	C	D	E	F	G	Variability in the index (S.D.)
OECD	Australia	68	85	58	86	61	96	78	0.91
	Austria	86	94	78	78	76	97	87	0.84
	Belgium	87	96	76	75	71	96	84	0.86
	Canada	86	89	75	88	62	94	86	0.82
	Chile	51	92	62	69	60	86	57	1.00
	Czech Republic	83	83	94	96	86	90	75	0.72
	Denmark	95	97	88	89	91	98	93	0.82
	Estonia	82	87	68	89	87	82	77	0.83
	Finland	94	88	67	80	84	97	86	0.69
	France	w	w	w	w	w	w	w	w
	Germany	82	93	77	78	70	96	89	0.75
	Greece	64	82	70	86	76	89	76	1.05
	Hungary	94	96	94	94	90	89	69	0.86
	Iceland	90	88	71	83	84	97	92	0.85
	Ireland	78	92	76	88	82	89	84	0.87
	Israel	73	86	67	71	80	90	80	0.86
	Italy	74	73	73	91	48	85	67	0.84
	Japan	76	85	71	97	63	81	61	0.87
	Korea	66	90	67	99	66	84	83	0.79
	Luxembourg	95	88	64	82	84	89	71	0.71
	Mexico	65	81	69	78	59	80	60	1.01
	Netherlands	66	90	44	62	61	86	45	0.67
	New Zealand	63	83	57	95	73	95	82	0.79
	Norway	80	90	52	75	79	98	77	0.71
	Poland	90	98	89	77	85	98	91	0.86
	Portugal	74	96	77	98	67	100	79	0.90
	Slovak Republic	87	94	88	80	79	75	78	0.79
	Slovenia	83	90	78	85	68	87	81	0.84
	Spain	75	91	85	91	67	92	74	0.92
	Sweden	77	93	64	87	67	99	75	0.83
	Switzerland	94	91	81	96	74	97	89	0.73
	Turkey	28	25	39	30	25	32	27	1.29
	United Kingdom	79	97	77	87	83	98	92	0.80
	United States	77	90	72	91	68	96	84	0.79
	OECD average	78	88	72	83	72	90	77	0.84
Partners	Albania	86	91	91	96	93	97	81	0.84
	Argentina	70	88	73	51	62	87	55	1.09
	Azerbaijan	67	67	80	82	81	91	76	1.09
	Brazil	56	89	58	70	64	92	65	0.95
	Bulgaria	73	84	70	73	87	88	72	1.13
	Colombia	66	93	66	79	49	81	63	1.09
	Croatia	79	90	75	94	58	90	72	0.82
	Dubai (UAE)	86	89	80	86	77	87	92	1.23
	Hong Kong-China	58	93	52	87	77	94	69	0.81
	Indonesia	86	96	90	97	90	92	69	0.87
	Jordan	60	62	64	58	61	86	69	1.08
	Kazakhstan	43	60	55	60	66	60	58	1.38
	Kyrgyzstan	54	71	69	66	64	65	59	1.37
	Latvia	90	93	81	91	93	89	77	0.83
	Liechtenstein	94	100	80	100	83	100	100	0.49
	Lithuania	94	99	93	98	96	99	96	0.68
	Macao-China	73	73	44	66	66	83	57	1.38
	Montenegro	85	95	73	88	88	93	58	0.71
	Panama	62	89	69	75	57	81	61	1.03
	Peru	64	91	72	85	69	83	63	0.95
	Qatar	77	80	82	88	84	88	85	1.07
	Romania	84	90	89	99	69	91	83	0.80
	Russian Federation	60	79	68	78	65	56	58	1.07
	Serbia	71	94	70	93	59	84	61	0.78
	Shanghai-China	58	59	45	71	60	73	47	1.33
	Singapore	64	83	59	84	83	90	90	0.92
	Chinese Taipei	52	57	54	70	56	67	52	1.42
	Thailand	67	82	72	90	90	68	87	0.86
	Trinidad and Tobago	45	66	34	41	54	91	71	0.94
	Tunisia	33	83	69	40	73	83	74	0.86
	Uruguay	53	92	68	35	57	94	33	1.03

Note: Higher values on the index indicate a positive teacher behaviour.
Source: OECD, *PISA 2009 Database*, Table IV.4.5.
StatLink http://dx.doi.org/10.1787/888932343418

Taking all these responses into account, among OECD countries, principals' reports suggest that teacher-related factors adversely affect the learning environment the most in Turkey, where the average student attends a school that is more than one-and-a-half standard deviations below the OECD average in the *index of teacher-related factors affecting school climate*. Teacher-related factors also adversely affect learning in the Netherlands, Chile and Mexico, where the average student attends a school that has an *index of teacher-related factors affecting school climate* of more than one-third of a standard deviation below the OECD average. In contrast, learning is less negatively influenced by teachers' attitudes and behaviours in Hungary, Poland, Denmark and Iceland, according to school principals. In these four countries, the average student is enrolled in a school that has an *index of teacher-related factors affecting school climate* of more than one-quarter of a standard deviation above the OECD average. Countries with high values on the *index of teacher-related factors affecting school climate* are generally also those with high values on the *index of student-related factors affecting school climate,* possibly indicating that these problems in the learning environment are not solely due to student or teacher behaviour, but may involve other factors in the school or the school system as well.

The degree to which teachers' attitudes and behaviour is reported to affect the learning environment also varies within a school system. Large variations in the way principals reported teacher-related factors affecting learning are observed in Turkey, Greece, Mexico and Chile; low levels of variation are observed in the Netherlands, Finland, Norway and Luxembourg.

Among the partner countries and economies, school principals reported that teachers' attitudes and behaviours adversely affect student learning the most in Trinidad and Tobago, Chinese Taipei, Shanghai-China, Kazakhstan, Kyrgyzstan, Uruguay and Jordan. The average student in these countries and economies attends a school that has an index value of at least half a standard deviation below the OECD average. In four other partner countries and economies, the average student attends a school with an index value of at least one-third of a standard deviation below the OECD average. Only in four partner countries and economies is the average *index of teacher-related factors affecting school climate* one-third of a standard deviation above the OECD average: Lithuania, Dubai (UAE), Albania and Indonesia. Variation within school systems is greatest in Chinese Taipei, Macao-China, Kazakhstan and Kyrgyzstan. Variation is the lowest in Liechtenstein, Lithuania, Montenegro and Serbia, indicating relative homogeneity in how teacher-related factors affect student learning.

PARENTS' INVOLVEMENT IN AND EXPECTATIONS OF SCHOOLING

Most countries provide formal and active channels for parents to be involved in schooling (OECD, 2010a). Parents' actions in this partnership include discussing educational matters with their children, supervising their children's educational progress, communicating with the school, and participating in school activities. While the first two forms of parental involvement entail interactions between parents and students, the latter two involve interactions between parents and the school (Ho and Willms, 1996).

Research suggests that students perform better when parents, teachers and schools have high expectations for them. A driving force behind school expectations is parental pressure for the school to set high academic standards for its students (Epstein, 2001). PISA asked school principals to report on the level of parental pressure for the school to set and achieve high standards for its students. It is important when comparing estimates across school systems to keep in mind that several factors beyond principal's experiences in schools may be determining the patterns in these responses, as described in Box IV.1.1.

In OECD countries, approximately 19% of students attend schools whose principals reported that many parents expect high academic standards from the school. In New Zealand, Ireland, the United States, the United Kingdom and Sweden, over one-third of students attend such a school, but in Finland, Austria, Germany, Switzerland, the Netherlands and Luxembourg, less than 10% of students attend such a school. Among partner countries and economies, expectations for high academic standards are greatest in Singapore, Qatar, Dubai (UAE) and Peru, and lowest in Liechtenstein, Macao-China, Hong Kong-China, Montenegro, Uruguay, Serbia, Croatia, Lithuania and Argentina. In all these countries, less than 10% of students attend schools whose principals reported that parents exert pressure on the school to raise academic standards (Table IV.4.7).

In a questionnaire addressed to parents in both OECD countries and partner countries and economies, PISA asked parents about their level of communication with the school and their participation in school activities, such as volunteering in sports or other extra-curricular activities or in the school library, assisting a teacher in school,

appearing as a guest speaker, or participating in the school government. Eight OECD countries – Italy, Germany, Denmark, Portugal, Hungary, Korea, Chile and New Zealand – administered the parent questionnaire. Among these countries, on average, 79% of parents reported having discussed their children's behaviour or progress with a teacher in the academic year, either at their own initiative or that of the teacher (Table IV.4.6). This proportion is highest in Portugal and Denmark, where 87% of parents reported having this form of communication with the school. In contrast, in Hungary, less than 64% of parents reported any communication with the school.

Among the six partner countries and economies that administered the parent questionnaire – Lithuania, Macao-China, Croatia, Panama, Hong Kong-China and Qatar – less than two-thirds of parents in Hong Kong-China and Macao-China discussed their children's behaviour or progress with a teacher, while more than 85% of parents in Croatia reported to have done so.

PRINCIPAL LEADERSHIP

School principals can shape teachers' professional development, define the school's educational goals, ensure that instructional practice is directed towards achieving these goals, suggest modifications to improve teaching practices, and help solve problems that may arise within the classroom or among teachers. They are also in a position to provide incentives and motivate teachers to improve the quality of instruction (Hallinger and Heck, 1998).

PISA asked principals to report on their level of involvement in and leadership of several issues, including making sure that teachers' work and development reflects the educational goals of the school, monitoring student performance and classroom activities, and working with teachers to resolve problems. An *index of school principal's leadership* combines their answers to evaluate whether or not principals are active in improving teaching practices and the working environment within the school. This index has a mean of zero and a standard deviation of one for the OECD countries. Higher values on the index indicate higher levels of principal leadership in the school. It is important when comparing estimates across school systems to keep in mind that several factors beyond principals' experiences in schools may be determining the patterns in these responses, as described in Box IV.1.1.

As in any organisation, decisions made at one level determine what actions can be taken at other levels. The degree to which principals can assume leadership roles in various domains may be constrained by external administrative agencies, regulatory frameworks, or the level of autonomy that is granted to individual schools. In federal education systems, the responsibility that principals have and the expected roles of principals differ across the administration units within a country. Thus, the results presented below must be interpreted in the context of the broader organisational configuration of the school system. In addition, the roles attributed to school principals and teachers may differ such that in some school systems, school principals are responsible for maintaining coherence between teacher development and the educational goals of the school, but they do not supervise classroom instruction or replace absent teachers. In these school systems, then, teachers are responsible for their daily work, and principal leadership is judged against other standards.

Among OECD countries, 93% of students attend schools whose principals reported that he or she ensures that teachers' work reflects the school's educational goals "quite often" or "very often"; over 86% of students attend schools whose principal "quite often" or "very often" takes the initiative to discuss a problem teachers may have in their classrooms; half of students attend schools whose principal "quite often" or "very often" observes classes; 61% of students attend schools whose principal "quite often" or "very often" considers exam results when making decisions regarding curriculum development; and over a quarter of OECD students attend schools whose principals "quite often" or "very often" take over lessons from teachers who are unexpectedly absent (see Figure IV.4.6).

Among OECD countries, the *index of principal's leadership* is highest in the United Kingdom, the United States, Chile and Poland. In these countries, the average student attends a school where the *index of principal leadership* is over half a standard deviation above the OECD average. Principal leadership is lowest in Japan, Finland and Korea. In particular, the average student in Japan attends a school that scores more than one standard deviation below the OECD average in the *index of principal's leadership*. In Finland, for example, very few students attend schools whose principals monitor teaching practices in the classroom or use examination results to make decisions about the curriculum. This could indicate different roles for teachers and principals in Finnish schools as compared to other school systems. Variation in principals' leadership role within the school system is greatest in Korea, Chile and the United States; principals' leadership roles are relatively more homogeneous across schools in Norway and Denmark.

■ Figure IV.4.6 ■

School principals' views of their involvement in school matters

Index of school principal's leadership based on school principals' reports

- **A** I make sure that the professional development activities of teachers are in accordance with the teaching goals of the school.
- **B** I ensure that teachers work according to the school's educational goals.
- **C** I observe instruction in classrooms.
- **D** I use student performance results to develop the school's educational goals.
- **E** I give teachers suggestions as to how they can improve their teaching.
- **F** I monitor students' work.
- **G** When a teacher has problems in his/her classroom, I take the initiative to discuss matters.
- **H** I inform teachers about possibilities for updating their knowledge and skills.
- **I** I check to see whether classroom activities are in keeping with our educational goals.
- **J** I take exam results into account in decisions regarding curriculum development.
- **K** I ensure that there is clarity concerning the responsibility for co-ordinating the curriculum.
- **L** When a teacher brings up a classroom problem, we solve the problem together.
- **M** I pay attention to disruptive behaviour in classrooms.
- **N** I take over lessons from teachers who are unexpectedly absent.

Percentage of students in schools whose principals reported that the following activities and behaviours occurred "quite often" or "very often" during the last school year

Legend: Range between top and bottom quarter; ◆ Average index

		A	B	C	D	E	F	G	H	I	J	K	L	M	N	Variability in the index (S.D.)
OECD	Australia	98	99	64	93	76	58	89	95	81	81	97	93	94	32	1.0
	Austria	89	92	41	60	67	86	84	79	67	22	75	92	87	53	0.8
	Belgium	95	97	43	42	68	33	89	90	82	46	74	98	96	4	0.8
	Canada	98	98	77	91	86	60	95	95	86	63	87	99	98	19	1.0
	Chile	97	98	55	93	95	73	90	96	82	84	94	97	97	62	1.1
	Czech Republic	95	98	57	81	79	93	86	98	83	59	93	96	75	23	0.8
	Denmark	86	89	25	44	53	39	94	91	76	25	76	99	95	29	0.6
	Estonia	92	94	59	84	58	75	72	93	57	62	87	83	79	24	0.9
	Finland	64	75	9	46	40	61	77	95	59	13	77	98	94	39	0.7
	France	w	w	w	w	w	w	w	w	w	w	w	w	w	w	w
	Germany	82	94	40	57	53	82	80	85	57	33	73	95	84	42	0.7
	Greece	40	78	12	61	53	46	97	96	67	34	69	98	96	63	1.0
	Hungary	93	99	54	84	62	84	89	91	65	73	86	94	91	41	0.8
	Iceland	88	89	39	78	77	69	87	96	54	58	87	100	75	26	0.7
	Ireland	88	88	14	64	41	50	88	92	62	78	88	97	97	39	0.9
	Israel	94	99	46	87	85	81	94	89	86	90	94	97	98	26	0.9
	Italy	97	99	39	86	75	87	96	98	88	77	92	98	98	18	0.9
	Japan	43	51	37	30	38	40	29	50	31	37	29	61	60	17	0.9
	Korea	80	85	42	64	68	56	75	69	60	46	63	79	68	7	1.2
	Luxembourg	87	98	32	65	52	64	96	67	74	32	47	98	98	23	1.0
	Mexico	95	97	68	94	89	90	95	91	92	62	90	97	96	43	1.0
	Netherlands	95	97	52	66	73	50	76	82	79	75	80	86	71	16	0.7
	New Zealand	99	98	68	98	73	42	78	84	74	87	97	83	94	12	1.0
	Norway	81	88	24	70	49	55	90	91	48	47	81	98	95	28	0.6
	Poland	94	97	93	95	89	96	91	99	92	71	80	97	93	37	0.8
	Portugal	93	97	9	94	65	49	91	89	48	82	97	99	97	7	0.7
	Slovak Republic	97	99	86	87	86	90	86	98	91	76	96	91	91	15	0.7
	Slovenia	99	100	77	78	85	90	90	95	85	65	93	98	94	23	0.8
	Spain	86	97	28	85	55	45	86	86	66	71	92	99	99	63	0.9
	Sweden	90	96	38	83	63	29	89	90	52	68	93	98	87	13	0.8
	Switzerland	72	82	64	34	60	61	85	80	59	17	54	92	83	31	0.8
	Turkey	85	95	70	93	85	90	75	90	87	78	93	97	99	36	0.9
	United Kingdom	100	100	93	100	92	88	90	96	95	97	99	96	97	29	0.9
	United States	98	98	95	96	94	72	95	97	94	88	90	97	96	16	1.1
	OECD average	88	93	50	75	69	66	86	89	72	61	82	94	90	29	0.9
Partners	Albania	97	100	98	99	94	94	90	88	93	87	93	96	96	47	0.8
	Argentina	95	98	63	90	96	84	94	91	86	66	87	98	96	43	0.9
	Azerbaijan	95	96	97	89	97	99	86	96	99	86	90	90	99	77	1.0
	Brazil	99	99	60	94	94	91	97	97	91	94	94	99	99	44	1.1
	Bulgaria	100	100	92	95	79	93	87	98	94	71	98	91	96	29	0.8
	Colombia	98	99	45	85	92	88	90	96	82	87	92	96	96	31	1.2
	Croatia	94	98	70	80	92	96	96	95	98	76	95	99	100	19	0.8
	Dubai (UAE)	100	100	95	97	98	93	98	99	98	90	93	98	97	39	1.2
	Hong Kong-China	99	99	99	97	100	93	96	98	95	92	97	96	96	45	0.9
	Indonesia	94	99	88	91	99	77	89	96	96	95	96	81	93	47	1.0
	Jordan	99	100	100	99	100	98	99	99	99	81	81	100	99	90	1.1
	Kazakhstan	96	98	98	95	97	97	85	98	99	60	87	86	89	17	0.8
	Kyrgyzstan	90	92	98	90	94	98	89	96	95	82	87	86	81	29	0.9
	Latvia	96	97	80	97	83	86	85	94	85	75	83	76	85	30	0.8
	Liechtenstein	53	21	3	15	14	46	82	16	10	0	13	96	58	44	0.7
	Lithuania	97	98	47	92	75	60	74	89	55	65	89	95	83	7	0.8
	Macao-China	100	100	88	74	82	86	93	76	86	52	88	90	90	45	0.9
	Montenegro	95	100	88	97	97	100	92	100	99	84	100	100	96	23	0.7
	Panama	91	95	86	88	95	84	90	92	95	85	88	97	94	43	1.1
	Peru	94	98	86	88	93	80	80	94	92	84	91	91	95	45	1.1
	Qatar	96	100	100	98	97	94	95	95	98	84	87	96	98	28	1.1
	Romania	98	100	87	98	90	90	96	98	99	91	99	100	99	40	0.8
	Russian Federation	99	99	92	89	87	95	80	99	97	55	97	96	86	31	0.9
	Serbia	97	100	67	90	91	82	97	99	87	93	91	97	97	44	0.8
	Shanghai-China	98	98	94	57	99	69	91	93	96	70	98	99	89	14	0.8
	Singapore	100	100	80	99	94	66	93	93	93	98	98	97	96	8	0.9
	Chinese Taipei	98	98	92	84	86	94	86	98	88	90	95	97	95	20	0.9
	Thailand	94	99	88	98	95	97	94	98	94	96	98	97	97	45	0.9
	Trinidad and Tobago	97	98	60	86	88	71	94	95	84	92	95	97	98	26	1.0
	Tunisia	84	97	92	92	97	60	97	82	84	40	59	99	99	45	1.1
	Uruguay	85	98	89	90	90	81	92	94	84	45	73	98	100	25	1.0

-3 -2 -1 0 1 2 3 4 Index points

Note: Higher values on the index indicate greater involvement of school principals in school matters.
Source: OECD, *PISA 2009 Database*, Table IV.4.8.
StatLink http://dx.doi.org/10.1787/888932343418

Among partner countries and economies, principal leadership is highest in Jordan, Dubai (UAE), Brazil, Qatar, Hong Kong-China and Romania. The average student in these countries attends a school in which the *index of principal's leadership* is more than one standard deviation above that of the OECD average. Students in Liechtenstein, in contrast, attend schools whose principals assume less active leadership roles in the domains examined by PISA.

RELATIONSHIP BETWEEN LEARNING ENVIRONMENT AND SCHOOL CLIMATE VARIABLES

Several of the indices discussed in this section are often inter-related: schools with a good disciplinary climate may also be schools with good relationships between teachers and students, or schools in which principals take an active leadership role. The correlation is a measure that captures the level of association between two variables. The correlation ranges from -1 to 1 with the extremes, indicating a perfect negative or positive relationship, and 0 indicating no association between the two variables. Generally, values above 0.3 or below -0.3 are considered moderate relationships, and values above 0.6 or below -0.6 are considered strong relationships.

In OECD countries, the different variables affecting the learning environment are, at most, moderately related to each other, which indicates that these characteristics may correspond to different aspects of the learning environment.

The most prominent exception is the relationship between the teacher-related and student-related factors that hinder student learning. In all OECD countries where data are available, school principals who reported that student-related factors hinder learning also tend to report that teacher-related factors do so as well. This relationship is not necessarily causal; it may indicate that there is a common underlying factor influencing student and teacher behaviour; or that when student-related factors begin to hinder learning, teacher-related factors also arise or vice versa; it may also reflect the way school principals assign responsibility for problems occurring within the school. The average OECD country has a correlation of 0.61 between student-related and teacher-related factors affecting student learning (Figure IV.4.7).

In 16 OECD countries, there is a moderate relationship between teacher-student relations and how teachers stimulate students' engagement with reading (Table IV.4.9). This relationship may indicate that, in these countries, the way teachers stimulate students' engagement with reading may benefit teacher-student relations and the learning environment. However, causality cannot be determined through these statistical analyses and this relationship may exist for different reasons. One may be that when relations between students and teachers are good, teachers are more likely to encourage their students to read. The average OECD country has a correlation of 0.29 between teacher-student relations and teachers' stimulation of students' engagement with reading.

■ Figure IV.4.7 ■

Relationship between student, teacher and principal behaviour

Values in the cells present correlation coefficients between pairs of measures

Correlation coefficients range from -1.00 (*i.e.* a perfect negative linear association) to +1.00 (*i.e.* a perfect positive linear association). When a correlation coefficients is 0, there is no linear relationship between two measures.

	Teacher-student relations	Disciplinary climate	Teachers' stimulation of students' reading engagement	Student-related factors affecting school climate	Teacher-related factors affecting school climate	School principals' leadership
Teacher-student relations		0.19	0.29	0.05	0.04	0.01
Disciplinary climate	0.17		0.17	0.10	0.05	0.01
Teachers' stimulation of students' reading engagement	0.30	0.15		0.03	0.03	0.02
Student-related factors affecting school climate	0.04	0.09	0.04		0.61	0.10
Teacher-related factors affecting school climate	0.03	0.05	0.02	0.65		0.18
School principals' leadership	0.01	0.01	0.01	0.11	0.19	

Upper triangle is the OECD average
Lower triangle is the average of all participating countries and economies

Note: Average coefficients are calculated as the arithmetic mean of the individual countries/economies' correlation coefficients. All countries and economies are weighted equally. Correlation coefficients that are statistically significant at the 5% level ($p < 0.05$) are indicated in bold.
Source: OECD, *PISA 2009 Database*, Table IV.4.9.
StatLink http://dx.doi.org/10.1787/888932343418

The leadership of school principals is positively associated with teacher-related factors affecting school climate in five OECD countries – Chile, Luxembourg, Korea, Ireland and Mexico – with a correlation of 0.30 or above. School principal leadership is also positively associated with student-related factors hindering learning in two OECD countries: Luxembourg and Chile. In these countries, schools whose principals reported that they assume an active leadership role in many areas are also schools in which learning is less often disrupted by teachers' or students' attitudes or behaviour. Again, the causal nature of this relationship cannot be established. The relationship may be the result of principals' involvement in guiding teacher development and helping to resolve problems among teachers or between students and teachers. Principal leadership may also be more likely to exist in schools where teachers work together to achieve the school's educational goals. The average OECD country has a correlation of 0.18 between the leadership of school principals and teachers' attitudes and behaviour that hinder student learning, and a correlation of 0.10 between school principals' leadership and students' attitudes and behaviour that disrupt learning.

These relationships are moderate in only a handful of OECD countries; they are weak or nonexistent in most OECD countries. While this analysis cannot explain the reasons behind the differences in the strength of these relationships across countries, the differences may be related to the way schools are organised or to the ambient attitudes concerning schooling and education in general.

Policy Implications

Many nations declare that they are committed to children and education. This is put to the test when these commitments come up against other considerations. How do such nations pay teachers compared to the way they pay other professionals with the same level of education? When people are being considered for jobs, how are education credentials weighed against other qualifications ? Would you want your child to be a teacher? How much attention do the media pay to schools and schooling? When it comes down to it, which matters more: a community's standing in the sports leagues or its standing in the school league tables? Are parents more likely to encourage their children to study longer and harder or would they want them to spend more time with their friends, participating in community activities, or taking part in sporting activities?

Some would argue that these are social and cultural matters, and that the substantial variation in the extent to which students in different countries acquire the knowledge and skills they will need to succeed in life is not often altered by public policy. However, in some of the high-performing countries that have very few natural resources, such as Finalnd, Singapore and Japan, education appears to have a high status at least in part because the general public understands that the country must live by its human resources, which depend on the quality of education. Moreover, over the last decade, the rapid improvements in learning outcomes that some countries demonstrated in PISA across diverse cultures, languages and geographic location, as reported in Volume V, *Learning Trends*, have shown that there is still room for improvement. Perhaps most important, this volume of the PISA 2009 series has, more than any previous internationally comparable analysis, shown that there is a range of resources, policies and practices that is strongly associated with student outcomes, both in combination with and aside from socio-economic factors. Together, the factors measured by PISA account for 88% of the observed differences in school performance across the participating countries.

It is not surprising that performance is influenced by social and economic advantage, with some of the lowest-performing countries also being among the poorest in the survey, and students within each country being more likely to succeed if they are from socio-economically advantaged backgrounds. However, this is only part of the story and one that is least affected by public policy, at least in the short term. PISA has therefore placed greater emphasis on the characteristics of schools and school systems: the resources invested in them, their policies and practices and the learning environments that they create.

Overall, Volume I, *What Students Know and Can Do,* notes that differences in per capita GDP explain only about 6% of differences in mean student performance across OECD countries. In other words, most of the country differences are due to students doing better or worse in PISA regardless of the economic well-being of their country. The factors identified in this volume go a long way towards explaining these differences. A school's resources, policies, practices and environment help account both for whether students are more likely to succeed at one school compared to another and for the strength of educational advantage that students obtain in schools with more advantaged socio-economic backgrounds. As well as contributing to overall performance, they contribute to equity, which is defined as students from different backgrounds having equal chances of performing well.

Chapter 2 of this volume gives a detailed breakdown of the strength of association between these different features of schools and performance both within and across school systems. Some conclusions can be drawn from these results.

A COMMITMENT TO CHILDREN MATTERS, AS DOES THE BELIEF THAT ALL STUDENTS CAN ATTAIN HIGH LEVELS OF ACHIEVEMENT

Placing a high value on education can only get a country so far if the teachers, parents and citizens of that country believe that only a segment of the nation's children can or need to meet high standards. From a national perspective, these belief systems have a powerful effect on student performance. Systems that show high performance and an equitable distribution of learning outcomes tend to be comprehensive, requiring teachers and schools to embrace diverse student populations through personalised educational pathways. In contrast, school systems that assume that students have different destinations, and that hold different expectations of students and group them into different schools, classes and grades often show less equitable outcomes without an overall performance advantage.

Earlier PISA assessments showed these expectations to be mirrored in how students perceived their own educational futures. The results can be seen in the distribution of student performance within countries and in the impact that socio-economic background has on learning outcomes:

- In countries, and in schools within countries, where more students repeat grades, overall results tend to be worse.
- In countries where more students repeat grades, socio-economic differences in performance tend to be wider, suggesting that people from socio-economically disadvantaged groups are more likely to be negatively affected by grade repetition.
- In countries where 15-year-olds are sorted into tracks based on their abilities, overall performance is not enhanced, and the younger the age at which selection for such tracks first occurs, the greater the impact of socio-economic background on student performance by age 15, without improved overall performance.
- In school systems where it is more common to transfer weak or disruptive students out of a school, performance and equity both tend to be lower. Individual schools that make more use of transfers also perform worse in some countries.

These associations account for a substantial amount of the differences in the outcomes of schooling systems. For example, the frequency with which students are transferred across schools is associated with a third of the variation in country performance. This does not necessarily mean that if transfer policies were changed, a third of country differences in reading performance would disappear, since PISA does not measure cause and effect. Transferring difficult students who do badly may be partly a symptom, rather than a cause, of schools and school systems that are not producing satisfactory results. It is worth noting that the schools with lower transfer rates tend to have greater autonomy and other means of addressing these challenges. The results listed above suggests that, in general, school systems that seek to cater to different students' needs through a high level of differentiation in the institutions, grade levels and classes have not succeeded in producing superior overall results, and in some respects they have lower-than-average and more socially inequitable performance.

In such countries, schools have a different framework of incentives than in countries where schools are required to educate students in a less differentiated way. In the latter case, schools must find ways of doing the best they can with students from across the spectrum. In differentiated systems, on the other hand, there may be incentives for schools to select the students whom they can educate to the best of their ability, and fewer incentives to persist in getting the best results from difficult students if there is an option of transferring them to other schools. These different incentives may help explain the greater level of equity achieved in less differentiated systems. School systems that continue to differentiate need to consider how to create appropriate incentives to ensure that some students are not "discarded" by the system.

SETTING STANDARDS AND SHOWING STUDENTS HOW TO MEET THEM MATTERS

Most of the high-performing countries have developed world-class academic standards for their students and almost all have incorporated those standards into a system of external examinations that are used to construct clear paths into the workforce and good jobs or to the next stage of education or both. Indeed, PISA shows that the existence of such external examinations is positively associated with the overall performance of school systems.

These examinations are often linked to national qualifications systems. In countries with such systems, one cannot go on to the next phase of one's education or begin a career in a particular field without a document showing that one is qualified to do so, according to a set of rules and standards laid down by the state. Everyone knows what is required to get any given qualification, in terms of both the content studied and the level of performance that has to

be demonstrated to obtain such a qualification. And the qualification earned, in turn, determines the opportunities available to students. The stakes are high. Students do not get to go on to the next stage simply because they have put in the requisite time; they get to move on only if they have met the requisite performance standards. Parents and students know that neither the teacher nor the administration can change the grade, and therefore the only way to improve the outcome for the student is for the student to work harder and do better work.

In some countries, after an examination has been conducted, newspapers may publish some of the exam questions that ask students to write short essays. The ministry of education then publishes examples of answers that earned the highest grades. In this way, students, parents and teachers all learn what is considered to be high-quality work and students can compare their own work to a clear example of work that meets those standards. Standards in such systems consist of narrative statements of what students should know and what they should be able to do, the questions asked in the exams and the responses given by students who earned good grades.

AUTONOMY MATTERS WHEN COMBINED WITH ACCOUNTABILITY

The incentive to deliver good results for all students is not just a matter of how a school's student body is defined; it also depends on the ways in which schools are held accountable for their results and what forms of autonomy they are allowed to have – and how that could help influence their performance. PISA has looked at accountability both in terms of the information that is made available about performance and how that information is used – whether by administrative authorities through rewards or control systems, or by parents, through their choice of school. Thus the issues of autonomy, evaluation, governance and choice interact in providing a framework in which schools are given the incentives and the capacity to improve.

In this context, PISA 2009 found that:

- In countries where schools have greater autonomy over what is taught and how students are assessed, students tend to perform better.
- Within countries where schools are held to account for their results through posting achievement data publicly, schools that enjoy greater autonomy in resource allocation tend to do better than those with less autonomy. However, in countries where there are no such accountability arrangements, the reverse is true.
- Countries that create a more competitive environment in which many schools compete for students do not systematically produce better results.
- Within many countries, schools that compete more for students tend to have higher performance levels, but this is often accounted for by the higher socio-economic status of students in these schools. Parents with a higher socio-economic status are more likely to take academic performance into consideration when choosing schools.
- In countries that use standards-based external examinations, students tend to do better overall, but there is no clear relationship between performance and the use of standardised tests or the public posting of results at the school level. However, performance differences between schools with students of different social backgrounds are, on average, lower in countries where more schools use standardised tests.

In recent years, many school systems have moved away from a model of purely administrative control and towards one where schools become more autonomous organisations, accountable to their users and to the public for outcomes. The PISA results suggest that some features of autonomy and accountability are associated with better performance. However, this is not a simple relationship under which any policy to increase autonomy, accountability or choice will improve student outcomes.

Some accountability systems publish data on the performance of students and schools to inform the public and the system managers about their performance. In systems that permit parents and students to choose among schools, this data can also influence those choices and thus hold schools accountable. However, some features, most notably the prevalence of private schools and competition for students, have no discernible relationship with overall performance once socio-economic background is accounted for. While students who attend schools that compete with other schools for student enrolment also perform better than students who attend schools that do not compete with other schools, the cross-country analysis suggests that systems as a whole do not benefit from higher rates of school competition. This may reflect the fact that socio-economically advantaged students, who tend to achieve higher scores, are also more likely to attend schools that compete for enrolment, even after accounting for location and attendance in private schools. More worryingly, in the countries that administered the PISA parent

questionnaire, socio-economically disadvantaged parents are significantly more likely than advantaged parents to report that they considered "low expenses" and "financial aid" to be very important determining factors in choosing a school. While parents from all backgrounds cite academic achievement as an important consideration when choosing a school for their children, socio-economically advantaged parents are, on average, 10 percentage points more likely than disadvantaged parents to cite this as "very important". These differences suggest that socio-economically disadvantaged parents may consider that they have more limited choices of schools for their children because of the cost of some schools. If children from socio-economically disadvantaged backgrounds cannot attend high-performing schools because of financial constraints, then school systems that offer parents more choice of schools for their children will necessarily be less effective in improving the performance of all students.

The combination of some forms of autonomy and accountability has closer associations with student results. For example, schools' autonomy in allocating resources is associated with good performance only in the systems where most of the schools post achievement data publicly. This suggests that it is combinations of these conditions, rather than each policy in isolation, that are related to better outcomes. The important thing about these PISA results is that they show differences in performance associated with both autonomy and accountability. These findings are compatible with the view that reforms in these directions can make a difference to outcomes, and should encourage countries to look at how a sound framework of autonomy and accountability can be implemented or strengthened.

HOW RESOURCES ARE ALLOCATED IN SCHOOLS MATTERS MORE THAN OVERALL SPENDING

Effective school systems require the right combination of trained and talented personnel, adequate educational resources and facilities and motivated students who are ready to learn. At the same time, demands for investments in education need to be balanced against other demands on public expenditure and the overall burden of taxation. School systems differ in the amount of time, human, material and financial resources they invest in education. Equally important, school systems also vary in how these resources are spent. Research usually shows a weak relationship between educational resources and student performance, with more variation explained by the quality of human resources (*i.e.* teachers and school principals) than by material and financial resources, particularly among industrialised nations. The generally weak relationship between resources and performance observed in past research is also seen in PISA:

- At the level of the school system and net of the level of national income, PISA shows that higher teachers' salaries, but not smaller class sizes, are associated with better student performance. Teachers' salaries are related to class size in that if spending levels are similar, school systems often make trade-offs between smaller classes and higher salaries for teachers. The findings from PISA suggest that systems prioritising higher teachers' salaries over smaller classes tend to perform better, which corresponds with research showing that raising teacher quality is a more effective route to improved student outcomes than creating smaller classes.
- Within countries, schools with better resources tend to do better only to the extent that they also tend to have more socio-economically advantaged students. Some countries show a strong relationship between schools' resources and their socio-economic and demographic background, which indicates that resources are inequitably distributed according to schools' socio-economic and demographic profiles.
- In other respects, the overall lack of a relationship between resources and outcomes does not show that resources are not important, but that their level does not have a systematic impact within the prevailing range. If most or all schools have the minimum resource requirements to allow effective teaching, additional material resources may make little difference to outcomes.

Recent research has emphasised the importance of teaching quality for learning outcomes. If there are ways in which higher investments can be used to recruit more qualified teachers or provide professional training that increases their effectiveness, this could be money well spent. The bottom line is that the quality of a school system cannot exceed the quality of its teachers.

THE SCHOOL CLIMATE AND TEACHER-STUDENT RELATIONS MATTER

A final important feature of schools is whether they create a conducive climate for teaching and learning. Education policies and practices can only be as good as how effectively they translate into learning in the classroom. Results from PISA suggest that schools and countries where students work in a climate characterised by expectations of high performance and a readiness to invest effort, good teacher-student relations, and high teacher morale tend

to achieve better results. Even after accounting for socio-economic background and other aspects of the learning environment measured by PISA, the results show that student performance is positively related to better teacher-student relations, a better disciplinary climate and favourable teacher-related factors that affects school climate:

- Across OECD countries, 13% of variation in student performance is associated with differences in school climate between schools. However, three-quarters of this effect is linked to the better school climate enjoyed by students from advantaged backgrounds, who also do better in reading, suggesting that this relationship is mediated by socio-economic background.
- Disciplinary climate has a relationship with performance that goes beyond the impact of social background. On the other hand, higher parental expectations of children are associated with stronger performance only to the extent that more socio-economically advantaged parents tend to have higher expectations.
- The learning environment is also shaped by parents and school principals. Parents who are interested in their children's education are more likely to support their school's efforts and participate in school activities, thus adding to available resources. School principals can define their schools' educational objectives and guide their schools towards them. PISA shows that school principals' perceptions of parents' pressure for high academic standards and achievement are positively related to higher school performance, even if much of this relationship is mediated by socio-economic factors.

PISA shows that the socio-economic background of students and schools and the learning environment are closely interrelated, and that both factors link to performance in important ways, perhaps because students from socio-economically advantaged backgrounds bring with them a higher level of discipline and more positive perceptions of school values, or perhaps because parental expectations of good classroom discipline and strong teacher commitment are higher in schools with advantaged socio-economic intake. Conversely, disadvantaged schools may not face as much parental pressure to reinforce effective disciplinary practices or ensure that absent or unmotivated teachers are replaced. In summary, students perform better in schools with a better school climate, partly because such schools tend to have more students from advantaged backgrounds who generally perform well, partly because the favourable socio-economic characteristics of students reinforce a favourable climate, and partly for reasons unrelated to socio-economic variables.

What these findings tell policy makers is that, while it is possible to improve features such as school discipline separately from socio-economic issues, policies that address these two issues in tandem could have a much bigger impact. School systems need to look at how they can influence the learning climate in schools with large proportaions of socio-economically disadvantaged students. This may be approached either through measures that change the social mix of students in some schools or by a change in attitudes and practices among teachers, students and parents in order to weaken the association between socio-economic disadvantage and a less favourable school climate.

References

Alexander, K., D. Entwisle and **S. Dauber** (2003), *On the Success of Failure: A Reassessment of the Effects of Retention in the Early Grades,* Cambridge University Press, Cambridge.

Berends, M. and **G. Zottola** (2009), "International Perspectives on School Choice", in M. Berends, *et al.* (eds.), *Handbook of School Choice,* Routledge, London.

Birch, S. and **G. Ladd** (1998), "Children's Interpersonal Behaviors and the Teacher-Child Relationship", *Developmental Psychology,* Vol. 34, No. 5, pp. 934-946.

Bishop, J. (1998), "Do Curriculum-based External Exit Exam Systems Enhance Student Achievement?", CPRE Research Report Series RR-40, Consortium for Policy Research in Education, University of Pennsylvania, Philadelphia.

Bishop, J. (2001), "How External Exit Exams Spur Achievement", in F. Mane and M. Bishop (eds.) *Educational Leadership,* Association for Supervision and Curriculum Development, Baltimore, Maryland.

Blair, C., *et al.* (2005), "Rising Mean IQ: Cognitive Demand of Mathematics Education for Young Children, Population Exposure to Formal Schooling, and the Neurobiology of the Prefrontal Cortex", *Intelligence,* Vol. 33, pp. 93-106.

Buchmann, C. and **E. Hannum** (2001), "Education and Stratification in Developing Countries: A Review of Theories and Research", *Annual Review of Sociology,* Vol. 27, pp. 77-102.

Bunar, N. (2010a), "The Controlled School Market and Urban Schools in Sweden", *Journal of School Choice,* Vol. 4, pp. 47-73.

Bunar, N. (2010b), "Choosing for Quality or Inequality", *Journal of Education Policy,* Vol. 25, pp. 1-18.

Carneiro, P. and **J. Heckman** (2005), "Human Capital Policy", in J. Heckman and A. Krueger (eds.), *Inequality in America: What Role for Human Capital Policies?,* MIT Press, Cambridge, Massachusetts.

Carnoy, M. (2000), "Globalization and Educational Reform", in N. Stromquist and K. Monkman (eds.), *Globalization and Education: Integration and Contestation across Cultures,* Rowman and Littlefield Publishers, Oxford.

Causa, O. and **C. Chapuis** (2009), "Equity in Student Achievement across OECD Countries: An Investigation of the Role of Policies", *OECD Economics Department Working Papers,* No. 708.

Ceci, S. (1991), "How Much Does Schooling Influence General Intelligence and Its Cognitive Components? A Reassessment of the Evidence", *Developmental Psychology,* Vol. 27, No. 5, pp. 703-722.

Coleman, J., *et al.* (1966), *Equality of Educational Opportunity,* US Government Printing Office, Washington, DC.

Covay, E. and **W. Carbonaro** (2009), "After the Bell: Participation in Extracurricular Activities, Classroom Behavior, and Academic Achievement", *Sociology of Education,* Vol. 83, No. 1, pp. 20-45.

Crosnoe, R., M. Johnson and **G. Elder** (2004), "Intergenerational Bonding in School: The Behavioral and Contextual Correlates of Student-Teacher Relationships", *Sociology of Education,* Vol. 77, No. 1, pp. 60-81.

Dempster, A.P., N.M. Laird and **D.B. Rubin** (1977), "Maximum likelihood from incomplete data via the EM algorithm", *Journal of the Royal Statistical Society, Series B,* Vol. 34, pp1-38.

Downey, D., P. Von Hippel and **B. Broh** (2004), "Are Schools the Great Equalizer? Cognitive Inequality over the Summer Months and the School Year", *American Sociological Review,* Vol. 69, No. 5, pp. 613-635.

Downey, D., P. Von Hippel and **M. Hughes** (2008), "Are 'Failing' Schools Really Failing? Using Seasonal Comparison to Evaluate School Effectiveness", *Sociology of Education,* Vol. 81, No. 3, pp. 242-270.

Ehrenberg, R., *et al.* (2001), "Class Size and Student Achievement", *Psychological Science in the Public Interest,* Vol. 2, No. 1, pp. 1-30.

Entwisle, D., K. Alexander and **L. Olson** (1997), *Children, Schools and Inequality,* Westview Press, Boulder, Colorado.

Epstein, J. (2001), *School, Family, and Community Partnerships: Preparing Educators and Improving Schools,* Westview Press, Boulder, Colorado.

Farkas, G. (2003), "Cognitive Skills and Non-cognitive Traits and Behaviors in Stratification Process", *Annual Review of Sociology,* Vol. 29, pp. 541-562.

Finn, J. (1998), "Class Size and Students at Risk: What is Known? What is Next?", US Department of Education, Office of Educational Research and Improvement, National Institute on the Education of At-Risk Students, Washington, DC.

Fuchs, T. and **L. Woessmann** (2007), "What Accounts for International Differences in Student Performance? A Re-Examination Using PISA Data", *Empirical Economics,* Vol. 32, No. 2-3, pp. 433-464.

Fuller, B. (1987), "What Factors Raise Achievement in the Third World?", *Review of Educational Research,* Vol. 57, No. 3, pp. 255-292.

Gamoran, A. (1993), "Alternative Uses of Ability Grouping in Secondary Schools: Can We Bring High-Quality Instruction to Low-Ability Classes?", *American Journal of Education,* Vol. 102, No. 1, pp. 1-12.

Gamoran, A. and **M. Nystrand** (1992), "Taking Students Seriously", in F. Newman (ed.), *Student Engagement and Achievement in American Secondary Schools,* Teachers College Press, New York City, New York.

Gamoran, A., W. Secada and **C. Marrett** (2000), "The Organizational Context of Teaching and Learning: Changing Theoretical Perspectives", in M. Hallinan (ed.), *Handbook of the Sociology of Education,* Springer, New York City, New York.

Gamoran, A., *et al.* (1997), "Upgrading High School Mathematics Instruction: Improving Learning Opportunities for Low-Achieving, Low-Income Youth", *Educational Evaluation and Policy Analysis,* Vol. 19, No. 4, pp. 325-338.

Ganzeboom, H. B. G., P. M. De Graaf and **D. J. Treiman** (1992), "A Standard International Socio-economic Index of Occupational Status", *Social Science Research* 2, pp. 1-56.

Gewirtz, S., S. Ball and **R. Bowe** (1995), *Markets, Choice and Equity in Education,* Open University Press, Buckingham.

Graue, E. and **J. DiPerna** (2000), "Redshirting and Early Retention: Who Gets the 'Gift of Time' and What are Its Outcomes?", *American Educational Research Journal,* Vol. 37, No. 2, pp. 509-534.

Greenwald, R., L. Hedges and **R. Laine** (1996), "The Effect of School Resources on Student Achievement", *Review of Educational Research,* Vol. 66, No. 3, pp. 361-396.

Hallinger, P. and **R. Heck** (1998), "Exploring the Principal's Contribution to School Effectiveness: 1980-1995", *School Effectiveness and School Improvement,* Vol. 9, pp. 157-191.

Hart, B. and **T. Risley** (1995), *Meaningful Differences in the Everyday Experiences of Young American Children,* Paul H. Brookes Publishing, Baltimore, Maryland.

Hauser, R (2004), "Progress in Schooling", in K. Neckerman (ed.), *Social Inequality,* Russell Sage Foundation, New York City, New York.

Heckman, J. (2000), "Policies to Foster Human Capital", *Research in Economics,* Vol. 54, No. 1, pp. 3-56.

Hess, F. and **T. Loveless** (2005), "How School Choice Affects Student Achievement", in J. Betts and T. Loveless (eds.), *Getting Choice Right: Ensuring Equity and Efficiency in Education Policy,* Brookings Institution Press, Washington, DC.

Heynemann, S. (2009), "International Perspectives on School Choice", in M. Berends, *et al.* (eds.), *Handbook of School Choice,* Routledge, London.

Heyneman, S. and **W. Loxley** (1983), "The Effect of Primary School Quality on Academic Achievement across Twenty-Nine High and Low Income Countries", *The American Journal of Sociology,* Vol. 88, No. 6, pp. 1162-1194.

Ho, E. and **D. Willms** (1996), "Effects of Parental Involvement on Eighth Grade Achievement", *Sociology of Education,* Vol. 69, No. 2, pp. 126-141.

Hsieh, H. and **M. Urquiola** (2006), "The Effects of Generalized School Choice on Achievement and Stratification: Evidence from Chile's Voucher Program", *Journal of Public Economics,* Vol. 90, No. 8-9, pp. 1477-1503.

ILO (International Labour Organization) (1990), *International Standard Classification of Occupations* (ISCO-88), Geneva.

Jacob, B. (2005), "Accountability, Incentives and Behavior: The Impact of High-Stakes Testing in Chicago Public Schools", *Journal of Public Economics,* Vol. 89, No. 5-6, pp. 761-796.

Jennings, J. (2005), "Below the Bubble: 'Educational Triage' and the Texas Accountability System", *American Educational Research Journal,* Vol. 42, No. 2, pp. 231-268.

Jennings, P. and **M. Greenberg** (2009), "The Prosocial Classroom: Teacher Social and Emotional Competence in Relation to Student and Classroom Outcomes", *Review of Educational Research,* Vol. 79, pp. 491-525.

Jussim, L. and **K. Harber** (2005), "Teacher Expectations and Self-Fulfilling Prophecies: Knowns and Unknowns, Resolved and Unresolved Controversies", *Personality and Social Psychology Review*, Vol. 9, No. 2, pp. 131-155.

Karsten, S. (1999), "Neoliberal Education Reform in the Netherlands", *Comparative Education,* Vol. 35, No. 3, pp. 303-317.

Kerckhoff, A. (2000), "Transitions from School to Work in Comparative Perspective", in M. Hallinan (ed.), *Handbook of the Sociology of Education*, Springer, New York City, New York.

Ladd, H. and **R. Walsh** (2002), "Implementing Value-Added Measures of School Effectiveness: Getting the Incentives Right", *Economics of Education Review,* Vol. 21, No. 1, pp. 1-17.

Lareau, A. (1987), "Social Class Differences in Family-School Relationships: The Importance of Cultural Capital", *Sociology of Education,* Vol. 60, No. 2, pp. 73-85.

Lee, V. and **J. Smith** (1995), "Effects of High School Restructuring and Size on Early Gains in Achievement and Engagement", *Sociology of Education,* Vol. 68, No. 4, pp. 241-270.

Lee, V. and **S. Loeb** (1995), "Where Do Head Start Attendees End Up? One Reason Why Preschool Effects Fade Out", *Educational Evaluation and Policy Analysis,* Vol. 17, No. 1, pp. 62-82.

LeTendre, G, B. Hofer and **H. Shimizu** (2003), "What is Tracking? Cultural Expectation in the United States, Germany, and Japan", *American Educational Research Journal,* Vol. 40, No. 1, pp. 43-89.

Lüdtke, O., A. Robitzsch, U. Trautwein and **O. Köller** (2007), "Umgang mit fehlenden Werten in der psychologischen Forschung: Probleme und Lösungen" ("Handling of Missing Data in Psychological Research"), *Psychologische Rundschau,* Vol. 58, Deutsche Gesellschaft für Psychologie, pp. 103-117.

Meyers, M., *et al.* (2004), "Inequality in Early Childhood Education and Care: What Do We Know?", in K. Neckerman (ed.), *Social Inequality,* Russell Sage Foundation, New York City, New York.

Muthén, L.K. and **B.O. Muthén** (2007), *Muplus User's Guide, Fifth Edition,* Muthén & Muthén, Los Angeles, California.

Nye, B., S. Konstantopoulos and **L. Hedges** (2004), "How Large Are Teacher Effects?", *Educational Evaluation and Policy Analysis,* Vol. 94, No. 6, pp. 237-257.

Nystrand, M. and **A. Gamoran** (1991), "Instructional Discourse Student Engagement, and Literature Achievement", *Research in the Teaching of English,* Vol. 25, No. 3, pp. 261-290.

OECD (1999), *Classifying Educational Programmes: Manual for ISCED-97 Implementation in OECD Countries,* OECD Publishing.

OECD (2007), *PISA 2006: Science Competencies for Tomorrow's World,* OECD Publishing.

OECD (2009a), *PISA 2009 Assessment Framework: Key Competencies in Reading, Mathematics and Science*, OECD Publishing.

OECD (2009b), *Creating Effective Teaching and Learning Environments: First Results from TALIS,* OECD Publishing.

OECD (2009c), *Education at a Glance 2009: OECD Indicators,* OECD Publishing.

OECD (2009d), *PISA 2006 Data Analysis Manual: SAS and SPSS, Second Edition,* OECD Publishing.

OECD (2010a), *Education at a Glance 2010: OECD Indicators,* OECD Publishing.

OECD (2010b), *PISA 2009 Database*, OECD Publishing.

OECD (2010c), *Quality Time for Students: Learning In and Out of Schools,* OECD Publishing.

OECD (forthcoming), "Volume VI: Students On Line: Reading and Using Digital Information", *PISA 2009 Initial Report,* OECD Publishing.

OECD (forthcoming), *PISA 2009 Technical Report,* OECD Publishing.

Pastor, D.A., K.E. Barron, B.J. Miller and **S.L. Davis** (2007), "A Latent Profile Analysis of College Students' Achievement Goal Orientation", *Contemporary Educational Psychology,* Vol. 32, No. 1, pp. 8-47.

Piketty, T. and **M. Valdenaire** (2006), *L'Impact de la taille des classes sur la réussite scolaire dans les écoles, collèges et lycées français : Estimations à partir du panel primaire 1997 et du panel secondaire 1995,* ministère de l'Éducation nationale, de l'Enseignement supérieur et de la Recherche, Direction de l'évaluation et de la prospective, Paris.

Plank, D. and **G. Sykes** (eds.) (2003), *Choosing Choice: School Choice in International Perspective,* Teachers College Press, New York City, New York.

Rivkin, S., E. Hanushek and **J. Kain** (2005), "Teachers, Schools and Academic Achievement", *Econometrica,* Vol. 73, No. 2, pp. 417-458.

Sammons, P. (1999), *School Effectiveness: Coming of Age in the Twenty-First Century,* Swets & Zeitlinger, Lisse.

Schafer, J.L. and **J.W. Graham** (2002), "Missing Data: Our View of the State of the Art", *Psychological Methods*, Vol. 7, No. 2, American Psychological Association, pp. 147-177.

Scheerens, J. and **R. Bosker** (1997), *The Foundations of Educational Effectiveness*, Pergamon Press, Oxford.

Schneider, M., P. Teske, and **M. Marschall** (2002), *Choosing Schools: Consumer Choice and the Quality of American Schools*, Princeton University Press, Princeton, New Jersey.

Schütz, G., M. West and **L. Woessmann** (2007), "School Accountability, Autonomy, Choice, and the Equity of Student Achievement: International Evidence form PISA 2003", *OECD Education Working Papers*, No. 14.

Sorensen, A. (1970), "Organizational Differentiation of Students and Educational Opportunity", *Sociology of Education*, Vol. 43, No. 3, pp. 355-376.

Taylor, B., M. Pressley and **P. Pearson** (2002), "Research-Supported Characteristics of Teachers and Schools that Promote Reading Achievement", in B. Taylor and P. Pearson (eds.), *Teaching Reading: Effective Schools, Accomplished Teachers*, CIERA, Mahwah, New Jersey.

Tyack, D. (1974), *The One Best System: A History of American Urban Education*, Harvard University Press, Cambridge, Massachusetts.

Viteritti, J. (1999), *Choosing Equality*, Brookings Institution Press, Washington, DC.

Whitty, G. (1997), "Creating Quasi-Markets in Education: A Review of Recent Research on Parental Choice and School Autonomy in Three Countries", *Review of Research in Education*, Vol. 22, pp. 3-47.

Whitty, G., S. Power and **D. Halpin** (1998), *Devolution and Choice in Education*, Open University Press, Buckingham.

Woessman, L. (2003), "Central Exit Exams and Student Achievement: International Evidence", in Peterson and M.R. West (eds.), *No Child Left Behind? The Politics and Practice of School Accountability*, Brookings Institution Press, Washington, DC.

Annex A

TECHNICAL BACKGROUND

All tables in Annex A are available on line

ANNEX A1
CONSTRUCTION OF READING SCALES AND INDICES FROM THE STUDENT, SCHOOL AND PARENT CONTEXT QUESTIONNAIRES

How the PISA 2009 reading assessments were designed, analysed and scaled

The development of the PISA 2009 reading tasks was co-ordinated by an international consortium of educational research institutions contracted by the OECD, under the guidance of a group of reading experts from participating countries. Participating countries contributed stimulus material and questions, which were reviewed, tried out and refined iteratively over the three years leading up to the administration of the assessment in 2009. The development process involved provisions for several rounds of commentary from participating countries, as well as small-scale piloting and a formal field trial in which samples of 15-year-olds from all participating countries took part. The reading expert group recommended the final selection of tasks, which included material submitted by 21 of the participating countries. The selection was made with regard to both their technical quality, assessed on the basis of their performance in the field trial, and their cultural appropriateness and interest level for 15-year-olds, as judged by the participating countries. Another essential criterion for selecting the set of material as a whole was its fit to the framework described in Volume I, *What Students Know and Can Do,* to maintain the balance across various categories of text, aspect and situation. Finally, it was carefully ensured that the set of questions covered a range of difficulty, allowing good measurement and description of the reading literacy of all 15-year-old students, from the least proficient to the highly able.

More than 130 print reading questions were used in PISA 2009, but each student in the sample only saw a fraction of the total pool because different sets of questions were given to different students. The reading questions selected for inclusion in PISA 2009 were organised into half-hour clusters. These, along with clusters of mathematics and science questions, were assembled into booklets containing four clusters each. Each participating student was then given a two-hour assessment. As reading was the focus of the PISA 2009 assessment, every booklet included at least one cluster of reading material. The clusters were rotated so that each cluster appeared in each of the four possible positions in the booklets, and each pair of clusters appeared in at least one of the 13 booklets that were used.

This design, similar to those used in previous PISA assessments, makes it possible to construct a single scale of reading proficiency, in which each question is associated with a particular point on the scale that indicates its difficulty, whereby each student's performance is associated with a particular point on the same scale that indicates his or her estimated proficiency. A description of the modelling technique used to construct this scale can be found in the *PISA 2009 Technical Report* (OECD, forthcoming).

The relative difficulty of tasks in a test is estimated by considering the proportion of test takers who answer each question correctly. The relative proficiency of students taking a particular test can be estimated by considering the proportion of test questions they answer correctly. A single continuous scale shows the relationship between the difficulty of questions and the proficiency of students. By constructing a scale that shows the difficulty of each question, it is possible to locate the level of reading literacy that the question represents. By showing the proficiency of each student on the same scale, it is possible to describe the level of reading literacy that the student possesses.

The location of student proficiency on this scale is set in relation to the particular group of questions used in the assessment. However, just as the sample of students taking PISA in 2009 is drawn to represent all the 15-year-olds in the participating countries, so the individual questions used in the assessment are designed to represent the definition of reading literacy adequately. Estimates of student proficiency reflect the kinds of tasks they would be expected to perform successfully. This means that students are likely to be able to complete questions successfully at or below the difficulty level associated with their own position on the scale (but they may not always do so). Conversely, they are unlikely to be able to successfully complete questions above the difficulty level associated with their position on the scale (but they may sometimes do so).

The further a student's proficiency is located above a given question, the more likely he or she is to successfully complete the question (and other questions of similar difficulty); the further the student's proficiency is located below a given question, the lower the probability that the student will be able to successfully complete the question, and other questions of similar difficulty.

How reading proficiency levels are defined in PISA 2009

PISA 2009 provides an overall reading literacy scale for the reading texts, drawing on all the questions in the reading assessment, as well as scales for three aspects and two text formats. The metric for the overall reading scale is based on a mean for OECD countries set at 500 in PISA 2000, with a standard deviation of 100. To help interpret what students' scores mean in substantive terms, the scale is divided into levels, based on a set of statistical principles, and then descriptions are generated, based on the tasks that are located within each level, to describe the kinds of skills and knowledge needed to successfully complete those tasks.

For PISA 2009, the range of difficulty of tasks allows for the description of seven levels of reading proficiency: Level 1b is the lowest described level, then Level 1a, Level 2, Level 3 and so on up to Level 6.

Students with a proficiency within the range of Level 1b are likely to be able to successfully complete Level 1b tasks (and others like them), but are unlikely to be able to complete tasks at higher levels. Level 6 reflects tasks that present the greatest challenge in terms of reading skills and knowledge. Students with scores in this range are likely to be able to complete reading tasks located at that level successfully, as well as all the other reading tasks in PISA.

PISA applies a standard methodology for constructing proficiency scales. Based on a student's performance on the tasks in the test, his or her score is generated and located in a specific part of the scale, thus allowing the score to be associated with a defined proficiency level. The level at which the student's score is located is the highest level for which he or she would be expected to answer correctly, most of a random selection of questions within the same level. Thus, for example, in an assessment composed of tasks spread uniformly across Level 3, students with a score located within Level 3 would be expected to complete at least 50% of the tasks successfully. Because a level covers a range of difficulty and proficiency, success rates across the band vary. Students near the bottom of the level would be likely to succeed on just over 50% of the tasks spread uniformly across the level, while students at the top of the level would be likely to succeed on well over 70% of the same tasks.

Figure I.2.12 in Volume I provides details of the nature of reading skills, knowledge and understanding required at each level of the reading scale.

Explanation of indices

This section explains the indices derived from the student, school and parent context questionnaires used in PISA 2009. Parent questionnaire indices are only available for the 14 countries that chose to administer the optional parent questionnaire.

Several PISA measures reflect indices that summarise responses from students, their parents or school representatives (typically principals) to a series of related questions. The questions were selected from a larger pool of questions on the basis of theoretical considerations and previous research. Structural equation modelling was used to confirm the theoretically expected behaviour of the indices and to validate their comparability across countries. For this purpose, a model was estimated separately for each country and collectively for all OECD countries.

For a detailed description of other PISA indices and details on the methods, see *PISA 2009 Technical Report* (OECD, forthcoming).

There are two types of indices: simple indices and scale indices.

Simple indices are the variables that are constructed through the arithmetic transformation or recoding of one or more items, in exactly the same way across assessments. Here, item responses are used to calculate meaningful variables, such as the recoding of the four-digit ISCO-88 codes into "Highest parents' socio-economic index (HISEI)" or, teacher-student ratio based on information from the school questionnaire.

Scale indices are the variables constructed through the scaling of multiple items. Unless otherwise indicated, the index was scaled using a weighted maximum likelihood estimate (WLE) (Warm, 1985), using a one-parameter item response model (a partial credit model was used in the case of items with more than two categories).

The scaling was done in three stages:

- The item parameters were estimated from equal-sized subsamples of students from each OECD country.
- The estimates were computed for all students and all schools by anchoring the item parameters obtained in the preceding step.
- The indices were then standardised so that the mean of the index value for the OECD student population was zero and the standard deviation was one (countries being given equal weight in the standardisation process).

Sequential codes were assigned to the different response categories of the questions in the sequence in which the latter appeared in the student, school or parent questionnaires. Where indicated in this section, these codes were inverted for the purpose of constructing indices or scales. It is important to note that negative values for an index do not necessarily imply that students responded negatively to the underlying questions. A negative value merely indicates that the respondents answered less positively than all respondents did on average across OECD countries. Likewise, a positive value on an index indicates that the respondents answered more favourably, or more positively, than respondents did, on average, in OECD countries. Terms enclosed in brackets < > in the following descriptions were replaced in the national versions of the student, school and parent questionnaires by the appropriate national equivalent. For example, the term <qualification at ISCED level 5A> was translated in the United States into "Bachelor's degree, post-graduate certificate program, Master's degree program or first professional degree program". Similarly the term <classes in the language of assessment> in Luxembourg was translated into "German classes" or "French classes" depending on whether students received the German or French version of the assessment instruments.

In addition to simple and scaled indices described in this annex, there are a number of variables from the questionnaires that correspond to single items not used to construct indices. These non-recoded variables have prefix of "ST" for the questionnaire items in the student questionnaire, "SC" for the items in the school questionnaire, and "PA" for the items in the parent questionnaire. All the context questionnaires as well as the PISA international database, including all variables, are available through *www.pisa.oecd.org*.

Student-level simple indices

Age

The variable AGE is calculated as the difference between the middle month and the year in which students were assessed and their month and year of birth, expressed in years and months.

Study programme

In PISA 2009, study programmes available to 15-year-old students in each country were collected both through the student tracking form and the student questionnaire (ST02). All study programmes were classified using ISCED (OECD, 1999). In the PISA international database, all national programmes are indicated in a variable (PROGN) where the first three digits are the ISO code for a country, the fourth digit the sub-national category and the last two digits the nationally specific programme code.

The following internationally comparable indices were derived from the data on study programmes:

- Programme level (ISCEDL) indicates whether students are (1) primary education level (ISCED 1); (2) lower secondary education level; or (3) upper secondary education level.
- Programme designation (ISCEDD) indicates the designation of the study programme: (1) = "A" (general programmes designed to give access to the next programme level); (2) = "B" (programmes designed to give access to vocational studies at the next programme level); (3) = "C" (programmes designed to give direct access to the labour market); or (4) = "M" (modular programmes that combine any or all of these characteristics).
- Programme orientation (ISCEDO) indicates whether the programme's curricular content is (1) general; (2) pre-vocational; (3) vocational; or (4) modular programmes that combine any or all of these characteristics.

Occupational status of parents

Occupational data for both a student's father and a student's mother were obtained by asking open-ended questions in the student questionnaire (ST9a, ST9b, ST12, ST13a, ST13b and ST16). The responses were coded to four-digit ISCO codes (ILO, 1990) and then mapped to Ganzeboom, *et al.*'s (1992) SEI index. Higher scores of SEI indicate higher levels of occupational status. The following three indices are obtained:

- Mother's occupational status (BMMJ).
- Father's occupational status (BFMJ).
- The highest occupational level of parents (HISEI) corresponds to the higher SEI score of either parent or to the only available parent's SEI score.

Educational level of parents

The educational level of parents is classified using ISCED (OECD, 1999) based on students' responses in the student questionnaire (ST10, ST11, ST14 and ST15). Please note that the question format for school education in PISA 2009 differs from the one used in PISA 2000, 2003 and 2006 but the method used to compute parental education is the same.

As in PISA 2000, 2003 and 2006, indices were constructed by selecting the highest level for each parent and then assigning them to the following categories: (0) None, (1) ISCED 1 (primary education), (2) ISCED 2 (lower secondary), (3) ISCED Level 3B or 3C (vocational/pre-vocational upper secondary), (4) ISCED 3A (upper secondary) and/or ISCED 4 (non-tertiary post-secondary), (5) ISCED 5B (vocational tertiary), (6) ISCED 5A, 6 (theoretically oriented tertiary and post-graduate). The following three indices with these categories are developed:

- Mother's educational level (MISCED).
- Father's educational level (FISCED).
- Highest educational level of parents (HISCED) corresponds to the higher ISCED level of either parent.

Highest educational level of parents was also converted into the number of years of schooling (PARED). For the conversion of level of education into years of schooling, see Table A1.1.

Immigration and language background

Information on the country of birth of students and their parents (ST17) is collected in a similar manner as in PISA 2000, PISA 2003 and PISA 2006 by using nationally specific ISO coded variables. The ISO codes of the country of birth for students and their parents are available in the PISA international database (COBN_S, COBN_M, and COBN_F).

The index on immigrant background (IMMIG) has the following categories: (1) native students (those students born in the country of assessment, or those with at least one parent born in that country; students who were born abroad with at least one parent born in the country of assessment are also classified as 'native' students), (2) second-generation students (those born in the country of assessment but whose parents were born in another country) and (3) first-generation students (those born outside the country of assessment and whose parents were also born in another country). Students with missing responses for either the student or for both parents, or for all three questions have been given missing values for this variable.

[Part 1/1]

Table A1.1 Levels of parental education converted into years of schooling

		Did not go to school	Completed ISCED Level 1 (primary education)	Completed ISCED Level 2 (lower secondary education)	Completed ISCED Levels3B or 3C (upper secondary education providing direct access to the labor market or to ISCED 5B programmes)	Completed ISCED Level 3A (upper secondary education providing access to ISCED 5A and 5B programmes) and/or ISCED Level 4 (non-tertiary post-secondary)	Completed ISCED Level 5A (university level tertiary education) or ISCED Level 6 (advanced research programmes)	Completed ISCED Level 5B (non-university tertiary education)
OECD	Australia	0.0	6.0	10.0	11.0	12.0	15.0	14.0
	Austria	0.0	4.0	9.0	12.0	12.5	17.0	15.0
	Belgium	0.0	6.0	9.0	12.0	12.0	17.0	14.5
	Canada	0.0	6.0	9.0	12.0	12.0	17.0	15.0
	Chile	0.0	6.0	8.0	12.0	12.0	17.0	16.0
	Czech Republic	0.0	5.0	9.0	11.0	13.0	16.0	16.0
	Denmark	0.0	6.0	9.0	12.0	12.0	17.0	15.0
	Estonia	0.0	4.0	9.0	12.0	12.0	16.0	15.0
	Finland	0.0	6.0	9.0	12.0	12.0	16.5	14.5
	France	0.0	5.0	9.0	12.0	12.0	15.0	14.0
	Germany	0.0	4.0	10.0	13.0	13.0	18.0	15.0
	Greece	0.0	6.0	9.0	11.5	12.0	17.0	15.0
	Hungary	0.0	4.0	8.0	10.5	12.0	16.5	13.5
	Iceland	0.0	7.0	10.0	13.0	14.0	18.0	16.0
	Ireland	0.0	6.0	9.0	12.0	12.0	16.0	14.0
	Israel	0.0	6.0	9.0	12.0	12.0	15.0	15.0
	Italy	0.0	5.0	8.0	12.0	13.0	17.0	16.0
	Japan	0.0	6.0	9.0	12.0	12.0	16.0	14.0
	Korea	0.0	6.0	9.0	12.0	12.0	16.0	14.0
	Luxembourg	0.0	6.0	9.0	12.0	13.0	17.0	16.0
	Mexico	0.0	6.0	9.0	12.0	12.0	16.0	14.0
	Netherlands	0.0	6.0	10.0	a	12.0	16.0	a
	New Zealand	0.0	5.5	10.0	11.0	12.0	15.0	14.0
	Norway	0.0	6.0	9.0	12.0	12.0	16.0	14.0
	Poland	0.0	a	8.0	11.0	12.0	16.0	15.0
	Portugal	0.0	6.0	9.0	12.0	12.0	17.0	15.0
	Scotland	0.0	7.0	11.0	13.0	13.0	16.0	16.0
	Slovak Republic	0.0	4.5	8.5	12.0	12.0	17.5	13.5
	Slovenia	0.0	4.0	8.0	11.0	12.0	16.0	15.0
	Spain	0.0	5.0	8.0	10.0	12.0	16.5	13.0
	Sweden	0.0	6.0	9.0	11.5	12.0	15.5	14.0
	Switzerland	0.0	6.0	9.0	12.5	12.5	17.5	14.5
	Turkey	0.0	5.0	8.0	11.0	11.0	15.0	13.0
	United Kingdom	0.0	6.0	9.0	12.0	13.0	16.0	15.0
	United States	0.0	6.0	9.0	a	12.0	16.0	14.0
Partners	Albania	0.0	6.0	9.0	12.0	12.0	16.0	16.0
	Argentina	0.0	6.0	10.0	12.0	12.0	17.0	14.5
	Azerbaijan	0.0	4.0	9.0	11.0	11.0	17.0	14.0
	Brazil	0.0	4.0	8.0	11.0	11.0	16.0	14.5
	Bulgaria	0.0	4.0	8.0	12.0	12.0	17.5	15.0
	Colombia	0.0	5.0	9.0	11.0	11.0	15.5	14.0
	Croatia	0.0	4.0	8.0	11.0	12.0	17.0	15.0
	Dubai (UAE)	0.0	5.0	9.0	12.0	12.0	16.0	15.0
	Hong Kong- China	0.0	6.0	9.0	11.0	13.0	16.0	14.0
	Indonesia	0.0	6.0	9.0	12.0	12.0	15.0	14.0
	Jordan	0.0	6.0	10.0	12.0	12.0	16.0	14.5
	Kazakhstan	0.0	4.0	9.0	11.5	12.5	15.0	14.0
	Kyrgyzstan	0.0	4.0	8.0	11.0	10.0	15.0	13.0
	Latvia	0.0	3.0	8.0	11.0	11.0	16.0	16.0
	Liechtenstein	0.0	5.0	9.0	11.0	13.0	17.0	14.0
	Lithuania	0.0	3.0	8.0	11.0	11.0	16.0	15.0
	Macao-China	0.0	6.0	9.0	11.0	12.0	16.0	15.0
	Montenegro	0.0	4.0	8.0	11.0	12.0	16.0	15.0
	Panama	0.0	6.0	9.0	12.0	12.0	16.0	a
	Peru	0.0	6.0	9.0	11.0	11.0	17.0	14.0
	Qatar	0.0	6.0	9.0	12.0	12.0	16.0	15.0
	Romania	0.0	4.0	8.0	11.5	12.5	16.0	14.0
	Russian Federation	0.0	4.0	9.0	11.5	12.0	15.0	a
	Serbia	0.0	4.0	8.0	11.0	12.0	17.0	14.5
	Shanghai-China	0.0	6.0	9.0	12.0	12.0	16.0	15.0
	Singapore	0.0	6.0	8.0	10.5	10.5	12.5	12.5
	Chinese Taipei	0.0	6.0	9.0	12.0	12.0	16.0	14.0
	Thailand	0.0	6.0	9.0	12.0	12.0	16.0	14.0
	Trinidad and Tobago	0.0	5.0	9.0	12.0	12.0	16.0	15.0
	Tunisia	0.0	6.0	9.0	12.0	13.0	17.0	16.0
	Uruguay	0.0	6.0	9.0	12.0	12.0	17.0	15.0

StatLink http://dx.doi.org/10.1787/888932343171

Students indicate the language they usually speak at home. The data are captured in nationally-specific language codes, which were recoded into variable ST19Q01 with the following two values: (1) language at home is the same as the language of assessment and (2) language at home is a different language than the language of assessment.

Family structure

The index of family structure (FAMSTRUC) is based on students' responses regarding people living at home with them (ST08). This index has the following three values: (1) single-parent family (students living with only one of the following: mother, father, male guardian, female guardian), (2) two-parent family (students living with a father or step/foster father and a mother or step/foster mother) and (3) other (except the non-responses, which are coded as missing or not applicable).

Relative grade

Data on the student's grade are obtained both from the student questionnaire (ST01) and from the student tracking form. As with all variables that are on both the tracking form and the questionnaire, inconsistencies between the two sources are reviewed and resolved during data-cleaning. In order to capture between-country variation, the relative grade index (GRADE) indicates whether students are at the modal grade in a country (value of 0), or whether they are below or above the modal grade level (+ x grades, - x grades).

The relationship between the grade and student performance was estimated through a multilevel model accounting for the following background variables: *i)* the ***PISA index of economic, social and cultural status***; *ii)* the ***PISA index of economic, social and cultural status*** squared; *iii)* the school mean of the ***PISA index of economic, social and cultural status***; *iv)* an indicator as to whether students were foreign born first-generation students; *v)* the percentage of first-generation students in the school; and *vi)* students' gender.

Table A1.2 presents the results of the multilevel model. Column 1 in Table A1.2 estimates the score point difference that is associated with one grade level (or school year). This difference can be estimated for the 32 OECD countries in which a sizeable number of 15-year-olds in the PISA samples were enrolled in at least two different grades. Since 15-year-olds cannot be assumed to be distributed at random across the grade levels, adjustments had to be made for the above-mentioned contextual factors that may relate to the assignment of students to the different grade levels. These adjustments are documented in columns 2 to 7 of the table. While it is possible to estimate the typical performance difference among students in two adjacent grades net of the effects of selection and contextual factors, this difference cannot automatically be equated with the progress that students have made over the last school year but should be interpreted as a lower boundary of the progress achieved. This is not only because different students were assessed but also because the content of the PISA assessment was not expressly designed to match what students had learned in the preceding school year but more broadly to assess the cumulative outcome of learning in school up to age 15. For example, if the curriculum of the grades in which 15-year-olds are enrolled mainly includes material other than that assessed by PISA (which, in turn, may have been included in earlier school years) then the observed performance difference will underestimate student progress.

Learning time

Learning time in test language (LMINS) was computed by multiplying students' responses on the number of minutes on average in the test language class by number of test language class periods per week (ST28 and ST29). Comparable indices are computed for mathematics (MMINS) and science (SMINS).

Student-level scale indices

Family wealth

The *index of family wealth* (WEALTH) is based on the students' responses on whether they had the following at home: a room of their own, a link to the Internet, a dishwasher (treated as a country-specific item), a DVD player, and three other country-specific items (some items in ST20); and their responses on the number of cellular phones, televisions, computers, cars and the rooms with a bath or shower (ST21).

Home educational resources

The *index of home educational resources* (HEDRES) is based on the items measuring the existence of educational resources at home including a desk and a quiet place to study, a computer that students can use for schoolwork, educational software, books to help with students' school work, technical reference books and a dictionary (some items in ST20).

Cultural possessions

The *index of cultural possessions* (CULTPOSS) is based on the students' responses to whether they had the following at home: classic literature, books of poetry and works of art (some items in ST20).

[Part 1/1]

Table A1.2 **A multilevel model to estimate grade effects in reading, accounting for some background variables**

		Grade		Index of economic, social and cultural status		PISA index of economic, social and cultural status squared		School mean PISA index of economic, social and cultural status		First generation students		School percentage of first generation students		Gender – student is a female		Intercept	
		Coef.	S.E.	Coef.	S.E.	Coef.	S.E.	Coef.	S.E.	Coef.	S.E.	Coef.	S.E.	Coef.	S.E.	Coef.	S.E.
OECD	Australia	33.2	(1.95)	30.0	(1.36)	-3.8	(1.05)	66.4	(1.87)	-7.4	(2.82)	0.1	(0.07)	32.9	(1.91)	466.0	(1.39)
	Austria	35.3	(2.18)	11.4	(1.66)	-0.5	(1.00)	89.7	(3.86)	-33.1	(6.11)	1.4	(0.13)	19.9	(2.67)	467.9	(2.45)
	Belgium	48.9	(1.98)	10.0	(1.12)	-0.1	(0.63)	79.9	(1.73)	-3.2	(5.18)	0.3	(0.11)	11.3	(1.81)	507.0	(1.70)
	Canada	45.0	(2.14)	19.4	(1.52)	1.5	(0.91)	33.9	(2.28)	-13.7	(3.18)	0.3	(0.04)	30.4	(1.60)	483.4	(1.76)
	Chile	35.5	(1.55)	8.6	(1.52)	0.3	(0.63)	37.4	(1.61)	c	c	c	c	13.8	(2.33)	478.6	(1.60)
	Czech Republic	44.6	(3.39)	13.4	(1.89)	-2.3	(1.47)	111.5	(3.12)	-8.9	(12.29)	0.4	(0.33)	32.3	(2.84)	460.7	(2.39)
	Denmark	36.1	(3.02)	27.9	(1.51)	-2.8	(1.10)	35.1	(2.91)	-37.5	(5.97)	0.0	(0.14)	25.5	(2.59)	474.0	(1.95)
	Estonia	44.4	(2.74)	14.1	(1.80)	1.6	(1.43)	52.1	(4.52)	-18.7	(14.08)	-3.3	(0.44)	36.7	(2.45)	485.8	(2.02)
	Finland	37.3	(3.60)	27.7	(1.66)	-2.5	(1.30)	10.4	(3.28)	-56.0	(13.09)	-0.1	(0.29)	51.5	(2.26)	500.6	(2.02)
	France	47.1	(5.14)	12.5	(1.70)	-1.9	(1.12)	81.6	(4.04)	-11.6	(9.24)	0.2	(0.15)	25.9	(2.67)	516.5	(2.35)
	Germany	34.4	(1.74)	9.2	(1.23)	-1.6	(0.74)	109.1	(2.16)	-13.2	(4.80)	0.2	(0.12)	27.2	(1.92)	458.0	(1.46)
	Greece	22.6	(10.86)	15.9	(1.46)	1.5	(1.07)	41.2	(2.84)	-15.0	(7.82)	0.0	(0.18)	36.2	(2.55)	469.0	(2.04)
	Hungary	25.6	(2.19)	8.3	(1.39)	0.9	(0.87)	74.8	(2.09)	2.8	(7.92)	0.0	(0.27)	21.4	(2.22)	494.1	(1.65)
	Iceland	c	c	29.8	(2.56)	-5.1	(1.56)	-3.8	(5.12)	-52.2	(11.45)	-1.3	(0.40)	44.9	(2.59)	469.1	(4.23)
	Ireland	18.2	(1.99)	29.7	(1.78)	-3.5	(1.44)	43.6	(2.68)	-32.8	(6.52)	-0.1	(0.20)	33.9	(3.62)	474.8	(2.77)
	Israel	36.6	(3.85)	19.9	(1.90)	3.4	(1.04)	104.7	(2.10)	-11.0	(6.13)	1.5	(0.08)	29.4	(2.81)	460.1	(2.13)
	Italy	36.1	(1.67)	4.5	(0.69)	-1.4	(0.42)	76.4	(1.07)	-29.7	(3.36)	0.2	(0.08)	24.0	(1.29)	491.4	(0.85)
	Japan	a	a	4.1	(1.51)	0.1	(1.47)	144.2	(2.40)	c	c	c	c	27.9	(2.43)	508.6	(1.58)
	Korea	31.2	(9.77)	12.9	(1.42)	1.9	(1.18)	64.9	(2.24)	a	a	a	a	30.6	(3.21)	537.7	(2.08)
	Luxembourg	45.3	(1.95)	16.6	(1.31)	-2.6	(1.08)	62.0	(2.89)	-10.4	(5.11)	-0.2	(0.10)	33.0	(2.22)	435.7	(2.40)
	Mexico	32.6	(1.59)	7.5	(0.92)	0.8	(0.34)	27.8	(0.80)	-41.9	(6.36)	-1.8	(0.15)	17.9	(1.03)	473.7	(1.02)
	Netherlands	26.6	(2.04)	6.0	(1.52)	-1.2	(1.02)	106.7	(2.32)	-11.6	(5.72)	1.7	(0.14)	15.3	(1.85)	484.5	(2.33)
	New Zealand	44.2	(4.15)	38.9	(1.82)	-1.7	(1.44)	56.3	(3.35)	-12.2	(3.84)	0.0	(0.10)	44.8	(2.62)	496.5	(2.44)
	Norway	37.6	(18.19)	34.2	(2.00)	-3.4	(1.62)	31.1	(4.32)	-33.4	(7.52)	0.4	(0.25)	48.3	(2.56)	453.2	(2.87)
	Poland	73.8	(4.44)	29.4	(1.59)	-1.8	(1.21)	19.4	(2.99)	c	c	c	c	44.2	(2.41)	498.9	(1.89)
	Portugal	48.9	(1.71)	12.0	(0.94)	1.0	(0.64)	21.3	(1.33)	-5.3	(5.75)	0.0	(0.23)	22.9	(1.84)	518.6	(1.92)
	Slovak Republic	34.2	(3.85)	14.7	(1.44)	-3.2	(0.98)	64.3	(6.30)	c	c	c	c	39.1	(2.58)	483.2	(2.33)
	Slovenia	22.8	(3.41)	4.8	(1.28)	0.0	(1.25)	100.2	(2.74)	-23.4	(7.48)	-0.2	(0.24)	27.7	(2.16)	452.4	(1.63)
	Spain	61.7	(1.22)	9.8	(0.83)	0.4	(0.64)	22.7	(1.25)	-29.7	(2.86)	0.4	(0.04)	18.0	(1.42)	511.3	(1.07)
	Sweden	63.8	(6.69)	31.4	(1.82)	-1.3	(1.04)	49.0	(6.55)	-38.8	(8.53)	0.3	(0.34)	43.2	(2.41)	454.4	(3.62)
	Switzerland	45.5	(2.75)	18.2	(1.27)	-1.0	(1.23)	59.5	(2.95)	-25.1	(3.99)	-0.7	(0.11)	27.0	(2.00)	488.8	(1.50)
	Turkey	33.7	(1.96)	7.7	(1.50)	0.3	(0.61)	46.3	(1.70)	c	c	c	c	27.9	(1.74)	524.0	(1.59)
	United Kingdom	35.9	(6.21)	27.7	(2.01)	-0.3	(1.51)	65.7	(2.49)	-13.6	(8.49)	-0.3	(0.13)	23.1	(2.48)	468.7	(1.73)
	United States	36.3	(2.17)	23.5	(1.70)	4.4	(1.15)	50.4	(2.56)	-5.6	(5.57)	0.8	(0.14)	25.4	(2.36)	463.5	(2.01)
Partners	Albania	11.9	(5.07)	20.8	(3.04)	3.2	(1.35)	43.0	(2.47)	c	c	c	c	56.5	(3.40)	421.5	(3.44)
	Argentina	33.6	(2.50)	11.2	(1.96)	0.9	(0.87)	52.6	(2.03)	-27.0	(10.55)	0.5	(0.20)	24.0	(2.38)	439.7	(2.32)
	Azerbaijan	13.2	(1.78)	10.5	(1.67)	1.3	(0.90)	36.4	(2.00)	-9.8	(12.34)	-0.3	(0.49)	22.6	(2.16)	390.9	(2.12)
	Brazil	36.1	(1.23)	7.7	(1.54)	1.3	(0.57)	38.3	(1.25)	-71.7	(17.16)	-0.9	(0.47)	20.2	(1.63)	445.5	(1.33)
	Bulgaria	27.8	(5.08)	15.7	(1.93)	0.2	(1.29)	75.7	(3.99)	c	c	c	c	42.1	(3.51)	423.7	(2.61)
	Colombia	33.2	(1.12)	6.9	(2.01)	0.9	(0.72)	39.4	(1.53)	c	c	c	c	3.2	(2.17)	477.7	(1.83)
	Croatia	31.8	(2.33)	10.3	(1.36)	-4.0	(0.99)	75.3	(2.01)	-13.0	(5.71)	-0.1	(0.22)	31.4	(2.56)	472.8	(1.69)
	Dubai (UAE)	34.6	(1.56)	15.2	(1.52)	3.2	(1.03)	25.9	(3.13)	21.5	(3.25)	1.1	(0.05)	28.2	(3.94)	362.4	(2.92)
	Hong Kong-China	33.6	(2.03)	-0.9	(1.70)	-1.0	(0.76)	41.9	(1.64)	23.4	(3.70)	-0.4	(0.06)	21.9	(2.42)	575.8	(1.83)
	Indonesia	14.4	(2.00)	4.7	(2.44)	0.9	(0.62)	29.1	(1.83)	c	c	c	c	28.0	(1.48)	430.8	(2.46)
	Jordan	47.6	(6.38)	17.7	(1.52)	0.7	(0.81)	26.9	(1.55)	-11.5	(7.50)	-0.2	(0.20)	48.1	(2.73)	415.5	(2.04)
	Kazakhstan	22.2	(2.42)	16.2	(2.12)	-1.7	(1.31)	55.7	(2.70)	-12.2	(6.78)	0.0	(0.10)	38.1	(2.23)	411.1	(1.57)
	Kyrgyzstan	20.8	(2.92)	18.3	(2.23)	1.7	(1.10)	75.2	(2.03)	-23.4	(21.78)	3.3	(0.50)	46.0	(2.45)	345.7	(1.83)
	Latvia	43.8	(3.07)	16.2	(1.89)	-0.8	(1.35)	37.0	(2.77)	c	c	c	c	38.9	(2.36)	479.6	(1.77)
	Liechtenstein	23.8	(7.40)	2.1	(4.18)	-5.3	(3.07)	112.5	(12.17)	-12.6	(10.22)	-0.7	(0.44)	20.3	(6.86)	499.8	(8.42)
	Lithuania	27.4	(2.87)	18.1	(1.56)	0.2	(1.04)	44.0	(2.45)	c	c	c	c	51.1	(2.34)	447.6	(1.87)
	Macao-China	36.7	(1.01)	1.8	(1.61)	-1.1	(0.78)	1.0	(4.75)	16.7	(2.17)	-0.1	(0.23)	14.1	(1.51)	511.0	(3.47)
	Montenegro	22.9	(3.44)	12.1	(1.38)	-0.3	(1.05)	64.2	(6.54)	-1.8	(6.69)	-1.2	(0.32)	39.3	(2.63)	409.5	(2.58)
	Panama	32.6	(3.41)	7.9	(2.42)	1.2	(0.79)	45.8	(2.60)	-3.4	(10.77)	-1.4	(0.16)	15.8	(4.48)	431.3	(3.22)
	Peru	27.5	(1.23)	10.5	(2.05)	0.9	(0.64)	47.2	(1.46)	c	c	c	c	8.3	(2.17)	445.6	(1.59)
	Qatar	30.7	(1.70)	5.3	(0.98)	0.4	(0.85)	12.7	(2.91)	31.5	(2.98)	1.7	(0.07)	31.4	(3.71)	302.5	(2.94)
	Romania	19.6	(4.19)	10.7	(1.63)	-0.3	(0.79)	63.9	(2.34)	c	c	c	c	13.7	(2.56)	446.4	(1.70)
	Russian Federation	31.0	(2.01)	18.2	(1.93)	-1.6	(1.40)	38.8	(3.32)	-9.1	(5.88)	-0.4	(0.22)	38.7	(2.28)	452.9	(1.89)
	Serbia	21.3	(4.48)	9.2	(1.25)	-0.8	(0.74)	55.1	(3.42)	1.2	(5.65)	0.3	(0.13)	27.1	(2.22)	425.1	(1.60)
	Shanghai-China	21.8	(3.34)	4.6	(1.41)	0.1	(0.85)	57.3	(1.48)	c	c	c	c	29.3	(1.98)	583.5	(2.04)
	Singapore	28.9	(2.09)	22.2	(2.19)	-2.8	(1.14)	104.7	(2.86)	0.4	(4.21)	-1.0	(0.13)	24.6	(2.57)	590.2	(2.76)
	Chinese Taipei	15.4	(4.12)	15.5	(1.50)	-1.2	(1.05)	82.8	(3.06)	c	c	c	c	36.8	(2.25)	515.6	(2.03)
	Thailand	22.1	(2.05)	10.4	(1.54)	2.4	(0.66)	28.8	(1.31)	a	a	a	a	31.3	(1.78)	454.6	(1.67)
	Trinidad and Tobago	35.3	(1.60)	-0.6	(2.00)	-0.2	(0.91)	123.2	(3.42)	-9.2	(13.59)	-0.7	(0.28)	40.4	(2.90)	484.9	(2.77)
	Tunisia	49.7	(1.57)	3.7	(1.76)	0.7	(0.56)	17.8	(1.25)	c	c	c	c	14.4	(1.84)	449.6	(1.63)
	Uruguay	41.4	(1.49)	12.4	(1.58)	0.5	(0.75)	29.7	(1.58)	c	c	c	c	30.1	(2.48)	464.2	(2.29)

StatLink http://dx.doi.org/10.1787/888932343171

Economic, social and cultural status

The *PISA index of economic, social and cultural status* (ESCS) was derived from the following three indices: highest occupational status of parents (HISEI), highest educational level of parents in years of education according to ISCED (PARED), and home possessions (HOMEPOS). The *index of home possessions* (HOMEPOS) comprises all items on the indices of WEALTH, CULTPOSS and HEDRES, as well as books in the home recoded into a four-level categorical variable (0-10 books, 11-25 or 26-100 books, 101-200 or 201-500 books, more than 500 books).

The *PISA index of economic, social and cultural status* (ESCS) was derived from a principal component analysis of standardised variables (each variable has an OECD mean of zero and a standard deviation of one), taking the factor scores for the first principal component as measures of the index of economic, social and cultural status.

Principal component analysis was also performed for each participating country to determine to what extent the components of the index operate in similar ways across countries. The analysis revealed that patterns of factor loading were very similar across countries, with all three components contributing to a similar extent to the index. For the occupational component, the average factor loading was 0.80, ranging from 0.66 to 0.87 across countries. For the educational component, the average factor loading was 0.79, ranging from 0.69 to 0.87 across countries. For the home possession component, the average factor loading was 0.73, ranging from 0.60 to 0.84 across countries. The reliability of the index ranged from 0.41 to 0.81. These results support the cross-national validity of the *PISA index of economic, social and cultural status.*

The imputation of components for students missing data on one component was done on the basis of a regression on the other two variables, with an additional random error component. The final values on the *PISA index of economic, social and cultural status* (ESCS) have an OECD mean of 0 and a standard deviation of 1.

Enjoyment of reading activities

The *index of enjoyment of reading* (ENJOY) activities was derived from students' level of agreement with the following statements (ST24): *i)* I read only if I have to; *ii)* reading is one of my favourite hobbies; *iii)* I like talking about books with other people; *iv)* I find it hard to finish books; *v)* I feel happy if I receive a book as a present; *vi)* for me, reading is a waste of time; *vii)* I enjoy going to a bookstore or a library; *viii)* I read only to get information that I need; *ix)* I cannot sit still and read for more than a few minutes; *x)* I like to express my opinions about books I have read; and *xi)* I like to exchange books with my friends.

As all items that are negatively phrased (items *i, iv, vi, viii* and *ix*) are inverted for scaling, the higher values on this index indicate higher levels of enjoyment of reading.

Diversity of reading materials

The *index of diversity of reading materials* (DIVREAD) was derived from the frequency with which students read the following materials because they want to (ST25): magazines, comic books, fiction, non-fiction books and newspapers. The higher values on this index indicate higher diversity in reading.

Online reading activities

The *index of online reading activities* (ONLNREAD) was derived from the frequency with which students involved in the following reading activities (ST26): reading emails, <chat on line>, reading online news, using an online dictionary or encyclopaedia, searching online information to learn about a particular topic, taking part in online group discussions or forums and searching for practical information online. The higher values on this index indicate more frequent online reading activities.

Approaches to learning

How students approach learning is based on student responses in ST27 and measured through the following three indices: memorisation (MEMOR), elaboration (ELAB) and control strategies (CSTRAT).

The *index of memorisation* (MEMOR) was derived from the frequency with which students did the following when they were studying: *i)* try to memorise everything that is covered in the text; *ii)* try to memorise as many details as possible; *iii)* read the text so many times that they can recite it; and *iv)* read the text over and over again.

The *index of elaboration* (ELAB) was derived from the frequency with which students did the following when they were studying: *i)* try to relate new information to prior knowledge acquired in other subjects; *ii)* figure out how the information might be useful outside school; *iii)* try to understand the material better by relating it to my own experiences; and *iv)* figure out how the text information fits in with what happens in real life.

The *index of control strategies* (CSTRAT) was derived from students' reports on how often they did the following statements: *i)* when I study, I start by figuring out what exactly I need to learn; *ii)* when I study, I check if I understand what I have read; *iii)* when I study, I try to figure out which concepts I still haven't really understood; *iv)* when I study, I make sure that I remember the most important points in the text; and *v)* when I study and I don't understand something, I look for additional information to clarify this.

Higher values on the index indicate higher importance attached to the given strategy.

Attitudes towards school

The *index of attitude towards school* (ATSCHL) was derived from students' level of agreement with the following statements in ST33: *i)* school has done little to prepare me for adult life when I leave school; *ii)* school has been a waste of time; *iii)* school has helped give me confidence to make decisions; *iv)* school has taught me things which could be useful in a job. As all items that are negatively phrased *i)* and *ii)* are inverted for scaling, higher values on this index indicate perception of a more positive school climate.

Teacher-student relations

The *index of teacher-student relations* (STUDREL) was derived from students' level of agreement with the following statements in ST34: *i)* I get along well with most of my teachers; *ii)* most of my teachers are interested in my well-being; *iii)* most of my teachers really listen to what I have to say; *iv)* if I need extra help, I will receive it from my teachers; and *v)* most of my teachers treat me fairly. Higher values on this index indicate positive teacher-student relations.

Disciplinary climate

The *index of disciplinary climate* (DISCLIMA) was derived from students' reports on how often the followings happened in their lessons of the language of instruction (ST36): *i)* students don't listen to what the teacher says; *ii)* there is noise and disorder; *iii)* the teacher has to wait a long time for the students to <quieten down>; *iv)* students cannot work well; and *v)* students don't start working for a long time after the lesson begins. As all items are inverted for scaling, higher values on this index indicate a better disciplinary climate.

Teachers' stimulation of students' reading engagement

The *index of teachers' stimulation of students' reading engagement* (STIMREAD) was derived from students' reports on how often the following occurred in their lessons of the language of instruction (ST37): *i)* the teacher asks students to explain the meaning of a text; *ii)* the teacher asks questions that challenge students to get a better understanding of a text; *iii)* the teacher gives students enough time to think about their answers; *iv)* the teacher recommends a book or author to read; *v)* the teacher encourages students to express their opinion about a text; *vi)* the teacher helps students relate the stories they read to their lives; and *vii)* the teacher shows students how the information in texts builds on what they already know. Higher values on this index indicate higher teachers' stimulation of students' reading engagement.

Use of structuring and scaffolding strategies

The *index of use of structuring and scaffolding strategies* (STRSTRAT) was derived from students reports on how often the following occurred in their lessons of the language of instruction (ST38): *i)* the teacher explains beforehand what is expected of the students; *ii)* the teacher checks that students are concentrating while working on the <reading assignment>; *iii)* the teacher discusses students' work, after they have finished the <reading assignment>; *iv)* the teacher tells students in advance how their work is going to be judged; *v)* the teacher asks whether every student has understood how to complete the <reading assignment>; *vi)* the teacher marks students' work; *vii)* the teacher gives students the chance to ask questions about the <reading assignment>; *viii)* the teacher poses questions that motivate students to participate actively; and *ix)* the teacher tells students how well they did on the <reading assignment> immediately after. Higher values on this index indicate a greater use of structured teaching.

Use of libraries

The *index of use of libraries* (LIBUSE) was derived from students' reports on the frequency for visiting a library for the following activities (ST39): *i)* borrow books to read for pleasure; *ii)* borrow books for school work; *iii)* work on homework, course assignments or research papers; *iv)* read magazines or newspapers; *v)* read books for fun; *vi)* learn about things that are not course-related, such as sports, hobbies, people or music; and *vii)* use the Internet. Higher values on this index indicate a great use of libraries.

Metacognition strategies: understanding and remembering

The *index of understanding and remembering* (UNDREM) was derived from students' reports on the usefulness of the following strategies for understanding and memorising the text (ST41): A) I concentrate on the parts of the text that are easy to understand; B) I quickly read through the text twice; C) After reading the text, I discuss its content with other people; D) I underline important parts of the text; E) I summarise the text in my own words; and F) I read the text aloud to another person.

This index was scored using a rater-scoring system. Through a variety of trial activities, both with reading experts and national centres, a preferred ordering of the strategies according to their effectiveness to achieve the intended goal was agreed. The experts' agreed order of the six items consisting this index is CDE > ABF. Scaling was conducted with two steps. First, a score was assigned to each student, which is a number that ranged from 0 to 1 and can be interpreted as the proportion of the total number of expert pair-wise relations that are consistent with the student ordering. For example, if the expert rule is (ABFD>CEG, 4´3=12 pair wise rules are created (i.e. A>C, A>E, A>G, B>C, B>E, B>G, F>C, F>E, F>G, D>C, D>E, D>G). If the responses of a student on this task follow 8 of the 12 rules, the student gets a score of 8/12 = 0.67. Second, these scores were standardised for the index to have a mean of 0 and a standard deviation of 1 across OECD countries. Higher values on this index indicate greater students' perception of usefulness of this strategy.

Metacognition strategies: summarising

The *index of summarising* (METASUM) was derived from students' reports on the usefulness of the following strategies for writing a summary of a long and rather difficult two-page text about fluctuations in the water levels of a lake in Africa (ST42): A) I write a summary. Then I check that each paragraph is covered in the summary, because the content of each paragraph should be included; B) I try to copy out accurately as many sentences as possible; C) before writing the summary, I read the text as many times as possible; D) I carefully check whether the most important facts in the text are represented in the summary; and E) I read through the text, underlining the most important sentences, then I write them in my own words as a summary.

This index was scored using a rater-scoring system. The experts' agreed order of the five items consisting this index is DE>AC>B. Higher values on this index indicate greater students' perception of usefulness of this strategy.

School-level simple indices

School and class size

The *index of school size* (SCHSIZE) was derived by summing up the number of girls and boys at a school (SC06).

Student-teacher ratio

Student-teacher ratio (STRATIO) was obtained by dividing the school size by the total number of teachers. The number of part-time teachers (SC09Q12) was weighted by 0.5 and the number of full-time teachers (SC09Q11) was weighted by 1.0 in the computation of this index.

Proportion of girls enrolled at school

The *index of the proportion of girls in the school* (PCGIRLS) was derived from the enrolment data (SC06).

School type

Schools are classified into as either public or private, according to whether a private entity or a public agency has the ultimate power to make decisions concerning its affairs (SC02). This information is combined with SC03 which provides information on the percentage of total funding which comes from government sources to create the *index of school type* (SCHTYPE). This index has three categories: (1) public schools controlled and managed by a public education authority or agency, (2) government-dependent private schools controlled by a non-government organisation or with a governing board not selected by a government agency that receive more than 50% of their core funding from government agencies, (3) government-independent private schools controlled by a non-government organisation or with a governing board not selected by a government agency that receive less than 50% of their core funding from government agencies.

Availability of computers

The *index of computer availability* (IRATCOMP) was derived from dividing the number of computers available for educational purposes available to students in the modal grade for 15-year-olds (SC10Q02) by the number of students in the modal grade for 15-year-olds (SC10Q01).

The *index of computers connected to the Internet* (COMPWEB) was derived from dividing the number of computers for educational purposes available to students in the modal grade for 15-year-olds that are connected to the web (SC10Q03) by the number of computers for educational purposes available to students in the modal grade for 15-year-olds (SC10Q02).

Quantity of teaching staff at school

The *proportion of fully certified teachers* (PROPCERT) was computed by dividing the number of fully certified teachers (SC09Q21 plus 0.5*SC09Q22) by the total number of teachers (SC09Q11 plus 0.5*SC09Q12). The proportion of teachers who have an ISCED 5A qualification (PROPQUAL) was calculated by dividing the number of these kind of teachers (SC09Q31 plus 0.5*SC09Q32) by the total number of teachers (SC09Q11 plus 0.5*SC09Q12).

Academic selectivity

The *index of academic selectivity* (SELSCH) was derived from school principals' responses on how frequently consideration was given to the following factors when students were admitted to the school, based on a scale from the response categories "never", "sometimes" and "always" (SC19Q02 and SC19Q03): student's record of academic performance (including placement tests); and recommendation of feeder schools. This index has the following three categories: (1) schools where these two factors are "never" considered for student admittance, (2) schools considering at least one of these two factors "sometimes" but neither factor "always", and (3) schools where at least one of these two factors is "always" considered for student admittance.

Ability grouping

The *index of ability grouping between classes* (ABGROUP) was derived from the two items of school principals' reports on whether school organises instruction differently for student with different abilities "for all subjects", "for some subjects", or "not for any

subject" (SC12Q01 for grouping into different classes and SC12Q02 for grouping within classes). This index has the following three categories: (1) schools that do not group students by ability in any subjects, either between or within classes; (2) schools that group students by ability for some, but not all, subjects, and that do so either between or within classes; and (3) schools that group students by ability in all subjects either between or within classes.

School-level scale indices

School responsibility for resource allocation

School principals were asked to report whether "principals", "teachers", "school governing board", "regional or local education authority" or "national education authority" has a considerable responsibility for the following tasks (SC24): *i)* selecting teachers for hire; *ii)* dismissing teachers; *iii)* establishing teachers' starting salaries; *iv)* determining teachers' salaries increases; *v)* formulating the school budget; and *vi)* deciding on budget allocations within the school. The *index of school responsibility for resource allocation* (RESPRES) was derived from these six items. The ratio of the number of responsibility that "principals" and/or "teachers" have for these six items to the number of responsibility that "regional or local education authority" and/or "national education authority" have for these six items was computed. Positive values on this index indicate relatively more responsibility for schools than local, regional or national education authority. This index has an OECD mean of 0 and a standard deviation of 1.

School responsibility for curriculum and assessment

School principals were asked to report whether "principals", "teachers", "school governing board", "regional or local education authority", or "national education authority" has a considerable responsibility for the following tasks (SC24): *i)* establishing student assessment policies; *ii)* choosing which textbooks are used; *iii)* determining course content; and *iv)* deciding which courses are offered. The *index of the school responsibility for curriculum and assessment* (RESPCURR) was derived from these four items. The ratio of the number of responsibility that "principals" and/or "teachers" have for these four items to the number of responsibility that "regional or local education authority" and/or "national education authority" have for these four items was computed. Positive values on this index indicate relatively more responsibility for schools than local, regional or national education authority. This index has an OECD mean of 0 and a standard deviation of 1.

Teacher participation

The *index of teacher participation* (TCHPARTI) was scaled based on all 12 items in SC24 using school principals' responses that "teachers" have considerable responsibility. Higher values on this index indicate greater teachers' participation.

School principal's leadership

The *index of school principal's leadership* (LDRSHP) was derived from school principals' responses about the frequency with which they were involved in the following school affairs in the previous school year (SC26): *i)* make sure that the professional development activities of teachers are in accordance with the teaching goals of the school; *ii)* ensure that teachers work according to the school's educational goals; *iii)* observe instruction in classrooms; *iv)* give teachers suggestions as to how they can improve their teaching; *v)* use student performance results to develop the school's educational goals; *vi)* monitor students' work; *vii)* take the initiative to discuss matters, when a teacher has problems in his/her classroom; *viii)* inform teachers about possibilities for updating their knowledge and skills; *ix)* check to see whether classroom activities are in keeping with our educational goals; *x)* take exam results into account in decisions regarding curriculum development; *xi)* ensure that there is clarity concerning the responsibility for coordinating the curriculum; *xii)* solve the problem together, when a teacher brings up a classroom problem; *xiii)* pay attention to disruptive behaviour in classrooms; and *xiv)* take over lessons from teachers who are unexpectedly absent. Higher values on this index indicate greater involvement of school principals in school affairs.

Teacher shortage

The *index of teacher shortage* (TCSHORT) was derived from four items measuring school principals' perceptions of potential factors hindering instruction at their school (SC11). These factors are a lack of: *i)* qualified science teachers; *ii)* a lack of qualified mathematics teachers; *iii)* qualified <test language> teachers; and *iv)* qualified teachers of other subjects. Higher values on this index indicate school principals' reports of higher teacher shortage at a school.

School's educational resources

The *index on the school's educational resources* (SCMATEDU) was derived from seven items measuring school principals' perceptions of potential factors hindering instruction at their school (SC11). These factors are: *i)* shortage or inadequacy of science laboratory equipment; *ii)* shortage or inadequacy of instructional materials; *iii)* shortage or inadequacy of computers for instruction; *iv)* lack or inadequacy of Internet connectivity; *v)* shortage or inadequacy of computer software for instruction; *vi)* shortage or inadequacy of library materials; and *vii)* shortage or inadequacy of audio-visual resources. As all items were inverted for scaling, higher values on this index indicate better quality of educational resources.

Extra-curricular activities offered by school

The *index of extra-curricular activities* (EXCURACT) was derived from school principals' reports on whether their schools offered the following activities to students in the national modal grade for 15-year-olds in the academic year of the PISA assessment (SC13):

i) band, orchestra or choir; *ii)* school play or school musical; *iii)* school yearbook, newspaper or magazine; *iv)* volunteering or service activities; *v)* book club; *vi)* debating club or debating activities; *vii)* school club or school competition for foreign language mathematics or science; *viii)* <academic club>; *ix)* art club or art activities; *x)* sporting team or sporting activities; *xi)* lectures and/ or seminars; *xii)* collaboration with local libraries; *xiii)* collaboration with local newspapers; and *xiv)* <country specific item>. Higher values on the index indicate higher levels of extra-curricular school activities.

Teacher behaviour

The *index on teacher-related factors affecting school climate* (TEACBEHA) was derived from school principals' reports on the extent to which the learning of students hindered by the following factors in their schools (SC17): *i)* teachers' low expectations of students; *ii)* poor student-teacher relations; *iii)* teachers not meeting individual students' needs; *iv)* teacher absenteeism; *v)* staff resisting change; *vi)* teachers being too strict with students; and *vii)* students not being encouraged to achieve their full potential. As all items were inverted for scaling, higher values on this index indicate a positive teacher behaviour.

Student behaviour

The *index of student-related factors affecting school climates* (STUBEHA) was derived from school principals' reports on the extent to which the learning of students hindered by the following factors in their schools (SC17): *i)* student absenteeism; *ii)* disruption of classes by students; *iii)* students skipping classes; *iv)* student lacking respect for teachers; *v)* student use of alcohol or illegal drugs; and *vi)* students intimidating or bullying other students. As all items were inverted for scaling higher values on this index indicate a positive student behaviour.

Parent questionnaire simple indices

Educational level of parents

The educational level of parents is classified using ISCED (OECD, 1999) based on parents' responses (PA09 and PA10). Three indices were constructed: educational level for mother (PQMISCED); educational level for father (PQFISCED); and the highest educational level of parents (PQHISCED), which corresponds to the higher ISCED level of either parent. These indices have the following categories: (0) None, (1) ISCED 3A (upper secondary), (2) ISCED 4 (non-tertiary post-secondary), (3) ISCED 5B (vocational tertiary), and (4) ISCED 5A, 6 (theoretically oriented tertiary and post-graduate).

Parent questionnaire scale indices

Parents' perception of school quality

The *index of parents' perception of school quality* (PQSCHOOL) was derived from parents' level of agreement with the following statements (PA14): *i)* most of my child's school teachers seem competent and dedicated; *ii)* standards of achievement are high in my child's schools; *iii)* I am happy with the content taught and the instructional methods used in my child's school; *iv)* I am satisfied with the disciplinary atmosphere in my child's school; *v)* my child's progress is carefully monitored by the school; *vi)* my child's school provides regular and useful information on my child's progress; and *vii)* my child's school does a good job in educating students. As all items were inverted for scaling, higher values on this index indicate parents' positive evaluations of the school's quality.

Parents' involvement in school

The *index of parents' involvement in school* (PARINVOL) was derived from parents' responses to whether they have participated in various school-related activities during the previous academic year (PA15). Parents were asked to report "yes" or "no" for the following statements: *i)* discuss my child's behaviour or progress with a teacher on my own initiative; *ii)* discuss my child's behaviour or progress on the initiative of one of my child's teachers; *iii)* volunteer in physical activities; *iv)* volunteer in extra-curricular activities; *v)* volunteer in school library or media centre; *vi)* assist a teacher in school; *vii)* appear as a guest speaker; and *viii)* participate in local school. Higher values on this index indicate greater parents' involvement in school.

Students reading resources at home

The *index of students' reading resources at home* (READRES) was derived from parents' reports on whether the followings are available for their children in their home (PA07): *i)* email; *ii)* online chat; *iii)* Internet connection; *iv)* daily newspaper; *v)* subscription to journal or magazine; and *vi)* books of his/her own (not school books). Higher values on this index indicate greater availability of reading resources at home.

Parents' current support of their child's reading literacy

The *index of parents' current support of their child's reading literary* (CURSUPP) was derived from parents' reports on the frequency with which they or someone else in their home did the following with their child (PA08): *i)* discuss political or social issues; *ii)* discuss books, films or television programmes; *iii)* discuss how well the child is doing at school; *iv)* go to a bookstore or library with the child; *v)* talk with the child about what he/she is reading; and *vi)* help the child with his/her homework. Higher values on this index indicate greater parental support of child's reading literacy.

Parents' support of their child's reading literacy at the beginning of primary school

The *index of parents' support of their child's reading literacy at the beginning of primary school* (PRESUPP) was derived from parents' reports on the frequency with which they or someone else in their home undertook the following activities with their child when the child attended the first year of primary school (PA03): *i)* read books; *ii)* tell stories; *iii)* sing songs; *iv)* play with alphabet toys; *v)* talk about what parent had read; *vi)* play word games; *vii)* wrote letters or words; and *viii)* read aloud signs and labels. Higher values on this index indicate greater levels of parents' support.

Motivational attributes of parents' own reading engagement

The *index of motivational attributes of parents' own reading engagement* (MOTREAD) was derived from parents' level of agreement with the following statements (PA06): *i)* reading is one of my favourite hobbies; *ii)* I feel happy if I receive a book as a present; *iii)* for me reading is a waste of time; and *iv)* I enjoy going to a bookstore or library. As the item iii was inverted for scaling, higher values on this index indicate greater parents' motivation to engage in reading activities.

ANNEX A2
THE PISA TARGET POPULATION, THE PISA SAMPLES AND THE DEFINITION OF SCHOOLS

Definition of the PISA target population

PISA 2009 provides an assessment of the cumulative yield of education and learning at a point at which most young adults are still enrolled in initial education.

A major challenge for an international survey is to ensure that international comparability of national target populations is guaranteed in such a venture.

Differences between countries in the nature and extent of pre-primary education and care, the age of entry into formal schooling and the institutional structure of educational systems do not allow the definition of internationally comparable grade levels of schooling. Consequently, international comparisons of educational performance typically define their populations with reference to a target age group. Some previous international assessments have defined their target population on the basis of the grade level that provides maximum coverage of a particular age cohort. A disadvantage of this approach is that slight variations in the age distribution of students across grade levels often lead to the selection of different target grades in different countries, or between education systems within countries, raising serious questions about the comparability of results across, and at times within, countries. In addition, because not all students of the desired age are usually represented in grade-based samples, there may be a more serious potential bias in the results if the unrepresented students are typically enrolled in the next higher grade in some countries and the next lower grade in others. This would exclude students with potentially higher levels of performance in the former countries and students with potentially lower levels of performance in the latter.

In order to address this problem, PISA uses an age-based definition for its target population, *i.e.* a definition that is not tied to the institutional structures of national education systems. PISA assesses students who were aged between 15 years and 3 (complete) months and 16 years and 2 (complete) months at the beginning of the assessment period, plus or minus a 1 month allowable variation, and who were enrolled in an educational institution with Grade 7 or higher, regardless of the grade levels or type of institution in which they were enrolled, and regardless of whether they were in full-time or part-time education. Educational institutions are generally referred to as schools in this publication, although some educational institutions (in particular, some types of vocational education establishments) may not be termed schools in certain countries. As expected from this definition, the average age of students across OECD countries was 15 years and 9 months. The range in country means was 2 months and 5 days (0.18 years), from the minimum country mean of 15 years and 8 months to the maximum country mean of 15 years and 10 months.

Given this definition of population, PISA makes statements about the knowledge and skills of a group of individuals who were born within a comparable reference period, but who may have undergone different educational experiences both in and outside of schools. In PISA, these knowledge and skills are referred to as the yield of education at an age that is common across countries. Depending on countries' policies on school entry, selection and promotion, these students may be distributed over a narrower or a wider range of grades across different education systems, tracks or streams. It is important to consider these differences when comparing PISA results across countries, as observed differences between students at age 15 may no longer appear as students' educational experiences converge later on.

If a country's scale scores in reading, scientific or mathematical literacy are significantly higher than those in another country, it cannot automatically be inferred that the schools or particular parts of the education system in the first country are more effective than those in the second. However, one can legitimately conclude that the cumulative impact of learning experiences in the first country, starting in early childhood and up to the age of 15, and embracing experiences both in school, home and beyond, have resulted in higher outcomes in the literacy domains that PISA measures.

The PISA target population did not include residents attending schools in a foreign country. It does, however, include foreign nationals attending schools in the country of assessment.

To accommodate countries that desired grade-based results for the purpose of national analyses, PISA 2009 provided a sampling option to supplement age-based sampling with grade-based sampling.

Population coverage

All countries attempted to maximise the coverage of 15-year-olds enrolled in education in their national samples, including students enrolled in special educational institutions. As a result, PISA 2009 reached standards of population coverage that are unprecedented in international surveys of this kind.

The sampling standards used in PISA permitted countries to exclude up to a total of 5% of the relevant population either by excluding schools or by excluding students within schools. All but 5 countries, Denmark (8.17%), Luxembourg (8.15%), Canada (6.00%), Norway (5.93%) and the United States (5.16%), achieved this standard, and in 36 countries and economies, the overall exclusion rate was less than 2%. When language exclusions were accounted for (*i.e.* removed from the overall exclusion rate), the United States no longer had an exclusion rate greater than 5%. For details, see *www.pisa.oecd.org*.

Exclusions within the above limits include:

- *At the school level: i)* schools that were geographically inaccessible or where the administration of the PISA assessment was not considered feasible; and *ii)* schools that provided teaching only for students in the categories defined under "within-school exclusions", such as schools for the blind. The percentage of 15-year-olds enrolled in such schools had to be less than 2.5% of the nationally desired target population [0.5% maximum for *i)* and 2% maximum for *ii)*]. The magnitude, nature and justification of school-level exclusions are documented in the *PISA 2009 Technical Report* (OECD, forthcoming).
- *At the student level: i)* students with an intellectual disability; *ii)* students with a functional disability; *iii)* students with limited assessment language proficiency; *iv)* other – a category defined by the national centres and approved by the international centre; and *v)* students taught in a language of instruction for the main domain for which no materials were available. Students could not be excluded solely because of low proficiency or common discipline problems. The percentage of 15-year-olds excluded within schools had to be less than 2.5% of the nationally desired target population.

Table A2.1 describes the target population of the countries participating in PISA 2009. Further information on the target population and the implementation of PISA sampling standards can be found in the *PISA 2009 Technical Report* (OECD, forthcoming).

- ***Column 1*** shows the **total number of 15-year-olds** according to the most recent available information, which in most countries meant the year 2008 as the year before the assessment.
- ***Column 2*** shows the number of 15-year-olds enrolled in schools in Grade 7 or above (as defined above), which is referred to as the **eligible population**.
- ***Column 3*** shows the **national desired target population**. Countries were allowed to exclude up to 0.5% of students *a priori* from the eligible population, essentially for practical reasons. The following *a priori* exclusions exceed this limit but were agreed with the PISA Consortium: Canada excluded 1.1% of its population from Territories and Aboriginal reserves; France excluded 1.7% of its students in its *territoires d'outre-mer* and other institutions; Indonesia excluded 4.7% of its students from four provinces because of security reasons; Kyrgyzstan excluded 2.3% of its population in remote, inaccessible schools; and Serbia excluded 2% of its students taught in Serbian in Kosovo.
- ***Column 4*** shows the **number of students enrolled in schools that were excluded from the national desired target population** either from the sampling frame or later in the field during data collection.
- ***Column 5*** shows the **size of the national desired target population after subtracting the students enrolled in excluded schools**. This is obtained by subtracting Column 4 from Column 3.
- ***Column 6*** shows the **percentage of students enrolled in excluded schools**. This is obtained by dividing Column 4 by Column 3 and multiplying by 100.
- ***Column 7*** shows the **number of students participating in PISA 2009**. Note that in some cases this number does not account for 15-year-olds assessed as part of additional national options.
- ***Column 8*** shows the **weighted number of participating students**, *i.e.* the number of students in the nationally defined target population that the PISA sample represents.
- Each country attempted to maximise the coverage of PISA's target population within the sampled schools. In the case of each sampled school, all eligible students, namely those 15 years of age, regardless of grade, were first listed. Sampled students who were to be excluded had still to be included in the sampling documentation, and a list drawn up stating the reason for their exclusion. ***Column 9*** indicates the **total number of excluded students,** which is further described and classified into specific categories in Table A2.2. ***Column 10*** indicates the **weighted number of excluded students,** *i.e.* the overall number of students in the nationally defined target population represented by the number of students excluded from the sample, which is also described and classified by exclusion categories in Table A2.2. Excluded students were excluded based on five categories: *i)* students with an intellectual disability – the student has a mental or emotional disability and is cognitively delayed such that he/she cannot perform in the PISA testing situation; *ii)* students with a functional disability – the student has a moderate to severe permanent physical disability such that he/she cannot perform in the PISA testing situation; *iii)* students with a limited assessment language proficiency – the student is unable to read or speak any of the languages of the assessment in the country and would be unable to overcome the language barrier in the testing situation (typically a student who has received less than one year of instruction in the languages of the assessment may be excluded); *iv)* other – a category defined by the national centres and approved by the international centre; and *v)* students taught in a language of instruction for the main domain for which no materials were available.
- ***Column 11*** shows the **percentage of students excluded within schools**. This is calculated as the weighted number of excluded students (Column 10), divided by the weighted number of excluded and participating students (Column 8 plus Column 10), then multiplied by 100.

[Part 1/2]

Table A2.1 PISA target populations and samples

		Population and sample information							
		Total population of 15-year-olds	Total enrolled population of 15-year-olds at Grade 7 or above	Total in national desired target population	Total school-level exclusions	Total in national desired target population after all school exclusions and before within-school exclusions	School-level exclusion rate (%)	Number of participating students	Weighted number of participating students
		(1)	(2)	(3)	(4)	(5)	(6)	(7)	(8)
OECD	Australia	286 334	269 669	269 669	7 057	262 612	2.62	14 251	240 851
	Austria	99 818	94 192	94 192	115	94 077	0.12	6 590	87 326
	Belgium	126 377	126 335	126 335	2 474	123 861	1.96	8 501	119 140
	Canada	430 791	426 590	422 052	2 370	419 682	0.56	23 207	360 286
	Chile	290 056	265 542	265 463	2 594	262 869	0.98	5 669	247 270
	Czech Republic	122 027	116 153	116 153	1 619	114 534	1.39	6 064	113 951
	Denmark	70 522	68 897	68 897	3 082	65 815	4.47	5 924	60 855
	Estonia	14 248	14 106	14 106	436	13 670	3.09	4 727	12 978
	Finland	66 198	66 198	66 198	1 507	64 691	2.28	5 810	61 463
	France	749 808	732 825	720 187	18 841	701 346	2.62	4 298	677 620
	Germany	852 044	852 044	852 044	7 138	844 906	0.84	4 979	766 993
	Greece	102 229	105 664	105 664	696	104 968	0.66	4 969	93 088
	Hungary	121 155	118 387	118 387	3 322	115 065	2.81	4 605	105 611
	Iceland	4 738	4 738	4 738	20	4 718	0.42	3 646	4 410
	Ireland	56 635	55 464	55 446	276	55 170	0.50	3 937	52 794
	Israel	122 701	112 254	112 254	1 570	110 684	1.40	5 761	103 184
	Italy	586 904	573 542	573 542	2 694	570 848	0.47	30 905	506 733
	Japan	1 211 642	1 189 263	1 189 263	22 955	1 166 308	1.93	6 088	1 113 403
	Korea	717 164	700 226	700 226	2 927	697 299	0.42	4 989	630 030
	Luxembourg	5 864	5 623	5 623	186	5 437	3.31	4 622	5 124
	Mexico	2 151 771	1 425 397	1 425 397	5 825	1 419 572	0.41	38 250	1 305 461
	Netherlands	199 000	198 334	198 334	6 179	192 155	3.12	4 760	183 546
	New Zealand	63 460	60 083	60 083	645	59 438	1.07	4 643	55 129
	Norway	63 352	62 948	62 948	1 400	61 548	2.22	4 660	57 367
	Poland	482 500	473 700	473 700	7 650	466 050	1.61	4 917	448 866
	Portugal	115 669	107 583	107 583	0	107 583	0.00	6 298	96 820
	Slovak Republic	72 826	72 454	72 454	1 803	70 651	2.49	4 555	69 274
	Slovenia	20 314	19 571	19 571	174	19 397	0.89	6 155	18 773
	Spain	433 224	425 336	425 336	3 133	422 203	0.74	25 887	387 054
	Sweden	121 486	121 216	121 216	2 323	118 893	1.92	4 567	113 054
	Switzerland	90 623	89 423	89 423	1 747	87 676	1.95	11 812	80 839
	Turkey	1 336 842	859 172	859 172	8 569	850 603	1.00	4 996	757 298
	United Kingdom	786 626	786 825	786 825	17 593	769 232	2.24	12 179	683 380
	United States	4 103 738	4 210 475	4 210 475	15 199	4 195 276	0.36	5 233	3 373 264
Partners	Albania	55 587	42 767	42 767	372	42 395	0.87	4 596	34 134
	Argentina	688 434	636 713	636 713	2 238	634 475	0.35	4 774	472 106
	Azerbaijan	185 481	184 980	184 980	1 886	183 094	1.02	4 727	105 886
	Brazil	3 292 022	2 654 489	2 654 489	15 571	2 638 918	0.59	20 127	2 080 159
	Bulgaria	80 226	70 688	70 688	1 369	69 319	1.94	4 507	57 833
	Colombia	893 057	582 640	582 640	412	582 228	0.07	7 921	522 388
	Croatia	48 491	46 256	46 256	535	45 721	1.16	4 994	43 065
	Dubai (UAE)	10 564	10 327	10 327	167	10 160	1.62	5 620	9 179
	Hong Kong-China	85 000	78 224	78 224	809	77 415	1.03	4 837	75 548
	Indonesia	4 267 801	3 158 173	3 010 214	10 458	2 999 756	0.35	5 136	2 259 118
	Jordan	117 732	107 254	107 254	0	107 254	0.00	6 486	104 056
	Kazakhstan	281 659	263 206	263 206	7 210	255 996	2.74	5 412	250 657
	Kyrgyzstan	116 795	93 989	91 793	1 149	90 644	1.25	4 986	78 493
	Latvia	28 749	28 149	28 149	943	27 206	3.35	4 502	23 362
	Liechtenstein	399	360	360	5	355	1.39	329	355
	Lithuania	51 822	43 967	43 967	522	43 445	1.19	4 528	40 530
	Macao-China	7 500	5 969	5 969	3	5 966	0.05	5 952	5 978
	Montenegro	8 500	8 493	8 493	10	8 483	0.12	4 825	7 728
	Panama	57 919	43 623	43 623	501	43 122	1.15	3 969	30 510
	Peru	585 567	491 514	490 840	984	489 856	0.20	5 985	427 607
	Qatar	10 974	10 665	10 665	114	10 551	1.07	9 078	9 806
	Romania	152 084	152 084	152 084	679	151 405	0.45	4 776	151 130
	Russian Federation	1 673 085	1 667 460	1 667 460	25 012	1 642 448	1.50	5 308	1 290 047
	Serbia	85 121	75 128	73 628	1 580	72 048	2.15	5 523	70 796
	Shanghai-China	112 000	100 592	100 592	1 287	99 305	1.28	5 115	97 045
	Singapore	54 982	54 212	54 212	633	53 579	1.17	5 283	51 874
	Chinese Taipei	329 249	329 189	329 189	1 778	327 411	0.54	5 831	297 203
	Thailand	949 891	763 679	763 679	8 438	755 241	1.10	6 225	691 916
	Trinidad and Tobago	19 260	17 768	17 768	0	17 768	0.00	4 778	14 938
	Tunisia	153 914	153 914	153 914	0	153 914	0.00	4 955	136 545
	Uruguay	53 801	43 281	43 281	30	43 251	0.07	5 957	33 971

Note: For a full explanation of the details in this table, please refer to the *PISA 2009 Technical Report* (OECD, forthcoming). The figure for total national population of 15-year-olds enrolled in Column 1 may occasionally be larger than the total number of 15-year-olds in Column 2 due to differing data sources. In Greece, Column 1 does not include immigrants but Column 2 does.

StatLink http://dx.doi.org/10.1787/888932343190

[Part 2/2]

Table A2.1 PISA target populations and samples

		Population and sample information				Coverage indices		
		Number of excluded students	Weighted number of excluded students	Within-school exclusion rate (%)	Overall exclusion rate (%)	Coverage index 1: Coverage of national desired population	Coverage index 2: Coverage of national enrolled population	Coverage index 3: Coverage of 15-year-old population
		(9)	(10)	(11)	(12)	(13)	(14)	(15)
OECD	Australia	313	4 389	1.79	4.36	0.956	0.956	0.841
	Austria	45	607	0.69	0.81	0.992	0.992	0.875
	Belgium	30	292	0.24	2.20	0.978	0.978	0.943
	Canada	1 607	20 837	5.47	6.00	0.940	0.930	0.836
	Chile	15	620	0.25	1.22	0.988	0.987	0.852
	Czech Republic	24	423	0.37	1.76	0.982	0.982	0.934
	Denmark	296	2 448	3.87	8.17	0.918	0.918	0.863
	Estonia	32	97	0.74	3.81	0.962	0.962	0.911
	Finland	77	717	1.15	3.40	0.966	0.966	0.928
	France	1	304	0.04	2.66	0.973	0.957	0.904
	Germany	28	3 591	0.47	1.30	0.987	0.987	0.900
	Greece	142	2 977	3.10	3.74	0.963	0.963	0.911
	Hungary	10	361	0.34	3.14	0.969	0.969	0.872
	Iceland	187	189	4.10	4.50	0.955	0.955	0.931
	Ireland	136	1 492	2.75	3.23	0.968	0.967	0.932
	Israel	86	1 359	1.30	2.68	0.973	0.973	0.841
	Italy	561	10 663	2.06	2.52	0.975	0.975	0.863
	Japan	0	0	0.00	1.93	0.981	0.981	0.919
	Korea	16	1 748	0.28	0.69	0.993	0.993	0.879
	Luxembourg	196	270	5.01	8.15	0.919	0.919	0.874
	Mexico	52	1 951	0.15	0.56	0.994	0.994	0.607
	Netherlands	19	648	0.35	3.46	0.965	0.965	0.922
	New Zealand	184	1 793	3.15	4.19	0.958	0.958	0.869
	Norway	207	2 260	3.79	5.93	0.941	0.941	0.906
	Poland	15	1 230	0.27	1.88	0.981	0.981	0.930
	Portugal	115	1 544	1.57	1.57	0.984	0.984	0.837
	Slovak Republic	106	1 516	2.14	4.58	0.954	0.954	0.951
	Slovenia	43	138	0.73	1.61	0.984	0.984	0.924
	Spain	775	12 673	3.17	3.88	0.961	0.961	0.893
	Sweden	146	3 360	2.89	4.75	0.953	0.953	0.931
	Switzerland	209	940	1.15	3.08	0.969	0.969	0.892
	Turkey	11	1 497	0.20	1.19	0.988	0.988	0.566
	United Kingdom	318	17 094	2.44	4.62	0.954	0.954	0.869
	United States	315	170 542	4.81	5.16	0.948	0.948	0.822
Partners	Albania	0	0	0.00	0.87	0.991	0.991	0.614
	Argentina	14	1 225	0.26	0.61	0.994	0.994	0.686
	Azerbaijan	0	0	0.00	1.02	0.990	0.990	0.571
	Brazil	24	2 692	0.13	0.72	0.993	0.993	0.632
	Bulgaria	0	0	0.00	1.94	0.981	0.981	0.721
	Colombia	11	490	0.09	0.16	0.998	0.998	0.585
	Croatia	34	273	0.63	1.78	0.982	0.982	0.888
	Dubai (UAE)	5	7	0.07	1.69	0.983	0.983	0.869
	Hong Kong-China	9	119	0.16	1.19	0.988	0.988	0.889
	Indonesia	0	0	0.00	0.35	0.997	0.950	0.529
	Jordan	24	443	0.42	0.42	0.996	0.996	0.884
	Kazakhstan	82	3 844	1.51	4.21	0.958	0.958	0.890
	Kyrgyzstan	86	1 384	1.73	2.96	0.970	0.948	0.672
	Latvia	19	102	0.43	3.77	0.962	0.962	0.813
	Liechtenstein	0	0	0.00	1.39	0.986	0.986	0.890
	Lithuania	74	632	1.53	2.70	0.973	0.973	0.782
	Macao-China	0	0	0.00	0.05	0.999	0.999	0.797
	Montenegro	0	0	0.00	0.12	0.999	0.999	0.909
	Panama	0	0	0.00	1.15	0.989	0.989	0.527
	Peru	9	558	0.13	0.33	0.997	0.995	0.730
	Qatar	28	28	0.28	1.35	0.986	0.986	0.894
	Romania	0	0	0.00	0.45	0.996	0.996	0.994
	Russian Federation	59	15 247	1.17	2.65	0.973	0.973	0.771
	Serbia	10	133	0.19	2.33	0.977	0.957	0.832
	Shanghai-China	7	130	0.13	1.41	0.986	0.986	0.866
	Singapore	48	417	0.80	1.96	0.980	0.980	0.943
	Chinese Taipei	32	1 662	0.56	1.09	0.989	0.989	0.903
	Thailand	6	458	0.07	1.17	0.988	0.988	0.728
	Trinidad and Tobago	11	36	0.24	0.24	0.998	0.998	0.776
	Tunisia	7	184	0.13	0.13	0.999	0.999	0.887
	Uruguay	14	67	0.20	0.26	0.997	0.997	0.631

Note: For a full explanation of the details in this table please refer to the *PISA 2009 Technical Report* (OECD, forthcoming). The figure for total national population of 15-year-olds enrolled in Column 1 may occasionally be larger than the total number of 15-year-olds in Column 2 due to differing data sources. In Greece, Column 1 does not include immigrants but Column 2 does include immigrants.

StatLink http://dx.doi.org/10.1787/888932343190

[Part 1/1]
Table A2.2 **Exclusions**

		Student exclusions (unweighted)						Student exclusion (weighted)					
		Number of excluded students with a disability (Code 1)	Number of excluded students with a disability (Code 2)	Number of excluded students because of language (Code 3)	Number of excluded students for other reasons (Code 4)	Number of excluded students because of no materials available in the language of instruction (Code 5)	Total number of excluded students	Weighted number of excluded students with a disability (Code 1)	Weighted number of excluded students with a disability (Code 2)	Weighted number of excluded students because of language (Code 3)	Weighted number of excluded students for other reasons (Code 4)	Number of excluded students because of no materials available in the language of instruction (Code 5)	Total weighted number of excluded students
		(1)	(2)	(3)	(4)	(5)	(6)	(7)	(8)	(9)	(10)	(11)	(12)
OECD	Australia	24	210	79	0	0	313	272	2 834	1 283	0	0	4 389
	Austria	0	26	19	0	0	45	0	317	290	0	0	607
	Belgium	3	17	10	0	0	30	26	171	95	0	0	292
	Canada	49	1 458	100	0	0	1 607	428	19 082	1 326	0	0	20 837
	Chile	5	10	0	0	0	15	177	443	0	0	0	620
	Czech Republic	8	7	9	0	0	24	117	144	162	0	0	423
	Denmark	13	182	35	66	0	296	165	1 432	196	656	0	2 448
	Estonia	3	28	1	0	0	32	8	87	2	0	0	97
	Finland	4	48	12	11	2	77	38	447	110	99	23	717
	France	1	0	0	0	0	1	304	0	0	0	0	304
	Germany	6	20	2	0	0	28	864	2 443	285	0	0	3 591
	Greece	7	11	7	117	0	142	172	352	195	2 257	0	2 977
	Hungary	0	1	0	9	0	10	0	48	0	313	0	361
	Iceland	3	78	64	38	1	187	3	78	65	39	1	189
	Ireland	4	72	25	35	0	136	51	783	262	396	0	1 492
	Israel	10	69	7	0	0	86	194	1 049	116	0	0	1 359
	Italy	45	348	168	0	0	561	748	6 241	3 674	0	0	10 663
	Japan	0	0	0	0	0	0	0	0	0	0	0	0
	Korea	7	9	0	0	0	16	994	753	0	0	0	1 748
	Luxembourg	2	132	62	0	0	196	2	206	62	0	0	270
	Mexico	25	25	2	0	0	52	1 010	905	36	0	0	1 951
	Netherlands	6	13	0	0	0	19	178	470	0	0	0	648
	New Zealand	19	84	78	0	3	184	191	824	749	0	29	1 793
	Norway	8	160	39	0	0	207	90	1 756	414	0	0	2 260
	Poland	2	13	0	0	0	15	169	1 061	0	0	0	1 230
	Portugal	2	100	13	0	0	115	25	1 322	197	0	0	1 544
	Slovak Republic	12	37	1	56	0	106	171	558	19	768	0	1 516
	Slovenia	6	10	27	0	0	43	40	32	66	0	0	138
	Spain	45	441	289	0	0	775	1 007	7 141	4 525	0	0	12 673
	Sweden	115	0	31	0	0	146	2 628	0	732	0	0	3 360
	Switzerland	11	106	92	0	0	209	64	344	532	0	0	940
	Turkey	3	3	5	0	0	11	338	495	665	0	0	1 497
	United Kingdom	40	247	31	0	0	318	2 438	13 482	1 174	0	0	17 094
	United States	29	236	40	10	0	315	15 367	127 486	21 718	5 971	0	170 542
Partners	Albania	0	0	0	0	0	0	0	0	0	0	0	0
	Argentina	4	10	0	0	0	14	288	937	0	0	0	1 225
	Azerbaijan	0	0	0	0	0	0	0	0	0	0	0	0
	Brazil	21	3	0	0	0	24	2 495	197	0	0	0	2 692
	Bulgaria	0	0	0	0	0	0	0	0	0	0	0	0
	Colombia	7	2	2	0	0	11	200	48	242	0	0	490
	Croatia	4	30	0	0	0	34	34	239	0	0	0	273
	Dubai (UAE)	1	1	3	0	0	5	2	2	3	0	0	7
	Hong Kong-China	0	9	0	0	0	9	0	119	0	0	0	119
	Indonesia	0	0	0	0	0	0	0	0	0	0	0	0
	Jordan	11	7	6	0	0	24	166	149	127	0	0	443
	Kazakhstan	10	17	0	0	55	82	429	828	0	0	2 587	3 844
	Kyrgyzstan	68	13	5	0	0	86	1 093	211	80	0	0	1 384
	Latvia	6	8	5	0	0	19	25	44	33	0	0	102
	Liechtenstein	0	0	0	0	0	0	0	0	0	0	0	0
	Lithuania	4	69	1	0	0	74	33	590	9	0	0	632
	Macao-China	0	0	0	0	0	0	0	0	0	0	0	0
	Montenegro	0	0	0	0	0	0	0	0	0	0	0	0
	Panama	0	0	0	0	0	0	0	0	0	0	0	0
	Peru	4	5	0	0	0	9	245	313	0	0	0	558
	Qatar	9	18	1	0	0	28	9	18	1	0	0	28
	Romania	0	0	0	0	0	0	0	0	0	0	0	0
	Russian Federation	11	47	1	0	0	59	2 081	13 010	157	0	0	15 247
	Serbia	4	5	0	0	1	10	66	53	0	0	13	133
	Shanghai-China	1	6	0	0	0	7	19	111	0	0	0	130
	Singapore	2	22	24	0	0	48	17	217	182	0	0	417
	Chinese Taipei	13	19	0	0	0	32	684	977	0	0	0	1 662
	Thailand	0	5	1	0	0	6	0	260	198	0	0	458
	Trinidad and Tobago	1	10	0	0	0	11	3	33	0	0	0	36
	Tunisia	4	1	2	0	0	7	104	21	58	0	0	184
	Uruguay	2	9	3	0	0	14	14	34	18	0	0	67

Exclusion codes:

Code 1 Functional disability – student has a moderate to severe permanent physical disability.

Code 2 Intellectual disability – student has a mental or emotional disability and has either been tested as cognitively delayed or is considered in the professional opinion of qualified staff to be cognitively delayed.

Code 3 Limited assessment language proficiency – student is not a native speaker of any of the languages of the assessment in the country and has been resident in the country for less than one year.

Code 4 Other defined by the national centres and approved by the international centre.

Code 5 No materials available in the language of instruction.

Note: For a full explanation of other details in this table, please refer to the *PISA 2009 Technical Report* (OECD, forthcoming).

StatLink http://dx.doi.org/10.1787/888932343190

- ***Column 12*** shows the **overall exclusion rate**, which represents the weighted percentage of the national desired target population excluded from PISA either through school-level exclusions or through the exclusion of students within schools. It is calculated as the school-level exclusion rate (Column 6 divided by 100) plus within-school exclusion rate (Column 11 divided by 100) multiplied by 1 minus the school-level exclusion rate (Column 6 divided by 100). This result is then multiplied by 100. Five countries, Denmark, Luxembourg, Canada, Norway and the United States, had exclusion rates higher than 5%. When language exclusions were accounted for (*i.e.* removed from the overall exclusion rate), the United States no longer had an exclusion rate greater than 5%.
- ***Column 13*** presents an **index of the extent to which the national desired target population is covered by the PISA sample**. Denmark, Luxembourg, Canada, Norway and the United States were the only countries where the coverage is below 95%.
- ***Column 14*** presents an **index of the extent to which 15-year-olds enrolled in schools are covered by the PISA sample**. The index measures the overall proportion of the national enrolled population that is covered by the non-excluded portion of the student sample. The index takes into account both school-level and student-level exclusions. Values close to 100 indicate that the PISA sample represents the entire education system as defined for PISA 2009. The index is the weighted number of participating students (Column 8) divided by the weighted number of participating and excluded students (Column 8 plus Column 10), times the nationally defined target population (Column 5) divided by the eligible population (Column 2) (times 100).
- ***Column 15*** presents an **index of the coverage of the 15-year-old population**. This index is the weighted number of participating students (Column 8) divided by the total population of 15-year-old students (Column 1).

This high level of coverage contributes to the comparability of the assessment results. For example, even assuming that the excluded students would have systematically scored worse than those who participated, and that this relationship is moderately strong, an exclusion rate in the order of 5% would likely lead to an overestimation of national mean scores of less than 5 score points (on a scale with an international mean of 500 score points and a standard deviation of 100 score points). This assessment is based on the following calculations: if the correlation between the propensity of exclusions and student performance is 0.3, resulting mean scores would likely be overestimated by 1 score point if the exclusion rate is 1%, by 3 score points if the exclusion rate is 5%, and by 6 score points if the exclusion rate is 10%. If the correlation between the propensity of exclusions and student performance is 0.5, resulting mean scores would be overestimated by 1 score point if the exclusion rate is 1%, by 5 score points if the exclusion rate is 5%, and by 10 score points if the exclusion rate is 10%. For this calculation, a model was employed that assumes a bivariate normal distribution for performance and the propensity to participate. For details, see the *PISA 2009 Technical Report* (OECD, forthcoming).

Sampling procedures and response rates

The accuracy of any survey results depends on the quality of the information on which national samples are based as well as on the sampling procedures. Quality standards, procedures, instruments and verification mechanisms were developed for PISA that ensured that national samples yielded comparable data and that the results could be compared with confidence.

Most PISA samples were designed as two-stage stratified samples (where countries applied different sampling designs, these are documented in the *PISA 2009 Technical Report* [OECD, forthcoming]). The first stage consisted of sampling individual schools in which 15-year-old students could be enrolled. Schools were sampled systematically with probabilities proportional to size, the measure of size being a function of the estimated number of eligible (15-year-old) students enrolled. A minimum of 150 schools were selected in each country (where this number existed), although the requirements for national analyses often required a somewhat larger sample. As the schools were sampled, replacement schools were simultaneously identified, in case a sampled school chose not to participate in PISA 2009.

In the case of Iceland, Liechtenstein, Luxembourg, Macao-China and Qatar, all schools and all eligible students within schools were included in the sample.

Experts from the PISA Consortium performed the sample selection process for most participating countries and monitored it closely in those countries that selected their own samples. The second stage of the selection process sampled students within sampled schools. Once schools were selected, a list of each sampled school's 15-year-old students was prepared. From this list, 35 students were then selected with equal probability (all 15-year-old students were selected if fewer than 35 were enrolled). The number of students to be sampled per school could deviate from 35, but could not be less than 20.

Data-quality standards in PISA required minimum participation rates for schools as well as for students. These standards were established to minimise the potential for response biases. In the case of countries meeting these standards, it was likely that any bias resulting from non-response would be negligible, *i.e.* typically smaller than the sampling error.

A minimum response rate of 85% was required for the schools initially selected. Where the initial response rate of schools was between 65 and 85%, however, an acceptable school response rate could still be achieved through the use of replacement schools. This procedure brought with it a risk of increased response bias. Participating countries were, therefore, encouraged to persuade as many of the schools in the original sample as possible to participate. Schools with a student participation rate between 25% and 50% were not regarded as participating schools, but data from these schools were included in the database and contributed to the various estimations. Data from schools with a student participation rate of less than 25% were excluded from the database.

[Part 1/2]
Table A2.3 **Response rates**

	Initial sample – before school replacement					Final sample – after school replacement		
	Weighted school participation rate before replacement (%)	Weighted number of responding schools (weighted also by enrolment)	Weighted number of schools sampled (responding and non-responding) (weighted also by enrolment)	Number of responding schools (unweighted)	Number of responding and non-responding schools (unweighted)	Weighted school participation rate after replacement (%)	Weighted number of responding schools (weighted also by enrolment)	Weighted number of schools sampled (responding and non-responding) (weighted also by enrolment)
	(1)	(2)	(3)	(4)	(5)	(6)	(7)	(8)
OECD								
Australia	97.78	265 659	271 696	342	357	98.85	268 780	271 918
Austria	93.94	88 551	94 261	280	291	93.94	88 551	94 261
Belgium	88.76	112 594	126 851	255	292	95.58	121 291	126 899
Canada	88.04	362 152	411 343	893	1 001	89.64	368 708	411 343
Chile	94.34	245 583	260 331	189	201	99.04	257 594	260 099
Czech Republic	83.09	94 696	113 961	226	270	97.40	111 091	114 062
Denmark	83.94	55 375	65 967	264	325	90.75	59 860	65 964
Estonia	100.00	13 230	13 230	175	175	100.00	13 230	13 230
Finland	98.65	62 892	63 751	201	204	100.00	63 748	63 751
France	94.14	658 769	699 776	166	177	94.14	658 769	699 776
Germany	98.61	826 579	838 259	223	226	100.00	838 259	838 259
Greece	98.19	98 710	100 529	181	184	99.40	99 925	100 529
Hungary	98.21	101 523	103 378	184	190	99.47	103 067	103 618
Iceland	98.46	4 488	4 558	129	141	98.46	4 488	4 558
Ireland	87.18	48 821	55 997	139	160	88.44	49 526	55 997
Israel	92.03	103 141	112 069	170	186	95.40	106 918	112 069
Italy	94.27	532 432	564 811	1 054	1 108	99.08	559 546	564 768
Japan	87.77	999 408	1 138 694	171	196	94.99	1 081 662	1 138 694
Korea	100.00	683 793	683 793	157	157	100.00	683 793	683 793
Luxembourg	100.00	5 437	5 437	39	39	100.00	5 437	5 437
Mexico	95.62	1 338 291	1 399 638	1 512	1 560	97.71	1 367 668	1 399 730
Netherlands	80.40	154 471	192 140	155	194	95.54	183 555	192 118
New Zealand	84.11	49 917	59 344	148	179	91.00	54 130	59 485
Norway	89.61	55 484	61 920	183	207	96.53	59 759	61 909
Poland	88.16	409 513	464 535	159	187	97.70	453 855	464 535
Portugal	93.61	102 225	109 205	201	216	98.43	107 535	109 251
Slovak Republic	93.33	67 284	72 092	180	191	99.01	71 388	72 105
Slovenia	98.36	19 798	20 127	337	352	98.36	19 798	20 127
Spain	99.53	422 692	424 705	888	892	99.53	422 692	424 705
Sweden	99.91	120 693	120 802	189	191	99.91	120 693	120 802
Switzerland	94.25	81 005	85 952	413	429	98.71	84 896	86 006
Turkey	100.00	849 830	849 830	170	170	100.00	849 830	849 830
United Kingdom	71.06	523 271	736 341	418	549	87.35	643 027	736 178
United States	67.83	2 673 852	3 941 908	140	208	77.50	3 065 651	3 955 606
Partners								
Albania	97.29	39 168	40 259	177	182	99.37	39 999	40 253
Argentina	97.18	590 215	607 344	194	199	99.42	603 817	607 344
Azerbaijan	99.86	168 646	168 890	161	162	100.00	168 890	168 890
Brazil	93.13	2 435 250	2 614 824	899	976	94.75	2 477 518	2 614 806
Bulgaria	98.16	56 922	57 991	173	178	99.10	57 823	58 346
Colombia	90.21	507 649	562 728	260	285	94.90	533 899	562 587
Croatia	99.19	44 561	44 926	157	159	99.86	44 862	44 926
Dubai (UAE)	100.00	10 144	10 144	190	190	100.00	10 144	10 144
Hong Kong-China	69.19	53 800	77 758	108	156	96.75	75 232	77 758
Indonesia	94.54	2 337 438	2 472 502	172	183	100.00	2 473 528	2 473 528
Jordan	100.00	105 906	105 906	210	210	100.00	105 906	105 906
Kazakhstan	100.00	257 427	257 427	199	199	100.00	257 427	257 427
Kyrgyzstan	98.53	88 412	89 733	171	174	99.47	89 260	89 733
Latvia	97.46	26 986	27 689	180	185	99.39	27 544	27 713
Liechtenstein	100.00	356	356	12	12	100.00	356	356
Lithuania	98.13	41 759	42 555	192	197	99.91	42 526	42 564
Macao-China	100.00	5 966	5 966	45	45	100.00	5 966	5 966
Montenegro	100.00	8 527	8 527	52	52	100.00	8 527	8 527
Panama	82.58	33 384	40 426	180	220	83.76	33 779	40 329
Peru	100.00	480 640	480 640	240	240	100.00	480 640	480 640
Qatar	97.30	10 223	10 507	149	154	97.30	10 223	10 507
Romania	100.00	150 114	150 114	159	159	100.00	150 114	150 114
Russian Federation	100.00	1 392 765	1 392 765	213	213	100.00	1 392 765	1 392 765
Serbia	99.21	70 960	71 524	189	191	99.97	71 504	71 524
Shanghai-China	99.32	98 841	99 514	151	152	100.00	99 514	99 514
Singapore	96.19	51 552	53 592	168	175	97.88	52 454	53 592
Chinese Taipei	99.34	322 005	324 141	157	158	100.00	324 141	324 141
Thailand	98.01	737 225	752 193	225	230	100.00	752 392	752 392
Trinidad and Tobago	97.21	17 180	17 673	155	160	97.21	17 180	17 673
Tunisia	100.00	153 198	153 198	165	165	100.00	153 198	153 198
Uruguay	98.66	42 820	43 400	229	233	98.66	42 820	43 400

StatLink http://dx.doi.org/10.1787/888932343190

[Part 2/2]

Table A2.3 Response rates

	Final sample – after school replacement		Final sample – students within schools after school replacement				
	Number of responding schools (unweighted)	Number of responding and non-responding schools (unweighted)	Weighted student participation rate after replacement (%)	Number of students assessed (weighted)	Number of students sampled (assessed and absent) (weighted)	Number of students assessed (unweighted)	Number of students sampled (assessed and absent) (unweighted)
	(9)	(10)	(11)	(12)	(13)	(14)	(15)
OECD							
Australia	345	357	86.05	205 234	238 498	14 060	16 903
Austria	280	291	88.63	72 793	82 135	6 568	7 587
Belgium	275	292	91.38	104 263	114 097	8 477	9 245
Canada	908	1 001	79.52	257 905	324 342	22 383	27 603
Chile	199	201	92.88	227 541	244 995	5 663	6 097
Czech Republic	260	270	90.75	100 685	110 953	6 049	6 656
Denmark	285	325	89.29	49 236	55 139	5 924	6 827
Estonia	175	175	94.06	12 208	12 978	4 727	5 023
Finland	203	204	92.27	56 709	61 460	5 810	6 309
France	166	177	87.12	556 054	638 284	4 272	4 900
Germany	226	226	93.93	720 447	766 993	4 979	5 309
Greece	183	184	95.95	88 875	92 631	4 957	5 165
Hungary	187	190	93.25	97 923	105 015	4 605	4 956
Iceland	129	141	83.91	3 635	4 332	3 635	4 332
Ireland	141	160	83.81	39 248	46 830	3 896	4 654
Israel	176	186	89.45	88 480	98 918	5 761	6 440
Italy	1 095	1 108	92.13	462 655	502 190	30 876	33 390
Japan	185	196	95.32	1 010 801	1 060 382	6 077	6 377
Korea	157	157	98.76	622 187	630 030	4 989	5 057
Luxembourg	39	39	95.57	4 897	5 124	4 622	4 833
Mexico	1 531	1 560	95.13	1 214 827	1 276 982	38 213	40 125
Netherlands	185	194	89.78	157 912	175 897	4 747	5 286
New Zealand	161	179	84.65	42 452	50 149	4 606	5 476
Norway	197	207	89.92	49 785	55 366	4 660	5 194
Poland	179	187	85.87	376 767	438 739	4 855	5 674
Portugal	212	216	87.11	83 094	95 386	6 263	7 169
Slovak Republic	189	191	93.03	63 854	68 634	4 555	4 898
Slovenia	337	352	90.92	16 777	18 453	6 135	6 735
Spain	888	892	89.60	345 122	385 164	25 871	28 280
Sweden	189	191	92.97	105 026	112 972	4 567	4 912
Switzerland	425	429	93.58	74 712	79 836	11 810	12 551
Turkey	170	170	97.85	741 029	757 298	4 996	5 108
United Kingdom	481	549	86.96	520 121	598 110	12 168	14 046
United States	160	208	86.99	2 298 889	2 642 598	5 165	5 951
Partners							
Albania	181	182	95.39	32 347	33 911	4 596	4 831
Argentina	198	199	88.25	414 166	469 285	4 762	5 423
Azerbaijan	162	162	99.14	105 095	106 007	4 691	4 727
Brazil	926	976	89.04	1 767 872	1 985 479	19 901	22 715
Bulgaria	176	178	97.34	56 096	57 630	4 499	4 617
Colombia	274	285	92.83	462 602	498 331	7 910	8 483
Croatia	158	159	93.76	40 321	43 006	4 994	5 326
Dubai (UAE)	190	190	90.39	8 297	9 179	5 620	6 218
Hong Kong-China	151	156	93.19	68 142	73 125	4 837	5 195
Indonesia	183	183	96.91	2 189 287	2 259 118	5 136	5 313
Jordan	210	210	95.85	99 734	104 056	6 486	6 777
Kazakhstan	199	199	98.49	246 872	250 657	5 412	5 489
Kyrgyzstan	173	174	98.04	76 523	78 054	4 986	5 086
Latvia	184	185	91.27	21 241	23 273	4 502	4 930
Liechtenstein	12	12	92.68	329	355	329	355
Lithuania	196	197	93.36	37 808	40 495	4 528	4 854
Macao-China	45	45	99.57	5 952	5 978	5 952	5 978
Montenegro	52	52	95.43	7 375	7 728	4 825	5 062
Panama	183	220	88.67	22 666	25 562	3 913	4 449
Peru	240	240	96.35	412 011	427 607	5 985	6 216
Qatar	149	154	93.63	8 990	9 602	8 990	9 602
Romania	159	159	99.47	150 331	151 130	4 776	4 803
Russian Federation	213	213	96.77	1 248 353	1 290 047	5 308	5 502
Serbia	190	191	95.37	67 496	70 775	5 522	5 804
Shanghai-China	152	152	98.89	95 966	97 045	5 115	5 175
Singapore	171	175	91.04	46 224	50 775	5 283	5 809
Chinese Taipei	158	158	95.30	283 239	297 203	5 831	6 108
Thailand	230	230	97.37	673 688	691 916	6 225	6 396
Trinidad and Tobago	155	160	85.92	12 275	14 287	4 731	5 518
Tunisia	165	165	96.93	132 354	136 545	4 955	5 113
Uruguay	229	233	87.03	29 193	33 541	5 924	6 815

StatLink http://dx.doi.org/10.1787/888932343190

PISA 2009 also required a minimum participation rate of 80% of students within participating schools. This minimum participation rate had to be met at the national level, not necessarily by each participating school. Follow-up sessions were required in schools in which too few students had participated in the original assessment sessions. Student participation rates were calculated over all original schools, and also over all schools, whether original sample or replacement schools, and from the participation of students in both the original assessment and any follow-up sessions. A student who participated in the original or follow-up cognitive sessions was regarded as a participant. Those who attended only the questionnaire session were included in the international database and contributed to the statistics presented in this publication if they provided at least a description of their father's or mother's occupation.

Table A2.3 shows the response rates for students and schools, before and after replacement.

- ***Column 1*** shows the **weighted participation rate of schools before replacement**. This is obtained by dividing Column 2 by Column 3.
- ***Column 2*** shows the **weighted number of responding schools before school replacement** (weighted by student enrolment).
- ***Column 3*** shows the **weighted number of sampled schools before school replacement** (including both responding and non-responding schools, weighted by student enrolment).
- ***Column 4*** shows the unweighted number **of responding schools before school replacement.**
- ***Column 5*** shows the unweighted **number of responding and non-responding schools before school replacement.**
- ***Column 6*** shows the **weighted participation rate of schools after replacement**. This is obtained by dividing Column 7 by Column 8.
- ***Column 7*** shows the **weighted number of responding schools after school replacement** (weighted by student enrolment).
- ***Column 8*** shows the **weighted number of schools sampled after school replacement** (including both responding and non-responding schools, weighted by student enrolment).
- ***Column 9*** shows the unweighted number of responding schools after school replacement.
- ***Column 10*** shows the unweighted number of responding and non-responding schools after school replacement.
- ***Column 11*** shows the **weighted student participation rate after replacement**. This is obtained by dividing Column 12 by Column 13.
- ***Column 12*** shows the **weighted number of students assessed**.
- ***Column 13*** shows the **weighted number of students sampled** (including both students who were assessed and students who were absent on the day of the assessment).
- ***Column 14*** shows the **unweighted number of students assessed.** Note that any students in schools with student-response rates less than 50% were not included in these rates (both weighted and unweighted).
- ***Column 15*** shows the **unweighted number of students sampled** (including both students that were assessed and students who were absent on the day of the assessment). Note that any students in schools where fewer than half of the eligible students were assessed were not included in these rates (neither weighted nor unweighted).

Definition of schools

In some countries, sub-units within schools were sampled instead of schools and this may affect the estimation of the between-school variance components. In Austria, the Czech Republic, Germany, Hungary, Japan, Romania and Slovenia, schools with more than one study programme were split into the units delivering these programmes. In the Netherlands, for schools with both lower and upper secondary programmes, schools were split into units delivering each programme level. In the Flemish Community of Belgium, in the case of multi-campus schools, implantations (campuses) were sampled, whereas in the French Community, in the case of multi-campus schools, the larger administrative units were sampled. In Australia, for schools with more than one campus, the individual campuses were listed for sampling. In Argentina, Croatia and Dubai (UAE), schools that had more than one campus had the locations listed for sampling. In Spain, the schools in the Basque region with multi-linguistic models were split into linguistic models for sampling.

Grade levels

Students assessed in PISA 2009 are at various grade levels. The percentage of students at each grade level is presented by country in Table A2.4a and by gender within each country in Table A2.4b.

[Part 1/1]
Table A2.4a Percentage of students at each grade level

		Grade level											
		7th grade		8th grade		9th grade		10th grade		11th grade		12th grade	
		%	S.E.	%	S.E.	%	S.E.	%	S.E.	%	S.E.	%	S.E.
OECD	Australia	0.0	(0.0)	0.1	(0.0)	10.4	(0.6)	70.8	(0.6)	18.6	(0.6)	0.1	(0.0)
	Austria	0.7	(0.2)	6.2	(1.0)	42.4	(0.9)	50.7	(1.0)	0.0	(0.0)	0.0	c
	Belgium	0.4	(0.2)	5.5	(0.5)	32.0	(0.6)	60.8	(0.7)	1.2	(0.1)	0.0	(0.0)
	Canada	0.0	(0.0)	1.2	(0.2)	13.6	(0.5)	84.1	(0.5)	1.1	(0.1)	0.0	(0.0)
	Chile	1.0	(0.2)	3.9	(0.5)	20.5	(0.8)	69.4	(1.0)	5.2	(0.3)	0.0	(0.0)
	Czech Republic	0.5	(0.2)	3.8	(0.3)	48.9	(1.0)	46.7	(1.1)	0.0	c	0.0	c
	Denmark	0.1	(0.0)	14.7	(0.6)	83.5	(0.8)	1.7	(0.5)	0.0	c	0.0	c
	Estonia	1.6	(0.3)	24.0	(0.7)	72.4	(0.9)	1.8	(0.3)	0.1	(0.1)	0.0	c
	Finland	0.5	(0.1)	11.8	(0.5)	87.3	(0.5)	0.0	c	0.4	(0.1)	0.0	c
	France	1.3	(0.9)	3.6	(0.7)	34.4	(1.2)	56.6	(1.5)	4.0	(0.7)	0.1	(0.0)
	Germany	1.2	(0.2)	11.0	(0.5)	54.8	(0.8)	32.5	(0.8)	0.4	(0.1)	0.0	(0.0)
	Greece	0.4	(0.2)	1.4	(0.5)	5.5	(0.8)	92.7	(1.0)	0.0	c	0.0	c
	Hungary	2.8	(0.6)	7.6	(1.1)	67.1	(1.4)	22.4	(0.9)	0.1	(0.1)	0.0	(0.0)
	Iceland	0.0	c	0.0	c	0.0	(0.0)	98.3	(0.1)	1.7	(0.1)	0.0	c
	Ireland	0.1	(0.0)	2.4	(0.3)	59.1	(1.0)	24.0	(1.4)	14.4	(1.1)	0.0	c
	Israel	0.0	c	0.3	(0.1)	17.9	(1.0)	81.3	(1.0)	0.5	(0.2)	0.0	(0.0)
	Italy	0.1	(0.1)	1.4	(0.3)	16.9	(0.4)	78.4	(0.6)	3.2	(0.3)	0.0	c
	Japan	0.0	c	0.0	c	0.0	c	100.0	(0.0)	0.0	c	0.0	c
	Korea	0.0	c	0.0	(0.0)	4.2	(0.9)	95.1	(0.9)	0.7	(0.1)	0.0	c
	Luxembourg	0.6	(0.1)	11.6	(0.2)	51.6	(0.3)	36.0	(0.2)	0.3	(0.0)	0.0	c
	Mexico	1.7	(0.1)	7.4	(0.3)	34.5	(0.8)	55.6	(0.9)	0.7	(0.2)	0.0	(0.0)
	Netherlands	0.2	(0.2)	2.7	(0.3)	46.2	(1.1)	50.5	(1.1)	0.5	(0.1)	0.0	c
	New Zealand	0.0	c	0.0	c	0.0	(0.0)	5.9	(0.4)	88.8	(0.5)	5.3	(0.3)
	Norway	0.0	c	0.0	c	0.5	(0.1)	99.3	(0.2)	0.2	(0.1)	0.0	c
	Poland	1.0	(0.2)	4.5	(0.4)	93.6	(0.6)	0.9	(0.3)	0.0	c	0.0	c
	Portugal	2.3	(0.3)	9.0	(0.8)	27.9	(1.6)	60.4	(2.2)	0.4	(0.1)	0.0	c
	Slovak Republic	1.0	(0.2)	2.6	(0.3)	35.7	(1.4)	56.9	(1.6)	3.8	(0.8)	0.0	(0.0)
	Slovenia	0.0	c	0.1	(0.1)	3.0	(0.7)	90.7	(0.7)	6.2	(0.2)	0.0	c
	Spain	0.1	(0.0)	9.9	(0.4)	26.5	(0.6)	63.4	(0.7)	0.0	(0.0)	0.0	c
	Sweden	0.1	(0.1)	3.2	(0.3)	95.1	(0.6)	1.6	(0.5)	0.0	c	0.0	c
	Switzerland	0.6	(0.1)	15.5	(0.9)	61.7	(1.3)	21.0	(1.1)	1.2	(0.5)	0.0	(0.0)
	Turkey	0.7	(0.1)	3.5	(0.8)	25.2	(1.3)	66.6	(1.5)	3.8	(0.3)	0.2	(0.1)
	United Kingdom	0.0	c	0.0	c	0.0	c	1.2	(0.1)	98.0	(0.1)	0.8	(0.0)
	United States	0.0	c	0.1	(0.1)	10.9	(0.8)	68.5	(1.0)	20.3	(0.7)	0.1	(0.1)
	OECD average	0.8	(0.1)	5.8	(0.1)	37.0	(0.2)	52.9	(0.2)	9.9	(0.1)	0.5	(0.0)
Partners	Albania	0.4	(0.1)	2.2	(0.3)	50.9	(2.0)	46.4	(2.0)	0.1	(0.0)	0.0	c
	Argentina	4.7	(0.9)	12.9	(1.3)	20.4	(1.2)	57.8	(2.1)	4.3	(0.5)	0.0	c
	Azerbaijan	0.6	(0.2)	5.3	(0.5)	49.4	(1.3)	44.3	(1.3)	0.4	(0.1)	0.0	c
	Brazil	6.8	(0.4)	18.0	(0.7)	37.5	(0.8)	35.7	(0.8)	2.1	(0.1)	0.0	c
	Bulgaria	1.5	(0.3)	6.1	(0.6)	88.7	(0.9)	3.8	(0.6)	0.0	c	0.0	c
	Colombia	4.4	(0.5)	10.3	(0.7)	22.1	(0.8)	42.3	(1.0)	21.0	(1.0)	0.0	c
	Croatia	0.0	c	0.2	(0.2)	77.5	(0.4)	22.3	(0.4)	0.0	c	0.0	c
	Dubai (UAE)	1.1	(0.1)	3.4	(0.1)	14.8	(0.4)	56.9	(0.5)	22.9	(0.4)	0.9	(0.1)
	Hong Kong-China	1.7	(0.2)	7.2	(0.5)	25.2	(0.5)	65.9	(0.9)	0.1	(0.0)	0.0	c
	Indonesia	1.5	(0.5)	6.5	(0.8)	46.0	(3.1)	40.5	(3.2)	5.0	(0.8)	0.5	(0.4)
	Jordan	0.1	(0.1)	1.3	(0.2)	7.0	(0.5)	91.6	(0.6)	0.0	c	0.0	c
	Kazakhstan	0.4	(0.1)	6.4	(0.4)	73.3	(1.9)	19.7	(2.0)	0.1	(0.0)	0.0	c
	Kyrgyzstan	0.2	(0.1)	7.9	(0.5)	71.4	(1.3)	19.8	(1.4)	0.7	(0.1)	0.0	c
	Latvia	2.7	(0.5)	15.5	(0.7)	79.4	(0.9)	2.4	(0.3)	0.1	(0.1)	0.0	(0.0)
	Liechtenstein	0.8	(0.5)	17.5	(1.1)	71.3	(0.8)	10.4	(1.0)	0.0	c	0.0	c
	Lithuania	0.5	(0.1)	10.2	(0.9)	80.9	(0.8)	8.4	(0.6)	0.0	(0.0)	0.0	c
	Macao-China	6.7	(0.1)	19.2	(0.2)	34.9	(0.1)	38.7	(0.1)	0.5	(0.1)	0.0	c
	Montenegro	0.0	c	2.5	(1.7)	82.7	(1.5)	14.8	(0.3)	0.0	c	0.0	c
	Panama	2.9	(0.8)	10.6	(1.6)	30.6	(3.3)	49.8	(4.5)	6.1	(1.4)	0.0	c
	Peru	4.0	(0.4)	8.9	(0.6)	17.1	(0.7)	44.6	(1.1)	25.4	(0.8)	0.0	c
	Qatar	1.7	(0.1)	3.6	(0.1)	13.5	(0.2)	62.6	(0.2)	18.2	(0.2)	0.4	(0.1)
	Romania	0.0	c	7.2	(1.0)	88.6	(1.1)	4.3	(0.6)	0.0	c	0.0	c
	Russian Federation	0.9	(0.2)	10.0	(0.7)	60.1	(1.8)	28.1	(1.6)	0.9	(0.2)	0.0	c
	Serbia	0.2	(0.1)	2.1	(0.5)	96.0	(0.6)	1.7	(0.2)	0.0	c	0.0	c
	Shanghai-China	1.0	(0.2)	4.1	(0.4)	37.4	(0.8)	57.1	(0.9)	0.4	(0.2)	0.0	(0.0)
	Singapore	1.0	(0.2)	2.6	(0.2)	34.7	(0.4)	61.6	(0.3)	0.0	c	0.0	(0.0)
	Chinese Taipei	0.0	c	0.1	(0.0)	34.4	(0.9)	65.5	(0.9)	0.0	(0.0)	0.0	c
	Thailand	0.1	(0.0)	0.5	(0.1)	23.2	(1.1)	73.5	(1.1)	2.7	(0.4)	0.0	c
	Trinidad and Tobago	2.1	(0.2)	8.8	(0.4)	25.3	(0.4)	56.1	(0.4)	7.7	(0.3)	0.0	c
	Tunisia	6.4	(0.4)	13.4	(0.6)	23.9	(0.9)	50.9	(1.4)	5.4	(0.4)	0.0	c
	Uruguay	7.1	(0.8)	10.6	(0.6)	21.5	(0.8)	56.2	(1.1)	4.6	(0.4)	0.0	c

StatLink http://dx.doi.org/10.1787/888932343190

[Part 1/2]
Table A2.4b **Percentage of students at each grade level, by gender**

		Boys – Grade level											
		7th grade		8th grade		9th grade		10th grade		11th grade		12th grade	
		%	S.E.	%	S.E.	%	S.E.	%	S.E.	%	S.E.	%	S.E.
OECD	Australia	0.0	c	0.1	(0.0)	13.1	(0.9)	69.6	(1.1)	17.1	(0.8)	0.1	(0.0)
	Austria	0.7	(0.2)	7.4	(1.2)	42.6	(1.3)	49.3	(1.3)	0.0	(0.0)	0.0	c
	Belgium	0.6	(0.2)	6.4	(0.7)	34.6	(0.9)	57.3	(1.0)	1.1	(0.2)	0.0	(0.0)
	Canada	0.0	(0.0)	1.4	(0.3)	14.6	(0.6)	82.9	(0.6)	1.1	(0.1)	0.0	(0.0)
	Chile	1.3	(0.3)	4.9	(0.6)	23.2	(1.0)	65.9	(1.3)	4.7	(0.3)	0.0	c
	Czech Republic	0.7	(0.2)	4.5	(0.5)	52.5	(2.2)	42.3	(2.4)	0.0	c	0.0	c
	Denmark	0.1	(0.0)	19.5	(0.9)	79.5	(1.0)	0.8	(0.3)	0.0	c	0.0	c
	Estonia	2.4	(0.5)	27.0	(1.0)	69.6	(1.1)	1.0	(0.3)	0.0	c	0.0	c
	Finland	0.6	(0.2)	14.0	(0.8)	85.2	(0.8)	0.0	c	0.2	(0.1)	0.0	c
	France	1.3	(0.9)	4.0	(0.6)	39.6	(1.5)	51.4	(1.9)	3.6	(0.8)	0.0	(0.0)
	Germany	1.4	(0.3)	13.1	(0.7)	56.1	(1.0)	28.8	(0.9)	0.6	(0.1)	0.0	c
	Greece	0.5	(0.2)	1.9	(0.5)	6.2	(1.2)	91.4	(1.5)	0.0	c	0.0	c
	Hungary	3.2	(0.8)	9.3	(1.3)	68.8	(1.6)	18.7	(0.9)	0.0	(0.0)	0.0	(0.0)
	Iceland	0.0	c	0.0	c	0.0	c	98.7	(0.2)	1.3	(0.2)	0.0	c
	Ireland	0.1	(0.0)	2.8	(0.5)	60.9	(1.3)	22.4	(1.5)	13.8	(1.4)	0.0	c
	Israel	0.0	c	0.5	(0.2)	19.9	(1.1)	78.7	(1.2)	1.0	(0.4)	0.0	c
	Italy	0.1	(0.1)	1.7	(0.4)	20.1	(0.6)	75.7	(0.7)	2.5	(0.3)	0.0	c
	Japan	0.0	c	0.0	c	0.0	c	100.0	(0.0)	0.0	c	0.0	c
	Korea	0.0	c	0.1	(0.1)	4.7	(1.3)	94.5	(1.4)	0.7	(0.2)	0.0	c
	Luxembourg	0.8	(0.2)	12.5	(0.4)	52.4	(0.5)	34.0	(0.4)	0.3	(0.1)	0.0	c
	Mexico	2.0	(0.2)	8.8	(0.5)	37.6	(0.9)	51.0	(0.9)	0.5	(0.2)	0.0	c
	Netherlands	0.4	(0.3)	3.0	(0.4)	48.9	(1.3)	47.3	(1.3)	0.3	(0.1)	0.0	c
	New Zealand	0.0	c	0.0	c	0.0	c	6.9	(0.5)	87.9	(0.6)	5.2	(0.5)
	Norway	0.0	c	0.0	c	0.5	(0.1)	99.2	(0.2)	0.3	(0.2)	0.0	c
	Poland	1.5	(0.3)	6.5	(0.6)	91.6	(0.7)	0.5	(0.2)	0.0	c	0.0	c
	Portugal	3.4	(0.5)	10.5	(0.9)	30.9	(2.0)	54.9	(2.6)	0.4	(0.1)	0.0	c
	Slovak Republic	1.4	(0.3)	3.7	(0.5)	40.1	(1.9)	51.6	(2.1)	3.3	(0.7)	0.0	c
	Slovenia	0.0	c	0.1	(0.1)	4.0	(1.2)	91.1	(1.2)	4.7	(0.4)	0.0	c
	Spain	0.1	(0.0)	12.2	(0.6)	28.7	(0.8)	58.9	(0.9)	0.0	(0.0)	0.0	c
	Sweden	0.0	(0.0)	4.1	(0.4)	94.7	(0.6)	1.1	(0.3)	0.0	c	0.0	c
	Switzerland	0.8	(0.2)	18.0	(1.2)	60.7	(1.8)	19.4	(1.8)	1.0	(0.4)	0.1	(0.1)
	Turkey	1.0	(0.2)	4.0	(0.9)	30.2	(1.4)	61.3	(1.7)	3.2	(0.3)	0.2	(0.1)
	United Kingdom	0.0	c	0.0	c	0.0	c	1.3	(0.2)	98.0	(0.2)	0.7	(0.1)
	United States	0.0	c	0.1	(0.0)	13.2	(1.0)	68.6	(1.4)	17.9	(0.9)	0.1	(0.1)
	OECD average	1.0	(0.1)	7.0	(0.1)	40.8	(0.2)	50.8	(0.2)	9.8	(0.1)	0.7	(0.0)
Partners	Albania	0.5	(0.2)	2.6	(0.4)	54.0	(2.0)	42.9	(2.1)	0.0	(0.0)	0.0	c
	Argentina	5.9	(1.1)	15.4	(1.4)	22.7	(1.5)	52.5	(2.4)	3.5	(0.5)	0.0	c
	Azerbaijan	0.6	(0.2)	4.7	(0.5)	47.8	(1.4)	46.5	(1.5)	0.3	(0.1)	0.0	c
	Brazil	8.4	(0.6)	21.0	(0.9)	37.8	(0.8)	31.1	(0.9)	1.7	(0.2)	0.0	c
	Bulgaria	2.0	(0.4)	7.4	(0.9)	86.9	(1.2)	3.7	(0.6)	0.0	c	0.0	c
	Colombia	5.5	(0.9)	11.5	(0.9)	21.9	(1.1)	42.4	(1.4)	18.7	(1.2)	0.0	c
	Croatia	0.0	c	0.1	(0.1)	79.1	(0.6)	20.7	(0.6)	0.0	c	0.0	c
	Dubai (UAE)	1.6	(0.2)	4.5	(0.3)	16.0	(0.6)	53.6	(0.7)	23.1	(0.6)	1.1	(0.2)
	Hong Kong-China	1.9	(0.3)	7.3	(0.6)	26.6	(0.7)	64.1	(1.0)	0.1	(0.1)	0.0	c
	Indonesia	1.8	(0.7)	8.2	(1.0)	49.3	(3.4)	36.2	(3.6)	4.0	(0.9)	0.5	(0.3)
	Jordan	0.1	(0.1)	1.2	(0.4)	7.5	(0.8)	91.2	(0.9)	0.0	c	0.0	c
	Kazakhstan	0.5	(0.1)	7.1	(0.6)	75.2	(2.2)	17.2	(2.3)	0.1	(0.0)	0.0	c
	Kyrgyzstan	0.2	(0.1)	8.9	(0.7)	72.9	(1.6)	17.4	(1.6)	0.5	(0.2)	0.0	c
	Latvia	3.6	(0.9)	19.9	(1.1)	74.7	(1.4)	1.6	(0.4)	0.1	(0.1)	0.0	(0.0)
	Liechtenstein	1.1	(0.7)	19.7	(1.6)	68.9	(1.2)	10.3	(1.2)	0.0	c	0.0	c
	Lithuania	0.6	(0.2)	12.3	(1.2)	80.0	(1.2)	7.2	(0.7)	0.0	c	0.0	c
	Macao-China	8.9	(0.2)	22.0	(0.2)	34.9	(0.2)	33.6	(0.2)	0.5	(0.1)	0.0	c
	Montenegro	0.0	c	3.0	(2.0)	85.0	(1.8)	12.0	(0.4)	0.0	c	0.0	c
	Panama	3.4	(1.1)	13.6	(2.5)	32.6	(4.4)	45.7	(5.5)	4.7	(1.8)	0.0	c
	Peru	4.9	(0.5)	11.2	(0.8)	18.8	(1.0)	42.3	(1.4)	22.9	(0.9)	0.0	c
	Qatar	1.9	(0.1)	4.3	(0.2)	14.8	(0.3)	60.4	(0.3)	18.2	(0.2)	0.4	(0.1)
	Romania	0.0	c	6.3	(1.1)	89.9	(1.3)	3.9	(0.7)	0.0	c	0.0	c
	Russian Federation	1.4	(0.3)	10.4	(0.9)	61.2	(1.9)	26.3	(1.9)	0.8	(0.2)	0.0	c
	Serbia	0.3	(0.1)	2.7	(0.7)	95.6	(0.8)	1.4	(0.2)	0.0	c	0.0	c
	Shanghai-China	1.2	(0.3)	5.1	(0.6)	38.8	(1.2)	54.7	(1.4)	0.2	(0.1)	0.0	c
	Singapore	0.8	(0.2)	2.9	(0.3)	35.7	(0.6)	60.6	(0.5)	0.0	c	0.0	c
	Chinese Taipei	0.0	c	0.2	(0.1)	35.2	(1.5)	64.7	(1.5)	0.0	c	0.0	c
	Thailand	0.2	(0.1)	0.8	(0.2)	26.3	(1.4)	70.5	(1.4)	2.2	(0.5)	0.0	c
	Trinidad and Tobago	2.7	(0.3)	10.7	(0.5)	28.4	(0.6)	51.0	(0.5)	7.1	(0.4)	0.0	c
	Tunisia	8.9	(0.6)	16.8	(0.9)	24.4	(1.1)	45.3	(1.5)	4.7	(0.5)	0.0	c
	Uruguay	9.1	(1.0)	12.0	(0.8)	24.9	(0.8)	50.4	(1.3)	3.6	(0.4)	0.0	c

StatLink http://dx.doi.org/10.1787/888932343190

[Part 2/2]
Table A2.4b Percentage of students at each grade level, by gender

		Girls – Grade level											
		7th grade		8th grade		9th grade		10th grade		11th grade		12th grade	
		%	S.E.	%	S.E.	%	S.E.	%	S.E.	%	S.E.	%	S.E.
OECD	Australia	0.0	(0.0)	0.1	(0.0)	7.9	(0.5)	72.0	(0.8)	20.0	(0.8)	0.1	(0.0)
	Austria	0.6	(0.4)	5.0	(1.2)	42.2	(1.4)	52.1	(1.5)	0.0	(0.0)	0.0	c
	Belgium	0.3	(0.1)	4.5	(0.5)	29.3	(1.1)	64.5	(1.1)	1.3	(0.2)	0.0	(0.0)
	Canada	0.0	(0.0)	1.0	(0.2)	12.5	(0.5)	85.3	(0.5)	1.1	(0.1)	0.0	(0.0)
	Chile	0.7	(0.1)	2.9	(0.5)	17.7	(0.9)	73.0	(1.1)	5.6	(0.4)	0.0	(0.0)
	Czech Republic	0.3	(0.2)	3.1	(0.4)	44.8	(1.9)	51.8	(1.9)	0.0	c	0.0	c
	Denmark	0.1	(0.0)	10.0	(0.7)	87.3	(0.9)	2.5	(0.8)	0.0	c	0.0	c
	Estonia	0.9	(0.3)	20.8	(0.9)	75.4	(1.1)	2.7	(0.5)	0.2	(0.2)	0.0	c
	Finland	0.4	(0.1)	9.6	(0.6)	89.4	(0.6)	0.0	c	0.6	(0.2)	0.0	c
	France	1.3	(0.9)	3.2	(0.9)	29.4	(1.5)	61.6	(1.7)	4.4	(0.8)	0.1	(0.1)
	Germany	1.1	(0.2)	8.8	(0.6)	53.4	(1.1)	36.4	(1.1)	0.3	(0.1)	0.0	(0.0)
	Greece	0.2	(0.2)	0.9	(0.5)	4.9	(0.7)	94.0	(0.9)	0.0	c	0.0	c
	Hungary	2.3	(0.7)	5.9	(1.1)	65.4	(1.6)	26.2	(1.2)	0.2	(0.1)	0.0	c
	Iceland	0.0	c	0.0	c	0.0	(0.1)	97.9	(0.2)	2.1	(0.2)	0.0	c
	Ireland	0.1	(0.1)	2.0	(0.4)	57.3	(1.5)	25.7	(2.0)	15.1	(1.5)	0.0	c
	Israel	0.0	c	0.1	(0.1)	15.9	(1.0)	83.8	(1.1)	0.2	(0.1)	0.0	(0.0)
	Italy	0.2	(0.1)	1.0	(0.2)	13.5	(0.6)	81.4	(0.7)	3.9	(0.3)	0.0	c
	Japan	0.0	c	0.0	c	0.0	c	100.0	(0.0)	0.0	c	0.0	c
	Korea	0.0	c	0.0	c	3.6	(1.0)	95.6	(1.0)	0.8	(0.1)	0.0	c
	Luxembourg	0.4	(0.1)	10.6	(0.3)	50.8	(0.4)	38.0	(0.3)	0.2	(0.1)	0.0	c
	Mexico	1.5	(0.2)	6.1	(0.4)	31.5	(0.9)	60.1	(1.0)	0.8	(0.3)	0.0	(0.0)
	Netherlands	0.1	(0.1)	2.3	(0.4)	43.4	(1.4)	53.5	(1.3)	0.7	(0.2)	0.0	c
	New Zealand	0.0	c	0.0	c	0.1	(0.1)	4.8	(0.5)	89.8	(0.6)	5.4	(0.5)
	Norway	0.0	c	0.0	c	0.4	(0.1)	99.4	(0.2)	0.1	(0.1)	0.0	c
	Poland	0.6	(0.2)	2.5	(0.3)	95.6	(0.7)	1.3	(0.6)	0.0	c	0.0	c
	Portugal	1.4	(0.2)	7.7	(0.8)	25.1	(1.4)	65.4	(1.9)	0.4	(0.1)	0.0	c
	Slovak Republic	0.7	(0.2)	1.5	(0.3)	31.4	(1.8)	62.1	(2.1)	4.3	(0.9)	0.0	(0.0)
	Slovenia	0.0	c	0.0	c	1.9	(0.7)	90.3	(0.8)	7.8	(0.5)	0.0	c
	Spain	0.1	(0.1)	7.6	(0.4)	24.2	(0.7)	68.0	(0.8)	0.0	(0.0)	0.0	c
	Sweden	0.1	(0.1)	2.3	(0.3)	95.4	(0.7)	2.2	(0.7)	0.0	c	0.0	c
	Switzerland	0.4	(0.1)	12.9	(0.9)	62.6	(1.8)	22.7	(2.0)	1.4	(0.6)	0.0	c
	Turkey	0.4	(0.2)	2.9	(0.8)	19.8	(1.3)	72.3	(1.6)	4.4	(0.4)	0.2	(0.1)
	United Kingdom	0.0	c	0.0	c	0.0	c	1.0	(0.1)	98.1	(0.1)	0.9	(0.1)
	United States	0.0	c	0.2	(0.2)	8.5	(0.7)	68.4	(1.1)	22.8	(1.0)	0.1	(0.1)
	OECD average	0.6	(0.1)	5.0	(0.1)	35.6	(0.2)	55.0	(0.2)	10.2	(0.1)	0.5	(0.0)
Partners	Albania	0.2	(0.1)	1.8	(0.4)	47.6	(2.3)	50.2	(2.3)	0.2	(0.1)	0.0	c
	Argentina	3.6	(0.9)	10.7	(1.5)	18.4	(1.2)	62.3	(2.2)	4.9	(0.6)	0.0	c
	Azerbaijan	0.6	(0.3)	5.8	(0.6)	51.0	(1.5)	42.1	(1.4)	0.4	(0.1)	0.0	c
	Brazil	5.4	(0.4)	15.3	(0.6)	37.1	(0.9)	39.7	(0.9)	2.5	(0.2)	0.0	c
	Bulgaria	0.9	(0.3)	4.6	(0.7)	90.6	(1.0)	3.9	(0.7)	0.0	c	0.0	c
	Colombia	3.3	(0.4)	9.1	(0.8)	22.4	(1.0)	42.2	(1.1)	23.0	(1.1)	0.0	c
	Croatia	0.0	c	0.2	(0.2)	75.8	(0.6)	24.1	(0.5)	0.0	c	0.0	c
	Dubai (UAE)	0.6	(0.1)	2.2	(0.2)	13.5	(0.5)	60.4	(0.6)	22.7	(0.7)	0.6	(0.1)
	Hong Kong-China	1.5	(0.2)	7.1	(0.6)	23.5	(0.6)	67.9	(1.0)	0.0	c	0.0	c
	Indonesia	1.2	(0.3)	4.9	(0.8)	42.7	(3.7)	44.6	(3.8)	6.0	(1.1)	0.6	(0.5)
	Jordan	0.1	(0.0)	1.3	(0.3)	6.5	(0.7)	92.1	(0.9)	0.0	c	0.0	c
	Kazakhstan	0.4	(0.1)	5.7	(0.5)	71.5	(2.0)	22.3	(2.1)	0.2	(0.1)	0.0	c
	Kyrgyzstan	0.1	(0.1)	7.1	(0.6)	69.9	(1.5)	22.0	(1.6)	0.9	(0.2)	0.0	c
	Latvia	1.7	(0.4)	11.2	(0.6)	83.9	(0.8)	3.1	(0.4)	0.1	(0.1)	0.0	c
	Liechtenstein	0.6	(0.6)	15.0	(1.5)	74.0	(1.2)	10.4	(1.6)	0.0	c	0.0	c
	Lithuania	0.3	(0.1)	8.1	(0.8)	81.9	(0.9)	9.6	(0.7)	0.0	(0.0)	0.0	c
	Macao-China	4.4	(0.1)	16.3	(0.2)	34.9	(0.2)	43.9	(0.2)	0.5	(0.1)	0.0	c
	Montenegro	0.0	c	2.0	(1.4)	80.3	(1.3)	17.8	(0.4)	0.0	c	0.0	c
	Panama	2.4	(0.6)	7.7	(1.1)	28.7	(3.0)	53.8	(4.0)	7.5	(1.6)	0.0	c
	Peru	3.2	(0.4)	6.5	(0.6)	15.4	(0.8)	47.0	(1.2)	27.9	(1.2)	0.0	c
	Qatar	1.4	(0.1)	3.0	(0.1)	12.1	(0.2)	64.9	(0.2)	18.1	(0.2)	0.5	(0.1)
	Romania	0.0	c	8.1	(1.5)	87.3	(1.5)	4.7	(0.6)	0.0	c	0.0	c
	Russian Federation	0.5	(0.1)	9.7	(0.8)	59.0	(2.0)	29.8	(1.8)	1.0	(0.2)	0.0	c
	Serbia	0.1	(0.1)	1.4	(0.5)	96.4	(0.6)	2.0	(0.2)	0.0	c	0.0	c
	Shanghai-China	0.8	(0.2)	3.0	(0.4)	36.1	(1.0)	59.5	(1.0)	0.6	(0.2)	0.0	(0.0)
	Singapore	1.2	(0.2)	2.3	(0.3)	33.7	(0.5)	62.7	(0.4)	0.0	c	0.0	(0.0)
	Chinese Taipei	0.0	c	0.0	(0.0)	33.7	(1.5)	66.3	(1.5)	0.0	(0.0)	0.0	c
	Thailand	0.0	c	0.3	(0.1)	20.9	(1.4)	75.8	(1.4)	3.0	(0.4)	0.0	c
	Trinidad and Tobago	1.5	(0.3)	6.9	(0.5)	22.3	(0.6)	61.0	(0.6)	8.3	(0.4)	0.0	c
	Tunisia	4.2	(0.4)	10.3	(0.5)	23.4	(1.0)	56.1	(1.4)	6.0	(0.5)	0.0	c
	Uruguay	5.4	(0.6)	9.4	(0.5)	18.5	(0.9)	61.4	(1.2)	5.4	(0.6)	0.0	c

StatLink http://dx.doi.org/10.1787/888932343190

Students in or out of the regular education system in Argentina

The low performance of 15-year-old students in Argentina is, to some extent, influenced by a fairly large proportion of 15-year-olds enrolled in programmes outside the regular education system. Table A2.5 shows the proportion of students inside and outside the regular education system, alongside their performance in PISA 2009.

Table A2.5 Percentage of students and mean scores in reading, mathematics and science, according to whether students are in or out of the regular education system in Argentina

	Percentage of students		Mean performance					
			Reading		Mathematics		Science	
	%	S.E.	Mean	S.E.	Mean	S.E.	Mean	S.E.
Students in the regular educational system[1]	60.9	2.2	439	5.1	421	4.8	439	4.9
Students out of the regular educational system[2]	39.1	2.2	335	8.0	337	6.7	341	8.3

1. Students who are not in grade 10 or 11 and in programme 3, 4, 5, 6, 7 or 8.
2. Students who are in grade 10 or 11 and in programme 3, 4, 5, 6, 7 or 8.
StatLink http://dx.doi.org/10.1787/888932343190

ANNEX A3
STANDARD ERRORS, SIGNIFICANCE TESTS AND SUB-GROUP COMPARISONS

The statistics in this report represent estimates of national performance based on samples of students, rather than values that could be calculated if every student in every country had answered every question. Consequently, it is important to measure the degree of uncertainty of the estimates. In PISA, each estimate has an associated degree of uncertainty, which is expressed through a standard error. The use of confidence intervals provides a way to make inferences about the population means and proportions in a manner that reflects the uncertainty associated with the sample estimates. From an observed sample statistic and assuming a normal distribution, it can be inferred that the corresponding population result would lie within the confidence interval in 95 out of 100 replications of the measurement on different samples drawn from the same population.

In many cases, readers are primarily interested in whether a given value in a particular country is different from a second value in the same or another country, *e.g.* whether females in a country perform better than males in the same country. In the tables and charts used in this report, differences are labelled as statistically significant when a difference of that size, smaller or larger, would be observed less than 5% of the time, if there were actually no difference in corresponding population values. Similarly, the risk of reporting a correlation as significant if there is, in fact, no correlation between two measures, is contained at 5%.

Throughout the report, significance tests were undertaken to assess the statistical significance of the comparisons made.

Gender differences

Gender differences in student performance or other indices were tested for statistical significance. Positive differences indicate higher scores for males while negative differences indicate higher scores for females. Generally, differences marked in bold in the tables in this volume are statistically significant at the 95% confidence level.

Performance differences between the top and bottom quartiles of PISA indices and scales

Differences in average performance between the top and bottom quarters of the PISA indices and scales were tested for statistical significance. Figures marked in bold indicate that performance between the top and bottom quarters of students on the respective index is statistically significantly different at the 95% confidence level.

Change in the performance per unit of the index

For many tables, the difference in student performance per unit of the index shown was calculated. Figures in bold indicate that the differences are statistically significantly different from zero at the 95% confidence level.

Relative risk or increased likelihood

The relative risk is a measure of association between an antecedent factor and an outcome factor. The relative risk is simply the ratio of two risks, i.e. the risk of observing the outcome when the antecedent is present and the risk of observing the outcome when the antecedent is not present. Figure A3.1 presents the notation that is used in the following.

■ Figure A3.1 ■

Labels used in a two-way table

p_{11}	p_{12}	$p_{1.}$
p_{21}	p_{22}	$p_{2.}$
$p_{.1}$	$p_{.2}$	$p_{..}$

$p_{..}$ is equal to $\frac{n_{..}}{n_{..}}$, with $n_{..}$ the total number of students and $p_{..}$ is therefore equal to 1, $p_{i.}$, $p_{.j}$ respectively represent the marginal probabilities for each row and for each column. The marginal probabilities are equal to the marginal frequencies divided by the total number of students. Finally, the p_{ij} represent the probabilities for each cell and are equal to the number of observations in a particular cell divided by the total number of observations.

In PISA, the rows represent the antecedent factor with the first row for "having the antecedent" and the second row for "not having the antecedent" and the columns represent the outcome with, the first column for "having the outcome" and the second column for "not having the outcome". The relative risk is then equal to:

$$RR = \frac{(p_{11} / p_{1.})}{(p_{21} / p_{2.})}$$

Figures in bold in the data tables presented in Annex B of this report indicate that the relative risk is statistically significantly different from 1 at the 95% confidence level.

Difference in reading performance between public and private schools

Differences in performance between public and private schools were tested for statistical significance. For this purpose, government-dependent and government-independent private schools were jointly considered as private schools. Positive differences represent higher scores for public schools while negative differences represent higher scores for private schools. Figures in bold in data tables presented in Annex B of this report indicate statistically significant different scores at the 95% confidence level.

Difference in reading performance between native students and students with an immigrant background

Differences in performance between native and non-native students were tested for statistical significance. For this purpose, first-generation and second-generation students were jointly considered as students with an immigrant background. Positive differences represent higher scores for native students, while negative differences represent higher scores for first-generation and second-generation students. Figures in bold in data tables presented in this volume indicate statistically significantly different scores at the 95% confidence level.

Differences in student and school characteristics by programme orientation, programme level and school type

Differences in some student and school characteristics were tested for statistical significance between lower- and upper-secondary schools, general and vocational programmes, or public and private schools. In comparing lower and upper secondary schools, positive differences represent higher values for lower secondary schools while negative differences represent higher values for upper secondary schools. In comparing general and vocational programmes, positive differences represent higher values for general programmes while negative differences represent higher values for vocational programmes. In comparing public and private schools, positive differences represent higher values for public schools while negative differences represent higher values for private schools. For this purpose, government-dependent and government-independent private schools were jointly considered as private schools. Figures in bold in data tables presented in Annex B of this report indicate statistically significant different scores at the 95% confidence level.

ANNEX A4
QUALITY ASSURANCE

Quality assurance procedures were implemented in all parts of PISA 2009, as was done for all previous PISA surveys.

The consistent quality and linguistic equivalence of the PISA 2009 assessment instruments were facilitated by providing countries with equivalent source versions of the assessment instruments in English and French, and requiring countries (other than those assessing students in English and French) to prepare and consolidate two independent translations using both source versions. Precise translation and adaptation guidelines were supplied, also including instructions for selecting and training the translators. For each country, the translation and format of the assessment instruments (including test materials, marking guides, questionnaires and manuals) were verified by expert translators appointed by the PISA Consortium before they were used in the PISA 2009 Field Trial and Main Study. These translators' mother tongue was the language of instruction in the country concerned and they were knowledgeable about education systems. For further information on the PISA translation procedures, see the *PISA 2009 Technical Report* (OECD, forthcoming).

The survey was implemented through standardised procedures. The PISA Consortium provided comprehensive manuals that explained the implementation of the survey, including precise instructions for the work of School Co-ordinators and scripts for Test Administrators to use during the assessment sessions. Proposed adaptations to survey procedures, or proposed modifications to the assessment session script, were submitted to the PISA Consortium for approval prior to verification. The PISA Consortium then verified the national translation and adaptation of these manuals.

To establish the credibility of PISA as valid and unbiased, and to encourage uniformity in administering the assessment sessions, Test Administrators in participating countries were selected using the following criteria: it was required that the Test Administrator not be the reading, mathematics or science instructor of any students in the sessions he or she would administer for PISA; it was recommended that the Test Administrator not be a member of the staff of any school where he or she would administer for PISA; and it was considered preferable that the Test Administrator not be a member of the staff of any school in the PISA sample. Participating countries organised an in-person training session for Test Administrators.

Participating countries were required to ensure that: Test Administrators worked with the School Co-ordinator to prepare the assessment session, including updating student tracking forms and identifying excluded students; no extra time was given for the cognitive items (while it was permissible to give extra time for the student questionnaire); no instrument was administered before the two one-hour parts of the cognitive session; Test Administrators recorded the student participation status on the student tracking forms and filled in a Session Report Form; no cognitive instrument was permitted to be photocopied; no cognitive instrument could be viewed by school staff before the assessment session; and Test Administrators returned the material to the National Centre immediately after the assessment sessions.

National Project Managers were encouraged to organise a follow-up session when more than 15% of the PISA sample was not able to attend the original assessment session.

National Quality Monitors from the PISA Consortium visited all National Centres to review data-collection procedures. Finally, School Quality Monitors from the PISA Consortium visited a sample of 15 schools during the assessment. For further information on the field operations, see the *PISA 2009 Technical Report* (OECD, forthcoming).

Marking procedures were designed to ensure consistent and accurate application of the marking guides outlined in the PISA Operations Manuals. National Project Managers were required to submit proposed modifications to these procedures to the Consortium for approval. Reliability studies to analyse the consistency of marking were implemented, these are discussed in more detail below.

Software specially designed for PISA facilitated data entry, detected common errors during data entry, and facilitated the process of data cleaning. Training sessions familiarised National Project Managers with these procedures.

For a description of the quality assurance procedures applied in PISA and in the results, see the *PISA 2009 Technical Report* (OECD, forthcoming).

The results of data adjudication show that the PISA Technical Standards were fully met in all countries and economies that participated in PISA 2009, though for one country, some serious doubts were raised. Analysis of the data for Azerbaijan suggest that the PISA Technical Standards may not have been fully met for the following four main reasons: *i)* the order of difficulty of the clusters is inconsistent with previous experience and the ordering varies across booklets; *ii)* the percentage correct on some items is higher than that of the highest scoring countries; *iii)* the difficulty of the clusters varies widely across booklets; and *iv)* the coding of items in Azerbaijan is at an extremely high level of agreement between independent coders, and was judged, on some items, to be too lenient. However, further investigation of the survey instruments, the procedures for test implementation and coding of student responses at the national level did not provide sufficient evidence of systematic errors or violations of the PISA Technical Standards. Azerbaijan's data are, therefore, included in the PISA 2009 international dataset.

For the PISA 2009 assessment in Austria, a dispute between teacher unions and the education minister has led to the announcement of a boycott of PISA which was withdrawn after the first week of testing. The boycott required the OECD to remove identifiable cases from the dataset. Although the Austrian dataset met the PISA 2009 technical standards after the removal of these cases, the negative atmosphere in regard to educational assessment has affected the conditions under which the assessment was administered and could have adversely affected student motivation to respond to the PISA tasks. The comparability of the 2009 data with data from earlier PISA assessments can therefore not be ensured and data for Austria have therefore been excluded from trend comparisons.

ANNEX A5
TECHNICAL NOTES ON ANALYSES IN VOLUME IV

Technical notes on multilevel models (within-country models)

Chapter 2 presents between- and within-country analyses of the relationship between performance and a range of variables in education policy and practice. The latter analyses, which examine the relationship between school and student characteristics and performance in each school system, are performed using two-level regression models (the student and school levels). These models take into account five **plausible values** estimated for each student's performance on the reading scale. **Sample weights** are applied at both the student and school levels and cases of missing data are assigned values through **multiple imputation**. Models were estimated using Mplus® software (Muthén and Muthén, 2007).

PISA reports student performance through **plausible values.** The main reason for using plausible values is to transform discontinuous variables, such as test scores, into a continuous latent feature, such as underlying ability. This reduces biased estimates when measuring underlying ability through a test using a relatively small number of items. To compute **plausible values, posterior distributions** are computed mathematically around the reported test scores. Five random values are then drawn from the **posterior distributions**, which are subsequently assigned to each student. The international *PISA Database* includes five **plausible values** for each of the performance scales. For a more detailed description on **plausible values** and their use, see *PISA Data Analysis Manual* (OECD, 2009d).

Weights are used at both the student and school levels. The purpose of these weights is to adjust the differences in the probabilities for students being selected in a sample. These differences are due to factors at both the school and the student levels, since PISA applies a two-stage sample design. A sample weight for a student i in a school j is the product of the following two base weights: a **school weight,** which is reciprocal to the probability of the school j being included in the sample, and a **student weight,** which is reciprocal to the probability of the selection of student i within school j. In practice, this weight is further multiplied by other factors, such as for non-participation and trimming of extreme school or student weights. A full description of the weighting methods used is in the *PISA 2009 Technical Report* (OECD, forthcoming). For the multilevel analysis, **student final weights** (W_FSTUWT) and **school weights** (W_FSCHWT) are used in Mplus® software. By default, Mplus® software transfers these weights into the within-school weights (W_{ij}) and between-school weights (W_j) with the following formulae, where n_j is the number of sampled students in school j and n is the number of sampled students in a country.

Within-school weights:

$$W_{ij} = (W\_FSTUWT)\frac{n_j}{\Sigma_i (W\_FSTUWT_{ij})}$$

Between-school weights:

$$W_j = (W\_FSCHWT)\frac{n}{\Sigma_{i,j} W_{ij} (W\_FSCHWT_j)}$$

Multiple imputation replaces each missing value with a set of plausible values that represent the uncertainty about the right value to impute. The multiple imputed data sets are then analysed by using standard procedures for complete data and by combining results from these analyses. Five imputed values are computed for each missing value. Different methods can be used according to the pattern of missing values. For arbitrary missing data patterns, the **MCMC (Monte Carlo Markov Chain) approach** can be used. This approach is used with the **SAS procedure MI** for the multilevel analyses in the multilevel analysis in this volume. **Multiple imputation** is conducted separately for each model and each country, except for the model with all variables (Tables IV.2.14a, IV.2.14b and IV.2.14c) in which the data were constructed from imputed data for the individual models, such as the model for learning environment, model for selecting and grouping students, etc. Where continuous values are generated for missing discrete variables, these are rounded to the nearest discrete value of the variable. Each of the five plausible value of readings is analysed by Mplus® software using one of the five imputed data sets, which were combined taking account of the between imputation variance.

The resulting estimates and standard errors take into account PISA's complex sampling design, the **measurement error** of reading performance by using five **plausible values** and the uncertainty of assigning values to missing data through **multiple imputation**.

In Volume IV, these **multilevel regression models** are estimated to assess the relationship between schools' features regarding four key organisational dimensions and their learning environment. More specifically, the five sets of models refer to schools' policies on selecting and grouping students (Tables IV.2.2b and IV.2.2c), governance (Tables IV.2.4b and IV.2.4c), assessment and accountability arrangements (Tables IV.2.9b and IV.2.9c), school resources (Tables IV.2.12b and IV.2.12c) and the learning environment (Tables IV.2.13b and IV.2.13c). A sixth model includes all these variables in addition to those related to students' reading habits, which are discussed in detail in Volume III, *Learning to Learn* (Tables IV.2.14b and IV.2.14c).

For each of these six within-country analyses, two models are estimated. The first model estimates the relationship between each group of variables and reading performance without accounting for the socio-economic and demographic background of students and schools; the second model estimates the same relationship after accounting for the socio-economic and demographic background of students and schools.

Occasionally in the models with many variables, the model does not converge due to an insufficient number of schools to fit the large number of school-level variables. Mplus® software usually indicates which variable is causing the problem (due possibly to near colinearity with other variables), and after omitting this variable, the model would converge successfully. These variables omitted from the models are given "c" in the tables for the multilevel regression results. This does not bias the estimates presented.

For example, the estimates presented in Table IV.2.2b result from a **two-level regression model** with five **plausible values** on reading performance as the dependent variable, and the variables related to the schools' policies on selecting and grouping students (including school selectivity, schools very likely to transfer students, schools with ability grouping for all subjects and the percentage of students that have repeated a grade) as independent variables. The models are weighted at both the student and school levels. If a variable is missing for a particular school or student, it is assigned values through multiple imputation. The estimates in Table IV.2.2c result from a similar model that also includes the students' gender, immigration background, language spoken at home, index of economic, social and economic status as a linear and a quadratic term; and a schools' average *PISA index of economic, social and economic status*, size as both a linear and a quadratic term and location. Table IV.2.2a provides the **variance decomposition** and **explained variance**, which are derived from the results of these models.

Technical notes on country fixed-effect regression models

Country fixed-effect regression models (Table IV.2.3, Table IV.2.5, Table IV.2.6, Table IV.2.8 and Table IV.2.10) are particularly useful for estimating the interaction between country-level variables and school- or student-level variables, such as the relationship between country-level selection policies (*e.g.* first age of selection) and how students' socio-economic background is related to performance (Table IV.2.3). These models pool the entire sample of cases and include **dummy variable** indicators for each country. These **dummy variables** absorb any differences between school systems so estimates are interpreted as the relationship in an average country. Students are weighed proportionally within each country/economy so that each school system contributes an equal number of weighed cases to the analysis. Models are run using **replicate weights** to account for the complex sampling design of PISA.

Technical notes on latent profile analysis

This section describes the methods used for classifying countries in Chapter 3. Four analyses were performed, each to identify country groupings with respect to how school systems select and sort students into schools and classrooms, the gouvernance of school systems, assessment and accountability policies and the amount and form of resources spent.

Method

A key aim of the report is to understand the similarities and differences among countries in terms of system-level policies and practices. Inevitably, each country has its own set of policies for selecting and sorting students into schools and classrooms, decision-making hierarchy, assessment and accountability policies, and budget to spend on education. **Latent profile analysis** is used to ascertain whether countries can be reliably assigned to a small number of groups that share similar profiles. Unlike traditional cluster analysis, **latent profile analysis** is model-based, and so provides the opportunity to asses the validity of the latent profile classes rigorously.

Latent profile analysis is a method that allows researchers to ascertain whether individual observations – in the context of this volume, students – can be reliably assigned to a small number of groups that share similar profiles. In a sense, **latent profile analysis** "clusters" students into unique profile groups. **Latent profile analysis** assumes that the population distribution of the observed variables is a mixture of several normal distributions. Thus, each variable y_i, given the model parameters, can be represented as a weighted mixture of K classes, where K is specified by the analyst according to theory, although exploratory studies of the number of latent profiles can also be conducted. The distribution for each class was defined by a mean vector and a covariance vector (Pastor et al, 2007).

In the report, **latent profile analysis** was conducted with *multiple categorical latent variables*. This model assumes that there are several dimensions, or latent variables, when classifying countries into groups. Given that **latent profile analysis** is model-based, several dimensions were hypothesised according to previous studies or researchers' models. This approach allows more groups to be extracted from the 34 OECD countries examined compared to using one categorical latent variable.

Figure A5.1 illustrates a two categorical latent variables model, that is, a model with two dimensions. In Figure A5.1, the first dimension, or categorical latent variable, C1 is measured by five variables and the second dimension C2 is measured by two variables. Their means are specified to vary only across the classes within each dimension. After grouping countries into a few classes within each dimension, these groups are assigned according to the combination of the two dimensions, C1 and C2. Thus, a model with two dimensions in which two classes are extracted in each dimension produces four groups. The models were estimated according to **maximum likelihood,** with robust standard errors. The number of dimensions estimated was decided based on the theory underlying the classification variables, and the number of classes to extract in each dimension was based on the theory and the model fit.

In the classification of school systems according to their assessment and accountability policies, two dimensions (or latent variables) were identified. The first one referred to assessments or achievement data used for information and benchmarking purposes; the second referred to assessments used for decision-making. For each dimension, two classes were extracted and, given the possible configurations of these two dimensions, four groups were produced.

Models were estimated for the 34 OECD countries. School data for France were not available because the school questionnaire was not administered. Partner countries and economies were grouped into each class using the estimates for the OECD countries. Once the estimates for the 34 OECD countries were obtained, these coefficients were applied to partner countries and economies to find their fit within the classes determined for OECD countries. The fit statistics for partner countries and economies using the OECD estimates were generally satisfactory, except for the **latent profile analysis** of selecting and sorting of students into schools and classrooms (Table A5.1).

Mplus® software was used to estimate the **latent profile analyses**.

■ Figure A5.1 ■

Latent profile analysis with two categorical latent variables

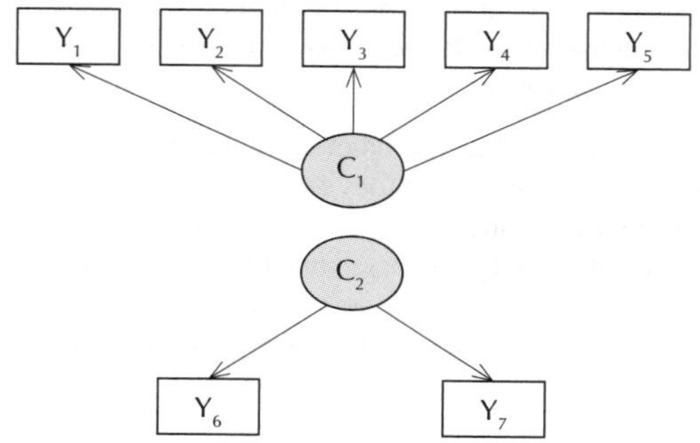

Missing data

Some information for the variables used in the **latent profile analysis** was not available for the entire sample of school systems. For estimating parameters in models with missing data, the model-based approach for categorical and continuous data, which is implemented in Mplus® software, is used. Model-based approaches can estimate parameters even when data are missing (Lüdtke, Robitzsch, Trautwein and Köller, 2007). Specifically, Mplus® software uses the **EM algorithm** (for a detailed description, see Dempster, Laird and Rubin, 1977) and assumes that the missing data are missing at random (MAR). MAR means missing values on an observed variable are not dependent on that variable but may be a function of other variables. For example, if a school system is missing data on "repetition rates", it is not assumed that this is due to the actual repetition rate of the school, but may be due to other variables measured in the school system (Schafer and Graham, 2002).

Models

In Chapter 3, **latent profile analysis** was conducted separately for each of the following sections:

- Selecting and grouping students into schools, grades and programmes
- Governance of school systems
- Assessment and accountability policies
- Resources invested in education

For each analysis, theory and model fit were combined to develop the final model presented in the report. For details on the rationale used to select the variables and dimensions applied in each analysis, see Chapter 3.

The model for "selecting and grouping students into schools, grades and programmes" has three dimensions, or categorical latent variables: vertical selection, horizontal selection at the system level and horizontal selection at the school level. The first dimension, vertical selection, has two variables: the proportion of students who did not start primary school within the two-year range most common in the country; and the average proportion of grade repetition. The second dimension, horizontal selection at the system level, has three variables: the number of programmes available to 15-year-old students, the age of first selection into these programmes, and the proportion of selective schools in the school system. The third dimension, horizontal selection at the school level, is composed of two variables: the proportion of schools that group students by ability in all subjects, and the proportion of schools that are very likely to transfer students with low academic achievement, behavioural problems or special learning needs. Given the model fit and the theory, two classes are extracted for vertical differentiation and horizontal differentiation at the school level. Three classes were extracted for horizontal differentiation at the system level. Given the combination of these classes, school systems were sorted into 12 groups (2 x 2 x 3).

The model for the governance of school systems has two dimensions: school autonomy and school competition. School autonomy comprises four variables measuring school autonomy in curricula and assessment policies: the proportion of schools for which principals and/or teachers have considerable responsibility in establishing students assessment policies, choosing which textbooks are used, determining course content, and deciding which courses are offered. School competition comprises

two variables: the proportion of schools that compete with other schools for student enrolment and the proportion of schools that are privately managed. Given the model fit for different models and the theory, the final model estimates two classes for each dimension. The combination of these classes renders four groups (2 x 2) into which school systems are classified.

The model for school systems' assessment and accountability policies has two dimensions: assessments used for information and benchmarking and assessments used for decision making. Assessments used for information and benchmarking has five variables: the proportion of schools informing parents about their child's standing with respect to a national or regional population of students, the proportion of schools that use achievement data to compare themselves to other schools, the proportion of schools that use achievement data to monitor their progress from year to year, the proportion of schools whose achievement data is tracked by administrative authorities, and the proportion of schools that make their achievement data public. The second dimension, assessments used for decision making, is measured by three variables: the proportion of schools that use achievement data to make changes about the curriculum and instruction, the proportion of schools that use achievement data to allocate resources and the proportion of schools that use achievement data to make judgments about teacher effectiveness. Given the model fit for different models and the theory, the final model estimates two classes for each dimension. The combination of these classes renders four groups (2 x 2) into which school systems are classified.

The model for resources invested in school systems has two dimensions: the amount of resources invested and the way resources are invested. The amount of resources invested in education uses one variable, which is the cumulative expenditure in education per student from age 6 to 15. The way resources are invested in education uses two variables: the average class size in the country and teachers' salaries relative to per capita GDP. Given the model fit for different models and the theory, the final model estimates three classes for the first dimension and two classes for the second dimension. The combination of these classes renders six potential groups (3 x 2) into which school systems are classified. However, given the observed data, countries are sorted into only five of these six groups.

Entropy index

Table A5.1 shows the entropy values for each **latent profile analysis**. The entropy is measured on a zero-to-one scale, with a value of one indicating that countries are perfectly classified. Higher values of entropy indicate better classification of countries.

Table IV.A5.1 Entropy value for each latent profile analysis

	Selecting and grouping students	Governance of school systems	Assessment and accountability policies	Resources invested in education
OECD countries	0.926	0.969	0.967	0.922
Partner countries	0.729	0.884	0.942	0.948

StatLink http://dx.doi.org/10.1787/888932343513

Results

Tables A5.2 to A5.5 show the values used to estimate the latent profile analyses and the resulting groups into which each country is classified.

[Part 1/1]
Table A5.2 **Data used for the "selecting and grouping students into schools, grades and programmes" latent profile analysis and latent class for each school system**

		Vertical differentiation		Horizontal differentiation at the system level			Horizontal differentiation at the school level		
		Students out of modal starting ages (proportion)	Students who repeated one or more grades (%)	First age of selection	Number of school types or distinct educational programmes	Selective schools (proportion)	Schools that transfer students to other schools due to low achievement, behavioural problems or special learning needs (proportion)	Schools that group students by ability in all subjects (proportion)	Latent class
OECD	Australia	0.17	8.4	16	1	0.34	0.03	0.04	1
	Austria	0.05	12.6	10	4	0.61	0.52	0.06	9
	Belgium	0.12	34.9	12	4	0.17	0.48	0.19	10
	Canada	0.28	8.4	16	1	0.29	0.13	0.13	1
	Chile	0.14	23.4	16	1	0.41	0.24	0.30	4
	Czech Republic	0.03	4.0	11	5	0.53	0.22	0.07	9
	Denmark	0.09	4.4	16	1	0.05	0.06	0.06	1
	Estonia	0.06	5.6	15	1	0.30	0.10	0.12	1
	Finland	0.01	2.8	16	1	0.04	0.02	0.01	1
	France	w	w	w	w	w	w	w	w
	Germany	0.04	21.4	10	4	0.72	0.24	0.11	10
	Greece	0.04	5.7	15	2	0.06	0.42	0.00	1
	Hungary	0.06	11.1	11	3	0.87	0.14	0.03	9
	Iceland	0.02	0.9	16	1	0.03	0.00	0.11	1
	Ireland	0.08	12.0	15	4	0.24	0.01	0.09	5
	Israel	0.07	7.5	15	2	0.55	0.23	0.23	5
	Italy	0.06	16.0	14	3	0.42	0.20	0.14	5
	Japan	0.00	c	15	2	0.88	0.08	0.11	5
	Korea	0.00	c	14	3	0.51	0.06	0.04	5
	Luxembourg	0.11	36.5	13	4	0.43	0.68	0.49	8
	Mexico	0.11	21.5	15	3	0.41	0.33	0.16	6
	Netherlands	0.15	26.7	12	7	0.88	0.15	0.44	12
	New Zealand	0.07	5.1	16	1	0.27	0.03	0.05	1
	Norway	0.05	c	16	1	0.06	0.01	0.05	1
	Poland	0.00	5.3	16	1	0.17	0.08	0.04	1
	Portugal	0.14	35.0	15	3	0.01	0.01	0.08	6
	Slovak Republic	0.02	3.8	11	5	0.63	0.30	0.07	9
	Slovenia	0.05	1.5	14	3	0.29	0.22	0.05	5
	Spain	0.09	35.3	16	1	0.03	0.07	0.07	2
	Sweden	0.09	4.6	16	1	0.04	0.03	0.09	1
	Switzerland	0.11	22.8	12	4	0.65	0.21	0.39	12
	Turkey	0.09	13.0	11	3	0.44	0.35	0.28	11
	United Kingdom	0.17	2.2	16	1	0.17	0.02	0.08	1
	United States	0.18	14.2	16	1	0.27	0.13	0.07	1
Partners	Albania	0.03	4.7	m	m	0.53	0.17	0.27	5
	Argentina	0.11	33.8	15	3	0.21	0.15	0.28	2
	Azerbaijan	0.07	1.7	15	2	0.64	0.15	0.24	5
	Brazil	0.28	40.2	17	1	0.11	0.14	0.21	2
	Bulgaria	0.05	5.6	13	3	0.76	0.35	0.19	11
	Colombia	0.23	33.9	15	2	0.33	0.41	0.19	4
	Croatia	0.02	2.8	15	5	0.94	0.18	0.21	9
	Dubai (UAE)	0.22	12.6	15	3	0.72	0.20	0.37	5
	Hong Kong-China	0.17	15.6	15	2	0.84	0.12	0.11	5
	Indonesia	0.12	18.0	15	1	0.71	0.41	0.20	7
	Jordan	0.09	6.6	16	1	0.35	0.46	0.46	3
	Kazakhstan	0.04	1.7	m	m	0.36	0.13	0.36	1
	Kyrgyzstan	0.08	4.3	15	4	0.61	0.38	0.19	7
	Latvia	0.05	11.1	16	1	0.25	0.15	0.10	1
	Liechtenstein	0.07	21.5	11	3	0.80	0.00	0.04	9
	Lithuania	0.06	3.9	15	2	0.14	0.07	0.15	1
	Macao-China	0.22	43.7	16	1	0.74	0.48	0.20	8
	Montenegro	0.02	1.8	15	3	0.59	0.07	0.29	5
	Panama	0.13	31.8	16	m	0.46	0.32	0.07	8
	Peru	0.20	28.1	m	m	0.23	0.27	0.33	4
	Qatar	0.30	14.9	15	4	0.44	0.45	0.37	7
	Romania	0.07	4.2	14	3	0.57	0.40	0.22	7
	Russian Federation	0.05	3.2	15	3	0.23	0.14	0.38	1
	Serbia	0.03	2.0	m	m	0.85	0.30	0.17	11
	Shanghai-China	0.19	7.5	14	4	0.57	0.15	0.13	5
	Singapore	0.05	5.4	12	4	0.84	0.01	0.14	9
	Chinese Taipei	0.17	1.6	15	3	0.53	0.37	0.06	7
	Thailand	0.05	3.5	15	2	0.70	0.10	0.19	5
	Trinidad and Tobago	0.20	28.8	11	4	0.61	0.14	0.15	10
	Tunisia	0.05	43.2	16	1	0.21	0.26	0.03	2
	Uruguay	0.09	38.0	12	1	0.10	0.09	0.12	2

StatLink http://dx.doi.org/10.1787/888932343513

[Part 1/1]

Table A5.3 **Data used for the "governance of school systems" latent profile analysis and latent class for each school system**

		School autonomy for curriculum and assessment				School competition		
		Establish student assessment policies (proportion)	Choose which textbooks are used (proportion)	Determine course content (proportion)	Decide which courses are offered (proportion)	Schools that compete with other schools for students in the same area (proportion)	Private schools (proportion)	Latent class
OECD	Australia	0.98	1.00	0.86	0.99	0.96	0.39	4
	Austria	0.85	0.99	0.77	0.71	0.57	0.01	3
	Belgium	0.96	0.99	0.74	0.87	0.95	w	4
	Canada	0.90	0.89	0.62	0.97	0.85	0.06	3
	Chile	0.94	0.93	0.65	0.84	0.79	0.53	4
	Czech Republic	1.00	0.99	0.99	0.99	0.84	0.03	3
	Denmark	0.89	1.00	0.88	0.86	0.78	0.2	3
	Estonia	0.97	0.98	0.97	0.98	0.81	0.03	3
	Finland	0.93	1.00	0.84	0.94	0.58	0.04	3
	France	w	w	w	w	w	w	w
	Germany	0.91	0.97	0.68	0.98	0.81	0.04	3
	Greece	0.32	0.15	0.04	0.12	0.6	0.03	1
	Hungary	1.00	1.00	0.85	0.71	0.8	0.12	3
	Iceland	0.99	0.97	0.87	0.90	0.51	0.01	3
	Ireland	1.00	1.00	0.66	0.99	0.82	0.57	4
	Israel	1.00	0.96	0.96	0.94	0.8	0.14	3
	Italy	0.99	1.00	0.86	0.73	0.88	0.05	3
	Japan	1.00	0.97	0.99	0.98	0.91	0.29	3
	Korea	0.98	1.00	0.98	0.96	0.87	0.36	4
	Luxembourg	0.42	0.93	0.80	0.79	0.77	0.13	3
	Mexico	0.71	0.74	0.21	0.09	0.86	0.11	1
	Netherlands	1.00	c	0.99	0.99	0.97	0.65	4
	New Zealand	0.98	1.00	0.99	1.00	0.87	0.05	3
	Norway	0.73	0.99	0.70	0.56	0.4	0.01	3
	Poland	1.00	1.00	1.00	0.71	0.68	0.02	3
	Portugal	0.72	1.00	0.08	0.14	0.79	0.14	1
	Slovak Republic	0.97	0.95	0.95	0.99	0.94	0.09	3
	Slovenia	0.95	0.99	0.94	0.80	0.49	0.03	3
	Spain	0.77	1.00	0.63	0.61	0.8	0.31	3
	Sweden	0.97	1.00	0.92	0.78	0.69	0.1	3
	Switzerland	0.84	0.80	0.62	0.73	0.38	0.06	3
	Turkey	0.70	0.32	0.24	0.35	0.66	0.01	1
	United Kingdom	1.00	1.00	0.98	1.00	0.89	0.06	3
	United States	0.87	0.90	0.82	0.96	0.79	0.08	3
Partners	Albania	0.67	0.99	0.43	0.47	0.68	0.11	1
	Argentina	0.94	0.97	0.71	0.39	0.85	0.35	3
	Azerbaijan	0.62	0.57	0.36	0.42	0.72	0	1
	Brazil	0.74	0.98	0.60	0.35	0.82	0.08	3
	Bulgaria	0.62	0.99	0.35	0.25	0.84	0.02	1
	Colombia	0.61	0.96	0.92	0.77	0.87	0.16	3
	Croatia	0.62	0.97	0.61	0.28	0.81	0.02	1
	Dubai (UAE)	0.87	0.73	0.74	0.75	0.9	0.69	4
	Hong Kong-China	1.00	1.00	0.98	1.00	0.98	0.93	4
	Indonesia	0.94	0.93	0.93	0.72	0.97	0.42	4
	Jordan	0.30	0.05	0.07	0.08	0.71	0.19	1
	Kazakhstan	0.53	0.30	0.29	0.63	0.75	0.03	1
	Kyrgyzstan	0.74	0.77	0.69	0.51	0.67	0.03	3
	Latvia	0.96	0.98	0.64	0.72	0.89	0.01	3
	Liechtenstein	0.94	0.60	c	0.62	0.52	0.06	3
	Lithuania	0.95	0.99	0.85	0.95	0.81	0	3
	Macao-China	c	c	1.00	0.96	1	0.96	4
	Montenegro	0.72	0.35	0.39	0.56	0.37	0.01	1
	Panama	0.66	0.78	0.64	0.49	0.71	0.17	3
	Peru	0.90	0.63	0.76	0.63	0.78	0.18	3
	Qatar	0.63	0.53	0.40	0.52	0.64	0.22	1
	Romania	0.78	0.99	0.80	0.71	0.83	0.01	3
	Russian Federation	0.88	0.92	0.61	0.93	0.74	0	3
	Serbia	0.93	0.77	0.43	0.13	0.79	0.01	1
	Shanghai-China	0.95	0.66	0.67	0.80	0.85	0.1	3
	Singapore	0.98	0.97	0.82	0.96	0.97	0.02	3
	Chinese Taipei	0.92	1.00	0.97	0.93	0.95	0.33	4
	Thailand	0.98	0.99	1.00	0.99	0.89	0.17	3
	Trinidad and Tobago	0.95	0.90	0.61	0.85	0.9	0.09	3
	Tunisia	0.22	0.01	0.17	0.13	0.66	0.02	1
	Uruguay	0.53	0.67	0.29	0.41	0.55	0.18	1

StatLink http://dx.doi.org/10.1787/888932343513

[Part 1/1]

Table A5.4 **Data used for the "assessment and accountability policies" latent profile analysis and latent class for each school system**

		Use of assessment or achievement data for benchmarking and information purposes				Use of assessment or achievement data for decision making			
		Provide information to parents relative to national/regional population (proportion)	Compare with other schools (proportion)	Monitor progress over time (proportion)	Post achievement data publicly (proportion)	Have their progress tracked by administrative authorities (proportion)	Make curricular decisions (proportion)	Allocate resources (proportion)	Monitor teacher practices (proportion)	Latent class
OECD	Australia	0.51	0.64	0.83	0.47	0.81	0.86	0.61	0.58	4
	Austria	0.09	0.26	0.49	0.06	0.49	0.63	0.16	0.82	1
	Belgium	0.36	0.13	0.51	0.02	0.45	0.61	0.22	0.37	1
	Canada	0.54	0.76	0.86	0.55	0.89	0.87	0.59	a	4
	Chile	0.83	0.53	0.89	0.36	0.77	0.92	0.77	0.72	4
	Czech Republic	0.63	0.72	0.89	0.31	0.56	0.84	0.04	0.71	4
	Denmark	0.46	0.36	0.35	0.45	0.57	0.85	0.36	0.41	2
	Estonia	0.58	0.74	0.85	0.32	0.87	0.78	0.16	0.64	4
	Finland	0.39	0.53	0.53	0.03	0.43	0.56	0.05	0.18	1
	France	w	w	w	w	w	w	w	w	w
	Germany	0.30	0.39	0.58	0.11	0.29	0.57	0.28	0.63	1
	Greece	0.25	0.30	0.62	0.31	0.55	0.47	0.04	0.27	1
	Hungary	0.46	0.73	0.87	0.33	0.50	0.65	0.13	0.64	3
	Iceland	0.39	0.56	0.92	0.23	0.75	0.92	0.01	0.52	4
	Ireland	0.25	0.47	0.67	0.19	0.49	0.65	0.54	0.52	1
	Israel	0.42	0.56	0.87	0.26	0.82	0.91	0.78	0.91	4
	Italy	0.16	0.41	0.72	0.30	0.26	0.89	0.39	0.48	2
	Japan	0.79	0.24	0.61	0.04	0.11	0.83	0.04	0.52	2
	Korea	0.84	0.78	0.83	0.33	0.76	0.88	0.39	0.77	4
	Luxembourg	0.38	0.58	0.40	0.37	0.74	0.60	0.33	0.49	1
	Mexico	0.63	0.80	0.89	0.34	0.87	0.92	0.32	0.83	4
	Netherlands	0.16	0.50	0.74	0.64	0.61	0.63	0.13	0.59	1
	New Zealand	0.78	0.94	0.97	0.78	0.93	0.98	0.68	0.68	4
	Norway	0.81	0.73	0.82	0.58	0.73	0.70	0.16	0.40	3
	Poland	0.77	0.63	0.95	0.53	0.90	0.92	0.14	0.97	4
	Portugal	0.46	0.54	0.89	0.30	0.69	0.80	0.55	0.50	4
	Slovak Republic	0.58	0.73	0.86	0.63	0.86	0.86	0.11	0.76	4
	Slovenia	0.43	0.62	0.92	0.36	0.69	0.75	0.15	0.41	3
	Spain	0.22	0.30	0.84	0.08	0.65	0.91	0.43	0.51	2
	Sweden	0.90	0.84	0.93	0.61	0.84	0.83	0.37	0.30	4
	Switzerland	0.29	0.43	0.41	0.03	0.33	0.50	0.24	0.23	1
	Turkey	0.81	0.83	0.84	0.50	0.77	0.55	0.31	0.84	3
	United Kingdom	0.70	0.92	0.97	0.80	0.94	0.93	0.58	0.85	4
	United States	0.88	0.97	0.98	0.89	0.96	0.98	0.72	0.81	4
Partners	Albania	0.51	0.88	1.00	0.34	0.81	0.89	0.79	0.97	4
	Argentina	0.22	0.31	0.81	0.06	0.67	0.94	0.35	0.72	2
	Azerbaijan	0.95	0.93	0.89	0.86	0.81	0.89	0.68	0.98	4
	Brazil	0.57	0.83	0.95	0.32	0.82	0.92	0.73	0.67	4
	Bulgaria	0.69	0.86	0.90	0.33	0.78	0.71	0.30	0.89	4
	Colombia	0.88	0.67	0.95	0.28	0.79	0.93	0.58	0.65	4
	Croatia	0.29	0.81	0.94	0.22	0.84	0.82	0.13	0.64	4
	Dubai (UAE)	0.58	0.65	0.93	0.47	0.89	0.92	0.75	0.87	4
	Hong Kong-China	0.14	0.36	0.95	0.48	0.61	0.97	0.49	0.80	4
	Indonesia	0.77	0.92	0.98	0.31	0.72	0.99	0.91	0.86	4
	Jordan	0.61	0.84	0.90	0.20	0.83	0.90	0.70	0.94	4
	Kazakhstan	0.85	0.95	1.00	0.83	0.99	0.99	0.83	0.98	4
	Kyrgyzstan	0.90	0.93	0.98	0.66	0.98	0.90	0.85	0.98	4
	Latvia	0.21	0.92	0.98	0.25	0.51	0.98	0.38	0.71	4
	Liechtenstein	0.53	0.53	0.43	0.26	0.34	0.59	0.37	0.11	1
	Lithuania	0.19	0.62	0.95	0.25	0.66	0.81	0.15	0.77	4
	Macao-China	0.01	0.24	0.78	0.14	0.39	1.00	0.38	0.67	2
	Montenegro	0.39	0.47	0.55	0.76	0.98	0.57	0.24	0.63	3
	Panama	0.51	0.43	0.77	0.06	0.78	0.74	0.51	0.59	4
	Peru	0.27	0.49	0.88	0.13	0.66	0.93	0.71	0.75	4
	Qatar	0.84	0.73	0.90	0.61	0.86	0.90	0.62	0.89	4
	Romania	0.81	0.92	0.97	0.62	0.75	0.92	0.66	0.92	4
	Russian Federation	0.84	0.98	0.99	0.76	0.99	1.00	0.65	0.99	4
	Serbia	0.47	0.63	0.96	0.56	0.84	0.79	0.19	0.59	4
	Shanghai-China	0.47	0.69	0.86	0.01	0.68	0.97	0.34	0.83	4
	Singapore	0.72	0.95	0.99	0.61	0.98	0.97	0.85	0.99	4
	Chinese Taipei	0.31	0.57	0.73	0.19	0.34	0.98	0.26	0.72	2
	Thailand	0.64	0.87	0.97	0.64	0.87	0.98	0.78	0.87	4
	Trinidad and Tobago	0.42	0.33	0.90	0.11	0.72	0.92	0.46	0.79	4
	Tunisia	0.53	0.90	0.95	0.07	0.82	0.52	0.59	0.86	3
	Uruguay	0.16	0.20	0.84	0.07	0.62	0.82	0.45	0.32	2

StatLink http://dx.doi.org/10.1787/888932343513

[Part 1/1]
Table A5.5 **Data used for the "resources invested in education" latent profile analysis and latent class for each school system**

		How resources are invested		Amount of resources	
		Teachers' salaries relative to GDP/capita: weighted average of upper and lower secondary school teachers (ratio)	Average class size for the language of instruction	Cumulative expenditure by educational institutions per student aged 6 to 15	Latent class
OECD	Australia	1.27	23.1	7.24	3
	Austria	1.13	20.8	9.78	3
	Belgium	1.45	18.5	8.01	3
	Canada	m	25.1	8.05	3
	Chile	m	36.5	2.36	2
	Czech Republic	0.94	24.0	4.48	1
	Denmark	1.16	19.4	8.76	3
	Estonia	m	22.5	4.30	1
	Finland	1.15	19.2	7.14	3
	France	1.05	26.9	7.47	3
	Germany	1.69	24.8	6.33	3
	Greece	1.13	22.6	4.84	1
	Hungary	0.92	28.5	4.43	1
	Iceland	0.75	18.7	9.49	3
	Ireland	1.26	22.9	7.59	3
	Israel	0.82	28.5	5.33	1
	Italy	1.13	20.9	7.73	3
	Japan	1.44	37.1	7.77	4
	Korea	2.01	35.9	6.11	4
	Luxembourg	1.18	21.0	15.56	5
	Mexico	m	34.7	2.12	2
	Netherlands	1.35	23.7	8.04	3
	New Zealand	1.42	24.2	4.86	1
	Norway	0.66	23.4	10.13	3
	Poland	0.96	22.5	4.00	1
	Portugal	1.55	22.3	5.68	1
	Slovak Republic	m	24.0	3.22	1
	Slovenia	1.18	28.2	7.79	3
	Spain	1.49	21.8	7.41	3
	Sweden	0.92	21.0	8.28	3
	Switzerland	1.58	18.6	10.44	3
	Turkey	m	26.8	1.27	1
	United Kingdom	1.28	25.0	8.49	3
	United States	m	24.4	10.58	3
Partners	Albania	m	26.1	m	1
	Argentina	m	28.1	m	1
	Azerbaijan	m	18.6	m	1
	Brazil	m	33.8	1.83	2
	Bulgaria	1.00	22.4	m	1
	Colombia	1.36	35.1	1.91	2
	Croatia	0.38	26.2	3.46	1
	Dubai (UAE)	m	24.8	m	1
	Hong Kong-China	2.34	35.6	m	2
	Indonesia	m	34.2	m	2
	Jordan	m	32.3	m	2
	Kazakhstan	m	22.5	m	1
	Kyrgyzstan	1.02	22.1	0.30	1
	Latvia	m	19.4	m	1
	Liechtenstein	m	16.2	m	1
	Lithuania	m	22.7	m	1
	Macao-China	1.23	38.4	m	2
	Montenegro	1.34	28.1	m	1
	Panama	m	28.5	m	1
	Peru	0.97	28.9	m	1
	Qatar	0.50	25.9	m	1
	Romania	m	24.4	m	1
	Russian Federation	m	21.1	1.75	1
	Serbia	m	26.7	m	1
	Shanghai-China	1.74	39.0	4.21	2
	Singapore	1.67	34.9	m	2
	Chinese Taipei	1.55	39.5	1.84	2
	Thailand	2.19	37.7	4.63	2
	Trinidad and Tobago	m	28.1	m	1
	Tunisia	m	28.3	m	1
	Uruguay	m	25.6	m	1

StatLink http://dx.doi.org/10.1787/888932343513

[Part 1/1]
Table A5.6 **Data source for variables used for latent profile analyses**

Section	Variable		Data source	
Selecting and grouping students into schools, grades and programmes	Vertical differentiation	Students out of modal starting ages	Table IV.3.1, 3rd to 7th column	(100 – highest two values among 3rd to 7th column) /100
		Students who repeated one or more grades	Table IV.3.1, 11th column	11th column/100
	Horizontal differentiation at the system level	First age of selection	Table IV.3.2a, 4th column	
		Number of school types or distinct educational programmes	Table IV.3.2a, 4th column	
		Selective schools	Table IV.3.2b, 26th column	(100 – 26th column)/100
	Horizontal differentiation at the school level	Schools that transfer students to other schools due to low achievement, behavioural problems or special learning needs	Table IV.3.3a, 8th column	8th column/100
		Schools that group students by ability in all subjects	Table IV.3.4, 4th column	4th column/100
Governance of school systems	School autonomy for curriculum and assessment	Establish students assessment policies	Figure IV.3.3b, 3rd column	3rd column/100
		Choose which textbooks are used	Figure IV.3.3b, 6th column	6th column/100
		Determine course content	Figure IV.3.3b, 9th column	9th column/100
		Decide which courses are offered	Figure IV.3.3b, 12th column	12th column/100
	School competition	Schools that compete with other schools for students in the same area	Table IV.3.8a, 4th column	(100 – 4th column)/100
		Private schools	Table IV.3.9, 6th and 10th columns	(6th + 10th column)/100
Assessment and accountability policies	Use of assessment or achievement data for benchmarking and information purposes	Provide information to parents relative to national/regional population	Table IV.3.14, 5th column	5th column/100
		Compare with other schools	Table IV.3.12, 10th column	10th column/100
		Monitor progress over time	Table IV.3.12, 6th column	6th column/100
		Post achievement data publicly	Table IV.3.13, 2nd column	2nd column/100
		Have their progress tracked by administrative authorities	Table IV.3.13, 6th column	6th column/100
	Use of assessment or achievement data for decision making	Make curricular decisions	Table IV.3.12, 8th column	8th column/100
		Allocate resources	Table IV.3.13, 5th column	5th column/100
		Monitoring teacher practices	Table IV.3.15, 2nd column	2nd column/100
Resources invested in education	How resources are invested	Teachers' salaries relative to GDP/capita	Table IV.3.21a, 4th and 5th columns	4th and 5th columns are weighted by proportion of students in lower and upper secondary schools within country
		Average class size of the language of instruction	Table IV.3.22, 2nd column	
	Amount of resources	Cumulative expenditure by educational institutions per student aged 6 to 15	Table IV 3.21b, 3rd column	3rd column/10000

StatLink http://dx.doi.org/10.1787/888932343513

ANNEX A6
TESTING RESULTS IN VOLUME IV

Annex A6 is available on line at *www.pisa.oecd.org*

Annex B

TABLES OF RESULTS

All tables in Annex B are available on line

Annex B1: Results for countries and economies

Annex B2: Results for regions within countries

Adjudicated regions
Data for which adherence to the PISA sampling standards and international comparability was internationally adjudicated.

Non-adjudicated regions
Data for which adherence to the PISA sampling standards at subnational levels was assessed by the countries concerned.

In these countries, adherence to the PISA sampling standards and international comparability was internationally adjudicated only for the combined set of all subnational entities.

Note: Unless otherwise specified, all the data contained in the following tables are drawn from the OECD PISA Database.

ANNEX B1
RESULTS FOR COUNTRIES AND ECONOMIES

[Part 1/1]

Table IV.1.1a Selected characteristics of school systems with reading performance at the OECD average

Four areas		
1. Selecting and grouping students (Figure IV.3.2)	V	High vertical differentiation
	v	Low vertical differentiation
	H	High horizontal differentiation at the system level
	h	Medium horizontal differentiation at the system level
	h	Low horizontal differentiation at the system level
	Hsc	High horizontal differentiation at the school level
	hsc	Low horizontal differentiation at the school level
2. Governance of schools (Figure IV.3.5)	A	More school autonomy for curriculum and assessment
	a	Less school autonomy for curriculum and assessment
	C	More school competition
	c	Less school competition
3. Assessment and accountability policies (Figure IV.3.6)	B	Frequent use of assessment or achievement data for benchmarking and information purposes
	b	Infrequent use of assessment or achievement data for benchmarking and information purposes
	D	Frequent use of assessment or achievement data for decision making
	d	Infrequent use of assessment or achievement data for decision making
4. Resources invested in education (Figure IV.3.7)	E	High cumulative expenditure by educational institutions per student aged 6 to 15
	e	Low cumulative expenditure by educational institutions per student aged 6 to 15
	S	Large class size and high teachers' salaries
	s	Small class size and/or low teachers' salaries

	Performance in reading (score points)	Strength of relationship between students' socio-economic background and reading performance (% variance explained)		Four areas: 1. Selecting and grouping students (Figure IV.3.2)	2. Governance of schools (Figure IV.3.5)	3. Assessment and accountability policies (Figure IV.3.6)	4. Resources invested in education (Figure IV.3.7)	Countries with similar system characteristics in the four areas
Chinese Taipei	495	Average impact of socio-economic background on reading performance	11.8	v + ***h*** + Hsc	A + C	b + D	e + S	–
Liechtenstein	499		8.4	v + H + hsc	A + c	b + d	e + s	–
Ireland	496		12.6	v + ***h*** + hsc	A + C	b + d	E + s	–
United Kingdom	494		13.7	v + h + hsc	A + c	B + D	E + s	Australia, Canada, Iceland, Sweden, United States
Sweden	497		13.4	v + h + hsc	A + c	B + D	E + s	Australia, Canada, Iceland, United Kingdom, United States
Denmark	495		14.5	v + h + hsc	A + c	b + D	E + s	–
Portugal	489		16.5	V + ***h*** + hsc	a + c	B + D	e + s	–
United States	500		16.8	v + h + hsc	A + c	B + D	E + s	Australia, Canada, Iceland, Sweden, United Kingdom
Germany	497	Above-average impact of socio-economic background on reading performance	17.9	V + H + hsc	A + c	b + d	E + s	–
Hungary	494		26.0	v + H + hsc	A + c	B + d	e + s	–

Note: Cells shaded in grey are the most prevailing patterns among school systems with above-average reading performance and a below-average impact of socio-economic background on reading performance within each of the four areas.
StatLink http://dx.doi.org/10.1787/888932343285

[Part 1/1]

Table IV.1.1b Selected characteristics of school systems with reading performance below the OECD average

Four areas		
1. Selecting and grouping students (Figure IV.3.2)	V	High vertical differentiation
	v	Low vertical differentiation
	H	High horizontal differentiation at the system level
	h	Medium horizontal differentiation at the system level
	h	Low horizontal differentiation at the system level
	Hsc	High horizontal differentiation at the school level
	hsc	Low horizontal differentiation at the school level
2. Governance of schools (Figure IV.3.5)	A	More school autonomy for curriculum and assessment
	a	Less school autonomy for curriculum and assessment
	C	More school competition
	c	Less school competition
3. Assessment and accountability policies (Figure IV.3.6)	B	Frequent use of assessment or achievement data for benchmarking and information purposes
	b	Infrequent use of assessment or achievement data for benchmarking and information purposes
	D	Frequent use of assessment or achievement data for decision making
	d	Infrequent use of assessment or achievement data for decision making
4. Resources invested in education (Figure IV.3.7)	E	High cumulative expenditure by educational institutions per student aged 6 to 15
	e	Low cumulative expenditure by educational institutions per student aged 6 to 15
	S	Large class size and high teachers' salaries
	s	Small class size and/or low teachers' salaries

	Performance in reading (score points)	Strength of relationship between students' socio-economic background and reading performance (% variance explained)		Four areas: 1. Selecting and grouping students (Figure IV.3.2)	2. Governance of schools (Figure IV.3.5)	3. Assessment and accountability policies (Figure IV.3.6)	4. Resources invested in education (Figure IV.3.7)	Countries with similar system characteristics in the four areas
Macao-China	487	Below-average impact of socio-economic background on reading performance	1.8	V + ***h*** + Hsc	A + C	b + D	e + S	–
Qatar	372		4.0	v + ***h*** + Hsc	a + c	B + D	e + s	
Azerbaijan	362		7.4	v + ***h*** + hsc	a + c	B + D	e + s	Albania
Indonesia	402		7.8	v + ***h*** + Hsc	A + C	B + D	e + S	–
Jordan	405		7.9	v + h + Hsc	a + c	B + D	e + S	–
Tunisia	404		8.1	V + h + hsc	a + c	B + d	e + s	–
Trinidad and Tobago	416		9.7	V + H + hsc	A + c	B + D	e + s	–
Serbia	442		9.8	v + H + Hsc	a + c	B + D	e + s	Bulgaria
Montenegro	408		10.0	v + ***h*** + hsc	a + c	B + d	e + s	–
Latvia	484		10.3	v + h + hsc	A + c	B + D	e + s	Estonia, New Zealand, Poland, Lithuania, Russian Federation
Croatia	476		11.0	v + H + hsc	a + c	B + D	e + s	–
Russian Federation	459		11.3	v + h + hsc	A + c	B + D	e + s	Estonia, New Zealand, Poland, Latvia, Lithuania
Italy	486		11.8	v + ***h*** + hsc	A + c	b + D	E + s	–
Albania	385	Average impact of socio-economic background on reading performance	10.7	v + ***h*** + hsc	a + c	B + D	e + s	Azerbaijan
Kazakhstan	390		12.0	v + h + hsc	a + c	B + D	e + s	
Israel	474		12.5	v + ***h*** + hsc	A + c	B + D	e + s	
Greece	483		12.5	v + h + hsc	a + c	b + d	e + s	–
Czech Republic	478		12.4	v + H + hsc	A + c	B + D	e + s	Slovak Republic
Brazil	412		13.0	V + h + hsc	A + c	B + D	e + S	–
Thailand	421		13.3	v + ***h*** + hsc	A + c	B + D	e + S	Shanghai-China
Romania	424		13.6	v + ***h*** + Hsc	A + c	B + D	e + s	Kyrgyzstan
Lithuania	468		13.6	v + h + hsc	A + c	B + D	e + s	Estonia, New Zealand, Poland, Latvia, Russian Federation
Dubai (UAE)	459		14.2	v + ***h*** + hsc	A + C	B + D	e + s	–
Spain	481		13.6	V + h + hsc	A + c	b + D	E + s	–
Mexico	425		14.5	V + ***h*** + hsc	a + c	B + D	e + S	–
Slovenia	483		14.3	v + ***h*** + hsc	A + c	B + d	E + s	–
Kyrgyzstan	314		14.6	v + ***h*** + Hsc	A + c	B + D	e + s	Romania
Slovak Republic	477		14.6	v + H + hsc	A + c	B + D	e + s	Czech Republic
Colombia	413		16.6	V + h + Hsc	A + c	B + D	e + S	–
Austria	470		16.6	v + H + hsc	A + c	b + d	E + s	–
Panama	371		18.1	V + ***h*** + Hsc	A + c	B + D	e + s	–
Chile	449	Above-average impact of socio-economic background on reading performance	18.7	V + h + Hsc	A + C	B + D	e + S	–
Luxembourg	472		18.0	V + ***h*** + Hsc	A + c	b + d	E + s	–
Turkey	464		19.0	v + H + Hsc	a + c	B + d	e + s	–
Argentina	398		19.6	V + h + hsc	A + c	b + D	e + s	–
Bulgaria	429		20.2	v + H + Hsc	a + c	B + D	e + s	Serbia
Uruguay	426		20.7	V + h + hsc	a + c	b + D	e + s	–
Peru	370		27.4	V + h + Hsc	A + c	B + D	e + s	–

Note: Cells shaded in grey are the most prevailing patterns among school systems with above-average reading performance and a below-average impact of socio-economic background on reading performance within each of the four areas.

StatLink http://dx.doi.org/10.1787/888932343285

[Part 1/4]
Table IV.2.1 Correlations between system-level characteristics and educational outcomes

			OECD countries							
			Reading performance		Variance in reading performance explained by the PISA index of economic, social and cultural status of students		Variance in reading performance explained by the PISA index of economic, social and cultural status of students and schools		Change in reading performance per unit increase in the PISA index of economic, social and cultural status of students	
			Without accounting for GDP/capita	With accounting for GDP/capita	Without accounting for GDP/capita	With accounting for GDP/capita	Without accounting for GDP/capita	With accounting for GDP/capita	Without accounting for GDP/capita	With accounting for GDP/capita
Selecting and grouping students	Vertical differentiation	Average age of entry into primary school	-0.21	-0.15	0.16	0.12	0.28	0.24	-0.17	-0.12
		Percentage of students who repeated one or more grades	*-0.32*	**-0.39**	**0.48**	**0.53**	**0.35**	**0.39**	0.00	-0.04
	Horizontal differentiation at the system level	Each additional year of selection prior to the age of 15	-0.19	-0.18	**0.50**	**0.50**	**0.76**	**0.76**	**0.38**	**0.40**
		Number of school types or distinct educational programmes available for 15-year-olds	-0.20	-0.23	0.29	*0.30*	**0.66**	**0.69**	0.20	0.18
		Percentage of students in selective schools	-0.08	-0.06	0.29	0.28	**0.69**	**0.69**	*0.32*	*0.34*
	Horizontal differentiation at the school level	Percentage of students in schools that group students by ability in all subjects	*-0.29*	**-0.42**	0.18	0.25	0.27	**0.36**	-0.11	-0.20
		Percentage of students in schools that transfer students to other schools due to low achievement, behavioural problems or special learning needs	**-0.53**	**-0.61**	**0.43**	**0.47**	**0.56**	**0.61**	0.13	0.10
School governance	School autonomy	Average index of school responsibility for curriculum and assessment	**0.45**	**0.49**	-0.21	-0.23	0.01	-0.01	**0.38**	**0.41**
		Average index of school responsibility for resource allocation	0.02	0.03	0.14	0.14	0.16	0.15	**0.36**	**0.38**
	School competition	Percentage of students in schools that compete with other schools for students in the same area	0.06	0.10	0.17	0.15	0.21	0.19	0.19	0.23
		Percentage of students in private schools	0.05	0.04	0.04	0.05	0.05	0.06	-0.03	-0.04
Assessment and accountability policies	Use of standardised assessments	Percentage of students in schools that assess students with standardised tests	0.15	0.14	-0.24	-0.23	**-0.47**	**-0.46**	-0.21	-0.23
		Existence of standards-based external examinations	*0.32*	*0.32*	-0.28	-0.27	-0.07	-0.06	0.07	0.06
	Percentage of students in schools that use assessment or achievement data to:	Provide comparative information to parents (relative to national/regional population)	0.08	0.15	-0.01	-0.04	-0.24	-0.29	0.01	0.07
		Compare the school with other schools	0.02	0.06	0.01	-0.01	-0.22	-0.25	0.02	0.05
		Monitor progress over time	-0.09	0.04	-0.05	-0.13	-0.17	-0.28	-0.09	0.02
		Post achievement data publicly	0.04	0.03	0.08	0.09	-0.17	-0.17	0.16	0.16
		Have their progress tracked by administrative authorities	-0.14	-0.12	-0.01	-0.03	**-0.38**	**-0.41**	-0.09	-0.07
		Make curricular decisions	-0.03	0.04	-0.20	-0.24	*-0.34*	**-0.40**	-0.06	0.00
		Allocate resources	-0.08	-0.09	0.21	0.22	-0.16	-0.16	0.11	0.11
		Monitor teacher practices	-0.17	-0.05	0.06	-0.01	0.11	0.03	0.03	0.18
Resources invested in education		Average number of minutes per week spent in regular school lessons on the language of instruction	-0.04	-0.02	-0.06	-0.07	*-0.30*	*-0.32*	-0.27	-0.25
	Percentage of students who take after-school lessons for:	enrichment	-0.22	-0.12	-0.07	-0.15	-0.06	-0.15	-0.22	-0.14
		remedial purposes	-0.07	0.00	-0.09	-0.14	0.12	0.08	-0.19	-0.14
		Average class size for the language of instruction	-0.22	-0.13	0.12	0.07	0.28	0.23	-0.11	-0.02
		Average index of extra-curricular activities	0.22	0.26	0.12	0.10	0.12	0.09	0.24	0.29
		Teachers' salaries relative to GDP/capita (weighted average of upper and lower secondary school teachers[1])	**0.40**	**0.39**	0.14	0.14	0.20	0.20	-0.08	-0.08
		Cumulative expenditure by educational institutions per student aged 6 to 15	*0.30*	0.21	-0.16	-0.10	-0.13	0.03	0.21	0.05

Note: Values that are statistically significant at the 10% level ($p < 0.10$) are indicated in italics and at the 5% level ($p < 0.05$) are in bold.
1. The average is computed by weighting teachers' salaries for upper and lower secondary school according to the respective 15-year-old students' enrolment (for countries with valid information on whether 15-year-old students are both at the upper and lower secondary levels).
StatLink http://dx.doi.org/10.1787/888932343285

[Part 2/4]
Table IV.2.1 Correlations between system-level characteristics and educational outcomes

			OECD countries							
			Change in reading performance per unit increase in the PISA index of economic, social and cultural status of schools		Change in reading performance per unit increase in the PISA index of economic, social and cultural status of students in the average school		Standard deviation of reading performance		Percentage of variance in reading performance that lies between schools	
			Without accounting for GDP/capita	With accounting for GDP/capita	Without accounting for GDP/capita	With accounting for GDP/capita	Without accounting for GDP/capita	With accounting for GDP/capita	Without accounting for GDP/capita	With accounting for GDP/capita
Selecting and grouping students	Vertical differentiation	Average age of entry into primary school	0.03	0.04	*-0.32*	-0.25	*-0.31*	-0.21	0.25	0.19
		Percentage of students who repeated one or more grades	0.08	0.08	-0.28	**-0.37**	0.12	0.04	*0.31*	**0.39**
	Horizontal differentiation at the system level	Each additional year of selection prior to the age of 15	**0.56**	**0.56**	**-0.46**	**-0.48**	0.02	0.04	**0.66**	**0.68**
		Number of school types or distinct educational programmes available for 15-year-olds	**0.55**	**0.55**	**-0.54**	**-0.60**	0.03	0.00	**0.69**	**0.74**
		Percentage of students in selective schools	**0.69**	**0.70**	**-0.59**	**-0.60**	0.10	0.16	**0.72**	**0.73**
	Horizontal differentiation at the school level	Percentage of students in schools that group students by ability in all subjects	0.19	0.19	-0.28	**-0.44**	0.11	-0.06	0.26	**0.40**
		Percentage of students in schools that transfer students to other schools due to low achievement, behavioural problems or special learning needs	*0.32*	*0.32*	**-0.49**	**-0.59**	0.25	0.19	**0.55**	**0.64**
School governance	School autonomy	Average index of school responsibility for curriculum and assessment	**0.40**	**0.41**	0.13	0.17	0.11	0.18	0.03	0.00
		Average index of school responsibility for resource allocation	0.25	0.25	0.06	0.07	-0.01	0.00	0.10	0.09
	School competition	Percentage of students in schools that compete with other schools for students in the same area	**0.38**	**0.39**	-0.12	-0.08	0.07	0.16	0.22	0.19
		Percentage of students in private schools	0.13	0.13	-0.09	-0.12	-0.12	-0.18	0.13	0.16
Assessment and accountability policies	Use of standardised assessments	Percentage of students in schools that assess students with standardised tests	**-0.35**	*-0.35*	**0.42**	**0.41**	-0.20	-0.26	**-0.45**	**-0.44**
		Existence of standards-based external examinations	0.09	0.09	0.11	0.10	-0.01	-0.04	-0.08	-0.07
	Percentage of students in schools that use assessment or achievement data to:	Provide comparative information to parents (relative to national/regional population)	-0.08	-0.08	*0.30*	**0.41**	-0.22	-0.13	*-0.33*	**-0.41**
		Compare the school with other schools	-0.26	-0.26	*0.32*	**0.39**	-0.18	-0.13	*-0.31*	**-0.37**
		Monitor progress over time	-0.20	-0.21	0.10	*0.31*	-0.13	0.11	-0.12	-0.30
		Post achievement data publicly	-0.19	-0.19	**0.35**	**0.36**	-0.04	-0.06	-0.28	-0.29
		Have their progress tracked by administrative authorities	**-0.46**	**-0.46**	**0.42**	**0.49**	-0.11	-0.06	**-0.43**	**-0.49**
		Make curricular decisions	-0.17	-0.17	0.25	**0.37**	0.00	0.14	-0.29	**-0.39**
		Allocate resources	-0.09	-0.09	*0.29*	*0.30*	0.17	0.18	-0.21	-0.21
		Monitor teacher practices	0.20	0.26	-0.16	0.02	-0.10	0.19	0.14	0.00
Resources invested in education		Average number of minutes per week spent in regular school lessons on the language of instruction	-0.29	-0.29	0.14	0.18	-0.15	-0.11	-0.27	*-0.31*
	Percentage of students who take after-school lessons for:	enrichment	-0.02	-0.01	-0.14	0.00	-0.03	0.21	0.09	-0.03
		remedial purposes	0.14	0.15	*-0.33*	-0.25	-0.15	-0.02	0.24	0.17
		Average class size for the language of instruction	0.27	*0.31*	**-0.46**	**-0.37**	-0.20	-0.03	**0.38**	*0.31*
		Average index of extra-curricular activities	0.13	0.14	0.07	0.13	0.11	0.21	0.02	-0.02
		Teachers' salaries relative to GDP/capita (weighted average of upper and lower secondary school teachers[1])	0.23	0.23	-0.14	-0.13	-0.31	-0.30	0.12	0.11
		Cumulative expenditure by educational institutions per student aged 6 to 15	0.02	-0.01	0.27	-0.07	**0.43**	0.09	-0.24	0.02

Note: Values that are statistically significant at the 10% level ($p < 0.10$) are indicated in italics and at the 5% level ($p < 0.05$) are in bold.
1. The average is computed by weighting teachers' salaries for upper and lower secondary school according to the respective 15-year-old students' enrolment (for countries with valid information on whether 15-year-old students are both at the upper and lower secondary levels).
StatLink http://dx.doi.org/10.1787/888932343285

[Part 3/4]
Table IV.2.1 Correlations between system-level characteristics and educational outcomes

			All countries and economies							
			Reading performance		Variance in reading performance explained by the PISA index of economic, social and cultural status of students		Variance in reading performance explained by the PISA index of economic, social and cultural status of students and schools		Change in reading performance per unit increase in the PISA index of economic, social and cultural status of students	
			Without accounting for GDP/capita	With accounting for GDP/capita	Without accounting for GDP/capita	With accounting for GDP/capita	Without accounting for GDP/capita	With accounting for GDP/capita	Without accounting for GDP/capita	With accounting for GDP/capita
Selecting and grouping students	Vertical differentiation	Average age of entry into primary school	-0.12	0.11	0.01	-0.03	0.12	0.06	-0.14	-0.03
		Percentage of students who repeated one or more grades	-0.18	**-0.34**	*0.24*	**0.27**	*0.23*	*0.23*	-0.17	-0.20
	Horizontal differentiation at the system level	Each additional year of selection prior to the age of 15	0.13	0.01	**0.40**	**0.47**	**0.71**	**0.73**	**0.38**	**0.44**
		Number of school types or distinct educational programmes available for 15-year-olds	-0.02	-0.04	0.21	**0.28**	**0.58**	**0.65**	**0.30**	**0.32**
		Percentage of students in selective schools	-0.04	-0.02	-0.10	-0.09	**0.35**	**0.34**	-0.02	-0.01
	Horizontal differentiation at the school level	Percentage of students in schools that group students by ability in all subjects	**-0.43**	**-0.45**	0.03	0.07	0.03	0.10	-0.07	-0.10
		Percentage of students in schools that transfer students to other schools due to low achievement, behavioural problems or special learning needs	**-0.38**	**-0.41**	0.11	0.14	0.20	**0.28**	-0.09	-0.08
School governance	School autonomy	Average index of school responsibility for curriculum and assessment	**0.46**	**0.39**	-0.14	-0.14	-0.07	-0.06	0.14	0.05
		Average index of school responsibility for resource allocation	*0.25*	0.22	0.00	0.04	0.04	0.06	0.14	0.08
	School competition	Percentage of students in schools that compete with other schools for students in the same area	0.16	0.18	0.03	-0.03	0.04	0.06	0.04	-0.04
		Percentage of students in private schools	0.14	0.01	-0.19	-0.19	-0.20	-0.16	*-0.21*	**-0.41**
Assessment and accountability policies	Use of standardised assessments	Percentage of students in schools that assess students with standardised tests	-0.05	0.01	**-0.29**	**-0.29**	**-0.47**	**-0.44**	-0.18	-0.20
		Existence of standards-based external examinations	0.16	0.21	*-0.24*	-0.21	-0.14	-0.14	0.05	0.07
	Percentage of students in schools that use assessment or achievement data to:	Provide comparative information to parents (relative to national/regional population)	*-0.23*	-0.04	-0.03	-0.03	-0.16	-0.18	0.06	0.17
		Compare the school with other schools	-0.21	0.01	-0.09	-0.13	*-0.24*	**-0.28**	-0.03	0.05
		Monitor progress over time	**-0.29**	0.06	-0.07	-0.18	*-0.23*	**-0.27**	-0.13	-0.08
		Post achievement data publicly	-0.11	-0.11	-0.10	-0.08	*-0.23*	-0.21	0.11	0.11
		Have their progress tracked by administrative authorities	**-0.36**	-0.22	0.01	-0.03	*-0.25*	*-0.25*	0.01	0.05
		Make curricular decisions	-0.15	0.05	-0.15	-0.21	**-0.33**	**-0.35**	-0.13	-0.12
		Allocate resources	**-0.47**	**-0.38**	0.03	0.03	-0.19	-0.21	-0.10	-0.06
		Monitor teacher practices	**-0.46**	-0.11	-0.12	*-0.24*	-0.12	-0.18	-0.17	-0.10
Resources invested in education		Average number of minutes per week spent in regular school lessons on the language of instruction	0.09	0.06	-0.03	-0.01	*-0.23*	-0.21	-0.10	-0.16
	Percentage of students who take after-school lessons for:	enrichment	**-0.51**	*-0.24*	*-0.21*	**-0.32**	-0.20	**-0.26**	**-0.31**	**-0.26**
		remedial purposes	**-0.35**	-0.09	-0.17	-0.21	-0.14	-0.14	**-0.24**	-0.18
		Average class size for the language of instruction	-0.05	0.14	-0.06	-0.13	0.02	0.03	**-0.33**	**-0.33**
		Average index of extra-curricular activities	0.01	0.16	*-0.22*	*-0.22*	-0.17	-0.15	-0.04	-0.04
		Teachers' salaries relative to GDP/capita (weighted average of upper and lower secondary school teachers[1])	**0.33**	*0.28*	-0.03	-0.14	0.02	-0.06	-0.25	**-0.33**
		Cumulative expenditure by educational institutions per student aged 6 to 15	**0.48**	0.22	-0.08	-0.05	-0.09	0.05	*0.30*	-0.10

Note: Values that are statistically significant at the 10% level (p < 0.10) are indicated in italics and at the 5% level (p < 0.05) are in bold.
1. The average is computed by weighting teachers' salaries for upper and lower secondary school according to the respective 15-year-old students' enrolment (for countries with valid information on whether 15-year-old students are both at the upper and lower secondary levels).
StatLink http://dx.doi.org/10.1787/888932343285

[Part 4/4]
Table IV.2.1 Correlations between system-level characteristics and educational outcomes

			All countries and economies							
			Change in reading performance per unit increase in the PISA index of economic, social and cultural status of schools		Change in reading performance per unit increase in the PISA index of economic, social and cultural status of students in the average school		Standard deviation of reading performance		Percentage of variance in reading performance that lies between schools	
			Without accounting for GDP/capita	With accounting for GDP/capita	Without accounting for GDP/capita	With accounting for GDP/capita	Without accounting for GDP/capita	With accounting for GDP/capita	Without accounting for GDP/capita	With accounting for GDP/capita
Selecting and grouping students	Vertical differentiation	Average age of entry into primary school	-0.11	-0.06	-0.19	-0.04	**-0.33**	*-0.25*	0.11	0.05
		Percentage of students who repeated one or more grades	0.05	0.01	**-0.36**	**-0.43**	0.11	0.12	**0.27**	**0.31**
	Horizontal differentiation at the system level	Each additional year of selection prior to the age of 15	**0.62**	**0.61**	*-0.22*	**-0.28**	0.16	*0.24*	**0.50**	**0.62**
		Number of school types or distinct educational programmes available for 15-year-olds	**0.58**	**0.58**	**-0.30**	**-0.36**	*0.23*	0.19	**0.60**	**0.64**
		Percentage of students in selective schools	**0.43**	**0.42**	**-0.49**	**-0.52**	-0.08	-0.09	**0.56**	**0.58**
	Horizontal differentiation at the school level	Percentage of students in schools that group students by ability in all subjects	0.01	0.02	-0.18	-0.20	0.17	0.06	*0.25*	0.21
		Percentage of students in schools that transfer students to other schools due to low achievement, behavioural problems or special learning needs	0.03	0.07	**-0.37**	**-0.41**	0.10	0.04	**0.46**	**0.47**
School governance	School autonomy	Average index of school responsibility for curriculum and assessment	0.18	0.14	0.14	0.02	-0.15	*-0.22*	-0.07	0.01
		Average index of school responsibility for resource allocation	0.15	0.08	0.01	-0.06	-0.04	-0.14	0.08	0.09
	School competition	Percentage of students in schools that compete with other schools for students in the same area	0.13	0.20	-0.10	-0.18	-0.10	-0.12	0.18	0.21
		Percentage of students in private schools	-0.06	-0.13	-0.14	**-0.33**	-0.11	**-0.30**	0.11	0.17
Assessment and accountability policies	Use of standardised assessments	Percentage of students in schools that assess students with standardised tests	**-0.30**	**-0.30**	*0.24*	**0.27**	-0.12	*-0.23*	**-0.31**	**-0.35**
		Existence of standards-based external examinations	0.04	-0.01	0.17	0.21	-0.10	-0.16	-0.09	-0.11
	Percentage of students in schools that use assessment or achievement data to:	Provide comparative information to parents (relative to national/regional population)	-0.05	-0.02	0.19	**0.38**	-0.07	-0.07	-0.15	**-0.30**
		Compare the school with other schools	**-0.29**	*-0.25*	0.19	**0.36**	*-0.21*	-0.21	*-0.21*	**-0.34**
		Monitor progress over time	**-0.30**	-0.19	-0.04	0.14	-0.08	-0.08	-0.02	-0.19
		Post achievement data publicly	-0.15	-0.16	**0.29**	**0.33**	-0.07	-0.14	*-0.23*	**-0.27**
		Have their progress tracked by administrative authorities	**-0.30**	*-0.24*	*0.21*	**0.36**	0.07	0.07	*-0.23*	**-0.37**
		Make curricular decisions	*-0.24*	-0.18	0.08	0.18	-0.09	-0.12	-0.14	*-0.25*
		Allocate resources	-0.19	-0.17	0.00	0.12	0.03	0.00	-0.01	-0.12
		Monitor teacher practices	-0.12	0.01	**-0.25**	-0.07	-0.11	-0.12	0.18	0.00
Resources invested in education		Average number of minutes per week spent in regular school lessons on the language of instruction	-0.14	-0.17	0.12	0.08	0.05	-0.01	-0.16	-0.16
	Percentage of students who take after-school lessons for:	enrichment	-0.18	-0.09	-0.23	-0.06	-0.12	-0.13	0.14	-0.02
		remedial purposes	-0.13	-0.04	*-0.24*	-0.12	-0.15	-0.18	0.17	0.09
		Average class size for the language of instruction	-0.05	0.05	**-0.41**	**-0.42**	**-0.25**	*-0.25*	**0.24**	*0.22*
		Average index of extra-curricular activities	-0.05	-0.05	0.03	0.09	-0.08	-0.18	0.02	-0.06
		Teachers' salaries relative to GDP/capita (weighted average of upper and lower secondary school teachers[1])	-0.08	-0.05	-0.17	-0.24	**-0.50**	**-0.44**	-0.01	0.05
		Cumulative expenditure by educational institutions per student aged 6 to 15	0.11	-0.05	**0.32**	-0.20	**0.40**	-0.12	-0.21	0.05

Note: Values that are statistically significant at the 10% level ($p < 0.10$) are indicated in italics and at the 5% level ($p < 0.05$) are in bold.
1. The average is computed by weighting teachers' salaries for upper and lower secondary school according to the respective 15-year-old students' enrolment (for countries with valid information on whether 15-year-old students are both at the upper and lower secondary levels).
StatLink http://dx.doi.org/10.1787/888932343285

[Part 1/2]

Table IV.2.2a **Within- and between-school variation in reading performance and variation explained by schools' policies on selecting and grouping students**

		Variance		Remaining variance						Variance decomposition expressed as a percentage of the average variance in student performance in reading across OECD countries		
		Empty (or fully unconditional) model[1]		Model with demographic and socio-economic background[2]		Model with school policies and practices[3]		Model with demographic and socio-economic background and with school policies and practices[4]		Total variance in student performance	Total variance within schools as a percentage of total variance	Total variance between schools as a percentage of total variance
		Within-school	Between-school	Within-school	Between-school	Within-school	Between-school	Within-school	Between-school	%	%	%
OECD	Australia	7 631	2 692	6 997	880	7 676	2 371	6 997	866	112	83	29
	Austria	4 454	5 588	4 255	2 262	4 441	3 996	4 257	1 840	109	48	61
	Belgium	4 833	5 343	4 612	1 643	4 831	5 688	4 612	1 618	111	52	58
	Canada	6 780	1 877	6 238	986	6 790	1 478	6 238	837	94	74	20
	Chile	4 005	4 893	3 886	1 219	4 007	1 177	3 877	484	97	43	53
	Czech Republic	4 428	4 249	4 136	1 135	4 458	3 154	4 138	997	94	48	46
	Denmark	6 012	1 134	5 254	328	5 999	908	5 249	236	78	65	12
	Estonia	5 595	1 557	4 991	681	5 591	1 130	4 972	570	78	61	17
	Finland	6 993	665	5 641	458	6 987	589	5 646	409	83	76	7
	France	w	w	w	w	w	w	w	w	w	w	w
	Germany	3 890	5 890	3 558	1 708	3 869	5 432	3 560	1 566	106	42	64
	Greece	5 558	4 745	5 126	2 165	5 575	3 280	5 139	1 968	112	60	52
	Hungary	2 923	5 846	2 792	1 717	2 919	2 514	2 789	1 089	95	32	63
	Iceland	8 186	1 348	7 186	1 015	8 186	1 215	7 192	882	104	89	15
	Ireland	6 966	2 805	6 408	1 145	7 014	1 826	6 403	870	106	76	30
	Israel	6 615	6 250	6 312	3 230	6 661	4 495	6 320	2 426	140	72	68
	Italy	4 085	6 695	3 905	2 880	4 090	3 721	3 910	2 380	117	44	73
	Japan	5 386	5 087	5 248	2 255	5 404	5 475	5 250	2 202	114	59	55
	Korea	5 283	2 741	4 829	1 038	5 284	2 722	4 827	892	87	57	30
	Luxembourg	6 906	5 335	6 112	610	6 956	1 150	6 107	288	133	75	58
	Mexico	3 869	3 583	3 723	1 964	3 887	2 413	3 728	1 508	81	42	39
	Netherlands	2 795	5 107	2 670	2 224	2 793	4 276	2 671	1 849	86	30	55
	New Zealand	8 228	2 622	6 974	530	8 241	2 165	6 978	459	118	89	28
	Norway	7 598	874	6 455	669	7 599	869	6 459	666	92	83	9
	Poland	6 869	1 585	5 582	458	6 835	973	5 580	370	92	75	17
	Portugal	5 191	2 565	4 666	883	5 194	804	4 661	408	84	56	28
	Slovak Republic	4 565	2 989	3 972	1 151	4 567	2 231	3 971	1 071	82	50	32
	Slovenia	3 102	4 142	2 941	1 818	3 084	3 929	2 944	1 677	79	34	45
	Spain	6 048	1 690	5 390	816	6 046	861	5 389	657	84	66	18
	Sweden	8 290	1 877	7 007	605	8 283	1 625	7 008	589	110	90	20
	Switzerland	5 652	2 740	5 115	1 100	5 667	1 633	5 115	717	91	61	30
	Turkey	3 245	6 536	2 958	1 375	3 242	2 692	2 959	913	106	35	71
	United Kingdom	6 684	2 775	6 275	635	6 737	1 867	6 283	594	103	73	30
	United States	6 476	3 638	6 041	838	6 493	1 771	6 019	672	110	70	40
	OECD average	5 591	3 616	5 068	1 285	5 618	2 437	5 068	1 048	100	61	39
Partners	Albania	7 105	3 127	6 150	1 339	7 107	2 184	6 147	1 143	111	77	34
	Argentina	5 523	8 456	5 201	3 238	5 527	3 571	5 204	1 775	152	60	92
	Azerbaijan	3 459	2 490	3 287	2 054	3 465	2 263	3 287	1 893	65	38	27
	Brazil	4 702	4 417	4 514	1 770	4 724	1 987	4 515	1 044	99	51	48
	Bulgaria	6 439	6 418	5 794	2 053	6 437	4 570	5 790	1 810	140	70	70
	Colombia	4 813	3 162	4 711	688	4 848	2 128	4 711	600	87	52	34
	Croatia	4 473	4 045	4 183	1 391	4 479	2 691	4 173	985	93	49	44
	Dubai (UAE)	5 439	5 732	5 121	2 472	5 414	4 005	5 102	2 001	121	59	62
	Hong Kong-China	4 360	3 143	4 183	1 270	4 362	1 707	4 183	1 078	81	47	34
	Indonesia	2 298	1 749	2 117	1 181	2 302	1 484	2 117	1 057	44	25	19
	Jordan	5 461	3 312	5 186	1 727	5 495	2 735	5 193	1 579	95	59	36
	Kazakhstan	5 078	2 887	4 456	1 542	5 081	2 776	4 456	1 490	87	55	31
	Kyrgyzstan	5 901	3 266	5 126	1 398	5 925	2 797	5 127	1 308	100	64	35
	Latvia	5 200	1 391	4 491	634	5 196	700	4 475	454	72	56	15
	Lithuania	5 190	1 864	4 263	828	5 193	1 504	4 267	802	77	56	20
	Macao-China	4 179	2 882	4 000	775	4 192	766	3 995	305	77	45	31
	Montenegro	5 587	3 150	5 124	683	5 602	1 883	5 122	631	95	61	34
	Panama	4 213	5 942	4 103	2 647	4 197	4 047	4 107	1 695	110	46	65
	Peru	4 623	5 886	4 524	1 316	4 634	3 147	4 528	1 004	114	50	64
	Qatar	5 891	6 676	5 520	3 383	5 859	4 786	5 501	2 799	137	64	73
	Romania	3 832	4 057	3 678	2 308	3 807	3 520	3 682	2 254	86	42	44
	Russian Federation	5 826	1 965	5 193	900	5 835	1 665	5 192	888	85	63	21
	Serbia	4 123	3 909	3 954	1 840	4 123	2 412	3 951	1 631	87	45	42
	Shanghai-China	4 095	2 551	3 813	701	4 124	1 447	3 817	532	72	44	28
	Singapore	6 195	3 387	5 612	782	6 236	2 801	5 624	753	104	67	37
	Chinese Taipei	5 808	2 772	5 070	1 306	5 857	1 835	5 073	1 069	93	63	30
	Thailand	3 052	1 231	2 706	816	3 053	1 007	2 708	704	47	33	13
	Trinidad and Tobago	5 148	8 320	4 720	2 527	5 126	2 895	4 723	1 582	146	56	90
	Tunisia	4 291	3 034	4 174	1 640	4 314	620	4 176	345	80	47	33
	Uruguay	5 835	4 807	5 342	968	5 875	1 439	5 347	607	116	63	52

1. Multilevel regression model consists of the student and school levels.
2. Multilevel regression model: Reading performance is regressed on the variables of demographic and socio-economic background.
3. Multilevel regression model: Reading performance is regressed on the variables of school policies and practices.
4. Multilevel regression model: Reading performance is regressed on the variables of demographic and socio-economic background and on the variables of school policies and practices.

StatLink http://dx.doi.org/10.1787/888932343285

[Part 2/2]

Table IV.2.2a **Within- and between-school variation in reading performance and variation explained by schools' policies on selecting and grouping students**

		Within-school variance expressed as a percentage of the average variance in student performance in reading across OECD countries				Between-school variance expressed as a percentage of the average variance in student performance in reading across OECD countries			
		Solely accounted for by students' and schools' socio-economic and demographic background	Solely accounted for by schools' policies on selecting and grouping students	Jointly accounted for by students' and schools' socio-economic and demographic background and schools' policies on selecting and grouping students	Remaining within-school variance	Solely accounted for by students' and schools' socio-economic and demographic background	Solely accounted for by schools' policies on selecting and grouping students	Jointly accounted for demographic and socio-economic background and schools' policies on selecting and grouping students	Remaining between-school variance
		%	%	%	%	%	%	%	%
OECD	Australia	7.4	0.0	-0.5	76.0	16.3	0.1	3.3	9.4
	Austria	2.0	0.0	0.2	46.2	23.4	4.6	12.7	20.0
	Belgium	2.4	0.0	0.0	50.1	44.2	0.3	-4.0	17.6
	Canada	6.0	0.0	-0.1	67.8	7.0	1.6	2.7	9.1
	Chile	1.4	0.1	-0.1	42.1	7.5	8.0	32.4	5.3
	Czech Republic	3.5	0.0	-0.3	44.9	23.4	1.5	10.4	10.8
	Denmark	8.1	0.1	0.1	57.0	7.3	1.0	1.5	2.6
	Estonia	6.7	0.2	-0.2	54.0	6.1	1.2	3.4	6.2
	Finland	14.6	-0.1	0.1	61.3	2.0	0.5	0.3	4.4
	France	w	w	w	w	w	w	w	w
	Germany	3.4	0.0	0.3	38.7	42.0	1.5	3.4	17.0
	Greece	4.7	-0.1	0.0	55.8	14.2	2.1	13.8	21.4
	Hungary	1.4	0.0	0.0	30.3	15.5	6.8	29.4	11.8
	Iceland	10.8	-0.1	0.1	78.1	3.6	1.4	0.0	9.6
	Ireland	6.6	0.1	-0.6	69.5	10.4	3.0	7.6	9.4
	Israel	3.7	-0.1	-0.4	68.6	22.5	8.7	10.3	26.4
	Italy	1.9	-0.1	0.0	42.5	14.6	5.4	26.9	25.8
	Japan	1.7	0.0	-0.2	57.0	35.5	0.6	-4.8	23.9
	Korea	5.0	0.0	0.0	52.4	19.9	1.6	-1.4	9.7
	Luxembourg	9.2	0.1	-0.6	66.3	9.4	3.5	42.0	3.1
	Mexico	1.7	-0.1	-0.1	40.5	9.8	5.0	7.8	16.4
	Netherlands	1.3	0.0	0.0	29.0	26.4	4.1	5.0	20.1
	New Zealand	13.7	0.0	-0.1	75.8	18.5	0.8	4.2	5.0
	Norway	12.4	0.0	0.0	70.2	2.2	0.0	0.0	7.2
	Poland	13.6	0.0	0.3	60.6	6.5	1.0	5.7	4.0
	Portugal	5.8	0.1	-0.1	50.6	4.3	5.1	14.0	4.4
	Slovak Republic	6.5	0.0	0.0	43.1	12.6	0.9	7.4	11.6
	Slovenia	1.5	0.0	0.2	32.0	24.5	1.5	0.8	18.2
	Spain	7.1	0.0	0.0	58.5	2.2	1.7	7.3	7.1
	Sweden	13.8	0.0	0.1	76.1	11.3	0.2	2.6	6.4
	Switzerland	6.0	0.0	-0.2	55.6	9.9	4.2	7.9	7.8
	Turkey	3.1	0.0	0.0	32.1	19.3	5.0	36.7	9.9
	United Kingdom	4.9	-0.1	-0.5	68.2	13.8	0.4	9.4	6.5
	United States	5.1	0.2	-0.4	65.4	11.9	1.8	18.5	7.3
	OECD average	6.0	0.0	-0.1	55.0	15.1	2.6	9.6	11.4
Partners	Albania	10.4	0.0	-0.1	66.8	11.3	2.1	8.1	12.4
	Argentina	3.5	0.0	0.0	56.5	19.5	15.9	37.2	19.3
	Azerbaijan	1.9	0.0	-0.1	35.7	4.0	1.8	0.7	20.6
	Brazil	2.3	0.0	-0.2	49.0	10.2	7.9	18.5	11.3
	Bulgaria	7.0	0.0	0.0	62.9	30.0	2.6	17.4	19.7
	Colombia	1.5	0.0	-0.4	51.2	16.6	1.0	10.3	6.5
	Croatia	3.3	0.1	-0.2	45.3	18.5	4.4	10.3	10.7
	Dubai (UAE)	3.4	0.2	0.1	55.4	21.8	5.1	13.7	21.7
	Hong Kong-China	1.9	0.0	0.0	45.4	6.8	2.1	13.5	11.7
	Indonesia	2.0	0.0	0.0	23.0	4.6	1.4	1.5	11.5
	Jordan	3.3	-0.1	-0.3	56.4	12.6	1.6	4.7	17.1
	Kazakhstan	6.8	0.0	0.0	48.4	14.0	0.6	0.6	16.2
	Kyrgyzstan	8.7	0.0	-0.3	55.7	16.2	1.0	4.1	14.2
	Latvia	7.8	0.2	-0.1	48.6	2.7	2.0	5.5	4.9
	Lithuania	10.1	0.0	0.0	46.3	7.6	0.3	3.6	8.7
	Macao-China	2.1	0.0	-0.2	43.4	5.0	5.1	17.9	3.3
	Montenegro	5.2	0.0	-0.2	55.6	13.6	0.6	13.2	6.9
	Panama	1.0	0.0	0.2	44.6	25.6	10.3	10.2	18.4
	Peru	1.1	0.0	-0.1	49.2	23.3	3.4	26.4	10.9
	Qatar	3.9	0.2	0.1	59.7	21.6	6.3	14.2	30.4
	Romania	1.4	-0.1	0.3	40.0	13.7	0.6	5.3	24.5
	Russian Federation	7.0	0.0	-0.1	56.4	8.4	0.1	3.1	9.6
	Serbia	1.9	0.0	0.0	42.9	8.5	2.3	14.0	17.7
	Shanghai-China	3.3	0.0	-0.3	41.5	9.9	1.8	10.2	5.8
	Singapore	6.7	-0.1	-0.3	61.1	22.2	0.3	6.1	8.2
	Chinese Taipei	8.5	0.0	-0.5	55.1	8.3	2.6	7.6	11.6
	Thailand	3.7	0.0	0.0	29.4	3.3	1.2	1.2	7.6
	Trinidad and Tobago	4.4	0.0	0.3	51.3	14.3	10.3	48.7	17.2
	Tunisia	1.5	0.0	-0.2	45.4	3.0	14.1	12.2	3.7
	Uruguay	5.7	-0.1	-0.4	58.1	9.0	3.9	32.7	6.6

1. Multilevel regression model consists of the student and school levels.
2. Multilevel regression model: Reading performance is regressed on the variables of demographic and socio-economic background.
3. Multilevel regression model: Reading performance is regressed on the variables of school policies and practices.
4. Multilevel regression model: Reading performance is regressed on the variables of demographic and socio-economic background and on the variables of school policies and practices.

StatLink http://dx.doi.org/10.1787/888932343285

[Part 1/1]

Table IV.2.2b Relationships between schools' policies on selecting and grouping students and reading performance

		Schools' policies on selecting and grouping students[1]							
		School with high academic selectivity for school admittance		School is very likely to transfer students with low achievement, behavioural problems or special learning needs		School with ability grouping for all subjects		Percentage of students who repeated one or more grades	
		Change in score	S.E.	Change in score	S.E.	Change in score	S.E.	Change in score	S.E.
OECD	Australia	-7.1	(8.7)	**-29.2**	(8.1)	**29.8**	(14.4)	-18.4	(31.0)
	Austria	**49.2**	(15.4)	**31.8**	(14.4)	-26.9	(19.3)	**-0.7**	(0.2)
	Belgium	-9.4	(15.6)	7.9	(11.7)	-20.8	(16.6)	**-1.2**	(0.3)
	Canada	**13.8**	(5.6)	4.2	(8.5)	-3.5	(6.9)	**-0.9**	(0.2)
	Chile	**27.7**	(8.3)	11.0	(8.7)	-1.5	(8.6)	**-1.5**	(0.1)
	Czech Republic	**45.7**	(10.6)	-10.7	(13.5)	**-21.3**	(9.3)	**-1.9**	(0.5)
	Denmark	21.3	(16.6)	5.3	(11.3)	**-31.1**	(7.3)	**-2.2**	(0.5)
	Estonia	15.0	(11.5)	-0.5	(11.2)	-0.9	(11.4)	**-1.6**	(0.3)
	Finland	**22.4**	(9.9)	c	c	-25.7	(28.0)	**-2.4**	(0.8)
	France	w	w	w	w	w	w	w	w
	Germany	28.3	(14.2)	12.9	(14.1)	-24.9	(17.9)	**-0.9**	(0.4)
	Greece	5.1	(19.3)	-8.8	(14.3)	**37.0**	(20.4)	-1.0	(0.3)
	Hungary	**31.1**	(19.4)	1.1	(12.7)	-34.5	(17.9)	**-1.1**	(0.2)
	Iceland	c	c	c	c	-18.4	(14.0)	-2.5	(2.4)
	Ireland	**-23.1**	(9.4)	c	c	-1.2	(12.8)	**-2.7**	(0.6)
	Israel	-3.9	(14.1)	-43.9	(22.8)	-10.7	(15.5)	**-2.3**	(0.4)
	Italy	-9.7	(8.7)	**24.3**	(8.5)	2.0	(9.0)	**-1.8**	(0.3)
	Japan	-11.5	(19.8)	**-53.6**	(16.5)	**32.1**	(16.0)	c	c
	Korea	3.1	(16.5)	-14.5	(19.6)	2.6	(21.2)	c	c
	Luxembourg	-13.3	(11.3)	2.3	(12.1)	-21.2	(11.6)	**-2.0**	(0.4)
	Mexico	10.1	(8.0)	9.3	(6.0)	1.1	(8.3)	**-1.0**	(0.1)
	Netherlands	**65.4**	(27.8)	**-48.9**	(15.0)	-5.8	(14.2)	-0.6	(0.5)
	New Zealand	-4.4	(11.6)	-50.4	(37.0)	25.9	(14.3)	**-2.9**	(0.8)
	Norway	4.6	(9.6)	c	c	6.7	(9.3)	c	c
	Poland	**43.5**	(10.2)	15.7	(13.4)	-1.6	(14.2)	**-2.1**	(0.2)
	Portugal	-36.7	(33.3)	c	c	**-16.3**	(9.2)	**-1.2**	(0.1)
	Slovak Republic	**20.0**	(8.8)	-10.5	(9.7)	**-18.4**	(11.8)	**-2.0**	(0.4)
	Slovenia	**46.7**	(11.9)	4.4	(13.2)	3.4	(15.5)	-0.3	(0.3)
	Spain	-2.3	(11.1)	**7.2**	(7.3)	9.8	(5.2)	**-1.6**	(0.1)
	Sweden	36.8	(19.2)	-6.2	(11.8)	23.6	(17.6)	-1.2	(0.9)
	Switzerland	**13.2**	(6.5)	**40.8**	(6.9)	-10.9	(6.7)	**-1.3**	(0.2)
	Turkey	**72.2**	(16.9)	1.1	(14.1)	4.1	(12.5)	**-1.6**	(0.4)
	United Kingdom	**42.5**	(11.6)	-17.8	(12.2)	0.1	(9.4)	**-5.4**	(1.5)
	United States	**57.4**	(20.7)	**-20.8**	(10.9)	17.0	(15.7)	**-1.7**	(0.3)
	OECD average	**17.3**	(2.7)	-4.9	(2.7)	-3.0	(2.5)	**-2.3**	(1.0)
Partners	Albania	7.3	(11.4)	19.1	(11.8)	-16.0	(13.2)	**-2.4**	(0.6)
	Argentina	15.0	(21.6)	36.0	(14.8)	-30.2	(13.7)	**-1.8**	(0.2)
	Azerbaijan	-4.2	(10.1)	23.5	(11.7)	-7.4	(12.5)	**-3.4**	(1.0)
	Brazil	-3.3	(9.4)	**25.0**	(11.0)	-2.9	(6.6)	**-1.6**	(0.1)
	Bulgaria	**36.1**	(14.5)	12.3	(15.4)	-14.2	(23.7)	**-1.3**	(0.2)
	Colombia	8.0	(10.8)	**25.9**	(10.3)	-19.5	(13.7)	**-1.7**	(0.3)
	Croatia	**58.3**	(19.0)	9.5	(13.8)	20.5	(17.5)	**-3.2**	(0.5)
	Dubai (UAE)	**40.9**	(11.9)	**-37.8**	(10.3)	-17.3	(10.8)	**-1.7**	(0.2)
	Hong Kong-China	**18.4**	(11.0)	-2.3	(8.7)	-21.2	(9.2)	**-2.8**	(0.4)
	Indonesia	11.1	(7.2)	**15.7**	(7.0)	-7.6	(7.3)	**-0.6**	(0.2)
	Jordan	-5.4	(11.6)	-3.4	(9.6)	6.7	(10.4)	**-2.9**	(0.8)
	Kazakhstan	-2.7	(10.1)	27.3	(15.5)	-5.3	(10.5)	-0.4	(1.2)
	Kyrgyzstan	-16.2	(9.9)	-10.3	(9.1)	**24.5**	(9.6)	**-1.0**	(0.6)
	Latvia	**18.6**	(7.3)	6.9	(8.6)	-17.6	(11.3)	**-1.5**	(0.3)
	Lithuania	19.4	(12.6)	7.0	(12.1)	-8.0	(9.2)	**-1.6**	(0.5)
	Macao-China	2.9	(10.5)	-14.1	(9.7)	3.9	(14.5)	**-1.4**	(0.2)
	Montenegro	-16.9	(15.9)	c	c	4.0	(13.8)	**-1.9**	(0.4)
	Panama	8.4	(16.6)	10.6	(17.7)	23.8	(13.8)	**-1.5**	(0.3)
	Peru	**30.2**	(11.2)	10.8	(12.9)	-7.6	(11.5)	**-2.1**	(0.2)
	Qatar	**44.9**	(12.1)	-7.9	(11.8)	-12.4	(12.1)	**-1.7**	(0.2)
	Romania	8.9	(13.3)	19.3	(15.5)	2.4	(19.8)	**-0.8**	(0.3)
	Russian Federation	**18.4**	(9.5)	15.0	(16.1)	-5.5	(7.0)	**-1.0**	(0.3)
	Serbia	-9.1	(14.6)	8.8	(12.0)	-10.1	(13.7)	**-1.3**	(0.2)
	Shanghai-China	**34.6**	(8.6)	-27.7	(15.8)	-11.9	(11.6)	-1.2	(0.5)
	Singapore	**31.0**	(11.7)	c	c	-2.6	(12.2)	**-3.0**	(1.1)
	Chinese Taipei	**33.1**	(10.8)	**-36.2**	(11.3)	13.6	(18.4)	-3.3	(2.7)
	Thailand	8.5	(6.3)	11.2	(8.3)	16.1	(9.4)	**-0.8**	(0.3)
	Trinidad and Tobago	11.9	(9.5)	-8.0	(12.0)	-29.0	(14.5)	**-3.7**	(0.2)
	Tunisia	7.0	(6.8)	-6.5	(6.6)	7.7	(9.4)	**-1.2**	(0.1)
	Uruguay	6.6	(12.1)	21.6	(10.1)	1.6	(11.2)	**-1.5**	(0.1)

Note: Values that are statistically significant are indicated in bold (see Annex A3).
1. Multilevel regression model (student and school levels): Reading performance is regressed on the variables of school policies and practices presented in this table.
StatLink http://dx.doi.org/10.1787/888932343285

[Part 1/2]

Table IV.2.2c **Relationships between schools' policies on selecting and grouping students and reading performance, accounting for students' and schools' socio-economic and demographic background**

		Schools' policies on selecting and grouping students[1]								Student socio-economic and demographic background[1]									
		School with high academic selectivity for school admittance		School is very likely to transfer students with low achievement, behavioural problems or special learning needs		School with ability grouping for all subjects		Percentage of students who repeated one or more grades		Student is a female		Student without an immigrant background		Student's language at home is the same as the language of assessment		PISA index of economic, social and cultural status of student (1 unit increase)		PISA index of economic, social and cultural status of student (squared)	
		Change in score	S.E.	Change in score	S.E.	Change in score	S.E.	Change in score	S.E.	Change in score	S.E.	Change in score	S.E.	Change in score	S.E.	Change in score	S.E.	Change in score	S.E.
OECD	Australia	0.5	(6.1)	-18.3	(11.4)	15.5	(15.9)	24.2	(35.9)	**37.7**	(2.3)	**-5.8**	(2.5)	**23.2**	(4.2)	**27.3**	(1.7)	**-3.0**	(1.0)
	Austria	**18.1**	(10.5)	19.0	(10.1)	-15.8	(12.3)	**-0.5**	(0.2)	**21.1**	(3.4)	**13.0**	(4.6)	**16.3**	(5.4)	**8.1**	(2.0)	0.1	(1.3)
	Belgium	7.1	(9.3)	0.8	(6.3)	-6.0	(7.7)	-0.1	(0.2)	**19.1**	(2.1)	**17.3**	(2.7)	**6.3**	(3.3)	**12.1**	(1.4)	1.5	(0.9)
	Canada	3.4	(3.8)	0.6	(5.5)	-3.4	(5.6)	**-0.7**	(0.1)	**35.2**	(2.0)	3.8	(2.6)	**18.2**	(4.4)	**19.0**	(1.3)	**3.2**	(1.0)
	Chile	8.7	(5.4)	8.2	(6.2)	-4.6	(5.7)	**-1.0**	(0.1)	**18.3**	(3.1)	0.7	(7.6)	**55.9**	(17.7)	**9.8**	(1.9)	0.6	(0.8)
	Czech Republic	**21.5**	(6.2)	-9.0	(8.2)	-7.7	(11.8)	**-0.5**	(0.5)	**35.1**	(2.6)	**13.0**	(3.8)	-1.2	(10.5)	**15.4**	(2.0)	-2.9	(1.6)
	Denmark	**20.7**	(8.4)	**13.1**	(5.1)	-5.6	(6.5)	**-1.5**	(0.3)	**29.3**	(2.9)	**13.9**	(3.6)	**20.3**	(5.9)	**27.2**	(1.7)	-0.3	(1.1)
	Estonia	5.2	(7.8)	-0.5	(12.1)	-11.8	(8.4)	**-1.3**	(0.3)	**43.4**	(2.9)	**14.4**	(3.5)	**27.1**	(7.0)	**17.0**	(2.1)	1.4	(1.9)
	Finland	11.2	(10.8)	c	c	c	c	**-1.8**	(0.7)	**56.5**	(2.5)	**13.4**	(5.6)	**46.9**	(7.3)	**27.2**	(1.9)	-1.1	(1.6)
	France	w	w	w	w	w	w	w	w	w	w	w	w	w	w	w	w	w	w
	Germany	15.2	(8.2)	11.3	(8.3)	-4.4	(11.0)	-0.2	(0.2)	**29.9**	(2.5)	**15.7**	(3.5)	3.5	(6.0)	**9.2**	(1.5)	-1.1	(0.9)
	Greece	-8.7	(14.9)	-1.0	(11.4)	c	c	-0.4	(0.3)	**36.2**	(3.1)	0.9	(3.6)	15.6	(13.9)	**15.8**	(1.7)	2.4	(1.3)
	Hungary	**27.2**	(13.4)	-10.6	(9.1)	c	c	**-0.5**	(0.2)	**24.1**	(2.6)	**-8.7**	(4.6)	16.7	(8.6)	**8.6**	(1.6)	0.8	(1.0)
	Iceland	c	c	c	c	-14.0	(10.5)	-2.7	(1.7)	**45.8**	(3.3)	4.4	(5.3)	**48.6**	(12.0)	**28.4**	(2.7)	**-3.8**	(1.6)
	Ireland	-10.9	(8.0)	c	c	-1.2	(12.9)	**-1.6**	(0.5)	**35.2**	(4.4)	-4.8	(3.9)	**31.3**	(10.3)	**26.9**	(2.1)	-1.9	(1.5)
	Israel	5.6	(11.0)	**-43.4**	(16.4)	-22.1	(12.2)	**-1.6**	(0.4)	**33.4**	(3.8)	-2.9	(4.0)	1.5	(6.1)	**22.1**	(2.6)	**3.9**	(1.3)
	Italy	-3.2	(8.1)	13.4	(7.7)	-2.2	(7.7)	**-0.9**	(0.2)	**27.3**	(1.7)	**15.6**	(2.6)	**5.8**	(2.6)	**5.3**	(0.8)	-0.9	(0.9)
	Japan	-14.8	(14.5)	-26.6	(13.9)	-11.8	(7.5)	c	c	**28.2**	(2.8)	3.4	(9.2)	**75.6**	(28.5)	4.4	(2.5)	-0.5	(2.3)
	Korea	**29.4**	(9.7)	-0.3	(13.5)	6.7	(15.2)	c	c	**43.1**	(5.7)	3.1	(11.6)	55.0	(37.1)	**18.8**	(2.7)	0.1	(1.4)
	Luxembourg	4.0	(7.4)	7.1	(7.8)	-0.5	(8.8)	**-1.1**	(0.2)	**37.1**	(3.2)	**28.6**	(3.5)	**24.2**	(4.9)	**16.7**	(2.9)	-1.6	(1.2)
	Mexico	2.6	(6.9)	-2.3	(4.9)	-3.7	(6.5)	**-0.7**	(0.1)	**21.7**	(1.9)	**24.6**	(3.5)	**20.1**	(5.4)	**8.5**	(1.4)	**1.6**	(0.5)
	Netherlands	**35.2**	(13.6)	-24.5	(12.9)	6.4	(9.5)	**-0.7**	(0.3)	**19.3**	(1.7)	**5.9**	(2.7)	12.2	(6.6)	**5.2**	(1.6)	0.2	(1.1)
	New Zealand	-9.2	(5.8)	c	c	11.2	(11.4)	0.7	(0.6)	**49.5**	(4.5)	-7.0	(3.6)	**46.5**	(5.6)	**34.9**	(2.8)	0.0	(2.4)
	Norway	3.1	(12.0)	c	c	1.1	(8.0)	c	c	**48.3**	(3.5)	**10.9**	(5.4)	**37.1**	(7.9)	**28.7**	(3.1)	-1.9	(2.0)
	Poland	3.9	(8.3)	-1.1	(6.6)	2.7	(10.0)	**-1.5**	(0.2)	**53.0**	(3.4)	22.0	(23.0)	**48.7**	(16.7)	**31.3**	(1.8)	**-3.5**	(1.4)
	Portugal	-25.9	(19.5)	c	c	-10.4	(6.8)	**-0.8**	(0.1)	**34.3**	(2.6)	-2.1	(3.1)	13.4	(8.1)	**18.0**	(1.4)	-0.7	(0.7)
	Slovak Republic	5.8	(6.9)	-5.0	(6.6)	-7.6	(10.8)	**-0.9**	(0.4)	**43.2**	(2.9)	1.0	(5.4)	**27.0**	(7.5)	**18.0**	(1.9)	**-3.5**	(1.2)
	Slovenia	**15.3**	(7.5)	8.5	(9.7)	-0.3	(17.0)	-0.4	(0.4)	**31.8**	(2.3)	**8.0**	(3.2)	5.7	(5.2)	**3.4**	(1.2)	1.1	(1.1)
	Spain	-1.6	(10.7)	4.7	(5.9)	5.0	(5.6)	**-0.9**	(0.1)	**29.7**	(1.7)	**23.6**	(2.4)	**11.5**	(3.5)	**19.8**	(1.0)	[illegible]	(0.6)
	Sweden	**20.9**	(10.6)	8.5	(13.7)	10.1	(8.8)	-0.1	(0.5)	**46.3**	(3.0)	7.6	(4.1)	**29.8**	(6.4)	**32.1**	(2.1)	[illegible]	(1.0)
	Switzerland	**12.4**	(5.0)	**24.3**	(6.1)	-7.2	(5.5)	**-0.9**	(0.1)	**32.1**	(2.3)	**11.3**	(2.8)	**19.6**	(3.5)	**18.3**	(1.6)	[illegible]	(1.4)
	Turkey	**24.5**	(9.9)	-15.3	(9.0)	9.4	(7.6)	**-1.0**	(0.3)	**30.7**	(2.9)	-2.2	(7.4)	3.4	(11.4)	**7.3**	(2.3)	[illegible]	(0.9)
	United Kingdom	8.7	(7.6)	-0.1	(6.0)	3.3	(6.2)	**-1.6**	(0.8)	**25.2**	(3.1)	-6.7	(4.4)	**17.7**	(6.6)	**26.0**	(2.0)	0.5	(1.6)
	United States	5.7	(8.8)	-1.2	(8.4)	**24.3**	(9.1)	**-1.0**	(0.3)	**28.2**	(4.1)	-3.2	(7.6)	6.5	(8.0)	**23.5**	(2.4)	-1.9	(3.0)
	OECD average	**7.6**	(1.7)	-1.5	(1.8)	-1.5	(1.8)	-0.1	(1.2)	**34.2**	(0.5)	**7.0**	(1.1)	**23.9**	(2.0)	**18.0**	(0.3)	-0.4	(0.2)
Partners	Albania	-3.2	(8.5)	18.6	(10.1)	-1.2	(10.9)	**-1.3**	(0.5)	**57.5**	(4.1)	23.4	(11.8)	15.6	(16.3)	**21.0**	(3.6)	**3.5**	(1.5)
	Argentina	-2.3	(10.2)	12.4	(9.1)	-18.5	(8.9)	**-1.2**	(0.2)	**30.8**	(3.2)	1.4	(5.3)	**44.9**	(17.2)	**12.5**	(2.1)	**1.6**	(1.0)
	Azerbaijan	-0.9	(10.1)	21.5	(11.5)	-12.5	(11.7)	**-2.9**	(1.0)	**22.7**	(2.4)	3.0	(5.0)	-1.8	(6.2)	**11.4**	(2.1)	1.6	(1.0)
	Brazil	-2.1	(7.4)	9.6	(5.8)	-3.3	(4.7)	**-1.0**	(0.1)	**28.3**	(2.0)	11.5	(9.1)	**31.9**	(12.6)	**8.2**	(1.9)	**1.5**	(0.7)
	Bulgaria	**20.3**	(9.9)	5.6	(9.5)	-15.4	(11.9)	-0.4	(0.2)	**47.6**	(3.8)	**28.4**	(8.0)	**28.3**	(6.8)	**13.6**	(2.3)	1.3	(1.4)
	Colombia	-11.8	(6.4)	4.3	(5.0)	-10.0	(7.8)	**-0.5**	(0.2)	**10.6**	(3.0)	**18.9**	(8.0)	**61.0**	(21.8)	**13.0**	(2.7)	1.3	(0.9)
	Croatia	**48.3**	(12.8)	-6.6	(8.1)	-1.4	(7.4)	**-1.9**	(0.4)	**35.7**	(3.5)	3.5	(2.5)	-7.3	(9.1)	**10.6**	(1.9)	**-3.6**	(1.2)
	Dubai (UAE)	8.8	(8.2)	**-22.0**	(8.6)	-15.9	(9.1)	**-0.9**	(0.2)	**28.1**	(4.6)	**-32.3**	(3.5)	**20.1**	(3.0)	**19.0**	(1.9)	**2.6**	(1.1)
	Hong Kong-China	14.3	(9.1)	8.8	(7.4)	-6.4	(8.7)	**-1.3**	(0.5)	**25.9**	(2.8)	**-8.9**	(2.4)	**25.4**	(6.8)	2.4	(2.1)	-1.3	(0.9)
	Indonesia	3.9	(6.6)	**12.4**	(6.5)	-7.2	(6.7)	**-0.5**	(0.2)	**28.9**	(1.8)	17.9	(11.2)	-5.2	(2.7)	**6.9**	(2.8)	1.4	(0.8)
	Jordan	-3.7	(9.3)	7.9	(7.5)	2.6	(8.1)	**-1.7**	(0.7)	**47.8**	(9.5)	-5.8	(3.8)	**25.4**	(8.4)	**20.2**	(2.3)	1.3	(1.1)
	Kazakhstan	-13.5	(8.0)	2.7	(10.9)	-7.1	(8.2)	-0.2	(1.4)	**41.5**	(2.6)	**-12.0**	(4.9)	2.0	(4.8)	**17.2**	(2.5)	-2.1	(1.4)
	Kyrgyzstan	-7.4	(8.7)	-5.3	(7.7)	13.0	(8.2)	**-0.7**	(0.6)	**50.5**	(3.0)	**-13.0**	(5.6)	-3.0	(4.9)	**19.9**	(2.4)	**2.6**	(1.2)
	Latvia	7.9	(5.9)	1.8	(7.3)	-17.0	(7.0)	**-1.0**	(0.3)	**46.4**	(2.9)	0.9	(3.3)	2.9	(9.0)	**19.6**	(2.5)	-0.6	(1.6)
	Lithuania	-4.3	(11.7)	6.7	(9.2)	-12.6	(7.8)	-0.2	(0.4)	**54.8**	(2.7)	-1.4	(4.8)	12.5	(7.9)	**19.1**	(1.7)	-0.1	(1.2)
	Macao-China	-0.4	(7.5)	-4.6	(7.6)	0.8	(12.7)	**-1.3**	(0.2)	**22.0**	(2.1)	**-10.1**	(2.7)	**55.1**	(6.8)	**7.1**	(2.1)	0.0	(1.0)
	Montenegro	**-15.4**	(9.0)	c	c	15.6	(9.6)	-0.3	(0.4)	**42.0**	(3.6)	**-6.8**	(2.8)	6.5	(11.2)	**13.1**	(1.5)	0.7	(1.4)
	Panama	10.8	(10.7)	-6.8	(12.3)	**26.5**	(9.3)	**-1.0**	(0.2)	**18.8**	(4.8)	3.2	(6.1)	13.5	(10.6)	**7.3**	(3.4)	**1.7**	(1.0)
	Peru	11.4	(8.8)	-1.4	(7.4)	-1.0	(6.6)	**-0.9**	(0.2)	**11.5**	(3.2)	**21.2**	(10.3)	**28.0**	(7.6)	**11.6**	(2.7)	1.1	(0.8)
	Qatar	19.5	(10.1)	-5.0	(9.2)	-8.7	(9.9)	**-1.0**	(0.2)	**36.3**	(6.2)	**-38.7**	(2.8)	**19.9**	(3.1)	**8.1**	(1.5)	**1.7**	(0.9)
	Romania	9.1	(9.7)	2.7	(12.1)	-13.2	(13.8)	**-0.1**	(0.3)	**16.1**	(3.9)	**20.0**	(10.0)	13.3	(7.8)	**11.2**	(2.2)	0.1	(1.2)
	Russian Federation	11.3	(7.6)	-0.4	(10.5)	-3.6	(5.9)	-0.1	(0.3)	**41.6**	(2.6)	1.4	(2.9)	**20.9**	(5.8)	**21.2**	(2.0)	-1.8	(1.7)
	Serbia	-10.2	(13.2)	10.4	(11.9)	-1.7	(12.4)	**-0.7**	(0.3)	**27.5**	(2.8)	-5.9	(3.5)	3.6	(10.3)	**7.8**	(1.8)	1.2	(1.2)
	Shanghai-China	**13.5**	(4.9)	3.1	(7.3)	3.8	(10.7)	-0.7	(0.3)	**33.5**	(2.3)	**21.0**	(8.7)	**31.2**	(9.5)	**5.3**	(1.8)	0.7	(1.2)
	Singapore	4.5	(7.4)	c	c	5.5	(6.3)	-1.2	(0.6)	**26.3**	(2.3)	-1.0	(3.0)	**25.2**	(3.4)	**17.4**	(2.6)	**-2.5**	(1.3)
	Chinese Taipei	13.6	(9.4)	-20.3	(10.6)	-3.7	(17.8)	-2.7	(1.7)	**45.9**	(4.2)	17.2	(10.2)	8.5	(5.0)	**20.3**	(3.0)	0.7	(1.8)
	Thailand	6.1	(7.2)	8.7	(7.6)	9.8	(7.8)	-0.6	(0.2)	**35.7**	(3.0)	**38.3**	(11.8)	**-15.9**	(4.1)	5.1	(2.9)	0.3	(1.0)
	Trinidad and Tobago	6.3	(7.5)	-2.6	(9.9)	-10.5	(12.2)	**-2.2**	(0.3)	**46.6**	(2.4)	-5.4	(3.3)	**31.8**	(7.5)	**4.5**	(2.2)	1.0	(1.1)
	Tunisia	4.1	(5.6)	-2.3	(5.1)	1.2	(8.6)	**-1.0**	(0.1)	**22.3**	(2.3)	**20.2**	(8.3)	-24.9	(18.3)	2.6	(2.6)	-0.3	(0.8)
	Uruguay	-1.5	(9.5)	-5.2	(9.8)	-5.9	(8.0)	**-0.7**	(0.1)	**39.0**	(3.0)	-2.7	(6.2)	14.3	(9.7)	**15.5**	(2.0)	0.0	(0.9)

Note: Values that are statistically significant are indicated in bold (see Annex A3).

1. Multilevel regression model (student and school levels): Reading performance is regressed on the variables of school policies and practices as well as on socio-economic and demographic background variables presented in this table.

StatLink http://dx.doi.org/10.1787/888932343285

[Part 2/2]

Table IV.2.2c Relationships between schools' policies on selecting and grouping students and reading performance, accounting for students' and schools' socio-economic and demographic background

		Student socio-economic and demographic background[1]									
		School average PISA index of economic, social and cultural status (1 unit increase)		School size (per 100 students)		School size (per 100 students) (squared)		School in a small town or village (15 000 or less people)		School in city (100 000 or more people)	
		Change in score	S.E.	Change in score	S.E.	Change in score	S.E.	Change in score	S.E.	Change in score	S.E.
OECD	Australia	**59.9**	(7.4)	0.3	(2.5)	0.0	(0.1)	2.9	(7.5)	7.3	(5.4)
	Austria	**51.4**	(12.2)	**8.9**	(3.1)	**-0.4**	(0.2)	-16.7	(10.8)	-0.6	(12.5)
	Belgium	**98.1**	(9.0)	**7.0**	(2.4)	**-0.3**	(0.1)	10.2	(8.1)	-7.3	(8.6)
	Canada	**24.3**	(6.5)	1.6	(1.2)	0.0	(0.1)	-0.1	(5.1)	1.0	(4.1)
	Chile	**26.1**	(3.7)	1.0	(1.0)	0.0	(0.0)	6.1	(9.2)	-1.9	(6.4)
	Czech Republic	**113.5**	(8.1)	4.2	(3.7)	-0.3	(0.3)	**14.4**	(6.7)	-12.0	(7.1)
	Denmark	**38.4**	(5.0)	2.4	(2.5)	-0.3	(0.2)	-5.8	(3.9)	8.1	(5.7)
	Estonia	**33.1**	(11.2)	1.6	(2.1)	**-0.1**	(0.1)	7.6	(9.0)	3.2	(9.4)
	Finland	**26.2**	(12.2)	-1.8	(1.8)	0.1	(0.0)	-1.4	(5.0)	0.4	(6.0)
	France	w	w	w	w	w	w	w	w	w	w
	Germany	**95.6**	(9.1)	**9.5**	(2.4)	**-0.3**	(0.1)	19.1	(9.5)	-1.8	(10.0)
	Greece	**44.8**	(11.7)	-25.8	(16.8)	3.7	(2.5)	17.9	(16.6)	-8.8	(18.5)
	Hungary	**50.1**	(8.1)	5.1	(2.7)	-0.2	(0.1)	-1.8	(10.5)	-4.0	(9.0)
	Iceland	23.9	(12.4)	-6.7	(6.2)	0.3	(0.8)	4.9	(9.1)	-3.4	(10.6)
	Ireland	**42.5**	(6.7)	2.6	(4.8)	-0.2	(0.3)	6.1	(6.5)	4.7	(8.2)
	Israel	**73.3**	(13.4)	**10.9**	(4.9)	**-0.5**	(0.2)	**37.5**	(15.1)	5.9	(14.9)
	Italy	**42.8**	(10.5)	**8.0**	(2.5)	**-0.2**	(0.1)	7.3	(11.6)	-1.6	(8.3)
	Japan	**140.7**	(20.9)	1.1	(4.6)	0.1	(0.2)	8.4	(13.8)	-22.3	(12.2)
	Korea	**63.4**	(8.6)	4.9	(4.4)	-0.2	(0.2)	-29.4	(16.5)	**-28.0**	(12.1)
	Luxembourg	**50.8**	(8.4)	-0.3	(1.9)	0.0	(0.1)	5.2	(7.6)	-34.7	(19.6)
	Mexico	**17.4**	(4.6)	0.8	(0.6)	0.0	(0.0)	-6.1	(7.0)	8.6	(6.6)
	Netherlands	**61.5**	(14.8)	**8.2**	(2.6)	**-0.2**	(0.1)	-20.5	(11.2)	7.9	(10.1)
	New Zealand	**58.2**	(9.7)	**4.5**	(1.8)	**-0.1**	(0.1)	12.3	(8.7)	5.9	(6.5)
	Norway	**31.6**	(16.0)	-3.3	(10.3)	0.2	(1.4)	-9.2	(6.7)	-3.2	(7.5)
	Poland	**20.5**	(6.7)	3.7	(4.9)	-0.1	(0.6)	-1.6	(7.0)	**-12.1**	(7.3)
	Portugal	**10.5**	(4.7)	0.4	(2.1)	0.0	(0.1)	1.0	(5.4)	10.7	(5.5)
	Slovak Republic	**55.6**	(12.8)	-0.8	(4.3)	0.2	(0.3)	-2.1	(7.8)	-5.4	(8.9)
	Slovenia	**61.1**	(11.5)	**17.4**	(4.2)	**-1.1**	(0.5)	7.3	(10.3)	-9.9	(8.0)
	Spain	**5.9**	(4.7)	-0.4	(1.3)	0.0	(0.1)	-2.8	(3.9)	**10.1**	(4.5)
	Sweden	**49.3**	(13.1)	-4.3	(3.3)	0.3	(0.2)	1.1	(7.4)	5.9	(9.0)
	Switzerland	**45.9**	(9.3)	**2.2**	(0.7)	**0.0**	(0.0)	-6.8	(7.7)	-10.2	(9.9)
	Turkey	**38.9**	(7.7)	**-6.1**	(2.7)	0.1	(0.1)	-12.9	(12.1)	14.2	(12.8)
	United Kingdom	**62.8**	(6.7)	1.7	(2.2)	0.0	(0.1)	8.0	(5.9)	0.8	(6.7)
	United States	**52.3**	(14.4)	-1.1	(1.7)	0.0	(0.0)	7.2	(16.2)	18.6	(19.7)
	OECD average	**50.6**	(1.8)	**1.7**	(0.8)	0.0	(0.1)	2.0	(1.7)	-1.6	(1.8)
Partners	Albania	**27.9**	(9.3)	**-8.5**	(3.8)	**0.7**	(0.3)	-4.1	(12.3)	12.5	(13.0)
	Argentina	**39.6**	(6.4)	2.9	(2.2)	-0.1	(0.1)	-7.2	(14.0)	10.6	(12.9)
	Azerbaijan	**25.5**	(11.4)	-3.1	(4.1)	0.2	(0.2)	-4.8	(16.0)	-11.8	(14.9)
	Brazil	**35.8**	(4.0)	-0.9	(0.9)	0.0	(0.0)	2.4	(7.1)	2.1	(5.5)
	Bulgaria	**52.8**	(10.2)	1.4	(3.7)	0.1	(0.3)	7.1	(10.6)	20.7	(11.4)
	Colombia	**43.2**	(3.8)	0.2	(0.7)	0.0	(0.0)	**17.2**	(7.2)	-3.2	(6.4)
	Croatia	**70.4**	(6.4)	**6.8**	(2.7)	-0.2	(0.2)	10.8	(8.3)	**-18.5**	(6.8)
	Dubai (UAE)	**52.2**	(9.1)	0.7	(0.5)	0.0	(0.0)	11.2	(19.8)	15.1	(18.1)
	Hong Kong-China	**25.7**	(8.6)	5.8	(7.9)	0.2	(0.4)	a	a	a	a
	Indonesia	**19.4**	(5.7)	3.1	(3.3)	0.0	(0.3)	2.4	(7.9)	13.2	(9.4)
	Jordan	6.1	(12.0)	-5.4	(4.1)	0.4	(0.2)	-9.5	(10.4)	-4.6	(9.4)
	Kazakhstan	**51.1**	(9.8)	**-6.0**	(1.5)	**0.1**	(0.1)	-17.3	(12.9)	9.3	(12.6)
	Kyrgyzstan	**37.8**	(11.2)	0.2	(2.6)	0.0	(0.1)	-2.5	(12.6)	**44.5**	(17.7)
	Latvia	**14.0**	(11.6)	-1.6	(3.1)	0.3	(0.2)	6.0	(8.2)	7.0	(9.9)
	Lithuania	**45.6**	(10.2)	-4.0	(3.4)	0.4	(0.2)	6.5	(9.7)	-12.2	(9.8)
	Macao-China	15.7	(8.1)	**1.7**	(1.3)	0.0	(0.0)	a	a	a	a
	Montenegro	**54.8**	(16.3)	-9.4	(5.0)	**0.6**	(0.3)	-6.0	(10.5)	-16.8	(12.3)
	Panama	**29.5**	(10.0)	**3.9**	(2.0)	**-0.1**	(0.1)	-24.5	(12.7)	14.1	(11.8)
	Peru	**38.1**	(6.2)	**3.1**	(1.3)	**-0.1**	(0.0)	-6.3	(8.6)	5.3	(8.9)
	Qatar	**44.1**	(11.8)	**3.8**	(1.1)	**0.0**	(0.0)	5.3	(13.3)	7.4	(13.6)
	Romania	**37.7**	(10.3)	-5.5	(5.5)	0.2	(0.3)	13.6	(10.8)	22.0	(13.2)
	Russian Federation	**46.3**	(8.9)	**-12.6**	(2.8)	**0.9**	(0.2)	7.3	(9.6)	8.0	(8.9)
	Serbia	**34.2**	(22.5)	-4.9	(2.7)	0.2	(0.1)	-1.0	(11.4)	0.8	(10.2)
	Shanghai-China	**45.6**	(4.9)	0.6	(0.7)	0.0	(0.0)	a	a	a	a
	Singapore	**84.1**	(8.1)	**8.4**	(3.3)	**-0.1**	(0.1)	a	a	a	a
	Chinese Taipei	**37.3**	(15.6)	0.5	(0.8)	0.0	(0.0)	-18.9	(16.4)	2.5	(8.1)
	Thailand	**17.9**	(6.7)	-0.3	(1.3)	0.0	(0.0)	-0.5	(15.6)	4.5	(10.0)
	Trinidad and Tobago	**77.6**	(9.8)	9.7	(6.8)	-0.7	(0.5)	-8.0	(7.0)	a	a
	Tunisia	**15.9**	(3.7)	**5.7**	(1.9)	**-0.3**	(0.1)	**0.3**	(4.8)	12.8	(7.7)
	Uruguay	**27.2**	(5.2)	1.1	(1.0)	0.0	(0.0)	**15.2**	(8.3)	**19.6**	(5.8)

Note: Values that are statistically significant are indicated in bold (see Annex A3).

1. Multilevel regression model (student and school levels): Reading performance is regressed on the variables of school policies and practices as well as on socio-economic and demographic background variables presented in this table.

StatLink http://dx.doi.org/10.1787/888932343285

[Part 1/1]

Table IV.2.3 **School systems' policies on transferring and grouping students and the relationship between reading performance and socio-economic background of students and schools**

	Model for first age of selection (OLS regression estimates)		Model for transferring of students (OLS regression estimates)	
	Coef.	**S.E.**	**Coef.**	**S.E.**
PISA index of economic, social and cultural status of student (ESCS)	**20.70**	(0.30)	**22.35**	(0.36)
x Each additional year of selection prior to age 15	**-2.53**	(0.15)		
x Percentage of students in schools that transfer students due to low achievement, behavioural problems or special learning needs (each additional 10%)			**-2.47**	(0.14)
School average PISA index of economic, social and cultural status	**43.80**	(1.13)	**47.32**	(1.27)
x Each additional year of selection prior to age 15	**10.83**	(0.56)		
x Percentage of students in schools that transfer students due to low achievement, behavioural problems or special learning needs (each additional 10%)			**5.08**	(0.44)
Student is a female	**35.88**	(0.51)	**36.14**	(0.50)
Student's language at home is the same as the language of assessment	**15.84**	(1.27)	**16.00**	(1.25)
Student without an immigrant background	**11.69**	(1.17)	**12.23**	(1.19)
School in a city (100 000 or more people)	-1.44	(1.21)	-1.96	(1.21)
School in a small town or village (15 000 or less people)	**2.81**	(1.14)	**2.97**	(1.15)
School size (per 100 students)	**1.63**	(0.14)	**1.66**	(0.14)
School size (per 100 students)(squared)	**-0.01**	(0.00)	**-0.02**	(0.00)
N	267 553		267 553	

Note: Estimates significant at the 5% level ($p < 0.05$) are in bold. Models include country fixed effects, estimate no intercept, are run for OECD countries only and use BRR weights to account for the sampling design. All countries are weighted equally.

StatLink http://dx.doi.org/10.1787/888932343285

[Part 1/2]

Table IV.2.4a Within- and between-school variation in reading performance and variation explained by school governance

		Variance		Remaining variance						Variance decomposition expressed as a percentage of the average variance in student performance in reading across OECD countries		
		Empty (or fully unconditional) model[1]		Model with demographic and socio-economic background[2]		Model with school policies and practices[3]		Model with demographic and socio-economic background and with school policies and practices[4]		Total variance in student performance	Total variance within schools as a percentage of total variance	Total variance between schools as a percentage of total variance
		Within-school	Between-school	Within-school	Between-school	Within-school	Between-school	Within-school	Between-school	%	%	%
OECD	Australia	7 631	2 692	6 997	880	7 702	1 849	6 998	847	112	83	29
	Austria	4 454	5 588	4 255	2 262	4 434	5 707	4 257	2 221	108	48	60
	Belgium	4 833	5 343	4 612	1 643	4 832	6 195	4 610	1 470	111	53	58
	Canada	6 780	1 877	6 238	986	6 784	1 582	6 233	940	94	74	20
	Chile	4 005	4 893	3 886	1 219	4 002	2 928	3 883	1 055	97	44	53
	Czech Republic	4 428	4 249	4 136	1 135	4 456	3 823	4 136	1 100	94	48	46
	Denmark	6 012	1 134	5 254	328	6 009	1 085	5 254	311	78	65	12
	Estonia	5 595	1 557	4 991	681	5 595	1 385	4 986	644	78	61	17
	Finland	6 993	665	5 641	458	6 994	609	5 645	445	83	76	7
	France	w	w	w	w	w	w	w	w	w	w	w
	Germany	3 890	5 890	3 558	1 708	3 868	4 193	3 563	1 474	106	42	64
	Greece	5 558	4 745	5 126	2 165	5 552	4 068	5 120	2 040	112	60	52
	Hungary	2 923	5 846	2 792	1 717	2 923	5 513	2 791	1 719	95	32	64
	Iceland	8 186	1 348	7 186	1 015	8 186	1 282	7 198	918	104	89	15
	Ireland	6 966	2 805	6 408	1 145	7 001	1 983	6 402	1 003	106	76	30
	Israel	6 615	6 250	6 312	3 230	6 648	6 550	6 320	3 251	140	72	68
	Italy	4 085	6 695	3 905	2 880	4 084	6 332	3 904	2 814	117	44	73
	Japan	5 386	5 087	5 248	2 255	5 420	5 486	5 252	1 797	114	59	55
	Korea	5 283	2 741	4 829	1 038	5 290	2 348	4 828	846	87	57	30
	Luxembourg	6 906	5 335	6 112	610	6 952	3 274	6 106	567	133	75	58
	Mexico	3 869	3 583	3 723	1 964	3 884	2 689	3 724	1 920	81	42	39
	Netherlands	2 795	5 107	2 670	2 224	2 795	4 821	2 670	2 034	86	30	55
	New Zealand	8 228	2 622	6 974	530	8 235	2 263	6 982	493	118	89	28
	Norway	7 598	874	6 455	669	7 585	833	6 440	634	92	83	9
	Poland	6 869	1 585	5 582	458	6 869	1 212	5 594	439	92	75	17
	Portugal	5 191	2 565	4 666	883	5 197	2 252	4 663	836	84	56	28
	Slovak Republic	4 565	2 989	3 972	1 151	4 566	2 815	3 973	1 148	82	50	32
	Slovenia	3 102	4 142	2 941	1 818	3 084	4 049	2 940	1 690	79	34	45
	Spain	6 048	1 690	5 390	816	6 053	1 323	5 393	796	84	66	18
	Sweden	8 290	1 877	7 007	605	8 280	1 558	7 017	590	110	90	20
	Switzerland	5 652	2 740	5 115	1 100	5 667	2 343	5 118	942	91	61	30
	Turkey	3 245	6 536	2 958	1 375	3 247	3 872	2 959	1 182	106	35	71
	United Kingdom	6 684	2 775	6 275	635	6 731	2 078	6 282	579	103	73	30
	United States	6 476	3 638	6 041	838	6 514	2 136	6 033	823	110	70	40
	OECD average	5 591	3 616	5 054	1 318	5 619	3 043	5 069	1 199	100	61	39
Partners	Albania	7 105	3 127	6 150	1 339	7 116	2 129	6 152	1 291	111	77	34
	Argentina	5 523	8 456	5 201	3 238	5 520	5 434	5 195	2 692	152	60	92
	Azerbaijan	3 459	2 490	3 287	2 054	3 464	2 306	3 288	1 989	65	38	27
	Brazil	4 702	4 417	4 514	1 770	4 727	2 829	4 510	1 637	99	51	48
	Bulgaria	6 439	6 418	5 794	2 053	6 437	5 366	5 787	1 804	140	70	70
	Colombia	4 813	3 162	4 711	688	4 845	2 079	4 710	574	87	52	34
	Croatia	4 473	4 045	4 183	1 391	4 488	3 602	4 176	1 013	93	49	44
	Dubai (UAE)	5 439	5 732	5 121	2 472	5 411	4 256	5 101	2 160	121	59	62
	Hong Kong-China	4 360	3 143	4 183	1 270	4 355	2 822	4 183	1 185	82	47	34
	Indonesia	2 298	1 749	2 117	1 181	2 301	1 656	2 117	1 173	44	25	19
	Jordan	5 461	3 312	5 186	1 727	5 487	2 915	5 194	1 423	95	59	36
	Kazakhstan	5 078	2 887	4 456	1 542	5 079	2 661	4 453	1 483	87	55	31
	Kyrgyzstan	5 901	3 266	5 126	1 398	5 922	2 259	5 119	1 208	100	64	35
	Latvia	5 200	1 391	4 491	634	5 201	1 336	4 490	596	72	57	15
	Lithuania	5 190	1 864	4 263	828	5 189	1 826	4 267	783	77	56	20
	Macao-China	4 179	2 882	4 000	775	4 188	1 916	3 992	670	77	45	31
	Montenegro	5 587	3 150	5 124	683	5 596	2 892	5 119	545	95	61	34
	Panama	4 213	5 942	4 103	2 647	4 200	4 206	4 101	2 343	110	46	65
	Peru	4 623	5 886	4 524	1 316	4 619	3 126	4 520	1 209	114	50	64
	Qatar	5 891	6 676	5 520	3 383	5 887	6 309	5 505	3 053	137	64	73
	Romania	3 832	4 057	3 678	2 308	3 810	3 860	3 682	2 183	86	42	44
	Russian Federation	5 826	1 965	5 193	900	5 837	1 874	5 193	903	85	63	21
	Serbia	4 123	3 909	3 954	1 840	4 121	3 123	3 955	1 789	87	45	42
	Shanghai-China	4 095	2 551	3 813	701	4 119	2 115	3 814	611	72	44	28
	Singapore	6 195	3 387	5 612	782	6 227	2 972	5 624	725	104	67	37
	Chinese Taipei	5 808	2 772	5 070	1 306	5 857	2 413	5 073	1 036	93	63	30
	Thailand	3 052	1 231	2 706	816	3 053	1 180	2 709	726	47	33	13
	Trinidad and Tobago	5 148	8 320	4 720	2 527	5 125	7 706	4 720	2 473	146	56	90
	Tunisia	4 291	3 034	4 174	1 640	4 311	2 474	4 173	1 424	80	47	33
	Uruguay	5 835	4 807	5 342	968	5 877	2 248	5 335	922	116	63	52

1. Multilevel regression model consists of the student- and school-levels.
2. Multilevel regression model: Reading performance is regressed on the variables of demographic and socio-economic background.
3. Multilevel regression model: Reading performance is regressed on the variables of school policies and practices.
4. Multilevel regression model: Reading performance is regressed on the variables of demographic and socio-economic background and on the variables of school policies and practices.

StatLink http://dx.doi.org/10.1787/888932343285

[Part 2/2]

Table IV.2.4a Within- and between-school variation in reading performance and variation explained by school governance

	Within-school variance expressed as a percentage of the average of within-school variance in student performance in reading across OECD countries				Between-school variance expressed as a percentage of the average of between-school variance in student performance in reading across OECD countries			
	Solely accounted for by students' and schools' socio-economic and demographic background	Solely accounted for by school school governance	Jointly accounted for by students' and schools' socio-economic and demographic background and school governance	Remaining within-school variance	Solely accounted for by students' and schools' socio-economic and demographic background	Solely accounted for by school governance	Jointly accounted for by students' and schools' socio-economic and demographic background and school governance	Remaining between-school variance
	%	%	%	%	%	%	%	%
OECD								
Australia	7.6	0.0	-0.8	76.0	10.9	0.4	8.8	9.2
Austria	1.9	0.0	0.2	46.2	37.9	0.4	-1.7	24.1
Belgium	2.4	-0.1	0.0	50.2	50.6	1.8	-10.2	15.9
Canada	6.0	0.0	-0.1	67.7	6.9	0.5	2.8	10.2
Chile	1.3	0.0	0.0	42.2	20.3	1.9	19.5	11.4
Czech Republic	3.5	0.0	-0.3	44.9	29.5	0.4	4.2	12.0
Denmark	8.2	0.0	0.0	57.0	8.3	0.2	0.4	3.4
Estonia	6.7	0.0	-0.1	54.1	7.9	0.4	1.5	7.1
Finland	14.6	-0.1	0.0	61.4	1.8	0.1	0.4	4.9
France	w	w	w	w	w	w	w	w
Germany	3.3	0.0	0.3	38.7	30.3	2.5	14.6	16.6
Greece	4.7	0.1	0.0	55.6	22.4	0.6	5.8	22.7
Hungary	1.5	-0.1	-0.1	30.4	41.1	0.0	3.6	18.8
Iceland	10.8	0.0	0.1	78.1	4.1	1.1	-0.5	10.0
Ireland	6.7	0.1	-0.4	69.3	10.7	1.5	7.5	10.8
Israel	3.5	0.2	-0.2	68.4	36.6	-0.3	-3.0	34.6
Italy	1.9	-0.1	0.0	42.5	39.5	0.6	2.5	30.1
Japan	1.8	0.0	-0.3	57.0	39.8	5.0	-9.3	19.7
Korea	5.1	0.0	-0.1	52.3	16.5	2.0	2.2	9.0
Luxembourg	9.2	0.1	-0.6	66.3	29.3	0.4	22.0	6.3
Mexico	1.7	0.0	-0.2	40.4	8.3	0.5	9.2	20.9
Netherlands	1.4	0.0	0.0	29.0	31.3	2.0	1.1	21.0
New Zealand	13.4	-0.1	0.0	76.0	19.5	0.4	3.4	5.2
Norway	12.4	0.2	0.0	70.0	2.1	0.3	0.1	6.9
Poland	13.8	-0.2	0.1	60.9	8.2	0.2	4.0	4.8
Portugal	5.8	0.0	-0.1	50.7	15.5	0.5	2.8	9.0
Slovak Republic	6.5	0.0	0.0	43.1	18.5	0.0	1.7	12.2
Slovenia	1.6	0.0	0.2	31.9	25.5	1.4	-0.4	18.5
Spain	7.2	-0.1	-0.1	58.6	5.8	0.2	3.7	8.6
Sweden	13.7	-0.2	0.3	76.2	10.2	0.1	3.7	6.4
Switzerland	6.1	-0.1	-0.2	55.6	15.2	1.7	2.5	10.4
Turkey	3.1	0.1	0.0	32.0	29.6	2.0	27.0	12.4
United Kingdom	5.1	0.0	-0.5	68.0	16.2	0.6	7.1	6.2
United States	5.3	0.0	-0.5	65.6	13.9	0.2	16.2	9.2
OECD average	6.0	0.0	-0.1	55.0	20.1	0.9	4.6	13.0
Partners								
Albania	10.6	0.2	-0.2	66.6	9.1	0.4	10.3	14.2
Argentina	3.5	-0.3	0.0	56.7	35.5	5.3	21.4	29.8
Azerbaijan	1.9	0.2	-0.1	35.5	3.9	0.0	0.8	22.3
Brazil	2.3	0.0	-0.3	49.0	13.1	1.4	15.8	17.7
Bulgaria	7.2	0.1	-0.2	62.9	38.9	2.9	8.5	19.4
Colombia	1.5	0.0	-0.4	51.1	16.3	1.2	10.5	6.3
Croatia	3.4	-0.1	-0.3	45.5	29.2	4.1	-0.4	11.0
Dubai (UAE)	3.3	0.2	0.1	55.5	23.5	3.8	11.6	23.3
Hong Kong-China	1.9	0.0	0.1	45.4	17.8	0.9	2.6	12.8
Indonesia	2.0	0.0	0.0	23.0	5.4	0.1	0.9	12.7
Jordan	3.0	-0.2	-0.1	56.6	16.1	3.0	1.3	15.6
Kazakhstan	7.0	0.0	0.0	48.2	12.9	0.6	1.9	16.0
Kyrgyzstan	8.5	0.0	-0.2	55.8	11.4	1.2	8.7	14.2
Latvia	7.5	0.0	0.0	48.9	8.0	0.4	0.2	6.5
Lithuania	10.1	-0.1	0.1	46.3	11.2	0.5	-0.2	8.6
Macao-China	2.1	0.1	-0.2	43.4	13.5	1.1	9.4	7.3
Montenegro	5.4	0.0	-0.2	55.5	23.7	0.6	3.3	6.6
Panama	1.1	0.0	0.1	44.5	21.4	2.9	16.0	24.3
Peru	1.1	0.0	0.0	49.1	20.4	1.3	28.7	13.5
Qatar	4.1	0.2	-0.2	59.8	34.7	3.5	0.5	33.8
Romania	1.4	-0.1	0.3	40.0	18.2	1.2	0.9	23.8
Russian Federation	7.0	0.0	-0.2	56.4	10.6	0.0	1.0	9.7
Serbia	1.8	-0.2	0.0	43.1	20.5	0.4	2.1	19.4
Shanghai-China	3.3	0.0	-0.3	41.4	16.3	1.0	3.8	6.6
Singapore	6.6	-0.1	-0.2	61.1	24.1	0.6	4.2	7.9
Chinese Taipei	8.5	-0.1	-0.5	55.2	15.1	2.7	1.2	11.1
Thailand	3.8	0.0	0.0	29.4	4.8	1.0	-0.3	7.9
Trinidad and Tobago	4.4	0.0	0.3	51.2	56.7	0.4	6.2	27.0
Tunisia	1.5	0.0	-0.2	45.4	11.7	2.3	3.5	15.4
Uruguay	5.9	0.1	-0.5	57.9	14.6	0.5	27.3	9.9

1. Multilevel regression model consists of the student and school levels.
2. Multilevel regression model: Reading performance is regressed on the variables of demographic and socio-economic background.
3. Multilevel regression model: Reading performance is regressed on the variables of school policies and practices.
4. Multilevel regression model: Reading performance is regressed on the variables of demographic and socio-economic background and on the variables of school policies and practices.

StatLink http://dx.doi.org/10.1787/888932343285

[Part 1/1]

Table IV.2.4b Relationships between school governance and reading performance

		School governance[1]							
		Index of school responsibility for resource allocation (higher values indicate more autonomy)		Index of school responsibility for curriculum and assessment (higher values indicate more autonomy)		School competes with other schools for students in the same area		Private school	
		Change in score	S.E.	Change in score	S.E.	Change in score	S.E.	Change in score	S.E.
OECD	Australia	6.7	(5.4)	-3.6	(3.9)	-6.9	(10.6)	**41.0**	(8.3)
	Austria	1.2	(17.0)	**-17.8**	(7.8)	-8.4	(15.1)	**42.3**	(21.8)
	Belgium	10.3	(32.1)	12.9	(8.3)	34.8	(30.1)	w	w
	Canada	1.2	(6.0)	-2.0	(4.8)	**19.7**	(5.1)	**38.6**	(11.8)
	Chile	**19.6**	(7.0)	8.7	(6.7)	3.8	(11.2)	**43.4**	(17.9)
	Czech Republic	-2.6	(3.7)	-2.2	(5.9)	**41.3**	(10.0)	**34.2**	(17.1)
	Denmark	4.5	(4.2)	3.1	(2.8)	-12.4	(8.1)	2.5	(8.7)
	Estonia	**-17.7**	(7.2)	-1.5	(5.1)	4.9	(9.7)	**40.3**	(20.3)
	Finland	6.9	(8.7)	1.9	(3.2)	10.8	(6.1)	-6.5	(17.3)
	France	w	w	w	w	w	w	w	w
	Germany	**25.4**	(12.2)	**-30.9**	(5.6)	**74.8**	(11.9)	-14.1	(36.5)
	Greece	**330.7**	(89.1)	5.8	(28.1)	1.5	(15.1)	33.3	(37.2)
	Hungary	1.4	(6.9)	9.0	(8.2)	15.7	(15.0)	**41.2**	(18.3)
	Iceland	-3.5	(5.6)	6.1	(3.8)	8.6	(8.5)	c	c
	Ireland	25.4	(25.5)	2.7	(6.5)	-12.1	(11.3)	**43.9**	(12.9)
	Israel	-2.6	(18.1)	2.8	(9.5)	13.7	(28.8)	8.8	(19.3)
	Italy	-9.6	(8.3)	-6.4	(6.4)	**47.4**	(14.0)	18.2	(19.0)
	Japan	17.6	(9.3)	-17.1	(11.1)	-21.2	(17.7)	-23.3	(23.3)
	Korea	**17.8**	(9.0)	10.2	(7.4)	10.7	(17.0)	9.1	(20.0)
	Luxembourg	**36.5**	(15.9)	**25.9**	(10.9)	3.9	(22.3)	**-94.9**	(33.3)
	Mexico	2.4	(4.7)	6.9	(4.9)	**22.0**	(9.2)	**61.4**	(13.1)
	Netherlands	6.8	(7.6)	18.1	(10.3)	20.4	(33.6)	0.1	(14.9)
	New Zealand	-12.7	(7.4)	2.2	(6.1)	2.2	(12.7)	**75.0**	(22.1)
	Norway	4.5	(3.8)	-6.5	(5.1)	5.6	(8.0)	c	c
	Poland	-2.5	(7.6)	-1.1	(4.8)	**33.1**	(8.4)	**43.6**	(19.3)
	Portugal	-6.6	(8.3)	**26.2**	(11.7)	**19.2**	(9.1)	19.2	(22.2)
	Slovak Republic	-0.7	(4.2)	-4.7	(4.5)	**33.0**	(11.5)	6.4	(16.4)
	Slovenia	-2.3	(13.9)	-6.4	(7.8)	9.8	(12.3)	**113.8**	(14.9)
	Spain	**9.4**	(4.7)	-0.2	(3.1)	**16.6**	(5.0)	**22.3**	(6.7)
	Sweden	6.8	(3.6)	-2.9	(3.8)	14.0	(8.0)	**29.4**	(11.8)
	Switzerland	**-17.4**	(5.6)	**20.1**	(6.2)	14.6	(8.3)	-3.0	(20.1)
	Turkey	-99.8	(90.0)	-5.1	(15.9)	**102.5**	(15.0)	c	c
	United Kingdom	1.4	(3.4)	-0.2	(5.1)	**-21.2**	(7.5)	**63.0**	(12.1)
	United States	-2.4	(7.7)	-0.4	(9.9)	-11.8	(13.7)	85.0	(22.4)
	OECD average	**10.8**	(4.3)	1.6	(1.5)	**14.9**	(2.6)	**26.6**	(3.6)
Partners	Albania	**-18.8**	(8.0)	1.9	(6.4)	10.5	(13.4)	**96.7**	(22.5)
	Argentina	**35.5**	(16.0)	**-26.4**	(10.9)	9.3	(16.9)	**98.9**	(20.7)
	Azerbaijan	**-21.1**	(10.4)	3.7	(6.1)	14.1	(11.4)	c	c
	Brazil	12.5	(7.9)	8.0	(5.1)	6.0	(8.2)	**77.3**	(19.5)
	Bulgaria	-10.4	(6.0)	**-34.3**	(14.0)	**55.1**	(14.5)	c	c
	Colombia	11.3	(7.3)	-5.4	(4.9)	12.9	(12.0)	**43.8**	(19.2)
	Croatia	**-68.1**	(24.6)	21.2	(20.7)	15.7	(15.6)	c	c
	Dubai (UAE)	8.4	(5.4)	**29.4**	(5.3)	-16.1	(20.2)	33.6	(17.1)
	Hong Kong-China	-4.9	(5.7)	-6.2	(6.8)	**87.6**	(30.2)	-11.9	(18.4)
	Indonesia	4.3	(3.9)	-0.1	(3.5)	9.2	(11.5)	**-19.9**	(8.9)
	Jordan	-7.7	(18.7)	-12.8	(12.7)	19.5	(13.0)	**38.3**	(12.4)
	Kazakhstan	13.3	(9.2)	**-20.5**	(8.0)	3.6	(10.3)	14.4	(25.7)
	Kyrgyzstan	5.3	(8.3)	-4.0	(3.7)	**22.1**	(8.0)	**107.7**	(26.5)
	Latvia	-2.9	(7.5)	3.0	(6.8)	16.5	(12.2)	c	c
	Lithuania	-10.3	(8.2)	1.4	(3.8)	4.6	(8.7)	c	c
	Macao-China	-12.7	(7.5)	12.0	(8.5)	-4.2	(16.6)	25.7	(23.7)
	Montenegro	16.4	(27.1)	-19.8	(11.2)	-23.8	(20.1)	c	c
	Panama	-6.9	(24.1)	**-25.2**	(11.4)	-11.5	(15.5)	**131.9**	(44.1)
	Peru	**18.1**	(7.9)	**-14.1**	(5.4)	**35.6**	(11.6)	**60.8**	(23.0)
	Qatar	0.2	(6.3)	1.0	(8.4)	-2.3	(13.4)	**100.7**	(16.9)
	Romania	82.3	(68.7)	-4.6	(9.5)	33.1	(21.3)	c	c
	Russian Federation	-1.1	(6.4)	-0.3	(4.4)	4.4	(7.4)	c	c
	Serbia	8.1	(14.2)	**-118.5**	(36.6)	33.9	(19.2)	c	c
	Shanghai-China	5.6	(4.7)	**-15.2**	(4.9)	9.1	(11.7)	19.2	(15.9)
	Singapore	**34.7**	(9.7)	-2.2	(5.0)	57.6	(52.3)	c	c
	Chinese Taipei	8.3	(8.2)	-13.0	(8.0)	-22.9	(12.3)	-16.5	(15.8)
	Thailand	-4.9	(3.4)	4.2	(4.0)	-4.0	(8.8)	19.6	(10.7)
	Trinidad and Tobago	22.5	(12.7)	12.6	(10.5)	**53.7**	(24.9)	**-64.9**	(31.6)
	Tunisia	1.7	(5.8)	-15.2	(32.7)	19.4	(11.0)	**-69.1**	(17.5)
	Uruguay	-8.8	(7.9)	8.4	(8.9)	16.5	(9.7)	**110.6**	(15.3)

Note: Values that are statistically significant are indicated in bold (see Annex A3).
1. Multilevel regression model (student and school levels): Reading performance is regressed on the variables of school policies and practices presented in this table.
StatLink http://dx.doi.org/10.1787/888932343285

[Part 1/2]

Table IV.2.4c Relationships between school governance and reading performance, accounting for students' and schools' socio-economic and demographic background

	School governance[1]								Student socio-economic and demographic background[1]									
	Index of school responsibility for resource allocation (higher values indicate more autonomy)		Index of school responsibility for curriculum and assessment (higher values indicate more autonomy)		School competes with other schools for students in the same area		Private school		Student is a female		Student without an immigrant background		Student's language at home is the same as the language of assessment		PISA index of economic, social and cultural status of student (1 unit increase)		PISA index of economic, social and cultural status of student (squared)	
	Change in score	S.E.	Change in score	S.E.	Change in score	S.E.	Change in score	S.E.	Change in score	S.E.	Change in score	S.E.	Change in score	S.E.	Change in score	S.E.	Change in score	S.E.
OECD																		
Australia	-3.8	(3.1)	-2.2	(3.2)	**-24.0**	(8.8)	4.9	(9.4)	**37.8**	(2.3)	**-6.0**	(2.5)	**23.0**	(4.2)	**27.3**	(1.7)	**-3.0**	(1.0)
Austria	4.2	(9.2)	-7.8	(5.0)	1.3	(9.5)	9.3	(17.4)	**21.4**	(3.4)	**13.6**	(4.7)	**15.3**	(5.7)	**8.1**	(2.0)	0.3	(1.4)
Belgium	23.5	(23.4)	**9.9**	(4.2)	2.7	(13.8)	w	w	**18.8**	(2.2)	**16.6**	(2.7)	**6.8**	(3.2)	**12.1**	(1.4)	1.4	(0.9)
Canada	-2.3	(4.4)	1.0	(3.8)	4.5	(5.6)	**28.4**	(9.2)	**35.5**	(2.0)	4.4	(2.6)	**17.4**	(4.4)	**19.3**	(1.3)	**2.8**	(0.9)
Chile	**8.6**	(4.0)	2.3	(4.3)	1.4	(9.8)	10.1	(12.6)	**18.7**	(3.1)	0.9	(7.9)	**54.5**	(17.7)	**9.6**	(1.8)	0.4	(0.8)
Czech Republic	1.8	(2.3)	-3.0	(3.7)	10.9	(6.7)	12.6	(12.0)	**35.2**	(2.7)	**12.9**	(3.8)	-1.4	(10.6)	**15.4**	(2.0)	-2.7	(1.6)
Denmark	3.0	(2.1)	0.7	(2.0)	**-12.4**	(5.6)	-7.4	(6.2)	**29.6**	(2.9)	**14.3**	(3.6)	**20.5**	(5.9)	**27.2**	(1.7)	-0.4	(1.1)
Estonia	-10.8	(6.0)	2.8	(3.7)	-5.8	(8.0)	19.0	(18.0)	**43.9**	(3.0)	**13.2**	(3.6)	**29.0**	(7.2)	**17.0**	(2.1)	1.4	(1.9)
Finland	1.3	(5.6)	-0.1	(2.8)	-5.2	(5.7)	12.5	(11.8)	**56.6**	(2.5)	**13.3**	(5.6)	**47.7**	(7.5)	**27.3**	(1.9)	-1.2	(1.6)
France	w	w	w	w	w	w	w	w	w	w	w	w	w	w	w	w	w	w
Germany	7.6	(6.6)	-9.0	(4.9)	**26.6**	(9.0)	-15.1	(14.4)	**29.7**	(2.5)	**15.7**	(3.4)	4.1	(5.7)	**9.1**	(1.5)	-1.1	(0.9)
Greece	**224.4**	(89.6)	-19.7	(17.5)	0.0	(12.9)	-16.9	(19.5)	**36.3**	(3.1)	2.4	(3.6)	17.0	(14.1)	**15.8**	(1.7)	2.2	(1.3)
Hungary	-2.5	(5.1)	1.4	(5.2)	-3.0	(10.4)	12.3	(15.2)	**24.8**	(2.5)	-7.1	(4.5)	**19.2**	(9.5)	**8.6**	(1.6)	0.6	(1.1)
Iceland	1.8	(5.8)	7.1	(3.7)	5.1	(7.9)	c	c	**45.9**	(3.3)	4.6	(5.3)	**49.3**	(11.8)	**28.3**	(2.7)	**-3.8**	(1.6)
Ireland	1.9	(16.4)	3.2	(5.5)	-11.4	(9.8)	**24.7**	(8.9)	**35.5**	(4.4)	-4.2	(3.9)	**31.8**	(10.4)	**26.9**	(2.1)	-1.8	(1.5)
Israel	-2.4	(14.8)	-2.9	(5.8)	25.0	(24.3)	11.8	(18.0)	**33.3**	(3.8)	-3.5	(4.0)	1.8	(6.2)	**21.9**	(2.6)	**3.7**	(1.2)
Italy	-5.3	(6.2)	**-8.6**	(4.3)	9.8	(13.3)	6.0	(17.5)	**27.6**	(1.7)	**16.4**	(2.6)	**6.7**	(2.6)	**5.2**	(0.8)	-1.0	(0.9)
Japan	6.7	(5.2)	-3.3	(6.1)	-24.9	(13.1)	**-53.3**	(14.9)	**28.4**	(2.8)	4.3	(9.3)	**74.5**	(27.9)	4.4	(2.5)	-0.4	(2.3)
Korea	**9.9**	(3.9)	-3.6	(4.7)	**-26.1**	(12.7)	15.1	(10.4)	**42.6**	(5.7)	2.7	(11.8)	**61.6**	(25.3)	**18.8**	(2.7)	0.2	(1.4)
Luxembourg	-0.3	(11.6)	**-10.6**	(5.0)	-15.5	(20.4)	9.0	(27.9)	**36.8**	(3.2)	**28.6**	(3.5)	**24.0**	(5.0)	**16.8**	(2.9)	-1.6	(1.2)
Mexico	2.9	(3.8)	2.2	(4.4)	2.6	(9.1)	17.2	(16.2)	**22.2**	(1.9)	**24.8**	(3.5)	**19.6**	(5.5)	**8.4**	(1.4)	**1.5**	(0.5)
Netherlands	1.1	(4.0)	**20.3**	(6.0)	19.4	(13.8)	2.3	(9.2)	**19.1**	(1.7)	**5.8**	(2.7)	12.0	(6.6)	**5.2**	(1.6)	0.3	(1.1)
New Zealand	-5.7	(3.6)	-1.4	(3.6)	12.0	(8.7)	-0.2	(12.4)	**49.4**	(4.5)	-6.8	(3.6)	**46.1**	(5.7)	**34.9**	(2.8)	0.3	(2.4)
Norway	-3.2	(3.5)	-5.1	(4.7)	-2.3	(8.0)	c	c	**48.8**	(3.5)	**10.8**	(5.4)	**38.0**	(7.7)	**28.5**	(3.2)	-1.5	(2.0)
Poland	3.9	(8.8)	-3.4	(2.7)	6.7	(4.6)	-0.8	(18.4)	**52.8**	(3.4)	22.7	(23.3)	**52.8**	(15.8)	**31.3**	(1.8)	**-3.4**	(1.4)
Portugal	10.2	(6.1)	-7.9	(8.9)	-2.3	(7.7)	7.3	(9.8)	**34.3**	(2.6)	-1.3	(3.2)	14.5	(8.2)	**18.0**	(1.4)	-0.7	(0.7)
Slovak Republic	1.1	(2.9)	-1.7	(3.4)	0.6	(11.4)	-4.8	(10.2)	**43.5**	(2.9)	1.2	(5.4)	**27.9**	(7.4)	**18.0**	(1.9)	**-3.5**	(1.3)
Slovenia	-16.8	(11.7)	6.0	(7.0)	-2.9	(11.1)	**45.8**	(18.1)	**31.8**	(2.4)	**8.2**	(3.2)	6.3	(5.0)	**3.3**	(1.2)	1.2	(1.1)
Spain	-0.7	(3.1)	1.7	(2.5)	7.4	(5.9)	5.6	(5.1)	**29.7**	(1.7)	**24.5**	(2.4)	**10.0**	(3.4)	**19.8**	(1.0)	-0.8	(0.6)
Sweden	2.8	(2.7)	0.8	(3.2)	6.8	(6.0)	1.5	(12.3)	**46.6**	(3.0)	7.4	(4.2)	**29.4**	(6.5)	**32.2**	(2.1)	-1.3	(1.0)
Switzerland	**-13.3**	(4.6)	**13.1**	(5.3)	-0.5	(6.4)	-17.4	(19.1)	**31.9**	(2.4)	**11.6**	(2.7)	**19.9**	(3.4)	**18.2**	(1.6)	-0.3	(1.4)
Turkey	-66.2	(65.3)	-10.2	(8.6)	**24.3**	(11.0)	c	c	**31.4**	(2.8)	-2.1	(7.7)	1.0	(11.3)	**7.8**	(2.2)	-0.1	(0.9)
United Kingdom	-1.8	(2.0)	1.1	(2.7)	0.7	(5.6)	**-31.4**	(12.7)	**26.1**	(3.1)	-6.8	(4.5)	**17.8**	(6.7)	**26.0**	(2.0)	0.6	(1.6)
United States	8.5	(6.2)	-5.0	(5.7)	-3.0	(9.4)	-10.1	(21.1)	**28.0**	(4.2)	-3.7	(7.5)	5.5	(8.1)	**23.6**	(2.4)	-1.8	(3.1)
OECD average	5.8	(3.6)	-1.0	(1.0)	0.9	(1.9)	3.4	(2.8)	**34.4**	(0.5)	**7.3**	(1.1)	**24.4**	(1.8)	**18.0**	(0.3)	-0.4	(0.2)
Partners																		
Albania	-8.6	(10.2)	2.4	(6.8)	-10.6	(10.7)	33.4	(30.6)	**58.3**	(4.1)	**23.0**	(11.6)	17.2	(16.5)	**20.3**	(3.8)	**3.1**	(1.6)
Argentina	16.9	(12.9)	**-16.1**	(7.6)	**-33.9**	(14.2)	**42.4**	(15.5)	**31.2**	(3.2)	1.8	(5.2)	**44.7**	(17.2)	**13.0**	(2.1)	1.9	(1.0)
Azerbaijan	-17.9	(12.0)	6.1	(6.1)	6.8	(12.4)	c	c	**22.7**	(2.4)	2.6	(5.1)	-2.0	(6.2)	**11.4**	(2.1)	1.6	(1.0)
Brazil	7.6	(4.4)	3.1	(3.7)	**-23.5**	(7.2)	17.7	(13.9)	**28.9**	(2.0)	12.0	(9.1)	**33.6**	(12.5)	**7.8**	(2.0)	1.3	(0.7)
Bulgaria	-4.3	(3.7)	**-30.7**	(10.9)	6.5	(11.4)	c	c	**47.5**	(3.8)	**29.1**	(8.0)	**29.1**	(6.8)	**13.4**	(2.3)	1.1	(1.4)
Colombia	**-11.9**	(2.9)	-2.2	(2.9)	**-23.0**	(8.0)	**15.9**	(6.1)	**10.5**	(3.0)	**19.3**	(8.0)	**58.3**	(21.9)	**13.2**	(2.7)	1.4	(0.9)
Croatia	**-41.6**	(12.3)	2.6	(8.5)	10.3	(10.7)	c	c	**35.1**	(3.4)	3.4	(2.5)	-5.5	(9.0)	**10.6**	(1.9)	**-3.5**	(1.2)
Dubai (UAE)	2.6	(3.6)	**18.1**	(4.1)	-23.3	(16.7)	0.7	(15.0)	**29.4**	(4.6)	**-31.7**	(3.5)	**20.0**	(3.1)	**19.0**	(1.9)	**2.6**	(1.1)
Hong Kong-China	-3.3	(4.8)	-4.7	(4.3)	24.9	(26.2)	**-21.3**	(9.1)	**25.9**	(2.9)	**-8.7**	(2.4)	**25.1**	(6.5)	2.3	(2.1)	-1.3	(0.9)
Indonesia	2.3	(3.4)	-1.6	(3.3)	-1.9	(12.3)	-4.8	(9.5)	**29.1**	(1.8)	18.6	(11.1)	-5.2	(2.7)	**7.0**	(2.9)	1.4	(0.8)
Jordan	-29.4	(18.8)	-22.4	(12.3)	11.5	(9.5)	18.3	(9.6)	**49.0**	(8.7)	-5.7	(3.7)	**24.8**	(8.3)	**20.3**	(2.3)	1.4	(1.1)
Kazakhstan	1.4	(7.0)	-2.7	(6.9)	-5.8	(8.2)	**-43.8**	(21.3)	**41.6**	(2.5)	**-11.8**	(4.9)	1.8	(4.7)	**17.3**	(2.5)	-2.1	(1.4)
Kyrgyzstan	**-24.8**	(5.9)	3.7	(3.6)	-6.2	(7.9)	**102.5**	(22.8)	**50.6**	(3.0)	**-12.0**	(5.6)	-3.0	(5.0)	**19.8**	(2.4)	**2.5**	(1.2)
Latvia	-4.3	(5.8)	2.4	(5.2)	15.5	(9.2)	c	c	**47.4**	(3.0)	1.0	(3.4)	4.6	(9.7)	**19.6**	(2.5)	-0.7	(1.6)
Lithuania	-5.1	(5.7)	**7.2**	(3.1)	-6.2	(7.3)	c	c	**54.8**	(2.7)	-1.1	(4.8)	12.9	(8.0)	**19.0**	(1.7)	-0.2	(1.2)
Macao-China	-7.3	(4.7)	6.3	(4.8)	**-55.4**	(19.9)	4.7	(14.1)	**21.9**	(2.1)	**-10.2**	(2.7)	**52.3**	(7.2)	**7.1**	(2.1)	0.0	(1.0)
Montenegro	26.1	(15.9)	-11.9	(6.7)	-6.8	(9.0)	c	c	**42.0**	(3.6)	**-6.7**	(2.8)	5.8	(11.2)	**13.1**	(1.5)	0.8	(1.4)
Panama	-3.1	(13.2)	-18.6	(9.7)	-9.5	(13.1)	38.2	(33.7)	**19.0**	(4.9)	3.5	(6.5)	12.3	(10.9)	**7.2**	(3.3)	1.7	(0.9)
Peru	**13.4**	(6.4)	**-9.2**	(3.9)	-4.0	(9.1)	1.8	(19.6)	**12.0**	(3.2)	**21.2**	(10.4)	**27.2**	(7.5)	**11.9**	(2.7)	1.2	(0.8)
Qatar	-0.8	(5.3)	0.6	(6.9)	-2.3	(11.2)	**52.8**	(20.5)	**36.7**	(6.3)	**-38.3**	(2.8)	**20.3**	(3.2)	**8.1**	(1.5)	1.7	(0.9)
Romania	28.0	(38.9)	-4.7	(6.4)	-15.9	(13.7)	c	c	**16.2**	(3.9)	18.2	(9.8)	13.2	(7.8)	**11.0**	(2.2)	-0.1	(1.2)
Russian Federation	-2.3	(4.3)	-1.4	(3.5)	3.8	(5.8)	c	c	**41.6**	(2.6)	1.4	(2.8)	**20.2**	(5.8)	**21.2**	(2.0)	-1.8	(1.7)
Serbia	-0.3	(10.4)	-29.0	(26.6)	10.9	(20.4)	c	c	**27.3**	(2.8)	-5.6	(3.5)	4.6	(9.4)	**7.7**	(1.8)	1.1	(1.2)
Shanghai-China	-0.1	(2.9)	**-8.0**	(2.8)	-10.3	(10.9)	11.8	(10.4)	**33.5**	(2.4)	**22.0**	(8.7)	**32.8**	(9.6)	**5.1**	(1.9)	0.6	(1.2)
Singapore	-3.4	(7.3)	3.7	(2.5)	27.7	(23.2)	c	c	**26.5**	(2.3)	-1.2	(3.0)	**25.4**	(3.5)	**17.3**	(2.6)	**-2.5**	(1.3)
Chinese Taipei	10.5	(6.0)	**-12.8**	(5.4)	**-23.3**	(10.1)	**-43.2**	(8.7)	**46.3**	(4.2)	17.5	(10.3)	8.1	(5.1)	**20.4**	(3.0)	0.8	(1.8)
Thailand	**-6.5**	(2.7)	6.4	(4.1)	-6.3	(8.0)	-5.1	(9.7)	**36.0**	(3.0)	**38.0**	(11.4)	**-16.3**	(3.9)	5.3	(2.8)	0.3	(1.0)
Trinidad and Tobago	6.4	(7.4)	0.0	(5.4)	1.6	(14.8)	-20.5	(17.9)	**46.4**	(2.4)	-5.1	(3.3)	**31.7**	(7.5)	**4.5**	(2.2)	0.9	(1.1)
Tunisia	-0.2	(5.3)	-3.6	(27.1)	5.6	(9.4)	**-66.3**	(18.3)	**22.4**	(2.3)	**20.7**	(8.5)	-20.4	(23.1)	2.9	(2.7)	-0.2	(0.8)
Uruguay	-9.0	(8.2)	4.3	(8.5)	-6.8	(6.9)	33.5	(17.5)	**39.6**	(3.0)	-2.0	(6.4)	14.4	(9.3)	**15.4**	(2.0)	-0.2	(0.9)

Note: Values that are statistically significant are indicated in bold (see Annex A3).

1. Multilevel regression model (student and school levels): Reading performance is regressed on the variables of school policies and practices as well as on socio-economic and demographic background variables presented in this table.

StatLink http://dx.doi.org/10.1787/888932343285

[Part 2/2]

Table IV.2.4c **Relationships between school governance and reading performance, accounting for students' and schools' socio-economic and demographic background**

		School socio-economic and demographic background[1]									
		School average PISA index of economic, social and cultural status (1 unit increase)		School size (per 100 students)		School size (per 100 students) (squared)		School in a small town or village (15 000 or less people)		School in city (100 000 or more people)	
		Change in score	S.E.	Change in score	S.E.	Change in score	S.E.	Change in score	S.E.	Change in score	S.E.
OECD	Australia	**64.0**	(12.3)	0.3	(2.5)	0.0	(0.1)	-2.5	(7.2)	6.2	(5.5)
	Austria	**59.4**	(14.8)	**12.1**	(3.7)	**-0.5**	(0.2)	-7.8	(10.1)	-8.2	(12.8)
	Belgium	**99.2**	(6.3)	**8.0**	(2.4)	**-0.3**	(0.1)	9.9	(7.3)	-4.5	(7.9)
	Canada	**22.4**	(7.0)	**3.0**	(1.2)	-0.1	(0.1)	7.5	(5.4)	2.6	(4.7)
	Chile	**39.8**	(4.7)	**4.4**	(1.5)	**-0.1**	(0.0)	22.3	(12.6)	-1.4	(10.1)
	Czech Republic	**120.9**	(8.2)	5.2	(4.1)	-0.2	(0.3)	**18.4**	(6.9)	-12.6	(7.2)
	Denmark	**40.9**	(5.8)	0.7	(3.1)	-0.2	(0.3)	**-13.1**	(5.0)	4.8	(6.0)
	Estonia	**28.5**	(13.6)	**4.7**	(2.0)	**-0.2**	(0.1)	3.9	(9.0)	0.2	(10.7)
	Finland	**30.5**	(12.9)	-1.5	(1.8)	0.1	(0.0)	-4.4	(5.9)	-3.7	(5.6)
	France	w	w	w	w	w	w	w	w	w	w
	Germany	**90.5**	(9.1)	**7.8**	(2.4)	**-0.3**	(0.1)	**18.3**	(9.1)	-0.3	(9.6)
	Greece	**49.9**	(9.7)	-24.3	(18.4)	3.9	(2.9)	27.0	(14.2)	-11.2	(12.7)
	Hungary	**72.7**	(9.2)	5.1	(3.8)	-0.1	(0.2)	-2.1	(15.5)	-8.0	(11.6)
	Iceland	23.4	(13.7)	-6.7	(6.5)	0.4	(0.8)	2.6	(9.2)	-9.7	(11.2)
	Ireland	**40.6**	(7.0)	6.7	(4.4)	-0.4	(0.3)	8.3	(7.0)	4.3	(8.1)
	Israel	**109.7**	(16.6)	8.5	(4.9)	-0.4	(0.2)	11.1	(18.8)	4.7	(18.0)
	Italy	**63.1**	(11.9)	**9.9**	(3.9)	-0.3	(0.2)	12.0	(10.7)	-12.2	(10.7)
	Japan	**159.5**	(13.9)	-3.1	(3.6)	0.3	(0.2)	4.5	(14.3)	-11.6	(11.7)
	Korea	**52.4**	(9.0)	3.7	(4.7)	-0.1	(0.2)	**-52.0**	(18.7)	**-38.6**	(14.4)
	Luxembourg	**82.2**	(9.4)	1.6	(2.4)	0.0	(0.1)	1.0	(15.1)	**-49.2**	(19.5)
	Mexico	**18.0**	(5.9)	**2.2**	(0.7)	0.0	(0.0)	-5.7	(7.6)	3.3	(6.9)
	Netherlands	**68.7**	(14.7)	**7.4**	(2.5)	-0.2	(0.1)	-21.3	(11.6)	-1.5	(12.5)
	New Zealand	**57.6**	(10.4)	2.7	(1.9)	-0.1	(0.1)	15.0	(10.0)	5.9	(8.3)
	Norway	**32.9**	(15.0)	-9.1	(9.2)	0.9	(1.2)	-9.0	(6.6)	2.3	(7.9)
	Poland	**27.9**	(7.8)	8.2	(5.4)	-0.6	(0.6)	5.5	(8.3)	**-18.8**	(8.7)
	Portugal	**32.8**	(6.0)	2.6	(3.3)	0.0	(0.1)	4.3	(7.3)	0.2	(6.6)
	Slovak Republic	**62.0**	(12.9)	-2.0	(5.0)	0.3	(0.4)	-11.2	(8.2)	-7.0	(9.4)
	Slovenia	**65.3**	(10.7)	**17.1**	(4.5)	-0.9	(0.5)	0.3	(10.2)	-10.2	(7.8)
	Spain	**21.8**	(4.7)	-0.6	(1.5)	0.0	(0.1)	-1.0	(4.9)	8.6	(4.8)
	Sweden	**48.4**	(15.3)	-2.4	(3.2)	0.2	(0.2)	3.4	(7.1)	2.0	(8.6)
	Switzerland	**62.5**	(9.2)	**2.1**	(0.8)	**0.0**	(0.0)	-8.9	(8.6)	-10.4	(13.0)
	Turkey	**51.9**	(6.5)	-4.8	(3.3)	0.0	(0.1)	-18.6	(14.0)	1.3	(14.9)
	United Kingdom	**85.8**	(8.2)	-2.0	(2.5)	0.1	(0.1)	5.0	(5.3)	3.3	(6.4)
	United States	**72.1**	(11.5)	-2.3	(1.5)	0.1	(0.0)	7.6	(11.3)	15.0	(15.4)
	OECD average	**59.3**	(1.9)	**2.0**	(0.8)	0.0	(0.1)	0.9	(1.8)	**-4.7**	(1.9)
Partners	Albania	**28.0**	(12.3)	-5.0	(4.4)	0.5	(0.3)	-2.3	(13.5)	12.1	(13.5)
	Argentina	**51.7**	(9.1)	**7.7**	(3.0)	-0.2	(0.1)	-5.9	(15.5)	9.6	(14.3)
	Azerbaijan	23.5	(14.1)	-5.8	(5.0)	0.4	(0.2)	-8.8	(15.9)	-17.1	(13.8)
	Brazil	**45.2**	(5.1)	1.2	(1.2)	0.0	(0.0)	-6.4	(8.1)	-7.7	(6.6)
	Bulgaria	**56.2**	(9.1)	7.6	(4.7)	-0.1	(0.3)	3.1	(10.2)	7.9	(10.2)
	Colombia	**54.1**	(3.6)	0.0	(0.7)	0.0	(0.0)	8.7	(7.9)	-5.4	(6.1)
	Croatia	**107.0**	(10.3)	1.2	(3.7)	0.0	(0.2)	5.5	(8.3)	**-36.4**	(9.3)
	Dubai (UAE)	**55.5**	(9.0)	**1.3**	(0.6)	0.0	(0.0)	-1.7	(21.7)	-3.2	(19.3)
	Hong Kong-China	**40.1**	(8.4)	11.4	(11.8)	0.0	(0.7)	a	a	a	a
	Indonesia	**21.8**	(6.2)	3.0	(3.4)	0.0	(0.3)	1.1	(8.2)	9.3	(10.1)
	Jordan	**30.0**	(7.7)	-3.3	(3.7)	0.2	(0.2)	-0.8	(10.1)	10.7	(8.2)
	Kazakhstan	**55.2**	(9.6)	**-7.2**	(1.6)	**0.2**	(0.1)	-20.4	(13.4)	15.8	(13.4)
	Kyrgyzstan	**35.7**	(11.1)	3.0	(2.3)	-0.1	(0.1)	-6.2	(13.5)	**42.5**	(17.0)
	Latvia	**27.8**	(11.3)	0.9	(3.0)	0.1	(0.2)	6.7	(8.6)	-2.1	(9.8)
	Lithuania	**50.1**	(8.4)	-4.5	(3.1)	0.4	(0.2)	9.9	(11.4)	-12.5	(10.1)
	Macao-China	**37.8**	(7.7)	**6.1**	(1.2)	**-0.1**	(0.0)	a	a	a	a
	Montenegro	**66.3**	(10.8)	**-12.1**	(4.9)	**0.7**	(0.3)	-7.7	(10.8)	-18.9	(11.7)
	Panama	**43.5**	(10.2)	**5.5**	(2.4)	-0.1	(0.1)	-3.5	(15.3)	-0.4	(17.6)
	Peru	**40.0**	(7.2)	**6.1**	(1.6)	**-0.1**	(0.1)	-2.1	(10.2)	5.5	(12.2)
	Qatar	**55.5**	(13.4)	**3.1**	(1.3)	**0.0**	(0.0)	-0.8	(15.6)	-12.2	(15.5)
	Romania	**41.7**	(9.9)	-5.0	(5.2)	0.2	(0.3)	5.0	(11.9)	19.9	(13.9)
	Russian Federation	**48.9**	(8.8)	**-13.1**	(2.9)	**0.9**	(0.2)	7.9	(9.3)	9.6	(8.8)
	Serbia	**43.3**	(19.4)	-8.3	(4.9)	0.4	(0.2)	-6.1	(13.7)	-2.9	(11.7)
	Shanghai-China	**52.6**	(5.8)	0.4	(0.7)	0.0	(0.0)	a	a	a	a
	Singapore	**89.1**	(9.1)	**11.4**	(2.5)	**-0.2**	(0.1)	a	a	a	a
	Chinese Taipei	**44.2**	(17.2)	0.9	(0.8)	0.0	(0.0)	-18.9	(15.6)	3.5	(7.7)
	Thailand	**19.2**	(5.9)	1.6	(1.3)	0.0	(0.0)	3.9	(15.3)	4.7	(11.0)
	Trinidad and Tobago	**127.1**	(9.0)	**23.9**	(7.4)	**-1.5**	(0.5)	-3.3	(8.4)	a	a
	Tunisia	**38.9**	(6.7)	1.2	(4.0)	0.1	(0.2)	**23.6**	(10.1)	13.1	(8.3)
	Uruguay	**42.7**	(7.0)	**3.0**	(1.3)	0.0	(0.0)	**25.4**	(8.4)	12.8	(7.4)

Note: Values that are statistically significant are indicated in bold (see Annex A3).
1. Multilevel regression model (student and school levels): Reading performance is regressed on the variables of school policies and practices as well as on socio-economic and demographic background variables presented in this table.

StatLink http://dx.doi.org/10.1787/888932343285

[Part 1/1]

Table IV.2.5 Ratio of schools' posting achievement data publicly and the relationship between school autonomy in allocating resources and reading performance

	Model for prevalence of schools' posting achievement data publicly (OLS regression estimates)			
	Gross model		Net model	
	Coef.	S.E.	Coef.	S.E.
School autonomy for resource allocation	**6.72**	(2.21)	**-3.24**	(1.45)
× Percentage of students in schools that post achievement data publicly (additional 10%)	-1.30	(4.34)	**0.58**	(0.28)
School autonomy for curriculum and assessment			0.04	(0.59)
Private school			-0.48	(1.49)
PISA index of economic, social and cultural status of student (ESCS)			**17.98**	(0.26)
PISA index of economic, social and cultural status of student (ESCS squared)			**2.06**	(0.22)
Student is a female			**36.23**	(0.51)
Student's language at home is the same as the language of assessment			**17.02**	(1.23)
Student without an immigrant background			**11.64**	(1.20)
School average PISA index of economic, social and cultural status			**58.13**	(0.97)
School in a city (100 000 or more people)			**-2.36**	(1.21)
School in a small town or village (15 000 or less people)			**2.93**	(1.14)
School size (100 students)			**1.61**	(0.13)
School size (100 students, squared)			**-0.01**	(0.00)
N	267 425		267 425	

Note: Estimates significant at the 5% level ($p < 0.05$) are in bold. Both net and gross models include country fixed effects, estimate no intercept, are run for OECD countries only and use BRR weights to account for the sampling design. All countries are weighted equally.

StatLink http://dx.doi.org/10.1787/888932343285

[Part 1/1]

Table IV.2.6 Likelihood of attending schools competing for students in the same area

	Logistic regression estimates			
	Student model		Student and school Model	
	Coef.	S.E.	Coef.	S.E.
PISA index of economic, social and cultural status of student (ESCS)	**0.31**	(0.02)	**0.01**	(0.01)
PISA index of economic, social and cultural status of student (ESCS squared)	0.00	(0.01)	0.01	(0.01)
Student is a female	**0.07**	(0.02)	0.03	(0.02)
Student's language at home is the same as the language of assessment	-0.06	(0.06)	-0.03	(0.07)
Student without an immigrant background	**-0.48**	(0.05)	**-0.15**	(0.06)
School average PISA index of economic, social and cultural status			**0.66**	(0.07)
School in a city (100 000 or more people)			**0.47**	(0.10)
School in a small town or village (15 000 or less people)			**-1.28**	(0.07)
School size (100 students)			-0.01	(0.01)
School size (squared)			0.00	(0.00)
Private school			**0.66**	(0.15)
N	267 553		267 553	

Note: Estimates indicate log-odds of attending a school that competes with other schools for enrolment. Estimates significant at the 5% level ($p < 0.05$) level are in bold. Both net and gross models include country fixed effects, do not estimate an intercept, are run for OECD countries only and use BRR weights to account for the sampling design. All countries are weighted equally.

StatLink http://dx.doi.org/10.1787/888932343285

[Part 1/1]

Table IV.2.7 Parents' reports on reasons for choosing schools for their children as "very important", by quarters of the PISA index of economic, social and cultural status of students (ESCS)

Results based on reports from students' parents

		Percentage of parents reporting the following reasons as "very important" in choosing a school for their child																							
		Distance (% of parents who reported "very important" when choosing schools)								Low expenses (% of parents who reported "very important" when choosing schools)								Financial aid (% of parents who reported "very important" when choosing schools)							
		Bottom ESCS quarter		Second ESCS quarter		Third ESCS quarter		Top ESCS quarter		Bottom ESCS quarter		Second ESCS quarter		Third ESCS quarter		Top ESCS quarter		Bottom ESCS quarter		Second ESCS quarter		Third ESCS quarter		Top ESCS quarter	
		%	S.E.	%	S.E.	%	S.E.	%	S.E.	%	S.E.	%	S.E.	%	S.E.	%	S.E.	%	S.E.	%	S.E.	%	S.E.	%	S.E.
OECD	Chile	**32.0**	(1.6)	28.0	(1.5)	23.3	(1.4)	**19.0**	(1.6)	**37.4**	(1.8)	34.4	(1.6)	29.1	(1.5)	**16.1**	(1.2)	**47.9**	(2.0)	47.2	(1.5)	40.9	(1.6)	**26.3**	(1.5)
	Denmark	16.2	(1.3)	16.1	(1.4)	17.0	(1.7)	17.0	(1.5)	**5.9**	(0.7)	3.5	(0.7)	1.8	(0.6)	**1.0**	(0.4)	**2.5**	(0.5)	1.4	(0.4)	1.2	(0.4)	**0.6**	(0.3)
	Germany	**21.9**	(1.4)	18.9	(1.7)	18.4	(1.5)	**15.7**	(1.5)	**16.1**	(1.3)	10.2	(1.3)	9.0	(1.1)	**4.6**	(0.8)	**12.6**	(1.4)	7.7	(1.0)	5.4	(0.9)	**3.1**	(0.7)
	Hungary	**19.9**	(1.9)	14.5	(1.6)	12.1	(1.5)	**10.6**	(1.3)	**19.2**	(1.8)	10.8	(1.3)	6.8	(0.9)	**3.5**	(0.6)	**15.4**	(1.7)	7.7	(0.9)	4.2	(0.6)	**2.2**	(0.4)
	Italy	**10.9**	(0.7)	8.7	(0.5)	6.7	(0.4)	**5.6**	(0.4)	**13.2**	(0.5)	11.2	(0.5)	9.3	(0.6)	**5.0**	(0.4)	a	a	a	a	a	a	a	a
	Korea	23.2	(1.4)	26.2	(1.3)	24.8	(1.4)	25.0	(1.5)	**20.7**	(1.3)	16.2	(1.2)	15.3	(1.1)	**10.1**	(0.9)	**27.3**	(1.3)	21.3	(1.3)	16.7	(1.1)	**13.1**	(1.1)
	New Zealand	**17.5**	(1.5)	10.7	(1.1)	10.1	(1.1)	**9.9**	(1.1)	**13.5**	(1.1)	7.3	(0.9)	5.2	(0.8)	**2.6**	(0.6)	**13.6**	(1.3)	7.7	(0.9)	5.3	(0.7)	**2.0**	(0.5)
	Portugal	27.0	(1.5)	31.3	(2.0)	31.1	(1.6)	26.3	(1.4)	**36.6**	(1.5)	33.1	(1.7)	25.3	(1.4)	**14.0**	(1.1)	**40.4**	(1.7)	38.1	(1.7)	27.1	(1.3)	**11.8**	(1.0)
	8 OECD countries average	**21.1**	(0.5)	19.3	(0.5)	17.9	(0.5)	**16.1**	(0.5)	**20.3**	(0.5)	15.8	(0.4)	12.7	(0.4)	**7.1**	(0.3)	**22.8**	(0.6)	18.7	(0.4)	14.4	(0.4)	**8.4**	(0.3)
Partners	Croatia	**18.6**	(1.3)	16.5	(1.4)	15.7	(1.3)	**11.9**	(1.2)	**16.4**	(1.0)	13.7	(1.0)	10.8	(1.0)	**5.0**	(0.6)	**15.3**	(1.2)	12.2	(1.1)	9.6	(1.0)	**5.2**	(0.7)
	Hong Kong-China	**12.6**	(0.8)	12.2	(1.0)	10.1	(1.0)	**7.9**	(0.8)	**13.2**	(0.9)	11.1	(1.0)	8.4	(0.9)	**5.4**	(0.6)	**17.5**	(1.0)	11.7	(1.1)	8.0	(0.8)	**3.9**	(0.5)
	Lithuania	**30.5**	(1.5)	30.7	(1.5)	27.7	(1.4)	**22.2**	(1.5)	**29.4**	(1.5)	23.8	(1.2)	19.3	(1.3)	**10.8**	(0.9)	**19.8**	(1.3)	15.2	(1.3)	11.6	(0.9)	**7.1**	(0.8)
	Macao-China	**15.0**	(0.9)	13.6	(0.9)	12.8	(0.9)	**12.4**	(1.0)	**23.1**	(1.2)	18.3	(1.2)	14.8	(0.8)	**9.0**	(0.7)	**29.2**	(1.3)	24.2	(1.1)	19.1	(0.9)	**11.3**	(0.9)
	Panama	**43.1**	(2.6)	43.2	(2.9)	44.1	(2.5)	**28.7**	(2.7)	**37.0**	(2.7)	37.9	(2.0)	38.4	(2.6)	**21.2**	(2.1)	**35.9**	(2.4)	37.2	(2.8)	27.6	(2.5)	**18.4**	(2.0)
	Qatar	**36.2**	(1.3)	27.5	(1.2)	25.3	(1.2)	**24.7**	(1.0)	**21.6**	(1.0)	21.9	(1.0)	15.4	(1.0)	**14.8**	(0.9)	**11.2**	(0.8)	12.8	(0.8)	9.4	(0.9)	**9.4**	(0.8)

		Percentage of parents reporting the following reasons as "very important" in choosing a school for their child															
		High academic achievement (% of parents who reported "very important" when choosing schools)								Safe environment (% of parents who reported "very important" when choosing schools)							
		Bottom ESCS quarter		Second ESCS quarter		Third ESCS quarter		Top ESCS quarter		Bottom ESCS quarter		Second ESCS quarter		Third ESCS quarter		Top ESCS quarter	
		%	S.E.	%	S.E.	%	S.E.	%	S.E.	%	S.E.	%	S.E.	%	S.E.	%	S.E.
OECD	Chile	**48.4**	(1.8)	54.4	(1.7)	57.7	(1.8)	**54.6**	(1.9)	**63.3**	(2.0)	67.6	(1.5)	71.8	(1.7)	**75.9**	(1.2)
	Denmark	**41.6**	(1.8)	45.9	(2.1)	40.5	(2.2)	45.5	(1.8)	**72.2**	(1.6)	73.4	(1.8)	75.8	(1.7)	**76.1**	(1.7)
	Germany	**32.6**	(2.0)	29.5	(1.6)	29.4	(2.0)	**19.7**	(1.2)	**57.6**	(1.8)	54.4	(2.0)	56.4	(2.1)	**45.5**	(2.0)
	Hungary	**19.2**	(1.6)	21.6	(1.5)	27.5	(1.6)	**37.9**	(1.9)	55.3	(2.0)	55.7	(1.9)	53.9	(1.8)	52.4	(1.6)
	Italy	**22.0**	(0.7)	23.1	(0.7)	25.0	(0.8)	**28.2**	(0.7)	57.6	(0.9)	59.8	(0.8)	60.4	(0.7)	59.0	(0.9)
	Korea	**37.7**	(1.5)	49.6	(1.5)	55.2	(1.9)	**65.6**	(1.7)	**55.6**	(1.4)	64.2	(1.4)	67.4	(1.4)	**73.9**	(1.6)
	New Zealand	**42.2**	(1.9)	45.4	(1.6)	53.1	(1.6)	**60.1**	(2.1)	**71.0**	(1.3)	73.0	(1.7)	79.5	(1.5)	**80.9**	(1.5)
	Portugal	**39.7**	(1.7)	48.7	(1.5)	53.5	(1.5)	**55.6**	(2.0)	**72.3**	(1.5)	73.8	(1.4)	79.7	(1.3)	**82.2**	(1.3)
	8 OECD countries average	**35.4**	(0.6)	39.8	(0.6)	42.7	(0.6)	**45.9**	(0.6)	**63.1**	(0.6)	65.2	(0.6)	68.1	(0.6)	**68.2**	(0.5)
Partners	Croatia	**26.2**	(1.3)	26.8	(1.3)	31.8	(1.4)	**35.8**	(1.7)	60.6	(1.4)	59.0	(1.3)	58.9	(1.8)	59.2	(1.8)
	Hong Kong-China	**25.1**	(1.3)	29.8	(1.3)	29.1	(1.2)	**36.4**	(1.7)	**59.0**	(1.5)	62.7	(1.6)	67.1	(1.4)	**73.0**	(1.2)
	Lithuania	**27.7**	(1.5)	32.9	(1.4)	44.7	(1.7)	**56.0**	(1.7)	**64.2**	(1.4)	70.0	(1.4)	76.0	(1.4)	**77.7**	(1.7)
	Macao-China	**30.6**	(1.2)	35.3	(1.2)	34.9	(1.2)	**38.0**	(1.2)	**60.0**	(1.2)	65.1	(1.1)	64.3	(1.3)	**69.9**	(1.2)
	Panama	**45.8**	(3.2)	44.3	(2.7)	46.1	(2.5)	**55.8**	(3.5)	**57.9**	(3.2)	59.7	(2.8)	67.5	(2.4)	**78.5**	(1.8)
	Qatar	**37.4**	(1.2)	45.3	(1.3)	49.3	(1.4)	**53.0**	(1.3)	**55.4**	(1.2)	62.9	(1.4)	63.5	(1.3)	**64.4**	(1.3)

Note: Estimates in bold indicate statistically significant differences between top and bottom ESCS quartile at the 5% level ($p < 0.05$). Average missing rates on these parent questionnaire items are 2% in Macao-China, 4% in Korea, Lithuania and Hong Kong-China, 5% in Hungary, 11% in Croatia and Chile, 13% in Italy, 21% in Panama, 25% in Portugal, 26% in New Zealand, 35% in Qatar, 38% in Germany, 41% in Denmark.

StatLink http://dx.doi.org/10.1787/888932343285

[Part 1/1]

Table IV.2.8 Systems' school competition rates and the relationship between reading performance and socio-economic background of students and schools

	Model for school competition (OLS regression estimates)	
	Coef.	S.E.
PISA index of economic, social and cultural status of student (ESCS)	**24.60**	(1.37)
x Percentage of students in schools that compete with other schools for students in the same area (additional 10%)	**-0.91**	(0.17)
School average PISA index of economic, social and cultural status	**36.14**	(5.19)
x Percentage of students in schools that compete with other schools for students in the same area (additional 10%)	**2.81**	(0.66)
Student is a female	**36.22**	(0.50)
Student's language at home is the same as the language of assessment	**16.73**	(1.24)
Student without an immigrant background	**11.17**	(1.19)
School in a city (100 000 or more people)	-2.26	(1.20)
School in a small town or village (15 000 or less people)	**2.89**	(1.15)
School size (100 students)	**1.61**	(0.14)
School size (100 students) (squared)	**-0.01**	(0.00)
N	267 553	

Note: Estimates significant at the 5% level ($p < 0.05$) are in bold. Models include country fixed effects, estimate no intercept, are run for OECD countries only and use BRR weights to account for the sampling design. All countries are weighted equally.

StatLink http://dx.doi.org/10.1787/888932343285

[Part 1/1]

Table IV.2.9a Within- and between-school variation in reading performance and variation explained by schools' assessment and accountability policies

		Variance		Remaining variance						Variance decomposition expressed as a percentage of the average variance in student performance in reading across OECD countries			Within-school variance expressed as a percentage of the average of within-school variance in student performance in reading across OECD countries				Between-school variance expressed as a percentage of the average of between-school variance in student performance in reading across OECD countries			
		Empty (or fully unconditional) model[1]		Model with demographic and socio-economic background[2]		Model with school policies and practices[3]		Model with demographic and socio-economic background and with school policies and practices[4]		Total variance in student performance	Total variance within schools as a percentage of total variance	Total variance between schools as a percentage of total variance	Solely accounted for by students' and schools' socio-economic and demographic background	Solely accounted for by schools' assessment and accountability policies	Jointly accounted for by students' and schools' socio-economic and demographic background and schools' assessment and accountability policies	Remaining within-school variance	Solely accounted for by students' and schools' socio-economic and demographic background	Solely accounted for by schools' assessment and accountability policies	Jointly accounted for by students' and schools' socio-economic and demographic background and schools' assessment and accountability policies	Remaining between-school variance
		Within-school	Between-school	Within-school	Between-school	Within-school	Between-school	Within-school	Between-school	%	%	%	%	%	%	%	%	%	%	%
OECD	Australia	7 631	2 692	6 997	880	7 698	2 229	7 000	767	112	83	29	7.6	0.0	-0.7	76.0	15.9	1.2	3.8	8.3
	Austria	4 454	5 588	4 255	2 262	4 434	5 117	4 252	1 866	108	48	60	2.0	0.0	0.2	46.2	35.3	4.3	0.8	20.3
	Belgium	4 833	5 343	4 612	1 643	4 832	5 282	4 610	1 390	111	53	58	2.4	0.0	0.0	50.1	42.3	2.7	-2.1	15.1
	Canada	6 780	1 877	6 238	986	6 780	1 814	6 240	962	94	74	20	5.9	0.0	0.0	67.8	9.3	0.3	0.4	10.5
	Chile	4 005	4 893	3 886	1 219	4 005	4 236	3 884	1 052	97	44	53	1.3	0.0	0.0	42.2	34.6	1.8	5.3	11.4
	Czech Republic	4 428	4 249	4 136	1 135	4 453	3 503	4 136	1 112	94	48	46	3.4	0.0	-0.3	44.9	26.0	0.3	7.8	12.1
	Denmark	6 012	1 134	5 254	328	6 003	1 011	5 257	309	78	65	12	8.1	0.0	0.1	57.1	7.6	0.2	1.1	3.4
	Estonia	5 595	1 557	4 991	681	5 596	1 288	4 979	529	78	61	17	6.7	0.1	-0.1	54.1	8.2	1.7	1.3	5.7
	Finland	6 993	665	5 641	458	6 989	593	5 640	412	83	76	7	14.7	0.0	0.0	61.3	2.0	0.5	0.3	4.5
	France	w	w	w	w	w	w	w	w	w	w	w	w	w	w	w	w	w	w	w
	Germany	3 890	5 890	3 558	1 708	3 867	5 224	3 562	1 436	106	42	64	3.3	0.0	0.3	38.7	41.1	2.9	4.3	15.6
	Greece	5 558	4 745	5 126	2 165	5 560	3 977	5 129	2 006	112	60	52	4.7	0.0	0.0	55.7	21.4	1.7	6.6	21.8
	Hungary	2 923	5 846	2 792	1 717	2 919	4 829	2 784	1 390	95	32	64	1.5	0.1	0.0	30.2	37.4	3.6	7.5	15.1
	Iceland	8 186	1 348	7 186	1 015	8 197	1 073	7 200	814	104	89	15	10.8	-0.1	0.0	78.2	2.8	2.2	0.8	8.8
	Ireland	6 966	2 805	6 408	1 145	6 975	2 490	6 402	1 051	106	76	30	6.2	0.1	-0.2	69.5	15.6	1.0	2.4	11.4
	Israel	6 615	6 250	6 312	3 230	6 656	4 936	6 317	2 501	140	72	68	3.7	-0.1	-0.4	68.6	26.4	7.9	6.4	27.2
	Italy	4 085	6 695	3 905	2 880	4 084	6 026	3 903	2 693	117	44	73	2.0	0.0	0.0	42.4	36.2	2.0	5.2	29.2
	Japan	5 386	5 087	5 248	2 255	5 418	4 830	5 251	1 934	114	59	55	1.8	0.0	-0.3	57.0	31.5	3.5	-0.7	21.0
	Korea	5 283	2 741	4 829	1 038	5 287	2 291	4 823	788	87	57	30	5.0	0.1	-0.1	52.4	16.3	2.7	2.2	8.6
	Luxembourg	6 906	5 335	6 112	610	6 951	2 742	6 104	360	133	75	58	9.2	0.1	-0.6	66.3	25.9	2.7	25.5	3.9
	Mexico	3 869	3 583	3 723	1 964	3 884	3 397	3 724	1 899	81	42	39	1.7	0.0	-0.2	40.5	16.3	0.7	1.3	20.6
	Netherlands	2 795	5 107	2 670	2 224	2 795	4 530	2 671	1 971	86	30	55	1.4	0.0	0.0	29.0	27.8	2.7	3.5	21.4
	New Zealand	8 228	2 622	6 974	530	8 234	2 290	6 978	515	118	89	28	13.6	0.0	0.0	75.8	19.3	0.2	3.4	5.6
	Norway	7 598	874	6 455	669	7 587	769	6 454	588	92	83	9	12.3	0.0	0.1	70.1	2.0	0.9	0.3	6.4
	Poland	6 869	1 585	5 582	458	6 864	1 517	5 600	397	92	75	17	13.7	-0.2	0.2	60.8	12.2	0.7	0.1	4.3
	Portugal	5 191	2 565	4 666	883	5 198	2 259	4 662	833	84	56	28	5.8	0.0	-0.1	50.6	15.5	0.5	2.8	9.1
	Slovak Republic	4 565	2 989	3 972	1 151	4 566	2 552	3 971	1 045	82	50	32	6.5	0.0	0.0	43.1	16.4	1.2	3.6	11.3
	Slovenia	3 102	4 142	2 941	1 818	3 079	3 826	2 931	1 650	79	34	45	1.6	0.1	0.1	31.8	23.6	1.8	1.6	17.9
	Spain	6 048	1 690	5 390	816	6 049	1 591	5 392	796	84	66	18	7.1	0.0	0.0	58.6	8.6	0.2	0.9	8.6
	Sweden	8 290	1 877	7 007	605	8 284	1 756	7 023	518	110	90	20	13.7	-0.2	0.2	76.3	13.5	1.0	0.4	5.6
	Switzerland	5 652	2 740	5 115	1 100	5 663	2 335	5 115	950	91	61	30	6.0	0.0	-0.1	55.6	15.0	1.6	2.8	10.3
	Turkey	3 245	6 536	2 958	1 375	3 243	4 757	2 954	1 210	106	35	71	3.1	0.0	0.0	32.1	38.5	1.8	17.5	13.1
	United Kingdom	6 684	2 775	6 275	635	6 723	2 218	6 282	531	103	73	30	4.8	-0.1	-0.4	68.2	18.3	1.1	4.9	5.8
	United States	6 476	3 638	6 041	838	6 519	2 597	6 044	610	110	70	40	5.2	0.0	-0.4	65.6	21.6	2.5	8.8	6.6
	OECD average	5 591	3 616	5 068	1 285	5 618	3 027	5 069	1 118	100	61	39	6.0	0.0	-0.1	55.1	20.7	1.8	4.0	12.1
Partners	Albania	7 105	3 127	6 150	1 339	7 112	2 350	6 149	1 163	111	77	34	10.5	0.0	-0.1	66.8	12.9	1.9	6.5	12.6
	Argentina	5 523	8 456	5 201	3 238	5 522	7 800	5 201	2 851	152	60	92	3.5	0.0	0.0	56.5	53.8	4.2	2.9	31.0
	Azerbaijan	3 459	2 490	3 287	2 054	3 463	1 944	3 285	1 497	65	38	27	1.9	0.0	-0.1	35.7	4.8	6.0	-0.1	16.3
	Brazil	4 702	4 417	4 514	1 770	4 721	3 812	4 514	1 671	99	51	48	2.3	0.0	-0.2	49.0	23.2	1.1	5.5	18.2
	Bulgaria	6 439	6 418	5 794	2 053	6 441	6 279	5 793	1 676	140	70	70	7.0	0.0	0.0	62.9	50.0	4.1	-2.6	18.2
	Colombia	4 813	3 162	4 711	688	4 836	2 657	4 710	552	87	52	34	1.4	0.0	-0.3	51.2	22.9	1.5	4.0	6.0
	Croatia	4 473	4 045	4 183	1 391	4 487	3 478	4 180	1 280	93	49	44	3.3	0.0	-0.2	45.4	23.9	1.2	5.0	13.9
	Dubai (UAE)	5 439	5 732	5 121	2 472	5 409	5 817	5 101	2 232	121	59	62	3.3	0.2	0.1	55.4	38.9	2.6	-3.5	24.2
	Hong Kong-China	4 360	3 143	4 183	1 270	4 352	2 329	4 183	987	82	47	34	1.8	0.0	0.1	45.4	14.6	3.1	5.8	10.7
	Indonesia	2 298	1 749	2 117	1 181	2 301	1 546	2 117	1 035	44	25	19	2.0	0.0	0.0	23.0	5.6	1.6	0.6	11.2
	Jordan	5 461	3 312	5 186	1 727	5 478	2 581	5 191	1 420	95	59	36	3.1	0.0	-0.1	56.4	12.6	3.3	4.6	15.4
	Kazakhstan	5 078	2 887	4 456	1 542	5 075	2 689	4 455	1 452	87	55	31	6.7	0.0	0.0	48.4	13.4	1.0	1.2	15.8
	Kyrgyzstan	5 901	3 266	5 126	1 398	5 922	2 702	5 124	1 227	100	64	35	8.7	0.0	-0.2	55.7	16.0	1.9	4.3	13.3
	Latvia	5 200	1 391	4 491	634	5 196	1 215	4 483	538	72	57	15	7.7	0.1	0.0	48.7	7.4	1.0	0.9	5.8
	Lithuania	5 190	1 864	4 263	828	3 451	492	4 823	788	77	56	20	-14.9	-6.1	25.0	52.4	-3.2	0.4	14.5	8.6
	Macao-China	4 179	2 882	4 000	775	4 181	2 019	3 992	627	77	45	31	2.0	0.1	-0.1	43.4	15.1	1.6	7.8	6.8
	Montenegro	5 587	3 150	5 124	683	5 607	2 022	5 120	390	95	61	34	5.3	0.0	-0.3	55.6	17.7	3.2	9.1	4.2
	Panama	4 213	5 942	4 103	2 647	4 196	5 464	4 104	2 137	110	46	65	1.0	0.0	0.2	44.6	36.1	5.5	-0.3	23.2
	Peru	4 623	5 886	4 524	1 316	4 621	4 711	4 521	1 146	114	50	64	1.1	0.0	0.0	49.1	38.7	1.9	10.9	12.4
	Qatar	5 891	6 676	5 520	3 383	5 868	5 814	5 506	2 773	137	64	73	3.9	0.2	0.1	59.8	33.0	6.6	2.7	30.1
	Romania	3 832	4 057	3 678	2 308	3 812	3 406	3 674	1 710	86	42	44	1.5	0.0	0.2	39.9	18.4	6.5	0.6	18.6
	Russian Federation	5 826	1 965	5 193	900	5 832	1 451	5 192	750	85	63	21	7.0	0.0	-0.1	56.4	7.6	1.6	4.0	8.1
	Serbia	4 123	3 909	3 954	1 840	4 122	3 366	3 956	1 646	87	45	42	1.8	0.0	0.0	43.0	18.7	2.1	3.8	17.9
	Shanghai-China	4 095	2 551	3 813	701	4 115	2 108	3 813	574	72	44	28	3.3	0.0	-0.2	41.4	16.7	1.4	3.4	6.2
	Singapore	6 195	3 387	5 612	782	6 231	2 759	5 624	739	104	67	37	6.6	-0.1	-0.3	61.1	21.9	0.5	6.4	8.0
	Chinese Taipei	5 808	2 772	5 070	1 306	5 856	1 864	5 072	890	93	63	30	8.5	0.0	-0.5	55.1	10.6	4.5	5.3	9.7
	Thailand	3 052	1 231	2 706	816	3 050	1 156	2 706	718	47	33	13	3.7	0.0	0.0	29.4	4.8	1.1	-0.3	7.8
	Trinidad and Tobago	5 148	8 320	4 720	2 527	5 120	7 270	4 720	2 276	146	56	90	4.3	0.0	0.3	51.3	54.2	2.7	8.7	24.7
	Tunisia	4 291	3 034	4 174	1 640	4 313	2 383	4 175	1 332	80	47	33	1.5	0.0	-0.2	45.3	11.4	3.4	3.7	14.5
	Uruguay	5 835	4 807	5 342	968	5 869	4 257	5 336	856	116	63	52	5.8	0.1	-0.4	58.0	36.9	1.2	4.8	9.3

1. Multilevel regression model consists of the student and school levels.
2. Multilevel regression model: Reading performance is regressed on the variables of demographic and socio-economic background.
3. Multilevel regression model: Reading performance is regressed on the variables of school policies and practices.
4. Multilevel regression model: Reading performance is regressed on the variables of demographic and socio-economic background and on the variables of school policies and practices.

StatLink http://dx.doi.org/10.1787/888932343285

[Part 1/1]
Table IV.2.9b Relationships between schools' assessment and accountability policies and reading performance

		Assessment and accountability policies[1]																					
		School uses standardised tests		School uses student assessments to monitor school's progress		School uses student assessments to improve instruction or curriculum		School uses student assessments to compare with other schools or district or national performance		Schools' accountability to parents: only relative to other students in the school		Schools' accountability to parents: at least relative to national or regional benchmark		School posts achievement data publicly		Achievement data are used in decisions about instructional resource allocation to the school		Achievement data are tracked over time by an administrative authority		School monitors teachers' practice through students' achievement test or assessments		School monitors teachers' practice through teacher peer review or observations of lessons by principal or inspectors	
		Change in score	S.E.	Change in score	S.E.	Change in score	S.E.	Change in score	S.E.	Change in score	S.E.	Change in score	S.E.	Change in score	S.E.	Change in score	S.E.	Change in score	S.E.	Change in score	S.E.	Change in score	S.E.
OECD	Australia	-7.3	(7.3)	**-23.8**	(8.5)	12.6	(10.9)	-6.5	(8.4)	5.1	(10.1)	7.2	(10.6)	**16.7**	(7.4)	11.7	(7.7)	-10.0	(9.9)	11.7	(7.0)	-12.6	(8.7)
	Austria	**-50.5**	(14.3)	-16.0	(14.7)	17.3	(14.1)	**38.6**	(13.6)	-1.7	(15.1)	5.1	(17.7)	21.2	(20.3)	-6.3	(13.3)	**43.2**	(11.7)	8.3	(18.3)	**-79.4**	(21.2)
	Belgium	**-34.8**	(11.0)	19.3	(11.3)	0.5	(11.7)	4.2	(13.6)	**71.2**	(12.9)	23.2	(13.9)	57.4	(31.9)	-5.7	(16.2)	12.0	(11.7)	**-25.9**	(10.9)	29.8	(18.2)
	Canada	8.3	(7.8)	5.4	(7.9)	-1.4	(6.3)	5.2	(8.4)	1.4	(8.1)	-2.6	(6.6)	5.4	(5.3)	**-10.3**	(4.8)	2.3	(8.5)	c	c	0.8	(5.7)
	Chile	**-47.2**	(16.1)	**60.0**	(23.3)	-17.0	(21.6)	**-44.8**	(14.0)	24.2	(28.4)	6.9	(23.9)	16.8	(15.7)	-3.5	(19.1)	-15.3	(17.9)	9.1	(18.8)	19.4	(25.2)
	Czech Republic	29.5	(17.8)	**34.9**	(13.6)	-13.9	(10.1)	7.8	(10.9)	12.5	(15.2)	18.8	(14.7)	14.7	(9.5)	5.8	(22.5)	13.6	(9.1)	-8.3	(10.0)	7.4	(15.5)
	Denmark	-23.4	(23.4)	-2.1	(6.2)	**14.2**	(7.2)	**13.4**	(6.0)	c	c	c	c	5.5	(5.7)	1.0	(6.2)	**-17.6**	(5.6)	1.3	(6.2)	-18.2	(9.8)
	Estonia	-0.1	(9.8)	-17.8	(17.1)	2.5	(9.3)	-10.2	(14.3)	-0.3	(13.9)	5.9	(10.4)	5.2	(8.5)	-17.6	(9.9)	-10.5	(13.8)	-8.9	(7.8)	-17.1	(19.6)
	Finland	-6.0	(19.2)	-9.4	(6.9)	7.4	(6.4)	1.5	(7.1)	-11.4	(22.3)	8.1	(6.3)	27.9	(16.1)	-5.4	(8.0)	-4.6	(6.9)	-9.2	(6.9)	-3.5	(6.0)
	France	w	w	w	w	w	w	w	w	w	w	w	w	w	w	w	w	w	w	w	w	w	w
	Germany	**-41.4**	(13.1)	-18.6	(12.9)	1.1	(12.7)	**41.8**	(11.5)	-0.8	(14.2)	-0.8	(15.6)	**44.5**	(21.5)	-8.0	(13.5)	8.7	(12.7)	-7.4	(12.0)	1.5	(14.8)
	Greece	4.6	(15.6)	-6.0	(17.4)	-14.2	(17.0)	**39.2**	(16.5)	27.9	(16.6)	25.9	(21.0)	**32.1**	(14.2)	17.9	(16.8)	-24.4	(16.0)	-10.7	(19.2)	8.4	(17.6)
	Hungary	**44.1**	(18.7)	29.2	(17.7)	-20.5	(14.6)	9.4	(14.9)	25.9	(19.4)	-4.4	(17.0)	10.1	(13.4)	-25.1	(17.1)	-6.0	(13.6)	**-51.0**	(16.9)	24.0	(28.0)
	Iceland	0.5	(9.8)	1.4	(15.0)	3.1	(18.6)	-3.7	(7.0)	-26.6	(15.7)	-12.5	(7.7)	-11.1	(8.2)	c	c	11.4	(7.8)	6.0	(7.4)	-2.3	(7.0)
	Ireland	-7.5	(11.5)	-17.7	(12.4)	18.7	(13.8)	-9.1	(10.4)	15.1	(12.0)	21.1	(12.0)	10.4	(15.2)	4.8	(10.3)	**-21.5**	(10.5)	9.6	(9.8)	8.4	(12.9)
	Israel	21.9	(20.6)	-17.6	(20.8)	-31.0	(22.9)	-1.0	(18.1)	**-107.1**	(25.9)	-26.7	(15.3)	21.9	(17.8)	5.3	(17.5)	10.3	(17.5)	5.9	(31.5)	-5.4	(23.4)
	Italy	**-28.3**	(9.7)	-12.7	(10.6)	**-26.9**	(11.7)	8.6	(12.6)	-6.4	(17.2)	9.0	(22.5)	**30.8**	(14.2)	**-23.8**	(11.3)	-16.6	(13.8)	-2.0	(10.7)	19.1	(12.6)
	Japan	25.5	(14.1)	16.7	(15.4)	-32.8	(17.8)	**37.8**	(19.0)	49.7	(26.5)	46.2	(27.5)	29.2	(30.7)	**-66.7**	(29.2)	-7.7	(16.2)	21.6	(15.6)	-14.3	(20.4)
	Korea	41.5	(26.6)	-22.1	(25.6)	13.5	(20.3)	12.8	(18.7)	-34.8	(28.4)	-32.3	(20.0)	11.6	(21.5)	-25.9	(19.0)	-11.9	(14.2)	15.3	(16.4)	**-61.6**	(27.9)
	Luxembourg	10.3	(28.2)	19.6	(19.5)	5.0	(17.5)	-36.0	(22.4)	-27.5	(27.7)	-45.0	(31.1)	21.3	(20.9)	36.3	(23.2)	-2.5	(21.9)	-21.5	(18.8)	8.7	(18.2)
	Mexico	9.5	(10.9)	**21.6**	(9.0)	16.1	(18.2)	-2.5	(10.4)	-6.9	(13.0)	-25.2	(13.0)	-3.1	(8.6)	10.8	(7.7)	13.6	(9.6)	13.5	(7.8)	1.7	(14.2)
	Netherlands	-7.6	(18.1)	-6.9	(17.1)	18.7	(12.9)	3.5	(12.9)	-2.4	(17.6)	-23.7	(25.1)	-3.7	(13.6)	12.3	(15.8)	25.1	(14.5)	**27.1**	(13.3)	-27.3	(15.8)
	New Zealand	5.4	(13.9)	5.4	(36.9)	0.3	(22.9)	-6.8	(14.3)	**70.2**	(23.5)	19.3	(14.4)	1.5	(12.5)	-15.9	(10.2)	27.8	(22.3)	-8.3	(11.9)	**-50.9**	(9.0)
	Norway	-15.1	(11.5)	-2.9	(9.0)	8.6	(6.4)	-8.9	(8.3)	8.9	(12.0)	7.8	(11.0)	10.4	(6.7)	-11.0	(9.0)	**20.8**	(8.5)	2.7	(6.7)	-8.8	(7.5)
	Poland	17.0	(12.4)	8.2	(34.3)	5.1	(9.5)	-9.0	(9.5)	3.8	(31.5)	-9.1	(10.5)	12.3	(8.3)	9.1	(13.0)	-15.8	(17.3)	-12.1	(13.7)	-9.7	(34.3)
	Portugal	**25.2**	(10.4)	15.7	(13.5)	-0.1	(11.5)	-3.3	(9.6)	15.9	(11.3)	-0.3	(11.3)	-10.6	(9.7)	-14.4	(8.5)	-9.2	(11.0)	8.9	(9.4)	-1.3	(11.1)
	Slovak Republic	**49.7**	(17.8)	-22.4	(12.8)	8.6	(12.3)	-0.1	(10.4)	-7.8	(18.3)	**-31.0**	(13.9)	**26.1**	(8.8)	-21.3	(12.6)	13.3	(11.0)	-18.4	(10.7)	-18.9	(18.3)
	Slovenia	-15.9	(10.3)	2.1	(16.1)	5.2	(12.8)	-0.6	(9.9)	4.0	(16.3)	-11.4	(9.8)	**20.9**	(10.6)	-34.3	(18.1)	**-36.4**	(12.0)	4.9	(10.3)	18.6	(17.3)
	Spain	5.4	(5.5)	-4.4	(6.4)	-3.2	(6.4)	**16.2**	(5.5)	-4.8	(5.7)	-6.7	(6.9)	5.7	(6.5)	-4.1	(5.2)	-2.5	(5.4)	1.5	(5.1)	6.9	(5.2)
	Sweden	-15.0	(17.1)	19.1	(17.4)	-14.0	(12.4)	5.8	(11.7)	**-46.8**	(23.3)	-15.7	(13.8)	-13.7	(9.5)	-6.6	(9.7)	3.2	(8.9)	2.9	(11.0)	10.9	(10.2)
	Switzerland	-7.3	(10.7)	**-17.7**	(8.2)	7.1	(7.7)	12.6	(8.8)	**-20.7**	(10.0)	**-19.4**	(9.5)	7.4	(10.2)	-0.9	(8.3)	**29.7**	(7.9)	-3.5	(8.6)	-5.6	(13.3)
	Turkey	0.1	(19.0)	**-73.4**	(13.3)	-4.8	(17.7)	**66.3**	(18.5)	**71.5**	(35.7)	**71.2**	(30.1)	**43.3**	(18.7)	-27.9	(20.9)	8.8	(16.9)	7.9	(19.9)	-41.5	(26.2)
	United Kingdom	**-16.5**	(8.1)	-37.8	(19.7)	2.0	(26.1)	20.5	(11.1)	16.7	(12.0)	4.5	(8.3)	-9.1	(12.5)	-15.2	(8.4)	**-27.3**	(11.0)	1.0	(12.1)	**-47.1**	(22.0)
	United States	**-73.8**	(28.3)	**74.5**	(19.6)	42.7	(23.1)	-22.9	(22.9)	36.6	(22.8)	9.6	(21.3)	-7.8	(26.7)	23.2	(21.1)	**-49.2**	(23.7)	-52.9	(34.1)	59.4	(39.3)
	OECD average	-3.0	(2.8)	0.1	(3.0)	0.9	(2.6)	**5.5**	(2.3)	4.8	(3.5)	0.7	(3.0)	**13.7**	(2.7)	**-6.6**	(2.6)	-1.4	(2.4)	-2.5	(2.6)	-6.1	(3.3)
Partners	Albania	4.2	(14.5)	**52.3**	(20.9)	6.5	(14.8)	**-29.3**	(11.5)	-7.9	(18.0)	-25.2	(16.6)	**41.7**	(16.1)	**-28.3**	(12.2)	18.6	(10.5)	-1.0	(14.5)	c	c
	Argentina	21.7	(18.5)	-19.8	(19.8)	0.5	(20.6)	1.2	(23.8)	-7.9	(24.5)	-5.0	(26.9)	**-45.4**	(20.8)	-8.0	(20.7)	-6.3	(22.1)	18.8	(18.0)	**81.9**	(29.9)
	Azerbaijan	**73.0**	(19.8)	14.0	(11.4)	2.1	(13.8)	29.6	(16.8)	19.0	(17.3)	c	c	**-24.8**	(12.6)	-1.3	(10.4)	-8.3	(11.7)	**-58.4**	(13.6)	-52.1	(37.6)
	Brazil	-3.1	(11.8)	3.8	(26.7)	10.1	(14.5)	**-56.5**	(15.3)	-7.3	(22.0)	**-30.9**	(9.8)	18.9	(9.7)	3.8	(8.1)	**21.1**	(9.9)	12.1	(8.5)	5.0	(10.5)
	Bulgaria	**-50.9**	(20.5)	29.1	(25.3)	**-32.9**	(16.6)	30.5	(23.3)	-12.4	(27.3)	-35.8	(25.3)	40.0	(20.4)	-4.4	(15.9)	-14.6	(23.3)	-4.0	(22.2)	66.2	(68.4)
	Colombia	**25.8**	(12.0)	-2.2	(19.0)	**-34.4**	(11.9)	**-25.6**	(12.2)	4.1	(20.9)	9.2	(14.4)	**22.9**	(9.9)	0.7	(9.6)	12.0	(14.3)	12.1	(10.4)	-6.7	(13.4)
	Croatia	5.2	(13.7)	5.5	(29.4)	-16.8	(18.3)	5.5	(15.3)	-24.1	(18.9)	c	c	**34.8**	(13.4)	4.9	(16.9)	-25.1	(13.6)	13.2	(14.2)	-35.0	(30.3)
	Dubai (UAE)	-6.2	(14.5)	-13.6	(23.6)	14.1	(23.9)	11.5	(14.8)	-14.5	(17.1)	**-36.2**	(17.0)	14.9	(13.2)	25.4	(14.7)	-5.7	(23.1)	**-57.8**	(20.5)	**114.3**	(32.2)
	Hong Kong-China	**81.4**	(20.9)	**-26.4**	(12.2)	**-47.2**	(18.5)	11.9	(8.9)	17.1	(12.1)	24.3	(13.3)	**40.4**	(9.4)	9.4	(9.8)	-0.2	(11.7)	**-43.5**	(10.9)	**-70.3**	(19.5)
	Indonesia	-11.4	(13.6)	1.0	(23.3)	23.5	(16.5)	**-38.3**	(12.0)	-6.9	(21.8)	-15.2	(20.5)	5.0	(8.7)	11.5	(15.9)	-10.1	(8.7)	-6.0	(10.2)	**68.7**	(13.6)
	Jordan	**-33.2**	(13.0)	-16.2	(16.2)	23.7	(20.1)	**35.9**	(17.3)	**-29.3**	(13.4)	**-43.0**	(11.1)	-20.1	(14.9)	5.9	(11.0)	22.8	(12.5)	-1.2	(16.0)	c	c
	Kazakhstan	16.9	(16.2)	**64.5**	(12.6)	-1.0	(53.4)	-4.8	(16.4)	**-44.8**	(21.8)	**-46.5**	(19.0)	**-27.7**	(10.1)	2.4	(10.6)	25.3	(20.3)	1.5	(23.8)	c	c
	Kyrgyzstan	-18.6	(19.3)	-4.3	(21.5)	20.5	(12.0)	**-74.0**	(16.9)	12.3	(28.8)	25.9	(24.2)	**27.1**	(10.1)	-22.9	(15.4)	-20.0	(25.0)	-8.4	(21.0)	c	c
	Latvia	-11.5	(14.1)	-12.1	(22.8)	-11.9	(9.9)	-7.5	(14.5)	-24.9	(14.5)	-7.0	(9.0)	14.4	(8.2)	-11.1	(8.8)	9.5	(7.8)	-1.9	(8.8)	**-46.2**	(10.1)
	Lithuania	**53.9**	(23.2)	**-155.4**	(22.4)	-17.3	(13.7)	41.5	(24.8)	13.4	(26.4)	c	c	**131.1**	(22.5)	27.6	(44.4)	**77.3**	(5.8)	**-93.6**	(20.6)	c	c
	Macao-China	-11.4	(18.0)	-1.2	(17.0)	c	c	-13.3	(16.1)	0.7	(16.7)	c	c	12.5	(20.7)	-10.8	(16.8)	6.2	(15.6)	-13.0	(15.6)	18.9	(15.2)
	Montenegro	0.5	(22.2)	33.8	(20.9)	-12.2	(16.8)	-17.5	(16.8)	21.4	(22.1)	**70.1**	(17.8)	**-39.8**	(18.2)	13.9	(15.6)	73.4	(39.5)	-5.7	(22.4)	**-103.5**	(42.7)
	Panama	-2.0	(18.6)	12.1	(15.1)	-1.5	(17.9)	-38.8	(20.1)	-46.9	(32.4)	-26.5	(22.7)	4.5	(22.4)	8.3	(18.9)	28.8	(29.8)	18.0	(21.0)	13.4	(32.2)
	Peru	-16.0	(12.7)	**52.2**	(19.8)	-22.0	(21.0)	-21.3	(14.1)	-22.4	(15.3)	-19.8	(17.8)	**40.7**	(19.9)	-5.2	(13.5)	14.7	(12.9)	**50.8**	(13.9)	38.3	(25.6)
	Qatar	29.7	(37.7)	39.6	(20.8)	**-35.1**	(15.7)	-33.0	(20.1)	-55.8	(30.2)	**-75.8**	(27.4)	**-28.6**	(13.5)	26.4	(14.3)	-40.0	(21.0)	-29.7	(24.5)	**-212.8**	(27.7)
	Romania	6.9	(17.1)	-54.9	(32.7)	6.7	(40.1)	5.9	(22.7)	45.6	(39.3)	34.1	(29.5)	**31.8**	(11.0)	0.8	(13.9)	22.5	(15.7)	51.9	(39.6)	**-93.7**	(33.4)
	Russian Federation	5.8	(7.0)	-4.6	(12.9)	c	c	**-23.6**	(11.1)	-4.7	(14.5)	18.3	(13.0)	14.1	(7.9)	1.8	(7.0)	**96.0**	(25.7)	23.3	(22.0)	**-211.2**	(35.3)
	Serbia	7.5	(16.7)	-59.6	(35.4)	-22.7	(17.1)	**-33.3**	(15.2)	-16.7	(25.1)	-13.5	(26.7)	17.3	(16.7)	-23.7	(19.8)	-6.8	(18.7)	5.3	(15.5)	23.4	(21.7)
	Shanghai-China	**53.8**	(19.1)	-19.7	(11.5)	**-57.0**	(22.9)	18.3	(11.0)	12.9	(10.6)	-5.6	(11.8)	c	c	-7.1	(10.4)	-6.6	(11.8)	-4.2	(11.1)	c	c
	Singapore	**-71.8**	(11.5)	1.9	(31.6)	15.9	(28.7)	14.9	(30.1)	32.9	(17.3)	-7.8	(14.1)	5.9	(9.0)	20.7	(10.9)	-28.0	(27.2)	-27.4	(41.1)	**68.0**	(14.0)
	Chinese Taipei	23.4	(27.1)	6.6	(10.3)	**29.0**	(14.8)	**-24.2**	(9.4)	4.8	(12.0)	**-27.6**	(9.7)	**27.9**	(12.1)	-16.9	(12.3)	3.4	(9.2)	**20.2**	(9.8)	**-29.2**	(10.8)
	Thailand	11.7	(12.0)	3.5	(17.2)	**-55.9**	(21.7)	1.4	(9.4)	4.3	(10.4)	3.0	(7.1)	-5.8	(7.4)	3.5	(10.7)	1.2	(11.2)	-8.6	(14.5)	37.9	(23.1)
	Trinidad and Tobago	14.7	(19.1)	6.9	(18.9)	-9.9	(20.4)	**38.8**	(14.7)	**71.5**	(17.1)	**55.9**	(17.2)	12.7	(27.9)	24.4	(15.8)	3.3	(18.6)	2.6	(15.0)	-19.8	(14.7)
	Tunisia	-6.0	(13.1)	28.2	(16.7)	4.6	(9.5)	**27.8**	(12.4)	12.3	(19.3)	-14.6	(19.4)	-2.8	(14.5)	-11.8	(9.9)	7.2	(11.3)	**-43.7**	(10.9)	-3.8	(24.5)
	Uruguay	**26.1**	(12.7)	6.0	(15.2)	22.0	(15.6)	**-53.7**	(15.6)	-9.2	(17.3)	-24.4	(15.3)	-9.6	(17.4)	9.1	(11.0)	7.1	(12.9)	2.4	(13.6)	1.6	(27.9)

Note: Values that are statistically significant are indicated in bold (see Annex A3).
1. Multilevel regression model (student and school levels): Reading performance is regressed on the variables of school policies and practices presented in this table.
StatLink http://dx.doi.org/10.1787/888932343285

[Part 1/2]

Table IV.2.9c Relationships between schools' assessment and accountability policies and reading performance, accounting for students' and schools' socio-economic and demographic background

		Assessment and accountability policies[1]																					
		School uses standardised tests		School uses student assessments to monitor school's progress		School uses student assessments to improve instruction or curriculum		School uses student assessments to compare with other schools or district or national performance		Schools' accountability to parents: only relative to other students in the school		Schools' accountability to parents: at least relative to national or regional benchmark		School posts achievement data publicly		Achievement data are used in decisions about instructional resource allocation to the school		Achievement data are tracked over time by an administrative authority		School monitors teachers' practice through students'[1] achievement test or assessments		School monitors teachers' practice through teacher peer review or observations of lessons by principal or inspectors	
		Change in score	S.E.	Change in score	S.E.	Change in score	S.E.	Change in score	S.E.	Change in score	S.E.	Change in score	S.E.	Change in score	S.E.	Change in score	S.E.	Change in score	S.E.	Change in score	S.E.	Change in score	S.E.
OECD	Australia	-5.1	(5.0)	2.5	(6.6)	-8.0	(6.2)	**-14.1**	(6.1)	**-16.6**	(8.2)	-0.5	(8.0)	0.8	(4.9)	2.8	(5.1)	1.3	(6.9)	**10.4**	(4.7)	-5.5	(5.4)
	Austria	**-36.7**	(8.5)	**-21.2**	(9.1)	6.6	(8.6)	**26.7**	(10.3)	2.6	(8.8)	-0.6	(11.1)	12.8	(14.5)	-13.5	(10.9)	16.5	(8.7)	0.3	(10.8)	**-34.1**	(13.0)
	Belgium	**-14.5**	(7.0)	7.7	(6.2)	-5.7	(7.0)	10.0	(7.9)	**25.6**	(7.9)	-2.2	(6.8)	3.3	(19.8)	-8.2	(9.2)	-0.9	(6.9)	2.5	(6.4)	8.9	(9.4)
	Canada	2.0	(6.6)	-2.6	(6.6)	-0.6	(6.6)	2.9	(6.4)	-4.2	(6.2)	-1.3	(5.4)	0.7	(4.5)	0.4	(3.6)	2.2	(5.4)	c	c	-7.3	(4.7)
	Chile	-15.5	(9.8)	23.1	(12.6)	-19.1	(13.7)	**-21.0**	(7.5)	21.8	(14.0)	12.6	(11.5)	5.7	(8.2)	0.8	(11.6)	0.2	(8.8)	-0.1	(9.5)	-4.7	(10.5)
	Czech Republic	9.7	(10.0)	-3.2	(8.4)	-2.3	(7.4)	2.6	(8.8)	1.4	(9.6)	-2.2	(10.7)	-1.2	(6.7)	-8.3	(12.9)	-1.0	(5.6)	1.3	(5.7)	16.8	(20.3)
	Denmark	-0.5	(15.1)	-1.7	(4.3)	4.5	(5.5)	7.1	(4.6)	c	c	c	c	1.4	(3.9)	1.9	(4.5)	-6.3	(3.9)	-1.0	(4.3)	-8.7	(5.8)
	Estonia	-4.0	(6.6)	-6.6	(10.8)	-5.1	(7.1)	-8.1	(8.5)	-4.6	(9.4)	6.8	(6.8)	6.2	(6.2)	-11.1	(8.3)	-8.8	(10.8)	-8.9	(6.0)	-26.1	(14.4)
	Finland	4.5	(16.5)	**-10.9**	(5.2)	4.0	(4.7)	2.8	(5.5)	-9.5	(14.8)	4.4	(5.1)	23.7	(16.9)	6.4	(6.9)	-2.2	(5.5)	-1.0	(6.4)	-6.9	(4.9)
	France	w	w	w	w	w	w	w	w	w	w	w	w	w	w	w	w	w	w	w	w	w	w
	Germany	6.8	(8.2)	-16.8	(8.8)	2.9	(9.1)	10.7	(7.8)	6.5	(9.5)	10.6	(9.0)	-8.4	(11.5)	-4.7	(9.3)	**21.0**	(7.4)	-6.3	(8.1)	4.7	(7.6)
	Greece	2.5	(12.3)	-3.2	(13.0)	-11.2	(13.6)	**26.1**	(13.3)	13.5	(11.9)	-7.1	(15.4)	8.8	(11.3)	6.8	(16.6)	-3.6	(12.1)	-5.8	(15.1)	10.8	(14.8)
	Hungary	15.9	(10.1)	8.1	(14.1)	-8.4	(7.8)	10.4	(9.4)	14.9	(10.3)	**-19.6**	(9.9)	3.8	(9.3)	-19.5	(11.5)	-8.9	(8.9)	-20.3	(10.4)	-17.5	(18.5)
	Iceland	6.6	(11.6)	0.6	(14.7)	4.7	(16.1)	-6.6	(6.7)	-20.5	(13.9)	-7.2	(6.1)	-15.5	(8.0)	c	c	10.8	(8.0)	-1.7	(6.9)	0.5	(6.9)
	Ireland	-0.4	(8.3)	-13.2	(8.2)	15.3	(8.9)	-5.4	(7.8)	3.2	(8.4)	8.2	(9.4)	-5.4	(12.0)	3.5	(7.7)	-4.1	(8.5)	6.0	(7.9)	-4.1	(10.0)
	Israel	13.5	(16.7)	-1.8	(15.7)	-16.1	(17.9)	21.1	(13.7)	**-60.7**	(21.0)	-7.8	(13.9)	-1.6	(14.2)	-14.2	(14.0)	11.4	(13.4)	-16.5	(24.4)	**-32.0**	(16.2)
	Italy	-11.0	(6.0)	-17.0	(9.9)	-9.7	(9.0)	-4.7	(12.2)	-16.0	(13.2)	-7.0	(13.3)	9.1	(8.5)	-8.0	(8.3)	-3.3	(8.8)	-0.4	(8.5)	10.0	(9.5)
	Japan	0.1	(9.8)	7.9	(10.1)	7.6	(10.2)	20.4	(13.2)	**34.3**	(11.5)	20.9	(13.4)	16.9	(23.5)	-36.1	(29.4)	**22.3**	(10.0)	-4.9	(11.4)	21.8	(13.2)
	Korea	11.3	(14.6)	**-32.7**	(9.0)	12.1	(10.2)	17.2	(9.5)	-15.0	(16.0)	-9.9	(14.6)	17.3	(13.1)	-14.8	(10.5)	-15.4	(9.3)	-7.9	(9.8)	**-46.3**	(15.8)
	Luxembourg	-36.9	(19.4)	8.0	(9.4)	8.3	(9.1)	-0.5	(11.9)	10.2	(15.3)	-10.6	(13.7)	0.5	(10.0)	10.5	(10.9)	**-18.2**	(9.2)	-6.8	(9.3)	-7.8	(10.8)
	Mexico	10.6	(8.9)	3.1	(8.7)	13.5	(15.5)	-9.0	(10.2)	4.0	(10.1)	2.7	(10.0)	-5.2	(7.5)	6.6	(6.6)	0.5	(8.6)	2.7	(6.4)	-7.1	(11.0)
	Netherlands	-0.2	(11.6)	-7.1	(10.5)	6.6	(12.4)	-9.4	(10.7)	1.0	(15.2)	2.2	(13.5)	4.4	(8.7)	11.8	(11.1)	13.7	(9.4)	**23.0**	(10.4)	-17.6	(9.1)
	New Zealand	-5.3	(9.6)	11.7	(11.7)	2.0	(14.6)	-9.9	(11.3)	-0.5	(12.1)	-2.5	(9.1)	3.1	(6.9)	6.3	(6.1)	3.1	(10.9)	2.5	(6.0)	-3.4	(8.1)
	Norway	-14.7	(11.3)	-2.8	(9.4)	10.0	(5.7)	-9.7	(8.0)	-0.4	(12.4)	6.1	(10.2)	8.9	(6.9)	-1.3	(8.7)	**15.5**	(7.8)	-0.9	(6.4)	-9.6	(7.6)
	Poland	16.1	(18.0)	-7.6	(10.8)	7.6	(7.0)	-4.8	(4.9)	-15.6	(17.0)	0.3	(5.0)	0.6	(4.3)	-4.3	(9.0)	8.6	(8.7)	-22.7	(17.3)	10.2	(19.8)
	Portugal	-2.4	(8.0)	7.0	(9.0)	4.3	(6.5)	-5.1	(6.3)	6.8	(7.1)	4.3	(6.9)	-2.0	(7.1)	-10.3	(6.3)	-9.0	(6.7)	-1.2	(6.2)	1.2	(8.5)
	Slovak Republic	-1.7	(15.6)	-10.8	(9.2)	-7.9	(9.8)	6.4	(7.7)	-11.1	(12.4)	**-20.0**	(9.1)	8.8	(6.8)	-5.1	(8.0)	1.1	(9.7)	-8.7	(7.4)	15.3	(17.4)
	Slovenia	7.2	(8.5)	-4.0	(14.5)	15.0	(12.0)	-1.9	(7.9)	-1.5	(11.0)	-6.5	(8.8)	5.6	(8.2)	-33.8	(19.8)	-18.2	(10.3)	-3.1	(8.6)	16.9	(10.9)
	Spain	-2.0	(4.1)	1.2	(5.5)	-3.1	(5.5)	4.7	(4.4)	-2.6	(4.2)	-5.2	(5.3)	2.4	(4.9)	-4.9	(3.9)	1.1	(4.3)	-5.7	(4.6)	2.8	(4.2)
	Sweden	6.9	(10.7)	**18.6**	(9.1)	-8.4	(7.0)	-5.2	(5.3)	-18.2	(20.1)	-8.8	(7.1)	-3.8	(6.1)	-4.5	(5.3)	-2.8	(7.3)	-8.6	(7.6)	5.8	(6.1)
	Switzerland	-2.4	(7.4)	-5.9	(6.2)	7.9	(5.8)	**15.8**	(6.2)	-9.7	(7.7)	**-18.6**	(7.2)	**-21.7**	(9.7)	0.1	(7.0)	**15.5**	(6.3)	-11.2	(7.1)	0.0	(9.9)
	Turkey	14.3	(13.2)	-25.3	(16.7)	-7.4	(9.5)	-15.3	(12.9)	28.6	(15.9)	21.1	(14.2)	**24.4**	(11.4)	-6.9	(9.0)	2.9	(11.0)	11.3	(14.1)	-5.2	(16.7)
	United Kingdom	3.3	(4.3)	**-28.1**	(11.9)	9.2	(10.5)	-2.2	(8.1)	12.4	(8.0)	0.7	(5.6)	-0.1	(5.4)	-4.7	(4.6)	**23.0**	(8.7)	-10.3	(5.8)	**41.8**	(13.8)
	United States	-18.0	(17.1)	**54.7**	(27.2)	5.0	(20.8)	6.5	(12.5)	-1.0	(14.3)	-8.5	(11.2)	28.5	(15.3)	-9.9	(9.2)	19.7	(25.8)	-2.6	(14.2)	27.9	(22.7)
	OECD average	-1.2	(2.0)	-2.1	(2.0)	1.0	(1.8)	1.8	(1.6)	-0.6	(2.2)	-1.4	(1.8)	**4.0**	(1.8)	**-5.2**	(1.9)	2.7	(1.7)	-3.0	(1.8)	-1.5	(2.2)
Partners	Albania	-11.7	(17.1)	**47.6**	(20.5)	5.6	(13.0)	-13.9	(12.3)	-0.3	(12.6)	-10.4	(13.3)	4.3	(10.6)	-25.8	(13.3)	11.1	(9.7)	-0.8	(16.2)	c	c
	Argentina	21.9	(12.4)	1.5	(13.6)	-8.7	(18.4)	-6.3	(14.1)	1.4	(15.2)	8.7	(11.8)	-12.3	(21.2)	1.2	(11.1)	-22.5	(12.7)	13.5	(11.9)	32.7	(26.4)
	Azerbaijan	**74.5**	(23.2)	4.0	(12.4)	2.7	(13.6)	**45.6**	(13.0)	5.4	(14.3)	c	c	**-25.0**	(11.9)	9.0	(9.7)	-11.2	(11.8)	**-68.6**	(9.8)	-34.3	(31.6)
	Brazil	-4.9	(7.0)	-9.3	(12.9)	2.6	(11.9)	-18.3	(9.9)	3.9	(15.9)	-6.9	(5.8)	10.6	(6.3)	-4.3	(5.7)	12.3	(6.3)	1.6	(6.8)	-7.7	(8.1)
	Bulgaria	-20.8	(11.7)	**36.3**	(16.1)	-12.3	(9.2)	8.9	(14.2)	-7.2	(15.8)	1.0	(16.3)	18.7	(10.0)	-6.1	(9.7)	1.5	(9.7)	0.4	(15.1)	78.3	(56.2)
	Colombia	4.7	(7.6)	2.8	(9.8)	-3.6	(7.6)	-4.3	(5.7)	**-32.7**	(13.2)	-9.7	(9.0)	**18.5**	(5.1)	**-10.0**	(5.0)	8.2	(6.0)	1.3	(5.4)	**-13.3**	(5.3)
	Croatia	-6.5	(8.7)	-5.7	(21.2)	-7.2	(7.7)	-4.1	(9.7)	-8.1	(8.7)	c	c	9.7	(9.1)	-3.7	(10.1)	11.4	(15.4)	2.2	(8.4)	19.0	(14.7)
	Dubai (UAE)	22.3	(11.8)	-10.7	(12.9)	-16.5	(12.6)	11.8	(9.6)	5.9	(9.7)	-14.7	(10.5)	6.5	(9.4)	8.4	(9.3)	-15.7	(12.7)	-21.7	(13.3)	**60.8**	(21.0)
	Hong Kong-China	**66.5**	(20.5)	-17.7	(11.1)	-13.1	(18.1)	10.8	(6.1)	8.6	(8.5)	**22.6**	(9.5)	**15.9**	(6.4)	**13.3**	(6.1)	-3.6	(6.1)	**-23.1**	(10.1)	**-42.0**	(16.6)
	Indonesia	-15.1	(11.9)	7.2	(15.9)	17.2	(13.7)	**-37.6**	(8.8)	0.5	(17.3)	-5.9	(16.3)	-1.7	(7.3)	20.1	(14.1)	-10.6	(7.1)	-1.9	(8.6)	**55.3**	(16.1)
	Jordan	-21.2	(12.2)	-7.9	(13.1)	12.4	(15.9)	28.8	(17.3)	-14.5	(11.8)	**-27.1**	(11.9)	-16.3	(12.4)	1.0	(9.5)	23.9	(13.7)	-0.3	(12.6)	c	c
	Kazakhstan	9.6	(11.0)	**30.6**	(12.3)	-30.5	(35.3)	-9.9	(11.5)	-6.3	(25.0)	-5.3	(23.3)	**-20.4**	(9.1)	-3.9	(9.1)	16.9	(16.6)	-13.7	(16.1)	c	c
	Kyrgyzstan	12.7	(15.8)	2.5	(12.3)	13.7	(10.5)	**-34.4**	(11.7)	23.7	(27.5)	21.7	(21.9)	**17.3**	(8.5)	-19.5	(10.3)	-28.9	(14.7)	15.6	(16.9)	c	c
	Latvia	-7.8	(14.1)	-8.5	(19.1)	-12.0	(9.6)	-2.0	(10.3)	-18.4	(11.2)	**-15.3**	(6.4)	2.2	(6.5)	-4.3	(6.2)	6.3	(6.5)	-4.7	(7.4)	**-28.7**	(14.3)
	Lithuania	11.3	(14.6)	**-32.7**	(9.0)	12.1	(10.2)	17.2	(9.5)	-15.0	(16.0)	c	c	17.3	(13.1)	-14.8	(10.5)	-15.4	(9.3)	-7.9	(9.8)	**-46.3**	(15.8)
	Macao-China	-7.5	(9.1)	-1.7	(9.7)	c	c	-0.1	(9.6)	0.5	(11.1)	c	c	17.9	(11.3)	**-16.8**	(8.4)	8.7	(8.6)	-7.8	(9.6)	-20.2	(12.4)
	Montenegro	-1.5	(9.4)	**23.4**	(10.6)	-12.5	(10.2)	-11.6	(9.3)	23.9	(13.2)	**36.6**	(12.4)	-0.6	(10.7)	0.7	(10.3)	-54.2	(34.5)	-10.2	(10.7)	-4.0	(35.1)
	Panama	-18.3	(12.9)	10.0	(9.7)	-20.2	(12.9)	**-25.6**	(13.0)	-31.8	(27.9)	16.4	(12.5)	3.5	(16.3)	-8.6	(14.7)	**38.0**	(15.8)	-11.9	(14.7)	0.9	(17.5)
	Peru	-4.6	(8.0)	13.1	(12.8)	11.5	(13.2)	-9.4	(6.7)	5.1	(7.8)	8.5	(9.7)	-0.1	(7.8)	0.7	(8.1)	**14.9**	(7.5)	5.0	(9.6)	14.0	(15.8)
	Qatar	-11.7	(17.8)	17.0	(15.3)	-12.9	(10.6)	-22.6	(13.4)	-3.2	(17.9)	**-33.8**	(14.9)	**-21.1**	(10.1)	9.6	(10.7)	-8.3	(15.9)	-12.8	(15.8)	**-126.4**	(21.5)
	Romania	6.2	(13.0)	-19.1	(24.5)	0.9	(16.9)	13.6	(23.1)	9.1	(24.5)	17.3	(21.9)	**30.1**	(9.4)	7.7	(10.5)	**27.1**	(11.3)	-17.0	(13.6)	**-55.4**	(16.8)
	Russian Federation	-4.9	(6.9)	-22.7	(14.3)	c	c	15.5	(10.7)	6.8	(12.3)	20.0	(10.4)	10.6	(6.1)	-2.1	(5.5)	**79.6**	(30.0)	9.0	(14.8)	**-86.1**	(32.1)
	Serbia	-0.6	(13.7)	**-37.7**	(17.7)	**-17.8**	(8.8)	-6.5	(10.2)	0.2	(23.7)	5.7	(29.2)	2.9	(11.7)	-16.6	(17.3)	-5.9	(9.6)	-2.2	(14.3)	17.4	(16.1)
	Shanghai-China	**27.8**	(14.1)	-11.6	(7.1)	**-33.8**	(13.8)	7.9	(6.1)	**20.5**	(6.6)	2.6	(6.8)	c	c	5.8	(5.8)	-1.6	(5.4)	-3.6	(6.9)	c	c
	Singapore	-13.8	(15.4)	14.5	(21.2)	-13.1	(28.1)	2.7	(19.9)	1.2	(13.6)	-5.2	(13.3)	-1.9	(5.4)	2.5	(6.3)	**-38.2**	(8.4)	1.1	(42.1)	**19.3**	(8.3)
	Chinese Taipei	20.7	(16.3)	2.8	(8.9)	-2.8	(12.4)	**-23.9**	(7.9)	**17.7**	(8.2)	-0.3	(7.5)	**21.4**	(7.5)	**-27.2**	(8.7)	**15.1**	(7.6)	**19.0**	(6.9)	**-25.7**	(6.9)
	Thailand	7.8	(10.6)	3.7	(14.7)	-39.9	(21.5)	13.9	(8.3)	12.4	(10.7)	14.5	(7.8)	-9.5	(7.5)	-1.7	(10.5)	-8.4	(9.8)	-13.5	(13.4)	37.3	(22.5)
	Trinidad and Tobago	9.7	(10.7)	16.9	(14.5)	-26.1	(14.6)	15.8	(8.7)	19.8	(13.4)	13.3	(13.2)	-16.6	(12.5)	7.0	(8.9)	10.1	(9.9)	-7.8	(9.8)	-20.4	(15.2)
	Tunisia	-18.6	(15.9)	14.2	(15.4)	9.6	(7.2)	**21.5**	(10.8)	14.7	(12.5)	4.3	(12.8)	-21.8	(11.7)	-6.4	(7.6)	6.9	(10.3)	**-37.1**	(9.4)	32.4	(19.7)
	Uruguay	-4.7	(6.0)	10.2	(8.2)	12.3	(8.4)	-9.8	(8.0)	6.4	(7.6)	4.7	(9.0)	3.4	(16.0)	-1.3	(6.1)	4.1	(6.7)	-14.6	(7.5)	4.5	(12.3)

Note: Values that are statistically significant are indicated in bold (see Annex A3).
1. Multilevel regression model (student and school levels): Reading performance is regressed on the variables of school policies and practices as well as socio-economic and demographic background variables presented in this table.

StatLink http://dx.doi.org/10.1787/888932343285

[Part 2/2]

Table IV.2.9c Relationships between schools' assessment and accountability policies and reading performance, accounting for students' and schools' socio-economic and demographic background

	Student socio-economic and demographic background[1]										School socio-economic and demographic background[1]									
	Student is a female		Student without an immigrant background		Student's language at home is the same as the language of assessment		PISA index of economic, social and cultural status of student (1 unit increase)		PISA index of economic, social and cultural status of student (squared)		School average PISA index of economic, social and cultural status (1 unit increase)		School size (per 100 students)		School size (per 100 students) (squared)		School in a small town or village (15 000 or less people)		School in city (100 000 or more people)	
	Change in score	S.E.	Change in score	S.E.	Change in score	S.E.	Change in score	S.E.	Change in score	S.E.	Change in score	S.E.	Change in score	S.E.	Change in score	S.E.	Change in score	S.E.	Change in score	S.E.
OECD																				
Australia	**37.5**	(2.3)	**-5.9**	(2.4)	**22.8**	(4.1)	**27.3**	(1.7)	**-3.0**	(1.0)	**64.2**	(7.2)	1.2	(2.1)	0.0	(0.1)	5.5	(7.2)	**10.0**	(4.9)
Austria	**21.0**	(3.3)	**13.4**	(4.6)	**14.8**	(5.7)	**8.2**	(2.0)	0.3	(1.4)	**65.6**	(10.0)	**9.0**	(2.8)	**-0.3**	(0.2)	-11.7	(9.8)	4.2	(11.6)
Belgium	**19.0**	(2.1)	**16.6**	(2.7)	**7.0**	(3.2)	**12.1**	(1.4)	1.4	(0.9)	**95.3**	(6.3)	**6.4**	(2.3)	**-0.2**	(0.1)	5.9	(6.5)	-1.4	(8.0)
Canada	**35.5**	(2.0)	3.9	(2.6)	**17.2**	(4.4)	**19.2**	(1.3)	**3.0**	(0.9)	**30.8**	(7.1)	1.7	(1.2)	0.0	(0.1)	2.4	(5.3)	2.4	(4.3)
Chile	**18.6**	(3.1)	0.7	(7.8)	**50.2**	(18.1)	**9.4**	(1.8)	0.3	(0.9)	**45.7**	(4.5)	**4.6**	(1.4)	**-0.1**	(0.0)	15.3	(12.2)	-4.1	(10.9)
Czech Republic	**35.3**	(2.7)	**12.9**	(3.8)	-1.9	(10.6)	**15.4**	(2.0)	-2.7	(1.6)	**124.9**	(8.9)	1.6	(3.3)	0.0	(0.3)	**14.0**	(7.0)	-12.4	(7.3)
Denmark	**29.3**	(2.9)	**14.3**	(3.6)	**20.6**	(5.9)	**27.2**	(1.7)	-0.3	(1.1)	**37.9**	(5.7)	3.5	(2.9)	-0.4	(0.3)	-8.4	(4.4)	4.7	(6.1)
Estonia	**43.9**	(3.0)	**13.3**	(3.7)	**28.4**	(7.2)	**17.0**	(2.1)	1.6	(1.9)	**32.5**	(13.4)	**4.4**	(1.9)	**-0.2**	(0.1)	1.8	(8.0)	-1.3	(8.6)
Finland	**56.6**	(2.5)	**13.3**	(5.3)	**46.8**	(7.4)	**27.3**	(1.9)	-1.2	(1.6)	**29.4**	(12.1)	-1.1	(1.8)	0.1	(0.0)	-1.0	(5.4)	-3.2	(6.4)
France	w	w	w	w	w	w	w	w	w	w	w	w	w	w	w	w	w	w	w	w
Germany	**29.9**	(2.5)	**15.3**	(3.4)	3.7	(5.8)	**9.2**	(1.5)	-1.1	(0.9)	**105.2**	(9.6)	**9.0**	(2.3)	**-0.3**	(0.1)	15.2	(9.3)	-10.7	(9.4)
Greece	**36.4**	(3.1)	1.8	(3.6)	16.9	(14.2)	**15.8**	(1.7)	2.3	(1.3)	**50.4**	(8.4)	-26.9	(20.3)	4.0	(3.0)	24.0	(13.2)	-14.3	(12.5)
Hungary	**24.4**	(2.5)	-7.0	(4.5)	18.2	(9.7)	**8.5**	(1.6)	0.4	(1.1)	**73.6**	(6.7)	5.0	(3.2)	-0.2	(0.2)	0.2	(11.6)	-9.7	(11.6)
Iceland	**45.8**	(3.3)	4.2	(5.3)	**47.6**	(12.4)	**28.5**	(2.7)	**-3.8**	(1.6)	22.1	(12.7)	-7.8	(6.7)	0.5	(0.9)	3.4	(9.6)	-4.8	(9.9)
Ireland	**35.7**	(4.5)	-4.3	(3.9)	**31.9**	(10.4)	**26.9**	(2.1)	-1.8	(1.5)	**49.2**	(7.5)	6.1	(4.2)	-0.4	(0.3)	9.2	(7.6)	10.6	(8.6)
Israel	**33.4**	(3.7)	-3.5	(4.0)	2.3	(6.1)	**22.1**	(2.6)	**3.9**	(1.3)	**99.4**	(12.6)	**8.8**	(4.1)	**-0.4**	(0.2)	7.5	(15.8)	1.3	(15.1)
Italy	**27.5**	(1.7)	**16.4**	(2.5)	**6.9**	(2.5)	**5.2**	(0.8)	-1.0	(0.9)	**60.6**	(10.2)	**12.4**	(2.6)	**-0.4**	(0.1)	7.9	(10.9)	-11.1	(8.7)
Japan	**28.2**	(2.8)	3.6	(9.2)	**73.1**	(28.3)	4.4	(2.5)	-0.4	(2.3)	**150.4**	(16.4)	-2.1	(3.8)	0.1	(0.2)	5.7	(14.3)	-12.8	(10.6)
Korea	**43.1**	(5.7)	3.9	(11.5)	**64.6**	(25.8)	**18.9**	(2.7)	0.4	(1.4)	**54.9**	(7.8)	5.3	(3.9)	-0.2	(0.2)	-32.1	(18.1)	**-35.6**	(12.6)
Luxembourg	**37.1**	(3.2)	**28.8**	(3.5)	**24.4**	(4.9)	**16.7**	(2.9)	-1.7	(1.2)	**78.6**	(8.6)	1.2	(3.0)	0.0	(0.1)	6.1	(9.5)	**-73.6**	(25.2)
Mexico	**22.2**	(1.9)	**24.8**	(3.5)	**19.3**	(5.6)	**8.5**	(1.4)	**1.5**	(0.5)	**23.6**	(4.4)	**1.5**	(0.6)	0.0	(0.0)	-9.3	(8.3)	3.5	(7.0)
Netherlands	**19.2**	(1.7)	**6.0**	(2.7)	11.9	(6.6)	**5.2**	(1.6)	0.2	(1.1)	**71.8**	(11.9)	5.4	(2.8)	-0.1	(0.1)	-23.0	(11.9)	7.0	(9.3)
New Zealand	**49.6**	(4.5)	-6.8	(3.6)	**46.5**	(5.7)	**34.9**	(2.8)	0.1	(2.4)	**56.7**	(9.6)	2.4	(2.2)	-0.1	(0.1)	10.8	(9.9)	5.1	(7.9)
Norway	**48.3**	(3.5)	**11.3**	(5.5)	**37.2**	(7.8)	**28.8**	(3.1)	-1.9	(2.0)	**29.6**	(14.7)	0.3	(9.0)	-0.3	(1.2)	-7.4	(6.1)	-9.0	(8.1)
Poland	**52.8**	(3.4)	21.5	(23.3)	**49.2**	(15.3)	**31.3**	(1.8)	**-3.3**	(1.4)	**32.1**	(7.1)	6.6	(5.3)	-0.3	(0.7)	3.8	(7.8)	**-17.3**	(8.6)
Portugal	**34.3**	(2.6)	-1.3	(3.1)	13.7	(8.2)	**18.0**	(1.4)	-0.6	(0.8)	**38.2**	(5.6)	-0.8	(2.8)	0.1	(0.1)	6.1	(7.5)	-0.6	(6.4)
Slovak Republic	**43.4**	(2.9)	1.5	(5.4)	**27.8**	(7.3)	**18.0**	(1.9)	**-3.6**	(1.2)	**62.6**	(10.6)	-2.7	(4.3)	0.3	(0.3)	-8.3	(7.7)	-3.9	(9.0)
Slovenia	**31.9**	(2.3)	**7.9**	(3.1)	6.3	(5.1)	**3.3**	(1.2)	1.2	(1.1)	**64.9**	(9.9)	**14.4**	(4.0)	-0.8	(0.4)	-10.3	(11.2)	-1.2	(8.0)
Spain	**29.7**	(1.7)	**24.6**	(2.4)	**10.3**	(3.5)	**19.8**	(1.0)	-0.8	(0.6)	**24.5**	(4.3)	-1.0	(1.5)	0.0	(0.1)	-4.5	(4.2)	**11.0**	(4.7)
Sweden	**46.4**	(3.0)	7.0	(4.1)	**29.3**	(6.3)	**32.2**	(2.1)	-1.2	(1.0)	**52.0**	(12.8)	-2.8	(3.2)	0.3	(0.2)	-1.6	(7.1)	1.2	(8.7)
Switzerland	**32.1**	(2.3)	**11.4**	(2.7)	**19.7**	(3.4)	**18.2**	(1.6)	-0.3	(1.4)	**62.6**	(9.6)	**2.3**	(0.9)	**0.0**	(0.0)	-3.1	(7.6)	-5.7	(13.5)
Turkey	**31.1**	(2.8)	-1.9	(7.7)	1.2	(11.5)	**7.2**	(2.3)	-0.4	(0.9)	**54.1**	(7.1)	**-7.8**	(3.0)	0.1	(0.1)	-13.2	(15.7)	13.1	(15.1)
United Kingdom	**25.7**	(3.1)	-6.9	(4.6)	**18.3**	(6.7)	**26.0**	(2.0)	0.4	(1.6)	**77.8**	(7.7)	1.1	(1.7)	0.0	(0.1)	6.1	(4.7)	-0.2	(5.8)
United States	**28.0**	(4.2)	-4.7	(7.6)	5.0	(8.1)	**23.7**	(2.4)	-1.9	(3.1)	**65.7**	(9.5)	-2.8	(1.8)	0.1	(0.0)	-7.8	(13.7)	3.5	(11.4)
OECD average	**34.3**	(0.5)	**7.2**	(1.1)	**24.0**	(1.8)	**18.0**	(0.3)	-0.4	(0.2)	**60.2**	(1.7)	**1.8**	(0.9)	0.0	(0.1)	0.3	(1.7)	**-4.7**	(1.8)
Partners																				
Albania	**57.9**	(4.1)	22.1	(11.6)	13.1	(16.7)	**20.7**	(3.7)	**3.3**	(1.5)	**30.1**	(10.2)	-6.3	(4.3)	0.5	(0.3)	-9.8	(14.7)	10.2	(12.9)
Argentina	**31.3**	(3.2)	1.3	(5.2)	**44.5**	(17.2)	**13.2**	(2.1)	**2.0**	(1.0)	**65.3**	(6.4)	**5.8**	(2.9)	**-0.2**	(0.1)	14.0	(16.3)	15.7	(16.2)
Azerbaijan	**22.6**	(2.4)	3.0	(5.0)	-2.8	(6.0)	**11.4**	(2.1)	1.6	(1.0)	**29.0**	(11.4)	**-7.9**	(3.6)	**0.5**	(0.2)	-18.3	(16.8)	-21.8	(13.2)
Brazil	**29.0**	(2.0)	12.4	(9.1)	**33.4**	(12.5)	**8.7**	(1.9)	**1.7**	(0.7)	**52.5**	(4.4)	-0.5	(1.1)	0.0	(0.0)	7.5	(7.6)	-7.6	(6.1)
Bulgaria	**47.7**	(3.8)	**28.7**	(8.0)	**28.7**	(6.7)	**13.5**	(2.3)	1.4	(1.4)	**65.7**	(8.5)	-0.2	(3.8)	0.2	(0.3)	-6.3	(10.5)	9.3	(11.2)
Colombia	**10.3**	(3.0)	**19.5**	(8.0)	**59.8**	(21.6)	**13.2**	(2.7)	1.4	(0.9)	**44.1**	(3.4)	0.0	(0.7)	0.0	(0.0)	10.8	(7.9)	-0.1	(6.2)
Croatia	**35.5**	(3.5)	3.0	(2.5)	-6.2	(9.3)	**10.6**	(1.9)	**-3.8**	(1.2)	**87.4**	(11.1)	**10.2**	(4.2)	-0.4	(0.2)	15.0	(8.7)	**-35.9**	(10.8)
Dubai (UAE)	**28.8**	(4.6)	**-31.8**	(3.5)	**18.9**	(3.0)	**19.1**	(1.9)	**2.6**	(1.1)	**72.3**	(9.0)	**1.5**	(0.6)	0.0	(0.0)	14.6	(21.9)	15.7	(20.1)
Hong Kong-China	**25.7**	(2.9)	**-8.4**	(2.4)	**23.9**	(6.6)	2.5	(2.1)	-1.2	(1.0)	**35.6**	(7.5)	**18.2**	(6.8)	-0.4	(0.4)	a	a	a	a
Indonesia	**29.0**	(1.8)	18.1	(11.0)	-5.0	(2.7)	**6.9**	(2.9)	1.4	(0.8)	**21.9**	(5.8)	3.3	(3.3)	0.0	(0.3)	0.3	(9.5)	10.8	(10.1)
Jordan	**43.5**	(8.3)	-5.8	(3.8)	**24.5**	(8.3)	**20.2**	(2.3)	1.3	(1.1)	14.5	(8.7)	-3.0	(3.8)	0.3	(0.2)	-5.6	(10.7)	-3.5	(9.1)
Kazakhstan	**41.6**	(2.6)	**-12.0**	(4.9)	2.0	(4.7)	**17.2**	(2.5)	-2.1	(1.4)	**48.7**	(9.7)	**-5.7**	(1.5)	**0.1**	(0.1)	-19.1	(13.5)	4.0	(13.3)
Kyrgyzstan	**50.6**	(3.0)	**-12.7**	(5.6)	-3.0	(4.9)	**19.7**	(2.4)	**2.4**	(1.2)	**37.2**	(10.8)	1.0	(2.3)	-0.1	(0.1)	-2.3	(11.6)	**48.7**	(14.4)
Latvia	**47.1**	(2.9)	0.5	(3.4)	3.4	(9.3)	**19.6**	(2.5)	-0.7	(1.6)	**32.0**	(10.9)	-0.5	(3.3)	0.2	(0.3)	6.2	(9.1)	-1.1	(10.9)
Lithuania	**43.1**	(5.7)	3.9	(11.5)	**64.6**	(25.8)	**18.9**	(2.7)	0.4	(1.4)	**54.9**	(7.8)	5.3	(3.9)	-0.2	(0.2)	-32.1	(18.1)	**-35.6**	(12.6)
Macao-China	**21.9**	(2.1)	**-10.2**	(2.7)	**52.6**	(7.3)	**7.0**	(2.1)	0.0	(1.0)	**38.5**	(7.8)	**6.5**	(1.2)	**-0.1**	(0.0)	a	a	a	a
Montenegro	**41.9**	(3.6)	**-7.1**	(2.8)	4.8	(11.8)	**12.9**	(1.5)	0.4	(1.4)	**66.1**	(10.4)	-7.5	(4.5)	0.4	(0.2)	-10.7	(10.8)	-16.6	(12.4)
Panama	**19.1**	(4.9)	3.5	(6.5)	12.8	(10.9)	**7.2**	(3.3)	1.6	(1.0)	**54.6**	(8.7)	4.4	(2.5)	-0.1	(0.1)	-9.0	(15.2)	-2.6	(19.6)
Peru	**11.9**	(3.2)	20.0	(10.7)	**27.3**	(7.2)	**12.2**	(2.7)	1.3	(0.8)	**47.4**	(4.8)	**4.0**	(1.4)	**-0.1**	(0.0)	-2.8	(10.5)	9.1	(10.6)
Qatar	**35.6**	(6.2)	**-38.4**	(2.8)	**19.8**	(3.2)	**8.1**	(1.5)	1.7	(0.9)	**61.0**	(11.7)	**4.0**	(1.0)	**0.0**	(0.0)	-4.5	(14.4)	-0.6	(13.1)
Romania	**16.3**	(3.9)	18.8	(10.0)	14.3	(7.5)	**11.0**	(2.2)	-0.1	(1.1)	**46.0**	(7.2)	-3.8	(3.7)	0.1	(0.2)	16.6	(9.8)	11.6	(10.6)
Russian Federation	**41.3**	(2.6)	1.6	(2.9)	**19.4**	(6.0)	**21.2**	(2.0)	-1.9	(1.7)	**42.9**	(8.2)	**-10.6**	(2.6)	**0.8**	(0.2)	9.0	(9.4)	11.2	(9.0)
Serbia	**27.5**	(2.8)	-5.5	(3.4)	5.1	(9.8)	**7.7**	(1.8)	1.2	(1.2)	**47.1**	(19.8)	-6.9	(4.3)	0.3	(0.2)	-5.1	(13.5)	-3.1	(10.3)
Shanghai-China	**33.5**	(2.4)	**20.8**	(8.9)	**30.9**	(9.9)	**5.1**	(1.9)	0.6	(1.2)	**53.2**	(4.8)	0.4	(0.6)	0.0	(0.0)	a	a	a	a
Singapore	**26.6**	(2.3)	-0.8	(3.0)	**25.4**	(3.5)	**17.3**	(2.6)	**-2.5**	(1.3)	**83.1**	(8.7)	**11.7**	(2.9)	**-0.2**	(0.1)	a	a	a	a
Chinese Taipei	**45.9**	(4.1)	17.2	(10.3)	8.4	(5.1)	**20.4**	(3.0)	0.8	(1.8)	**47.3**	(11.6)	0.8	(0.6)	0.0	(0.0)	**-28.8**	(10.1)	-6.0	(7.8)
Thailand	**36.3**	(3.0)	**35.4**	(12.0)	**-16.0**	(3.8)	4.8	(2.8)	0.2	(1.0)	**19.5**	(5.7)	1.4	(1.1)	0.0	(0.0)	9.3	(11.8)	11.3	(10.9)
Trinidad and Tobago	**46.4**	(2.4)	-5.2	(3.2)	**31.6**	(7.3)	**4.5**	(2.2)	0.9	(1.1)	**124.5**	(9.0)	**24.3**	(6.9)	**-1.4**	(0.5)	-1.7	(8.5)	a	a
Tunisia	**22.6**	(2.4)	**21.1**	(8.4)	-20.3	(23.9)	3.1	(2.7)	-0.2	(0.8)	**33.7**	(6.0)	**10.7**	(2.9)	**-0.3**	(0.1)	18.3	(9.5)	6.0	(9.7)
Uruguay	**39.6**	(3.0)	-2.3	(6.4)	14.0	(9.5)	**15.4**	(2.0)	-0.2	(0.9)	**50.8**	(4.6)	1.6	(1.1)	0.0	(0.0)	**25.1**	(8.0)	12.2	(7.1)

Note: Values that are statistically significant are indicated in bold (see Annex A3).

1. Multilevel regression model (student and school levels): Reading performance is regressed on the variables of school policies and practices as well as socio-economic and demographic background variables presented in this table.

StatLink http://dx.doi.org/10.1787/888932343285

[Part 1/1]
Table IV.2.10 Systems' assessment and accountability policies and the relationship between reading performance and socio-economic background of students and schools

	Model for using standardised tests (OLS regression estimates)		Model for using student assessments (OLS regression estimates)		Model for using student achievement data (OLS regression estimates)	
	Coef.	S.E.	Coef.	S.E.	Coef.	S.E.
PISA index of economic, social and cultural status of student (ESCS)	**6.73**	(0.82)	**6.82**	(1.38)	**7.11**	(0.76)
x Percentage of students in schools that use standardised tests (additional 10%)	**1.45**	(0.11)				
x Percentage of students in schools that use student assessments to improve instruction or curriculum (additional 10%)			**14.18**	(1.76)		
x Percentage of students in schools in which achievement data are tracked over time by an administrative authority (additional 10%)					**15.84**	(1.12)
School's average PISA index of economic, social and cultural status	**92.28**	(3.17)	**111.71**	(5.79)	**109.87**	(3.26)
x Percentage of students in schools that use standardised tests (additional 10%)	**-4.65**	(0.42)				
x Percentage of students in schools that use student assessments to improve instruction or curriculum (additional 10%)			**-69.86**	(7.31)		
x Percentage of students in schools in which achievement data are tracked over time by an administrative authority (additional 10%)					**-77.06**	(4.72)
Student is a female	**36.04**	(0.50)	**36.08**	(0.50)	**35.95**	(0.50)
Student's language at home is the same as the language of assessment	**16.91**	(1.29)	**16.40**	(1.24)	**16.46**	(1.22)
Student without an immigrant background	**10.99**	(1.18)	**11.25**	(1.18)	**11.05**	(1.17)
School in a city (100 000 or more people)	-2.09	(1.22)	-1.90	(1.20)	-1.97	(1.19)
School in a small town or village (15 000 or less people)	**2.45**	(1.16)	**3.17**	(1.15)	**2.49**	(1.15)
School size (100 students)	**1.54**	(0.14)	**1.63**	(0.14)	**1.49**	(0.14)
School size (100 students) (squared)	**-0.01**	(0.00)	**-0.01**	(0.00)	**-0.01**	(0.00)
N	267 553		267 553		267 553	

Note: Estimates significant at the 5% level ($p < 0.05$) are in bold. Models include country fixed effects, estimate no intercept, are run for OECD countries only and use BRR weights to account for the sampling design. All countries are weighted equally.
StatLink http://dx.doi.org/10.1787/888932343285

[Part 1/1]

Table IV.2.11 Relationship between schools' average PISA index of economic, social and cultural status and school resources

		Correlation between schools' average PISA index of economic, social and cultural status and resources invested in education									
		School average class size		Students' learning time at school in language of instruction lessons		Index of schools' extra-curricular activities (higher values indicate more activities)		Index of teacher shortage (higher values indicate higher shortage)		Index of quality of schools' educational resources (higher values indicate better resources)	
		Correlation	S.E.	Correlation	S.E.	Correlation	S.E.	Correlation	S.E.	Correlation	S.E.
OECD	Australia	**0.26**	(0.0)	**-0.11**	(0.1)	**0.26**	(0.0)	**-0.28**	(0.1)	**0.31**	(0.0)
	Austria	**0.40**	(0.1)	0.00	(0.1)	**0.41**	(0.1)	-0.01	(0.1)	0.03	(0.1)
	Belgium	**0.71**	(0.0)	**0.24**	(0.1)	**0.29**	(0.1)	**-0.17**	(0.1)	0.02	(0.1)
	Canada	**0.23**	(0.1)	**-0.09**	(0.0)	**0.26**	(0.0)	**-0.15**	(0.0)	**0.18**	(0.0)
	Chile	-0.01	(0.1)	0.00	(0.1)	**0.30**	(0.1)	-0.06	(0.1)	**0.36**	(0.1)
	Czech Republic	**0.38**	(0.0)	**-0.23**	(0.0)	**0.24**	(0.1)	**-0.34**	(0.1)	0.00	(0.1)
	Denmark	**0.30**	(0.1)	-0.03	(0.1)	**0.16**	(0.1)	**-0.23**	(0.1)	0.04	(0.1)
	Estonia	**0.61**	(0.1)	0.00	(0.1)	0.06	(0.1)	-0.05	(0.1)	0.10	(0.1)
	Finland	**0.17**	(0.1)	**0.19**	(0.1)	0.06	(0.1)	0.03	(0.1)	0.13	(0.1)
	France	**0.72**	(0.0)	**0.18**	(0.1)	w	w	w	w	w	w
	Germany	**0.48**	(0.0)	**-0.49**	(0.0)	**0.40**	(0.1)	-0.11	(0.1)	0.06	(0.1)
	Greece	**0.39**	(0.1)	0.00	(0.1)	**0.29**	(0.1)	**-0.19**	(0.0)	0.16	(0.1)
	Hungary	**0.46**	(0.1)	0.12	(0.1)	**0.30**	(0.1)	-0.08	(0.1)	0.11	(0.1)
	Iceland	**0.47**	(0.0)	**0.07**	(0.0)	**0.30**	(0.0)	**-0.38**	(0.0)	**0.06**	(0.0)
	Ireland	**0.47**	(0.1)	**-0.20**	(0.1)	0.08	(0.1)	**-0.16**	(0.1)	0.16	(0.1)
	Israel	**0.30**	(0.1)	**-0.30**	(0.1)	**0.34**	(0.1)	-0.07	(0.1)	**0.25**	(0.1)
	Italy	**0.41**	(0.0)	**-0.28**	(0.0)	**0.34**	(0.0)	0.02	(0.0)	**0.15**	(0.0)
	Japan	**0.35**	(0.1)	**0.61**	(0.0)	**0.46**	(0.1)	-0.04	(0.1)	**0.17**	(0.1)
	Korea	**0.40**	(0.1)	**0.23**	(0.1)	0.13	(0.1)	-0.02	(0.1)	-0.04	(0.1)
	Luxembourg	**0.52**	(0.0)	**0.01**	(0.0)	**0.56**	(0.0)	**-0.33**	(0.0)	**0.13**	(0.0)
	Mexico	**0.31**	(0.0)	**0.09**	(0.0)	**0.31**	(0.0)	**-0.26**	(0.0)	**0.59**	(0.0)
	Netherlands	**0.62**	(0.0)	**-0.47**	(0.1)	**0.35**	(0.1)	0.06	(0.1)	0.06	(0.1)
	New Zealand	**0.22**	(0.1)	-0.07	(0.1)	**0.29**	(0.1)	**-0.19**	(0.1)	**0.16**	(0.1)
	Norway	**0.26**	(0.1)	0.05	(0.1)	0.15	(0.1)	**-0.23**	(0.1)	0.14	(0.1)
	Poland	**0.18**	(0.1)	0.13	(0.1)	0.12	(0.1)	-0.05	(0.1)	0.06	(0.1)
	Portugal	**0.54**	(0.0)	**-0.20**	(0.1)	0.01	(0.1)	-0.09	(0.1)	**0.24**	(0.1)
	Slovak Republic	**0.36**	(0.1)	**-0.24**	(0.1)	0.13	(0.1)	**-0.20**	(0.1)	-0.05	(0.1)
	Slovenia	**0.38**	(0.0)	**0.37**	(0.0)	**0.29**	(0.0)	**-0.02**	(0.0)	**0.13**	(0.0)
	Spain	**0.48**	(0.0)	**-0.12**	(0.1)	**0.22**	(0.1)	-0.02	(0.0)	**0.10**	(0.0)
	Sweden	**0.32**	(0.1)	**-0.15**	(0.1)	-0.01	(0.1)	-0.12	(0.1)	**0.26**	(0.1)
	Switzerland	**0.43**	(0.1)	0.00	(0.1)	**0.34**	(0.1)	**-0.16**	(0.1)	0.10	(0.1)
	Turkey	-0.10	(0.1)	**0.28**	(0.1)	**0.38**	(0.1)	0.01	(0.1)	0.05	(0.1)
	United Kingdom	0.01	(0.1)	**-0.19**	(0.1)	**0.14**	(0.1)	**-0.15**	(0.1)	0.00	(0.1)
	United States	**-0.18**	(0.1)	0.10	(0.1)	**0.16**	(0.1)	**-0.28**	(0.1)	**0.22**	(0.1)
	OECD average	**0.35**	(0.0)	-0.02	(0.0)	**0.25**	(0.0)	**-0.13**	(0.0)	**0.13**	(0.0)
Partners	Albania	**0.24**	(0.1)	0.03	(0.1)	**0.42**	(0.1)	**-0.38**	(0.1)	**0.44**	(0.1)
	Argentina	**0.22**	(0.1)	-0.06	(0.1)	**0.34**	(0.1)	**-0.21**	(0.1)	**0.51**	(0.1)
	Azerbaijan	**0.48**	(0.1)	0.02	(0.1)	-0.02	(0.1)	-0.10	(0.1)	**0.19**	(0.1)
	Brazil	**0.25**	(0.0)	-0.03	(0.0)	**0.40**	(0.0)	**-0.37**	(0.0)	**0.52**	(0.0)
	Bulgaria	**0.27**	(0.1)	**-0.19**	(0.1)	**0.28**	(0.1)	**0.19**	(0.1)	0.09	(0.1)
	Colombia	0.01	(0.1)	-0.11	(0.1)	**0.29**	(0.1)	**-0.30**	(0.1)	**0.53**	(0.1)
	Croatia	**0.20**	(0.1)	0.14	(0.1)	**0.41**	(0.1)	**-0.19**	(0.1)	0.09	(0.1)
	Dubai (UAE)	**-0.29**	(0.0)	**0.04**	(0.0)	**-0.04**	(0.0)	**-0.20**	(0.0)	**0.35**	(0.0)
	Hong Kong-China	-0.15	(0.1)	**-0.26**	(0.1)	0.14	(0.1)	**-0.17**	(0.1)	0.06	(0.1)
	Indonesia	0.11	(0.1)	-0.04	(0.1)	**0.37**	(0.1)	**-0.35**	(0.1)	**0.44**	(0.1)
	Jordan	-0.12	(0.1)	0.14	(0.1)	**0.25**	(0.1)	**-0.24**	(0.1)	**0.26**	(0.1)
	Kazakhstan	**0.42**	(0.1)	**0.18**	(0.1)	**0.14**	(0.1)	-0.07	(0.1)	**0.21**	(0.1)
	Kyrgyzstan	**0.37**	(0.1)	**0.35**	(0.1)	**0.20**	(0.1)	0.07	(0.1)	**0.26**	(0.1)
	Latvia	**0.71**	(0.0)	**0.16**	(0.1)	0.09	(0.1)	0.07	(0.1)	**0.15**	(0.1)
	Lithuania	**0.56**	(0.0)	0.10	(0.1)	**0.31**	(0.1)	-0.06	(0.1)	-0.01	(0.1)
	Macao-China	**0.04**	(0.0)	**0.25**	(0.0)	**0.27**	(0.0)	**-0.01**	(0.0)	**0.26**	(0.0)
	Montenegro	**0.33**	(0.0)	**0.56**	(0.1)	**0.27**	(0.0)	**-0.12**	(0.0)	**-0.11**	(0.0)
	Panama	**0.31**	(0.1)	**0.27**	(0.1)	0.16	(0.1)	**-0.24**	(0.1)	**0.67**	(0.1)
	Peru	**0.27**	(0.1)	-0.04	(0.1)	**0.35**	(0.1)	**-0.35**	(0.1)	**0.52**	(0.1)
	Qatar	**-0.29**	(0.0)	**-0.04**	(0.0)	**0.02**	(0.0)	**0.02**	(0.0)	**0.23**	(0.0)
	Romania	**0.46**	(0.1)	**0.45**	(0.1)	**0.28**	(0.1)	**-0.18**	(0.1)	**0.20**	(0.1)
	Russian Federation	**0.51**	(0.1)	0.12	(0.1)	**0.27**	(0.1)	-0.12	(0.1)	**0.26**	(0.1)
	Serbia	**0.32**	(0.1)	**0.56**	(0.0)	**0.19**	(0.1)	**-0.27**	(0.0)	-0.01	(0.1)
	Shanghai-China	**0.15**	(0.1)	-0.05	(0.1)	**0.32**	(0.1)	**-0.18**	(0.1)	**0.16**	(0.1)
	Singapore	**-0.30**	(0.0)	**-0.30**	(0.0)	**0.23**	(0.0)	**-0.29**	(0.0)	**0.10**	(0.0)
	Chinese Taipei	0.13	(0.1)	**0.28**	(0.1)	**0.25**	(0.1)	-0.17	(0.1)	**0.19**	(0.1)
	Thailand	**0.57**	(0.0)	**-0.25**	(0.0)	**0.38**	(0.1)	-0.08	(0.1)	**0.39**	(0.1)
	Trinidad and Tobago	**0.55**	(0.0)	**-0.01**	(0.0)	**0.45**	(0.0)	**-0.21**	(0.0)	**0.11**	(0.0)
	Tunisia	**0.30**	(0.1)	**-0.31**	(0.1)	0.10	(0.1)	0.07	(0.1)	0.13	(0.1)
	Uruguay	0.11	(0.1)	**-0.19**	(0.0)	**0.22**	(0.1)	**-0.25**	(0.0)	**0.33**	(0.1)

Notes: Values that are statistically significant are indicated in bold (see Annex A3). Correlations that are greater than 0.3 are considered moderate and highlighted in blue. Correlations that are below -0.3 are considered moderate and highlighted in grey.

StatLink http://dx.doi.org/10.1787/888932343285

[Part 1/1]

Table IV.2.12a Within- and between-school variation in reading performance and variation explained by resources invested in education

	Variance		Remaining variance						Variance decomposition expressed as a percentage of the average variance in student performance in reading across OECD countries			Within-school variance expressed as a percentage of the average of within-school variance in student performance in reading across OECD countries				Between-school variance expressed as a percentage of the average of between-school variance in student performance in reading across OECD countries			
	Empty (or fully unconditional) model[1]		Model with demographic and socio-economic background[2]		Model with resources invested in education[3]		Model with demographic and socio-economic background and with school-level variables[4]		Total variance in student performance	Total variance within schools as a percentage of total variance	Total variance between schools as a percentage of total variance	Solely accounted for by students' and schools' socio-economic and demographic background	Solely accounted for by resources invested in education	Jointly accounted for by students' and schools' socio-economic and demographic background and resources invested in education	Remaining between-school variance	Solely accounted for by students' and schools' socio-economic and demographic background	Solely accounted for by resources invested in education	Jointly accounted for by students' and schools' socio-economic and demographic background and resources invested in education	Remaining between-school variance
	Within-school	Between-school	Within-school	Between-school	Within-school	Between-school	Within-school	Between-school	%	%	%	%	%	%	%	%	%	%	%
OECD																			
Australia	7 631	2 692	6 997	880	7 569	1 246	6 914	710	112	83	29	7.1	0.9	-0.2	75.1	5.8	1.8	13.9	7.7
Austria	4 454	5 588	4 255	2 262	4 433	3 773	4 254	1 942	108	48	60	1.9	0.0	0.2	46.2	19.9	3.5	16.2	21.1
Belgium	4 833	5 343	4 612	1 643	4 725	2 221	4 530	1 131	111	53	58	2.1	0.9	0.3	49.2	11.8	5.6	28.4	12.3
Canada	6 780	1 877	6 238	986	6 722	1 271	6 192	832	94	74	20	5.8	0.5	0.1	67.2	4.8	1.7	4.9	9.0
Chile	4 005	4 893	3 886	1 219	3 997	1 339	3 863	605	97	44	53	1.5	0.2	-0.2	42.0	8.0	6.7	31.9	6.6
Czech Republic	4 428	4 249	4 136	1 135	4 459	1 871	4 138	777	94	48	46	3.5	0.0	-0.3	44.9	11.9	3.9	21.9	8.4
Denmark	6 012	1 134	5 254	328	5 991	620	5 249	240	78	65	12	8.1	0.1	0.2	57.0	4.1	1.0	4.6	2.6
Estonia	5 595	1 557	4 991	681	5 469	888	4 907	491	78	61	17	6.1	0.9	0.5	53.3	4.3	2.1	5.2	5.3
Finland	6 993	665	5 641	458	6 744	389	5 533	256	83	76	7	13.2	1.2	1.5	60.1	1.4	2.2	0.8	2.8
France	w	w	w	w	w	w	w	w	w	w	w	w	w	w	w	w	w	w	w
Germany	3 890	5 890	3 558	1 708	3 871	3 207	3 556	1 400	106	42	64	3.4	0.0	0.2	38.6	19.6	3.3	25.8	15.2
Greece	5 558	4 745	5 126	2 165	5 570	2 170	5 122	1 655	112	60	52	4.9	0.1	-0.2	55.6	5.6	5.5	22.4	18.0
Hungary	2 923	5 846	2 792	1 717	2 925	2 758	2 792	1 088	95	32	64	1.4	0.0	0.0	30.3	18.1	6.8	26.7	11.8
Iceland	8 186	1 348	7 186	1 015	7 844	998	6 999	775	104	89	15	9.2	2.0	1.7	76.0	2.4	2.6	1.2	8.4
Ireland	6 966	2 805	6 408	1 145	6 676	1 477	6 178	929	106	76	30	5.4	2.5	0.7	67.1	6.0	2.3	12.1	10.1
Israel	6 615	6 250	6 312	3 230	6 547	2 425	6 236	1 636	140	72	68	3.4	0.8	-0.1	67.7	8.6	17.3	24.2	17.8
Italy	4 085	6 695	3 905	2 880	4 079	2 816	3 896	2 065	117	44	73	2.0	0.1	0.0	42.3	8.2	8.9	33.3	22.4
Japan	5 386	5 087	5 248	2 255	5 380	2 205	5 209	1 767	114	59	55	1.9	0.4	-0.4	56.6	4.8	5.3	26.0	19.2
Korea	5 283	2 741	4 829	1 038	5 277	1 340	4 810	751	87	57	30	5.1	0.2	-0.1	52.2	6.4	3.1	12.1	8.2
Luxembourg	6 906	5 335	6 112	610	6 694	1 470	5 941	208	133	75	58	8.2	1.9	0.4	64.5	13.7	4.4	37.6	2.3
Mexico	3 869	3 583	3 723	1 964	3 888	1 432	3 722	1 172	81	42	39	1.8	0.0	-0.2	40.4	2.8	8.6	14.8	12.7
Netherlands	2 795	5 107	2 670	2 224	2 764	1 384	2 645	1 169	86	30	55	1.3	0.3	0.1	28.7	2.3	11.5	29.0	12.7
New Zealand	8 228	2 622	6 974	530	7 963	1 466	6 820	343	118	89	28	12.4	1.7	1.2	74.1	12.2	2.0	10.5	3.7
Norway	7 598	874	6 455	669	7 525	517	6 420	468	92	83	9	12.0	0.4	0.4	69.7	0.5	2.2	1.7	5.1
Poland	6 869	1 585	5 582	458	6 817	703	5 578	361	92	75	17	13.4	0.0	0.5	60.6	3.7	1.1	8.5	3.9
Portugal	5 191	2 565	4 666	883	4 983	765	4 520	550	84	56	28	5.0	1.6	0.7	49.1	2.3	3.6	15.9	6.0
Slovak Republic	4 565	2 989	3 972	1 151	4 565	1 269	3 965	844	82	50	32	6.5	0.1	-0.1	43.1	4.6	3.3	15.3	9.2
Slovenia	3 102	4 142	2 941	1 818	3 073	1 482	2 922	881	79	34	45	1.6	0.2	0.1	31.7	6.5	10.2	18.7	9.6
Spain	6 048	1 690	5 390	816	5 950	1 286	5 330	788	84	66	18	6.7	0.7	0.4	57.9	5.4	0.3	4.1	8.6
Sweden	8 290	1 877	7 007	605	8 099	1 075	6 919	451	110	90	20	12.8	1.0	1.1	75.1	6.8	1.7	7.0	4.9
Switzerland	5 652	2 740	5 115	1 100	5 464	1 550	4 978	779	91	61	30	5.3	1.5	0.5	54.1	8.4	3.5	9.4	8.5
Turkey	3 245	6 536	2 958	1 375	3 236	1 917	2 940	832	106	35	71	3.2	0.2	-0.1	31.9	11.8	5.9	44.3	9.0
United Kingdom	6 684	2 775	6 275	635	6 073	1 215	5 787	490	103	73	30	3.1	5.3	1.3	62.9	7.9	1.6	15.4	5.3
United States	6 476	3 638	6 041	838	6 459	1 192	5 975	460	110	70	40	5.2	0.7	-0.5	64.9	8.0	4.1	22.5	5.0
OECD average	5 591	3 616	5 068	1 285	5 510	1 568	4 995	874	100	61	39	5.6	0.8	0.3	54.3	7.5	4.5	17.2	9.5
Partners																			
Albania	7 105	3 127	6 150	1 339	7 067	1 595	6 129	1 113	111	77	34	10.2	0.2	0.2	66.6	5.2	2.5	14.2	12.1
Argentina	5 523	8 456	5 201	3 238	5 525	3 569	5 201	2 181	152	60	92	3.5	0.0	0.0	56.5	15.1	11.5	41.6	23.7
Azerbaijan	3 459	2 490	3 287	2 054	3 464	1 868	3 285	1 694	65	38	27	2.0	0.0	-0.1	35.7	1.9	3.9	2.8	18.4
Brazil	4 702	4 417	4 514	1 770	4 724	2 194	4 511	1 372	99	51	48	2.3	0.0	-0.3	49.0	8.9	4.3	19.8	14.9
Bulgaria	6 439	6 418	5 794	2 053	6 423	3 634	5 770	1 384	140	70	70	7.1	0.3	-0.1	62.7	24.4	7.3	23.0	15.0
Colombia	4 813	3 162	4 711	688	4 814	784	4 682	528	87	52	34	1.4	0.3	-0.3	50.9	2.8	1.7	24.1	5.7
Croatia	4 473	4 045	4 183	1 391	4 455	917	4 158	506	93	49	44	3.2	0.3	-0.1	45.2	4.5	9.6	24.4	5.5
Dubai (UAE)	5 439	5 732	5 121	2 472	5 409	2 334	5 118	1 598	121	59	62	3.2	0.0	0.3	55.6	8.0	9.5	27.4	17.4
Hong Kong-China	4 360	3 143	4 183	1 270	4 230	1 237	4 066	803	82	47	34	1.8	1.3	0.1	44.2	4.7	5.1	15.6	8.7
Indonesia	2 298	1 749	2 117	1 181	2 293	933	2 111	819	44	25	19	2.0	0.1	0.0	22.9	1.2	3.9	4.9	8.9
Jordan	5 461	3 312	5 186	1 727	5 469	1 344	5 165	1 103	95	59	36	3.3	0.2	-0.3	56.1	2.6	6.8	14.6	12.0
Kazakhstan	5 078	2 887	4 456	1 542	5 065	1 579	4 437	1 099	87	55	31	6.8	0.2	-0.1	48.2	5.2	4.8	9.4	11.9
Kyrgyzstan	5 901	3 266	5 126	1 398	5 921	921	5 116	746	100	64	35	8.7	0.1	-0.3	55.6	1.9	7.1	18.4	8.1
Latvia	5 200	1 391	4 491	634	5 187	591	4 466	431	72	57	15	7.8	0.3	-0.1	48.5	1.7	2.2	6.5	4.7
Lithuania	5 190	1 864	4 263	828	5 167	1 322	4 257	774	77	56	20	9.9	0.1	0.2	46.2	6.0	0.6	5.3	8.4
Macao-China	4 179	2 882	4 000	775	4 105	580	3 928	428	77	45	31	1.9	0.8	0.0	42.7	1.6	3.8	21.2	4.7
Montenegro	5 587	3 150	5 124	683	5 456	608	5 043	354	95	61	34	4.5	0.9	0.5	54.8	2.8	3.6	24.0	3.8
Panama	4 213	5 942	4 103	2 647	4 190	1 717	4 095	1 390	110	46	65	1.0	0.1	0.2	44.5	3.6	13.7	32.2	15.1
Peru	4 623	5 886	4 524	1 316	4 608	2 149	4 500	805	114	50	64	1.2	0.3	-0.1	48.9	14.6	5.6	35.0	8.7
Qatar	5 891	6 676	5 520	3 383	5 856	2 721	5 515	1 850	137	64	73	3.7	0.1	0.3	59.9	9.5	16.7	26.3	20.1
Romania	3 832	4 057	3 678	2 308	3 770	1 475	3 647	890	86	42	44	1.3	0.3	0.3	39.6	6.4	15.4	12.6	9.7
Russian Federation	5 826	1 965	5 193	900	5 838	1 402	5 196	770	85	63	21	7.0	0.0	-0.1	56.4	6.9	1.4	4.7	8.4
Serbia	4 123	3 909	3 954	1 840	4 076	2 083	3 915	1 265	87	45	42	1.8	0.4	0.1	42.5	8.9	6.2	13.6	13.7
Shanghai-China	4 095	2 551	3 813	701	4 061	664	3 769	458	72	44	28	3.2	0.5	-0.1	40.9	2.2	2.6	17.9	5.0
Singapore	6 195	3 387	5 612	782	6 050	994	5 471	497	104	67	37	6.3	1.5	0.1	59.4	5.4	3.1	22.9	5.4
Chinese Taipei	5 808	2 772	5 070	1 306	5 826	951	5 044	695	93	63	30	8.5	0.3	-0.5	54.8	2.8	6.6	13.1	7.5
Thailand	3 052	1 231	2 706	816	3 056	762	2 707	657	47	33	13	3.8	0.0	0.0	29.4	1.1	1.7	3.4	7.1
Trinidad and Tobago	5 148	8 320	4 720	2 527	5 124	2 065	4 719	1 537	146	56	90	4.4	0.0	0.3	51.3	5.7	10.8	57.2	16.7
Tunisia	4 291	3 034	4 174	1 640	4 310	439	4 173	353	80	47	33	1.5	0.0	-0.2	45.3	0.9	14.0	14.2	3.8
Uruguay	5 835	4 807	5 342	968	5 852	1 355	5 308	657	116	63	52	5.9	0.4	-0.6	57.7	7.6	3.4	34.1	7.1

1. Multilevel regression model consists of the student and school levels.
2. Multilevel regression model: Reading performance is regressed on the variables of demographic and socio-economic background.
3. Multilevel regression model: Reading performance is regressed on the variables of resources invested in education.
4. Multilevel regression model: Reading performance is regressed on the variables of demographic and socio-economic background and on the variables of resources invested in education.

StatLink http://dx.doi.org/10.1787/888932343285

[Part 1/2]
Table IV.2.12b Relationships between resources invested in education and reading performance

		Resources invested in education (student level)[1]		Resources invested in education (school level)[1]									
		Class size		Students' learning time at school in language of instruction lessons		Students' learning time at school in mathematics and science lessons		Percentage of students attending after-school lessons (enrichment)		Percentage of students attending after-school lessons (remedial)		Percentage of students who attended pre-primary education for one year or less	
		Change in score	S.E.	Change in score	S.E.	Change in score	S.E.	Change in score	S.E.	Change in score	S.E.	Change in score	S.E.
OECD	Australia	**2.7**	(0.3)	**-0.5**	(0.2)	0.2	(0.1)	0.2	(0.5)	-0.1	(0.6)	**2.1**	(0.7)
	Austria	-0.3	(0.4)	**-0.5**	(0.2)	0.1	(0.1)	-0.3	(0.6)	0.3	(0.4)	-1.2	(0.9)
	Belgium	**2.8**	(0.4)	**-0.6**	(0.1)	**0.3**	(0.1)	**-1.0**	(0.3)	**1.1**	(0.4)	-0.9	(0.7)
	Canada	**1.7**	(0.2)	-0.1	(0.1)	0.0	(0.0)	0.0	(0.2)	-0.5	(0.3)	**0.7**	(0.3)
	Chile	-0.4	(0.4)	**-0.4**	(0.1)	**0.4**	(0.1)	**-0.8**	(0.3)	-0.2	(0.3)	-0.5	(0.3)
	Czech Republic	0.2	(0.4)	**-0.7**	(0.1)	**0.3**	(0.0)	**-0.7**	(0.3)	0.2	(0.3)	0.1	(0.8)
	Denmark	-0.4	(0.5)	**-0.2**	(0.1)	**0.1**	(0.0)	-0.6	(0.3)	-0.7	(0.4)	0.9	(0.6)
	Estonia	**2.8**	(0.4)	0.1	(0.2)	0.0	(0.1)	-0.3	(0.3)	-0.2	(0.3)	0.6	(0.5)
	Finland	**4.4**	(0.6)	0.0	(0.1)	**0.1**	(0.0)	**-1.1**	(0.4)	**-1.2**	(0.2)	**-1.3**	(0.3)
	France	w	w	w	w	w	w	w	w	w	w	w	w
	Germany	0.4	(0.4)	**-0.6**	(0.2)	**0.2**	(0.1)	-0.5	(0.5)	-0.7	(0.5)	1.6	(1.4)
	Greece	0.1	(0.8)	0.1	(0.1)	**0.3**	(0.2)	**1.4**	(0.4)	-0.2	(0.6)	-0.6	(0.8)
	Hungary	-0.2	(0.3)	0.1	(0.2)	0.1	(0.1)	0.5	(0.3)	**-0.6**	(0.3)	**2.5**	(1.1)
	Iceland	**4.4**	(0.7)	-0.2	(0.1)	**0.2**	(0.1)	**-0.8**	(0.3)	-0.2	(0.4)	0.3	(0.9)
	Ireland	**4.0**	(0.4)	**-0.8**	(0.3)	0.2	(0.2)	**1.0**	(0.5)	-1.2	(0.7)	0.2	(0.5)
	Israel	**1.4**	(0.3)	-0.1	(0.1)	**0.2**	(0.1)	**1.0**	(0.5)	**-3.9**	(0.5)	-1.2	(1.2)
	Italy	**-0.5**	(0.2)	**-0.2**	(0.1)	**-0.1**	(0.0)	0.3	(0.3)	**-0.4**	(0.2)	1.1	(0.6)
	Japan	**-2.0**	(0.8)	0.0	(0.1)	**0.3**	(0.1)	0.3	(0.5)	0.6	(0.3)	-3.0	(3.1)
	Korea	1.6	(2.3)	0.1	(0.2)	**0.2**	(0.1)	0.4	(0.3)	0.3	(0.2)	0.8	(1.2)
	Luxembourg	**4.4**	(1.4)	-0.1	(0.3)	0.1	(0.1)	-2.3	(1.6)	-0.1	(0.8)	2.1	(2.4)
	Mexico	-0.1	(0.2)	0.0	(0.1)	**0.1**	(0.0)	**-0.8**	(0.3)	-0.4	(0.3)	**0.6**	(0.2)
	Netherlands	**1.3**	(0.3)	**-1.0**	(0.2)	**0.5**	(0.1)	**-1.6**	(0.4)	0.6	(0.4)	0.3	(1.2)
	New Zealand	**3.7**	(0.4)	**-1.2**	(0.4)	**0.5**	(0.1)	0.0	(0.6)	**-1.6**	(0.8)	-0.2	(0.7)
	Norway	**1.1**	(0.5)	c	c	c	c	0.1	(0.3)	**-2.2**	(0.5)	0.7	(0.6)
	Poland	**2.1**	(0.8)	-0.3	(0.2)	**0.1**	(0.1)	**0.5**	(0.2)	**-0.6**	(0.2)	0.7	(0.9)
	Portugal	**3.7**	(0.5)	**-0.2**	(0.1)	**0.2**	(0.0)	0.1	(0.3)	-0.4	(0.2)	0.4	(0.4)
	Slovak Republic	-0.1	(0.5)	**-0.7**	(0.1)	**0.2**	(0.0)	0.0	(0.2)	0.2	(0.2)	**1.2**	(0.4)
	Slovenia	0.5	(0.4)	**0.6**	(0.1)	**0.5**	(0.1)	**-0.5**	(0.2)	**-0.6**	(0.2)	0.0	(0.2)
	Spain	**2.0**	(0.3)	-0.2	(0.1)	0.0	(0.0)	**0.4**	(0.2)	-0.2	(0.2)	-0.1	(0.4)
	Sweden	**3.3**	(0.4)	**-0.4**	(0.1)	0.1	(0.1)	0.3	(0.3)	**-1.3**	(0.6)	1.2	(0.7)
	Switzerland	**4.1**	(0.6)	-0.1	(0.1)	0.0	(0.1)	**-1.1**	(0.2)	**0.6**	(0.3)	1.8	(1.3)
	Turkey	0.2	(0.3)	**0.7**	(0.2)	0.1	(0.1)	**1.5**	(0.6)	**-1.9**	(0.6)	1.1	(0.9)
	United Kingdom	**5.1**	(0.3)	**-0.3**	(0.1)	**0.4**	(0.1)	0.4	(0.3)	**-1.2**	(0.2)	**1.9**	(0.6)
	United States	**0.8**	(0.3)	0.0	(0.2)	0.0	(0.1)	**-2.4**	(0.5)	0.2	(0.4)	**-7.8**	(3.1)
	OECD average	**1.7**	(0.1)	**-0.2**	(0.0)	**0.2**	(0.0)	**-0.2**	(0.1)	**-0.5**	(0.1)	0.2	(0.2)
Partners	Albania	**0.9**	(0.3)	-0.2	(0.2)	0.2	(0.1)	**1.0**	(0.3)	**-1.0**	(0.3)	-0.7	(0.4)
	Argentina	-0.4	(0.3)	**-0.3**	(0.1)	0.1	(0.1)	**-2.3**	(0.7)	**1.4**	(0.6)	**1.2**	(0.4)
	Azerbaijan	0.0	(0.3)	0.1	(0.1)	**0.2**	(0.1)	0.8	(0.5)	**-1.4**	(0.4)	**1.1**	(0.5)
	Brazil	-0.3	(0.2)	-0.2	(0.2)	**0.2**	(0.1)	-0.1	(0.2)	**-0.6**	(0.2)	0.3	(0.3)
	Bulgaria	**1.1**	(0.5)	-0.3	(0.3)	-0.1	(0.2)	-0.4	(0.5)	-0.7	(0.4)	0.3	(0.7)
	Colombia	**-1.1**	(0.3)	-0.2	(0.1)	**0.1**	(0.0)	-0.2	(0.3)	**-0.8**	(0.3)	**1.0**	(0.3)
	Croatia	1.1	(0.7)	0.1	(0.1)	**0.3**	(0.0)	0.0	(0.4)	**-0.8**	(0.3)	0.0	(0.4)
	Dubai (UAE)	0.2	(0.3)	**-0.7**	(0.1)	**0.2**	(0.0)	**-1.0**	(0.3)	**-0.8**	(0.3)	**0.9**	(0.4)
	Hong Kong-China	**2.2**	(0.3)	**-0.7**	(0.2)	**0.4**	(0.1)	0.3	(0.2)	0.1	(0.3)	**2.6**	(1.2)
	Indonesia	**0.5**	(0.2)	**-0.2**	(0.1)	**0.1**	(0.0)	**-0.5**	(0.2)	-0.3	(0.2)	**0.3**	(0.2)
	Jordan	**-1.1**	(0.5)	**0.8**	(0.2)	-0.2	(0.1)	-0.1	(0.3)	**-1.7**	(0.3)	**1.2**	(0.2)
	Kazakhstan	**-1.4**	(0.5)	0.0	(0.1)	0.1	(0.1)	-0.4	(0.3)	0.3	(0.3)	0.5	(0.4)
	Kyrgyzstan	-0.3	(0.4)	**0.4**	(0.1)	0.0	(0.1)	**0.9**	(0.2)	**-0.9**	(0.2)	0.1	(0.2)
	Latvia	**1.2**	(0.5)	-0.2	(0.1)	0.0	(0.1)	0.2	(0.2)	**-1.0**	(0.4)	0.3	(0.3)
	Lithuania	**1.3**	(0.4)	0.1	(0.1)	0.0	(0.0)	0.2	(0.2)	0.2	(0.3)	0.0	(0.4)
	Macao-China	**2.3**	(0.5)	**-0.4**	(0.2)	**0.4**	(0.1)	**1.7**	(0.8)	**-1.6**	(0.5)	-1.8	(1.1)
	Montenegro	**2.6**	(0.6)	**1.6**	(0.4)	0.0	(0.1)	**1.3**	(0.6)	**-2.0**	(0.3)	0.3	(0.5)
	Panama	-0.8	(0.5)	-0.4	(0.3)	**0.2**	(0.1)	**-1.2**	(0.6)	0.2	(0.4)	0.2	(0.4)
	Peru	**-0.7**	(0.3)	0.0	(0.1)	0.0	(0.0)	0.2	(0.4)	**-1.1**	(0.3)	**0.9**	(0.5)
	Qatar	0.4	(0.3)	0.1	(0.1)	0.1	(0.1)	-0.3	(0.4)	**-1.5**	(0.4)	0.3	(0.3)
	Romania	**1.2**	(0.3)	**0.5**	(0.2)	0.2	(0.1)	-0.1	(0.3)	-0.5	(0.3)	-1.5	(0.9)
	Russian Federation	0.2	(0.5)	-0.1	(0.1)	**0.1**	(0.0)	0.3	(0.2)	0.0	(0.2)	-0.1	(0.5)
	Serbia	**1.4**	(0.4)	-0.2	(0.3)	**0.2**	(0.1)	0.3	(0.5)	**-0.7**	(0.3)	0.5	(0.3)
	Shanghai-China	**1.6**	(0.5)	**-0.4**	(0.1)	0.1	(0.1)	0.1	(0.2)	**0.6**	(0.2)	0.3	(0.5)
	Singapore	**2.1**	(0.4)	**-0.5**	(0.1)	**0.3**	(0.0)	**0.5**	(0.2)	**-0.7**	(0.2)	1.6	(1.1)
	Chinese Taipei	**1.1**	(0.6)	-0.1	(0.2)	0.0	(0.1)	**2.1**	(0.3)	**-0.7**	(0.3)	-2.1	(1.2)
	Thailand	0.0	(0.3)	0.0	(0.1)	**0.1**	(0.0)	0.3	(0.2)	-0.2	(0.2)	0.2	(0.6)
	Trinidad and Tobago	0.1	(0.2)	**-0.8**	(0.1)	**0.6**	(0.1)	0.4	(0.3)	-0.3	(0.4)	**2.3**	(0.7)
	Tunisia	0.2	(0.4)	**0.7**	(0.3)	**0.8**	(0.1)	0.0	(0.2)	0.0	(0.2)	0.2	(0.1)
	Uruguay	**-1.1**	(0.4)	**-0.9**	(0.1)	**0.4**	(0.1)	**0.8**	(0.4)	**-0.8**	(0.3)	0.5	(0.3)

Note: Values that are statistically significant are indicated in bold (see Annex A3).
1. Multilevel regression model (student and school levels): Reading performance is regressed on the school resource variables presented in this table.
StatLink http://dx.doi.org/10.1787/888932343285

[Part 2/2]

Table IV.2.12b Relationships between resources invested in education and reading performance

		Resources invested in education (school level)[1]											
		Percentage of students who attended pre-primary education for more than one year		School average class size		Index of library use in or outside school (higher values indicate more use)		Index of schools' extra-curricular activities (higher values indicate more activities)		Index of teacher shortage (higher values indicate higher shortage)		Index of quality of schools' educational resources (higher values indicate better resources)	
		Change in score	S.E.	Change in score	S.E.	Change in score	S.E.	Change in score	S.E.	Change in score	S.E.	Change in score	S.E.
OECD	Australia	**3.0**	(0.6)	**3.3**	(1.3)	**52.4**	(11.8)	-3.5	(3.5)	**5.8**	(2.9)	1.6	(2.5)
	Austria	0.6	(0.8)	**4.8**	(1.4)	-18.3	(12.4)	**-16.0**	(6.5)	**20.0**	(6.0)	**12.0**	(6.0)
	Belgium	0.6	(0.5)	**9.5**	(1.2)	-2.8	(11.4)	1.6	(4.0)	5.8	(4.1)	4.7	(5.7)
	Canada	**1.1**	(0.2)	**1.6**	(0.5)	-1.2	(7.1)	-1.4	(2.7)	**9.5**	(3.2)	**8.2**	(2.8)
	Chile	0.6	(0.3)	**1.3**	(0.6)	-23.8	(13.1)	-4.9	(4.0)	**11.3**	(3.9)	**8.6**	(3.8)
	Czech Republic	0.9	(0.6)	**4.1**	(0.9)	**26.3**	(9.6)	**-11.2**	(5.1)	9.7	(5.3)	-1.2	(4.5)
	Denmark	**1.6**	(0.5)	**3.2**	(0.9)	-13.8	(11.7)	-3.4	(3.7)	-0.5	(2.3)	2.0	(3.0)
	Estonia	0.1	(0.3)	**3.6**	(0.8)	-21.0	(20.1)	-4.2	(4.3)	-5.6	(4.6)	2.0	(7.0)
	Finland	**-0.9**	(0.3)	**2.4**	(0.9)	20.6	(11.4)	0.4	(3.7)	3.1	(2.7)	5.2	(3.0)
	France	w	w	w	w	w	w	w	w	w	w	w	w
	Germany	**3.1**	(1.2)	**6.5**	(2.2)	-12.6	(22.6)	-4.0	(6.7)	6.3	(6.5)	2.9	(6.6)
	Greece	0.2	(0.6)	-1.0	(1.4)	**-28.9**	(13.2)	9.4	(6.4)	10.9	(5.6)	**11.1**	(5.3)
	Hungary	**2.7**	(1.2)	**5.9**	(0.9)	-23.2	(15.4)	-4.7	(7.7)	**21.8**	(6.9)	-3.0	(7.4)
	Iceland	0.1	(0.6)	1.1	(1.0)	**33.9**	(15.2)	-0.3	(4.6)	4.7	(5.1)	1.2	(4.1)
	Ireland	0.4	(0.4)	**7.7**	(1.3)	14.5	(12.0)	-1.0	(5.9)	3.5	(3.6)	-2.8	(3.4)
	Israel	0.0	(1.1)	**4.1**	(1.2)	6.2	(14.4)	-0.7	(6.4)	-0.1	(6.6)	8.5	(4.7)
	Italy	**2.5**	(0.4)	**5.2**	(1.0)	**-26.5**	(10.0)	-0.8	(3.5)	**18.1**	(3.3)	**9.6**	(3.0)
	Japan	1.0	(2.3)	**1.9**	(0.9)	18.6	(18.0)	1.3	(5.4)	**13.6**	(6.3)	-1.1	(5.1)
	Korea	**2.1**	(1.0)	1.7	(1.1)	-16.7	(23.9)	10.3	(5.8)	-4.7	(8.1)	6.6	(8.3)
	Luxembourg	-0.1	(1.3)	**7.3**	(2.9)	12.0	(19.2)	-11.3	(10.9)	21.6	(11.7)	-4.1	(8.0)
	Mexico	**0.8**	(0.2)	0.4	(0.3)	-6.3	(7.6)	3.2	(2.3)	3.0	(2.8)	**11.6**	(2.9)
	Netherlands	0.0	(0.6)	**6.9**	(1.9)	20.6	(16.3)	**12.5**	(5.4)	**12.4**	(5.8)	5.2	(4.8)
	New Zealand	0.2	(0.5)	**2.0**	(0.9)	-3.8	(23.2)	-4.7	(5.4)	3.0	(3.3)	8.5	(5.0)
	Norway	**0.8**	(0.3)	**1.1**	(0.5)	13.1	(8.5)	-3.1	(3.6)	3.8	(3.0)	6.4	(4.5)
	Poland	1.5	(0.9)	1.3	(0.8)	**-33.2**	(12.3)	-11.0	(6.4)	3.0	(4.0)	-1.4	(3.5)
	Portugal	**1.0**	(0.2)	**4.2**	(0.8)	-8.7	(8.8)	6.3	(6.7)	4.3	(3.3)	4.1	(3.2)
	Slovak Republic	**1.4**	(0.3)	**1.8**	(0.7)	**-38.5**	(9.5)	**-15.2**	(6.6)	6.5	(4.2)	-0.6	(4.3)
	Slovenia	**0.5**	(0.2)	**3.1**	(0.7)	9.2	(12.8)	0.2	(6.8)	7.6	(6.3)	3.1	(4.7)
	Spain	**0.6**	(0.3)	**2.5**	(0.7)	-13.6	(7.4)	-0.4	(3.6)	**7.6**	(2.7)	0.4	(2.5)
	Sweden	1.3	(0.7)	1.9	(1.4)	6.5	(9.1)	2.2	(5.0)	6.2	(4.6)	**20.3**	(5.9)
	Switzerland	1.7	(1.3)	**6.0**	(1.1)	4.4	(11.2)	-4.7	(4.1)	5.5	(4.3)	6.4	(4.4)
	Turkey	0.8	(0.7)	**-2.7**	(1.0)	**-30.9**	(10.1)	**-13.6**	(6.4)	15.8	(8.1)	-11.6	(9.0)
	United Kingdom	**2.8**	(0.5)	0.6	(1.0)	17.7	(11.5)	**-8.3**	(3.3)	2.1	(3.7)	-2.0	(3.3)
	United States	**-6.7**	(3.0)	**-4.0**	(1.2)	-11.0	(16.8)	**-15.4**	(7.0)	15.6	(8.2)	-3.7	(5.8)
	OECD average	**0.8**	(0.2)	**3.0**	(0.2)	-2.4	(2.4)	**-2.9**	(1.0)	**7.6**	(0.9)	**3.6**	(0.9)
Partners	Albania	0.4	(0.3)	-0.8	(0.9)	0.9	(13.6)	0.7	(6.6)	**18.4**	(6.6)	11.4	(6.8)
	Argentina	**1.3**	(0.4)	-0.8	(1.1)	**-55.9**	(15.3)	0.0	(7.1)	**18.0**	(6.0)	4.1	(5.3)
	Azerbaijan	**0.8**	(0.4)	-3.6	(2.1)	4.1	(14.4)	2.8	(5.0)	6.6	(4.6)	0.0	(5.3)
	Brazil	**0.8**	(0.2)	0.9	(0.5)	-12.6	(9.7)	-4.4	(3.4)	**14.3**	(3.3)	**16.0**	(3.7)
	Bulgaria	**1.6**	(0.4)	-0.3	(2.6)	-38.9	(22.1)	14.6	(10.8)	**24.4**	(6.4)	8.5	(7.4)
	Colombia	**1.4**	(0.3)	-0.3	(0.5)	**-40.4**	(9.3)	-0.5	(3.0)	5.5	(3.4)	**6.6**	(2.6)
	Croatia	**1.0**	(0.2)	**4.2**	(0.9)	**39.5**	(15.1)	**-9.9**	(3.6)	**14.7**	(3.1)	-2.1	(3.5)
	Dubai (UAE)	**1.5**	(0.3)	-1.1	(0.7)	4.4	(11.0)	6.3	(5.4)	9.0	(5.1)	8.5	(5.4)
	Hong Kong-China	**2.5**	(0.8)	1.4	(0.9)	9.2	(15.1)	**-11.1**	(4.9)	5.2	(5.0)	-3.8	(3.8)
	Indonesia	**0.5**	(0.2)	0.2	(0.4)	11.5	(9.6)	0.8	(3.8)	-1.2	(3.1)	5.5	(3.1)
	Jordan	**1.1**	(0.3)	0.5	(0.5)	**32.9**	(15.7)	0.0	(2.9)	**15.3**	(4.0)	**-11.2**	(4.6)
	Kazakhstan	**1.0**	(0.3)	-1.0	(0.7)	**-45.8**	(10.7)	-2.0	(3.4)	-1.1	(5.2)	-1.0	(4.1)
	Kyrgyzstan	**1.7**	(0.2)	-0.4	(0.9)	**-32.6**	(8.8)	-0.9	(3.0)	2.5	(3.6)	**9.2**	(3.6)
	Latvia	**0.6**	(0.2)	**3.6**	(0.6)	6.3	(11.0)	-1.9	(4.5)	2.3	(4.1)	1.7	(4.7)
	Lithuania	0.3	(0.1)	**2.3**	(0.8)	-9.9	(11.0)	4.7	(6.2)	7.0	(5.5)	-0.7	(7.1)
	Macao-China	0.1	(0.7)	-0.2	(0.7)	35.9	(23.2)	-0.6	(4.3)	**11.4**	(4.4)	2.2	(5.5)
	Montenegro	0.2	(0.4)	-2.5	(1.4)	**-39.0**	(14.8)	-6.2	(5.8)	7.7	(5.3)	1.9	(10.0)
	Panama	0.6	(0.4)	**4.2**	(0.9)	-48.2	(25.7)	-4.6	(5.6)	0.2	(5.3)	**19.6**	(4.2)
	Peru	**1.2**	(0.3)	0.7	(0.5)	-18.9	(18.8)	**-10.0**	(4.6)	**17.5**	(5.3)	**12.5**	(4.6)
	Qatar	**2.1**	(0.3)	0.0	(0.9)	3.7	(15.8)	**-11.9**	(5.1)	-3.8	(5.0)	-9.3	(5.5)
	Romania	0.1	(0.6)	**2.0**	(1.0)	26.6	(18.6)	-20.3	(11.4)	1.6	(5.2)	0.0	(5.5)
	Russian Federation	**0.5**	(0.2)	0.8	(0.6)	8.2	(11.4)	-3.5	(3.6)	-3.8	(4.0)	9.2	(5.1)
	Serbia	0.8	(0.4)	**4.2**	(1.1)	-5.8	(21.3)	**-17.3**	(7.1)	11.8	(7.0)	1.4	(6.8)
	Shanghai-China	**1.3**	(0.4)	**1.7**	(0.4)	**-84.7**	(14.9)	-1.8	(2.6)	**5.7**	(2.6)	3.5	(3.1)
	Singapore	**3.4**	(0.8)	-1.1	(0.7)	-26.2	(17.0)	**-8.9**	(3.5)	5.8	(4.3)	-1.2	(3.9)
	Chinese Taipei	-1.4	(0.7)	**3.6**	(0.9)	18.3	(15.0)	-0.5	(3.8)	8.1	(5.0)	3.6	(4.0)
	Thailand	**1.0**	(0.5)	0.6	(0.5)	-2.6	(20.7)	-0.3	(3.0)	3.4	(3.8)	4.7	(5.2)
	Trinidad and Tobago	**2.4**	(0.7)	**4.2**	(0.9)	-7.5	(14.0)	-4.1	(4.7)	**12.0**	(4.6)	3.2	(5.4)
	Tunisia	**0.7**	(0.2)	**1.8**	(0.7)	3.4	(7.7)	-0.3	(3.7)	1.4	(1.7)	-0.1	(3.1)
	Uruguay	**0.6**	(0.3)	0.6	(0.7)	-3.5	(15.8)	-1.7	(4.1)	6.3	(4.5)	**8.6**	(3.7)

Note: Values that are statistically significant are indicated in bold (see Annex A3).
1. Multilevel regression model (student and school levels): Reading performance is regressed on the school resource variables presented in this table.
StatLink http://dx.doi.org/10.1787/888932343285

[Part 1/3]

Table IV.2.12c **Relationships between resources invested in education and reading performance, accounting for students' and schools' socio-economic and demographic background**

		Resources invested in education (student level)[1]		Resources invested in education (school level)[1]									
		Class size		Students' learning time at school in language of instruction lessons		Students' learning time at school in mathematics and science lessons		Percentage of students attending after-school lessons (enrichment)		Percentage of students attending after-school lessons (remedial)		Percentage of students who attended pre-primary education for one year or less	
		Change in score	S.E.	Change in score	S.E.	Change in score	S.E.	Change in score	S.E.	Change in score	S.E.	Change in score	S.E.
OECD	Australia	**2.1**	(0.3)	-0.3	(0.2)	0.1	(0.1)	-0.1	(0.5)	-0.2	(0.5)	0.7	(0.6)
	Austria	-0.4	(0.4)	-0.2	(0.1)	0.0	(0.0)	-0.4	(0.4)	0.4	(0.3)	-0.7	(0.7)
	Belgium	**2.4**	(0.4)	**-0.4**	(0.1)	**0.2**	(0.1)	-0.4	(0.4)	0.2	(0.3)	**-1.2**	(0.6)
	Canada	**1.3**	(0.2)	-0.1	(0.1)	0.0	(0.0)	**-0.4**	(0.2)	-0.3	(0.3)	**0.5**	(0.2)
	Chile	-0.3	(0.3)	-0.2	(0.1)	**0.2**	(0.0)	**-0.6**	(0.3)	-0.1	(0.2)	**-0.6**	(0.2)
	Czech Republic	-0.2	(0.4)	**-0.4**	(0.1)	**0.1**	(0.0)	-0.4	(0.2)	-0.2	(0.2)	0.0	(0.7)
	Denmark	-0.3	(0.5)	-0.1	(0.1)	0.0	(0.0)	-0.3	(0.2)	**-0.7**	(0.3)	-0.1	(0.5)
	Estonia	**2.1**	(0.4)	0.1	(0.2)	0.0	(0.1)	-0.3	(0.2)	-0.2	(0.2)	**1.0**	(0.4)
	Finland	**3.0**	(0.6)	-0.1	(0.1)	0.0	(0.0)	**-1.2**	(0.4)	**-0.9**	(0.2)	**-0.9**	(0.3)
	France	w	w	w	w	w	w	w	w	w	w	w	w
	Germany	0.3	(0.3)	0.2	(0.2)	0.1	(0.1)	-0.4	(0.3)	-0.4	(0.3)	-0.4	(0.9)
	Greece	-0.2	(0.7)	0.1	(0.1)	0.2	(0.1)	**1.0**	(0.4)	-0.4	(0.5)	-0.9	(0.6)
	Hungary	-0.2	(0.3)	0.2	(0.2)	0.0	(0.1)	0.1	(0.2)	0.0	(0.2)	**2.9**	(1.1)
	Iceland	**3.3**	(0.6)	-0.1	(0.1)	0.2	(0.1)	**-0.7**	(0.2)	-0.3	(0.3)	-0.3	(0.8)
	Ireland	**3.3**	(0.4)	-0.5	(0.3)	0.2	(0.2)	0.1	(0.3)	-0.8	(0.5)	0.2	(0.3)
	Israel	**1.1**	(0.3)	0.0	(0.1)	0.1	(0.1)	**0.9**	(0.4)	**-3.1**	(0.4)	-2.0	(1.4)
	Italy	**-0.5**	(0.2)	-0.1	(0.1)	**-0.1**	(0.0)	-0.1	(0.2)	**-0.4**	(0.2)	0.0	(0.6)
	Japan	**-2.0**	(0.8)	-0.1	(0.1)	**0.3**	(0.1)	-0.2	(0.5)	**0.6**	(0.3)	-2.1	(3.0)
	Korea	0.1	(2.1)	0.0	(0.1)	0.1	(0.0)	-0.4	(0.2)	0.3	(0.2)	0.0	(0.9)
	Luxembourg	**3.5**	(1.2)	**0.3**	(0.1)	-0.1	(0.1)	**-1.7**	(0.7)	0.6	(0.4)	-1.3	(1.4)
	Mexico	-0.2	(0.2)	0.0	(0.1)	0.1	(0.0)	**-0.7**	(0.3)	-0.3	(0.3)	**0.5**	(0.2)
	Netherlands	**1.2**	(0.3)	**-0.8**	(0.2)	**0.4**	(0.1)	**-1.4**	(0.5)	0.2	(0.4)	0.3	(1.3)
	New Zealand	**2.7**	(0.4)	**-0.3**	(0.2)	0.1	(0.1)	**-0.6**	(0.3)	-0.7	(0.4)	-0.2	(0.3)
	Norway	0.5	(0.4)	c	c	c	c	0.0	(0.4)	**-1.9**	(0.5)	0.1	(0.6)
	Poland	**1.4**	(0.7)	-0.3	(0.1)	0.0	(0.0)	**0.3**	(0.1)	**-0.3**	(0.1)	1.0	(0.6)
	Portugal	**3.0**	(0.4)	**-0.2**	(0.1)	**0.1**	(0.0)	-0.2	(0.2)	-0.3	(0.2)	0.2	(0.3)
	Slovak Republic	-0.2	(0.4)	**-0.4**	(0.1)	**0.1**	(0.0)	-0.1	(0.2)	0.1	(0.2)	0.8	(0.4)
	Slovenia	0.3	(0.3)	**0.6**	(0.1)	**0.2**	(0.1)	**-0.4**	(0.2)	**-0.7**	(0.2)	0.1	(0.3)
	Spain	**1.5**	(0.2)	-0.1	(0.1)	0.0	(0.0)	0.1	(0.1)	-0.1	(0.1)	0.3	(0.3)
	Sweden	**2.0**	(0.4)	-0.2	(0.1)	0.1	(0.0)	0.2	(0.3)	-0.7	(0.4)	0.3	(0.5)
	Switzerland	**3.3**	(0.5)	0.0	(0.1)	0.0	(0.0)	**-0.9**	(0.2)	0.2	(0.2)	**1.8**	(0.8)
	Turkey	0.2	(0.2)	**0.3**	(0.1)	0.1	(0.0)	**0.9**	(0.3)	**-1.0**	(0.3)	0.1	(0.4)
	United Kingdom	**4.5**	(0.3)	-0.1	(0.1)	**0.1**	(0.1)	0.0	(0.2)	**-0.4**	(0.1)	0.4	(0.4)
	United States	**0.6**	(0.3)	-0.1	(0.1)	**0.1**	(0.1)	**-1.7**	(0.4)	0.4	(0.4)	**-2.3**	(1.1)
	OECD average	**1.2**	(0.1)	**-0.1**	(0.0)	**0.1**	(0.0)	**-0.3**	(0.1)	**-0.3**	(0.1)	-0.1	(0.2)
Partners	Albania	0.4	(0.3)	-0.2	(0.2)	0.1	(0.1)	**0.8**	(0.2)	**-0.8**	(0.3)	-0.5	(0.3)
	Argentina	-0.4	(0.3)	**-0.2**	(0.1)	0.1	(0.0)	**-2.0**	(0.5)	0.8	(0.4)	0.6	(0.4)
	Azerbaijan	-0.2	(0.3)	0.1	(0.1)	**0.2**	(0.1)	0.2	(0.5)	-0.8	(0.5)	0.8	(0.6)
	Brazil	-0.3	(0.2)	0.0	(0.1)	0.0	(0.1)	**-0.3**	(0.1)	**-0.4**	(0.2)	0.2	(0.2)
	Bulgaria	**0.9**	(0.4)	0.0	(0.2)	0.0	(0.1)	**-1.4**	(0.4)	0.2	(0.3)	-0.5	(0.5)
	Colombia	**-1.0**	(0.3)	-0.1	(0.1)	**0.1**	(0.0)	-0.3	(0.3)	-0.4	(0.2)	0.4	(0.3)
	Croatia	0.9	(0.6)	0.0	(0.1)	**0.3**	(0.0)	**-0.7**	(0.3)	-0.3	(0.2)	0.2	(0.3)
	Dubai (UAE)	0.1	(0.2)	**-0.5**	(0.1)	**0.2**	(0.0)	**-0.6**	(0.3)	-0.5	(0.2)	0.1	(0.3)
	Hong Kong-China	**2.0**	(0.3)	**-0.5**	(0.1)	**0.3**	(0.1)	-0.2	(0.2)	-0.1	(0.3)	1.4	(1.0)
	Indonesia	**0.4**	(0.2)	**-0.1**	(0.1)	**0.1**	(0.0)	**-0.4**	(0.2)	-0.3	(0.2)	0.2	(0.1)
	Jordan	**-0.9**	(0.4)	**0.8**	(0.3)	-0.2	(0.1)	0.3	(0.2)	**-1.2**	(0.3)	**1.1**	(0.2)
	Kazakhstan	**-1.4**	(0.5)	-0.1	(0.1)	0.0	(0.1)	-0.5	(0.3)	0.4	(0.2)	-0.1	(0.4)
	Kyrgyzstan	-0.3	(0.3)	**0.3**	(0.1)	0.0	(0.0)	**0.6**	(0.2)	**-0.5**	(0.2)	-0.1	(0.2)
	Latvia	0.9	(0.5)	-0.2	(0.1)	0.0	(0.1)	0.0	(0.2)	**-0.8**	(0.3)	0.3	(0.3)
	Lithuania	**0.8**	(0.4)	0.1	(0.1)	**-0.1**	(0.0)	-0.1	(0.2)	0.1	(0.3)	-0.1	(0.3)
	Macao-China	**2.0**	(0.5)	-0.3	(0.1)	**0.2**	(0.1)	1.3	(0.7)	**-1.0**	(0.4)	-0.8	(1.1)
	Montenegro	**1.9**	(0.5)	**1.0**	(0.4)	0.0	(0.1)	0.3	(0.6)	**-1.1**	(0.4)	-0.5	(0.5)
	Panama	-0.7	(0.5)	-0.4	(0.3)	**0.2**	(0.1)	**-1.2**	(0.5)	0.0	(0.4)	-0.2	(0.5)
	Peru	**-0.8**	(0.3)	0.0	(0.1)	**0.0**	(0.0)	0.1	(0.2)	**-0.7**	(0.2)	0.3	(0.3)
	Qatar	0.4	(0.2)	0.1	(0.1)	0.1	(0.1)	-0.2	(0.3)	**-1.2**	(0.3)	-0.5	(0.4)
	Romania	**1.1**	(0.3)	0.3	(0.2)	**0.2**	(0.1)	**-0.5**	(0.2)	0.0	(0.2)	**-2.3**	(0.6)
	Russian Federation	0.1	(0.5)	-0.1	(0.1)	0.1	(0.0)	0.1	(0.2)	0.2	(0.2)	-0.1	(0.4)
	Serbia	**1.0**	(0.4)	0.0	(0.2)	**0.1**	(0.1)	0.1	(0.5)	-0.3	(0.3)	0.0	(0.4)
	Shanghai-China	**1.4**	(0.4)	**-0.3**	(0.1)	0.1	(0.1)	-0.2	(0.2)	**0.4**	(0.2)	0.3	(0.4)
	Singapore	**1.9**	(0.3)	**-0.3**	(0.1)	**0.1**	(0.0)	-0.3	(0.2)	-0.1	(0.1)	0.5	(0.9)
	Chinese Taipei	**1.1**	(0.5)	-0.2	(0.2)	0.0	(0.1)	**1.7**	(0.3)	-0.4	(0.3)	-0.7	(1.1)
	Thailand	-0.2	(0.3)	0.1	(0.1)	**0.1**	(0.0)	0.2	(0.2)	0.0	(0.2)	0.2	(0.5)
	Trinidad and Tobago	0.1	(0.2)	**-0.5**	(0.1)	**0.4**	(0.1)	0.2	(0.3)	**-0.7**	(0.3)	**1.5**	(0.7)
	Tunisia	0.1	(0.4)	**0.9**	(0.3)	**0.8**	(0.0)	0.0	(0.2)	0.0	(0.2)	0.0	(0.2)
	Uruguay	**-1.0**	(0.3)	**-0.5**	(0.1)	**0.2**	(0.1)	0.0	(0.3)	-0.5	(0.3)	0.1	(0.3)

Note: Values that are statistically significant are indicated in bold (see Annex A3).
1. Multilevel regression model (student and school levels): Reading performance is regressed on the school resource variables as well as on socio-economic and demographic background variables presented in this table.
StatLink http://dx.doi.org/10.1787/888932343285

[Part 2/3]

Table IV.2.12c Relationships between resources invested in education and reading performance, accounting for students' and schools' socio-economic and demographic background

		Resources invested in education (school level)[1]											
		Percentage of students who attended pre-primary education for more than one year		School average class size		Index of library use in or outside school (higher values indicate more use)		Index of schools' extra-curricular activities (higher values indicate more activities)		Index of teacher shortage (higher values indicate higher shortage)		Index of quality of schools' educational resources (higher values indicate better resources)	
		Change in score	S.E.	Change in score	S.E.	Change in score	S.E.	Change in score	S.E.	Change in score	S.E.	Change in score	S.E.
OECD	Australia	0.8	(0.5)	**3.1**	(1.0)	**29.3**	(9.5)	-3.4	(2.9)	-1.0	(2.5)	-2.8	(2.0)
	Austria	-0.3	(0.5)	**3.2**	(1.0)	-4.2	(8.9)	-7.5	(5.7)	4.4	(4.5)	3.3	(4.3)
	Belgium	0.0	(0.4)	**2.7**	(1.1)	**29.8**	(9.4)	-2.2	(2.9)	1.5	(3.4)	2.3	(3.9)
	Canada	**0.7**	(0.2)	0.8	(0.5)	2.9	(6.1)	-1.2	(2.4)	2.0	(2.7)	3.6	(2.2)
	Chile	-0.3	(0.3)	**1.2**	(0.6)	-14.3	(9.9)	-3.8	(2.6)	**7.2**	(3.5)	0.5	(3.0)
	Czech Republic	0.3	(0.5)	**1.5**	(0.7)	**34.3**	(7.9)	-4.7	(3.7)	-1.6	(3.5)	1.5	(3.5)
	Denmark	0.1	(0.5)	1.2	(0.7)	-6.6	(8.9)	-2.3	(2.6)	-1.2	(1.9)	1.1	(2.3)
	Estonia	-0.2	(0.2)	**2.3**	(0.9)	-3.9	(17.0)	-3.7	(3.6)	-6.3	(3.6)	2.4	(4.2)
	Finland	**-0.8**	(0.2)	1.4	(0.8)	**22.4**	(7.5)	-1.0	(3.0)	2.7	(2.2)	4.4	(2.6)
	France	w	w	w	w	w	w	w	w	w	w	w	w
	Germany	0.5	(0.8)	2.4	(1.4)	**-27.5**	(13.4)	-2.1	(4.1)	-2.1	(4.3)	0.7	(4.4)
	Greece	-0.3	(0.5)	-1.1	(1.7)	-17.0	(11.1)	10.3	(5.5)	4.9	(5.3)	4.8	(4.9)
	Hungary	**2.7**	(1.1)	**3.2**	(0.8)	-6.3	(11.8)	-1.3	(5.2)	5.0	(5.0)	-7.0	(5.5)
	Iceland	-0.6	(0.6)	1.3	(1.0)	**27.0**	(12.5)	5.0	(4.9)	3.4	(5.0)	6.3	(4.1)
	Ireland	-0.2	(0.3)	**5.0**	(1.6)	14.3	(11.2)	1.3	(4.9)	0.6	(3.2)	**-5.8**	(2.8)
	Israel	-0.5	(1.1)	1.7	(1.0)	-0.5	(10.5)	-4.0	(6.4)	-7.3	(6.5)	4.0	(4.9)
	Italy	**1.3**	(0.5)	**3.5**	(0.9)	-14.3	(10.1)	-2.6	(3.0)	5.1	(3.1)	**7.9**	(2.8)
	Japan	0.3	(2.0)	1.6	(0.9)	4.1	(18.1)	-1.8	(5.2)	8.9	(6.1)	-6.0	(4.8)
	Korea	0.9	(0.7)	-0.4	(1.2)	-22.5	(21.1)	4.5	(4.9)	-7.1	(6.8)	7.4	(4.6)
	Luxembourg	0.9	(0.7)	0.2	(1.7)	9.5	(11.5)	-11.4	(5.9)	-10.2	(6.0)	**-6.7**	(3.3)
	Mexico	**0.6**	(0.2)	0.1	(0.3)	7.6	(7.2)	4.0	(2.2)	1.9	(2.6)	3.9	(2.6)
	Netherlands	-0.5	(0.7)	**4.5**	(2.0)	22.2	(14.3)	9.3	(5.3)	10.5	(5.6)	1.3	(5.3)
	New Zealand	-0.1	(0.3)	-0.1	(1.0)	7.2	(10.7)	3.8	(2.8)	-3.6	(3.2)	**6.2**	(2.8)
	Norway	0.4	(0.3)	0.3	(0.5)	12.3	(8.4)	-1.0	(4.0)	1.9	(3.3)	7.2	(4.6)
	Poland	**1.3**	(0.6)	0.4	(0.6)	-1.6	(10.0)	**-11.2**	(5.4)	1.1	(3.3)	-3.8	(2.8)
	Portugal	**0.5**	(0.2)	**3.2**	(0.9)	10.7	(10.1)	5.7	(5.6)	3.6	(3.0)	-0.3	(2.3)
	Slovak Republic	0.6	(0.3)	0.6	(0.9)	**-20.8**	(10.2)	-12.8	(6.8)	-0.1	(3.6)	0.9	(4.0)
	Slovenia	0.3	(0.2)	**1.4**	(0.6)	23.1	(12.2)	-0.2	(5.0)	2.7	(4.1)	2.3	(3.9)
	Spain	**0.5**	(0.2)	0.6	(0.7)	3.4	(6.5)	-1.0	(2.9)	3.0	(2.2)	0.2	(2.0)
	Sweden	0.7	(0.5)	-0.1	(1.0)	6.8	(7.1)	6.9	(3.7)	6.5	(3.7)	**10.3**	(3.8)
	Switzerland	1.5	(0.8)	**2.8**	(1.1)	1.8	(9.9)	-1.7	(3.4)	-3.1	(3.3)	1.3	(3.8)
	Turkey	**-1.6**	(0.4)	**-1.7**	(0.7)	-4.0	(9.3)	-7.9	(4.3)	-0.7	(4.8)	-2.8	(5.9)
	United Kingdom	0.5	(0.3)	**3.1**	(0.9)	9.4	(7.4)	-1.7	(2.2)	0.5	(2.9)	2.3	(2.3)
	United States	**-2.5**	(1.0)	**-2.6**	(1.0)	22.4	(12.4)	-5.6	(4.3)	**10.1**	(5.1)	-2.7	(3.4)
	OECD average	**0.2**	(0.1)	**1.4**	(0.2)	**4.8**	(1.9)	-1.4	(0.8)	1.3	(0.7)	**1.5**	(0.7)
Partners	Albania	0.2	(0.2)	-0.7	(1.1)	6.4	(10.9)	2.9	(6.4)	11.1	(6.3)	2.2	(6.3)
	Argentina	0.4	(0.4)	-1.4	(1.0)	**-30.4**	(11.2)	4.3	(5.9)	4.0	(4.9)	-3.1	(5.2)
	Azerbaijan	0.5	(0.4)	**-5.2**	(2.1)	1.1	(15.1)	3.7	(4.6)	7.0	(4.5)	-3.8	(5.2)
	Brazil	0.3	(0.2)	0.4	(0.5)	-9.0	(6.9)	-1.7	(3.0)	**5.3**	(2.3)	**8.5**	(2.9)
	Bulgaria	-0.1	(0.3)	2.8	(1.8)	-3.5	(14.9)	1.1	(6.2)	**10.7**	(4.0)	-4.8	(4.7)
	Colombia	0.3	(0.3)	0.6	(0.6)	-16.0	(8.5)	0.0	(2.9)	0.7	(3.2)	4.4	(2.4)
	Croatia	0.1	(0.2)	**4.9**	(0.8)	17.8	(12.9)	-5.8	(3.0)	3.5	(3.0)	-2.3	(2.9)
	Dubai (UAE)	**0.8**	(0.3)	-1.1	(0.9)	2.1	(10.5)	3.7	(4.6)	8.2	(4.8)	2.7	(4.8)
	Hong Kong-China	1.2	(0.7)	**1.9**	(0.9)	8.3	(12.4)	-7.3	(4.0)	-0.4	(4.3)	-0.6	(3.3)
	Indonesia	**0.5**	(0.2)	-0.2	(0.6)	13.9	(9.3)	2.0	(4.1)	-1.8	(2.9)	3.6	(2.8)
	Jordan	**0.8**	(0.3)	1.0	(0.5)	15.4	(15.9)	-0.9	(2.7)	**12.1**	(3.7)	**-11.1**	(4.5)
	Kazakhstan	0.2	(0.2)	-1.3	(0.8)	**-38.4**	(9.8)	-1.7	(3.2)	-0.1	(4.4)	-3.1	(3.7)
	Kyrgyzstan	**0.9**	(0.3)	-0.1	(1.1)	**-32.8**	(9.7)	-0.4	(2.9)	-1.3	(3.5)	**8.3**	(3.3)
	Latvia	**0.5**	(0.2)	**1.8**	(0.9)	12.9	(10.8)	0.6	(4.4)	2.7	(3.9)	0.4	(3.8)
	Lithuania	-0.1	(0.2)	1.4	(0.9)	-0.2	(10.2)	2.2	(5.0)	2.5	(4.9)	0.8	(5.2)
	Macao-China	0.5	(0.7)	0.1	(0.9)	23.7	(21.6)	-2.8	(4.0)	3.2	(4.2)	-0.1	(5.6)
	Montenegro	0.2	(0.4)	0.0	(1.5)	-9.6	(14.9)	-4.0	(7.4)	6.4	(4.0)	-0.4	(7.5)
	Panama	-0.2	(0.4)	**2.6**	(1.3)	-22.7	(26.2)	-2.3	(5.9)	-0.1	(5.0)	**12.4**	(4.6)
	Peru	0.3	(0.3)	-0.6	(0.5)	-12.5	(10.8)	-4.8	(3.7)	6.7	(3.7)	**5.9**	(2.8)
	Qatar	**1.0**	(0.4)	-1.7	(1.0)	-0.3	(13.5)	**-14.6**	(4.1)	-2.3	(4.4)	**-11.9**	(4.8)
	Romania	**-0.9**	(0.5)	**2.2**	(0.9)	-6.2	(14.5)	-8.0	(8.6)	**9.2**	(3.8)	-6.0	(4.3)
	Russian Federation	0.2	(0.2)	0.8	(0.8)	9.6	(11.7)	-2.7	(3.0)	-4.3	(2.9)	4.8	(4.0)
	Serbia	0.3	(0.4)	**3.6**	(1.4)	-23.5	(14.4)	-11.6	(6.6)	**12.4**	(5.7)	-8.0	(5.9)
	Shanghai-China	**0.8**	(0.3)	**1.5**	(0.5)	**-57.6**	(14.7)	-0.4	(2.2)	3.0	(2.3)	3.6	(2.5)
	Singapore	**1.7**	(0.7)	-0.8	(0.8)	4.2	(13.4)	-4.2	(2.8)	0.7	(3.0)	0.2	(2.9)
	Chinese Taipei	0.1	(0.8)	**2.7**	(0.9)	1.4	(14.2)	-1.1	(3.7)	1.5	(4.0)	-0.3	(3.7)
	Thailand	0.8	(0.5)	-0.4	(0.6)	-1.7	(19.0)	0.4	(3.3)	2.1	(3.8)	1.8	(5.1)
	Trinidad and Tobago	1.2	(0.7)	**3.6**	(0.8)	5.7	(15.3)	-1.3	(4.1)	3.6	(4.0)	0.5	(4.5)
	Tunisia	0.3	(0.2)	**2.0**	(0.7)	3.9	(9.1)	-0.5	(3.6)	2.2	(1.8)	0.7	(2.9)
	Uruguay	-0.2	(0.2)	0.3	(0.6)	4.8	(10.0)	2.9	(3.3)	4.7	(3.5)	3.9	(2.8)

Note: Values that are statistically significant are indicated in bold (see Annex A3).
1. Multilevel regression model (student and school levels): Reading performance is regressed on the school resource variables as well as on socio-economic and demographic background variables presented in this table.
StatLink http://dx.doi.org/10.1787/888932343285

[Part 3/3]

Table IV.2.12c **Relationships between resources invested in education and reading performance, accounting for students' and schools' socio-economic and demographic background**

		Student socio-economic and demographic background[1]										School socio-economic and demographic background[1]									
		Student is a female		Student without an immigrant background		Student's language at home is the same as the language of assessment		PISA index of economic, social and cultural status of student (1 unit increase)		PISA index of economic, social and cultural status of student (squared)		School average PISA index of economic, social and cultural status (1 unit increase)		School size (per 100 students)		School size (per 100 students) (squared)		School in a small town or village (15000 or less people)		School in city (100000 or more people)	
		Change in score	S.E.	Change in score	S.E.	Change in score	S.E.	Change in score	S.E.	Change in score	S.E.	Change in score	S.E.	Change in score	S.E.	Change in score	S.E.	Change in score	S.E.	Change in score	S.E.
OECD	Australia	**36.4**	(2.3)	**-6.0**	(2.5)	**22.9**	(4.2)	**29.4**	(1.8)	**-3.1**	(1.1)	**51.5**	(10.6)	-0.8	(1.8)	0.0	(0.1)	7.0	(7.1)	5.5	(5.0)
	Austria	**21.4**	(3.5)	**12.8**	(4.7)	**15.9**	(5.8)	**8.2**	(2.0)	0.1	(1.4)	**51.9**	(14.3)	**8.8**	(2.9)	**-0.4**	(0.2)	-12.4	(10.5)	-3.4	(13.2)
	Belgium	**17.6**	(2.2)	**17.0**	(2.7)	5.2	(3.1)	**11.0**	(1.3)	1.5	(0.9)	**74.3**	(9.4)	**6.9**	(2.1)	**-0.3**	(0.1)	6.9	(6.8)	-3.5	(6.2)
	Canada	**34.6**	(2.0)	4.1	(2.6)	**18.1**	(4.4)	**18.4**	(1.3)	**3.1**	(0.9)	**25.4**	(6.3)	0.1	(1.2)	0.0	(0.1)	-0.2	(4.7)	-1.1	(4.4)
	Chile	**18.1**	(3.0)	0.5	(7.7)	**55.7**	(17.9)	**9.8**	(1.8)	0.5	(0.9)	**34.0**	(5.2)	1.0	(1.3)	0.0	(0.0)	11.4	(9.2)	0.4	(6.8)
	Czech Republic	**34.4**	(2.7)	**13.3**	(3.8)	-1.7	(10.7)	**15.3**	(2.0)	-2.9	(1.6)	**98.1**	(8.6)	3.7	(4.2)	-0.2	(0.4)	**14.4**	(6.1)	-5.4	(6.3)
	Denmark	**29.3**	(2.9)	**13.0**	(3.6)	**22.3**	(6.0)	**27.1**	(1.7)	-0.2	(1.1)	**29.8**	(5.9)	3.6	(2.8)	-0.4	(0.3)	-7.0	(4.2)	9.0	(5.5)
	Estonia	**42.5**	(2.9)	**9.8**	(4.3)	**29.6**	(6.6)	**16.2**	(2.1)	1.3	(1.9)	**41.7**	(13.9)	0.9	(3.1)	-0.1	(0.1)	5.8	(7.8)	-6.6	(8.8)
	Finland	**54.8**	(2.6)	**14.7**	(4.9)	**41.7**	(7.1)	**25.8**	(2.0)	-0.8	(1.6)	**19.4**	(7.9)	-0.6	(1.3)	0.1	(0.0)	-4.7	(5.1)	-1.7	(6.0)
	France	w	w	w	w	w	w	w	w	w	w	w	w	w	w	w	w	w	w	w	w
	Germany	**30.2**	(2.5)	**15.9**	(3.2)	3.3	(5.3)	**9.1**	(1.6)	-1.0	(0.9)	**91.7**	(11.5)	**7.4**	(2.6)	**-0.2**	(0.1)	16.3	(9.5)	-3.0	(9.8)
	Greece	**36.1**	(3.1)	2.2	(3.5)	18.0	(13.8)	**15.8**	(1.7)	2.0	(1.3)	**28.5**	(11.1)	-7.5	(19.0)	1.7	(2.7)	**27.4**	(13.3)	-2.0	(14.5)
	Hungary	**24.8**	(2.5)	-8.1	(4.7)	**22.7**	(8.6)	**8.7**	(1.6)	1.0	(1.1)	**59.9**	(9.0)	2.5	(2.9)	-0.1	(0.2)	4.2	(11.4)	2.5	(9.0)
	Iceland	**42.8**	(3.2)	3.6	(5.3)	**47.3**	(11.7)	**26.2**	(2.6)	**-3.5**	(1.6)	24.5	(14.6)	-11.2	(7.3)	1.0	(0.9)	1.3	(8.5)	-6.4	(12.0)
	Ireland	**32.1**	(4.8)	-4.5	(3.8)	**32.6**	(10.3)	**24.5**	(2.2)	-1.1	(1.6)	**42.9**	(7.9)	-1.2	(5.8)	-0.2	(0.3)	**-20.3**	(10.1)	-13.4	(10.8)
	Israel	**31.8**	(3.7)	-3.5	(4.3)	0.5	(6.1)	**20.9**	(2.5)	**3.7**	(1.3)	**42.8**	(19.3)	10.4	(5.9)	-0.5	(0.3)	16.5	(11.0)	-14.7	(10.9)
	Italy	**27.4**	(1.6)	**14.3**	(2.5)	**7.3**	(2.6)	**5.2**	(0.8)	-1.0	(0.8)	**37.7**	(7.8)	**7.8**	(2.4)	-0.3	(0.1)	8.0	(8.3)	-5.0	(7.6)
	Japan	**28.9**	(2.8)	3.3	(9.1)	**67.8**	(29.5)	4.7	(2.5)	-0.3	(2.1)	**81.3**	(18.8)	-6.3	(4.0)	0.3	(0.2)	3.9	(15.3)	-11.2	(10.6)
	Korea	**42.3**	(5.4)	2.8	(10.6)	18.4	(55.4)	**19.2**	(2.9)	0.7	(1.4)	**53.2**	(11.7)	0.3	(4.9)	0.1	(0.2)	-26.8	(19.3)	**-34.8**	(15.7)
	Luxembourg	**35.2**	(3.2)	**28.4**	(3.5)	**27.4**	(5.5)	**15.1**	(2.2)	-1.3	(1.2)	**67.6**	(11.4)	1.2	(2.1)	0.0	(0.1)	**15.9**	(7.7)	-4.8	(34.3)
	Mexico	**21.7**	(1.9)	**24.6**	(3.5)	**18.8**	(5.2)	**9.0**	(1.3)	**1.7**	(0.5)	**11.0**	(4.1)	0.3	(0.5)	0.0	(0.0)	-5.5	(7.4)	4.6	(6.8)
	Netherlands	**19.1**	(1.7)	**5.5**	(2.7)	**12.2**	(6.2)	**5.0**	(1.6)	0.3	(1.1)	**32.6**	(13.2)	0.2	(2.3)	0.0	(0.1)	-4.2	(9.2)	9.3	(9.3)
	New Zealand	**46.1**	(4.4)	**-7.0**	(3.6)	**42.5**	(5.8)	**33.3**	(2.8)	0.4	(2.5)	**52.0**	(8.7)	**3.7**	(1.6)	-0.1	(0.1)	13.6	(7.7)	9.4	(6.9)
	Norway	**48.0**	(3.5)	10.5	(5.4)	**37.7**	(7.6)	**28.5**	(3.1)	-1.9	(2.0)	10.4	(12.6)	1.8	(7.7)	-0.4	(1.1)	-7.0	(5.5)	4.7	(7.5)
	Poland	**52.5**	(3.4)	25.7	(25.3)	**52.6**	(15.8)	**30.9**	(1.8)	**-3.3**	(1.4)	**22.3**	(7.0)	1.6	(4.9)	0.0	(0.6)	-0.7	(7.9)	**-17.1**	(7.1)
	Portugal	**33.0**	(2.6)	-2.5	(3.0)	11.7	(8.4)	**16.6**	(1.4)	-0.1	(0.7)	**16.2**	(7.8)	-1.6	(2.6)	0.1	(0.1)	4.3	(6.7)	7.0	(5.9)
	Slovak Republic	**43.3**	(2.9)	1.2	(5.4)	**26.9**	(7.3)	**17.9**	(1.9)	**-3.7**	(1.2)	**37.7**	(13.1)	-2.3	(4.5)	0.2	(0.3)	-1.0	(8.1)	-3.3	(8.1)
	Slovenia	**29.8**	(2.3)	**8.8**	(3.1)	5.7	(5.2)	**3.1**	(1.2)	0.9	(1.2)	**51.5**	(10.0)	5.8	(3.9)	-0.4	(0.4)	1.5	(7.6)	-2.0	(6.0)
	Spain	**29.2**	(1.7)	**23.7**	(2.4)	**11.0**	(3.7)	**19.1**	(1.0)	-0.7	(0.6)	**21.5**	(4.8)	-1.1	(1.6)	0.0	(0.1)	-5.2	(4.1)	**10.0**	(5.0)
	Sweden	**44.4**	(2.9)	7.3	(4.0)	**28.5**	(6.4)	**31.4**	(2.1)	-1.0	(1.0)	**40.8**	(13.5)	-3.2	(3.3)	0.3	(0.2)	1.9	(6.7)	9.5	(9.2)
	Switzerland	**30.9**	(2.4)	**11.2**	(2.6)	**18.9**	(3.2)	**16.8**	(1.5)	0.2	(1.3)	**50.7**	(9.4)	1.7	(0.9)	**0.0**	(0.0)	-6.4	(7.1)	-0.9	(11.8)
	Turkey	**31.1**	(2.9)	-2.2	(7.5)	2.3	(11.1)	**7.2**	(2.3)	-0.3	(0.9)	**50.1**	(8.1)	-1.6	(2.5)	-0.1	(0.1)	**-24.3**	(11.1)	3.5	(10.4)
	United Kingdom	**19.0**	(3.3)	-6.0	(4.1)	11.7	(6.3)	**22.3**	(1.9)	0.8	(1.4)	**63.0**	(7.9)	-3.3	(2.0)	0.1	(0.1)	3.5	(4.0)	-0.3	(5.5)
	United States	**28.0**	(4.2)	-4.9	(7.4)	6.3	(7.9)	**23.1**	(2.5)	-1.6	(3.1)	**50.2**	(11.3)	-0.4	(1.0)	0.0	(0.0)	10.5	(10.8)	**20.9**	(9.9)
	OECD average	**33.2**	(0.5)	**7.0**	(1.1)	**22.5**	(2.4)	**17.4**	(0.3)	-0.3	(0.2)	**44.4**	(1.9)	0.9	(0.8)	0.0	(0.1)	1.5	(1.6)	-1.3	(1.9)
Partners	Albania	**57.3**	(4.0)	**24.5**	(11.8)	17.4	(16.7)	**20.8**	(3.7)	**3.4**	(1.5)	20.8	(10.7)	-7.6	(4.1)	**0.6**	(0.3)	1.4	(11.9)	11.0	(13.9)
	Argentina	**31.6**	(3.2)	1.3	(5.3)	**46.2**	(17.2)	**13.0**	(2.1)	2.0	(1.0)	**46.5**	(9.2)	**7.4**	(2.9)	**-0.2**	(0.1)	11.9	(14.7)	8.0	(12.5)
	Azerbaijan	**22.6**	(2.4)	3.8	(5.0)	-1.8	(6.2)	**11.5**	(2.1)	1.6	(1.0)	16.3	(12.4)	-2.1	(3.9)	0.2	(0.2)	-12.3	(13.5)	-20.0	(12.6)
	Brazil	**28.9**	(2.0)	12.5	(9.0)	**33.2**	(12.5)	**8.2**	(2.0)	**1.5**	(0.7)	**43.0**	(4.8)	-0.9	(1.2)	0.0	(0.0)	3.3	(7.4)	**-13.7**	(5.7)
	Bulgaria	**46.6**	(3.8)	**29.5**	(8.1)	**28.2**	(6.8)	**13.2**	(2.3)	1.6	(1.4)	**69.5**	(9.4)	-4.4	(3.7)	**0.5**	(0.2)	9.3	(9.1)	6.1	(10.3)
	Colombia	**10.5**	(3.0)	**19.2**	(8.0)	**58.4**	(22.0)	**13.4**	(2.7)	1.5	(0.8)	**28.1**	(5.3)	0.0	(0.7)	0.0	(0.0)	**17.6**	(7.3)	-2.1	(6.7)
	Croatia	**35.0**	(3.3)	3.4	(2.5)	-8.1	(9.3)	**10.2**	(1.9)	**-3.5**	(1.2)	**54.2**	(9.7)	-3.4	(2.6)	0.1	(0.1)	**17.4**	(6.1)	-12.8	(7.6)
	Dubai (UAE)	**25.1**	(4.3)	**-30.3**	(3.6)	**17.5**	(3.2)	**18.8**	(1.9)	**2.7**	(1.1)	**23.3**	(10.4)	1.1	(0.6)	**0.0**	(0.0)	12.0	(16.2)	15.7	(12.2)
	Hong Kong-China	**25.1**	(2.9)	**-8.5**	(2.4)	**21.7**	(6.3)	2.2	(2.1)	-1.2	(0.9)	**31.3**	(5.7)	2.5	(6.3)	0.2	(0.3)	a	a	a	a
	Indonesia	**28.7**	(1.8)	18.0	(11.1)	-4.3	(2.7)	**6.9**	(2.8)	1.4	(0.8)	6.3	(6.2)	1.3	(3.9)	0.1	(0.3)	1.9	(7.7)	12.4	(8.8)
	Jordan	**30.0**	(8.6)	-6.8	(3.6)	**25.4**	(8.4)	**20.2**	(2.3)	1.5	(1.1)	-0.3	(8.5)	**-8.6**	(3.7)	**0.5**	(0.2)	-5.9	(9.4)	6.9	(8.6)
	Kazakhstan	**41.1**	(2.6)	**-11.8**	(4.8)	3.1	(4.6)	**17.2**	(2.4)	-2.2	(1.4)	**45.7**	(11.3)	-2.4	(2.1)	0.1	(0.1)	-10.6	(10.8)	-1.0	(10.9)
	Kyrgyzstan	**50.4**	(2.9)	-10.5	(5.5)	-3.2	(4.7)	**19.7**	(2.4)	**2.5**	(1.2)	15.5	(9.5)	0.3	(2.3)	-0.1	(0.1)	0.1	(8.6)	**23.2**	(11.5)
	Latvia	**47.1**	(2.9)	0.7	(3.3)	3.1	(9.2)	**19.4**	(2.5)	-0.6	(1.6)	14.5	(13.5)	-3.5	(3.7)	0.3	(0.3)	1.4	(7.8)	4.3	(10.3)
	Lithuania	**54.8**	(2.7)	-1.3	(4.8)	10.6	(8.0)	**18.9**	(1.7)	-0.2	(1.2)	**44.7**	(10.8)	-7.4	(4.0)	0.5	(0.3)	10.0	(11.1)	-12.1	(10.3)
	Macao-China	**21.3**	(2.0)	**-9.8**	(2.7)	**44.8**	(7.4)	**7.0**	(2.1)	0.1	(0.9)	**28.6**	(10.1)	2.9	(1.9)	-0.1	(0.0)	a	a	a	a
	Montenegro	**39.3**	(3.3)	**-7.3**	(2.7)	5.5	(11.5)	**12.5**	(1.5)	0.7	(1.5)	**33.1**	(14.5)	-4.9	(3.5)	0.3	(0.2)	-6.6	(12.7)	-4.3	(17.5)
	Panama	**18.5**	(4.8)	4.2	(6.5)	15.3	(10.8)	**6.9**	(3.3)	1.4	(1.0)	12.7	(13.4)	2.4	(2.0)	-0.1	(0.1)	-15.7	(14.2)	8.1	(14.2)
	Peru	**12.2**	(3.2)	20.3	(10.4)	**32.4**	(7.9)	**11.9**	(2.7)	1.1	(0.8)	**34.7**	(5.6)	**4.2**	(1.4)	**-0.1**	(0.0)	-4.2	(8.0)	3.2	(7.6)
	Qatar	**35.9**	(6.2)	**-37.0**	(2.7)	**19.7**	(3.4)	**8.1**	(1.5)	**1.7**	(0.9)	**36.2**	(15.8)	**3.9**	(1.2)	**0.0**	(0.0)	-1.3	(11.3)	-3.5	(11.1)
	Romania	**15.9**	(3.9)	**19.2**	(9.7)	**16.5**	(7.7)	**11.0**	(2.1)	0.1	(1.0)	**40.9**	(8.9)	-3.8	(3.7)	0.2	(0.2)	**28.8**	(8.9)	11.5	(9.2)
	Russian Federation	**41.4**	(2.6)	1.9	(2.8)	**19.3**	(5.7)	**21.4**	(2.0)	-1.5	(1.7)	**41.5**	(8.9)	**-13.6**	(3.7)	**0.9**	(0.2)	8.5	(8.8)	10.7	(7.6)
	Serbia	**26.0**	(2.8)	-5.6	(3.4)	2.8	(10.6)	**7.4**	(1.7)	1.3	(1.2)	**38.8**	(17.8)	**-9.0**	(4.2)	0.3	(0.2)	9.4	(9.6)	-2.0	(8.8)
	Shanghai-China	**33.0**	(2.5)	**22.2**	(9.2)	**31.4**	(9.6)	**4.7**	(1.8)	0.6	(1.2)	**26.1**	(7.4)	-0.4	(0.6)	0.0	(0.0)	a	a	a	a
	Singapore	**25.7**	(2.2)	-2.1	(2.9)	**26.2**	(3.4)	**16.2**	(2.7)	-2.4	(1.2)	**49.7**	(10.7)	**7.0**	(2.3)	-0.1	(0.1)	a	a	a	a
	Chinese Taipei	**46.4**	(4.2)	16.8	(10.1)	8.4	(5.1)	**20.6**	(3.0)	0.9	(1.8)	15.5	(15.9)	-0.8	(0.6)	0.0	(0.0)	-1.4	(11.4)	10.8	(7.0)
	Thailand	**36.4**	(3.1)	**32.9**	(11.5)	**-14.4**	(3.7)	4.1	(2.9)	-0.1	(1.1)	9.8	(7.2)	1.2	(1.1)	0.0	(0.0)	1.4	(12.9)	16.4	(9.2)
	Trinidad and Tobago	**46.3**	(2.4)	-5.5	(3.3)	**31.4**	(7.3)	**4.6**	(2.2)	1.0	(1.1)	**63.4**	(12.1)	6.0	(5.8)	-0.5	(0.4)	-5.0	(7.6)	a	a
	Tunisia	**22.2**	(2.3)	**20.0**	(8.4)	-26.3	(18.3)	2.8	(2.6)	-0.3	(0.8)	**13.7**	(6.0)	1.5	(2.2)	-0.1	(0.1)	3.0	(5.5)	10.4	(7.4)
	Uruguay	**39.1**	(3.0)	-1.7	(6.3)	15.1	(9.1)	**15.4**	(2.0)	0.0	(0.9)	**33.0**	(5.7)	1.3	(1.1)	0.0	(0.0)	**19.8**	(7.4)	**21.2**	(7.0)

Note: Values that are statistically significant are indicated in bold (see Annex A3).
1. Multilevel regression model (student and school levels): Reading performance is regressed on the school resource variables as well as on socio-economic and demographic background variables presented in this table.

StatLink http://dx.doi.org/10.1787/888932343285

[Part 1/1]

Table IV.2.13a Within- and between-school variation in reading performance and variation explained by the learning environment

		Variance		Remaining variance						Variance decomposition expressed as a percentage of the average variance in student performance in reading across OECD countries			Within-school variance expressed as a percentage of the average variance in student performance in reading across OECD countries				Between-school variance expressed as a percentage of the average variance in student performance in reading across OECD countries			
		Empty (or fully unconditional) model[1]		Model with demographic and socio-economic background[2]		Model with learning environment and school climate[3]		Model with demographic and socio-economic background and with learning environment and school climate[4]		Total variance in student performance	Total variance within schools as a percentage of total variance	Total variance between schools as a percentage of total variance	Solely accounted for by students' and schools' socio-economic and demographic background	Solely accounted for by the learning environment	Jointly accounted for by students' and schools' socio-economic and demographic background and the learning environment	Remaining within-school variance	Solely accounted for by students' and schools' socio-economic and demographic background	Solely accounted for by the learning environment	Jointly accounted for by students' and schools' socio-economic and demographic background and the learning environment	Remaining between-school variance
		Within-school	Between-school	Within-school	Between-school	Within-school	Between-school	Within-school	Between-school	%	%	%	%	%	%	%	%	%	%	%
OECD	Australia	7 631	2 692	6 997	880	7 207	1 169	6 608	717	112	83	29	6.5	4.2	0.4	71.8	4.9	1.8	14.8	7.8
	Austria	4 454	5 588	4 255	2 262	4 385	4 722	4 213	1 926	108	48	60	1.9	0.5	0.3	45.8	30.4	3.7	5.8	20.9
	Belgium	4 833	5 343	4 612	1 643	4 793	4 492	4 575	1 447	111	53	58	2.4	0.4	0.0	49.7	33.1	2.1	7.1	15.7
	Canada	6 780	1 877	6 238	986	6 476	1 471	6 005	880	94	74	20	5.1	2.5	0.8	65.2	6.4	1.2	3.2	9.6
	Chile	4 005	4 893	3 886	1 219	3 965	3 185	3 847	894	97	44	53	1.3	0.4	0.0	41.8	24.9	3.5	15.0	9.7
	Czech Republic	4 428	4 249	4 136	1 135	4 404	2 477	4 100	829	94	48	46	3.3	0.4	-0.1	44.5	17.9	3.3	15.9	9.0
	Denmark	6 012	1 134	5 254	328	5 733	612	5 059	258	78	65	12	7.3	2.1	0.9	54.9	3.8	0.8	4.9	2.8
	Estonia	5 595	1 557	4 991	681	5 310	1 113	4 765	440	78	61	17	5.9	2.4	0.6	51.8	7.3	2.6	2.2	4.8
	Finland	6 993	665	5 641	458	6 668	520	5 464	387	83	76	7	13.1	1.9	1.6	59.3	1.4	0.8	0.8	4.2
	France	w	w	w	w	w	w	w	w	w	w	w	w	w	w	w	w	w	w	w
	Germany	3 890	5 890	3 558	1 708	3 789	3 397	3 509	1 509	106	42	64	3.0	0.5	0.6	38.1	20.5	2.2	24.9	16.4
	Greece	5 558	4 745	5 126	2 165	5 487	3 612	5 073	1 630	112	60	52	4.5	0.6	0.2	55.1	21.5	5.8	6.5	17.7
	Hungary	2 923	5 846	2 792	1 717	2 916	4 984	2 777	1 582	95	32	64	1.5	0.2	-0.1	30.2	37.0	1.5	7.9	17.2
	Iceland	8 186	1 348	7 186	1 015	7 696	879	6 866	741	104	89	15	9.0	3.5	1.8	74.6	1.5	3.0	2.1	8.0
	Ireland	6 966	2 805	6 408	1 145	6 689	1 438	6 157	703	106	76	30	5.8	2.7	0.3	66.9	8.0	4.8	10.0	7.6
	Israel	6 615	6 250	6 312	3 230	6 591	4 199	6 263	2 059	140	72	68	3.6	0.5	-0.3	68.0	23.2	12.7	9.6	22.4
	Italy	4 085	6 695	3 905	2 880	4 048	4 414	3 879	2 198	117	44	73	1.8	0.3	0.1	42.1	24.1	7.4	17.4	23.9
	Japan	5 386	5 087	5 248	2 255	5 299	1 804	5 143	1 091	114	59	55	1.7	1.2	-0.2	55.9	7.7	12.6	23.0	11.8
	Korea	5 283	2 741	4 829	1 038	5 197	1 683	4 745	711	87	57	30	4.9	0.9	0.0	51.5	10.6	3.6	7.9	7.7
	Luxembourg	6 906	5 335	6 112	610	6 811	2 148	5 977	541	133	75	58	9.1	1.5	-0.4	64.9	17.5	0.7	33.9	5.9
	Mexico	3 869	3 583	3 723	1 964	3 782	3 173	3 644	1 451	81	42	39	1.5	0.9	0.1	39.6	18.7	5.6	-1.1	15.8
	Netherlands	2 795	5 107	2 670	2 224	2 768	3 860	2 650	1 740	86	30	55	1.3	0.2	0.1	28.8	23.0	5.3	8.3	18.9
	New Zealand	8 228	2 622	6 974	530	7 805	1 234	6 677	441	118	89	28	12.3	3.2	1.4	72.5	8.6	1.0	14.1	4.8
	Norway	7 598	874	6 455	669	7 084	593	6 056	447	92	83	9	11.2	4.3	1.3	65.8	1.6	2.4	0.6	4.9
	Poland	6 869	1 585	5 582	458	6 601	1 363	5 470	423	92	75	17	12.3	1.2	1.7	59.4	10.2	0.4	2.0	4.6
	Portugal	5 191	2 565	4 666	883	5 084	2 282	4 591	781	84	56	28	5.4	0.8	0.3	49.9	16.3	1.1	2.0	8.5
	Slovak Republic	4 565	2 989	3 972	1 151	4 486	2 402	3 922	1 016	82	50	32	6.1	0.5	0.3	42.6	15.1	1.5	4.9	11.0
	Slovenia	3 102	4 142	2 941	1 818	3 051	3 205	2 895	1 322	79	34	45	1.7	0.5	0.1	31.4	20.4	5.4	4.8	14.4
	Spain	6 048	1 690	5 390	816	5 890	1 277	5 293	750	84	66	18	6.5	1.1	0.7	57.5	5.7	0.7	3.8	8.1
	Sweden	8 290	1 877	7 007	605	7 987	1 226	6 804	561	110	90	20	12.8	2.2	1.1	73.9	7.2	0.5	6.6	6.1
	Switzerland	5 652	2 740	5 115	1 100	5 609	2 219	5 087	1 041	91	61	30	5.7	0.3	0.1	55.2	12.8	0.6	5.0	11.3
	Turkey	3 245	6 536	2 958	1 375	3 180	4 235	2 913	1 013	106	35	71	2.9	0.5	0.2	31.6	35.0	3.9	21.1	11.0
	United Kingdom	6 684	2 775	6 275	635	6 292	1 651	5 939	622	103	73	30	3.8	3.7	0.6	64.5	11.2	0.1	12.1	6.8
	United States	6 476	3 638	6 041	838	6 260	2 100	5 860	585	110	70	40	4.3	2.0	0.4	63.6	16.4	2.7	14.0	6.4
	OECD average	5 591	3 616	5 068	1 285	5 435	2 398	4 934	992	100	61	39	5.4	1.5	0.4	53.6	15.3	3.2	9.4	10.8
Partners	Albania	7 105	3 127	6 150	1 339	6 796	2 641	5 964	1 208	111	77	34	9.0	2.0	1.3	64.8	15.6	1.4	3.9	13.1
	Argentina	5 523	8 456	5 201	3 238	5 525	5 961	5 198	2 871	152	60	92	3.6	0.0	-0.1	56.5	33.6	4.0	23.1	31.2
	Azerbaijan	3 459	2 490	3 287	2 054	3 376	1 931	3 201	1 484	65	38	27	1.9	0.9	0.0	34.8	4.9	6.2	-0.1	16.1
	Brazil	4 702	4 417	4 514	1 770	4 651	3 602	4 447	1 516	99	51	48	2.2	0.7	-0.2	48.3	22.7	2.8	6.1	16.5
	Bulgaria	6 439	6 418	5 794	2 053	6 317	5 855	5 705	1 780	140	70	70	6.7	1.0	0.4	62.0	44.3	3.0	3.1	19.3
	Colombia	4 813	3 162	4 711	688	4 704	2 034	4 580	598	87	52	34	1.3	1.4	-0.2	49.7	15.6	1.0	11.3	6.5
	Croatia	4 473	4 045	4 183	1 391	4 384	1 756	4 109	974	93	49	44	3.0	0.8	0.2	44.6	8.5	4.5	20.3	10.6
	Dubai (UAE)	5 439	5 732	5 121	2 472	5 248	4 834	4 980	1 968	121	59	62	2.9	1.5	0.5	54.1	31.1	5.5	4.3	21.4
	Hong Kong-China	4 360	3 143	4 183	1 270	4 257	1 666	4 097	804	82	47	34	1.7	0.9	0.2	44.5	9.4	5.1	11.0	8.7
	Indonesia	2 298	1 749	2 117	1 181	2 294	1 445	2 108	991	44	25	19	2.0	0.1	-0.1	22.9	4.9	2.1	1.2	10.8
	Jordan	5 461	3 312	5 186	1 727	5 221	2 299	4 977	1 308	95	59	36	2.7	2.3	0.3	54.1	10.8	4.6	6.4	14.2
	Kazakhstan	5 078	2 887	4 456	1 542	4 866	2 287	4 303	1 272	87	55	31	6.1	1.7	0.6	46.7	11.0	2.9	3.6	13.8
	Kyrgyzstan	5 901	3 266	5 126	1 398	5 667	2 143	4 915	1 169	100	64	35	8.2	2.3	0.2	53.4	10.6	2.5	9.7	12.7
	Latvia	5 200	1 391	4 491	634	5 004	1 133	4 374	415	72	57	15	6.9	1.3	0.9	47.5	7.8	2.4	0.4	4.5
	Lithuania	5 190	1 864	4 263	828	5 072	1 532	4 179	708	77	56	20	9.7	0.9	0.4	45.4	8.9	1.3	2.3	7.7
	Macao-China	4 179	2 882	4 000	775	4 166	1 051	3 986	330	77	45	31	2.0	0.1	0.0	43.3	7.8	4.8	15.1	3.6
	Montenegro	5 587	3 150	5 124	683	5 423	1 356	4 983	471	95	61	34	4.8	1.5	0.3	54.1	9.6	2.3	17.2	5.1
	Panama	4 213	5 942	4 103	2 647	4 120	4 826	4 026	2 334	110	46	65	1.0	0.8	0.2	43.7	27.1	3.4	8.7	25.4
	Peru	4 623	5 886	4 524	1 316	4 441	4 893	4 351	1 026	114	50	64	1.0	1.9	0.1	47.3	42.0	3.2	7.6	11.1
	Qatar	5 891	6 676	5 520	3 383	5 704	5 602	5 408	2 757	137	64	73	3.2	1.2	0.8	58.7	30.9	6.8	4.9	29.9
	Romania	3 832	4 057	3 678	2 308	3 680	2 797	3 559	1 610	86	42	44	1.3	1.3	0.4	38.7	12.9	7.6	6.1	17.5
	Russian Federation	5 826	1 965	5 193	900	5 618	1 562	5 052	761	85	63	21	6.1	1.5	0.7	54.9	8.7	1.5	2.9	8.3
	Serbia	4 123	3 909	3 954	1 840	4 043	2 926	3 883	1 654	87	45	42	1.7	0.8	0.1	42.2	13.8	2.0	8.7	18.0
	Shanghai-China	4 095	2 551	3 813	701	4 034	1 539	3 745	592	72	44	28	3.1	0.7	-0.1	40.7	10.3	1.2	9.8	6.4
	Singapore	6 195	3 387	5 612	782	5 977	1 631	5 445	665	104	67	37	5.8	1.8	0.6	59.1	10.5	1.3	17.8	7.2
	Chinese Taipei	5 808	2 772	5 070	1 306	5 597	2 070	4 920	898	93	63	30	7.4	1.6	0.7	53.4	12.7	4.4	3.2	9.8
	Thailand	3 052	1 231	2 706	816	2 920	1 062	2 626	657	47	33	13	3.2	0.9	0.6	28.5	4.4	1.7	0.1	7.1
	Trinidad and Tobago	5 148	8 320	4 720	2 527	5 011	4 749	4 640	2 135	146	56	90	4.0	0.9	0.6	50.4	28.4	4.3	34.5	23.2
	Tunisia	4 291	3 034	4 174	1 640	4 254	2 547	4 133	1 402	80	47	33	1.3	0.4	0.0	44.9	12.4	2.6	2.7	15.2
	Uruguay	5 835	4 807	5 342	968	5 843	2 841	5 314	828	116	63	52	5.7	0.3	-0.4	57.7	21.9	1.5	19.8	9.0

1. Multilevel regression model consists of the student and school levels.
2. Multilevel regression model: Reading performance is regressed on the variables of demographic and socio-economic background.
3. Multilevel regression model: Reading performance is regressed on the variables of leaning environment and school climate.
4. Multilevel regression model: Reading performance is regressed on the variables of demographic and socio-economic background and on the variables of learning environment and school climate.

StatLink http://dx.doi.org/10.1787/888932343285

[Part 1/1]

Table IV.2.13b Relationships between the learning environment and reading performance

		Learning environment and school climate (student level)[1]						Learning environment and school climate (school level)[1]													
		Index of teacher-student relations (higher values indicate better relationships)		Index of disciplinary climate (higher values indicate better climate)		Index of teachers' stimulation of reading engagement (higher values indicate more stimulation)		Index of teacher-student relations (school average)		Index of disciplinary climate (school average)		Index of student-related factors affecting school climate (higher values indicate a positive student behaviour)		Index of teacher-related factors affecting school climate (higher values indicate a positive teacher behaviour)		Index of teachers' stimulation of reading engagement (school average)		Parents expect the school to set high academic standards and pressure for students to achieve them		Index of school principal's leadership (higher values indicate more leadership roles are taken)	
		Change in score	S.E.	Change in score	S.E.	Change in score	S.E.	Change in score	S.E.	Change in score	S.E.	Change in score	S.E.	Change in score	S.E.	Change in score	S.E.	Change in score	S.E.	Change in score	S.E.
OECD	Australia	**19.3**	(1.1)	**9.6**	(1.3)	0.0	(1.1)	**49.5**	(13.4)	**44.7**	(10.4)	-4.2	(4.5)	**15.5**	(4.4)	2.5	(17.3)	9.0	(7.9)	-1.1	(2.5)
	Austria	**5.1**	(1.3)	**4.3**	(1.2)	-2.5	(1.5)	**-31.8**	(14.3)	**52.4**	(9.2)	-8.8	(6.4)	**16.3**	(7.1)	**34.0**	(12.0)	1.6	(34.1)	0.0	(6.6)
	Belgium	**4.2**	(1.4)	**3.9**	(1.3)	2.4	(1.3)	-0.8	(20.4)	**35.4**	(16.5)	-11.3	(8.6)	**43.9**	(5.9)	-7.8	(22.2)	**66.8**	(19.2)	-11.2	(9.1)
	Canada	**14.6**	(1.1)	**5.7**	(1.4)	**3.0**	(1.1)	5.3	(6.9)	7.3	(7.8)	-0.5	(3.0)	**8.4**	(3.8)	11.3	(7.2)	**26.7**	(5.0)	-0.6	(2.4)
	Chile	**6.1**	(1.4)	2.5	(1.5)	-1.2	(1.4)	12.1	(13.4)	-12.4	(18.7)	-11.3	(7.1)	**28.8**	(7.5)	-12.3	(12.6)	**66.0**	(16.8)	-0.4	(6.2)
	Czech Republic	**8.0**	(1.6)	2.5	(1.5)	**-3.3**	(1.6)	-1.7	(12.4)	**31.8**	(7.2)	**-18.7**	(6.0)	**31.4**	(6.3)	26.6	(14.8)	**39.5**	(9.5)	0.4	(4.8)
	Denmark	**16.8**	(1.6)	2.8	(1.9)	-0.1	(1.8)	**29.2**	(11.4)	**24.4**	(6.6)	-1.6	(2.8)	**11.0**	(3.2)	**-24.8**	(10.0)	**30.2**	(5.5)	-0.5	(5.2)
	Estonia	**17.4**	(1.9)	**9.6**	(2.5)	**-6.3**	(2.0)	32.3	(17.0)	11.3	(11.8)	**-9.4**	(4.6)	**21.9**	(6.4)	-9.4	(16.1)	-4.6	(19.7)	2.8	(3.2)
	Finland	**20.5**	(1.8)	-0.7	(2.0)	**-7.7**	(2.2)	**30.6**	(11.7)	12.2	(7.0)	7.4	(4.2)	-0.7	(4.1)	19.6	(14.7)	12.6	(13.1)	**-7.3**	(2.9)
	France	w	w	w	w	w	w	w	w	w	w	w	w	w	w	w	w	w	w	w	w
	Germany	**6.3**	(1.4)	**5.7**	(1.5)	0.5	(1.6)	**-52.0**	(16.1)	2.0	(18.3)	**-24.7**	(7.4)	**60.5**	(7.0)	**40.1**	(18.4)	24.2	(19.5)	-7.9	(7.2)
	Greece	**6.9**	(1.9)	2.3	(2.1)	3.4	(2.2)	38.1	(23.4)	28.8	(16.7)	-11.4	(7.9)	**23.9**	(8.1)	-24.0	(21.4)	**43.3**	(18.2)	-11.8	(7.2)
	Hungary	1.1	(1.4)	-0.1	(1.7)	3.1	(1.6)	-23.5	(17.7)	23.3	(18.9)	-13.0	(9.5)	**22.4**	(8.0)	-24.7	(21.0)	26.8	(23.9)	-5.7	(7.9)
	Iceland	**19.5**	(1.8)	**7.6**	(2.7)	**-4.5**	(1.7)	**33.4**	(9.0)	**28.2**	(12.2)	-5.6	(5.5)	10.5	(7.5)	-2.5	(12.0)	-6.4	(8.9)	-7.0	(4.0)
	Ireland	**14.9**	(2.3)	**9.5**	(2.0)	-3.2	(2.0)	**82.3**	(21.9)	**32.8**	(10.2)	1.6	(4.9)	12.0	(6.2)	-22.5	(17.8)	**26.1**	(8.2)	-4.7	(4.2)
	Israel	**7.4**	(1.6)	2.8	(2.2)	-3.2	(1.8)	**51.4**	(25.4)	22.9	(22.1)	-12.1	(12.6)	19.0	(9.9)	**-95.2**	(14.8)	**39.3**	(14.5)	**-24.0**	(8.7)
	Italy	**3.8**	(0.9)	**5.5**	(0.9)	-0.7	(0.9)	-24.2	(18.3)	**43.3**	(12.6)	**-15.7**	(6.5)	**34.8**	(6.4)	-13.2	(13.6)	**36.2**	(15.1)	**-16.3**	(5.0)
	Japan	**10.1**	(1.6)	**4.3**	(1.8)	0.5	(1.4)	**87.4**	(20.0)	**30.4**	(15.1)	**-17.1**	(6.9)	**30.4**	(7.0)	2.8	(15.3)	**47.6**	(9.2)	-7.9	(5.0)
	Korea	**12.2**	(3.2)	0.3	(3.0)	-1.4	(3.0)	27.2	(31.9)	40.1	(21.6)	-13.2	(9.0)	**26.8**	(8.3)	-40.8	(31.6)	**39.2**	(14.0)	-4.1	(5.2)
	Luxembourg	**3.1**	(1.6)	**9.5**	(2.2)	0.5	(1.6)	-64.7	(34.6)	54.8	(33.1)	**-27.5**	(13.6)	**35.6**	(12.4)	76.1	(48.2)	-0.1	(22.0)	12.9	(7.7)
	Mexico	**6.9**	(0.9)	**7.0**	(1.1)	**2.7**	(1.1)	**29.0**	(9.6)	15.9	(12.1)	-6.5	(5.0)	**10.4**	(5.3)	-8.4	(10.6)	4.8	(11.1)	**11.3**	(3.5)
	Netherlands	**4.8**	(1.4)	1.1	(1.2)	**-5.6**	(1.4)	34.0	(27.4)	**54.6**	(20.1)	**-44.8**	(16.0)	**46.9**	(8.7)	-5.4	(20.4)	29.0	(17.1)	12.6	(12.2)
	New Zealand	**16.2**	(2.0)	**10.6**	(2.5)	**3.7**	(1.8)	24.3	(15.0)	**37.8**	(12.8)	-4.2	(6.5)	**11.4**	(5.3)	-10.0	(15.3)	**52.6**	(8.4)	-5.8	(3.9)
	Norway	**21.2**	(1.9)	**6.2**	(2.1)	-1.3	(2.2)	16.9	(14.3)	12.2	(6.9)	4.2	(5.1)	-1.4	(5.8)	10.7	(15.7)	**30.7**	(6.5)	-2.2	(5.0)
	Poland	**4.8**	(2.2)	**7.2**	(2.1)	**12.6**	(1.9)	16.8	(17.3)	16.3	(10.7)	-2.7	(4.5)	9.2	(5.2)	-19.7	(23.5)	**31.2**	(10.2)	-4.6	(5.1)
	Portugal	**5.6**	(1.6)	**9.5**	(1.7)	0.6	(1.9)	20.0	(13.9)	8.0	(14.8)	5.3	(6.1)	2.0	(5.9)	10.0	(23.3)	**39.1**	(17.1)	-7.8	(6.4)
	Slovak Republic	**7.9**	(1.6)	**5.8**	(1.8)	0.9	(1.7)	16.1	(14.0)	**41.5**	(10.1)	**-14.7**	(6.0)	**14.6**	(6.8)	**-34.6**	(11.9)	18.0	(13.3)	**-13.9**	(5.7)
	Slovenia	**3.8**	(1.2)	1.5	(1.1)	**3.2**	(1.1)	-16.5	(15.8)	**21.5**	(9.4)	10.2	(7.2)	1.2	(8.3)	23.4	(13.9)	**27.4**	(10.2)	-1.5	(5.5)
	Spain	**7.9**	(1.0)	**8.8**	(1.1)	0.7	(1.2)	**-16.9**	(8.1)	**24.5**	(6.1)	-3.3	(3.1)	**15.3**	(2.5)	2.2	(6.2)	10.0	(7.7)	**7.3**	(2.3)
	Sweden	**15.8**	(1.9)	1.4	(2.0)	2.2	(2.4)	2.5	(12.7)	**27.6**	(12.5)	2.8	(4.5)	11.0	(6.0)	28.7	(16.6)	**14.5**	(7.1)	-6.0	(4.4)
	Switzerland	**3.9**	(1.1)	**5.6**	(1.7)	**-5.1**	(1.8)	**-24.2**	(9.2)	**39.3**	(12.5)	1.8	(6.5)	**10.5**	(5.1)	13.3	(17.0)	-7.1	(10.5)	3.4	(4.5)
	Turkey	**4.8**	(1.3)	2.7	(1.7)	2.7	(1.7)	-24.0	(24.8)	**76.6**	(20.2)	15.4	(16.2)	-13.9	(13.5)	8.1	(22.4)	**76.3**	(31.4)	18.7	(10.1)
	United Kingdom	**14.2**	(1.6)	**12.7**	(1.5)	**3.7**	(1.8)	-17.0	(17.1)	28.6	(15.3)	-1.3	(7.4)	**17.5**	(7.9)	18.8	(14.3)	**27.4**	(9.6)	-5.5	(3.4)
	United States	**6.9**	(2.1)	**12.6**	(2.0)	3.2	(1.8)	-9.2	(24.5)	24.0	(23.7)	-20.7	(12.2)	**40.8**	(12.5)	31.9	(24.0)	10.9	(19.3)	-10.7	(8.9)
	OECD average	**9.8**	(0.3)	**5.5**	(0.3)	0.1	(0.3)	**10.1**	(3.2)	**28.6**	(2.7)	**-7.7**	(1.4)	**19.0**	(1.3)	0.1	(3.3)	**26.9**	(2.7)	**-3.0**	(1.1)
Partners	Albania	**15.2**	(2.3)	**10.3**	(2.6)	2.3	(2.1)	21.5	(27.2)	-1.1	(21.7)	-3.3	(8.7)	-3.8	(9.1)	9.7	(23.5)	**39.4**	(14.5)	-5.2	(5.4)
	Argentina	-1.6	(1.8)	2.3	(1.6)	1.4	(2.0)	**-62.9**	(27.6)	6.6	(17.8)	-11.4	(9.0)	**33.9**	(8.4)	-22.0	(26.4)	47.0	(31.7)	2.8	(10.0)
	Azerbaijan	1.1	(1.5)	**8.3**	(1.7)	**4.1**	(1.0)	-15.9	(16.4)	**61.2**	(16.9)	-1.7	(5.1)	3.8	(6.0)	-12.6	(11.3)	**-23.1**	(10.4)	2.2	(3.1)
	Brazil	**6.8**	(1.1)	**6.6**	(1.5)	-0.7	(1.2)	11.6	(12.2)	9.6	(12.0)	-1.2	(3.8)	**18.4**	(4.5)	**-23.8**	(11.5)	**37.9**	(13.7)	6.9	(3.7)
	Bulgaria	**5.3**	(1.8)	**7.9**	(2.1)	3.5	(1.8)	-19.6	(24.6)	15.6	(21.4)	-18.1	(9.6)	**25.5**	(10.4)	24.2	(25.5)	42.7	(24.3)	-3.9	(10.7)
	Colombia	0.2	(1.7)	**15.0**	(1.9)	**4.4**	(1.8)	**-85.8**	(11.7)	28.0	(18.1)	3.8	(5.5)	8.4	(5.3)	24.1	(17.1)	-23.1	(14.8)	5.1	(4.8)
	Croatia	-2.9	(1.8)	**8.9**	(1.8)	**5.5**	(1.5)	**-43.4**	(18.0)	**72.9**	(12.1)	**-16.5**	(5.9)	**34.5**	(6.6)	-53.8	(37.8)	**33.3**	(16.9)	7.6	(5.1)
	Dubai (UAE)	**9.9**	(1.2)	**7.4**	(1.5)	**-2.4**	(1.1)	-17.0	(17.8)	**61.3**	(12.8)	3.1	(8.1)	**16.4**	(7.5)	-13.1	(15.5)	-0.8	(11.2)	-1.1	(5.6)
	Hong Kong-China	**5.4**	(1.7)	**7.2**	(1.7)	**4.7**	(1.5)	**88.4**	(20.0)	**83.7**	(15.3)	3.9	(7.0)	**17.2**	(5.6)	**-52.6**	(17.3)	c	c	**-8.4**	(3.5)
	Indonesia	0.3	(1.5)	**3.1**	(1.5)	-0.8	(1.1)	-22.3	(16.0)	-9.2	(8.8)	-3.1	(5.4)	**16.3**	(6.2)	**-24.9**	(10.1)	7.5	(8.1)	-3.2	(3.8)
	Jordan	**11.7**	(1.4)	**3.8**	(1.8)	**3.4**	(1.5)	**80.1**	(22.5)	4.6	(11.0)	-1.2	(6.1)	5.0	(6.6)	6.7	(17.1)	0.1	(10.8)	**12.8**	(4.3)
	Kazakhstan	**8.1**	(1.8)	**13.3**	(1.8)	1.6	(1.4)	**-52.0**	(13.1)	**29.2**	(13.4)	7.7	(6.2)	-2.4	(5.4)	13.2	(9.7)	**36.9**	(13.8)	-4.8	(5.8)
	Kyrgyzstan	**5.6**	(1.7)	**17.3**	(1.7)	2.3	(1.5)	**-56.0**	(15.8)	**65.9**	(19.0)	4.3	(5.6)	8.0	(5.1)	-23.5	(14.0)	-8.3	(8.7)	5.6	(5.7)
	Latvia	**13.6**	(2.0)	**7.3**	(2.4)	0.9	(2.1)	5.5	(13.7)	-1.2	(9.4)	-3.6	(7.1)	12.2	(7.4)	-1.7	(9.7)	**51.9**	(10.1)	-4.0	(5.8)
	Lithuania	**6.8**	(1.3)	**7.9**	(1.9)	0.7	(1.7)	-10.0	(9.0)	**33.8**	(9.0)	-11.7	(6.5)	11.1	(7.0)	-8.2	(13.4)	**25.8**	(11.4)	-8.3	(5.0)
	Macao-China	2.6	(1.6)	**5.8**	(1.9)	-0.9	(1.6)	20.6	(32.7)	**108.3**	(15.0)	0.5	(10.2)	5.7	(8.3)	-12.6	(28.7)	c	c	-0.3	(6.0)
	Montenegro	**-4.3**	(1.4)	**11.7**	(1.9)	**7.5**	(1.3)	**-84.5**	(25.3)	**80.5**	(19.8)	21.5	(12.4)	-9.4	(10.8)	9.2	(29.5)	c	c	6.1	(9.1)
	Panama	**4.9**	(1.9)	**8.8**	(2.4)	0.5	(1.7)	**-58.9**	(23.7)	**49.9**	(20.2)	16.2	(9.3)	-0.5	(10.8)	-9.1	(32.8)	-1.5	(27.3)	**15.6**	(7.1)
	Peru	**5.5**	(1.7)	**15.6**	(1.9)	0.6	(1.7)	-3.2	(19.2)	44.0	(23.8)	0.3	(7.1)	12.8	(7.3)	10.5	(20.9)	12.9	(13.2)	**22.1**	(5.8)
	Qatar	**9.7**	(0.9)	**5.0**	(1.1)	**-1.8**	(0.8)	**41.0**	(18.8)	**59.3**	(19.0)	6.9	(10.1)	-2.6	(10.0)	-1.2	(15.7)	27.5	(14.7)	-0.5	(5.7)
	Romania	**7.4**	(1.7)	**9.1**	(2.4)	**3.3**	(1.6)	9.0	(14.7)	**73.6**	(18.9)	-11.7	(9.5)	7.8	(8.4)	23.0	(21.8)	32.8	(18.2)	0.8	(7.3)
	Russian Federation	**12.6**	(1.6)	**5.2**	(1.7)	**5.3**	(1.5)	-15.7	(15.7)	**28.4**	(7.3)	-0.1	(4.9)	7.2	(4.1)	11.4	(10.2)	**23.7**	(9.6)	0.4	(5.0)
	Serbia	**-5.7**	(1.4)	**9.0**	(1.7)	**3.8**	(1.3)	**-46.5**	(20.7)	**46.0**	(21.9)	12.7	(12.8)	0.1	(11.6)	-1.8	(17.6)	28.0	(21.4)	-4.6	(9.9)
	Shanghai-China	**7.7**	(1.5)	3.7	(2.0)	2.1	(1.8)	**70.0**	(19.3)	**51.0**	(8.1)	-3.0	(7.6)	2.6	(5.8)	-8.7	(21.4)	2.6	(14.6)	0.0	(5.5)
	Singapore	**8.7**	(1.7)	**15.7**	(1.8)	**-4.3**	(1.4)	38.8	(20.0)	**83.8**	(15.4)	-0.3	(6.4)	**18.1**	(6.9)	**-40.1**	(17.3)	**23.1**	(7.9)	-7.1	(4.1)
	Chinese Taipei	**11.0**	(1.6)	**12.5**	(2.8)	-0.9	(1.9)	-22.6	(38.5)	34.0	(22.6)	13.8	(8.6)	0.6	(6.4)	2.8	(33.4)	4.1	(15.3)	-3.4	(5.6)
	Thailand	**4.8**	(1.8)	**10.9**	(1.6)	**5.6**	(1.9)	4.3	(10.3)	25.6	(14.6)	0.6	(5.0)	1.0	(4.6)	8.9	(8.9)	8.0	(7.4)	5.3	(4.2)
	Trinidad and Tobago	**8.2**	(1.1)	**4.4**	(1.4)	1.7	(1.2)	3.3	(28.3)	**79.5**	(20.3)	**-17.7**	(7.5)	**39.6**	(8.8)	-5.1	(21.6)	**82.5**	(14.2)	-5.7	(5.8)
	Tunisia	**6.4**	(1.1)	**3.2**	(1.4)	1.6	(1.3)	**48.4**	(17.2)	-0.5	(19.6)	-13.6	(8.3)	12.7	(8.3)	**-31.5**	(14.0)	27.7	(16.0)	-6.2	(3.8)
	Uruguay	0.8	(1.5)	**4.5**	(1.8)	**3.6**	(1.6)	**-94.0**	(15.2)	**21.7**	(10.4)	**-13.5**	(5.6)	**22.1**	(5.2)	29.9	(17.4)	**68.1**	(25.8)	1.2	(5.0)

Note: Values that are statistically significant are indicated in bold (see Annex A3).
1. Multilevel regression model (student and school levels): Reading performance is regressed on the learning environment variables presented in this table.
StatLink http://dx.doi.org/10.1787/888932343285

[Part 1/2]

Table IV.2.13c Relationships between the learning environment and reading performance, accounting for students' and schools' socio-economic and demographic background

		Learning environment and school climate (student level)[1]						Learning environment and school climate (school level)[1]													
		Index of teacher-student relations (higher values indicate better relationships)		Index of disciplinary climate (higher values indicate better climate)		Index of teachers' stimulation of reading engagement (higher values indicate more stimulation)		Index of teacher-student relations (school average)		Index of disciplinary climate (school average)		Index of student-related factors affecting school climate (higher values indicate a positive student behaviour)		Index of teacher-related factors affecting school climate (higher values indicate a positive teacher behaviour)		Index of teachers' stimulation of reading engagement (school average)		Parents expect the school to set high academic standards and pressure for students to achieve them		Index of school principal's leadership (higher values indicate more leadership roles are taken)	
		Change in score	S.E.	Change in score	S.E.	Change in score	S.E.	Change in score	S.E.	Change in score	S.E.	Change in score	S.E.	Change in score	S.E.	Change in score	S.E.	Change in score	S.E.	Change in score	S.E.
OECD	Australia	**17.8**	(1.0)	**8.2**	(1.1)	-0.7	(1.1)	**24.4**	(11.8)	**29.7**	(9.5)	-2.0	(3.2)	4.1	(3.7)	-2.9	(12.9)	2.0	(5.8)	2.0	(2.2)
	Austria	**4.1**	(1.3)	**4.0**	(1.2)	-1.6	(1.5)	**-19.4**	(9.4)	**23.2**	(7.8)	-6.9	(5.7)	**11.0**	(4.4)	20.4	(11.8)	-19.5	(23.4)	-2.9	(4.3)
	Belgium	**3.7**	(1.3)	**4.1**	(1.3)	2.3	(1.2)	7.4	(13.7)	7.5	(11.4)	-1.5	(4.7)	**14.4**	(4.6)	-4.0	(12.4)	11.4	(8.8)	-6.4	(4.9)
	Canada	**12.6**	(1.1)	**4.8**	(1.3)	**2.1**	(1.1)	11.5	(6.0)	5.6	(7.4)	1.4	(2.4)	5.6	(3.1)	2.2	(6.0)	**10.5**	(4.2)	2.5	(2.2)
	Chile	**6.1**	(1.3)	2.0	(1.4)	-1.2	(1.4)	15.4	(10.3)	6.8	(10.4)	2.4	(4.5)	**9.8**	(3.8)	-18.0	(10.1)	8.5	(8.6)	0.6	(3.2)
	Czech Republic	**6.9**	(1.5)	1.8	(1.4)	-2.7	(1.5)	**23.3**	(7.4)	**14.9**	(5.1)	-6.4	(3.8)	**11.8**	(4.0)	13.7	(8.7)	7.3	(5.9)	0.3	(3.1)
	Denmark	**14.5**	(1.5)	2.6	(1.8)	-1.1	(1.7)	11.6	(7.7)	**17.2**	(5.5)	3.1	(2.8)	-0.3	(3.3)	-10.8	(7.4)	2.8	(4.9)	5.0	(3.5)
	Estonia	**13.7**	(1.9)	**9.6**	(2.3)	**-6.6**	(1.8)	**42.4**	(10.8)	7.1	(7.0)	-3.2	(3.9)	**12.8**	(4.4)	-14.3	(13.1)	-7.5	(9.3)	-1.9	(3.4)
	Finland	**15.8**	(1.7)	0.1	(1.8)	**-4.4**	(1.9)	20.3	(10.6)	8.0	(5.8)	5.3	(3.7)	-1.2	(3.6)	14.6	(12.2)	-2.7	(8.9)	-5.1	(2.7)
	France	w	w	w	w	w	w	w	w	w	w	w	w	w	w	w	w	w	w	w	w
	Germany	**4.3**	(1.3)	**4.8**	(1.4)	1.1	(1.5)	-8.1	(14.6)	1.8	(14.3)	-7.5	(4.9)	**18.3**	(5.8)	2.7	(16.2)	11.6	(10.2)	-0.3	(5.6)
	Greece	**5.6**	(1.8)	1.8	(2.0)	3.2	(2.0)	**47.7**	(20.6)	**35.7**	(13.9)	-6.8	(5.9)	**18.0**	(7.2)	-15.2	(15.6)	1.3	(9.1)	-5.9	(5.1)
	Hungary	0.6	(1.4)	-0.3	(1.6)	**3.5**	(1.6)	-17.7	(14.5)	14.3	(14.5)	-9.8	(6.0)	4.7	(5.2)	19.4	(13.4)	3.2	(15.0)	3.6	(5.1)
	Iceland	**15.9**	(1.7)	**6.8**	(2.4)	**-5.0**	(1.7)	**26.7**	(8.8)	21.2	(10.9)	-5.8	(5.1)	12.5	(6.7)	-4.0	(12.8)	-6.6	(7.4)	-5.8	(4.9)
	Ireland	**12.6**	(2.1)	**8.6**	(1.8)	-3.5	(1.9)	**77.6**	(16.7)	9.0	(7.8)	0.4	(3.5)	1.6	(5.3)	-20.2	(14.4)	11.3	(6.7)	-2.0	(3.5)
	Israel	**6.2**	(1.5)	2.0	(2.1)	**-3.6**	(1.8)	**40.2**	(20.2)	**28.7**	(12.0)	**-18.0**	(8.7)	**21.1**	(8.1)	**-68.2**	(13.8)	7.1	(9.6)	**-21.3**	(5.9)
	Italy	**3.0**	(0.9)	**4.8**	(0.8)	-0.7	(1.0)	-12.0	(13.8)	**22.1**	(9.6)	0.0	(5.5)	**18.4**	(4.6)	6.0	(11.3)	**18.9**	(9.5)	**-16.9**	(3.6)
	Japan	**9.6**	(1.5)	3.1	(1.8)	1.1	(1.4)	**60.7**	(15.0)	**34.0**	(9.5)	-9.0	(5.9)	**22.4**	(6.1)	-14.0	(13.7)	11.5	(7.9)	-0.3	(3.5)
	Korea	**11.1**	(2.9)	0.0	(2.8)	-0.7	(2.9)	32.3	(28.8)	13.7	(14.6)	3.5	(6.3)	**11.4**	(5.5)	-45.7	(23.9)	23.8	(14.3)	-5.9	(3.2)
	Luxembourg	**3.1**	(1.4)	**9.1**	(1.9)	-0.1	(1.3)	29.1	(22.7)	-6.5	(19.4)	-4.0	(9.1)	0.8	(8.9)	-47.9	(25.5)	-15.8	(9.2)	0.1	(3.4)
	Mexico	**5.7**	(0.9)	**6.5**	(1.1)	**2.7**	(1.1)	**19.5**	(8.0)	**36.5**	(9.7)	-4.8	(3.5)	**11.3**	(4.3)	2.7	(7.6)	2.6	(8.4)	1.3	(2.7)
	Netherlands	**4.5**	(1.4)	0.8	(1.2)	**-4.9**	(1.4)	18.9	(25.0)	**60.2**	(19.3)	-11.5	(9.3)	**17.6**	(7.3)	-20.1	(16.1)	-16.0	(13.4)	7.2	(5.9)
	New Zealand	**13.2**	(1.9)	**8.6**	(2.0)	3.1	(1.7)	15.6	(12.7)	**19.8**	(8.7)	-0.6	(4.9)	4.2	(4.7)	**-19.0**	(9.2)	**16.4**	(5.7)	-3.4	(2.6)
	Norway	**18.1**	(1.9)	**5.6**	(1.9)	-0.1	(2.1)	18.5	(11.6)	**16.0**	(6.2)	5.8	(4.3)	0.8	(5.4)	5.3	(12.8)	**21.4**	(5.5)	-4.1	(4.6)
	Poland	**3.8**	(1.9)	**5.1**	(1.9)	**8.3**	(1.7)	-1.0	(8.4)	**12.3**	(6.2)	-1.9	(2.6)	5.8	(3.8)	1.7	(12.2)	-0.2	(6.8)	-1.8	(3.0)
	Portugal	**4.0**	(1.6)	**8.1**	(1.5)	-1.1	(1.9)	**32.7**	(11.3)	17.3	(9.9)	1.5	(3.9)	-0.2	(3.9)	-14.8	(10.9)	-2.2	(8.1)	-6.1	(3.6)
	Slovak Republic	**6.2**	(1.5)	**4.7**	(1.6)	0.3	(1.6)	6.5	(10.5)	**27.1**	(7.5)	-8.4	(4.9)	3.8	(5.6)	-8.6	(9.4)	-1.3	(10.9)	-5.6	(4.3)
	Slovenia	**3.9**	(1.1)	1.4	(1.1)	**2.3**	(1.0)	4.3	(13.2)	**13.1**	(6.4)	**16.2**	(5.9)	-0.6	(6.1)	16.0	(10.2)	16.9	(8.7)	1.6	(4.3)
	Spain	**6.1**	(1.0)	**7.2**	(1.0)	0.7	(1.1)	-3.6	(5.7)	**20.7**	(5.4)	-2.4	(2.7)	**4.8**	(2.3)	-4.4	(5.3)	-4.7	(6.7)	1.0	(2.2)
	Sweden	**12.1**	(1.7)	1.8	(1.8)	2.7	(2.1)	-1.2	(9.9)	9.0	(8.8)	0.8	(3.3)	3.8	(4.1)	24.4	(14.9)	-2.5	(5.8)	-4.1	(3.1)
	Switzerland	**3.1**	(1.0)	**4.1**	(1.6)	-3.1	(1.8)	-2.4	(9.0)	16.0	(9.2)	2.8	(5.1)	3.3	(3.9)	-3.4	(14.2)	-10.9	(6.9)	-1.4	(3.3)
	Turkey	**4.3**	(1.3)	2.8	(1.5)	1.8	(1.6)	24.8	(15.2)	20.8	(13.9)	0.3	(6.7)	0.5	(6.2)	15.6	(9.7)	-1.8	(17.5)	0.8	(4.2)
	United Kingdom	**12.5**	(1.5)	**11.6**	(1.4)	2.9	(1.8)	-2.8	(9.7)	-0.7	(8.5)	0.9	(4.2)	-0.5	(4.6)	8.4	(9.8)	8.3	(6.5)	-1.4	(2.7)
	United States	**4.6**	(2.0)	**11.9**	(2.0)	2.2	(1.8)	8.0	(17.2)	26.5	(17.9)	-5.7	(6.9)	8.1	(7.5)	3.1	(17.6)	-10.8	(8.3)	-3.2	(3.8)
	OECD average	**8.2**	(0.3)	**4.8**	(0.3)	0.0	(0.3)	**16.7**	(2.5)	**17.8**	(1.9)	**-2.2**	(0.9)	**7.9**	(0.9)	**-5.4**	(2.3)	2.9	(1.7)	**-2.4**	(0.7)
Partners	Albania	**10.9**	(2.2)	**9.7**	(2.6)	1.7	(2.0)	7.1	(21.0)	19.9	(13.2)	-6.7	(5.8)	-1.4	(6.6)	8.1	(22.7)	15.1	(12.5)	3.2	(4.9)
	Argentina	-2.0	(1.7)	2.3	(1.6)	1.1	(1.8)	-0.9	(20.8)	24.8	(12.8)	-7.1	(6.0)	**16.9**	(6.7)	-13.6	(18.6)	-2.3	(21.4)	3.0	(6.4)
	Azerbaijan	0.5	(1.4)	**8.7**	(1.7)	**3.8**	(1.0)	-6.9	(16.6)	**61.0**	(17.0)	-1.3	(5.0)	2.5	(6.1)	-5.6	(10.7)	**-20.4**	(9.0)	0.1	(2.8)
	Brazil	**6.4**	(1.0)	**6.3**	(1.5)	-0.8	(1.2)	**21.8**	(9.6)	**19.1**	(8.0)	**-8.3**	(2.7)	**12.0**	(3.4)	**-23.7**	(8.0)	6.5	(8.2)	2.1	(2.1)
	Bulgaria	**3.9**	(1.7)	**7.1**	(2.1)	2.5	(1.6)	**30.9**	(12.4)	14.7	(11.0)	-3.9	(5.6)	4.9	(5.4)	-1.0	(15.3)	**24.4**	(10.3)	1.5	(6.2)
	Colombia	0.0	(1.7)	**14.7**	(1.8)	**3.5**	(1.7)	-9.5	(9.5)	**23.3**	(9.8)	-1.9	(3.0)	3.9	(3.4)	4.7	(10.2)	-13.1	(7.7)	-2.9	(2.5)
	Croatia	-1.9	(1.7)	**7.6**	(1.7)	**4.4**	(1.5)	-17.8	(14.6)	**40.2**	(11.3)	**-9.3**	(4.0)	**18.6**	(5.2)	-21.8	(22.6)	-5.2	(11.6)	-1.3	(4.5)
	Dubai (UAE)	**9.3**	(1.2)	**6.8**	(1.4)	**-2.8**	(1.1)	9.4	(13.1)	**47.8**	(8.9)	1.4	(5.3)	5.3	(5.4)	-16.5	(11.4)	1.3	(7.6)	-3.5	(3.7)
	Hong Kong-China	**5.4**	(1.6)	**6.2**	(1.7)	**4.3**	(1.6)	**37.8**	(11.0)	**63.8**	(6.1)	-0.5	(4.0)	11.5	(15.7)	**-54.0**	(15.7)	c	c	-5.0	(103.9)
	Indonesia	-0.5	(1.4)	**3.4**	(1.4)	-0.5	(1.0)	-22.7	(16.9)	14.9	(9.1)	-3.9	(4.9)	11.0	(6.1)	**-18.8**	(8.6)	2.1	(7.2)	-5.6	(3.3)
	Jordan	**10.2**	(1.4)	**4.1**	(1.7)	2.8	(1.5)	**62.1**	(19.6)	**20.1**	(10.2)	1.5	(4.3)	-0.4	(4.2)	-8.1	(12.4)	0.4	(10.2)	6.5	(4.3)
	Kazakhstan	**5.3**	(1.7)	**12.8**	(1.8)	0.2	(1.2)	**-38.5**	(11.8)	**22.1**	(11.1)	6.7	(5.0)	-3.3	(4.2)	7.2	(8.1)	**25.3**	(12.0)	-2.2	(4.8)
	Kyrgyzstan	**4.1**	(1.5)	**16.3**	(1.6)	1.4	(1.4)	**-28.2**	(12.9)	**51.6**	(15.3)	3.2	(4.4)	2.4	(3.9)	-0.3	(13.4)	-8.4	(7.3)	1.1	(4.0)
	Latvia	**9.1**	(1.7)	**7.9**	(2.2)	-0.1	(1.9)	20.0	(12.0)	**16.2**	(7.7)	1.6	(5.0)	7.1	(5.8)	**-16.2**	(7.7)	**19.5**	(7.1)	-2.9	(4.3)
	Lithuania	**4.7**	(1.2)	**8.5**	(1.6)	-0.2	(1.6)	-3.2	(8.0)	**25.0**	(7.5)	-5.3	(4.1)	3.1	(4.9)	-13.8	(10.4)	**20.5**	(10.0)	-2.1	(3.5)
	Macao-China	1.6	(1.4)	**4.0**	(1.9)	-1.2	(1.5)	15.0	(13.9)	**75.1**	(6.0)	**-10.6**	(4.8)	10.8	(20.1)	-24.0	(17.2)	c	c	-0.8	(73.6)
	Montenegro	**-3.6**	(1.3)	**9.9**	(1.8)	**6.7**	(1.2)	-39.7	(23.9)	22.2	(17.9)	16.3	(9.5)	-11.7	(9.0)	**44.2**	(17.8)	c	c	3.7	(6.5)
	Panama	**4.5**	(1.8)	**9.3**	(2.4)	0.5	(1.7)	-1.4	(20.9)	**41.1**	(18.0)	6.8	(6.8)	9.8	(8.0)	1.9	(21.1)	-4.4	(16.8)	-3.9	(4.6)
	Peru	**5.0**	(1.7)	**15.3**	(1.9)	0.1	(1.7)	**25.6**	(11.3)	**35.9**	(12.6)	2.0	(4.0)	0.1	(4.4)	-0.9	(12.2)	8.5	(6.1)	-1.3	(3.0)
	Qatar	**8.5**	(0.8)	**4.8**	(1.0)	**-1.8**	(0.8)	**34.6**	(15.2)	**45.1**	(14.6)	5.0	(8.1)	-4.3	(7.6)	-2.5	(12.5)	7.3	(10.6)	-0.1	(4.1)
	Romania	**7.4**	(1.5)	**9.1**	(2.3)	2.4	(1.5)	12.9	(13.5)	**60.1**	(16.3)	-12.7	(7.5)	**12.3**	(6.2)	8.2	(18.1)	24.2	(13.3)	4.6	(6.3)
	Russian Federation	**10.0**	(1.4)	**5.1**	(1.6)	**3.6**	(1.4)	-3.5	(10.5)	**28.8**	(7.1)	-2.7	(4.3)	3.1	(3.6)	7.7	(7.9)	3.7	(7.1)	-1.2	(2.9)
	Serbia	**-5.2**	(1.4)	**8.3**	(1.7)	**3.3**	(1.3)	17.8	(28.1)	8.9	(21.6)	4.8	(10.6)	7.0	(7.9)	-3.7	(14.5)	1.0	(17.3)	-6.4	(7.0)
	Shanghai-China	**7.7**	(1.4)	1.6	(1.8)	2.2	(1.7)	13.7	(9.1)	**16.6**	(4.4)	**-6.8**	(3.1)	7.4	(15.2)	-2.7	(10.0)	1.0	(3.8)	-1.6	(108.4)
	Singapore	**8.3**	(1.5)	**12.6**	(1.6)	**-4.5**	(1.4)	13.9	(10.7)	**39.1**	(4.0)	-0.6	(4.8)	4.5	(11.8)	**-18.7**	(5.7)	5.7	(3.4)	-2.6	(99.7)
	Chinese Taipei	**8.7**	(1.7)	**9.9**	(2.8)	-1.5	(1.5)	-8.3	(27.7)	**58.1**	(15.7)	**18.4**	(6.3)	**-11.7**	(5.7)	-28.0	(18.8)	10.1	(10.7)	**-11.4**	(3.8)
	Thailand	**3.9**	(1.8)	**8.3**	(1.6)	**4.4**	(1.7)	15.3	(8.4)	14.1	(12.3)	-3.5	(5.0)	**9.2**	(4.3)	7.1	(9.0)	-5.2	(5.4)	4.6	(4.3)
	Trinidad and Tobago	**6.9**	(1.0)	**3.6**	(1.3)	1.1	(1.2)	1.1	(17.1)	**52.1**	(16.1)	-6.3	(5.2)	10.3	(6.7)	-4.7	(15.8)	**21.3**	(9.4)	-3.2	(4.0)
	Tunisia	**5.2**	(1.1)	**3.4**	(1.3)	0.9	(1.3)	**41.9**	(13.5)	17.5	(14.6)	-11.9	(6.7)	10.6	(6.2)	-11.5	(12.8)	12.4	(10.5)	-2.9	(3.1)
	Uruguay	0.0	(1.4)	**4.2**	(1.7)	2.3	(1.5)	-14.1	(13.5)	**18.3**	(6.4)	**-10.2**	(4.0)	**8.5**	(4.1)	1.5	(10.8)	6.6	(15.4)	3.3	(2.4)

Note: Values that are statistically significant are indicated in bold (see Annex A3).

1. Multilevel regression model (student and school levels): Reading performance is regressed on the school resource variables and practices as well as on socio-economic and demographic background variables presented in this table.

StatLink http://dx.doi.org/10.1787/888932343285

[Part 2/2]

Table IV.2.13c **Relationships between the learning environment and reading performance, accounting for students' and schools' socio-economic and demographic background**

		Student socio-economic and demographic background[1]										School socio-economic and demographic background[1]									
		Student is a female		Student without an immigrant background		Student's language at home is the same as the language of assessment		PISA index of economic, social and cultural status of student (1 unit increase)		PISA index of economic, social and cultural status of student (squared)		School average PISA index of economic, social and cultural status (1 unit increase)		School size (per 100 students)		School size (per 100 students) (squared)		School in a small town or village (15 000 or less people)		School in city (100 000 or more people)	
		Change in score	S.E.	Change in score	S.E.	Change in score	S.E.	Change in score	S.E.	Change in score	S.E.	Change in score	S.E.	Change in score	S.E.	Change in score	S.E.	Change in score	S.E.	Change in score	S.E.
OECD	Australia	**34.9**	(2.3)	**-6.0**	(2.5)	**26.8**	(4.1)	**27.5**	(1.7)	**-3.4**	(1.2)	**42.8**	(9.7)	1.0	(2.3)	0.0	(0.1)	-3.2	(7.0)	0.9	(4.9)
	Austria	**20.7**	(3.4)	**11.7**	(4.9)	**17.5**	(6.0)	**8.1**	(2.0)	0.4	(1.4)	**57.6**	(12.9)	**9.3**	(2.9)	**-0.4**	(0.2)	-13.1	(9.9)	-10.4	(11.6)
	Belgium	**19.0**	(2.2)	**17.7**	(2.8)	5.5	(3.2)	**12.2**	(1.4)	1.4	(0.9)	**88.8**	(9.4)	**6.8**	(3.1)	**-0.3**	(0.1)	11.2	(8.1)	0.1	(8.5)
	Canada	**33.4**	(2.0)	4.3	(2.6)	**18.2**	(4.5)	**17.6**	(1.3)	**2.1**	(0.9)	**21.1**	(7.0)	**3.9**	(1.3)	-0.1	(0.1)	3.6	(4.9)	-1.2	(4.8)
	Chile	**18.6**	(3.1)	0.4	(7.7)	**48.9**	(17.9)	**9.8**	(1.8)	0.3	(0.9)	**39.8**	(5.2)	**5.4**	(1.4)	**-0.1**	(0.0)	11.3	(11.2)	-4.4	(8.2)
	Czech Republic	**34.0**	(2.6)	**12.1**	(3.8)	-1.7	(10.9)	**15.5**	(2.0)	-2.7	(1.6)	**102.5**	(7.9)	4.7	(3.4)	-0.1	(0.3)	**11.7**	(5.3)	-12.3	(6.7)
	Denmark	**28.2**	(2.8)	**14.8**	(3.5)	**21.1**	(5.8)	**25.4**	(1.7)	-0.2	(1.1)	**34.6**	(7.2)	2.8	(3.2)	-0.3	(0.3)	-5.6	(4.4)	6.1	(5.1)
	Estonia	**41.0**	(2.8)	**9.1**	(3.9)	**27.1**	(7.1)	**16.1**	(2.1)	0.4	(1.9)	**41.8**	(12.7)	3.8	(2.0)	**-0.2**	(0.1)	9.7	(7.2)	-1.0	(6.4)
	Finland	**54.4**	(2.6)	**13.9**	(5.4)	**48.5**	(7.2)	**25.6**	(2.0)	-1.5	(1.6)	**21.5**	(10.4)	-0.6	(1.8)	0.0	(0.0)	-1.0	(5.2)	-2.4	(5.7)
	France	w	w	w	w	w	w	w	w	w	w	w	w	w	w	w	w	w	w	w	w
	Germany	**28.5**	(2.5)	**15.1**	(3.2)	3.8	(5.4)	**8.9**	(1.5)	-1.2	(0.9)	**85.6**	(10.3)	**7.9**	(2.4)	**-0.3**	(0.1)	15.6	(8.8)	-3.1	(10.5)
	Greece	**35.0**	(3.1)	1.9	(3.6)	15.8	(13.5)	**15.8**	(1.7)	1.8	(1.3)	**44.9**	(8.8)	5.3	(16.1)	0.0	(2.5)	10.7	(12.5)	-11.5	(12.5)
	Hungary	**24.8**	(2.5)	-6.7	(4.4)	**20.1**	(9.8)	**8.7**	(1.6)	0.6	(1.0)	**74.2**	(8.5)	3.9	(3.3)	-0.1	(0.2)	-8.3	(13.4)	-10.4	(11.3)
	Iceland	**41.6**	(3.3)	2.7	(5.3)	**52.2**	(11.7)	**25.5**	(2.8)	-3.2	(1.7)	14.3	(11.4)	-2.3	(5.3)	0.2	(0.8)	1.4	(8.2)	-5.2	(10.4)
	Ireland	**31.9**	(4.5)	-5.3	(3.9)	**32.0**	(10.5)	**25.7**	(2.0)	-1.7	(1.5)	**36.1**	(7.5)	6.1	(4.2)	-0.5	(0.3)	**19.5**	(7.3)	**23.3**	(8.6)
	Israel	**31.3**	(3.7)	-4.0	(4.3)	3.1	(6.0)	**21.9**	(2.5)	**3.8**	(1.3)	**84.0**	(13.1)	**11.2**	(4.4)	**-0.5**	(0.2)	-15.5	(15.4)	-7.7	(14.2)
	Italy	**26.0**	(1.6)	**16.6**	(2.7)	**6.8**	(2.5)	**5.0**	(0.8)	-1.1	(0.8)	**53.1**	(9.1)	**10.6**	(2.5)	**-0.4**	(0.1)	2.5	(10.1)	-9.8	(9.1)
	Japan	**26.5**	(2.7)	2.7	(9.0)	**83.3**	(29.5)	4.4	(2.5)	-0.5	(2.3)	**82.4**	(13.1)	0.8	(2.3)	-0.1	(0.1)	-12.9	(13.3)	-1.6	(6.8)
	Korea	**42.7**	(5.6)	3.8	(11.4)	**69.8**	(26.6)	**18.2**	(2.5)	0.8	(1.4)	**41.2**	(9.0)	5.2	(3.7)	-0.1	(0.1)	-25.9	(19.1)	**-26.4**	(13.3)
	Luxembourg	**34.9**	(3.1)	**28.6**	(3.6)	**25.2**	(5.1)	**17.1**	(2.8)	-1.6	(1.2)	**87.9**	(11.3)	0.4	(2.2)	0.1	(0.1)	4.1	(9.3)	**-58.6**	(19.6)
	Mexico	**20.8**	(1.9)	**22.9**	(3.4)	**17.4**	(5.7)	**8.1**	(1.4)	**1.4**	(0.5)	**27.1**	(3.5)	**2.5**	(0.5)	**0.0**	(0.0)	-8.7	(6.8)	1.2	(6.7)
	Netherlands	**18.7**	(1.7)	**5.9**	(2.6)	11.3	(6.7)	**5.3**	(1.6)	0.3	(1.1)	**63.6**	(14.2)	**7.9**	(2.4)	**-0.2**	(0.1)	**-25.4**	(11.0)	6.6	(9.6)
	New Zealand	**47.2**	(4.4)	-6.1	(3.5)	**46.3**	(5.7)	**32.3**	(2.7)	-0.4	(2.4)	**34.4**	(11.3)	**4.2**	(1.5)	**-0.1**	(0.1)	10.6	(8.7)	5.4	(6.7)
	Norway	**46.7**	(3.5)	**11.0**	(5.5)	**37.3**	(7.9)	**25.1**	(3.1)	-0.9	(2.0)	**29.4**	(12.0)	5.8	(6.9)	-1.0	(0.9)	-7.7	(5.1)	-7.5	(6.8)
	Poland	**49.8**	(3.2)	23.2	(24.3)	**44.8**	(16.9)	**30.1**	(1.9)	**-3.2**	(1.5)	**29.0**	(7.5)	7.6	(6.1)	-0.5	(0.7)	2.9	(7.2)	-13.9	(8.0)
	Portugal	**31.8**	(2.5)	-2.0	(3.1)	13.9	(8.2)	**17.9**	(1.3)	-0.6	(0.8)	**36.7**	(6.0)	0.7	(2.9)	0.0	(0.1)	0.4	(7.4)	6.7	(6.8)
	Slovak Republic	**42.3**	(2.9)	0.8	(5.4)	**28.3**	(7.4)	**17.5**	(1.8)	**-3.5**	(1.2)	**56.8**	(12.0)	-2.1	(4.5)	0.3	(0.4)	-7.3	(7.3)	1.6	(8.3)
	Slovenia	**30.6**	(2.2)	**7.7**	(3.1)	4.5	(5.1)	**3.4**	(1.2)	0.7	(1.1)	**64.5**	(7.4)	**13.9**	(4.0)	-0.8	(0.4)	-9.9	(8.0)	0.0	(6.8)
	Spain	**27.2**	(1.7)	**24.6**	(2.4)	**8.7**	(3.4)	**19.2**	(1.0)	-0.8	(0.6)	**21.6**	(4.7)	-0.7	(1.4)	0.0	(0.1)	-3.5	(4.2)	**9.0**	(4.5)
	Sweden	**44.6**	(2.9)	5.7	(4.2)	**31.3**	(6.1)	**31.4**	(2.0)	-0.9	(1.1)	**41.7**	(12.3)	-3.6	(3.0)	0.3	(0.2)	1.8	(6.1)	2.0	(8.2)
	Switzerland	**30.8**	(2.4)	**10.8**	(2.7)	**19.8**	(3.3)	**18.2**	(1.5)	-0.4	(1.4)	**54.6**	(11.4)	**2.9**	(0.9)	**0.0**	(0.0)	-7.0	(9.2)	-7.1	(14.8)
	Turkey	**29.7**	(2.9)	-0.6	(7.7)	0.3	(11.8)	**7.1**	(2.3)	-0.4	(0.9)	**59.0**	(6.8)	-3.3	(3.0)	0.0	(0.1)	**-26.1**	(12.7)	-10.7	(14.0)
	United Kingdom	**23.8**	(3.0)	-5.8	(4.1)	**18.2**	(6.2)	**22.9**	(1.9)	0.3	(1.5)	**68.4**	(7.6)	1.3	(2.1)	0.0	(0.1)	8.4	(5.8)	-0.6	(6.4)
	United States	**25.4**	(4.5)	-1.3	(7.1)	5.2	(7.2)	**21.8**	(2.3)	-1.7	(2.9)	**66.6**	(9.5)	-0.1	(1.0)	0.0	(0.0)	**16.7**	(7.1)	6.6	(8.3)
	OECD average	**32.6**	(0.5)	**7.0**	(1.1)	**24.6**	(1.9)	**17.3**	(0.3)	**-0.5**	(0.2)	**51.7**	(1.7)	**3.7**	(0.7)	-0.2	(0.1)	-1.2	(1.6)	**-4.1**	(1.7)
Partners	Albania	**54.9**	(4.1)	19.3	(11.4)	12.8	(16.9)	**18.5**	(3.6)	2.6	(1.5)	**35.0**	(10.0)	-6.7	(4.3)	0.5	(0.3)	-7.8	(12.5)	3.2	(13.5)
	Argentina	**31.4**	(3.2)	1.6	(5.1)	**43.9**	(16.9)	**13.1**	(2.1)	**2.0**	(1.0)	**58.4**	(7.6)	**7.3**	(3.0)	**-0.2**	(0.1)	-2.5	(15.6)	12.8	(15.8)
	Azerbaijan	**22.9**	(2.3)	1.0	(4.7)	-4.6	(6.2)	**10.5**	(2.1)	1.3	(1.0)	**32.9**	(10.0)	-2.6	(3.4)	0.2	(0.1)	-12.2	(15.0)	-17.9	(12.7)
	Brazil	**28.2**	(2.0)	10.9	(9.3)	**31.9**	(12.7)	**8.1**	(1.9)	1.3	(0.7)	**49.6**	(4.2)	0.8	(1.1)	0.0	(0.0)	-1.1	(8.1)	-5.9	(6.0)
	Bulgaria	**46.1**	(3.9)	**26.9**	(8.1)	**27.9**	(6.8)	**13.0**	(2.3)	1.2	(1.3)	**66.7**	(9.3)	7.3	(4.1)	-0.2	(0.3)	-5.8	(10.1)	9.4	(11.5)
	Colombia	**9.2**	(3.0)	**18.1**	(7.9)	**54.5**	(21.2)	**12.6**	(2.7)	1.2	(0.8)	**44.3**	(3.9)	0.4	(0.8)	0.0	(0.0)	**16.2**	(6.6)	-5.1	(6.0)
	Croatia	**33.8**	(3.2)	2.1	(2.4)	-8.5	(8.3)	**9.9**	(1.9)	**-3.8**	(1.2)	**54.5**	(14.7)	6.1	(3.9)	-0.2	(0.2)	4.9	(7.7)	**-26.9**	(8.5)
	Dubai (UAE)	**25.1**	(4.5)	**-29.0**	(3.5)	**18.8**	(2.8)	**17.7**	(2.0)	**2.6**	(1.1)	**71.4**	(8.3)	**1.1**	(0.5)	0.0	(0.0)	0.8	(20.3)	0.4	(18.4)
	Hong Kong-China	**24.8**	(2.9)	**-8.3**	(2.4)	**22.3**	(6.9)	2.0	(2.0)	-1.0	(0.9)	**38.7**	(6.9)	**11.2**	(0.9)	-0.2	(15.8)	a	a	a	a
	Indonesia	**29.1**	(1.8)	18.9	(11.0)	-4.7	(2.6)	**6.8**	(2.8)	1.3	(0.8)	**23.1**	(5.7)	5.5	(3.4)	-0.2	(0.3)	-7.7	(8.1)	-2.3	(10.8)
	Jordan	**40.9**	(9.5)	-4.1	(3.6)	**24.5**	(8.8)	**19.1**	(2.3)	1.6	(1.1)	9.2	(10.4)	-2.9	(3.2)	0.2	(0.2)	-6.9	(8.9)	5.8	(9.5)
	Kazakhstan	**40.2**	(2.5)	**-11.6**	(4.8)	1.8	(4.7)	**15.8**	(2.4)	-2.1	(1.3)	**43.5**	(10.1)	**-5.0**	(1.6)	**0.1**	(0.0)	-15.4	(11.4)	9.6	(11.3)
	Kyrgyzstan	**49.9**	(2.9)	**-12.3**	(5.7)	-2.2	(4.8)	**18.1**	(2.4)	2.3	(1.2)	**39.4**	(9.5)	0.6	(2.5)	0.0	(0.1)	-0.5	(10.8)	30.3	(16.1)
	Latvia	**44.9**	(2.9)	-0.1	(3.3)	9.0	(9.2)	**18.8**	(2.4)	-1.1	(1.6)	**29.6**	(9.9)	4.9	(3.2)	-0.2	(0.3)	0.8	(7.7)	-3.5	(9.7)
	Lithuania	**54.4**	(2.7)	-1.2	(4.6)	11.2	(7.4)	**18.5**	(1.7)	0.0	(1.2)	**42.6**	(8.6)	-2.1	(3.1)	0.2	(0.2)	5.2	(9.1)	-13.9	(8.3)
	Macao-China	**21.2**	(2.1)	**-10.1**	(2.6)	**51.1**	(6.2)	**6.8**	(2.2)	0.1	(1.0)	**32.3**	(1.6)	**6.0**	(0.2)	-0.1	(23.0)	a	a	a	a
	Montenegro	**39.9**	(3.5)	**-7.8**	(2.8)	5.5	(11.1)	**12.3**	(1.4)	0.5	(1.4)	**63.6**	(16.1)	-0.7	(4.7)	0.0	(0.2)	-4.0	(15.2)	**-28.0**	(13.0)
	Panama	**18.6**	(4.7)	1.7	(6.5)	15.5	(10.8)	**7.1**	(3.1)	1.6	(1.0)	**41.8**	(12.4)	**4.8**	(2.2)	-0.1	(0.1)	-24.4	(15.3)	-3.8	(18.0)
	Peru	**10.4**	(3.2)	18.9	(10.3)	**20.4**	(7.2)	**12.0**	(2.7)	1.1	(0.8)	**47.2**	(5.3)	**3.7**	(1.4)	-0.1	(0.1)	-9.0	(9.8)	12.4	(10.3)
	Qatar	**34.6**	(6.0)	**-34.5**	(2.6)	**18.4**	(3.2)	**7.8**	(1.5)	1.4	(0.9)	**72.0**	(10.3)	**3.6**	(1.1)	**0.0**	(0.0)	11.6	(13.1)	0.8	(14.3)
	Romania	**15.4**	(3.9)	17.9	(10.1)	10.3	(8.0)	**11.4**	(2.1)	0.0	(1.1)	**27.4**	(9.0)	1.2	(3.8)	-0.1	(0.2)	-10.8	(13.0)	9.4	(12.1)
	Russian Federation	**39.1**	(2.7)	0.6	(2.9)	**21.8**	(5.7)	**20.0**	(2.0)	-1.7	(1.7)	**44.2**	(8.7)	**-8.2**	(2.8)	**0.6**	(0.2)	2.8	(9.0)	7.3	(8.3)
	Serbia	**26.9**	(2.9)	-5.7	(3.4)	0.4	(10.3)	**7.4**	(1.8)	0.8	(1.1)	**53.2**	(23.0)	0.3	(2.9)	0.0	(0.2)	-2.6	(12.4)	-8.4	(9.8)
	Shanghai-China	**33.2**	(2.4)	**24.2**	(8.3)	**30.8**	(9.4)	**4.4**	(1.9)	0.7	(1.3)	**48.3**	(1.3)	**0.7**	(0.2)	0.0	(12.9)	a	a	a	a
	Singapore	**22.7**	(2.3)	-2.1	(2.8)	**23.4**	(3.3)	**17.0**	(2.7)	-2.4	(1.3)	**66.1**	(3.4)	**9.0**	(0.3)	-0.1	(14.4)	a	a	a	a
	Chinese Taipei	**42.8**	(4.3)	13.2	(8.9)	8.3	(4.9)	**18.2**	(2.8)	-0.1	(1.8)	**58.3**	(10.2)	0.2	(0.9)	0.0	(0.0)	-23.1	(15.3)	8.9	(7.8)
	Thailand	**33.3**	(2.9)	**31.1**	(10.4)	**-15.3**	(3.9)	4.9	(2.9)	0.1	(1.0)	**19.7**	(5.5)	1.7	(1.2)	0.0	(0.0)	4.6	(14.5)	5.7	(10.1)
	Trinidad and Tobago	**43.9**	(2.4)	-6.1	(3.2)	**29.4**	(7.1)	**4.7**	(2.2)	1.1	(1.0)	**103.7**	(10.9)	**23.9**	(6.6)	**-1.5**	(0.5)	-9.0	(8.8)	a	a
	Tunisia	**21.1**	(2.4)	**21.0**	(8.4)	-24.1	(18.5)	3.0	(2.8)	-0.1	(0.8)	**31.6**	(6.2)	**11.3**	(2.7)	**-0.3**	(0.1)	**22.5**	(8.8)	11.0	(10.4)
	Uruguay	**39.1**	(3.0)	-1.6	(6.3)	15.4	(9.4)	**15.1**	(2.0)	-0.3	(0.9)	**44.4**	(4.9)	1.4	(1.1)	0.0	(0.0)	**20.7**	(8.2)	**15.3**	(6.9)

Note: Values that are statistically significant are indicated in bold (see Annex A3).
1. Multilevel regression model (student and school levels): Reading performance is regressed on the school resource variables and practices as well as on socio-economic and demographic background variables presented in this table.

StatLink http://dx.doi.org/10.1787/888932343285

[Part 1/1]

Table IV.2.14a Within- and between-school variation in reading performance and variation explained jointly by student and school characteristics

		Variance		Remaining variance						Variance decomposition expressed as a percentage of the average variance in student performance in reading across OECD countries			Within-school variance expressed as a percentage of the average of within-school variance in student performance in reading across OECD countries				Between-school variance expressed as a percentage of the average of between-school variance in student performance in reading across OECD countries			
		Empty (or fully unconditional) model[1]		Model with demographic and socio-economic background[2]		Model with student- and school-level variables[3]		Model with demographic and socio-economic background and with student- and school-level variables[4]		Total variance in student performance	Total variance within schools as a percentage of total variance	Total variance between schools as a percentage of total variance	Solely accounted for by students' and schools' socio-economic and demographic background	Solely accounted for by the students' and schools' characteristics	Jointly accounted for by students' and schools' socio-economic and demographic background and the students' and schools' characteristics	Remaining within-school variance	Solely accounted for by students' and schools' socio-economic and demographic background	Solely accounted for by the students' and schools' characteristics	Jointly accounted for by students' and schools' socio-economic and demographic background and the students' and schools' characteristics	Remaining between-school variance
		Within-school	Between-school	Within-school	Between-school	Within-school	Between-school	Within-school	Between-school	%	%	%	%	%	%	%	%	%	%	%
OECD	Australia	7 631	2 692	6 997	880	4 883	366	4 746	315	112	83	29	1.5	24.5	5.4	51.5	0.6	6.1	19.1	3.4
	Austria	4 454	5 588	4 255	2 262	3 605	1 576	3 517	894	108	48	60	1.0	8.0	1.2	38.2	7.4	14.9	28.7	9.7
	Belgium	4 833	5 343	4 612	1 643	3 549	979	3 477	707	111	53	58	0.8	12.3	1.6	37.8	3.0	10.2	37.2	7.7
	Canada	6 780	1 877	6 238	986	4 579	606	4 473	509	94	74	20	1.1	19.2	4.7	48.6	1.0	5.2	8.6	5.5
	Chile	4 005	4 893	3 886	1 219	3 228	276	3 194	200	97	44	53	0.4	7.5	0.9	34.7	0.8	11.1	39.1	2.2
	Czech Republic	4 428	4 249	4 136	1 135	3 299	647	3 222	374	94	48	46	0.8	9.9	2.3	35.0	3.0	8.3	30.9	4.1
	Denmark	6 012	1 134	5 254	328	3 768	236	3 569	142	78	65	12	2.2	18.3	6.1	38.8	1.0	2.0	7.7	1.5
	Estonia	5 595	1 557	4 991	681	3 741	179	3 639	118	78	61	17	1.1	14.7	5.5	39.5	0.7	6.1	8.8	1.3
	Finland	6 993	665	5 641	458	4 026	147	3 827	125	83	76	7	2.2	19.7	12.5	41.6	0.2	3.6	2.0	1.4
	France	w	w	w	w	w	w	w	w	w	w	w	w	w	w	w	w	w	w	w
	Germany	3 890	5 890	3 558	1 708	3 089	1 050	3 006	687	106	42	64	0.9	6.0	2.7	32.6	3.9	11.1	41.5	7.5
	Greece	5 558	4 745	5 126	2 165	4 429	1 181	4 278	979	112	60	52	1.6	9.2	3.1	46.5	2.2	12.9	25.8	10.6
	Hungary	2 923	5 846	2 792	1 717	2 364	645	2 317	341	95	32	64	0.5	5.2	0.9	25.2	3.3	14.9	41.5	3.7
	Iceland	8 186	1 348	7 186	1 015	5 176	194	5 025	165	104	89	15	1.6	23.5	9.2	54.6	0.3	9.2	3.3	1.8
	Ireland	6 966	2 805	6 408	1 145	4 727	419	4 561	412	106	76	30	1.8	20.1	4.3	49.5	0.1	8.0	17.9	4.5
	Israel	6 615	6 250	6 312	3 230	5 364	881	5 283	674	140	72	68	0.9	11.2	2.4	57.4	2.2	27.8	30.6	7.3
	Italy	4 085	6 695	3 905	2 880	3 367	1 048	3 302	992	117	44	73	0.7	6.6	1.2	35.9	0.6	20.5	40.8	10.8
	Japan	5 386	5 087	5 248	2 255	3 980	551	3 952	448	114	59	55	0.3	14.1	1.2	42.9	1.1	19.6	29.6	4.9
	Korea	5 283	2 741	4 829	1 038	3 305	214	3 158	167	87	57	30	1.6	18.1	3.3	34.3	0.5	9.5	18.0	1.8
	Luxembourg	6 906	5 335	c	c	c	c	c	c	133	75	58	c	c	c	c	c	c	c	c
	Mexico	3 869	3 583	3 723	1 964	3 237	867	3 170	720	81	42	39	0.7	6.0	0.9	34.4	1.6	13.5	16.0	7.8
	Netherlands	2 795	5 107	2 670	2 224	2 213	639	2 190	514	86	30	55	0.3	5.2	1.1	23.8	1.4	18.6	30.0	5.6
	New Zealand	8 228	2 622	6 974	530	5 074	280	4 794	139	118	89	28	3.0	23.7	10.6	52.1	1.5	4.2	21.2	1.5
	Norway	7 598	874	6 455	669	4 705	232	4 449	198	92	83	9	2.8	21.8	9.6	48.3	0.4	5.1	1.9	2.1
	Poland	6 869	1 585	5 582	458	4 444	217	4 163	174	92	75	17	3.1	15.4	10.9	45.2	0.5	3.1	11.8	1.9
	Portugal	5 191	2 565	4 666	883	3 588	314	3 465	246	84	56	28	1.3	13.0	4.4	37.6	0.7	6.9	17.5	2.7
	Slovak Republic	4 565	2 989	3 972	1 151	3 348	548	3 136	479	82	50	32	2.3	9.1	4.1	34.1	0.7	7.3	19.2	5.2
	Slovenia	3 102	4 142	2 941	1 818	2 613	898	2 542	549	79	34	45	0.8	4.3	1.0	27.6	3.8	13.8	21.5	6.0
	Spain	6 048	1 690	5 390	816	4 103	429	3 914	414	84	66	18	2.1	16.0	5.1	42.5	0.2	4.4	9.3	4.5
	Sweden	8 290	1 877	7 007	605	5 318	276	4 988	165	110	90	20	3.6	21.9	10.4	54.2	1.2	4.8	12.6	1.8
	Switzerland	5 652	2 740	5 115	1 100	3 924	364	3 768	242	91	61	30	1.7	14.6	4.1	40.9	1.3	9.3	16.5	2.6
	Turkey	3 245	6 536	2 958	1 375	2 724	516	2 571	221	106	35	71	1.7	4.2	1.5	27.9	3.2	12.5	52.8	2.4
	United Kingdom	6 684	2 775	6 275	635	4 339	455	4 271	314	103	73	30	0.7	21.8	3.7	46.4	1.5	3.5	21.7	3.4
	United States	6 476	3 638	6 041	838	4 550	98	4 444	46	110	70	40	1.2	17.3	3.6	48.3	0.6	8.6	29.9	0.5
	OECD average	5 591	3 616	5 036	1 307	3 896	541	3 763	396	100	61	39	1.4	13.8	4.4	40.9	1.6	9.9	22.3	4.3
Partners	Albania	7 105	3 127	6 150	1 339	5 337	699	5 095	630	111	77	34	2.6	11.5	7.7	55.3	0.8	7.7	18.7	6.8
	Argentina	5 523	8 456	5 201	3 238	4 731	1 175	4 579	849	152	60	92	1.7	6.8	1.8	49.7	3.5	26.0	53.1	9.2
	Azerbaijan	3 459	2 490	3 287	2 054	3 121	955	3 017	778	65	38	27	1.1	2.9	0.7	32.8	1.9	13.9	2.8	8.4
	Brazil	4 702	4 417	4 514	1 770	4 123	866	4 027	670	99	51	48	1.0	5.3	1.0	43.7	2.1	11.9	26.6	7.3
	Bulgaria	6 439	6 418	5 794	2 053	5 435	1 190	5 075	624	140	70	70	3.9	7.8	3.1	55.1	6.1	15.5	41.3	6.8
	Colombia	4 813	3 162	4 711	688	3 972	332	3 909	249	87	52	34	0.7	8.7	0.4	42.5	0.9	4.8	26.0	2.7
	Croatia	4 473	4 045	4 183	1 391	3 512	228	3 411	189	93	49	44	1.1	8.4	2.1	37.0	0.4	13.1	28.4	2.1
	Dubai (UAE)	5 439	5 732	5 121	2 472	4 308	791	4 162	605	121	59	62	1.6	10.4	1.9	45.2	2.0	20.3	33.4	6.6
	Hong Kong-China	4 360	3 143	4 183	1 270	3 327	395	3 281	323	82	47	34	0.5	9.8	1.4	35.6	0.8	10.3	19.6	3.5
	Indonesia	2 298	1 749	2 117	1 181	2 027	588	1 918	541	44	25	19	1.2	2.2	0.8	20.8	0.5	7.0	5.7	5.9
	Jordan	5 461	3 312	5 186	1 727	4 523	675	4 412	590	95	59	36	1.2	8.4	1.8	47.9	0.9	12.4	16.3	6.4
	Kazakhstan	5 078	2 887	4 456	1 542	3 895	984	3 556	692	87	55	31	3.7	9.8	3.1	38.6	3.2	9.2	11.4	7.5
	Kyrgyzstan	5 901	3 266	5 126	1 398	5 018	579	4 570	512	100	64	35	4.9	6.0	3.6	49.6	0.7	9.6	19.6	5.6
	Latvia	5 200	1 391	4 491	634	3 613	222	3 461	198	72	57	15	1.7	11.2	6.1	37.6	0.3	4.7	7.9	2.1
	Lithuania	5 190	1 864	4 263	828	3 695	511	3 440	413	77	56	20	2.8	8.9	7.3	37.4	1.1	4.5	10.2	4.5
	Macao-China	4 179	2 882	c	c	c	c	c	c	77	45	31	c	c	c	c	c	c	c	c
	Montenegro	5 587	3 150	c	c	c	c	c	c	95	61	34	c	c	c	c	c	c	c	c
	Panama	4 213	5 942	4 103	2 647	3 795	682	3 733	576	110	46	65	0.7	4.0	0.5	40.5	1.2	22.5	34.6	6.3
	Peru	4 623	5 886	4 524	1 316	3 972	827	3 907	390	114	50	64	0.7	6.7	0.4	42.4	4.7	10.1	44.9	4.2
	Qatar	5 891	6 676	5 520	3 383	5 122	1 337	4 929	1 019	137	64	73	2.1	6.4	1.9	53.5	3.5	25.7	32.3	11.1
	Romania	3 832	4 057	3 678	2 308	3 210	492	3 157	384	86	42	44	0.6	5.7	1.1	34.3	1.2	20.9	17.8	4.2
	Russian Federation	5 826	1 965	5 193	900	4 359	580	4 186	436	85	63	21	1.9	10.9	5.0	45.5	1.6	5.0	10.0	4.7
	Serbia	4 123	3 909	3 954	1 840	3 296	497	3 230	455	87	45	42	0.7	7.9	1.1	35.1	0.5	15.0	22.0	4.9
	Shanghai-China	4 095	2 551	3 813	701	3 238	157	3 089	115	72	44	28	1.6	7.9	1.4	33.5	0.5	6.4	19.6	1.2
	Singapore	6 195	3 387	5 612	782	4 325	337	4 165	223	104	67	37	1.7	15.7	4.6	45.2	1.2	6.1	27.1	2.4
	Chinese Taipei	5 808	2 772	5 070	1 306	4 020	112	3 797	70	93	63	30	2.4	13.8	5.6	41.2	0.5	13.4	15.5	0.8
	Thailand	3 052	1 231	2 706	816	2 516	436	2 360	351	47	33	13	1.7	3.8	2.1	25.6	0.9	5.1	3.6	3.8
	Trinidad and Tobago	5 148	8 320	4 720	2 527	4 387	921	4 220	837	146	56	90	1.8	5.4	2.8	45.8	0.9	18.4	62.0	9.1
	Tunisia	4 291	3 034	4 174	1 640	3 999	220	3 916	162	80	47	33	0.9	2.8	0.4	42.5	0.6	16.1	14.5	1.8
	Uruguay	5 835	4 807	5 342	968	4 831	336	4 616	269	116	63	52	2.3	7.9	3.0	50.1	0.7	7.6	41.0	2.9

1. Multilevel regression model consists of the student and school levels.
2. Multilevel regression model: Reading performance is regressed on the variables of demographic and socio-economic background.
3. Multilevel regression model: Reading performance is regressed on the student- and school-level variables.
4. Multilevel regression model: Reading performance is regressed on the variables of demographic and socio-economic background and on the student- and school-level variables.

StatLink http://dx.doi.org/10.1787/888932343285

[Part 1/5]

Table IV.2.14b Relationships between reading performance and students' reading engagement and approaches to learning, the learning environment, resources, policies and practices

		Students' reading engagement and approaches to learning[1]																Learning environment and school climate (student level)[1]					
		Index of enjoyment of reading (higer values indicate more enjoyment)		Index of diversity in reading (higer values indicate more diversity)		Index of online reading activities (higer values indicate more activities)		Index of memorisation strategies (higer values indicate higher importance attached to this strategy)		Index of elaboration strategies (higer values indicate higher importance attached to this strategy)		Index of control strategies (higer values indicate higher importance attached to this strategy)		Index of understanding and remembering (higer values indicate greater students' perception of usefulness of this strategy)		Index of summarising (higer values indicate greater students' perception of usefulness of this strategy)		Index of teacher-student relations (higher values indicate better relationships)		Index of disciplinary climate (higher values indicate better climate)		Index of teachers' stimulation of reading engagement (higher values indicate more stimulation)	
		Change in score	S.E.	Change in score	S.E.	Change in score	S.E.	Change in score	S.E.	Change in score	S.E.	Change in score	S.E.	Change in score	S.E.	Change in score	S.E.	Change in score	S.E.	Change in score	S.E.	Change in score	S.E.
OECD	Australia	**28.3**	(0.9)	**-5.0**	(1.2)	**10.8**	(1.0)	**-13.4**	(1.2)	**-8.2**	(0.9)	**18.7**	(1.3)	**11.3**	(1.3)	**17.8**	(1.0)	**6.1**	(1.0)	**3.0**	(1.1)	**-4.1**	(0.9)
	Austria	**17.9**	(1.4)	-1.5	(1.6)	**5.2**	(1.4)	**-6.4**	(1.5)	**-3.3**	(1.4)	2.7	(1.5)	**9.9**	(1.6)	**14.7**	(1.7)	1.6	(1.2)	1.3	(1.1)	**-3.5**	(1.4)
	Belgium	**18.0**	(1.2)	**4.5**	(1.1)	**4.9**	(1.3)	**-9.9**	(1.2)	**-7.1**	(1.2)	**10.7**	(1.3)	**10.8**	(1.2)	**17.5**	(1.3)	-1.2	(1.2)	0.5	(1.1)	-0.2	(1.1)
	Canada	**25.3**	(0.9)	-1.1	(1.1)	**4.5**	(1.1)	**-9.2**	(0.9)	**-10.2**	(0.8)	**16.6**	(1.1)	**6.9**	(1.0)	**17.6**	(0.9)	**5.2**	(1.0)	0.7	(1.2)	-0.9	(1.0)
	Chile	**15.9**	(1.5)	2.0	(1.4)	**6.5**	(1.2)	-1.8	(1.4)	**-6.7**	(1.4)	**9.3**	(1.6)	**11.4**	(1.2)	**13.4**	(1.3)	**3.1**	(1.2)	1.0	(1.3)	**-3.4**	(1.3)
	Czech Republic	**20.5**	(1.4)	1.5	(1.4)	**5.7**	(1.1)	**-5.2**	(1.2)	**-2.6**	(1.3)	**9.6**	(1.5)	**9.2**	(1.3)	**19.8**	(1.3)	0.4	(1.5)	-0.5	(1.3)	**-5.1**	(1.5)
	Denmark	**26.9**	(1.6)	**4.9**	(1.4)	**4.7**	(1.6)	**-19.2**	(1.6)	**-4.8**	(1.5)	**8.3**	(1.7)	**15.9**	(1.6)	**18.4**	(1.3)	**7.8**	(1.3)	-0.3	(1.5)	-2.3	(1.6)
	Estonia	**29.2**	(1.6)	4.1	(2.2)	**7.9**	(1.9)	**-14.9**	(1.9)	1.5	(1.8)	2.6	(2.1)	**13.5**	(1.3)	**17.1**	(1.8)	**7.6**	(1.5)	**6.0**	(2.3)	**-9.5**	(2.0)
	Finland	**26.1**	(1.4)	**10.2**	(1.6)	**4.3**	(1.7)	**-14.0**	(1.7)	-1.3	(1.5)	**10.2**	(2.0)	**11.0**	(1.4)	**20.6**	(1.7)	**3.8**	(1.5)	-1.8	(1.5)	**-9.0**	(1.7)
	France	w	w	w	w	w	w	w	w	w	w	w	w	w	w	w	w	w	w	w	w	w	w
	Germany	**15.5**	(1.1)	**3.8**	(1.2)	**4.6**	(1.4)	**-5.0**	(1.7)	**-5.7**	(1.4)	**5.7**	(1.7)	**9.2**	(1.5)	**12.4**	(1.6)	2.2	(1.3)	1.9	(1.3)	-0.3	(1.4)
	Greece	**29.5**	(2.1)	2.0	(2.0)	1.7	(1.3)	**-9.0**	(1.6)	-3.0	(1.6)	**9.4**	(1.9)	**3.6**	(1.6)	**16.9**	(1.7)	0.0	(1.8)	-2.4	(2.1)	1.1	(1.9)
	Hungary	**16.9**	(1.4)	0.4	(1.1)	**5.7**	(1.3)	1.2	(1.8)	**-6.9**	(1.7)	1.1	(1.7)	**8.4**	(1.5)	**13.5**	(1.2)	-2.3	(1.3)	-2.6	(1.4)	2.1	(1.5)
	Iceland	**24.1**	(1.4)	**8.4**	(1.7)	**4.3**	(1.8)	**-19.2**	(1.9)	-2.8	(1.7)	**17.8**	(2.1)	**8.1**	(1.5)	**21.5**	(1.7)	**6.4**	(1.4)	3.7	(2.1)	**-5.0**	(1.4)
	Ireland	**29.9**	(1.9)	**-4.7**	(2.1)	**7.9**	(1.7)	**-5.6**	(1.8)	**-4.8**	(1.4)	**8.7**	(1.9)	**12.6**	(1.9)	**17.4**	(1.5)	**5.3**	(2.0)	**5.5**	(1.7)	**-4.9**	(1.7)
	Israel	**18.2**	(2.3)	**4.3**	(1.6)	**8.5**	(1.6)	**-11.0**	(1.9)	**-6.5**	(1.7)	**12.2**	(2.1)	**6.5**	(1.9)	**15.8**	(1.9)	2.3	(1.5)	1.1	(2.0)	**-4.4**	(1.8)
	Italy	**16.5**	(0.9)	**3.8**	(1.0)	**4.2**	(0.7)	**-9.7**	(0.8)	**-3.1**	(0.8)	**7.6**	(1.0)	**7.8**	(0.9)	**14.7**	(0.9)	0.3	(0.8)	**1.7**	(0.7)	-1.5	(0.9)
	Japan	**19.7**	(1.5)	0.5	(1.2)	**5.2**	(1.8)	**-6.4**	(1.4)	**-3.9**	(1.5)	**11.9**	(1.8)	**8.3**	(1.4)	**18.9**	(1.7)	**5.0**	(1.3)	2.7	(1.6)	-1.8	(1.4)
	Korea	**22.4**	(3.7)	0.9	(3.0)	**5.9**	(2.8)	1.7	(2.8)	1.6	(2.3)	**9.9**	(2.7)	**11.2**	(2.3)	**21.4**	(1.9)	4.4	(2.4)	1.3	(2.1)	-3.8	(2.3)
	Luxembourg	c	c	c	c	c	c	c	c	c	c	c	c	c	c	c	c	c	c	c	c	c	c
	Mexico	**11.6**	(1.1)	-1.1	(0.8)	**2.4**	(1.0)	**-7.7**	(1.0)	**-5.1**	(1.0)	**10.8**	(1.2)	**6.6**	(0.8)	**15.3**	(0.9)	**4.5**	(0.9)	**4.2**	(1.0)	1.8	(1.0)
	Netherlands	**12.3**	(1.5)	**6.7**	(1.0)	**2.9**	(1.4)	**-11.0**	(1.1)	**-3.4**	(1.2)	**6.2**	(1.4)	**7.0**	(1.1)	**9.6**	(1.0)	0.8	(1.3)	-0.8	(1.1)	**-4.8**	(1.1)
	New Zealand	**33.1**	(1.8)	**-7.7**	(2.5)	**10.9**	(2.1)	**-13.1**	(1.9)	**-11.8**	(2.1)	**18.6**	(2.3)	**8.3**	(1.8)	**22.0**	(1.4)	2.6	(1.8)	**4.7**	(2.0)	-0.3	(1.8)
	Norway	**27.2**	(1.9)	**5.8**	(1.8)	-0.9	(1.8)	**-16.8**	(2.0)	1.5	(1.9)	**12.8**	(2.6)	**12.4**	(1.5)	**23.3**	(1.7)	**7.4**	(1.6)	0.9	(1.6)	**-4.3**	(1.8)
	Poland	**19.6**	(1.4)	**7.0**	(1.8)	**7.6**	(1.4)	**-6.9**	(2.1)	**-7.5**	(2.1)	**15.3**	(1.7)	**8.8**	(1.6)	**25.2**	(1.5)	-1.1	(1.6)	1.0	(1.6)	**4.7**	(1.6)
	Portugal	**14.7**	(1.6)	-0.8	(1.6)	**3.2**	(1.4)	**-7.9**	(1.5)	**-5.2**	(1.9)	**17.9**	(1.9)	**9.9**	(1.2)	**18.5**	(1.3)	-1.2	(1.3)	**4.0**	(1.4)	-1.9	(1.4)
	Slovak Republic	**17.9**	(1.6)	**4.2**	(1.4)	**9.3**	(1.4)	**-10.0**	(1.1)	**-6.9**	(1.7)	**11.4**	(1.9)	**7.3**	(1.5)	**18.1**	(1.4)	1.4	(1.4)	1.5	(1.4)	-2.9	(1.6)
	Slovenia	**10.7**	(1.3)	**4.3**	(1.3)	**3.5**	(0.9)	**-10.8**	(1.3)	**-4.9**	(1.2)	**8.3**	(1.4)	**5.4**	(1.1)	**10.6**	(1.0)	1.1	(1.1)	-0.4	(1.0)	**2.5**	(1.1)
	Spain	**21.8**	(0.9)	**4.7**	(0.9)	**7.0**	(1.0)	**-2.1**	(0.8)	**-5.4**	(1.1)	**13.2**	(1.0)	**9.0**	(0.8)	**21.6**	(0.9)	0.0	(0.8)	**4.6**	(0.9)	**-2.3**	(0.9)
	Sweden	**25.5**	(1.9)	**11.4**	(1.6)	**3.8**	(1.9)	-2.1	(1.5)	**-7.1**	(2.1)	**7.4**	(2.2)	**15.3**	(1.5)	**21.1**	(1.7)	**4.5**	(1.6)	-0.8	(1.5)	-2.2	(2.0)
	Switzerland	**19.5**	(1.1)	**6.3**	(1.2)	**3.8**	(1.2)	**-8.7**	(1.5)	**-5.7**	(1.6)	**4.8**	(1.4)	**14.2**	(1.2)	**18.3**	(1.4)	-1.4	(1.1)	1.2	(1.3)	**-4.3**	(1.3)
	Turkey	**12.0**	(1.8)	**-5.4**	(1.9)	**3.2**	(1.5)	**-6.3**	(1.7)	0.3	(1.8)	**10.4**	(2.4)	**7.8**	(1.3)	**10.8**	(1.6)	1.4	(1.2)	-0.4	(1.5)	1.3	(1.6)
	United Kingdom	**29.6**	(1.5)	**-3.7**	(1.5)	**8.2**	(1.5)	**-11.4**	(1.6)	**-5.9**	(1.5)	**15.1**	(1.8)	**8.1**	(1.5)	**15.9**	(1.3)	**4.9**	(1.4)	**5.5**	(1.3)	-1.3	(1.5)
	United States	**25.9**	(2.0)	-2.3	(2.5)	**6.3**	(2.2)	**-12.6**	(2.2)	**-9.8**	(2.3)	**17.2**	(2.3)	**8.3**	(2.0)	**13.8**	(2.1)	1.0	(1.6)	**7.9**	(1.6)	0.0	(1.6)
	OECD average	**21.3**	(0.3)	**2.1**	(0.3)	**5.4**	(0.3)	**-8.9**	(0.3)	**-4.8**	(0.3)	**10.7**	(0.3)	**9.5**	(0.3)	**17.3**	(0.3)	**2.6**	(0.2)	**1.7**	(0.3)	**-2.2**	(0.3)
Partners	Albania	**27.6**	(2.9)	-0.8	(2.6)	0.1	(1.6)	0.8	(2.4)	**-5.9**	(2.7)	**18.8**	(3.0)	**19.0**	(2.0)	**11.5**	(2.1)	**5.4**	(2.1)	**5.2**	(2.2)	-1.1	(2.0)
	Argentina	**18.9**	(2.6)	**2.8**	(1.3)	**3.4**	(1.4)	**-3.9**	(1.7)	**-4.4**	(1.7)	**14.1**	(1.8)	**8.5**	(2.0)	**14.9**	(1.9)	-3.2	(1.7)	0.0	(1.7)	-1.9	(1.8)
	Azerbaijan	**14.2**	(2.0)	0.9	(0.9)	0.0	(0.6)	-0.1	(1.6)	-1.2	(1.8)	**8.0**	(1.7)	**7.7**	(1.8)	1.4	(1.5)	-1.6	(1.5)	**6.1**	(1.6)	**2.5**	(1.0)
	Brazil	**15.1**	(1.3)	-0.8	(1.2)	**3.1**	(0.8)	**-2.9**	(1.4)	**-5.8**	(1.2)	**11.3**	(1.5)	**8.9**	(1.0)	**14.1**	(1.2)	**3.7**	(1.0)	**4.1**	(1.4)	-2.0	(1.2)
	Bulgaria	**10.8**	(2.9)	**3.2**	(1.5)	**9.0**	(1.3)	-3.7	(2.0)	**-8.4**	(1.8)	**11.0**	(2.2)	**10.5**	(1.9)	**18.4**	(1.9)	1.0	(1.4)	**5.0**	(1.8)	1.8	(1.6)
	Colombia	**11.4**	(2.1)	-0.5	(1.3)	**6.3**	(1.5)	**-8.0**	(1.5)	-2.3	(2.0)	**8.7**	(1.7)	**12.5**	(2.0)	**15.6**	(1.9)	-1.7	(1.5)	**12.1**	(1.8)	1.2	(1.8)
	Croatia	**14.1**	(1.4)	**5.1**	(1.5)	**4.2**	(1.1)	-3.2	(1.7)	**-6.6**	(2.1)	2.1	(2.0)	**11.0**	(1.3)	**17.6**	(1.3)	**-4.7**	(1.6)	**4.5**	(1.6)	2.8	(1.5)
	Dubai (UAE)	**22.4**	(1.5)	**-3.4**	(1.0)	**3.9**	(1.0)	**-8.8**	(1.5)	**-3.9**	(1.4)	**11.8**	(1.4)	**10.6**	(1.2)	**15.1**	(1.2)	**5.4**	(1.2)	**3.8**	(1.3)	**-2.7**	(1.1)
	Hong Kong-China	**22.6**	(2.0)	0.9	(1.4)	2.4	(1.4)	**-8.0**	(2.0)	**-8.4**	(1.4)	**14.4**	(1.7)	**9.4**	(1.0)	**10.8**	(1.0)	0.8	(1.4)	**3.5**	(1.5)	1.4	(1.5)
	Indonesia	**17.2**	(2.1)	**1.9**	(0.8)	-0.9	(0.8)	**3.2**	(1.5)	0.6	(1.6)	**4.3**	(1.6)	**8.4**	(1.0)	**5.9**	(1.0)	**-3.2**	(1.4)	1.2	(1.4)	**-2.1**	(1.1)
	Jordan	**12.2**	(2.0)	-0.4	(1.1)	**4.3**	(1.0)	0.6	(2.0)	2.4	(2.0)	**11.4**	(1.9)	**7.1**	(1.4)	**12.6**	(1.5)	**6.4**	(1.3)	**4.7**	(1.7)	0.4	(1.4)
	Kazakhstan	**16.0**	(2.4)	**-5.0**	(1.3)	**3.0**	(0.8)	**-6.2**	(2.2)	**-5.8**	(1.9)	**10.3**	(2.1)	**15.7**	(1.2)	**18.4**	(1.6)	2.3	(1.6)	**10.0**	(1.6)	**3.3**	(1.3)
	Kyrgyzstan	**24.7**	(2.8)	1.7	(1.4)	-1.0	(0.8)	2.1	(1.8)	**-4.4**	(2.2)	**11.0**	(2.1)	**12.9**	(1.8)	**10.3**	(1.7)	1.3	(1.7)	**13.3**	(1.7)	1.1	(1.4)
	Latvia	**26.2**	(2.3)	1.9	(2.5)	**4.6**	(2.0)	**-11.3**	(2.3)	**-4.4**	(2.1)	**9.0**	(2.2)	**11.4**	(1.6)	**19.9**	(1.7)	**5.3**	(1.7)	**4.8**	(2.0)	-2.9	(1.8)
	Lithuania	**20.4**	(1.4)	**4.3**	(1.4)	**9.1**	(1.2)	**-13.7**	(2.1)	**-9.4**	(1.6)	**11.4**	(2.0)	**11.3**	(1.6)	**16.6**	(1.6)	2.1	(1.1)	**4.6**	(1.6)	-1.5	(1.6)
	Macao-China	c	c	c	c	c	c	c	c	c	c	c	c	c	c	c	c	c	c	c	c	c	c
	Montenegro	c	c	c	c	c	c	c	c	c	c	c	c	c	c	c	c	c	c	c	c	c	c
	Panama	**9.4**	(3.1)	3.1	(1.6)	1.1	(1.3)	1.5	(2.0)	-4.6	(2.7)	**10.1**	(2.6)	**5.9**	(2.4)	**10.4**	(2.0)	**3.6**	(1.8)	**6.9**	(2.4)	-1.7	(1.7)
	Peru	**15.7**	(2.1)	1.6	(1.4)	**2.4**	(1.2)	**-9.3**	(1.8)	-1.4	(1.9)	**5.8**	(1.9)	**7.6**	(1.7)	**13.0**	(1.8)	**3.4**	(1.6)	**11.5**	(2.0)	0.4	(1.6)
	Qatar	**17.6**	(1.4)	1.1	(0.8)	**4.3**	(0.8)	**-4.1**	(1.3)	**-5.9**	(1.3)	**13.1**	(1.3)	**7.8**	(1.1)	**9.3**	(1.2)	**6.0**	(0.8)	**4.1**	(1.0)	**-3.7**	(0.8)
	Romania	2.5	(2.6)	-1.0	(1.7)	**7.2**	(1.1)	-3.3	(1.9)	**-4.1**	(1.9)	**12.2**	(2.5)	**10.0**	(1.9)	**10.2**	(1.9)	**5.3**	(1.6)	**5.9**	(2.0)	0.8	(1.5)
	Russian Federation	**29.4**	(2.2)	-0.8	(1.5)	**5.9**	(0.9)	**-9.8**	(1.7)	**-6.9**	(1.7)	**9.0**	(1.9)	**14.2**	(1.5)	**17.0**	(1.6)	**5.3**	(1.4)	**3.2**	(1.6)	**2.8**	(1.3)
	Serbia	**11.2**	(1.5)	0.6	(2.2)	**6.3**	(1.1)	**-7.1**	(1.4)	**-3.2**	(1.4)	**5.8**	(1.7)	**10.8**	(1.4)	**16.3**	(1.7)	**-4.7**	(1.1)	**5.4**	(1.7)	1.9	(1.1)
	Shanghai-China	**19.7**	(2.5)	0.0	(1.3)	-1.2	(1.5)	**-8.6**	(2.2)	**-4.6**	(2.0)	**13.1**	(2.4)	**10.0**	(1.2)	**15.9**	(1.7)	**2.7**	(1.3)	1.3	(1.9)	0.5	(1.5)
	Singapore	**23.3**	(1.5)	1.0	(1.0)	**4.9**	(1.1)	**-9.2**	(1.4)	**-8.3**	(1.3)	**11.3**	(1.6)	**6.5**	(1.1)	**23.2**	(1.5)	1.8	(1.3)	**7.1**	(1.5)	**-4.7**	(1.4)
	Chinese Taipei	**24.9**	(1.7)	1.0	(1.5)	-1.4	(2.4)	-2.8	(2.0)	-1.9	(2.5)	**18.9**	(3.1)	**11.8**	(1.9)	**13.6**	(1.4)	2.3	(1.2)	**8.3**	(1.6)	**-4.4**	(1.7)
	Thailand	**13.3**	(2.3)	**6.5**	(1.2)	-0.8	(0.9)	**9.6**	(2.1)	-4.9	(3.2)	**5.3**	(2.7)	**8.6**	(1.4)	**4.0**	(1.5)	0.1	(1.8)	**6.8**	(1.4)	1.2	(1.7)
	Trinidad and Tobago	**16.2**	(1.8)	2.3	(1.3)	**3.0**	(1.0)	**2.9**	(1.4)	**-8.6**	(1.4)	**10.7**	(1.5)	**7.0**	(1.3)	**12.3**	(1.5)	**4.1**	(1.0)	**2.8**	(1.3)	-0.3	(1.2)
	Tunisia	**5.5**	(2.1)	-0.1	(1.6)	0.4	(1.1)	**-7.3**	(1.6)	1.1	(1.4)	**13.3**	(1.7)	**4.4**	(1.5)	**9.3**	(1.4)	**3.5**	(1.1)	**3.2**	(1.2)	-0.1	(1.2)
	Uruguay	**13.7**	(1.7)	**5.1**	(1.2)	**6.1**	(1.3)	**-4.7**	(1.4)	**-7.9**	(1.5)	**11.9**	(1.6)	**7.6**	(1.4)	**18.3**	(1.4)	**-3.0**	(1.4)	0.8	(1.5)	0.7	(1.4)

Note: Values that are statistically significant are indicated in bold (see Annex A3).

1. Multilevel regression model (student and school levels): Reading performance is regressed on all the variables presented in this table.

StatLink http://dx.doi.org/10.1787/888932343285

[Part 2/5]

Table IV.2.14b Relationships between reading performance and students' reading engagement and approaches to learning, the learning environment, resources, policies and practices

		Learning environment and school climate (school level)[1]														School policies on selecting and grouping students[1]							
		Index of teacher-student relations (school average)		Index of disciplinary climate (school average)		Index of student-related factors affecting school climate (higher values indicate a positive student behaviour)		Index of teacher-related factors affecting school climate (higher values indicate a positive teacher behaviour)		Index of teachers'[1] stimulation of reading engagement (school average)		Parents expect the school to set high academic standards and pressure for students to achieve them		Index of school principal's leadership (higher values indicate more leadership roles are taken)		School with high academic selectivity for school admittance		School is very likely to transfer students with low achievement, behavioural problems or special learning needs		School with ability grouping for all subjects		Percentage of students that repeated one or more grades	
		Change in score	S.E.	Change in score	S.E.	Change in score	S.E.	Change in score	S.E.	Change in score	S.E.	Change in score	S.E.	Change in score	S.E.	Change in score	S.E.	Change in score	S.E.	Change in score	S.E.	Change in score	S.E.
OECD	Australia	**21.1**	(8.3)	**21.9**	(6.8)	3.1	(2.5)	1.7	(2.9)	-10.0	(10.6)	6.7	(4.9)	1.5	(1.4)	3.7	(3.7)	6.8	(7.5)	**-16.1**	(8.1)	**-0.9**	(0.2)
	Austria	-1.8	(9.8)	14.1	(8.0)	-5.8	(4.8)	8.7	(5.1)	12.3	(8.8)	-17.2	(28.2)	-6.6	(6.2)	**25.8**	(8.9)	**16.4**	(8.3)	-21.7	(13.7)	**-0.4**	(0.2)
	Belgium	-15.4	(10.1)	**20.0**	(6.7)	-1.2	(3.7)	**10.6**	(3.7)	6.7	(11.3)	9.9	(9.0)	-6.4	(4.2)	1.0	(7.2)	3.0	(4.9)	-12.0	(7.1)	**0.8**	(0.2)
	Canada	2.3	(5.1)	8.2	(4.4)	4.6	(2.3)	3.0	(2.7)	-5.9	(5.6)	6.6	(3.6)	-2.0	(1.9)	3.5	(4.3)	-2.2	(5.4)	2.5	(5.9)	**-0.4**	(0.1)
	Chile	7.7	(6.2)	-4.3	(6.2)	**-7.1**	(3.1)	**6.5**	(2.1)	10.3	(6.0)	8.3	(6.0)	-0.5	(2.1)	8.4	(4.6)	4.4	(5.6)	-3.8	(5.6)	**-0.8**	(0.1)
	Czech Republic	-10.9	(7.4)	**12.0**	(4.6)	**-12.0**	(3.8)	**15.9**	(3.4)	9.5	(8.3)	**11.3**	(5.7)	-2.6	(2.7)	**21.1**	(7.7)	-1.8	(6.3)	-6.8	(6.1)	-0.1	(0.4)
	Denmark	0.8	(6.5)	7.6	(4.6)	-1.2	(2.4)	5.4	(3.0)	-4.6	(6.1)	**16.1**	(4.0)	**5.2**	(2.5)	13.4	(6.9)	5.3	(5.3)	-9.4	(5.5)	-0.4	(0.3)
	Estonia	**24.9**	(7.4)	**13.0**	(4.6)	-1.2	(2.8)	5.5	(3.9)	**-28.3**	(8.3)	5.4	(5.0)	1.1	(1.9)	**11.0**	(3.8)	0.1	(6.1)	0.5	(7.7)	-0.3	(0.3)
	Finland	13.0	(8.4)	5.9	(4.6)	4.8	(2.6)	0.7	(2.8)	-4.4	(9.0)	4.7	(7.5)	-2.0	(2.5)	**20.1**	(8.9)	c	c	7.2	(8.7)	-1.0	(0.6)
	France	w	w	w	w	w	w	w	w	w	w	w	w	w	w	w	w	w	w	w	w	w	w
	Germany	-3.0	(10.7)	-0.4	(11.3)	**-15.5**	(5.2)	**25.2**	(6.0)	**46.6**	(13.3)	-20.2	(15.4)	-3.8	(4.6)	**16.3**	(7.1)	8.3	(6.9)	-5.3	(9.4)	0.1	(0.2)
	Greece	21.6	(18.4)	**24.4**	(10.9)	-8.8	(5.7)	**14.4**	(6.4)	0.3	(11.8)	-1.6	(13.6)	-1.2	(4.8)	-11.7	(16.6)	6.5	(8.6)	**-113.4**	(46.6)	-0.3	(0.2)
	Hungary	2.9	(10.5)	9.5	(8.6)	-2.7	(5.1)	**10.2**	(4.6)	0.8	(9.9)	4.2	(11.7)	-3.5	(3.9)	15.1	(13.2)	0.0	(8.2)	-3.3	(14.5)	**-0.8**	(0.2)
	Iceland	**13.6**	(6.6)	18.7	(9.7)	-6.8	(4.4)	7.4	(5.4)	-0.5	(8.4)	-2.7	(8.2)	-1.2	(3.4)	c	c	c	c	**-15.0**	(7.4)	-1.2	(1.3)
	Ireland	**35.6**	(12.8)	**16.6**	(6.1)	-0.8	(4.0)	10.5	(5.7)	-13.9	(11.1)	5.3	(5.7)	1.6	(3.5)	-7.7	(5.8)	c	c	-12.5	(11.7)	**-1.2**	(0.4)
	Israel	17.8	(11.4)	7.6	(8.4)	-6.1	(5.4)	4.8	(5.1)	**-59.6**	(11.0)	4.2	(6.3)	**-14.3**	(4.5)	**-14.4**	(6.4)	**-25.1**	(9.9)	5.4	(9.6)	-0.1	(0.4)
	Italy	**-19.0**	(6.8)	**28.8**	(4.7)	-4.6	(3.3)	**11.8**	(3.2)	12.4	(7.5)	**20.6**	(5.8)	**-6.8**	(2.6)	-2.7	(4.2)	**14.5**	(4.7)	-1.2	(4.9)	**-0.5**	(0.2)
	Japan	**47.8**	(14.5)	**26.3**	(8.8)	-3.5	(3.6)	**12.3**	(4.3)	-4.5	(9.4)	6.3	(6.9)	-0.8	(3.0)	-16.1	(9.4)	-5.8	(8.1)	-6.9	(7.7)	c	c
	Korea	-0.1	(15.4)	**25.8**	(8.2)	-9.0	(4.8)	**12.8**	(3.4)	**-39.0**	(12.3)	**17.8**	(5.9)	-2.1	(2.5)	**14.3**	(4.9)	2.1	(7.9)	-12.8	(10.2)	c	c
	Luxembourg	c	c	c	c	c	c	c	c	c	c	c	c	c	c	c	c	c	c	c	c	c	c
	Mexico	4.3	(6.9)	**19.1**	(7.1)	-2.4	(2.8)	**5.9**	(3.0)	**13.8**	(6.0)	-1.9	(5.7)	1.5	(1.8)	2.9	(4.0)	0.4	(3.4)	-5.2	(4.9)	**-0.3**	(0.1)
	Netherlands	-17.1	(16.3)	**26.4**	(11.3)	**-11.3**	(5.0)	**14.1**	(4.8)	1.9	(13.1)	5.8	(9.5)	1.2	(4.3)	12.8	(8.7)	**-14.8**	(7.5)	-0.8	(5.3)	0.1	(0.2)
	New Zealand	-4.7	(9.3)	**31.6**	(7.6)	-6.2	(3.9)	**9.7**	(3.2)	-14.8	(7.7)	**27.7**	(5.1)	-1.7	(2.4)	6.7	(5.8)	-19.9	(13.9)	0.7	(8.4)	-0.5	(0.6)
	Norway	4.0	(8.1)	8.4	(6.3)	-1.2	(3.7)	-0.8	(3.7)	3.8	(8.1)	**15.0**	(4.2)	-2.3	(3.8)	15.3	(7.8)	c	c	2.8	(9.1)	c	c
	Poland	-4.5	(7.9)	4.0	(5.5)	4.2	(2.3)	-3.3	(2.8)	-1.6	(8.2)	4.0	(5.8)	**-5.5**	(2.8)	4.9	(5.7)	4.7	(5.4)	-0.2	(7.9)	**-1.5**	(0.2)
	Portugal	-4.0	(10.1)	10.2	(6.2)	-0.1	(3.1)	-0.3	(2.9)	-8.6	(8.4)	10.4	(7.0)	1.1	(3.0)	**-45.3**	(14.7)	c	c	3.9	(7.4)	**-0.6**	(0.1)
	Slovak Republic	5.7	(9.0)	**14.3**	(7.1)	-5.3	(4.1)	7.5	(3.9)	3.6	(8.4)	0.5	(8.6)	-3.3	(3.8)	1.7	(7.8)	-9.9	(5.5)	-7.3	(7.5)	**-1.0**	(0.3)
	Slovenia	-8.2	(8.4)	8.4	(6.1)	0.9	(4.1)	4.4	(3.7)	14.2	(8.1)	8.5	(5.8)	0.0	(2.9)	11.1	(5.8)	2.4	(5.5)	-16.9	(10.2)	-0.3	(0.2)
	Spain	**-14.9**	(4.5)	**11.0**	(3.6)	-0.8	(2.1)	3.5	(2.0)	3.4	(4.2)	2.9	(5.0)	0.7	(1.6)	10.1	(7.1)	4.2	(5.0)	5.7	(4.7)	**-0.9**	(0.1)
	Sweden	2.1	(8.2)	4.9	(6.6)	-3.3	(2.9)	5.2	(3.9)	**19.1**	(9.3)	6.1	(5.2)	**-9.7**	(2.6)	4.8	(8.3)	14.8	(11.8)	-0.5	(8.4)	-0.3	(0.4)
	Switzerland	-2.2	(6.1)	**20.7**	(5.5)	-2.2	(2.8)	4.8	(3.0)	-9.0	(8.1)	1.6	(6.0)	-0.3	(2.3)	3.1	(4.1)	**14.1**	(4.6)	-6.0	(3.2)	**-0.6**	(0.1)
	Turkey	-0.9	(10.9)	3.9	(10.3)	-3.1	(5.7)	-0.6	(4.5)	6.2	(10.7)	5.3	(8.9)	1.7	(3.4)	**22.5**	(6.3)	-1.9	(5.9)	**-16.7**	(7.1)	**-1.3**	(0.2)
	United Kingdom	**-21.3**	(8.7)	14.4	(8.5)	-3.5	(3.6)	8.6	(4.4)	**25.3**	(8.0)	8.0	(4.5)	-1.3	(1.8)	**10.3**	(5.2)	-10.7	(5.9)	4.3	(5.3)	**-1.7**	(0.8)
	United States	-4.0	(8.1)	**26.9**	(8.0)	-7.1	(4.1)	5.1	(3.1)	9.8	(8.4)	**11.0**	(4.8)	**-4.0**	(2.0)	2.8	(4.5)	**11.6**	(5.6)	15.2	(8.4)	**-0.7**	(0.3)
	OECD average	2.9	(1.7)	**14.4**	(1.3)	**-3.6**	(0.7)	**7.2**	(0.7)	-0.1	(1.6)	**6.0**	(1.6)	**-2.1**	(0.6)	**5.3**	(1.4)	1.0	(1.4)	**-7.7**	(2.0)	**-0.6**	(0.1)
Partners	Albania	-7.7	(12.7)	-0.4	(9.8)	-0.9	(5.5)	-3.9	(5.3)	13.8	(12.7)	14.5	(8.1)	6.7	(4.1)	-11.1	(6.0)	13.3	(7.8)	-6.3	(8.4)	**-1.6**	(0.4)
	Argentina	-5.9	(12.6)	7.8	(8.5)	-5.3	(4.7)	-0.8	(5.0)	1.8	(11.7)	7.4	(12.0)	1.7	(5.6)	13.0	(10.2)	**18.4**	(8.3)	-14.0	(9.3)	**-1.0**	(0.1)
	Azerbaijan	1.3	(14.0)	**38.1**	(13.2)	-8.5	(4.4)	**9.2**	(4.1)	7.5	(9.3)	**-34.0**	(8.7)	-0.5	(3.2)	-8.4	(7.8)	**19.6**	(8.6)	-0.9	(8.3)	**-2.6**	(1.0)
	Brazil	7.4	(7.1)	8.5	(6.7)	**-5.8**	(2.9)	**6.4**	(2.8)	**-15.1**	(7.2)	-2.4	(6.8)	**5.2**	(2.0)	3.0	(6.0)	**14.4**	(5.6)	2.8	(4.9)	**-0.8**	(0.1)
	Bulgaria	-1.5	(9.9)	6.2	(10.3)	-6.3	(5.4)	**10.8**	(5.1)	15.3	(12.1)	13.8	(12.4)	0.8	(4.3)	13.8	(9.4)	-2.0	(9.7)	-3.3	(10.7)	-0.3	(0.2)
	Colombia	-10.3	(7.6)	6.4	(7.8)	0.8	(3.2)	3.1	(2.4)	1.7	(8.0)	2.1	(6.0)	-3.5	(2.0)	2.8	(5.3)	-0.5	(4.8)	**-12.1**	(5.8)	**-0.6**	(0.2)
	Croatia	1.4	(8.9)	**15.7**	(5.7)	-5.0	(2.9)	**8.4**	(3.0)	**33.8**	(8.4)	**20.0**	(8.9)	-3.0	(3.0)	**28.4**	(6.2)	2.6	(5.1)	0.1	(5.1)	**-1.7**	(0.5)
	Dubai (UAE)	7.1	(11.3)	**24.7**	(6.1)	4.1	(4.2)	3.2	(4.0)	-5.3	(8.4)	-0.2	(6.0)	-3.6	(2.9)	7.8	(6.9)	-12.5	(6.4)	-7.2	(7.0)	**-0.6**	(0.2)
	Hong Kong-China	21.5	(11.5)	**36.2**	(8.8)	0.4	(4.3)	5.4	(2.9)	-12.4	(10.3)	7.2	(14.1)	**-6.4**	(2.2)	4.1	(6.5)	3.7	(5.3)	-3.1	(7.5)	**-0.6**	(0.2)
	Indonesia	-18.8	(11.5)	-9.4	(7.9)	0.1	(4.4)	**11.4**	(4.6)	**-18.1**	(8.5)	-2.1	(6.4)	-4.3	(2.9)	0.2	(5.1)	**11.7**	(5.3)	-1.9	(6.6)	**-0.3**	(0.2)
	Jordan	17.9	(14.1)	**19.4**	(8.0)	0.8	(4.0)	2.1	(3.4)	-9.9	(10.8)	-1.0	(6.4)	4.3	(2.9)	6.1	(6.4)	**12.6**	(6.1)	-2.7	(6.0)	-0.8	(0.4)
	Kazakhstan	**-42.2**	(12.0)	12.5	(9.2)	4.9	(5.4)	0.5	(4.0)	**37.2**	(7.9)	17.1	(8.8)	-2.7	(4.3)	-9.3	(6.6)	2.7	(12.2)	-7.2	(6.3)	-0.4	(1.2)
	Kyrgyzstan	**-30.1**	(9.0)	12.3	(13.2)	5.1	(3.8)	2.8	(3.5)	-4.5	(9.6)	-1.3	(6.0)	-3.3	(2.9)	**-11.9**	(5.5)	5.5	(5.5)	**14.8**	(6.0)	0.0	(0.6)
	Latvia	**21.7**	(8.7)	7.0	(6.4)	**-9.7**	(3.8)	**12.0**	(3.0)	-10.4	(6.6)	**20.7**	(5.8)	3.0	(3.1)	-1.0	(5.2)	2.8	(6.5)	-4.4	(5.4)	**-0.5**	(0.2)
	Lithuania	1.4	(6.7)	**21.5**	(6.9)	**-7.9**	(3.6)	4.8	(3.7)	-4.9	(8.9)	14.9	(9.0)	-2.1	(3.4)	8.8	(7.6)	10.6	(8.5)	-11.1	(6.3)	**-0.8**	(0.4)
	Macao-China	c	c	c	c	c	c	c	c	c	c	c	c	c	c	c	c	c	c	c	c	c	c
	Montenegro	c	c	c	c	c	c	c	c	c	c	c	c	c	c	c	c	c	c	c	c	c	c
	Panama	-5.1	(9.9)	**51.8**	(10.1)	0.6	(5.6)	0.5	(5.8)	7.7	(12.0)	2.2	(9.4)	-0.5	(3.5)	-11.4	(6.4)	**16.1**	(7.0)	**22.6**	(10.6)	**-0.4**	(0.2)
	Peru	-2.7	(8.1)	17.1	(13.6)	0.4	(4.0)	0.1	(4.0)	13.0	(10.3)	3.3	(7.6)	1.2	(3.2)	**14.5**	(6.9)	-6.0	(6.5)	-9.8	(5.8)	**-0.9**	(0.2)
	Qatar	10.3	(10.0)	**34.2**	(10.9)	-0.7	(6.0)	3.4	(6.1)	7.5	(11.0)	12.4	(8.2)	4.1	(3.3)	2.0	(8.4)	-7.3	(7.8)	-4.2	(8.6)	**-0.6**	(0.2)
	Romania	-21.7	(13.4)	**46.2**	(12.4)	**-11.2**	(4.9)	**16.4**	(4.0)	18.1	(13.5)	**27.2**	(8.5)	**-8.3**	(3.7)	**-16.9**	(5.7)	-5.0	(6.6)	-1.7	(7.3)	0.1	(0.2)
	Russian Federation	-14.8	(8.9)	**22.4**	(6.5)	**-7.7**	(3.5)	**9.1**	(2.7)	**15.7**	(7.7)	2.1	(7.0)	-0.8	(3.3)	3.5	(6.5)	10.7	(8.8)	-4.0	(4.6)	0.0	(0.2)
	Serbia	-3.5	(11.9)	**30.4**	(7.8)	5.8	(6.3)	5.6	(3.9)	-4.1	(8.0)	-1.8	(11.6)	-3.2	(3.2)	-15.6	(8.6)	**10.9**	(5.1)	-0.8	(6.7)	**-0.8**	(0.2)
	Shanghai-China	15.5	(9.1)	**20.9**	(6.9)	-1.8	(2.4)	2.9	(1.9)	7.7	(9.0)	5.2	(4.1)	-2.0	(2.3)	**16.8**	(3.9)	-1.0	(4.3)	**-14.6**	(4.9)	**-0.8**	(0.2)
	Singapore	20.8	(10.8)	**29.8**	(8.6)	2.6	(3.1)	1.5	(4.1)	-16.3	(12.3)	**9.6**	(4.4)	-2.6	(2.5)	8.8	(5.9)	c	c	7.9	(5.5)	**-1.2**	(0.4)
	Chinese Taipei	**16.5**	(8.3)	**13.1**	(6.0)	-2.3	(2.2)	**4.1**	(1.8)	5.9	(6.9)	0.1	(3.5)	-2.2	(2.1)	7.6	(4.1)	**-12.5**	(3.4)	-5.5	(9.2)	0.3	(0.5)
	Thailand	6.0	(7.7)	9.1	(10.5)	-1.0	(4.6)	1.7	(4.8)	7.7	(7.8)	5.2	(6.2)	**7.4**	(3.2)	0.1	(5.6)	13.2	(8.7)	8.8	(7.7)	-0.4	(0.3)
	Trinidad and Tobago	-25.0	(17.1)	**24.2**	(11.7)	-3.1	(4.1)	**10.1**	(5.0)	14.4	(11.0)	8.5	(8.2)	-3.1	(3.8)	-3.1	(7.5)	-2.3	(9.0)	-6.1	(12.1)	**-1.5**	(0.2)
	Tunisia	-10.0	(8.3)	9.3	(8.2)	3.3	(3.2)	1.0	(3.3)	**24.4**	(7.8)	**19.3**	(5.6)	**-3.7**	(1.9)	**11.0**	(5.5)	3.2	(4.7)	3.1	(8.7)	**-0.6**	(0.2)
	Uruguay	-13.2	(9.1)	**11.8**	(4.9)	-4.1	(2.8)	-1.3	(3.2)	0.9	(7.0)	14.6	(10.0)	-0.8	(2.1)	5.0	(6.4)	**-19.5**	(6.9)	2.3	(6.3)	**-0.7**	(0.1)

Note: Values that are statistically significant are indicated in bold (see Annex A3).

1. Multilevel regression model (student and school levels): Reading performance is regressed on all the variables presented in this table.

StatLink http://dx.doi.org/10.1787/888932343285

[Part 3/5]

Table IV.2.14b Relationships between reading performance and students' reading engagement and approaches to learning, the learning environment, resources, policies and practices

		School governance[1]								School assessment and accountability policies[1]							
		Index of school responsibility for resource allocation (higher values indicate more autonomy)		Index of school responsibility for curriculum and assessment (higher values indicate more autonomy)		School competes with schools for students in the same area		Private school		School uses standardised tests		School uses student assessments to monitor school's progress		School uses student assessments to improve instruction or curriculum		School uses student assessments to compare with other schools or district or national performance	
		Change in score	S.E.	Change in score	S.E.	Change in score	S.E.	Change in score	S.E.	Change in score	S.E.	Change in score	S.E.	Change in score	S.E.	Change in score	S.E.
OECD	Australia	**4.8**	(1.9)	-0.9	(1.9)	-10.3	(7.4)	1.1	(4.9)	-3.5	(3.3)	**-9.9**	(4.5)	0.1	(4.9)	-4.8	(3.7)
	Austria	13.5	(8.9)	-8.4	(5.7)	-4.7	(8.2)	8.5	(15.0)	**-25.1**	(11.0)	-0.6	(10.7)	-6.4	(8.5)	13.1	(9.9)
	Belgium	-6.5	(21.8)	2.3	(3.7)	11.3	(10.9)	w	w	**-20.6**	(6.1)	7.7	(5.5)	-9.1	(5.3)	1.7	(9.1)
	Canada	3.6	(4.1)	-1.8	(3.2)	5.4	(4.1)	6.3	(9.8)	4.8	(4.6)	-1.7	(5.2)	1.8	(4.3)	2.3	(4.9)
	Chile	2.6	(2.1)	-0.4	(2.4)	8.9	(5.2)	-2.9	(6.9)	0.5	(7.6)	13.3	(7.5)	-10.7	(10.1)	**-13.6**	(4.7)
	Czech Republic	**4.3**	(2.0)	**-6.6**	(3.3)	5.7	(6.6)	16.9	(9.1)	**20.0**	(9.9)	13.7	(8.7)	-6.9	(7.2)	6.4	(5.9)
	Denmark	-0.6	(2.1)	0.1	(1.9)	-5.0	(4.1)	-5.9	(5.5)	-1.2	(8.8)	-2.1	(3.5)	3.5	(4.8)	3.3	(3.9)
	Estonia	-4.4	(3.1)	-0.1	(2.3)	2.6	(4.9)	-2.9	(9.0)	-2.9	(4.9)	-2.4	(6.4)	-10.1	(5.4)	2.7	(5.4)
	Finland	1.0	(5.0)	1.8	(2.0)	0.4	(3.7)	-11.6	(10.1)	19.9	(12.1)	-1.4	(3.6)	-3.3	(3.6)	0.4	(4.1)
	France	w	w	w	w	w	w	w	w	w	w	w	w	w	w	w	w
	Germany	12.3	(6.4)	-5.7	(4.9)	**35.4**	(7.6)	-8.9	(13.3)	-5.3	(7.0)	-8.5	(6.6)	2.2	(7.0)	12.6	(6.6)
	Greece	**125.7**	(58.7)	-2.3	(19.5)	-2.9	(9.7)	-7.1	(35.0)	-2.8	(8.7)	-3.9	(9.7)	**-23.8**	(12.0)	5.6	(10.2)
	Hungary	**-6.0**	(3.0)	1.5	(3.5)	5.6	(6.9)	1.7	(9.3)	**23.6**	(7.9)	**24.0**	(8.7)	**-15.5**	(6.5)	**-18.9**	(7.9)
	Iceland	-4.2	(3.5)	**5.6**	(2.4)	7.8	(4.8)	c	c	-12.9	(7.5)	-3.6	(10.9)	11.4	(9.1)	-6.4	(4.1)
	Ireland	4.5	(11.2)	-0.7	(4.3)	-8.1	(8.8)	5.3	(6.8)	-0.2	(5.9)	0.3	(5.5)	0.8	(5.3)	-11.1	(6.8)
	Israel	-1.4	(8.3)	-6.0	(4.2)	13.7	(10.4)	-1.8	(14.0)	23.5	(16.0)	-2.3	(9.4)	-19.9	(11.5)	9.1	(8.7)
	Italy	-3.3	(4.7)	-3.5	(2.1)	1.9	(5.6)	12.2	(11.4)	**-11.8**	(4.1)	-2.7	(4.5)	2.5	(5.4)	0.0	(5.2)
	Japan	0.7	(3.9)	-0.2	(3.3)	-0.1	(7.9)	**-22.0**	(10.9)	2.5	(5.2)	-3.1	(5.5)	-7.9	(8.1)	-1.6	(5.5)
	Korea	**7.3**	(3.5)	1.4	(2.9)	4.3	(7.8)	2.5	(6.3)	**-22.4**	(11.4)	**-26.7**	(6.0)	**26.4**	(5.8)	-1.3	(5.2)
	Luxembourg	c	c	c	c	c	c	c	c	c	c	c	c	c	c	c	c
	Mexico	-3.4	(3.6)	-2.5	(2.7)	10.6	(5.8)	**22.3**	(10.6)	8.8	(5.7)	4.4	(6.1)	8.1	(8.1)	0.0	(5.7)
	Netherlands	-0.8	(2.8)	6.9	(4.5)	17.2	(15.6)	0.2	(4.8)	-6.9	(6.4)	-9.4	(5.9)	**13.0**	(6.1)	0.7	(5.7)
	New Zealand	-1.4	(4.3)	-4.8	(2.9)	**16.3**	(5.1)	-4.6	(13.6)	1.8	(5.4)	1.5	(14.5)	**46.2**	(14.5)	4.0	(8.4)
	Norway	4.9	(3.3)	1.0	(3.1)	1.9	(3.9)	c	c	-10.9	(9.9)	-3.2	(6.0)	0.7	(5.0)	-1.2	(6.0)
	Poland	5.6	(6.1)	0.4	(2.5)	7.8	(4.8)	-1.4	(17.2)	-2.1	(9.6)	-6.6	(6.4)	0.3	(7.1)	-0.8	(3.8)
	Portugal	1.2	(4.2)	5.4	(7.2)	6.5	(4.9)	-2.4	(9.1)	9.6	(5.8)	9.3	(7.1)	-9.8	(5.1)	-3.0	(4.6)
	Slovak Republic	0.2	(2.4)	-2.0	(2.8)	3.6	(8.3)	1.5	(9.5)	1.6	(12.6)	-12.7	(7.6)	4.0	(6.9)	-0.5	(5.8)
	Slovenia	-3.3	(4.9)	**-8.5**	(4.2)	10.0	(5.3)	**28.3**	(14.0)	-2.8	(6.2)	-13.5	(8.7)	-9.2	(6.1)	-5.1	(5.4)
	Spain	-2.0	(2.5)	-1.0	(1.8)	**7.8**	(3.8)	8.3	(4.4)	**-7.5**	(3.2)	2.0	(3.3)	-5.3	(3.9)	6.0	(3.2)
	Sweden	2.2	(2.1)	0.2	(2.2)	**10.0**	(4.9)	6.4	(9.2)	6.0	(9.5)	13.4	(8.7)	-7.5	(6.3)	5.9	(5.5)
	Switzerland	**-5.3**	(2.6)	2.2	(2.6)	3.8	(3.7)	-8.7	(8.4)	3.6	(4.4)	-6.2	(4.4)	3.7	(3.5)	2.5	(4.4)
	Turkey	-24.5	(14.7)	**-14.3**	(6.0)	**15.1**	(6.3)	c	c	**-22.1**	(8.7)	-14.8	(9.4)	-9.1	(5.6)	7.1	(12.4)
	United Kingdom	-1.1	(2.0)	-0.4	(2.3)	**-15.5**	(5.1)	22.6	(12.7)	-0.4	(3.8)	-15.4	(11.0)	5.7	(8.1)	-4.0	(7.4)
	United States	-2.7	(3.0)	**-8.6**	(3.0)	-0.3	(5.4)	c	c	**-28.6**	(12.0)	20.1	(16.2)	9.5	(7.6)	-5.7	(10.0)
	OECD average	3.9	(2.2)	-1.6	(0.9)	**5.2**	(1.2)	2.4	(2.3)	-2.0	(1.5)	-1.3	(1.4)	-0.5	(1.3)	0.2	(1.2)
Partners	Albania	-10.8	(7.2)	-0.6	(3.6)	-1.3	(7.9)	**55.4**	(19.7)	-13.1	(13.2)	c	c	6.4	(11.7)	-16.4	(8.7)
	Argentina	3.8	(8.5)	-9.4	(7.4)	0.7	(9.7)	**34.3**	(9.1)	-6.7	(8.5)	-6.0	(9.5)	-2.7	(12.8)	-1.1	(8.8)
	Azerbaijan	-1.5	(7.5)	-2.2	(4.3)	**18.4**	(7.9)	c	c	**53.4**	(15.7)	-2.3	(10.1)	-3.3	(11.6)	**48.7**	(12.0)
	Brazil	**8.7**	(4.1)	0.9	(3.0)	-10.0	(5.4)	19.1	(10.9)	-4.0	(5.7)	-2.3	(11.1)	-1.3	(7.1)	**-16.1**	(5.8)
	Bulgaria	-7.2	(3.8)	**-22.3**	(10.8)	0.7	(9.3)	c	c	-9.6	(13.3)	17.1	(14.5)	-11.1	(8.5)	-4.5	(12.4)
	Colombia	**6.3**	(3.0)	-3.0	(2.6)	-2.6	(6.5)	-0.1	(8.8)	10.2	(6.4)	10.5	(11.5)	-3.3	(7.5)	1.3	(5.2)
	Croatia	**-17.3**	(8.5)	3.1	(4.7)	10.3	(6.1)	c	c	1.3	(4.3)	-12.1	(8.2)	6.0	(5.7)	5.2	(4.9)
	Dubai (UAE)	0.7	(2.9)	**8.8**	(3.3)	-5.3	(12.1)	5.3	(12.6)	15.5	(10.0)	-5.6	(9.4)	-19.3	(10.7)	1.3	(7.0)
	Hong Kong-China	-4.3	(2.3)	2.4	(2.8)	2.7	(22.0)	5.6	(10.6)	c	c	12.4	(10.1)	4.8	(10.1)	0.2	(4.1)
	Indonesia	1.5	(3.4)	-4.8	(2.7)	-2.4	(9.1)	-10.5	(7.7)	-5.0	(10.6)	-12.8	(14.5)	**31.9**	(12.1)	-1.7	(8.6)
	Jordan	-4.0	(10.2)	-10.5	(6.8)	-4.1	(6.3)	14.2	(9.0)	-3.8	(8.5)	**-16.5**	(7.8)	-8.9	(15.2)	**26.0**	(8.8)
	Kazakhstan	-0.2	(6.6)	-3.1	(6.6)	2.7	(7.5)	-5.9	(20.5)	-1.1	(13.1)	c	c	-8.7	(34.9)	-3.5	(12.6)
	Kyrgyzstan	-1.7	(6.0)	3.5	(3.0)	-3.2	(6.9)	28.0	(19.8)	28.8	(17.4)	2.8	(16.1)	11.6	(8.9)	**-22.7**	(8.9)
	Latvia	-5.6	(4.1)	2.6	(4.0)	-4.4	(6.4)	c	c	-5.3	(7.1)	-3.3	(12.2)	c	c	3.1	(9.5)
	Lithuania	0.3	(4.9)	3.7	(2.6)	-1.5	(5.9)	c	c	-8.7	(6.5)	0.1	(9.7)	-7.1	(5.9)	-8.7	(6.2)
	Macao-China	c	c	c	c	c	c	c	c	c	c	c	c	c	c	c	c
	Montenegro	c	c	c	c	c	c	c	c	c	c	c	c	c	c	c	c
	Panama	10.3	(7.8)	**-10.7**	(4.1)	-12.2	(7.1)	25.6	(21.6)	-9.5	(6.8)	-11.0	(9.1)	-6.3	(9.1)	-1.5	(7.2)
	Peru	7.9	(4.9)	-3.1	(3.5)	**20.6**	(7.1)	11.4	(14.0)	-10.3	(6.8)	-2.5	(10.9)	-13.9	(13.5)	-10.3	(7.0)
	Qatar	2.6	(4.6)	-5.4	(5.6)	2.3	(7.8)	**34.1**	(12.1)	17.0	(21.7)	-5.3	(12.5)	**-24.0**	(7.5)	-12.1	(11.2)
	Romania	6.7	(27.0)	-3.8	(3.4)	-2.6	(10.1)	c	c	-4.4	(7.4)	**51.6**	(17.3)	-12.3	(8.4)	-21.4	(12.5)
	Russian Federation	-1.1	(3.5)	1.3	(3.6)	1.7	(4.9)	c	c	-8.1	(6.3)	c	c	c	c	**-30.1**	(14.6)
	Serbia	9.8	(8.5)	-25.6	(20.9)	**-17.2**	(6.3)	c	c	1.3	(5.9)	-11.5	(10.4)	-6.9	(7.2)	-2.6	(7.8)
	Shanghai-China	0.4	(1.8)	-2.5	(1.7)	1.0	(4.9)	**12.0**	(6.1)	5.9	(9.6)	-5.0	(7.5)	-14.3	(12.6)	**8.7**	(4.3)
	Singapore	7.4	(3.9)	-1.9	(2.2)	-18.6	(11.8)	c	c	-16.9	(15.1)	10.0	(17.3)	-21.1	(13.5)	-2.6	(11.8)
	Chinese Taipei	-0.8	(2.7)	-1.7	(1.6)	**-19.5**	(7.7)	**-21.1**	(7.3)	11.3	(5.9)	4.6	(4.5)	10.6	(5.8)	**-17.0**	(3.6)
	Thailand	-1.5	(3.0)	4.3	(3.2)	5.7	(7.5)	-11.6	(8.9)	16.0	(8.5)	1.0	(14.8)	-1.1	(18.4)	-13.8	(7.9)
	Trinidad and Tobago	**14.0**	(5.8)	3.2	(4.8)	6.0	(9.8)	-24.5	(13.9)	4.9	(7.8)	22.9	(12.1)	-17.1	(12.7)	-1.8	(6.6)
	Tunisia	-3.9	(6.6)	6.8	(18.6)	3.5	(4.6)	**-29.5**	(14.2)	**-16.2**	(7.8)	4.5	(9.4)	0.3	(4.0)	11.5	(6.7)
	Uruguay	-5.8	(4.7)	4.9	(5.7)	4.1	(4.7)	**41.0**	(10.4)	-7.3	(4.5)	**14.2**	(5.3)	1.9	(6.3)	**-16.5**	(5.7)

Note: Values that are statistically significant are indicated in bold (see Annex A3).
1. Multilevel regression model (student and school levels): Reading performance is regressed on all the variables presented in this table.
StatLink http://dx.doi.org/10.1787/888932343285

[Part 4/5]

Table IV.2.14b Relationships between reading performance and students' reading engagement and approaches to learning, the learning environment, resources, policies and practices

		School assessment and accountability policies[1]														Resources invested in education (student level)[1]	
		Schools' accountability to parents: only relative to other students in the school		Schools' accountability to parents: at least relative to national or regional benchmark		School posts achievement data publicly		Achievement data are used in decisions about instructional resource allocation to the school		Achievement data are tracked over time by an administrative authority		School monitors teachers' practice through students' achievement test or assessments		School monitors teachers' practice through teacher peer review or observations of lessons by principal or inspectors		Class size	
		Change in score	S.E.	Change in score	S.E.	Change in score	S.E.	Change in score	S.E.	Change in score	S.E.	Change in score	S.E.	Change in score	S.E.	Change in score	S.E.
OECD	Australia	-8.1	(4.7)	-0.8	(5.6)	1.0	(3.6)	1.4	(3.6)	0.2	(4.3)	6.1	(3.5)	1.0	(3.9)	**1.4**	(0.2)
	Austria	-7.6	(8.9)	8.0	(12.8)	-5.0	(16.4)	11.7	(12.6)	11.9	(8.8)	1.1	(15.8)	-33.4	(23.4)	-0.1	(0.4)
	Belgium	**27.9**	(7.3)	-12.0	(7.8)	35.9	(22.7)	5.1	(6.5)	4.0	(5.1)	-11.4	(5.9)	14.2	(8.5)	**2.1**	(0.4)
	Canada	0.5	(4.4)	-4.0	(4.1)	3.3	(3.5)	-3.9	(3.3)	5.1	(4.4)	c	c	-1.7	(4.3)	**0.7**	(0.2)
	Chile	-13.5	(13.5)	-8.8	(11.2)	-2.2	(4.4)	**-13.5**	(5.5)	3.8	(5.1)	0.3	(4.9)	-5.2	(9.7)	-0.4	(0.3)
	Czech Republic	13.9	(9.4)	12.2	(9.5)	4.1	(5.0)	3.2	(13.2)	2.0	(5.0)	-5.4	(5.6)	4.9	(9.6)	-0.3	(0.3)
	Denmark	c	c	c	c	-0.9	(3.3)	5.8	(3.8)	-4.0	(4.2)	-3.2	(3.7)	-3.2	(4.6)	-0.3	(0.4)
	Estonia	5.1	(6.5)	2.6	(4.0)	-1.3	(4.0)	-3.6	(5.0)	0.9	(5.3)	**-8.7**	(4.2)	-5.6	(8.1)	**1.2**	(0.4)
	Finland	-5.2	(7.6)	4.1	(3.7)	9.7	(9.4)	-0.8	(6.8)	3.6	(3.4)	0.8	(4.4)	-2.4	(3.3)	**2.5**	(0.5)
	France	w	w	w	w	w	w	w	w	w	w	w	w	w	w	w	w
	Germany	**15.5**	(7.3)	0.5	(8.9)	-7.4	(10.2)	-0.3	(6.3)	**16.4**	(6.6)	1.3	(7.1)	-0.9	(8.4)	0.2	(0.3)
	Greece	4.9	(10.3)	-12.8	(14.6)	13.0	(9.2)	11.5	(16.5)	**-21.3**	(8.5)	-2.1	(9.1)	12.6	(10.2)	0.1	(0.7)
	Hungary	-7.1	(8.8)	-0.4	(7.1)	-3.6	(6.4)	-15.2	(10.4)	-4.0	(5.9)	**-19.2**	(7.3)	**-44.3**	(21.6)	0.0	(0.3)
	Iceland	-8.1	(8.7)	-1.2	(5.9)	-1.8	(5.9)	c	c	7.9	(5.8)	5.7	(4.5)	4.9	(5.9)	**2.3**	(0.4)
	Ireland	1.8	(6.7)	1.4	(7.2)	5.4	(8.3)	**-11.3**	(5.7)	0.2	(6.0)	9.7	(5.6)	-4.5	(6.1)	**2.4**	(0.4)
	Israel	-20.2	(14.4)	-0.1	(7.2)	-1.5	(8.4)	9.9	(8.0)	0.7	(9.3)	15.4	(14.6)	-3.8	(12.3)	**0.9**	(0.2)
	Italy	1.0	(8.1)	2.2	(6.8)	7.1	(5.4)	-5.0	(4.5)	-4.3	(4.4)	-0.1	(4.5)	-1.8	(5.1)	**-0.5**	(0.2)
	Japan	-10.8	(13.6)	-13.6	(13.3)	18.2	(10.0)	-21.8	(17.5)	-6.2	(7.4)	1.8	(7.1)	-7.9	(8.6)	**-1.7**	(0.6)
	Korea	7.0	(8.0)	-9.2	(6.2)	**9.4**	(4.8)	**-20.7**	(5.1)	-0.6	(5.7)	5.8	(5.2)	-13.9	(11.3)	0.0	(1.7)
	Luxembourg	c	c	c	c	c	c	c	c	c	c	c	c	c	c	c	c
	Mexico	-5.6	(6.1)	-5.3	(6.4)	1.2	(4.1)	1.7	(4.3)	2.7	(4.9)	-0.7	(3.9)	-5.3	(6.4)	-0.1	(0.2)
	Netherlands	4.5	(7.8)	0.9	(9.3)	7.7	(5.3)	-3.2	(6.4)	9.5	(5.8)	3.3	(5.7)	-10.5	(6.1)	**1.1**	(0.2)
	New Zealand	2.9	(9.2)	-5.6	(6.5)	-4.0	(6.2)	-0.3	(4.9)	8.5	(8.3)	-6.9	(5.2)	-11.5	(16.8)	**2.1**	(0.3)
	Norway	10.1	(7.8)	7.5	(6.7)	4.2	(4.6)	-4.6	(5.4)	4.1	(5.2)	-0.5	(4.5)	-5.8	(5.3)	0.7	(0.4)
	Poland	-5.9	(10.4)	-0.3	(5.8)	-5.8	(4.4)	-3.5	(5.7)	-1.0	(5.7)	-14.3	(7.4)	**-40.7**	(13.0)	1.1	(0.6)
	Portugal	7.3	(5.9)	-0.1	(5.2)	-5.5	(4.6)	-4.2	(4.5)	1.2	(4.6)	0.4	(5.0)	7.6	(6.9)	**2.5**	(0.4)
	Slovak Republic	6.7	(10.0)	-6.2	(8.8)	-1.0	(6.1)	-1.2	(7.3)	2.8	(7.1)	-0.5	(6.8)	c	c	-0.4	(0.4)
	Slovenia	6.7	(8.7)	-1.6	(5.3)	**13.0**	(5.4)	**-16.9**	(6.2)	-5.7	(6.8)	0.5	(5.8)	4.1	(9.1)	0.5	(0.3)
	Spain	0.2	(2.9)	-0.8	(4.0)	-7.0	(4.2)	-4.6	(2.8)	-5.9	(3.2)	0.8	(2.9)	0.1	(3.0)	**1.5**	(0.2)
	Sweden	17.3	(23.5)	-0.6	(7.7)	-2.3	(4.6)	-7.0	(4.7)	-6.6	(4.9)	-5.9	(5.6)	2.3	(5.4)	**1.7**	(0.4)
	Switzerland	-7.4	(4.4)	0.1	(4.9)	-1.6	(11.3)	-2.2	(4.1)	2.8	(4.1)	0.5	(4.3)	-0.2	(5.0)	**2.5**	(0.4)
	Turkey	-0.6	(16.9)	-13.8	(16.6)	**13.4**	(6.8)	-1.0	(6.9)	**19.1**	(6.4)	0.6	(10.0)	**-28.0**	(10.7)	0.1	(0.2)
	United Kingdom	10.0	(6.2)	-1.8	(4.6)	-1.2	(4.5)	-0.9	(4.3)	**11.4**	(5.4)	-5.8	(5.5)	15.0	(12.5)	**3.2**	(0.3)
	United States	7.9	(18.3)	5.3	(8.6)	**30.9**	(8.1)	**11.9**	(4.3)	-4.1	(12.6)	**-11.8**	(5.6)	24.3	(14.8)	0.5	(0.3)
	OECD average	1.6	(1.8)	-1.7	(1.5)	**3.9**	(1.4)	**-2.7**	(1.4)	1.7	(1.1)	-1.4	(1.2)	**-4.5**	(1.8)	**0.9**	(0.1)
Partners	Albania	-22.1	(12.8)	**-26.5**	(12.4)	12.4	(6.7)	**-18.7**	(8.0)	8.7	(8.3)	-10.6	(14.8)	c	c	**0.5**	(0.2)
	Argentina	**-21.7**	(10.8)	**-27.4**	(10.7)	-9.0	(16.9)	4.3	(8.6)	-15.9	(9.3)	11.9	(7.8)	22.4	(15.4)	-0.4	(0.3)
	Azerbaijan	-9.3	(16.2)	c	c	-6.7	(11.1)	6.0	(8.5)	-7.7	(9.0)	**-62.2**	(16.2)	-8.7	(28.3)	-0.1	(0.3)
	Brazil	1.8	(9.2)	-3.6	(5.1)	8.2	(4.5)	**-12.6**	(4.9)	5.9	(5.7)	3.7	(4.9)	-7.4	(6.1)	-0.2	(0.2)
	Bulgaria	-12.9	(14.3)	3.6	(15.5)	13.1	(9.8)	-8.4	(9.7)	10.4	(10.7)	-19.4	(13.2)	16.9	(30.2)	0.3	(0.4)
	Colombia	**-34.1**	(14.2)	-16.2	(10.3)	**16.0**	(4.6)	-3.6	(4.4)	7.3	(5.9)	1.4	(4.7)	-4.1	(5.6)	**-0.7**	(0.3)
	Croatia	**-8.4**	(4.1)	c	c	3.0	(4.9)	9.5	(5.3)	-0.4	(6.8)	-7.0	(4.5)	-1.9	(12.4)	0.8	(0.5)
	Dubai (UAE)	-11.2	(7.6)	**-18.4**	(7.5)	4.2	(5.6)	6.5	(6.2)	-2.9	(8.6)	-6.8	(9.6)	**51.7**	(21.4)	0.3	(0.2)
	Hong Kong-China	5.7	(5.1)	**12.5**	(6.2)	9.1	(4.9)	**14.5**	(4.5)	-3.4	(4.7)	**-16.2**	(8.3)	-7.8	(11.6)	**1.6**	(0.2)
	Indonesia	-16.7	(13.1)	-18.1	(12.6)	3.2	(6.3)	11.6	(10.1)	-6.6	(5.6)	-1.2	(7.4)	32.8	(17.7)	**0.4**	(0.2)
	Jordan	6.5	(10.2)	c	c	-4.9	(9.7)	-7.4	(7.3)	-2.2	(7.4)	3.8	(8.9)	c	c	**-0.9**	(0.4)
	Kazakhstan	-27.5	(22.3)	-22.4	(20.6)	**-15.5**	(7.9)	-6.6	(7.9)	c	c	-3.5	(10.6)	c	c	**-0.8**	(0.4)
	Kyrgyzstan	9.3	(21.5)	11.0	(18.1)	**14.1**	(6.7)	-2.0	(9.3)	-25.1	(14.2)	-23.0	(16.9)	c	c	-0.2	(0.3)
	Latvia	-7.1	(5.6)	-4.2	(5.3)	5.8	(4.3)	-3.9	(4.6)	2.8	(4.7)	-6.4	(5.3)	c	c	0.7	(0.4)
	Lithuania	1.6	(5.6)	c	c	-6.6	(6.3)	14.2	(8.0)	-4.2	(5.3)	7.5	(6.3)	c	c	**0.8**	(0.4)
	Macao-China	c	c	c	c	c	c	c	c	c	c	c	c	c	c	c	c
	Montenegro	c	c	c	c	c	c	c	c	c	c	c	c	c	c	c	c
	Panama	**-27.3**	(11.3)	-2.4	(7.6)	26.0	(13.7)	-7.0	(7.4)	-0.3	(7.9)	9.5	(7.8)	-15.7	(12.5)	-0.5	(0.5)
	Peru	-1.9	(8.5)	-0.8	(9.2)	8.1	(11.0)	6.8	(6.7)	6.2	(6.8)	-4.5	(9.8)	31.7	(18.8)	**-0.6**	(0.2)
	Qatar	30.4	(18.3)	8.8	(15.1)	**-17.4**	(7.7)	-5.7	(8.0)	-19.3	(13.3)	-8.2	(13.4)	c	c	0.3	(0.2)
	Romania	0.9	(15.0)	13.9	(11.9)	-9.3	(6.7)	-0.7	(7.4)	**27.2**	(7.3)	**-16.1**	(7.9)	-1.4	(13.5)	**0.8**	(0.3)
	Russian Federation	-11.5	(11.2)	4.9	(8.9)	3.1	(6.2)	-5.6	(4.6)	**91.1**	(18.7)	-1.1	(9.7)	c	c	0.2	(0.4)
	Serbia	-5.0	(13.6)	-1.1	(19.8)	2.0	(6.9)	**-15.1**	(6.4)	4.5	(7.4)	8.3	(5.2)	0.5	(7.8)	**1.2**	(0.3)
	Shanghai-China	10.3	(6.2)	-2.7	(5.6)	c	c	2.9	(3.3)	-4.8	(4.4)	5.2	(6.1)	c	c	**1.0**	(0.4)
	Singapore	**26.0**	(10.0)	18.8	(9.9)	1.6	(4.1)	4.4	(5.1)	-23.9	(15.7)	-9.5	(12.2)	17.6	(16.4)	**1.3**	(0.3)
	Chinese Taipei	**11.3**	(4.8)	3.9	(3.7)	3.1	(4.5)	-5.5	(4.1)	-1.3	(3.5)	5.9	(3.7)	0.5	(4.5)	**0.8**	(0.4)
	Thailand	11.0	(9.4)	**11.9**	(5.8)	**-11.6**	(5.3)	6.8	(8.7)	**-16.2**	(8.2)	-7.6	(9.4)	14.8	(16.5)	-0.2	(0.3)
	Trinidad and Tobago	10.0	(9.7)	14.9	(9.3)	-17.6	(9.8)	5.3	(7.2)	5.2	(7.4)	**-13.8**	(6.5)	9.3	(11.8)	0.0	(0.2)
	Tunisia	-0.9	(8.2)	-1.0	(7.8)	1.8	(7.9)	-2.3	(4.1)	1.5	(4.6)	-7.6	(7.4)	-1.6	(9.5)	0.0	(0.4)
	Uruguay	0.6	(5.0)	-2.9	(6.3)	3.6	(9.5)	-0.5	(4.0)	-2.8	(4.8)	**-13.5**	(4.6)	-3.3	(9.9)	**-0.8**	(0.3)

Note: Values that are statistically significant are indicated in bold (see Annex A3).
1. Multilevel regression model (student and school levels): Reading performance is regressed on all the variables presented in this table.
StatLink http://dx.doi.org/10.1787/888932343285

Table IV.2.14b [Part 5/5]
Relationships between reading performance and students' reading engagement and approaches to learning, the learning environment, resources, policies and practices

		Resources invested in education (school level)[1]																				
		Students' learning time at school in language of instruction lessons		Students' learning time at school in mathematics and science lessons		Percentage of students attending after-school lessons (enrichment)		Percentage of students attending after-school lessons (remedial)		Percentage of students who attended pre-primary education for one year or less		Percentage of students who attended pre-primary education for more than one year		School average class size		Index of library use in or outside school (higher values indicate more use)		Index of schools' extra-curricular activities (higher values indicate more activities)		Index of teacher shortage (higher values indicate higher shortage)		Index of quality of schools' educational resources (higher values indicate better resources)	
		Change in score	S.E.	Change in score	S.E.	Change in score	S.E.	Change in score	S.E.	Change in score	S.E.	Change in score	S.E.	Change in score	S.E.	Change in score	S.E.	Change in score	S.E.	Change in score	S.E.	Change in score	S.E.
OECD	Australia	-0.2	(0.1)	0.1	(0.1)	-0.2	(0.3)	0.1	(0.4)	**1.1**	(0.4)	**1.3**	(0.4)	**3.2**	(0.8)	-0.2	(2.1)	0.0	(1.9)	6.9	(7.0)	-2.2	(1.6)
	Austria	-0.1	(0.1)	0.1	(0.0)	0.0	(0.4)	-0.2	(0.3)	-1.0	(0.6)	-0.2	(0.5)	**2.2**	(1.1)	5.2	(4.7)	**10.2**	(4.0)	-17.1	(9.4)	**12.3**	(5.0)
	Belgium	**-0.4**	(0.1)	**0.2**	(0.1)	**-1.0**	(0.3)	**0.7**	(0.3)	-0.5	(0.5)	**1.2**	(0.4)	**5.4**	(1.0)	-1.5	(3.0)	5.8	(3.4)	-12.6	(10.9)	2.6	(2.6)
	Canada	0.0	(0.0)	0.0	(0.0)	0.0	(0.2)	**-0.6**	(0.2)	**0.6**	(0.2)	**0.7**	(0.2)	**1.3**	(0.4)	-0.1	(2.1)	3.9	(2.1)	-5.5	(5.6)	3.2	(1.9)
	Chile	**-0.2**	(0.1)	**0.1**	(0.0)	**-0.7**	(0.2)	**0.3**	(0.2)	-0.1	(0.2)	0.3	(0.2)	-0.4	(0.4)	1.2	(2.0)	2.6	(2.9)	**-17.7**	(7.4)	**5.3**	(2.4)
	Czech Republic	-0.2	(0.1)	**0.1**	(0.0)	-0.3	(0.2)	-0.1	(0.2)	0.2	(0.5)	0.7	(0.4)	**2.5**	(0.7)	-6.4	(3.7)	-1.4	(4.3)	7.0	(7.3)	-0.7	(3.3)
	Denmark	-0.1	(0.1)	0.0	(0.0)	**-0.4**	(0.2)	-0.4	(0.2)	0.2	(0.5)	0.7	(0.5)	0.8	(0.6)	-1.7	(2.4)	-0.9	(1.8)	**-26.2**	(7.8)	-1.7	(2.3)
	Estonia	-0.1	(0.1)	0.0	(0.0)	-0.2	(0.1)	0.0	(0.1)	0.0	(0.3)	-0.1	(0.1)	**2.4**	(0.4)	-3.3	(2.6)	-2.5	(2.5)	-7.8	(10.0)	1.5	(2.6)
	Finland	0.0	(0.1)	0.0	(0.0)	-0.7	(0.3)	**-0.7**	(0.2)	**-0.7**	(0.2)	**-0.5**	(0.2)	1.1	(0.8)	3.0	(3.1)	-0.1	(2.4)	-10.3	(6.5)	2.0	(2.5)
	France	w	w	w	w	w	w	w	w	w	w	w	w	w	w	w	w	w	w	w	w	w	w
	Germany	**-0.5**	(0.2)	**0.2**	(0.1)	-0.3	(0.3)	**-0.6**	(0.3)	0.4	(0.7)	**1.4**	(0.6)	1.5	(1.0)	-1.9	(3.6)	2.8	(3.9)	**-26.0**	(10.2)	0.0	(3.6)
	Greece	0.1	(0.1)	**0.2**	(0.1)	0.6	(0.3)	0.1	(0.4)	-0.5	(0.5)	0.0	(0.4)	0.2	(1.1)	4.2	(4.6)	**10.5**	(5.0)	**-32.5**	(12.4)	**8.9**	(4.0)
	Hungary	-0.1	(0.1)	**0.2**	(0.1)	0.3	(0.2)	0.1	(0.2)	**2.3**	(0.7)	**2.3**	(0.7)	**2.8**	(0.6)	-3.8	(5.1)	**13.6**	(5.3)	-17.8	(9.7)	-1.6	(3.1)
	Iceland	-0.1	(0.1)	0.1	(0.1)	-0.2	(0.2)	-0.2	(0.2)	0.4	(0.5)	-0.1	(0.4)	0.6	(0.7)	-2.2	(3.4)	-1.9	(3.7)	2.8	(7.4)	4.0	(3.8)
	Ireland	**-0.4**	(0.2)	0.0	(0.2)	**0.6**	(0.2)	-0.6	(0.4)	0.1	(0.3)	0.2	(0.2)	**3.8**	(0.9)	**6.2**	(2.9)	0.9	(3.4)	7.4	(9.1)	**-6.2**	(2.7)
	Israel	0.1	(0.1)	**0.1**	(0.0)	**0.8**	(0.3)	**-2.5**	(0.4)	1.1	(0.7)	1.2	(0.6)	**3.4**	(0.6)	-0.4	(4.5)	-2.2	(4.0)	4.2	(12.0)	**10.0**	(3.0)
	Italy	**-0.1**	(0.0)	0.0	(0.0)	-0.2	(0.2)	-0.2	(0.2)	0.5	(0.4)	**1.2**	(0.3)	**3.1**	(0.7)	2.9	(2.4)	**5.7**	(2.4)	**-25.7**	(6.7)	**7.3**	(2.4)
	Japan	0.0	(0.1)	**0.2**	(0.0)	0.4	(0.2)	0.0	(0.1)	-1.8	(1.8)	-0.9	(1.3)	**1.6**	(0.4)	3.4	(3.3)	2.9	(3.7)	-6.1	(10.0)	-1.2	(2.8)
	Korea	0.0	(0.1)	**0.1**	(0.0)	**0.3**	(0.1)	**0.3**	(0.1)	**1.6**	(0.6)	**1.6**	(0.5)	**1.7**	(0.5)	-5.5	(3.0)	-0.1	(3.2)	-11.3	(11.4)	1.9	(3.4)
	Luxembourg	c	c	c	c	c	c	c	c	c	c	c	c	c	c	c	c	c	c	c	c	c	c
	Mexico	0.0	(0.1)	**0.1**	(0.0)	**-0.6**	(0.2)	-0.3	(0.2)	**0.4**	(0.2)	**0.4**	(0.1)	**0.6**	(0.2)	**4.9**	(1.9)	0.4	(2.0)	**-14.2**	(6.0)	**5.4**	(2.3)
	Netherlands	**-0.7**	(0.1)	**0.3**	(0.1)	**-1.0**	(0.3)	0.5	(0.3)	-0.2	(1.1)	0.1	(0.5)	**5.2**	(1.2)	**11.2**	(3.5)	6.5	(5.2)	0.4	(11.8)	2.9	(3.1)
	New Zealand	**-0.7**	(0.2)	**0.2**	(0.1)	-0.2	(0.3)	**-1.1**	(0.5)	-0.2	(0.3)	0.4	(0.2)	0.3	(0.8)	1.7	(3.2)	3.2	(2.6)	-16.8	(10.4)	1.2	(2.8)
	Norway	c	c	c	c	0.3	(0.3)	**-1.8**	(0.3)	0.2	(0.5)	0.3	(0.2)	**0.8**	(0.4)	-2.2	(2.7)	2.5	(2.8)	-7.7	(6.8)	0.0	(3.8)
	Poland	-0.2	(0.1)	0.0	(0.0)	**0.2**	(0.1)	-0.1	(0.1)	-0.2	(0.5)	0.2	(0.5)	0.7	(0.5)	1.3	(4.5)	2.3	(2.8)	**-25.0**	(8.9)	-3.5	(2.4)
	Portugal	0.0	(0.1)	0.0	(0.0)	0.0	(0.2)	0.1	(0.2)	-0.1	(0.3)	**0.5**	(0.2)	**1.5**	(0.7)	**12.3**	(3.8)	3.1	(3.1)	-2.0	(7.4)	1.5	(2.4)
	Slovak Republic	**-0.4**	(0.1)	**0.1**	(0.0)	-0.1	(0.1)	0.2	(0.1)	**0.9**	(0.3)	**1.1**	(0.2)	1.0	(0.6)	-5.4	(5.3)	3.9	(3.0)	**-28.7**	(8.9)	-1.0	(3.9)
	Slovenia	**0.5**	(0.1)	**0.3**	(0.1)	**-0.3**	(0.1)	-0.3	(0.2)	0.1	(0.1)	**0.4**	(0.2)	**2.2**	(0.5)	4.5	(4.8)	3.0	(3.6)	-5.5	(9.8)	3.7	(3.8)
	Spain	0.1	(0.1)	0.0	(0.0)	0.1	(0.1)	0.0	(0.1)	0.3	(0.3)	**0.6**	(0.2)	0.1	(0.4)	-0.4	(2.1)	**4.2**	(1.8)	-4.3	(4.5)	-2.2	(1.7)
	Sweden	-0.1	(0.1)	0.0	(0.0)	-0.4	(0.2)	**-0.8**	(0.3)	**1.0**	(0.4)	**1.0**	(0.4)	**1.6**	(0.8)	4.0	(3.4)	**7.6**	(2.9)	-0.2	(6.5)	**7.8**	(3.7)
	Switzerland	0.0	(0.1)	0.0	(0.0)	-0.3	(0.2)	0.0	(0.2)	**1.6**	(0.6)	**1.6**	(0.6)	**3.0**	(0.6)	-2.3	(2.2)	**6.9**	(2.7)	**-15.7**	(6.2)	1.5	(1.9)
	Turkey	**0.6**	(0.1)	**0.1**	(0.0)	0.7	(0.4)	**-0.9**	(0.3)	-0.2	(0.4)	**0.9**	(0.4)	-0.6	(0.6)	**-15.5**	(4.3)	**12.4**	(4.0)	**-23.4**	(8.0)	**-14.2**	(5.0)
	United Kingdom	**-0.2**	(0.1)	**0.1**	(0.0)	0.0	(0.2)	**-0.6**	(0.1)	**1.2**	(0.3)	**1.5**	(0.3)	**2.8**	(0.9)	-1.4	(2.4)	1.5	(2.5)	-4.8	(7.0)	0.3	(2.3)
	United States	**0.2**	(0.1)	-0.1	(0.0)	**-1.5**	(0.3)	0.2	(0.3)	-1.1	(0.8)	-0.7	(0.8)	**-2.1**	(0.7)	**-6.3**	(2.5)	**8.5**	(2.7)	-5.1	(6.9)	0.8	(1.9)
	OECD average	**-0.1**	(0.0)	**0.1**	(0.0)	**-0.1**	(0.0)	**-0.3**	(0.0)	**0.2**	(0.1)	**0.6**	(0.1)	**1.7**	(0.1)	0.2	(0.6)	**3.6**	(0.6)	**-10.7**	(1.5)	**1.5**	(0.5)
Partners	Albania	0.1	(0.1)	-0.1	(0.1)	**1.0**	(0.2)	**-0.8**	(0.2)	**-1.1**	(0.3)	-0.4	(0.2)	1.1	(0.7)	-2.8	(4.6)	**11.4**	(4.4)	-3.5	(8.0)	4.9	(5.7)
	Argentina	-0.1	(0.1)	**0.1**	(0.0)	**-1.4**	(0.4)	**0.6**	(0.3)	**1.1**	(0.3)	**1.1**	(0.4)	-0.1	(0.8)	1.5	(5.2)	7.5	(5.7)	**-18.4**	(8.6)	4.3	(3.9)
	Azerbaijan	0.0	(0.1)	0.1	(0.0)	0.3	(0.4)	-0.3	(0.4)	**1.4**	(0.4)	0.1	(0.3)	-0.8	(1.5)	-2.8	(4.0)	**-10.1**	(3.4)	**-29.3**	(14.0)	0.6	(4.5)
	Brazil	0.0	(0.1)	0.0	(0.1)	-0.1	(0.1)	**-0.4**	(0.1)	0.2	(0.2)	**0.3**	(0.1)	0.5	(0.3)	-1.7	(2.3)	**6.6**	(2.2)	0.9	(6.8)	**7.2**	(2.4)
	Bulgaria	0.0	(0.2)	-0.1	(0.1)	**-0.7**	(0.3)	-0.2	(0.3)	-0.2	(0.5)	0.5	(0.3)	**4.4**	(1.6)	**16.4**	(6.9)	8.7	(4.8)	-17.6	(13.6)	-6.4	(5.3)
	Colombia	-0.1	(0.1)	**0.1**	(0.0)	-0.3	(0.2)	-0.3	(0.2)	**0.7**	(0.2)	**0.8**	(0.2)	0.0	(0.4)	-0.6	(2.3)	1.6	(2.7)	**-32.9**	(7.5)	0.9	(2.1)
	Croatia	-0.1	(0.1)	**0.2**	(0.0)	-0.3	(0.2)	-0.3	(0.2)	**-0.5**	(0.2)	**0.5**	(0.1)	**2.6**	(0.5)	**-6.1**	(2.6)	**8.8**	(2.2)	-8.3	(9.3)	-3.1	(2.4)
	Dubai (UAE)	**-0.3**	(0.1)	0.1	(0.0)	**-0.7**	(0.2)	**-0.7**	(0.2)	-0.1	(0.3)	**0.6**	(0.2)	-0.1	(0.5)	3.4	(4.1)	**12.2**	(3.4)	-11.4	(8.7)	1.0	(3.5)
	Hong Kong-China	**-0.3**	(0.1)	**0.2**	(0.0)	0.1	(0.2)	0.1	(0.2)	1.1	(0.7)	**1.3**	(0.5)	**1.8**	(0.6)	-5.6	(3.1)	2.1	(2.8)	-7.5	(9.6)	0.3	(2.9)
	Indonesia	-0.1	(0.1)	**0.1**	(0.0)	-0.3	(0.2)	-0.2	(0.2)	0.2	(0.1)	**0.5**	(0.1)	0.2	(0.4)	0.8	(3.0)	-2.1	(2.7)	13.9	(8.4)	4.1	(2.8)
	Jordan	**0.5**	(0.2)	-0.2	(0.1)	-0.2	(0.2)	**-1.2**	(0.2)	**0.5**	(0.2)	**0.5**	(0.2)	0.2	(0.5)	-2.4	(2.8)	**13.4**	(3.1)	23.7	(14.6)	**-8.3**	(3.7)
	Kazakhstan	0.0	(0.1)	0.1	(0.1)	-0.3	(0.3)	0.1	(0.3)	0.0	(0.4)	**0.8**	(0.2)	-0.4	(0.6)	-0.7	(3.0)	-1.2	(3.5)	**-34.9**	(11.0)	-1.2	(5.2)
	Kyrgyzstan	**0.4**	(0.1)	-0.1	(0.0)	**0.6**	(0.2)	**-0.6**	(0.2)	-0.1	(0.2)	**1.3**	(0.2)	-0.3	(0.9)	4.0	(2.8)	1.2	(3.4)	**-19.9**	(8.8)	4.6	(3.4)
	Latvia	-0.1	(0.1)	0.0	(0.0)	-0.1	(0.2)	**-0.7**	(0.2)	0.0	(0.2)	**0.4**	(0.1)	**1.7**	(0.6)	-0.4	(3.3)	-0.3	(2.9)	-2.1	(8.0)	3.4	(2.9)
	Lithuania	0.1	(0.1)	0.0	(0.0)	-0.1	(0.2)	0.2	(0.2)	0.0	(0.3)	**0.3**	(0.1)	0.8	(0.5)	-2.4	(4.9)	4.4	(3.7)	-17.1	(10.2)	-2.4	(5.1)
	Macao-China	c	c	c	c	c	c	c	c	c	c	c	c	c	c	c	c	c	c	c	c	c	c
	Montenegro	c	c	c	c	c	c	c	c	c	c	c	c	c	c	c	c	c	c	c	c	c	c
	Panama	0.0	(0.2)	0.1	(0.1)	**-0.9**	(0.3)	-0.2	(0.3)	0.0	(0.3)	0.3	(0.3)	**2.9**	(0.7)	5.9	(5.1)	-2.3	(3.8)	**-30.9**	(15.7)	**14.7**	(2.8)
	Peru	0.0	(0.0)	0.0	(0.0)	0.0	(0.3)	**-0.6**	(0.2)	**0.8**	(0.3)	**0.7**	(0.3)	0.2	(0.4)	-3.8	(3.5)	**10.8**	(3.5)	-11.0	(14.8)	3.5	(2.9)
	Qatar	0.1	(0.1)	0.1	(0.1)	**-0.6**	(0.3)	**-0.6**	(0.3)	-0.2	(0.3)	**1.1**	(0.3)	0.4	(0.7)	**-9.1**	(4.3)	6.6	(4.5)	-10.7	(12.5)	**-11.6**	(4.2)
	Romania	0.2	(0.1)	0.0	(0.1)	0.3	(0.2)	**-1.3**	(0.2)	-1.0	(0.6)	-0.7	(0.4)	**3.4**	(0.9)	-9.6	(5.8)	4.7	(3.6)	-7.3	(14.1)	-4.0	(3.9)
	Russian Federation	-0.1	(0.1)	0.0	(0.0)	0.1	(0.1)	-0.1	(0.1)	-0.1	(0.4)	0.3	(0.2)	0.7	(0.5)	-3.7	(2.8)	-1.9	(2.8)	-11.5	(8.1)	3.8	(3.8)
	Serbia	**0.5**	(0.2)	**0.1**	(0.0)	-0.1	(0.3)	-0.4	(0.2)	**0.8**	(0.2)	**0.9**	(0.3)	**2.2**	(1.0)	0.2	(4.3)	6.5	(4.1)	**-22.0**	(9.8)	-7.9	(4.7)
	Shanghai-China	**-0.2**	(0.1)	0.1	(0.0)	0.3	(0.1)	0.1	(0.1)	-0.1	(0.3)	0.2	(0.3)	**0.9**	(0.2)	-1.8	(1.5)	1.3	(1.8)	**-41.4**	(9.4)	0.4	(1.7)
	Singapore	**-0.2**	(0.1)	**0.1**	(0.0)	0.3	(0.2)	-0.2	(0.1)	1.4	(0.8)	**2.5**	(0.6)	-0.6	(0.7)	**-6.8**	(2.8)	1.8	(2.7)	-22.1	(12.6)	-0.9	(2.5)
	Chinese Taipei	-0.1	(0.1)	0.0	(0.0)	**1.0**	(0.1)	**-0.4**	(0.1)	1.1	(0.6)	**1.2**	(0.5)	**3.3**	(0.5)	-0.8	(2.0)	0.1	(2.2)	-6.7	(7.7)	2.7	(2.2)
	Thailand	0.1	(0.1)	0.0	(0.0)	**0.4**	(0.2)	-0.3	(0.2)	0.3	(0.4)	**0.8**	(0.4)	**0.8**	(0.4)	-1.2	(2.4)	0.9	(2.8)	**-37.9**	(11.3)	**7.4**	(3.3)
	Trinidad and Tobago	**-0.3**	(0.1)	**0.3**	(0.1)	0.1	(0.3)	0.0	(0.2)	0.7	(0.6)	1.0	(0.5)	**2.2**	(0.8)	-1.7	(3.7)	**8.6**	(3.6)	-10.3	(14.5)	2.9	(3.7)
	Tunisia	0.2	(0.4)	0.3	(0.2)	-0.2	(0.2)	0.1	(0.1)	**0.5**	(0.1)	**0.6**	(0.2)	0.5	(0.7)	3.6	(3.1)	0.3	(1.7)	-10.8	(6.9)	-0.8	(2.3)
	Uruguay	-0.1	(0.1)	**0.1**	(0.0)	0.0	(0.2)	0.2	(0.2)	0.5	(0.3)	0.2	(0.2)	**1.3**	(0.3)	0.5	(2.9)	2.2	(2.7)	**-20.1**	(7.1)	1.4	(2.0)

Note: Values that are statistically significant are indicated in bold (see Annex A3).
1. Multilevel regression model (student and school levels): Reading performance is regressed on all the variables presented in this table.
StatLink http://dx.doi.org/10.1787/888932343285

[Part 1/6]

Table IV.2.14c Relationships between reading performance and students' reading engagement and approaches to learning, the learning environment, resources, policies and practices, accounting for students' and schools' socio-economic and demographic background

		Students' reading engagement and approaches to learning[1]																Learning environment and school climate (student level)[1]					
		Index of enjoyment of reading (higer values indicate more enjoyment)		Index of diversity in reading (higer values indicate more diversity)		Index of online reading activities (higer values indicate more activities)		Index of memorisation strategies (higer values indicate higher importance attached to this strategy)		Index of elaboration strategies (higer values indicate higher importance attached to this strategy)		Index of control strategies (higer values indicate higher importance attached to this strategy)		Index of understanding and remembering (higer values indicate greater students' perception of usefulness of this strategy)		Index of summarising (higer values indicate greater students' perception of usefulness of this strategy)		Index of teacher-student relations (higher values indicate better relationships)		Index of disciplinary climate (higher values indicate better climate)		Index of teachers' stimulation of reading engagement (higher values indicate more stimulation)	
		Change in score	S.E.	Change in score	S.E.	Change in score	S.E.	Change in score	S.E.	Change in score	S.E.	Change in score	S.E.	Change in score	S.E.	Change in score	S.E.	Change in score	S.E.	Change in score	S.E.	Change in score	S.E.
OECD	Australia	**26.9**	(1.0)	**-4.7**	(1.1)	**9.3**	(1.0)	**-13.2**	(1.2)	**-7.8**	(0.9)	**18.0**	(1.2)	**10.6**	(1.2)	**17.3**	(1.0)	**6.2**	(1.0)	**2.8**	(1.0)	**-3.9**	(0.9)
	Austria	**18.0**	(1.4)	-1.6	(1.6)	**5.1**	(1.4)	**-6.3**	(1.5)	**-4.1**	(1.4)	2.5	(1.4)	**9.8**	(1.6)	**13.7**	(1.6)	1.3	(1.2)	1.3	(1.1)	**-2.9**	(1.4)
	Belgium	**18.0**	(1.2)	**3.8**	(1.1)	**5.0**	(1.3)	**-8.8**	(1.1)	**-7.2**	(1.2)	**10.0**	(1.3)	**10.4**	(1.3)	**16.9**	(1.3)	-1.1	(1.2)	0.7	(1.1)	-0.1	(1.1)
	Canada	**25.1**	(0.9)	-1.4	(1.1)	**3.6**	(1.1)	**-8.5**	(0.8)	**-10.6**	(0.8)	**15.9**	(1.1)	**6.7**	(1.0)	**17.3**	(0.9)	**4.8**	(1.0)	0.7	(1.2)	-1.1	(1.0)
	Chile	**14.9**	(1.5)	2.1	(1.4)	**5.1**	(1.3)	-1.7	(1.4)	**-6.3**	(1.4)	**8.7**	(1.6)	**11.2**	(1.2)	**12.8**	(1.3)	**3.3**	(1.1)	0.7	(1.3)	**-3.2**	(1.3)
	Czech Republic	**17.9**	(1.4)	1.3	(1.4)	**4.8**	(1.1)	**-5.6**	(1.2)	-1.8	(1.3)	**8.5**	(1.4)	**8.8**	(1.3)	**19.1**	(1.2)	0.7	(1.5)	-0.6	(1.3)	**-4.5**	(1.5)
	Denmark	**24.4**	(1.6)	**4.1**	(1.4)	**4.6**	(1.6)	**-17.9**	(1.6)	**-5.6**	(1.5)	**8.2**	(1.7)	**14.4**	(1.5)	**17.3**	(1.4)	**7.4**	(1.2)	0.0	(1.5)	-2.3	(1.5)
	Estonia	**24.5**	(1.9)	3.7	(2.2)	**7.6**	(1.9)	**-15.1**	(2.0)	2.5	(1.9)	2.0	(2.1)	**12.9**	(1.4)	**16.1**	(1.8)	**7.5**	(1.5)	**6.3**	(2.2)	**-9.0**	(2.0)
	Finland	**22.5**	(1.4)	**9.2**	(1.5)	**4.1**	(1.7)	**-14.0**	(1.5)	-0.8	(1.4)	**9.8**	(1.8)	**9.8**	(1.4)	**18.7**	(1.6)	**4.1**	(1.5)	-1.6	(1.5)	**-8.2**	(1.6)
	France	w	w	w	w	w	w	w	w	w	w	w	w	w	w	w	w	w	w	w	w	w	w
	Germany	**13.1**	(1.2)	**4.2**	(1.3)	**3.8**	(1.4)	**-4.6**	(1.7)	**-5.1**	(1.5)	**5.2**	(1.7)	**8.4**	(1.4)	**11.6**	(1.5)	1.7	(1.2)	1.8	(1.3)	0.2	(1.4)
	Greece	**24.7**	(2.0)	2.3	(1.9)	0.7	(1.3)	**-9.2**	(1.5)	-2.4	(1.6)	**8.2**	(1.8)	**3.5**	(1.6)	**16.3**	(1.7)	0.4	(1.7)	-2.1	(2.0)	1.5	(1.8)
	Hungary	**14.6**	(1.5)	0.4	(1.1)	**5.1**	(1.3)	1.1	(1.8)	**-6.2**	(1.6)	1.2	(1.7)	**8.4**	(1.4)	**13.2**	(1.2)	-2.1	(1.3)	-2.6	(1.4)	2.5	(1.5)
	Iceland	**22.9**	(1.4)	**7.8**	(1.7)	**3.9**	(1.7)	**-18.6**	(2.0)	-2.4	(1.7)	**16.5**	(2.0)	**7.6**	(1.5)	**20.0**	(1.6)	**6.2**	(1.4)	3.6	(2.0)	**-5.2**	(1.4)
	Ireland	**28.1**	(1.8)	**-4.8**	(2.1)	**7.5**	(1.6)	**-5.7**	(1.7)	**-4.9**	(1.4)	**7.8**	(1.9)	**11.5**	(1.8)	**17.0**	(1.4)	**5.0**	(1.9)	**5.3**	(1.6)	**-4.6**	(1.7)
	Israel	**16.8**	(2.3)	**4.0**	(1.6)	**7.0**	(1.6)	**-10.8**	(1.9)	**-6.6**	(1.7)	**11.5**	(2.1)	**6.6**	(1.9)	**15.0**	(1.9)	2.3	(1.5)	0.7	(2.0)	**-4.2**	(1.8)
	Italy	**14.5**	(0.9)	**4.0**	(1.0)	**3.7**	(0.7)	**-9.9**	(0.8)	**-2.1**	(0.8)	**6.6**	(1.0)	**7.6**	(0.9)	**14.3**	(0.8)	0.2	(0.8)	**1.5**	(0.7)	-1.3	(0.9)
	Japan	**18.9**	(1.6)	0.8	(1.2)	**4.8**	(1.8)	**-6.4**	(1.4)	**-3.1**	(1.5)	**11.6**	(1.8)	**8.1**	(1.4)	**18.4**	(1.7)	**4.8**	(1.3)	2.3	(1.6)	-1.5	(1.3)
	Korea	**21.5**	(3.5)	0.6	(3.0)	4.1	(2.6)	1.3	(2.7)	2.3	(2.3)	**8.5**	(2.5)	**10.8**	(2.3)	**20.1**	(1.9)	**4.5**	(2.3)	0.9	(2.0)	-3.2	(2.3)
	Luxembourg	c	c	c	c	c	c	c	c	c	c	c	c	c	c	c	c	c	c	c	c	c	c
	Mexico	**10.1**	(1.2)	-1.1	(0.8)	1.6	(0.9)	**-7.9**	(1.0)	**-4.6**	(1.0)	**10.2**	(1.2)	**6.6**	(0.8)	**14.3**	(0.9)	**4.0**	(0.9)	**3.9**	(1.0)	**2.1**	(1.0)
	Netherlands	**11.6**	(1.7)	**6.5**	(1.1)	**3.3**	(1.4)	**-10.2**	(1.1)	**-3.1**	(1.2)	**5.7**	(1.4)	**6.7**	(1.1)	**9.5**	(1.0)	0.9	(1.3)	-0.7	(1.1)	**-4.7**	(1.1)
	New Zealand	**29.5**	(1.8)	**-6.3**	(2.4)	**9.2**	(1.9)	**-12.3**	(2.0)	**-10.3**	(2.1)	**16.9**	(2.1)	**7.3**	(1.7)	**20.2**	(1.5)	2.9	(1.8)	**4.0**	(1.8)	0.0	(1.8)
	Norway	**25.2**	(1.9)	**4.7**	(1.8)	-1.3	(1.8)	**-14.8**	(1.9)	1.7	(1.9)	**11.2**	(2.5)	**11.3**	(1.6)	**20.8**	(1.7)	**7.1**	(1.6)	1.1	(1.6)	-3.4	(1.8)
	Poland	**15.3**	(1.5)	**5.4**	(1.7)	**5.5**	(1.4)	**-7.9**	(2.0)	**-5.3**	(2.0)	**12.4**	(1.5)	**7.2**	(1.5)	**23.5**	(1.4)	-0.2	(1.6)	0.7	(1.6)	**4.2**	(1.5)
	Portugal	**12.5**	(1.7)	-0.8	(1.6)	2.3	(1.4)	**-7.7**	(1.4)	**-4.9**	(1.9)	**15.5**	(1.9)	**9.5**	(1.2)	**17.8**	(1.3)	-0.8	(1.3)	**4.0**	(1.3)	-2.3	(1.4)
	Slovak Republic	**14.2**	(1.5)	2.6	(1.4)	**7.7**	(1.4)	**-10.4**	(1.0)	**-4.5**	(1.5)	**9.0**	(1.7)	**6.6**	(1.4)	**16.4**	(1.3)	1.6	(1.3)	1.5	(1.4)	-2.4	(1.6)
	Slovenia	**8.1**	(1.2)	**4.7**	(1.3)	**3.5**	(0.9)	**-11.0**	(1.3)	**-3.5**	(1.2)	**7.2**	(1.4)	**5.3**	(1.0)	**9.8**	(1.0)	1.6	(1.1)	-0.3	(1.0)	1.9	(1.0)
	Spain	**20.7**	(0.9)	**4.0**	(0.9)	**5.5**	(1.0)	**-1.9**	(0.8)	**-5.6**	(1.0)	**11.8**	(1.0)	**8.8**	(0.8)	**20.5**	(0.9)	0.2	(0.7)	**4.0**	(0.9)	-1.8	(0.9)
	Sweden	**23.5**	(2.0)	**9.5**	(1.6)	2.7	(1.7)	-2.6	(1.5)	**-6.4**	(2.0)	**7.3**	(2.1)	**13.5**	(1.5)	**19.8**	(1.7)	**4.1**	(1.5)	-0.6	(1.5)	-1.5	(1.9)
	Switzerland	**18.6**	(1.2)	**5.5**	(1.2)	**3.7**	(1.3)	**-7.9**	(1.5)	**-6.1**	(1.6)	**4.6**	(1.4)	**13.0**	(1.2)	**17.4**	(1.4)	-1.2	(1.1)	0.9	(1.2)	**-3.3**	(1.4)
	Turkey	**8.7**	(1.8)	**-5.5**	(1.8)	0.9	(1.4)	**-6.6**	(1.7)	1.7	(1.7)	**9.5**	(2.3)	**8.0**	(1.3)	**9.1**	(1.6)	1.7	(1.2)	0.0	(1.4)	1.0	(1.5)
	United Kingdom	**29.0**	(1.6)	**-3.4**	(1.5)	**7.7**	(1.6)	**-10.8**	(1.6)	**-6.2**	(1.5)	**14.2**	(1.7)	**7.8**	(1.4)	**15.4**	(1.3)	**4.6**	(1.4)	**5.4**	(1.3)	-1.3	(1.5)
	United States	**25.4**	(2.1)	-3.1	(2.3)	**5.0**	(2.2)	**-12.3**	(2.4)	**-9.9**	(2.3)	**16.0**	(2.3)	**8.1**	(2.1)	**13.6**	(2.1)	0.4	(1.6)	**8.1**	(1.6)	0.0	(1.6)
	OECD average	**19.4**	(0.3)	**1.8**	(0.3)	**4.6**	(0.3)	**-8.7**	(0.3)	**-4.4**	(0.3)	**9.7**	(0.3)	**9.0**	(0.3)	**16.3**	(0.3)	**2.6**	(0.2)	**1.7**	(0.3)	**-2.0**	(0.3)
Partners	Albania	**18.0**	(3.1)	-2.0	(2.6)	0.2	(1.7)	0.0	(2.3)	-4.4	(2.6)	**16.4**	(3.0)	**17.9**	(2.0)	**10.5**	(2.0)	**5.3**	(2.1)	**5.6**	(2.2)	-0.4	(2.0)
	Argentina	**15.9**	(2.6)	2.2	(1.2)	**3.0**	(1.4)	**-4.2**	(1.6)	**-3.4**	(1.7)	**12.4**	(1.7)	**8.5**	(1.9)	**13.6**	(1.8)	-3.1	(1.6)	0.2	(1.6)	-1.5	(1.8)
	Azerbaijan	**12.2**	(1.9)	0.5	(0.8)	-0.1	(0.7)	-0.4	(1.6)	-1.0	(1.8)	**6.9**	(1.6)	**7.8**	(1.7)	0.8	(1.5)	-1.5	(1.4)	**6.7**	(1.6)	**2.5**	(1.0)
	Brazil	**12.1**	(1.3)	-1.9	(1.1)	**2.9**	(0.8)	**-3.5**	(1.4)	**-4.8**	(1.2)	**11.0**	(1.5)	**8.5**	(1.0)	**13.3**	(1.2)	**3.9**	(1.0)	**4.1**	(1.4)	-1.6	(1.2)
	Bulgaria	**5.6**	(2.7)	1.1	(1.4)	**8.2**	(1.2)	**-5.0**	(1.9)	**-5.9**	(1.7)	**9.9**	(2.1)	**9.1**	(1.8)	**16.7**	(1.7)	1.0	(1.4)	**5.0**	(1.9)	1.7	(1.6)
	Colombia	**11.1**	(2.2)	-0.5	(1.3)	**5.1**	(1.4)	**-7.8**	(1.5)	-1.7	(1.9)	**7.8**	(1.7)	**12.3**	(2.0)	**15.1**	(1.9)	-1.7	(1.6)	**11.8**	(1.8)	1.0	(1.7)
	Croatia	**10.0**	(1.5)	**5.1**	(1.5)	**3.5**	(1.1)	**-4.0**	(1.8)	**-5.2**	(2.1)	1.2	(2.0)	**11.4**	(1.3)	**16.4**	(1.3)	**-3.5**	(1.5)	**4.4**	(1.6)	2.6	(1.4)
	Dubai (UAE)	**20.5**	(1.4)	**-3.5**	(1.0)	**2.4**	(1.0)	**-8.6**	(1.5)	**-3.9**	(1.4)	**11.4**	(1.4)	**10.0**	(1.2)	**14.6**	(1.2)	**5.5**	(1.2)	**3.5**	(1.3)	**-2.8**	(1.1)
	Hong Kong-China	**20.8**	(1.9)	0.9	(1.5)	2.1	(1.3)	**-8.7**	(2.0)	**-7.5**	(1.4)	**14.5**	(1.6)	**8.8**	(1.0)	**10.6**	(1.0)	1.0	(1.4)	3.1	(1.6)	1.4	(1.5)
	Indonesia	**12.9**	(2.1)	**1.6**	(0.8)	-0.6	(0.8)	**3.0**	(1.5)	1.4	(1.6)	2.6	(1.5)	**7.9**	(0.9)	**5.6**	(0.9)	**-3.0**	(1.3)	1.8	(1.4)	-1.6	(1.0)
	Jordan	**12.6**	(2.0)	-0.8	(1.1)	**2.4**	(1.0)	0.8	(2.0)	2.5	(1.9)	**10.2**	(1.9)	**6.9**	(1.4)	**11.9**	(1.5)	**6.0**	(1.3)	**4.6**	(1.6)	0.4	(1.4)
	Kazakhstan	**9.0**	(2.3)	**-5.7**	(1.2)	1.0	(0.8)	**-5.0**	(2.3)	**-5.3**	(1.9)	**7.3**	(1.9)	**15.3**	(1.1)	**16.3**	(1.5)	2.4	(1.6)	**10.2**	(1.6)	**2.9**	(1.2)
	Kyrgyzstan	**16.1**	(2.7)	-0.1	(1.3)	**-1.8**	(0.8)	1.9	(1.7)	-3.6	(2.0)	**7.3**	(2.0)	**10.9**	(1.8)	**9.9**	(1.6)	1.9	(1.5)	**13.8**	(1.6)	1.5	(1.3)
	Latvia	**19.2**	(2.4)	1.0	(2.5)	2.6	(1.8)	**-11.0**	(2.3)	-3.3	(2.1)	**7.9**	(2.3)	**10.8**	(1.5)	**18.5**	(1.7)	**4.8**	(1.6)	**5.5**	(2.0)	-2.5	(1.7)
	Lithuania	**13.8**	(1.5)	2.8	(1.5)	**7.6**	(1.2)	**-14.1**	(2.1)	**-6.4**	(1.7)	**8.7**	(1.9)	**10.1**	(1.5)	**14.6**	(1.5)	**2.4**	(1.0)	**5.7**	(1.5)	-1.2	(1.6)
	Macao-China	c	c	c	c	c	c	c	c	c	c	c	c	c	c	c	c	c	c	c	c	c	c
	Montenegro	c	c	c	c	c	c	c	c	c	c	c	c	c	c	c	c	c	c	c	c	c	c
	Panama	**7.6**	(3.1)	2.9	(1.6)	0.4	(1.4)	1.7	(1.9)	-3.7	(2.7)	**10.0**	(2.5)	**6.0**	(2.3)	**10.1**	(2.0)	**3.4**	(1.8)	**7.4**	(2.4)	-1.6	(1.7)
	Peru	**15.7**	(2.1)	1.0	(1.4)	0.7	(1.2)	**-9.2**	(1.7)	-1.5	(1.9)	**5.4**	(1.9)	**7.6**	(1.7)	**12.4**	(1.7)	**3.3**	(1.5)	**11.1**	(2.0)	0.3	(1.5)
	Qatar	**15.6**	(1.3)	1.5	(0.8)	**3.5**	(0.7)	**-4.0**	(1.3)	**-5.1**	(1.2)	**11.5**	(1.3)	**7.6**	(1.1)	**8.7**	(1.1)	**5.5**	(0.8)	**3.9**	(1.0)	**-3.4**	(0.8)
	Romania	0.0	(2.5)	-1.6	(1.7)	**6.5**	(1.1)	**-3.9**	(1.8)	**-4.3**	(1.9)	**11.8**	(2.4)	**9.7**	(1.8)	**10.2**	(1.8)	**5.7**	(1.6)	**6.3**	(2.0)	0.8	(1.5)
	Russian Federation	**23.5**	(2.2)	-1.3	(1.5)	**4.2**	(1.0)	**-9.5**	(1.7)	**-5.0**	(1.6)	**7.4**	(1.9)	**13.3**	(1.5)	**15.3**	(1.5)	**5.1**	(1.4)	**3.3**	(1.5)	2.3	(1.3)
	Serbia	**7.8**	(1.7)	0.4	(2.2)	**6.6**	(1.2)	**-8.3**	(1.4)	-1.4	(1.4)	**4.8**	(1.7)	**10.4**	(1.4)	**15.8**	(1.7)	**-4.4**	(1.2)	**5.3**	(1.6)	2.0	(1.1)
	Shanghai-China	**14.8**	(2.6)	1.3	(1.2)	-0.8	(1.5)	**-9.7**	(2.1)	-2.0	(2.0)	**13.1**	(2.4)	**9.5**	(1.2)	**15.5**	(1.7)	**3.1**	(1.2)	0.5	(1.7)	0.7	(1.5)
	Singapore	**20.4**	(1.5)	0.4	(1.0)	**3.2**	(1.1)	**-8.8**	(1.4)	**-7.6**	(1.3)	**10.0**	(1.5)	**6.4**	(1.1)	**22.4**	(1.4)	2.4	(1.2)	**6.3**	(1.4)	**-4.4**	(1.3)
	Chinese Taipei	**18.8**	(1.8)	1.1	(1.5)	-1.9	(2.2)	**-5.1**	(1.9)	-0.5	(2.2)	**18.9**	(3.1)	**10.4**	(1.9)	**12.9**	(1.3)	2.2	(1.3)	**7.5**	(1.7)	**-4.1**	(1.5)
	Thailand	**10.7**	(2.4)	**5.0**	(1.1)	-0.5	(0.9)	**7.5**	(2.1)	-3.6	(3.0)	**5.2**	(2.6)	**7.1**	(1.4)	**3.9**	(1.5)	0.1	(1.8)	**5.7**	(1.4)	1.1	(1.6)
	Trinidad and Tobago	**12.6**	(1.8)	1.9	(1.3)	**2.7**	(1.1)	2.0	(1.3)	**-7.0**	(1.4)	**9.6**	(1.5)	**6.2**	(1.3)	**11.5**	(1.5)	**3.9**	(1.0)	2.4	(1.2)	-0.3	(1.2)
	Tunisia	3.5	(2.1)	-0.7	(1.7)	0.2	(1.1)	**-7.0**	(1.6)	1.3	(1.4)	**12.4**	(1.6)	**4.7**	(1.4)	**8.9**	(1.4)	**3.1**	(1.1)	**3.5**	(1.2)	-0.4	(1.2)
	Uruguay	**10.0**	(1.7)	**3.9**	(1.1)	**4.2**	(1.3)	**-5.0**	(1.4)	**-6.3**	(1.4)	**10.6**	(1.6)	**6.9**	(1.3)	**16.9**	(1.3)	**-2.7**	(1.3)	1.0	(1.5)	0.5	(1.4)

Note: Values that are statistically significant are indicated in bold (see Annex A3).
1. Multilevel regression model (student and school levels): Reading performance is regressed on all the variables presented in this table.
StatLink http://dx.doi.org/10.1787/888932343285

[Part 2/6]

Table IV.2.14c **Relationships between reading performance and students' reading engagement and approaches to learning, the learning environment, resources, policies and practices, accounting for students' and schools' socio-economic and demographic background**

		Learning environment and school climate (school level)[1]														School policies on selecting and grouping students[1]							
		Index of teacher-student relations (school average)		Index of disciplinary climate (school average)		Index of student-related factors affecting school climate (higher values indicate a positive student behaviour)		Index of teacher-related factors affecting school climate (higher values indicate a positive teacher behaviour)		Index of teachers' stimulation of reading engagement (school average)		Parents expect the school to set high academic standards and pressure for students to achieve them		Index of school principal's leadership (higher values indicate more leadership roles are taken)		School with high academic selectivity for school admittance		School is very likely to transfer students with low achievement, behavioural problems or special learning needs		School with ability grouping for all subjects		Percentage of students that repeated one or more grades	
		Change in score	S.E.	Change in score	S.E.	Change in score	S.E.	Change in score	S.E.	Change in score	S.E.	Change in score	S.E.	Change in score	S.E.	Change in score	S.E.	Change in score	S.E.	Change in score	S.E.	Change in score	S.E.
OECD	Australia	12.0	(7.7)	**20.6**	(6.0)	3.7	(2.4)	0.0	(2.8)	-11.0	(9.1)	5.0	(4.2)	2.6	(1.4)	5.6	(3.4)	7.4	(7.4)	**-13.7**	(6.7)	**-1.0**	(0.2)
	Austria	-8.7	(7.6)	2.4	(6.8)	-4.5	(4.2)	**10.4**	(4.1)	13.9	(9.0)	-17.1	(22.0)	-2.2	(4.9)	12.1	(7.7)	10.2	(6.9)	-15.9	(12.2)	**-0.6**	(0.2)
	Belgium	-10.4	(8.8)	9.6	(6.4)	0.7	(3.0)	**6.1**	(3.0)	9.5	(9.3)	2.5	(6.7)	-5.5	(3.4)	4.3	(6.2)	0.0	(4.2)	-9.8	(6.1)	**0.7**	(0.2)
	Canada	3.0	(4.9)	7.1	(4.4)	**4.7**	(2.2)	1.7	(2.6)	-4.6	(5.3)	4.5	(3.2)	-0.6	(1.8)	2.2	(4.0)	-1.1	(4.8)	0.8	(5.5)	**-0.4**	(0.1)
	Chile	**13.3**	(6.0)	-2.9	(5.4)	-4.4	(2.7)	**6.4**	(1.9)	2.1	(5.8)	-0.8	(5.4)	0.6	(1.9)	6.9	(4.1)	4.5	(5.2)	-3.0	(4.3)	**-0.6**	(0.1)
	Czech Republic	5.2	(6.3)	7.3	(3.9)	-5.3	(3.4)	**10.1**	(3.0)	4.6	(7.4)	2.3	(4.4)	-0.6	(2.4)	**12.6**	(6.3)	-5.7	(5.9)	1.7	(8.3)	0.1	(0.3)
	Denmark	-3.9	(5.7)	7.0	(4.0)	0.5	(2.3)	2.6	(2.7)	-3.0	(6.1)	4.4	(4.0)	**6.1**	(2.2)	**16.5**	(6.1)	7.0	(4.8)	-3.1	(5.2)	-0.5	(0.3)
	Estonia	**20.3**	(6.8)	**10.2**	(3.8)	-1.6	(2.8)	5.9	(3.2)	**-19.1**	(7.6)	5.1	(4.3)	0.1	(1.7)	**10.1**	(3.5)	-2.6	(5.8)	-2.6	(6.5)	-0.4	(0.3)
	Finland	11.9	(8.6)	4.4	(4.5)	4.7	(2.7)	-0.8	(2.9)	-5.1	(8.2)	0.1	(8.2)	-1.4	(2.4)	17.3	(10.3)	c	c	6.2	(9.0)	-0.8	(0.6)
	France	w	w	w	w	w	w	w	w	w	w	w	w	w	w	w	w	w	w	w	w	w	w
	Germany	8.7	(9.4)	3.4	(9.4)	**-9.5**	(4.3)	**13.5**	(5.1)	18.4	(12.1)	-18.6	(10.3)	-0.7	(4.7)	**16.3**	(6.1)	4.0	(5.6)	-9.7	(7.8)	0.0	(0.2)
	Greece	**35.9**	(18.2)	**24.2**	(10.2)	-3.2	(5.7)	11.0	(6.6)	-0.4	(10.5)	0.3	(12.2)	0.5	(4.3)	-6.7	(16.8)	6.4	(7.6)	**-167.4**	(48.8)	-0.2	(0.2)
	Hungary	-1.5	(8.2)	4.4	(7.4)	-3.9	(4.0)	**7.1**	(3.5)	11.6	(8.4)	-6.0	(8.8)	1.2	(2.9)	14.3	(9.9)	-4.6	(6.6)	1.1	(13.0)	**-0.5**	(0.2)
	Iceland	10.9	(6.8)	14.2	(8.7)	-7.2	(4.3)	9.5	(5.4)	-1.3	(9.0)	-3.1	(7.3)	-0.6	(3.5)	c	c	c	c	-11.8	(6.9)	-1.3	(1.2)
	Ireland	**39.2**	(14.1)	11.7	(6.8)	-1.1	(4.2)	9.4	(6.1)	-8.9	(10.9)	6.1	(5.9)	2.4	(3.6)	-10.2	(5.8)	c	c	-10.0	(12.6)	**-1.0**	(0.4)
	Israel	4.9	(11.4)	14.5	(8.6)	-6.8	(5.0)	5.8	(4.9)	**-44.1**	(11.5)	-1.9	(6.0)	**-9.8**	(4.2)	-10.8	(6.2)	**-24.2**	(8.4)	1.8	(7.4)	-0.2	(0.4)
	Italy	**-16.4**	(7.7)	**24.9**	(5.1)	-2.2	(3.3)	**10.8**	(3.1)	14.2	(7.6)	**18.6**	(6.2)	**-7.0**	(2.5)	-0.9	(4.2)	**13.5**	(4.8)	-1.1	(4.7)	**-0.4**	(0.2)
	Japan	**41.1**	(12.3)	**24.6**	(8.6)	-4.5	(3.3)	**14.9**	(3.8)	-7.4	(8.3)	-0.1	(6.4)	-0.7	(2.6)	-7.1	(9.2)	-2.7	(7.5)	-5.8	(7.4)	c	c
	Korea	19.0	(13.9)	**15.8**	(7.6)	1.7	(4.4)	**5.5**	(2.8)	**-36.7**	(10.5)	**19.1**	(6.3)	-3.9	(2.4)	**13.4**	(4.4)	-7.3	(7.0)	-13.0	(9.4)	c	c
	Luxembourg	c	c	c	c	c	c	c	c	c	c	c	c	c	c	c	c	c	c	c	c	c	c
	Mexico	5.0	(6.7)	**20.9**	(6.8)	-1.6	(2.6)	**7.3**	(2.8)	**12.2**	(5.7)	-0.6	(5.3)	0.6	(1.7)	-0.9	(3.8)	-2.3	(3.5)	-4.3	(4.8)	**-0.3**	(0.1)
	Netherlands	-14.0	(15.5)	**32.0**	(11.6)	-7.5	(4.7)	**8.8**	(4.4)	-14.0	(11.8)	-8.1	(8.3)	2.2	(3.5)	12.2	(7.8)	-11.6	(6.7)	-0.5	(4.6)	-0.2	(0.2)
	New Zealand	-3.5	(8.8)	**20.1**	(6.8)	-3.1	(3.4)	0.9	(3.0)	-8.6	(7.3)	**15.8**	(4.8)	-1.5	(2.0)	2.6	(4.4)	**-31.6**	(12.9)	4.1	(7.2)	0.3	(0.5)
	Norway	7.1	(7.7)	**11.8**	(6.0)	1.2	(3.3)	-1.3	(3.5)	-0.3	(7.9)	**15.0**	(4.2)	-3.9	(3.4)	**14.9**	(7.3)	c	c	1.6	(8.7)	c	c
	Poland	-5.4	(7.1)	4.6	(5.2)	3.2	(2.1)	-1.0	(2.7)	-2.1	(7.6)	0.1	(5.7)	-5.0	(2.7)	-1.6	(6.6)	4.5	(5.5)	3.1	(7.5)	**-1.3**	(0.2)
	Portugal	-0.7	(9.7)	**11.6**	(5.7)	0.3	(2.8)	1.5	(2.9)	-16.0	(8.5)	0.5	(6.7)	2.1	(2.8)	**-38.6**	(13.3)	c	c	3.2	(6.9)	**-0.6**	(0.1)
	Slovak Republic	5.2	(8.9)	**14.8**	(7.1)	-4.6	(4.1)	5.1	(4.0)	6.8	(8.3)	-0.7	(9.2)	-2.4	(3.6)	-1.7	(7.2)	-9.1	(5.3)	-0.2	(7.9)	**-0.8**	(0.3)
	Slovenia	4.6	(7.7)	8.1	(5.0)	5.2	(3.6)	2.4	(3.1)	5.1	(7.0)	6.6	(5.1)	2.9	(2.5)	3.1	(4.9)	4.8	(4.5)	-4.5	(8.7)	-0.3	(0.2)
	Spain	**-10.1**	(4.4)	**10.9**	(3.6)	-1.3	(2.1)	2.2	(2.0)	0.5	(4.2)	1.1	(5.0)	-0.1	(1.7)	7.4	(7.6)	3.0	(5.1)	3.2	(4.6)	**-0.7**	(0.1)
	Sweden	1.9	(7.2)	-0.6	(6.1)	-2.4	(2.7)	3.6	(3.5)	16.6	(9.2)	-0.6	(4.5)	**-7.2**	(2.3)	1.4	(7.0)	16.8	(10.2)	0.3	(6.8)	0.0	(0.4)
	Switzerland	2.5	(5.9)	**12.1**	(5.0)	-0.6	(2.6)	2.6	(2.6)	-11.2	(7.1)	-1.5	(4.8)	-0.6	(2.2)	5.4	(4.0)	**9.7**	(4.4)	-5.7	(3.1)	**-0.4**	(0.1)
	Turkey	16.3	(9.1)	10.9	(8.2)	1.9	(3.7)	-3.8	(3.1)	10.7	(6.8)	1.3	(6.1)	1.3	(2.8)	**14.9**	(4.4)	-6.4	(4.6)	-3.4	(4.6)	**-1.0**	(0.2)
	United Kingdom	**-16.1**	(7.0)	8.2	(6.9)	-1.4	(3.1)	4.3	(3.7)	11.4	(7.2)	3.3	(3.9)	-1.0	(1.6)	7.2	(4.4)	-8.6	(5.9)	2.5	(5.1)	-1.0	(0.7)
	United States	-1.6	(7.2)	**24.6**	(7.7)	-6.5	(3.7)	4.2	(2.5)	9.2	(8.0)	2.5	(4.3)	-2.6	(1.7)	5.0	(4.1)	7.7	(5.4)	14.9	(7.7)	**-0.8**	(0.2)
	OECD average	**5.5**	(1.6)	**12.3**	(1.2)	**-1.7**	(0.6)	**5.2**	(0.6)	-1.5	(1.5)	1.7	(1.3)	**-1.1**	(0.5)	**4.1**	(1.3)	-0.7	(1.2)	**-7.5**	(2.0)	**-0.5**	(0.1)
Partners	Albania	-7.2	(12.9)	1.6	(10.8)	1.7	(5.5)	-3.9	(5.3)	13.9	(13.4)	15.3	(8.1)	4.1	(3.8)	-7.2	(5.9)	**17.6**	(7.5)	-3.7	(8.8)	**-1.4**	(0.4)
	Argentina	19.6	(12.6)	6.9	(7.3)	-4.6	(3.7)	1.8	(4.1)	-5.1	(10.2)	-8.0	(12.1)	5.6	(5.2)	10.8	(8.6)	12.1	(7.9)	-4.7	(8.9)	**-0.8**	(0.1)
	Azerbaijan	10.6	(14.4)	**36.1**	(13.6)	-7.4	(4.3)	**8.0**	(3.8)	9.5	(9.2)	**-31.2**	(7.6)	-1.2	(2.6)	-4.0	(7.2)	14.9	(8.2)	-0.2	(7.9)	**-2.5**	(0.9)
	Brazil	**16.4**	(6.8)	10.3	(6.2)	**-5.5**	(2.7)	**7.2**	(2.7)	**-12.4**	(6.3)	-4.2	(5.7)	**4.0**	(1.8)	1.1	(5.4)	**10.6**	(4.7)	4.1	(4.1)	**-0.7**	(0.1)
	Bulgaria	**22.3**	(8.6)	5.7	(7.5)	-3.0	(3.9)	6.1	(3.7)	-5.0	(9.8)	3.2	(8.0)	-3.7	(3.5)	**18.8**	(7.8)	1.7	(7.8)	-6.9	(7.5)	0.2	(0.2)
	Colombia	0.4	(7.9)	11.1	(6.8)	-0.2	(2.9)	3.4	(2.6)	-2.7	(7.1)	-6.7	(5.6)	-1.8	(1.9)	1.3	(4.6)	2.4	(4.1)	**-11.0**	(5.4)	**-0.4**	(0.2)
	Croatia	3.2	(9.0)	**11.5**	(5.4)	-4.8	(2.9)	**7.5**	(2.9)	**32.1**	(7.6)	12.9	(8.7)	-1.7	(3.1)	**23.8**	(5.7)	0.4	(4.7)	-1.5	(4.9)	**-1.6**	(0.4)
	Dubai (UAE)	5.4	(10.6)	**25.8**	(6.0)	3.9	(3.9)	3.2	(3.7)	-3.0	(8.0)	-1.1	(5.5)	-3.3	(2.8)	3.5	(6.4)	-11.1	(5.9)	-5.7	(6.9)	**-0.5**	(0.2)
	Hong Kong-China	19.3	(11.5)	**36.8**	(8.8)	-1.8	(4.5)	5.6	(2.9)	**-20.0**	(10.0)	-3.2	(14.4)	**-6.1**	(2.0)	5.8	(5.9)	7.3	(4.8)	-3.7	(6.9)	-0.4	(0.3)
	Indonesia	-19.6	(12.6)	0.4	(8.6)	1.0	(4.4)	7.4	(4.9)	**-17.5**	(8.1)	-0.9	(6.1)	-4.8	(2.8)	2.0	(5.2)	10.1	(5.3)	-1.6	(7.0)	-0.2	(0.2)
	Jordan	24.0	(13.2)	**22.0**	(7.3)	0.4	(3.9)	1.9	(3.6)	-16.4	(9.4)	0.2	(5.9)	3.3	(3.2)	1.8	(6.4)	**13.0**	(5.8)	-1.3	(6.0)	-0.6	(0.4)
	Kazakhstan	**-27.9**	(9.4)	10.7	(8.3)	6.3	(4.6)	-1.8	(3.4)	**24.1**	(7.6)	11.2	(8.3)	0.9	(4.0)	-7.5	(5.9)	-5.8	(8.8)	-5.6	(5.3)	-0.4	(1.1)
	Kyrgyzstan	**-20.3**	(9.8)	9.2	(13.0)	5.1	(3.7)	1.6	(3.3)	4.0	(9.2)	-2.0	(5.8)	-2.6	(2.7)	-8.9	(5.5)	4.6	(5.1)	**14.0**	(6.1)	0.0	(0.6)
	Latvia	**22.6**	(8.6)	9.6	(6.1)	**-7.9**	(3.9)	**10.2**	(3.4)	-11.0	(6.8)	**17.1**	(5.8)	2.2	(2.9)	-1.6	(4.9)	3.6	(6.7)	-6.7	(5.2)	**-0.5**	(0.2)
	Lithuania	-7.8	(6.4)	**18.5**	(6.4)	-5.7	(3.3)	1.9	(3.6)	0.7	(8.7)	**18.9**	(7.7)	-1.6	(3.2)	3.4	(8.3)	6.9	(8.1)	-9.2	(6.0)	0.0	(0.4)
	Macao-China	c	c	c	c	c	c	c	c	c	c	c	c	c	c	c	c	c	c	c	c	c	c
	Montenegro	c	c	c	c	c	c	c	c	c	c	c	c	c	c	c	c	c	c	c	c	c	c
	Panama	-1.5	(9.4)	**40.3**	(9.4)	1.0	(5.2)	4.1	(5.3)	6.8	(10.7)	2.3	(9.1)	-1.5	(3.1)	-8.7	(6.4)	6.0	(7.1)	18.9	(9.8)	**-0.4**	(0.2)
	Peru	6.6	(7.6)	16.6	(9.8)	-0.1	(2.9)	0.9	(2.8)	**16.5**	(8.2)	3.5	(5.1)	-3.6	(2.2)	9.1	(5.5)	-1.8	(5.0)	**-9.8**	(4.4)	**-0.5**	(0.2)
	Qatar	7.2	(9.0)	**32.0**	(9.8)	0.4	(5.5)	1.1	(5.3)	9.3	(9.8)	12.5	(7.5)	3.7	(3.1)	-1.6	(8.1)	-4.2	(7.1)	-5.3	(7.9)	**-0.6**	(0.2)
	Romania	-8.4	(12.9)	**35.3**	(11.0)	-7.0	(4.7)	**14.2**	(3.6)	14.5	(13.4)	**14.6**	(7.4)	-6.7	(3.6)	-10.3	(5.4)	-8.6	(6.0)	-2.8	(6.4)	0.2	(0.1)
	Russian Federation	-6.2	(8.5)	**23.1**	(6.8)	**-7.3**	(3.2)	**6.7**	(2.6)	8.7	(7.3)	-1.9	(5.9)	0.1	(2.8)	0.2	(6.0)	5.7	(7.9)	-3.3	(4.2)	0.4	(0.2)
	Serbia	-2.8	(11.9)	**28.9**	(9.2)	4.3	(5.5)	4.1	(3.8)	-3.0	(7.8)	-0.1	(10.9)	-2.0	(3.1)	-14.1	(8.5)	**13.3**	(5.7)	-3.5	(6.9)	**-0.8**	(0.2)
	Shanghai-China	16.1	(8.2)	**19.2**	(6.3)	-4.0	(2.1)	**4.0**	(1.6)	2.7	(8.4)	3.2	(4.1)	-2.6	(2.1)	**13.9**	(3.6)	3.3	(4.3)	-6.1	(5.0)	**-0.7**	(0.2)
	Singapore	15.2	(8.3)	**22.8**	(8.6)	1.6	(2.7)	-2.0	(3.8)	-15.5	(10.7)	4.1	(4.1)	-1.2	(2.2)	4.3	(4.8)	c	c	7.4	(4.8)	**-0.8**	(0.4)
	Chinese Taipei	11.6	(8.8)	**22.0**	(6.0)	1.6	(2.3)	0.4	(1.9)	-6.6	(7.0)	5.7	(3.4)	**-3.8**	(1.7)	4.2	(3.6)	-6.3	(3.2)	-2.2	(8.2)	0.0	(0.6)
	Thailand	3.9	(7.7)	3.4	(10.3)	1.0	(4.4)	2.9	(4.6)	10.3	(8.3)	0.7	(6.1)	4.7	(2.9)	0.1	(5.4)	**20.4**	(9.0)	7.8	(7.5)	**-0.6**	(0.3)
	Trinidad and Tobago	-25.8	(16.9)	**25.7**	(11.2)	-5.9	(4.1)	6.2	(4.9)	13.4	(11.8)	5.1	(7.9)	-2.3	(3.5)	-1.4	(7.2)	1.0	(9.4)	-4.0	(11.8)	**-1.3**	(0.3)
	Tunisia	-5.5	(8.1)	11.4	(7.6)	4.3	(3.0)	-2.0	(3.5)	**16.0**	(6.9)	**15.4**	(5.3)	-3.2	(1.8)	**11.0**	(4.9)	2.2	(4.2)	5.9	(8.0)	**-0.5**	(0.2)
	Uruguay	-5.7	(7.8)	**12.2**	(4.8)	-1.7	(2.7)	-1.2	(2.9)	-0.7	(6.5)	9.4	(10.0)	1.6	(2.0)	-1.0	(6.7)	**-17.4**	(6.3)	-1.5	(6.2)	**-0.5**	(0.1)

Note: Values that are statistically significant are indicated in bold (see Annex A3).
1. Multilevel regression model (student and school levels): Reading performance is regressed on all the variables presented in this table.
StatLink http://dx.doi.org/10.1787/888932343285

[Part 3/6]

Table IV.2.14c Relationships between reading performance and students' reading engagement and approaches to learning, the learning environment, resources, policies and practices, accounting for students' and schools' socio-economic and demographic background

		School governance[1]								School assessment and accountability policies[1]							
		Index of school responsibility for resource allocation (higher values indicate more autonomy)		Index of school responsibility for curriculum and assessment (higher values indicate more autonomy)		School competes with other schools for students in the same area		Private school		School uses standardised tests		School uses student assessments to monitor school's progress		School uses student assessments to improve instruction or curriculum		School uses student assessments to compare with other schools or district or national performance	
		Change in score	S.E.	Change in score	S.E.	Change in score	S.E.	Change in score	S.E.	Change in score	S.E.	Change in score	S.E.	Change in score	S.E.	Change in score	S.E.
OECD	Australia	1.0	(2.1)	-0.5	(1.8)	-10.7	(6.9)	-8.1	(5.2)	-4.2	(3.1)	-2.2	(4.7)	-6.4	(5.0)	**-7.8**	(3.7)
	Austria	2.3	(7.3)	-2.4	(4.2)	-1.9	(6.1)	-5.2	(12.2)	**-25.2**	(8.5)	-9.7	(8.1)	-1.2	(6.9)	**17.4**	(7.8)
	Belgium	-3.4	(20.6)	5.3	(3.1)	1.9	(8.8)	w	w	**-13.9**	(5.4)	6.2	(4.8)	-7.8	(5.0)	1.8	(6.6)
	Canada	1.6	(3.8)	-0.5	(3.0)	4.7	(4.4)	4.1	(8.8)	2.5	(4.2)	-2.5	(4.8)	0.0	(4.0)	1.4	(4.3)
	Chile	**4.1**	(2.0)	-1.2	(2.3)	6.0	(5.3)	-12.1	(6.2)	-0.7	(6.5)	9.5	(6.0)	-7.2	(8.4)	**-11.9**	(4.2)
	Czech Republic	**3.7**	(1.7)	-5.2	(2.8)	2.4	(5.5)	10.9	(8.3)	6.4	(8.2)	5.3	(6.5)	-7.3	(6.0)	4.9	(5.8)
	Denmark	0.2	(1.6)	0.4	(1.5)	-7.2	(4.2)	-1.8	(5.2)	1.5	(11.0)	-2.7	(3.3)	1.7	(4.4)	1.9	(3.5)
	Estonia	-2.1	(2.7)	0.1	(1.9)	0.2	(4.4)	**-17.3**	(7.7)	-1.8	(4.5)	-2.6	(5.5)	**-11.4**	(4.6)	4.0	(4.9)
	Finland	1.0	(4.6)	1.4	(1.9)	-3.6	(3.9)	-5.4	(10.2)	20.3	(13.0)	-3.6	(3.7)	-2.2	(3.6)	1.4	(4.1)
	France	w	w	w	w	w	w	w	w	w	w	w	w	w	w	w	w
	Germany	**15.0**	(5.7)	-2.5	(4.0)	**27.0**	(6.8)	**-27.4**	(10.2)	6.1	(6.0)	**-15.5**	(6.2)	7.7	(6.2)	7.7	(5.2)
	Greece	**112.8**	(52.1)	-9.9	(17.1)	-2.1	(12.0)	-27.8	(27.2)	-2.4	(8.5)	-3.9	(9.4)	-20.9	(10.9)	10.5	(9.4)
	Hungary	**-5.6**	(2.2)	1.2	(2.7)	0.5	(5.2)	0.9	(7.4)	8.3	(5.9)	11.9	(8.0)	-6.5	(5.7)	-9.6	(5.9)
	Iceland	-3.6	(3.3)	**7.4**	(2.6)	4.9	(4.7)	c	c	-11.2	(8.1)	-2.7	(11.0)	12.5	(8.2)	-7.8	(4.4)
	Ireland	1.7	(10.4)	0.5	(4.4)	-8.1	(9.3)	1.9	(6.8)	-1.3	(5.7)	4.5	(5.7)	-0.6	(5.3)	-12.0	(6.8)
	Israel	0.0	(6.7)	-5.8	(3.5)	15.6	(8.6)	2.7	(11.8)	14.0	(11.3)	5.5	(9.7)	-8.1	(10.2)	12.8	(7.9)
	Italy	-2.7	(4.5)	-3.8	(2.1)	-1.4	(5.6)	6.0	(11.5)	**-10.4**	(4.0)	-3.4	(5.0)	3.5	(5.8)	-1.3	(5.1)
	Japan	0.0	(3.7)	-2.1	(3.1)	0.4	(7.0)	**-23.0**	(10.5)	1.4	(4.7)	1.8	(4.8)	-6.3	(7.3)	-2.8	(5.9)
	Korea	**8.4**	(2.9)	-1.1	(2.8)	-6.3	(7.0)	0.8	(6.1)	-10.8	(12.2)	**-29.1**	(5.8)	**17.1**	(7.3)	-1.8	(5.4)
	Luxembourg	c	c	c	c	c	c	c	c	c	c	c	c	c	c	c	c
	Mexico	-2.3	(3.5)	-2.5	(2.6)	6.1	(5.4)	3.2	(11.7)	**10.3**	(5.2)	1.0	(5.7)	7.9	(7.3)	-0.3	(5.3)
	Netherlands	-0.9	(2.4)	**8.9**	(4.1)	0.8	(14.3)	2.5	(4.4)	-2.9	(5.8)	-7.6	(5.4)	7.8	(5.7)	-7.2	(5.5)
	New Zealand	-3.3	(3.3)	**-4.9**	(2.4)	**18.8**	(5.1)	-14.9	(11.9)	-1.0	(4.8)	1.9	(9.1)	**35.8**	(10.2)	2.7	(7.9)
	Norway	2.1	(3.3)	0.9	(2.9)	0.0	(4.3)	c	c	-9.8	(8.6)	-5.3	(6.0)	2.1	(5.1)	-2.1	(5.7)
	Poland	7.5	(7.1)	-0.3	(2.4)	4.4	(4.6)	-12.6	(17.4)	2.5	(10.1)	-5.3	(6.1)	1.9	(6.3)	-2.6	(3.6)
	Portugal	4.5	(3.8)	7.2	(6.7)	4.2	(5.1)	-7.5	(7.7)	1.2	(5.2)	5.8	(6.9)	-6.9	(5.2)	-2.7	(4.3)
	Slovak Republic	0.0	(2.4)	-2.4	(2.8)	3.4	(9.4)	-4.8	(8.9)	-4.6	(11.8)	-10.4	(7.0)	-2.1	(6.9)	1.5	(6.1)
	Slovenia	**-8.2**	(3.9)	-2.8	(3.3)	1.6	(4.6)	1.0	(14.0)	3.5	(5.3)	-8.4	(7.1)	-5.1	(5.3)	-7.0	(4.5)
	Spain	-2.6	(2.2)	-0.2	(1.7)	7.6	(4.3)	5.3	(4.1)	**-6.9**	(3.3)	2.5	(3.3)	-4.9	(4.0)	5.0	(3.2)
	Sweden	0.5	(1.8)	2.2	(2.0)	7.9	(4.4)	-3.2	(9.0)	8.4	(10.5)	15.3	(9.0)	-4.6	(5.7)	-0.2	(4.6)
	Switzerland	-4.8	(2.6)	1.6	(2.2)	1.4	(3.8)	-15.1	(8.0)	3.0	(4.0)	-1.9	(3.9)	2.9	(3.1)	5.6	(3.9)
	Turkey	**-23.0**	(9.2)	-7.3	(4.6)	1.5	(5.3)	c	c	**-12.5**	(5.6)	0.3	(7.4)	-3.4	(4.3)	-11.6	(7.7)
	United Kingdom	-1.6	(1.8)	0.5	(2.0)	-6.2	(4.5)	-7.9	(11.5)	2.3	(3.6)	**-21.6**	(10.6)	7.6	(7.3)	-1.8	(6.4)
	United States	-0.6	(2.6)	**-6.2**	(2.8)	0.1	(4.7)	c	c	**-26.2**	(10.0)	6.0	(13.1)	7.1	(7.9)	-5.1	(8.3)
	OECD average	3.2	(1.9)	-0.8	(0.8)	**2.3**	(1.2)	**-5.7**	(2.1)	-1.7	(1.3)	-1.9	(1.3)	0.1	(1.1)	-0.5	(1.0)
Partners	Albania	-8.4	(8.1)	-2.3	(3.7)	-7.3	(7.7)	32.3	(23.5)	-8.7	(13.7)	c	c	5.6	(11.3)	-13.7	(9.5)
	Argentina	-3.7	(7.6)	-2.0	(6.7)	-13.7	(9.3)	**19.2**	(9.2)	-2.5	(9.0)	-4.4	(8.0)	2.0	(11.8)	0.3	(7.4)
	Azerbaijan	-0.1	(7.9)	-0.1	(3.9)	11.7	(7.5)	c	c	**59.9**	(15.0)	-2.1	(8.6)	-4.9	(9.5)	**54.9**	(9.7)
	Brazil	5.5	(3.4)	-1.1	(2.7)	**-18.2**	(5.2)	1.6	(10.0)	-2.4	(4.9)	0.2	(9.6)	-1.2	(7.5)	**-12.1**	(5.2)
	Bulgaria	**-6.2**	(3.0)	**-29.9**	(8.7)	-14.0	(8.6)	c	c	-7.3	(10.5)	13.0	(12.4)	-4.7	(6.9)	-6.3	(9.3)
	Colombia	-1.6	(2.9)	-2.4	(2.3)	-11.6	(6.9)	0.5	(7.7)	5.6	(5.6)	7.2	(10.4)	1.8	(7.7)	0.8	(4.4)
	Croatia	**-15.2**	(7.5)	2.5	(4.5)	9.5	(5.7)	c	c	-0.5	(3.9)	-12.7	(8.1)	6.9	(5.3)	3.0	(4.5)
	Dubai (UAE)	-0.7	(2.5)	**7.6**	(3.1)	-17.1	(11.7)	-2.5	(13.4)	16.4	(9.0)	-3.0	(8.3)	-18.2	(9.4)	2.1	(6.6)
	Hong Kong-China	**-4.3**	(2.2)	0.6	(2.8)	10.5	(21.1)	1.5	(8.7)	c	c	12.4	(9.8)	5.7	(11.4)	2.2	(3.8)
	Indonesia	1.6	(3.1)	-4.4	(2.7)	-5.6	(8.4)	-9.2	(8.4)	-3.8	(10.3)	-6.3	(16.1)	25.3	(18.7)	-11.9	(9.5)
	Jordan	-5.4	(10.4)	-10.6	(7.3)	-3.4	(6.4)	7.3	(8.7)	-4.7	(7.9)	-8.7	(7.5)	-4.6	(15.5)	**20.0**	(9.7)
	Kazakhstan	-2.8	(5.6)	5.7	(5.8)	0.1	(6.1)	**-36.8**	(18.6)	-0.1	(10.0)	c	c	-16.7	(25.2)	6.6	(11.6)
	Kyrgyzstan	**-13.2**	(5.5)	3.4	(2.8)	-3.1	(6.9)	27.2	(17.2)	20.6	(16.8)	-1.2	(15.1)	8.3	(8.7)	**-17.9**	(8.9)
	Latvia	-7.1	(3.9)	3.8	(3.9)	-1.0	(6.4)	c	c	-4.8	(6.5)	-3.5	(11.0)	c	c	2.9	(8.5)
	Lithuania	1.6	(4.3)	**5.7**	(2.5)	-2.1	(5.6)	c	c	**-13.3**	(6.0)	1.1	(9.3)	-7.7	(5.2)	-6.4	(5.5)
	Macao-China	c	c	c	c	c	c	c	c	c	c	c	c	c	c	c	c
	Montenegro	c	c	c	c	c	c	c	c	c	c	c	c	c	c	c	c
	Panama	9.4	(7.7)	**-10.2**	(4.1)	**-16.0**	(6.9)	8.4	(20.9)	-9.1	(6.7)	-10.3	(9.0)	-12.1	(8.8)	-1.1	(6.9)
	Peru	7.4	(4.2)	-3.5	(2.3)	6.5	(5.6)	-18.0	(13.3)	-1.9	(5.4)	-2.7	(8.3)	-1.1	(10.1)	-6.7	(5.3)
	Qatar	1.7	(4.2)	-5.9	(5.0)	0.6	(7.1)	25.2	(13.4)	2.8	(21.4)	-5.3	(11.6)	**-23.1**	(6.8)	-15.3	(10.3)
	Romania	0.4	(23.3)	-2.6	(2.9)	-6.8	(9.3)	c	c	-4.0	(6.3)	**46.6**	(19.7)	-7.3	(8.4)	-17.7	(12.8)
	Russian Federation	-1.0	(3.4)	1.3	(3.1)	2.1	(4.6)	c	c	-10.6	(5.8)	c	c	**-25.4**	(10.9)	-4.8	(11.1)
	Serbia	6.6	(7.3)	-24.5	(17.0)	**-16.0**	(5.7)	c	c	-0.4	(5.9)	-15.1	(10.4)	-7.6	(6.1)	-0.6	(8.0)
	Shanghai-China	0.4	(1.7)	**-3.2**	(1.5)	-0.8	(4.9)	3.6	(5.5)	14.2	(9.6)	-6.1	(6.2)	-16.0	(11.5)	5.8	(4.1)
	Singapore	-0.1	(3.8)	0.1	(2.0)	-2.2	(10.9)	c	c	-10.2	(17.5)	10.7	(16.1)	-5.5	(13.6)	-9.4	(10.6)
	Chinese Taipei	2.2	(2.5)	**-3.2**	(1.5)	**-19.9**	(6.6)	**-26.0**	(6.1)	**12.5**	(5.3)	1.6	(4.2)	-3.7	(5.4)	**-11.7**	(3.9)
	Thailand	-3.0	(2.7)	3.8	(3.0)	2.7	(6.6)	-12.4	(8.8)	**20.9**	(8.1)	3.9	(14.4)	-11.2	(16.5)	-10.7	(7.8)
	Trinidad and Tobago	9.2	(5.7)	1.3	(4.8)	2.1	(9.7)	-22.9	(14.7)	4.8	(7.7)	19.7	(11.3)	-17.0	(12.2)	-2.5	(6.4)
	Tunisia	-3.7	(5.9)	3.5	(18.2)	-1.4	(4.8)	**-46.6**	(14.9)	**-17.9**	(7.9)	2.3	(8.9)	2.0	(3.7)	**11.6**	(5.7)
	Uruguay	-7.0	(4.3)	2.5	(5.3)	2.1	(4.4)	**37.0**	(10.9)	**-9.7**	(4.1)	**13.2**	(4.9)	4.2	(6.0)	**-12.6**	(5.4)

Note: Values that are statistically significant are indicated in bold (see Annex A3).

1. Multilevel regression model (student and school levels): Reading performance is regressed on all the variables presented in this table.

StatLink http://dx.doi.org/10.1787/888932343285

[Part 4/6]

Table IV.2.14c **Relationships between reading performance and students' reading engagement and approaches to learning, the learning environment, resources, policies and practices, accounting for students' and schools' socio-economic and demographic background**

		School assessment and accountability policies[1]														Resources invested in education (student level)[1]	
		Schools' accountability to parents: only relative to other students in the school		Schools' accountability to parents: at least relative to national or regional benchmark		School posts achievement data publicly		Achievement data are used in decisions about instructional resource allocation to the school		Achievement data are tracked over time by an administrative authority		School monitors teachers' practice through students' achievement test or assessments		School monitors teachers' practice through teacher peer review or observations of lessons by principal or inspectors		Class size	
		Change in score	S.E.	Change in score	S.E.	Change in score	S.E.	Change in score	S.E.	Change in score	S.E.	Change in score	S.E.	Change in score	S.E.	Change in score	S.E.
OECD	Australia	-8.7	(4.6)	1.5	(5.3)	1.5	(3.6)	1.3	(3.3)	-1.4	(4.2)	**6.7**	(3.3)	0.1	(3.7)	**1.3**	(0.2)
	Austria	1.5	(7.4)	-2.5	(10.5)	-1.1	(13.5)	-0.3	(10.8)	9.7	(7.3)	3.8	(11.0)	-20.3	(13.8)	-0.1	(0.4)
	Belgium	**18.3**	(6.1)	-11.2	(6.1)	22.9	(21.6)	0.4	(5.9)	1.9	(4.4)	-5.0	(5.0)	8.2	(6.8)	**1.9**	(0.3)
	Canada	-1.1	(4.0)	-2.6	(3.7)	3.4	(3.2)	0.3	(3.0)	4.3	(4.1)	c	c	-3.1	(4.0)	**0.7**	(0.2)
	Chile	-4.9	(12.2)	-3.9	(9.1)	-1.6	(3.9)	-10.3	(5.3)	5.0	(4.7)	0.4	(5.0)	-3.3	(7.4)	-0.4	(0.3)
	Czech Republic	8.1	(7.3)	5.2	(7.8)	0.2	(4.5)	-0.5	(9.3)	-2.3	(4.1)	-0.5	(4.5)	14.6	(10.3)	-0.5	(0.3)
	Denmark	c	c	c	c	-1.7	(2.7)	3.8	(3.1)	-2.3	(3.4)	-3.4	(3.3)	-1.9	(4.2)	-0.3	(0.4)
	Estonia	4.4	(5.2)	2.4	(3.6)	1.2	(3.6)	-1.6	(4.7)	-2.3	(5.3)	**-8.0**	(3.6)	-3.6	(7.4)	**1.1**	(0.4)
	Finland	-5.2	(6.9)	3.5	(3.7)	11.4	(9.5)	5.2	(6.6)	3.6	(3.4)	0.8	(3.9)	-3.5	(3.2)	**2.1**	(0.5)
	France	w	w	w	w	w	w	w	w	w	w	w	w	w	w	w	w
	Germany	10.8	(6.4)	5.2	(7.3)	-13.9	(8.3)	-7.0	(5.5)	**16.3**	(5.7)	-0.8	(5.8)	5.3	(6.4)	0.1	(0.3)
	Greece	8.0	(9.4)	-18.2	(12.4)	3.4	(8.3)	3.5	(16.6)	-10.7	(7.5)	-2.2	(8.0)	16.4	(9.3)	-0.2	(0.7)
	Hungary	-2.2	(7.2)	-9.6	(5.9)	2.0	(5.0)	-8.4	(7.9)	-3.6	(5.3)	**-12.5**	(5.7)	**-46.5**	(22.8)	0.0	(0.3)
	Iceland	-3.5	(9.2)	1.3	(5.4)	-4.2	(5.7)	c	c	6.0	(6.1)	4.9	(4.5)	5.1	(5.9)	**2.0**	(0.4)
	Ireland	3.4	(6.3)	1.4	(7.0)	2.4	(9.2)	-7.6	(6.6)	-0.3	(6.0)	7.0	(5.5)	-5.5	(5.9)	**2.2**	(0.4)
	Israel	-25.6	(13.1)	4.5	(6.7)	-2.5	(8.7)	-0.7	(7.0)	1.6	(7.9)	7.3	(14.9)	-12.3	(11.1)	**0.8**	(0.2)
	Italy	0.1	(7.6)	-1.5	(6.8)	6.0	(5.0)	-4.5	(4.3)	-3.0	(4.5)	-1.0	(4.3)	-1.9	(5.1)	**-0.5**	(0.2)
	Japan	3.5	(15.0)	1.6	(14.6)	**19.3**	(8.3)	-27.8	(16.0)	3.1	(6.8)	1.5	(6.7)	-2.9	(8.3)	**-1.7**	(0.6)
	Korea	16.0	(8.6)	3.0	(7.5)	**11.0**	(4.7)	**-15.4**	(4.6)	-1.9	(5.3)	1.2	(4.8)	-7.4	(8.2)	-0.7	(1.6)
	Luxembourg	c	c	c	c	c	c	c	c	c	c	c	c	c	c	c	c
	Mexico	-0.9	(5.8)	1.1	(6.1)	1.7	(4.0)	3.5	(3.9)	1.0	(4.5)	-0.9	(3.6)	-3.3	(5.9)	-0.2	(0.2)
	Netherlands	6.8	(7.8)	6.0	(8.5)	**10.4**	(4.8)	0.6	(6.3)	5.1	(4.9)	7.0	(5.2)	-8.2	(5.3)	**1.0**	(0.2)
	New Zealand	-6.3	(7.3)	-9.4	(5.7)	-2.7	(5.3)	-0.8	(4.4)	-2.4	(7.4)	-2.2	(4.5)	-16.1	(14.9)	**1.8**	(0.3)
	Norway	9.8	(7.9)	8.2	(6.5)	6.5	(4.8)	0.2	(5.4)	4.3	(5.0)	0.0	(4.1)	-6.7	(5.4)	0.4	(0.3)
	Poland	-7.8	(9.7)	2.8	(5.4)	-3.7	(3.9)	-6.8	(5.8)	3.4	(5.8)	-14.2	(8.8)	**-32.1**	(13.8)	0.9	(0.6)
	Portugal	6.3	(5.5)	3.7	(4.9)	-5.5	(4.4)	-3.7	(4.3)	-0.4	(4.1)	-0.1	(4.4)	6.8	(6.4)	**2.2**	(0.4)
	Slovak Republic	2.0	(9.4)	-5.8	(8.3)	-2.8	(6.0)	-0.1	(6.8)	1.5	(6.8)	-2.9	(6.4)			-0.4	(0.3)
	Slovenia	-0.8	(7.1)	-3.1	(4.3)	**9.3**	(4.3)	**-13.1**	(6.0)	-1.8	(5.8)	-2.1	(4.7)	1.3	(6.9)	0.4	(0.3)
	Spain	-0.4	(2.8)	-1.7	(4.0)	-5.8	(3.9)	-3.9	(2.9)	-4.9	(3.2)	-1.6	(3.0)	0.4	(3.0)	**1.2**	(0.2)
	Sweden	0.5	(17.9)	-1.8	(6.2)	-1.1	(4.1)	-3.7	(3.9)	-5.5	(4.4)	-8.5	(4.9)	3.0	(4.7)	**1.3**	(0.4)
	Switzerland	-6.7	(3.9)	-3.5	(4.2)	-5.8	(9.9)	0.8	(3.8)	0.0	(3.9)	-2.4	(4.1)	0.8	(4.2)	**2.1**	(0.4)
	Turkey	-7.9	(12.8)	-1.1	(12.2)	10.0	(5.3)	-3.6	(4.8)	8.0	(5.4)	8.9	(6.3)	-8.7	(8.4)	0.2	(0.2)
	United Kingdom	5.0	(6.4)	-0.5	(4.4)	-1.6	(4.1)	-0.9	(3.8)	7.0	(5.1)	-8.7	(5.3)	22.1	(11.7)	**3.0**	(0.3)
	United States	3.9	(10.3)	5.7	(6.3)	**25.3**	(7.4)	6.6	(4.0)	-2.9	(10.1)	**-10.5**	(5.0)	19.9	(11.7)	0.4	(0.3)
	OECD average	0.9	(1.6)	-0.6	(1.3)	**2.9**	(1.3)	**-3.1**	(1.2)	1.1	(1.0)	-1.2	(1.1)	-2.7	(1.6)	**0.7**	(0.1)
Partners	Albania	-15.4	(12.1)	-16.8	(11.9)	9.8	(7.2)	**-22.1**	(8.2)	8.3	(8.2)	-9.3	(14.7)	c	c	0.3	(0.2)
	Argentina	-15.8	(9.0)	**-16.9**	(8.1)	-0.1	(14.7)	3.1	(6.7)	**-22.0**	(8.9)	**15.9**	(7.1)	11.5	(14.3)	-0.4	(0.3)
	Azerbaijan	-12.1	(14.9)	c	c	-14.4	(9.3)	12.9	(7.4)	-13.1	(8.5)	**-82.5**	(15.6)	22.2	(23.4)	-0.2	(0.3)
	Brazil	1.8	(8.1)	-1.9	(4.4)	8.2	(4.2)	**-9.0**	(4.3)	5.3	(4.7)	3.6	(4.2)	-7.5	(5.7)	-0.2	(0.2)
	Bulgaria	0.5	(11.7)	11.0	(11.5)	14.4	(7.6)	-7.9	(7.7)	-1.2	(7.7)	-13.5	(10.5)	11.6	(25.1)	0.4	(0.4)
	Colombia	-22.6	(14.3)	-8.8	(9.3)	**13.7**	(4.3)	-3.9	(4.1)	4.7	(4.9)	0.1	(4.3)	-2.0	(4.8)	**-0.7**	(0.3)
	Croatia	-7.5	(3.8)	c	c	2.6	(4.6)	5.5	(5.1)	2.1	(7.0)	-4.6	(4.3)	-7.0	(11.8)	0.7	(0.5)
	Dubai (UAE)	-3.6	(6.6)	**-16.7**	(7.4)	1.5	(5.3)	6.2	(5.8)	-3.3	(7.8)	-5.3	(8.5)	39.1	(20.1)	0.2	(0.2)
	Hong Kong-China	4.0	(5.2)	11.5	(6.1)	6.9	(4.4)	**9.4**	(4.4)	-2.6	(4.5)	-12.2	(7.5)	-8.5	(11.4)	**1.6**	(0.2)
	Indonesia	-11.0	(11.8)	-13.8	(11.0)	3.0	(6.3)	18.6	(11.8)	-8.5	(6.1)	1.5	(7.2)	29.4	(20.5)	0.3	(0.2)
	Jordan	9.4	(10.5)			-0.4	(9.6)	-6.9	(7.2)	-0.4	(6.9)	5.1	(8.3)	c	c	**-0.9**	(0.4)
	Kazakhstan	-27.0	(17.6)	-27.7	(16.2)	-11.9	(6.7)	-8.7	(6.6)	c	c	-16.2	(10.6)	c	c	**-0.9**	(0.4)
	Kyrgyzstan	11.1	(21.2)	9.2	(17.8)	11.2	(6.1)	-6.6	(9.5)	-18.4	(12.2)	2.0	(17.3)	c	c	-0.3	(0.3)
	Latvia	-7.2	(5.7)	-6.3	(4.9)	5.5	(4.2)	-3.8	(4.4)	3.0	(4.4)	-5.1	(5.1)	c	c	0.6	(0.4)
	Lithuania	-2.3	(5.0)	c	c	-7.4	(5.4)	13.5	(7.0)	-2.0	(4.8)	9.1	(5.6)	c	c	0.6	(0.4)
	Macao-China	c	c	c	c	c	c	c	c	c	c	c	c	c	c	c	c
	Montenegro	c	c	c	c	c	c	c	c	c	c	c	c	c	c	c	c
	Panama	**-22.8**	(11.0)	1.8	(7.1)	18.9	(12.0)	-3.3	(7.6)	6.4	(7.8)	3.4	(7.7)	-9.2	(12.7)	-0.5	(0.5)
	Peru	8.9	(6.1)	6.1	(6.5)	8.8	(6.4)	8.8	(5.1)	6.5	(5.1)	-8.2	(7.8)	**27.2**	(13.1)	**-0.6**	(0.3)
	Qatar	26.6	(16.7)	8.0	(13.9)	**-14.1**	(6.9)	-0.4	(7.4)	-12.9	(12.3)	-11.4	(11.2)	c	c	0.3	(0.2)
	Romania	-1.4	(13.8)	12.7	(12.6)	-5.2	(6.4)	0.8	(6.8)	**24.5**	(6.8)	-9.4	(7.7)	-6.9	(14.9)	**0.8**	(0.2)
	Russian Federation	-1.8	(10.0)	5.6	(7.3)	2.3	(5.7)	-4.0	(4.4)	**91.1**	(17.5)	5.6	(10.9)	c	c	0.1	(0.4)
	Serbia	-5.5	(13.6)	-3.9	(18.7)	1.9	(6.7)	**-18.3**	(6.9)	4.0	(7.7)	8.4	(5.2)	4.4	(8.4)	**1.0**	(0.3)
	Shanghai-China	7.1	(5.4)	-4.8	(5.0)	c	c	1.8	(3.1)	-3.4	(3.7)	5.0	(5.3)	c	c	**1.0**	(0.4)
	Singapore	11.9	(6.3)	9.2	(6.2)	-0.3	(3.9)	0.2	(4.3)	**-28.6**	(7.4)	0.0	(13.9)	12.4	(12.0)	**1.2**	(0.3)
	Chinese Taipei	**11.9**	(4.5)	6.3	(3.5)	2.0	(4.2)	**-8.4**	(3.9)	5.4	(3.6)	**6.6**	(3.2)	-0.7	(4.0)	**0.8**	(0.3)
	Thailand	13.4	(7.9)	**11.3**	(5.3)	-7.2	(5.2)	7.3	(8.3)	**-15.4**	(7.1)	-14.4	(8.6)	17.3	(15.4)	-0.3	(0.3)
	Trinidad and Tobago	8.4	(9.4)	11.3	(8.7)	-18.2	(10.7)	7.8	(7.1)	6.6	(6.7)	**-13.1**	(6.1)	6.0	(11.9)	0.0	(0.2)
	Tunisia	3.9	(7.9)	3.2	(7.4)	1.9	(7.2)	-3.2	(3.9)	-0.9	(4.3)	-9.4	(5.6)	2.2	(7.8)	0.0	(0.4)
	Uruguay	2.2	(4.9)	-3.9	(6.1)	4.8	(9.9)	-1.2	(3.8)	-0.8	(4.4)	**-12.9**	(4.5)	1.8	(9.4)	**-0.8**	(0.3)

Note: Values that are statistically significant are indicated in bold (see Annex A3).
1. Multilevel regression model (student and school levels): Reading performance is regressed on all the variables presented in this table.
StatLink http://dx.doi.org/10.1787/888932343285

[Part 5/6]

Table IV.2.14c **Relationships between reading performance and students' reading engagement and approaches to learning, the learning environment, resources, policies and practices, accounting for students' and schools' socio-economic and demographic background**

		Resources invested in education (school level)[1]																					
		Students' learning time at school in language of instruction lessons		Students' learning time at school in mathematics and science lessons		Percentage of students attending after-school lessons (enrichment)		Percentage of students attending after-school lessons (remedial)		Percentage of students that attended pre-primary education for one year or less		Percentage of students that attended pre-primary education for more than one year		School average class size		Index of library use in or outside school (higher values indicate more use)		Index of schools' extra-curricular activities (higher values indicate more activities)		Index of teacher shortage (higher values indicate higher shortage)		Index of quality of schools' educational resources (higher values indicate better resources)	
		Change in score	S.E.	Change in score	S.E.	Change in score	S.E.	Change in score	S.E.	Change in score	S.E.	Change in score	S.E.	Change in score	S.E.	Change in score	S.E.	Change in score	S.E.	Change in score	S.E.	Change in score	S.E.
OECD	Australia	-0.1	(0.1)	0.0	(0.1)	-0.4	(0.3)	0.1	(0.3)	0.4	(0.4)	0.4	(0.3)	**2.7**	(0.8)	-0.1	(2.0)	-1.0	(1.9)	7.4	(6.5)	-2.2	(1.6)
	Austria	0.1	(0.1)	0.0	(0.0)	-0.2	(0.3)	0.1	(0.2)	-0.5	(0.5)	-0.5	(0.4)	**1.9**	(0.8)	4.9	(4.0)	-2.3	(3.6)	-0.6	(8.1)	5.4	(3.8)
	Belgium	**-0.2**	(0.1)	**0.1**	(0.0)	**-0.7**	(0.2)	0.4	(0.3)	-0.7	(0.4)	**0.8**	(0.3)	**2.5**	(0.9)	-3.3	(2.7)	3.9	(2.7)	8.9	(8.8)	1.0	(2.4)
	Canada	0.0	(0.0)	0.0	(0.0)	-0.2	(0.2)	**-0.5**	(0.2)	**0.5**	(0.2)	**0.5**	(0.2)	**0.9**	(0.4)	-0.3	(1.9)	1.3	(2.1)	-0.7	(5.3)	2.0	(1.8)
	Chile	-0.1	(0.1)	0.1	(0.0)	**-0.7**	(0.2)	0.3	(0.2)	-0.3	(0.2)	-0.1	(0.3)	0.0	(0.4)	-0.4	(1.8)	1.9	(2.7)	**-16.5**	(7.1)	2.6	(2.3)
	Czech Republic	**-0.2**	(0.1)	0.0	(0.0)	-0.3	(0.2)	-0.2	(0.2)	0.2	(0.5)	0.4	(0.3)	1.1	(0.6)	-2.6	(3.3)	-4.2	(3.1)	**16.6**	(6.6)	1.1	(2.8)
	Denmark	-0.1	(0.0)	0.0	(0.0)	-0.3	(0.2)	-0.3	(0.2)	-0.4	(0.4)	-0.2	(0.4)	0.2	(0.5)	-2.3	(2.2)	-0.9	(1.7)	**-21.3**	(7.1)	-1.9	(2.0)
	Estonia	0.0	(0.1)	0.0	(0.0)	-0.3	(0.1)	-0.1	(0.1)	0.2	(0.2)	-0.2	(0.1)	**1.8**	(0.5)	-3.3	(2.4)	-1.5	(2.6)	-4.0	(9.0)	2.9	(2.2)
	Finland	0.0	(0.1)	0.0	(0.0)	**-0.7**	(0.3)	**-0.5**	(0.2)	**-0.6**	(0.2)	**-0.6**	(0.2)	1.1	(0.8)	1.7	(3.0)	0.2	(2.2)	-7.8	(6.3)	2.3	(2.4)
	France	w	w	w	w	w	w	w	w	w	w	w	w	w	w	w	w	w	w	w	w	w	w
	Germany	0.0	(0.1)	**0.2**	(0.1)	-0.4	(0.3)	-0.4	(0.2)	-0.6	(0.6)	0.1	(0.5)	1.2	(0.9)	-2.2	(3.1)	0.1	(3.4)	**-25.9**	(9.1)	-1.3	(2.8)
	Greece	0.1	(0.1)	0.1	(0.1)	0.4	(0.3)	0.1	(0.4)	-0.9	(0.5)	-0.5	(0.4)	-1.0	(1.4)	**7.9**	(4.0)	4.6	(5.1)	**-27.4**	(11.7)	5.7	(4.0)
	Hungary	0.0	(0.1)	0.1	(0.1)	0.2	(0.2)	0.3	(0.1)	**2.7**	(0.7)	**2.5**	(0.7)	**1.5**	(0.5)	-2.5	(4.1)	4.7	(4.0)	-3.4	(8.3)	-2.1	(2.6)
	Iceland	-0.1	(0.1)	0.0	(0.1)	-0.2	(0.2)	-0.2	(0.2)	0.3	(0.5)	-0.4	(0.4)	0.1	(0.8)	1.1	(3.6)	-2.9	(3.6)	6.4	(6.9)	4.5	(3.7)
	Ireland	-0.3	(0.2)	0.0	(0.1)	0.3	(0.3)	-0.4	(0.4)	0.2	(0.3)	0.2	(0.3)	**4.1**	(1.0)	5.5	(3.5)	2.2	(3.5)	5.7	(9.4)	**-6.9**	(2.8)
	Israel	0.1	(0.1)	0.0	(0.0)	**0.6**	(0.3)	**-2.1**	(0.4)	0.2	(0.8)	0.6	(0.7)	**2.1**	(0.8)	-1.8	(3.9)	-3.6	(3.8)	-7.8	(11.3)	**8.0**	(2.8)
	Italy	-0.1	(0.1)	0.0	(0.0)	-0.3	(0.2)	-0.2	(0.1)	0.1	(0.4)	**0.9**	(0.3)	**2.6**	(0.7)	3.0	(2.4)	2.4	(2.5)	**-20.4**	(7.1)	**6.2**	(2.4)
	Japan	-0.1	(0.1)	**0.2**	(0.0)	0.2	(0.2)	0.0	(0.1)	-1.0	(1.8)	-1.0	(1.1)	**1.1**	(0.4)	3.4	(3.2)	-0.4	(3.7)	-11.3	(9.8)	-2.6	(2.8)
	Korea	0.0	(0.1)	**0.1**	(0.0)	0.0	(0.1)	**0.3**	(0.1)	0.9	(0.6)	0.8	(0.5)	-0.3	(0.7)	-4.2	(2.7)	-2.3	(3.1)	-5.4	(9.1)	1.7	(3.1)
	Luxembourg	c	c	c	c	c	c	c	c	c	c	c	c	c	c	c	c	c	c	c	c	c	c
	Mexico	0.0	(0.1)	**0.1**	(0.0)	**-0.5**	(0.2)	-0.2	(0.2)	**0.3**	(0.2)	**0.3**	(0.2)	0.2	(0.2)	**5.5**	(1.8)	-1.1	(1.9)	-5.5	(5.8)	0.9	(2.2)
	Netherlands	**-0.5**	(0.1)	**0.2**	(0.1)	**-0.8**	(0.3)	0.1	(0.3)	-0.7	(1.0)	-0.5	(0.5)	**3.4**	(1.3)	**9.0**	(3.6)	8.1	(4.8)	-3.7	(10.9)	0.5	(3.2)
	New Zealand	**-0.5**	(0.1)	**0.2**	(0.1)	-0.2	(0.3)	**-1.0**	(0.4)	-0.3	(0.3)	0.1	(0.2)	0.4	(0.9)	2.7	(2.6)	-0.7	(2.7)	-10.3	(9.5)	4.4	(2.6)
	Norway	c	c	c	c	0.4	(0.3)	**-1.6**	(0.3)	0.0	(0.5)	0.1	(0.2)	0.2	(0.4)	0.9	(2.8)	0.9	(2.6)	-6.0	(6.6)	2.6	(3.5)
	Poland	-0.2	(0.1)	0.0	(0.0)	**0.2**	(0.1)	-0.1	(0.1)	0.1	(0.5)	0.4	(0.5)	0.4	(0.5)	1.8	(4.1)	1.3	(2.9)	-13.9	(8.4)	-3.7	(2.2)
	Portugal	0.1	(0.1)	0.0	(0.0)	-0.2	(0.2)	0.2	(0.2)	0.0	(0.2)	0.2	(0.2)	0.6	(0.8)	**10.1**	(3.7)	1.7	(3.0)	15.8	(8.4)	-1.2	(2.1)
	Slovak Republic	**-0.3**	(0.1)	**0.1**	(0.0)	-0.1	(0.1)	0.1	(0.1)	0.7	(0.4)	**0.7**	(0.3)	0.6	(0.7)	-3.6	(5.4)	2.3	(3.1)	**-21.2**	(9.5)	1.7	(3.9)
	Slovenia	**0.5**	(0.1)	**0.1**	(0.1)	**-0.2**	(0.1)	**-0.4**	(0.2)	0.2	(0.2)	0.3	(0.2)	**1.1**	(0.5)	5.0	(4.0)	-0.6	(2.9)	1.8	(8.1)	3.0	(3.3)
	Spain	0.0	(0.1)	0.0	(0.0)	0.1	(0.1)	0.0	(0.1)	0.3	(0.3)	**0.5**	(0.2)	0.0	(0.4)	-0.8	(2.1)	**4.1**	(1.8)	-0.5	(4.6)	-1.4	(1.7)
	Sweden	-0.1	(0.1)	0.0	(0.0)	-0.2	(0.2)	**-0.5**	(0.3)	0.7	(0.3)	**0.8**	(0.3)	0.5	(0.7)	5.0	(2.9)	**7.9**	(2.9)	-1.8	(5.8)	**6.6**	(3.0)
	Switzerland	0.0	(0.1)	0.0	(0.0)	-0.3	(0.1)	0.0	(0.1)	**1.3**	(0.5)	**1.2**	(0.5)	**1.7**	(0.6)	-1.8	(2.2)	3.0	(2.4)	**-12.5**	(6.1)	0.1	(1.8)
	Turkey	**0.2**	(0.1)	**0.1**	(0.0)	0.3	(0.2)	**-0.5**	(0.2)	-0.4	(0.2)	**-0.6**	(0.3)	-1.0	(0.5)	**-6.4**	(2.9)	-2.2	(3.0)	-7.0	(7.2)	-6.3	(3.6)
	United Kingdom	-0.1	(0.1)	0.1	(0.0)	0.0	(0.2)	**-0.3**	(0.1)	0.6	(0.3)	**0.6**	(0.3)	**2.1**	(0.8)	-1.4	(2.2)	0.4	(2.4)	-0.4	(6.0)	0.9	(2.0)
	United States	0.1	(0.1)	0.0	(0.0)	**-1.0**	(0.3)	0.2	(0.2)	-1.1	(0.8)	-1.2	(0.7)	-1.5	(0.8)	-2.2	(1.9)	**6.7**	(2.6)	0.5	(6.2)	0.2	(1.7)
	OECD average	**-0.1**	(0.0)	**0.1**	(0.0)	**-0.2**	(0.0)	**-0.2**	(0.0)	0.1	(0.1)	**0.2**	(0.1)	**1.0**	(0.1)	0.9	(0.6)	**1.1**	(0.5)	**-5.4**	(1.4)	**1.1**	(0.5)
Partners	Albania	0.0	(0.1)	0.0	(0.1)	**0.9**	(0.2)	**-0.7**	(0.2)	**-1.0**	(0.3)	-0.3	(0.2)	0.5	(0.7)	-3.3	(4.7)	7.3	(4.6)	4.3	(8.4)	2.3	(5.5)
	Argentina	**-0.1**	(0.1)	**0.1**	(0.0)	**-1.6**	(0.4)	**0.7**	(0.3)	**0.9**	(0.3)	0.6	(0.3)	-1.1	(0.9)	4.5	(4.4)	-0.1	(5.1)	**-19.4**	(7.5)	-1.3	(3.9)
	Azerbaijan	0.0	(0.1)	0.0	(0.0)	-0.4	(0.4)	0.4	(0.5)	**1.0**	(0.4)	-0.2	(0.2)	-2.9	(2.0)	-0.5	(3.7)	**-10.0**	(3.2)	**-36.6**	(15.9)	-3.2	(4.5)
	Brazil	0.0	(0.1)	0.0	(0.0)	-0.2	(0.1)	**-0.3**	(0.1)	0.1	(0.1)	0.0	(0.1)	-0.1	(0.3)	-0.6	(2.2)	2.0	(1.9)	-2.4	(5.5)	**5.7**	(2.1)
	Bulgaria	0.1	(0.1)	0.1	(0.1)	**-1.4**	(0.3)	0.2	(0.2)	-0.5	(0.4)	0.0	(0.3)	**3.9**	(1.2)	6.9	(5.3)	6.8	(3.7)	-5.6	(11.2)	**-9.8**	(3.9)
	Colombia	-0.1	(0.1)	0.1	(0.0)	-0.2	(0.2)	-0.1	(0.2)	0.2	(0.2)	0.1	(0.2)	0.2	(0.4)	-1.3	(2.1)	-1.4	(2.6)	**-23.1**	(7.2)	0.5	(1.9)
	Croatia	-0.1	(0.1)	**0.1**	(0.0)	**-0.4**	(0.2)	-0.2	(0.2)	-0.4	(0.2)	0.2	(0.2)	**2.6**	(0.6)	-4.4	(2.4)	**5.1**	(2.3)	-12.3	(9.2)	-3.4	(2.3)
	Dubai (UAE)	**-0.2**	(0.1)	0.1	(0.0)	**-0.5**	(0.2)	**-0.6**	(0.2)	-0.3	(0.3)	0.4	(0.2)	-0.2	(0.7)	1.0	(3.6)	**11.8**	(3.4)	-9.2	(8.0)	-1.4	(3.4)
	Hong Kong-China	-0.2	(0.1)	**0.2**	(0.0)	0.0	(0.2)	0.1	(0.2)	0.9	(0.7)	0.8	(0.5)	**1.9**	(0.6)	**-5.8**	(2.9)	0.9	(2.8)	0.0	(9.1)	0.1	(2.6)
	Indonesia	-0.1	(0.1)	**0.1**	(0.0)	-0.2	(0.2)	-0.2	(0.2)	0.1	(0.1)	**0.4**	(0.1)	0.1	(0.5)	1.5	(3.2)	-2.2	(2.7)	**15.9**	(7.6)	2.3	(2.5)
	Jordan	**0.5**	(0.2)	**-0.2**	(0.1)	0.1	(0.2)	**-0.9**	(0.2)	**0.4**	(0.2)	0.4	(0.2)	0.5	(0.5)	-3.0	(2.7)	**11.9**	(3.0)	15.8	(14.3)	**-7.5**	(3.5)
	Kazakhstan	-0.1	(0.1)	0.1	(0.1)	-0.4	(0.2)	0.1	(0.2)	-0.3	(0.4)	0.0	(0.2)	-0.5	(0.8)	1.2	(2.8)	-1.5	(3.1)	**-29.5**	(9.2)	-1.3	(4.2)
	Kyrgyzstan	**0.4**	(0.1)	0.0	(0.0)	**0.5**	(0.2)	**-0.4**	(0.2)	-0.1	(0.2)	**0.8**	(0.2)	-0.4	(1.0)	3.8	(2.7)	-2.2	(3.6)	**-20.8**	(8.4)	5.6	(3.2)
	Latvia	-0.1	(0.1)	0.0	(0.1)	-0.1	(0.2)	**-0.6**	(0.2)	-0.1	(0.2)	**0.3**	(0.1)	1.0	(0.8)	0.2	(3.2)	0.5	(2.9)	2.0	(9.2)	3.5	(2.7)
	Lithuania	0.0	(0.1)	-0.1	(0.0)	-0.3	(0.2)	0.1	(0.2)	0.1	(0.2)	0.0	(0.2)	0.8	(0.7)	0.3	(4.5)	1.5	(3.8)	-9.6	(8.9)	0.6	(4.5)
	Macao-China	c	c	c	c	c	c	c	c	c	c	c	c	c	c	c	c	c	c	c	c	c	c
	Montenegro	c	c	c	c	c	c	c	c	c	c	c	c	c	c	c	c	c	c	c	c	c	c
	Panama	0.1	(0.2)	0.1	(0.1)	**-1.1**	(0.3)	-0.1	(0.3)	-0.1	(0.3)	-0.1	(0.3)	**1.6**	(0.8)	5.6	(5.2)	-2.0	(3.7)	-15.7	(16.0)	**9.4**	(3.2)
	Peru	0.0	(0.0)	**0.0**	(0.0)	-0.1	(0.2)	**-0.5**	(0.1)	0.4	(0.2)	0.2	(0.2)	-0.7	(0.4)	-4.4	(2.4)	5.0	(2.8)	-14.2	(10.0)	1.8	(2.0)
	Qatar	0.1	(0.1)	0.0	(0.1)	**-0.5**	(0.3)	-0.5	(0.3)	**-0.6**	(0.3)	**0.7**	(0.3)	-0.8	(0.8)	**-10.9**	(3.8)	6.3	(4.0)	-10.6	(11.3)	**-12.1**	(4.1)
	Romania	0.1	(0.1)	0.1	(0.1)	0.0	(0.2)	**-0.7**	(0.2)	**-1.7**	(0.6)	**-1.1**	(0.4)	**3.6**	(0.8)	-6.1	(5.3)	6.1	(3.5)	-17.6	(11.8)	**-7.2**	(3.2)
	Russian Federation	-0.1	(0.1)	0.0	(0.0)	0.1	(0.1)	0.0	(0.1)	-0.2	(0.3)	0.2	(0.2)	0.9	(0.7)	-2.8	(2.5)	-1.7	(2.4)	-5.2	(8.6)	2.9	(3.5)
	Serbia	**0.5**	(0.2)	**0.1**	(0.0)	-0.2	(0.3)	-0.3	(0.2)	**0.7**	(0.3)	**0.9**	(0.3)	**2.6**	(0.9)	0.0	(4.5)	**8.3**	(4.1)	**-20.5**	(9.0)	-7.6	(4.7)
	Shanghai-China	-0.1	(0.1)	0.0	(0.0)	0.1	(0.2)	0.0	(0.1)	0.0	(0.3)	0.1	(0.3)	**1.0**	(0.3)	-1.8	(1.4)	0.1	(1.6)	**-28.0**	(8.8)	-0.2	(1.7)
	Singapore	**-0.2**	(0.0)	**0.1**	(0.0)	-0.2	(0.2)	0.0	(0.1)	0.4	(0.7)	1.1	(0.6)	-0.7	(0.8)	-4.4	(2.5)	0.5	(2.4)	-5.4	(10.4)	0.6	(2.3)
	Chinese Taipei	**-0.2**	(0.1)	0.0	(0.0)	**0.7**	(0.1)	-0.2	(0.1)	**1.6**	(0.6)	**1.7**	(0.5)	**2.6**	(0.6)	-1.8	(1.9)	-2.7	(1.9)	-9.0	(7.7)	0.0	(2.1)
	Thailand	**0.1**	(0.1)	**0.1**	(0.0)	0.2	(0.2)	0.1	(0.2)	0.3	(0.4)	0.5	(0.4)	-0.3	(0.5)	-1.0	(2.3)	-1.5	(2.6)	**-32.2**	(9.9)	2.7	(3.6)
	Trinidad and Tobago	**-0.2**	(0.1)	**0.2**	(0.1)	0.1	(0.2)	-0.3	(0.2)	0.5	(0.6)	0.6	(0.5)	**2.7**	(0.8)	-1.8	(3.5)	4.1	(3.6)	-1.6	(16.7)	2.5	(4.0)
	Tunisia	0.4	(0.4)	0.3	(0.2)	-0.2	(0.1)	0.0	(0.1)	**0.3**	(0.1)	0.2	(0.2)	0.3	(0.7)	3.0	(2.9)	0.4	(1.5)	-11.5	(7.0)	-0.3	(2.3)
	Uruguay	-0.1	(0.1)	**0.1**	(0.0)	0.0	(0.2)	0.0	(0.2)	0.4	(0.2)	0.1	(0.2)	**1.0**	(0.4)	2.9	(2.8)	1.4	(2.6)	-12.0	(7.2)	1.1	(2.0)

Note: Values that are statistically significant are indicated in bold (see Annex A3).

1. Multilevel regression model (student and school levels): Reading performance is regressed on all the variables presented in this table.

StatLink http://dx.doi.org/10.1787/888932343285

[Part 6/6]

Table IV.2.14c

Relationships between reading performance and students' reading engagement and approaches to learning, the learning environment, resources, policies and practices, accounting for students' and schools' socio-economic and demographic background

		Student socio-economic and demographic background[1]										School socio-economic and demographic background[1]									
		Student is a female		Student without an immigrant background		Student's language at home is the same as the language of assessment		PISA index of economic, social and cultural status of student (1 unit increase)		PISA index of economic, social and cultural status of student (squared)		School average PISA index of economic, social and cultural status (1 unit increase)		School size (per 100 students)		School size (per 100 students) (squared)		School in a small town or village (15 000 or less people)		School in city (100 000 or more people)	
		Change in score	S.E.	Change in score	S.E.	Change in score	S.E.	Change in score	S.E.	Change in score	S.E.	Change in score	S.E.	Change in score	S.E.	Change in score	S.E.	Change in score	S.E.	Change in score	S.E.
OECD	Australia	**4.8**	(2.1)	-1.0	(2.0)	**23.9**	(3.7)	**15.1**	(1.4)	**-2.9**	(1.0)	**31.7**	(9.1)	-1.6	(1.4)	0.0	(0.0)	-2.6	(5.2)	3.0	(4.1)
	Austria	2.7	(3.1)	**12.6**	(4.6)	**16.0**	(5.3)	**4.7**	(1.9)	0.0	(1.3)	**42.6**	(10.2)	4.2	(2.3)	-0.2	(0.1)	-10.1	(7.6)	8.9	(9.7)
	Belgium	2.0	(2.3)	**14.6**	(2.3)	5.0	(2.7)	**5.5**	(1.1)	0.9	(0.8)	**42.1**	(6.7)	**5.2**	(2.2)	**-0.3**	(0.1)	7.8	(4.8)	-8.4	(5.6)
	Canada	-1.3	(1.9)	**6.0**	(2.1)	**16.5**	(3.8)	**10.2**	(1.3)	**2.1**	(0.9)	**11.0**	(5.2)	0.2	(1.2)	0.0	(0.0)	2.6	(4.0)	-1.4	(3.9)
	Chile	**5.8**	(2.9)	1.3	(6.8)	**45.8**	(17.6)	**5.8**	(1.7)	0.6	(0.8)	**16.6**	(4.5)	0.1	(1.0)	0.0	(0.0)	4.6	(6.6)	-2.4	(4.4)
	Czech Republic	**15.2**	(2.5)	**12.0**	(3.4)	-6.0	(9.5)	**8.8**	(1.7)	-1.9	(1.5)	**61.7**	(7.7)	5.3	(3.6)	-0.3	(0.3)	6.6	(4.9)	-4.3	(5.4)
	Denmark	**6.1**	(2.5)	**13.6**	(3.1)	**24.0**	(5.1)	**14.1**	(1.5)	-0.5	(1.0)	**16.7**	(5.9)	**7.0**	(2.7)	**-0.7**	(0.2)	-4.6	(3.5)	6.4	(4.9)
	Estonia	**16.4**	(3.4)	5.3	(3.7)	**28.4**	(6.1)	**7.2**	(1.8)	1.3	(1.5)	**25.3**	(8.5)	-2.2	(1.6)	0.1	(0.1)	-0.7	(4.1)	-1.0	(5.2)
	Finland	**15.2**	(2.1)	**11.9**	(4.3)	**35.9**	(6.2)	**14.0**	(1.7)	-1.3	(1.4)	**15.6**	(6.4)	-0.2	(1.0)	0.0	(0.0)	-1.9	(4.5)	-0.9	(5.0)
	France	w	w	w	w	w	w	w	w	w	w	w	w	w	w	w	w	w	w	w	w
	Germany	**11.2**	(2.5)	**13.4**	(3.0)	3.1	(4.9)	**4.7**	(1.4)	-1.1	(0.8)	**63.7**	(9.1)	2.5	(1.9)	-0.1	(0.1)	14.6	(7.7)	-5.1	(6.9)
	Greece	**19.4**	(3.0)	2.5	(3.3)	18.6	(11.1)	**10.8**	(1.5)	1.0	(1.2)	**27.2**	(9.7)	1.0	(15.8)	0.6	(2.4)	9.9	(12.3)	5.1	(10.2)
	Hungary	**10.9**	(2.4)	-6.9	(4.6)	**26.1**	(9.7)	**6.5**	(1.4)	0.7	(0.9)	**33.1**	(5.9)	3.2	(1.8)	-0.1	(0.1)	-3.4	(6.5)	3.7	(5.5)
	Iceland	**9.1**	(3.1)	4.1	(4.7)	**40.5**	(9.6)	**12.5**	(2.6)	-1.9	(1.5)	15.0	(8.8)	-0.4	(5.2)	0.1	(0.7)	0.8	(5.8)	-0.4	(7.2)
	Ireland	**10.8**	(4.7)	0.1	(3.3)	**28.8**	(10.1)	**14.1**	(1.7)	-1.4	(1.5)	5.1	(9.5)	-4.1	(5.2)	0.1	(0.3)	-6.4	(9.0)	-4.2	(8.2)
	Israel	**12.1**	(3.8)	-0.9	(3.7)	2.0	(5.6)	**12.3**	(2.4)	**2.8**	(1.2)	**31.8**	(12.8)	5.3	(2.8)	**-0.3**	(0.1)	10.6	(9.5)	**-16.6**	(7.4)
	Italy	**13.8**	(1.7)	**13.7**	(2.5)	4.4	(2.6)	**2.4**	(0.8)	-0.5	(0.8)	**12.9**	(5.8)	**4.0**	(1.8)	-0.2	(0.1)	-1.8	(4.9)	4.4	(5.2)
	Japan	**11.4**	(2.7)	6.3	(7.5)	31.0	(33.5)	0.4	(1.9)	1.4	(1.7)	**52.0**	(14.6)	**-3.8**	(1.7)	**0.2**	(0.1)	-17.7	(9.6)	1.5	(5.1)
	Korea	**23.4**	(4.4)	4.2	(12.4)	-10.4	(36.1)	**8.8**	(1.9)	-1.4	(1.3)	11.8	(7.2)	4.3	(2.8)	-0.1	(0.1)	**-33.0**	(12.1)	**-24.2**	(8.2)
	Luxembourg	c	c	c	c	c	c	c	c	c	c	c	c	c	c	c	c	c	c	c	c
	Mexico	**12.6**	(1.9)	**19.0**	(3.2)	**16.3**	(5.0)	**6.3**	(1.3)	**1.3**	(0.5)	**9.7**	(3.7)	0.6	(0.4)	0.0	(0.0)	-8.0	(5.8)	8.7	(5.6)
	Netherlands	**5.1**	(2.0)	**5.3**	(2.7)	10.2	(6.5)	2.3	(1.6)	-0.3	(1.0)	**32.2**	(8.4)	2.1	(1.5)	-0.1	(0.1)	1.3	(5.9)	9.2	(5.5)
	New Zealand	**12.2**	(3.7)	1.7	(3.0)	**34.5**	(5.8)	**16.9**	(2.3)	0.6	(2.5)	**31.6**	(10.3)	2.3	(1.5)	-0.1	(0.0)	**17.9**	(6.8)	5.9	(5.5)
	Norway	**14.8**	(3.2)	**11.1**	(5.4)	**32.4**	(7.3)	**14.6**	(2.4)	-2.1	(1.7)	12.8	(8.4)	8.3	(5.7)	-1.3	(0.8)	**-9.3**	(3.7)	-6.0	(6.1)
	Poland	**26.0**	(3.1)	25.3	(21.3)	**41.1**	(20.8)	**17.6**	(1.8)	-1.3	(1.3)	5.7	(6.5)	0.9	(4.6)	0.0	(0.5)	-1.2	(5.6)	-1.2	(5.7)
	Portugal	**11.6**	(2.6)	-1.5	(3.0)	**16.7**	(7.1)	**11.3**	(1.1)	0.3	(0.7)	**11.9**	(5.9)	2.8	(1.7)	-0.1	(0.1)	2.1	(4.7)	7.9	(5.1)
	Slovak Republic	**26.7**	(2.6)	-1.7	(4.8)	**23.6**	(6.1)	**10.7**	(1.7)	-1.8	(1.0)	18.4	(10.5)	-1.2	(3.8)	0.2	(0.3)	8.1	(7.3)	7.5	(6.4)
	Slovenia	**19.4**	(2.2)	**6.5**	(2.7)	5.6	(4.9)	0.9	(1.1)	0.4	(1.1)	**49.3**	(6.5)	**10.4**	(3.1)	**-0.8**	(0.3)	1.8	(5.5)	1.3	(4.8)
	Spain	**5.4**	(1.6)	**21.6**	(2.2)	**8.7**	(2.8)	**11.4**	(1.0)	0.1	(0.6)	3.4	(4.0)	-1.4	(1.2)	0.0	(0.1)	0.6	(3.7)	**7.7**	(3.4)
	Sweden	**10.2**	(2.8)	6.0	(3.6)	**31.4**	(6.4)	**18.8**	(2.0)	-0.3	(1.1)	19.9	(10.3)	-3.1	(2.2)	**0.3**	(0.1)	4.9	(5.0)	5.6	(5.0)
	Switzerland	**5.1**	(2.1)	**10.6**	(2.4)	**17.0**	(2.8)	**9.6**	(1.4)	0.0	(1.1)	**25.3**	(5.9)	**1.2**	(0.5)	**0.0**	(0.0)	-0.1	(3.8)	1.7	(5.6)
	Turkey	**19.6**	(2.9)	-2.0	(6.6)	5.8	(11.0)	**7.7**	(1.9)	-0.1	(0.7)	**40.9**	(6.5)	-0.4	(1.2)	0.0	(0.0)	-3.9	(6.6)	-0.6	(5.9)
	United Kingdom	-0.4	(2.7)	0.8	(3.4)	**17.4**	(5.7)	**10.9**	(1.7)	0.3	(1.2)	**43.1**	(7.0)	-1.0	(1.5)	0.0	(0.1)	3.2	(3.7)	3.3	(4.3)
	United States	0.9	(3.6)	-1.2	(5.6)	4.4	(5.9)	**13.9**	(2.0)	-2.6	(2.5)	**19.0**	(6.9)	0.3	(0.8)	0.0	(0.0)	6.1	(4.6)	-7.5	(5.9)
	OECD average	**11.2**	(0.5)	**6.7**	(1.0)	**18.7**	(2.1)	**9.7**	(0.3)	-0.2	(0.2)	**26.2**	(1.4)	**1.6**	(0.7)	-0.1	(0.1)	0.0	(1.2)	0.2	(1.1)
Partners	Albania	**31.3**	(4.0)	12.8	(11.7)	7.1	(19.0)	**13.9**	(3.2)	2.2	(1.3)	2.3	(10.2)	-3.8	(3.7)	0.4	(0.3)	-8.7	(9.8)	9.3	(10.4)
	Argentina	**19.8**	(3.1)	1.4	(4.9)	**48.3**	(15.9)	**8.7**	(2.1)	1.6	(1.0)	**30.9**	(7.3)	**6.7**	(2.6)	**-0.2**	(0.1)	5.9	(10.7)	10.2	(9.2)
	Azerbaijan	**18.3**	(2.3)	2.8	(4.4)	-6.3	(5.9)	**9.0**	(2.1)	**2.1**	(1.0)	**28.9**	(11.6)	-1.7	(3.4)	0.2	(0.1)	-16.7	(11.8)	-16.3	(11.4)
	Brazil	**19.9**	(2.1)	7.3	(9.2)	**26.4**	(12.5)	**4.9**	(2.0)	1.3	(0.7)	**26.4**	(4.2)	0.5	(0.8)	0.0	(0.0)	-9.7	(5.8)	-6.2	(4.5)
	Bulgaria	**35.7**	(3.3)	**23.9**	(8.5)	**26.6**	(6.6)	**7.8**	(2.2)	**2.5**	(1.2)	**48.2**	(9.0)	1.5	(3.5)	0.1	(0.2)	3.1	(8.2)	3.4	(7.9)
	Colombia	5.3	(2.7)	**18.0**	(7.7)	**65.6**	(19.8)	**7.5**	(2.5)	0.9	(0.8)	**26.3**	(6.1)	0.1	(0.5)	0.0	(0.0)	9.2	(6.1)	-4.6	(5.6)
	Croatia	**21.3**	(3.5)	2.6	(2.1)	-5.9	(8.2)	**6.1**	(1.7)	**-2.8**	(1.0)	18.3	(9.4)	-0.4	(2.0)	0.1	(0.1)	4.7	(4.3)	-6.7	(5.0)
	Dubai (UAE)	6.7	(3.9)	**-23.2**	(3.3)	**14.9**	(2.9)	**13.1**	(1.8)	**2.1**	(1.0)	8.6	(9.6)	0.7	(0.6)	0.0	(0.0)	-3.5	(14.1)	15.6	(12.8)
	Hong Kong-China	**11.8**	(2.4)	-2.7	(2.4)	**21.1**	(6.1)	-1.2	(2.0)	-0.8	(0.8)	**19.0**	(5.5)	-5.6	(7.4)	0.4	(0.4)	a	a	a	a
	Indonesia	**22.5**	(1.7)	18.0	(10.5)	-2.7	(2.4)	5.4	(2.8)	1.5	(0.8)	8.5	(5.3)	-0.2	(4.1)	0.1	(0.3)	-5.3	(8.5)	8.7	(9.6)
	Jordan	**19.5**	(8.3)	-2.4	(3.6)	**22.5**	(7.6)	**13.8**	(2.4)	1.7	(1.1)	1.2	(8.1)	-4.2	(3.1)	0.2	(0.2)	-1.1	(8.6)	11.6	(7.2)
	Kazakhstan	**32.0**	(2.3)	-6.8	(4.0)	3.1	(4.1)	**13.0**	(2.1)	-2.2	(1.2)	**48.1**	(10.0)	**-3.8**	(1.7)	0.1	(0.1)	**-20.9**	(8.7)	-7.2	(8.8)
	Kyrgyzstan	**40.3**	(2.8)	**-11.7**	(5.4)	-2.6	(4.6)	**15.7**	(2.3)	2.3	(1.2)	14.4	(8.5)	1.0	(2.0)	-0.1	(0.1)	2.5	(8.5)	**29.8**	(11.0)
	Latvia	**22.0**	(2.9)	-1.9	(3.1)	4.6	(7.5)	**11.9**	(2.2)	-1.1	(1.5)	0.4	(11.6)	1.9	(3.4)	-0.1	(0.3)	7.3	(5.7)	7.1	(7.4)
	Lithuania	**32.7**	(2.9)	0.4	(4.4)	9.8	(6.8)	**11.4**	(1.6)	0.7	(1.1)	**34.1**	(9.2)	-4.1	(3.4)	0.2	(0.2)	4.5	(7.2)	-11.9	(7.6)
	Macao-China	c	c	c	c	c	c	c	c	c	c	c	c	c	c	c	c	c	c	c	c
	Montenegro	c	c	c	c	c	c	c	c	c	c	c	c	c	c	c	c	c	c	c	c
	Panama	**13.8**	(4.4)	-2.1	(6.1)	14.3	(10.6)	**6.8**	(2.9)	1.5	(0.9)	10.3	(8.7)	2.5	(1.5)	-0.1	(0.0)	-15.9	(9.2)	6.7	(9.8)
	Peru	3.4	(3.3)	14.9	(9.6)	**30.4**	(7.6)	**9.6**	(2.7)	0.8	(0.8)	**28.4**	(5.9)	**3.5**	(1.2)	**-0.1**	(0.0)	-0.1	(6.4)	7.5	(6.9)
	Qatar	**19.1**	(6.0)	**-30.4**	(2.5)	**18.6**	(3.3)	**4.0**	(1.4)	1.5	(0.8)	19.3	(11.5)	1.6	(1.0)	0.0	(0.0)	-14.3	(10.4)	-4.2	(10.4)
	Romania	**13.3**	(3.6)	**18.6**	(9.4)	12.2	(7.2)	**6.3**	(2.0)	0.8	(0.9)	**27.0**	(7.9)	-1.4	(2.4)	0.0	(0.1)	10.0	(6.8)	3.6	(6.0)
	Russian Federation	**21.9**	(2.6)	1.8	(2.6)	**16.4**	(5.0)	**12.3**	(1.8)	-0.4	(1.6)	**27.1**	(7.4)	**-7.5**	(2.9)	**0.5**	(0.2)	8.2	(7.8)	7.4	(6.4)
	Serbia	**18.9**	(2.9)	-4.9	(2.9)	-0.5	(9.1)	1.7	(1.9)	0.9	(1.0)	-0.7	(16.5)	**-5.9**	(2.5)	**0.3**	(0.1)	-1.2	(8.2)	2.9	(6.2)
	Shanghai-China	**23.7**	(2.7)	**25.2**	(8.2)	**23.1**	(9.1)	3.2	(1.7)	2.4	(1.5)	**17.4**	(5.1)	-0.6	(0.5)	0.0	(0.0)	a	a	a	a
	Singapore	**5.1**	(2.3)	0.5	(2.6)	**17.9**	(2.9)	**7.4**	(2.7)	-2.5	(1.3)	**37.4**	(9.5)	**4.8**	(1.8)	-0.1	(0.0)	a	a	a	a
	Chinese Taipei	**27.8**	(3.5)	11.2	(7.4)	5.6	(3.5)	**7.6**	(2.1)	-0.4	(1.4)	**20.6**	(5.7)	-0.5	(0.3)	0.0	(0.0)	-3.4	(4.7)	6.6	(4.0)
	Thailand	**24.1**	(2.9)	**26.8**	(12.7)	**-12.2**	(3.4)	**6.0**	(2.5)	0.9	(0.9)	**15.1**	(5.0)	1.3	(0.9)	0.0	(0.0)	-2.0	(7.9)	15.1	(8.4)
	Trinidad and Tobago	**29.7**	(2.5)	-4.3	(3.2)	**25.2**	(6.7)	2.2	(2.0)	1.3	(1.0)	**33.0**	(10.9)	-2.0	(5.0)	0.0	(0.4)	-11.7	(6.6)	a	a
	Tunisia	**17.3**	(2.3)	**19.0**	(8.1)	-20.0	(22.8)	2.0	(2.7)	-0.2	(0.8)	**15.6**	(4.3)	-0.5	(2.1)	0.0	(0.1)	-4.0	(5.0)	8.7	(5.1)
	Uruguay	**26.0**	(3.1)	-1.7	(5.9)	**19.6**	(8.4)	**10.2**	(2.1)	0.4	(0.9)	8.1	(5.8)	0.8	(0.9)	0.0	(0.0)	**14.3**	(6.1)	**13.6**	(4.8)

Note: Values that are statistically significant are indicated in bold (see Annex A3).
1. Multilevel regression model (student and school levels): Reading performance is regressed on all the variables presented in this table.
StatLink http://dx.doi.org/10.1787/888932343285

[Part 1/2]

Table IV.3.1 Vertical differentiation of school systems

Results based on students' self-reports

		Average age of entry into primary school		Percentage of students who started primary school:										Percentage of students reporting that they have repeated a grade in:							
				4-year-olds		5-year-olds		6-year-olds		7-year-olds		8-year-olds or older		Primary schools		Lower secondary schools		Upper secondary schools		Primary, lower secondary or upper secondary schools	
		Mean age	S.E.	%	S.E.	%	S.E.	%	S.E.	%	S.E.	%	S.E.	%	S.E.	%	S.E.	%	S.E.	%	S.E.
OECD	Australia	5.2	(0.01)	11.9	(0.4)	57.9	(0.7)	26.0	(0.6)	3.5	(0.3)	0.8	(0.1)	7.3	(0.3)	1.4	(0.2)	0.1	(0.0)	8.4	(0.4)
	Austria	6.2	(0.01)	0.0	c	3.4	(0.2)	72.6	(0.9)	22.4	(0.8)	1.6	(0.3)	4.9	(0.4)	5.7	(0.5)	4.4	(0.4)	12.6	(0.9)
	Belgium	5.9	(0.01)	1.5	(0.3)	16.9	(0.5)	71.2	(0.8)	8.9	(0.4)	1.5	(0.2)	18.4	(0.6)	15.0	(0.6)	9.9	(0.4)	34.9	(0.7)
	Canada	5.2	(0.02)	23.0	(0.6)	48.0	(0.7)	24.3	(0.7)	3.1	(0.2)	1.7	(0.2)	4.4	(0.3)	4.3	(0.2)	0.6	(0.1)	8.4	(0.3)
	Chile	6.0	(0.01)	0.0	c	16.2	(0.6)	70.0	(0.8)	13.8	(0.6)	0.0	c	10.3	(0.7)	7.3	(0.6)	10.8	(0.6)	23.4	(0.9)
	Czech Republic	6.4	(0.01)	0.1	(0.0)	0.9	(0.2)	58.6	(0.9)	38.3	(0.9)	2.2	(0.3)	2.1	(0.3)	2.3	(0.3)	0.0	c	4.0	(0.3)
	Denmark	6.6	(0.01)	0.2	(0.1)	3.6	(0.3)	37.2	(0.9)	53.7	(0.9)	5.3	(0.4)	3.6	(0.3)	1.0	(0.2)	0.1	(0.1)	4.4	(0.3)
	Estonia	6.9	(0.01)	0.1	(0.0)	0.3	(0.1)	13.7	(0.7)	80.3	(0.7)	5.6	(0.4)	3.9	(0.5)	2.5	(0.4)	0.0	c	5.6	(0.6)
	Finland	6.7	(0.01)	0.0	c	0.1	(0.1)	28.1	(0.7)	70.9	(0.6)	0.8	(0.1)	2.4	(0.2)	0.5	(0.1)	c	c	2.8	(0.3)
	France	5.9	(0.02)	3.2	(0.4)	14.8	(0.7)	71.6	(1.1)	8.8	(0.6)	1.5	(0.3)	17.8	(0.9)	23.5	(1.2)	1.0	(0.2)	36.9	(1.0)
	Germany	6.3	(0.01)	0.0	c	2.9	(0.3)	67.1	(0.9)	29.0	(0.8)	1.1	(0.1)	9.2	(0.6)	14.2	(0.6)	0.0	c	21.4	(0.7)
	Greece	6.3	(0.02)	0.2	(0.1)	2.5	(0.3)	66.6	(1.5)	29.7	(1.4)	1.0	(0.2)	2.0	(0.4)	4.2	(0.8)	0.4	(0.1)	5.7	(0.8)
	Hungary	6.8	(0.02)	0.1	(0.0)	0.4	(0.1)	31.8	(0.8)	61.7	(0.8)	6.0	(0.6)	6.2	(0.9)	5.8	(0.9)	2.4	(0.3)	11.1	(1.2)
	Iceland	5.8	(0.01)	0.4	(0.1)	22.2	(0.6)	75.6	(0.7)	1.6	(0.2)	0.2	(0.1)	0.7	(0.1)	0.4	(0.1)	0.0	c	0.9	(0.2)
	Ireland	4.5	(0.01)	59.0	(1.0)	36.2	(0.9)	4.8	(0.4)	0.0	c	0.0	c	11.0	(0.6)	1.7	(0.3)	0.2	(0.1)	12.0	(0.6)
	Israel	6.3	(0.01)	0.0	c	5.0	(0.4)	67.2	(0.9)	25.7	(0.9)	2.1	(0.3)	4.3	(0.3)	4.9	(0.4)	3.6	(0.3)	7.5	(0.5)
	Italy	5.9	(0.00)	0.0	c	12.2	(0.4)	82.3	(0.4)	4.8	(0.2)	0.7	(0.1)	1.0	(0.1)	4.7	(0.3)	11.7	(0.4)	16.0	(0.4)
	Japan	6.0	(0.00)	0.0	c	0.0	c	100.0	(0.0)	0.0	c	0.0	c	0.0	c	0.0	c	0.0	c	0.0	c
	Korea	6.0	(0.00)	0.0	c	0.7	(0.1)	98.9	(0.2)	0.3	(0.1)	0.0	c	0.0	c	0.0	c	0.0	c	0.0	c
	Luxembourg	6.2	(0.01)	1.4	(0.2)	5.9	(0.3)	65.4	(0.7)	24.0	(0.7)	3.3	(0.3)	22.2	(0.5)	20.2	(0.6)	2.0	(0.2)	36.5	(0.5)
	Mexico	6.2	(0.01)	0.7	(0.1)	8.1	(0.2)	70.0	(0.5)	19.1	(0.5)	2.1	(0.1)	17.3	(0.7)	5.9	(0.3)	1.2	(0.1)	21.5	(0.7)
	Netherlands	6.0	(0.02)	2.3	(0.3)	11.2	(0.7)	69.1	(1.0)	16.2	(1.1)	1.2	(0.2)	22.4	(1.2)	5.3	(0.5)	0.6	(0.1)	26.7	(1.1)
	New Zealand	5.1	(0.01)	4.4	(0.3)	85.9	(0.6)	6.7	(0.4)	2.6	(0.2)	0.4	(0.1)	3.9	(0.3)	1.7	(0.2)	0.9	(0.1)	5.1	(0.3)
	Norway	5.8	(0.01)	0.3	(0.1)	24.4	(0.7)	70.5	(0.7)	4.2	(0.4)	0.6	(0.1)	0.0	c	0.0	c	c	c	0.0	c
	Poland	7.0	(0.00)	0.0	c	0.0	c	0.0	c	100.0	(0.0)	0.0	c	1.9	(0.2)	3.9	(0.4)	c	c	5.3	(0.4)
	Portugal	6.0	(0.02)	0.6	(0.1)	22.8	(0.7)	63.6	(0.7)	8.2	(0.4)	4.9	(0.3)	22.4	(1.5)	20.9	(1.5)	1.9	(0.3)	35.0	(1.9)
	Slovak Republic	6.3	(0.01)	0.0	(0.0)	1.0	(0.1)	67.6	(1.2)	30.4	(1.2)	1.0	(0.2)	1.9	(0.3)	2.0	(0.3)	0.3	(0.1)	3.8	(0.5)
	Slovenia	6.7	(0.01)	0.2	(0.1)	2.0	(0.2)	32.8	(0.7)	62.2	(0.7)	2.8	(0.2)	0.0	c	1.5	(0.4)	0.0	c	1.5	(0.4)
	Spain	5.9	(0.01)	0.0	c	23.5	(0.9)	67.2	(0.9)	5.3	(0.3)	3.9	(0.3)	12.2	(0.4)	31.9	(0.7)	c	c	35.3	(0.7)
	Sweden	6.6	(0.03)	0.6	(0.1)	4.6	(0.4)	46.2	(1.5)	44.8	(1.7)	3.8	(0.4)	3.8	(0.3)	1.4	(0.2)	0.3	(0.1)	4.6	(0.4)
	Switzerland	6.5	(0.01)	0.1	(0.0)	6.0	(0.4)	42.8	(1.0)	46.8	(1.0)	4.4	(0.3)	14.9	(0.7)	9.3	(0.6)	1.4	(0.2)	22.8	(0.9)
	Turkey	6.9	(0.01)	0.0	(0.0)	1.1	(0.2)	19.2	(0.8)	72.2	(0.9)	7.5	(0.6)	3.8	(0.5)	0.0	c	10.5	(0.8)	13.0	(0.8)
	United Kingdom	5.0	(0.02)	22.4	(1.3)	60.9	(1.4)	15.1	(1.1)	1.4	(0.2)	0.2	(0.1)	1.6	(0.1)	0.8	(0.1)	0.7	(0.1)	2.2	(0.2)
	United States	5.9	(0.01)	3.0	(0.3)	24.5	(0.7)	58.0	(0.8)	13.3	(0.5)	1.2	(0.2)	11.2	(0.8)	4.2	(0.4)	1.6	(0.2)	14.2	(0.9)
	OECD average	6.1	(0.00)	4.0	(0.1)	15.5	(0.1)	51.8	(0.1)	26.7	(0.1)	2.0	(0.1)	7.3	(0.1)	6.1	(0.1)	2.2	(0.1)	13.0	(0.1)
Partners	Albania	6.6	(0.02)	0.1	(0.1)	1.1	(0.2)	47.7	(1.5)	48.8	(1.4)	2.4	(0.4)	2.9	(0.4)	2.5	(0.3)	2.3	(0.4)	4.7	(0.5)
	Argentina	6.0	(0.01)	0.8	(0.2)	16.4	(0.8)	72.4	(1.0)	8.8	(0.6)	1.6	(0.2)	15.9	(0.9)	24.1	(1.6)	4.8	(0.5)	33.8	(1.6)
	Azerbaijan	6.6	(0.02)	0.0	c	1.0	(0.2)	43.0	(1.4)	50.0	(1.4)	6.0	(0.5)	0.8	(0.2)	1.0	(0.3)	0.5	(0.2)	1.7	(0.3)
	Brazil	7.4	(0.04)	0.0	c	8.4	(0.4)	32.0	(0.7)	38.2	(0.9)	21.5	(0.8)	21.0	(0.7)	25.7	(0.8)	8.2	(0.4)	40.1	(0.9)
	Bulgaria	6.9	(0.01)	0.0	(0.0)	0.1	(0.1)	12.2	(0.7)	82.6	(0.9)	5.0	(0.6)	2.7	(0.3)	4.1	(0.4)	1.5	(0.3)	5.6	(0.5)
	Colombia	6.0	(0.02)	0.0	c	25.9	(0.9)	50.9	(1.1)	17.9	(0.7)	5.3	(0.5)	22.1	(1.1)	18.2	(0.9)	3.0	(0.3)	33.9	(1.1)
	Croatia	6.7	(0.01)	0.0	c	0.1	(0.1)	29.0	(0.6)	68.9	(0.5)	1.9	(0.2)	1.2	(0.2)	1.4	(0.2)	2.3	(0.2)	2.8	(0.2)
	Dubai (UAE)	5.8	(0.02)	5.8	(0.4)	31.2	(0.8)	46.4	(0.8)	13.7	(0.5)	2.9	(0.2)	7.1	(0.3)	6.3	(0.3)	1.3	(0.2)	12.6	(0.3)
	Hong Kong-China	6.1	(0.01)	2.1	(0.2)	12.1	(0.6)	66.8	(0.8)	15.9	(0.7)	3.1	(0.3)	10.5	(0.5)	6.3	(0.5)	0.2	(0.1)	15.6	(0.7)
	Indonesia	6.3	(0.03)	0.0	c	9.3	(0.8)	52.0	(1.7)	36.4	(1.9)	2.3	(0.3)	16.5	(1.2)	6.1	(0.6)	4.7	(0.7)	18.0	(1.2)
	Jordan	6.1	(0.02)	0.6	(0.1)	6.2	(0.5)	80.6	(1.2)	10.0	(0.8)	2.5	(0.4)	3.9	(0.4)	4.9	(0.4)	c	c	6.6	(0.5)
	Kazakhstan	6.6	(0.02)	0.0	(0.0)	1.6	(0.2)	38.5	(1.6)	56.9	(1.6)	2.9	(0.3)	1.5	(0.2)	0.7	(0.1)	0.0	c	1.7	(0.2)
	Kyrgyzstan	6.8	(0.02)	0.0	(0.0)	0.5	(0.1)	23.3	(1.4)	69.1	(1.2)	7.1	(0.5)	3.0	(0.3)	3.0	(0.3)	0.0	c	4.3	(0.4)
	Latvia	6.8	(0.01)	0.0	c	0.0	c	25.1	(1.1)	69.8	(1.2)	5.1	(0.4)	6.0	(0.6)	6.1	(0.9)	1.5	(0.3)	11.1	(1.0)
	Liechtenstein	6.5	(0.03)	0.0	c	1.5	(0.7)	48.1	(2.5)	45.4	(2.5)	5.0	(1.2)	10.2	(1.7)	12.5	(1.6)	c	c	21.5	(2.0)
	Lithuania	6.8	(0.01)	0.1	(0.1)	1.1	(0.2)	28.3	(0.8)	65.6	(0.9)	4.8	(0.3)	2.1	(0.3)	2.2	(0.3)	c	c	3.9	(0.4)
	Macao-China	6.1	(0.01)	7.1	(0.4)	10.7	(0.4)	53.6	(0.7)	24.6	(0.5)	4.0	(0.3)	23.1	(0.5)	32.3	(0.5)	0.6	(0.1)	43.7	(0.5)
	Montenegro	6.7	(0.01)	0.0	c	0.1	(0.0)	31.6	(0.8)	66.6	(0.6)	1.7	(0.4)	0.6	(0.2)	1.1	(0.4)	0.5	(0.1)	1.8	(0.5)
	Panama	5.7	(0.02)	0.0	c	42.2	(1.8)	44.7	(1.8)	11.9	(1.0)	1.2	(0.2)	17.6	(1.9)	21.8	(2.1)	6.5	(0.9)	31.8	(2.7)
	Peru	6.0	(0.01)	2.3	(0.2)	18.1	(0.6)	61.7	(0.7)	15.8	(0.6)	2.1	(0.3)	20.6	(1.0)	11.6	(0.8)	3.1	(0.3)	28.1	(1.2)
	Qatar	6.2	(0.02)	6.0	(0.2)	18.5	(0.4)	51.1	(0.5)	17.5	(0.4)	6.8	(0.3)	8.7	(0.3)	7.7	(0.3)	4.1	(0.2)	14.8	(0.3)
	Romania	6.9	(0.01)	0.0	(0.0)	0.1	(0.0)	12.2	(0.5)	80.9	(0.9)	6.9	(0.8)	2.3	(0.4)	2.7	(0.5)	c	c	4.2	(0.7)
	Russian Federation	6.7	(0.01)	0.0	(0.0)	0.7	(0.1)	29.3	(1.1)	65.5	(1.2)	4.5	(0.4)	2.3	(0.3)	1.3	(0.3)	0.0	c	3.2	(0.5)
	Serbia	6.9	(0.01)	0.0	c	0.0	c	10.3	(0.5)	86.9	(0.5)	2.8	(0.3)	0.4	(0.1)	1.5	(0.4)	0.4	(0.1)	2.0	(0.5)
	Shanghai-China	6.8	(0.01)	0.9	(0.1)	3.2	(0.3)	28.2	(0.9)	53.1	(0.9)	14.6	(0.6)	4.4	(0.6)	3.5	(0.5)	0.2	(0.1)	7.5	(0.7)
	Singapore	6.7	(0.01)	0.6	(0.1)	1.9	(0.2)	27.2	(0.8)	68.3	(0.9)	2.0	(0.2)	2.3	(0.2)	1.7	(0.2)	2.1	(0.2)	5.4	(0.3)
	Chinese Taipei	6.9	(0.01)	0.0	c	0.0	c	25.0	(0.9)	58.5	(0.9)	16.6	(0.7)	0.9	(0.1)	0.9	(0.1)	0.5	(0.1)	1.6	(0.2)
	Thailand	6.4	(0.01)	0.0	c	1.4	(0.3)	58.1	(1.1)	36.7	(1.2)	3.8	(0.4)	2.3	(0.2)	1.3	(0.2)	0.2	(0.1)	3.5	(0.3)
	Trinidad and Tobago	5.2	(0.02)	16.2	(0.5)	63.0	(0.8)	13.0	(0.6)	3.9	(0.3)	3.9	(0.3)	27.4	(0.6)	3.1	(0.3)	1.3	(0.2)	28.8	(0.6)
	Tunisia	5.9	(0.01)	0.0	c	10.6	(0.6)	84.5	(0.7)	4.9	(0.4)	0.0	c	23.2	(1.2)	32.8	(1.1)	3.3	(0.4)	43.2	(1.2)
	Uruguay	5.9	(0.01)	1.3	(0.2)	11.7	(0.6)	79.2	(0.7)	7.4	(0.4)	0.3	(0.1)	21.3	(0.9)	25.8	(0.9)	0.7	(0.1)	38.0	(1.1)

StatLink http://dx.doi.org/10.1787/888932343285

[Part 2/2]
Vertical differentiation of school systems
Table IV.3.1 *Results based on students' self-reports*

		Percentage of students at:						Percentage of students enrolled in:			
		Grades below the modal grade		The modal grade		Grade above the modal grade		Lower secondary education (ISCED 2)		Upper secondary education (ISCED 3)	
		%	S.E.	%	S.E.	%	S.E.	%	S.E.	%	S.E.
OECD	Australia	10.5	(0.6)	70.8	(0.6)	18.6	(0.6)	81.4	(0.7)	18.6	(0.7)
	Austria	49.2	(1.0)	50.7	(1.0)	0.0	(0.0)	6.8	(1.1)	93.2	(1.1)
	Belgium	37.9	(0.8)	60.8	(0.7)	1.2	(0.1)	8.9	(0.6)	91.1	(0.6)
	Canada	14.8	(0.5)	84.1	(0.5)	1.1	(0.1)	14.8	(0.5)	85.2	(0.5)
	Chile	25.4	(1.0)	69.4	(1.0)	5.2	(0.3)	4.9	(0.6)	95.1	(0.6)
	Czech Republic	4.4	(0.3)	48.9	(1.0)	46.7	(1.1)	53.8	(1.1)	46.2	(1.1)
	Denmark	14.8	(0.6)	83.5	(0.8)	1.7	(0.5)	99.1	(0.5)	0.9	(0.5)
	Estonia	25.7	(0.8)	72.4	(0.9)	1.9	(0.2)	98.1	(0.2)	1.9	(0.2)
	Finland	12.3	(0.5)	87.3	(0.5)	0.4	(0.1)	99.6	(0.1)	0.4	(0.1)
	France	39.2	(1.5)	56.6	(1.5)	4.1	(0.7)	36.8	(1.4)	63.2	(1.4)
	Germany	12.2	(0.5)	54.8	(0.8)	33.0	(0.8)	96.6	(0.4)	3.4	(0.4)
	Greece	7.3	(1.0)	92.7	(1.0)	0.0	c	7.3	(1.0)	92.7	(1.0)
	Hungary	10.4	(1.6)	67.1	(1.4)	22.5	(0.9)	10.4	(1.6)	89.6	(1.6)
	Iceland	0.0	(0.0)	98.3	(0.1)	1.7	(0.1)	98.3	(0.1)	1.7	(0.1)
	Ireland	2.5	(0.3)	59.1	(1.0)	38.4	(1.0)	61.6	(1.0)	38.4	(1.0)
	Israel	18.2	(1.0)	81.3	(1.0)	0.6	(0.2)	14.4	(1.1)	85.6	(1.1)
	Italy	18.4	(0.5)	78.4	(0.6)	3.2	(0.3)	1.5	(0.3)	98.5	(0.3)
	Japan	0.0	c	100.0	(0.0)	0.0	c	0.0	c	100.0	(0.0)
	Korea	4.2	(0.9)	95.1	(0.9)	0.7	(0.1)	4.2	(0.9)	95.8	(0.9)
	Luxembourg	12.2	(0.2)	51.6	(0.3)	36.2	(0.2)	61.8	(0.2)	38.2	(0.2)
	Mexico	43.7	(0.9)	55.6	(0.9)	0.7	(0.2)	43.5	(1.0)	56.5	(1.0)
	Netherlands	49.0	(1.2)	50.5	(1.1)	0.5	(0.1)	74.5	(1.9)	25.5	(1.9)
	New Zealand	5.9	(0.4)	88.8	(0.5)	5.3	(0.3)	5.9	(0.4)	94.1	(0.4)
	Norway	0.5	(0.1)	99.3	(0.2)	0.2	(0.1)	99.8	(0.1)	0.2	(0.1)
	Poland	5.5	(0.5)	93.6	(0.6)	0.9	(0.3)	99.1	(0.3)	0.9	(0.3)
	Portugal	39.2	(2.2)	60.4	(2.2)	0.4	(0.1)	43.6	(2.1)	56.4	(2.1)
	Slovak Republic	39.3	(1.4)	56.9	(1.6)	3.8	(0.8)	38.7	(1.4)	61.3	(1.4)
	Slovenia	3.1	(0.8)	90.7	(0.7)	6.2	(0.2)	3.1	(0.8)	96.9	(0.8)
	Spain	36.6	(0.7)	63.4	(0.7)	0.0	(0.0)	100.0	(0.0)	0.0	(0.0)
	Sweden	3.3	(0.3)	95.1	(0.6)	1.6	(0.5)	98.4	(0.5)	1.6	(0.5)
	Switzerland	16.1	(1.0)	61.7	(1.3)	22.2	(1.1)	79.3	(1.1)	20.7	(1.1)
	Turkey	29.4	(1.5)	66.6	(1.5)	4.0	(0.3)	4.2	(0.9)	95.8	(0.9)
	United Kingdom	1.2	(0.1)	98.0	(0.1)	0.8	(0.0)	0.1	(0.1)	99.9	(0.1)
	United States	11.0	(0.8)	68.5	(1.0)	20.4	(0.7)	11.0	(0.8)	89.0	(0.8)
	OECD average	17.7	(0.2)	73.9	(0.0)	8.4	(0.1)	45.9	(0.2)	54.1	(0.2)
Partners	Albania	2.5	(0.4)	50.9	(2.0)	46.6	(2.0)	53.4	(2.0)	46.6	(2.0)
	Argentina	38.0	(2.2)	57.8	(2.1)	4.3	(0.5)	38.7	(2.1)	61.3	(2.1)
	Azerbaijan	5.9	(0.5)	49.4	(1.3)	44.7	(1.3)	55.3	(1.3)	44.7	(1.3)
	Brazil	24.8	(0.9)	37.5	(0.8)	37.8	(0.9)	24.8	(0.9)	75.2	(0.9)
	Bulgaria	7.5	(0.7)	88.7	(0.9)	3.8	(0.6)	7.2	(0.7)	92.8	(0.7)
	Colombia	36.8	(1.4)	42.3	(1.0)	21.0	(1.0)	36.8	(1.4)	63.2	(1.4)
	Croatia	0.2	(0.2)	77.5	(0.4)	22.3	(0.4)	0.2	(0.2)	99.8	(0.2)
	Dubai (UAE)	19.3	(0.4)	56.9	(0.5)	23.8	(0.4)	19.3	(0.4)	80.7	(0.4)
	Hong Kong-China	34.0	(0.9)	65.9	(0.9)	0.1	(0.0)	34.0	(0.9)	66.0	(0.9)
	Indonesia	8.0	(1.0)	46.0	(3.1)	46.0	(3.5)	54.0	(3.5)	46.0	(3.5)
	Jordan	8.4	(0.6)	91.6	(0.6)	0.0	c	100.0	(0.0)	0.0	c
	Kazakhstan	6.9	(0.5)	73.3	(1.9)	19.8	(2.1)	80.2	(2.1)	19.8	(2.1)
	Kyrgyzstan	8.1	(0.5)	71.4	(1.3)	20.5	(1.5)	79.5	(1.5)	20.5	(1.5)
	Latvia	18.1	(0.8)	79.4	(0.9)	2.5	(0.4)	97.0	(0.5)	3.0	(0.5)
	Liechtenstein	18.3	(1.1)	71.3	(0.8)	10.4	(1.0)	94.0	(0.9)	6.0	(0.9)
	Lithuania	10.7	(0.9)	80.9	(0.8)	8.4	(0.6)	100.0	(0.0)	0.0	(0.0)
	Macao-China	60.8	(0.1)	38.7	(0.1)	0.5	(0.1)	60.8	(0.1)	39.2	(0.1)
	Montenegro	2.5	(1.7)	82.7	(1.5)	14.8	(0.3)	2.5	(1.7)	97.5	(1.7)
	Panama	44.1	(4.6)	49.8	(4.5)	6.1	(1.4)	44.1	(4.6)	55.9	(4.6)
	Peru	30.0	(1.3)	44.6	(1.1)	25.4	(0.8)	30.3	(1.4)	69.7	(1.4)
	Qatar	18.8	(0.1)	62.6	(0.2)	18.6	(0.2)	18.8	(0.1)	81.2	(0.1)
	Romania	7.2	(1.0)	88.6	(1.1)	4.3	(0.6)	100.0	(0.0)	0.0	c
	Russian Federation	11.0	(0.8)	60.1	(1.8)	29.0	(1.7)	71.0	(1.7)	29.0	(1.7)
	Serbia	2.3	(0.6)	96.0	(0.6)	1.7	(0.2)	2.3	(0.6)	97.7	(0.6)
	Shanghai-China	42.5	(0.8)	57.1	(0.9)	0.4	(0.2)	42.2	(0.8)	57.8	(0.8)
	Singapore	38.4	(0.3)	61.6	(0.3)	0.0	(0.0)	3.6	(0.2)	96.4	(0.2)
	Chinese Taipei	34.5	(0.9)	65.5	(0.9)	0.0	(0.0)	34.5	(0.9)	65.5	(0.9)
	Thailand	23.8	(1.1)	73.5	(1.1)	2.7	(0.4)	23.8	(1.1)	76.2	(1.1)
	Trinidad and Tobago	36.2	(0.3)	56.1	(0.4)	7.7	(0.3)	36.2	(0.3)	63.8	(0.3)
	Tunisia	43.7	(1.4)	50.9	(1.4)	5.4	(0.4)	43.7	(1.4)	56.3	(1.4)
	Uruguay	39.2	(1.2)	56.2	(1.1)	4.6	(0.4)	39.2	(1.2)	60.8	(1.2)

StatLink http://dx.doi.org/10.1787/888932343285

[Part 1/1]

Table IV.3.2a Horizontal differentiation of school systems

		Number of school types or distinct educational programmes available to 15-year-old students	First age of selection in the education system
OECD	Australia[a]	1	16.0
	Austria[a]	4	10.0
	Belgium[a]	4	12.0
	Canada[a]	1	16.0
	Chile[a]	1	16.0
	Czech Republic[a]	5	11.0
	Denmark[a]	1	16.0
	Estonia[a]	1	15.0
	Finland[a]	1	16.0
	France	w	w
	Germany[a]	4	10.0
	Greece[a]	2	15.0
	Hungary[a]	3	11.0
	Iceland[a]	1	16.0
	Ireland[a]	4	15.0
	Israel[a]	2	15.0
	Italy[a]	3	14.0
	Japan[a]	2	15.0
	Korea[a]	3	14.0
	Luxembourg[a]	4	13.0
	Mexico[a]	3	15.0
	Netherlands[a]	7	12.0
	New Zealand[a]	1	16.0
	Norway[a]	1	16.0
	Poland[a]	1	16.0
	Portugal[a]	3	15.0
	Slovak Republic[a]	5	11.0
	Slovenia[a]	3	14.0
	Spain[a]	1	16.0
	Sweden[a]	1	16.0
	Switzerland[a]	4	12.0
	Turkey[a]	3	11.0
	United Kingdom[a]	1	16.0
	United States[a]	1	16.0
	OECD average	2.5	14.0
Partners	Albania	m	m
	Argentina[b]	3	15.0
	Azerbaijan[a]	2	15.0
	Brazil[a]	1	17.0
	Bulgaria[b]	3	13.0
	Colombia[b]	2	15.0
	Croatia[b]	5	14-15
	Dubai (UAE)[b]	3	15.0
	Hong Kong-China[b]	2	15.0
	Indonesia[a]	1	15.0
	Jordan[a]	1	16.0
	Kazakhstan	m	m
	Kyrgyzstan[b]	4	14-15
	Latvia[b]	1	16.0
	Liechtenstein[a]	3	11.0
	Lithuania[b]	2	14-15
	Macao-China[b]	1	16.0
	Montenegro[b]	3	15.0
	Panama[b]	m	15-16
	Peru	m	m
	Qatar[b]	4	15.0
	Romania[a]	3	14.0
	Russian Federation[a]	3	14.5
	Serbia	m	m
	Shanghai-China[b]	4	14.0
	Singapore[b]	4	12.0
	Chinese Taipei[b]	3	15.0
	Thailand[b]	2	15.0
	Trinidad and Tobago[b]	4	11.0
	Tunisia[a]	1	16.0
	Uruguay[a]	1	12.0

Sources: a. *PISA 2006: Science Competencies for Tomorrow's World* (OECD, 2007).
b. PISA system-level data collection in 2010.

StatLink http://dx.doi.org/10.1787/888932343285

[Part 1/3]
School admittance policies
Table IV.3.2b *Results based on school principals' reports*

		Percentage of students in schools where the principal reported the following factors to be "never", "sometimes" or "always" considered for admittance at school																	
		Residence in a particular area						Students' records of academic performance						Recommendations of feeder schools					
		Never		Sometimes		Always		Never		Sometimes		Always		Never		Sometimes		Always	
		%	S.E.	%	S.E.	%	S.E.	%	S.E.	%	S.E.	%	S.E.	%	S.E.	%	S.E.	%	S.E.
OECD	Australia	32.7	(2.0)	22.1	(2.4)	45.2	(2.5)	39.6	(2.7)	36.9	(2.7)	23.5	(2.7)	26.6	(2.5)	48.0	(2.7)	25.3	(2.5)
	Austria	49.1	(4.2)	19.5	(3.5)	31.5	(3.2)	26.0	(1.7)	12.6	(2.3)	61.4	(2.7)	64.1	(3.7)	31.4	(3.7)	4.5	(1.9)
	Belgium	86.2	(2.1)	11.6	(2.1)	2.3	(0.9)	48.1	(3.1)	36.9	(2.8)	15.0	(2.3)	58.0	(3.7)	38.8	(3.6)	3.3	(1.2)
	Canada	12.2	(1.1)	14.8	(1.4)	73.0	(1.6)	46.6	(2.3)	37.6	(2.1)	15.8	(1.5)	31.3	(2.1)	46.8	(2.3)	21.9	(1.6)
	Chile	78.1	(3.6)	17.8	(3.3)	4.1	(1.6)	29.9	(3.3)	36.4	(4.0)	33.7	(3.6)	40.2	(4.2)	45.4	(4.2)	14.4	(2.5)
	Czech Republic	67.1	(2.8)	19.9	(2.7)	13.0	(2.3)	31.4	(2.8)	16.4	(2.7)	52.2	(2.4)	47.5	(3.8)	42.8	(4.0)	9.6	(2.2)
	Denmark	32.3	(2.8)	18.0	(2.2)	49.7	(2.9)	76.0	(3.2)	21.4	(3.0)	2.6	(1.1)	58.5	(3.2)	38.1	(3.2)	3.4	(1.2)
	Estonia	22.8	(3.3)	20.0	(2.9)	57.3	(3.2)	27.0	(2.6)	46.0	(3.2)	27.0	(2.7)	45.1	(3.6)	49.8	(3.7)	5.1	(1.7)
	Finland	19.3	(2.8)	6.5	(2.0)	74.2	(3.4)	82.2	(3.2)	16.8	(3.2)	0.9	(0.8)	73.1	(3.6)	23.9	(3.4)	3.0	(1.3)
	France	w	w	w	w	w	w	w	w	w	w	w	w	w	w	w	w	w	w
	Germany	19.3	(2.7)	20.2	(2.8)	60.5	(3.5)	23.2	(2.2)	33.7	(3.1)	43.1	(2.9)	21.5	(2.5)	14.5	(2.5)	63.9	(3.0)
	Greece	16.6	(3.1)	12.8	(2.8)	70.7	(3.7)	72.8	(3.1)	23.7	(3.2)	3.5	(1.0)	66.6	(3.4)	30.5	(3.5)	3.0	(1.2)
	Hungary	74.2	(3.3)	16.4	(2.8)	9.5	(2.2)	9.5	(2.0)	4.1	(1.2)	86.4	(2.1)	51.4	(4.0)	43.8	(4.2)	4.8	(1.7)
	Iceland	12.5	(0.2)	23.1	(0.2)	64.4	(0.2)	92.0	(0.1)	8.0	(0.1)	0.0	c	67.9	(0.2)	29.0	(0.2)	3.1	(0.1)
	Ireland	49.4	(4.5)	18.5	(3.4)	32.1	(4.0)	76.5	(3.9)	13.3	(3.0)	10.2	(2.8)	50.1	(4.3)	29.2	(3.9)	20.7	(3.7)
	Israel	52.0	(3.6)	18.7	(2.7)	29.2	(3.0)	21.9	(3.1)	31.1	(3.7)	47.0	(3.8)	19.7	(2.6)	47.5	(3.9)	32.7	(4.0)
	Italy	49.5	(2.0)	21.2	(1.7)	29.3	(1.9)	44.6	(1.8)	23.6	(1.8)	31.8	(1.9)	37.5	(1.9)	35.8	(2.0)	26.7	(1.8)
	Japan	61.9	(3.0)	16.6	(2.8)	21.5	(2.7)	1.1	(0.8)	10.9	(2.1)	88.0	(2.3)	31.6	(3.4)	47.3	(3.6)	21.1	(3.1)
	Korea	72.2	(3.7)	14.7	(3.3)	13.1	(2.3)	38.7	(3.4)	11.3	(2.8)	50.0	(3.9)	70.1	(3.4)	21.1	(3.0)	8.8	(2.1)
	Luxembourg	14.2	(0.1)	38.5	(0.1)	47.3	(0.1)	4.6	(0.0)	56.8	(0.1)	38.6	(0.1)	25.1	(0.1)	56.0	(0.1)	18.9	(0.1)
	Mexico	75.5	(1.4)	13.4	(1.1)	11.0	(1.3)	40.8	(2.0)	22.1	(1.6)	37.1	(1.7)	72.0	(1.6)	19.2	(1.3)	8.8	(1.2)
	Netherlands	63.9	(4.3)	17.7	(3.7)	18.4	(3.8)	3.3	(1.3)	19.3	(3.6)	77.4	(3.8)	1.9	(1.2)	14.0	(3.1)	84.1	(3.1)
	New Zealand	36.3	(3.2)	13.8	(2.5)	49.9	(3.0)	57.1	(3.2)	21.8	(3.1)	21.1	(2.8)	39.6	(3.2)	38.4	(3.5)	22.0	(2.7)
	Norway	19.5	(2.6)	9.3	(2.0)	71.1	(3.1)	92.6	(2.0)	5.8	(1.8)	1.6	(0.9)	75.2	(3.4)	18.9	(3.0)	5.9	(2.0)
	Poland	11.9	(2.3)	7.5	(1.9)	80.5	(2.7)	50.9	(3.1)	34.3	(3.5)	14.8	(2.3)	43.5	(3.8)	52.0	(3.9)	4.5	(1.4)
	Portugal	22.0	(3.6)	21.3	(3.2)	56.7	(3.6)	84.3	(2.4)	14.7	(2.4)	1.0	(0.7)	76.3	(3.2)	23.4	(3.2)	0.3	(0.2)
	Slovak Republic	73.2	(2.6)	10.1	(2.2)	16.7	(2.1)	27.1	(2.4)	14.6	(2.9)	58.3	(2.7)	42.8	(4.1)	41.5	(4.0)	15.6	(3.0)
	Slovenia	75.5	(0.6)	15.5	(0.3)	9.0	(0.7)	32.2	(0.5)	43.5	(0.4)	24.3	(0.2)	54.7	(0.4)	38.4	(0.4)	6.9	(0.1)
	Spain	21.9	(1.9)	12.3	(1.9)	65.8	(2.6)	88.9	(1.6)	9.9	(1.6)	1.1	(0.6)	84.3	(1.9)	13.9	(1.9)	1.8	(0.6)
	Sweden	45.6	(3.7)	5.6	(1.8)	48.8	(3.6)	95.2	(1.4)	3.0	(1.2)	1.8	(0.7)	78.6	(3.3)	19.5	(3.1)	1.9	(1.1)
	Switzerland	12.6	(2.3)	12.1	(2.2)	75.3	(2.7)	30.0	(2.8)	9.4	(1.4)	60.6	(2.8)	35.0	(2.9)	28.0	(3.3)	37.0	(2.8)
	Turkey	42.3	(3.6)	13.9	(2.5)	43.8	(3.3)	34.1	(3.7)	33.2	(3.9)	32.7	(3.5)	33.5	(4.3)	50.1	(3.9)	16.4	(3.4)
	United Kingdom	21.3	(2.5)	23.7	(3.0)	55.0	(2.8)	80.4	(2.3)	7.7	(2.0)	11.8	(1.8)	67.7	(2.9)	21.4	(2.8)	10.9	(1.9)
	United States	13.6	(2.1)	8.9	(2.0)	77.6	(2.7)	54.6	(3.4)	22.5	(3.0)	22.9	(2.8)	56.4	(3.7)	24.5	(3.6)	19.2	(3.0)
	OECD average	41.1	(0.5)	16.2	(0.4)	42.6	(0.5)	47.4	(0.4)	22.4	(0.5)	30.2	(0.4)	49.9	(0.5)	34.0	(0.6)	16.1	(0.4)
Partners	Albania	33.1	(3.3)	25.1	(3.3)	41.8	(3.6)	41.4	(4.1)	28.3	(3.5)	30.3	(4.1)	25.2	(3.3)	31.9	(3.7)	42.9	(3.6)
	Argentina	71.1	(4.2)	17.6	(3.1)	11.3	(2.9)	62.8	(3.5)	17.7	(2.8)	19.4	(3.0)	59.8	(3.6)	34.7	(3.6)	5.6	(2.1)
	Azerbaijan	23.7	(3.7)	12.8	(3.4)	63.5	(4.6)	22.3	(3.7)	34.6	(3.8)	43.1	(4.5)	16.9	(3.3)	31.4	(4.2)	51.8	(5.1)
	Brazil	43.0	(2.5)	25.8	(2.3)	31.2	(2.8)	80.2	(2.1)	12.2	(1.9)	7.6	(1.1)	66.8	(2.6)	27.5	(2.4)	5.7	(1.2)
	Bulgaria	55.6	(4.4)	25.6	(4.0)	18.8	(3.8)	7.9	(1.7)	15.8	(2.5)	76.3	(2.9)	67.0	(4.8)	30.8	(4.6)	2.2	(1.3)
	Colombia	53.5	(4.3)	30.2	(4.1)	16.3	(2.3)	34.8	(4.0)	34.2	(4.1)	31.0	(3.6)	42.8	(4.2)	43.4	(3.8)	13.8	(3.1)
	Croatia	66.4	(3.7)	24.0	(3.2)	9.7	(2.4)	0.8	(0.0)	5.7	(1.8)	93.5	(1.8)	49.8	(3.8)	45.1	(4.0)	5.0	(1.8)
	Dubai (UAE)	41.0	(0.1)	36.0	(0.1)	22.9	(0.1)	2.6	(0.0)	26.3	(0.1)	71.1	(0.1)	23.5	(0.1)	40.8	(0.1)	35.8	(0.1)
	Hong Kong-China	67.5	(4.0)	31.7	(4.1)	0.7	(0.7)	1.5	(1.0)	16.7	(2.7)	81.8	(2.9)	5.0	(1.5)	77.9	(3.5)	17.1	(3.2)
	Indonesia	47.8	(3.8)	30.2	(4.2)	22.1	(3.3)	18.1	(3.0)	21.5	(3.0)	60.4	(3.8)	45.9	(4.0)	21.3	(3.4)	32.8	(4.0)
	Jordan	16.4	(3.0)	32.5	(3.8)	51.1	(3.8)	33.0	(3.8)	43.2	(4.1)	23.7	(3.1)	35.0	(3.2)	43.2	(4.0)	21.8	(3.3)
	Kazakhstan	29.7	(3.5)	20.1	(3.0)	50.2	(3.9)	39.7	(3.5)	30.6	(3.4)	29.7	(3.3)	41.2	(3.7)	39.1	(3.6)	19.7	(2.7)
	Kyrgyzstan	29.1	(3.6)	18.6	(3.3)	52.3	(4.1)	26.0	(3.6)	23.6	(3.4)	50.4	(3.6)	26.5	(3.5)	37.2	(3.7)	36.3	(3.9)
	Latvia	62.4	(3.4)	17.4	(2.8)	20.2	(2.6)	50.0	(2.9)	25.9	(3.1)	24.2	(2.9)	67.5	(3.3)	29.4	(3.3)	3.1	(1.2)
	Liechtenstein	36.3	(0.1)	0.0	c	63.7	(0.1)	21.2	(0.4)	10.0	(0.2)	68.7	(0.4)	6.0	(0.3)	19.4	(0.4)	74.5	(0.5)
	Lithuania	25.0	(2.7)	29.4	(3.3)	45.6	(3.3)	51.1	(3.2)	37.8	(3.7)	11.1	(2.3)	59.8	(3.8)	36.5	(3.8)	3.7	(1.0)
	Macao-China	81.7	(0.0)	12.5	(0.0)	5.8	(0.0)	7.7	(0.0)	27.4	(0.0)	64.9	(0.0)	10.3	(0.0)	45.8	(0.0)	44.0	(0.0)
	Montenegro	69.8	(1.3)	21.4	(0.4)	8.8	(1.6)	29.0	(0.6)	17.0	(0.3)	54.0	(0.8)	47.0	(0.9)	36.8	(0.6)	16.2	(0.4)
	Panama	56.0	(4.3)	23.4	(5.0)	20.7	(4.7)	39.7	(5.4)	23.7	(3.8)	36.6	(4.7)	31.3	(4.8)	42.1	(4.7)	26.6	(4.5)
	Peru	60.0	(3.3)	27.0	(3.2)	13.0	(1.9)	56.3	(3.5)	24.6	(3.2)	19.1	(2.8)	69.1	(3.3)	24.0	(3.3)	6.9	(1.9)
	Qatar	26.8	(0.1)	27.5	(0.1)	45.6	(0.1)	30.1	(0.1)	26.2	(0.1)	43.7	(0.1)	46.0	(0.1)	39.1	(0.1)	14.8	(0.1)
	Romania	60.2	(4.0)	25.2	(3.6)	14.6	(2.7)	22.6	(3.5)	21.3	(3.1)	56.0	(3.4)	51.9	(4.2)	40.3	(4.4)	7.7	(2.2)
	Russian Federation	42.3	(2.9)	30.3	(3.9)	27.5	(3.5)	58.1	(3.5)	26.7	(2.9)	15.3	(2.6)	47.4	(3.5)	38.5	(3.9)	14.1	(2.5)
	Serbia	60.0	(3.5)	34.9	(3.7)	5.1	(1.5)	4.2	(1.4)	12.2	(2.4)	83.5	(2.7)	44.1	(4.4)	47.5	(4.8)	8.3	(2.7)
	Shanghai-China	25.4	(3.2)	33.4	(3.2)	41.2	(3.0)	20.0	(2.3)	26.2	(3.1)	53.9	(3.4)	25.4	(3.3)	61.8	(3.6)	12.8	(2.9)
	Singapore	33.9	(0.6)	40.0	(0.8)	26.1	(0.3)	1.2	(0.0)	16.9	(0.2)	81.9	(0.2)	44.5	(0.6)	43.2	(0.8)	12.3	(0.3)
	Chinese Taipei	31.1	(3.9)	28.3	(3.9)	40.7	(4.1)	25.1	(2.8)	28.0	(3.4)	47.0	(3.2)	36.7	(3.8)	49.0	(3.8)	14.3	(2.9)
	Thailand	33.4	(3.6)	28.5	(3.5)	38.0	(3.5)	14.6	(2.2)	31.6	(3.7)	53.9	(3.6)	13.1	(2.9)	24.4	(3.5)	62.5	(3.8)
	Trinidad and Tobago	23.3	(0.2)	60.3	(0.3)	16.4	(0.3)	8.2	(0.2)	34.6	(0.3)	57.2	(0.3)	22.7	(0.3)	62.6	(0.3)	14.7	(0.2)
	Tunisia	5.6	(1.9)	5.5	(2.3)	88.9	(2.9)	36.5	(4.2)	45.9	(4.3)	17.5	(3.7)	55.8	(3.9)	37.0	(3.8)	7.2	(2.0)
	Uruguay	48.8	(2.7)	17.2	(2.3)	33.9	(2.6)	76.3	(2.4)	13.5	(1.8)	10.2	(1.9)	70.3	(2.6)	28.1	(2.6)	1.5	(0.9)

StatLink http://dx.doi.org/10.1787/888932343285

[Part 2/3]
School admittance policies
Table IV.3.2b *Results based on school principals' reports*

		Percentage of students in schools where the principal reported the following factors to be "never", "sometimes" or "always" considered for admittance at school																	
		Parents' endorsement of the instructional or religious philosophy of the school						Whether the student requires or is interested in a special programme						Preference given to family members of current or former students					
		Never		Sometimes		Always		Never		Sometimes		Always		Never		Sometimes		Always	
		%	S.E.	%	S.E.	%	S.E.	%	S.E.	%	S.E.	%	S.E.	%	S.E.	%	S.E.	%	S.E.
OECD	Australia	47.3	(2.4)	22.4	(2.4)	30.4	(1.9)	25.1	(2.6)	61.2	(2.6)	13.7	(2.1)	23.3	(2.2)	33.6	(2.3)	43.1	(2.4)
	Austria	82.5	(2.7)	12.4	(2.3)	5.1	(1.6)	29.4	(3.8)	30.4	(3.8)	40.2	(3.7)	47.6	(3.6)	31.3	(3.0)	21.2	(3.0)
	Belgium	44.6	(3.3)	20.3	(2.5)	35.1	(3.1)	47.4	(3.3)	37.6	(3.1)	15.0	(2.1)	52.8	(2.6)	31.1	(2.8)	16.1	(2.0)
	Canada	63.2	(2.2)	22.4	(2.1)	14.4	(1.5)	15.5	(1.5)	66.2	(2.2)	18.3	(2.1)	53.8	(2.0)	33.7	(1.9)	12.5	(1.2)
	Chile	68.4	(3.2)	14.7	(3.0)	16.9	(2.7)	46.6	(4.2)	30.3	(3.7)	23.1	(3.1)	33.0	(4.0)	44.0	(4.2)	23.0	(3.6)
	Czech Republic	73.8	(3.4)	9.3	(2.6)	17.0	(2.6)	36.6	(3.1)	45.6	(3.1)	17.7	(2.8)	82.1	(2.3)	12.2	(2.4)	5.6	(1.8)
	Denmark	60.4	(3.7)	26.7	(3.1)	12.8	(2.4)	45.2	(3.7)	46.2	(3.8)	8.6	(1.6)	40.3	(2.9)	41.0	(3.2)	18.7	(2.8)
	Estonia	59.2	(3.6)	22.8	(3.1)	17.9	(2.9)	18.1	(2.8)	65.0	(3.4)	16.9	(2.7)	52.4	(2.9)	34.2	(3.1)	13.3	(2.5)
	Finland	82.1	(2.8)	16.6	(2.8)	1.3	(0.9)	47.7	(3.2)	44.8	(3.5)	7.5	(2.0)	72.9	(3.0)	24.4	(3.1)	2.7	(1.1)
	France	w	w	w	w	w	w	w	w	w	w	w	w	w	w	w	w	w	w
	Germany	84.6	(2.6)	10.7	(2.2)	4.7	(1.5)	31.3	(3.3)	43.2	(3.3)	25.5	(3.2)	57.2	(2.8)	30.0	(2.8)	12.8	(2.4)
	Greece	86.3	(2.7)	6.4	(1.9)	7.3	(2.0)	53.7	(3.6)	32.5	(3.7)	13.8	(3.0)	39.2	(3.7)	39.1	(3.6)	21.7	(3.1)
	Hungary	58.2	(4.2)	17.6	(3.1)	24.2	(3.5)	10.2	(2.4)	11.6	(2.6)	78.1	(3.4)	34.4	(3.7)	57.3	(4.2)	8.3	(2.2)
	Iceland	88.0	(0.1)	11.5	(0.1)	0.6	(0.1)	60.7	(0.2)	37.7	(0.2)	1.6	(0.1)	95.4	(0.1)	4.6	(0.1)	0.0	c
	Ireland	47.0	(4.8)	26.4	(4.2)	26.6	(3.9)	44.1	(4.4)	45.0	(4.4)	10.9	(2.8)	30.4	(3.6)	15.9	(3.2)	53.7	(3.9)
	Israel	48.4	(3.4)	20.6	(3.4)	31.1	(3.0)	18.7	(3.1)	54.0	(3.8)	27.3	(3.6)	56.9	(3.4)	35.2	(3.7)	7.9	(2.1)
	Italy	46.2	(2.0)	18.4	(1.4)	35.4	(1.9)	18.0	(1.7)	31.5	(1.7)	50.5	(1.8)	31.6	(1.5)	40.7	(1.8)	27.7	(1.5)
	Japan	77.0	(3.3)	12.7	(2.6)	10.3	(2.4)	33.0	(3.2)	40.1	(3.9)	26.9	(3.1)	81.5	(2.5)	17.0	(2.4)	1.5	(0.9)
	Korea	83.2	(3.4)	11.4	(2.7)	5.5	(2.0)	51.6	(4.2)	29.9	(3.6)	18.5	(3.2)	76.5	(3.5)	20.0	(3.2)	3.5	(1.5)
	Luxembourg	48.0	(0.1)	36.1	(0.1)	15.9	(0.1)	8.4	(0.1)	77.3	(0.1)	14.3	(0.1)	11.9	(0.1)	31.0	(0.1)	57.1	(0.1)
	Mexico	69.8	(1.8)	15.5	(1.3)	14.7	(1.4)	56.4	(1.7)	28.5	(1.6)	15.1	(1.3)	76.0	(1.7)	16.8	(1.5)	7.1	(1.1)
	Netherlands	43.8	(5.0)	35.5	(4.6)	20.7	(3.7)	21.7	(3.8)	69.2	(4.7)	9.2	(2.7)	76.8	(3.5)	15.0	(2.9)	8.1	(2.5)
	New Zealand	66.6	(2.8)	13.1	(2.5)	20.3	(2.1)	34.7	(2.9)	52.5	(3.3)	12.8	(2.1)	30.6	(3.0)	34.4	(3.2)	35.0	(3.0)
	Norway	95.0	(1.6)	3.6	(1.4)	1.4	(0.9)	82.8	(2.4)	13.7	(2.1)	3.5	(1.4)	69.2	(3.1)	25.5	(2.9)	5.2	(1.7)
	Poland	76.7	(2.9)	19.5	(3.0)	3.7	(1.2)	49.8	(3.4)	39.0	(3.6)	11.2	(2.1)	84.3	(2.7)	12.6	(2.6)	3.1	(1.2)
	Portugal	52.3	(3.9)	24.9	(3.3)	22.7	(3.1)	8.8	(1.9)	37.4	(3.6)	53.8	(3.7)	20.1	(2.8)	56.0	(3.6)	23.9	(3.2)
	Slovak Republic	73.2	(3.3)	8.0	(1.8)	18.9	(3.0)	25.9	(3.7)	30.9	(3.9)	43.2	(3.9)	89.0	(2.3)	9.0	(1.8)	2.0	(1.4)
	Slovenia	90.0	(0.2)	3.1	(0.1)	6.9	(0.1)	8.3	(0.5)	15.4	(0.4)	76.3	(0.6)	90.0	(0.3)	9.3	(0.2)	0.7	(0.3)
	Spain	75.9	(2.1)	13.3	(1.9)	10.8	(1.7)	51.1	(2.9)	35.3	(2.8)	13.6	(2.2)	39.4	(2.6)	28.9	(2.3)	31.7	(2.5)
	Sweden	79.6	(3.1)	14.9	(2.9)	5.5	(1.7)	67.5	(3.6)	27.3	(3.6)	5.2	(1.8)	66.7	(3.4)	16.6	(2.8)	16.7	(2.4)
	Switzerland	88.8	(2.2)	8.2	(1.9)	3.0	(1.2)	47.9	(2.9)	34.2	(3.4)	17.9	(2.7)	78.1	(2.8)	20.7	(2.9)	1.2	(0.4)
	Turkey	a	a	a	a	a	a	36.7	(3.9)	40.5	(3.7)	22.8	(3.3)	65.0	(3.5)	26.1	(3.4)	8.9	(2.1)
	United Kingdom	77.1	(2.8)	10.2	(1.9)	12.7	(2.3)	64.2	(3.4)	32.7	(3.3)	3.0	(1.2)	24.8	(3.0)	36.4	(3.3)	38.9	(3.5)
	United States	78.7	(2.8)	11.6	(2.4)	9.7	(2.3)	40.3	(4.1)	46.7	(4.1)	12.9	(2.7)	75.0	(2.9)	20.0	(2.7)	5.0	(1.5)
	OECD average	69.2	(0.5)	16.3	(0.4)	14.5	(0.4)	37.5	(0.5)	40.4	(3.0)	22.1	(0.4)	56.3	(0.5)	27.4	(0.5)	16.3	(0.4)
Partners	Albania	71.1	(3.7)	11.5	(2.7)	17.4	(2.7)	47.6	(4.3)	33.0	(4.1)	19.4	(2.6)	40.3	(4.2)	44.3	(4.5)	15.3	(2.9)
	Argentina	56.9	(3.8)	7.6	(1.8)	35.5	(3.9)	37.4	(3.6)	35.7	(3.7)	26.9	(3.4)	34.3	(3.0)	17.2	(3.1)	48.4	(3.5)
	Azerbaijan	9.3	(2.6)	17.1	(3.2)	73.6	(3.7)	14.2	(3.5)	42.9	(4.6)	42.9	(4.6)	34.4	(4.2)	34.3	(4.0)	31.4	(3.9)
	Brazil	58.3	(2.5)	21.2	(2.1)	20.5	(2.2)	57.2	(2.8)	29.9	(2.8)	12.9	(1.4)	67.9	(2.6)	21.6	(2.2)	10.5	(2.0)
	Bulgaria	14.9	(2.6)	31.4	(4.0)	53.6	(4.4)	27.8	(5.0)	49.8	(5.0)	22.4	(4.2)	63.2	(3.9)	23.1	(3.2)	13.7	(2.6)
	Colombia	64.9	(4.2)	15.9	(3.4)	19.2	(3.1)	45.6	(4.5)	31.3	(4.4)	23.2	(4.1)	39.5	(4.0)	41.8	(3.7)	18.7	(3.5)
	Croatia	65.8	(3.6)	18.4	(2.9)	15.8	(2.6)	21.8	(3.4)	51.6	(3.9)	26.6	(3.5)	68.1	(3.5)	29.0	(3.3)	2.9	(1.2)
	Dubai (UAE)	40.8	(0.1)	22.5	(0.1)	36.7	(0.1)	31.1	(0.1)	56.9	(0.1)	12.0	(0.1)	17.6	(0.1)	33.8	(0.2)	48.6	(0.2)
	Hong Kong-China	35.5	(4.0)	37.6	(4.4)	26.9	(3.6)	45.6	(4.1)	44.3	(4.1)	10.0	(2.5)	23.1	(3.5)	66.6	(4.0)	10.3	(1.9)
	Indonesia	50.6	(4.3)	14.9	(3.3)	34.5	(3.6)	28.0	(3.8)	29.7	(4.2)	42.3	(4.1)	39.9	(4.0)	43.9	(4.4)	16.1	(3.0)
	Jordan	49.4	(3.3)	24.4	(3.2)	26.3	(3.1)	39.2	(3.4)	39.8	(3.2)	21.0	(3.0)	50.1	(3.8)	29.1	(3.6)	20.8	(2.6)
	Kazakhstan	15.3	(2.4)	30.4	(3.5)	54.3	(3.7)	20.6	(2.6)	44.3	(3.5)	35.0	(3.4)	68.2	(3.4)	24.6	(3.1)	7.2	(1.9)
	Kyrgyzstan	46.3	(4.2)	27.0	(3.6)	26.8	(3.8)	12.2	(2.6)	24.0	(3.6)	63.9	(4.1)	52.5	(4.0)	28.7	(3.7)	18.7	(3.1)
	Latvia	83.2	(3.0)	10.5	(2.4)	6.3	(1.6)	27.7	(3.7)	40.3	(3.8)	31.9	(3.8)	57.0	(3.2)	26.0	(2.9)	17.1	(2.7)
	Liechtenstein	90.0	(0.1)	6.8	(0.2)	3.1	(0.2)	39.6	(0.4)	60.4	(0.4)	0.0	c	74.8	(0.3)	25.2	(0.3)	0.0	c
	Lithuania	55.7	(3.6)	19.2	(2.9)	25.1	(3.4)	24.2	(3.3)	37.3	(3.6)	38.6	(3.8)	41.6	(3.0)	28.7	(3.8)	29.7	(3.4)
	Macao-China	33.1	(0.0)	59.1	(0.0)	7.8	(0.0)	34.4	(0.0)	65.6	(0.0)	0.0	c	9.3	(0.0)	66.2	(0.0)	24.5	(0.0)
	Montenegro	73.7	(0.5)	13.1	(0.3)	13.1	(0.2)	26.6	(0.5)	19.5	(1.4)	53.9	(0.9)	75.1	(0.5)	23.0	(0.5)	1.9	(0.1)
	Panama	69.4	(4.9)	16.6	(4.0)	14.0	(3.4)	44.2	(5.3)	41.3	(5.6)	14.6	(3.6)	57.9	(5.1)	23.6	(5.0)	18.5	(4.0)
	Peru	68.9	(3.7)	14.0	(2.2)	17.1	(2.8)	50.5	(3.8)	34.6	(3.5)	14.9	(2.4)	54.0	(3.9)	30.0	(3.3)	16.0	(2.6)
	Qatar	32.1	(0.1)	24.2	(0.1)	43.6	(0.1)	37.0	(0.1)	45.9	(0.1)	17.1	(0.1)	24.8	(0.1)	31.6	(0.1)	43.6	(0.1)
	Romania	56.6	(4.2)	29.4	(4.1)	14.0	(2.9)	26.9	(3.4)	38.8	(3.5)	34.4	(3.2)	65.4	(3.9)	28.9	(3.5)	5.7	(2.0)
	Russian Federation	17.6	(2.7)	31.5	(3.3)	50.9	(3.5)	18.0	(2.9)	34.6	(3.7)	47.4	(4.2)	58.7	(3.8)	28.4	(3.2)	12.9	(2.5)
	Serbia	56.0	(4.0)	29.7	(3.8)	14.3	(3.4)	5.8	(1.8)	24.5	(2.9)	69.8	(3.0)	74.9	(3.8)	23.6	(3.6)	1.4	(0.9)
	Shanghai-China	16.3	(2.6)	40.0	(3.8)	43.7	(3.8)	25.4	(3.2)	62.7	(4.0)	11.9	(2.6)	61.7	(4.0)	31.8	(3.5)	6.6	(2.2)
	Singapore	53.9	(0.8)	34.7	(0.4)	11.4	(1.1)	21.1	(0.4)	69.9	(0.9)	9.1	(1.0)	45.6	(0.7)	49.0	(0.8)	5.4	(0.1)
	Chinese Taipei	35.1	(3.8)	35.9	(3.8)	29.0	(3.9)	23.9	(3.0)	39.9	(4.2)	36.3	(3.9)	51.7	(4.0)	32.4	(3.7)	15.8	(2.8)
	Thailand	33.5	(3.5)	31.6	(3.8)	34.9	(3.6)	19.5	(2.7)	40.5	(4.1)	40.0	(3.9)	36.3	(3.2)	49.8	(3.8)	13.9	(2.8)
	Trinidad and Tobago	48.0	(0.3)	45.3	(0.3)	6.7	(0.1)	39.6	(0.4)	52.7	(0.4)	7.7	(0.2)	38.3	(0.3)	58.3	(0.3)	3.3	(0.1)
	Tunisia	80.0	(3.6)	18.2	(3.5)	1.8	(1.1)	76.6	(3.5)	18.9	(3.2)	4.5	(2.0)	46.5	(4.4)	43.7	(4.2)	9.8	(2.3)
	Uruguay	78.4	(1.9)	8.0	(1.7)	13.6	(2.1)	59.5	(2.9)	25.7	(2.7)	14.8	(2.4)	61.5	(2.6)	23.1	(2.7)	15.4	(2.3)

StatLink http://dx.doi.org/10.1787/888932343285

[Part 3/3]

School admittance policies

Table IV.3.2b *Results based on school principals' reports*

	Percentage of students in schools where the principal reported the following factors to be "never", "sometimes" or "always" considered for admittance at school						Percentage of students in schools where principals reported whether "students' records of academic performance" and "recommendations of feeder schools" are considered for student admittance					
	Other											
	Never		Sometimes		Always		These two factors are "never" considered		At least one of these two factors "sometimes" considered but neither factor "always" considered		At least one of these two factors is "always" considered	
	%	S.E.	%	S.E.	%	S.E.	%	S.E.	%	S.E.	%	S.E.
OECD												
Australia	43.1	(2.8)	45.7	(3.3)	11.3	(1.9)	18.4	(2.1)	48.1	(2.9)	33.5	(2.9)
Austria	61.9	(4.5)	31.0	(3.8)	7.1	(2.7)	23.8	(1.7)	15.2	(2.4)	61.0	(2.7)
Belgium	52.9	(4.1)	40.3	(4.0)	6.8	(2.0)	38.8	(3.1)	44.4	(3.0)	16.8	(2.4)
Canada	47.1	(2.8)	46.4	(3.2)	6.5	(1.6)	25.3	(2.0)	45.4	(2.2)	29.3	(1.6)
Chile	42.8	(5.7)	40.0	(5.9)	17.2	(3.8)	19.5	(2.9)	39.6	(3.9)	40.9	(3.8)
Czech Republic	64.2	(3.2)	30.6	(3.0)	5.2	(1.4)	25.7	(3.0)	21.8	(2.8)	52.5	(2.4)
Denmark	32.5	(3.7)	55.6	(4.1)	11.9	(2.7)	51.2	(3.6)	43.6	(3.7)	5.3	(1.5)
Estonia	37.4	(5.0)	58.2	(5.0)	4.4	(2.1)	14.1	(2.6)	56.2	(3.8)	29.7	(2.9)
Finland	51.2	(4.4)	48.0	(4.4)	0.8	(0.7)	68.3	(4.0)	27.7	(3.7)	4.0	(1.5)
France	w	w	w	w	w	w	w	w	w	w	w	w
Germany	51.8	(4.9)	32.2	(4.2)	16.0	(3.8)	11.3	(1.9)	16.6	(2.2)	72.2	(2.3)
Greece	38.5	(3.6)	57.7	(3.6)	3.9	(1.4)	57.1	(3.5)	36.7	(3.6)	6.1	(1.7)
Hungary	49.3	(4.6)	46.6	(4.6)	4.2	(2.1)	7.1	(1.8)	6.1	(1.5)	86.9	(2.1)
Iceland	66.0	(0.4)	32.3	(0.3)	1.7	(0.1)	66.4	(0.2)	30.5	(0.2)	3.1	(0.1)
Ireland	29.2	(4.5)	48.4	(4.5)	22.4	(3.5)	49.7	(4.4)	26.5	(3.7)	23.8	(3.8)
Israel	30.0	(4.4)	51.6	(5.0)	18.4	(4.1)	12.2	(2.4)	32.5	(3.7)	55.2	(4.0)
Italy	42.5	(2.3)	45.7	(2.4)	11.8	(1.8)	29.0	(1.8)	28.8	(2.1)	42.2	(2.0)
Japan	67.6	(3.4)	29.2	(3.2)	3.2	(1.2)	1.1	(0.8)	10.9	(2.1)	88.0	(2.3)
Korea	79.7	(3.8)	17.4	(3.4)	2.9	(1.7)	37.5	(3.4)	11.1	(2.7)	51.4	(3.8)
Luxembourg	6.2	(0.1)	78.6	(0.1)	15.1	(0.1)	1.8	(0.0)	55.4	(0.1)	42.8	(0.1)
Mexico	62.8	(2.5)	25.3	(2.3)	11.9	(1.9)	34.3	(2.0)	24.4	(1.6)	41.3	(1.8)
Netherlands	55.9	(5.9)	43.1	(5.9)	1.0	(0.8)	0.6	(0.6)	11.0	(2.5)	88.3	(2.6)
New Zealand	31.0	(4.7)	46.6	(5.5)	22.4	(4.6)	37.4	(3.1)	35.9	(3.5)	26.6	(3.0)
Norway	58.3	(3.6)	37.8	(3.5)	3.9	(1.5)	74.3	(3.4)	19.8	(3.1)	5.9	(2.0)
Poland	60.8	(4.4)	37.0	(4.4)	2.2	(0.9)	34.6	(3.1)	48.7	(3.5)	16.7	(2.5)
Portugal	33.9	(4.4)	62.3	(4.8)	3.8	(1.9)	71.1	(3.4)	27.7	(3.4)	1.3	(0.7)
Slovak Republic	51.6	(5.0)	40.9	(4.9)	7.5	(2.6)	18.6	(2.6)	18.5	(2.9)	62.9	(2.8)
Slovenia	69.4	(0.7)	28.1	(0.7)	2.5	(0.1)	25.2	(0.5)	46.2	(0.4)	28.6	(0.3)
Spain	46.6	(3.0)	31.1	(3.2)	22.2	(3.3)	78.2	(1.9)	19.4	(2.0)	2.5	(0.6)
Sweden	64.5	(3.5)	25.7	(3.6)	9.8	(2.6)	77.0	(3.3)	19.3	(3.1)	3.7	(1.4)
Switzerland	68.5	(3.8)	29.5	(3.7)	2.0	(0.8)	23.2	(2.4)	11.6	(1.8)	65.2	(2.8)
Turkey	52.2	(4.0)	36.7	(4.0)	11.1	(2.4)	15.1	(2.9)	41.5	(4.1)	43.5	(4.3)
United Kingdom	47.9	(4.5)	38.3	(4.2)	13.7	(2.8)	63.8	(3.0)	18.8	(2.8)	17.4	(2.2)
United States	65.7	(5.8)	25.2	(4.9)	9.1	(4.2)	45.5	(3.6)	27.3	(3.6)	27.3	(3.0)
OECD average	50.4	(0.7)	40.7	(0.7)	8.9	(0.4)	35.1	(0.5)	29.3	(0.5)	35.6	(0.4)
Partners												
Albania	44.8	(4.2)	42.8	(4.6)	12.4	(3.2)	20.0	(3.0)	26.7	(3.0)	53.2	(3.8)
Argentina	43.3	(4.2)	40.0	(4.1)	16.7	(3.0)	49.3	(3.6)	29.9	(3.3)	20.8	(3.1)
Azerbaijan	35.5	(5.4)	45.9	(5.6)	18.6	(4.3)	8.7	(2.2)	27.1	(4.0)	64.1	(4.5)
Brazil	38.6	(3.2)	39.9	(3.0)	21.5	(2.9)	61.2	(2.6)	28.3	(2.4)	10.5	(1.3)
Bulgaria	42.5	(5.2)	52.5	(5.0)	5.0	(3.5)	7.0	(1.7)	16.7	(2.5)	76.3	(2.9)
Colombia	33.9	(5.1)	51.9	(5.5)	14.2	(3.1)	24.4	(3.3)	42.7	(3.9)	32.9	(3.7)
Croatia	32.8	(3.7)	64.0	(3.9)	3.2	(1.6)	0.0	c	6.5	(1.8)	93.5	(1.8)
Dubai (UAE)	34.3	(0.2)	52.8	(0.2)	12.9	(0.1)	1.9	(0.0)	26.3	(0.1)	71.8	(0.1)
Hong Kong-China	46.4	(5.8)	17.9	(4.5)	35.7	(6.0)	0.0	c	16.0	(2.8)	84.0	(2.8)
Indonesia	42.0	(4.4)	44.3	(4.8)	13.7	(3.3)	11.4	(2.3)	17.7	(3.3)	70.9	(3.7)
Jordan	39.5	(4.9)	51.2	(5.4)	9.4	(3.0)	20.3	(2.8)	45.2	(3.9)	34.5	(3.6)
Kazakhstan	50.3	(4.1)	42.8	(3.9)	6.9	(2.1)	27.6	(3.0)	36.3	(3.5)	36.1	(3.6)
Kyrgyzstan	39.8	(5.3)	40.0	(4.8)	20.2	(4.1)	16.1	(3.0)	23.2	(3.1)	60.7	(3.7)
Latvia	43.7	(5.1)	55.4	(5.2)	0.9	(0.9)	44.4	(3.1)	30.8	(3.4)	24.8	(3.0)
Liechtenstein	83.3	(0.5)	9.9	(0.5)	6.8	(0.0)	6.0	(0.3)	13.8	(0.4)	80.2	(0.5)
Lithuania	29.2	(5.8)	60.8	(6.4)	9.9	(2.7)	38.7	(3.4)	47.9	(3.8)	13.5	(2.3)
Macao-China	31.7	(0.0)	67.3	(0.0)	1.0	(0.0)	5.4	(0.0)	20.8	(0.0)	73.8	(0.0)
Montenegro	28.0	(1.2)	64.9	(1.1)	7.1	(0.1)	15.1	(0.4)	25.6	(0.5)	59.3	(0.7)
Panama	37.6	(7.2)	55.5	(7.2)	6.9	(2.8)	18.8	(4.0)	35.2	(4.6)	46.0	(5.1)
Peru	51.3	(4.9)	35.9	(4.0)	12.8	(2.9)	47.9	(3.5)	29.1	(3.7)	23.0	(2.9)
Qatar	42.8	(0.1)	46.6	(0.1)	10.6	(0.1)	24.5	(0.1)	31.7	(0.1)	43.8	(0.1)
Romania	39.7	(4.0)	53.2	(3.9)	7.1	(2.0)	17.0	(3.1)	26.2	(3.1)	56.7	(3.5)
Russian Federation	50.4	(4.2)	42.3	(4.0)	7.3	(2.5)	37.8	(3.7)	39.1	(4.0)	23.2	(2.6)
Serbia	45.3	(4.7)	51.1	(4.2)	3.6	(1.3)	2.7	(1.0)	12.9	(2.5)	84.4	(2.9)
Shanghai-China	45.6	(4.4)	50.8	(4.5)	3.6	(1.4)	13.8	(2.5)	29.2	(3.3)	57.0	(3.2)
Singapore	47.5	(0.8)	46.0	(0.6)	6.5	(1.2)	1.2	(0.0)	14.5	(0.2)	84.3	(0.2)
Chinese Taipei	46.9	(4.6)	49.1	(4.5)	4.0	(2.1)	16.9	(2.6)	29.7	(3.5)	53.3	(3.6)
Thailand	38.8	(5.6)	50.3	(6.0)	10.9	(3.5)	8.9	(2.1)	21.5	(3.1)	69.6	(3.2)
Trinidad and Tobago	24.6	(0.4)	64.9	(0.5)	10.6	(0.3)	4.3	(0.2)	34.6	(0.4)	61.2	(0.3)
Tunisia	26.2	(3.9)	72.1	(4.1)	1.7	(1.0)	27.2	(3.5)	51.3	(4.1)	21.4	(3.9)
Uruguay	52.7	(3.3)	40.1	(3.2)	7.2	(1.5)	60.7	(2.4)	29.1	(2.3)	10.2	(1.9)

StatLink http://dx.doi.org/10.1787/888932343285

[Part 1/2]

Table IV.3.2c School admittance policies, by lower or upper secondary level of education

Results based on school principals' reports

		Lower secondary education (ISCED 2)													
		Percentage of students in schools where the principal reported the following factors to be "always" considered for admittance at school													
		Residence in a particular area		Students' academic records		Recommendations of feeder schools		Parents' endorsement of the instructional or religious philosophy of the school		Students' needs or desires for a special programme		Attendance of other family members at the school		Other	
		%	S.E.	%	S.E.	%	S.E.	%	S.E.	%	S.E.	%	S.E.	%	S.E.
OECD	Australia	48.7	(2.7)	23.0	(3.0)	25.3	(2.5)	31.5	(2.3)	13.3	(2.3)	45.5	(2.6)	11.2	(2.0)
	Austria	62.7	(10.9)	15.4	(5.4)	4.2	(1.8)	0.8	(0.4)	35.3	(11.7)	32.5	(11.8)	1.2	(0.9)
	Belgium	10.3	(5.6)	21.3	(4.5)	3.2	(1.2)	24.3	(4.6)	33.5	(7.8)	10.2	(3.4)	17.6	(7.1)
	Canada	69.1	(2.4)	13.1	(1.6)	21.6	(1.6)	9.5	(1.2)	14.4	(2.3)	10.5	(2.3)	4.6	(1.6)
	Chile	3.2	(2.8)	8.5	(4.7)	13.5	(2.4)	6.4	(2.9)	6.1	(3.1)	34.2	(10.6)	15.9	(7.8)
	Czech Republic	23.3	(4.0)	15.4	(2.4)	9.0	(2.0)	24.6	(4.3)	21.4	(3.7)	10.3	(3.3)	4.1	(1.2)
	Denmark	49.7	(2.9)	2.0	(1.0)	3.4	(1.2)	13.0	(2.4)	8.6	(1.7)	18.9	(2.8)	11.9	(2.7)
	Estonia	57.6	(3.2)	26.8	(2.7)	5.0	(1.6)	17.9	(2.9)	16.9	(2.7)	13.2	(2.5)	4.1	(2.1)
	Finland	74.5	(3.4)	0.8	(0.8)	3.0	(1.3)	1.3	(0.9)	7.4	(2.0)	2.7	(1.1)	0.8	(0.7)
	France	w	w	w	w	w	w	w	w	w	w	w	w	w	w
	Germany	60.9	(3.6)	43.5	(3.0)	59.3	(2.9)	4.8	(1.6)	25.0	(3.1)	13.1	(2.4)	15.9	(3.9)
	Greece	88.0	(4.7)	0.0	c	2.9	(1.2)	0.0	c	9.8	(6.7)	34.2	(11.9)	6.2	(6.0)
	Hungary	68.0	(8.8)	3.0	(2.1)	4.8	(1.7)	30.0	(9.1)	27.8	(8.4)	11.1	(5.5)	0.0	c
	Iceland	64.4	(0.2)	0.0	c	2.8	(0.1)	0.6	(0.1)	1.6	(0.1)	0.0	c	1.7	(0.1)
	Ireland	32.9	(4.2)	11.6	(3.2)	17.9	(3.2)	26.3	(3.9)	11.5	(3.1)	53.9	(4.1)	22.0	(3.5)
	Israel	32.3	(6.6)	28.1	(6.3)	31.2	(3.8)	24.4	(4.9)	22.9	(5.5)	7.2	(3.3)	20.2	(7.1)
	Italy	33.4	(12.6)	19.6	(7.7)	26.2	(1.8)	16.3	(7.3)	27.9	(10.5)	37.8	(11.3)	0.0	c
	Japan	c	c	c	c	c	c	c	c	c	c	c	c	c	c
	Korea	24.9	(6.1)	3.4	(2.6)	8.6	(2.0)	1.1	(1.1)	11.2	(9.4)	2.3	(2.4)	0.0	c
	Luxembourg	50.3	(0.3)	37.2	(0.3)	18.9	(0.1)	17.2	(0.2)	16.6	(0.2)	55.4	(0.2)	19.1	(0.2)
	Mexico	15.7	(2.3)	19.1	(2.1)	8.7	(1.2)	15.8	(2.5)	7.0	(1.7)	12.7	(2.1)	8.2	(3.0)
	Netherlands	18.9	(4.4)	76.0	(4.3)	82.3	(3.1)	22.0	(4.3)	10.4	(3.4)	9.0	(3.0)	1.4	(1.1)
	New Zealand	39.8	(4.1)	21.8	(4.0)	20.9	(2.6)	23.6	(3.7)	15.4	(3.4)	34.2	(4.4)	27.1	(7.8)
	Norway	71.1	(3.1)	1.6	(0.9)	5.6	(1.9)	1.4	(0.9)	3.5	(1.4)	5.2	(1.7)	3.9	(1.5)
	Poland	81.3	(2.7)	14.1	(2.4)	4.5	(1.4)	3.5	(1.2)	10.5	(2.1)	2.8	(1.2)	2.3	(1.0)
	Portugal	66.7	(4.0)	1.9	(1.5)	0.3	(0.2)	15.9	(2.7)	42.1	(4.4)	18.3	(2.8)	6.2	(3.2)
	Slovak Republic	41.3	(4.7)	7.3	(2.8)	15.6	(3.0)	17.3	(4.4)	28.9	(4.8)	5.2	(3.6)	1.8	(1.8)
	Slovenia	86.6	(7.3)	0.0	c	6.8	(0.1)	0.0	c	17.6	(8.2)	13.4	(9.1)	3.1	(3.2)
	Spain	65.8	(2.6)	1.1	(0.6)	1.7	(0.6)	10.9	(1.7)	13.6	(2.2)	31.7	(2.5)	22.2	(3.3)
	Sweden	49.6	(3.6)	0.6	(0.6)	1.9	(1.1)	5.6	(1.8)	4.2	(1.7)	16.9	(2.4)	9.8	(2.6)
	Switzerland	79.2	(2.6)	60.7	(3.2)	36.0	(2.8)	3.3	(1.4)	12.6	(2.3)	1.5	(0.5)	1.7	(0.8)
	Turkey	c	c	c	c	c	c	c	c	c	c	c	c	c	c
	United Kingdom	26.8	(15.4)	3.0	(2.6)	9.9	(1.7)	22.2	(18.9)	4.0	(3.8)	66.8	(17.7)	25.5	(22.4)
	United States	81.9	(3.4)	17.3	(3.5)	19.0	(3.0)	7.4	(2.6)	18.2	(4.5)	6.2	(3.5)	4.8	(2.3)
	OECD average	50.9	(1.0)	16.0	(0.6)	15.3	(0.4)	12.9	(0.9)	16.1	(0.9)	19.9	(1.1)	8.9	(1.1)
Partners	Albania	43.7	(5.1)	30.0	(5.8)	42.6	(3.6)	16.1	(3.7)	13.9	(3.2)	15.4	(3.9)	12.4	(3.8)
	Argentina	11.7	(3.6)	12.9	(3.5)	5.5	(2.1)	20.3	(3.3)	16.0	(2.9)	40.9	(4.3)	17.2	(4.4)
	Azerbaijan	61.3	(4.9)	42.6	(4.8)	49.6	(5.0)	75.0	(3.8)	44.4	(5.0)	29.5	(4.1)	18.3	(4.5)
	Brazil	32.8	(3.4)	6.0	(1.0)	5.5	(1.1)	14.6	(2.2)	9.9	(1.8)	8.7	(1.7)	22.7	(3.2)
	Bulgaria	47.1	(8.0)	16.9	(5.2)	2.2	(1.3)	37.9	(8.0)	22.3	(7.7)	26.0	(6.8)	6.4	(4.0)
	Colombia	16.2	(2.7)	27.7	(4.2)	13.5	(3.0)	14.8	(2.5)	22.0	(4.3)	19.6	(4.1)	11.4	(2.9)
	Croatia	c	c	c	c	c	c	c	c	c	c	c	c	c	c
	Dubai (UAE)	26.8	(0.5)	58.9	(0.8)	34.8	(0.1)	32.6	(0.8)	12.0	(0.8)	48.2	(0.9)	13.9	(0.5)
	Hong Kong-China	0.7	(0.7)	78.1	(3.9)	16.8	(3.2)	27.0	(3.9)	10.9	(3.1)	13.8	(2.4)	41.3	(7.4)
	Indonesia	20.6	(3.9)	52.5	(5.3)	32.5	(4.0)	36.6	(5.0)	33.6	(4.8)	18.7	(4.1)	13.1	(4.1)
	Jordan	51.1	(3.8)	23.7	(3.1)	21.8	(3.3)	26.3	(3.1)	21.0	(3.0)	20.8	(2.6)	9.4	(3.0)
	Kazakhstan	53.1	(3.9)	25.4	(3.0)	19.7	(2.7)	51.7	(3.9)	32.4	(3.5)	5.9	(1.8)	6.4	(2.1)
	Kyrgyzstan	54.7	(4.3)	49.4	(3.7)	35.6	(3.8)	25.6	(3.8)	63.4	(4.1)	18.9	(3.2)	19.9	(4.0)
	Latvia	20.0	(2.7)	23.5	(3.0)	3.1	(1.2)	6.4	(1.6)	31.8	(3.9)	16.9	(2.7)	0.9	(0.9)
	Liechtenstein	67.7	(0.7)	66.7	(0.5)	74.5	(0.5)	3.3	(0.2)	0.0	c	0.0	c	7.3	(0.1)
	Lithuania	45.6	(3.3)	11.1	(2.3)	3.6	(1.0)	25.1	(3.4)	38.6	(3.8)	29.7	(3.4)	9.9	(2.7)
	Macao-China	6.4	(0.0)	67.2	(0.1)	44.0	(0.0)	9.2	(0.1)	0.0	c	25.7	(0.1)	1.3	(0.1)
	Montenegro	c	c	c	c	c	c	c	c	c	c	c	c	c	c
	Panama	22.5	(6.6)	27.9	(6.1)	25.5	(4.3)	11.1	(5.0)	19.2	(6.2)	15.1	(4.2)	9.2	(4.9)
	Peru	16.8	(2.4)	13.3	(3.2)	6.8	(1.9)	9.6	(2.6)	13.9	(2.9)	14.9	(2.9)	11.0	(3.3)
	Qatar	47.2	(0.4)	48.7	(0.4)	14.7	(0.1)	37.5	(0.4)	14.9	(0.3)	42.2	(0.4)	4.0	(0.3)
	Romania	14.6	(2.7)	56.0	(3.4)	7.7	(2.2)	14.0	(2.9)	34.4	(3.2)	5.7	(2.0)	7.1	(2.0)
	Russian Federation	27.8	(4.0)	13.5	(2.8)	13.9	(2.5)	47.8	(3.7)	43.8	(4.8)	12.3	(2.8)	6.4	(2.9)
	Serbia	54.2	(17.0)	27.6	(17.9)	8.0	(2.6)	0.0	c	18.4	(19.0)	28.6	(16.6)	0.0	c
	Shanghai-China	58.6	(4.5)	24.6	(4.8)	12.6	(2.9)	40.5	(5.5)	6.8	(2.6)	7.9	(3.3)	1.6	(1.6)
	Singapore	29.0	(3.4)	80.1	(2.8)	12.1	(0.3)	10.6	(2.6)	6.7	(1.9)	3.8	(1.4)	4.0	(1.0)
	Chinese Taipei	55.4	(7.1)	20.0	(4.6)	14.1	(2.8)	28.0	(6.9)	19.2	(5.7)	11.6	(4.5)	1.3	(1.3)
	Thailand	37.7	(5.6)	48.7	(4.6)	62.5	(3.8)	37.1	(4.9)	34.2	(5.4)	13.2	(4.8)	8.7	(4.0)
	Trinidad and Tobago	22.3	(0.7)	51.4	(0.7)	13.8	(0.2)	6.3	(0.4)	9.9	(0.4)	2.1	(0.2)	9.1	(0.7)
	Tunisia	89.5	(3.2)	20.8	(5.3)	7.1	(2.0)	0.2	(0.1)	0.0	c	12.0	(3.5)	3.8	(2.3)
	Uruguay	42.5	(4.3)	7.5	(2.6)	1.5	(0.9)	5.0	(1.6)	16.2	(3.2)	9.3	(2.8)	11.9	(2.9)

StatLink http://dx.doi.org/10.1787/888932343285

[Part 2/2]

School admittance policies, by lower or upper secondary level of education

Table IV.3.2c *Results based on school principals' reports*

		Upper secondary education (ISCED 3)													
		Percentage of students in schools where the principal reported the following factors to be "always" considered for admittance at school													
		Residence in a particular area		Students' academic records		Recommendations of feeder schools		Parents' endorsement of the instructional or religious philosophy of the school		Students' needs or desires for a special programme		Attendance of other family members at the school		Other	
		%	S.E.	%	S.E.	%	S.E.	%	S.E.	%	S.E.	%	S.E.	%	S.E.
OECD	Australia	29.1	(3.8)	24.4	(4.1)	19.3	(3.6)	27.4	(3.5)	16.2	(3.6)	35.8	(4.2)	13.6	(3.5)
	Austria	29.0	(3.3)	64.9	(2.8)	4.7	(2.0)	5.4	(1.7)	40.7	(3.9)	20.3	(3.1)	7.6	(3.0)
	Belgium	1.5	(0.8)	14.4	(2.3)	3.4	(1.3)	36.1	(3.2)	13.2	(2.0)	16.6	(2.0)	5.8	(2.0)
	Canada	73.7	(1.7)	16.3	(1.6)	23.6	(1.8)	15.3	(1.7)	19.0	(2.2)	12.9	(1.3)	6.8	(1.7)
	Chile	4.1	(1.7)	34.9	(3.7)	14.5	(2.6)	17.4	(2.8)	23.9	(3.3)	22.4	(3.7)	17.3	(3.9)
	Czech Republic	1.4	(1.0)	94.1	(2.9)	16.7	(4.2)	8.4	(2.6)	13.5	(4.4)	0.4	(0.4)	6.4	(2.6)
	Denmark	58.4	(27.6)	73.1	(25.4)	66.2	(26.0)	0.0	c	0.0	c	0.0	c	10.1	(15.9)
	Estonia	41.5	(8.7)	40.7	(7.7)	9.5	(5.3)	20.1	(5.3)	16.2	(4.8)	21.9	(6.8)	16.4	(8.4)
	Finland	c	c	c	c	c	c	c	c	c	c	c	c	c	c
	France	w	w	w	w	w	w	w	w	w	w	w	w	w	w
	Germany	47.0	(14.2)	32.5	(14.2)	13.4	(5.1)	0.0	c	40.0	(15.9)	2.3	(1.4)	16.9	(14.8)
	Greece	69.3	(3.9)	3.8	(1.1)	2.7	(1.2)	7.9	(2.1)	14.1	(3.1)	20.8	(3.4)	3.7	(1.4)
	Hungary	3.0	(1.5)	95.5	(1.4)	5.2	(1.9)	23.6	(3.7)	83.6	(3.6)	8.0	(2.4)	4.6	(2.3)
	Iceland	c	c	c	c	c	c	c	c	c	c	c	c	c	c
	Ireland	30.8	(4.2)	8.0	(2.4)	19.2	(3.7)	27.1	(4.3)	9.8	(2.6)	53.5	(4.0)	23.1	(3.9)
	Israel	28.7	(2.9)	50.1	(3.9)	33.5	(4.1)	32.1	(3.2)	28.0	(3.7)	8.0	(2.2)	18.1	(4.2)
	Italy	29.3	(1.9)	32.0	(2.0)	26.5	(1.9)	35.6	(2.0)	50.9	(1.8)	27.6	(1.5)	11.8	(1.8)
	Japan	21.5	(2.7)	88.0	(2.3)	21.1	(3.1)	10.3	(2.4)	26.9	(3.1)	1.5	(0.9)	3.2	(1.2)
	Korea	12.6	(2.4)	52.1	(4.1)	9.1	(2.1)	5.7	(2.1)	18.8	(3.4)	3.5	(1.6)	3.1	(1.8)
	Luxembourg	42.3	(0.3)	40.7	(0.3)	18.8	(0.3)	13.7	(0.3)	10.5	(0.2)	59.9	(0.3)	9.6	(0.2)
	Mexico	7.4	(1.7)	51.0	(2.4)	7.3	(1.4)	13.9	(1.6)	21.2	(1.9)	2.8	(1.0)	14.3	(2.5)
	Netherlands	16.7	(4.7)	81.6	(4.9)	90.3	(3.8)	16.8	(4.7)	5.4	(2.1)	5.7	(2.7)	0.0	c
	New Zealand	50.5	(3.0)	21.1	(2.8)	21.8	(2.7)	20.1	(2.1)	12.6	(2.1)	35.1	(3.0)	22.1	(4.5)
	Norway	c	c	c	c	c	c	c	c	c	c	c	c	c	c
	Poland	c	c	c	c	c	c	c	c	c	c	c	c	c	c
	Portugal	49.0	(4.3)	0.3	(0.2)	0.4	(0.3)	28.0	(4.2)	62.9	(4.4)	28.1	(4.3)	2.1	(1.5)
	Slovak Republic	1.2	(1.2)	89.8	(3.4)	17.5	(4.4)	19.8	(4.1)	52.3	(6.1)	0.0	c	11.3	(4.1)
	Slovenia	6.6	(0.1)	25.1	(0.2)	7.1	(0.1)	7.2	(0.1)	78.2	(0.2)	0.3	(0.0)	2.4	(0.0)
	Spain	c	c	c	c	c	c	c	c	c	c	c	c	c	c
	Sweden	0.0	c	77.4	(14.4)	0.0	c	0.0	c	63.6	(19.0)	0.0	c	7.7	(6.0)
	Switzerland	59.9	(8.6)	60.1	(6.8)	10.9	(3.6)	1.9	(2.7)	38.5	(9.3)	0.0	c	3.2	(2.4)
	Turkey	41.3	(3.4)	34.1	(3.7)	17.1	(3.5)	0.0	c	23.1	(3.5)	8.3	(2.2)	11.6	(2.5)
	United Kingdom	55.5	(2.9)	10.2	(2.1)	10.7	(1.9)	12.7	(2.4)	3.1	(1.2)	38.4	(3.7)	13.7	(2.9)
	United States	77.0	(2.8)	23.6	(2.9)	19.6	(3.1)	10.0	(2.4)	12.3	(2.7)	4.8	(1.5)	9.7	(4.6)
	OECD average	31.7	(1.3)	44.3	(1.3)	18.2	(1.1)	14.9	(0.6)	28.5	(1.1)	15.7	(0.6)	9.9	(1.0)
Partners	Albania	39.7	(5.0)	30.6	(5.1)	40.5	(4.3)	18.9	(4.3)	25.6	(3.6)	15.3	(3.8)	12.5	(4.0)
	Argentina	11.1	(2.9)	23.5	(4.0)	7.1	(2.9)	44.8	(5.1)	33.8	(4.3)	53.2	(4.3)	16.3	(3.5)
	Azerbaijan	66.2	(4.5)	43.6	(4.6)	54.0	(5.2)	71.8	(4.0)	41.0	(4.7)	33.6	(4.3)	19.0	(4.5)
	Brazil	30.7	(3.2)	8.2	(1.3)	5.7	(1.3)	22.4	(2.5)	13.9	(1.6)	11.0	(2.4)	21.1	(3.3)
	Bulgaria	16.6	(4.0)	80.6	(3.0)	2.4	(1.4)	54.8	(4.7)	22.4	(4.5)	12.8	(2.7)	4.9	(3.7)
	Colombia	16.3	(2.4)	33.0	(3.7)	12.8	(2.8)	21.7	(3.6)	23.8	(4.4)	18.2	(3.5)	15.8	(3.5)
	Croatia	9.7	(2.4)	93.5	(1.8)	5.0	(1.8)	15.8	(2.6)	26.6	(3.5)	2.9	(1.2)	3.2	(1.6)
	Dubai (UAE)	22.0	(0.1)	74.1	(0.2)	38.0	(0.2)	37.6	(0.2)	12.0	(0.2)	48.7	(0.3)	12.6	(0.1)
	Hong Kong-China	0.7	(0.7)	83.7	(2.7)	17.4	(3.4)	26.8	(3.6)	9.6	(2.4)	8.4	(1.8)	32.7	(5.6)
	Indonesia	23.8	(5.2)	69.7	(5.2)	31.9	(6.2)	32.0	(5.6)	52.6	(5.9)	13.1	(3.8)	14.5	(5.7)
	Jordan	c	c	c	c	c	c	c	c	c	c	c	c	c	c
	Kazakhstan	38.6	(6.3)	47.3	(6.8)	25.4	(6.4)	64.8	(5.8)	45.9	(6.6)	12.7	(4.6)	9.1	(4.0)
	Kyrgyzstan	43.1	(5.8)	54.1	(6.1)	41.5	(6.7)	31.5	(5.6)	65.4	(6.3)	18.3	(4.5)	21.4	(6.6)
	Latvia	27.4	(7.6)	44.4	(8.9)	1.5	(1.0)	2.1	(1.5)	37.2	(9.3)	21.0	(6.2)	0.0	c
	Liechtenstein	c	c	c	c	c	c	c	c	c	c	c	c	c	c
	Lithuania	c	c	c	c	c	c	c	c	c	c	c	c	c	c
	Macao-China	5.0	(0.1)	61.3	(0.2)	45.3	(0.2)	5.5	(0.1)	0.0	c	22.8	(0.2)	0.7	(0.1)
	Montenegro	6.7	(0.0)	53.4	(0.1)	16.1	(0.1)	13.5	(0.1)	55.0	(0.1)	2.0	(0.0)	7.3	(0.0)
	Panama	19.2	(5.7)	43.4	(6.2)	25.0	(5.5)	16.2	(4.7)	10.9	(2.9)	21.1	(5.4)	5.4	(1.8)
	Peru	11.3	(1.9)	21.7	(3.3)	5.4	(1.8)	20.3	(3.4)	15.4	(2.6)	16.5	(2.8)	13.5	(3.2)
	Qatar	45.3	(0.1)	42.6	(0.1)	15.8	(0.1)	45.0	(0.1)	17.5	(0.1)	43.9	(0.1)	11.8	(0.1)
	Romania	c	c	c	c	c	c	c	c	c	c	c	c	c	c
	Russian Federation	26.7	(3.8)	19.6	(4.7)	10.4	(3.4)	58.6	(5.5)	56.1	(5.3)	14.3	(3.8)	9.5	(3.4)
	Serbia	4.3	(1.5)	84.1	(2.7)	8.3	(2.8)	14.5	(3.4)	70.2	(3.0)	1.1	(0.9)	3.6	(1.3)
	Shanghai-China	28.4	(3.9)	75.2	(4.0)	17.4	(4.4)	46.0	(5.0)	15.6	(3.8)	5.6	(2.4)	5.2	(2.2)
	Singapore	26.0	(0.3)	82.0	(0.2)	12.4	(0.3)	11.4	(1.1)	9.1	(1.0)	5.4	(0.1)	6.6	(1.3)
	Chinese Taipei	33.1	(4.7)	60.9	(3.7)	14.7	(3.5)	29.5	(4.5)	45.2	(4.9)	18.0	(3.3)	5.2	(2.8)
	Thailand	38.1	(3.8)	55.5	(4.1)	61.5	(4.4)	34.2	(3.9)	41.9	(4.3)	14.1	(3.1)	11.5	(3.7)
	Trinidad and Tobago	13.3	(0.3)	60.4	(0.4)	13.5	(0.3)	7.0	(0.2)	6.5	(0.2)	4.0	(0.1)	11.4	(0.4)
	Tunisia	88.5	(4.2)	15.0	(5.0)	7.1	(2.2)	3.2	(1.9)	8.0	(3.6)	8.0	(3.0)	0.0	c
	Uruguay	28.6	(2.7)	11.9	(2.5)	2.0	(1.3)	19.0	(3.1)	14.0	(2.7)	19.3	(3.1)	4.3	(1.3)

StatLink http://dx.doi.org/10.1787/888932343285

[Part 1/1]

Table IV.3.3a Horizontal differentiation at the school level: school transfer policies

Results based on school principals' reports

		Percentage of students in schools where the principal reported that a student in national modal grade for 15-year-olds in the school would be "likely" or "very likely" transferred to another school because of the following reasons:												Percentage of students in schools where the principal reported that a student in national modal grade for 15-year-olds in the school would be "very likely" transferred to another school because of one of the following reasons: "low academic achievement", "behavioural problems" or "special learning needs"	
		Low academic achievement		High academic achievement		Behavioural problems		Special learning needs		Parents' or guardians' request		Other			
		%	S.E.	%	S.E.	%	S.E.	%	S.E.	%	S.E.	%	S.E.	%	S.E.
OECD	Australia	5.5	(1.4)	9.3	(1.7)	34.5	(3.0)	14.0	(2.3)	47.0	(2.9)	14.8	(2.6)	2.9	(1.1)
	Austria	68.1	(2.9)	9.8	(2.6)	57.8	(4.2)	33.1	(4.2)	56.5	(4.1)	34.4	(5.4)	52.2	(3.8)
	Belgium	63.8	(2.9)	6.0	(1.5)	73.6	(2.6)	65.0	(3.0)	64.4	(2.9)	32.5	(4.2)	48.3	(3.1)
	Canada	13.6	(1.5)	1.7	(0.6)	41.2	(2.3)	33.4	(2.1)	61.8	(2.5)	29.7	(3.1)	12.6	(1.4)
	Chile	29.9	(3.6)	22.5	(3.0)	75.1	(3.6)	49.8	(4.8)	88.0	(2.9)	55.9	(7.4)	24.0	(3.8)
	Czech Republic	35.7	(2.8)	12.2	(2.5)	35.7	(3.5)	13.4	(2.7)	60.1	(4.5)	18.6	(2.7)	22.1	(2.6)
	Denmark	13.2	(2.5)	6.5	(1.6)	67.1	(3.7)	38.5	(3.7)	74.9	(3.0)	47.0	(4.0)	6.1	(1.7)
	Estonia	19.2	(2.9)	12.9	(2.5)	44.4	(4.2)	64.5	(4.1)	91.1	(2.2)	52.4	(5.2)	9.9	(2.3)
	Finland	6.2	(2.0)	1.3	(1.0)	20.7	(3.3)	21.7	(3.4)	54.3	(3.9)	22.9	(3.7)	1.7	(1.1)
	France	w	w	w	w	w	w	w	w	w	w	w	w	w	w
	Germany	40.2	(3.4)	5.8	(1.8)	34.8	(3.8)	27.0	(3.2)	46.0	(3.8)	22.6	(4.2)	24.0	(3.4)
	Greece	38.8	(4.3)	10.4	(3.2)	88.0	(2.4)	67.9	(3.6)	90.1	(2.5)	81.2	(3.5)	42.2	(4.2)
	Hungary	54.3	(3.9)	9.5	(1.7)	61.1	(3.6)	17.7	(2.9)	69.4	(3.7)	30.8	(4.4)	14.1	(3.2)
	Iceland	0.4	(0.1)	7.7	(0.1)	38.0	(0.2)	26.2	(0.2)	78.7	(0.2)	5.2	(0.3)	0.0	(0.0)
	Ireland	3.1	(1.5)	2.5	(1.4)	26.8	(4.4)	6.2	(2.1)	45.6	(5.1)	27.7	(4.9)	0.8	(0.7)
	Israel	38.5	(4.2)	6.5	(1.8)	76.2	(3.3)	67.7	(3.7)	80.0	(2.5)	57.9	(4.8)	23.1	(3.6)
	Italy	69.3	(1.9)	5.3	(0.9)	41.0	(2.1)	31.9	(2.1)	88.7	(1.1)	41.7	(2.3)	20.1	(2.0)
	Japan	66.5	(3.1)	1.4	(0.8)	53.4	(3.5)	25.5	(3.5)	49.0	(4.0)	65.3	(3.9)	8.4	(2.1)
	Korea	35.9	(4.2)	15.7	(3.2)	69.8	(3.9)	23.8	(3.8)	81.0	(3.3)	52.1	(4.5)	6.3	(2.2)
	Luxembourg	54.7	(0.1)	32.8	(0.1)	81.7	(0.1)	77.1	(0.1)	94.6	(0.1)	67.8	(0.1)	68.0	(0.1)
	Mexico	40.9	(1.9)	22.7	(1.7)	62.5	(2.0)	47.3	(2.0)	90.0	(1.1)	52.3	(2.7)	32.8	(2.1)
	Netherlands	30.4	(2.8)	17.1	(2.6)	57.0	(4.3)	61.2	(3.7)	55.1	(3.9)	25.6	(5.1)	15.2	(2.8)
	New Zealand	1.5	(0.6)	4.7	(1.4)	21.3	(2.8)	7.2	(1.7)	31.6	(3.2)	14.2	(3.5)	2.7	(0.8)
	Norway	1.5	(0.9)	0.1	(0.1)	39.3	(3.7)	36.7	(3.4)	56.8	(4.0)	27.9	(2.8)	1.4	(1.0)
	Poland	6.6	(2.1)	5.9	(2.2)	43.2	(3.9)	56.5	(4.4)	93.7	(2.1)	51.6	(5.5)	8.2	(2.4)
	Portugal	14.3	(2.7)	5.9	(1.9)	39.6	(4.1)	16.9	(3.0)	90.2	(2.4)	59.2	(5.2)	0.8	(0.6)
	Slovak Republic	49.7	(3.4)	12.5	(3.2)	60.8	(3.8)	42.3	(4.6)	88.5	(2.7)	43.1	(4.7)	30.2	(4.2)
	Slovenia	88.8	(0.5)	21.9	(0.2)	75.9	(0.3)	29.1	(0.4)	68.3	(0.3)	53.4	(0.5)	21.8	(0.2)
	Spain	8.8	(1.7)	2.7	(0.9)	38.5	(2.7)	38.3	(2.8)	59.0	(3.2)	33.2	(3.7)	7.3	(1.6)
	Sweden	1.9	(1.1)	0.7	(0.8)	15.6	(2.8)	37.8	(4.1)	73.1	(3.8)	17.1	(3.6)	3.4	(1.5)
	Switzerland	33.9	(3.2)	32.0	(3.3)	59.4	(4.2)	50.5	(3.5)	50.8	(3.7)	34.1	(4.4)	21.3	(2.5)
	Turkey	56.4	(4.0)	48.5	(4.1)	87.8	(2.8)	71.4	(3.3)	98.2	(1.0)	82.8	(3.5)	35.1	(4.1)
	United Kingdom	4.1	(1.2)	4.8	(1.7)	31.3	(3.3)	16.0	(2.7)	43.1	(3.0)	11.2	(2.9)	2.2	(0.9)
	United States	12.3	(3.1)	2.2	(1.2)	42.3	(4.0)	18.5	(3.4)	44.3	(4.1)	14.7	(4.3)	12.6	(2.9)
	OECD average	30.5	(0.5)	11.0	(0.4)	51.4	(0.6)	37.4	(0.6)	68.6	(0.5)	38.8	(0.7)	17.6	(0.4)
Partners	Albania	41.0	(3.8)	32.8	(3.6)	44.4	(3.9)	80.7	(3.6)	99.0	(0.9)	72.4	(4.4)	17.4	(3.1)
	Argentina	27.2	(3.7)	10.2	(2.7)	63.3	(4.2)	56.6	(4.0)	91.9	(2.7)	55.8	(5.1)	14.6	(3.3)
	Azerbaijan	14.6	(4.1)	20.2	(5.5)	23.3	(5.0)	33.3	(6.1)	46.0	(5.3)	28.2	(4.9)	15.4	(4.1)
	Brazil	25.0	(2.8)	2.9	(0.6)	59.9	(3.9)	22.0	(2.8)	91.5	(1.9)	74.1	(3.0)	13.8	(2.0)
	Bulgaria	47.6	(5.6)	13.8	(3.8)	93.4	(2.8)	52.2	(5.2)	98.4	(1.1)	82.5	(4.5)	34.5	(5.8)
	Colombia	46.3	(5.7)	14.7	(3.8)	73.6	(4.7)	63.8	(5.5)	94.1	(2.2)	83.2	(3.8)	41.3	(5.0)
	Croatia	69.7	(4.0)	10.2	(2.6)	56.9	(4.2)	55.1	(4.1)	89.6	(2.8)	51.7	(4.4)	18.3	(2.8)
	Dubai (UAE)	26.0	(0.1)	12.8	(0.1)	53.5	(0.1)	49.4	(0.2)	67.8	(0.2)	45.7	(0.2)	20.1	(0.1)
	Hong Kong-China	76.1	(3.9)	38.4	(4.1)	77.1	(3.7)	59.4	(3.9)	82.8	(3.3)	41.9	(6.6)	12.1	(3.0)
	Indonesia	39.4	(4.5)	10.1	(2.7)	79.7	(3.8)	56.8	(5.0)	94.6	(2.0)	80.8	(3.9)	40.5	(4.0)
	Jordan	33.2	(3.5)	38.3	(3.7)	92.3	(2.2)	63.6	(4.2)	93.4	(2.0)	74.8	(4.9)	46.0	(4.2)
	Kazakhstan	19.2	(3.6)	32.1	(4.0)	37.2	(4.0)	57.6	(4.5)	81.1	(3.5)	53.6	(4.5)	12.9	(2.5)
	Kyrgyzstan	66.6	(4.5)	55.7	(4.8)	72.8	(3.6)	81.4	(3.7)	92.7	(2.5)	65.8	(5.5)	38.2	(4.3)
	Latvia	30.7	(4.3)	31.3	(4.4)	51.5	(4.6)	87.2	(2.8)	96.4	(1.8)	77.8	(4.3)	14.7	(4.2)
	Liechtenstein	36.5	(0.4)	52.3	(0.4)	63.0	(0.4)	41.8	(0.3)	66.8	(0.4)	48.5	(0.6)	0.0	c
	Lithuania	33.5	(4.2)	28.3	(3.9)	60.2	(4.5)	26.2	(3.5)	94.5	(1.8)	66.6	(6.4)	6.8	(2.1)
	Macao-China	96.5	(0.0)	43.3	(0.0)	99.6	(0.0)	73.8	(0.0)	80.9	(0.0)	72.5	(0.0)	47.7	(0.0)
	Montenegro	31.4	(0.3)	23.7	(0.2)	39.2	(0.3)	65.1	(0.3)	87.9	(0.1)	80.0	(0.1)	7.1	(0.1)
	Panama	45.1	(5.7)	5.2	(1.8)	78.7	(4.5)	37.5	(4.5)	89.8	(1.6)	71.4	(6.8)	32.4	(5.6)
	Peru	24.2	(3.4)	19.1	(3.0)	63.6	(4.1)	43.4	(3.7)	93.7	(1.8)	59.2	(4.2)	26.8	(3.7)
	Qatar	34.6	(0.1)	24.9	(0.1)	71.3	(0.1)	56.5	(0.1)	88.3	(0.1)	60.9	(0.1)	44.9	(0.1)
	Romania	34.9	(3.7)	20.7	(3.7)	57.6	(3.9)	71.1	(3.8)	97.9	(1.3)	73.9	(4.1)	40.1	(4.0)
	Russian Federation	23.9	(3.2)	19.6	(3.2)	22.4	(3.4)	55.6	(4.7)	77.1	(3.4)	47.8	(6.1)	13.6	(2.5)
	Serbia	77.8	(3.7)	53.3	(3.7)	89.7	(2.1)	78.6	(3.4)	99.2	(0.5)	78.7	(4.5)	29.8	(3.8)
	Shanghai-China	40.3	(4.0)	26.5	(3.7)	49.1	(3.7)	61.7	(4.8)	84.0	(3.4)	66.9	(4.3)	15.3	(3.0)
	Singapore	1.7	(0.5)	12.7	(0.4)	10.1	(0.2)	11.8	(0.3)	36.9	(0.7)	14.5	(0.7)	0.7	(0.0)
	Chinese Taipei	82.7	(3.0)	39.0	(3.7)	94.4	(1.9)	82.5	(3.5)	91.5	(2.0)	81.4	(3.6)	37.2	(3.9)
	Thailand	47.8	(3.6)	30.0	(3.3)	88.1	(2.1)	41.4	(3.6)	94.3	(1.6)	69.6	(4.8)	9.8	(2.6)
	Trinidad and Tobago	7.0	(0.2)	29.0	(0.3)	39.6	(0.4)	41.0	(0.3)	86.0	(0.2)	47.0	(0.5)	13.8	(0.2)
	Tunisia	13.9	(2.8)	36.7	(3.1)	68.1	(4.2)	55.2	(4.6)	98.8	(1.1)	74.2	(3.8)	26.0	(3.7)
	Uruguay	6.8	(1.7)	2.3	(0.9)	36.8	(3.1)	39.0	(3.1)	90.3	(2.1)	46.1	(4.1)	8.5	(2.0)

StatLink http://dx.doi.org/10.1787/888932343285

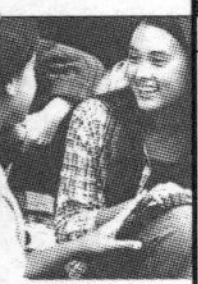

[Part 1/2]

Horizontal differentiation at the school level: school transfer policies, by lower or upper secondary level of education

Table IV.3.3b *Results based on school principals' reports*

	Lower secondary education (ISCED 2)											
	Percentage of students in schools where the principal reports that a student in national modal grade for 15-year-olds in the school would be "likely" or "very likely" transferred to another school because of the following reasons:											
	Low academic achievement		High academic achievement		Behavioural problems		Special learning needs		Parents' or guardians' request		Other	
	%	S.E.	%	S.E.	%	S.E.	%	S.E.	%	S.E.	%	S.E.
OECD												
Australia	5.1	(1.4)	9.5	(1.9)	35.8	(3.2)	15.0	(2.5)	48.8	(3.1)	15.9	(2.8)
Austria	35.4	(12.6)	28.3	(13.0)	83.3	(5.9)	43.5	(13.8)	79.0	(8.3)	47.2	(15.0)
Belgium	40.9	(8.0)	20.9	(7.2)	80.2	(6.0)	75.5	(6.4)	60.1	(7.9)	30.0	(8.5)
Canada	14.9	(2.1)	1.1	(0.6)	58.2	(3.2)	57.7	(2.8)	66.0	(3.5)	33.1	(4.7)
Chile	20.4	(5.6)	16.3	(4.3)	81.8	(7.9)	44.0	(8.2)	85.8	(7.4)	70.3	(11.4)
Czech Republic	9.4	(2.2)	18.0	(4.2)	27.3	(4.4)	19.8	(4.3)	57.8	(6.6)	15.6	(3.2)
Denmark	13.3	(2.5)	6.5	(1.6)	67.5	(3.7)	38.7	(3.7)	75.3	(3.0)	47.4	(4.0)
Estonia	19.1	(2.9)	12.9	(2.5)	44.3	(4.2)	64.7	(4.1)	91.1	(2.2)	52.4	(5.2)
Finland	6.2	(2.0)	1.3	(0.9)	20.8	(3.3)	21.7	(3.4)	54.3	(3.9)	22.9	(3.7)
France	w	w	w	w	w	w	w	w	w	w	w	w
Germany	40.1	(3.4)	5.9	(1.8)	35.1	(3.9)	26.9	(3.3)	46.5	(3.8)	22.9	(4.2)
Greece	26.1	(11.1)	23.0	(10.9)	89.9	(7.1)	76.9	(8.9)	96.5	(3.5)	74.8	(10.9)
Hungary	5.0	(4.3)	26.4	(9.7)	17.0	(7.0)	8.0	(4.8)	54.9	(11.1)	33.8	(12.3)
Iceland	0.4	(0.1)	7.7	(0.1)	38.0	(0.2)	26.2	(0.2)	78.7	(0.2)	5.2	(0.3)
Ireland	2.7	(1.4)	2.8	(1.6)	27.2	(4.5)	5.7	(2.0)	46.4	(5.3)	28.5	(5.1)
Israel	33.4	(6.3)	11.2	(4.9)	73.5	(7.3)	76.1	(5.1)	88.4	(3.1)	69.5	(8.1)
Italy	15.6	(23.1)	84.4	(23.1)	0.0	c	0.0	c	0.0	c	0.0	c
Japan	c	c	c	c	c	c	c	c	c	c	c	c
Korea	2.3	(2.4)	34.7	(10.1)	80.6	(14.0)	11.4	(8.0)	92.5	(6.1)	23.3	(16.3)
Luxembourg	48.0	(0.2)	39.8	(0.2)	85.7	(0.2)	80.4	(0.2)	94.8	(0.1)	71.1	(0.3)
Mexico	45.6	(3.9)	20.3	(3.5)	73.9	(2.9)	48.1	(4.1)	89.4	(2.2)	51.0	(4.8)
Netherlands	26.3	(3.2)	21.9	(3.4)	60.8	(4.9)	64.5	(4.2)	56.4	(4.4)	27.3	(5.9)
New Zealand	0.4	(0.4)	2.6	(1.7)	19.5	(4.5)	5.3	(1.7)	31.2	(5.1)	10.2	(4.8)
Norway	1.5	(0.9)	0.1	(0.1)	39.3	(3.7)	36.7	(3.4)	56.8	(4.0)	27.9	(2.8)
Poland	6.2	(2.1)	5.8	(2.2)	43.1	(3.9)	57.0	(4.4)	93.8	(2.1)	51.7	(5.6)
Portugal	8.0	(1.8)	5.1	(2.1)	38.0	(4.6)	15.9	(4.4)	89.1	(3.2)	57.2	(6.5)
Slovak Republic	7.4	(3.1)	15.6	(5.2)	43.1	(5.9)	43.0	(6.2)	90.0	(3.7)	48.9	(7.3)
Slovenia	24.1	(12.0)	0.0	c	69.0	(11.7)	45.1	(14.9)	72.4	(11.3)	68.4	(16.2)
Spain	8.8	(1.7)	2.7	(0.9)	38.5	(2.7)	38.3	(2.8)	59.0	(3.2)	33.2	(3.7)
Sweden	1.9	(1.1)	0.7	(0.8)	15.8	(2.9)	38.0	(4.1)	74.2	(3.9)	17.4	(3.7)
Switzerland	27.0	(3.2)	34.9	(3.4)	62.2	(3.9)	49.2	(3.5)	51.6	(3.8)	33.7	(4.6)
Turkey	c	c	c	c	c	c	c	c	c	c	c	c
United Kingdom	0.0	c	38.1	(26.6)	53.7	(23.6)	3.1	(2.8)	54.3	(22.7)	47.7	(29.0)
United States	11.2	(3.7)	3.7	(2.4)	48.8	(5.7)	21.6	(4.7)	44.4	(5.5)	14.5	(6.0)
OECD average	16.3	(1.2)	16.2	(1.5)	50.1	(1.3)	37.4	(1.1)	67.1	(1.2)	37.2	(1.7)
Partners												
Albania	30.2	(4.4)	26.3	(4.7)	34.1	(4.7)	85.2	(4.1)	98.2	(1.8)	69.6	(6.3)
Argentina	22.3	(4.0)	15.3	(4.6)	58.8	(5.1)	56.6	(5.9)	95.2	(1.8)	54.0	(6.4)
Azerbaijan	14.5	(4.3)	20.6	(5.8)	23.0	(5.4)	32.4	(6.4)	44.5	(5.7)	28.6	(5.4)
Brazil	13.7	(2.7)	4.8	(1.6)	58.0	(4.7)	20.8	(3.7)	91.5	(2.7)	75.4	(4.4)
Bulgaria	46.2	(12.2)	40.9	(14.0)	96.9	(3.2)	63.5	(11.1)	100.0	(0.0)	81.8	(10.3)
Colombia	43.9	(6.0)	12.5	(3.3)	70.8	(5.0)	61.3	(6.0)	93.3	(2.6)	81.7	(4.8)
Croatia	c	c	c	c	c	c	c	c	c	c	c	c
Dubai (UAE)	17.5	(0.9)	12.7	(0.7)	47.6	(1.5)	34.3	(1.2)	70.2	(1.4)	41.8	(1.3)
Hong Kong-China	75.3	(4.5)	41.7	(4.5)	79.9	(3.7)	60.4	(4.2)	83.9	(3.3)	44.3	(7.5)
Indonesia	22.5	(5.3)	6.4	(3.2)	68.9	(6.0)	46.5	(6.9)	91.7	(3.2)	76.0	(5.3)
Jordan	33.2	(3.5)	38.3	(3.7)	92.3	(2.2)	63.6	(4.2)	93.4	(2.0)	74.8	(4.9)
Kazakhstan	17.0	(3.5)	31.8	(4.4)	32.7	(4.2)	57.8	(4.9)	80.5	(3.7)	53.0	(4.6)
Kyrgyzstan	65.2	(4.7)	54.6	(4.8)	71.7	(3.9)	82.1	(3.9)	93.4	(2.5)	66.1	(5.6)
Latvia	30.9	(4.3)	31.5	(4.4)	52.1	(4.6)	87.5	(2.8)	96.6	(1.8)	78.1	(4.3)
Liechtenstein	32.4	(0.8)	55.6	(0.7)	60.6	(0.6)	38.1	(0.7)	64.6	(0.6)	44.5	(0.9)
Lithuania	33.5	(4.2)	28.3	(3.9)	60.2	(4.5)	26.2	(3.5)	94.5	(1.8)	66.6	(6.4)
Macao-China	95.9	(0.0)	45.2	(0.1)	99.7	(0.0)	72.3	(0.1)	81.6	(0.1)	73.8	(0.1)
Montenegro	c	c	c	c	c	c	c	c	c	c	c	c
Panama	23.8	(4.6)	4.8	(1.7)	77.3	(5.7)	26.4	(4.8)	85.2	(3.8)	72.8	(7.8)
Peru	16.6	(3.2)	17.3	(3.5)	59.1	(4.8)	42.6	(4.3)	91.9	(2.6)	56.7	(5.7)
Qatar	40.6	(0.5)	26.7	(0.4)	76.0	(0.4)	70.3	(0.4)	94.8	(0.3)	88.8	(0.4)
Romania	34.9	(3.7)	20.7	(3.7)	57.6	(3.9)	71.1	(3.8)	97.9	(1.3)	73.9	(4.1)
Russian Federation	21.2	(3.3)	18.1	(3.3)	20.3	(3.8)	56.5	(5.2)	76.9	(3.5)	46.4	(7.2)
Serbia	0.0	c	0.0	c	0.0	c	0.0	c	0.0	c	0.0	c
Shanghai-China	31.6	(4.8)	32.5	(5.8)	31.0	(4.6)	54.7	(7.1)	81.5	(5.3)	60.2	(6.3)
Singapore	1.2	(0.9)	14.2	(2.9)	9.4	(2.2)	12.1	(2.3)	43.6	(3.9)	23.4	(3.8)
Chinese Taipei	65.7	(6.9)	42.2	(6.8)	92.0	(3.7)	80.8	(5.9)	96.9	(2.5)	92.6	(4.0)
Thailand	27.7	(5.1)	20.9	(3.8)	72.4	(4.7)	40.9	(5.8)	86.8	(4.2)	79.5	(5.4)
Trinidad and Tobago	6.9	(0.4)	36.7	(0.8)	44.5	(0.7)	47.9	(0.8)	89.8	(0.5)	46.8	(1.1)
Tunisia	16.9	(4.2)	73.2	(4.6)	73.7	(5.8)	54.3	(6.2)	97.8	(1.8)	74.9	(5.2)
Uruguay	2.8	(1.3)	1.2	(0.7)	38.0	(5.4)	43.6	(4.7)	92.3	(2.4)	40.7	(5.3)

StatLink http://dx.doi.org/10.1787/888932343285

[Part 2/2]

Table IV.3.3b Horizontal differentiation at the school level: school transfer policies, by lower or upper secondary level of education

Results based on school principals' reports

	Upper secondary education (ISCED 3)											
	Percentage of students in schools where the principal reports that a student in national modal grade for 15-year-olds in the school would be "likely" or "very likely" transferred to another school because of the following reasons:											
	Low academic achievement		High academic achievement		Behavioural problems		Special learning needs		Parents' or guardians' request		Other	
	%	S.E.	%	S.E.	%	S.E.	%	S.E.	%	S.E.	%	S.E.
OECD												
Australia	7.0	(2.6)	8.3	(2.8)	34.9	(5.0)	12.9	(3.5)	40.4	(5.0)	12.6	(3.8)
Austria	70.3	(2.9)	8.5	(2.4)	56.2	(4.3)	32.5	(4.4)	55.0	(4.3)	33.5	(5.5)
Belgium	65.8	(3.0)	4.8	(1.4)	73.1	(2.8)	64.0	(3.1)	64.8	(3.1)	32.7	(4.3)
Canada	13.4	(1.6)	1.8	(0.7)	38.3	(2.4)	29.3	(2.2)	61.1	(2.7)	29.1	(3.2)
Chile	30.4	(3.7)	22.8	(3.1)	74.8	(3.8)	50.1	(4.9)	88.1	(2.9)	55.0	(7.7)
Czech Republic	64.0	(4.6)	6.0	(2.3)	44.8	(5.0)	6.4	(2.5)	62.6	(5.9)	21.8	(4.5)
Denmark	c	c	c	c	c	c	c	c	c	c	c	c
Estonia	22.3	(8.4)	15.1	(3.2)	51.6	(10.2)	51.7	(9.8)	89.2	(7.9)	57.0	(13.5)
Finland	c	c	c	c	c	c	c	c	c	c	c	c
France	w	w	w	w	w	w	w	w	w	w	w	w
Germany	49.5	(19.3)	0.0	c	20.4	(16.1)	29.1	(20.8)	9.4	(7.7)	12.4	(11.5)
Greece	39.6	(4.5)	9.6	(3.4)	87.9	(2.5)	67.2	(3.8)	89.6	(2.7)	81.7	(3.7)
Hungary	59.5	(4.3)	7.7	(1.4)	65.7	(3.7)	18.7	(3.1)	70.9	(4.0)	30.5	(4.8)
Iceland	c	c	c	c	c	c	c	c	c	c	c	c
Ireland	3.8	(1.8)	2.1	(1.3)	26.1	(4.6)	7.1	(2.4)	44.2	(5.2)	26.4	(5.0)
Israel	39.2	(4.3)	5.8	(1.7)	76.5	(3.3)	66.6	(3.8)	78.8	(2.7)	56.6	(4.9)
Italy	69.4	(1.9)	5.2	(0.9)	41.1	(2.0)	31.9	(2.1)	88.6	(1.1)	41.7	(2.3)
Japan	66.5	(3.1)	1.4	(0.8)	53.4	(3.5)	25.5	(3.5)	49.0	(4.0)	65.3	(3.9)
Korea	37.4	(4.4)	14.8	(3.3)	69.3	(4.0)	24.3	(4.0)	80.4	(3.4)	53.8	(4.6)
Luxembourg	66.2	(0.3)	21.5	(0.2)	75.0	(0.3)	71.7	(0.3)	94.2	(0.1)	62.7	(0.4)
Mexico	37.9	(2.2)	24.2	(1.8)	54.9	(2.7)	46.8	(2.2)	90.4	(1.1)	53.0	(3.3)
Netherlands	42.4	(5.5)	2.5	(1.8)	45.8	(6.6)	51.4	(5.8)	51.5	(6.4)	20.6	(7.2)
New Zealand	1.6	(0.6)	4.8	(1.5)	21.4	(2.8)	7.3	(1.7)	31.7	(3.2)	14.5	(3.5)
Norway	c	c	c	c	c	c	c	c	c	c	c	c
Poland	c	c	c	c	c	c	c	c	c	c	c	c
Portugal	19.0	(3.6)	6.5	(2.4)	40.8	(5.3)	17.6	(3.7)	91.0	(2.7)	60.8	(6.4)
Slovak Republic	74.5	(4.2)	10.7	(4.2)	71.4	(5.4)	41.9	(6.1)	87.6	(3.7)	39.4	(6.4)
Slovenia	90.1	(0.1)	22.3	(0.2)	76.0	(0.1)	28.8	(0.2)	68.2	(0.2)	53.1	(0.2)
Spain	c	c	c	c	c	c	c	c	c	c	c	c
Sweden	0.0	c	0.0	c	0.0	c	24.4	(17.2)	3.9	(3.8)	2.0	(1.7)
Switzerland	63.9	(9.8)	19.4	(10.3)	47.8	(12.9)	56.1	(11.1)	47.6	(10.8)	36.2	(12.6)
Turkey	58.3	(4.2)	47.7	(4.2)	88.7	(2.8)	70.5	(3.4)	98.1	(1.0)	82.3	(3.6)
United Kingdom	4.0	(1.3)	3.8	(1.5)	31.9	(3.5)	16.2	(2.8)	43.6	(3.2)	11.1	(3.0)
United States	12.5	(3.2)	2.0	(1.1)	41.5	(4.0)	18.1	(3.6)	44.2	(4.2)	14.8	(4.3)
OECD average	41.1	(1.1)	10.3	(0.6)	52.2	(1.1)	35.9	(1.3)	63.9	(0.9)	39.3	(1.1)
Partners												
Albania	53.2	(6.5)	40.2	(5.7)	55.8	(6.0)	75.9	(5.4)	100.0	(0.0)	75.3	(5.3)
Argentina	30.4	(4.9)	6.9	(2.5)	66.1	(5.2)	56.7	(4.7)	89.8	(3.9)	56.9	(6.3)
Azerbaijan	14.7	(4.2)	19.8	(5.7)	23.6	(5.6)	34.4	(6.3)	47.9	(5.5)	27.6	(5.2)
Brazil	27.0	(3.0)	2.6	(0.6)	60.2	(4.0)	22.2	(2.8)	91.5	(1.9)	73.9	(3.0)
Bulgaria	47.7	(5.7)	13.4	(3.8)	93.3	(2.9)	52.0	(5.3)	98.4	(1.1)	82.5	(4.5)
Colombia	47.7	(6.0)	16.0	(4.3)	75.3	(4.8)	65.2	(5.5)	94.5	(2.2)	83.9	(3.6)
Croatia	69.7	(4.0)	10.2	(2.6)	56.9	(4.2)	55.1	(4.1)	89.6	(2.8)	51.7	(4.4)
Dubai (UAE)	27.4	(0.2)	12.8	(0.1)	54.4	(0.3)	51.9	(0.3)	67.4	(0.3)	46.4	(0.3)
Hong Kong-China	76.6	(3.9)	36.6	(4.0)	75.6	(3.9)	58.8	(4.0)	82.2	(3.6)	40.7	(6.6)
Indonesia	58.9	(6.9)	14.5	(4.9)	91.9	(3.8)	68.9	(7.2)	97.9	(1.7)	88.0	(5.2)
Jordan	c	c	c	c	c	c	c	c	c	c	c	c
Kazakhstan	26.9	(7.4)	33.2	(7.4)	53.5	(7.1)	56.9	(7.7)	83.3	(5.2)	56.0	(7.6)
Kyrgyzstan	73.0	(6.6)	60.5	(8.0)	77.8	(5.0)	78.4	(5.4)	89.9	(3.8)	64.2	(8.8)
Latvia	23.9	(8.3)	24.9	(7.7)	33.6	(9.4)	75.0	(10.3)	91.4	(5.6)	67.3	(12.8)
Liechtenstein	c	c	c	c	c	c	c	c	c	c	c	c
Lithuania	c	c	c	c	c	c	c	c	c	c	c	c
Macao-China	97.6	(0.1)	40.4	(0.2)	99.5	(0.0)	76.0	(0.1)	79.9	(0.2)	70.3	(0.2)
Montenegro	31.2	(0.1)	23.8	(0.1)	39.1	(0.1)	65.3	(0.1)	87.8	(0.1)	79.9	(0.1)
Panama	65.6	(6.0)	5.7	(2.7)	80.0	(5.4)	48.4	(7.2)	93.9	(2.5)	70.3	(9.4)
Peru	27.3	(3.9)	19.8	(3.4)	65.5	(4.3)	43.7	(4.2)	94.5	(1.6)	60.2	(4.6)
Qatar	33.3	(0.1)	24.5	(0.1)	70.2	(0.1)	53.5	(0.1)	86.8	(0.1)	54.3	(0.2)
Romania	c	c	c	c	c	c	c	c	c	c	c	c
Russian Federation	30.4	(5.6)	23.4	(5.4)	27.4	(5.3)	53.5	(6.4)	77.4	(4.7)	51.0	(6.8)
Serbia	77.8	(3.7)	53.3	(3.7)	89.6	(2.1)	78.6	(3.4)	99.2	(0.5)	78.7	(4.5)
Shanghai-China	47.8	(5.6)	21.3	(4.6)	64.4	(5.5)	67.6	(6.0)	86.2	(3.7)	73.0	(5.4)
Singapore	1.7	(0.5)	12.6	(0.4)	10.1	(0.2)	11.8	(0.3)	36.6	(0.8)	14.2	(0.6)
Chinese Taipei	91.8	(2.6)	37.3	(4.3)	95.6	(1.9)	83.4	(4.2)	88.7	(2.7)	76.1	(5.0)
Thailand	54.1	(3.8)	32.8	(3.7)	93.0	(2.1)	41.6	(4.0)	96.6	(1.5)	66.7	(5.4)
Trinidad and Tobago	7.1	(0.2)	24.9	(0.4)	37.1	(0.4)	37.3	(0.4)	84.0	(0.2)	47.1	(0.6)
Tunisia	11.5	(3.3)	8.5	(3.6)	63.8	(5.8)	55.9	(6.3)	99.5	(0.7)	73.7	(5.1)
Uruguay	9.4	(2.4)	3.1	(1.1)	36.1	(3.3)	36.0	(3.5)	88.9	(2.8)	49.5	(4.8)

StatLink http://dx.doi.org/10.1787/888932343285

[Part 1/1]

Table IV.3.4 Horizontal differentiation at the school level: ability grouping and reading performance

Results based on school principals' reports

		Percentage of students in schools where the principal reported within school (between and/or within classes)						Performance on the reading scale							
		No ability grouping		Ability grouping for some subjects		Ability grouping for all subjects		No ability grouping or ability grouping for some subjects		Ability grouping for all subjects		Observed difference (Ability grouping for all subjects – No ability grouping or Ability grouping for some subjects)		After accounting for the students' and schools' socio-economic background	
		%	S.E.	%	S.E.	%	S.E.	Mean score	S.E.	Mean score	S.E.	Score dif.	S.E.	Score dif.	S.E.
OECD	Australia	4.6	(1.1)	91.7	(1.5)	3.7	(1.1)	515	(2.4)	521	(13.3)	6.3	(13.8)	-3.0	(5.7)
	Austria	53.6	(3.3)	40.4	(3.1)	6.0	(1.7)	473	(3.2)	418	(27.5)	-54.9	(28.0)	-20.9	(12 .1)
	Belgium	54.3	(2.6)	27.1	(2.6)	18.7	(2.2)	507	(2.8)	508	(8.5)	1.2	(9.5)	4.8	(5.0)
	Canada	9.7	(1.0)	77.4	(1.9)	12.9	(1.6)	526	(1.7)	517	(5.8)	-8.7	(6.3)	-3.2	(4.8)
	Chile	35.1	(4.1)	34.6	(3.8)	30.3	(3.7)	447	(4.1)	454	(6.6)	7.0	(8.3)	5.5	(6.2)
	Czech Republic	31.2	(3.5)	61.5	(3.5)	7.3	(1.8)	480	(3.3)	440	(4.9)	**-40.1**	(6.4)	**-22.6**	(10.2)
	Denmark	50.4	(3.5)	43.8	(3.5)	5.8	(1.7)	496	(2.0)	468	(8.2)	**-28.0**	(8.3)	-5.0	(5.3)
	Estonia	43.8	(3.6)	44.2	(3.5)	12.0	(2.3)	501	(3.0)	496	(7.9)	-5.1	(8.8)	-6.4	(6.6)
	Finland	42.5	(4.0)	56.2	(4.2)	1.4	(0.9)	536	(2.2)	539	(34.8)	3.0	(34.9)	3.2	(32.7)
	France	w	w	w	w	w	w	w	w	w	w	w	w	w	w
	Germany	49.4	(2.9)	39.6	(3.0)	11.0	(2.3)	503	(3.1)	477	(16.8)	-26.0	(17.7)	-6.2	(11.5)
	Greece	85.2	(2.7)	14.4	(2.7)	0.4	(0.4)	482	(4.4)	518	(4.0)	**35.0**	(6.1)	**-42.9**	(6.7)
	Hungary	32.3	(3.5)	64.8	(3.9)	2.9	(1.6)	496	(3.5)	457	(64.2)	-38.8	(65.8)	-2.5	(19.9)
	Iceland	25.2	(0.2)	63.4	(0.2)	11.3	(0.2)	500	(1.5)	485	(4.6)	**-15.4**	(4.9)	-5.0	(5.0)
	Ireland	3.6	(1.8)	87.3	(3.3)	9.0	(2.8)	494	(3.6)	498	(13.8)	4.6	(14.9)	11.4	(11.8)
	Israel	2.8	(1.2)	74.0	(2.9)	23.2	(2.9)	487	(4.7)	437	(9.3)	**-50.3**	(11.1)	-19.0	(10.0)
	Italy	44.4	(1.9)	41.7	(1.8)	13.9	(1.6)	489	(2.0)	485	(8.3)	-3.6	(9.5)	7.5	(5.8)
	Japan	33.3	(3.6)	55.9	(3.8)	10.8	(2.1)	518	(4.1)	536	(9.6)	17.9	(11.6)	**-15.5**	(7.3)
	Korea	9.9	(2.8)	86.2	(3.2)	3.9	(1.6)	539	(3.6)	541	(12.7)	2.0	(13.6)	7.7	(10.5)
	Luxembourg	29.3	(0.1)	19.7	(0.1)	51.0	(0.1)	507	(1.6)	434	(1.8)	**-72.4**	(2.2)	**-17.1**	(3.0)
	Mexico	30.9	(1.7)	52.8	(1.7)	16.3	(1.4)	425	(2.3)	428	(5.4)	2.4	(6.3)	2.7	(4.7)
	Netherlands	19.8	(3.0)	36.2	(3.6)	44.0	(4.3)	507	(7.4)	510	(8.1)	2.8	(11.2)	13.4	(7.1)
	New Zealand	1.5	(1.0)	93.6	(1.6)	4.8	(1.3)	522	(2.7)	534	(12.0)	12.5	(12.9)	-1.3	(8.0)
	Norway	26.6	(3.1)	68.8	(3.0)	4.6	(1.4)	502	(2.6)	517	(11.8)	14.7	(11.9)	5.0	(8.9)
	Poland	54.2	(3.2)	42.2	(3.3)	3.6	(1.4)	500	(2.7)	517	(9.4)	17.3	(9.5)	10.6	(5.6)
	Portugal	68.5	(4.1)	23.8	(3.7)	7.7	(2.0)	491	(3.2)	469	(13.2)	-22.4	(13.7)	-9.1	(10.9)
	Slovak Republic	26.6	(3.8)	66.2	(4.0)	7.2	(2.0)	480	(2.6)	439	(10.5)	**-40.9**	(10.7)	-16.2	(11.3)
	Slovenia	45.0	(0.4)	50.2	(0.4)	4.7	(0.5)	484	(0.9)	468	(10.0)	-16.3	(10.0)	-11.2	(10.3)
	Spain	39.6	(2.7)	53.6	(3.0)	6.8	(1.6)	480	(2.0)	501	(5.4)	**21.1**	(5.6)	**12.0**	(4.5)
	Sweden	25.8	(2.9)	65.5	(3.2)	8.7	(2.0)	496	(3.1)	516	(9.8)	19.9	(10.2)	10.6	(5.8)
	Switzerland	25.1	(2.7)	35.8	(3.2)	39.1	(3.4)	510	(3.9)	485	(4.5)	**-25.3**	(7.0)	-8.4	(5.4)
	Turkey	37.6	(4.1)	34.9	(3.8)	27.6	(3.7)	462	(4.7)	468	(8.4)	6.0	(10.6)	4.1	(6.5)
	United Kingdom	0.9	(0.9)	91.5	(1.9)	7.6	(1.9)	496	(2.7)	494	(9.2)	-1.8	(10.0)	-2.0	(7.6)
	United States	8.8	(2.2)	83.8	(3.1)	7.4	(2.2)	499	(4.3)	507	(16.1)	7.9	(18.2)	9.4	(7. 7)
	OECD average	31.9	(0.5)	55.2	(0.5)	12.9	(0.4)	495	(0.6)	487	(2.9)	**-8.1**	(3.0)	-3.3	(1.8)
Partners	Albania	33.5	(3.6)	39.6	(3.9)	26.9	(3.2)	383	(5.5)	389	(6.7)	5.8	(9.4)	6.0	(6.2)
	Argentina	39.3	(3.9)	32.9	(3.5)	27.8	(4.2)	401	(6.5)	398	(11.8)	-2.6	(15.0)	-5.0	(8.1)
	Azerbaijan	8.9	(2.6)	67.2	(4.3)	23.9	(4.1)	360	(3.9)	367	(8.4)	7.4	(9.6)	-3.4	(7.4)
	Brazil	55.2	(3.2)	23.9	(2.9)	20.9	(2.2)	425	(3.9)	414	(5.5)	-11.5	(7.6)	-5.9	(4.4)
	Bulgaria	45.3	(5.3)	35.8	(5.2)	19.0	(4.2)	440	(7.2)	423	(23.0)	-16.7	(24.7)	-14.6	(12.1)
	Colombia	40.5	(4.9)	42.1	(4.4)	17.3	(3.4)	417	(4.2)	408	(7.3)	-8.8	(8.4)	-9.6	(7.9)
	Croatia	51.4	(3.9)	28.0	(4.0)	20.6	(3.1)	474	(3.8)	485	(7.9)	10.7	(9.8)	10.5	(7.2)
	Dubai (UAE)	14.9	(0.1)	48.2	(0.1)	36.9	(0.1)	473	(1.6)	457	(2.2)	**-16.8**	(2.8)	**-12.6**	(2.8)
	Hong Kong-China	23.9	(3.0)	65.2	(3.7)	10.9	(2.6)	536	(2.8)	511	(13.7)	-25.1	(15.1)	-10.3	(14.0)
	Indonesia	60.4	(4.1)	19.3	(3.2)	20.3	(3.4)	404	(4.6)	393	(6.7)	-10.8	(8.6)	-5.5	(6.8)
	Jordan	16.9	(2.9)	37.2	(4.0)	45.9	(4.0)	399	(4.7)	412	(6.1)	12.2	(8.4)	10.9	(7.9)
	Kazakhstan	22.8	(3.6)	41.5	(3.9)	35.7	(3.5)	395	(4.2)	383	(7.2)	-12.4	(9.4)	-9.5	(8.2)
	Kyrgyzstan	27.7	(3.8)	52.9	(3.6)	19.4	(2.5)	309	(3.5)	336	(9.5)	**26.8**	(10.6)	12.2	(7.1)
	Latvia	55.4	(4.2)	34.6	(4.1)	10.0	(2.2)	485	(3.2)	474	(7.9)	-10.7	(8.5)	**-12.1**	(5.7)
	Liechtenstein	28.8	(0.3)	66.8	(0.2)	4.4	(0.1)	497	(2.9)	542	(19.2)	**44.3**	(19.9)	10.5	(20.3)
	Lithuania	23.0	(3.1)	62.0	(3.5)	14.9	(2.6)	471	(2.7)	452	(8.2)	**-19.2**	(8.9)	**-18.2**	(7.5)
	Macao-China	36.1	(0.0)	43.8	(0.0)	20.1	(0.0)	487	(1.1)	487	(1.6)	0.2	(2.0)	3.7	(2.0)
	Montenegro	52.1	(0.9)	18.8	(1.4)	29.1	(0.6)	412	(2.4)	397	(2.3)	**-14.4**	(3.5)	**9.7**	(2.7)
	Panama	42.4	(5.4)	50.3	(5.8)	7.3	(2.7)	370	(7.6)	391	(16.6)	20.6	(19.2)	**20.1**	(9.2)
	Peru	25.5	(3.0)	41.2	(3.6)	33.2	(3.5)	372	(5.3)	364	(7.1)	-8.1	(9.9)	-0.1	(5.2)
	Qatar	16.1	(0.1)	46.4	(0.1)	37.5	(0.1)	375	(1.1)	355	(1.4)	**-20.0**	(1.9)	**-5.9**	(1.8)
	Romania	28.0	(3.3)	50.5	(3.5)	21.6	(3.5)	424	(5.5)	427	(11.2)	3.8	(14.1)	0.6	(9.0)
	Russian Federation	22.7	(2.9)	39.6	(3.9)	37.8	(3.3)	462	(3.8)	455	(5.5)	-7.4	(6.2)	-2.2	(3.8)
	Serbia	52.4	(4.1)	30.4	(3.7)	17.3	(3.1)	445	(2.7)	437	(9.7)	-7.6	(11.0)	-4.6	(7.7)
	Shanghai-China	36.3	(4.1)	50.7	(4.5)	13.0	(2.7)	556	(3.0)	552	(12.1)	-4.7	(13.8)	2.0	(7.9)
	Singapore	0.0	c	86.4	(0.5)	13.6	(0.5)	527	(1.0)	521	(3.6)	-5.4	(3.7)	-2.3	(3.5)
	Chinese Taipei	48.3	(3.9)	46.1	(3.9)	5.6	(1.8)	494	(2.9)	514	(13.8)	20.1	(15.0)	-5.0	(12.5)
	Thailand	30.6	(3.5)	50.6	(3.5)	18.8	(2.6)	417	(3.0)	440	(6.6)	**23.5**	(7.5)	**12.0**	(5.8)
	Trinidad and Tobago	38.9	(0.4)	46.4	(0.3)	14.7	(0.2)	426	(1.4)	385	(3.4)	**-41.2**	(3.7)	-6.2	(3.8)
	Tunisia	96.2	(1.4)	0.6	(0.6)	3.2	(1.4)	402	(3.1)	443	(38.9)	40.8	(39.7)	8.8	(28.4)
	Uruguay	61.8	(3.1)	26.7	(3.0)	11.5	(2.5)	426	(2.8)	423	(12.1)	-2.9	(12.9)	-6.8	(8.6)

Note: Values that are statistically significant are indicated in bold (see Annex A3).

StatLink http://dx.doi.org/10.1787/888932343285

[Part 1/3]
Index of school responsibility for resource allocation and reading performance, by national quarters of this index

Table IV.3.5 *Results based on school principals' reports*

		Index of school responsibility for resource allocation															
		All students		Bottom quarter		Second quarter		Third quarter		Top quarter		In lower secondary education (ISCED 2)		In upper secondary education (ISCED 3)		Difference between lower and upper secondary education	
		Mean index	S.E.	Mean index	S.E.	Mean index	S.E.	Mean index	S.E.	Mean index	S.E.	Mean index	S.E.	Mean index	S.E.	Dif.	S.E.
OECD	Australia	-0.07	(0.03)	-0.66	(0.01)	-0.51	(0.01)	-0.20	(0.01)	1.09	(0.12)	-0.04	(0.04)	-0.12	(0.07)	0.08	(0.06)
	Austria	-0.61	(0.02)	-0.76	(0.01)	-0.72	(0.00)	-0.62	(0.00)	-0.35	(0.06)	-0.72	(0.01)	-0.61	(0.02)	**-0.11**	(0.02)
	Belgium	-0.36	(0.01)	-0.73	(0.01)	-0.49	(0.01)	-0.18	(0.01)	-0.04	(0.03)	-0.40	(0.08)	-0.36	(0.01)	-0.04	(0.08)
	Canada	-0.39	(0.02)	-0.68	(0.00)	-0.59	(0.00)	-0.48	(0.00)	0.19	(0.07)	-0.39	(0.03)	-0.39	(0.02)	0.00	(0.03)
	Chile	0.45	(0.07)	-0.77	(0.01)	-0.45	(0.02)	0.77	(0.06)	2.27	(0.05)	-0.22	(0.11)	0.49	(0.07)	**-0.71**	(0.12)
	Czech Republic	1.12	(0.08)	-0.20	(0.02)	0.33	(0.02)	1.92	(0.09)	2.45	(0.00)	1.10	(0.09)	1.15	(0.12)	-0.06	(0.15)
	Denmark	0.18	(0.06)	-0.47	(0.01)	-0.23	(0.01)	-0.06	(0.01)	1.49	(0.13)	0.18	(0.07)	0.98	(0.58)	-0.81	(0.59)
	Estonia	-0.04	(0.05)	-0.39	(0.01)	-0.26	(0.01)	-0.12	(0.00)	0.61	(0.13)	-0.05	(0.04)	0.54	(0.24)	**-0.59**	(0.23)
	Finland	-0.39	(0.03)	-0.69	(0.01)	-0.56	(0.00)	-0.44	(0.00)	0.15	(0.09)	-0.39	(0.02)	c	c	c	c
	France	w	w	w	w	w	w	w	w	w	w	w	w	w	w	w	w
	Germany	-0.53	(0.03)	-0.75	(0.00)	-0.68	(0.00)	-0.58	(0.00)	-0.10	(0.11)	-0.53	(0.03)	-0.49	(0.08)	-0.04	(0.09)
	Greece	-0.77	(0.01)	-0.82	(0.00)	-0.81	(0.00)	-0.80	(0.00)	-0.64	(0.01)	-0.78	(0.01)	-0.77	(0.01)	-0.01	(0.02)
	Hungary	0.82	(0.09)	-0.41	(0.02)	-0.01	(0.02)	1.27	(0.08)	2.45	(0.00)	0.51	(0.19)	0.86	(0.10)	-0.35	(0.21)
	Iceland	-0.06	(0.00)	-0.44	(0.00)	-0.25	(0.00)	-0.11	(0.00)	0.54	(0.01)	-0.06	(0.00)	c	c	c	c
	Ireland	-0.42	(0.02)	-0.73	(0.01)	-0.52	(0.01)	-0.32	(0.01)	-0.13	(0.02)	-0.43	(0.02)	-0.42	(0.02)	-0.01	(0.01)
	Israel	-0.25	(0.05)	-0.66	(0.01)	-0.54	(0.00)	-0.43	(0.00)	0.62	(0.20)	-0.38	(0.07)	-0.23	(0.06)	**-0.15**	(0.06)
	Italy	-0.65	(0.02)	-0.83	(0.00)	-0.82	(0.00)	-0.74	(0.00)	-0.23	(0.06)	-0.68	(0.06)	-0.65	(0.02)	-0.03	(0.06)
	Japan	-0.18	(0.06)	-0.77	(0.01)	-0.75	(0.00)	-0.57	(0.01)	1.36	(0.13)	c	c	-0.18	(0.06)	c	c
	Korea	-0.44	(0.07)	-0.81	(0.00)	-0.74	(0.00)	-0.60	(0.01)	0.40	(0.20)	-0.72	(0.03)	-0.42	(0.07)	**-0.29**	(0.07)
	Luxembourg	-0.27	(0.00)	-0.75	(0.00)	-0.61	(0.00)	-0.54	(0.00)	0.81	(0.01)	-0.30	(0.00)	-0.23	(0.00)	**-0.08**	(0.01)
	Mexico	-0.37	(0.03)	-0.82	(0.00)	-0.72	(0.00)	-0.54	(0.00)	0.59	(0.07)	-0.56	(0.04)	-0.23	(0.03)	**-0.33**	(0.05)
	Netherlands	1.30	(0.10)	-0.03	(0.03)	0.70	(0.06)	2.07	(0.04)	2.45	(0.00)	1.27	(0.11)	1.37	(0.14)	-0.11	(0.15)
	New Zealand	0.11	(0.04)	-0.34	(0.01)	-0.14	(0.00)	-0.05	(0.01)	0.96	(0.11)	0.10	(0.05)	0.11	(0.04)	-0.01	(0.04)
	Norway	-0.23	(0.04)	-0.60	(0.01)	-0.45	(0.00)	-0.28	(0.01)	0.43	(0.13)	-0.23	(0.04)	c	c	c	c
	Poland	-0.36	(0.02)	-0.63	(0.00)	-0.51	(0.01)	-0.39	(0.01)	0.07	(0.07)	-0.36	(0.02)	c	c	c	c
	Portugal	-0.44	(0.06)	-0.78	(0.00)	-0.69	(0.00)	-0.57	(0.01)	0.27	(0.20)	-0.51	(0.05)	-0.40	(0.08)	-0.11	(0.06)
	Slovak Republic	0.50	(0.09)	-0.40	(0.02)	-0.15	(0.01)	0.17	(0.03)	2.37	(0.05)	0.38	(0.13)	0.57	(0.13)	-0.19	(0.19)
	Slovenia	-0.13	(0.01)	-0.49	(0.00)	-0.35	(0.00)	-0.20	(0.00)	0.51	(0.03)	0.36	(0.26)	-0.15	(0.00)	**0.51**	(0.26)
	Spain	-0.47	(0.03)	-0.82	(0.00)	-0.77	(0.00)	-0.53	(0.01)	0.24	(0.09)	-0.47	(0.03)	c	c	c	c
	Sweden	0.81	(0.07)	-0.34	(0.02)	0.14	(0.03)	0.99	(0.07)	2.45	(0.00)	0.81	(0.07)	0.61	(0.34)	0.20	(0.35)
	Switzerland	-0.18	(0.06)	-0.63	(0.01)	-0.46	(0.01)	-0.32	(0.01)	0.69	(0.16)	-0.19	(0.06)	-0.15	(0.19)	-0.04	(0.20)
	Turkey	-0.74	(0.01)	-0.83	(0.00)	-0.81	(0.00)	-0.75	(0.00)	-0.57	(0.05)	c	c	-0.74	(0.01)	c	c
	United Kingdom	0.83	(0.07)	-0.37	(0.02)	0.11	(0.02)	1.14	(0.07)	2.45	(0.00)	0.55	(0.55)	0.86	(0.07)	-0.31	(0.55)
	United States	0.40	(0.06)	-0.54	(0.01)	-0.24	(0.02)	0.72	(0.04)	1.67	(0.07)	0.38	(0.07)	0.41	(0.06)	-0.03	(0.06)
	OECD average	-0.06	(0.01)	-0.60	(0.00)	-0.41	(0.00)	-0.04	(0.01)	0.83	(0.02)	-0.09	(0.02)	0.05	(0.03)	-0.14	(0.04)
Partners	Albania	-0.60	(0.04)	-0.83	(0.00)	-0.81	(0.00)	-0.68	(0.01)	-0.07	(0.13)	-0.63	(0.05)	-0.56	(0.06)	-0.07	(0.07)
	Argentina	-0.56	(0.04)	-0.81	(0.00)	-0.74	(0.00)	-0.62	(0.01)	-0.06	(0.10)	-0.65	(0.03)	-0.50	(0.05)	**-0.16**	(0.05)
	Azerbaijan	-0.54	(0.02)	-0.78	(0.01)	-0.66	(0.01)	-0.56	(0.00)	-0.17	(0.06)	-0.55	(0.02)	-0.53	(0.03)	-0.02	(0.02)
	Brazil	-0.52	(0.02)	-0.84	(0.00)	-0.83	(0.00)	-0.77	(0.00)	0.36	(0.10)	-0.72	(0.02)	-0.45	(0.03)	**-0.26**	(0.03)
	Bulgaria	1.38	(0.09)	-0.09	(0.05)	0.74	(0.04)	2.41	(0.02)	2.45	(0.00)	1.46	(0.16)	1.37	(0.09)	0.09	(0.18)
	Colombia	-0.29	(0.07)	-0.82	(0.00)	-0.80	(0.00)	-0.67	(0.01)	1.13	(0.18)	-0.40	(0.06)	-0.23	(0.08)	**-0.17**	(0.06)
	Croatia	-0.39	(0.03)	-0.65	(0.01)	-0.49	(0.01)	-0.37	(0.01)	-0.06	(0.08)	c	c	-0.39	(0.03)	c	c
	Dubai (UAE)	0.82	(0.00)	-0.70	(0.00)	0.29	(0.00)	1.25	(0.01)	2.44	(0.00)	0.57	(0.02)	0.88	(0.01)	**-0.31**	(0.02)
	Hong Kong-China	0.20	(0.05)	-0.44	(0.02)	-0.15	(0.01)	-0.03	(0.01)	1.41	(0.15)	0.24	(0.06)	0.18	(0.06)	0.06	(0.05)
	Indonesia	0.04	(0.06)	-0.72	(0.01)	-0.60	(0.01)	-0.05	(0.05)	1.53	(0.09)	-0.07	(0.07)	0.17	(0.12)	-0.25	(0.15)
	Jordan	-0.63	(0.03)	-0.82	(0.00)	-0.80	(0.00)	-0.66	(0.01)	-0.24	(0.10)	-0.63	(0.03)	c	c	c	c
	Kazakhstan	-0.35	(0.05)	-0.65	(0.01)	-0.60	(0.00)	-0.48	(0.01)	0.33	(0.15)	-0.40	(0.04)	-0.15	(0.12)	**-0.25**	(0.12)
	Kyrgyzstan	-0.43	(0.04)	-0.77	(0.01)	-0.63	(0.00)	-0.50	(0.01)	0.20	(0.13)	-0.47	(0.04)	-0.27	(0.08)	**-0.20**	(0.05)
	Latvia	0.05	(0.05)	-0.47	(0.01)	-0.19	(0.01)	-0.04	(0.01)	0.90	(0.13)	0.05	(0.05)	0.09	(0.21)	-0.04	(0.21)
	Liechtenstein	0.15	(0.01)	-0.75	(0.00)	-0.62	(0.00)	0.36	(0.03)	1.61	(0.01)	0.07	(0.02)	c	c	c	c
	Lithuania	-0.28	(0.03)	-0.60	(0.00)	-0.46	(0.01)	-0.34	(0.01)	0.30	(0.10)	-0.28	(0.03)	c	c	c	c
	Macao-China	1.61	(0.00)	0.09	(0.00)	1.43	(0.00)	2.45	(0.00)	2.45	(0.00)	1.64	(0.00)	1.55	(0.00)	**0.09**	(0.01)
	Montenegro	-0.39	(0.00)	-0.60	(0.00)	-0.49	(0.00)	-0.41	(0.00)	-0.05	(0.00)	c	c	-0.38	(0.00)	c	c
	Panama	-0.33	(0.07)	-0.82	(0.00)	-0.76	(0.00)	-0.58	(0.01)	0.82	(0.20)	-0.47	(0.09)	-0.23	(0.14)	-0.25	(0.21)
	Peru	0.02	(0.07)	-0.81	(0.00)	-0.67	(0.01)	-0.48	(0.01)	2.03	(0.12)	-0.37	(0.06)	0.19	(0.09)	**-0.56**	(0.11)
	Qatar	0.27	(0.00)	-0.84	(0.00)	-0.55	(0.00)	0.37	(0.00)	2.09	(0.00)	0.41	(0.01)	0.23	(0.00)	**0.18**	(0.01)
	Romania	-0.75	(0.01)	-0.83	(0.00)	-0.82	(0.00)	-0.76	(0.00)	-0.57	(0.02)	-0.75	(0.01)	c	c	c	c
	Russian Federation	-0.08	(0.05)	-0.59	(0.01)	-0.40	(0.01)	-0.14	(0.01)	0.84	(0.09)	-0.10	(0.00)	-0.02	(0.00)	-0.08	(0.05)
	Serbia	-0.39	(0.03)	-0.63	(0.01)	-0.47	(0.01)	-0.40	(0.01)	-0.04	(0.08)	-0.54	(0.04)	-0.38	(0.03)	**-0.15**	(0.05)
	Shanghai-China	0.83	(0.07)	-0.35	(0.02)	0.10	(0.04)	1.21	(0.04)	2.36	(0.03)	0.78	(0.09)	0.86	(0.10)	-0.08	(0.13)
	Singapore	-0.43	(0.01)	-0.76	(0.00)	-0.62	(0.00)	-0.51	(0.00)	0.17	(0.04)	-0.52	(0.03)	-0.42	(0.01)	**-0.10**	(0.03)
	Chinese Taipei	0.05	(0.06)	-0.70	(0.01)	-0.47	(0.01)	-0.21	(0.02)	1.57	(0.14)	-0.39	(0.05)	0.28	(0.08)	**-0.68**	(0.07)
	Thailand	0.28	(0.07)	-0.59	(0.01)	-0.37	(0.01)	0.07	(0.03)	1.99	(0.10)	0.05	(0.12)	0.35	(0.08)	**-0.29**	(0.13)
	Trinidad and Tobago	-0.50	(0.00)	-0.77	(0.00)	-0.66	(0.00)	-0.61	(0.00)	0.02	(0.01)	-0.51	(0.01)	-0.50	(0.00)	0.00	(0.01)
	Tunisia	-0.71	(0.01)	-0.81	(0.00)	-0.75	(0.00)	-0.74	(0.00)	-0.53	(0.03)	-0.65	(0.01)	-0.75	(0.01)	**0.10**	(0.02)
	Uruguay	-0.51	(0.03)	-0.84	(0.00)	-0.77	(0.00)	-0.72	(0.00)	0.27	(0.13)	-0.70	(0.01)	-0.39	(0.05)	**-0.31**	(0.05)

Note: Values that are statistically significant are indicated in bold (see Annex A3).
StatLink http://dx.doi.org/10.1787/888932343285

[Part 2/3]

Table IV.3.5 Index of school responsibility for resource allocation and reading performance, by national quarters of this index

Results based on school principals' reports

		Index of school responsibility for resource allocation												Variability in the index of school responsibility for resource allocation	
		In general programmes		In vocational programmes		Difference between general and vocational programmes		In public schools		In private schools		Difference between public and private schools			
		Mean index	S.E.	Mean index	S.E.	Dif.	S.E.	Mean index	S.E.	Mean index	S.E.	Dif.	S.E.	Standard deviation	S.E.
OECD	Australia	-0.02	(0.04)	-0.55	(0.07)	**0.53**	(0.09)	-0.50	(0.01)	0.59	(0.09)	**-1.08**	(0.09)	0.89	(0.05)
	Austria	-0.67	(0.01)	-0.59	(0.03)	**-0.08**	(0.03)	-0.64	(0.01)	-0.41	(0.13)	-0.24	(0.13)	0.30	(0.08)
	Belgium	-0.40	(0.01)	-0.32	(0.02)	**-0.08**	(0.02)	-0.46	(0.03)	-0.32	(0.01)	**-0.14**	(0.03)	0.31	(0.03)
	Canada	a	a	a	a	a	a	-0.49	(0.01)	0.87	(0.18)	**-1.37**	(0.18)	0.55	(0.05)
	Chile	0.46	(0.07)	0.34	(0.16)	0.12	(0.14)	-0.66	(0.03)	1.25	(0.10)	**-1.91**	(0.11)	1.23	(0.04)
	Czech Republic	1.13	(0.09)	1.11	(0.14)	0.03	(0.16)	1.11	(0.08)	1.66	(0.41)	-0.55	(0.42)	1.17	(0.02)
	Denmark	0.18	(0.06)	c	c	c	c	-0.04	(0.05)	0.93	(0.19)	**-0.96**	(0.19)	0.90	(0.06)
	Estonia	-0.05	(0.05)	c	c	c	c	-0.07	(0.04)	0.87	(0.45)	**-0.94**	(0.45)	0.59	(0.08)
	Finland	-0.39	(0.03)	c	c	c	c	-0.44	(0.03)	0.93	(0.55)	**-1.37**	(0.56)	0.50	(0.04)
	France	w	w	w	w	w	w	w	w	w	w	w	w	w	w
	Germany	-0.53	(0.03)	-0.46	(0.09)	-0.07	(0.10)	-0.60	(0.02)	0.77	(0.39)	**-1.36**	(0.39)	0.49	(0.09)
	Greece	-0.76	(0.01)	-0.80	(0.01)	**0.04**	(0.01)	-0.78	(0.01)	-0.65	(0.04)	**-0.13**	(0.04)	0.08	(0.01)
	Hungary	0.81	(0.10)	0.90	(0.18)	-0.08	(0.21)	0.72	(0.10)	1.54	(0.24)	**-0.82**	(0.27)	1.17	(0.03)
	Iceland	-0.06	(0.00)	c	c	c	c	-0.08	(0.00)	c	c	c	c	0.50	(0.01)
	Ireland	-0.42	(0.02)	c	c	c	c	-0.60	(0.03)	-0.32	(0.02)	**-0.28**	(0.03)	0.24	(0.02)
	Israel	-0.25	(0.05)	c	c	c	c	-0.43	(0.04)	0.58	(0.22)	**-1.01**	(0.22)	0.75	(0.10)
	Italy	-0.62	(0.03)	-0.69	(0.02)	0.07	(0.04)	-0.76	(0.01)	0.93	(0.23)	**-1.69**	(0.23)	0.52	(0.05)
	Japan	-0.57	(0.06)	0.92	(0.17)	**-1.49**	(0.18)	-0.67	(0.00)	0.99	(0.00)	**-1.66**	(0.18)	1.01	(0.07)
	Korea	-0.41	(0.08)	-0.52	(0.08)	0.10	(0.11)	-0.73	(0.01)	0.06	(0.15)	**-0.80**	(0.15)	0.75	(0.11)
	Luxembourg	-0.25	(0.00)	-0.31	(0.01)	**0.05**	(0.01)	-0.60	(0.00)	1.59	(0.00)	**-2.18**	(0.00)	0.84	(0.00)
	Mexico	-0.37	(0.04)	-0.40	(0.03)	0.03	(0.05)	-0.59	(0.01)	1.29	(0.12)	**-1.88**	(0.12)	0.77	(0.04)
	Netherlands	1.35	(0.10)	1.06	(0.56)	0.29	(0.58)	1.26	(0.14)	1.32	(0.14)	-0.06	(0.20)	1.04	(0.03)
	New Zealand	0.11	(0.04)	c	c	c	c	0.01	(0.04)	1.88	(0.33)	**-1.86**	(0.33)	0.72	(0.06)
	Norway	-0.23	(0.04)	c	c	c	c	-0.25	(0.04)	c	c	c	c	0.60	(0.08)
	Poland	-0.36	(0.02)	c	c	c	c	-0.41	(0.02)	1.58	(0.25)	**-1.99**	(0.25)	0.44	(0.06)
	Portugal	-0.52	(0.04)	0.15	(0.28)	**-0.67**	(0.27)	-0.65	(0.01)	0.80	(0.31)	**-1.46**	(0.31)	0.71	(0.11)
	Slovak Republic	0.50	(0.12)	0.35	(0.23)	0.15	(0.26)	0.45	(0.09)	0.99	(0.34)	-0.54	(0.36)	1.12	(0.06)
	Slovenia	-0.14	(0.02)	-0.13	(0.00)	0.00	(0.02)	-0.14	(0.01)	0.18	(0.01)	**-0.33**	(0.02)	0.58	(0.02)
	Spain	-0.47	(0.03)	c	c	c	c	-0.74	(0.01)	0.06	(0.07)	**-0.80**	(0.07)	0.58	(0.06)
	Sweden	0.81	(0.07)	c	c	c	c	0.65	(0.08)	2.28	(0.07)	**-1.63**	(0.11)	1.12	(0.03)
	Switzerland	-0.18	(0.06)	-0.19	(0.21)	0.01	(0.22)	-0.31	(0.03)	1.13	(0.33)	**-1.44**	(0.33)	0.73	(0.10)
	Turkey	-0.73	(0.02)	-0.75	(0.01)	0.03	(0.03)	-0.75	(0.01)	c	c	c	c	0.21	(0.07)
	United Kingdom	0.86	(0.07)	c	c	**c**	c	0.78	(0.08)	2.08	(0.12)	**-1.30**	(0.15)	1.14	(0.03)
	United States	0.40	(0.06)	c	c	c	c	0.34	(0.06)	1.09	(0.29)	**-0.75**	(0.29)	0.92	(0.04)
	OECD average	-0.06	(0.01)	-0.05	(0.04)	-0.05	(0.04)	-0.21	(0.01)	0.88	(0.04)	**-1.08**	(0.05)	0.71	(0.01)
Partners	Albania	-0.61	(0.03)	-0.42	(0.22)	-0.19	(0.21)	-0.73	(0.01)	0.49	(0.26)	**-1.22**	(0.26)	0.54	(0.10)
	Argentina	-0.54	(0.04)	-0.68	(0.03)	**0.14**	(0.05)	-0.71	(0.01)	-0.28	(0.10)	**-0.43**	(0.10)	0.41	(0.07)
	Azerbaijan	-0.54	(0.02)	-0.50	(0.11)	-0.05	(0.11)	-0.55	(0.02)	c	c	c	c	0.32	(0.05)
	Brazil	-0.52	(0.02)	c	c	c	c	-0.78	(0.01)	1.33	(0.15)	**-2.11**	(0.15)	0.79	(0.05)
	Bulgaria	1.28	(0.10)	1.54	(0.18)	-0.26	(0.23)	1.36	(0.09)	c	c	c	c	1.12	(0.03)
	Colombia	-0.26	(0.07)	-0.41	(0.20)	0.15	(0.20)	-0.71	(0.03)	1.48	(0.22)	**-2.20**	(0.22)	1.05	(0.08)
	Croatia	-0.30	(0.08)	-0.43	(0.02)	0.13	(0.09)	-0.43	(0.01)	c	c	c	c	0.36	(0.08)
	Dubai (UAE)	0.82	(0.00)	c	c	c	c	-0.71	(0.00)	1.23	(0.00)	**-1.94**	(0.00)	1.20	(0.00)
	Hong Kong-China	0.20	(0.05)	c	c	c	c	-0.53	(0.05)	0.26	(0.06)	**-0.79**	(0.08)	0.88	(0.06)
	Indonesia	-0.04	(0.06)	0.53	(0.28)	**-0.57**	(0.29)	-0.60	(0.02)	0.90	(0.11)	**-1.51**	(0.11)	0.98	(0.05)
	Jordan	-0.63	(0.03)	c	c	c	c	-0.73	(0.01)	-0.19	(0.14)	**-0.55**	(0.14)	0.44	(0.09)
	Kazakhstan	-0.39	(0.05)	0.12	(0.30)	-0.51	(0.30)	-0.42	(0.04)	1.62	(0.53)	**-2.04**	(0.53)	0.66	(0.09)
	Kyrgyzstan	-0.45	(0.04)	0.41	(0.28)	**-0.86**	(0.28)	-0.50	(0.03)	1.96	(0.34)	**-2.46**	(0.33)	0.60	(0.09)
	Latvia	0.05	(0.05)	c	c	c	c	0.05	(0.05)	c	c	c	c	0.66	(0.07)
	Liechtenstein	0.15	(0.01)	c	c	c	c	0.07	(0.01)	c	c	c	c	1.01	(0.01)
	Lithuania	-0.28	(0.03)	c	c	c	c	-0.28	(0.03)	c	c	c	c	0.49	(0.07)
	Macao-China	1.61	(0.00)	c	c	c	c	-0.66	(0.00)	1.70	(0.00)	c	c	1.02	(0.00)
	Montenegro	-0.35	(0.01)	-0.41	(0.00)	**0.06**	(0.01)	-0.39	(0.00)	c	c	c	c	0.25	(0.00)
	Panama	-0.33	(0.07)	c	c	c	c	-0.71	(0.02)	0.97	(0.21)	**-1.68**	(0.21)	0.87	(0.09)
	Peru	0.02	(0.07)	c	c	c	c	-0.56	(0.04)	2.07	(0.12)	**-2.63**	(0.13)	1.25	(0.05)
	Qatar	0.27	(0.00)	c	c	c	c	0.07	(0.00)	0.54	(0.01)	**-0.47**	(0.01)	1.18	(0.00)
	Romania	-0.75	(0.01)	-0.72	(0.02)	-0.03	(0.03)	-0.75	(0.01)	c	c	c	c	0.13	(0.01)
	Russian Federation	-0.09	(0.00)	0.16	(0.00)	-0.24	(0.16)	-0.08	(0.05)	c	c	c	c	0.69	(0.06)
	Serbia	-0.43	(0.04)	-0.41	(0.02)	-0.02	(0.04)	-0.40	(0.02)	c	c	c	c	0.33	(0.09)
	Shanghai-China	0.71	(0.08)	1.26	(0.14)	**-0.55**	(0.16)	0.69	(0.07)	1.99	(0.16)	**-1.30**	(0.18)	1.08	(0.03)
	Singapore	-0.43	(0.01)	c	c	c	c	-0.44	(0.00)	c	c	c	c	0.63	(0.02)
	Chinese Taipei	-0.18	(0.07)	0.40	(0.10)	**-0.58**	(0.12)	-0.49	(0.02)	1.00	(0.16)	**-1.49**	(0.16)	1.02	(0.06)
	Thailand	0.11	(0.08)	0.89	(0.20)	**-0.78**	(0.20)	-0.02	(0.07)	1.73	(0.21)	**-1.75**	(0.23)	1.07	(0.05)
	Trinidad and Tobago	-0.49	(0.00)	-0.59	(0.00)	**0.10**	(0.00)	-0.63	(0.00)	0.54	(0.01)	**-1.17**	(0.01)	0.56	(0.00)
	Tunisia	-0.71	(0.01)	c	c	c	c	-0.74	(0.01)	1.19	(0.64)	**-1.93**	(0.64)	0.29	(0.05)
	Uruguay	-0.51	(0.04)	-0.76	(0.01)	**0.26**	(0.04)	-0.76	(0.00)	0.61	(0.17)	**-1.37**	(0.17)	0.64	(0.08)

Note: Values that are statistically significant are indicated in bold (see Annex A3).

StatLink http://dx.doi.org/10.1787/888932343285

[Part 3/3]

Index of school responsibility for resource allocation and reading performance, by national quarters of this index

Table IV.3.5 *Results based on school principals' reports*

		Performance on the reading scale by national quarters of this index								Change in the reading score per unit of this index		Increased likelihood of students in the bottom quarter of this index scoring in the bottom quarter of the national reading performance distribution		Explained variance in student performance (r-squared X 100)	
		Bottom quarter		Second quarter		Third quarter		Top quarter							
		Mean score	S.E.	Mean score	S.E.	Mean score	S.E.	Mean score	S.E.	Effect	S.E.	Ratio	S.E.	%	S.E.
OECD	Australia	**498**	(5.3)	503	(5.2)	517	(3.5)	**541**	(4.3)	**20.5**	(2.29)	**1.4**	(0.09)	3.4	(0.70)
	Austria	**489**	(9.1)	446	(9.5)	479	(8.8)	**465**	(8.3)	-13.1	(9.71)	**0.7**	(0.13)	0.2	(0.24)
	Belgium	**480**	(8.4)	507	(7.0)	517	(4.3)	**519**	(5.5)	36.6	(18.93)	**1.6**	(0.17)	1.2	(1.18)
	Canada	**516**	(3.3)	523	(3.1)	523	(3.3)	**535**	(3.5)	**17.5**	(2.92)	**1.1**	(0.07)	1.1	(0.45)
	Chile	**415**	(6.6)	438	(7.0)	467	(6.1)	**477**	(5.9)	**18.8**	(2.72)	**2.0**	(0.23)	7.9	(2.20)
	Czech Republic	**494**	(7.0)	461	(8.0)	476	(5.1)	**478**	(6.3)	-1.5	(3.65)	**0.7**	(0.12)	0.0	(0.25)
	Denmark	493	(4.5)	491	(3.1)	494	(4.5)	502	(5.3)	6.0	(3.32)	1.0	(0.09)	0.4	(0.47)
	Estonia	493	(5.4)	508	(4.8)	499	(5.1)	503	(7.0)	-5.5	(5.86)	1.2	(0.13)	0.2	(0.33)
	Finland	**529**	(4.4)	533	(4.2)	536	(4.6)	**546**	(5.1)	7.2	(7.79)	1.1	(0.10)	0.2	(0.40)
	France	w	w	w	w	w	w	w	w	w	w	w	w	w	w
	Germany	**483**	(8.1)	493	(8.1)	506	(7.6)	**508**	(6.1)	9.0	(5.22)	**1.4**	(0.18)	0.2	(0.24)
	Greece	**477**	(6.8)	475	(8.1)	475	(7.1)	**503**	(6.5)	**170.1**	(32.30)	1.1	(0.13)	2.3	(0.92)
	Hungary	507	(9.3)	490	(10.7)	485	(9.7)	495	(9.0)	-2.0	(4.48)	0.8	(0.17)	0.1	(0.52)
	Iceland	**501**	(2.7)	496	(4.2)	502	(3.6)	**493**	(3.6)	0.0	(3.14)	1.0	(0.08)	0.0	(0.03)
	Ireland	**475**	(8.2)	487	(9.5)	508	(5.7)	**506**	(7.3)	**58.1**	(16.79)	**1.4**	(0.21)	2.1	(1.27)
	Israel	**448**	(10.6)	470	(10.0)	478	(10.3)	**502**	(8.7)	13.8	(8.65)	**1.5**	(0.23)	0.9	(1.22)
	Italy	**492**	(3.7)	488	(3.6)	488	(5.8)	**476**	(4.6)	**-13.8**	(5.24)	**0.9**	(0.07)	0.6	(0.40)
	Japan	523	(5.5)	513	(6.7)	508	(12.8)	535	(9.0)	2.2	(5.78)	0.9	(0.11)	0.0	(0.43)
	Korea	**534**	(6.5)	534	(8.3)	538	(9.9)	**551**	(6.8)	**13.2**	(4.19)	1.1	(0.19)	1.6	(1.05)
	Luxembourg	**432**	(2.7)	458	(3.2)	503	(2.7)	**496**	(2.3)	**7.9**	(1.23)	**1.9**	(0.09)	0.4	(0.13)
	Mexico	**392**	(5.0)	410	(3.9)	438	(3.6)	**461**	(2.7)	**23.4**	(2.71)	**1.9**	(0.13)	4.6	(0.80)
	Netherlands	501	(13.7)	510	(9.5)	506	(7.4)	515	(9.7)	3.1	(5.65)	1.4	(0.27)	0.1	(0.62)
	New Zealand	512	(6.5)	523	(4.4)	524	(4.7)	525	(5.5)	6.1	(4.91)	1.2	(0.11)	0.2	(0.33)
	Norway	503	(4.5)	496	(4.7)	504	(4.5)	508	(4.9)	2.5	(4.38)	1.0	(0.09)	0.0	(0.11)
	Poland	497	(6.0)	509	(5.8)	497	(4.7)	498	(5.4)	**10.6**	(4.99)	1.0	(0.12)	0.3	(0.24)
	Portugal	490	(5.9)	491	(5.7)	480	(6.6)	496	(6.6)	8.8	(6.44)	0.9	(0.12)	0.5	(0.73)
	Slovak Republic	**456**	(7.3)	484	(7.5)	488	(8.8)	**482**	(10.3)	4.0	(4.78)	**1.5**	(0.19)	0.3	(0.53)
	Slovenia	**478**	(2.4)	484	(3.0)	505	(2.7)	**465**	(3.7)	**-11.5**	(3.23)	1.0	(0.06)	0.5	(0.32)
	Spain	**469**	(3.8)	466	(3.7)	482	(4.5)	**507**	(4.4)	**24.8**	(3.52)	**1.3**	(0.09)	2.7	(0.55)
	Sweden	**484**	(5.9)	490	(6.1)	502	(6.7)	**514**	(5.4)	**11.6**	(2.64)	**1.3**	(0.14)	1.7	(0.78)
	Switzerland	488	(6.3)	517	(7.4)	506	(5.1)	490	(7.2)	-3.8	(6.40)	1.2	(0.13)	0.1	(0.35)
	Turkey	469	(7.1)	461	(7.3)	465	(8.2)	461	(7.8)	24.4	(12.49)	0.9	(0.14)	0.4	(0.57)
	United Kingdom	493	(4.5)	486	(7.5)	507	(6.2)	497	(5.8)	3.6	(2.57)	1.0	(0.10)	0.2	(0.28)
	United States	495	(7.8)	494	(7.0)	505	(6.0)	506	(7.8)	3.2	(4.83)	1.1	(0.11)	0.1	(0.30)
	OECD average	**485**	(1.2)	489	(1.2)	497	(1.1)	**502**	(1.1)	**13.8**	(1.53)	**1.2**	(0.02)	1.0	(0.12)
Partners	Albania	**381**	(6.2)	373	(6.5)	377	(10.1)	**409**	(7.7)	**18.0**	(8.66)	1.0	(0.11)	0.9	(0.64)
	Argentina	**359**	(11.3)	374	(9.8)	407	(10.6)	**452**	(11.5)	**77.0**	(13.96)	**1.7**	(0.27)	8.5	(2.23)
	Azerbaijan	368	(7.2)	367	(6.4)	358	(9.0)	352	(6.9)	-18.2	(10.13)	0.8	(0.16)	0.6	(0.74)
	Brazil	**394**	(3.5)	395	(3.8)	401	(5.1)	**457**	(7.3)	**45.7**	(2.60)	**1.2**	(0.08)	14.8	(1.74)
	Bulgaria	**451**	(10.9)	427	(11.9)	420	(12.4)	**418**	(13.8)	-12.6	(7.06)	**0.7**	(0.13)	1.5	(1.77)
	Colombia	**394**	(6.5)	397	(6.4)	406	(6.3)	**455**	(9.4)	**23.9**	(3.42)	**1.4**	(0.15)	8.4	(1.99)
	Croatia	484	(7.1)	489	(7.4)	467	(5.9)	463	(10.5)	-3.4	(15.71)	**0.7**	(0.13)	0.0	(0.36)
	Dubai (UAE)	**392**	(1.8)	478	(2.4)	497	(2.7)	**470**	(2.5)	**24.8**	(0.93)	**2.6**	(0.11)	7.8	(0.56)
	Hong Kong-China	**541**	(7.3)	538	(5.6)	532	(7.0)	**522**	(6.9)	-9.1	(4.80)	0.9	(0.14)	0.9	(0.93)
	Indonesia	411	(7.5)	405	(7.8)	396	(6.3)	394	(6.6)	-6.0	(3.51)	0.8	(0.14)	0.8	(0.92)
	Jordan	400	(6.9)	404	(6.2)	407	(6.2)	408	(6.7)	9.5	(12.17)	1.1	(0.15)	0.2	(0.59)
	Kazakhstan	395	(5.7)	390	(5.5)	384	(8.2)	392	(8.2)	**13.0**	(6.58)	0.9	(0.11)	0.9	(0.88)
	Kyrgyzstan	**293**	(7.6)	322	(7.0)	310	(7.1)	**332**	(9.6)	**26.5**	(11.89)	1.3	(0.18)	2.6	(2.34)
	Latvia	489	(7.1)	478	(5.8)	491	(5.7)	478	(5.1)	-2.9	(4.36)	0.9	(0.14)	0.1	(0.21)
	Liechtenstein	**466**	(7.2)	442	(7.1)	522	(7.1)	**568**	(7.1)	**47.4**	(3.37)	1.7	(0.38)	33.6	(3.66)
	Lithuania	468	(6.8)	480	(5.5)	469	(6.0)	456	(6.0)	-10.7	(7.49)	1.1	(0.14)	0.4	(0.50)
	Macao-China	**490**	(1.6)	496	(1.6)	480	(2.1)	**482**	(2.0)	**-1.7**	(0.79)	1.0	(0.05)	0.1	(0.05)
	Montenegro	**398**	(2.8)	403	(5.6)	418	(2.7)	**412**	(2.0)	1.3	(4.92)	1.2	(0.09)	0.0	(0.02)
	Panama	**357**	(10.5)	331	(13.1)	352	(9.7)	**443**	(14.2)	**42.9**	(6.91)	1.1	(0.23)	14.2	(6.12)
	Peru	**351**	(6.6)	343	(6.5)	354	(10.1)	**431**	(9.1)	**28.4**	(3.51)	1.2	(0.16)	13.1	(3.00)
	Qatar	**373**	(1.5)	361	(1.8)	376	(1.8)	**377**	(1.9)	**4.4**	(0.75)	**0.6**	(0.03)	0.2	(0.07)
	Romania	414	(9.6)	426	(7.5)	429	(8.0)	429	(12.1)	31.2	(55.54)	1.3	(0.21)	0.2	(0.81)
	Russian Federation	450	(6.9)	464	(4.6)	461	(6.7)	462	(7.7)	1.1	(5.77)	1.2	(0.12)	0.0	(0.16)
	Serbia	444	(7.6)	440	(6.2)	438	(5.5)	445	(8.4)	-13.8	(13.79)	1.0	(0.17)	0.3	(0.61)
	Shanghai-China	555	(7.5)	564	(6.5)	551	(7.2)	553	(7.1)	-4.2	(3.71)	1.0	(0.16)	0.3	(0.60)
	Singapore	**516**	(2.3)	508	(2.3)	521	(2.9)	**558**	(2.9)	**35.5**	(3.22)	**1.2**	(0.06)	5.3	(0.82)
	Chinese Taipei	**503**	(6.0)	508	(6.7)	503	(6.9)	**466**	(6.4)	**-16.0**	(3.67)	**0.8**	(0.10)	3.6	(1.46)
	Thailand	411	(6.2)	425	(6.1)	436	(6.2)	414	(7.7)	-3.3	(3.09)	1.2	(0.15)	0.2	(0.46)
	Trinidad and Tobago	**409**	(2.2)	410	(3.7)	416	(3.7)	**449**	(2.4)	**19.2**	(1.84)	**1.2**	(0.07)	0.9	(0.17)
	Tunisia	408	(6.7)	410	(5.6)	411	(5.7)	386	(11.7)	**-34.0**	(9.60)	0.8	(0.14)	1.4	(0.43)
	Uruguay	**399**	(5.8)	407	(6.6)	415	(4.1)	**482**	(5.7)	**46.9**	(6.76)	**1.5**	(0.15)	9.2	(1.57)

Note: Values that are statistically significant are indicated in bold (see Annex A3).

StatLink http://dx.doi.org/10.1787/888932343285

[Part 1/3]
Index of school responsibility for curriculum and assessment and reading performance, by national quarters of this index
Table IV.3.6 *Results based on school principals' reports*

		Index of school responsibility for curriculum and assessment															
		All students		Bottom quarter		Second quarter		Third quarter		Top quarter		In lower secondary education (ISCED 2)		In upper secondary education (ISCED 3)		Difference between lower and upper secondary education	
		Mean index	S.E.	Mean index	S.E.	Mean index	S.E.	Mean index	S.E.	Mean index	S.E.	Mean index	S.E.	Mean index	S.E.	Dif.	S.E.
OECD	Australia	0.17	(0.05)	-0.76	(0.01)	-0.40	(0.01)	0.47	(0.06)	1.36	(0.00)	0.20	(0.06)	0.12	(0.07)	0.09	(0.07)
	Austria	-0.31	(0.06)	-1.03	(0.02)	-0.78	(0.01)	-0.36	(0.03)	0.92	(0.08)	0.16	(0.19)	-0.35	(0.06)	**0.51**	(0.20)
	Belgium	-0.17	(0.05)	-0.92	(0.02)	-0.60	(0.01)	-0.25	(0.02)	1.09	(0.05)	-0.36	(0.07)	-0.15	(0.05)	**-0.20**	(0.08)
	Canada	-0.66	(0.03)	-1.07	(0.01)	-0.91	(0.00)	-0.76	(0.00)	0.11	(0.07)	-0.59	(0.04)	-0.67	(0.03)	0.08	(0.04)
	Chile	-0.09	(0.08)	-1.01	(0.02)	-0.75	(0.02)	0.06	(0.07)	1.36	(0.00)	-0.41	(0.11)	-0.07	(0.08)	**-0.34**	(0.12)
	Czech Republic	0.92	(0.06)	-0.40	(0.06)	1.36	(0.00)	1.36	(0.00)	1.36	(0.00)	1.05	(0.06)	0.78	(0.10)	**0.27**	(0.12)
	Denmark	0.05	(0.06)	-0.90	(0.02)	-0.59	(0.01)	0.34	(0.06)	1.36	(0.00)	0.06	(0.06)	-0.43	(0.17)	**0.49**	(0.18)
	Estonia	0.22	(0.07)	-0.81	(0.02)	-0.29	(0.03)	0.60	(0.07)	1.36	(0.00)	0.22	(0.07)	-0.04	(0.16)	0.26	(0.17)
	Finland	-0.15	(0.06)	-0.86	(0.02)	-0.62	(0.01)	-0.28	(0.03)	1.16	(0.05)	-0.15	(0.06)	c	c	c	c
	France	w	w	w	w	w	w	w	w	w	w	w	w	w	w	w	w
	Germany	-0.25	(0.05)	-0.91	(0.02)	-0.60	(0.01)	-0.24	(0.02)	0.74	(0.06)	-0.25	(0.05)	-0.34	(0.16)	0.09	(0.16)
	Greece	-1.25	(0.02)	-1.37	(0.00)	-1.37	(0.00)	-1.28	(0.01)	-0.98	(0.05)	-1.30	(0.02)	-1.25	(0.02)	-0.05	(0.03)
	Hungary	0.11	(0.08)	-0.87	(0.02)	-0.48	(0.01)	0.41	(0.06)	1.36	(0.00)	-0.02	(0.15)	0.12	(0.08)	-0.15	(0.17)
	Iceland	0.23	(0.00)	-0.77	(0.00)	-0.30	(0.00)	0.63	(0.01)	1.36	(0.00)	0.23	(0.00)	c	c	c	c
	Ireland	0.01	(0.07)	-0.69	(0.03)	-0.35	(0.00)	-0.10	(0.01)	1.18	(0.04)	0.02	(0.07)	-0.01	(0.08)	0.03	(0.04)
	Israel	-0.01	(0.08)	-0.93	(0.01)	-0.68	(0.01)	0.19	(0.06)	1.36	(0.00)	0.02	(0.14)	-0.02	(0.08)	0.04	(0.12)
	Italy	0.20	(0.04)	-0.79	(0.01)	-0.37	(0.01)	0.59	(0.03)	1.36	(0.00)	0.29	(0.17)	0.20	(0.04)	0.09	(0.18)
	Japan	1.06	(0.05)	0.15	(0.09)	1.36	(0.00)	1.36	(0.00)	1.36	(0.00)	c	c	1.06	(0.05)	c	c
	Korea	0.79	(0.08)	-0.40	(0.06)	0.82	(0.06)	1.36	(0.00)	1.36	(0.00)	1.11	(0.08)	0.77	(0.08)	**0.34**	(0.11)
	Luxembourg	-0.86	(0.00)	-1.19	(0.00)	-1.03	(0.00)	-0.96	(0.00)	-0.26	(0.01)	-0.93	(0.00)	-0.74	(0.00)	**-0.20**	(0.00)
	Mexico	-0.92	(0.02)	-1.29	(0.00)	-1.16	(0.00)	-0.96	(0.00)	-0.29	(0.05)	-1.02	(0.02)	-0.85	(0.03)	**-0.17**	(0.04)
	Netherlands	1.04	(0.05)	0.06	(0.08)	1.36	(0.00)	1.36	(0.00)	1.36	(0.00)	1.00	(0.07)	1.14	(0.06)	-0.14	(0.09)
	New Zealand	0.81	(0.04)	-0.35	(0.03)	0.88	(0.05)	1.36	(0.00)	1.36	(0.00)	0.92	(0.07)	0.81	(0.04)	**0.12**	(0.05)
	Norway	-0.57	(0.05)	-1.11	(0.01)	-0.87	(0.01)	-0.62	(0.01)	0.32	(0.12)	-0.57	(0.05)	c	c	c	c
	Poland	0.31	(0.06)	-0.55	(0.03)	-0.20	(0.02)	0.63	(0.07)	1.36	(0.00)	0.31	(0.06)	c	c	c	c
	Portugal	-0.93	(0.03)	-1.21	(0.00)	-1.07	(0.00)	-0.96	(0.01)	-0.50	(0.08)	-0.97	(0.02)	-0.91	(0.04)	**-0.06**	(0.03)
	Slovak Republic	0.08	(0.08)	-0.89	(0.01)	-0.71	(0.02)	0.55	(0.08)	1.36	(0.00)	0.00	(0.11)	0.13	(0.11)	-0.12	(0.16)
	Slovenia	-0.38	(0.01)	-0.96	(0.00)	-0.79	(0.00)	-0.50	(0.00)	0.75	(0.01)	-0.31	(0.16)	-0.38	(0.00)	0.07	(0.16)
	Spain	-0.48	(0.04)	-1.11	(0.01)	-0.87	(0.01)	-0.57	(0.01)	0.62	(0.07)	-0.48	(0.04)	c	c	c	c
	Sweden	0.21	(0.07)	-0.86	(0.02)	-0.41	(0.02)	0.73	(0.08)	1.36	(0.00)	0.21	(0.07)	-0.24	(0.26)	0.46	(0.29)
	Switzerland	-0.62	(0.05)	-1.17	(0.01)	-0.95	(0.01)	-0.74	(0.01)	0.38	(0.10)	-0.73	(0.04)	-0.20	(0.16)	-0.53	(0.17)
	Turkey	-1.04	(0.03)	-1.36	(0.00)	-1.25	(0.01)	-1.06	(0.01)	-0.51	(0.09)	c	c	-1.04	(0.03)	c	c
	United Kingdom	0.83	(0.05)	-0.39	(0.03)	0.98	(0.05)	1.36	(0.00)	1.36	(0.00)	0.46	(0.27)	0.85	(0.05)	-0.39	(0.27)
	United States	-0.20	(0.06)	-1.02	(0.01)	-0.82	(0.01)	-0.28	(0.04)	1.30	(0.02)	-0.25	(0.08)	-0.20	(0.07)	-0.05	(0.07)
	OECD average	-0.06	(0.01)	-0.84	(0.01)	-0.38	(0.00)	0.11	(0.01)	0.88	(0.01)	-0.07	(0.02)	-0.07	(0.02)	0.02	(0.03)
Partners	Albania	-0.42	(0.07)	-1.15	(0.01)	-0.91	(0.00)	-0.48	(0.03)	0.86	(0.09)	-0.45	(0.09)	-0.38	(0.10)	-0.07	(0.13)
	Argentina	-0.57	(0.05)	-1.05	(0.02)	-0.87	(0.01)	-0.61	(0.01)	0.25	(0.11)	-0.63	(0.05)	-0.53	(0.06)	-0.10	(0.06)
	Azerbaijan	-0.64	(0.08)	-1.31	(0.01)	-1.10	(0.01)	-0.71	(0.03)	0.58	(0.10)	-0.68	(0.08)	-0.58	(0.09)	**-0.10**	(0.04)
	Brazil	-0.56	(0.03)	-1.16	(0.01)	-0.94	(0.01)	-0.69	(0.01)	0.55	(0.06)	-0.74	(0.03)	-0.50	(0.03)	**-0.24**	(0.04)
	Bulgaria	-0.91	(0.04)	-1.23	(0.01)	-1.07	(0.00)	-0.93	(0.01)	-0.40	(0.08)	-0.82	(0.08)	-0.91	(0.04)	0.09	(0.09)
	Colombia	-0.21	(0.07)	-1.00	(0.02)	-0.76	(0.02)	-0.17	(0.03)	1.09	(0.05)	-0.23	(0.09)	-0.20	(0.07)	-0.04	(0.06)
	Croatia	-0.93	(0.02)	-1.21	(0.01)	-1.04	(0.01)	-0.91	(0.00)	-0.54	(0.08)	c	c	-0.93	(0.02)	c	c
	Dubai (UAE)	0.15	(0.00)	-1.27	(0.00)	-0.62	(0.00)	1.11	(0.00)	1.36	(0.00)	-0.03	(0.02)	0.19	(0.01)	**-0.22**	(0.03)
	Hong Kong-China	0.92	(0.06)	-0.39	(0.05)	1.32	(0.01)	1.36	(0.00)	1.36	(0.00)	0.95	(0.06)	0.90	(0.06)	0.06	(0.04)
	Indonesia	0.13	(0.08)	-0.94	(0.03)	-0.45	(0.02)	0.57	(0.08)	1.36	(0.00)	0.09	(0.10)	0.18	(0.13)	-0.08	(0.16)
	Jordan	-1.20	(0.03)	-1.37	(0.00)	-1.37	(0.00)	-1.30	(0.01)	-0.77	(0.12)	-1.20	(0.03)	c	c	c	c
	Kazakhstan	-0.98	(0.04)	-1.35	(0.00)	-1.22	(0.01)	-1.02	(0.01)	-0.33	(0.09)	-0.99	(0.04)	-0.93	(0.06)	-0.06	(0.05)
	Kyrgyzstan	-0.25	(0.08)	-1.24	(0.01)	-0.90	(0.02)	-0.16	(0.05)	1.30	(0.02)	-0.28	(0.08)	-0.14	(0.13)	-0.13	(0.12)
	Latvia	-0.54	(0.05)	-1.03	(0.01)	-0.83	(0.01)	-0.61	(0.01)	0.30	(0.11)	-0.54	(0.05)	-0.67	(0.07)	**0.14**	(0.07)
	Liechtenstein	-0.05	(0.01)	-1.26	(0.00)	-0.97	(0.01)	0.63	(0.03)	1.36	(0.00)	-0.14	(0.02)	c	c	c	c
	Lithuania	0.13	(0.06)	-0.89	(0.02)	-0.32	(0.03)	0.39	(0.06)	1.36	(0.00)	0.13	(0.06)	c	c	c	c
	Macao-China	0.86	(0.00)	-0.46	(0.00)	1.16	(0.00)	1.36	(0.00)	1.36	(0.00)	0.81	(0.00)	0.94	(0.00)	**-0.13**	(0.00)
	Montenegro	-0.97	(0.00)	-1.34	(0.00)	-1.19	(0.00)	-0.98	(0.00)	-0.37	(0.01)	c	c	-0.97	(0.00)	c	c
	Panama	-0.60	(0.07)	-1.28	(0.02)	-0.98	(0.01)	-0.71	(0.03)	0.56	(0.14)	-0.60	(0.09)	-0.60	(0.10)	0.00	(0.12)
	Peru	-0.19	(0.08)	-1.22	(0.02)	-0.85	(0.01)	-0.05	(0.06)	1.36	(0.00)	-0.23	(0.09)	-0.17	(0.09)	-0.06	(0.10)
	Qatar	-0.61	(0.00)	-1.36	(0.00)	-1.17	(0.00)	-0.79	(0.00)	0.87	(0.00)	-0.30	(0.01)	-0.69	(0.00)	**0.39**	(0.01)
	Romania	-0.36	(0.06)	-1.00	(0.02)	-0.78	(0.01)	-0.47	(0.02)	0.80	(0.07)	-0.36	(0.06)	c	c	c	c
	Russian Federation	-0.36	(0.06)	-1.07	(0.03)	-0.78	(0.01)	-0.39	(0.02)	0.80	(0.09)	-0.42	(0.00)	-0.20	(0.00)	**-0.23**	(0.10)
	Serbia	-1.03	(0.01)	-1.24	(0.01)	-1.08	(0.01)	-0.97	(0.01)	-0.82	(0.02)	-0.88	(0.05)	-1.03	(0.02)	**0.15**	(0.05)
	Shanghai-China	-0.09	(0.08)	-1.17	(0.01)	-0.80	(0.02)	0.25	(0.08)	1.36	(0.00)	-0.12	(0.12)	-0.06	(0.09)	-0.05	(0.15)
	Singapore	-0.09	(0.01)	-0.95	(0.00)	-0.69	(0.00)	-0.10	(0.00)	1.36	(0.00)	-0.08	(0.06)	-0.09	(0.02)	0.02	(0.07)
	Chinese Taipei	0.38	(0.08)	-0.85	(0.02)	-0.16	(0.05)	1.15	(0.03)	1.36	(0.00)	0.27	(0.15)	0.44	(0.09)	-0.17	(0.16)
	Thailand	0.76	(0.06)	-0.52	(0.05)	0.83	(0.06)	1.36	(0.00)	1.36	(0.00)	0.68	(0.08)	0.79	(0.07)	-0.11	(0.09)
	Trinidad and Tobago	-0.61	(0.00)	-1.09	(0.00)	-0.91	(0.00)	-0.74	(0.00)	0.31	(0.01)	-0.64	(0.01)	-0.59	(0.01)	**-0.05**	(0.01)
	Tunisia	-1.29	(0.01)	-1.37	(0.00)	-1.37	(0.00)	-1.29	(0.01)	-1.14	(0.02)	-1.28	(0.01)	-1.30	(0.01)	0.02	(0.02)
	Uruguay	-0.99	(0.03)	-1.34	(0.01)	-1.18	(0.00)	-0.99	(0.01)	-0.45	(0.08)	-1.09	(0.02)	-0.92	(0.04)	**-0.17**	(0.04)

Note: Values that are statistically significant are indicated in bold (see Annex A3).
StatLink http://dx.doi.org/10.1787/888932343285

[Part 2/3]

Table IV.3.6 **Index of school responsibility for curriculum and assessment and reading performance, by national quarters of this index**

Results based on school principals' reports

		Index of school responsibility for curriculum and assessment												Variability in the index of school responsibility for curriculum and assessment	
		In general programmes		In vocational programmes		Difference between general and vocational programmes		In public schools		In private schools		Difference between public and private schools			
		Mean index	S.E.	Mean index	S.E.	Dif.	S.E.	Mean index	S.E.	Mean index	S.E.	Dif.	S.E.	Standard deviation	S.E.
OECD	Australia	0.20	(0.06)	0.14	(0.22)	0.06	(0.21)	0.05	(0.07)	0.38	(0.08)	**-0.34**	(0.11)	0.90	(0.02)
	Austria	-0.33	(0.10)	-0.34	(0.08)	0.01	(0.13)	-0.33	(0.06)	-0.27	(0.15)	-0.07	(0.17)	0.81	(0.04)
	Belgium	-0.21	(0.06)	-0.14	(0.06)	-0.07	(0.08)	-0.36	(0.07)	-0.09	(0.06)	**-0.27**	(0.09)	0.82	(0.03)
	Canada	a	a	a	a	a	a	-0.73	(0.02)	0.23	(0.16)	**-0.96**	(0.16)	0.60	(0.04)
	Chile	-0.09	(0.08)	0.00	(0.16)	-0.09	(0.13)	-0.50	(0.10)	0.24	(0.12)	**-0.75**	(0.16)	0.96	(0.03)
	Czech Republic	1.07	(0.05)	0.65	(0.14)	**0.42**	(0.14)	0.91	(0.06)	1.07	(0.21)	-0.15	(0.21)	0.79	(0.04)
	Denmark	0.05	(0.06)	c	c	c	c	-0.08	(0.08)	0.50	(0.14)	**-0.57**	(0.17)	0.94	(0.02)
	Estonia	0.22	(0.07)	c	c	c	c	0.23	(0.07)	-0.26	(0.24)	0.50	(0.26)	0.91	(0.02)
	Finland	-0.15	(0.06)	c	c	c	c	-0.17	(0.06)	0.38	(0.42)	-0.56	(0.42)	0.83	(0.04)
	France	w	w	w	w	w	w	w	w	w	w	w	w	w	w
	Germany	-0.26	(0.05)	-0.30	(0.18)	0.04	(0.18)	-0.27	(0.05)	0.13	(0.25)	-0.41	(0.26)	0.69	(0.03)
	Greece	-1.24	(0.02)	-1.31	(0.03)	0.07	(0.04)	-1.27	(0.01)	-0.83	(0.20)	**-0.45**	(0.20)	0.28	(0.06)
	Hungary	0.15	(0.08)	-0.15	(0.20)	0.30	(0.21)	0.03	(0.08)	0.64	(0.21)	**-0.61**	(0.22)	0.91	(0.03)
	Iceland	0.23	(0.00)	c	c	c	c	0.23	(0.00)	c	c	c	c	0.91	(0.00)
	Ireland	0.01	(0.07)	c	c	c	c	0.01	(0.13)	0.01	(0.09)	0.00	(0.15)	0.74	(0.04)
	Israel	-0.01	(0.08)	c	c	c	c	-0.10	(0.08)	0.34	(0.19)	**-0.44**	(0.20)	0.96	(0.03)
	Italy	0.29	(0.05)	0.12	(0.04)	**0.17**	(0.07)	0.21	(0.04)	0.05	(0.11)	0.16	(0.13)	0.90	(0.01)
	Japan	1.01	(0.07)	1.21	(0.07)	**-0.20**	(0.09)	0.98	(0.00)	1.26	(0.00)	**-0.28**	(0.08)	0.66	(0.05)
	Korea	0.90	(0.08)	0.44	(0.17)	**0.46**	(0.18)	0.74	(0.10)	0.87	(0.11)	-0.13	(0.14)	0.78	(0.04)
	Luxembourg	-0.83	(0.00)	-0.96	(0.00)	**0.12**	(0.00)	-0.93	(0.00)	-0.44	(0.00)	**-0.49**	(0.00)	0.56	(0.00)
	Mexico	-0.93	(0.02)	-0.91	(0.04)	-0.02	(0.04)	-0.97	(0.02)	-0.53	(0.10)	**-0.44**	(0.10)	0.52	(0.03)
	Netherlands	1.07	(0.05)	0.88	(0.40)	0.20	(0.41)	1.04	(0.09)	1.04	(0.07)	0.01	(0.11)	0.63	(0.04)
	New Zealand	0.81	(0.04)	c	c	c	c	0.81	(0.05)	0.92	(0.06)	-0.12	(0.08)	0.78	(0.02)
	Norway	-0.57	(0.05)	c	c	c	c	-0.57	(0.05)	c	c	c	c	0.67	(0.06)
	Poland	0.31	(0.06)	c	c	c	c	0.30	(0.06)	0.67	(0.18)	-0.36	(0.19)	0.83	(0.02)
	Portugal	-0.96	(0.02)	-0.70	(0.13)	**-0.26**	(0.12)	-1.05	(0.01)	-0.21	(0.12)	**-0.84**	(0.12)	0.39	(0.06)
	Slovak Republic	-0.01	(0.09)	0.53	(0.21)	**-0.54**	(0.22)	0.11	(0.08)	-0.18	(0.25)	0.29	(0.25)	1.00	(0.02)
	Slovenia	-0.48	(0.01)	-0.28	(0.00)	**-0.20**	(0.01)	-0.38	(0.01)	-0.38	(0.01)	0.01	(0.01)	0.76	(0.01)
	Spain	-0.48	(0.04)	c	c	c	c	-0.67	(0.04)	-0.11	(0.07)	**-0.56**	(0.08)	0.77	(0.03)
	Sweden	0.21	(0.07)	c	c	c	c	0.17	(0.07)	0.53	(0.19)	-0.35	(0.20)	0.95	(0.02)
	Switzerland	-0.65	(0.05)	-0.34	(0.29)	-0.30	(0.30)	-0.68	(0.05)	0.34	(0.28)	**-1.02**	(0.28)	0.71	(0.05)
	Turkey	-1.01	(0.05)	-1.09	(0.05)	0.07	(0.06)	-1.05	(0.03)	c	c	c	c	0.44	(0.06)
	United Kingdom	0.85	(0.05)	c	c	c	c	0.82	(0.05)	1.34	(0.02)	**-0.53**	(0.05)	0.80	(0.03)
	United States	-0.20	(0.06)	c	c	c	c	-0.29	(0.06)	0.68	(0.40)	**-0.97**	(0.41)	0.93	(0.03)
	OECD average	-0.03	(0.01)	-0.13	(0.04)	0.01	(0.04)	-0.11	(0.01)	0.28	(0.03)	**-0.36**	(0.04)	0.76	(0.01)
Partners	Albania	-0.42	(0.07)	-0.37	(0.24)	-0.05	(0.25)	-0.50	(0.07)	0.21	(0.16)	**-0.71**	(0.18)	0.84	(0.05)
	Argentina	-0.58	(0.05)	-0.52	(0.15)	-0.06	(0.15)	-0.69	(0.05)	-0.37	(0.09)	**-0.32**	(0.11)	0.62	(0.06)
	Azerbaijan	-0.63	(0.08)	-0.85	(0.17)	0.22	(0.19)	-0.63	(0.08)	c	c	c	c	0.81	(0.07)
	Brazil	-0.56	(0.03)	c	c	c	c	-0.72	(0.03)	0.63	(0.11)	**-1.35**	(0.11)	0.77	(0.03)
	Bulgaria	-0.87	(0.05)	-0.97	(0.04)	0.11	(0.07)	-0.91	(0.04)	c	c	c	c	0.39	(0.06)
	Colombia	-0.21	(0.08)	-0.21	(0.12)	0.00	(0.13)	-0.33	(0.08)	0.35	(0.12)	**-0.68**	(0.14)	0.84	(0.04)
	Croatia	-0.91	(0.05)	-0.93	(0.03)	0.02	(0.06)	-0.95	(0.02)	c	c	c	c	0.37	(0.07)
	Dubai (UAE)	0.15	(0.00)	c	c	c	c	-1.19	(0.00)	0.51	(0.00)	**-1.70**	(0.00)	1.15	(0.00)
	Hong Kong-China	0.92	(0.06)	c	c	c	c	0.38	(0.15)	0.96	(0.06)	**-0.58**	(0.16)	0.78	(0.04)
	Indonesia	0.14	(0.08)	0.09	(0.25)	0.05	(0.27)	-0.10	(0.11)	0.44	(0.12)	**-0.53**	(0.17)	0.95	(0.03)
	Jordan	-1.20	(0.03)	c	c	c	c	-1.28	(0.01)	-0.86	(0.17)	**-0.42**	(0.17)	0.49	(0.08)
	Kazakhstan	-0.99	(0.04)	-0.80	(0.08)	**-0.20**	(0.09)	-0.98	(0.04)	-0.96	(0.13)	-0.02	(0.14)	0.52	(0.06)
	Kyrgyzstan	-0.26	(0.08)	-0.03	(0.34)	-0.23	(0.35)	-0.27	(0.08)	0.51	(0.38)	**-0.78**	(0.39)	1.00	(0.04)
	Latvia	-0.54	(0.05)	c	c	c	c	-0.54	(0.05)	c	c	c	c	0.64	(0.06)
	Liechtenstein	-0.05	(0.01)	c	c	c	c	-0.14	(0.01)	c	c	c	c	1.14	(0.00)
	Lithuania	0.13	(0.06)	c	c	c	c	0.13	(0.06)	c	c	c	c	0.88	(0.03)
	Macao-China	0.86	(0.00)	c	c	c	c	c	c	0.93	(0.00)	c	c	0.81	(0.00)
	Montenegro	-0.83	(0.01)	-1.05	(0.00)	**0.22**	(0.01)	-0.97	(0.00)	c	c	c	c	0.57	(0.01)
	Panama	-0.60	(0.07)	c	c	c	c	-0.68	(0.09)	-0.25	(0.18)	**-0.43**	(0.20)	0.81	(0.07)
	Peru	-0.19	(0.08)	c	c	c	c	-0.44	(0.07)	0.72	(0.15)	**-1.16**	(0.15)	1.02	(0.04)
	Qatar	-0.61	(0.00)	c	c	c	c	-0.88	(0.00)	0.04	(0.01)	**-0.91**	(0.01)	0.94	(0.00)
	Romania	-0.42	(0.07)	-0.16	(0.12)	-0.26	(0.13)	-0.36	(0.06)	c	c	c	c	0.74	(0.04)
	Russian Federation	-0.40	(0.00)	0.35	(0.00)	**-0.74**	(0.36)	-0.36	(0.06)	c	c	c	c	0.79	(0.04)
	Serbia	-1.06	(0.01)	-1.02	(0.02)	-0.04	(0.03)	-1.03	(0.02)	c	c	c	c	0.18	(0.02)
	Shanghai-China	-0.28	(0.09)	0.59	(0.17)	**-0.87**	(0.19)	-0.14	(0.08)	0.39	(0.28)	-0.53	(0.29)	1.05	(0.03)
	Singapore	-0.09	(0.01)	c	c	c	c	-0.12	(0.00)	c	c	c	c	0.91	(0.01)
	Chinese Taipei	0.36	(0.11)	0.40	(0.10)	-0.04	(0.15)	0.24	(0.11)	0.62	(0.12)	**-0.38**	(0.16)	0.94	(0.02)
	Thailand	0.81	(0.07)	0.58	(0.14)	0.22	(0.16)	0.73	(0.07)	0.90	(0.17)	-0.17	(0.18)	0.85	(0.03)
	Trinidad and Tobago	-0.61	(0.01)	-0.56	(0.01)	**-0.05**	(0.01)	-0.67	(0.01)	-0.13	(0.01)	**-0.54**	(0.01)	0.68	(0.01)
	Tunisia	-1.29	(0.01)	c	c	c	c	-1.30	(0.01)	-1.08	(0.06)	**-0.21**	(0.06)	0.11	(0.01)
	Uruguay	-0.99	(0.03)	-1.08	(0.04)	0.09	(0.05)	-1.10	(0.02)	-0.49	(0.12)	**-0.61**	(0.12)	0.45	(0.06)

Note: Values that are statistically significant are indicated in bold (see Annex A3).

StatLink http://dx.doi.org/10.1787/888932343285

[Part 3/3]
Index of school responsibility for curriculum and assessment and reading performance, by national quarters of this index

Table IV.3.6 *Results based on school principals' reports*

		Performance on the reading scale by national quarters of this index								Change in the reading score per unit of this index		Increased likelihood of students in the bottom quarter of this index scoring in the bottom quarter of the national reading performance distribution		Explained variance in student performance (r-squared X 100)	
		Bottom quarter		Second quarter		Third quarter		Top quarter							
		Mean score	S.E.	Mean score	S.E.	Mean score	S.E.	Mean score	S.E.	Effect	S.E.	Ratio	S.E.	%	S.E.
OECD	Australia	513	(3.5)	521	(7.9)	509	(4.2)	517	(5.1)	0.6	(3.5)	1.0	(0.1)	0.0	(0.1)
	Austria	470	(10.5)	472	(10.9)	484	(9.4)	452	(8.0)	-11.7	(6.1)	1.0	(0.2)	0.9	(1.0)
	Belgium	**477**	(7.3)	507	(6.9)	521	(5.5)	**519**	(7.1)	**17.6**	(4.3)	**1.6**	(0.2)	2.0	(1.0)
	Canada	521	(3.4)	525	(3.5)	523	(2.9)	528	(3.8)	6.8	(3.6)	1.1	(0.1)	0.2	(0.2)
	Chile	**440**	(7.6)	445	(6.4)	452	(8.2)	**461**	(7.6)	8.2	(4.4)	1.2	(0.2)	0.9	(1.1)
	Czech Republic	482	(6.6)	476	(5.7)	476	(5.1)	475	(4.9)	-3.4	(4.7)	0.8	(0.1)	0.1	(0.2)
	Denmark	492	(4.5)	493	(4.0)	492	(4.3)	503	(4.9)	**4.9**	(2.5)	1.1	(0.1)	0.3	(0.3)
	Estonia	494	(5.4)	505	(3.1)	504	(4.1)	501	(6.4)	1.4	(3.5)	1.2	(0.1)	0.0	(0.2)
	Finland	536	(3.7)	540	(4.5)	528	(4.5)	539	(4.1)	1.9	(2.4)	1.0	(0.1)	0.0	(0.1)
	France	w	w	w	w	w	w	w	w	w	w	w	w	w	w
	Germany	**514**	(7.6)	514	(6.1)	492	(8.4)	**469**	(7.7)	**-29.5**	(5.8)	**0.7**	(0.1)	4.7	(2.0)
	Greece	**478**	(7.7)	477	(7.2)	474	(6.9)	**503**	(7.2)	**33.9**	(12.6)	1.1	(0.1)	1.0	(0.5)
	Hungary	491	(9.3)	490	(10.4)	488	(12.1)	508	(8.1)	9.0	(6.0)	1.1	(0.2)	0.8	(1.1)
	Iceland	**491**	(3.1)	492	(3.4)	503	(4.9)	**507**	(4.5)	**7.6**	(1.7)	1.1	(0.1)	0.5	(0.2)
	Ireland	510	(6.9)	495	(7.3)	472	(7.2)	499	(10.4)	-2.1	(7.9)	**0.7**	(0.1)	0.0	(0.3)
	Israel	476	(11.3)	483	(10.2)	461	(9.4)	478	(9.6)	1.1	(6.0)	1.0	(0.2)	0.0	(0.2)
	Italy	489	(4.6)	492	(5.0)	478	(4.4)	486	(5.2)	-3.2	(3.0)	0.9	(0.1)	0.1	(0.2)
	Japan	523	(9.1)	519	(5.4)	518	(4.8)	519	(5.2)	-3.3	(8.3)	1.0	(0.2)	0.0	(0.3)
	Korea	**522**	(8.8)	536	(5.6)	549	(4.9)	**550**	(4.6)	**16.5**	(5.7)	1.5	(0.3)	2.6	(1.7)
	Luxembourg	**479**	(3.1)	432	(3.6)	478	(4.2)	**499**	(3.1)	**21.2**	(2.2)	**0.8**	(0.0)	1.3	(0.3)
	Mexico	**418**	(3.5)	409	(4.6)	428	(3.8)	**446**	(4.1)	**23.4**	(4.0)	1.1	(0.1)	2.1	(0.7)
	Netherlands	493	(10.7)	513	(7.3)	513	(6.7)	514	(6.9)	14.2	(9.4)	1.3	(0.3)	1.0	(1.3)
	New Zealand	524	(5.5)	521	(4.2)	520	(6.1)	521	(5.3)	-2.3	(4.2)	1.0	(0.1)	0.0	(0.1)
	Norway	504	(5.6)	500	(4.3)	504	(4.1)	503	(5.2)	-0.8	(4.2)	1.0	(0.1)	0.0	(0.1)
	Poland	506	(4.7)	502	(4.9)	497	(4.6)	497	(5.0)	-4.3	(3.5)	0.9	(0.1)	0.2	(0.3)
	Portugal	**485**	(7.7)	484	(6.2)	485	(5.0)	**503**	(6.3)	**25.5**	(10.2)	1.1	(0.2)	1.3	(0.9)
	Slovak Republic	466	(7.8)	499	(7.9)	480	(9.0)	465	(7.4)	-6.8	(4.7)	1.2	(0.2)	0.6	(0.9)
	Slovenia	**496**	(2.1)	489	(2.0)	486	(2.7)	**461**	(2.1)	**-13.2**	(1.6)	**0.7**	(0.0)	1.2	(0.3)
	Spain	**464**	(4.3)	483	(4.6)	489	(4.5)	**487**	(5.0)	**8.2**	(3.1)	**1.4**	(0.1)	0.5	(0.4)
	Sweden	500	(7.2)	486	(5.8)	504	(4.7)	500	(5.2)	3.0	(3.4)	1.0	(0.1)	0.1	(0.2)
	Switzerland	**475**	(4.3)	483	(5.5)	509	(7.4)	**533**	(5.9)	**23.8**	(4.9)	**1.5**	(0.1)	3.3	(1.4)
	Turkey	475	(8.6)	454	(6.0)	466	(7.3)	462	(6.5)	-4.1	(9.5)	0.8	(0.1)	0.0	(0.3)
	United Kingdom	491	(5.0)	495	(4.1)	498	(4.8)	499	(4.5)	4.4	(3.5)	1.1	(0.1)	0.1	(0.2)
	United States	498	(7.5)	499	(8.0)	490	(6.5)	513	(7.0)	6.9	(4.5)	1.0	(0.1)	0.4	(0.6)
	OECD average	**491**	(1.2)	492	(1.1)	493	(1.1)	**497**	(1.1)	**4.7**	(1.0)	**1.1**	(0.0)	0.8	(0.1)
Partners	Albania	386	(7.0)	391	(8.9)	381	(8.8)	382	(8.2)	-0.3	(5.1)	1.0	(0.1)	0.0	(0.1)
	Argentina	**377**	(7.9)	385	(9.7)	424	(10.3)	**407**	(12.0)	**21.2**	(9.9)	**1.3**	(0.2)	1.5	(1.4)
	Azerbaijan	361	(8.0)	366	(5.6)	363	(7.4)	356	(7.4)	-1.9	(5.1)	1.0	(0.2)	0.0	(0.3)
	Brazil	**401**	(7.5)	400	(4.7)	398	(4.1)	**448**	(5.7)	**33.1**	(3.8)	1.1	(0.1)	7.3	(1.6)
	Bulgaria	448	(18.4)	435	(13.3)	408	(14.2)	425	(11.4)	-23.4	(20.3)	0.8	(0.2)	0.7	(1.1)
	Colombia	**403**	(6.9)	410	(7.0)	416	(7.1)	**424**	(8.4)	8.7	(5.1)	1.2	(0.2)	0.7	(0.9)
	Croatia	483	(8.7)	475	(8.6)	474	(7.0)	471	(8.1)	-13.4	(12.5)	0.8	(0.1)	0.3	(0.6)
	Dubai (UAE)	**386**	(2.0)	447	(2.7)	503	(3.4)	**501**	(3.1)	**39.8**	(0.9)	**2.9**	(0.1)	18.3	(0.8)
	Hong Kong-China	**546**	(8.4)	528	(4.4)	529	(4.3)	**529**	(4.7)	-9.4	(6.1)	0.8	(0.2)	0.8	(1.0)
	Indonesia	409	(7.2)	395	(7.2)	402	(9.4)	400	(6.4)	-2.3	(3.9)	0.8	(0.1)	0.1	(0.5)
	Jordan	405	(6.3)	405	(6.2)	401	(5.8)	409	(7.3)	-4.5	(9.8)	1.0	(0.1)	0.1	(0.3)
	Kazakhstan	374	(7.6)	404	(6.7)	400	(7.3)	384	(9.7)	-9.5	(9.2)	1.3	(0.2)	0.3	(0.6)
	Kyrgyzstan	314	(8.8)	333	(9.0)	308	(7.8)	302	(8.1)	-7.8	(4.4)	1.0	(0.1)	0.6	(0.7)
	Latvia	479	(6.3)	485	(5.1)	483	(5.0)	489	(6.8)	3.7	(5.1)	1.2	(0.1)	0.1	(0.3)
	Liechtenstein	**469**	(6.9)	472	(7.2)	491	(8.5)	**565**	(8.0)	**36.0**	(2.8)	1.5	(0.4)	24.4	(3.3)
	Lithuania	474	(6.0)	466	(7.8)	467	(4.8)	466	(6.2)	-2.9	(4.0)	1.0	(0.1)	0.1	(0.3)
	Macao-China	**481**	(1.7)	479	(2.4)	493	(2.4)	**493**	(2.7)	**9.2**	(1.0)	1.1	(0.1)	0.9	(0.2)
	Montenegro	393	(2.2)	422	(2.9)	419	(6.5)	397	(2.7)	**-16.2**	(2.0)	**1.3**	(0.1)	1.0	(0.2)
	Panama	375	(14.1)	371	(8.7)	379	(13.8)	358	(17.6)	-3.5	(11.6)	0.7	(0.2)	0.1	(0.9)
	Peru	**359**	(6.2)	361	(9.1)	372	(10.3)	**386**	(11.9)	8.4	(5.0)	1.0	(0.2)	0.8	(0.9)
	Qatar	**370**	(1.4)	375	(1.8)	330	(1.7)	**412**	(2.0)	**28.1**	(1.1)	**0.6**	(0.0)	5.3	(0.4)
	Romania	432	(9.3)	425	(8.8)	430	(10.4)	411	(9.0)	**-13.4**	(5.8)	0.9	(0.2)	1.2	(1.0)
	Russian Federation	446	(6.3)	463	(6.1)	473	(5.3)	455	(7.4)	-2.4	(4.1)	1.3	(0.2)	0.0	(0.2)
	Serbia	**463**	(5.3)	443	(7.4)	440	(6.3)	**421**	(6.8)	**-94.5**	(19.5)	**0.6**	(0.1)	4.3	(1.8)
	Shanghai-China	**564**	(6.0)	568	(8.2)	560	(6.6)	**532**	(6.7)	**-13.0**	(3.6)	**0.7**	(0.1)	2.9	(1.6)
	Singapore	**523**	(2.2)	529	(2.1)	512	(2.1)	**540**	(2.8)	**6.9**	(1.4)	1.0	(0.1)	0.4	(0.2)
	Chinese Taipei	**504**	(6.9)	500	(8.5)	489	(5.5)	**488**	(6.1)	-7.6	(4.6)	0.8	(0.1)	0.7	(0.9)
	Thailand	419	(5.4)	422	(5.0)	423	(4.6)	421	(4.7)	1.9	(4.0)	1.0	(0.1)	0.1	(0.3)
	Trinidad and Tobago	**400**	(2.8)	429	(3.1)	430	(3.1)	**425**	(3.2)	**17.1**	(2.1)	**1.3**	(0.1)	1.1	(0.3)
	Tunisia	406	(5.5)	406	(5.2)	398	(8.2)	404	(9.8)	-28.7	(43.5)	0.9	(0.1)	0.1	(0.5)
	Uruguay	**397**	(4.4)	420	(5.6)	427	(7.1)	**460**	(6.2)	**47.3**	(8.3)	**1.6**	(0.2)	4.5	(1.0)

Note: Values that are statistically significant are indicated in bold (see Annex A3).
StatLink http://dx.doi.org/10.1787/888932343285

[Part 1/3]

Table IV.3.7 School choice: system level

		Year of reference	Indicators of school choice (lower secondary)													
			Freedom for parents to choose a public school for their child(ren)							Financial incentives and disincentives for school choice					Responsibility for informing parents about school choices available to them	
			Public schools							School vouchers (also referred to as scholarships) are available and applicable			Tuition tax credits are available to help families offset costs of private schooling			
			Initial assignment based on geographical area schools	Families are given a general right to enrol in any traditional public school they wish	Choice of other public schools is restricted to the district or municipality	Choice of other public schools is restricted by region	Families must apply to enrol in a public school other than the one assigned to their child(ren)	There is free choice of other public schools if there are places available	Others restrictions or conditions	Public schools	Government-dependent private schools	Independent private schools	Government-dependent private schools	Independent private schools	Government is responsible for providing detailed information on specific school choice alternatives within families' location	The information contains performance data
			(1)	(2)	(3)	(4)	(5)	(6)	(7)	(8)	(9)	(10)	(11)	(12)	(13)	(14)
OECD	Austria[a]	2008	yes	yes	no	no	yes	yes	yes	no	no	no	no	no	yes	no
	Belgium (Fl.)[a]	2008	no	yes	no	no	no	yes	no	yes	yes	no	no	m	no	a
	Belgium (Fr.)[a]	2008	no	yes	no	no	no	yes	no	yes	yes	no	no	m	yes	no
	Chile[a]	2008	no	yes	no	no	no	no	no	yes	yes	m	no	no	yes	yes
	Czech Republic[a]	2008	yes	yes	no	no	no	yes	no	no	no	a	no	a	yes	no
	Denmark[a]	2008	yes	yes	no	no	yes	yes	no	no	no	no	no	no	no	a
	England[a, 1]	2008	yes	yes	no	no	yes	yes	no	a	a	no	no	no	yes	yes
	Estonia[a]	2008	yes	yes	no	no	yes	yes	no	yes	a	yes	a	yes	no	a
	Finland[a]	2008	yes	no	no	no	yes	no	yes	a	a	a	no	a	no	a
	France[a]	2008	yes	no	no	no	yes	yes	no	yes	yes	yes	no	no	yes	no
	Germany[a]	2008	yes	no	no	no	yes	yes	yes	yes	yes	m	yes	yes	yes	no
	Greece[a]	2008	yes	no	no	no	no	no	no	no	a	no	a	no	yes	m
	Hungary[a]	2008	yes	yes	no	no	yes	yes	no	no	no	no	m	m	yes	yes
	Iceland[a]	2008	yes	no	yes	yes	yes	yes	no	no	no	no	no	no	yes	m
	Ireland[a, 2]	2008	yes	yes	no	no	yes	yes	no	no	a	no	a	m	no	a
	Israel[a]	2008	yes	yes	yes	yes	no	yes	no	a	a	a	no	no	yes	no
	Italy[a]	2008	yes	yes	no	no	yes	yes	m	yes	a	no	a	yes	no	a
	Japan[a]	2008	yes	no	no	yes	yes	no	no	no	a	no	a	no	no	a
	Korea[a]	2008	yes	no	no	no	no	no	no	no	no	a	yes	a	no	a
	Luxembourg[a]	2008	yes	yes	no	no	yes	yes	no	no	no	no	yes	yes	yes	no
	Mexico[a, 1]	2008	yes	yes	no	no	yes	yes	no	a	a	no	a	no	yes	no
	Netherlands[a]	2008	no	no	no	no	no	no	yes	no	no	no	no	no	yes	no
	New Zealand[a]	2008	no	yes	no	no	yes	yes	no	yes	yes	yes	no	no	yes	yes
	Norway[a]	2008	yes	no	yes	yes	yes	no	m	no	no	no	no	no	no	a
	Poland[a, 1]	2008	yes	no	yes	yes	yes	yes	yes	yes	yes	yes	no	no	yes	no
	Portugal[a, 1]	2008	yes	yes	no	no	yes	yes	no	a	a	a	yes	yes	yes	no
	Scotland[a]	2008	yes	no	no	no	yes	yes	yes	no	no	no	no	yes	yes	no
	Slovak Republic[a]	2008	yes	yes	no	no	no	yes	no	yes	no	a	no	a	yes	no
	Slovenia[a]	2008	yes	no	no	no	yes	yes	no	no	no	no	no	no	no	a
	Spain[a, 1]	2008	yes	yes	no	no	yes	yes	no	yes	yes	a	no	yes	yes	no
	Sweden[a]	2008	yes	no	no	no	no	yes	no	no	no	a	no	a	no	a
	Switzerland[a]	2008	yes	no	yes	yes	yes	no	no	no	no	no	no	no	no	a
	United States[a, 1]	2008	yes	m	yes	yes	yes	no	yes	a	a	yes	a	yes	yes	yes
Partners	Argentina[b]	2008	yes	yes	no	yes	no	yes	yes	yes	no	no	m	m	yes	no
	Azerbaijan		m	m	m	m	m	m	m	m	m	m	m	m	m	m
	Brazil[a]	2008	yes	yes	yes	yes	yes	yes	yes	a	a	a	a	yes	no	a
	Bulgaria[b]	2008	no	yes	no	no	no	yes	no	no	a	no	a	no	yes	yes
	Chinese Taipei[b, 1]	2008	yes	no	yes	yes	yes	no	yes	yes	a	yes	a	no	yes	no
	Colombia[b]	2008	yes	no	no	no	yes	yes	no	no	no	no	no	no	no	a
	Croatia[b, 1]	2008	yes	no	yes	yes	yes	yes	no	no	a	no	a	no	yes	no
	Dubai (UAE)[b]	2008	yes	yes	m	yes	yes	yes	no	m	m	m	m	m	no	a
	Hong Kong-China[b]	2008	yes	yes	no	no	yes	yes	no	no	no	no	no	no	yes	no
	Indonesia		m	m	m	m	m	m	m	m	m	m	m	m	m	m
	Jordan		m	m	m	m	m	m	m	m	m	m	m	m	m	m
	Kazakhstan		m	m	m	m	m	m	m	m	m	m	m	m	m	m
	Kyrgyzstan[b]	2008	yes	yes	no	no	yes	yes	no	no	a	no	a	no	no	a
	Latvia[b]	2008	yes	no	yes	no	no	yes	no	no	no	no	no	no	no	a
	Liechtenstein		m	m	m	m	m	m	m	m	m	m	m	m	m	m
	Lithuania[b, 1]	2008	yes	no	no	no	no	no	no	yes	yes	yes	no	no	yes	no
	Macao-China[b]	2008	no	yes	no	no	no	yes	no	no	no	yes	no	no	yes	no
	Montenegro[b, 1]	2008	yes	yes	no	no	yes	yes	no	yes	a	a	a	a	yes	no
	Panama[b]	2008	yes	yes	no	no	no	yes	yes	m	m	a	m	m	m	m
	Peru[b]	2008	no	yes	no	no	no	yes	no	a	a	a	no	no	no	a
	Qatar[b]	2008	yes	no	no	no	yes	yes	no	no	a	yes	a	no	yes	yes
	Romania		m	m	m	m	m	m	m	m	m	m	m	m	m	m
	Shanghai-China[b]	2008	yes	no	no	no	no	no	no	no	a	no	a	no	yes	no
	Singapore[b, 1]	2008	no	yes	no	no	no	yes	no	yes	a	no	a	no	yes	yes
	Thailand[b]	2008	yes	yes	yes	yes	yes	yes	yes	yes	yes	yes	yes	yes	yes	yes
	Trinidad and Tobago		m	m	m	m	m	m	m	m	m	m	m	m	m	m
	Tunisia		m	m	m	m	m	m	m	m	m	m	m	m	m	m
	Uruguay		m	m	m	m	m	m	m	m	m	m	m	m	m	m

1. Colum (13): Yes, but information is limited to public forms of school choice
2. Schools which are publicly funded and privately managed are included in the category of "public schools".

Sources: a. *Education at a Glance 2010: OECD Indicators* (OECD, 2010a). For further notes, see *Education at a Glance* (OECD, 2010a) Annex 3, available on line: *www.oecd.org/edu/eag2010*

b. PISA system-level data collection in 2010.

StatLink http://dx.doi.org/10.1787/888932343285

[Part2/3]

Table IV.3.7 **School choice: system level**

		Changes in school choice over 25 years (lower secondary)										
		Expansion of school choice within the public school sector over the past 25 years					Government-dependent private schools and their role in providing compulsory education at the lower secondary level					
		Public schools					Government-dependent private schools					
		Opportunities for school choice among public schools have expanded since 1985	Reforms have reduced restrictions to school choice among existing public schools	Reforms have included the creation of new autonomous public schools, to offer new options from which parents can choose	Reforms have permitted greater autonomy for existing public schools, including decisions about enrolment procedures and policies, which can increase school choice	Reforms have included new funding mechanisms that promote school choice	Government-dependent private schools are permitted to operate and provide compulsory education	Opportunities for families to choose a government-dependent private school have been expanded since 1985	Reforms have reduced restrictions to school choice among existing government-dependent private schools	Reforms have promoted the creation of additional government-dependent private schools, to offer new options from which parents can choose	Reforms have permitted greater autonomy for existing government-dependent private schools, including decisions about enrolment procedures and policies, which can increase school choice	Reforms have included new funding mechanisms that promote school choice
	Year of reference	(15)	(16)	(17)	(18)	(19)	(20)	(21)	(22)	(23)	(24)	(25)
OECD												
Austria[a]	2008	no	a	a	a	a	yes	no	a	a	a	a
Belgium (Fl.)[a]	2008	no	a	a	a	a	yes	no	a	a	a	a
Belgium (Fr.)[a]	2008	yes	yes	no	no	no	yes	yes	yes	no	no	no
Chile[a]	2008	no	a	a	a	a	yes	no	a	a	a	a
Czech Republic[a]	2008	yes	no	yes	m	no	yes	yes	no	no	no	yes
Denmark[a]	2008	yes	yes	no	yes	no	yes	no	a	a	a	a
England[a, 1]	2008	yes	yes	yes	yes	yes	yes	yes	yes	yes	yes	yes
Estonia[a]	2008	yes	yes	yes	yes	yes	no	a	a	a	a	a
Finland[a]	2008	yes	yes	no	yes	yes	yes	yes	yes	yes	yes	yes
France[a]	2008	yes	yes	no	no	no	yes	no	a	a	a	a
Germany[a]	2008	yes	yes	yes	yes	no	yes	yes	no	yes	no	no
Greece[a]	2008	no	a	a	a	a	no	a	a	a	a	a
Hungary[a]	2008	yes	yes	yes	yes	yes	yes	yes	yes	yes	yes	yes
Iceland[a]	2008	yes	yes	yes	no	no	yes	yes	yes	yes	no	no
Ireland[a, 2]	2008	no	a	a	a	a	no	a	a	a	a	a
Israel[a]	2008	yes	yes	yes	yes	yes	yes	yes	yes	yes	yes	yes
Italy[a]	2008	yes	yes	yes	yes	yes	no	a	a	a	a	a
Japan[a]	2008	no	a	a	a	a	no	a	a	a	a	a
Korea[a]	2008	no	a	a	a	a	yes	no	a	a	a	a
Luxembourg[a]	2008	yes	yes	yes	yes	yes	yes	no	a	a	a	a
Mexico[a, 1]	2008	no	a	a	a	a	no	a	a	a	a	a
Netherlands[a]	2008	no	a	a	a	a	yes	no	a	a	a	a
New Zealand[a]	2008	yes	yes	yes	yes	no	yes	no	a	a	a	a
Norway[a]	2008	no	a	a	a	a	yes	yes	yes	yes	no	no
Poland[a, 1]	2008	yes	no	no	no	yes	yes	yes	yes	no	no	yes
Portugal[a, 1]	2008	yes	yes	yes	no	yes	yes	no	a	a	a	a
Scotland[a]	2008	no	a	a	a	a	yes	no	no	no	no	no
Slovak Republic[a]	2008	yes	yes	yes	yes	yes	yes	yes	yes	yes	yes	yes
Slovenia[a]	2008	no	a	a	a	a	yes	yes	no	yes	no	yes
Spain[a, 1]	2008	yes	no	no	no	no	yes	yes	no	yes	no	no
Sweden[a]	2008	yes	yes	no	no	yes	yes	yes	yes	yes	no	yes
Switzerland[a]	2008	no	a	a	a	a	yes	no	a	a	a	a
United States[a, 1]	2008	yes	yes	yes	yes	yes	no	a	a	a	a	a
Partners												
Argentina[b]	2008	yes	yes	no	no	no	yes	yes	yes	yes	no	no
Azerbaijan		m	m	m	m	m	m	m	m	m	m	m
Brazil[a]	2008	no	a	a	a	a	no	a	a	a	a	a
Bulgaria[b]	2008	yes	yes	no	yes	yes	no	a	a	a	a	a
Chinese Taipei[b, 1]	2008	yes	no	no	no	no	a	a	a	a	a	a
Colombia[b]	2008	no	a	a	a	a	yes	no	a	a	a	a
Croatia[b, 1]	2008	no	a	a	a	a	no	a	a	a	a	a
Dubai (UAE)[b]	2008	yes	no	no	no	no	yes	no	a	a	a	a
Hong Kong-China[b]	2008	yes	no	yes	no	yes	yes	yes	yes	yes	yes	yes
Indonesia		m	m	m	m	m	m	m	m	m	m	m
Jordan		m	m	m	m	m	m	m	m	m	m	m
Kazakhstan		m	m	m	m	m	m	m	m	m	m	m
Kyrgyzstan[b]	2008	yes	no	no	yes	yes	no	a	a	a	a	a
Latvia[b]	2008	no	a	a	a	a	yes	yes	no	yes	no	no
Liechtenstein		m	m	m	m	m	m	m	m	m	m	m
Lithuania[b, 1]	2008	yes	no	no	no	no	yes	yes	no	no	no	yes
Macao-China[b]	2008	no	a	a	a	a	yes	no	a	a	a	a
Montenegro[b, 1]	2008	no	a	a	a	a	no	a	a	a	a	a
Panama[b]	2008	no	a	a	a	a	yes	no	a	a	a	a
Peru[b]	2008	yes	no	yes	yes	no	yes	yes	no	no	yes	no
Qatar[b]	2008	yes	no	yes	no	yes	no	a	a	a	a	a
Romania		m	m	m	m	m	m	m	m	m	m	m
Shanghai-China[b]	2008	no	a	a	a	a	no	a	a	a	a	a
Singapore[b, 1]	2008	yes	yes	yes	yes	no	no	a	a	a	a	a
Thailand[b]	2008	yes	yes	yes	yes	yes	yes	no	a	a	a	a
Trinidad and Tobago		m	m	m	m	m	m	m	m	m	m	m
Tunisia		m	m	m	m	m	m	m	m	m	m	m
Uruguay		m	m	m	m	m	m	m	m	m	m	m

1. Colum (13): Yes, but information is limited to public forms of school choice
2. Schools which are publicly funded and privately managed are included in the category of "public schools".

Sources: a. *Education at a Glance 2010: OECD Indicators* (OECD, 2010a). For further notes, see *Education at a Glance* (OECD, 2010a) Annex 3, available on line: *www.oecd.org/edu/eag2010*

b. PISA system-level data collection in 2010.

StatLink http://dx.doi.org/10.1787/888932343285

[Part 3/3]
Table IV.3.7 School choice: system level

		Changes in school choice over 25 years (lower secondary)						A standard curriculum or partially standardised curriculum is required according to government regulations (lower secondary)			
		Independent private schools and their role in providing compulsory education at the lower secondary level									
		Independent private schools									
	Year of reference	Independent private schools are permitted to operate and provide compulsory education	Opportunities for families to choose an independent private school have been expanded by legislation since 1985	Reforms have reduced restrictions to school choice among existing independent private schools	Reforms have promoted the creation of additional independent private schools, to offer new options from which parents can choose	Reforms have permitted greater autonomy for existing independent private schools, including decisions about enrolment procedures and policies, which can increase school choice	Reforms have included new funding mechanisms that promote school choice	Public schools	Government-dependent private schools	Independent private schools	Homeschooling
		(26)	(27)	(28)	(29)	(30)	(31)	(32)	(33)	(34)	(35)
OECD											
Austria[a]	2008	yes	no	a	a	a	a	yes	yes	no	yes
Belgium (Fl.)[a]	2008	no	a	a	a	a	a	yes	yes	m	a
Belgium (Fr.)[a]	2008	no	a	a	a	a	a	yes	yes	m	yes
Chile[a]	2008	yes	no	a	a	a	a	yes	yes	yes	no
Czech Republic[a]	2008	no	a	a	a	a	a	yes	yes	a	a
Denmark[a]	2008	yes	no	a	a	a	a	yes	no	no	no
England[a, 1]	2008	yes	no	a	a	a	a	yes	yes	no	no
Estonia[a]	2008	yes	yes	yes	yes	yes	yes	yes	a	yes	yes
Finland[a]	2008	no	a	a	a	a	a	yes	yes	a	yes
France[a]	2008	yes	no	a	a	a	a	yes	yes	yes	yes
Germany[a]	2008	yes	m	m	m	m	m	yes	yes	m	a
Greece[a]	2008	yes	no	a	a	a	a	yes	a	yes	a
Hungary[a]	2008	yes	m	m	m	m	m	no	no	no	no
Iceland[a]	2008	yes	yes	no	yes	no	no	yes	yes	yes	yes
Ireland[a, 2]	2008	yes	no	a	a	a	a	yes	a	yes	a
Israel[a]	2008	yes	no	a	a	a	a	yes	yes	yes	yes
Italy[a]	2008	yes	yes	yes	no	no	yes	yes	a	yes	a
Japan[a]	2008	yes	yes	yes	yes	no	no	yes	a	yes	a
Korea[a]	2008	no	a	a	a	a	a	yes	yes	a	a
Luxembourg[a]	2008	yes	yes	no	yes	yes	yes	yes	yes	no	yes
Mexico[a, 1]	2008	yes	no	a	a	a	a	yes	a	yes	a
Netherlands[a]	2008	yes	no	a	a	a	a	no	no	no	no
New Zealand[a]	2008	yes	no	a	a	a	a	yes	yes	no	no
Norway[a]	2008	yes	no	a	a	a	a	yes	no	no	yes
Poland[a, 1]	2008	yes	yes	yes	no	no	yes	yes	yes	yes	yes
Portugal[a, 1]	2008	yes	no	a	a	a	a	yes	yes	yes	yes
Scotland[a]	2008	yes	yes	no	yes	no	no	m	m	no	no
Slovak Republic[a]	2008	no	a	a	a	a	a	yes	yes	a	yes
Slovenia[a]	2008	yes	no	a	a	a	a	yes	yes	no	yes
Spain[a, 1]	2008	yes	no	a	a	a	a	yes	yes	yes	a
Sweden[a]	2008	no	a	a	a	a	a	yes	yes	a	yes
Switzerland[a]	2008	yes	no	a	a	a	a	yes	yes	yes	yes
United States[a, 1]	2008	yes	no	a	a	a	a	no	a	no	no
Partners											
Argentina[b]	2008	yes	yes	yes	yes	yes	no	yes	yes	yes	a
Azerbaijan		m	m	m	m	m	m	m	m	m	m
Brazil[a]	2008	yes	no	a	a	a	a	yes	a	yes	a
Bulgaria[b]	2008	yes	yes	no	no	no	no	yes	a	yes	a
Chinese Taipei[b, 1]	2008	yes	yes	yes	yes	yes	yes	yes	a	yes	no
Colombia[b]	2008	yes	no	a	a	a	a	yes	yes	yes	a
Croatia[b, 1]	2008	yes	yes	no	yes	yes	yes	yes	a	yes	a
Dubai (UAE)[b]	2008	yes	yes	no	yes	yes	yes	m	m	m	a
Hong Kong-China[b]	2008	yes	yes	yes	yes	yes	yes	yes	yes	no	a
Indonesia		m	m	m	m	m	m	m	m	m	m
Jordan		m	m	m	m	m	m	m	m	m	m
Kazakhstan		m	m	m	m	m	m	m	m	m	m
Kyrgyzstan[b]	2008	yes	yes	no	yes	no	no	yes	a	yes	a
Latvia[b]	2008	yes	yes	no	yes	no	no	yes	yes	yes	a
Liechtenstein		m	m	m	m	m	m	m	m	m	m
Lithuania[b, 1]	2008	yes	yes	no	yes	no	yes	yes	yes	yes	a
Macao-China[b]	2008	yes	no	a	a	a	a	yes	yes	yes	a
Montenegro[b, 1]	2008	no	a	a	a	a	a	yes	a	a	yes
Panama[b]	2008	yes	no	a	a	a	a	m	m	m	a
Peru[b]	2008	yes	yes	no	yes	no	no	yes	yes	yes	a
Qatar[b]	2008	yes	yes	no	yes	no	yes	yes	a	no	yes
Romania		m	m	m	m	m	m	m	m	m	m
Shanghai-China[b]	2008	yes	yes	no	yes	yes	no	yes	a	yes	a
Singapore[b, 1]	2008	yes	no	a	a	a	a	yes	a	no	a
Thailand[b]	2008	yes	no	a	a	a	a	yes	yes	yes	yes
Trinidad and Tobago		m	m	m	m	m	m	m	m	m	m
Tunisia		m	m	m	m	m	m	m	m	m	m
Uruguay		m	m	m	m	m	m	m	m	m	m

1. Colum (13): Yes, but information is limited to public forms of school choice
2. Schools which are publicly funded and privately managed are included in the category of "public schools".

Sources: a. *Education at a Glance 2010: OECD Indicators* (OECD, 2010a). For further notes, see *Education at a Glance* (OECD, 2010a) Annex 3, available on line: *www.oecd.org/edu/eag2010*
b. PISA system-level data collection in 2010.

StatLink http://dx.doi.org/10.1787/888932343285

[Part 1/1]
Table IV.3.8a **School choice: school level**
Results based on school principals' reports

		Percentage of students in schools where the principal reported the number of schools competing for students in the same area					
		Two or more other schools		One other school		No other schools	
		%	S.E.	%	S.E.	%	S.E.
OECD	Australia	90.2	(1.2)	5.6	(1.1)	4.3	(1.1)
	Austria	43.1	(3.7)	14.0	(2.9)	42.8	(3.8)
	Belgium	81.9	(2.4)	12.7	(1.9)	5.3	(1.4)
	Canada	66.5	(1.9)	18.1	(1.9)	15.4	(1.0)
	Chile	68.1	(3.9)	10.9	(2.5)	21.0	(3.2)
	Czech Republic	70.8	(3.0)	12.7	(2.2)	16.4	(2.6)
	Denmark	66.7	(3.1)	11.1	(2.4)	22.2	(2.7)
	Estonia	57.5	(2.7)	23.7	(2.8)	18.9	(2.4)
	Finland	43.9	(3.3)	13.6	(3.0)	42.5	(3.2)
	France	w	w	w	w	w	w
	Germany	64.1	(2.9)	17.2	(2.4)	18.7	(2.5)
	Greece	40.1	(3.7)	19.7	(2.8)	40.2	(3.8)
	Hungary	57.9	(4.3)	22.1	(3.3)	20.0	(3.4)
	Iceland	35.8	(0.2)	15.0	(0.1)	49.2	(0.2)
	Ireland	70.3	(4.2)	11.5	(3.1)	18.1	(3.6)
	Israel	62.3	(3.7)	17.9	(3.0)	19.8	(2.7)
	Italy	78.2	(1.6)	9.9	(1.2)	11.9	(1.2)
	Japan	85.0	(2.2)	5.8	(1.8)	9.2	(1.8)
	Korea	72.3	(3.6)	14.5	(3.1)	13.3	(2.6)
	Luxembourg	52.1	(0.1)	24.5	(0.1)	23.4	(0.1)
	Mexico	73.8	(1.3)	12.4	(1.2)	13.8	(1.1)
	Netherlands	76.2	(3.0)	21.0	(2.8)	2.9	(1.1)
	New Zealand	74.8	(2.5)	11.8	(2.2)	13.4	(2.2)
	Norway	22.3	(3.3)	17.8	(2.9)	59.9	(3.4)
	Poland	43.4	(3.0)	24.2	(3.4)	32.3	(3.4)
	Portugal	57.4	(3.6)	22.0	(3.1)	20.6	(2.9)
	Slovak Republic	79.0	(3.1)	14.4	(2.8)	6.5	(1.8)
	Slovenia	39.9	(0.3)	8.8	(0.3)	51.2	(0.4)
	Spain	65.0	(2.1)	14.6	(2.0)	20.5	(2.3)
	Sweden	52.1	(3.4)	17.2	(2.8)	30.7	(3.5)
	Switzerland	29.0	(3.2)	8.9	(1.7)	62.1	(3.2)
	Turkey	52.0	(4.0)	10.9	(2.5)	37.1	(3.7)
	United Kingdom	78.0	(2.5)	10.9	(2.0)	11.2	(1.8)
	United States	69.7	(3.1)	8.9	(2.1)	21.4	(3.3)
	OECD average	61.2	(0.5)	14.7	(0.4)	24.1	(0.4)
Partners	Albania	51.1	(3.9)	17.3	(3.0)	31.6	(3.1)
	Argentina	76.5	(3.4)	8.6	(2.1)	14.9	(3.2)
	Azerbaijan	49.0	(4.6)	23.1	(3.6)	27.8	(3.8)
	Brazil	69.2	(2.3)	12.9	(1.5)	17.8	(2.2)
	Bulgaria	71.6	(3.6)	11.9	(3.3)	16.5	(2.3)
	Colombia	75.8	(3.7)	10.7	(2.9)	13.5	(3.1)
	Croatia	70.7	(3.6)	10.3	(2.4)	19.0	(3.1)
	Dubai (UAE)	84.9	(0.1)	5.0	(0.1)	10.1	(0.0)
	Hong Kong-China	94.0	(1.8)	4.0	(1.7)	2.0	(1.2)
	Indonesia	87.4	(2.3)	9.3	(2.3)	3.3	(1.2)
	Jordan	49.0	(3.6)	21.6	(3.0)	29.4	(3.6)
	Kazakhstan	64.6	(3.6)	10.5	(2.3)	24.9	(3.5)
	Kyrgyzstan	53.0	(3.5)	14.3	(3.0)	32.8	(3.7)
	Latvia	69.3	(3.7)	19.8	(3.1)	10.9	(2.4)
	Liechtenstein	10.2	(0.4)	41.8	(0.4)	48.1	(0.5)
	Lithuania	55.1	(3.3)	25.4	(3.1)	19.5	(2.9)
	Macao-China	92.2	(0.0)	7.7	(0.0)	0.1	(0.0)
	Montenegro	27.2	(1.3)	10.2	(0.2)	62.6	(1.1)
	Panama	53.1	(4.5)	17.6	(3.8)	29.3	(4.8)
	Peru	60.5	(3.2)	17.3	(3.0)	22.2	(2.6)
	Qatar	51.2	(0.1)	13.1	(0.1)	35.8	(0.1)
	Romania	61.5	(4.0)	21.7	(3.5)	16.7	(3.0)
	Russian Federation	59.1	(3.8)	14.4	(2.5)	26.4	(3.6)
	Serbia	58.2	(3.9)	20.4	(3.7)	21.4	(2.6)
	Shanghai-China	68.8	(3.8)	16.1	(2.9)	15.1	(3.1)
	Singapore	90.3	(0.8)	6.4	(1.1)	3.4	(0.3)
	Chinese Taipei	85.1	(3.2)	10.1	(2.5)	4.8	(1.7)
	Thailand	71.2	(3.2)	17.8	(2.9)	10.9	(1.8)
	Trinidad and Tobago	76.2	(0.2)	13.6	(0.2)	10.2	(0.2)
	Tunisia	34.2	(3.6)	31.4	(4.0)	34.4	(3.5)
	Uruguay	42.0	(2.7)	12.9	(2.1)	45.1	(2.9)

StatLink http://dx.doi.org/10.1787/888932343285

[Part 1/1]
School choice, by lower or upper secondary level of education
Table IV.3.8b *Results based on school principals' reports*

		Lower secondary education (ISCED 2)						Upper secondary education (ISCED 3)						Difference between lower and upper secondary education in the percentages of schools competing for students in the same area with at least one other school	
		Number of schools competing for students in the same area						Number of schools competing for students in the same area							
		Two or more other schools		One other school		No other schools		Two or more other schools		One other school		No other schools			
		%	S.E.	%	S.E.	%	S.E.	%	S.E.	%	S.E.	%	S.E.	Dif. in %	S.E.
OECD	Australia	90.3	(1.3)	5.7	(1.2)	4.0	(1.1)	87.5	(2.1)	6.2	(2.1)	6.4	(2.4)	2.4	(2.2)
	Austria	69.0	(9.0)	9.5	(4.8)	21.5	(7.7)	41.2	(3.9)	14.4	(3.2)	44.5	(4.0)	**22.9**	(9.0)
	Belgium	70.0	(7.7)	16.1	(5.5)	13.9	(6.7)	83.1	(2.4)	12.4	(1.9)	4.5	(1.4)	-9.4	(6.8)
	Canada	60.7	(3.1)	14.3	(2.2)	25.1	(2.8)	67.5	(2.0)	18.7	(2.1)	13.8	(0.9)	**-11.3**	(2.5)
	Chile	56.3	(8.7)	24.2	(6.9)	19.5	(6.0)	68.7	(4.0)	10.2	(2.6)	21.1	(3.4)	1.6	(6.5)
	Czech Republic	55.0	(5.0)	17.3	(3.6)	27.7	(4.5)	89.9	(3.0)	7.3	(2.3)	2.8	(1.7)	**-24.9**	(4.7)
	Denmark	66.9	(3.1)	11.2	(2.4)	21.9	(2.7)	44.5	(24.7)	0.0	c	55.5	(24.7)	33.6	(24.8)
	Estonia	57.1	(2.7)	23.7	(2.8)	19.2	(2.5)	74.1	(6.0)	23.0	(6.1)	2.9	(1.5)	**-16.3**	(2.4)
	Finland	43.8	(3.3)	13.6	(3.0)	42.7	(3.2)	c	c	c	c	c	c	c	c
	France	w	w	w	w	w	w	w	w	w	w	w	w	w	w
	Germany	64.8	(3.0)	17.7	(2.4)	17.5	(2.6)	41.5	(14.3)	0.8	(0.7)	57.7	(14.3)	**40.3**	(15.1)
	Greece	41.8	(14.4)	16.8	(10.9)	41.4	(14.6)	40.0	(3.8)	19.9	(2.9)	40.1	(4.0)	-1.3	(15.3)
	Hungary	66.0	(8.7)	8.5	(3.8)	25.5	(8.0)	57.0	(4.5)	23.6	(3.6)	19.4	(3.7)	-6.1	(8.7)
	Iceland	35.8	(0.2)	15.0	(0.1)	49.2	(0.2)	c	c	c	c	c	c	c	c
	Ireland	69.3	(4.5)	11.9	(3.2)	18.8	(3.8)	72.1	(4.1)	11.0	(3.0)	16.9	(3.6)	-1.9	(2.3)
	Israel	54.6	(6.7)	21.2	(6.4)	24.2	(5.7)	63.6	(3.8)	17.4	(3.1)	19.0	(2.7)	-5.2	(5.5)
	Italy	47.1	(13.2)	10.1	(3.7)	42.8	(12.4)	78.6	(1.7)	9.9	(1.2)	11.5	(1.2)	**-31.3**	(12.6)
	Japan	c	c	c	c	c	c	85.0	(2.2)	5.8	(1.8)	9.2	(1.8)	c	c
	Korea	83.1	(12.3)	0.7	(0.7)	16.3	(12.3)	71.8	(3.7)	15.1	(3.2)	13.1	(2.6)	-3.1	(12.7)
	Luxembourg	49.9	(0.3)	26.2	(0.2)	23.9	(0.2)	55.8	(0.3)	21.7	(0.2)	22.5	(0.2)	**-1.4**	(0.4)
	Mexico	61.9	(2.6)	16.1	(2.1)	22.0	(2.1)	83.0	(1.5)	9.5	(1.1)	7.5	(1.1)	**-14.5**	(2.4)
	Netherlands	75.5	(3.6)	21.1	(3.3)	3.3	(1.3)	78.0	(5.3)	20.4	(5.2)	1.5	(1.5)	-1.8	(1.8)
	New Zealand	75.5	(4.1)	10.9	(3.8)	13.5	(3.4)	74.8	(2.5)	11.9	(2.2)	13.4	(2.1)	-0.1	(2.4)
	Norway	22.3	(3.3)	17.8	(2.9)	59.9	(3.4)	c	c	c	c	c	c	c	c
	Poland	42.9	(3.1)	24.5	(3.4)	32.6	(3.4)	c	c	c	c	c	c	c	c
	Portugal	48.4	(4.9)	24.2	(4.4)	27.4	(4.5)	64.4	(4.3)	20.3	(3.6)	15.4	(3.2)	**-12.0**	(5.2)
	Slovak Republic	66.5	(5.3)	20.3	(4.8)	13.2	(3.6)	86.9	(3.6)	10.7	(3.2)	2.3	(1.7)	**-10.9**	(4.0)
	Slovenia	30.0	(10.0)	21.7	(9.8)	48.3	(11.8)	40.3	(0.2)	8.4	(0.1)	51.3	(0.2)	3.0	(11.8)
	Spain	65.0	(2.1)	14.6	(2.0)	20.5	(2.3)	c	c	c	c	c	c	c	c
	Sweden	51.4	(3.4)	17.4	(2.8)	31.2	(3.6)	95.1	(5.0)	4.9	(5.0)	0.0	c	**-31.2**	(3.6)
	Switzerland	23.2	(3.3)	10.5	(1.9)	66.2	(3.4)	50.8	(7.3)	2.9	(1.2)	46.3	(7.3)	**-19.9**	(7.9)
	Turkey	c	c	c	c	c	c	54.2	(4.2)	11.4	(2.6)	34.4	(3.9)	c	c
	United Kingdom	89.2	(8.1)	7.7	(5.7)	3.1	(3.5)	77.5	(2.6)	11.1	(2.0)	11.4	(1.9)	**8.4**	(3.8)
	United States	63.4	(4.7)	11.4	(3.0)	25.1	(5.0)	70.5	(3.1)	8.5	(2.0)	21.0	(3.2)	-4.1	(3.7)
	OECD average	58.0	(1.2)	15.5	(0.8)	26.5	(1.1)	67.8	(1.2)	12.1	(0.6)	20.2	(1.2)	**-3.6**	(1.7)
Partners	Albania	59.0	(5.0)	16.9	(4.2)	24.1	(3.8)	42.0	(5.5)	17.7	(3.9)	40.2	(4.4)	**16.1**	(5.5)
	Argentina	75.1	(4.2)	7.0	(2.0)	17.9	(4.3)	77.4	(3.8)	9.6	(2.5)	13.0	(3.2)	-5.0	(3.8)
	Azerbaijan	52.1	(5.0)	21.7	(3.8)	26.2	(4.0)	45.3	(4.8)	24.9	(3.8)	29.8	(4.3)	3.6	(3.1)
	Brazil	64.5	(3.1)	13.9	(2.1)	21.6	(2.7)	70.7	(2.6)	12.6	(1.6)	16.6	(2.4)	-5.0	(2.9)
	Bulgaria	51.8	(7.5)	14.2	(5.5)	34.0	(6.2)	73.2	(3.8)	11.8	(3.5)	15.1	(2.4)	**-18.9**	(6.7)
	Colombia	72.7	(4.2)	11.3	(3.1)	16.1	(4.0)	77.6	(3.7)	10.3	(2.9)	12.1	(2.9)	-4.0	(2.4)
	Croatia	c	c	c	c	c	c	70.8	(3.6)	10.1	(2.4)	19.1	(3.1)	c	c
	Dubai (UAE)	87.8	(0.4)	6.3	(0.3)	5.9	(0.3)	84.2	(0.1)	4.7	(0.1)	11.2	(0.1)	**5.3**	(0.3)
	Hong Kong-China	94.4	(2.0)	2.9	(1.3)	2.7	(1.6)	93.8	(1.8)	4.6	(1.9)	1.6	(1.0)	-1.1	(1.0)
	Indonesia	87.6	(3.3)	8.5	(3.2)	3.9	(2.0)	87.1	(3.5)	10.3	(3.2)	2.6	(1.3)	-1.3	(2.4)
	Jordan	49.0	(3.6)	21.6	(3.0)	29.4	(3.6)	c	c	c	c	c	c	c	c
	Kazakhstan	65.7	(3.6)	8.9	(2.2)	25.4	(3.7)	60.4	(6.9)	16.9	(5.7)	22.7	(5.9)	-2.8	(6.0)
	Kyrgyzstan	51.5	(3.6)	13.0	(3.0)	35.5	(3.9)	58.5	(6.0)	19.3	(5.1)	22.2	(4.8)	**-13.2**	(4.1)
	Latvia	68.9	(3.8)	19.9	(3.2)	11.1	(2.4)	80.6	(7.8)	16.0	(7.6)	3.4	(1.9)	**-7.8**	(2.3)
	Liechtenstein	10.8	(0.4)	38.1	(0.7)	51.1	(0.8)	c	c	c	c	c	c	c	c
	Lithuania	55.1	(3.3)	25.4	(3.1)	19.5	(2.9)	c	c	c	c	c	c	c	c
	Macao-China	93.0	(0.1)	6.9	(0.1)	0.1	(0.0)	91.0	(0.1)	9.0	(0.1)	0.0	c	c	c
	Montenegro	c	c	c	c	c	c	25.6	(0.1)	10.5	(0.1)	64.0	(0.1)	c	c
	Panama	49.6	(6.7)	15.8	(2.7)	34.6	(6.9)	55.9	(6.7)	19.0	(5.8)	25.0	(5.5)	-9.5	(8.2)
	Peru	48.3	(3.8)	15.7	(3.2)	36.0	(4.2)	65.8	(3.4)	17.9	(3.2)	16.2	(2.2)	**-19.8**	(3.5)
	Qatar	49.4	(0.4)	15.4	(0.2)	35.1	(0.3)	51.5	(0.1)	12.5	(0.1)	35.9	(0.1)	**0.8**	(0.4)
	Romania	61.5	(4.0)	21.7	(3.5)	16.7	(3.0)	c	c	c	c	c	c	c	c
	Russian Federation	60.1	(4.1)	11.7	(2.8)	28.2	(4.1)	56.8	(5.1)	21.1	(3.5)	22.1	(4.0)	-6.1	(4.0)
	Serbia	37.7	(13.2)	18.4	(9.9)	43.9	(14.6)	58.7	(4.0)	20.5	(3.7)	20.8	(2.6)	-23.1	(14.8)
	Shanghai-China	68.5	(6.2)	15.1	(4.9)	16.4	(4.9)	69.0	(4.4)	16.7	(3.1)	14.3	(3.9)	-2.1	(6.2)
	Singapore	92.7	(1.8)	4.0	(1.7)	3.3	(1.6)	90.2	(0.9)	6.5	(1.1)	3.4	(0.2)	0.0	(1.4)
	Chinese Taipei	76.4	(6.4)	16.6	(5.2)	7.0	(3.4)	89.6	(3.3)	6.6	(2.5)	3.7	(1.7)	-3.2	(3.8)
	Thailand	67.8	(4.5)	17.7	(3.6)	14.6	(3.4)	72.3	(3.6)	17.9	(3.3)	9.8	(1.9)	-4.8	(3.4)
	Trinidad and Tobago	76.0	(0.5)	12.6	(0.5)	11.3	(0.4)	76.3	(0.3)	14.2	(0.2)	9.6	(0.2)	**-1.7**	(0.5)
	Tunisia	33.3	(4.3)	23.7	(4.0)	43.0	(5.8)	34.9	(5.3)	37.3	(6.0)	27.8	(3.9)	**-15.2**	(6.7)
	Uruguay	37.5	(3.6)	12.7	(3.1)	49.8	(3.8)	45.0	(3.3)	13.0	(2.6)	42.0	(3.2)	-7.8	(4.1)

Note: Values that are statistically significant are indicated in bold (see Annex A3).
StatLink http://dx.doi.org/10.1787/888932343285

[Part 1/3]

Table IV.3.9 Percentage of students and performance in reading, mathematics and science, by type of school

Results based on school principals' reports

		Government or public schools[1]								Government-dependent private schools[2]							
		Percentage of students		Performance on the reading scale		Performance on the mathematics scale		Performance on the science scale		Percentage of students		Performance on the reading scale		Performance on the mathematics scale		Performance on the science scale	
			S.E.	Mean score	S.E.	Mean score	S.E.	Mean score	S.E.		S.E.	Mean score	S.E.	Mean score	S.E.	Mean score	S.E.
OECD	Australia	61.0	(0.9)	497	(3.9)	499	(4.0)	511	(4.3)	23.9	(1.5)	530	(3.8)	522	(4.0)	539	(3.3)
	Austria	87.4	(2.4)	465	(3.5)	493	(3.4)	491	(3.9)	10.8	(2.7)	513	(15.4)	518	(16.0)	520	(14.8)
	Belgium	w	w	w	w	w	w	w	w	w	w	w	w	w	w	w	w
	Canada	93.6	(0.8)	521	(1.5)	522	(1.7)	526	(1.7)	3.5	(0.5)	569	(8.5)	602	(7.3)	572	(8.4)
	Chile	47.3	(1.9)	423	(5.2)	398	(4.7)	425	(4.5)	49.2	(2.4)	454	(4.1)	421	(4.3)	450	(4.1)
	Czech Republic	97.1	(0.9)	477	(3.0)	492	(3.0)	499	(3.2)	2.9	(0.9)	512	(24.5)	517	(20.2)	541	(19.0)
	Denmark	79.6	(2.9)	491	(2.2)	500	(2.7)	495	(2.5)	17.8	(2.8)	512	(6.7)	516	(7.8)	518	(8.3)
	Estonia	97.1	(1.1)	501	(2.7)	512	(2.6)	528	(2.7)	2.3	(1.0)	c	c	c	c	c	c
	Finland	96.1	(1.2)	536	(2.2)	541	(2.1)	554	(2.3)	3.9	(1.2)	542	(18.7)	535	(14.1)	564	(17.2)
	France	w	w	w	w	w	w	w	w	w	w	w	w	w	w	w	w
	Germany	96.0	(1.4)	497	(3.2)	512	(3.5)	520	(3.6)	4.0	(1.4)	514	(24.9)	538	(30.7)	535	(26.1)
	Greece	96.6	(0.8)	480	(4.5)	464	(4.0)	467	(4.2)	0.0	c	c	c	c	c	c	c
	Hungary	88.4	(2.5)	492	(3.7)	488	(3.9)	501	(3.7)	11.5	(2.5)	508	(13.3)	506	(16.5)	517	(11.8)
	Iceland	99.1	(0.1)	498	(1.5)	504	(1.5)	493	(1.4)	0.9	(0.1)	c	c	c	c	c	c
	Ireland	43.4	(1.3)	474	(4.9)	472	(4.3)	489	(5.7)	49.5	(2.3)	504	(4.5)	493	(3.7)	514	(4.8)
	Israel	85.8	(2.7)	470	(4.5)	443	(3.9)	451	(4.1)	10.2	(2.5)	521	(14.8)	491	(19.0)	498	(14.7)
	Italy	94.7	(0.6)	489	(1.6)	486	(2.0)	492	(1.9)	1.9	(0.4)	403	(8.7)	431	(8.6)	428	(8.1)
	Japan	71.4	(1.1)	522	(4.0)	531	(3.8)	542	(3.8)	1.9	(1.1)	c	c	c	c	c	c
	Korea	64.5	(4.3)	533	(5.2)	542	(6.5)	535	(5.5)	18.4	(3.3)	529	(8.4)	534	(10.0)	525	(9.2)
	Luxembourg	87.5	(0.1)	472	(1.3)	491	(1.2)	485	(1.3)	10.9	(0.1)	471	(3.6)	480	(3.0)	471	(3.5)
	Mexico	89.4	(1.1)	420	(2.1)	414	(1.9)	411	(1.8)	0.1	(0.1)	c	c	c	c	c	c
	Netherlands	35.3	(4.0)	515	(9.6)	531	(9.8)	526	(11.7)	64.7	(4.0)	502	(8.5)	521	(7.6)	518	(8.3)
	New Zealand	95.1	(0.5)	517	(2.3)	516	(2.4)	529	(2.6)	0.0	c	c	c	c	c	c	c
	Norway	98.6	(0.4)	503	(2.6)	498	(2.4)	500	(2.6)	1.4	(0.4)	c	c	c	c	c	c
	Poland	97.9	(0.1)	499	(2.7)	493	(2.9)	507	(2.5)	0.6	(0.2)	527	(23.8)	530	(22.9)	537	(22.0)
	Portugal	86.1	(2.8)	485	(3.3)	482	(3.1)	489	(3.1)	8.8	(2.6)	498	(9.2)	493	(9.1)	495	(8.0)
	Slovak Republic	91.0	(2.4)	475	(3.0)	495	(3.5)	489	(3.3)	9.0	(2.4)	499	(14.3)	512	(15.5)	505	(12.7)
	Slovenia	97.3	(0.1)	481	(1.1)	499	(1.2)	509	(1.2)	2.7	(0.1)	561	(6.0)	596	(7.3)	598	(7.3)
	Spain	69.1	(1.1)	469	(2.3)	473	(2.4)	478	(2.4)	25.7	(1.5)	503	(4.0)	501	(4.0)	507	(3.8)
	Sweden	90.0	(0.8)	494	(2.8)	491	(2.9)	492	(2.7)	10.0	(0.8)	529	(11.1)	521	(11.4)	521	(11.5)
	Switzerland	94.0	(1.6)	500	(2.6)	534	(3.5)	516	(3.0)	2.3	(0.9)	546	(7.5)	566	(14.6)	548	(6.3)
	Turkey	99.2	(0.6)	464	(3.6)	444	(4.5)	453	(3.6)	0.0	c	c	c	c	c	c	c
	United Kingdom	93.7	(1.1)	492	(2.5)	490	(2.7)	510	(2.8)	0.0	c	c	c	c	c	c	c
	United States	93.1	(1.9)	494	(3.4)	482	(3.5)	496	(3.4)	0.0	c	c	c	c	c	c	c
	OECD average	84.9	(0.3)	489	(0.6)	492	(0.6)	497	(0.7)	10.9	(0.4)	511	(2.8)	516	(2.9)	519	(2.6)
Partners	Albania	88.9	(2.1)	378	(4.2)	371	(4.0)	384	(3.8)	0.0	c	c	c	c	c	c	c
	Argentina	64.7	(2.1)	367	(5.6)	363	(4.5)	372	(5.7)	19.9	(2.9)	451	(10.4)	428	(10.5)	448	(10.5)
	Azerbaijan	99.6	(0.1)	361	(3.3)	431	(2.8)	373	(3.1)	0.0	c	c	c	c	c	c	c
	Brazil	91.6	(1.1)	398	(3.2)	373	(2.6)	393	(2.8)	0.2	(0.1)	c	c	c	c	c	c
	Bulgaria	98.1	(0.8)	428	(6.8)	426	(6.0)	438	(6.0)	0.0	c	c	c	c	c	c	c
	Colombia	83.7	(2.5)	400	(4.0)	369	(3.5)	389	(3.8)	3.0	(0.9)	429	(10.0)	386	(8.2)	415	(10.5)
	Croatia	98.1	(1.1)	475	(3.1)	460	(3.2)	486	(3.0)	0.0	c	c	c	c	c	c	c
	Dubai (UAE)	31.5	(0.1)	386	(1.9)	373	(2.0)	395	(2.3)	0.0	c	c	c	c	c	c	c
	Hong Kong-China	7.5	(0.2)	553	(10.1)	587	(14.4)	576	(10.9)	89.9	(1.1)	532	(2.3)	551	(2.9)	547	(3.0)
	Indonesia	57.9	(2.8)	409	(5.0)	379	(5.2)	391	(5.4)	14.7	(2.4)	360	(5.8)	331	(4.6)	345	(5.2)
	Jordan	81.4	(0.7)	401	(3.6)	380	(3.9)	410	(3.8)	0.1	(0.0)	c	c	c	c	c	c
	Kazakhstan	96.8	(1.4)	389	(3.2)	404	(3.1)	399	(3.2)	0.0	c	c	c	c	c	c	c
	Kyrgyzstan	97.4	(1.1)	310	(3.2)	328	(2.8)	326	(2.9)	0.0	c	c	c	c	c	c	c
	Latvia	99.2	(0.5)	484	(2.9)	482	(3.1)	494	(3.1)	0.5	(0.4)	c	c	c	c	c	c
	Liechtenstein	94.4	(0.0)	498	(2.9)	537	(4.1)	520	(3.6)	0.0	c	c	c	c	c	c	c
	Lithuania	99.6	(0.4)	468	(2.4)	476	(2.6)	491	(2.9)	0.4	(0.4)	c	c	c	c	c	c
	Macao-China	4.0	(0.0)	c	c	c	c	c	c	83.8	(0.0)	487	(0.9)	524	(1.0)	512	(1.2)
	Montenegro	99.5	(0.0)	408	(1.7)	402	(2.0)	401	(2.0)	0.0	c	c	c	c	c	c	c
	Panama	83.1	(3.1)	343	(6.6)	338	(5.0)	352	(6.1)	0.0	c	c	c	c	c	c	c
	Peru	82.4	(2.6)	350	(3.5)	346	(3.4)	351	(3.1)	0.4	(0.4)	c	c	c	c	c	c
	Qatar	77.7	(0.1)	339	(1.0)	336	(0.9)	348	(1.1)	0.2	(0.0)	c	c	c	c	c	c
	Romania	99.5	(0.5)	425	(4.1)	427	(3.4)	428	(3.4)	0.0	c	c	c	c	c	c	c
	Russian Federation	99.9	(0.1)	459	(3.3)	468	(3.3)	478	(3.3)	0.0	c	c	c	c	c	c	c
	Serbia	98.8	(0.9)	441	(2.6)	442	(3.1)	442	(2.5)	0.0	c	c	c	c	c	c	c
	Shanghai-China	90.4	(1.1)	554	(2.4)	596	(2.8)	572	(2.4)	0.6	(0.6)	c	c	c	c	c	c
	Singapore	98.5	(1.1)	527	(1.0)	563	(1.4)	543	(1.3)	0.0	c	c	c	c	c	c	c
	Chinese Taipei	66.8	(1.4)	510	(3.4)	567	(4.6)	540	(3.4)	1.3	(0.8)	c	c	c	c	c	c
	Thailand	82.9	(0.7)	423	(2.9)	421	(3.6)	428	(3.2)	12.9	(1.5)	406	(10.3)	399	(11.0)	405	(11.8)
	Trinidad and Tobago	91.1	(0.1)	417	(1.4)	415	(1.5)	411	(1.3)	6.4	(0.1)	422	(4.3)	428	(3.6)	428	(4.9)
	Tunisia	98.3	(0.4)	405	(2.9)	373	(3.0)	402	(2.7)	0.0	c	c	c	c	c	c	c
	Uruguay	82.5	(0.9)	409	(2.7)	411	(2.6)	411	(2.7)	0.0	c	c	c	c	c	c	c

Note: Values that are statistically significant are indicated in bold (see Annex A3).

1. Schools which are directly controlled or managed by: i) a public education authority or agency or ii) a government agency directly or a governing body, most of whose members are either appointed by a public authority or elected by public franchise.
2. Schools which receive 50% or more of their core funding (*i.e.* funding that supports the basic educational services of the institution) from government agencies.
3. Schools which receive less than 50% of their core funding (*i.e.* funding that supports the basic educational services of the institution) from government agencies.

StatLink http://dx.doi.org/10.1787/888932343285

[Part 2/3]

Table IV.3.9 Percentage of students and performance in reading, mathematics and science, by type of school
Results based on school principals' reports

	Government-independent private schools[3]								Difference in performance on the reading scale between public and private schools (government-dependent and government-independent schools combined)	
			Performance on the reading scale		Performance on the mathematics scale		Performance on the science scale			
	Percentage of students	S.E.	Mean score	S.E.	Mean score	S.E.	Mean score	S.E.	Dif. (Pub. – Priv.)	S.E.
OECD										
Australia	15.1	(1.4)	558	(5.6)	557	(4.9)	570	(5.1)	**-44**	(5.5)
Austria	1.8	(0.9)	398	(16.1)	429	(15.8)	440	(12.5)	-31	(15.0)
Belgium	w	w	w	w	w	w	w	w	w	w
Canada	2.9	(0.7)	574	(11.7)	576	(11.0)	572	(9.9)	**-50**	(7.2)
Chile	3.6	(1.6)	519	(11.2)	499	(12.2)	507	(15.1)	**-36**	(6.6)
Czech Republic	0.0	c	c	c	c	c	c	c	-36	(24.9)
Denmark	2.6	(1.2)	495	(13.2)	500	(8.9)	503	(14.1)	**-18**	(6.6)
Estonia	0.6	(0.6)	c	c	c	c	c	c	-11	(21.0)
Finland	0.0	c	c	c	c	c	c	c	-7	(18.7)
France	w	w	w	w	w	w	w	w	w	w
Germany	0.0	c	c	c	c	c	c	c	-18	(25.9)
Greece	3.4	(0.8)	534	(25.6)	508	(18.7)	523	(22.0)	**-55**	(26.5)
Hungary	0.0	(0.0)	c	c	c	c	c	c	-15	(14.5)
Iceland	0.0	c	c	c	c	c	c	c	c	c
Ireland	7.1	(2.0)	548	(12.7)	527	(8.1)	552	(8.9)	**-35**	(6.5)
Israel	3.9	(1.4)	446	(35.3)	433	(20.7)	449	(26.7)	-30	(18.5)
Italy	3.3	(0.6)	478	(10.6)	459	(7.4)	475	(8.6)	**38**	(7.9)
Japan	26.7	(1.6)	517	(9.3)	529	(8.7)	537	(8.5)	8	(9.8)
Korea	17.2	(3.1)	571	(7.0)	579	(9.5)	565	(7.2)	-16	(8.9)
Luxembourg	1.6	(0.0)	c	c	c	c	c	c	-9	(3.4)
Mexico	10.5	(1.1)	470	(4.7)	458	(4.9)	457	(4.4)	**-49**	(5.3)
Netherlands	0.0	c	c	c	c	c	c	c	13	(14.5)
New Zealand	4.9	(0.5)	580	(7.8)	574	(8.3)	582	(9.4)	**-63**	(7.9)
Norway	0.0	c	c	c	c	c	c	c	c	c
Poland	1.5	(0.2)	568	(10.9)	569	(12.5)	575	(10.0)	**-57**	(12.5)
Portugal	5.1	(1.3)	538	(22.4)	538	(24.9)	545	(21.9)	**-28**	(10.6)
Slovak Republic	0.0	c	c	c	c	c	c	c	-24	(15.8)
Slovenia	0.0	c	c	c	c	c	c	c	**-80**	(6.2)
Spain	5.2	(1.1)	519	(10.8)	516	(10.2)	525	(7.9)	**-37**	(3.9)
Sweden	0.0	c	c	c	c	c	c	c	**-35**	(11.3)
Switzerland	3.7	(1.4)	502	(17.2)	526	(17.8)	517	(15.2)	-19	(10.9)
Turkey	0.8	(0.6)	c	c	c	c	c	c	c	c
United Kingdom	6.3	(1.1)	553	(5.4)	546	(5.7)	583	(6.8)	**-62**	(6.0)
United States	6.9	(1.9)	559	(19.9)	545	(16.5)	559	(24.8)	**-65**	(20.2)
OECD average	4.2	(0.3)	523	(3.6)	519	(3.0)	528	(3.3)	**-30**	(2.6)
Partners										
Albania	11.1	(2.1)	442	(10.9)	426	(15.3)	445	(12.9)	**-65**	(11.7)
Argentina	15.3	(2.9)	458	(18.2)	441	(18.1)	457	(16.7)	**-87**	(11.0)
Azerbaijan	0.4	(0.1)	c	c	c	c	c	c	c	c
Brazil	8.1	(1.1)	519	(8.9)	490	(8.3)	508	(7.3)	**-116**	(9.8)
Bulgaria	1.9	(0.8)	c	c	c	c	c	c	c	c
Colombia	13.3	(2.5)	473	(8.7)	434	(7.9)	461	(6.4)	**-65**	(7.6)
Croatia	1.9	(1.1)	c	c	c	c	c	c	c	c
Dubai (UAE)	68.5	(0.1)	463	(1.7)	459	(1.6)	468	(1.7)	**-77**	(2.5)
Hong Kong-China	2.6	(1.2)	c	c	c	c	c	c	**22**	(10.4)
Indonesia	27.4	(3.1)	408	(7.2)	378	(7.8)	386	(6.9)	**18**	(7.3)
Jordan	18.5	(0.7)	423	(8.8)	414	(10.6)	439	(10.1)	**-23**	(9.5)
Kazakhstan	3.2	(1.4)	439	(24.4)	442	(17.0)	444	(19.9)	**-50**	(25.1)
Kyrgyzstan	2.6	(1.1)	432	(16.6)	443	(18.6)	436	(13.1)	**-121**	(17.2)
Latvia	0.2	(0.2)	c	c	c	c	c	c	c	c
Liechtenstein	5.6	(0.0)	c	c	c	c	c	c	c	c
Lithuania	0.0	c	c	c	c	c	c	c	c	c
Macao-China	12.2	(0.0)	500	(2.4)	550	(3.0)	524	(2.5)	c	c
Montenegro	0.5	(0.0)	c	c	c	c	c	c	c	c
Panama	16.9	(3.1)	475	(14.8)	443	(12.3)	464	(12.7)	**-131**	(16.2)
Peru	17.1	(2.5)	433	(11.5)	429	(10.9)	428	(10.1)	**-82**	(12.0)
Qatar	22.1	(0.1)	458	(2.4)	452	(2.0)	464	(2.4)	**-117**	(2.8)
Romania	0.5	(0.5)	c	c	c	c	c	c	c	c
Russian Federation	0.1	(0.1)	c	c	c	c	c	c	c	c
Serbia	1.2	(0.9)	c	c	c	c	c	c	c	c
Shanghai-China	9.0	(1.2)	583	(11.1)	646	(12.8)	605	(8.8)	-20	(12.8)
Singapore	1.5	(1.1)	c	c	c	c	c	c	c	c
Chinese Taipei	31.9	(1.7)	475	(4.4)	507	(5.0)	491	(4.1)	**37**	(5.4)
Thailand	4.1	(1.5)	445	(21.7)	433	(21.2)	432	(20.6)	7	(7.6)
Trinidad and Tobago	2.5	(0.0)	435	(5.0)	416	(4.3)	413	(5.0)	**-8**	(3.8)
Tunisia	1.7	(0.4)	326	(6.0)	306	(10.6)	348	(11.4)	**79**	(6.7)
Uruguay	17.5	(0.9)	505	(5.4)	501	(6.3)	502	(6.0)	**-96**	(6.0)

Note: Values that are statistically significant are indicated in bold (see Annex A3).
1. Schools which are directly controlled or managed by: i) a public education authority or agency or ii) a government agency directly or a governing body, most of whose members are either appointed by a public authority or elected by public franchise.
2. Schools which receive 50% or more of their core funding (*i.e.* funding that supports the basic educational services of the institution) from government agencies.
3. Schools which receive less than 50% of their core funding (*i.e.* funding that supports the basic educational services of the institution) from government agencies.
StatLink http://dx.doi.org/10.1787/888932343285

[Part 3/3]

Table IV.3.9 Percentage of students and performance in reading, mathematics and science, by type of school

Results based on school principals' reports

		PISA index of economic, social and cultural status						Difference in performance on the reading scale between public and private schools after accounting for the PISA index of economic, social and cultural status of:			
		Public schools		Private schools (Government-dependent and government-independent)		Difference		Students		Students and schools	
		Mean index	S.E.	Mean index	S.E.	Dif. (Pub. – Priv.)	S.E.	Dif. (Pub. – Priv.)	S.E.	Dif. (Pub. – Priv.)	S.E.
OECD	Australia	0.15	(0.02)	0.61	(0.02)	**-0.46**	(0.03)	**-23**	(5.3)	3	(6.9)
	Austria	0.01	(0.03)	0.36	(0.09)	**-0.34**	(0.10)	-18	(12.3)	9	(12.0)
	Belgium	w	w	w	w	w	w	w	w	w	w
	Canada	0.46	(0.02)	1.04	(0.06)	**-0.58**	(0.06)	**-31**	(6.4)	-11	(6.3)
	Chile	-1.01	(0.06)	-0.46	(0.06)	**-0.55**	(0.08)	**-22**	(5.8)	-5	(6.3)
	Czech Republic	-0.10	(0.01)	0.18	(0.12)	**-0.28**	(0.12)	-23	(20.1)	5	(14.2)
	Denmark	0.25	(0.03)	0.49	(0.05)	**-0.24**	(0.06)	-10	(5.4)	-2	(5.1)
	Estonia	0.14	(0.02)	0.36	(0.16)	-0.22	(0.16)	-5	(18.0)	6	(14.4)
	Finland	0.36	(0.02)	0.52	(0.16)	-0.16	(0.16)	-1	(14.7)	1	(13.8)
	France	w	w	w	w	w	w	w	w	w	w
	Germany	0.17	(0.03)	0.44	(0.17)	-0.28	(0.18)	-4	(19.8)	**20**	(11.2)
	Greece	-0.08	(0.03)	0.85	(0.26)	**-0.93**	(0.26)	**-25**	(21.1)	17	(19.4)
	Hungary	-0.24	(0.03)	0.09	(0.13)	**-0.33**	(0.15)	1	(9.1)	**18**	(7.5)
	Iceland	0.71	(0.02)	c	c	c	c	c	c	c	c
	Ireland	-0.14	(0.03)	0.15	(0.04)	**-0.29**	(0.05)	**-21**	(5.9)	**-12**	(5.7)
	Israel	-0.03	(0.03)	0.11	(0.10)	-0.15	(0.11)	-23	(14.1)	-12	(11.2)
	Italy	-0.13	(0.01)	0.09	(0.11)	**-0.23**	(0.11)	**46**	(6.0)	**60**	(7.3)
	Japan	-0.07	(0.02)	0.15	(0.03)	**-0.22**	(0.04)	**17**	(8.2)	**45**	(6.7)
	Korea	-0.17	(0.04)	-0.13	(0.06)	-0.04	(0.08)	**-15**	(7.1)	**-13**	(6.0)
	Luxembourg	0.20	(0.02)	0.22	(0.04)	**-0.02**	(0.04)	-7	(3.7)	**-6**	(3.5)
	Mexico	-1.38	(0.02)	0.02	(0.10)	**-1.40**	(0.10)	**-16**	(4.4)	**23**	(5.5)
	Netherlands	0.32	(0.07)	0.23	(0.04)	0.09	(0.09)	10	(12.2)	3	(9.4)
	New Zealand	0.04	(0.01)	0.78	(0.04)	**-0.74**	(0.04)	**-23**	(6.7)	14	(7.6)
	Norway	0.47	(0.02)	c	c	c	c	c	c	c	c
	Poland	-0.30	(0.02)	0.74	(0.10)	**-1.05**	(0.11)	-16	(10.5)	5	(10.5)
	Portugal	-0.39	(0.04)	0.02	(0.16)	**-0.41**	(0.17)	**-16**	(7.3)	-4	(6.6)
	Slovak Republic	-0.11	(0.02)	0.07	(0.10)	-0.18	(0.10)	-16	(12.8)	-3	(9.4)
	Slovenia	0.06	(0.01)	0.69	(0.06)	**-0.63**	(0.06)	**-57**	(6.7)	-5	(6.8)
	Spain	-0.55	(0.03)	0.07	(0.06)	**-0.62**	(0.05)	**-19**	(3.6)	-7	(4.3)
	Sweden	0.29	(0.02)	0.71	(0.08)	**-0.43**	(0.08)	**-17**	(8.5)	2	(7.5)
	Switzerland	0.06	(0.03)	0.47	(0.14)	**-0.41**	(0.15)	-2	(10.6)	28	(16.4)
	Turkey	-1.19	(0.05)	c	c	c	c	c	c	c	c
	United Kingdom	0.16	(0.02)	0.92	(0.05)	**-0.76**	(0.05)	**-27**	(6.1)	20	(7.1)
	United States	0.09	(0.04)	0.93	(0.15)	**-0.84**	(0.16)	**-31**	(16.1)	-1	(14.3)
	OECD average	-0.06	(0.01)	0.37	(0.02)	**-0.44**	(0.02)	**-14**	(2.1)	**7**	(1.8)
Partners	Albania	-1.05	(0.04)	-0.21	(0.10)	**-0.84**	(0.11)	**-40**	(12.0)	-13	(13.0)
	Argentina	-0.95	(0.05)	-0.02	(0.12)	**-0.93**	(0.13)	**-56**	(9.2)	**-20**	(9.1)
	Azerbaijan	-0.65	(0.03)	c	c	c	c	c	c	c	c
	Brazil	-1.35	(0.03)	0.28	(0.10)	**-1.64**	(0.10)	**-87**	(9.1)	**-29**	(9.1)
	Bulgaria	-0.13	(0.04)	c	c	c	c	c	c	c	c
	Colombia	-1.43	(0.04)	-0.08	(0.10)	**-1.35**	(0.11)	**-35**	(6.6)	8	(6.8)
	Croatia	-0.20	(0.02)	c	c	c	c	c	c	c	c
	Dubai (UAE)	-0.13	(0.02)	0.57	(0.01)	**-0.70**	(0.03)	**-53**	(2.9)	**-12**	(3.4)
	Hong Kong-China	-0.89	(0.17)	-0.82	(0.04)	-0.08	(0.18)	**23**	(7.7)	**25**	(4.9)
	Indonesia	-1.49	(0.08)	-1.61	(0.09)	0.12	(0.12)	**16**	(6.6)	**13**	(6.4)
	Jordan	-0.66	(0.03)	-0.14	(0.09)	**-0.52**	(0.10)	-10	(8.2)	-1	(8.1)
	Kazakhstan	-0.53	(0.03)	0.01	(0.21)	**-0.54**	(0.21)	-30	(18.3)	-7	(12.7)
	Kyrgyzstan	-0.68	(0.03)	0.46	(0.27)	**-1.14**	(0.28)	**-78**	(11.4)	-16	(18.1)
	Latvia	-0.13	(0.03)	c	c	c	c	c	c	c	c
	Liechtenstein	0.07	(0.05)	c	c	c	c	c	c	c	c
	Lithuania	-0.05	(0.02)	c	c	c	c	c	c	c	c
	Macao-China	c	c	-0.69	(0.01)	c	c	c	c	c	c
	Montenegro	-0.25	(0.02)	c	c	c	c	c	c	c	c
	Panama	-1.20	(0.07)	0.57	(0.19)	**-1.77**	(0.20)	**-99**	(15.4)	-27	(18.2)
	Peru	-1.62	(0.04)	-0.32	(0.14)	**-1.29**	(0.15)	**-38**	(8.4)	10	(8.5)
	Qatar	0.38	(0.01)	0.79	(0.01)	**-0.41**	(0.02)	**-114**	(2.9)	**-107**	(3.2)
	Romania	-0.35	(0.03)	c	c	c	c	c	c	c	c
	Russian Federation	-0.21	(0.02)	c	c	c	c	c	c	c	c
	Serbia	0.06	(0.02)	c	c	c	c	c	c	c	c
	Shanghai-China	-0.53	(0.03)	-0.19	(0.21)	-0.34	(0.21)	-11	(8.9)	3	(9.0)
	Singapore	-0.43	(0.01)	c	c	c	c	c	c	c	c
	Chinese Taipei	-0.29	(0.03)	-0.37	(0.05)	**0.09**	(0.06)	**34**	(4.5)	**29**	(5.1)
	Thailand	-1.36	(0.04)	-1.09	(0.12)	**-0.27**	(0.13)	**13**	(6.2)	**18**	(6.0)
	Trinidad and Tobago	-0.59	(0.02)	-0.39	(0.03)	**-0.20**	(0.04)	**-2**	(4.0)	**21**	(3.6)
	Tunisia	-1.21	(0.05)	-0.67	(0.07)	**-0.54**	(0.09)	**89**	(6.8)	**104**	(7.5)
	Uruguay	-0.99	(0.03)	0.64	(0.07)	**-1.63**	(0.08)	**-47**	(5.0)	**34**	(6.7)

Note: Values that are statistically significant are indicated in bold (see Annex A3).

1. Schools which are directly controlled or managed by: i) a public education authority or agency or ii) a government agency directly or a governing body, most of whose members are either appointed by a public authority or elected by public franchise.

2. Schools which receive 50% or more of their core funding (*i.e.* funding that supports the basic educational services of the institution) from government agencies.

3. Schools which receive less than 50% of their core funding (*i.e.* funding that supports the basic educational services of the institution) from government agencies.

StatLink http://dx.doi.org/10.1787/888932343285

[Part 1/2]
Assessment practices
Table IV.3.10 *Results based on school principals' reports*

		Percentage of students in schools with the following assessment practices:																	
		Standardised tests						Teacher-developed tests						Teachers' judgmental ratings					
		Never		1 to 5 times a year		At least once a month		Never		1 to 5 times a year		At least once a month		Never		1 to 5 times a year		At least once a month	
		%	S.E.	%	S.E.	%	S.E.	%	S.E.	%	S.E.	%	S.E.	%	S.E.	%	S.E.	%	S.E.
OECD	Australia	29.9	(2.8)	68.4	(2.8)	1.7	(0.7)	1.2	(0.5)	41.5	(2.8)	57.2	(2.7)	5.3	(1.2)	48.4	(2.8)	46.3	(3.0)
	Austria	67.6	(3.8)	29.7	(3.8)	2.7	(1.3)	0.6	(0.7)	49.6	(4.4)	49.7	(4.3)	0.0	(0.0)	17.8	(3.1)	82.2	(3.1)
	Belgium	73.2	(2.9)	22.5	(2.8)	4.3	(1.3)	0.0	c	22.3	(2.4)	77.7	(2.4)	3.8	(1.1)	27.3	(2.8)	68.8	(3.0)
	Canada	12.0	(0.8)	85.3	(1.1)	2.8	(0.7)	0.0	c	8.2	(1.1)	91.8	(1.1)	14.5	(1.4)	30.4	(2.2)	55.1	(2.2)
	Chile	13.6	(2.4)	70.1	(3.6)	16.3	(2.9)	0.0	c	6.8	(2.1)	93.2	(2.1)	36.6	(4.3)	29.2	(3.5)	34.2	(4.2)
	Czech Republic	11.1	(2.1)	86.8	(2.4)	2.1	(1.0)	1.3	(0.8)	50.3	(3.4)	48.5	(3.4)	5.6	(1.7)	34.2	(3.3)	60.2	(3.5)
	Denmark	3.4	(1.4)	87.2	(2.3)	9.4	(2.0)	2.4	(1.1)	62.7	(3.3)	34.8	(3.3)	0.2	(0.2)	69.5	(2.9)	30.3	(2.8)
	Estonia	17.2	(2.8)	80.4	(2.9)	2.4	(1.0)	0.0	c	15.0	(2.6)	85.0	(2.6)	0.5	(0.5)	3.7	(1.2)	95.9	(1.3)
	Finland	1.5	(0.8)	96.3	(1.5)	2.1	(1.2)	0.0	c	51.4	(3.6)	48.6	(3.6)	0.0	c	17.7	(3.1)	82.3	(3.1)
	France	w	w	w	w	w	w	w	w	w	w	w	w	w	w	w	w	w	w
	Germany	60.0	(3.3)	40.0	(3.3)	0.0	c	0.0	c	34.3	(3.6)	65.7	(3.6)	0.6	(0.5)	22.1	(2.9)	77.4	(2.9)
	Greece	34.9	(4.4)	47.2	(4.2)	17.9	(3.3)	0.0	c	51.5	(4.1)	48.5	(4.1)	5.2	(2.3)	54.7	(4.2)	40.1	(4.0)
	Hungary	23.9	(3.4)	75.9	(3.4)	0.2	(0.2)	1.8	(1.1)	48.7	(4.2)	49.5	(4.3)	1.0	(0.8)	13.5	(3.1)	85.5	(3.0)
	Iceland	13.7	(0.2)	86.3	(0.2)	0.0	c	0.0	c	44.5	(0.2)	55.5	(0.2)	0.0	c	17.4	(0.2)	82.6	(0.2)
	Ireland	35.0	(4.2)	59.2	(4.2)	5.8	(1.5)	0.0	c	57.0	(4.7)	43.0	(4.7)	2.4	(1.4)	55.9	(4.6)	41.8	(4.4)
	Israel	13.2	(2.6)	65.6	(4.1)	21.2	(3.4)	0.0	c	35.1	(4.2)	64.9	(4.2)	2.1	(1.1)	40.0	(3.9)	57.9	(3.8)
	Italy	29.2	(2.0)	55.4	(2.1)	15.4	(1.3)	0.5	(0.3)	26.9	(1.9)	72.6	(1.9)	6.5	(1.1)	21.9	(1.8)	71.5	(2.1)
	Japan	34.6	(3.6)	63.1	(3.3)	2.3	(1.2)	0.0	c	80.5	(3.2)	19.5	(3.2)	2.8	(1.3)	72.9	(3.0)	24.3	(2.9)
	Korea	2.1	(1.5)	96.5	(1.8)	1.4	(1.0)	34.5	(4.1)	58.3	(4.2)	7.2	(2.2)	14.5	(2.9)	64.7	(3.8)	20.8	(3.1)
	Luxembourg	1.0	(0.0)	96.4	(0.0)	2.6	(0.0)	3.6	(0.1)	12.7	(0.1)	83.7	(0.1)	17.5	(0.1)	39.7	(0.1)	42.9	(0.1)
	Mexico	20.8	(1.5)	64.5	(1.9)	14.7	(1.4)	0.9	(0.3)	62.1	(1.7)	37.0	(1.7)	20.9	(1.3)	45.6	(1.7)	33.6	(1.7)
	Netherlands	13.9	(3.1)	52.1	(4.7)	34.0	(3.7)	0.1	(0.2)	9.0	(2.1)	90.9	(2.1)	13.3	(3.1)	52.6	(4.2)	34.1	(4.1)
	New Zealand	18.9	(2.8)	63.3	(3.0)	17.7	(2.2)	0.7	(0.7)	29.7	(3.0)	69.6	(3.0)	2.7	(1.0)	47.1	(3.7)	50.2	(3.6)
	Norway	4.7	(1.6)	94.4	(1.8)	0.9	(0.6)	0.4	(0.4)	13.8	(2.3)	85.8	(2.3)	0.6	(0.6)	31.9	(3.3)	67.5	(3.4)
	Poland	3.2	(1.5)	82.6	(2.7)	14.2	(2.5)	0.0	c	28.4	(3.6)	71.6	(3.6)	2.6	(1.2)	24.0	(3.3)	73.4	(3.3)
	Portugal	12.1	(2.4)	80.4	(3.0)	7.4	(1.9)	0.0	c	29.6	(3.7)	70.4	(3.7)	0.0	c	3.2	(1.4)	96.8	(1.4)
	Slovak Republic	6.4	(2.1)	84.7	(2.9)	8.9	(2.4)	0.3	(0.2)	43.8	(3.8)	56.0	(3.8)	0.0	c	10.8	(2.1)	89.2	(2.1)
	Slovenia	76.4	(0.6)	23.3	(0.6)	0.3	(0.0)	0.9	(0.0)	64.0	(0.4)	35.2	(0.4)	0.4	(0.0)	55.4	(0.4)	44.1	(0.4)
	Spain	71.1	(2.6)	27.5	(2.6)	1.4	(0.5)	0.1	(0.1)	12.2	(1.7)	87.7	(1.7)	3.4	(1.1)	22.8	(2.1)	73.8	(2.4)
	Sweden	3.4	(1.4)	93.2	(2.0)	3.4	(1.4)	0.0	c	19.1	(2.7)	80.9	(2.7)	0.0	c	11.4	(2.4)	88.6	(2.4)
	Switzerland	33.1	(2.9)	62.7	(3.0)	4.2	(1.5)	2.1	(1.0)	14.0	(2.5)	84.0	(2.7)	3.9	(1.5)	28.5	(2.7)	67.6	(2.6)
	Turkey	28.3	(3.7)	64.3	(3.9)	7.5	(1.7)	1.0	(0.8)	56.9	(4.0)	42.1	(3.9)	4.2	(1.7)	71.5	(3.5)	24.3	(3.4)
	United Kingdom	32.5	(3.1)	66.6	(3.1)	0.9	(0.6)	0.1	(0.1)	69.2	(2.7)	30.8	(2.7)	1.2	(0.5)	62.4	(3.1)	36.4	(3.0)
	United States	2.5	(1.2)	95.3	(1.6)	2.1	(1.1)	0.2	(0.3)	3.8	(1.8)	96.0	(1.8)	17.1	(2.7)	21.0	(3.5)	61.9	(3.9)
	OECD average	24.4	(0.4)	68.7	(0.5)	6.9	(0.3)	1.6	(0.3)	36.8	(0.5)	61.7	(0.5)	5.7	(0.3)	35.4	(0.5)	58.8	(0.5)
Partners	Albania	5.2	(1.8)	92.2	(2.3)	2.6	(1.3)	1.7	(1.3)	44.0	(4.0)	54.3	(3.9)	55.1	(3.9)	24.6	(3.9)	20.4	(3.7)
	Argentina	28.6	(3.5)	42.6	(3.9)	28.7	(3.5)	0.0	c	8.0	(2.0)	92.0	(2.0)	19.2	(3.2)	18.1	(3.1)	62.7	(3.7)
	Azerbaijan	2.1	(1.0)	63.9	(4.4)	33.9	(4.3)	0.6	(0.6)	44.1	(4.9)	55.3	(4.9)	9.2	(2.0)	27.3	(3.9)	63.5	(4.5)
	Brazil	18.0	(2.0)	65.4	(2.6)	16.6	(1.9)	0.2	(0.1)	21.3	(2.3)	78.5	(2.3)	1.6	(0.5)	14.7	(2.0)	83.7	(2.1)
	Bulgaria	7.7	(2.5)	58.6	(4.6)	33.7	(4.3)	0.0	c	37.0	(4.3)	63.0	(4.3)	2.9	(1.2)	32.1	(4.0)	65.0	(4.2)
	Colombia	18.5	(3.7)	68.8	(3.9)	12.7	(2.5)	1.1	(1.0)	32.6	(4.2)	66.3	(4.3)	6.4	(2.0)	40.0	(4.5)	53.7	(4.5)
	Croatia	32.3	(3.6)	62.2	(3.8)	5.5	(1.7)	0.0	c	62.0	(3.8)	38.0	(3.8)	3.1	(1.5)	38.6	(3.3)	58.3	(3.3)
	Dubai (UAE)	13.5	(0.1)	62.1	(0.2)	24.4	(0.1)	0.8	(0.0)	23.1	(0.2)	76.1	(0.2)	14.0	(0.1)	22.9	(0.1)	63.1	(0.2)
	Hong Kong-China	1.6	(0.8)	98.4	(0.8)	0.0	c	0.0	c	39.6	(3.9)	60.4	(3.9)	1.2	(0.9)	51.5	(3.8)	47.2	(3.8)
	Indonesia	4.9	(1.7)	74.7	(3.7)	20.4	(3.4)	1.5	(1.1)	29.5	(3.8)	68.9	(4.0)	19.7	(3.8)	48.3	(4.3)	32.0	(4.2)
	Jordan	12.8	(2.7)	64.7	(4.3)	22.5	(3.8)	0.8	(0.8)	34.7	(3.7)	64.6	(3.7)	1.5	(1.0)	39.5	(3.6)	59.0	(3.8)
	Kazakhstan	5.2	(1.5)	53.3	(3.9)	41.5	(3.9)	0.0	c	13.6	(2.8)	86.4	(2.8)	3.4	(1.0)	49.1	(3.6)	47.5	(3.7)
	Kyrgyzstan	2.2	(1.0)	48.2	(3.9)	49.6	(3.8)	1.0	(0.8)	34.3	(3.4)	64.7	(3.5)	7.6	(2.3)	25.9	(3.5)	66.5	(3.7)
	Latvia	3.9	(1.6)	60.9	(4.1)	35.1	(3.9)	0.0	c	32.3	(4.1)	67.7	(4.1)	1.2	(0.9)	7.4	(1.9)	91.4	(2.1)
	Liechtenstein	42.3	(0.4)	57.7	(0.4)	0.0	c	0.0	c	4.5	(0.2)	95.5	(0.2)	0.0	c	35.0	(0.1)	65.0	(0.1)
	Lithuania	14.9	(2.7)	74.4	(3.2)	10.7	(2.3)	0.0	c	30.9	(3.6)	69.1	(3.6)	1.2	(1.1)	15.2	(2.5)	83.6	(2.4)
	Macao-China	19.6	(0.0)	61.3	(0.0)	19.1	(0.0)	0.0	c	16.2	(0.0)	83.8	(0.0)	26.9	(0.0)	43.5	(0.0)	29.6	(0.0)
	Montenegro	40.9	(0.8)	57.4	(0.8)	1.7	(0.0)	0.0	c	76.2	(1.3)	23.8	(1.3)	0.0	c	44.0	(1.0)	56.0	(1.0)
	Panama	37.5	(5.1)	41.2	(5.4)	21.3	(4.7)	3.8	(2.1)	28.8	(4.4)	67.4	(4.7)	10.9	(2.9)	27.8	(4.5)	61.3	(5.2)
	Peru	31.0	(3.7)	39.2	(3.4)	29.7	(3.8)	0.0	c	11.5	(2.1)	88.5	(2.1)	27.3	(3.6)	17.6	(2.6)	55.1	(3.8)
	Qatar	0.8	(0.0)	82.7	(0.1)	16.5	(0.1)	2.4	(0.0)	27.1	(0.1)	70.5	(0.1)	7.9	(0.1)	31.9	(0.1)	60.2	(0.1)
	Romania	17.6	(2.9)	71.5	(3.5)	10.9	(2.1)	0.0	c	18.7	(3.6)	81.3	(3.6)	3.9	(1.6)	25.2	(3.5)	70.9	(3.6)
	Russian Federation	16.2	(3.1)	65.2	(3.1)	18.6	(2.1)	0.1	(0.1)	21.1	(3.5)	78.8	(3.5)	9.6	(2.0)	55.5	(3.4)	34.8	(3.1)
	Serbia	53.9	(4.0)	42.4	(4.1)	3.6	(1.6)	0.5	(0.3)	71.2	(3.9)	28.3	(3.9)	0.9	(0.5)	39.2	(4.2)	59.9	(4.2)
	Shanghai-China	7.8	(1.8)	90.9	(2.1)	1.3	(0.9)	0.8	(0.8)	19.7	(3.2)	79.5	(3.2)	8.5	(2.4)	76.5	(3.5)	14.9	(2.9)
	Singapore	0.9	(0.2)	87.3	(0.3)	11.9	(0.2)	0.0	c	27.3	(1.0)	72.7	(1.0)	22.0	(0.5)	54.1	(0.8)	23.9	(1.0)
	Chinese Taipei	10.0	(2.5)	63.2	(4.0)	26.8	(3.5)	1.2	(0.9)	19.1	(3.1)	79.7	(3.1)	3.5	(1.6)	20.4	(3.2)	76.1	(3.6)
	Thailand	19.3	(2.9)	80.7	(2.9)	0.0	c	0.0	c	49.2	(3.2)	50.8	(3.2)	0.0	c	33.3	(3.8)	66.7	(3.8)
	Trinidad and Tobago	18.2	(0.2)	71.7	(0.2)	10.0	(0.2)	0.0	c	27.8	(0.3)	72.2	(0.3)	22.7	(0.3)	41.8	(0.3)	35.5	(0.3)
	Tunisia	5.0	(1.8)	89.7	(2.4)	5.3	(1.6)	1.3	(0.9)	56.6	(4.1)	42.1	(4.1)	29.3	(4.3)	54.0	(4.3)	16.6	(2.8)
	Uruguay	64.9	(2.9)	31.1	(2.6)	3.9	(1.1)	0.0	c	14.9	(2.2)	85.1	(2.2)	2.3	(0.2)	42.4	(3.2)	55.4	(3.2)

StatLink http://dx.doi.org/10.1787/888932343285

[Part 2/2]
Assessment practices
Table IV.3.10 *Results based on school principals' reports*

		Percentage of students in schools with the following assessment practices:											
		Student portfolios						Student assignments/projects/homework					
		Never		1 to 5 times a year		At least once a month		Never		1 to 5 times a year		At least once a month	
		%	S.E.	%	S.E.	%	S.E.	%	S.E.	%	S.E.	%	S.E.
OECD	Australia	17.7	(2.1)	66.5	(2.9)	15.8	(2.2)	1.0	(0.4)	23.2	(2.4)	75.8	(2.4)
	Austria	13.6	(2.2)	64.5	(3.9)	21.9	(3.6)	1.7	(1.1)	10.8	(2.1)	87.4	(2.2)
	Belgium	26.2	(3.0)	63.5	(3.0)	10.3	(1.8)	0.1	(0.0)	15.9	(2.3)	84.1	(2.3)
	Canada	15.0	(1.3)	64.8	(2.2)	20.3	(2.1)	0.7	(0.4)	2.9	(0.6)	96.4	(0.8)
	Chile	0.0	c	52.7	(4.4)	47.3	(4.4)	0.0	c	34.6	(3.8)	65.4	(3.8)
	Czech Republic	43.9	(4.1)	45.4	(3.5)	10.7	(2.4)	0.6	(0.3)	29.6	(3.0)	69.8	(3.0)
	Denmark	5.1	(1.5)	39.8	(3.5)	55.2	(3.7)	0.2	(0.2)	24.1	(2.9)	75.7	(2.9)
	Estonia	26.5	(3.5)	69.1	(3.7)	4.3	(1.4)	0.0	c	11.5	(2.2)	88.5	(2.2)
	Finland	16.9	(3.2)	79.6	(3.5)	3.5	(1.4)	0.0	c	25.2	(3.4)	74.8	(3.4)
	France	w	w	w	w	w	w	w	w	w	w	w	w
	Germany	4.1	(1.3)	75.0	(3.2)	20.9	(3.1)	0.0	c	7.3	(1.9)	92.7	(1.9)
	Greece	42.4	(3.8)	47.6	(3.8)	10.0	(2.3)	11.7	(2.6)	71.8	(3.4)	16.6	(3.2)
	Hungary	38.3	(4.4)	59.0	(4.6)	2.7	(1.8)	0.6	(0.4)	47.2	(4.1)	52.2	(4.1)
	Iceland	0.0	c	44.4	(0.2)	55.6	(0.2)	0.1	(0.0)	13.2	(0.2)	86.7	(0.2)
	Ireland	39.0	(4.3)	53.8	(4.2)	7.2	(2.8)	0.8	(0.9)	1.0	(0.9)	98.1	(1.2)
	Israel	22.4	(3.0)	67.0	(3.8)	10.6	(2.3)	0.6	(0.6)	24.0	(3.3)	75.4	(3.4)
	Italy	6.1	(1.0)	40.1	(2.0)	53.9	(2.0)	4.5	(0.7)	32.2	(1.9)	63.4	(2.0)
	Japan	1.0	(0.7)	66.3	(3.7)	32.7	(3.7)	0.0	c	54.6	(3.9)	45.4	(3.9)
	Korea	17.0	(3.4)	69.8	(3.9)	13.2	(2.8)	2.6	(1.3)	56.1	(4.2)	41.3	(4.4)
	Luxembourg	39.3	(0.1)	52.8	(0.1)	7.9	(0.1)	0.0	c	36.4	(0.1)	63.6	(0.1)
	Mexico	4.4	(0.7)	45.4	(1.8)	50.2	(1.9)	1.3	(0.6)	31.7	(1.6)	67.1	(1.6)
	Netherlands	42.8	(3.7)	48.8	(4.0)	8.4	(2.2)	1.4	(0.9)	29.1	(3.1)	69.5	(3.3)
	New Zealand	18.6	(2.8)	70.4	(3.0)	11.0	(2.1)	0.0	c	17.4	(2.7)	82.6	(2.7)
	Norway	44.7	(3.4)	43.0	(3.7)	12.3	(2.7)	0.6	(0.6)	43.6	(3.3)	55.8	(3.2)
	Poland	28.6	(3.5)	59.6	(3.9)	11.8	(2.5)	0.0	c	12.3	(2.6)	87.7	(2.6)
	Portugal	12.5	(2.6)	76.1	(3.3)	11.4	(2.7)	1.3	(0.8)	18.5	(3.4)	80.2	(3.5)
	Slovak Republic	38.0	(3.9)	51.0	(4.2)	11.0	(2.6)	0.2	(0.2)	36.3	(3.6)	63.5	(3.6)
	Slovenia	45.7	(0.4)	45.7	(0.4)	8.6	(0.3)	0.5	(0.0)	28.1	(0.4)	71.4	(0.4)
	Spain	1.4	(0.5)	22.2	(2.4)	76.4	(2.4)	0.4	(0.2)	14.0	(2.0)	85.7	(2.0)
	Sweden	59.6	(3.9)	27.4	(3.3)	13.0	(2.6)	0.6	(0.6)	32.0	(3.5)	67.4	(3.5)
	Switzerland	42.1	(3.4)	53.4	(3.4)	4.5	(1.1)	1.8	(0.8)	26.5	(2.8)	71.7	(2.9)
	Turkey	14.6	(3.0)	76.7	(3.1)	8.7	(2.0)	1.0	(1.0)	79.5	(3.1)	19.5	(3.1)
	United Kingdom	14.5	(2.4)	64.3	(3.4)	21.2	(2.9)	0.0	c	35.9	(3.4)	64.1	(3.4)
	United States	31.1	(4.0)	56.4	(4.0)	12.4	(2.6)	0.0	c	3.4	(1.4)	96.6	(1.4)
	OECD average	23.4	(0.5)	56.4	(0.6)	20.1	(0.4)	1.0	(0.2)	28.2	(0.5)	70.8	(0.5)
Partners	Albania	31.0	(4.1)	51.7	(4.3)	17.3	(3.2)	3.2	(1.7)	27.8	(3.5)	69.1	(3.8)
	Argentina	34.5	(4.2)	32.0	(4.2)	33.5	(3.8)	0.0	c	9.0	(2.2)	91.0	(2.2)
	Azerbaijan	28.6	(4.2)	36.5	(4.3)	34.9	(4.0)	3.9	(1.8)	16.0	(3.6)	80.0	(3.7)
	Brazil	23.5	(2.4)	59.2	(2.7)	17.3	(2.4)	0.2	(0.2)	7.0	(1.3)	92.8	(1.3)
	Bulgaria	51.7	(5.7)	44.7	(5.6)	3.6	(2.0)	1.5	(1.0)	14.0	(3.1)	84.5	(3.2)
	Colombia	22.3	(4.0)	42.3	(4.5)	35.3	(4.2)	2.5	(1.5)	9.2	(3.0)	88.2	(3.4)
	Croatia	56.0	(4.1)	37.6	(4.2)	6.4	(1.9)	0.0	c	20.7	(2.9)	79.3	(2.9)
	Dubai (UAE)	17.0	(0.1)	50.6	(0.2)	32.4	(0.1)	0.0	c	18.2	(0.1)	81.8	(0.1)
	Hong Kong-China	34.9	(4.2)	58.8	(4.1)	6.4	(2.1)	0.0	c	22.6	(3.4)	77.4	(3.4)
	Indonesia	17.1	(3.2)	49.3	(4.2)	33.6	(4.0)	1.9	(1.2)	10.2	(2.5)	87.9	(2.5)
	Jordan	7.8	(2.3)	39.9	(3.6)	52.3	(3.7)	2.1	(1.2)	31.0	(3.3)	66.9	(3.2)
	Kazakhstan	7.7	(2.3)	64.2	(3.8)	28.1	(3.4)	1.1	(0.8)	27.9	(3.0)	71.0	(3.0)
	Kyrgyzstan	8.3	(2.1)	52.4	(3.6)	39.3	(3.5)	1.7	(1.1)	28.3	(3.8)	70.1	(3.9)
	Latvia	10.3	(2.6)	70.8	(3.6)	18.8	(3.0)	2.9	(1.3)	13.9	(2.7)	83.2	(3.1)
	Liechtenstein	12.7	(0.2)	68.0	(0.4)	19.3	(0.4)	0.0	c	8.8	(0.2)	91.2	(0.2)
	Lithuania	39.3	(3.8)	53.3	(3.8)	7.4	(2.0)	0.8	(0.6)	32.6	(3.8)	66.6	(3.8)
	Macao-China	46.3	(0.0)	33.6	(0.0)	20.1	(0.0)	0.0	c	4.1	(0.0)	95.9	(0.0)
	Montenegro	52.4	(0.9)	46.8	(0.9)	0.8	(0.0)	0.0	c	36.8	(0.7)	63.2	(0.7)
	Panama	34.7	(5.9)	30.5	(5.8)	34.7	(5.1)	2.8	(2.0)	24.8	(4.8)	72.5	(5.1)
	Peru	6.0	(1.5)	26.4	(3.4)	67.6	(3.6)	0.4	(0.4)	7.1	(1.7)	92.5	(1.7)
	Qatar	6.5	(0.1)	42.4	(0.1)	51.1	(0.1)	0.2	(0.0)	19.7	(0.1)	80.1	(0.1)
	Romania	1.1	(0.8)	63.8	(3.9)	35.1	(3.8)	2.1	(1.1)	9.4	(2.5)	88.5	(2.8)
	Russian Federation	11.5	(2.3)	76.5	(2.7)	11.9	(2.3)	1.3	(0.7)	43.4	(3.5)	55.3	(3.6)
	Serbia	62.6	(4.2)	32.8	(4.2)	4.6	(1.5)	1.3	(1.0)	70.4	(3.4)	28.2	(3.4)
	Shanghai-China	2.7	(1.3)	82.1	(3.0)	15.3	(2.8)	1.3	(0.9)	5.2	(1.8)	93.5	(2.0)
	Singapore	16.1	(0.2)	81.2	(1.0)	2.7	(1.1)	0.0	c	21.7	(1.0)	78.3	(1.0)
	Chinese Taipei	8.6	(2.4)	60.6	(3.5)	30.8	(3.1)	1.4	(1.0)	22.6	(3.7)	76.0	(3.9)
	Thailand	0.0	c	66.9	(3.7)	33.1	(3.7)	0.0	c	30.0	(3.2)	70.0	(3.2)
	Trinidad and Tobago	19.0	(0.2)	69.5	(0.3)	11.4	(0.1)	0.3	(0.0)	9.5	(0.2)	90.1	(0.2)
	Tunisia	40.4	(4.7)	46.2	(4.7)	13.4	(3.0)	8.1	(3.0)	39.1	(4.1)	52.8	(4.2)
	Uruguay	56.9	(3.0)	30.7	(2.9)	12.4	(2.0)	1.1	(0.8)	22.9	(2.5)	75.9	(2.5)

StatLink http://dx.doi.org/10.1787/888932343285

[Part 1/1]
Table IV.3.11 Evaluation and accountability: system level

		Existence of standards-based external examinations
OECD	Australia[a]	0.81
	Austria[a]	0.00
	Belgium[a]	0.00
	Canada[a]	0.51
	Chile[b]	0.00
	Czech Republic[a]	1.00
	Denmark[a]	1.00
	Estonia[b]	1.00
	Finland[a]	1.00
	France	w
	Germany[a]	0.35
	Greece[a]	0.00
	Hungary[a]	1.00
	Iceland[a]	1.00
	Ireland[a]	1.00
	Israel[b]	1.00
	Italy[a]	1.00
	Japan[a]	1.00
	Korea[a]	1.00
	Luxembourg[a]	1.00
	Mexico[a]	0.00
	Netherlands[a]	1.00
	New Zealand[a]	1.00
	Norway[a]	1.00
	Poland[a]	1.00
	Portugal[a]	0.00
	Slovak Republic[a]	1.00
	Slovenia[b]	1.00
	Spain[a]	0.00
	Sweden[a]	0.00
	Switzerland[a]	0.00
	Turkey[a]	1.00
	United Kingdom[a]	1.00
	United States[a]	0.07
	OECD average	0.66
Partners	Albania	m
	Argentina[b]	0.00
	Azerbaijan[b]	1.00
	Brazil[b]	0.00
	Bulgaria[c]	1.00
	Colombia[c]	1.00
	Croatia[c]	1.00
	Dubai (UAE)[c]	1.00
	Hong Kong-China[c]	1.00
	Indonesia[b]	1.00
	Jordan[b]	1.00
	Kazakhstan	m
	Kyrgyzstan[c]	1.00
	Latvia[c]	1.00
	Liechtenstein[b]	1.00
	Lithuania[c]	1.00
	Macao-China[c]	0.00
	Montenegro[c]	1.00
	Panama[c]	0.00
	Peru[c]	0.00
	Qatar[c]	0.00
	Romania[b]	0.78
	Russian Federation[b]	1.00
	Serbia[b]	0.26
	Shanghai-China[c]	1.00
	Singapore[c]	1.00
	Chinese Taipei[c]	1.00
	Thailand[c]	0.79
	Trinidad and Tobago[c]	1.00
	Tunisia[b]	0.00
	Uruguay[b]	0.00

Note: This indicates the extent to which standards-based external examinations for students at the secondary education level exist in the system. Where there is a value between 0 and 1, standards-based external examinations exist in some parts of the system concerned, but not throughout the system (*e.g.* regional variation or variation between different types of education programmes). The data from source "a" concern the existence of such examinations for at least one of the following subjects: mathematics or science, while the data from sources "b" and "c" concern the existence of such examinations for at least one of any subjects including the language of instruction, mathematics, science and other subjects.

Sources: a. *PISA 2006: Science Competencies for Tomorrow's World* (OECD, 2007) and Woessman (2003).
b. PISA system-level data collection in 2007.
c. PISA system-level data collection in 2010.

StatLink http://dx.doi.org/10.1787/888932343285

[Part 1/1]
Assessment purposes
Table IV.3.12 *Results based on school principals' reports*

Percentage of students in schools where the principal reported assessments of students in national modal grade for 15-year-olds are used for the following purposes:

		To inform parents about their child's progress		To make decisions about students' retention or promotion		To group students for instructional purposes		To compare the school to <district or national> performance		To monitor the school's progress from year to year		To make judgements about teachers' effectiveness		To identify aspects of instruction or the curriculum that could be improved		To compare the school with other schools		To compare the school with other schools or with national/regional performance	
		%	S.E.	%	S.E.	%	S.E.	%	S.E.	%	S.E.	%	S.E.	%	S.E.	%	S.E.	%	S.E.
OECD	Australia	99.0	(0.4)	67.9	(2.9)	81.2	(2.3)	60.4	(3.0)	82.9	(2.2)	44.3	(2.7)	86.1	(2.2)	43.5	(2.9)	64.0	(2.9)
	Austria	92.9	(2.3)	94.0	(1.7)	31.9	(2.2)	9.5	(2.1)	48.7	(3.6)	26.0	(3.5)	62.6	(4.2)	21.1	(3.2)	26.0	(3.7)
	Belgium	99.4	(0.5)	99.0	(0.7)	16.1	(2.3)	11.4	(2.0)	50.7	(3.5)	31.0	(2.6)	60.9	(3.2)	6.5	(1.3)	13.1	(2.0)
	Canada	99.8	(0.2)	93.9	(1.3)	76.5	(1.9)	73.4	(1.6)	86.2	(1.5)	34.7	(2.0)	86.7	(1.4)	57.0	(2.4)	76.4	(1.6)
	Chile	96.9	(1.5)	86.7	(2.8)	45.1	(3.9)	48.7	(4.5)	89.4	(2.6)	58.2	(3.5)	91.7	(2.2)	43.0	(4.4)	52.5	(4.3)
	Czech Republic	97.3	(1.2)	89.1	(2.4)	40.1	(3.6)	65.2	(3.1)	89.1	(2.0)	60.4	(4.0)	84.2	(2.6)	62.4	(3.8)	71.6	(3.4)
	Denmark	96.8	(1.1)	8.7	(2.0)	53.5	(3.2)	33.0	(3.1)	34.9	(3.4)	8.1	(1.9)	85.2	(2.3)	28.1	(3.0)	35.8	(3.3)
	Estonia	97.9	(1.1)	81.7	(2.8)	25.8	(3.0)	67.2	(3.4)	85.0	(2.8)	71.9	(3.0)	77.9	(3.0)	61.0	(3.4)	74.0	(3.0)
	Finland	98.2	(0.8)	94.4	(1.7)	16.3	(3.0)	49.7	(3.9)	52.5	(3.6)	23.7	(3.9)	56.3	(3.8)	27.2	(2.7)	53.4	(3.7)
	France	w	w	w	w	w	w	w	w	w	w	w	w	w	w	w	w	w	w
	Germany	98.3	(0.9)	96.7	(1.2)	34.3	(2.7)	33.2	(3.4)	58.0	(3.3)	21.8	(2.5)	56.8	(3.6)	21.8	(3.1)	39.3	(3.6)
	Greece	100.0	(0.0)	97.7	(1.1)	8.2	(1.7)	20.7	(2.9)	62.3	(4.1)	22.2	(3.3)	47.4	(3.7)	24.8	(3.2)	30.2	(3.4)
	Hungary	97.5	(1.3)	82.6	(3.3)	51.9	(3.5)	68.6	(3.8)	86.9	(2.5)	59.6	(4.2)	64.8	(4.1)	61.1	(4.3)	73.0	(3.6)
	Iceland	100.0	(0.0)	4.6	(0.1)	37.7	(0.3)	55.0	(0.2)	92.0	(0.1)	29.3	(0.2)	92.3	(0.2)	47.0	(0.2)	56.1	(0.2)
	Ireland	100.0	(0.0)	a	a	73.8	(4.3)	44.3	(4.8)	67.1	(4.3)	37.0	(4.3)	64.8	(4.6)	23.8	(4.0)	46.5	(4.9)
	Israel	99.2	(0.5)	82.4	(2.8)	96.1	(1.5)	53.9	(3.8)	87.4	(2.3)	84.9	(2.9)	90.7	(2.1)	29.0	(3.6)	56.3	(3.7)
	Italy	99.1	(0.3)	87.0	(1.4)	64.0	(2.2)	34.0	(1.8)	72.1	(1.6)	20.3	(1.7)	88.8	(1.3)	23.2	(1.5)	40.8	(1.8)
	Japan	99.5	(0.5)	91.3	(2.1)	41.5	(3.8)	22.3	(2.9)	61.1	(3.8)	78.3	(2.7)	83.3	(2.4)	19.6	(2.8)	23.7	(3.0)
	Korea	95.3	(1.7)	36.9	(4.0)	78.1	(3.5)	75.2	(3.7)	83.4	(2.9)	66.4	(4.7)	88.3	(2.3)	62.3	(3.8)	77.8	(3.5)
	Luxembourg	100.0	(0.0)	99.6	(0.0)	45.4	(0.1)	53.5	(0.1)	40.3	(0.1)	21.7	(0.1)	60.0	(0.1)	34.7	(0.1)	58.2	(0.1)
	Mexico	98.4	(0.4)	93.4	(0.9)	67.8	(1.6)	72.6	(1.7)	88.5	(1.2)	80.1	(1.4)	92.0	(0.9)	70.4	(1.8)	79.6	(1.6)
	Netherlands	99.4	(0.5)	96.9	(1.3)	54.2	(3.7)	42.5	(4.4)	73.5	(4.1)	50.1	(4.1)	62.9	(4.2)	39.8	(4.1)	50.2	(4.5)
	New Zealand	99.3	(0.6)	77.2	(2.7)	91.1	(1.9)	92.2	(2.0)	97.2	(1.4)	60.8	(3.3)	98.3	(1.0)	82.5	(2.8)	93.5	(1.8)
	Norway	98.0	(1.1)	1.1	(0.6)	58.6	(3.5)	68.7	(3.4)	82.0	(2.9)	24.4	(2.8)	69.8	(3.5)	52.1	(3.5)	73.0	(3.4)
	Poland	99.4	(0.6)	98.4	(1.0)	32.6	(3.7)	57.0	(3.7)	95.0	(1.7)	78.7	(3.1)	92.2	(2.0)	57.0	(3.8)	63.1	(3.7)
	Portugal	99.4	(0.6)	97.6	(1.0)	22.8	(3.6)	48.0	(4.3)	88.8	(2.3)	34.7	(4.0)	79.6	(3.0)	40.0	(3.9)	53.8	(4.3)
	Slovak Republic	100.0	(0.0)	96.9	(1.4)	47.5	(3.7)	51.8	(4.4)	86.4	(2.7)	79.7	(3.3)	85.9	(2.9)	67.8	(3.3)	73.2	(3.1)
	Slovenia	98.5	(0.0)	95.7	(0.3)	24.1	(0.6)	53.5	(0.4)	92.3	(0.3)	40.4	(0.4)	74.9	(0.4)	43.2	(0.4)	62.1	(0.4)
	Spain	99.5	(0.4)	99.7	(0.1)	49.1	(2.6)	24.0	(2.2)	84.2	(1.9)	43.7	(2.8)	90.7	(1.5)	23.3	(1.9)	29.9	(2.2)
	Sweden	98.9	(0.8)	38.8	(3.7)	38.5	(3.8)	78.3	(3.3)	93.1	(2.0)	21.8	(2.8)	83.0	(2.8)	75.5	(3.3)	83.5	(2.8)
	Switzerland	89.7	(2.1)	86.9	(2.6)	25.1	(2.7)	38.2	(3.2)	41.1	(3.5)	40.6	(3.5)	49.5	(3.6)	22.7	(2.7)	43.0	(3.2)
	Turkey	93.6	(1.8)	71.4	(3.1)	72.5	(3.7)	72.9	(3.8)	83.9	(3.0)	71.4	(3.6)	55.0	(3.9)	72.1	(3.4)	83.4	(3.1)
	United Kingdom	99.6	(0.4)	69.8	(3.5)	94.8	(1.3)	91.3	(2.1)	97.1	(1.3)	82.7	(2.6)	92.7	(1.6)	82.2	(2.8)	92.1	(1.9)
	United States	96.9	(1.3)	70.4	(3.3)	69.1	(4.2)	95.3	(1.5)	97.7	(1.1)	58.0	(4.1)	98.1	(1.1)	90.3	(2.4)	96.8	(1.3)
	OECD average	98.1	(0.2)	77.8	(0.4)	50.5	(0.5)	53.5	(0.5)	76.7	(0.5)	47.5	(0.5)	77.4	(0.5)	45.9	(0.5)	59.0	(0.5)
Partners	Albania	97.0	(2.0)	87.7	(2.9)	68.2	(3.9)	77.6	(3.2)	99.7	(0.2)	89.9	(2.4)	88.5	(2.5)	76.9	(3.4)	87.7	(2.6)
	Argentina	95.0	(1.7)	89.8	(2.3)	23.1	(3.5)	26.1	(3.7)	80.9	(3.2)	53.1	(4.0)	93.5	(1.7)	15.4	(3.0)	30.9	(3.7)
	Azerbaijan	96.9	(1.6)	96.2	(1.8)	81.2	(3.6)	81.6	(3.5)	89.3	(2.8)	94.4	(1.9)	89.0	(2.4)	84.8	(3.6)	92.6	(2.7)
	Brazil	97.3	(0.8)	95.3	(1.6)	51.6	(3.1)	79.1	(2.8)	94.7	(1.4)	80.2	(2.0)	91.6	(1.4)	54.7	(3.5)	82.5	(2.5)
	Bulgaria	100.0	(0.0)	78.6	(4.3)	41.8	(5.0)	83.8	(3.4)	89.7	(2.6)	92.1	(3.0)	70.5	(4.6)	78.1	(3.6)	86.4	(3.1)
	Colombia	100.0	(0.0)	95.4	(2.1)	41.4	(4.1)	62.7	(4.3)	94.8	(2.1)	62.6	(4.0)	92.8	(2.4)	53.8	(4.7)	67.1	(4.3)
	Croatia	98.8	(0.9)	88.7	(2.8)	59.5	(3.9)	72.5	(3.4)	94.4	(1.9)	55.3	(3.9)	82.4	(3.2)	66.0	(4.0)	81.1	(3.2)
	Dubai (UAE)	99.4	(0.0)	87.8	(0.1)	84.1	(0.1)	57.5	(0.2)	93.3	(0.1)	87.1	(0.1)	91.8	(0.1)	60.9	(0.2)	65.2	(0.2)
	Hong Kong-China	98.6	(1.0)	99.4	(0.6)	80.4	(3.2)	34.3	(3.7)	95.4	(1.6)	75.7	(3.5)	96.5	(1.6)	22.3	(3.5)	35.9	(3.8)
	Indonesia	99.9	(0.1)	93.1	(2.2)	86.6	(2.8)	78.8	(3.4)	98.2	(1.1)	97.6	(1.2)	98.5	(0.9)	86.2	(2.8)	91.7	(2.3)
	Jordan	99.2	(0.8)	92.8	(2.0)	87.5	(2.4)	77.4	(3.4)	90.0	(2.4)	82.1	(2.5)	89.5	(1.9)	67.1	(4.0)	84.1	(3.0)
	Kazakhstan	99.3	(0.7)	95.9	(1.5)	55.9	(3.8)	92.8	(1.9)	99.5	(0.5)	99.4	(0.4)	99.0	(0.7)	89.1	(2.5)	95.4	(1.7)
	Kyrgyzstan	94.4	(2.0)	78.1	(3.2)	63.1	(4.1)	83.6	(3.0)	97.5	(1.2)	99.2	(0.7)	90.3	(2.3)	84.6	(2.8)	93.2	(2.0)
	Latvia	98.8	(0.4)	94.4	(1.7)	34.2	(3.4)	91.7	(2.1)	98.2	(0.7)	92.5	(2.0)	97.5	(0.9)	81.6	(2.9)	92.4	(2.0)
	Liechtenstein	73.7	(0.2)	78.4	(0.3)	71.2	(0.3)	53.3	(0.4)	42.5	(0.3)	21.7	(0.4)	58.7	(0.5)	7.0	(0.3)	53.3	(0.4)
	Lithuania	98.8	(0.9)	94.1	(1.8)	55.5	(3.6)	55.1	(3.9)	95.0	(1.7)	71.0	(3.7)	81.1	(2.8)	47.9	(3.7)	62.4	(3.7)
	Macao-China	100.0	(0.0)	93.7	(0.0)	61.7	(0.0)	9.1	(0.0)	78.3	(0.0)	73.6	(0.0)	100.0	(0.0)	23.3	(0.0)	23.8	(0.0)
	Montenegro	40.0	(1.1)	11.8	(0.2)	20.6	(0.4)	37.6	(0.7)	54.8	(1.0)	55.6	(1.0)	56.7	(1.0)	44.9	(0.8)	47.4	(0.8)
	Panama	90.2	(3.6)	86.9	(4.4)	47.8	(5.4)	32.1	(5.2)	77.2	(4.4)	58.2	(5.4)	74.3	(5.2)	32.6	(5.9)	42.8	(5.7)
	Peru	98.7	(0.6)	88.6	(2.3)	53.7	(3.8)	39.6	(3.7)	87.6	(2.4)	79.6	(2.8)	93.0	(1.8)	35.9	(3.3)	49.4	(3.8)
	Qatar	94.5	(0.0)	77.7	(0.1)	77.1	(0.1)	60.7	(0.1)	89.9	(0.1)	84.0	(0.1)	90.4	(0.1)	69.4	(0.1)	72.7	(0.1)
	Romania	99.3	(0.6)	89.1	(2.8)	66.0	(4.1)	87.1	(3.0)	97.4	(1.3)	85.4	(3.2)	92.4	(2.3)	83.1	(3.2)	92.3	(2.1)
	Russian Federation	100.0	(0.0)	95.7	(1.6)	52.4	(4.7)	82.6	(2.6)	98.6	(0.8)	97.6	(1.1)	100.0	(0.0)	95.0	(1.6)	97.9	(1.2)
	Serbia	95.3	(2.0)	84.4	(3.2)	61.4	(3.9)	34.6	(3.6)	96.3	(1.7)	62.9	(3.8)	78.6	(3.8)	57.4	(4.2)	62.9	(3.8)
	Shanghai-China	91.8	(1.9)	45.7	(4.0)	42.8	(4.2)	60.2	(4.1)	85.7	(2.8)	83.4	(3.0)	96.7	(1.3)	63.7	(4.0)	69.4	(3.9)
	Singapore	100.0	(0.0)	88.2	(0.2)	95.1	(0.1)	93.4	(0.9)	98.8	(0.1)	85.2	(1.0)	97.4	(1.1)	81.7	(0.8)	95.1	(1.0)
	Chinese Taipei	95.3	(1.8)	49.3	(3.8)	48.1	(3.9)	46.7	(3.3)	72.7	(3.8)	57.9	(4.0)	97.6	(1.2)	46.5	(3.9)	56.8	(3.7)
	Thailand	100.0	(0.0)	99.4	(0.6)	91.8	(1.9)	82.8	(2.6)	96.7	(1.4)	94.7	(1.6)	98.0	(1.1)	81.7	(3.0)	86.7	(2.4)
	Trinidad and Tobago	100.0	(0.0)	52.7	(0.3)	50.5	(0.3)	31.3	(0.3)	89.7	(0.2)	67.7	(0.3)	92.0	(0.3)	20.9	(0.2)	32.5	(0.3)
	Tunisia	97.1	(1.4)	95.7	(1.7)	64.6	(4.4)	87.2	(2.9)	94.8	(1.9)	75.7	(3.8)	52.4	(3.7)	83.1	(2.9)	90.3	(2.5)
	Uruguay	95.6	(1.2)	97.5	(1.0)	30.4	(2.9)	17.6	(2.5)	83.6	(2.7)	37.2	(2.5)	82.4	(2.2)	8.6	(1.6)	19.9	(2.5)

StatLink http://dx.doi.org/10.1787/888932343285

[Part 1/1]
Table IV.3.13 **Use of achievement data for accountability purposes**
Results based on school principals' reports

		Percentage of students in schools with the following uses of achievement data:									
		Posted publicly		Used in evaluation of the principal's performance		Used in evaluation of teachers' performance		Used in decisions about instructional resource allocation to the school		Tracked over time by an administrative authority	
		%	S.E.	%	S.E.	%	S.E.	%	S.E.	%	S.E.
OECD	Australia	46.6	(2.6)	42.7	(2.6)	41.3	(3.0)	61.4	(3.2)	81.0	(2.2)
	Austria	6.3	(2.5)	21.4	(3.2)	24.1	(3.4)	16.2	(2.9)	49.1	(3.6)
	Belgium	1.9	(0.9)	11.1	(1.9)	19.1	(2.5)	22.4	(2.2)	45.0	(3.0)
	Canada	55.2	(2.3)	17.1	(1.6)	14.7	(1.4)	58.5	(2.0)	89.0	(1.2)
	Chile	35.5	(3.9)	37.0	(4.2)	53.2	(4.0)	77.4	(3.5)	76.7	(3.9)
	Czech Republic	30.6	(3.2)	54.2	(3.1)	79.1	(3.1)	4.0	(1.3)	56.0	(3.6)
	Denmark	45.3	(3.3)	30.5	(3.4)	38.2	(3.6)	35.8	(3.7)	56.5	(3.3)
	Estonia	32.3	(3.4)	43.5	(3.1)	73.8	(3.2)	16.2	(2.6)	87.0	(2.4)
	Finland	2.5	(1.4)	5.2	(1.8)	10.9	(2.6)	5.2	(1.9)	43.4	(4.1)
	France	w	w	w	w	w	w	w	w	w	w
	Germany	10.6	(2.4)	18.3	(2.9)	23.7	(2.9)	27.9	(3.1)	28.9	(3.0)
	Greece	31.3	(3.5)	18.8	(3.4)	27.3	(3.9)	3.5	(1.4)	54.5	(4.4)
	Hungary	33.2	(4.3)	56.0	(3.8)	82.3	(3.1)	13.4	(2.7)	50.4	(4.7)
	Iceland	22.5	(0.2)	13.9	(0.1)	21.9	(0.2)	1.2	(0.1)	75.4	(0.2)
	Ireland	18.7	(3.7)	5.3	(2.2)	21.0	(4.0)	54.2	(4.6)	49.1	(4.7)
	Israel	25.7	(3.5)	78.4	(3.1)	86.8	(2.3)	77.5	(3.2)	82.1	(2.5)
	Italy	30.3	(1.8)	16.1	(1.6)	24.0	(1.7)	38.8	(2.1)	25.7	(1.9)
	Japan	3.7	(1.4)	9.0	(2.2)	23.6	(2.9)	3.9	(1.5)	10.8	(2.0)
	Korea	33.0	(4.4)	27.6	(4.1)	45.3	(4.4)	39.2	(4.0)	75.8	(3.8)
	Luxembourg	37.0	(0.1)	19.9	(0.1)	8.2	(0.0)	32.9	(0.1)	74.4	(0.1)
	Mexico	33.8	(1.8)	42.9	(1.9)	78.5	(1.6)	32.1	(1.9)	86.7	(1.4)
	Netherlands	63.5	(3.7)	34.4	(3.8)	71.1	(4.0)	12.9	(2.3)	60.7	(3.9)
	New Zealand	77.7	(2.9)	49.6	(3.4)	48.0	(3.2)	67.9	(3.1)	93.4	(1.6)
	Norway	58.1	(3.6)	52.3	(3.4)	51.0	(3.6)	15.9	(2.8)	73.0	(3.5)
	Poland	53.4	(3.9)	79.9	(3.0)	85.8	(2.7)	14.0	(2.7)	89.6	(2.5)
	Portugal	30.2	(3.5)	11.9	(2.6)	17.4	(3.2)	54.6	(4.1)	68.5	(3.6)
	Slovak Republic	62.7	(4.0)	51.5	(4.1)	73.5	(3.6)	11.1	(2.4)	86.1	(2.3)
	Slovenia	36.2	(0.4)	73.5	(0.3)	37.7	(0.5)	14.9	(0.3)	69.0	(0.4)
	Spain	7.8	(1.5)	16.7	(2.0)	34.3	(2.4)	42.7	(2.5)	65.3	(2.6)
	Sweden	61.4	(3.2)	43.4	(3.7)	43.4	(3.5)	36.5	(3.8)	84.0	(2.6)
	Switzerland	3.2	(1.2)	7.5	(1.7)	11.5	(2.0)	24.3	(2.8)	32.7	(2.7)
	Turkey	49.7	(4.0)	46.0	(4.0)	71.7	(3.5)	31.4	(3.6)	76.9	(3.1)
	United Kingdom	80.1	(2.8)	93.1	(1.6)	94.2	(1.0)	57.7	(3.3)	93.7	(1.7)
	United States	89.3	(2.5)	62.5	(3.9)	41.0	(3.7)	72.0	(4.2)	95.5	(1.8)
	OECD average	36.6	(0.5)	36.1	(0.5)	44.8	(0.5)	32.7	(0.5)	66.2	(0.5)
Partners	Albania	34.4	(3.7)	86.1	(2.8)	97.4	(1.2)	78.7	(3.4)	80.8	(3.6)
	Argentina	6.2	(2.0)	18.7	(3.3)	49.1	(4.2)	34.6	(3.7)	66.5	(4.0)
	Azerbaijan	86.0	(3.1)	90.9	(2.5)	96.5	(1.6)	68.4	(4.0)	80.9	(3.5)
	Brazil	32.3	(2.4)	56.3	(2.3)	72.8	(2.2)	72.8	(2.5)	81.7	(1.8)
	Bulgaria	32.7	(4.9)	58.2	(4.7)	87.5	(3.2)	30.2	(4.1)	78.4	(4.5)
	Colombia	27.8	(4.1)	25.6	(3.7)	55.2	(4.3)	57.7	(4.8)	79.3	(3.5)
	Croatia	21.8	(3.6)	19.5	(3.1)	45.3	(3.7)	13.3	(2.5)	84.3	(2.9)
	Dubai (UAE)	47.4	(0.1)	52.1	(0.2)	87.5	(0.1)	74.6	(0.2)	88.8	(0.1)
	Hong Kong-China	48.4	(4.0)	17.0	(3.2)	55.0	(3.8)	48.8	(3.6)	60.9	(3.9)
	Indonesia	30.7	(4.2)	85.2	(3.0)	96.6	(1.9)	90.9	(2.8)	72.1	(4.2)
	Jordan	20.1	(2.9)	55.1	(3.4)	83.9	(2.5)	70.2	(3.4)	82.8	(2.4)
	Kazakhstan	82.5	(2.6)	77.5	(3.0)	97.5	(1.2)	83.1	(2.6)	99.2	(0.8)
	Kyrgyzstan	65.9	(3.5)	86.1	(2.7)	96.4	(1.5)	84.5	(3.1)	98.3	(0.8)
	Latvia	25.1	(3.7)	31.6	(3.9)	80.9	(3.0)	37.8	(4.1)	50.9	(3.8)
	Liechtenstein	26.3	(0.2)	8.6	(0.3)	0.0	c	37.0	(0.5)	34.4	(0.4)
	Lithuania	25.0	(3.2)	37.8	(3.8)	72.6	(3.9)	15.3	(2.8)	65.5	(4.0)
	Macao-China	13.9	(0.0)	12.2	(0.0)	29.6	(0.0)	37.6	(0.0)	38.9	(0.0)
	Montenegro	75.8	(0.5)	81.5	(1.4)	95.6	(0.1)	24.3	(0.5)	98.4	(0.2)
	Panama	6.3	(2.5)	35.7	(4.8)	53.8	(5.6)	51.1	(6.0)	77.5	(4.6)
	Peru	13.2	(2.4)	26.2	(3.2)	65.0	(3.2)	71.1	(3.6)	66.4	(3.3)
	Qatar	60.8	(0.1)	60.3	(0.1)	86.6	(0.1)	61.9	(0.1)	86.2	(0.1)
	Romania	61.9	(3.8)	88.6	(2.7)	92.2	(2.3)	65.9	(3.7)	74.5	(4.0)
	Russian Federation	76.0	(3.5)	82.4	(2.3)	97.1	(0.9)	65.4	(3.8)	99.3	(0.5)
	Serbia	55.7	(4.0)	49.8	(3.6)	77.5	(3.8)	19.4	(3.1)	83.9	(3.8)
	Shanghai-China	0.6	(0.6)	44.8	(4.2)	80.2	(3.0)	34.3	(3.6)	68.3	(3.6)
	Singapore	61.2	(0.9)	72.8	(0.3)	84.6	(0.5)	84.8	(0.2)	98.0	(0.1)
	Chinese Taipei	19.4	(3.4)	15.9	(3.1)	25.5	(3.5)	25.6	(3.9)	33.5	(4.4)
	Thailand	64.1	(3.8)	73.7	(3.1)	87.1	(2.7)	78.1	(3.1)	87.3	(2.4)
	Trinidad and Tobago	10.8	(0.2)	30.1	(0.2)	51.9	(0.4)	46.0	(0.3)	71.6	(0.3)
	Tunisia	6.8	(2.0)	55.9	(4.1)	71.5	(4.1)	58.7	(4.5)	81.9	(3.0)
	Uruguay	6.9	(1.9)	15.8	(2.1)	35.0	(2.7)	44.5	(2.9)	61.9	(2.7)

StatLink http://dx.doi.org/10.1787/888932343285

[Part 1/1]
Table IV.3.14 School accountability to parents
Results based on school principals' reports

		Percentage of students in schools where the school provides information to parents on student performance:							
		Relative to other students in the same school		Relative to national or regional benchmarks		As a group relative to students in the same grade in other schools		Relative to national or regional benchmarks or as a group relative to students in the same grade in other schools	
		%	S.E.	%	S.E.	%	S.E.	%	S.E.
OECD	Australia	69.5	(2.5)	46.4	(2.5)	21.3	(2.5)	50.6	(2.6)
	Austria	30.3	(3.9)	4.3	(1.4)	7.2	(1.9)	9.1	(2.1)
	Belgium	36.5	(2.4)	35.0	(1.9)	1.3	(0.7)	35.5	(2.0)
	Canada	65.3	(2.0)	51.0	(2.4)	23.6	(2.1)	53.5	(2.3)
	Chile	56.0	(4.6)	79.2	(2.8)	29.3	(4.1)	82.9	(3.0)
	Czech Republic	61.9	(3.5)	61.3	(3.5)	32.4	(3.4)	63.3	(3.4)
	Denmark	a	a	38.2	(3.5)	31.4	(3.4)	45.6	(3.6)
	Estonia	26.7	(3.2)	52.5	(3.4)	25.2	(3.2)	57.7	(3.5)
	Finland	12.6	(2.6)	29.3	(3.4)	17.8	(3.1)	38.9	(3.6)
	France	w	w	w	w	w	w	w	w
	Germany	46.5	(3.8)	25.7	(2.9)	15.5	(2.1)	29.9	(2.9)
	Greece	68.3	(3.3)	12.3	(2.8)	21.1	(3.3)	25.3	(3.1)
	Hungary	62.0	(4.0)	39.6	(3.6)	21.0	(3.2)	45.5	(3.7)
	Iceland	23.0	(0.2)	37.7	(0.2)	21.1	(0.2)	38.9	(0.2)
	Ireland	39.3	(4.2)	23.1	(4.0)	4.4	(2.1)	24.7	(4.2)
	Israel	35.5	(3.3)	33.4	(3.4)	19.1	(2.9)	42.2	(3.3)
	Italy	13.3	(1.5)	14.3	(1.4)	4.2	(0.7)	15.7	(1.4)
	Japan	60.0	(3.4)	78.4	(3.2)	3.6	(1.3)	78.8	(3.3)
	Korea	71.1	(4.0)	82.8	(3.0)	38.7	(4.4)	83.6	(3.1)
	Luxembourg	83.4	(0.1)	33.0	(0.1)	10.2	(0.0)	37.7	(0.1)
	Mexico	83.3	(1.4)	57.4	(1.8)	38.7	(1.9)	63.0	(1.6)
	Netherlands	18.8	(3.9)	15.8	(3.9)	3.7	(2.0)	15.9	(3.9)
	New Zealand	45.1	(3.5)	71.6	(3.3)	43.8	(3.1)	77.9	(3.1)
	Norway	39.2	(3.5)	73.2	(3.3)	48.6	(3.7)	80.9	(3.1)
	Poland	58.6	(3.8)	74.0	(3.2)	49.4	(4.0)	76.9	(3.4)
	Portugal	36.7	(3.7)	41.9	(4.1)	11.5	(2.8)	46.2	(4.1)
	Slovak Republic	60.6	(3.5)	53.8	(3.7)	26.5	(3.2)	58.0	(3.6)
	Slovenia	16.4	(0.2)	41.0	(0.4)	4.0	(0.4)	42.7	(0.4)
	Spain	38.4	(2.8)	18.6	(2.6)	10.9	(2.5)	21.8	(2.7)
	Sweden	11.2	(2.5)	87.9	(2.5)	20.4	(3.1)	89.8	(2.2)
	Switzerland	45.6	(3.5)	25.6	(2.9)	12.0	(1.8)	28.9	(3.0)
	Turkey	90.5	(2.3)	71.6	(4.1)	70.1	(3.5)	80.7	(3.3)
	United Kingdom	34.6	(3.5)	66.9	(3.1)	28.9	(2.9)	70.0	(3.0)
	United States	53.0	(4.0)	85.0	(3.1)	57.9	(3.2)	87.8	(2.7)
	OECD average	46.7	(0.6)	47.6	(0.5)	23.5	(0.5)	51.7	(0.5)
Partners	Albania	86.4	(2.8)	41.8	(4.1)	39.8	(3.8)	51.3	(4.0)
	Argentina	45.3	(4.2)	19.7	(3.1)	7.2	(1.9)	21.9	(3.2)
	Azerbaijan	98.9	(0.7)	91.8	(2.2)	83.2	(3.4)	95.4	(1.8)
	Brazil	31.3	(2.6)	54.8	(2.8)	15.7	(2.2)	56.5	(2.8)
	Bulgaria	88.2	(2.8)	64.8	(4.8)	56.2	(5.0)	69.1	(4.7)
	Colombia	64.4	(4.2)	82.4	(4.0)	17.1	(3.3)	88.1	(3.1)
	Croatia	62.7	(4.2)	a	a	28.5	(3.6)	28.5	(3.6)
	Dubai (UAE)	62.6	(0.1)	53.4	(0.2)	18.0	(0.2)	57.9	(0.2)
	Hong Kong-China	77.2	(3.5)	9.8	(2.6)	7.2	(2.0)	14.2	(3.0)
	Indonesia	91.0	(1.9)	65.6	(4.2)	62.8	(4.2)	77.4	(3.5)
	Jordan	85.7	(2.7)	57.5	(4.1)	27.1	(3.8)	61.4	(3.9)
	Kazakhstan	93.9	(1.6)	74.5	(3.3)	72.9	(3.2)	84.9	(2.3)
	Kyrgyzstan	91.1	(2.4)	83.9	(2.9)	62.5	(4.2)	90.1	(2.4)
	Latvia	22.4	(3.6)	10.8	(2.6)	18.2	(3.2)	21.4	(3.4)
	Liechtenstein	68.1	(0.2)	45.7	(0.4)	25.7	(0.4)	52.6	(0.3)
	Lithuania	41.3	(3.8)	a	a	18.6	(2.9)	18.6	(2.9)
	Macao-China	31.9	(0.0)	1.0	(0.0)	0.6	(0.0)	1.0	(0.0)
	Montenegro	86.5	(0.4)	35.1	(0.7)	26.5	(0.5)	38.7	(0.7)
	Panama	60.7	(5.8)	49.0	(5.2)	21.5	(4.8)	51.1	(5.2)
	Peru	58.2	(3.5)	18.2	(2.4)	21.1	(3.0)	27.3	(3.0)
	Qatar	81.9	(0.1)	78.2	(0.1)	45.3	(0.1)	84.1	(0.1)
	Romania	72.0	(3.6)	70.7	(4.0)	47.8	(3.8)	81.2	(3.2)
	Russian Federation	68.9	(3.2)	76.9	(2.5)	51.2	(3.1)	84.3	(2.3)
	Serbia	93.1	(2.1)	27.4	(3.8)	35.6	(3.8)	47.4	(3.8)
	Shanghai-China	69.8	(3.5)	39.5	(3.6)	28.1	(3.3)	46.5	(3.5)
	Singapore	87.6	(0.3)	68.0	(0.4)	31.4	(0.7)	72.3	(0.3)
	Chinese Taipei	48.6	(4.5)	27.0	(3.5)	16.1	(2.8)	30.5	(3.6)
	Thailand	64.6	(4.2)	54.2	(4.2)	44.9	(3.9)	63.5	(3.7)
	Trinidad and Tobago	78.3	(0.3)	32.7	(0.3)	25.6	(0.3)	42.0	(0.3)
	Tunisia	89.5	(2.5)	36.1	(4.2)	41.5	(3.8)	52.8	(3.7)
	Uruguay	31.3	(2.9)	12.6	(2.0)	4.6	(1.7)	15.7	(2.3)

StatLink http://dx.doi.org/10.1787/888932343285

[Part 1/1]

Table IV.3.15 Schools' methods for monitoring teachers' practices

Results based on school principals' reports

		Percentage of students in schools where the methods used to monitor the practice of teacher for language of instruction are:							
		Tests or assessments of student achievement		Teacher peer review (of lesson plans, assessment instruments, lessons)		Principal or senior staff observations of lessons		Observation of classes by inspectors or other persons external to the school	
		%	S.E.	%	S.E.	%	S.E.	%	S.E.
OECD	Australia	58.2	(2.5)	65.2	(2.8)	62.3	(2.8)	5.9	(1.4)
	Austria	82.1	(3.0)	83.0	(2.9)	86.1	(3.0)	41.7	(3.8)
	Belgium	36.8	(3.4)	65.3	(3.1)	68.7	(2.8)	50.0	(3.2)
	Canada	a	a	a	a	81.6	(1.6)	13.2	(1.5)
	Chile	72.1	(3.7)	82.0	(3.1)	72.3	(3.4)	20.7	(3.6)
	Czech Republic	71.4	(3.1)	57.1	(3.4)	96.0	(1.4)	29.4	(3.2)
	Denmark	40.8	(3.1)	32.5	(3.3)	69.3	(3.0)	34.3	(3.2)
	Estonia	63.7	(3.2)	56.4	(3.0)	91.0	(2.4)	16.1	(2.4)
	Finland	18.2	(3.1)	19.1	(2.9)	23.2	(3.1)	2.0	(1.1)
	France	w	w	w	w	w	w	w	w
	Germany	63.0	(3.6)	22.5	(3.0)	72.2	(3.0)	27.2	(2.8)
	Greece	26.6	(3.3)	31.2	(4.3)	15.3	(2.9)	26.4	(3.5)
	Hungary	63.8	(3.9)	75.2	(3.4)	96.2	(1.7)	20.8	(3.5)
	Iceland	52.3	(0.3)	18.9	(0.2)	53.4	(0.3)	5.3	(0.1)
	Ireland	51.9	(5.0)	37.2	(4.7)	18.0	(3.7)	42.7	(4.9)
	Israel	91.2	(2.3)	52.4	(3.6)	82.4	(3.0)	46.7	(3.8)
	Italy	48.1	(1.9)	86.2	(1.4)	20.5	(1.4)	0.9	(0.3)
	Japan	52.0	(3.6)	43.1	(3.8)	85.8	(2.7)	23.2	(2.7)
	Korea	76.7	(3.9)	88.2	(2.9)	89.5	(2.5)	62.5	(4.0)
	Luxembourg	49.3	(0.1)	38.0	(0.1)	53.9	(0.1)	10.0	(0.1)
	Mexico	82.6	(1.2)	79.2	(1.5)	79.1	(1.3)	48.4	(1.7)
	Netherlands	58.5	(4.2)	49.0	(4.9)	71.0	(4.3)	33.1	(3.3)
	New Zealand	67.6	(3.6)	89.5	(2.1)	95.5	(1.5)	51.2	(3.8)
	Norway	40.1	(3.0)	45.3	(3.5)	40.4	(3.2)	13.3	(2.4)
	Poland	97.0	(1.4)	92.3	(1.7)	97.4	(1.2)	20.0	(3.0)
	Portugal	49.6	(3.5)	79.6	(2.9)	20.6	(2.9)	1.6	(0.8)
	Slovak Republic	75.5	(3.8)	90.0	(2.5)	98.8	(0.8)	30.6	(3.7)
	Slovenia	41.2	(0.4)	51.5	(0.4)	90.7	(0.2)	3.6	(0.1)
	Spain	50.5	(2.4)	26.7	(2.7)	13.1	(1.9)	25.4	(2.4)
	Sweden	30.2	(3.6)	14.9	(2.7)	63.5	(3.7)	23.7	(3.4)
	Switzerland	22.6	(2.5)	58.0	(3.3)	83.1	(1.9)	37.1	(3.1)
	Turkey	84.3	(2.4)	46.3	(4.2)	87.8	(2.7)	47.0	(4.1)
	United Kingdom	84.7	(2.6)	86.9	(2.5)	98.3	(0.9)	66.3	(3.3)
	United States	80.8	(3.4)	55.9	(3.9)	98.0	(1.2)	53.2	(4.0)
	OECD average	58.9	(0.5)	56.8	(0.5)	68.9	(0.4)	28.3	(0.5)
Partners	Albania	96.6	(1.3)	95.7	(1.6)	100.0	(0.0)	81.5	(2.9)
	Argentina	72.1	(3.5)	63.6	(3.9)	86.3	(2.6)	31.0	(4.2)
	Azerbaijan	98.2	(1.2)	98.7	(0.8)	99.1	(0.8)	95.0	(1.9)
	Brazil	67.1	(2.6)	77.5	(2.2)	45.3	(2.7)	17.3	(2.1)
	Bulgaria	89.2	(3.2)	21.0	(3.2)	98.8	(1.0)	64.6	(5.2)
	Colombia	65.4	(4.0)	64.5	(3.6)	46.5	(4.0)	7.3	(2.4)
	Croatia	64.0	(4.2)	56.8	(4.2)	91.3	(2.2)	50.9	(4.0)
	Dubai (UAE)	87.3	(0.2)	96.8	(0.1)	94.6	(0.1)	79.4	(0.2)
	Hong Kong-China	80.4	(3.1)	81.5	(3.4)	97.3	(1.3)	31.1	(3.4)
	Indonesia	86.3	(3.0)	90.6	(2.6)	94.8	(1.9)	83.0	(3.3)
	Jordan	93.6	(1.8)	94.0	(2.0)	100.0	(0.0)	99.4	(0.6)
	Kazakhstan	98.2	(1.1)	100.0	(0.0)	100.0	(0.0)	87.9	(2.3)
	Kyrgyzstan	97.5	(1.2)	97.7	(1.1)	100.0	(0.0)	95.0	(1.8)
	Latvia	71.1	(3.4)	93.3	(2.1)	94.7	(1.8)	35.4	(3.4)
	Liechtenstein	11.1	(0.4)	34.8	(0.5)	5.6	(0.0)	82.0	(0.4)
	Lithuania	77.4	(3.1)	71.9	(3.5)	97.3	(1.3)	37.0	(3.9)
	Macao-China	66.8	(0.0)	96.7	(0.0)	96.8	(0.0)	52.8	(0.0)
	Montenegro	63.1	(1.1)	67.2	(1.2)	98.4	(0.1)	74.9	(1.3)
	Panama	58.8	(5.0)	86.9	(3.2)	84.3	(3.9)	40.6	(4.8)
	Peru	75.1	(2.9)	59.2	(3.5)	82.4	(2.7)	48.5	(3.5)
	Qatar	88.7	(0.1)	94.0	(0.1)	97.9	(0.0)	86.4	(0.1)
	Romania	91.5	(2.3)	89.2	(2.4)	94.7	(1.8)	80.8	(3.1)
	Russian Federation	98.5	(0.6)	96.4	(1.2)	99.7	(0.3)	72.1	(3.6)
	Serbia	59.2	(4.3)	59.9	(4.4)	80.8	(3.3)	59.0	(3.2)
	Shanghai-China	82.6	(3.0)	89.0	(2.4)	99.4	(0.6)	87.9	(2.2)
	Singapore	98.7	(0.0)	76.8	(0.3)	97.6	(0.1)	18.0	(1.1)
	Chinese Taipei	71.9	(3.7)	48.5	(3.7)	65.9	(3.8)	19.5	(3.3)
	Thailand	86.8	(2.6)	92.6	(2.3)	89.8	(2.6)	50.9	(3.6)
	Trinidad and Tobago	78.7	(0.3)	73.9	(0.3)	81.5	(0.2)	18.6	(0.2)
	Tunisia	85.9	(2.8)	62.4	(4.3)	80.5	(3.7)	95.6	(1.4)
	Uruguay	31.9	(2.9)	63.4	(2.8)	86.0	(2.2)	78.4	(2.4)

StatLink http://dx.doi.org/10.1787/888932343285

[Part 1/1]

Table IV.3.16a **Students' learning time at school**
Results based on students' self-reports

		Regular lessons at school in language of instruction					Regular lessons at school in mathematics					Regular lessons at school in science					Regular lessons at school in mathematics and science				
		Time student spent for learning per week (minutes)		Variability in learning time		School variability in the distribution of learning time	Time student spent for learning per week (minutes)		Variability in learning time		School variability in the distribution of learning time	Time student spent for learning per week (minutes)		Variability in learning time		School variability in the distribution of learning time	Time student spent for learning per week (minutes)		Variability in learning time		School variability in the distribution of learning time
		Mean	S.E.	S.D.	S.E.	Proportion of the index variance between schools	Mean	S.E.	S.D.	S.E.	Proportion of the index variance between schools	Mean	S.E.	S.D.	S.E.	Proportion of the index variance between schools	Mean	S.E.	S.D.	S.E.	Proportion of the index variance between schools
OECD	Australia	242.9	(1.9)	70.5	(2.3)	0.19	245.6	(1.9)	78.8	(2.4)	0.15	219.0	(2.7)	106.6	(2.6)	0.14	440.9	(4.1)	165.0	(3.3)	0.38
	Austria	140.8	(1.6)	48.0	(1.9)	0.53	154.8	(2.4)	70.2	(1.9)	0.45	194.6	(6.4)	146.0	(7.4)	0.46	346.0	(6.9)	169.8	(6.7)	0.45
	Belgium	216.0	(1.8)	58.1	(2.1)	0.27	210.2	(1.8)	73.9	(1.7)	0.27	185.2	(2.8)	111.0	(2.6)	0.31	377.7	(3.8)	162.2	(2.9)	0.31
	Canada	326.4	(2.8)	123.6	(2.3)	0.32	322.6	(2.7)	118.7	(2.1)	0.31	317.5	(2.9)	125.9	(2.0)	0.35	632.9	(5.4)	230.6	(3.8)	0.33
	Chile	312.7	(4.9)	144.6	(4.3)	0.19	316.5	(5.2)	146.4	(4.2)	0.21	291.3	(4.8)	160.4	(3.7)	0.15	588.0	(8.0)	270.1	(6.3)	0.35
	Czech Republic	181.2	(1.5)	39.0	(1.1)	0.62	187.0	(2.0)	42.4	(1.2)	0.65	237.5	(5.0)	128.0	(2.8)	0.43	409.6	(5.5)	149.4	(3.8)	0.45
	Denmark	312.1	(3.4)	99.3	(3.4)	0.21	216.5	(2.9)	77.3	(3.3)	0.25	173.5	(2.5)	79.2	(3.1)	0.28	376.2	(4.3)	133.2	(4.9)	0.24
	Estonia	201.9	(1.3)	38.8	(1.5)	0.25	225.8	(1.2)	29.5	(1.4)	0.42	193.5	(2.9)	105.4	(1.5)	0.13	416.6	(3.4)	113.9	(1.7)	0.14
	Finland	150.3	(2.0)	36.5	(1.5)	0.57	171.7	(2.1)	38.6	(2.0)	0.47	194.4	(3.2)	76.5	(3.2)	0.28	364.5	(4.7)	94.0	(5.4)	0.43
	France	229.9	(2.1)	74.4	(2.1)	0.12	210.8	(1.9)	68.9	(2.1)	0.12	189.6	(3.3)	111.2	(2.3)	0.28	383.4	(4.6)	158.1	(2.7)	0.19
	Germany	184.4	(1.7)	60.7	(4.0)	0.24	191.5	(2.2)	73.5	(4.9)	0.29	239.3	(3.1)	90.2	(2.8)	0.40	418.4	(4.9)	136.3	(6.3)	0.40
	Greece	195.5	(2.3)	81.4	(3.3)	0.18	196.5	(1.9)	48.5	(3.0)	0.23	214.6	(2.0)	55.9	(2.7)	0.27	409.2	(3.2)	91.1	(5.1)	0.26
	Hungary	173.5	(2.1)	74.2	(3.9)	0.10	156.0	(2.2)	58.5	(3.0)	0.17	157.3	(3.2)	90.1	(2.7)	0.21	303.3	(4.7)	122.6	(3.9)	0.22
	Iceland	233.2	(1.0)	65.5	(2.0)	0.20	238.7	(0.9)	67.2	(1.7)	0.16	145.1	(1.0)	69.3	(1.5)	0.18	376.6	(1.7)	113.8	(2.8)	0.15
	Ireland	179.9	(1.4)	33.4	(0.8)	0.27	185.9	(1.3)	33.9	(0.9)	0.18	146.8	(1.4)	44.6	(1.3)	0.12	303.8	(3.1)	86.4	(1.7)	0.15
	Israel	216.6	(4.8)	128.1	(6.0)	0.19	261.5	(3.7)	126.4	(4.4)	0.13	203.2	(4.8)	148.1	(4.2)	0.20	417.5	(6.1)	216.5	(6.5)	0.17
	Italy	284.5	(1.6)	78.0	(1.8)	0.66	228.4	(1.2)	56.6	(1.3)	0.62	158.4	(2.3)	93.2	(2.2)	0.62	381.8	(3.1)	129.0	(3.2)	0.54
	Japan	211.3	(2.7)	61.5	(2.3)	0.67	234.5	(3.3)	79.3	(3.0)	0.79	148.0	(2.0)	52.3	(1.8)	0.57	380.7	(3.8)	110.1	(3.5)	0.75
	Korea	212.0	(3.7)	44.1	(7.1)	1.00	217.4	(3.8)	46.6	(6.3)	0.98	179.7	(4.4)	55.3	(12.1)	0.99	397.1	(6.8)	84.0	(13.2)	0.99
	Luxembourg	193.5	(0.9)	70.2	(2.8)	0.37	203.7	(0.7)	56.0	(1.4)	0.22	168.0	(1.4)	125.5	(2.3)	0.36	366.9	(1.7)	142.5	(2.4)	0.36
	Mexico	236.3	(2.1)	100.2	(1.6)	0.18	255.6	(2.1)	94.6	(1.6)	0.22	251.0	(1.6)	119.1	(1.9)	0.23	478.0	(2.4)	185.4	(2.9)	0.22
	Netherlands	161.7	(1.8)	40.0	(1.2)	0.29	165.7	(1.4)	41.3	(2.0)	0.20	217.2	(4.4)	123.4	(3.4)	0.19	318.7	(5.1)	153.9	(3.2)	0.18
	New Zealand	243.4	(1.3)	39.9	(2.0)	0.28	241.7	(1.5)	42.6	(1.8)	0.28	243.9	(2.4)	96.2	(3.2)	0.11	477.5	(3.5)	123.2	(3.1)	0.17
	Norway	240.0	(0.0)	0.0	(0.0)	c	180.0	(0.0)	0.0	(0.0)	c	120.0	(0.0)	0.0	(0.0)	c	300.0	(0.0)	0.0	(0.0)	c
	Poland	229.0	(1.3)	21.6	(1.4)	0.71	204.2	(1.6)	27.4	(0.8)	0.77	188.1	(2.7)	42.0	(2.2)	0.86	392.1	(3.3)	51.5	(2.6)	0.80
	Portugal	225.3	(2.4)	108.3	(3.4)	0.13	263.4	(2.7)	109.6	(3.1)	0.12	229.8	(5.5)	165.2	(4.8)	0.49	428.7	(5.8)	225.3	(4.0)	0.15
	Slovak Republic	176.3	(1.8)	49.1	(1.2)	0.87	169.4	(2.7)	64.6	(1.9)	0.90	215.8	(3.6)	114.3	(3.4)	0.75	374.4	(4.6)	160.7	(4.0)	0.78
	Slovenia	175.6	(0.5)	33.9	(2.5)	0.38	163.3	(0.4)	32.1	(2.1)	0.43	200.1	(1.3)	94.3	(2.0)	0.31	355.1	(1.5)	112.7	(2.3)	0.35
	Spain	200.5	(1.0)	46.6	(1.4)	0.32	206.5	(0.8)	44.7	(1.4)	0.27	216.8	(2.1)	103.2	(2.0)	0.20	394.7	(2.3)	137.9	(2.4)	0.20
	Sweden	184.6	(3.4)	86.7	(4.0)	0.19	191.7	(3.7)	88.5	(5.4)	0.22	192.5	(3.3)	86.0	(4.3)	0.29	371.7	(5.5)	149.2	(10.3)	0.24
	Switzerland	201.3	(1.6)	56.1	(1.7)	0.42	207.0	(1.8)	59.4	(1.8)	0.43	181.5	(3.1)	100.5	(2.2)	0.41	374.0	(3.8)	129.4	(2.5)	0.37
	Turkey	236.7	(2.2)	80.8	(2.0)	0.20	182.8	(2.4)	81.8	(1.9)	0.26	128.9	(5.3)	137.9	(5.5)	0.26	307.6	(6.7)	183.6	(6.6)	0.31
	United Kingdom	219.4	(2.3)	56.7	(2.2)	0.29	212.5	(2.3)	58.3	(3.0)	0.35	280.4	(2.4)	90.2	(2.2)	0.18	480.0	(3.8)	130.9	(4.2)	0.21
	United States	257.7	(3.2)	117.6	(4.6)	0.18	258.5	(3.3)	115.0	(4.7)	0.18	258.3	(3.1)	123.3	(5.1)	0.15	509.1	(5.4)	212.7	(7.1)	0.15
	OECD average	217.2	(0.4)	66.7	(0.5)	0.35	214.1	(0.4)	66.2	(0.5)	0.36	202.4	(0.6)	99.1	(0.6)	0.34	401.6	(0.8)	142.2	(0.8)	0.35
Partners	Albania	208.9	(2.0)	70.1	(4.4)	0.14	193.1	(2.0)	72.4	(4.4)	0.06	240.2	(4.4)	143.5	(4.5)	0.10	425.8	(5.1)	174.7	(5.5)	0.08
	Argentina	293.1	(6.9)	163.4	(5.0)	0.40	354.6	(7.4)	181.4	(3.4)	0.33	341.5	(8.9)	207.5	(5.1)	0.32	558.5	(12.2)	319.6	(8.3)	0.44
	Azerbaijan	169.2	(3.8)	86.4	(3.2)	0.27	220.0	(3.5)	91.2	(2.7)	0.29	310.6	(3.8)	95.1	(2.6)	0.19	529.0	(5.1)	135.5	(3.7)	0.24
	Brazil	216.7	(1.1)	47.3	(0.9)	0.38	213.9	(1.1)	47.6	(0.8)	0.40	169.9	(2.1)	70.6	(0.9)	0.39	377.3	(3.1)	106.4	(1.4)	0.42
	Bulgaria	144.5	(2.0)	49.8	(2.1)	0.33	143.3	(2.9)	50.1	(2.9)	0.41	254.6	(3.2)	76.5	(3.8)	0.29	392.6	(5.0)	103.6	(5.3)	0.30
	Colombia	218.0	(3.2)	91.9	(2.7)	0.15	239.8	(3.4)	110.9	(4.4)	0.14	197.5	(4.0)	107.6	(3.4)	0.23	425.4	(6.0)	189.3	(5.8)	0.36
	Croatia	166.0	(2.0)	38.6	(2.0)	0.41	149.3	(2.1)	46.5	(1.1)	0.44	155.6	(4.6)	116.0	(2.4)	0.50	298.6	(5.4)	141.9	(2.9)	0.50
	Dubai (UAE)	251.0	(1.3)	82.3	(2.0)	0.33	278.5	(1.4)	102.8	(2.1)	0.25	303.8	(2.4)	156.8	(2.7)	0.39	536.4	(2.9)	216.3	(3.4)	0.39
	Hong Kong-China	274.3	(2.5)	67.1	(1.8)	0.16	269.0	(2.6)	77.5	(1.6)	0.15	301.8	(4.7)	157.0	(3.2)	0.17	444.2	(5.2)	221.1	(3.8)	0.36
	Indonesia	199.2	(4.8)	142.6	(5.2)	0.18	238.5	(5.2)	161.9	(6.1)	0.37	239.3	(7.9)	185.6	(6.1)	0.40	466.0	(10.7)	303.1	(8.9)	0.19
	Jordan	269.5	(1.3)	44.0	(2.1)	0.16	223.5	(1.2)	37.8	(1.9)	0.11	300.4	(2.3)	81.5	(1.8)	0.22	521.8	(2.8)	99.7	(3.0)	0.17
	Kazakhstan	198.3	(4.6)	72.6	(16.3)	0.53	174.0	(2.9)	55.2	(2.9)	0.40	289.9	(3.9)	77.3	(6.6)	0.42	461.0	(5.7)	108.1	(7.3)	0.43
	Kyrgyzstan	216.3	(3.6)	100.6	(3.9)	0.18	231.4	(4.1)	110.6	(3.9)	0.20	234.8	(5.1)	131.4	(4.5)	0.42	428.3	(8.1)	201.6	(6.8)	0.42
	Latvia	163.6	(1.8)	49.4	(1.0)	0.20	221.2	(2.0)	43.0	(3.0)	0.18	265.4	(2.8)	105.3	(2.6)	0.09	481.1	(3.6)	122.3	(3.3)	0.12
	Liechtenstein	205.0	(1.8)	45.6	(3.9)	0.31	222.2	(2.5)	52.0	(4.4)	0.41	177.3	(5.2)	87.0	(6.9)	0.07	395.6	(5.8)	112.5	(10.1)	0.16
	Lithuania	206.8	(2.8)	73.9	(4.6)	0.09	179.1	(2.6)	75.0	(6.1)	0.29	213.1	(4.3)	121.1	(7.1)	0.19	378.3	(4.2)	142.3	(6.1)	0.18
	Macao-China	265.1	(0.1)	36.3	(0.1)	0.77	275.8	(0.1)	35.5	(0.1)	0.77	259.6	(0.5)	96.1	(0.3)	0.42	503.2	(0.6)	132.7	(0.3)	0.40
	Montenegro	158.5	(0.3)	24.3	(0.1)	0.47	155.4	(0.3)	24.1	(0.1)	0.50	134.7	(1.7)	74.8	(1.2)	0.35	275.9	(1.5)	88.2	(1.3)	0.35
	Panama	191.6	(2.4)	65.7	(5.2)	0.14	205.4	(3.0)	70.9	(5.7)	0.13	225.8	(10.7)	142.9	(9.6)	0.29	374.3	(12.7)	196.7	(10.0)	0.26
	Peru	282.8	(5.2)	161.9	(5.3)	0.18	295.6	(4.4)	160.2	(4.1)	0.23	234.1	(4.4)	152.8	(5.7)	0.38	502.5	(7.0)	268.3	(7.5)	0.40
	Qatar	238.8	(0.9)	93.3	(1.7)	0.20	256.6	(1.2)	110.0	(2.1)	0.38	271.8	(1.5)	141.8	(2.2)	0.23	509.9	(2.5)	228.2	(3.4)	0.26
	Romania	184.3	(2.0)	54.8	(2.8)	0.44	142.3	(2.8)	64.0	(1.9)	0.44	150.5	(3.6)	85.4	(2.3)	0.33	251.3	(3.6)	111.7	(2.8)	0.41
	Russian Federation	237.8	(3.2)	61.8	(3.7)	0.41	204.9	(2.8)	61.3	(1.9)	0.40	278.4	(5.1)	151.6	(4.3)	0.38	458.4	(7.7)	188.6	(4.2)	0.40
	Serbia	144.8	(0.6)	30.2	(0.7)	0.48	154.8	(1.2)	35.2	(0.7)	0.61	228.9	(5.1)	159.9	(4.4)	0.37	357.2	(5.2)	175.2	(4.4)	0.39
	Shanghai-China	256.1	(3.0)	94.2	(2.8)	0.48	274.1	(3.5)	102.2	(3.4)	0.49	201.9	(7.2)	118.6	(4.2)	0.34	375.6	(6.7)	171.0	(6.2)	0.39
	Singapore	283.2	(2.1)	141.1	(2.6)	0.18	343.5	(2.1)	171.8	(2.1)	0.36	345.1	(2.8)	181.9	(2.6)	0.34	660.2	(4.4)	302.2	(4.0)	0.36
	Chinese Taipei	249.3	(2.9)	80.9	(2.0)	0.47	231.8	(3.7)	85.7	(2.1)	0.51	200.1	(3.7)	113.9	(3.8)	0.48	414.0	(6.0)	183.4	(4.7)	0.52
	Thailand	148.8	(1.7)	54.5	(1.1)	0.69	207.3	(3.1)	86.2	(1.6)	0.43	266.6	(6.1)	175.1	(3.9)	0.26	459.7	(8.1)	243.9	(5.0)	0.31
	Trinidad and Tobago	226.7	(1.8)	104.4	(2.5)	0.18	232.3	(1.9)	107.1	(3.0)	0.17	235.0	(2.5)	154.5	(2.6)	0.16	442.4	(3.6)	218.7	(4.4)	0.16
	Tunisia	272.9	(0.2)	10.5	(0.5)	0.33	220.8	(0.3)	15.3	(0.9)	0.04	230.9	(1.8)	68.1	(1.2)	0.67	451.8	(1.9)	76.3	(1.9)	0.56
	Uruguay	184.3	(1.5)	66.2	(2.5)	0.25	191.6	(1.7)	67.8	(3.7)	0.26	319.9	(3.6)	147.3	(1.8)	0.32	494.2	(4.2)	180.1	(4.2)	0.33

StatLink http://dx.doi.org/10.1787/888932343285

[Part 1/1]

Table IV.3.16b Students' learning time at school, by lower or upper secondary level of education
Results based on students' self-reports

		Lower secondary education (ISCED 2)						Upper secondary education (ISCED 3)						Difference between lower and upper secondary education in time student spent for learning per week (minutes)					
		Time student spent for learning per week (minutes)						Time student spent for learning per week (minutes)											
		Regular lessons at school in language of instruction		Regular lessons at school in mathematics		Regular lessons at school in science		Regular lessons at school in language of instruction		Regular lessons at school in mathematics		Regular lessons at school in science		Regular lessons at school in language of instruction		Regular lessons at school in mathematics		Regular lessons at school in science	
		Mean	S.E.	Mean	S.E.	Mean	S.E.	Mean	S.E.	Mean	S.E.	Mean	S.E.	Dif.	S.E.	Dif.	S.E.	Dif.	S.E.
OECD	Australia	237.2	(2.1)	238.1	(2.1)	218.5	(2.5)	236.3	(2.8)	246.8	(2.9)	222.4	(7.3)	0.9	(2.9)	**-8.7**	(3.2)	-3.9	(7.0)
	Austria	194.3	(3.0)	192.4	(4.4)	331.4	(13.3)	138.5	(1.6)	153.2	(2.4)	188.5	(6.4)	**55.9**	(3.5)	**39.2**	(5.1)	**142.9**	(14.3)
	Belgium	239.4	(7.2)	214.7	(6.3)	131.4	(6.4)	211.1	(1.4)	209.4	(1.7)	187.6	(2.9)	**28.3**	(7.2)	5.4	(6.3)	**-56.1**	(6.6)
	Canada	340.8	(4.9)	301.4	(4.3)	267.1	(3.9)	324.5	(3.1)	326.3	(3.1)	326.1	(3.2)	**16.3**	(5.7)	**-24.8**	(5.4)	**-59.0**	(5.0)
	Chile	301.8	(20.0)	298.5	(16.8)	255.4	(20.6)	313.1	(5.0)	317.1	(5.3)	292.5	(4.8)	-11.2	(20.5)	-18.6	(17.5)	-37.1	(21.0)
	Czech Republic	202.7	(2.0)	205.1	(2.0)	251.2	(5.2)	157.4	(1.6)	166.9	(3.3)	222.7	(8.8)	**45.3**	(2.5)	**38.2**	(3.7)	**28.5**	(10.4)
	Denmark	312.8	(3.4)	216.3	(2.9)	173.2	(2.5)	208.2	(18.9)	215.9	(8.7)	c	c	**104.6**	(19.2)	0.4	(9.4)	c	c
	Estonia	202.0	(1.3)	226.4	(1.2)	193.0	(3.0)	195.9	(9.1)	191.5	(9.5)	208.5	(17.5)	6.0	(9.3)	**34.9**	(9.4)	-15.5	(17.7)
	Finland	150.2	(2.0)	171.5	(2.0)	194.4	(3.2)	c	c	c	c	c	c	c	c	c	c	c	c
	France	231.7	(3.4)	212.4	(2.4)	142.1	(4.0)	229.8	(2.4)	210.6	(2.5)	214.9	(4.9)	2.0	(4.0)	1.8	(3.4)	**-72.8**	(6.6)
	Germany	185.3	(1.6)	192.3	(2.0)	239.8	(3.1)	155.8	(14.9)	164.2	(29.1)	210.9	(21.6)	**29.5**	(14.9)	28.1	(29.0)	28.9	(21.4)
	Greece	193.6	(18.6)	176.6	(6.5)	186.8	(11.5)	195.5	(2.2)	197.8	(2.0)	216.4	(1.9)	-2.0	(18.9)	**-21.1**	(6.8)	**-29.6**	(11.6)
	Hungary	174.6	(5.8)	166.0	(6.5)	161.3	(8.6)	173.8	(2.3)	155.5	(2.2)	157.0	(3.4)	0.8	(6.2)	10.4	(6.6)	4.2	(8.9)
	Iceland	234.0	(1.0)	238.7	(0.9)	144.0	(1.0)	191.0	(4.2)	237.5	(7.8)	217.6	(12.8)	**43.0**	(4.3)	1.2	(7.9)	**-73.7**	(12.9)
	Ireland	185.3	(1.5)	192.8	(1.3)	153.9	(1.2)	171.3	(2.5)	175.1	(2.5)	134.1	(3.0)	**14.0**	(2.8)	**17.7**	(2.7)	**19.9**	(3.0)
	Israel	189.9	(5.4)	255.9	(4.6)	190.4	(5.8)	218.5	(5.4)	256.9	(3.9)	204.4	(5.2)	**-28.6**	(7.2)	-1.0	(5.9)	**-14.0**	(7.0)
	Italy	459.8	(33.1)	290.4	(22.5)	141.6	(25.4)	282.7	(1.6)	227.5	(1.3)	158.7	(2.3)	**177.1**	(33.1)	**62.9**	(22.9)	-17.1	(25.6)
	Japan	c	c	c	c	c	c	211.3	(2.7)	234.5	(3.3)	148.0	(2.0)	c	c	c	c	c	c
	Korea	186.1	(7.1)	169.3	(6.6)	181.4	(2.9)	213.1	(3.9)	219.5	(4.0)	179.6	(4.6)	**-27.0**	(8.1)	**-50.3**	(7.7)	1.8	(5.5)
	Luxembourg	201.7	(1.3)	214.0	(0.9)	139.4	(1.6)	180.3	(1.1)	187.5	(0.8)	214.4	(2.4)	**21.4**	(1.7)	**26.5**	(1.2)	**-75.1**	(2.7)
	Mexico	232.3	(2.2)	242.0	(2.2)	257.6	(2.7)	229.0	(1.8)	253.3	(1.8)	239.2	(1.8)	3.3	(2.8)	**-11.2**	(3.2)	**18.4**	(3.1)
	Netherlands	166.3	(2.0)	168.2	(1.6)	190.1	(3.7)	149.4	(2.6)	159.5	(2.2)	294.6	(7.9)	**16.9**	(3.3)	**8.6**	(2.7)	**-104.4**	(8.5)
	New Zealand	227.2	(3.3)	225.8	(3.1)	215.2	(3.2)	244.3	(1.4)	242.6	(1.5)	245.5	(2.5)	**-17.1**	(3.2)	**-16.8**	(2.8)	**-30.3**	(3.6)
	Norway	240.0	(0.0)	180.0	(0.0)	120.0	(0.0)	c	c	c	c	c	c	c	c	c	c	c	c
	Poland	229.1	(1.3)	204.3	(1.6)	187.4	(2.8)	c	c	c	c	c	c	c	c	c	c	c	c
	Portugal	244.5	(5.0)	255.6	(5.2)	133.9	(3.2)	210.6	(2.5)	269.6	(2.3)	350.5	(7.4)	**33.9**	(5.8)	**-14.0**	(5.7)	**-216.6**	(8.4)
	Slovak Republic	230.2	(1.6)	231.7	(2.1)	250.0	(2.5)	142.9	(1.8)	131.0	(3.2)	193.7	(5.5)	**87.4**	(2.4)	**100.7**	(3.9)	**56.4**	(6.0)
	Slovenia	208.1	(4.4)	179.0	(3.2)	201.2	(17.4)	174.7	(0.4)	162.8	(0.3)	200.0	(1.3)	**33.3**	(4.5)	**16.3**	(3.2)	1.2	(17.6)
	Spain	200.6	(1.0)	206.5	(0.8)	216.8	(2.1)	c	c	c	c	c	c	c	c	c	c	c	c
	Sweden	183.8	(3.4)	188.7	(3.4)	190.0	(3.2)	169.3	(10.4)	201.1	(32.1)	179.6	(21.7)	14.5	(11.3)	-12.4	(32.2)	10.4	(22.1)
	Switzerland	206.3	(1.5)	216.8	(1.6)	176.1	(2.6)	181.1	(5.3)	167.5	(5.3)	207.9	(10.0)	**25.3**	(5.5)	**49.3**	(5.8)	**-31.8**	(10.0)
	Turkey	c	c	c	c	c	c	237.6	(2.2)	183.4	(2.5)	127.7	(5.5)	c	c	c	c	c	c
	United Kingdom	c	c	c	c	c	c	218.5	(2.2)	211.6	(2.4)	280.1	(2.5)	c	c	c	c	c	c
	United States	235.1	(7.0)	249.2	(8.7)	228.6	(6.4)	260.5	(3.2)	259.4	(3.2)	261.4	(3.1)	**-25.4**	(6.7)	-10.2	(8.0)	**-32.9**	(6.3)
	OECD average	226.7	(1.5)	216.8	(1.1)	195.6	(1.5)	207.5	(1.0)	211.2	(1.6)	216.7	(1.6)	**24.0**	(2.1)	**9.3**	(2.2)	**-21.4**	(2.4)
Partners	Albania	231.1	(1.5)	192.9	(2.3)	218.8	(4.9)	183.5	(3.4)	192.0	(3.4)	265.2	(6.3)	**47.6**	(3.7)	1.0	(4.3)	**-46.4**	(7.7)
	Argentina	325.3	(10.5)	336.3	(10.5)	326.7	(12.5)	279.1	(8.7)	364.3	(10.4)	349.8	(11.7)	**46.2**	(13.7)	-28.0	(15.3)	-23.1	(16.4)
	Azerbaijan	167.5	(5.0)	230.2	(3.7)	334.8	(3.1)	171.3	(4.7)	207.4	(5.4)	280.7	(5.9)	-3.8	(6.2)	**22.8**	(5.7)	**54.1**	(5.4)
	Brazil	223.2	(1.8)	221.2	(1.9)	177.7	(2.9)	214.7	(1.3)	211.5	(1.2)	167.3	(2.4)	**8.5**	(2.1)	**9.7**	(2.2)	**10.5**	(3.3)
	Bulgaria	197.2	(5.9)	177.3	(3.7)	274.8	(8.1)	141.1	(2.0)	141.1	(3.0)	253.9	(3.4)	**56.1**	(6.2)	**36.2**	(4.7)	**21.0**	(9.1)
	Colombia	232.5	(3.9)	248.1	(4.5)	207.0	(3.7)	210.1	(3.5)	235.3	(4.2)	192.2	(5.2)	**22.4**	(3.9)	**12.8**	(5.5)	**14.8**	(5.4)
	Croatia	c	c	c	c	c	c	166.0	(2.0)	149.2	(2.1)	155.5	(4.6)	c	c	c	c	c	c
	Dubai (UAE)	257.8	(2.3)	264.4	(3.0)	237.9	(3.6)	248.8	(1.2)	280.4	(1.6)	313.5	(2.7)	**9.0**	(2.5)	**-16.0**	(3.5)	**-75.6**	(4.5)
	Hong Kong-China	275.5	(3.2)	254.1	(3.1)	207.0	(3.9)	273.6	(2.7)	276.7	(3.1)	398.2	(7.4)	1.8	(2.9)	**-22.6**	(3.5)	**-191.2**	(8.6)
	Indonesia	220.7	(7.1)	245.3	(8.9)	222.8	(7.1)	176.1	(5.5)	232.2	(5.5)	259.0	(14.2)	**44.6**	(9.2)	13.1	(10.6)	**-36.2**	(15.2)
	Jordan	269.3	(1.3)	223.0	(1.1)	300.2	(2.3)	c	c	c	c	c	c	c	c	c	c	c	c
	Kazakhstan	195.9	(2.7)	173.0	(2.3)	283.5	(2.5)	208.2	(19.7)	177.9	(9.7)	316.9	(16.3)	-12.3	(19.7)	-4.9	(9.6)	**-33.4**	(16.4)
	Kyrgyzstan	219.3	(3.8)	243.6	(4.3)	234.8	(5.3)	209.4	(5.6)	190.2	(4.8)	239.0	(8.2)	9.9	(5.7)	**53.4**	(5.4)	-4.1	(7.9)
	Latvia	163.5	(1.9)	221.2	(1.9)	264.8	(3.0)	159.7	(8.2)	210.6	(7.2)	238.8	(16.0)	3.9	(8.3)	10.6	(6.7)	26.0	(16.2)
	Liechtenstein	209.5	(2.0)	226.7	(2.5)	171.2	(5.1)	c	c	c	c	c	c	c	c	c	c	c	c
	Lithuania	204.2	(2.0)	177.9	(2.2)	210.4	(4.1)	c	c	c	c	c	c	c	c	c	c	c	c
	Macao-China	260.1	(0.1)	269.0	(0.1)	222.0	(0.3)	272.9	(0.2)	286.3	(0.2)	344.9	(1.0)	**-12.8**	(0.2)	**-17.3**	(0.2)	**-122.9**	(1.0)
	Montenegro	c	c	c	c	c	c	158.2	(0.2)	155.0	(0.2)	133.3	(0.9)	c	c	c	c	c	c
	Panama	196.4	(4.2)	204.2	(4.5)	196.7	(8.1)	184.1	(2.9)	202.8	(3.9)	243.0	(16.3)	**12.3**	(5.5)	1.4	(6.2)	**-46.3**	(18.5)
	Peru	285.5	(8.1)	293.6	(7.3)	227.0	(8.1)	283.1	(5.1)	295.6	(5.1)	231.4	(4.1)	2.4	(7.3)	-2.0	(8.4)	-4.4	(8.2)
	Qatar	238.9	(2.7)	243.9	(3.2)	241.8	(3.7)	239.5	(1.0)	259.5	(1.3)	278.1	(1.8)	-0.5	(3.1)	**-15.5**	(3.4)	**-36.3**	(4.4)
	Romania	184.2	(2.0)	143.2	(2.8)	151.7	(3.7)	c	c	c	c	c	c	c	c	c	c	c	c
	Russian Federation	238.7	(3.3)	203.4	(2.8)	274.9	(6.1)	235.5	(6.6)	208.6	(6.6)	286.7	(11.0)	3.2	(6.8)	-5.2	(7.1)	-11.8	(12.8)
	Serbia	177.2	(3.5)	179.6	(4.3)	228.3	(27.1)	144.0	(0.6)	154.2	(1.2)	227.7	(5.2)	**33.1**	(3.6)	**25.5**	(4.5)	0.6	(27.6)
	Shanghai-China	324.6	(5.4)	345.9	(6.4)	218.8	(13.2)	206.2	(2.1)	222.7	(2.6)	190.6	(7.2)	**118.4**	(5.5)	**123.2**	(6.2)	28.2	(14.5)
	Singapore	284.3	(11.8)	262.7	(8.8)	253.1	(10.7)	282.2	(2.1)	346.3	(2.2)	347.0	(2.9)	2.2	(11.7)	**-83.6**	(9.2)	**-93.9**	(10.9)
	Chinese Taipei	301.8	(4.4)	267.6	(4.5)	268.2	(4.8)	221.7	(3.3)	213.0	(4.6)	159.7	(4.7)	**80.1**	(5.4)	**54.6**	(6.3)	**108.5**	(6.5)
	Thailand	199.0	(2.8)	209.9	(3.6)	194.4	(3.0)	132.9	(1.7)	206.5	(3.6)	290.6	(7.3)	**66.1**	(2.9)	3.5	(4.3)	**-96.2**	(6.8)
	Trinidad and Tobago	212.4	(3.3)	217.1	(3.3)	171.5	(2.8)	232.2	(1.9)	239.2	(2.1)	268.9	(3.5)	**-19.9**	(3.7)	**-22.1**	(3.7)	**-97.4**	(4.6)
	Tunisia	274.9	(0.1)	220.0	(0.1)	166.4	(0.6)	271.4	(0.4)	221.5	(0.5)	280.9	(1.2)	**3.5**	(0.4)	**-1.5**	(0.5)	**-114.5**	(1.3)
	Uruguay	215.3	(2.7)	202.6	(2.2)	271.3	(4.4)	166.8	(1.4)	184.9	(2.1)	343.9	(4.4)	**48.5**	(3.0)	**17.8**	(2.8)	**-72.7**	(6.0)

Note: Values that are statistically significant are indicated in bold (see Annex A3).

StatLink http://dx.doi.org/10.1787/888932343285

[Part 1/1]

Table IV.3.17a **Percentage of students attending after-school lessons, by enrichment or remedial lessons**
Results based on students' self-reports

		Language of instruction				Mathematics				Science				Attend after-school lessons for at least one of the three subjects			
		Enrichment lessons		Remedial lessons		Enrichment lessons		Remedial lessons		Enrichment lessons		Remedial lessons		Enrichment lessons		Remedial lessons	
		%	S.E.	%	S.E.	%	S.E.	%	S.E.	%	S.E.	%	S.E.	%	S.E.	%	S.E.
OECD	Australia	7.8	(0.3)	5.0	(0.3)	13.9	(0.5)	7.7	(0.3)	5.9	(0.3)	3.6	(0.2)	21.1	(0.6)	11.3	(0.4)
	Austria	2.6	(0.3)	5.4	(0.5)	4.4	(0.4)	17.2	(0.8)	1.8	(0.2)	2.7	(0.3)	10.6	(0.6)	26.7	(1.1)
	Belgium	3.8	(0.2)	2.4	(0.2)	9.2	(0.4)	11.3	(0.6)	3.6	(0.3)	3.4	(0.2)	14.7	(0.5)	16.8	(0.6)
	Canada	5.9	(0.3)	4.5	(0.2)	11.9	(0.4)	8.4	(0.3)	6.4	(0.3)	4.3	(0.2)	18.6	(0.5)	11.8	(0.4)
	Chile	9.0	(0.6)	10.1	(0.7)	15.3	(0.8)	20.8	(0.9)	9.8	(0.6)	8.5	(0.7)	25.6	(1.0)	28.4	(1.0)
	Czech Republic	8.2	(0.5)	4.6	(0.4)	14.1	(0.7)	15.5	(0.7)	11.5	(0.6)	3.6	(0.4)	34.8	(0.7)	24.7	(0.8)
	Denmark	2.9	(0.3)	3.4	(0.3)	5.3	(0.5)	4.9	(0.4)	3.2	(0.3)	1.4	(0.2)	9.8	(0.6)	8.8	(0.5)
	Estonia	2.8	(0.4)	11.0	(0.7)	11.2	(0.7)	26.6	(0.9)	6.0	(0.4)	14.2	(0.8)	23.9	(1.0)	35.2	(1.0)
	Finland	1.3	(0.1)	2.2	(0.2)	2.5	(0.2)	9.2	(0.5)	1.8	(0.2)	2.0	(0.2)	5.4	(0.3)	12.6	(0.7)
	France	8.7	(0.4)	16.2	(0.8)	18.8	(0.7)	25.1	(0.9)	6.4	(0.4)	2.8	(0.3)	25.5	(0.8)	33.0	(1.0)
	Germany	5.4	(0.4)	6.7	(0.4)	11.0	(0.6)	18.8	(0.7)	3.5	(0.3)	3.7	(0.3)	19.3	(0.7)	28.8	(0.9)
	Greece	30.4	(1.0)	17.6	(0.6)	51.7	(1.4)	36.8	(1.1)	41.6	(1.3)	28.7	(1.0)	66.3	(1.3)	49.7	(1.1)
	Hungary	3.6	(0.5)	4.3	(0.7)	16.0	(0.7)	16.9	(0.9)	5.8	(0.5)	4.8	(0.5)	30.0	(1.0)	23.2	(1.0)
	Iceland	7.7	(0.4)	8.8	(0.4)	17.6	(0.6)	17.5	(0.7)	6.7	(0.4)	3.4	(0.3)	29.1	(0.8)	22.5	(0.7)
	Ireland	5.0	(0.4)	3.6	(0.3)	16.0	(0.8)	8.2	(0.6)	3.8	(0.4)	1.9	(0.2)	24.1	(0.9)	12.4	(0.6)
	Israel	20.1	(0.7)	12.7	(0.6)	40.7	(1.0)	22.4	(0.7)	16.6	(0.7)	10.2	(0.6)	57.1	(0.9)	31.8	(0.8)
	Italy	5.2	(0.2)	7.0	(0.3)	16.5	(0.4)	19.9	(0.4)	3.5	(0.2)	4.5	(0.2)	29.8	(0.5)	33.9	(0.6)
	Japan	14.8	(0.6)	21.6	(1.1)	29.8	(0.9)	34.2	(1.2)	14.1	(0.6)	15.3	(0.7)	38.7	(0.9)	42.0	(1.2)
	Korea	27.0	(1.4)	54.4	(2.4)	37.9	(1.5)	61.2	(2.2)	17.2	(1.2)	44.8	(2.5)	47.6	(1.5)	69.3	(1.8)
	Luxembourg	5.5	(0.3)	4.1	(0.3)	10.6	(0.4)	17.1	(0.6)	4.7	(0.3)	3.6	(0.3)	14.9	(0.5)	23.3	(0.6)
	Mexico	24.5	(0.5)	17.5	(0.5)	26.7	(0.5)	21.2	(0.5)	24.1	(0.5)	16.6	(0.5)	41.4	(0.6)	32.7	(0.6)
	Netherlands	7.4	(0.6)	4.2	(0.5)	10.8	(0.7)	10.1	(0.6)	5.3	(0.4)	4.2	(0.4)	17.6	(0.7)	17.8	(0.7)
	New Zealand	7.2	(0.5)	5.4	(0.4)	11.8	(0.6)	7.2	(0.4)	6.4	(0.4)	4.2	(0.3)	21.8	(0.8)	11.6	(0.5)
	Norway	8.5	(0.5)	3.8	(0.3)	17.1	(0.7)	8.2	(0.5)	8.5	(0.4)	2.6	(0.3)	23.8	(0.7)	10.6	(0.5)
	Poland	15.8	(1.1)	13.0	(0.9)	20.8	(1.1)	23.0	(1.1)	18.2	(1.1)	11.8	(0.9)	56.5	(1.2)	34.8	(1.2)
	Portugal	15.7	(1.0)	11.3	(0.9)	31.7	(1.0)	18.3	(1.0)	9.0	(0.6)	4.0	(0.4)	43.0	(1.1)	26.8	(1.1)
	Slovak Republic	14.5	(1.0)	12.4	(0.9)	20.5	(1.3)	20.2	(1.1)	4.1	(0.3)	2.6	(0.2)	31.4	(1.4)	29.9	(1.1)
	Slovenia	7.7	(0.4)	6.4	(0.5)	15.0	(0.6)	20.2	(0.6)	10.8	(0.5)	9.8	(0.5)	25.0	(0.8)	26.6	(0.8)
	Spain	10.5	(0.5)	13.0	(0.9)	24.0	(0.6)	27.9	(0.7)	11.9	(0.4)	11.9	(0.5)	37.9	(0.7)	36.5	(0.9)
	Sweden	5.1	(0.4)	4.9	(0.3)	8.4	(0.6)	8.9	(0.5)	3.0	(0.3)	2.2	(0.3)	16.1	(0.7)	13.6	(0.6)
	Switzerland	5.5	(0.3)	5.2	(0.4)	10.0	(0.5)	12.3	(0.5)	3.0	(0.2)	2.2	(0.2)	17.5	(0.7)	18.1	(0.7)
	Turkey	11.8	(0.7)	9.6	(0.6)	21.2	(1.2)	14.4	(0.9)	14.0	(1.2)	10.2	(0.8)	29.6	(1.3)	21.5	(1.0)
	United Kingdom	8.6	(0.5)	16.9	(0.8)	17.2	(0.9)	23.6	(0.9)	11.8	(0.6)	19.0	(0.9)	33.4	(1.0)	47.8	(1.0)
	United States	9.8	(0.5)	6.6	(0.4)	14.8	(0.5)	8.7	(0.6)	11.1	(0.6)	7.2	(0.5)	24.8	(0.8)	14.3	(0.7)
	OECD average	9.7	(0.1)	9.9	(0.1)	17.8	(0.1)	18.3	(0.1)	9.3	(0.1)	8.1	(0.1)	28.4	(0.1)	26.1	(0.2)
Partners	Albania	32.8	(1.5)	37.6	(1.4)	40.0	(1.4)	43.6	(1.5)	28.0	(1.2)	31.0	(1.3)	61.6	(1.4)	60.4	(1.5)
	Argentina	9.2	(0.6)	8.9	(0.6)	18.6	(0.8)	25.4	(1.0)	9.8	(0.7)	7.9	(0.7)	29.6	(0.9)	33.0	(1.1)
	Azerbaijan	44.7	(1.1)	41.6	(1.2)	49.7	(1.2)	43.9	(1.3)	45.2	(1.2)	45.5	(1.3)	68.4	(1.2)	61.2	(1.4)
	Brazil	10.1	(0.4)	10.3	(0.4)	16.4	(0.6)	13.5	(0.5)	6.4	(0.3)	7.4	(0.3)	23.8	(0.7)	19.7	(0.6)
	Bulgaria	10.4	(1.1)	10.4	(0.9)	14.9	(0.9)	17.7	(1.0)	10.2	(0.8)	10.3	(0.9)	28.8	(1.2)	24.9	(1.2)
	Colombia	26.5	(1.2)	24.8	(1.1)	35.6	(1.2)	31.4	(1.1)	28.3	(1.1)	23.6	(1.0)	56.5	(1.1)	44.4	(1.1)
	Croatia	4.4	(0.3)	5.6	(0.4)	22.8	(0.7)	31.4	(0.9)	9.6	(0.6)	10.3	(0.6)	33.6	(0.8)	38.4	(0.9)
	Dubai (UAE)	18.6	(0.5)	13.0	(0.5)	41.5	(0.7)	25.5	(0.6)	27.9	(0.6)	17.7	(0.5)	53.6	(0.7)	34.9	(0.6)
	Hong Kong-China	18.8	(0.8)	12.0	(0.6)	30.0	(1.0)	22.4	(0.8)	17.0	(0.8)	12.6	(0.7)	48.9	(1.1)	38.7	(0.9)
	Indonesia	52.6	(2.4)	35.7	(1.6)	64.1	(1.8)	44.9	(1.5)	59.1	(2.1)	40.7	(1.5)	74.9	(1.6)	55.5	(1.4)
	Jordan	32.3	(0.9)	25.7	(0.8)	32.1	(1.0)	30.4	(0.9)	35.3	(0.9)	24.3	(0.7)	54.8	(1.0)	43.9	(1.0)
	Kazakhstan	47.5	(1.5)	54.3	(1.4)	56.4	(1.3)	62.0	(1.3)	55.3	(1.3)	62.3	(1.3)	79.0	(1.2)	80.6	(1.0)
	Kyrgyzstan	31.5	(1.4)	23.9	(1.0)	36.9	(1.4)	26.4	(1.1)	29.7	(1.2)	21.7	(0.8)	62.4	(1.5)	40.3	(1.2)
	Latvia	12.4	(0.7)	4.9	(0.5)	33.1	(1.3)	9.8	(0.7)	12.2	(0.8)	4.7	(0.5)	54.5	(1.2)	14.2	(0.8)
	Liechtenstein	2.8	(1.0)	6.4	(1.2)	9.7	(1.8)	15.3	(1.9)	4.0	(1.2)	2.8	(0.8)	17.4	(2.5)	17.4	(2.0)
	Lithuania	9.4	(0.8)	8.7	(0.5)	17.1	(0.9)	14.9	(0.8)	7.9	(0.5)	5.5	(0.4)	30.8	(1.0)	22.1	(0.9)
	Macao-China	8.7	(0.3)	4.5	(0.3)	16.1	(0.5)	16.7	(0.4)	11.3	(0.4)	7.6	(0.3)	36.8	(0.7)	28.5	(0.5)
	Montenegro	7.1	(0.7)	5.8	(0.7)	30.6	(0.7)	13.5	(0.6)	10.9	(0.6)	7.0	(0.7)	39.9	(0.8)	19.7	(0.7)
	Panama	36.9	(2.1)	26.9	(1.7)	45.4	(1.7)	39.8	(1.2)	33.3	(1.7)	25.5	(1.6)	58.0	(1.7)	51.8	(1.4)
	Peru	26.2	(1.0)	21.5	(0.9)	39.2	(0.9)	26.8	(0.9)	23.9	(0.8)	20.5	(0.9)	52.3	(1.0)	39.0	(1.0)
	Qatar	34.1	(0.5)	23.1	(0.4)	36.2	(0.5)	36.2	(0.4)	36.7	(0.5)	31.5	(0.5)	57.3	(0.6)	49.0	(0.5)
	Romania	20.0	(1.5)	16.6	(1.2)	23.0	(1.4)	18.1	(1.2)	12.7	(0.7)	8.9	(0.8)	41.6	(1.4)	27.9	(1.5)
	Russian Federation	36.2	(1.5)	42.5	(1.3)	47.8	(1.7)	54.7	(1.3)	24.5	(1.4)	28.7	(1.0)	65.5	(1.4)	66.1	(1.3)
	Serbia	5.5	(0.4)	5.4	(0.6)	25.3	(0.9)	20.1	(1.1)	8.3	(0.5)	8.8	(0.7)	34.1	(1.0)	28.1	(1.2)
	Shanghai-China	13.0	(0.8)	17.9	(0.9)	28.1	(1.0)	37.7	(0.9)	9.3	(0.8)	6.6	(0.7)	46.7	(1.1)	51.4	(1.0)
	Singapore	27.1	(0.7)	30.3	(0.6)	48.5	(0.7)	49.1	(0.6)	34.2	(0.7)	41.7	(0.6)	60.5	(0.6)	60.7	(0.7)
	Chinese Taipei	28.8	(0.9)	18.6	(1.1)	48.7	(1.0)	26.6	(1.0)	32.3	(0.7)	18.3	(0.6)	61.9	(0.9)	36.5	(1.1)
	Thailand	22.6	(1.0)	10.3	(0.7)	41.5	(1.2)	20.3	(0.8)	35.5	(1.1)	20.9	(0.7)	61.8	(1.2)	37.4	(1.0)
	Trinidad and Tobago	29.9	(0.6)	11.3	(0.5)	55.2	(0.8)	17.0	(0.5)	26.9	(0.7)	9.3	(0.5)	67.5	(0.8)	23.1	(0.6)
	Tunisia	16.3	(1.0)	16.3	(1.1)	41.3	(1.3)	38.9	(1.2)	23.7	(1.0)	23.4	(1.0)	55.5	(1.3)	53.4	(1.3)
	Uruguay	4.5	(0.4)	3.8	(0.3)	17.0	(0.7)	11.4	(0.5)	10.8	(0.5)	4.3	(0.4)	27.0	(0.7)	16.3	(0.6)

StatLink http://dx.doi.org/10.1787/888932343285

[Part 1/2]

Table IV.3.17b Percentage of students attending after-school lessons, by hours per week
Results based on students' self-reports

		Language of instruction						Mathematics					
		No attendance		Less than 4 hours a week		4 hours a week or more		No attendance		Less than 4 hours a week		4 hours a week or more	
		%	S.E.	%	S.E.	%	S.E.	%	S.E.	%	S.E.	%	S.E.
OECD	Australia	88.7	(0.5)	9.5	(0.5)	1.9	(0.2)	80.9	(0.7)	16.5	(0.6)	2.6	(0.2)
	Austria	94.8	(0.4)	4.6	(0.4)	0.6	(0.1)	83.0	(0.9)	15.7	(0.9)	1.3	(0.2)
	Belgium	85.5	(0.5)	11.6	(0.4)	3.0	(0.2)	74.6	(0.6)	20.6	(0.5)	4.8	(0.3)
	Canada	90.8	(0.3)	6.9	(0.3)	2.3	(0.1)	81.5	(0.5)	14.9	(0.5)	3.5	(0.2)
	Chile	80.8	(0.9)	10.9	(0.6)	8.3	(0.6)	70.4	(1.1)	21.2	(0.9)	8.5	(0.6)
	Czech Republic	78.1	(0.9)	17.6	(0.8)	4.4	(0.4)	69.6	(1.0)	25.2	(0.9)	5.2	(0.4)
	Denmark	71.9	(1.2)	21.0	(1.0)	7.1	(0.5)	70.5	(1.2)	24.5	(1.0)	4.9	(0.4)
	Estonia	47.9	(1.1)	41.8	(1.0)	10.4	(0.5)	36.8	(1.0)	47.3	(0.9)	15.9	(0.9)
	Finland	92.1	(0.5)	6.6	(0.4)	1.3	(0.2)	89.8	(0.6)	7.6	(0.5)	2.6	(0.3)
	France	73.8	(0.9)	21.5	(0.8)	4.7	(0.4)	62.3	(0.9)	32.1	(0.9)	5.6	(0.4)
	Germany	89.2	(0.7)	9.2	(0.6)	1.6	(0.2)	74.3	(0.8)	22.8	(0.8)	2.9	(0.4)
	Greece	61.0	(1.1)	32.6	(1.1)	6.4	(0.4)	32.6	(1.1)	52.6	(1.0)	14.8	(0.9)
	Hungary	92.7	(0.7)	6.3	(0.6)	1.0	(0.2)	70.0	(1.1)	28.3	(1.0)	1.7	(0.2)
	Iceland	91.1	(0.6)	6.7	(0.4)	2.3	(0.3)	78.6	(0.8)	18.5	(0.7)	3.0	(0.3)
	Ireland	92.1	(0.5)	6.4	(0.5)	1.5	(0.2)	79.7	(0.8)	18.3	(0.8)	2.0	(0.3)
	Israel	72.4	(0.9)	21.0	(0.8)	6.7	(0.5)	47.2	(1.2)	40.4	(1.0)	12.5	(0.6)
	Italy	74.0	(0.5)	16.2	(0.4)	9.8	(0.3)	57.4	(0.6)	32.4	(0.5)	10.2	(0.3)
	Japan	35.6	(1.0)	58.6	(0.9)	5.7	(0.5)	23.6	(1.0)	55.0	(1.1)	21.4	(1.1)
	Korea	32.4	(2.0)	51.8	(1.8)	15.8	(0.9)	23.4	(1.6)	47.0	(1.7)	29.7	(1.3)
	Luxembourg	85.1	(0.7)	11.7	(0.6)	3.2	(0.3)	71.3	(0.8)	23.6	(0.8)	5.1	(0.4)
	Mexico	57.8	(0.9)	26.9	(0.6)	15.3	(0.5)	49.4	(0.9)	33.0	(0.7)	17.6	(0.5)
	Netherlands	89.3	(0.8)	9.1	(0.6)	1.7	(0.3)	82.2	(0.8)	15.3	(0.7)	2.5	(0.3)
	New Zealand	88.9	(0.6)	8.8	(0.5)	2.3	(0.3)	83.2	(0.7)	13.9	(0.6)	2.9	(0.3)
	Norway	70.0	(1.0)	24.4	(0.9)	5.6	(0.4)	65.0	(1.1)	28.7	(0.9)	6.2	(0.5)
	Poland	73.3	(1.6)	22.0	(1.5)	4.7	(0.4)	58.1	(1.4)	37.1	(1.4)	4.8	(0.4)
	Portugal	79.6	(1.0)	18.3	(0.9)	2.1	(0.3)	59.5	(1.1)	36.8	(1.0)	3.7	(0.3)
	Slovak Republic	80.8	(1.6)	16.8	(1.4)	2.4	(0.4)	72.6	(1.9)	25.0	(1.9)	2.4	(0.3)
	Slovenia	88.5	(0.6)	8.9	(0.5)	2.6	(0.3)	68.6	(0.8)	26.7	(0.8)	4.7	(0.4)
	Spain	80.7	(0.7)	13.9	(0.6)	5.4	(0.3)	59.7	(0.8)	31.8	(0.7)	8.4	(0.5)
	Sweden	88.0	(0.7)	10.0	(0.6)	2.0	(0.3)	84.4	(0.9)	13.9	(0.8)	1.7	(0.2)
	Switzerland	87.2	(0.6)	10.4	(0.6)	2.3	(0.2)	78.1	(0.9)	19.2	(0.8)	2.7	(0.2)
	Turkey	68.4	(1.4)	22.2	(1.2)	9.4	(0.7)	55.3	(1.9)	28.2	(1.5)	16.5	(0.9)
	United Kingdom	80.3	(0.8)	16.0	(0.8)	3.7	(0.3)	70.1	(1.1)	25.5	(1.0)	4.4	(0.3)
	United States	85.7	(0.6)	10.3	(0.5)	4.0	(0.3)	78.6	(0.8)	16.3	(0.7)	5.1	(0.4)
	OECD average	77.9	(0.2)	17.4	(0.1)	4.7	(0.1)	66.0	(0.2)	26.9	(0.2)	7.1	(0.1)
Partners	Albania	51.8	(2.2)	25.2	(1.5)	22.9	(1.5)	42.1	(2.3)	35.2	(1.7)	22.7	(1.4)
	Argentina	79.8	(0.9)	15.2	(0.9)	5.0	(0.4)	62.9	(1.2)	31.5	(1.0)	5.6	(0.5)
	Azerbaijan	45.6	(1.8)	30.3	(1.4)	24.2	(1.3)	34.2	(1.8)	35.4	(1.3)	30.4	(1.5)
	Brazil	62.1	(0.9)	25.0	(0.8)	12.9	(0.7)	53.0	(1.0)	33.1	(0.9)	13.9	(0.6)
	Bulgaria	82.4	(1.0)	11.8	(0.8)	5.8	(0.6)	67.3	(1.2)	27.0	(1.2)	5.7	(0.5)
	Colombia	54.0	(1.6)	30.8	(1.3)	15.2	(1.1)	45.4	(1.4)	38.0	(1.2)	16.6	(0.9)
	Croatia	88.5	(0.6)	8.5	(0.5)	3.0	(0.3)	59.4	(1.0)	35.7	(1.0)	4.9	(0.3)
	Dubai (UAE)	71.9	(0.7)	20.4	(0.7)	7.7	(0.5)	49.6	(0.7)	28.9	(0.8)	21.5	(0.7)
	Hong Kong-China	69.6	(1.1)	28.1	(1.1)	2.3	(0.3)	51.4	(1.1)	42.0	(1.1)	6.6	(0.4)
	Indonesia	47.2	(2.7)	35.2	(2.2)	17.6	(1.2)	31.6	(1.9)	43.5	(1.5)	24.8	(1.4)
	Jordan	63.6	(1.9)	22.8	(1.3)	13.7	(0.9)	55.9	(2.0)	27.9	(1.3)	16.2	(1.2)
	Kazakhstan	51.1	(1.8)	41.0	(1.6)	7.8	(0.7)	35.5	(1.6)	54.1	(1.6)	10.4	(0.7)
	Kyrgyzstan	58.1	(2.1)	27.4	(1.5)	14.5	(1.3)	47.6	(2.1)	38.9	(1.9)	13.5	(0.9)
	Latvia	71.6	(1.3)	23.7	(1.2)	4.6	(0.5)	49.2	(1.7)	44.3	(1.7)	6.5	(0.6)
	Liechtenstein	93.1	(1.4)	5.0	(1.2)	1.9	(0.7)	84.4	(2.2)	14.2	(2.1)	1.5	(0.8)
	Lithuania	74.3	(1.0)	19.3	(0.9)	6.4	(0.5)	58.8	(1.4)	34.1	(1.4)	7.1	(0.5)
	Macao-China	68.3	(0.7)	23.1	(0.6)	8.5	(0.4)	53.7	(0.7)	28.8	(0.7)	17.4	(0.5)
	Montenegro	84.0	(0.9)	10.8	(0.7)	5.2	(0.5)	55.4	(0.8)	36.6	(0.8)	7.9	(0.6)
	Panama	59.3	(3.3)	20.1	(1.8)	20.6	(2.1)	38.9	(1.7)	36.5	(2.0)	24.6	(2.3)
	Peru	42.5	(1.5)	33.9	(1.3)	23.6	(0.9)	33.5	(1.3)	39.6	(1.0)	27.0	(1.0)
	Qatar	57.7	(0.7)	30.8	(0.7)	11.5	(0.4)	35.9	(0.6)	40.6	(0.6)	23.5	(0.5)
	Romania	62.4	(2.2)	25.5	(1.9)	12.1	(1.1)	49.6	(2.0)	40.8	(2.0)	9.6	(1.1)
	Russian Federation	45.6	(1.5)	48.9	(1.5)	5.6	(0.4)	31.9	(1.6)	59.5	(1.5)	8.6	(0.5)
	Serbia	81.0	(0.8)	14.8	(0.8)	4.2	(0.4)	55.8	(1.1)	36.0	(1.0)	8.1	(0.5)
	Shanghai-China	45.8	(0.8)	39.5	(0.8)	14.7	(0.6)	29.0	(0.9)	47.4	(0.8)	23.6	(0.7)
	Singapore	56.6	(0.7)	35.7	(0.8)	7.7	(0.4)	29.8	(0.7)	48.6	(0.8)	21.6	(0.6)
	Chinese Taipei	56.2	(1.0)	31.8	(1.0)	12.0	(0.6)	37.8	(1.1)	41.0	(0.8)	21.2	(0.8)
	Thailand	75.2	(1.3)	18.3	(1.2)	6.5	(0.6)	47.3	(1.6)	36.0	(1.3)	16.7	(0.9)
	Trinidad and Tobago	66.3	(1.0)	23.4	(0.8)	10.3	(0.6)	37.2	(0.9)	45.4	(1.0)	17.4	(0.8)
	Tunisia	44.2	(1.5)	34.2	(0.9)	21.5	(0.9)	25.1	(1.6)	44.3	(1.0)	30.5	(1.3)
	Uruguay	94.5	(0.5)	4.4	(0.4)	1.1	(0.2)	78.3	(0.8)	18.5	(0.8)	3.2	(0.3)

StatLink http://dx.doi.org/10.1787/888932343285

[Part 2/2]
Table IV.3.17b Percentage of students attending after-school lessons, by hours per week
Results based on students' self-reports

		Science						Other subjects					
		No attendance		Less than 4 hours a week		Four hours a week or more		No attendance		Less than 4 hours a week		Four hours a week or more	
		%	S.E.	%	S.E.	%	S.E.	%	S.E.	%	S.E.	%	S.E.
OECD	Australia	90.5	(0.5)	7.9	(0.5)	1.7	(0.1)	85.2	(0.4)	10.9	(0.4)	3.8	(0.2)
	Austria	96.1	(0.3)	3.2	(0.3)	0.7	(0.2)	86.9	(0.6)	11.6	(0.6)	1.5	(0.2)
	Belgium	84.2	(0.5)	13.5	(0.4)	2.3	(0.2)	82.2	(0.5)	14.0	(0.5)	3.8	(0.2)
	Canada	89.4	(0.3)	8.0	(0.3)	2.6	(0.2)	87.0	(0.4)	9.4	(0.4)	3.6	(0.2)
	Chile	78.5	(1.0)	15.6	(0.8)	5.9	(0.4)	81.8	(0.9)	12.7	(0.8)	5.4	(0.4)
	Czech Republic	75.3	(1.0)	19.4	(0.8)	5.2	(0.4)	70.8	(0.9)	23.8	(0.8)	5.4	(0.5)
	Denmark	77.0	(0.9)	21.3	(0.8)	1.8	(0.2)	74.3	(1.1)	20.4	(0.9)	5.4	(0.4)
	Estonia	43.1	(1.0)	46.4	(1.1)	10.5	(0.6)	42.9	(1.0)	45.4	(1.1)	11.7	(0.6)
	Finland	92.2	(0.4)	5.9	(0.4)	1.9	(0.3)	87.6	(0.6)	9.1	(0.5)	3.3	(0.3)
	France	78.7	(0.8)	18.1	(0.7)	3.2	(0.3)	79.3	(0.8)	15.8	(0.7)	4.9	(0.5)
	Germany	91.7	(0.6)	6.9	(0.5)	1.4	(0.2)	76.6	(0.7)	18.1	(0.7)	5.3	(0.4)
	Greece	44.2	(1.2)	42.6	(1.1)	13.1	(0.8)	63.3	(1.1)	19.8	(0.7)	16.9	(0.8)
	Hungary	89.7	(0.8)	8.7	(0.7)	1.6	(0.2)	78.5	(1.0)	17.9	(0.9)	3.6	(0.3)
	Iceland	93.1	(0.5)	5.5	(0.4)	1.4	(0.2)	85.2	(0.7)	11.6	(0.6)	3.2	(0.4)
	Ireland	93.2	(0.5)	5.2	(0.5)	1.6	(0.2)	84.4	(0.6)	12.6	(0.6)	3.0	(0.3)
	Israel	74.3	(1.2)	19.3	(1.0)	6.4	(0.5)	64.3	(1.1)	25.1	(1.0)	10.7	(0.6)
	Italy	75.3	(0.5)	19.1	(0.4)	5.7	(0.2)	62.4	(0.6)	26.3	(0.5)	11.3	(0.3)
	Japan	38.6	(1.1)	57.0	(1.0)	4.4	(0.3)	24.2	(0.9)	59.7	(0.9)	16.2	(0.8)
	Korea	43.3	(2.3)	47.1	(2.2)	9.6	(0.8)	33.0	(1.7)	46.7	(1.8)	20.2	(1.2)
	Luxembourg	83.8	(0.7)	11.8	(0.6)	4.4	(0.3)	82.5	(0.7)	12.9	(0.6)	4.6	(0.3)
	Mexico	52.3	(0.9)	30.4	(0.8)	17.3	(0.5)	65.2	(0.7)	18.0	(0.6)	16.7	(0.6)
	Netherlands	89.7	(0.5)	8.5	(0.5)	1.8	(0.3)	85.0	(0.7)	11.7	(0.6)	3.3	(0.4)
	New Zealand	88.9	(0.6)	8.3	(0.5)	2.8	(0.3)	84.7	(0.7)	11.3	(0.5)	4.0	(0.3)
	Norway	69.0	(1.0)	26.8	(0.9)	4.2	(0.3)	68.2	(0.9)	23.9	(0.9)	7.9	(0.5)
	Poland	67.5	(1.5)	27.4	(1.4)	5.1	(0.4)	52.8	(1.2)	36.7	(1.1)	10.4	(0.6)
	Portugal	86.5	(0.8)	11.4	(0.7)	2.0	(0.3)	75.2	(1.0)	21.9	(0.9)	2.9	(0.3)
	Slovak Republic	92.1	(0.9)	6.1	(0.7)	1.7	(0.3)	80.6	(1.2)	16.4	(1.1)	3.0	(0.4)
	Slovenia	79.8	(0.8)	16.2	(0.6)	4.0	(0.4)	79.9	(0.8)	14.4	(0.7)	5.7	(0.5)
	Spain	76.0	(0.6)	18.3	(0.5)	5.7	(0.3)	67.0	(0.7)	25.8	(0.6)	7.1	(0.4)
	Sweden	87.6	(0.7)	10.7	(0.7)	1.6	(0.2)	84.8	(0.9)	11.4	(0.7)	3.8	(0.4)
	Switzerland	90.4	(0.6)	8.1	(0.5)	1.5	(0.2)	81.5	(0.6)	16.1	(0.6)	2.4	(0.2)
	Turkey	65.7	(1.9)	19.3	(1.2)	15.0	(1.0)	73.0	(1.3)	15.8	(1.0)	11.2	(0.9)
	United Kingdom	75.5	(1.0)	18.9	(0.9)	5.7	(0.4)	60.8	(1.0)	32.2	(0.9)	7.0	(0.4)
	United States	83.3	(0.9)	12.3	(0.8)	4.5	(0.4)	79.6	(0.9)	13.1	(0.6)	7.4	(0.6)
	OECD average	77.6	(0.2)	17.8	(0.1)	4.6	(0.1)	72.7	(0.2)	20.4	(0.1)	7.0	(0.1)
Partners	Albania	47.8	(2.3)	31.7	(1.6)	20.5	(1.3)	57.2	(2.0)	25.9	(1.4)	16.9	(1.2)
	Argentina	77.3	(1.1)	17.2	(1.0)	5.6	(0.5)	71.9	(1.0)	19.4	(1.0)	8.7	(0.7)
	Azerbaijan	37.8	(1.6)	21.8	(1.0)	40.4	(1.3)	53.2	(1.7)	25.9	(1.3)	20.8	(1.1)
	Brazil	59.4	(1.0)	29.0	(0.9)	11.6	(0.5)	62.7	(1.1)	22.3	(0.9)	15.0	(0.7)
	Bulgaria	79.3	(1.3)	14.6	(1.1)	6.1	(0.5)	73.2	(1.3)	15.3	(0.9)	11.6	(0.8)
	Colombia	47.3	(1.5)	38.1	(1.2)	14.6	(0.9)	49.6	(1.2)	30.9	(1.0)	19.6	(1.0)
	Croatia	81.0	(0.7)	15.5	(0.6)	3.5	(0.4)	81.6	(0.7)	12.8	(0.6)	5.6	(0.4)
	Dubai (UAE)	58.7	(0.7)	22.1	(0.6)	19.2	(0.6)	68.2	(0.9)	19.8	(0.8)	12.0	(0.6)
	Hong Kong-China	72.2	(1.0)	21.1	(0.8)	6.8	(0.6)	44.8	(1.1)	40.2	(1.0)	15.0	(0.6)
	Indonesia	35.6	(2.2)	40.5	(1.7)	23.9	(1.3)	46.9	(1.4)	28.0	(1.3)	25.0	(1.2)
	Jordan	52.5	(1.9)	26.2	(1.5)	21.3	(1.1)	67.1	(1.8)	17.4	(1.4)	15.6	(1.0)
	Kazakhstan	42.7	(1.7)	33.1	(1.3)	24.1	(1.1)	48.1	(1.5)	37.5	(1.4)	14.5	(0.8)
	Kyrgyzstan	52.2	(2.2)	33.5	(1.7)	14.3	(1.0)	53.3	(2.1)	27.1	(1.5)	19.6	(1.4)
	Latvia	71.7	(1.1)	22.6	(1.0)	5.7	(0.5)	59.1	(1.2)	32.6	(1.2)	8.3	(0.6)
	Liechtenstein	92.9	(1.5)	6.3	(1.4)	0.7	(0.5)	85.6	(2.3)	12.9	(2.0)	1.5	(0.9)
	Lithuania	76.4	(0.9)	17.7	(0.8)	5.9	(0.4)	71.8	(1.0)	17.9	(0.9)	10.3	(0.6)
	Macao-China	68.0	(0.7)	22.9	(0.6)	9.1	(0.5)	56.4	(0.7)	29.2	(0.8)	14.4	(0.6)
	Montenegro	72.3	(1.1)	19.4	(0.9)	8.3	(0.6)	75.4	(1.3)	15.5	(1.2)	9.1	(0.5)
	Panama	49.3	(1.7)	31.1	(2.3)	19.6	(1.9)	57.4	(2.3)	19.3	(2.2)	23.3	(3.5)
	Peru	37.6	(1.5)	45.0	(1.4)	17.4	(0.6)	52.5	(1.3)	27.3	(1.1)	20.2	(0.9)
	Qatar	38.4	(0.6)	35.3	(0.6)	26.3	(0.5)	56.0	(0.7)	21.7	(0.6)	22.2	(0.6)
	Romania	58.2	(1.9)	25.9	(1.5)	15.9	(1.5)	60.7	(2.1)	19.9	(1.6)	19.5	(1.4)
	Russian Federation	61.5	(1.7)	32.6	(1.6)	5.9	(0.4)	59.7	(1.1)	31.4	(1.1)	9.0	(0.5)
	Serbia	70.7	(1.0)	21.1	(0.9)	8.2	(0.6)	70.6	(1.0)	16.9	(0.8)	12.5	(0.7)
	Shanghai-China	71.2	(1.3)	22.3	(0.9)	6.5	(0.6)	38.1	(0.8)	43.0	(0.7)	18.9	(0.6)
	Singapore	43.1	(0.7)	41.5	(0.6)	15.3	(0.5)	56.7	(0.9)	34.2	(0.7)	9.1	(0.5)
	Chinese Taipei	56.2	(0.9)	30.5	(0.8)	13.3	(0.5)	48.7	(0.9)	35.6	(0.9)	15.7	(0.5)
	Thailand	47.0	(1.7)	32.1	(1.5)	20.9	(1.0)	57.6	(1.5)	27.5	(1.4)	14.9	(0.9)
	Trinidad and Tobago	60.9	(0.8)	27.0	(0.8)	12.1	(0.6)	60.3	(1.0)	25.5	(0.9)	14.2	(0.8)
	Tunisia	28.1	(1.5)	50.7	(1.1)	21.2	(1.0)	44.8	(1.7)	33.0	(1.3)	22.3	(0.9)
	Uruguay	83.8	(0.7)	13.1	(0.7)	3.1	(0.4)	84.4	(0.8)	10.3	(0.6)	5.3	(0.4)

StatLink http://dx.doi.org/10.1787/888932343285

[Part 1/1]
Table IV.3.18 **Percentage of students attending pre-primary education**
Results based on students' self-reports

		Percentage of students reporting that they have attended pre-primary education (ISCED 0)					
		No attendance		For one year or less		For more than one year	
		%	S.E.	%	S.E.	%	S.E.
OECD	Australia	4.4	(0.3)	45.3	(0.6)	50.3	(0.7)
	Austria	2.3	(0.3)	12.5	(0.7)	85.2	(0.7)
	Belgium	2.5	(0.3)	3.8	(0.3)	93.6	(0.4)
	Canada	9.5	(0.3)	42.3	(0.7)	48.2	(0.7)
	Chile	15.0	(0.8)	52.8	(0.8)	32.2	(0.9)
	Czech Republic	3.9	(0.3)	9.5	(0.5)	86.6	(0.6)
	Denmark	2.2	(0.2)	28.1	(0.8)	69.8	(0.8)
	Estonia	10.3	(0.6)	10.0	(0.5)	79.7	(0.7)
	Finland	5.0	(0.5)	28.9	(0.9)	66.1	(1.0)
	France	1.7	(0.2)	5.2	(0.4)	93.1	(0.4)
	Germany	4.9	(0.4)	10.4	(0.6)	84.7	(0.7)
	Greece	5.4	(0.4)	28.5	(1.0)	66.1	(1.1)
	Hungary	1.4	(0.2)	4.1	(0.4)	94.5	(0.5)
	Iceland	3.0	(0.3)	3.6	(0.3)	93.4	(0.4)
	Ireland	17.4	(0.7)	41.5	(1.0)	41.2	(1.1)
	Israel	5.5	(0.4)	20.1	(0.8)	74.5	(0.9)
	Italy	5.2	(0.2)	8.7	(0.3)	86.1	(0.4)
	Japan	0.9	(0.1)	2.2	(0.2)	96.9	(0.3)
	Korea	5.9	(0.5)	15.9	(0.7)	78.1	(1.0)
	Luxembourg	4.5	(0.3)	10.4	(0.5)	85.0	(0.5)
	Mexico	10.3	(0.4)	19.5	(0.4)	70.2	(0.5)
	Netherlands	3.5	(0.6)	1.9	(0.2)	94.6	(0.6)
	New Zealand	9.3	(0.5)	21.9	(0.7)	68.8	(0.8)
	Norway	9.3	(0.5)	6.4	(0.4)	84.3	(0.7)
	Poland	2.3	(0.3)	47.8	(1.4)	49.9	(1.5)
	Portugal	19.1	(0.9)	20.7	(0.8)	60.2	(1.1)
	Slovak Republic	5.0	(0.4)	12.2	(0.7)	82.8	(0.9)
	Slovenia	17.3	(0.7)	14.3	(0.6)	68.4	(0.8)
	Spain	4.6	(0.3)	8.5	(0.4)	86.8	(0.5)
	Sweden	9.8	(0.4)	24.1	(0.9)	66.1	(1.0)
	Switzerland	2.3	(0.2)	26.5	(1.8)	71.3	(1.8)
	Turkey	71.6	(1.3)	20.2	(0.9)	8.2	(0.7)
	United Kingdom	5.8	(0.5)	28.2	(0.7)	66.0	(0.8)
	United States	1.8	(0.2)	27.7	(0.9)	70.6	(1.0)
	OECD average	8.3	(0.1)	19.5	(0.1)	72.2	(0.1)
Partners	Albania	24.5	(1.3)	22.7	(1.0)	52.7	(1.3)
	Argentina	4.7	(0.6)	29.1	(1.4)	66.2	(1.4)
	Azerbaijan	68.7	(1.5)	14.6	(0.9)	16.7	(1.0)
	Brazil	21.3	(0.7)	33.4	(0.8)	45.3	(1.1)
	Bulgaria	11.4	(0.6)	14.8	(0.7)	73.8	(1.0)
	Colombia	18.5	(1.2)	53.3	(1.3)	28.2	(1.2)
	Croatia	26.8	(1.2)	21.2	(0.7)	52.1	(1.1)
	Dubai (UAE)	12.9	(0.4)	27.8	(0.7)	59.2	(0.7)
	Hong Kong-China	2.8	(0.4)	4.9	(0.3)	92.3	(0.5)
	Indonesia	46.0	(2.1)	29.9	(1.4)	24.1	(1.5)
	Jordan	28.0	(1.2)	45.3	(1.0)	26.7	(0.9)
	Kazakhstan	58.1	(1.5)	14.9	(0.7)	27.0	(1.3)
	Kyrgyzstan	62.7	(1.6)	17.8	(1.2)	19.5	(1.0)
	Latvia	21.5	(1.2)	12.8	(0.7)	65.7	(1.3)
	Liechtenstein	1.2	(0.6)	6.1	(1.4)	92.7	(1.5)
	Lithuania	37.6	(1.0)	11.8	(0.5)	50.6	(0.9)
	Macao-China	3.2	(0.2)	9.9	(0.4)	86.9	(0.4)
	Montenegro	35.8	(0.6)	22.3	(0.8)	41.9	(0.8)
	Panama	22.0	(1.4)	45.3	(1.6)	32.7	(1.4)
	Peru	15.1	(0.7)	26.3	(0.8)	58.6	(1.1)
	Qatar	38.3	(0.5)	38.7	(0.5)	23.0	(0.4)
	Romania	4.8	(0.4)	7.6	(0.6)	87.6	(0.9)
	Russian Federation	21.4	(1.1)	11.2	(0.6)	67.4	(1.3)
	Serbia	13.0	(0.7)	50.1	(0.9)	36.9	(0.9)
	Shanghai-China	2.5	(0.5)	10.7	(0.7)	86.8	(1.0)
	Singapore	2.3	(0.2)	6.6	(0.4)	91.1	(0.4)
	Chinese Taipei	1.6	(0.2)	13.7	(0.5)	84.7	(0.5)
	Thailand	2.1	(0.2)	9.2	(0.5)	88.7	(0.6)
	Trinidad and Tobago	9.6	(0.5)	28.8	(0.7)	61.6	(0.8)
	Tunisia	48.1	(2.0)	31.3	(1.4)	20.6	(1.0)
	Uruguay	12.8	(0.7)	15.9	(0.6)	71.3	(0.8)

StatLink http://dx.doi.org/10.1787/888932343285

Table IV.3.19

[Part 1/2]

Index of schools' extra-curricular activities and reading performance, by national quarters of this index

Results based on reports from school principals and reported proportionate to the number of 15-year-olds enrolled in the school

		Index of schools' extra-curricular activities										Variability in the index of schools' extra-curricular activities	
		All students		Bottom quarter		Second quarter		Third quarter		Top quarter			
		Mean index	S.E.	Mean index	S.E.	Mean index	S.E.	Mean index	S.E.	Mean index	S.E.	Standard deviation	S.E.
OECD	Australia	0.67	(0.04)	-0.29	(0.07)	0.41	(0.01)	0.88	(0.02)	1.68	(0.06)	0.85	(0.05)
	Austria	-0.04	(0.07)	-1.17	(0.07)	-0.36	(0.02)	0.15	(0.03)	1.22	(0.12)	0.97	(0.07)
	Belgium	-0.32	(0.05)	-1.39	(0.08)	-0.55	(0.02)	-0.01	(0.02)	0.66	(0.06)	0.86	(0.05)
	Canada	0.71	(0.03)	-0.14	(0.02)	0.43	(0.01)	0.86	(0.01)	1.71	(0.05)	0.75	(0.03)
	Chile	-0.13	(0.07)	-1.29	(0.06)	-0.44	(0.02)	0.15	(0.02)	1.08	(0.11)	0.96	(0.06)
	Czech Republic	0.03	(0.05)	-0.88	(0.05)	-0.12	(0.02)	0.25	(0.02)	0.86	(0.05)	0.70	(0.03)
	Denmark	-0.99	(0.06)	-2.17	(0.08)	-1.24	(0.02)	-0.69	(0.02)	0.12	(0.07)	0.94	(0.05)
	Estonia	0.44	(0.05)	-0.42	(0.06)	0.23	(0.02)	0.63	(0.01)	1.30	(0.06)	0.69	(0.05)
	Finland	-0.28	(0.05)	-1.24	(0.06)	-0.49	(0.02)	-0.04	(0.01)	0.66	(0.06)	0.76	(0.04)
	France	w	w	w	w	w	w	w	w	w	w	w	w
	Germany	0.30	(0.06)	-0.81	(0.09)	0.07	(0.02)	0.57	(0.02)	1.38	(0.07)	0.91	(0.06)
	Greece	-0.23	(0.08)	-1.37	(0.09)	-0.56	(0.02)	-0.02	(0.02)	1.04	(0.11)	0.99	(0.07)
	Hungary	0.09	(0.06)	-0.82	(0.06)	-0.10	(0.02)	0.25	(0.02)	1.04	(0.09)	0.76	(0.06)
	Iceland	0.02	(0.00)	-0.82	(0.00)	-0.23	(0.00)	0.19	(0.00)	0.95	(0.00)	0.72	(0.00)
	Ireland	-0.09	(0.08)	-1.00	(0.06)	-0.46	(0.02)	0.05	(0.02)	1.06	(0.12)	0.85	(0.07)
	Israel	0.11	(0.06)	-0.94	(0.06)	-0.18	(0.02)	0.32	(0.02)	1.22	(0.10)	0.90	(0.06)
	Italy	0.13	(0.03)	-0.90	(0.03)	-0.19	(0.01)	0.37	(0.01)	1.23	(0.04)	0.86	(0.02)
	Japan	0.01	(0.05)	-0.78	(0.05)	-0.21	(0.02)	0.17	(0.01)	0.85	(0.07)	0.67	(0.05)
	Korea	1.01	(0.07)	0.03	(0.05)	0.75	(0.02)	1.20	(0.03)	2.06	(0.09)	0.82	(0.05)
	Luxembourg	0.27	(0.00)	-0.78	(0.00)	0.11	(0.00)	0.47	(0.00)	1.28	(0.00)	0.81	(0.00)
	Mexico	-0.14	(0.03)	-1.34	(0.04)	-0.45	(0.01)	0.11	(0.01)	1.13	(0.04)	0.99	(0.03)
	Netherlands	-0.31	(0.06)	-1.16	(0.06)	-0.58	(0.01)	-0.10	(0.02)	0.59	(0.06)	0.71	(0.04)
	New Zealand	1.21	(0.05)	0.29	(0.05)	0.88	(0.01)	1.40	(0.02)	2.25	(0.07)	0.79	(0.04)
	Norway	-0.60	(0.06)	-1.65	(0.08)	-0.76	(0.02)	-0.34	(0.01)	0.35	(0.07)	0.81	(0.06)
	Poland	0.46	(0.06)	-0.46	(0.04)	0.21	(0.02)	0.65	(0.02)	1.44	(0.08)	0.76	(0.05)
	Portugal	0.29	(0.06)	-0.71	(0.08)	0.00	(0.02)	0.51	(0.02)	1.35	(0.08)	0.85	(0.06)
	Slovak Republic	0.71	(0.06)	-0.26	(0.06)	0.43	(0.02)	0.92	(0.01)	1.75	(0.10)	0.81	(0.05)
	Slovenia	0.91	(0.01)	-0.12	(0.00)	0.69	(0.00)	1.19	(0.00)	1.88	(0.01)	0.79	(0.01)
	Spain	-0.18	(0.05)	-1.26	(0.07)	-0.40	(0.01)	0.04	(0.02)	0.91	(0.06)	0.89	(0.05)
	Sweden	-0.34	(0.06)	-1.28	(0.10)	-0.51	(0.02)	-0.10	(0.02)	0.51	(0.05)	0.75	(0.07)
	Switzerland	-0.52	(0.04)	-1.38	(0.04)	-0.69	(0.01)	-0.32	(0.02)	0.32	(0.05)	0.70	(0.04)
	Turkey	0.38	(0.06)	-0.75	(0.07)	0.10	(0.03)	0.69	(0.01)	1.49	(0.10)	0.91	(0.06)
	United Kingdom	1.01	(0.06)	0.14	(0.04)	0.60	(0.02)	1.16	(0.02)	2.13	(0.08)	0.84	(0.05)
	United States	1.02	(0.06)	0.10	(0.05)	0.75	(0.01)	1.17	(0.03)	2.07	(0.07)	0.78	(0.05)
	OECD average	0.17	(0.01)	-0.82	(0.01)	-0.09	(0.00)	0.39	(0.00)	1.20	(0.01)	0.82	(0.01)
Partners	Albania	0.20	(0.10)	-1.07	(0.06)	-0.22	(0.02)	0.45	(0.03)	1.65	(0.10)	1.07	(0.06)
	Argentina	-0.63	(0.07)	-1.77	(0.08)	-0.82	(0.02)	-0.34	(0.02)	0.41	(0.09)	0.92	(0.05)
	Azerbaijan	0.90	(0.09)	-0.25	(0.07)	0.51	(0.03)	1.05	(0.04)	2.30	(0.10)	1.01	(0.06)
	Brazil	-0.43	(0.06)	-1.85	(0.06)	-0.80	(0.02)	-0.05	(0.02)	0.96	(0.06)	1.11	(0.04)
	Bulgaria	0.10	(0.08)	-1.00	(0.08)	-0.17	(0.02)	0.31	(0.03)	1.24	(0.11)	0.92	(0.08)
	Colombia	0.11	(0.08)	-0.97	(0.06)	-0.23	(0.03)	0.27	(0.03)	1.37	(0.13)	0.97	(0.08)
	Croatia	0.25	(0.06)	-0.74	(0.06)	-0.01	(0.02)	0.46	(0.02)	1.28	(0.07)	0.81	(0.05)
	Dubai (UAE)	0.96	(0.00)	-0.06	(0.00)	0.65	(0.00)	1.25	(0.00)	1.98	(0.00)	0.84	(0.00)
	Hong Kong-China	1.26	(0.07)	0.32	(0.05)	0.97	(0.01)	1.39	(0.01)	2.33	(0.08)	0.82	(0.05)
	Indonesia	-0.11	(0.09)	-1.26	(0.06)	-0.51	(0.03)	0.12	(0.02)	1.20	(0.12)	1.00	(0.07)
	Jordan	0.63	(0.08)	-0.65	(0.10)	0.31	(0.03)	0.95	(0.02)	1.91	(0.07)	1.03	(0.07)
	Kazakhstan	1.30	(0.07)	0.11	(0.07)	1.04	(0.02)	1.59	(0.03)	2.43	(0.06)	0.92	(0.05)
	Kyrgyzstan	0.72	(0.07)	-0.28	(0.05)	0.35	(0.02)	0.89	(0.02)	1.92	(0.07)	0.87	(0.04)
	Latvia	0.77	(0.06)	-0.03	(0.10)	0.53	(0.02)	0.92	(0.02)	1.67	(0.08)	0.75	(0.09)
	Liechtenstein	0.02	(0.00)	-0.65	(0.01)	-0.31	(0.01)	0.05	(0.02)	1.00	(0.00)	0.64	(0.00)
	Lithuania	0.47	(0.05)	-0.39	(0.05)	0.20	(0.02)	0.67	(0.01)	1.39	(0.08)	0.74	(0.04)
	Macao-China	0.75	(0.00)	-0.40	(0.00)	0.41	(0.00)	1.00	(0.00)	2.00	(0.00)	0.97	(0.00)
	Montenegro	0.62	(0.01)	-0.54	(0.01)	0.05	(0.01)	0.99	(0.00)	1.99	(0.00)	1.02	(0.01)
	Panama	0.10	(0.09)	-1.04	(0.08)	-0.23	(0.03)	0.30	(0.03)	1.36	(0.12)	0.96	(0.08)
	Peru	0.14	(0.07)	-0.98	(0.06)	-0.12	(0.02)	0.35	(0.02)	1.31	(0.08)	0.92	(0.05)
	Qatar	1.13	(0.00)	0.02	(0.00)	0.89	(0.00)	1.47	(0.00)	2.14	(0.00)	0.84	(0.00)
	Romania	1.01	(0.08)	-0.17	(0.07)	0.66	(0.03)	1.26	(0.03)	2.28	(0.08)	0.97	(0.06)
	Russian Federation	0.72	(0.06)	-0.31	(0.05)	0.42	(0.02)	0.94	(0.03)	1.84	(0.08)	0.88	(0.05)
	Serbia	0.23	(0.06)	-0.69	(0.06)	0.01	(0.01)	0.41	(0.02)	1.20	(0.09)	0.78	(0.05)
	Shanghai-China	0.94	(0.07)	-0.45	(0.08)	0.60	(0.03)	1.23	(0.03)	2.38	(0.08)	1.12	(0.06)
	Singapore	1.07	(0.01)	0.10	(0.00)	0.76	(0.00)	1.26	(0.00)	2.16	(0.00)	0.82	(0.00)
	Chinese Taipei	0.95	(0.05)	-0.02	(0.06)	0.60	(0.02)	1.14	(0.03)	2.08	(0.09)	0.86	(0.05)
	Thailand	1.00	(0.07)	-0.14	(0.04)	0.60	(0.02)	1.17	(0.03)	2.38	(0.10)	1.00	(0.05)
	Trinidad and Tobago	0.25	(0.01)	-0.91	(0.01)	-0.03	(0.00)	0.51	(0.00)	1.45	(0.00)	0.95	(0.00)
	Tunisia	0.33	(0.10)	-0.93	(0.08)	-0.11	(0.01)	0.44	(0.03)	1.90	(0.15)	1.18	(0.07)
	Uruguay	-0.44	(0.05)	-1.44	(0.06)	-0.68	(0.01)	-0.17	(0.01)	0.53	(0.05)	0.81	(0.04)

StatLink http://dx.doi.org/10.1787/888932343285

[Part 2/2]
Table IV.3.19 Index of schools' extra-curricular activities and reading performance, by national quarters of this index
Results based on school principals' reports

		Performance on the reading scale by national quarters of this index								Change in the reading score per unit of this index		Increased likelihood of students in the bottom quarter of this index scoring in the bottom quarter of the national reading performance distribution		Explained variance in student performance (r-squared x 100)	
		Bottom quarter		Second quarter		Third quarter		Top quarter							
		Mean score	S.E.	Mean score	S.E.	Mean score	S.E.	Mean score	S.E.	Effect	S.E.	Ratio	S.E.	%	S.E.
OECD	Australia	**498**	(6.9)	513	(5.5)	518	(5.4)	**531**	(4.2)	**13.1**	(3.23)	**1.3**	(0.12)	1.3	(0.56)
	Austria	**440**	(7.5)	461	(9.0)	470	(8.8)	**510**	(11.1)	**30.2**	(3.87)	**1.6**	(0.22)	8.8	(2.54)
	Belgium	**460**	(7.8)	502	(7.8)	532	(6.4)	**529**	(7.8)	**29.1**	(5.02)	**2.0**	(0.23)	6.1	(1.88)
	Canada	**508**	(3.1)	521	(3.4)	531	(3.3)	**537**	(3.3)	**14.2**	(2.28)	**1.3**	(0.08)	1.4	(0.45)
	Chile	**422**	(6.7)	436	(7.2)	461	(7.7)	**478**	(7.3)	**21.6**	(4.13)	**1.5**	(0.21)	6.3	(2.05)
	Czech Republic	**458**	(8.0)	471	(8.4)	479	(7.7)	**502**	(7.4)	**21.3**	(6.35)	1.4	(0.19)	2.6	(1.57)
	Denmark	489	(4.3)	496	(4.4)	496	(4.2)	498	(4.9)	3.8	(2.39)	1.2	(0.11)	0.2	(0.24)
	Estonia	498	(5.6)	503	(4.9)	500	(5.8)	502	(5.2)	1.3	(4.56)	1.1	(0.14)	0.0	(0.17)
	Finland	534	(4.3)	534	(4.5)	538	(3.6)	538	(4.3)	1.7	(2.51)	1.0	(0.09)	0.0	(0.09)
	France	w	w	w	w	w	w	w	w	w	w	w	w	w	w
	Germany	**467**	(8.1)	488	(8.1)	514	(7.8)	**530**	(7.8)	**28.4**	(3.96)	**1.8**	(0.23)	7.7	(2.07)
	Greece	**457**	(11.2)	496	(5.5)	482	(9.2)	**495**	(6.0)	**11.0**	(5.08)	**1.7**	(0.27)	1.3	(1.19)
	Hungary	**462**	(11.7)	481	(7.4)	508	(8.7)	**526**	(8.4)	**31.0**	(6.75)	**2.0**	(0.36)	6.7	(2.79)
	Iceland	**494**	(3.6)	494	(4.2)	502	(3.7)	**503**	(3.0)	**8.9**	(2.46)	1.1	(0.09)	0.4	(0.26)
	Ireland	**493**	(6.9)	498	(9.2)	490	(8.5)	**495**	(7.5)	-1.6	(4.28)	1.0	(0.12)	0.0	(0.15)
	Israel	**431**	(10.3)	484	(8.8)	483	(9.4)	**500**	(8.9)	**28.8**	(5.48)	**1.8**	(0.28)	5.3	(2.05)
	Italy	**452**	(4.9)	476	(4.2)	502	(4.2)	**524**	(4.3)	**32.7**	(2.98)	**1.9**	(0.16)	8.9	(1.52)
	Japan	**484**	(7.4)	501	(10.0)	532	(7.3)	**562**	(8.5)	**43.4**	(6.52)	**1.8**	(0.21)	8.4	(2.22)
	Korea	**520**	(10.2)	542	(6.2)	540	(6.0)	**555**	(6.5)	**13.2**	(5.36)	1.5	(0.25)	1.9	(1.36)
	Luxembourg	**433**	(2.5)	467	(2.5)	462	(3.6)	**527**	(2.5)	**35.2**	(1.38)	**1.9**	(0.09)	7.6	(0.56)
	Mexico	**404**	(5.0)	417	(4.0)	429	(3.4)	**453**	(3.4)	**19.7**	(2.11)	**1.6**	(0.12)	5.3	(1.11)
	Netherlands	**465**	(8.5)	478	(8.3)	533	(8.8)	**557**	(8.4)	**50.8**	(6.74)	**2.1**	(0.37)	16.3	(3.64)
	New Zealand	**504**	(7.5)	522	(6.3)	521	(6.2)	**537**	(4.7)	**13.4**	(3.55)	**1.3**	(0.16)	1.1	(0.57)
	Norway	502	(4.9)	497	(5.1)	504	(4.5)	509	(5.0)	4.3	(3.75)	1.1	(0.11)	0.1	(0.30)
	Poland	498	(5.7)	494	(5.2)	504	(5.6)	505	(5.2)	3.2	(3.79)	1.0	(0.11)	0.1	(0.23)
	Portugal	482	(6.0)	490	(8.0)	491	(7.2)	495	(7.0)	4.2	(3.84)	1.1	(0.14)	0.2	(0.34)
	Slovak Republic	465	(10.5)	471	(8.7)	489	(7.3)	485	(8.0)	11.9	(6.30)	1.2	(0.20)	1.1	(1.19)
	Slovenia	**437**	(1.6)	470	(2.9)	506	(2.3)	**519**	(2.3)	**40.7**	(1.29)	**2.1**	(0.11)	12.5	(0.72)
	Spain	**475**	(3.7)	479	(4.6)	476	(4.2)	**495**	(5.7)	**9.2**	(2.61)	1.2	(0.10)	0.9	(0.50)
	Sweden	490	(5.9)	498	(6.9)	504	(5.0)	499	(6.5)	4.8	(4.67)	1.2	(0.12)	0.1	(0.25)
	Switzerland	**478**	(4.5)	489	(7.7)	502	(6.1)	**531**	(6.6)	**28.4**	(4.71)	**1.3**	(0.13)	4.5	(1.48)
	Turkey	**441**	(6.1)	466	(7.4)	468	(8.0)	**483**	(8.9)	**17.4**	(4.60)	**1.5**	(0.21)	3.8	(2.00)
	United Kingdom	490	(5.2)	494	(5.6)	498	(6.7)	500	(5.4)	**7.2**	(3.27)	1.1	(0.10)	0.4	(0.35)
	United States	**484**	(10.1)	506	(6.4)	499	(6.0)	**511**	(6.1)	**12.8**	(4.70)	**1.4**	(0.17)	1.1	(0.80)
	OECD average	**473**	(1.2)	489	(1.2)	499	(1.1)	**513**	(1.1)	**18.0**	(0.76)	**1.5**	(0.03)	3.7	(0.25)
Partners	Albania	**361**	(7.2)	370	(8.5)	396	(9.0)	**412**	(10.6)	**17.5**	(5.41)	**1.4**	(0.19)	3.5	(2.14)
	Argentina	**358**	(10.2)	401	(9.8)	415	(9.1)	**425**	(10.7)	**27.8**	(6.78)	**1.9**	(0.25)	5.7	(2.75)
	Azerbaijan	**363**	(6.4)	360	(6.1)	372	(8.3)	**350**	(7.1)	-1.7	(3.20)	1.0	(0.16)	0.1	(0.24)
	Brazil	**396**	(4.7)	414	(6.5)	423	(6.1)	**457**	(6.2)	**21.1**	(2.53)	**1.5**	(0.12)	6.6	(1.59)
	Bulgaria	**406**	(15.4)	416	(12.6)	442	(17.1)	**483**	(10.0)	**34.2**	(7.14)	1.6	(0.33)	8.2	(3.65)
	Colombia	**387**	(6.7)	412	(6.1)	418	(9.9)	**438**	(6.3)	**16.1**	(4.23)	**1.7**	(0.21)	3.2	(1.66)
	Croatia	**427**	(6.6)	469	(6.9)	498	(7.4)	**509**	(6.8)	**39.0**	(5.05)	**2.5**	(0.30)	13.0	(3.12)
	Dubai (UAE)	**440**	(2.6)	466	(2.7)	486	(3.2)	**475**	(2.9)	**16.8**	(1.33)	**1.5**	(0.09)	1.9	(0.30)
	Hong Kong-China	**502**	(7.0)	539	(7.2)	546	(6.4)	**545**	(6.9)	**19.4**	(5.43)	**1.9**	(0.25)	3.6	(1.97)
	Indonesia	**379**	(6.1)	398	(5.2)	399	(7.2)	**430**	(8.7)	**16.9**	(3.79)	**1.7**	(0.27)	6.5	(2.75)
	Jordan	**374**	(8.0)	399	(6.6)	410	(6.8)	**437**	(6.9)	**22.8**	(3.70)	**1.7**	(0.22)	6.7	(2.25)
	Kazakhstan	400	(6.9)	384	(7.3)	383	(7.6)	395	(7.3)	0.5	(4.29)	0.9	(0.12)	0.0	(0.17)
	Kyrgyzstan	313	(7.2)	305	(5.6)	306	(7.8)	333	(9.9)	9.8	(5.66)	1.0	(0.14)	0.8	(0.90)
	Latvia	481	(7.5)	482	(5.4)	486	(5.9)	486	(5.7)	3.7	(4.30)	1.1	(0.18)	0.1	(0.31)
	Liechtenstein	**477**	(7.4)	473	(8.0)	473	(7.9)	**574**	(6.5)	**58.7**	(5.53)	1.2	(0.31)	20.6	(3.34)
	Lithuania	**448**	(5.1)	467	(7.0)	467	(7.2)	**493**	(6.5)	**22.4**	(4.04)	**1.4**	(0.14)	3.6	(1.31)
	Macao-China	**463**	(2.1)	489	(2.3)	485	(2.8)	**510**	(2.0)	**15.3**	(0.94)	**1.6**	(0.08)	3.8	(0.46)
	Montenegro	**393**	(2.7)	401	(4.8)	402	(2.5)	**434**	(2.5)	**17.5**	(1.45)	**1.3**	(0.10)	3.6	(0.57)
	Panama	**358**	(18.2)	341	(17.1)	382	(13.4)	**396**	(12.9)	**19.2**	(7.36)	1.3	(0.34)	3.4	(2.86)
	Peru	**334**	(8.5)	354	(7.9)	384	(8.1)	**404**	(8.9)	**28.2**	(4.57)	**1.8**	(0.24)	6.9	(2.06)
	Qatar	**376**	(1.8)	372	(1.6)	389	(1.6)	**350**	(1.9)	**-14.7**	(1.06)	**0.7**	(0.04)	1.2	(0.17)
	Romania	**403**	(10.6)	401	(8.4)	443	(9.8)	**451**	(10.3)	**24.7**	(5.87)	1.4	(0.25)	7.0	(3.21)
	Russian Federation	**447**	(8.2)	462	(8.1)	465	(7.8)	**463**	(4.7)	**7.8**	(3.40)	**1.3**	(0.15)	0.6	(0.52)
	Serbia	**427**	(9.0)	431	(8.6)	453	(6.3)	**464**	(8.3)	**22.7**	(6.13)	1.4	(0.22)	4.5	(2.41)
	Shanghai-China	**539**	(5.2)	538	(7.8)	563	(6.8)	**583**	(6.6)	**16.4**	(2.91)	1.3	(0.16)	5.3	(1.84)
	Singapore	**507**	(2.4)	522	(3.1)	521	(3.1)	**553**	(2.7)	**19.4**	(1.32)	**1.2**	(0.06)	2.7	(0.36)
	Chinese Taipei	**475**	(5.4)	485	(6.0)	512	(5.8)	**510**	(7.7)	**14.8**	(4.46)	**1.4**	(0.14)	2.2	(1.23)
	Thailand	**404**	(5.1)	408	(5.7)	425	(6.7)	**448**	(5.8)	**19.0**	(3.04)	**1.4**	(0.16)	7.0	(2.30)
	Trinidad and Tobago	**373**	(3.0)	389	(3.7)	439	(2.9)	**479**	(2.8)	**45.0**	(1.27)	**1.9**	(0.12)	14.8	(0.72)
	Tunisia	389	(7.6)	403	(8.7)	418	(8.4)	404	(7.9)	5.5	(3.39)	1.3	(0.20)	0.6	(0.73)
	Uruguay	**396**	(6.0)	423	(5.4)	448	(7.5)	**437**	(7.6)	**18.3**	(4.73)	**1.7**	(0.17)	2.2	(1.19)

Note: Values that are statistically significant are indicated in bold (see Annex A3).
StatLink http://dx.doi.org/10.1787/888932343285

Table IV.3.20 [Part 1/2]
Index of teacher shortage and reading performance, by national quarters of this index
Results based on school principals' reports

		Index of teacher shortage										Performance on the reading scale by national quarters of this index							
		All students		Bottom quarter		Second quarter		Third quarter		Top quarter		Bottom quarter		Second quarter		Third quarter		Top quarter	
		Mean index	S.E.	Mean index	S.E.	Mean index	S.E.	Mean index	S.E.	Mean index	S.E.	Mean score	S.E.	Mean score	S.E.	Mean score	S.E.	Mean score	S.E.
OECD	Australia	0.14	(0.06)	-1.02	(0.00)	-0.44	(0.04)	0.62	(0.02)	1.39	(0.04)	**530**	(5.3)	524	(3.6)	511	(6.7)	**494**	(4.6)
	Austria	-0.35	(0.06)	-1.02	(0.00)	-1.02	(0.00)	-0.20	(0.05)	0.84	(0.06)	473	(6.6)	473	(7.0)	461	(9.9)	473	(9.1)
	Belgium	0.51	(0.05)	-0.75	(0.04)	0.30	(0.02)	0.86	(0.02)	1.63	(0.04)	**533**	(6.7)	513	(7.1)	500	(6.6)	**486**	(7.2)
	Canada	-0.23	(0.03)	-1.02	(0.00)	-0.88	(0.01)	0.00	(0.02)	0.97	(0.03)	**529**	(3.4)	529	(3.0)	524	(2.9)	**515**	(2.8)
	Chile	0.29	(0.09)	-1.02	(0.00)	-0.26	(0.05)	0.79	(0.02)	1.67	(0.08)	454	(7.3)	445	(6.0)	461	(7.7)	438	(8.0)
	Czech Republic	-0.02	(0.04)	-0.86	(0.03)	-0.26	(0.00)	0.18	(0.01)	0.87	(0.05)	**513**	(7.8)	493	(6.4)	457	(7.9)	**449**	(5.8)
	Denmark	-0.12	(0.04)	-1.01	(0.01)	-0.26	(0.00)	0.07	(0.02)	0.71	(0.03)	**507**	(5.0)	495	(4.0)	493	(4.3)	**485**	(4.4)
	Estonia	-0.11	(0.05)	-1.02	(0.00)	-0.31	(0.01)	0.10	(0.01)	0.81	(0.07)	509	(5.6)	506	(4.8)	489	(5.0)	500	(6.0)
	Finland	-0.42	(0.04)	-1.02	(0.00)	-0.80	(0.03)	-0.25	(0.00)	0.39	(0.04)	538	(4.5)	538	(3.6)	536	(4.6)	532	(4.3)
	France	w	w	w	w	w	w	w	w	w	w	w	w	w	w	w	w	w	w
	Germany	0.53	(0.06)	-0.67	(0.05)	0.28	(0.02)	0.92	(0.03)	1.61	(0.05)	511	(9.5)	506	(8.3)	478	(9.0)	496	(9.4)
	Greece	-0.47	(0.07)	-1.02	(0.00)	-1.02	(0.00)	-0.31	(0.03)	0.49	(0.16)	483	(8.1)	484	(7.3)	478	(7.6)	485	(6.5)
	Hungary	-0.55	(0.05)	-1.02	(0.00)	-1.02	(0.00)	-0.49	(0.03)	0.33	(0.05)	495	(7.5)	494	(7.5)	497	(7.9)	490	(9.6)
	Iceland	-0.24	(0.00)	-1.02	(0.00)	-0.81	(0.00)	0.03	(0.00)	0.84	(0.00)	**503**	(4.8)	504	(5.4)	494	(3.2)	**491**	(3.1)
	Ireland	-0.29	(0.07)	-1.02	(0.00)	-0.90	(0.03)	-0.01	(0.03)	0.79	(0.09)	500	(7.6)	501	(6.7)	489	(7.5)	485	(7.8)
	Israel	0.19	(0.08)	-1.02	(0.00)	-0.22	(0.05)	0.52	(0.02)	1.48	(0.08)	484	(8.8)	470	(10.1)	475	(9.6)	467	(9.2)
	Italy	0.13	(0.03)	-1.02	(0.00)	-0.19	(0.02)	0.57	(0.01)	1.16	(0.03)	**479**	(5.5)	483	(5.6)	494	(5.1)	**492**	(5.0)
	Japan	-0.53	(0.05)	-1.02	(0.00)	-1.02	(0.00)	-0.57	(0.04)	0.49	(0.06)	521	(7.1)	520	(6.9)	528	(6.7)	511	(8.1)
	Korea	-0.02	(0.09)	-1.02	(0.00)	-0.64	(0.05)	0.51	(0.03)	1.08	(0.09)	540	(8.7)	537	(6.9)	539	(5.9)	542	(6.2)
	Luxembourg	1.15	(0.00)	-0.06	(0.00)	1.12	(0.00)	1.56	(0.00)	1.98	(0.00)	**499**	(2.3)	457	(2.2)	468	(3.4)	**460**	(3.2)
	Mexico	0.46	(0.03)	-0.90	(0.02)	0.27	(0.01)	0.81	(0.01)	1.66	(0.03)	**442**	(3.6)	425	(3.4)	421	(5.1)	**413**	(4.5)
	Netherlands	0.51	(0.06)	-0.61	(0.06)	0.34	(0.02)	0.85	(0.02)	1.46	(0.04)	506	(12.6)	520	(11.0)	494	(12.5)	513	(10.4)
	New Zealand	0.07	(0.05)	-1.02	(0.00)	-0.29	(0.03)	0.44	(0.03)	1.14	(0.03)	**537**	(5.1)	535	(4.7)	509	(8.0)	**508**	(5.7)
	Norway	0.31	(0.06)	-0.69	(0.05)	0.15	(0.02)	0.65	(0.01)	1.13	(0.03)	**518**	(5.2)	501	(4.8)	494	(4.5)	**499**	(4.4)
	Poland	-0.78	(0.04)	-1.02	(0.00)	-1.02	(0.00)	-1.02	(0.00)	-0.04	(0.05)	502	(4.2)	503	(4.5)	499	(5.6)	497	(5.9)
	Portugal	-0.80	(0.03)	-1.02	(0.00)	-1.02	(0.00)	-1.02	(0.00)	-0.14	(0.05)	491	(4.5)	490	(4.2)	490	(4.5)	487	(9.1)
	Slovak Republic	-0.29	(0.05)	-1.02	(0.00)	-0.57	(0.04)	-0.04	(0.02)	0.46	(0.06)	**501**	(7.3)	488	(6.4)	465	(6.3)	**456**	(7.4)
	Slovenia	-0.72	(0.00)	-1.02	(0.00)	-1.02	(0.00)	-0.88	(0.01)	0.06	(0.01)	484	(5.3)	481	(3.7)	484	(4.1)	483	(2.7)
	Spain	-0.78	(0.02)	-1.02	(0.00)	-1.02	(0.00)	-1.02	(0.00)	-0.06	(0.03)	480	(3.2)	482	(3.1)	481	(3.0)	481	(3.6)
	Sweden	-0.34	(0.05)	-1.02	(0.00)	-0.80	(0.03)	-0.09	(0.02)	0.56	(0.05)	501	(6.5)	500	(5.0)	495	(6.1)	495	(6.0)
	Switzerland	-0.09	(0.05)	-1.02	(0.00)	-0.63	(0.04)	0.28	(0.02)	1.01	(0.05)	509	(6.5)	507	(7.0)	487	(5.5)	495	(7.1)
	Turkey	2.05	(0.10)	0.41	(0.13)	1.89	(0.04)	2.61	(0.01)	3.29	(0.01)	468	(7.5)	458	(8.3)	468	(7.1)	463	(9.9)
	United Kingdom	-0.08	(0.06)	-1.02	(0.00)	-0.80	(0.03)	0.29	(0.04)	1.22	(0.06)	**507**	(4.7)	497	(4.5)	487	(5.6)	**492**	(5.7)
	United States	-0.45	(0.06)	-1.02	(0.00)	-1.02	(0.00)	-0.55	(0.06)	0.79	(0.05)	**510**	(6.7)	513	(6.6)	502	(5.7)	**476**	(6.6)
	OECD average	-0.04	(0.01)	-0.90	(0.01)	-0.42	(0.00)	0.19	(0.00)	0.97	(0.01)	**502**	(1.1)	496	(1.1)	489	(1.1)	**486**	(1.2)
Partners	Albania	-0.06	(0.06)	-1.02	(0.00)	-0.54	(0.04)	0.16	(0.04)	1.18	(0.08)	**404**	(6.7)	388	(8.4)	384	(9.1)	**363**	(8.8)
	Argentina	-0.17	(0.06)	-1.02	(0.00)	-0.90	(0.03)	0.14	(0.03)	1.10	(0.07)	**414**	(10.9)	415	(8.9)	397	(9.4)	**373**	(9.8)
	Azerbaijan	-0.02	(0.09)	-1.02	(0.00)	-0.63	(0.05)	0.24	(0.04)	1.32	(0.10)	367	(7.5)	358	(6.8)	360	(7.6)	362	(9.0)
	Brazil	0.12	(0.05)	-1.02	(0.00)	-0.42	(0.03)	0.55	(0.02)	1.38	(0.04)	**439**	(6.3)	419	(4.0)	404	(4.5)	**388**	(5.4)
	Bulgaria	-0.64	(0.05)	-1.02	(0.00)	-1.02	(0.00)	-0.59	(0.05)	0.08	(0.08)	**420**	(11.2)	426	(10.4)	423	(8.7)	**449**	(9.5)
	Colombia	0.16	(0.10)	-1.02	(0.00)	-0.46	(0.05)	0.53	(0.04)	1.60	(0.14)	**433**	(7.8)	420	(6.4)	410	(5.8)	**390**	(7.8)
	Croatia	-0.19	(0.06)	-1.02	(0.00)	-0.81	(0.04)	0.07	(0.04)	1.01	(0.06)	**490**	(6.6)	488	(5.9)	471	(6.5)	**457**	(8.2)
	Dubai (UAE)	-0.43	(0.00)	-1.02	(0.00)	-1.02	(0.00)	-0.56	(0.01)	0.89	(0.00)	**463**	(3.4)	463	(3.6)	464	(3.2)	**450**	(2.8)
	Hong Kong-China	-0.50	(0.07)	-1.02	(0.00)	-1.02	(0.00)	-0.57	(0.05)	0.59	(0.10)	**542**	(4.8)	539	(5.3)	539	(6.3)	**512**	(8.7)
	Indonesia	0.30	(0.08)	-0.90	(0.03)	-0.04	(0.03)	0.59	(0.02)	1.54	(0.09)	**422**	(6.9)	399	(5.7)	394	(8.8)	**392**	(7.5)
	Jordan	0.76	(0.10)	-0.90	(0.04)	0.27	(0.03)	1.08	(0.04)	2.60	(0.09)	**422**	(8.0)	402	(7.2)	392	(8.4)	**404**	(6.5)
	Kazakhstan	0.47	(0.09)	-1.02	(0.00)	0.06	(0.04)	0.90	(0.03)	1.95	(0.08)	385	(8.9)	403	(9.1)	402	(8.5)	371	(4.0)
	Kyrgyzstan	0.92	(0.09)	-0.42	(0.09)	0.63	(0.03)	1.32	(0.03)	2.17	(0.08)	**299**	(8.2)	313	(8.1)	319	(9.2)	**326**	(7.8)
	Latvia	-0.43	(0.06)	-1.02	(0.00)	-1.01	(0.01)	-0.21	(0.01)	0.54	(0.08)	**481**	(5.7)	482	(5.5)	487	(5.0)	**486**	(5.7)
	Liechtenstein	-0.06	(0.01)	-1.02	(0.00)	-0.79	(0.01)	0.48	(0.01)	1.10	(0.00)	**489**	(8.9)	465	(9.8)	470	(8.4)	**573**	(7.1)
	Lithuania	-0.37	(0.05)	-1.02	(0.00)	-0.77	(0.03)	-0.20	(0.01)	0.53	(0.06)	471	(6.1)	471	(4.8)	460	(5.5)	470	(7.5)
	Macao-China	0.36	(0.00)	-1.02	(0.00)	-0.34	(0.01)	0.68	(0.00)	2.13	(0.00)	**497**	(1.8)	486	(2.3)	494	(2.2)	**470**	(1.9)
	Montenegro	-0.36	(0.01)	-1.02	(0.00)	-0.65	(0.01)	-0.21	(0.00)	0.44	(0.00)	**426**	(5.8)	410	(5.0)	392	(2.9)	**403**	(2.7)
	Panama	-0.14	(0.09)	-1.02	(0.00)	-0.80	(0.06)	0.20	(0.04)	1.08	(0.10)	387	(14.2)	376	(11.5)	360	(12.8)	370	(8.9)
	Peru	0.37	(0.06)	-0.92	(0.03)	0.13	(0.04)	0.76	(0.02)	1.52	(0.05)	**406**	(9.8)	368	(9.0)	366	(9.2)	**334**	(8.0)
	Qatar	-0.25	(0.00)	-1.02	(0.00)	-1.02	(0.00)	-0.24	(0.00)	1.27	(0.00)	**399**	(3.0)	399	(2.7)	344	(2.0)	**344**	(1.7)
	Romania	-0.74	(0.03)	-1.02	(0.00)	-1.02	(0.00)	-0.85	(0.03)	-0.09	(0.04)	**435**	(5.3)	436	(5.4)	428	(5.7)	**399**	(10.3)
	Russian Federation	0.13	(0.08)	-1.02	(0.00)	-0.44	(0.04)	0.41	(0.03)	1.57	(0.07)	**466**	(7.6)	466	(4.7)	459	(5.6)	**445**	(5.9)
	Serbia	-0.64	(0.05)	-1.02	(0.00)	-1.02	(0.00)	-0.77	(0.04)	0.26	(0.08)	**446**	(4.2)	448	(4.3)	444	(4.6)	**429**	(5.6)
	Shanghai-China	0.55	(0.11)	-1.02	(0.00)	-0.08	(0.06)	0.93	(0.03)	2.38	(0.12)	**570**	(6.2)	567	(6.1)	540	(6.5)	**546**	(7.7)
	Singapore	0.10	(0.01)	-1.02	(0.00)	-0.20	(0.01)	0.53	(0.00)	1.08	(0.01)	**558**	(2.4)	521	(2.1)	518	(2.3)	**506**	(2.6)
	Chinese Taipei	-0.09	(0.10)	-1.02	(0.00)	-1.02	(0.00)	-0.21	(0.04)	1.88	(0.18)	**509**	(5.1)	507	(5.2)	484	(6.1)	**481**	(7.8)
	Thailand	0.79	(0.08)	-0.60	(0.07)	0.62	(0.03)	1.23	(0.02)	1.91	(0.06)	425	(6.9)	421	(6.6)	418	(6.4)	421	(7.8)
	Trinidad and Tobago	0.49	(0.01)	-0.84	(0.00)	0.23	(0.00)	0.86	(0.00)	1.72	(0.01)	**448**	(2.8)	437	(3.0)	400	(2.8)	**399**	(2.6)
	Tunisia	-0.60	(0.04)	-1.02	(0.00)	-1.02	(0.00)	-0.58	(0.04)	0.21	(0.05)	406	(5.4)	411	(5.6)	399	(5.9)	398	(7.1)
	Uruguay	0.11	(0.05)	-1.02	(0.00)	-0.39	(0.03)	0.51	(0.03)	1.35	(0.03)	**438**	(7.1)	428	(7.8)	425	(6.9)	**411**	(4.7)

Note: Values that are statistically significant are indicated in bold (see Annex A3).
StatLink http://dx.doi.org/10.1787/888932343285

[Part 2/2]

Table IV.3.20 Index of teacher shortage and reading performance, by national quarters of this index

Results based on school principals' reports

		Variability in the index of teacher shortage		Change in the reading score per unit of this index		Increased likelihood of students in the top quarter of this index scoring in the bottom quarter of the national reading performance distribution		Explained variance in student performance (r-squared x 100)	
		Standard deviation	S.E.	Effect	S.E.	Ratio	S.E.	%	S.E.
OECD	Australia	1.0	(0.0)	**-14.5**	(3.05)	**0.8**	(0.07)	2.1	(0.89)
	Austria	0.8	(0.0)	-0.3	(6.32)	0.9	(0.11)	0.0	(0.23)
	Belgium	0.9	(0.0)	**-20.5**	(4.23)	**0.6**	(0.09)	3.6	(1.43)
	Canada	0.9	(0.0)	**-6.0**	(1.86)	0.9	(0.06)	0.3	(0.21)
	Chile	1.1	(0.1)	-5.3	(3.72)	0.9	(0.13)	0.5	(0.72)
	Czech Republic	0.7	(0.0)	**-38.3**	(5.19)	**0.6**	(0.10)	8.3	(2.22)
	Denmark	0.6	(0.0)	**-12.4**	(3.72)	**0.8**	(0.08)	0.9	(0.55)
	Estonia	0.7	(0.0)	-7.5	(4.25)	0.9	(0.11)	0.4	(0.46)
	Finland	0.6	(0.0)	-6.3	(3.70)	1.0	(0.08)	0.2	(0.23)
	France	w	w	w	w	w	w	w	w
	Germany	0.9	(0.0)	-8.3	(5.90)	0.7	(0.15)	0.6	(0.91)
	Greece	0.8	(0.1)	-2.1	(4.66)	1.0	(0.13)	0.0	(0.20)
	Hungary	0.6	(0.0)	-8.3	(10.33)	1.1	(0.16)	0.3	(0.82)
	Iceland	0.8	(0.0)	**-5.9**	(1.79)	0.9	(0.07)	0.2	(0.14)
	Ireland	0.8	(0.1)	-7.1	(5.35)	0.9	(0.10)	0.3	(0.56)
	Israel	1.0	(0.0)	-6.1	(4.92)	0.9	(0.14)	0.3	(0.50)
	Italy	0.9	(0.0)	**7.4**	(3.62)	1.2	(0.13)	0.4	(0.42)
	Japan	0.7	(0.0)	-4.3	(7.42)	1.0	(0.11)	0.1	(0.33)
	Korea	0.9	(0.0)	0.9	(4.85)	1.0	(0.16)	0.0	(0.24)
	Luxembourg	0.9	(0.0)	**-24.3**	(1.32)	**0.6**	(0.05)	4.1	(0.43)
	Mexico	1.0	(0.0)	**-10.3**	(1.96)	**0.7**	(0.07)	1.4	(0.55)
	Netherlands	0.8	(0.0)	-1.2	(8.33)	1.1	(0.25)	0.0	(0.51)
	New Zealand	0.8	(0.0)	**-16.0**	(3.37)	**0.7**	(0.07)	1.8	(0.74)
	Norway	0.7	(0.0)	**-12.0**	(3.63)	**0.8**	(0.09)	0.9	(0.54)
	Poland	0.5	(0.0)	-5.6	(6.13)	1.0	(0.12)	0.1	(0.24)
	Portugal	0.5	(0.0)	-4.7	(7.28)	0.9	(0.07)	0.1	(0.26)
	Slovak Republic	0.6	(0.0)	**-27.3**	(9.02)	**0.6**	(0.11)	3.6	(2.16)
	Slovenia	0.5	(0.0)	-1.9	(2.69)	1.0	(0.08)	0.0	(0.03)
	Spain	0.5	(0.0)	-0.4	(3.97)	1.0	(0.06)	0.0	(0.05)
	Sweden	0.7	(0.0)	-3.6	(4.56)	0.9	(0.09)	0.1	(0.17)
	Switzerland	0.8	(0.0)	-7.7	(4.05)	**0.8**	(0.09)	0.5	(0.51)
	Turkey	1.2	(0.1)	-2.0	(4.07)	0.9	(0.14)	0.1	(0.43)
	United Kingdom	1.0	(0.0)	**-6.6**	(3.04)	0.9	(0.07)	0.4	(0.41)
	United States	0.8	(0.0)	**-18.5**	(4.98)	0.8	(0.09)	2.4	(1.20)
	OECD average	0.8	(0.0)	**-8.7**	(0.88)	**0.9**	(0.02)	1.0	(0.14)
Partners	Albania	0.9	(0.0)	**-16.1**	(4.51)	**0.7**	(0.11)	2.1	(1.15)
	Argentina	0.9	(0.0)	**-16.8**	(7.02)	0.8	(0.14)	2.1	(1.66)
	Azerbaijan	1.0	(0.1)	-3.1	(5.47)	0.9	(0.15)	0.2	(0.58)
	Brazil	1.0	(0.0)	**-20.7**	(3.34)	**0.7**	(0.07)	4.6	(1.41)
	Bulgaria	0.5	(0.0)	**24.7**	(12.40)	1.1	(0.16)	1.3	(1.29)
	Colombia	1.1	(0.1)	**-16.5**	(4.22)	**0.7**	(0.12)	4.3	(2.39)
	Croatia	0.9	(0.0)	**-15.6**	(5.80)	**0.8**	(0.11)	2.4	(1.86)
	Dubai (UAE)	0.9	(0.0)	**-9.9**	(1.21)	1.0	(0.07)	0.7	(0.18)
	Hong Kong-China	0.8	(0.1)	**-17.9**	(5.72)	0.8	(0.11)	2.6	(1.78)
	Indonesia	1.0	(0.1)	**-14.0**	(3.68)	**0.6**	(0.13)	4.1	(2.19)
	Jordan	1.3	(0.1)	-3.8	(2.93)	**0.7**	(0.13)	0.3	(0.50)
	Kazakhstan	1.1	(0.1)	-2.6	(3.29)	1.1	(0.18)	0.1	(0.30)
	Kyrgyzstan	1.0	(0.1)	6.1	(4.55)	1.3	(0.17)	0.4	(0.64)
	Latvia	0.7	(0.0)	2.8	(4.43)	1.1	(0.13)	0.1	(0.22)
	Liechtenstein	0.9	(0.0)	**27.1**	(3.75)	1.2	(0.25)	9.0	(2.36)
	Lithuania	0.7	(0.0)	1.1	(6.59)	0.9	(0.11)	0.0	(0.25)
	Macao-China	1.3	(0.0)	**-7.6**	(0.63)	**0.8**	(0.06)	1.7	(0.28)
	Montenegro	0.6	(0.0)	**-14.6**	(3.76)	**0.7**	(0.09)	0.9	(0.45)
	Panama	0.9	(0.1)	-10.1	(8.07)	0.9	(0.21)	0.9	(1.47)
	Peru	0.9	(0.0)	**-28.4**	(5.46)	**0.5**	(0.11)	7.3	(2.84)
	Qatar	1.0	(0.0)	**-22.6**	(0.86)	**0.6**	(0.05)	4.1	(0.31)
	Romania	0.4	(0.0)	**-37.0**	(11.72)	**0.8**	(0.10)	3.3	(1.93)
	Russian Federation	1.1	(0.0)	-6.2	(4.11)	0.9	(0.12)	0.5	(0.71)
	Serbia	0.6	(0.1)	**-15.1**	(5.00)	1.0	(0.14)	1.3	(0.85)
	Shanghai-China	1.4	(0.1)	**-6.3**	(2.81)	**0.7**	(0.12)	1.1	(1.02)
	Singapore	0.8	(0.0)	**-24.3**	(1.34)	**0.5**	(0.05)	4.4	(0.47)
	Chinese Taipei	1.3	(0.1)	**-7.8**	(3.40)	**0.7**	(0.09)	1.4	(1.21)
	Thailand	1.0	(0.0)	-4.2	(4.77)	0.9	(0.14)	0.3	(0.85)
	Trinidad and Tobago	1.0	(0.0)	**-19.9**	(1.37)	**0.7**	(0.05)	3.2	(0.44)
	Tunisia	0.6	(0.0)	-9.2	(7.89)	0.9	(0.10)	0.4	(0.64)
	Uruguay	0.9	(0.0)	**-10.3**	(3.21)	0.8	(0.12)	1.0	(0.59)

Note: Values that are statistically significant are indicated in bold (see Annex A3).

StatLink http://dx.doi.org/10.1787/888932343285

[Part 1/1]
Table IV.3.21a **Teachers' salaries: system level**

		Reference year for 2008 salary data	Ratio of teachers' salaries after 15 years of experience (minimum training) to GDP per capita			
			Primary education	Lower secondary education	Upper secondary education, general programmes	Adjustments for inflation (2008)
OECD	Australia[a]	2008	1.25	1.27	1.27	0.98
	Austria[a]	2007/2008	1.02	1.10	1.13	1.00
	Belgium (Fl.)[a]	2007/2008	1.17	1.17	1.51	1.00
	Belgium (Fr.)[a]	2007/2008	1.13	1.13	1.44	1.00
	Chile		m	m	m	m
	Czech Republic[a]	2007/2008	0.89	0.91	0.97	1.00
	Denmark[a]	2007/2008	1.16	1.16	1.40	1.00
	England[a]	2007/2008	1.26	1.26	1.26	1.00
	Estonia[a]	2007/2008	0.61	0.61	0.61	1.00
	Finland[a]	2007	1.07	1.15	1.26	1.00
	France[a]	2007/2008	0.97	1.05	1.05	1.00
	Germany[a]	2007/2008	1.55	1.69	1.82	1.00
	Greece[a]	2007	1.13	1.13	1.13	1.02
	Hungary[a]	2008	0.78	0.78	0.94	0.98
	Iceland[a]	2007/2008	0.74	0.74	0.87	1.00
	Ireland[a]	2007/2008	1.26	1.26	1.26	1.00
	Israel[a]	2007/2008	0.73	0.82	0.82	1.00
	Italy[a]	2007/2008	1.01	1.10	1.13	1.00
	Japan[a]	2007/2008	1.44	1.44	1.44	1.00
	Korea[a]	2008	2.01	2.01	2.01	0.99
	Luxembourg[a]	2007/2008	0.81	1.18	1.18	1.00
	Mexico[a]	2007/2008	1.33	1.69	m	1.00
	Netherlands[a]	2007/2008	1.14	1.25	1.66	1.00
	New Zealand[a]	2008	1.42	1.42	1.42	0.98
	Norway[a]	2007	0.66	0.66	0.69	0.91
	Poland[a]	2007/2008	0.84	0.96	1.10	1.00
	Portugal[a]	2007/2008	1.55	1.55	1.55	1.00
	Scotland[a]	2007/2008	1.38	1.38	1.38	1.00
	Slovak Republic		m	m	m	m
	Slovenia[a]	2007/2008	1.18	1.18	1.18	1.00
	Spain[a]	2007/2008	1.36	1.49	1.56	1.00
	Sweden[a]	2007	0.90	0.92	0.98	1.02
	Switzerland[a]	2007/2008	1.34	1.53	1.80	1.00
	Turkey		m	m	m	m
	United States[a]	2007/2008	0.94	0.94	1.01	1.00
	OECD average		1.13	1.18	1.25	
Partners	Albania		m	m	m	m
	Argentina[b, 1]	2007	m	m	m	1.09
	Azerbaijan		m	m	m	m
	Brazil		m	m	m	m
	Bulgaria[b, 1]	2007/2008	1.00	1.00	1.00	1.00
	Colombia[b, 1]	2008	1.07	1.20	1.46	0.96
	Croatia[b, 1]	2007/2008	0.34	0.34	0.38	1.00
	Dubai (UAE)[b, 1]	2007/2008	m	m	m	m
	Hong Kong-China[b, 1]	2007/2008	1.86	2.34	2.34	1.00
	Indonesia		m	m	m	m
	Jordan		m	m	m	m
	Kazakhstan		m	m	m	m
	Kyrgyzstan[b, 1]	2007/2008	1.02	1.02	1.02	1.00
	Latvia[b, 1]	07-août-07	m	m	m	m
	Liechtenstein		m	m	m	m
	Lithuania[b, 1]	2007/2008	m	m	m	m
	Macao-China[b, 1]	2007/2008	1.02	1.23	1.23	1.00
	Montenegro[b, 1]	2007	1.34	1.34	1.34	1.00
	Panama		m	m	m	m
	Peru[b, 1]	2008	0.98	0.97	0.97	1.00
	Qatar[b, 1]	2007/2008	0.50	0.50	0.50	1.00
	Romania		m	m	m	m
	Russian Federation[a]		m	m	m	m
	Serbia		m	m	m	m
	Shanghai-China[b, 1]	2007/2008	1.39	1.71	1.75	1.00
	Singapore[b, 1]	2007	1.67	1.67	1.67	1.00
	Chinese Taipei[b, 1]	2007	1.55	1.55	1.55	1.00
	Thailand[b, 1]	2007/2008	2.19	2.19	2.19	1.00
	Trinidad and Tobago		m	m	m	m
	Tunisia		m	m	m	m
	Uruguay		m	m	m	m

1. GDPs for countries participating in PISA system level data collection 2010 were provided by the UNESCO Institute for Statistics database for dissemination 27-05-2010.
Sources: a. *Education at a Glance 2010*: OECD Indicators (OECD, 2010a). For further notes, see *Education at a Glance* (OECD, 2010a) Annex 3, available on line: *www.oecd.org/edu/eag2010*.
b. PISA system-level data collection in 2010.
StatLink http://dx.doi.org/10.1787/888932343285

[Part 1/1]

Table IV.3.21b **Cumulative expenditure by educational institutions: system level**

		Cumulative expenditure by educational institutions per student aged 6 to 15	
		Year of reference	In equivalent USD converted using PPPs
OECD	Australia[a]	2007	72 386
	Austria[a]	2007	97 789
	Belgium[a]	2007	80 145
	Canada[a 1]	2006	80 451
	Chile[a]	2008	23 597
	Czech Republic[a]	2007	44 761
	Denmark[a]	2007	87 642
	Estonia[a]	2007	43 037
	Finland[a]	2007	71 385
	France[a]	2007	74 659
	Germany[a]	2007	63 296
	Greece[a]	2005	48 422
	Hungary[a, 1]	2007	44 342
	Iceland[a]	2007	94 847
	Ireland[a]	2007	75 924
	Israel[a]	2007	53 321
	Italy[a, 1]	2007	77 310
	Japan[a]	2007	77 681
	Korea[a]	2007	61 104
	Luxembourg[a, 1]	2007	155 624
	Mexico[a]	2007	21 175
	Netherlands[a]	2007	80 348
	New Zealand[a]	2007	48 633
	Norway[a]	2007	101 265
	Poland[a, 1]	2007	39 964
	Portugal[a, 1]	2007	56 803
	Slovak Republic[a]	2007	32 200
	Slovenia[a]	2007	77 898
	Spain[a]	2007	74 119
	Sweden[a]	2007	82 753
	Switzerland[a, 1]	2007	104 352
	Turkey[a, 1]	2006	12 708
	United Kingdom[a]	2007	84 899
	United States[a]	2007	105 752
	OECD average		69 135
Partners	Albania	m	m
	Argentina[b]	2007	m
	Azerbaijan	2007	m
	Brazil[a, 1]	2007	18 261
	Bulgaria[b]	2007	m
	Colombia[b]	2007	19 067
	Croatia[b]	2007	34 569
	Dubai (UAE)[b]	2007	m
	Hong Kong-China[b,]	2007	m
	Indonesia	2007	m
	Jordan	2007	m
	Kazakhstan		m
	Kyrgyzstan[b]	2007	3 010
	Latvia[b]	2007	m
	Liechtenstein	m	m
	Lithuania[b]	2007	m
	Macao-China[b]	2007	m
	Montenegro[b]	2007	m
	Panama[b]	2007	m
	Peru[b]	2007	m
	Qatar[b]	2007	m
	Romania	m	m
	Russian Federation[a,1]	2007	17 499
	Serbia	m	m
	Shanghai-China[b]	2007	42 064
	Singapore[b]	2007	m
	Chinese Taipei[b]	2007	18 370
	Thailand[b]	2007	46 331
	Trinidad and Tobago[b]	2007	m
	Tunisia	m	m
	Uruguay	m	m

1. Public institutions only.

Sources: a. Based on *Education at a Glance 2010* (OECD, 2010a) Table B1.3.a. For further notes, see *Education at a Glance 2010* (OECD, 2010a) Annex 3, available on line: *www.oecd.org/edu/eag2010.*

b. PISA system-level data collection in 2010.

StatLink http://dx.doi.org/10.1787/888932343285

[Part 1/1]
Table IV.3.21c **GDP per capita: system level**

		GDP per capita	
		Year of reference	In equivalent USD converted using PPPs
OECD	Australia[a]	2007	37 615
	Austria[a]	2007	36 839
	Belgium[a]	2007	34 662
	Canada[a]	2006	36 397
	Chile[a]	2008	14 106
	Czech Republic[a]	2007	23 995
	Denmark[a]	2007	36 326
	Estonia[a]	2007	20 620
	Finland[a]	2007	35 322
	France[a]	2007	32 495
	Germany[a]	2007	34 683
	Greece[a]	2007	27 793
	Hungary[a]	2007	18 763
	Iceland[a]	2007	36 325
	Ireland[a]	2007	44 381
	Israel[a]	2007	26 444
	Italy[a]	2007	31 016
	Japan[a]	2007	33 635
	Korea[a]	2007	26 574
	Luxembourg[a]	2007	82 456
	Mexico[a]	2007	14 128
	Netherlands[a]	2007	39 594
	New Zealand[a]	2007	27 020
	Norway[a]	2007	53 672
	Poland[a]	2007	16 312
	Portugal[a]	2007	22 638
	Slovak Republic[a]	2007	20 270
	Slovenia[a]	2007	26 557
	Spain[a]	2007	31 469
	Sweden[a]	2007	36 785
	Switzerland[a]	2007	41 800
	Turkey[a]	2007	13 362
	United Kingdom[a]	2007	34 957
	United States[a]	2007	46 434
	OECD average		32 219
Partners	Albania		m
	Argentina[b]	2007	13 243
	Azerbaijan[b]	2007	8 090
	Brazil[a]	2007	10 770
	Bulgaria[b]	2007	11 249
	Colombia[b]	2007	8 515
	Croatia[b]	2007	18 337
	Dubai (UAE)		m
	Hong Kong-China[b]	2007	42 178
	Indonesia[b]	2007	3 727
	Jordan[b]	2007	5 007
	Kazakhstan[b]	2007	10 917
	Kyrgyzstan[b]	2007	1 994
	Latvia[b]	2007	17 397
	Liechtenstein		m
	Lithuania[b]	2007	17 933
	Macao-China[b]	2007	52 691
	Montenegro[b]	2007	12 476
	Panama[b]	2007	11 381
	Peru[b]	2007	7 682
	Qatar		m
	Romania[b]	2007	11 673
	Russian Federation[a]	2007	14 765
	Serbia[b]	2007	10 270
	Shanghai-China[b]	2007	5 340
	Singapore[b]	2007	51 462
	Chinese Taipei[c]	2007	17 154
	Thailand[b]	2007	7 722
	Trinidad and Tobago[b]	2007	24 541
	Tunisia[b]	2007	7 637
	Uruguay[b]	2007	11 429

1. Data in China.

Sources: a. *Education at a Glance 2010*: OECD Indicators (OECD, 2010a). For further notes, see *Education at a Glance* (OECD, 2010a) Annex 3, available on line: *www.oecd.org/edu/eag2010.*

b. UNESCO Institute of Statistics.

c. National Statistics in Chinese Taipei (2010).

StatLink http://dx.doi.org/10.1787/888932343285

[Part 1/1]
Table IV.3.22 Class size for the language of instruction lessons
Results based on students' self-reports

		Class size		Variability in class size		School variability in the distribution of class size
		Mean	S.E.	Standard deviation	S.E.	Proportion of the index variance between schools
OECD	Australia	22.9	(0.1)	5.1	(0.1)	0.35
	Austria	20.8	(0.2)	6.3	(0.1)	0.40
	Belgium	18.5	(0.1)	5.3	(0.1)	0.55
	Canada	25.1	(0.1)	6.0	(0.1)	0.66
	Chile	36.5	(0.4)	7.3	(0.2)	0.75
	Czech Republic	24.0	(0.2)	5.2	(0.1)	0.66
	Denmark	19.4	(0.2)	4.2	(0.2)	0.62
	Estonia	22.5	(0.3)	7.3	(0.2)	0.78
	Finland	19.2	(0.2)	4.1	(0.1)	0.50
	France	26.9	(0.3)	6.6	(0.2)	0.56
	Germany	24.8	(0.2)	5.1	(0.1)	0.61
	Greece	22.6	(0.3)	4.5	(0.2)	0.85
	Hungary	28.5	(0.3)	6.9	(0.2)	0.70
	Iceland	18.7	(0.1)	5.6	(0.1)	0.60
	Ireland	22.7	(0.2)	5.4	(0.1)	0.33
	Israel	28.5	(0.3)	9.8	(0.3)	0.47
	Italy	20.9	(0.1)	4.6	(0.1)	0.56
	Japan	37.1	(0.2)	5.9	(0.3)	0.92
	Korea	35.9	(0.3)	5.1	(0.3)	0.93
	Luxembourg	21.0	(0.0)	4.7	(0.1)	0.47
	Mexico	34.7	(0.2)	11.4	(0.2)	0.78
	Netherlands	23.7	(0.3)	5.3	(0.1)	0.37
	New Zealand	24.2	(0.1)	5.3	(0.1)	0.51
	Norway	23.4	(0.3)	6.8	(0.4)	0.69
	Poland	22.5	(0.2)	4.4	(0.1)	0.79
	Portugal	22.3	(0.2)	4.9	(0.1)	0.46
	Slovak Republic	24.0	(0.3)	5.6	(0.2)	0.64
	Slovenia	28.2	(0.1)	5.1	(0.1)	0.82
	Spain	21.8	(0.2)	6.6	(0.1)	0.40
	Sweden	21.0	(0.2)	5.3	(0.1)	0.47
	Switzerland	18.6	(0.1)	4.3	(0.1)	0.51
	Turkey	27.0	(0.4)	9.9	(0.3)	0.32
	United Kingdom	25.0	(0.1)	5.9	(0.1)	0.38
	United States	24.4	(0.3)	7.4	(0.2)	0.34
	OECD average	24.6	(0.0)	6.0	(0.0)	0.58
Partners	Albania	26.1	(0.5)	10.8	(0.7)	0.53
	Argentina	28.1	(0.5)	8.4	(0.3)	0.60
	Azerbaijan	18.6	(0.3)	5.6	(0.2)	0.39
	Brazil	33.8	(0.2)	9.0	(0.2)	0.50
	Bulgaria	22.4	(0.3)	5.2	(0.2)	0.47
	Colombia	35.1	(0.5)	7.9	(0.3)	0.67
	Croatia	26.2	(0.3)	5.7	(0.2)	0.62
	Dubai (UAE)	24.8	(0.1)	7.9	(0.1)	0.52
	Hong Kong-China	35.6	(0.3)	6.9	(0.2)	0.49
	Indonesia	34.2	(0.5)	8.6	(0.4)	0.61
	Jordan	32.3	(0.5)	9.4	(0.3)	0.82
	Kazakhstan	22.5	(0.3)	6.2	(0.2)	0.84
	Kyrgyzstan	22.1	(0.3)	6.8	(0.2)	0.45
	Latvia	19.4	(0.3)	6.4	(0.2)	0.61
	Liechtenstein	16.2	(0.2)	4.4	(0.1)	0.58
	Lithuania	22.7	(0.3)	6.1	(0.2)	0.77
	Macao-China	38.4	(0.0)	6.8	(0.1)	0.83
	Montenegro	28.1	(0.1)	6.0	(0.1)	0.56
	Panama	28.5	(0.6)	7.4	(0.3)	0.63
	Peru	28.9	(0.5)	9.9	(0.3)	0.71
	Qatar	25.9	(0.1)	8.0	(0.1)	0.54
	Romania	24.4	(0.3)	6.6	(0.2)	0.66
	Russian Federation	21.1	(0.3)	6.6	(0.2)	0.82
	Serbia	26.7	(0.2)	5.8	(0.2)	0.54
	Shanghai-China	39.0	(0.4)	8.1	(0.3)	0.71
	Singapore	34.9	(0.1)	7.1	(0.1)	0.31
	Chinese Taipei	39.5	(0.3)	8.0	(0.2)	0.70
	Thailand	37.7	(0.4)	9.1	(0.3)	0.81
	Trinidad and Tobago	28.1	(0.1)	8.8	(0.1)	0.45
	Tunisia	28.3	(0.2)	5.4	(0.2)	0.43
	Uruguay	25.6	(0.3)	7.6	(0.2)	0.59

StatLink http://dx.doi.org/10.1787/888932343285

[Part 1/2]

Index of quality of schools' educational resources and reading performance, by national quarters of this index

Table IV.3.23 *Results based on school principals' reports*

		Index of the quality of the schools' educational resources										Performance on the reading scale by national quarters of this index							
		All students		Bottom quarter		Second quarter		Third quarter		Top quarter		Bottom quarter		Second quarter		Third quarter		Top quarter	
		Mean index	S.E.	Mean index	S.E.	Mean index	S.E.	Mean index	S.E.	Mean index	S.E.	Mean score	S.E.	Mean score	S.E.	Mean score	S.E.	Mean score	S.E.
OECD	Australia	0.44	(0.06)	-0.85	(0.05)	-0.04	(0.02)	0.75	(0.04)	1.90	(0.01)	**499**	(4.2)	509	(7.1)	523	(6.1)	**528**	(4.6)
	Austria	0.26	(0.06)	-0.84	(0.05)	-0.10	(0.02)	0.43	(0.03)	1.54	(0.06)	469	(9.9)	462	(9.7)	472	(9.6)	476	(9.5)
	Belgium	0.10	(0.06)	-1.07	(0.07)	-0.30	(0.02)	0.31	(0.02)	1.47	(0.06)	**493**	(7.5)	504	(8.3)	512	(7.2)	**517**	(8.1)
	Canada	0.39	(0.04)	-0.74	(0.04)	-0.04	(0.01)	0.57	(0.02)	1.78	(0.03)	**521**	(3.9)	517	(3.3)	526	(3.0)	**532**	(3.2)
	Chile	-0.42	(0.09)	-1.85	(0.08)	-0.77	(0.03)	-0.15	(0.03)	1.10	(0.10)	**427**	(9.1)	442	(5.5)	455	(7.1)	**476**	(6.7)
	Czech Republic	-0.12	(0.05)	-0.93	(0.05)	-0.36	(0.01)	0.05	(0.02)	0.78	(0.05)	483	(8.3)	475	(7.9)	475	(6.6)	479	(8.8)
	Denmark	0.14	(0.05)	-0.65	(0.04)	-0.20	(0.01)	0.23	(0.02)	1.18	(0.07)	494	(4.0)	496	(4.8)	495	(5.0)	496	(5.1)
	Estonia	0.04	(0.05)	-0.70	(0.07)	-0.22	(0.01)	0.14	(0.01)	0.94	(0.07)	**492**	(5.3)	499	(4.7)	508	(6.4)	**506**	(6.0)
	Finland	-0.18	(0.07)	-1.08	(0.05)	-0.48	(0.01)	-0.06	(0.02)	0.88	(0.10)	**531**	(3.9)	534	(3.5)	539	(4.7)	**541**	(4.3)
	France	w	w	w	w	w	w	w	w	w	w	w	w	w	w	w	w	w	w
	Germany	-0.01	(0.07)	-1.09	(0.06)	-0.30	(0.02)	0.14	(0.02)	1.20	(0.07)	**487**	(10.2)	498	(8.8)	503	(8.1)	**503**	(8.3)
	Greece	-0.09	(0.07)	-1.21	(0.09)	-0.37	(0.02)	0.12	(0.03)	1.08	(0.09)	**474**	(6.8)	480	(9.5)	483	(12.8)	**493**	(7.8)
	Hungary	0.26	(0.07)	-0.70	(0.06)	-0.09	(0.02)	0.38	(0.03)	1.45	(0.07)	486	(11.1)	492	(8.9)	512	(8.7)	487	(10.8)
	Iceland	0.43	(0.00)	-0.62	(0.00)	0.03	(0.00)	0.69	(0.00)	1.61	(0.00)	**498**	(3.5)	492	(3.0)	494	(3.0)	**509**	(3.0)
	Ireland	-0.34	(0.10)	-1.54	(0.09)	-0.75	(0.02)	-0.25	(0.03)	1.18	(0.13)	**500**	(7.3)	497	(7.6)	471	(9.1)	**508**	(8.2)
	Israel	-0.03	(0.08)	-1.36	(0.09)	-0.40	(0.02)	0.24	(0.03)	1.38	(0.07)	**455**	(10.5)	465	(11.1)	470	(8.9)	**508**	(7.1)
	Italy	-0.09	(0.03)	-1.15	(0.03)	-0.40	(0.01)	0.09	(0.01)	1.09	(0.05)	**466**	(5.1)	482	(4.2)	500	(4.9)	**498**	(5.5)
	Japan	0.50	(0.08)	-0.75	(0.07)	0.17	(0.02)	0.73	(0.02)	1.86	(0.02)	**500**	(7.6)	537	(8.0)	516	(10.4)	**526**	(10.4)
	Korea	0.06	(0.07)	-0.78	(0.04)	-0.22	(0.02)	0.02	(0.02)	1.23	(0.12)	**541**	(7.4)	548	(8.0)	536	(7.1)	**533**	(8.3)
	Luxembourg	0.31	(0.00)	-0.64	(0.00)	-0.09	(0.00)	0.24	(0.00)	1.73	(0.00)	495	(2.4)	444	(2.7)	447	(2.9)	497	(2.3)
	Mexico	-0.82	(0.04)	-2.20	(0.04)	-1.22	(0.01)	-0.52	(0.01)	0.66	(0.05)	**396**	(5.4)	408	(3.3)	431	(3.8)	**466**	(3.3)
	Netherlands	0.32	(0.07)	-0.65	(0.06)	-0.06	(0.02)	0.52	(0.03)	1.48	(0.07)	495	(10.0)	525	(8.9)	515	(8.0)	498	(15.5)
	New Zealand	0.20	(0.06)	-0.77	(0.04)	-0.18	(0.01)	0.23	(0.02)	1.53	(0.07)	**512**	(6.0)	517	(7.4)	527	(5.0)	**533**	(6.6)
	Norway	-0.24	(0.05)	-0.98	(0.04)	-0.53	(0.01)	-0.10	(0.02)	0.67	(0.07)	**493**	(4.2)	497	(5.0)	512	(5.1)	**509**	(5.2)
	Poland	0.29	(0.05)	-0.66	(0.06)	-0.01	(0.02)	0.41	(0.02)	1.41	(0.07)	**502**	(5.8)	503	(4.2)	500	(5.2)	**496**	(6.4)
	Portugal	-0.17	(0.06)	-1.01	(0.04)	-0.55	(0.01)	-0.08	(0.03)	0.95	(0.08)	**480**	(7.7)	488	(6.1)	486	(6.8)	**504**	(5.8)
	Slovak Republic	-0.46	(0.06)	-1.34	(0.06)	-0.74	(0.02)	-0.28	(0.02)	0.52	(0.07)	**476**	(7.4)	469	(8.6)	480	(9.4)	**485**	(9.6)
	Slovenia	0.48	(0.01)	-0.40	(0.00)	0.12	(0.00)	0.66	(0.00)	1.56	(0.01)	**457**	(2.0)	478	(2.9)	507	(2.0)	**490**	(2.1)
	Spain	0.01	(0.05)	-0.99	(0.05)	-0.27	(0.01)	0.18	(0.02)	1.10	(0.07)	480	(3.8)	476	(4.4)	485	(4.8)	483	(4.3)
	Sweden	0.01	(0.06)	-0.90	(0.05)	-0.28	(0.02)	0.17	(0.02)	1.04	(0.08)	**484**	(6.4)	493	(5.2)	504	(6.4)	**511**	(6.8)
	Switzerland	0.53	(0.07)	-0.47	(0.06)	0.15	(0.02)	0.71	(0.02)	1.72	(0.03)	**499**	(7.2)	495	(6.4)	495	(6.9)	**512**	(7.0)
	Turkey	-1.35	(0.06)	-2.23	(0.08)	-1.53	(0.01)	-1.18	(0.01)	-0.48	(0.06)	**457**	(5.6)	465	(9.4)	463	(8.4)	**472**	(7.0)
	United Kingdom	0.45	(0.07)	-0.64	(0.04)	-0.03	(0.02)	0.63	(0.03)	1.85	(0.02)	497	(5.1)	498	(6.2)	489	(6.4)	500	(5.7)
	United States	0.51	(0.08)	-0.74	(0.05)	-0.03	(0.03)	0.87	(0.05)	1.93	(0.00)	**490**	(11.2)	491	(6.2)	505	(5.4)	**513**	(7.8)
	OECD average	0.04	(0.01)	-0.99	(0.01)	-0.31	(0.00)	0.21	(0.00)	1.25	(0.01)	**486**	(1.2)	490	(1.2)	495	(1.2)	**503**	(1.3)
Partners	Albania	-0.74	(0.06)	-1.75	(0.06)	-1.00	(0.02)	-0.53	(0.02)	0.32	(0.10)	**359**	(7.2)	371	(7.4)	399	(9.3)	**410**	(10.2)
	Argentina	-0.63	(0.11)	-2.26	(0.08)	-1.02	(0.03)	-0.25	(0.03)	0.99	(0.13)	**348**	(12.0)	389	(9.7)	404	(10.5)	**454**	(9.3)
	Azerbaijan	-0.58	(0.07)	-1.50	(0.06)	-0.90	(0.02)	-0.45	(0.02)	0.54	(0.11)	368	(7.1)	345	(7.1)	362	(9.1)	371	(7.9)
	Brazil	-0.73	(0.04)	-1.90	(0.04)	-1.15	(0.01)	-0.60	(0.02)	0.72	(0.06)	**382**	(5.7)	403	(4.6)	406	(7.0)	**459**	(6.3)
	Bulgaria	-0.10	(0.07)	-0.88	(0.05)	-0.41	(0.02)	0.04	(0.02)	0.86	(0.12)	435	(15.7)	423	(10.3)	428	(14.6)	432	(16.1)
	Colombia	-1.10	(0.11)	-2.51	(0.11)	-1.52	(0.03)	-0.89	(0.04)	0.51	(0.16)	**390**	(7.9)	392	(6.6)	413	(6.8)	**457**	(5.5)
	Croatia	-0.21	(0.07)	-1.18	(0.05)	-0.54	(0.02)	-0.04	(0.02)	0.93	(0.10)	473	(7.6)	485	(9.6)	473	(5.7)	473	(9.3)
	Dubai (UAE)	0.89	(0.00)	-0.51	(0.00)	0.54	(0.00)	1.58	(0.00)	1.93	(0.00)	**418**	(2.3)	455	(2.0)	482	(2.8)	**485**	(2.8)
	Hong Kong-China	0.83	(0.08)	-0.42	(0.07)	0.44	(0.03)	1.37	(0.05)	1.93	(0.00)	**525**	(8.5)	527	(7.5)	530	(7.1)	**551**	(6.6)
	Indonesia	-1.19	(0.09)	-2.50	(0.07)	-1.61	(0.03)	-0.82	(0.04)	0.16	(0.09)	**374**	(5.1)	395	(7.2)	412	(6.2)	**426**	(7.3)
	Jordan	-0.33	(0.08)	-1.64	(0.09)	-0.61	(0.03)	-0.06	(0.02)	0.99	(0.09)	**402**	(6.9)	405	(5.8)	399	(7.3)	**414**	(8.8)
	Kazakhstan	-0.76	(0.07)	-1.96	(0.07)	-1.14	(0.02)	-0.53	(0.02)	0.61	(0.12)	**383**	(7.2)	386	(7.2)	385	(9.1)	**407**	(8.4)
	Kyrgyzstan	-1.72	(0.08)	-2.79	(0.05)	-2.03	(0.02)	-1.48	(0.03)	-0.58	(0.09)	**298**	(8.1)	300	(6.7)	311	(6.8)	**347**	(10.7)
	Latvia	-0.11	(0.05)	-0.93	(0.05)	-0.33	(0.01)	0.04	(0.01)	0.79	(0.07)	**478**	(5.3)	483	(4.9)	484	(6.3)	**491**	(7.0)
	Liechtenstein	0.97	(0.01)	-0.43	(0.00)	0.57	(0.03)	1.82	(0.02)	1.93	(0.00)	**569**	(6.7)	499	(8.7)	468	(10.3)	**462**	(9.4)
	Lithuania	-0.18	(0.04)	-0.96	(0.06)	-0.36	(0.01)	-0.02	(0.02)	0.63	(0.06)	**473**	(6.3)	477	(6.4)	466	(6.7)	**458**	(7.0)
	Macao-China	0.03	(0.00)	-1.23	(0.00)	-0.24	(0.00)	0.22	(0.00)	1.35	(0.00)	**466**	(1.6)	497	(1.5)	478	(1.6)	**506**	(1.7)
	Montenegro	-0.79	(0.00)	-1.46	(0.00)	-0.96	(0.00)	-0.68	(0.00)	-0.04	(0.00)	**431**	(2.6)	382	(4.3)	433	(2.7)	**384**	(1.9)
	Panama	-0.84	(0.12)	-2.31	(0.15)	-1.31	(0.03)	-0.68	(0.07)	0.94	(0.11)	**331**	(14.0)	336	(10.9)	361	(12.4)	**453**	(10.2)
	Peru	-1.10	(0.08)	-2.64	(0.06)	-1.50	(0.03)	-0.79	(0.03)	0.54	(0.14)	**315**	(7.3)	344	(6.7)	396	(5.2)	**419**	(12.3)
	Qatar	0.57	(0.00)	-0.93	(0.00)	0.26	(0.00)	1.01	(0.00)	1.93	(0.00)	**377**	(1.7)	354	(1.8)	359	(2.1)	**395**	(2.1)
	Romania	0.09	(0.06)	-0.88	(0.06)	-0.29	(0.02)	0.22	(0.02)	1.29	(0.09)	**419**	(11.1)	434	(10.3)	409	(7.5)	**435**	(11.4)
	Russian Federation	-0.63	(0.07)	-1.81	(0.07)	-0.92	(0.03)	-0.34	(0.03)	0.54	(0.08)	**437**	(6.4)	460	(6.8)	466	(7.5)	**475**	(7.7)
	Serbia	-0.38	(0.07)	-1.31	(0.06)	-0.64	(0.02)	-0.19	(0.03)	0.62	(0.10)	447	(6.5)	429	(7.0)	439	(8.2)	453	(9.1)
	Shanghai-China	0.16	(0.10)	-1.51	(0.11)	-0.14	(0.03)	0.59	(0.03)	1.69	(0.05)	**551**	(6.8)	547	(7.2)	555	(7.6)	**570**	(7.8)
	Singapore	1.06	(0.01)	-0.15	(0.01)	0.61	(0.01)	1.86	(0.00)	1.93	(0.00)	**519**	(2.8)	513	(2.6)	537	(2.6)	**535**	(2.8)
	Chinese Taipei	0.27	(0.09)	-1.40	(0.12)	0.00	(0.03)	0.68	(0.03)	1.78	(0.04)	**479**	(7.1)	504	(7.9)	492	(6.7)	**505**	(7.4)
	Thailand	-0.45	(0.07)	-1.47	(0.06)	-0.87	(0.01)	-0.35	(0.02)	0.88	(0.13)	**409**	(5.7)	414	(5.0)	424	(6.6)	**439**	(6.6)
	Trinidad and Tobago	-0.65	(0.01)	-1.75	(0.01)	-1.00	(0.00)	-0.40	(0.00)	0.53	(0.01)	419	(2.8)	411	(3.8)	431	(2.5)	423	(2.3)
	Tunisia	-0.49	(0.07)	-1.41	(0.06)	-0.74	(0.02)	-0.38	(0.02)	0.57	(0.11)	**392**	(9.0)	404	(7.9)	413	(9.9)	**406**	(8.0)
	Uruguay	0.13	(0.06)	-1.15	(0.07)	-0.24	(0.02)	0.37	(0.02)	1.55	(0.06)	**407**	(6.2)	420	(6.8)	429	(7.2)	**447**	(8.7)

Note: Values that are statistically significant are indicated in bold (see Annex A3).

StatLink http://dx.doi.org/10.1787/888932343285

[Part 2/2]

Table IV.3.23 **Index of quality of schools' educational resources and reading performance, by national quarters of this index**
Results based on school principals' reports

		Variability in the index of quality of schools' educational resources		Change in the reading score per unit of this index		Increased likelihood of students in the top quarter of this index scoring in the bottom quarter of the national reading performance distribution		Explained variance in student performance (r-squared x 100)	
		Standard deviation	S.E.	Effect	S.E.	Ratio	S.E.	%	S.E.
OECD	Australia	1.1	(0.0)	**11.8**	(2.34)	**1.3**	(0.10)	1.6	(0.64)
	Austria	0.9	(0.0)	6.8	(5.69)	1.2	(0.22)	0.4	(0.76)
	Belgium	1.0	(0.0)	8.9	(4.67)	1.3	(0.17)	0.8	(0.79)
	Canada	1.0	(0.0)	**5.4**	(1.99)	1.1	(0.08)	0.3	(0.25)
	Chile	1.2	(0.1)	**16.6**	(2.72)	**1.7**	(0.22)	5.5	(1.85)
	Czech Republic	0.7	(0.0)	3.7	(6.84)	1.0	(0.14)	0.1	(0.30)
	Denmark	0.7	(0.0)	1.3	(3.12)	1.0	(0.09)	0.0	(0.09)
	Estonia	0.7	(0.1)	7.9	(4.57)	1.1	(0.13)	0.5	(0.52)
	Finland	0.8	(0.1)	**5.5**	(2.61)	1.1	(0.10)	0.3	(0.26)
	France	w	w	w	w	w	w	w	w
	Germany	0.9	(0.0)	4.8	(5.82)	1.3	(0.23)	0.2	(0.59)
	Greece	0.9	(0.1)	7.4	(4.38)	1.1	(0.18)	0.5	(0.63)
	Hungary	0.8	(0.0)	3.0	(7.49)	1.2	(0.24)	0.1	(0.56)
	Iceland	0.9	(0.0)	**4.8**	(1.73)	1.0	(0.08)	0.2	(0.14)
	Ireland	1.1	(0.1)	1.6	(3.82)	0.8	(0.12)	0.0	(0.24)
	Israel	1.1	(0.1)	**18.8**	(4.46)	1.3	(0.20)	3.3	(1.56)
	Italy	0.9	(0.0)	**14.4**	(2.85)	**1.5**	(0.13)	1.8	(0.76)
	Japan	1.0	(0.0)	6.7	(5.30)	1.4	(0.21)	0.4	(0.70)
	Korea	0.8	(0.1)	-4.6	(6.47)	0.9	(0.19)	0.2	(0.79)
	Luxembourg	0.9	(0.0)	**10.8**	(1.20)	**0.6**	(0.04)	0.9	(0.20)
	Mexico	1.1	(0.0)	**24.6**	(1.94)	**1.7**	(0.14)	11.2	(1.71)
	Netherlands	0.8	(0.0)	-4.0	(8.42)	1.5	(0.29)	0.1	(0.80)
	New Zealand	0.9	(0.0)	**9.6**	(3.80)	1.2	(0.12)	0.8	(0.60)
	Norway	0.7	(0.0)	**11.0**	(3.71)	1.1	(0.10)	0.7	(0.46)
	Poland	0.8	(0.0)	-2.3	(4.05)	1.0	(0.11)	0.0	(0.15)
	Portugal	0.8	(0.0)	**12.5**	(3.94)	1.2	(0.16)	1.4	(0.87)
	Slovak Republic	0.8	(0.0)	0.1	(5.66)	0.9	(0.15)	0.0	(0.21)
	Slovenia	0.8	(0.0)	**17.7**	(1.50)	**1.5**	(0.08)	2.3	(0.37)
	Spain	0.8	(0.0)	**4.8**	(2.28)	1.0	(0.07)	0.2	(0.21)
	Sweden	0.8	(0.0)	**18.0**	(4.63)	**1.3**	(0.13)	2.0	(1.13)
	Switzerland	0.9	(0.0)	5.0	(4.83)	1.1	(0.12)	0.2	(0.42)
	Turkey	0.7	(0.0)	5.4	(6.09)	1.1	(0.14)	0.2	(0.54)
	United Kingdom	1.0	(0.0)	1.2	(3.35)	1.0	(0.10)	0.0	(0.11)
	United States	1.0	(0.0)	**10.3**	(4.32)	1.2	(0.18)	1.2	(1.10)
	OECD average	0.9	(0.0)	**7.6**	(0.78)	**1.2**	(0.03)	1.1	(0.13)
Partners	Albania	0.8	(0.1)	**26.3**	(4.57)	**1.6**	(0.21)	4.9	(1.76)
	Argentina	1.3	(0.1)	**32.7**	(4.68)	**2.1**	(0.36)	15.1	(4.00)
	Azerbaijan	0.8	(0.1)	6.0	(5.57)	0.9	(0.15)	0.4	(0.90)
	Brazil	1.1	(0.0)	**30.3**	(3.13)	**1.7**	(0.15)	11.7	(2.18)
	Bulgaria	0.7	(0.1)	7.8	(7.77)	1.0	(0.21)	0.3	(0.58)
	Colombia	1.2	(0.1)	**21.6**	(3.03)	**1.5**	(0.21)	9.4	(2.11)
	Croatia	0.9	(0.1)	-1.9	(5.41)	1.0	(0.16)	0.0	(0.35)
	Dubai (UAE)	1.0	(0.0)	**26.7**	(1.19)	**2.0**	(0.09)	6.3	(0.54)
	Hong Kong-China	0.9	(0.0)	**12.1**	(5.02)	1.3	(0.21)	1.8	(1.67)
	Indonesia	1.1	(0.1)	**18.0**	(2.90)	**1.9**	(0.26)	8.3	(2.40)
	Jordan	1.1	(0.1)	4.5	(4.44)	1.1	(0.15)	0.3	(0.59)
	Kazakhstan	1.0	(0.1)	4.5	(4.26)	1.1	(0.13)	0.3	(0.44)
	Kyrgyzstan	0.9	(0.1)	**24.4**	(6.53)	1.2	(0.15)	4.8	(2.43)
	Latvia	0.7	(0.0)	8.4	(4.61)	1.1	(0.13)	0.5	(0.55)
	Liechtenstein	1.0	(0.0)	**-42.0**	(3.11)	**0.1**	(0.07)	26.7	(3.36)
	Lithuania	0.7	(0.0)	-3.2	(7.21)	0.9	(0.13)	0.1	(0.33)
	Macao-China	1.0	(0.0)	**12.5**	(0.76)	**1.5**	(0.08)	2.8	(0.33)
	Montenegro	0.6	(0.0)	**-22.4**	(2.16)	**0.6**	(0.05)	1.8	(0.36)
	Panama	1.3	(0.1)	**39.2**	(6.28)	1.7	(0.39)	25.8	(6.47)
	Peru	1.3	(0.1)	**31.1**	(4.79)	**2.4**	(0.32)	16.0	(4.65)
	Qatar	1.1	(0.0)	**6.7**	(0.81)	**0.8**	(0.04)	0.4	(0.10)
	Romania	0.9	(0.0)	11.0	(6.09)	1.1	(0.23)	1.1	(1.32)
	Russian Federation	0.9	(0.1)	**15.7**	(4.14)	**1.5**	(0.15)	2.8	(1.38)
	Serbia	0.8	(0.1)	6.6	(5.69)	0.9	(0.15)	0.4	(0.75)
	Shanghai-China	1.2	(0.1)	**7.1**	(3.26)	1.1	(0.16)	1.2	(1.11)
	Singapore	0.9	(0.0)	**10.7**	(1.37)	**1.2**	(0.06)	1.0	(0.25)
	Chinese Taipei	1.2	(0.1)	5.4	(2.95)	**1.5**	(0.20)	0.6	(0.65)
	Thailand	1.0	(0.1)	**13.5**	(3.58)	1.3	(0.17)	3.4	(1.73)
	Trinidad and Tobago	0.9	(0.0)	**12.1**	(1.28)	0.9	(0.07)	1.0	(0.21)
	Tunisia	0.8	(0.1)	5.7	(6.24)	1.3	(0.25)	0.3	(0.67)
	Uruguay	1.1	(0.0)	**14.5**	(3.83)	1.3	(0.15)	2.4	(1.19)

Note: Values that are statistically significant are indicated in bold (see Annex A3).
StatLink http://dx.doi.org/10.1787/888932343285

[Part 1/1]

Table IV.3.24 Percentage of students using the library

Results based on student' self-reports and school principals' reports

		Percentage of students in school where there is a library		Percentage of students in schools where the principal reported lack of library materials		Percentage of students using a library to borrow books for pleasure		Percentage of students using library to borrow books for schoolwork		In schools without a library:				In schools with a library:							
														Where the principal reported lack of library materials				Where the principal reported adequacy of library materials			
										Percentage of students using library to borrow books for pleasure		Percentage of students using library to borrow books for schoolwork		Percentage of students using library to borrow books for pleasure		Percentage of students using library to borrow books for schoolwork		Percentage of students using library to borrow books for pleasure		Percentage of students using library to borrow books for schoolwork	
		%	S.E.	%	S.E.	%	S.E.	%	S.E.	%	S.E.	%	S.E.	%	S.E.	%	S.E.	%	S.E.	%	S.E.
OECD	Australia	99.3	(0.1)	13.0	(1.8)	55.5	(0.8)	69.5	(0.7)	37.9	(6.4)	46.0	(6.7)	53.4	(2.2)	64.7	(1.8)	56.1	(0.9)	70.4	(0.8)
	Austria	81.3	(1.4)	16.4	(2.6)	38.6	(1.1)	43.1	(1.3)	22.3	(1.7)	23.1	(1.7)	40.6	(4.0)	39.4	(4.2)	42.6	(1.6)	48.9	(1.6)
	Belgium	65.8	(2.2)	33.1	(3.0)	48.0	(0.9)	72.7	(1.0)	47.3	(1.8)	71.9	(1.8)	45.1	(2.5)	66.0	(2.9)	50.7	(1.4)	77.2	(1.3)
	Canada	97.0	(0.2)	15.4	(1.6)	59.4	(0.7)	71.0	(0.6)	58.0	(2.9)	62.9	(3.0)	59.6	(1.8)	67.5	(2.2)	59.7	(0.7)	71.9	(0.6)
	Chile	96.0	(0.8)	45.5	(4.0)	39.3	(1.0)	67.6	(1.2)	30.9	(4.2)	54.0	(4.6)	38.4	(1.4)	68.3	(1.6)	41.6	(1.6)	69.3	(2.0)
	Czech Republic	76.6	(1.9)	38.4	(4.1)	46.2	(1.0)	56.1	(1.2)	38.5	(2.1)	46.9	(2.5)	51.1	(2.1)	58.8	(2.4)	46.8	(1.8)	60.0	(2.0)
	Denmark	87.8	(1.9)	13.2	(2.5)	54.0	(1.0)	85.5	(0.8)	53.4	(3.8)	77.6	(3.0)	51.2	(2.4)	85.0	(1.3)	54.4	(1.0)	86.9	(0.8)
	Estonia	97.3	(0.9)	25.6	(3.0)	66.3	(0.8)	85.0	(0.6)	66.3	(4.3)	89.1	(5.0)	65.8	(1.5)	87.2	(1.5)	66.6	(1.0)	84.0	(0.9)
	Finland	72.3	(2.9)	42.3	(3.8)	65.3	(0.8)	63.3	(1.0)	66.2	(1.6)	63.2	(1.7)	66.4	(1.4)	61.4	(2.1)	64.4	(1.4)	64.7	(1.5)
	France	98.7	(0.2)	w	w	48.1	(1.2)	50.1	(1.1)	36.3	(6.8)	47.6	(7.8)	w	w	w	w	w	w	w	w
	Germany	79.9	(2.1)	30.8	(3.1)	36.5	(0.8)	34.8	(0.9)	34.1	(2.1)	34.1	(2.3)	34.8	(1.9)	32.2	(2.0)	37.6	(1.2)	35.3	(1.3)
	Greece	66.6	(2.6)	50.0	(4.1)	46.8	(1.0)	55.5	(1.1)	40.6	(1.6)	47.9	(1.5)	49.9	(1.6)	56.3	(1.7)	49.7	(2.0)	60.6	(2.1)
	Hungary	96.5	(1.0)	14.1	(3.1)	56.5	(1.0)	67.0	(1.1)	54.8	(10.6)	54.8	(11.0)	57.7	(3.3)	62.6	(3.2)	56.7	(1.1)	68.3	(1.2)
	Iceland	97.9	(0.2)	8.8	(0.1)	53.3	(0.8)	63.3	(0.8)	58.8	(4.9)	59.3	(5.0)	48.9	(2.5)	58.5	(2.8)	53.0	(0.9)	63.4	(0.9)
	Ireland	80.6	(2.6)	59.6	(4.3)	39.7	(1.0)	37.3	(1.2)	36.3	(2.2)	31.4	(2.2)	37.5	(1.7)	33.9	(2.0)	43.3	(1.8)	42.9	(2.3)
	Israel	89.9	(1.2)	33.4	(3.6)	50.7	(1.0)	65.4	(0.9)	45.1	(3.3)	45.8	(2.7)	54.6	(2.9)	63.7	(2.3)	49.9	(1.5)	67.4	(1.1)
	Italy	86.0	(0.8)	41.0	(1.9)	42.9	(0.6)	49.3	(0.6)	33.7	(1.4)	40.8	(1.2)	42.7	(1.2)	47.2	(1.2)	45.8	(0.9)	52.5	(0.9)
	Japan	93.8	(0.3)	19.0	(2.9)	48.2	(0.9)	36.4	(1.0)	53.6	(2.9)	42.3	(3.0)	47.8	(2.3)	36.2	(2.6)	47.8	(1.1)	35.9	(1.3)
	Korea	98.5	(0.2)	38.8	(4.4)	73.1	(0.9)	63.9	(1.0)	67.3	(6.7)	73.0	(6.0)	70.7	(1.4)	61.5	(1.4)	74.6	(1.3)	65.1	(1.6)
	Luxembourg	97.8	(0.2)	25.1	(0.1)	39.8	(0.7)	49.9	(0.6)	24.2	(5.2)	32.9	(4.5)	32.8	(1.4)	42.2	(1.4)	42.2	(0.8)	52.7	(0.8)
	Mexico	89.0	(0.9)	52.5	(1.9)	60.7	(0.7)	81.5	(0.7)	50.6	(2.4)	67.4	(3.1)	63.8	(0.8)	84.5	(0.7)	58.7	(1.0)	81.7	(1.1)
	Netherlands	81.9	(3.1)	10.2	(2.5)	47.9	(1.5)	71.3	(2.1)	36.3	(3.4)	51.3	(4.0)	41.5	(6.8)	74.0	(6.2)	51.5	(1.3)	76.2	(1.6)
	New Zealand	97.6	(0.3)	11.8	(1.9)	71.9	(0.8)	78.4	(0.7)	77.3	(3.5)	81.4	(3.5)	70.9	(2.5)	77.1	(1.9)	72.4	(0.9)	78.6	(0.8)
	Norway	92.2	(1.4)	43.1	(3.3)	49.6	(1.0)	64.6	(1.4)	44.5	(4.0)	51.9	(5.8)	44.8	(1.5)	58.0	(1.8)	53.4	(1.3)	70.5	(1.7)
	Poland	96.9	(0.8)	19.1	(2.8)	65.1	(1.0)	82.2	(0.7)	56.9	(5.2)	72.1	(3.5)	66.6	(2.4)	85.2	(1.7)	65.1	(1.1)	82.4	(0.7)
	Portugal	96.1	(0.8)	30.2	(3.4)	51.9	(0.9)	69.6	(0.9)	44.3	(5.1)	57.3	(4.2)	52.0	(1.6)	68.9	(1.7)	52.0	(1.2)	70.2	(1.1)
	Slovak Republic	87.0	(1.8)	48.6	(4.0)	46.2	(0.9)	58.9	(1.0)	44.5	(2.7)	55.6	(3.0)	46.9	(1.8)	59.0	(1.8)	46.8	(1.5)	60.8	(1.6)
	Slovenia	97.2	(0.2)	7.3	(0.3)	66.8	(0.7)	86.7	(0.5)	56.3	(3.7)	80.7	(2.5)	57.4	(3.1)	78.4	(2.6)	68.1	(0.8)	87.7	(0.5)
	Spain	95.6	(0.6)	33.8	(2.6)	39.9	(0.7)	52.4	(0.8)	37.2	(2.6)	46.8	(2.8)	39.9	(1.3)	51.1	(1.1)	39.9	(1.0)	52.9	(1.2)
	Sweden	91.8	(1.2)	27.7	(3.3)	52.0	(1.0)	71.4	(1.3)	54.5	(3.7)	65.1	(4.6)	48.6	(2.1)	65.3	(2.9)	52.8	(1.2)	73.9	(1.5)
	Switzerland	81.5	(2.2)	12.6	(2.5)	54.1	(1.1)	60.1	(1.1)	51.4	(3.0)	53.7	(3.4)	56.6	(4.5)	59.5	(3.5)	54.8	(1.4)	62.1	(1.2)
	Turkey	94.1	(1.4)	74.7	(3.3)	68.2	(0.8)	77.0	(0.8)	60.1	(3.2)	68.4	(3.8)	68.3	(1.1)	76.5	(1.1)	69.3	(1.5)	78.1	(1.5)
	United Kingdom	95.9	(0.5)	17.5	(2.6)	42.0	(0.9)	49.0	(1.0)	32.0	(4.1)	45.3	(4.0)	40.4	(2.4)	46.5	(2.0)	43.4	(1.1)	49.9	(1.2)
	United States	95.6	(1.3)	16.2	(3.1)	57.0	(1.2)	72.2	(1.0)	50.5	(5.3)	67.6	(8.2)	60.3	(2.9)	74.6	(2.8)	56.7	(1.3)	71.9	(1.0)
	OECD average	89.8	(0.3)	29.4	(0.5)	52.4	(0.2)	63.6	(0.2)	47.1	(0.7)	56.1	(0.8)	51.7	(0.4)	62.2	(0.4)	53.6	(0.2)	65.9	(0.2)
Partners	Albania	86.2	(2.1)	70.5	(3.8)	84.4	(1.2)	78.9	(1.1)	69.9	(5.3)	69.9	(5.0)	85.3	(1.1)	79.4	(1.3)	88.9	(1.6)	81.5	(1.8)
	Argentina	92.1	(1.6)	43.9	(4.0)	37.7	(1.2)	73.8	(1.1)	31.1	(4.4)	54.2	(5.2)	40.4	(1.8)	76.0	(1.8)	35.2	(1.8)	74.7	(1.7)
	Azerbaijan	97.7	(0.3)	36.5	(4.7)	81.3	(1.0)	86.9	(0.8)	66.3	(4.8)	75.5	(4.5)	84.4	(1.2)	89.1	(1.2)	80.3	(1.7)	85.1	(1.2)
	Brazil	92.0	(0.6)	55.6	(2.4)	64.0	(0.9)	79.0	(0.8)	53.1	(2.0)	71.1	(2.4)	66.1	(1.2)	80.0	(1.0)	64.3	(1.1)	78.8	(1.1)
	Bulgaria	85.8	(2.1)	34.6	(4.6)	60.3	(1.3)	70.7	(1.3)	54.8	(2.7)	62.2	(3.3)	57.8	(2.5)	68.6	(2.6)	63.0	(1.7)	74.0	(1.5)
	Colombia	92.3	(1.8)	69.5	(3.5)	57.3	(1.3)	83.6	(0.9)	43.5	(3.9)	73.8	(6.3)	59.4	(1.6)	86.5	(1.2)	54.5	(1.9)	79.1	(1.5)
	Croatia	98.0	(0.6)	35.6	(3.6)	56.8	(1.1)	88.3	(0.6)	43.5	(8.9)	76.9	(8.8)	57.4	(1.7)	90.1	(0.9)	57.4	(1.5)	88.2	(0.9)
	Dubai (UAE)	71.9	(0.3)	13.1	(0.1)	64.8	(0.6)	67.7	(0.7)	54.6	(1.3)	66.4	(1.4)	63.6	(2.6)	63.1	(2.5)	69.5	(0.8)	68.2	(0.9)
	Hong Kong-China	94.1	(0.3)	16.8	(3.2)	84.6	(0.7)	84.6	(0.8)	83.8	(2.2)	87.7	(1.7)	84.8	(1.3)	84.8	(2.0)	84.6	(0.8)	84.3	(0.9)
	Indonesia	89.1	(1.8)	68.7	(3.9)	75.6	(1.0)	88.5	(0.8)	55.9	(4.2)	73.7	(2.7)	78.1	(1.0)	91.4	(0.7)	76.6	(1.9)	88.5	(1.6)
	Jordan	94.7	(1.1)	31.7	(4.0)	66.9	(1.0)	75.2	(0.9)	44.0	(3.2)	55.4	(4.1)	69.9	(2.0)	78.2	(1.6)	68.4	(1.4)	74.4	(1.3)
	Kazakhstan	97.8	(0.2)	52.8	(3.6)	85.2	(0.7)	95.8	(0.4)	64.5	(4.6)	86.5	(3.5)	85.8	(1.0)	96.4	(0.5)	85.4	(1.2)	95.6	(0.7)
	Kyrgyzstan	95.6	(0.6)	76.2	(3.3)	81.0	(0.8)	89.8	(0.7)	64.8	(6.2)	67.6	(4.4)	82.2	(1.2)	90.4	(0.9)	79.9	(1.5)	91.4	(0.9)
	Latvia	97.7	(0.7)	14.6	(2.7)	63.0	(1.2)	80.1	(0.8)	75.3	(7.4)	86.2	(4.9)	63.9	(2.3)	81.2	(2.5)	62.4	(1.4)	79.4	(1.0)
	Liechtenstein	93.7	(1.0)	28.8	(0.3)	44.7	(2.4)	55.7	(2.7)	45.6	(10.1)	58.6	(7.6)	62.9	(5.4)	72.4	(5.4)	38.3	(2.9)	48.6	(3.4)
	Lithuania	98.2	(0.4)	18.8	(2.4)	65.6	(0.9)	74.5	(0.9)	61.7	(5.3)	72.2	(5.4)	65.3	(2.6)	73.0	(2.4)	65.7	(1.0)	74.7	(1.0)
	Macao-China	98.1	(0.2)	36.3	(0.0)	74.6	(0.6)	72.7	(0.5)	67.2	(4.4)	64.5	(4.6)	74.5	(1.0)	68.4	(0.9)	75.0	(0.8)	75.5	(0.7)
	Montenegro	97.5	(0.2)	39.2	(1.1)	62.4	(0.6)	73.0	(0.6)	42.2	(4.3)	59.4	(4.8)	65.9	(1.1)	76.0	(1.0)	61.1	(0.9)	70.5	(0.9)
	Panama	88.0	(2.6)	67.4	(4.8)	50.3	(1.5)	79.2	(1.6)	42.4	(4.8)	71.8	(2.8)	52.8	(2.4)	84.2	(2.3)	46.2	(2.4)	73.6	(2.9)
	Peru	79.7	(2.4)	68.5	(3.2)	66.3	(0.9)	78.4	(0.8)	54.0	(2.3)	63.8	(1.8)	70.7	(1.0)	84.4	(0.9)	66.6	(2.3)	77.5	(2.1)
	Qatar	90.9	(0.3)	14.9	(0.1)	57.7	(0.5)	62.4	(0.5)	43.5	(1.9)	47.5	(1.8)	54.4	(1.4)	54.0	(1.6)	59.5	(0.6)	61.9	(0.6)
	Romania	98.0	(0.3)	24.0	(3.3)	69.0	(1.0)	79.7	(0.9)	61.2	(5.3)	64.9	(6.6)	67.0	(2.8)	76.6	(2.2)	69.9	(1.2)	81.1	(1.1)
	Russian Federation	98.6	(0.3)	49.1	(4.2)	69.8	(0.8)	91.3	(0.5)	66.4	(6.5)	75.8	(5.5)	69.8	(1.4)	91.2	(0.8)	69.7	(1.6)	91.7	(0.7)
	Serbia	96.9	(0.6)	30.7	(3.8)	58.2	(1.0)	82.9	(0.7)	52.1	(5.1)	71.1	(5.1)	57.9	(1.5)	84.2	(1.0)	58.1	(1.2)	82.7	(0.9)
	Shanghai-China	97.3	(0.4)	30.4	(3.7)	75.3	(0.7)	59.8	(0.8)	68.1	(3.1)	54.2	(3.5)	75.8	(1.5)	59.1	(1.6)	75.4	(0.9)	60.2	(1.0)
	Singapore	96.8	(0.2)	5.9	(0.1)	81.2	(0.6)	65.5	(0.6)	75.1	(3.6)	58.6	(3.9)	78.5	(1.8)	60.1	(2.5)	81.5	(0.6)	65.9	(0.6)
	Chinese Taipei	97.1	(0.4)	28.0	(3.9)	77.7	(0.7)	66.3	(1.0)	62.2	(5.3)	53.2	(4.4)	75.0	(1.3)	61.8	(1.8)	79.3	(0.9)	68.4	(1.2)
	Thailand	100.0	(0.0)	60.7	(3.9)	79.4	(0.7)	84.1	(0.7)	c	c	c	c	80.6	(1.0)	85.7	(0.7)	76.9	(1.2)	81.3	(1.3)
	Trinidad and Tobago	96.1	(0.3)	49.1	(0.4)	63.9	(0.8)	67.5	(0.7)	59.6	(4.0)	61.7	(3.8)	63.0	(1.2)	65.3	(1.2)	64.5	(1.2)	68.1	(1.1)
	Tunisia	72.9	(2.9)	65.6	(4.1)	70.7	(1.1)	82.7	(0.9)	69.5	(1.4)	80.9	(1.1)	72.5	(1.6)	84.4	(1.4)	68.2	(2.4)	80.7	(2.0)
	Uruguay	95.8	(0.5)	22.5	(2.8)	36.1	(0.8)	61.8	(0.9)	30.3	(3.6)	50.7	(4.1)	36.2	(1.5)	62.0	(2.3)	35.6	(1.0)	62.1	(1.0)

StatLink http://dx.doi.org/10.1787/888932343285

[Part 1/2]

Table IV.4.1 Index of teacher-student relations and reading performance, by national quarters of this index
Results based on students' self-reports

		Index of teacher-student relations										Variability in this index		School variability in the distribution of this index
		All students		Bottom quarter		Second quarter		Third quarter		Top quarter				
		Mean index	S.E.	Mean index	S.E.	Mean index	S.E.	Mean index	S.E.	Mean index	S.E.	Standard deviation	S.E.	Proportion of the index variance between schools
OECD	Australia	0.11	(0.01)	-1.07	(0.01)	-0.09	(0.00)	0.19	(0.00)	1.40	(0.01)	0.99	(0.0)	0.04
	Austria	0.00	(0.03)	-1.33	(0.02)	-0.45	(0.01)	0.36	(0.01)	1.42	(0.02)	1.09	(0.0)	0.07
	Belgium	-0.04	(0.01)	-1.07	(0.01)	-0.35	(0.00)	0.17	(0.00)	1.07	(0.02)	0.87	(0.0)	0.04
	Canada	0.32	(0.01)	-0.89	(0.01)	0.04	(0.00)	0.42	(0.00)	1.72	(0.01)	1.03	(0.0)	0.07
	Chile	0.09	(0.02)	-1.12	(0.02)	-0.26	(0.01)	0.32	(0.01)	1.42	(0.02)	1.02	(0.0)	0.06
	Czech Republic	-0.24	(0.02)	-1.26	(0.01)	-0.50	(0.00)	0.06	(0.00)	0.76	(0.02)	0.85	(0.0)	0.06
	Denmark	0.18	(0.02)	-1.04	(0.02)	-0.07	(0.01)	0.34	(0.01)	1.49	(0.02)	1.01	(0.0)	0.06
	Estonia	-0.04	(0.02)	-1.04	(0.01)	-0.35	(0.00)	0.17	(0.00)	1.07	(0.02)	0.85	(0.0)	0.04
	Finland	-0.16	(0.02)	-1.19	(0.01)	-0.46	(0.00)	0.08	(0.00)	0.93	(0.02)	0.87	(0.0)	0.03
	France	-0.15	(0.02)	-1.21	(0.02)	-0.47	(0.01)	0.09	(0.00)	0.99	(0.02)	0.90	(0.0)	0.05
	Germany	0.01	(0.02)	-1.25	(0.02)	-0.42	(0.01)	0.33	(0.01)	1.38	(0.02)	1.05	(0.0)	0.05
	Greece	-0.18	(0.02)	-1.30	(0.02)	-0.55	(0.01)	0.04	(0.01)	1.09	(0.02)	0.96	(0.0)	0.06
	Hungary	-0.01	(0.02)	-1.05	(0.02)	-0.30	(0.01)	0.17	(0.00)	1.13	(0.02)	0.88	(0.0)	0.05
	Iceland	0.17	(0.02)	-1.16	(0.02)	-0.12	(0.01)	0.32	(0.01)	1.65	(0.02)	1.12	(0.0)	0.09
	Ireland	-0.08	(0.02)	-1.23	(0.02)	-0.37	(0.01)	0.17	(0.00)	1.09	(0.02)	0.96	(0.0)	0.03
	Israel	0.05	(0.03)	-1.30	(0.02)	-0.41	(0.01)	0.32	(0.01)	1.60	(0.02)	1.15	(0.0)	0.10
	Italy	-0.06	(0.01)	-1.23	(0.01)	-0.38	(0.00)	0.18	(0.00)	1.18	(0.01)	0.97	(0.0)	0.08
	Japan	-0.42	(0.02)	-1.55	(0.02)	-0.76	(0.00)	-0.21	(0.00)	0.83	(0.01)	0.97	(0.0)	0.05
	Korea	-0.27	(0.02)	-1.19	(0.01)	-0.51	(0.00)	0.01	(0.01)	0.62	(0.02)	0.78	(0.0)	0.06
	Luxembourg	-0.04	(0.02)	-1.35	(0.01)	-0.48	(0.00)	0.24	(0.00)	1.42	(0.02)	1.10	(0.0)	0.04
	Mexico	0.14	(0.01)	-1.03	(0.01)	-0.18	(0.00)	0.32	(0.00)	1.48	(0.01)	1.00	(0.0)	0.05
	Netherlands	-0.11	(0.02)	-1.01	(0.02)	-0.39	(0.00)	0.13	(0.00)	0.83	(0.02)	0.78	(0.0)	0.02
	New Zealand	0.19	(0.02)	-0.93	(0.01)	-0.03	(0.01)	0.29	(0.01)	1.44	(0.02)	0.95	(0.0)	0.04
	Norway	-0.17	(0.02)	-1.38	(0.02)	-0.55	(0.00)	0.06	(0.00)	1.19	(0.02)	1.03	(0.0)	0.06
	Poland	-0.35	(0.02)	-1.42	(0.02)	-0.69	(0.00)	-0.13	(0.01)	0.85	(0.02)	0.93	(0.0)	0.04
	Portugal	0.37	(0.02)	-0.71	(0.01)	0.13	(0.00)	0.43	(0.01)	1.64	(0.02)	0.93	(0.0)	0.03
	Slovak Republic	-0.16	(0.02)	-1.14	(0.02)	-0.40	(0.00)	0.17	(0.00)	0.76	(0.02)	0.82	(0.0)	0.08
	Slovenia	-0.42	(0.01)	-1.44	(0.02)	-0.73	(0.00)	-0.22	(0.00)	0.71	(0.02)	0.88	(0.0)	0.08
	Spain	-0.03	(0.02)	-1.24	(0.01)	-0.40	(0.00)	0.22	(0.00)	1.32	(0.01)	1.03	(0.0)	0.09
	Sweden	0.15	(0.02)	-1.05	(0.02)	-0.13	(0.01)	0.30	(0.01)	1.50	(0.02)	1.02	(0.0)	0.07
	Switzerland	0.24	(0.02)	-1.13	(0.02)	-0.14	(0.01)	0.55	(0.01)	1.68	(0.01)	1.11	(0.0)	0.07
	Turkey	0.44	(0.03)	-0.96	(0.01)	0.01	(0.01)	0.67	(0.01)	2.03	(0.01)	1.16	(0.0)	0.04
	United Kingdom	0.12	(0.02)	-1.00	(0.01)	-0.10	(0.01)	0.24	(0.00)	1.35	(0.02)	0.94	(0.0)	0.04
	United States	0.32	(0.02)	-0.90	(0.01)	0.02	(0.00)	0.39	(0.01)	1.77	(0.02)	1.05	(0.0)	0.08
	OECD average	0.00	(0.00)	-1.15	(0.00)	-0.32	(0.00)	0.21	(0.00)	1.26	(0.00)	0.97	(0.0)	0.06
Partners	Albania	0.67	(0.02)	-0.50	(0.01)	0.29	(0.01)	0.96	(0.01)	1.94	(0.02)	0.97	(0.0)	0.06
	Argentina	0.04	(0.03)	-1.11	(0.02)	-0.35	(0.01)	0.23	(0.00)	1.41	(0.02)	1.01	(0.0)	0.08
	Azerbaijan	0.53	(0.02)	-0.85	(0.02)	0.16	(0.00)	0.85	(0.01)	1.96	(0.02)	1.11	(0.0)	0.06
	Brazil	0.19	(0.02)	-0.98	(0.01)	-0.11	(0.01)	0.33	(0.01)	1.52	(0.01)	1.00	(0.0)	0.05
	Bulgaria	-0.01	(0.03)	-1.31	(0.02)	-0.43	(0.01)	0.26	(0.01)	1.43	(0.03)	1.09	(0.0)	0.07
	Colombia	0.34	(0.02)	-0.85	(0.01)	-0.03	(0.01)	0.54	(0.01)	1.68	(0.02)	1.01	(0.0)	0.06
	Croatia	-0.17	(0.02)	-1.25	(0.01)	-0.53	(0.00)	0.07	(0.00)	1.03	(0.02)	0.94	(0.0)	0.05
	Dubai (UAE)	0.36	(0.01)	-0.93	(0.02)	0.00	(0.01)	0.61	(0.01)	1.76	(0.01)	1.06	(0.0)	0.04
	Hong Kong-China	-0.03	(0.02)	-1.03	(0.01)	-0.19	(0.01)	0.17	(0.00)	0.95	(0.02)	0.85	(0.0)	0.03
	Indonesia	0.13	(0.02)	-0.73	(0.01)	-0.12	(0.01)	0.25	(0.00)	1.14	(0.02)	0.75	(0.0)	0.04
	Jordan	0.26	(0.02)	-1.19	(0.02)	-0.12	(0.01)	0.57	(0.01)	1.76	(0.02)	1.16	(0.0)	0.04
	Kazakhstan	0.41	(0.02)	-0.68	(0.01)	0.13	(0.00)	0.58	(0.01)	1.63	(0.02)	0.92	(0.0)	0.14
	Kyrgyzstan	0.27	(0.02)	-0.84	(0.02)	-0.05	(0.01)	0.44	(0.01)	1.52	(0.02)	0.94	(0.0)	0.06
	Latvia	-0.03	(0.02)	-1.04	(0.01)	-0.30	(0.00)	0.17	(0.00)	1.07	(0.02)	0.85	(0.0)	0.06
	Liechtenstein	0.08	(0.06)	-1.42	(0.07)	-0.32	(0.03)	0.47	(0.03)	1.58	(0.05)	1.18	(0.0)	0.11
	Lithuania	0.14	(0.02)	-1.20	(0.01)	-0.31	(0.01)	0.50	(0.01)	1.56	(0.02)	1.09	(0.0)	0.06
	Macao-China	-0.24	(0.01)	-1.24	(0.01)	-0.53	(0.00)	0.01	(0.00)	0.81	(0.02)	0.87	(0.0)	0.03
	Montenegro	0.13	(0.02)	-1.11	(0.01)	-0.21	(0.01)	0.30	(0.01)	1.52	(0.02)	1.05	(0.0)	0.10
	Panama	0.46	(0.03)	-0.87	(0.02)	0.04	(0.01)	0.71	(0.01)	1.94	(0.02)	1.10	(0.0)	0.04
	Peru	0.29	(0.02)	-0.87	(0.02)	0.01	(0.00)	0.45	(0.01)	1.58	(0.02)	0.98	(0.0)	0.08
	Qatar	0.18	(0.01)	-1.32	(0.01)	-0.22	(0.00)	0.45	(0.01)	1.83	(0.01)	1.23	(0.0)	0.05
	Romania	0.02	(0.02)	-1.05	(0.02)	-0.32	(0.00)	0.21	(0.00)	1.25	(0.02)	0.93	(0.0)	0.04
	Russian Federation	0.07	(0.02)	-0.95	(0.01)	-0.19	(0.01)	0.21	(0.00)	1.22	(0.02)	0.87	(0.0)	0.07
	Serbia	0.16	(0.02)	-1.00	(0.01)	-0.15	(0.01)	0.29	(0.01)	1.49	(0.02)	0.99	(0.0)	0.03
	Shanghai-China	0.21	(0.02)	-0.87	(0.02)	0.04	(0.00)	0.23	(0.00)	1.44	(0.02)	0.93	(0.0)	0.03
	Singapore	0.24	(0.01)	-0.85	(0.01)	0.00	(0.01)	0.30	(0.00)	1.51	(0.02)	0.95	(0.0)	0.04
	Chinese Taipei	0.03	(0.01)	-1.04	(0.01)	-0.21	(0.01)	0.17	(0.00)	1.22	(0.02)	0.93	(0.0)	0.03
	Thailand	0.10	(0.01)	-0.84	(0.01)	-0.03	(0.01)	0.17	(0.00)	1.12	(0.02)	0.80	(0.0)	0.14
	Trinidad and Tobago	0.16	(0.02)	-1.11	(0.02)	-0.20	(0.01)	0.35	(0.01)	1.61	(0.02)	1.08	(0.0)	0.03
	Tunisia	0.02	(0.02)	-1.17	(0.01)	-0.40	(0.00)	0.31	(0.01)	1.33	(0.01)	0.99	(0.0)	0.06
	Uruguay	0.03	(0.02)	-1.09	(0.01)	-0.33	(0.00)	0.23	(0.00)	1.29	(0.02)	0.96	(0.0)	0.04

Note: Values that are statistically significant are indicated in bold (see Annex A3).
StatLink http://dx.doi.org/10.1787/888932343285

[Part 2/2]

Table IV.4.1 Index of teacher-student relations and reading performance, by national quarters of this index

Results based on students' self-reports

		Performance on the reading scale by national quarters of this index								Change in the reading score per unit of this index		Increased likelihood of students in the bottom quarter of this index scoring in the bottom quarter of the national reading performance distribution		Explained variance in student performance (r-squared x 100)	
		Bottom quarter		Second quarter		Third quarter		Top quarter							
		Mean score	S.E.	Mean score	S.E.	Mean score	S.E.	Mean score	S.E.	Effect	S.E.	Ratio	S.E.	%	S.E.
OECD	Australia	**477**	(2.6)	513	(2.8)	529	(3.0)	**550**	(2.8)	**27.4**	(1.10)	**1.9**	(0.08)	7.7	(0.56)
	Austria	**462**	(3.6)	481	(4.4)	488	(3.9)	**474**	(5.0)	3.8	(1.96)	**1.3**	(0.09)	0.2	(0.21)
	Belgium	**499**	(3.5)	517	(3.2)	525	(3.1)	**510**	(3.5)	**4.3**	(1.74)	**1.2**	(0.06)	0.1	(0.12)
	Canada	**503**	(2.1)	524	(2.1)	532	(2.2)	**544**	(2.4)	**15.7**	(1.07)	**1.5**	(0.05)	3.3	(0.43)
	Chile	**439**	(4.5)	448	(3.9)	459	(3.5)	**457**	(4.2)	**7.7**	(1.66)	**1.3**	(0.10)	0.9	(0.39)
	Czech Republic	**461**	(3.5)	479	(3.5)	493	(4.9)	**495**	(4.2)	**13.7**	(1.60)	**1.5**	(0.10)	1.7	(0.40)
	Denmark	**465**	(3.0)	493	(3.3)	508	(3.3)	**517**	(3.1)	**19.2**	(1.30)	**1.8**	(0.09)	5.4	(0.69)
	Estonia	**478**	(3.9)	495	(3.8)	509	(3.5)	**523**	(3.6)	**19.6**	(2.11)	**1.5**	(0.11)	4.0	(0.83)
	Finland	**512**	(3.4)	531	(4.0)	546	(3.3)	**556**	(3.2)	**20.1**	(1.44)	**1.5**	(0.10)	4.1	(0.58)
	France	**468**	(5.8)	506	(4.3)	509	(4.6)	**508**	(4.7)	**15.2**	(2.95)	**1.6**	(0.13)	1.7	(0.63)
	Germany	498	(4.0)	510	(4.0)	513	(3.7)	499	(3.4)	1.5	(1.65)	1.1	(0.08)	0.0	(0.07)
	Greece	**464**	(6.4)	480	(5.7)	492	(5.0)	**496**	(4.8)	**11.0**	(2.16)	**1.4**	(0.12)	1.3	(0.46)
	Hungary	**484**	(3.9)	492	(4.1)	503	(4.7)	**500**	(4.9)	**6.9**	(2.35)	**1.2**	(0.10)	0.5	(0.32)
	Iceland	**469**	(3.5)	497	(3.9)	509	(4.5)	**532**	(2.6)	**22.0**	(1.29)	**1.7**	(0.12)	6.6	(0.72)
	Ireland	**465**	(5.2)	500	(4.2)	511	(3.9)	**517**	(3.9)	**21.1**	(2.23)	**1.7**	(0.12)	4.7	(0.94)
	Israel	**467**	(4.7)	484	(4.8)	484	(4.3)	**482**	(4.9)	**4.1**	(1.82)	**1.2**	(0.08)	0.2	(0.17)
	Italy	**476**	(2.1)	491	(2.1)	495	(2.4)	**485**	(2.2)	**3.8**	(0.98)	**1.2**	(0.04)	0.2	(0.08)
	Japan	**483**	(6.1)	520	(3.9)	537	(3.6)	**542**	(3.9)	**22.9**	(2.13)	**2.0**	(0.11)	5.0	(0.79)
	Korea	**526**	(4.0)	544	(4.2)	543	(4.2)	**545**	(4.9)	**11.4**	(2.23)	**1.2**	(0.10)	1.3	(0.52)
	Luxembourg	**462**	(2.8)	481	(3.2)	485	(2.9)	**470**	(3.1)	**3.0**	(1.49)	**1.2**	(0.10)	0.1	(0.11)
	Mexico	**412**	(3.0)	425	(2.9)	433	(2.3)	**432**	(1.9)	**7.8**	(0.91)	**1.4**	(0.06)	0.9	(0.19)
	Netherlands	**498**	(5.4)	520	(5.2)	513	(6.8)	**516**	(7.0)	**7.0**	(2.72)	1.2	(0.12)	0.4	(0.32)
	New Zealand	**490**	(3.3)	522	(3.7)	531	(3.6)	**547**	(4.3)	**22.7**	(1.97)	**1.6**	(0.10)	4.5	(0.81)
	Norway	**468**	(3.3)	500	(3.2)	513	(3.7)	**535**	(3.8)	**23.9**	(1.37)	**1.8**	(0.10)	7.4	(0.86)
	Poland	**489**	(3.7)	497	(3.1)	508	(3.6)	**512**	(3.9)	**9.0**	(1.74)	**1.3**	(0.09)	0.9	(0.36)
	Portugal	**477**	(4.3)	491	(3.8)	496	(4.0)	**496**	(3.8)	**7.4**	(1.63)	**1.2**	(0.08)	0.7	(0.29)
	Slovak Republic	**464**	(4.1)	480	(3.5)	485	(4.1)	**483**	(4.2)	**9.3**	(2.35)	**1.3**	(0.10)	0.7	(0.36)
	Slovenia	**473**	(3.1)	490	(2.8)	492	(2.8)	**489**	(3.0)	**6.5**	(1.66)	**1.2**	(0.07)	0.4	(0.22)
	Spain	**465**	(3.1)	485	(2.9)	493	(2.8)	**484**	(2.6)	**7.3**	(1.26)	**1.4**	(0.08)	0.7	(0.26)
	Sweden	**471**	(4.1)	497	(4.4)	510	(4.4)	**519**	(4.1)	**17.8**	(1.73)	**1.7**	(0.11)	3.5	(0.69)
	Switzerland	**483**	(3.2)	513	(3.3)	510	(3.8)	**499**	(4.0)	**4.4**	(1.31)	**1.4**	(0.08)	0.3	(0.16)
	Turkey	**456**	(5.1)	463	(4.6)	469	(4.2)	**470**	(4.3)	**5.6**	(1.49)	**1.4**	(0.09)	0.6	(0.34)
	United Kingdom	**466**	(3.3)	496	(3.1)	506	(2.9)	**515**	(3.7)	**17.7**	(1.68)	**1.6**	(0.09)	3.1	(0.59)
	United States	**472**	(4.1)	505	(4.5)	511	(4.8)	**516**	(4.9)	**14.9**	(1.83)	**1.6**	(0.08)	2.7	(0.60)
	OECD average	**475**	(0.7)	496	(0.7)	504	(0.7)	**506**	(0.7)	**12.2**	(0.31)	**1.4**	(0.02)	2.2	(0.09)
Partners	Albania	**366**	(6.0)	389	(5.4)	396	(5.9)	**402**	(5.2)	**15.3**	(2.16)	**1.5**	(0.12)	2.3	(0.64)
	Argentina	**420**	(6.1)	413	(5.9)	399	(5.1)	**381**	(5.8)	**-13.5**	(2.33)	**0.8**	(0.07)	1.7	(0.54)
	Azerbaijan	359	(4.6)	363	(4.1)	372	(4.4)	365	(3.5)	2.2	(1.38)	1.2	(0.10)	0.1	(0.15)
	Brazil	**397**	(3.4)	412	(3.1)	421	(3.5)	**423**	(3.8)	**10.0**	(1.35)	**1.4**	(0.08)	1.1	(0.29)
	Bulgaria	427	(7.8)	446	(7.7)	433	(6.9)	423	(8.3)	-3.1	(2.45)	1.1	(0.10)	0.1	(0.15)
	Colombia	**415**	(4.5)	420	(4.3)	422	(4.6)	**403**	(4.2)	**-4.1**	(1.65)	1.0	(0.09)	0.2	(0.19)
	Croatia	473	(4.7)	481	(3.8)	476	(4.0)	475	(3.6)	-0.8	(1.71)	1.0	(0.09)	0.0	(0.05)
	Dubai (UAE)	**441**	(3.3)	468	(3.3)	470	(3.0)	**466**	(3.1)	**8.6**	(1.49)	**1.4**	(0.08)	0.7	(0.26)
	Hong Kong-China	**515**	(3.6)	536	(2.8)	538	(3.1)	**544**	(3.1)	**12.8**	(1.83)	**1.4**	(0.09)	1.7	(0.48)
	Indonesia	**405**	(4.5)	404	(4.7)	405	(4.7)	**395**	(3.9)	**-4.7**	(1.88)	0.9	(0.11)	0.3	(0.22)
	Jordan	**384**	(4.1)	402	(4.3)	414	(4.1)	**432**	(3.3)	**16.5**	(1.42)	**1.6**	(0.10)	4.7	(0.75)
	Kazakhstan	394	(4.8)	382	(4.1)	394	(4.0)	393	(4.2)	0.7	(2.11)	1.0	(0.07)	0.0	(0.04)
	Kyrgyzstan	317	(4.0)	322	(4.4)	322	(5.2)	311	(5.1)	-2.0	(1.91)	1.0	(0.07)	0.0	(0.08)
	Latvia	**466**	(4.4)	480	(4.0)	494	(4.1)	**497**	(4.1)	**13.3**	(1.89)	**1.4**	(0.11)	2.0	(0.56)
	Liechtenstein	484	(9.7)	501	(10.4)	515	(9.4)	498	(9.9)	5.2	(3.97)	1.3	(0.27)	0.6	(0.86)
	Lithuania	**454**	(3.5)	465	(3.6)	477	(3.6)	**478**	(3.8)	**8.0**	(1.41)	**1.3**	(0.09)	1.0	(0.36)
	Macao-China	**480**	(2.1)	485	(1.8)	491	(2.2)	**491**	(2.2)	**5.5**	(1.31)	**1.2**	(0.06)	0.4	(0.18)
	Montenegro	**421**	(3.1)	413	(2.6)	407	(3.7)	**397**	(4.4)	**-8.9**	(1.77)	**0.8**	(0.06)	1.1	(0.42)
	Panama	377	(8.9)	381	(7.0)	384	(7.6)	364	(7.7)	-3.1	(2.16)	1.2	(0.14)	0.1	(0.16)
	Peru	**359**	(5.2)	376	(5.2)	377	(5.4)	**376**	(5.1)	**6.2**	(2.03)	**1.3**	(0.09)	0.4	(0.25)
	Qatar	**337**	(2.3)	375	(2.5)	396	(2.3)	**393**	(2.1)	**17.0**	(0.88)	**1.8**	(0.08)	3.4	(0.35)
	Romania	**417**	(5.3)	428	(4.8)	426	(4.7)	**431**	(4.9)	**6.3**	(2.14)	**1.2**	(0.10)	0.4	(0.30)
	Russian Federation	**442**	(4.4)	456	(4.1)	462	(4.7)	**480**	(4.7)	**14.8**	(1.71)	**1.4**	(0.10)	2.1	(0.46)
	Serbia	**448**	(3.2)	448	(4.5)	443	(3.7)	**432**	(3.9)	**-7.3**	(1.59)	**0.9**	(0.06)	0.8	(0.32)
	Shanghai-China	**536**	(3.6)	557	(3.1)	559	(3.4)	**572**	(3.4)	**14.5**	(1.53)	**1.4**	(0.09)	2.9	(0.58)
	Singapore	**504**	(2.8)	531	(4.2)	537	(3.9)	**533**	(2.8)	**10.8**	(1.57)	**1.5**	(0.08)	1.1	(0.33)
	Chinese Taipei	**482**	(3.3)	496	(3.7)	496	(3.5)	**508**	(3.0)	**11.5**	(1.27)	**1.3**	(0.07)	1.5	(0.34)
	Thailand	**417**	(3.6)	422	(3.2)	420	(3.4)	**427**	(3.0)	**3.5**	(1.43)	**1.2**	(0.07)	0.1	(0.12)
	Trinidad and Tobago	**402**	(3.9)	415	(4.4)	435	(3.5)	**430**	(3.7)	**10.8**	(1.73)	**1.4**	(0.10)	1.1	(0.34)
	Tunisia	**399**	(3.9)	397	(4.1)	408	(3.5)	**415**	(3.6)	**7.3**	(1.53)	**1.1**	(0.07)	0.7	(0.31)
	Uruguay	**429**	(3.6)	429	(3.7)	435	(4.1)	**417**	(3.7)	**-5.6**	(1.58)	1.0	(0.08)	0.3	(0.18)

Note: Values that are statistically significant are indicated in bold (see Annex A3).

StatLink http://dx.doi.org/10.1787/888932343285

[Part 1/2]

Table IV.4.2 **Index of disciplinary climate and reading performance, by national quarters of this index**
Results based on students' self-reports

		Index of disciplinary climate										Variability in this index		School variability in the distribution of this index
		All students		Bottom quarter		Second quarter		Third quarter		Top quarter				
		Mean index	S.E.	Mean index	S.E.	Mean index	S.E.	Mean index	S.E.	Mean index	S.E.	Standard deviation	S.E.	Proportion of the index variance between schools
OECD	Australia	-0.07	(0.02)	-1.41	(0.01)	-0.31	(0.00)	0.30	(0.00)	1.12	(0.01)	1.01	(0.0)	0.12
	Austria	0.11	(0.04)	-1.48	(0.03)	-0.19	(0.01)	0.62	(0.01)	1.48	(0.01)	1.17	(0.0)	0.17
	Belgium	-0.07	(0.02)	-1.39	(0.02)	-0.31	(0.01)	0.30	(0.00)	1.13	(0.01)	1.01	(0.0)	0.10
	Canada	-0.08	(0.01)	-1.34	(0.01)	-0.31	(0.00)	0.25	(0.00)	1.07	(0.01)	0.96	(0.0)	0.14
	Chile	-0.10	(0.02)	-1.29	(0.02)	-0.37	(0.00)	0.23	(0.00)	1.01	(0.01)	0.91	(0.0)	0.13
	Czech Republic	-0.18	(0.04)	-1.62	(0.03)	-0.43	(0.01)	0.25	(0.01)	1.10	(0.01)	1.08	(0.0)	0.22
	Denmark	0.01	(0.02)	-1.06	(0.02)	-0.20	(0.01)	0.28	(0.01)	1.02	(0.02)	0.83	(0.0)	0.16
	Estonia	0.05	(0.03)	-1.17	(0.01)	-0.24	(0.01)	0.34	(0.01)	1.28	(0.02)	0.96	(0.0)	0.24
	Finland	-0.29	(0.02)	-1.51	(0.02)	-0.57	(0.01)	0.06	(0.00)	0.85	(0.02)	0.94	(0.0)	0.14
	France	-0.20	(0.03)	-1.59	(0.02)	-0.55	(0.01)	0.23	(0.01)	1.12	(0.01)	1.07	(0.0)	0.15
	Germany	0.25	(0.02)	-1.05	(0.03)	0.05	(0.01)	0.61	(0.00)	1.40	(0.01)	0.98	(0.0)	0.13
	Greece	-0.40	(0.02)	-1.49	(0.02)	-0.65	(0.00)	-0.11	(0.00)	0.64	(0.01)	0.85	(0.0)	0.15
	Hungary	-0.02	(0.03)	-1.29	(0.02)	-0.24	(0.01)	0.32	(0.01)	1.12	(0.01)	0.96	(0.0)	0.16
	Iceland	-0.05	(0.01)	-1.18	(0.02)	-0.20	(0.01)	0.17	(0.00)	0.99	(0.01)	0.87	(0.0)	0.12
	Ireland	-0.03	(0.03)	-1.51	(0.02)	-0.29	(0.01)	0.41	(0.01)	1.27	(0.01)	1.10	(0.0)	0.10
	Israel	0.08	(0.02)	-1.22	(0.02)	-0.20	(0.00)	0.37	(0.01)	1.35	(0.01)	1.01	(0.0)	0.19
	Italy	0.03	(0.02)	-1.40	(0.01)	-0.26	(0.00)	0.53	(0.00)	1.25	(0.01)	1.05	(0.0)	0.23
	Japan	0.75	(0.02)	-0.43	(0.02)	0.56	(0.00)	1.11	(0.00)	1.77	(0.00)	0.88	(0.0)	0.27
	Korea	0.38	(0.03)	-0.65	(0.02)	0.12	(0.00)	0.67	(0.00)	1.38	(0.01)	0.82	(0.0)	0.08
	Luxembourg	-0.21	(0.02)	-1.77	(0.02)	-0.53	(0.01)	0.25	(0.01)	1.21	(0.01)	1.17	(0.0)	0.05
	Mexico	0.11	(0.01)	-1.00	(0.01)	-0.12	(0.00)	0.43	(0.00)	1.13	(0.01)	0.85	(0.0)	0.12
	Netherlands	-0.28	(0.02)	-1.43	(0.02)	-0.54	(0.01)	0.02	(0.00)	0.84	(0.02)	0.91	(0.0)	0.08
	New Zealand	-0.12	(0.02)	-1.36	(0.02)	-0.36	(0.00)	0.20	(0.01)	1.05	(0.01)	0.96	(0.0)	0.09
	Norway	-0.24	(0.02)	-1.43	(0.02)	-0.51	(0.01)	0.09	(0.00)	0.88	(0.02)	0.93	(0.0)	0.17
	Poland	0.07	(0.03)	-1.23	(0.02)	-0.17	(0.01)	0.41	(0.01)	1.27	(0.01)	0.99	(0.0)	0.17
	Portugal	0.19	(0.03)	-1.08	(0.02)	-0.05	(0.00)	0.56	(0.01)	1.32	(0.01)	0.96	(0.0)	0.10
	Slovak Republic	-0.02	(0.03)	-1.26	(0.02)	-0.24	(0.01)	0.33	(0.01)	1.10	(0.01)	0.94	(0.0)	0.16
	Slovenia	-0.11	(0.02)	-1.61	(0.02)	-0.38	(0.01)	0.29	(0.01)	1.28	(0.01)	1.13	(0.0)	0.23
	Spain	0.09	(0.02)	-1.30	(0.02)	-0.17	(0.00)	0.51	(0.00)	1.31	(0.01)	1.04	(0.0)	0.14
	Sweden	-0.03	(0.03)	-1.19	(0.02)	-0.26	(0.01)	0.23	(0.00)	1.08	(0.01)	0.90	(0.0)	0.18
	Switzerland	0.09	(0.03)	-1.25	(0.03)	-0.16	(0.00)	0.50	(0.00)	1.28	(0.01)	1.01	(0.0)	0.10
	Turkey	0.03	(0.02)	-1.15	(0.02)	-0.14	(0.01)	0.31	(0.01)	1.12	(0.01)	0.91	(0.0)	0.08
	United Kingdom	0.11	(0.03)	-1.26	(0.02)	-0.13	(0.01)	0.53	(0.00)	1.30	(0.01)	1.02	(0.0)	0.14
	United States	0.16	(0.02)	-1.10	(0.02)	-0.08	(0.00)	0.48	(0.01)	1.34	(0.01)	0.97	(0.0)	0.14
	OECD average	0.00	(0.00)	-1.28	(0.00)	-0.25	(0.00)	0.35	(0.00)	1.17	(0.00)	0.97	(0.0)	0.15
Partners	Albania	0.53	(0.03)	-0.57	(0.02)	0.30	(0.01)	0.85	(0.00)	1.53	(0.01)	0.84	(0.0)	0.13
	Argentina	-0.26	(0.03)	-1.57	(0.02)	-0.55	(0.01)	0.12	(0.01)	0.97	(0.02)	1.00	(0.0)	0.17
	Azerbaijan	0.57	(0.03)	-0.66	(0.02)	0.25	(0.01)	0.94	(0.01)	1.73	(0.01)	0.96	(0.0)	0.12
	Brazil	-0.18	(0.02)	-1.26	(0.01)	-0.47	(0.00)	0.10	(0.00)	0.93	(0.01)	0.87	(0.0)	0.12
	Bulgaria	0.02	(0.04)	-1.33	(0.03)	-0.21	(0.01)	0.40	(0.01)	1.20	(0.01)	1.01	(0.0)	0.09
	Colombia	0.19	(0.02)	-0.86	(0.02)	-0.03	(0.01)	0.49	(0.00)	1.15	(0.02)	0.81	(0.0)	0.11
	Croatia	-0.13	(0.03)	-1.47	(0.02)	-0.39	(0.00)	0.25	(0.01)	1.10	(0.01)	1.02	(0.0)	0.14
	Dubai (UAE)	0.13	(0.01)	-1.21	(0.02)	-0.14	(0.01)	0.56	(0.00)	1.32	(0.01)	1.01	(0.0)	0.17
	Hong Kong-China	0.37	(0.02)	-0.69	(0.02)	0.09	(0.00)	0.63	(0.00)	1.46	(0.01)	0.89	(0.0)	0.08
	Indonesia	0.26	(0.02)	-0.83	(0.02)	-0.02	(0.00)	0.54	(0.00)	1.35	(0.01)	0.86	(0.0)	0.12
	Jordan	0.23	(0.03)	-1.13	(0.02)	-0.07	(0.01)	0.64	(0.01)	1.48	(0.01)	1.03	(0.0)	0.14
	Kazakhstan	0.78	(0.03)	-0.49	(0.02)	0.57	(0.00)	1.19	(0.01)	1.84	(0.00)	0.93	(0.0)	0.17
	Kyrgyzstan	0.35	(0.02)	-0.75	(0.02)	0.10	(0.00)	0.67	(0.00)	1.40	(0.01)	0.86	(0.0)	0.05
	Latvia	0.25	(0.03)	-0.93	(0.02)	-0.01	(0.01)	0.58	(0.01)	1.35	(0.02)	0.90	(0.0)	0.21
	Liechtenstein	0.13	(0.05)	-1.14	(0.06)	-0.07	(0.01)	0.47	(0.02)	1.24	(0.04)	0.94	(0.0)	0.14
	Lithuania	0.30	(0.03)	-0.92	(0.02)	0.03	(0.00)	0.62	(0.01)	1.47	(0.01)	0.95	(0.0)	0.13
	Macao-China	0.11	(0.01)	-0.84	(0.01)	-0.05	(0.00)	0.32	(0.00)	1.02	(0.01)	0.76	(0.0)	0.12
	Montenegro	0.28	(0.01)	-0.97	(0.02)	0.02	(0.01)	0.65	(0.01)	1.41	(0.01)	0.95	(0.0)	0.08
	Panama	0.04	(0.03)	-1.11	(0.03)	-0.18	(0.01)	0.38	(0.01)	1.08	(0.02)	0.88	(0.0)	0.07
	Peru	0.19	(0.02)	-0.83	(0.01)	-0.02	(0.00)	0.50	(0.00)	1.11	(0.01)	0.79	(0.0)	0.06
	Qatar	-0.02	(0.01)	-1.39	(0.01)	-0.36	(0.00)	0.34	(0.00)	1.33	(0.01)	1.07	(0.0)	0.09
	Romania	0.43	(0.03)	-0.62	(0.02)	0.17	(0.01)	0.74	(0.00)	1.44	(0.01)	0.83	(0.0)	0.13
	Russian Federation	0.44	(0.02)	-0.83	(0.02)	0.20	(0.00)	0.80	(0.00)	1.57	(0.01)	0.96	(0.0)	0.14
	Serbia	-0.02	(0.03)	-1.22	(0.02)	-0.27	(0.01)	0.29	(0.01)	1.13	(0.01)	0.93	(0.0)	0.14
	Shanghai-China	0.45	(0.02)	-0.64	(0.02)	0.20	(0.00)	0.75	(0.00)	1.47	(0.01)	0.86	(0.0)	0.18
	Singapore	0.12	(0.01)	-1.09	(0.02)	-0.07	(0.00)	0.45	(0.00)	1.20	(0.01)	0.91	(0.0)	0.07
	Chinese Taipei	0.09	(0.02)	-1.01	(0.02)	-0.08	(0.00)	0.28	(0.00)	1.18	(0.01)	0.87	(0.0)	0.08
	Thailand	0.33	(0.01)	-0.56	(0.02)	0.11	(0.00)	0.53	(0.00)	1.22	(0.01)	0.74	(0.0)	0.07
	Trinidad and Tobago	-0.02	(0.02)	-1.33	(0.02)	-0.31	(0.01)	0.34	(0.01)	1.23	(0.01)	1.01	(0.0)	0.09
	Tunisia	-0.19	(0.02)	-1.29	(0.02)	-0.50	(0.00)	0.10	(0.01)	0.93	(0.01)	0.88	(0.0)	0.06
	Uruguay	-0.01	(0.02)	-1.35	(0.02)	-0.26	(0.01)	0.37	(0.01)	1.18	(0.01)	1.00	(0.0)	0.13

Note: Values that are statistically significant are indicated in bold (see Annex A3).
StatLink http://dx.doi.org/10.1787/888932343285

[Part 2/2]

Table IV.4.2 Index of disciplinary climate and reading performance, by national quarters of this index

Results based on students' self-reports

		Performance on the reading scale by national quarters of this index								Change in the reading score per unit of this index		Increased likelihood of students in the bottom quarter of this index scoring in the bottom quarter of the national reading performance distribution		Explained variance in student performance (r-squared x 100)	
		Bottom quarter		Second quarter		Third quarter		Top quarter							
		Mean score	S.E.	Mean score	S.E.	Mean score	S.E.	Mean score	S.E.	Effect	S.E.	Ratio	S.E.	%	S.E.
OECD	Australia	**486**	(2.5)	509	(2.7)	525	(3.1)	**548**	(3.7)	**22.8**	(1.18)	**1.7**	(0.06)	5.6	(0.55)
	Austria	**455**	(4.7)	463	(4.3)	487	(3.8)	**502**	(4.3)	**14.9**	(1.99)	**1.6**	(0.12)	3.2	(0.83)
	Belgium	**499**	(4.3)	508	(3.7)	519	(3.9)	**526**	(3.7)	**10.2**	(2.07)	**1.3**	(0.10)	1.1	(0.44)
	Canada	**509**	(2.4)	524	(2.6)	529	(2.5)	**541**	(2.4)	**12.3**	(1.18)	**1.4**	(0.05)	1.7	(0.33)
	Chile	**439**	(4.2)	445	(4.3)	454	(4.1)	**464**	(4.0)	**10.0**	(2.04)	**1.3**	(0.10)	1.2	(0.48)
	Czech Republic	**465**	(4.3)	471	(3.8)	486	(4.1)	**507**	(4.3)	**14.1**	(1.89)	**1.4**	(0.09)	2.9	(0.73)
	Denmark	**482**	(3.2)	493	(3.1)	497	(3.8)	**511**	(3.4)	**13.2**	(1.58)	**1.4**	(0.10)	1.7	(0.42)
	Estonia	**487**	(4.3)	492	(3.8)	504	(3.8)	**521**	(3.6)	**12.9**	(2.10)	**1.3**	(0.11)	2.2	(0.72)
	Finland	**532**	(3.0)	535	(3.3)	532	(3.7)	**546**	(3.6)	**4.0**	(1.61)	1.1	(0.06)	0.2	(0.15)
	France	**482**	(5.0)	490	(5.1)	500	(4.2)	**519**	(5.2)	**12.7**	(2.60)	**1.3**	(0.11)	1.7	(0.69)
	Germany	**487**	(4.4)	506	(4.6)	514	(3.5)	**513**	(3.6)	**9.1**	(1.85)	**1.4**	(0.11)	1.0	(0.39)
	Greece	**475**	(5.5)	474	(6.0)	485	(5.2)	**498**	(5.2)	**11.4**	(2.67)	1.1	(0.09)	1.1	(0.48)
	Hungary	**479**	(4.8)	485	(4.4)	492	(4.3)	**522**	(4.4)	**15.6**	(2.27)	**1.3**	(0.12)	2.8	(0.78)
	Iceland	**485**	(3.7)	497	(3.9)	506	(3.6)	**519**	(2.9)	**15.4**	(2.31)	**1.4**	(0.09)	2.0	(0.61)
	Ireland	**476**	(5.2)	490	(4.4)	508	(4.2)	**519**	(3.5)	**14.7**	(1.93)	**1.5**	(0.13)	3.0	(0.76)
	Israel	**463**	(5.0)	473	(4.1)	488	(4.1)	**493**	(4.9)	**10.8**	(2.18)	**1.4**	(0.09)	1.0	(0.41)
	Italy	**453**	(2.2)	473	(2.3)	503	(2.3)	**518**	(1.9)	**23.6**	(1.06)	**1.8**	(0.06)	6.8	(0.53)
	Japan	**470**	(6.5)	518	(4.1)	543	(3.6)	**551**	(3.7)	**35.1**	(2.94)	**2.3**	(0.17)	9.6	(1.36)
	Korea	**530**	(3.8)	531	(4.5)	544	(4.4)	**554**	(4.4)	**13.3**	(2.43)	**1.2**	(0.10)	1.9	(0.63)
	Luxembourg	**462**	(2.9)	460	(3.2)	479	(3.1)	**501**	(3.0)	**13.3**	(1.38)	**1.2**	(0.07)	2.3	(0.47)
	Mexico	**415**	(2.7)	419	(2.3)	428	(2.1)	**442**	(2.2)	**11.7**	(1.22)	**1.3**	(0.05)	1.4	(0.28)
	Netherlands	502	(6.1)	511	(6.3)	515	(5.9)	518	(7.0)	**6.6**	(2.49)	1.2	(0.11)	0.5	(0.35)
	New Zealand	**498**	(4.1)	513	(4.3)	526	(3.9)	**554**	(3.5)	**20.7**	(2.09)	**1.4**	(0.10)	3.8	(0.76)
	Norway	**484**	(3.5)	505	(3.1)	512	(3.9)	**516**	(3.9)	**14.1**	(1.74)	**1.4**	(0.08)	2.1	(0.51)
	Poland	**491**	(3.6)	495	(3.4)	503	(3.5)	**516**	(3.6)	**10.3**	(1.73)	**1.2**	(0.07)	1.3	(0.43)
	Portugal	**481**	(4.2)	479	(3.9)	493	(3.9)	**506**	(4.0)	**9.7**	(1.94)	**1.2**	(0.08)	1.2	(0.46)
	Slovak Republic	**465**	(4.4)	471	(4.1)	481	(4.1)	**495**	(3.6)	**11.6**	(2.19)	**1.3**	(0.10)	1.5	(0.53)
	Slovenia	**460**	(3.0)	477	(3.1)	492	(3.2)	**516**	(3.3)	**17.9**	(1.21)	**1.6**	(0.11)	5.2	(0.66)
	Spain	**465**	(3.0)	476	(3.1)	493	(2.7)	**494**	(2.1)	**10.9**	(1.12)	**1.5**	(0.07)	1.7	(0.35)
	Sweden	**487**	(4.0)	494	(4.7)	503	(4.1)	**514**	(4.5)	**11.4**	(2.23)	**1.3**	(0.09)	1.1	(0.44)
	Switzerland	**485**	(4.2)	493	(3.3)	507	(3.5)	**519**	(3.9)	**12.3**	(2.04)	**1.4**	(0.08)	1.8	(0.57)
	Turkey	**445**	(4.4)	460	(4.3)	473	(4.6)	**480**	(4.0)	**13.4**	(1.81)	**1.5**	(0.09)	2.2	(0.58)
	United Kingdom	**464**	(3.4)	489	(3.4)	511	(3.1)	**519**	(3.0)	**21.1**	(1.64)	**1.8**	(0.10)	5.2	(0.79)
	United States	**465**	(4.1)	491	(4.4)	517	(5.6)	**532**	(3.5)	**25.6**	(1.66)	**1.9**	(0.13)	6.6	(0.74)
	OECD average	**477**	(0.7)	489	(0.7)	501	(0.7)	**515**	(0.7)	**14.3**	(0.33)	**1.4**	(0.02)	2.6	(0.10)
Partners	Albania	**368**	(4.5)	390	(5.4)	395	(6.5)	**399**	(6.8)	**14.2**	(3.47)	**1.3**	(0.12)	1.5	(0.72)
	Argentina	405	(6.5)	398	(6.7)	401	(5.4)	411	(5.2)	1.3	(2.49)	1.0	(0.08)	0.0	(0.08)
	Azerbaijan	**342**	(4.3)	365	(4.1)	378	(5.1)	**376**	(4.4)	**14.8**	(1.93)	**1.7**	(0.14)	3.6	(0.97)
	Brazil	**400**	(3.5)	406	(3.1)	417	(4.0)	**431**	(4.3)	**13.3**	(2.19)	**1.2**	(0.07)	1.6	(0.50)
	Bulgaria	**409**	(7.6)	423	(7.2)	450	(7.4)	**447**	(9.8)	**15.9**	(3.34)	**1.4**	(0.14)	2.1	(0.85)
	Colombia	**397**	(4.9)	410	(4.1)	421	(3.6)	**433**	(4.8)	**17.3**	(2.44)	**1.6**	(0.12)	2.7	(0.77)
	Croatia	**448**	(4.1)	465	(4.0)	483	(3.7)	**509**	(3.8)	**21.7**	(1.78)	**1.7**	(0.12)	6.5	(1.02)
	Dubai (UAE)	**427**	(2.8)	448	(3.2)	480	(3.2)	**489**	(3.4)	**23.7**	(1.75)	**1.8**	(0.10)	5.1	(0.73)
	Hong Kong-China	**515**	(4.1)	520	(3.2)	547	(3.2)	**551**	(3.0)	**16.4**	(2.15)	**1.5**	(0.10)	3.0	(0.76)
	Indonesia	392	(4.1)	410	(4.9)	410	(3.9)	399	(4.9)	2.8	(2.09)	1.3	(0.11)	0.1	(0.21)
	Jordan	**390**	(3.9)	401	(3.9)	423	(4.0)	**418**	(4.1)	**10.6**	(1.70)	**1.4**	(0.09)	1.5	(0.48)
	Kazakhstan	**366**	(5.0)	393	(4.1)	401	(4.1)	**402**	(4.2)	**15.2**	(2.66)	**1.8**	(0.11)	2.4	(0.81)
	Kyrgyzstan	**290**	(4.5)	317	(4.1)	335	(4.0)	**333**	(5.4)	**21.4**	(2.67)	**1.8**	(0.14)	3.7	(0.90)
	Latvia	**478**	(3.9)	474	(4.2)	484	(4.9)	**501**	(5.0)	**9.6**	(2.15)	1.1	(0.10)	1.2	(0.54)
	Liechtenstein	494	(8.8)	492	(9.1)	502	(8.6)	510	(9.1)	6.0	(5.01)	1.1	(0.24)	0.5	(0.82)
	Lithuania	**449**	(3.4)	459	(3.2)	474	(3.6)	**494**	(4.3)	**17.1**	(1.90)	**1.5**	(0.09)	3.6	(0.78)
	Macao-China	**472**	(2.2)	477	(2.4)	489	(2.4)	**509**	(2.1)	**17.0**	(1.39)	**1.4**	(0.08)	2.9	(0.47)
	Montenegro	**380**	(3.2)	406	(3.2)	423	(2.8)	**430**	(4.9)	**19.8**	(2.17)	**1.7**	(0.11)	4.3	(0.88)
	Panama	**359**	(10.6)	369	(7.1)	392	(7.2)	**386**	(7.2)	**12.1**	(3.85)	**1.5**	(0.18)	1.2	(0.77)
	Peru	**350**	(4.9)	366	(4.3)	383	(4.6)	**389**	(4.8)	**19.7**	(2.32)	**1.6**	(0.09)	2.5	(0.63)
	Qatar	**352**	(2.5)	359	(2.5)	392	(3.0)	**398**	(2.2)	**15.7**	(1.08)	**1.3**	(0.06)	2.2	(0.30)
	Romania	**397**	(4.7)	411	(4.5)	441	(4.8)	**452**	(5.6)	**26.6**	(2.50)	**1.8**	(0.12)	6.1	(1.09)
	Russian Federation	**441**	(4.4)	461	(4.4)	474	(3.8)	**464**	(4.6)	**9.7**	(1.64)	**1.5**	(0.09)	1.1	(0.35)
	Serbia	**422**	(3.8)	434	(3.2)	445	(3.5)	**471**	(3.8)	**19.3**	(2.04)	**1.5**	(0.10)	4.7	(0.99)
	Shanghai-China	**530**	(4.1)	548	(3.5)	570	(2.9)	**576**	(3.7)	**21.3**	(1.93)	**1.8**	(0.12)	5.2	(0.91)
	Singapore	**498**	(3.0)	509	(2.7)	537	(2.6)	**562**	(2.5)	**26.7**	(1.32)	**1.7**	(0.10)	6.2	(0.60)
	Chinese Taipei	**475**	(3.5)	487	(3.2)	498	(3.9)	**522**	(4.2)	**20.3**	(2.13)	**1.5**	(0.09)	4.2	(0.81)
	Thailand	**407**	(3.9)	416	(2.9)	432	(3.2)	**431**	(3.5)	**13.3**	(1.91)	**1.5**	(0.10)	1.9	(0.56)
	Trinidad and Tobago	**405**	(3.3)	402	(4.3)	430	(4.5)	**447**	(3.3)	**15.8**	(1.72)	**1.3**	(0.08)	2.1	(0.44)
	Tunisia	403	(3.6)	401	(4.0)	406	(3.7)	408	(3.8)	0.3	(1.78)	1.1	(0.07)	0.0	(0.04)
	Uruguay	**416**	(3.9)	420	(3.5)	437	(3.6)	**442**	(3.6)	**10.0**	(1.68)	**1.2**	(0.08)	1.1	(0.34)

Note: Values that are statistically significant are indicated in bold (see Annex A3).

StatLink http://dx.doi.org/10.1787/888932343285

[Part 1/2]
Index of teachers' stimulation of students' reading engagement and reading skills and performance, by national quarters of this index
Table IV.4.3 *Results based on students' self-reports*

		Index of teachers' stimulation of students' reading engagement										Variability in this index		School variability in the distribution of this index
		All students		Bottom quarter		Second quarter		Third quarter		Top quarter				
		Mean index	S.E.	Mean index	S.E.	Mean index	S.E.	Mean index	S.E.	Mean index	S.E.	Standard deviation	S.E.	Proportion of the index variance between schools
OECD	Australia	0.13	(0.01)	-1.07	(0.01)	-0.15	(0.00)	0.41	(0.00)	1.34	(0.01)	1.00	(0.0)	0.07
	Austria	-0.30	(0.02)	-1.57	(0.02)	-0.57	(0.00)	0.01	(0.01)	0.95	(0.02)	1.03	(0.0)	0.07
	Belgium	-0.16	(0.01)	-1.23	(0.02)	-0.42	(0.00)	0.09	(0.00)	0.90	(0.02)	0.89	(0.0)	0.05
	Canada	0.23	(0.01)	-1.02	(0.01)	-0.06	(0.00)	0.53	(0.00)	1.49	(0.01)	1.05	(0.0)	0.10
	Chile	0.17	(0.02)	-1.02	(0.02)	-0.14	(0.00)	0.43	(0.00)	1.40	(0.02)	0.99	(0.0)	0.09
	Czech Republic	-0.12	(0.02)	-1.15	(0.02)	-0.39	(0.00)	0.13	(0.01)	0.95	(0.02)	0.88	(0.0)	0.07
	Denmark	0.23	(0.02)	-0.82	(0.01)	-0.03	(0.00)	0.46	(0.00)	1.32	(0.02)	0.89	(0.0)	0.07
	Estonia	0.06	(0.02)	-0.96	(0.02)	-0.19	(0.00)	0.30	(0.00)	1.08	(0.02)	0.84	(0.0)	0.08
	Finland	-0.33	(0.02)	-1.32	(0.02)	-0.55	(0.00)	-0.08	(0.00)	0.62	(0.01)	0.79	(0.0)	0.07
	France	0.13	(0.02)	-0.92	(0.02)	-0.15	(0.00)	0.37	(0.00)	1.22	(0.02)	0.88	(0.0)	0.06
	Germany	-0.15	(0.02)	-1.26	(0.02)	-0.42	(0.00)	0.11	(0.00)	0.95	(0.02)	0.91	(0.0)	0.04
	Greece	0.00	(0.02)	-1.14	(0.03)	-0.24	(0.00)	0.26	(0.00)	1.11	(0.02)	0.93	(0.0)	0.07
	Hungary	0.23	(0.02)	-0.86	(0.02)	-0.02	(0.00)	0.48	(0.00)	1.30	(0.02)	0.89	(0.0)	0.10
	Iceland	-0.41	(0.02)	-1.69	(0.02)	-0.67	(0.00)	-0.08	(0.01)	0.82	(0.02)	1.03	(0.0)	0.09
	Ireland	0.06	(0.02)	-1.20	(0.02)	-0.21	(0.00)	0.35	(0.00)	1.31	(0.02)	1.03	(0.0)	0.04
	Israel	-0.29	(0.03)	-1.68	(0.02)	-0.63	(0.00)	0.01	(0.00)	1.13	(0.03)	1.15	(0.0)	0.15
	Italy	0.06	(0.01)	-1.06	(0.01)	-0.19	(0.00)	0.33	(0.00)	1.17	(0.01)	0.92	(0.0)	0.10
	Japan	-0.13	(0.02)	-1.38	(0.02)	-0.44	(0.01)	0.15	(0.00)	1.15	(0.02)	1.05	(0.0)	0.08
	Korea	-0.43	(0.02)	-1.68	(0.03)	-0.70	(0.00)	-0.15	(0.01)	0.79	(0.02)	1.02	(0.0)	0.05
	Luxembourg	-0.02	(0.02)	-1.17	(0.02)	-0.28	(0.00)	0.24	(0.00)	1.15	(0.02)	0.98	(0.0)	0.01
	Mexico	0.08	(0.01)	-1.09	(0.01)	-0.22	(0.00)	0.33	(0.00)	1.32	(0.01)	0.99	(0.0)	0.07
	Netherlands	-0.38	(0.02)	-1.44	(0.02)	-0.61	(0.01)	-0.11	(0.00)	0.65	(0.02)	0.87	(0.0)	0.05
	New Zealand	0.12	(0.02)	-1.11	(0.02)	-0.18	(0.00)	0.42	(0.00)	1.36	(0.02)	1.02	(0.0)	0.04
	Norway	-0.37	(0.02)	-1.52	(0.02)	-0.64	(0.00)	-0.09	(0.00)	0.76	(0.02)	0.93	(0.0)	0.08
	Poland	0.29	(0.02)	-0.88	(0.02)	0.04	(0.01)	0.56	(0.00)	1.43	(0.02)	0.97	(0.0)	0.06
	Portugal	0.24	(0.02)	-0.83	(0.01)	-0.06	(0.00)	0.46	(0.00)	1.37	(0.02)	0.91	(0.0)	0.03
	Slovak Republic	-0.04	(0.03)	-1.13	(0.03)	-0.32	(0.00)	0.22	(0.00)	1.09	(0.02)	0.93	(0.0)	0.09
	Slovenia	0.22	(0.02)	-0.95	(0.02)	-0.07	(0.01)	0.50	(0.00)	1.38	(0.02)	0.98	(0.0)	0.07
	Spain	-0.11	(0.02)	-1.26	(0.02)	-0.39	(0.00)	0.16	(0.00)	1.05	(0.01)	0.96	(0.0)	0.09
	Sweden	-0.16	(0.02)	-1.26	(0.02)	-0.44	(0.00)	0.12	(0.00)	0.92	(0.01)	0.91	(0.0)	0.07
	Switzerland	-0.14	(0.02)	-1.19	(0.02)	-0.41	(0.00)	0.11	(0.00)	0.93	(0.02)	0.89	(0.0)	0.05
	Turkey	0.60	(0.03)	-0.66	(0.02)	0.24	(0.00)	0.80	(0.00)	2.04	(0.03)	1.11	(0.0)	0.06
	United Kingdom	0.12	(0.02)	-1.01	(0.02)	-0.14	(0.00)	0.38	(0.00)	1.27	(0.02)	0.95	(0.0)	0.07
	United States	0.51	(0.03)	-0.86	(0.02)	0.11	(0.01)	0.72	(0.00)	2.07	(0.03)	1.20	(0.0)	0.07
	OECD average	0.00	(0.00)	-1.16	(0.00)	-0.28	(0.00)	0.26	(0.00)	1.17	(0.00)	0.96	(0.0)	0.07
Partners	Albania	0.59	(0.02)	-0.50	(0.02)	0.29	(0.00)	0.81	(0.01)	1.76	(0.03)	0.93	(0.0)	0.06
	Argentina	0.13	(0.02)	-1.03	(0.03)	-0.20	(0.00)	0.36	(0.00)	1.37	(0.02)	0.98	(0.0)	0.08
	Azerbaijan	0.72	(0.03)	-0.71	(0.03)	0.36	(0.01)	0.92	(0.01)	2.30	(0.04)	1.23	(0.0)	0.10
	Brazil	0.12	(0.01)	-1.02	(0.01)	-0.20	(0.00)	0.37	(0.00)	1.33	(0.02)	0.97	(0.0)	0.04
	Bulgaria	0.32	(0.03)	-1.02	(0.04)	-0.01	(0.01)	0.58	(0.01)	1.72	(0.03)	1.14	(0.0)	0.04
	Colombia	0.27	(0.03)	-0.83	(0.03)	-0.03	(0.01)	0.50	(0.00)	1.45	(0.02)	0.95	(0.0)	0.09
	Croatia	0.29	(0.02)	-0.88	(0.02)	0.01	(0.01)	0.56	(0.00)	1.48	(0.02)	0.98	(0.0)	0.05
	Dubai (UAE)	0.43	(0.01)	-0.91	(0.02)	0.13	(0.01)	0.72	(0.01)	1.79	(0.02)	1.10	(0.0)	0.06
	Hong Kong-China	-0.03	(0.02)	-1.05	(0.02)	-0.33	(0.00)	0.20	(0.00)	1.05	(0.02)	0.89	(0.0)	0.09
	Indonesia	0.42	(0.03)	-0.72	(0.02)	0.03	(0.00)	0.60	(0.01)	1.75	(0.03)	1.02	(0.0)	0.07
	Jordan	0.41	(0.03)	-1.08	(0.03)	0.06	(0.01)	0.71	(0.01)	1.93	(0.03)	1.24	(0.0)	0.08
	Kazakhstan	1.22	(0.03)	-0.10	(0.02)	0.79	(0.00)	1.42	(0.01)	2.78	(0.02)	1.15	(0.0)	0.11
	Kyrgyzstan	0.89	(0.03)	-0.33	(0.02)	0.53	(0.00)	1.07	(0.01)	2.30	(0.03)	1.07	(0.0)	0.09
	Latvia	0.24	(0.03)	-0.76	(0.02)	-0.04	(0.00)	0.43	(0.00)	1.31	(0.02)	0.86	(0.0)	0.10
	Liechtenstein	-0.32	(0.05)	-1.50	(0.06)	-0.61	(0.02)	0.00	(0.01)	0.81	(0.06)	0.95	(0.0)	0.18
	Lithuania	0.31	(0.02)	-0.76	(0.01)	0.01	(0.00)	0.54	(0.00)	1.46	(0.02)	0.92	(0.0)	0.04
	Macao-China	-0.23	(0.01)	-1.20	(0.01)	-0.51	(0.00)	-0.02	(0.00)	0.82	(0.02)	0.85	(0.0)	0.06
	Montenegro	0.59	(0.02)	-0.75	(0.02)	0.26	(0.01)	0.82	(0.00)	2.04	(0.02)	1.14	(0.0)	0.07
	Panama	0.26	(0.03)	-0.95	(0.03)	-0.05	(0.01)	0.48	(0.01)	1.58	(0.04)	1.05	(0.0)	0.04
	Peru	0.50	(0.02)	-0.62	(0.01)	0.17	(0.00)	0.69	(0.00)	1.74	(0.03)	0.97	(0.0)	0.06
	Qatar	0.27	(0.01)	-1.26	(0.02)	-0.08	(0.00)	0.59	(0.00)	1.83	(0.02)	1.28	(0.0)	0.06
	Romania	0.28	(0.02)	-0.78	(0.02)	-0.03	(0.00)	0.50	(0.00)	1.45	(0.03)	0.93	(0.0)	0.05
	Russian Federation	1.14	(0.03)	-0.19	(0.02)	0.69	(0.00)	1.33	(0.01)	2.73	(0.03)	1.16	(0.0)	0.08
	Serbia	0.37	(0.02)	-0.79	(0.02)	0.03	(0.00)	0.59	(0.00)	1.66	(0.03)	1.02	(0.0)	0.05
	Shanghai-China	0.14	(0.02)	-0.92	(0.02)	-0.09	(0.00)	0.38	(0.00)	1.18	(0.02)	0.88	(0.0)	0.04
	Singapore	-0.04	(0.01)	-1.14	(0.01)	-0.34	(0.00)	0.23	(0.00)	1.10	(0.02)	0.94	(0.0)	0.05
	Chinese Taipei	-0.04	(0.02)	-1.18	(0.02)	-0.41	(0.00)	0.21	(0.00)	1.23	(0.02)	1.03	(0.0)	0.03
	Thailand	0.33	(0.02)	-0.79	(0.01)	-0.01	(0.01)	0.55	(0.00)	1.57	(0.03)	0.97	(0.0)	0.07
	Trinidad and Tobago	0.38	(0.02)	-0.99	(0.02)	0.04	(0.00)	0.66	(0.00)	1.82	(0.02)	1.15	(0.0)	0.05
	Tunisia	0.49	(0.03)	-0.76	(0.02)	0.19	(0.00)	0.76	(0.01)	1.76	(0.03)	1.03	(0.0)	0.06
	Uruguay	0.06	(0.02)	-1.10	(0.02)	-0.24	(0.00)	0.32	(0.00)	1.26	(0.02)	0.97	(0.0)	0.04

Note: Values that are statistically significant are indicated in bold (see Annex A3).
StatLink http://dx.doi.org/10.1787/888932343285

[Part 2/2]

Index of teachers' stimulation of students' reading engagement and reading skills and performance, by national quarters of this index

Table IV.4.3 *Results based on students' self-reports*

		Performance on the reading scale by national quarters of this index								Change in the reading score per unit of this index		Increased likelihood of students in the bottom quarter of this index scoring in the bottom quarter of the national reading performance distribution		Explained variance in student performance (r-squared x 100)	
		Bottom quarter		Second quarter		Third quarter		Top quarter							
		Mean score	S.E.	Mean score	S.E.	Mean score	S.E.	Mean score	S.E.	Effect	S.E.	Ratio	S.E.	%	S.E.
OECD	Australia	**490**	(2.6)	518	(3.0)	528	(2.6)	**534**	(3.4)	**14.6**	(1.27)	**1.5**	(0.06)	2.3	(0.36)
	Austria	**468**	(4.5)	476	(4.2)	480	(4.2)	**481**	(4.6)	**4.7**	(1.81)	1.1	(0.09)	0.3	(0.19)
	Belgium	**494**	(3.0)	513	(3.3)	528	(3.0)	**517**	(4.0)	**8.7**	(2.02)	**1.4**	(0.07)	0.6	(0.29)
	Canada	**507**	(2.0)	525	(2.1)	532	(2.0)	**540**	(2.8)	**10.4**	(1.21)	**1.4**	(0.05)	1.5	(0.34)
	Chile	**445**	(3.9)	448	(3.9)	452	(3.4)	**459**	(4.2)	**4.0**	(1.60)	1.1	(0.07)	0.2	(0.19)
	Czech Republic	**475**	(3.9)	479	(3.8)	489	(3.4)	**486**	(3.9)	**5.2**	(2.00)	1.1	(0.08)	0.3	(0.21)
	Denmark	**481**	(3.4)	496	(3.2)	505	(3.2)	**503**	(3.5)	**7.4**	(1.81)	**1.4**	(0.09)	0.6	(0.30)
	Estonia	**502**	(4.1)	499	(3.1)	503	(3.8)	**502**	(3.7)	-0.7	(1.99)	1.0	(0.08)	0.0	(0.05)
	Finland	536	(3.1)	528	(3.2)	539	(3.2)	542	(3.4)	**3.7**	(1.82)	1.0	(0.06)	0.1	(0.12)
	France	**475**	(5.1)	501	(4.4)	511	(4.3)	**508**	(4.9)	**13.5**	(2.86)	**1.5**	(0.11)	1.3	(0.55)
	Germany	**495**	(4.4)	507	(3.6)	513	(3.2)	**507**	(4.3)	4.0	(2.11)	1.1	(0.09)	0.2	(0.17)
	Greece	478	(5.5)	479	(5.5)	489	(5.4)	488	(5.4)	3.3	(2.24)	1.1	(0.11)	0.1	(0.15)
	Hungary	**479**	(4.7)	494	(4.5)	501	(4.2)	**505**	(5.3)	**8.0**	(3.10)	**1.4**	(0.12)	0.6	(0.47)
	Iceland	502	(3.5)	491	(3.5)	510	(3.0)	507	(3.0)	**4.6**	(1.72)	1.0	(0.08)	0.3	(0.19)
	Ireland	487	(4.5)	501	(4.2)	508	(4.0)	497	(4.5)	3.2	(2.27)	**1.2**	(0.09)	0.1	(0.19)
	Israel	**503**	(4.1)	482	(4.7)	473	(4.8)	**461**	(4.5)	**-13.7**	(1.64)	**0.6**	(0.05)	2.2	(0.52)
	Italy	**480**	(2.1)	485	(2.4)	491	(2.3)	**491**	(2.4)	**3.4**	(1.20)	**1.1**	(0.04)	0.1	(0.07)
	Japan	**503**	(4.9)	518	(5.0)	533	(3.4)	**529**	(3.7)	**11.6**	(2.16)	**1.4**	(0.08)	1.5	(0.53)
	Korea	**531**	(5.0)	536	(4.2)	549	(3.9)	**542**	(4.5)	**4.9**	(1.89)	**1.2**	(0.08)	0.4	(0.29)
	Luxembourg	**462**	(3.1)	478	(3.2)	482	(3.1)	**483**	(2.9)	**5.6**	(1.86)	**1.2**	(0.07)	0.3	(0.19)
	Mexico	**418**	(2.8)	422	(2.3)	431	(2.3)	**433**	(2.5)	**4.7**	(0.98)	**1.2**	(0.04)	0.3	(0.13)
	Netherlands	509	(6.0)	512	(5.1)	516	(5.9)	510	(7.1)	0.6	(2.29)	1.0	(0.07)	0.0	(0.05)
	New Zealand	**501**	(3.9)	525	(3.2)	533	(3.7)	**533**	(3.4)	**10.4**	(1.66)	**1.4**	(0.08)	1.1	(0.36)
	Norway	**496**	(3.3)	495	(3.5)	512	(3.1)	**514**	(3.8)	**9.4**	(1.71)	1.1	(0.07)	0.9	(0.33)
	Poland	**486**	(4.2)	498	(3.0)	504	(3.4)	**518**	(4.3)	**11.7**	(1.85)	**1.4**	(0.09)	1.6	(0.51)
	Portugal	**475**	(3.7)	496	(4.2)	496	(3.6)	**492**	(4.1)	**5.5**	(1.52)	**1.4**	(0.09)	0.3	(0.18)
	Slovak Republic	475	(4.1)	476	(3.6)	482	(3.8)	481	(4.0)	2.4	(2.28)	**1.2**	(0.09)	0.1	(0.14)
	Slovenia	**467**	(3.2)	486	(2.8)	495	(3.0)	**497**	(2.8)	**10.7**	(1.65)	**1.6**	(0.08)	1.4	(0.44)
	Spain	**476**	(3.0)	482	(2.6)	487	(2.8)	**484**	(2.6)	**3.3**	(1.69)	1.1	(0.06)	0.1	(0.13)
	Sweden	**487**	(3.6)	495	(3.5)	508	(4.0)	**510**	(4.4)	**10.0**	(2.01)	**1.2**	(0.08)	0.9	(0.36)
	Switzerland	**494**	(3.3)	501	(3.3)	504	(3.1)	**506**	(4.1)	**5.1**	(1.93)	1.0	(0.07)	0.2	(0.18)
	Turkey	**448**	(4.4)	464	(4.5)	470	(4.1)	**475**	(3.9)	**7.5**	(1.43)	**1.4**	(0.08)	1.0	(0.39)
	United Kingdom	**469**	(3.3)	501	(3.6)	510	(3.1)	**504**	(3.6)	**12.6**	(1.81)	**1.6**	(0.09)	1.6	(0.47)
	United States	**476**	(5.0)	500	(4.3)	510	(5.1)	**520**	(5.1)	**11.0**	(1.67)	**1.6**	(0.09)	1.9	(0.59)
	OECD average	**484**	(0.7)	494	(0.6)	502	(0.6)	**502**	(0.7)	**6.2**	(0.33)	**1.2**	(0.01)	0.7	(0.06)
Partners	Albania	**365**	(4.8)	393	(4.6)	400	(5.4)	**394**	(5.3)	**10.0**	(2.00)	**1.4**	(0.11)	0.9	(0.37)
	Argentina	404	(5.6)	412	(5.5)	402	(5.4)	400	(6.2)	-4.0	(2.29)	1.0	(0.07)	0.1	(0.16)
	Azerbaijan	**348**	(4.6)	371	(4.8)	374	(4.3)	**368**	(3.1)	**5.7**	(1.33)	**1.5**	(0.14)	0.9	(0.43)
	Brazil	**404**	(3.0)	414	(3.0)	420	(3.9)	**416**	(3.7)	**3.1**	(1.44)	**1.1**	(0.06)	0.1	(0.10)
	Bulgaria	**411**	(7.6)	436	(7.2)	445	(7.2)	**438**	(9.0)	**6.7**	(2.55)	**1.3**	(0.11)	0.5	(0.34)
	Colombia	**404**	(4.2)	417	(4.4)	424	(4.4)	**419**	(5.4)	**4.6**	(2.23)	**1.2**	(0.08)	0.3	(0.27)
	Croatia	**461**	(4.4)	477	(3.8)	482	(3.7)	**486**	(3.8)	**8.8**	(1.78)	**1.4**	(0.09)	1.0	(0.39)
	Dubai (UAE)	**449**	(2.9)	457	(3.2)	473	(2.8)	**466**	(2.8)	**5.7**	(1.40)	1.2	(0.09)	0.4	(0.18)
	Hong Kong-China	**514**	(3.3)	533	(3.6)	550	(3.1)	**537**	(3.7)	**9.0**	(2.11)	**1.5**	(0.11)	0.9	(0.43)
	Indonesia	404	(4.6)	407	(4.1)	406	(4.4)	394	(4.0)	**-4.9**	(1.44)	1.0	(0.07)	0.6	(0.31)
	Jordan	**384**	(4.0)	403	(3.7)	425	(4.1)	**421**	(3.8)	**11.2**	(1.33)	**1.6**	(0.11)	2.5	(0.56)
	Kazakhstan	383	(4.5)	392	(3.9)	398	(4.2)	390	(4.3)	1.7	(1.69)	**1.2**	(0.08)	0.0	(0.09)
	Kyrgyzstan	316	(4.3)	323	(4.1)	327	(4.6)	310	(5.2)	-2.7	(1.89)	**1.2**	(0.11)	0.1	(0.14)
	Latvia	**471**	(4.7)	485	(3.7)	490	(3.6)	**490**	(4.5)	**5.7**	(2.15)	**1.3**	(0.10)	0.4	(0.28)
	Liechtenstein	**479**	(10.2)	494	(10.0)	512	(9.0)	**517**	(8.9)	**17.0**	(5.20)	1.4	(0.36)	3.8	(2.32)
	Lithuania	**458**	(3.7)	469	(3.5)	478	(3.6)	**472**	(4.0)	**4.1**	(1.88)	**1.3**	(0.10)	0.2	(0.19)
	Macao-China	**486**	(2.0)	481	(2.7)	489	(2.2)	**492**	(2.0)	**2.8**	(1.25)	1.1	(0.06)	0.1	(0.09)
	Montenegro	**391**	(2.6)	414	(2.9)	416	(3.9)	**419**	(3.9)	**8.3**	(1.90)	**1.4**	(0.10)	1.1	(0.49)
	Panama	376	(7.6)	376	(9.8)	381	(7.5)	371	(6.5)	-3.2	(2.63)	1.0	(0.14)	0.1	(0.20)
	Peru	**364**	(5.5)	372	(4.9)	378	(4.3)	**377**	(4.7)	3.4	(1.97)	**1.2**	(0.09)	0.1	(0.13)
	Qatar	**360**	(2.8)	367	(2.4)	387	(2.1)	**386**	(2.2)	**7.2**	(1.02)	**1.2**	(0.07)	0.6	(0.18)
	Romania	**398**	(5.3)	425	(5.2)	440	(4.7)	**439**	(5.2)	**13.1**	(2.27)	**1.7**	(0.13)	1.9	(0.61)
	Russian Federation	**442**	(4.3)	457	(4.0)	472	(4.7)	**470**	(4.1)	**9.0**	(1.47)	**1.5**	(0.10)	1.4	(0.42)
	Serbia	**432**	(3.4)	440	(3.3)	445	(3.2)	**457**	(3.3)	**7.3**	(1.48)	**1.2**	(0.09)	0.8	(0.34)
	Shanghai-China	**540**	(3.2)	553	(3.6)	565	(3.6)	**566**	(3.4)	**10.7**	(1.69)	**1.3**	(0.10)	1.4	(0.44)
	Singapore	**517**	(2.9)	528	(3.0)	533	(2.8)	**528**	(2.7)	2.1	(1.57)	**1.2**	(0.08)	0.0	(0.07)
	Chinese Taipei	**484**	(3.4)	491	(3.1)	509	(3.6)	**499**	(3.5)	**4.2**	(1.48)	**1.3**	(0.08)	0.3	(0.18)
	Thailand	**405**	(3.2)	420	(3.3)	430	(3.1)	**431**	(3.3)	**8.0**	(1.47)	**1.5**	(0.10)	1.2	(0.42)
	Trinidad and Tobago	**409**	(3.8)	421	(3.9)	425	(3.8)	**434**	(3.7)	**8.0**	(1.75)	**1.2**	(0.10)	0.7	(0.30)
	Tunisia	**404**	(3.4)	403	(4.1)	407	(4.2)	**406**	(3.8)	0.0	(1.74)	1.0	(0.06)	0.0	(0.04)
	Uruguay	**414**	(3.9)	431	(3.7)	442	(3.7)	**430**	(4.0)	**5.6**	(2.18)	**1.3**	(0.09)	0.3	(0.25)

Note: Values that are statistically significant are indicated in bold (see Annex A3).
StatLink http://dx.doi.org/10.1787/888932343285

[Part 1/2]

Index of student-related factors affecting school climate and reading performance, by national quarters of this index

Table IV.4.4 *Results based on school principals' reports*

		Index of student-related factors affecting school climate										Variability in this index	
		All students		Bottom quarter		Second quarter		Third quarter		Top quarter			
		Mean index	S.E.	Mean index	S.E.	Mean index	S.E.	Mean index	S.E.	Mean index	S.E.	Standard deviation	S.E.
OECD	Australia	0.01	(0.04)	-1.20	(0.04)	-0.29	(0.02)	0.28	(0.02)	1.24	(0.07)	0.96	(0.0)
	Austria	-0.22	(0.07)	-1.39	(0.05)	-0.48	(0.03)	0.12	(0.02)	0.89	(0.07)	0.91	(0.0)
	Belgium	0.27	(0.05)	-0.97	(0.04)	-0.04	(0.02)	0.56	(0.02)	1.52	(0.06)	0.98	(0.0)
	Canada	-0.41	(0.03)	-1.37	(0.04)	-0.70	(0.01)	-0.25	(0.01)	0.67	(0.06)	0.85	(0.0)
	Chile	-0.10	(0.08)	-1.52	(0.09)	-0.44	(0.02)	0.21	(0.04)	1.34	(0.09)	1.12	(0.1)
	Czech Republic	-0.18	(0.06)	-1.15	(0.05)	-0.47	(0.02)	0.05	(0.02)	0.84	(0.06)	0.80	(0.0)
	Denmark	0.27	(0.05)	-0.71	(0.04)	-0.03	(0.02)	0.48	(0.02)	1.34	(0.07)	0.81	(0.0)
	Estonia	-0.10	(0.05)	-1.02	(0.06)	-0.38	(0.02)	0.13	(0.02)	0.88	(0.04)	0.78	(0.0)
	Finland	-0.43	(0.06)	-1.33	(0.05)	-0.66	(0.02)	-0.16	(0.02)	0.45	(0.05)	0.71	(0.0)
	France	w	w	w	w	w	w	w	w	w	w	w	w
	Germany	0.11	(0.05)	-1.00	(0.07)	-0.08	(0.02)	0.35	(0.01)	1.16	(0.07)	0.86	(0.0)
	Greece	0.02	(0.08)	-1.32	(0.12)	-0.14	(0.03)	0.38	(0.01)	1.15	(0.08)	1.00	(0.1)
	Hungary	0.18	(0.07)	-1.14	(0.08)	-0.18	(0.03)	0.49	(0.03)	1.53	(0.07)	1.04	(0.1)
	Iceland	0.13	(0.00)	-0.87	(0.01)	-0.14	(0.00)	0.39	(0.00)	1.12	(0.00)	0.79	(0.0)
	Ireland	-0.25	(0.08)	-1.30	(0.09)	-0.51	(0.02)	-0.04	(0.02)	0.84	(0.08)	0.85	(0.1)
	Israel	0.05	(0.06)	-1.04	(0.06)	-0.21	(0.02)	0.33	(0.02)	1.13	(0.06)	0.86	(0.0)
	Italy	-0.02	(0.03)	-1.17	(0.03)	-0.36	(0.01)	0.31	(0.01)	1.14	(0.04)	0.92	(0.0)
	Japan	0.60	(0.06)	-0.56	(0.07)	0.31	(0.03)	0.88	(0.02)	1.75	(0.06)	0.91	(0.0)
	Korea	0.40	(0.07)	-0.72	(0.08)	0.07	(0.03)	0.67	(0.02)	1.57	(0.08)	0.92	(0.1)
	Luxembourg	-0.13	(0.00)	-1.02	(0.00)	-0.45	(0.00)	0.07	(0.00)	0.89	(0.00)	0.76	(0.0)
	Mexico	0.23	(0.03)	-0.94	(0.03)	-0.10	(0.01)	0.50	(0.01)	1.45	(0.03)	0.94	(0.0)
	Netherlands	-0.17	(0.05)	-1.08	(0.06)	-0.39	(0.02)	0.02	(0.01)	0.75	(0.09)	0.75	(0.1)
	New Zealand	-0.16	(0.04)	-1.21	(0.04)	-0.39	(0.02)	0.02	(0.01)	0.96	(0.06)	0.88	(0.0)
	Norway	-0.08	(0.05)	-0.86	(0.04)	-0.35	(0.02)	0.09	(0.01)	0.78	(0.07)	0.67	(0.0)
	Poland	0.05	(0.06)	-0.90	(0.05)	-0.20	(0.02)	0.26	(0.02)	1.04	(0.07)	0.77	(0.0)
	Portugal	0.04	(0.08)	-1.14	(0.04)	-0.32	(0.02)	0.29	(0.02)	1.32	(0.13)	0.98	(0.1)
	Slovak Republic	-0.25	(0.05)	-1.14	(0.05)	-0.45	(0.02)	-0.06	(0.02)	0.66	(0.08)	0.72	(0.0)
	Slovenia	-0.39	(0.01)	-1.51	(0.00)	-0.78	(0.00)	-0.17	(0.01)	0.88	(0.01)	0.97	(0.0)
	Spain	0.12	(0.05)	-1.09	(0.05)	-0.23	(0.02)	0.40	(0.02)	1.39	(0.05)	0.98	(0.0)
	Sweden	-0.12	(0.05)	-0.99	(0.04)	-0.37	(0.02)	0.06	(0.01)	0.83	(0.07)	0.74	(0.0)
	Switzerland	0.13	(0.06)	-0.87	(0.03)	-0.11	(0.02)	0.31	(0.01)	1.19	(0.07)	0.82	(0.0)
	Turkey	-1.66	(0.12)	-3.15	(0.05)	-2.41	(0.03)	-1.55	(0.05)	0.47	(0.13)	1.44	(0.1)
	United Kingdom	0.19	(0.04)	-0.61	(0.04)	0.00	(0.01)	0.25	(0.01)	1.11	(0.06)	0.70	(0.0)
	United States	-0.16	(0.06)	-1.10	(0.05)	-0.39	(0.02)	0.01	(0.01)	0.85	(0.10)	0.79	(0.1)
	OECD average	-0.06	(0.01)	-1.13	(0.01)	-0.35	(0.00)	0.17	(0.00)	1.07	(0.01)	0.88	(0.0)
Partners	Albania	0.84	(0.07)	-0.24	(0.07)	0.53	(0.02)	1.07	(0.02)	1.98	(0.05)	0.87	(0.0)
	Argentina	0.44	(0.08)	-0.98	(0.05)	0.02	(0.04)	0.90	(0.03)	1.82	(0.08)	1.10	(0.0)
	Azerbaijan	0.83	(0.09)	-0.62	(0.11)	0.66	(0.03)	1.28	(0.02)	2.00	(0.06)	1.04	(0.1)
	Brazil	-0.33	(0.06)	-1.57	(0.07)	-0.66	(0.02)	-0.02	(0.02)	0.94	(0.06)	1.01	(0.0)
	Bulgaria	-0.11	(0.15)	-1.82	(0.15)	-0.41	(0.06)	0.44	(0.03)	1.35	(0.10)	1.26	(0.1)
	Colombia	-0.04	(0.09)	-1.39	(0.06)	-0.40	(0.03)	0.35	(0.03)	1.26	(0.07)	1.03	(0.1)
	Croatia	-0.51	(0.07)	-1.61	(0.04)	-0.90	(0.02)	-0.27	(0.03)	0.73	(0.05)	0.91	(0.0)
	Dubai (UAE)	0.87	(0.00)	-0.74	(0.00)	0.69	(0.00)	1.33	(0.00)	2.18	(0.00)	1.21	(0.0)
	Hong Kong-China	0.48	(0.07)	-0.66	(0.10)	0.29	(0.02)	0.67	(0.02)	1.64	(0.07)	0.93	(0.1)
	Indonesia	0.62	(0.07)	-0.38	(0.07)	0.44	(0.02)	0.82	(0.02)	1.61	(0.08)	0.80	(0.1)
	Jordan	-0.04	(0.09)	-1.61	(0.12)	-0.30	(0.03)	0.38	(0.03)	1.36	(0.05)	1.18	(0.1)
	Kazakhstan	-0.51	(0.12)	-2.62	(0.09)	-1.22	(0.06)	0.30	(0.05)	1.52	(0.08)	1.63	(0.1)
	Kyrgyzstan	-0.31	(0.11)	-2.26	(0.08)	-0.67	(0.07)	0.28	(0.05)	1.42	(0.09)	1.43	(0.1)
	Latvia	0.03	(0.07)	-0.95	(0.08)	-0.19	(0.02)	0.23	(0.02)	1.03	(0.08)	0.81	(0.1)
	Liechtenstein	0.20	(0.01)	-0.89	(0.00)	-0.25	(0.00)	0.66	(0.02)	1.28	(0.00)	0.87	(0.0)
	Lithuania	0.20	(0.05)	-0.64	(0.07)	0.00	(0.01)	0.37	(0.01)	1.06	(0.06)	0.72	(0.1)
	Macao-China	0.16	(0.00)	-2.49	(0.00)	-0.12	(0.00)	1.22	(0.00)	2.02	(0.00)	1.78	(0.0)
	Montenegro	0.08	(0.01)	-0.87	(0.02)	-0.25	(0.01)	0.33	(0.00)	1.10	(0.01)	0.82	(0.0)
	Panama	0.21	(0.08)	-0.96	(0.04)	-0.01	(0.03)	0.49	(0.04)	1.33	(0.06)	0.89	(0.0)
	Peru	0.35	(0.07)	-0.97	(0.09)	0.08	(0.03)	0.79	(0.02)	1.49	(0.05)	1.00	(0.1)
	Qatar	0.36	(0.00)	-1.35	(0.01)	0.26	(0.00)	0.84	(0.00)	1.68	(0.00)	1.22	(0.0)
	Romania	0.21	(0.07)	-0.91	(0.07)	-0.08	(0.02)	0.48	(0.03)	1.35	(0.09)	0.90	(0.1)
	Russian Federation	-0.19	(0.08)	-1.81	(0.11)	-0.34	(0.03)	0.23	(0.02)	1.17	(0.06)	1.18	(0.1)
	Serbia	-0.32	(0.05)	-1.31	(0.06)	-0.62	(0.02)	-0.07	(0.03)	0.72	(0.07)	0.82	(0.0)
	Shanghai-China	0.11	(0.13)	-2.36	(0.09)	-0.28	(0.10)	0.99	(0.05)	2.08	(0.06)	1.72	(0.1)
	Singapore	0.36	(0.01)	-0.65	(0.01)	0.10	(0.00)	0.41	(0.00)	1.61	(0.00)	0.89	(0.0)
	Chinese Taipei	-0.14	(0.14)	-2.51	(0.07)	-0.68	(0.09)	0.64	(0.04)	1.97	(0.06)	1.72	(0.1)
	Thailand	-0.03	(0.06)	-0.99	(0.05)	-0.20	(0.02)	0.17	(0.02)	0.92	(0.06)	0.76	(0.0)
	Trinidad and Tobago	-0.52	(0.00)	-1.58	(0.01)	-0.90	(0.00)	-0.27	(0.00)	0.68	(0.01)	0.92	(0.0)
	Tunisia	-0.05	(0.07)	-1.07	(0.06)	-0.23	(0.02)	0.19	(0.02)	0.92	(0.07)	0.80	(0.1)
	Uruguay	0.40	(0.06)	-0.96	(0.05)	0.00	(0.02)	0.71	(0.03)	1.86	(0.06)	1.09	(0.0)

Note: Values that are statistically significant are indicated in bold (see Annex A3).

StatLink http://dx.doi.org/10.1787/888932343285

[Part 2/2]

Table IV.4.4 Index of student-related factors affecting school climate and reading performance, by national quarters of this index

Results based on school principals' reports

		Performance on the reading scale by national quarters of this index								Change in the reading score per unit of this index		Increased likelihood of students in the bottom quarter of this index scoring in the bottom quarter of the national reading performance distribution		Explained variance in student performance (r-squared x 100)	
		Bottom quarter		Second quarter		Third quarter		Top quarter							
		Mean score	S.E.	Mean score	S.E.	Mean score	S.E.	Mean score	S.E.	Effect	S.E.	Ratio	S.E.	%	S.E.
OECD	Australia	**475**	(4.0)	506	(5.7)	535	(5.2)	**544**	(4.0)	**29.6**	(2.32)	**2.0**	(0.15)	8.2	(1.21)
	Austria	**446**	(10.7)	464	(8.6)	483	(8.5)	**488**	(9.0)	**23.2**	(6.01)	**1.6**	(0.26)	4.5	(2.36)
	Belgium	**440**	(7.3)	506	(7.5)	525	(6.7)	**558**	(5.8)	**44.5**	(3.24)	**3.0**	(0.32)	18.6	(2.57)
	Canada	**514**	(3.7)	522	(3.3)	521	(2.8)	**539**	(3.4)	**14.0**	(2.16)	**1.2**	(0.07)	1.7	(0.57)
	Chile	**414**	(7.0)	437	(7.6)	461	(6.1)	**486**	(6.0)	**25.1**	(3.02)	**2.0**	(0.26)	11.7	(2.77)
	Czech Republic	**442**	(7.3)	461	(8.5)	489	(7.4)	**518**	(6.2)	**39.5**	(4.53)	**1.8**	(0.23)	11.8	(2.76)
	Denmark	**478**	(3.9)	483	(3.8)	500	(3.8)	**519**	(4.2)	**18.8**	(2.54)	**1.4**	(0.11)	3.4	(0.85)
	Estonia	**483**	(5.6)	499	(4.8)	507	(4.7)	**515**	(6.4)	**18.3**	(3.66)	**1.5**	(0.18)	2.9	(1.22)
	Finland	531	(4.0)	539	(3.7)	533	(4.9)	541	(4.5)	5.2	(2.93)	1.1	(0.09)	0.2	(0.20)
	France	w	w	w	w	w	w	w	w	w	w	w	w	w	w
	Germany	**447**	(8.8)	487	(8.2)	510	(7.9)	**546**	(5.5)	**44.8**	(4.34)	**2.5**	(0.36)	17.0	(3.09)
	Greece	**458**	(13.3)	476	(9.1)	491	(7.9)	**506**	(4.7)	**14.1**	(5.86)	**1.6**	(0.30)	2.2	(1.69)
	Hungary	**440**	(8.2)	492	(7.6)	517	(9.9)	**528**	(8.6)	**33.0**	(3.73)	**2.7**	(0.38)	14.4	(3.36)
	Iceland	**492**	(3.3)	504	(4.0)	488	(3.7)	**510**	(3.2)	**9.7**	(1.95)	**1.2**	(0.08)	0.7	(0.26)
	Ireland	**476**	(8.3)	475	(7.0)	499	(8.8)	**525**	(5.8)	**23.6**	(4.22)	**1.5**	(0.21)	4.3	(1.59)
	Israel	**452**	(12.0)	478	(8.3)	485	(8.0)	**481**	(12.1)	**18.4**	(7.89)	1.4	(0.24)	2.0	(1.72)
	Italy	**438**	(5.4)	479	(4.4)	498	(4.7)	**529**	(3.6)	**37.3**	(2.51)	**2.3**	(0.19)	12.7	(1.58)
	Japan	**458**	(7.9)	523	(8.8)	538	(6.8)	**561**	(6.9)	**40.0**	(3.90)	**2.7**	(0.28)	13.2	(2.23)
	Korea	**518**	(6.9)	521	(8.1)	554	(5.1)	**563**	(5.4)	**19.5**	(4.96)	**1.7**	(0.24)	5.1	(2.39)
	Luxembourg	**424**	(3.1)	490	(2.5)	487	(2.8)	**488**	(2.1)	**31.7**	(1.40)	**2.1**	(0.12)	5.4	(0.45)
	Mexico	**406**	(4.7)	427	(3.6)	435	(3.9)	**433**	(4.2)	**11.7**	(2.27)	**1.5**	(0.11)	1.7	(0.65)
	Netherlands	**456**	(8.4)	508	(10.4)	520	(8.8)	**548**	(9.9)	**44.5**	(6.48)	**2.6**	(0.35)	14.1	(4.00)
	New Zealand	**493**	(6.1)	503	(5.6)	534	(4.4)	**556**	(3.8)	**24.4**	(2.25)	**1.6**	(0.15)	4.5	(0.71)
	Norway	**493**	(4.6)	500	(4.1)	505	(4.4)	**514**	(6.4)	**10.5**	(4.25)	1.2	(0.10)	0.6	(0.48)
	Poland	**493**	(4.4)	503	(4.5)	501	(5.6)	**505**	(5.0)	**7.6**	(3.07)	1.1	(0.10)	0.4	(0.35)
	Portugal	483	(5.9)	485	(5.5)	492	(7.9)	497	(8.2)	**7.0**	(3.53)	1.1	(0.15)	0.6	(0.66)
	Slovak Republic	**460**	(7.7)	483	(6.2)	476	(8.0)	**491**	(7.9)	**15.7**	(6.33)	1.3	(0.19)	1.6	(1.26)
	Slovenia	**453**	(1.8)	458	(2.7)	504	(2.7)	**517**	(3.2)	**29.1**	(1.01)	**1.5**	(0.08)	9.6	(0.66)
	Spain	**464**	(3.3)	469	(3.7)	488	(3.6)	**504**	(5.0)	**15.3**	(2.18)	**1.4**	(0.11)	2.9	(0.80)
	Sweden	**481**	(6.8)	488	(5.5)	506	(6.0)	**517**	(4.8)	**18.1**	(4.67)	**1.3**	(0.14)	1.9	(0.85)
	Switzerland	**478**	(6.4)	501	(7.7)	508	(8.1)	**514**	(7.3)	**19.4**	(4.26)	**1.4**	(0.14)	2.9	(1.28)
	Turkey	476	(8.9)	464	(7.2)	449	(7.8)	467	(8.2)	-0.1	(3.44)	0.8	(0.16)	0.0	(0.26)
	United Kingdom	**477**	(5.1)	491	(4.8)	496	(6.8)	**518**	(6.1)	**24.8**	(4.28)	**1.4**	(0.12)	3.3	(1.09)
	United States	**479**	(6.8)	481	(5.8)	512	(6.1)	**528**	(8.4)	**25.3**	(4.43)	**1.4**	(0.16)	4.3	(1.38)
	OECD average	**467**	(1.2)	488	(1.1)	501	(1.1)	**517**	(1.1)	**22.5**	(0.71)	**1.7**	(0.04)	5.7	(0.30)
Partners	Albania	380	(5.9)	385	(7.5)	382	(8.6)	392	(10.8)	2.7	(5.75)	1.1	(0.11)	0.1	(0.33)
	Argentina	**356**	(11.3)	386	(8.3)	412	(8.1)	**443**	(13.4)	**30.9**	(5.92)	**1.7**	(0.29)	9.9	(3.65)
	Azerbaijan	364	(7.7)	351	(7.4)	363	(8.0)	368	(6.5)	2.2	(3.59)	0.9	(0.16)	0.1	(0.28)
	Brazil	**399**	(4.4)	392	(3.9)	400	(4.8)	**458**	(7.0)	**24.3**	(3.03)	1.1	(0.09)	6.9	(1.79)
	Bulgaria	**395**	(13.5)	404	(11.4)	447	(14.0)	**473**	(11.5)	**22.7**	(5.87)	1.5	(0.28)	6.4	(3.21)
	Colombia	**400**	(6.2)	408	(6.7)	418	(10.5)	**427**	(8.7)	**11.9**	(3.35)	1.3	(0.18)	2.0	(1.18)
	Croatia	**442**	(7.3)	460	(6.6)	485	(7.9)	**517**	(6.6)	**31.2**	(3.88)	**1.8**	(0.25)	10.5	(2.47)
	Dubai (UAE)	**413**	(2.2)	461	(3.4)	479	(2.5)	**485**	(2.8)	**22.0**	(0.95)	**1.9**	(0.11)	6.2	(0.53)
	Hong Kong-China	**493**	(7.5)	533	(5.7)	544	(6.7)	**561**	(6.3)	**23.3**	(4.29)	**2.2**	(0.31)	6.7	(2.40)
	Indonesia	**392**	(6.8)	394	(7.9)	395	(5.1)	**426**	(7.4)	**17.3**	(5.24)	1.3	(0.23)	4.3	(2.77)
	Jordan	**394**	(6.4)	400	(6.5)	405	(8.2)	**421**	(8.2)	6.7	(3.80)	1.2	(0.15)	0.8	(0.83)
	Kazakhstan	**370**	(7.3)	392	(8.7)	399	(7.7)	**400**	(8.5)	**6.0**	(2.62)	**1.4**	(0.18)	1.1	(0.98)
	Kyrgyzstan	**287**	(7.0)	314	(9.4)	326	(8.7)	**329**	(10.5)	**11.2**	(3.38)	**1.4**	(0.17)	2.6	(1.47)
	Latvia	**477**	(5.3)	480	(5.8)	480	(5.0)	**499**	(7.5)	**10.7**	(4.53)	1.2	(0.14)	1.2	(0.99)
	Liechtenstein	**486**	(5.7)	456	(7.6)	487	(7.5)	**568**	(5.9)	**41.3**	(3.57)	1.0	(0.24)	18.7	(3.09)
	Lithuania	**447**	(6.4)	462	(6.0)	473	(6.1)	**491**	(6.9)	**21.8**	(6.46)	**1.4**	(0.18)	3.3	(1.71)
	Macao-China	**476**	(1.4)	464	(1.8)	489	(1.9)	**517**	(1.5)	**8.9**	(0.36)	**1.1**	(0.05)	4.4	(0.34)
	Montenegro	404	(4.5)	421	(3.4)	407	(2.5)	403	(2.6)	**-8.2**	(1.81)	1.1	(0.09)	0.5	(0.24)
	Panama	**337**	(8.3)	365	(10.2)	361	(16.3)	**418**	(16.1)	**33.9**	(7.94)	1.3	(0.31)	9.0	(4.55)
	Peru	**346**	(6.1)	360	(7.0)	377	(8.2)	**392**	(11.6)	**19.4**	(5.01)	**1.4**	(0.17)	3.9	(1.87)
	Qatar	**344**	(1.7)	385	(2.2)	367	(2.2)	**390**	(2.5)	**11.5**	(0.64)	**1.3**	(0.04)	1.5	(0.16)
	Romania	**406**	(9.6)	415	(9.4)	422	(9.7)	**455**	(10.8)	**19.4**	(6.32)	1.3	(0.27)	3.7	(2.33)
	Russian Federation	**457**	(8.4)	445	(5.0)	453	(6.5)	**483**	(7.1)	**8.9**	(3.77)	1.0	(0.17)	1.4	(1.23)
	Serbia	**428**	(7.1)	432	(4.5)	442	(8.2)	**465**	(6.7)	**15.9**	(4.96)	**1.3**	(0.15)	2.4	(1.41)
	Shanghai-China	**542**	(6.7)	530	(7.0)	568	(7.1)	**583**	(6.9)	**8.7**	(2.26)	**1.4**	(0.18)	3.5	(1.77)
	Singapore	**492**	(2.6)	514	(2.5)	530	(2.7)	**568**	(3.1)	**32.9**	(1.48)	**1.6**	(0.09)	8.9	(0.74)
	Chinese Taipei	**482**	(5.8)	484	(7.3)	500	(8.0)	**513**	(7.9)	**7.9**	(2.27)	1.3	(0.17)	2.5	(1.41)
	Thailand	**410**	(6.6)	422	(5.0)	425	(5.5)	**429**	(7.2)	**13.0**	(5.44)	1.2	(0.16)	1.9	(1.53)
	Trinidad and Tobago	**375**	(2.6)	394	(2.9)	426	(2.5)	**489**	(2.6)	**51.4**	(1.26)	**1.9**	(0.10)	17.9	(0.76)
	Tunisia	**387**	(8.0)	407	(6.6)	409	(6.8)	**411**	(10.9)	10.6	(7.41)	1.4	(0.24)	1.0	(1.29)
	Uruguay	**402**	(5.3)	416	(5.5)	436	(8.0)	**449**	(7.9)	**19.4**	(2.79)	**1.4**	(0.14)	4.5	(1.36)

Note: Values that are statistically significant are indicated in bold (see Annex A3).

StatLink http://dx.doi.org/10.1787/888932343285

[Part 1/2]
Index of teacher-related factors affecting school climate and reading performance, by national quarters of this index
Table IV.4.5 *Results based on school principals' reports*

		Index of teacher-related factors affecting school climate										Variability in this index	
		All students		Bottom quarter		Second quarter		Third quarter		Top quarter			
		Mean index	S.E.	Mean index	S.E.	Mean index	S.E.	Mean index	S.E.	Mean index	S.E.	Standard deviation	S.E.
OECD	Australia	-0.23	(0.04)	-1.32	(0.04)	-0.55	(0.02)	-0.03	(0.02)	1.00	(0.06)	0.91	(0.04)
	Austria	0.08	(0.06)	-0.85	(0.07)	-0.24	(0.01)	0.22	(0.02)	1.19	(0.08)	0.84	(0.05)
	Belgium	0.09	(0.04)	-0.98	(0.04)	-0.18	(0.02)	0.35	(0.02)	1.19	(0.05)	0.86	(0.04)
	Canada	-0.08	(0.03)	-1.04	(0.05)	-0.35	(0.01)	0.10	(0.01)	0.97	(0.05)	0.82	(0.03)
	Chile	-0.48	(0.08)	-1.65	(0.08)	-0.86	(0.02)	-0.27	(0.03)	0.86	(0.09)	1.00	(0.06)
	Czech Republic	0.02	(0.06)	-0.83	(0.03)	-0.26	(0.01)	0.19	(0.02)	0.98	(0.07)	0.72	(0.04)
	Denmark	0.43	(0.06)	-0.54	(0.04)	0.07	(0.02)	0.71	(0.03)	1.50	(0.05)	0.82	(0.03)
	Estonia	0.09	(0.06)	-0.93	(0.05)	-0.23	(0.02)	0.35	(0.02)	1.17	(0.05)	0.83	(0.04)
	Finland	-0.06	(0.06)	-0.92	(0.05)	-0.27	(0.02)	0.19	(0.01)	0.78	(0.06)	0.69	(0.05)
	France	w	w	w	w	w	w	w	w	w	w	w	w
	Germany	-0.04	(0.05)	-0.92	(0.05)	-0.28	(0.01)	0.12	(0.02)	0.92	(0.08)	0.75	(0.05)
	Greece	-0.08	(0.09)	-1.43	(0.10)	-0.36	(0.02)	0.28	(0.02)	1.17	(0.08)	1.05	(0.06)
	Hungary	0.51	(0.07)	-0.55	(0.06)	0.21	(0.01)	0.75	(0.03)	1.64	(0.07)	0.86	(0.05)
	Iceland	0.29	(0.00)	-0.80	(0.00)	0.06	(0.00)	0.55	(0.00)	1.34	(0.01)	0.85	(0.00)
	Ireland	0.10	(0.08)	-0.95	(0.08)	-0.19	(0.02)	0.27	(0.02)	1.26	(0.09)	0.87	(0.06)
	Israel	-0.21	(0.06)	-1.22	(0.07)	-0.44	(0.02)	-0.06	(0.02)	0.89	(0.07)	0.86	(0.05)
	Italy	-0.30	(0.03)	-1.29	(0.03)	-0.62	(0.01)	-0.11	(0.01)	0.81	(0.04)	0.84	(0.03)
	Japan	-0.20	(0.06)	-1.21	(0.05)	-0.50	(0.02)	-0.07	(0.02)	0.97	(0.08)	0.87	(0.05)
	Korea	-0.14	(0.07)	-0.99	(0.06)	-0.38	(0.02)	-0.09	(0.01)	0.88	(0.11)	0.79	(0.07)
	Luxembourg	-0.16	(0.00)	-0.94	(0.00)	-0.44	(0.00)	-0.05	(0.00)	0.80	(0.00)	0.71	(0.00)
	Mexico	-0.41	(0.04)	-1.62	(0.03)	-0.75	(0.01)	-0.20	(0.01)	0.93	(0.05)	1.01	(0.03)
	Netherlands	-0.68	(0.05)	-1.47	(0.04)	-0.96	(0.02)	-0.48	(0.02)	0.19	(0.08)	0.67	(0.04)
	New Zealand	-0.20	(0.05)	-1.14	(0.03)	-0.45	(0.02)	-0.05	(0.02)	0.83	(0.06)	0.79	(0.03)
	Norway	-0.24	(0.05)	-1.05	(0.03)	-0.49	(0.01)	-0.14	(0.02)	0.70	(0.09)	0.71	(0.05)
	Poland	0.47	(0.07)	-0.64	(0.05)	0.17	(0.02)	0.77	(0.03)	1.57	(0.05)	0.86	(0.04)
	Portugal	0.14	(0.07)	-0.94	(0.10)	-0.16	(0.02)	0.27	(0.03)	1.37	(0.06)	0.90	(0.06)
	Slovak Republic	-0.06	(0.05)	-0.97	(0.08)	-0.34	(0.01)	0.07	(0.02)	0.98	(0.08)	0.79	(0.06)
	Slovenia	0.02	(0.01)	-1.06	(0.01)	-0.18	(0.00)	0.34	(0.00)	1.00	(0.01)	0.84	(0.00)
	Spain	0.10	(0.05)	-1.00	(0.04)	-0.23	(0.01)	0.30	(0.02)	1.32	(0.06)	0.92	(0.04)
	Sweden	-0.03	(0.05)	-1.07	(0.04)	-0.29	(0.02)	0.23	(0.02)	1.00	(0.08)	0.83	(0.05)
	Switzerland	0.17	(0.05)	-0.74	(0.05)	-0.03	(0.01)	0.35	(0.01)	1.10	(0.05)	0.73	(0.03)
	Turkey	-1.82	(0.11)	-3.18	(0.06)	-2.47	(0.03)	-1.69	(0.06)	0.06	(0.11)	1.29	(0.07)
	United Kingdom	0.07	(0.05)	-0.90	(0.05)	-0.20	(0.01)	0.28	(0.02)	1.09	(0.06)	0.80	(0.04)
	United States	-0.17	(0.06)	-1.11	(0.06)	-0.36	(0.02)	-0.03	(0.02)	0.84	(0.08)	0.79	(0.05)
	OECD average	-0.09	(0.01)	-1.10	(0.01)	-0.38	(0.00)	0.10	(0.00)	1.01	(0.01)	0.84	(0.01)
Partners	Albania	0.51	(0.07)	-0.55	(0.05)	0.22	(0.02)	0.77	(0.03)	1.60	(0.06)	0.84	(0.04)
	Argentina	-0.21	(0.08)	-1.58	(0.06)	-0.63	(0.03)	0.13	(0.04)	1.22	(0.07)	1.09	(0.06)
	Azerbaijan	0.14	(0.10)	-1.28	(0.08)	-0.25	(0.04)	0.57	(0.03)	1.52	(0.08)	1.09	(0.05)
	Brazil	-0.37	(0.04)	-1.50	(0.04)	-0.69	(0.02)	-0.15	(0.02)	0.88	(0.06)	0.95	(0.03)
	Bulgaria	0.07	(0.13)	-1.51	(0.11)	-0.13	(0.05)	0.53	(0.02)	1.39	(0.09)	1.13	(0.08)
	Colombia	-0.23	(0.09)	-1.52	(0.09)	-0.66	(0.03)	0.03	(0.03)	1.23	(0.12)	1.09	(0.07)
	Croatia	-0.13	(0.07)	-1.10	(0.06)	-0.40	(0.02)	0.05	(0.02)	0.92	(0.08)	0.82	(0.05)
	Dubai (UAE)	0.55	(0.00)	-1.08	(0.00)	0.28	(0.00)	1.01	(0.00)	1.98	(0.00)	1.23	(0.00)
	Hong Kong-China	-0.32	(0.06)	-1.26	(0.06)	-0.61	(0.02)	-0.15	(0.02)	0.74	(0.09)	0.81	(0.06)
	Indonesia	0.48	(0.08)	-0.61	(0.06)	0.19	(0.03)	0.74	(0.03)	1.60	(0.06)	0.87	(0.05)
	Jordan	-0.51	(0.09)	-1.96	(0.07)	-0.73	(0.04)	-0.18	(0.02)	0.81	(0.11)	1.08	(0.06)
	Kazakhstan	-0.54	(0.10)	-2.25	(0.10)	-1.10	(0.04)	-0.06	(0.03)	1.25	(0.09)	1.38	(0.07)
	Kyrgyzstan	-0.53	(0.12)	-2.37	(0.11)	-0.88	(0.04)	-0.02	(0.04)	1.14	(0.11)	1.37	(0.07)
	Latvia	0.21	(0.07)	-0.73	(0.05)	-0.15	(0.02)	0.38	(0.02)	1.34	(0.08)	0.83	(0.05)
	Liechtenstein	0.13	(0.00)	-0.50	(0.01)	0.07	(0.00)	0.26	(0.00)	0.70	(0.01)	0.49	(0.00)
	Lithuania	0.60	(0.05)	-0.21	(0.05)	0.34	(0.02)	0.83	(0.02)	1.43	(0.05)	0.68	(0.04)
	Macao-China	-0.33	(0.00)	-2.15	(0.00)	-0.71	(0.00)	0.24	(0.00)	1.30	(0.00)	1.38	(0.00)
	Montenegro	-0.05	(0.01)	-0.89	(0.00)	-0.26	(0.01)	0.11	(0.01)	0.83	(0.01)	0.71	(0.01)
	Panama	-0.46	(0.10)	-1.71	(0.09)	-0.82	(0.03)	-0.21	(0.03)	0.89	(0.09)	1.03	(0.06)
	Peru	-0.27	(0.06)	-1.43	(0.08)	-0.52	(0.02)	-0.06	(0.02)	0.93	(0.08)	0.95	(0.06)
	Qatar	0.26	(0.00)	-1.10	(0.01)	-0.04	(0.00)	0.62	(0.00)	1.55	(0.00)	1.07	(0.00)
	Romania	0.21	(0.06)	-0.76	(0.05)	-0.05	(0.02)	0.38	(0.02)	1.28	(0.06)	0.80	(0.04)
	Russian Federation	-0.31	(0.08)	-1.70	(0.08)	-0.58	(0.03)	0.03	(0.02)	1.01	(0.09)	1.07	(0.05)
	Serbia	-0.21	(0.06)	-1.15	(0.05)	-0.45	(0.02)	-0.03	(0.02)	0.78	(0.07)	0.78	(0.05)
	Shanghai-China	-0.60	(0.11)	-2.41	(0.09)	-1.00	(0.05)	0.03	(0.03)	0.97	(0.08)	1.33	(0.06)
	Singapore	-0.13	(0.01)	-1.17	(0.00)	-0.45	(0.00)	-0.04	(0.00)	1.13	(0.00)	0.92	(0.00)
	Chinese Taipei	-0.65	(0.12)	-2.49	(0.09)	-1.13	(0.06)	-0.15	(0.04)	1.18	(0.09)	1.42	(0.07)
	Thailand	0.02	(0.07)	-1.03	(0.05)	-0.25	(0.02)	0.27	(0.02)	1.09	(0.07)	0.86	(0.04)
	Trinidad and Tobago	-0.82	(0.00)	-1.88	(0.01)	-1.21	(0.00)	-0.57	(0.00)	0.37	(0.01)	0.94	(0.00)
	Tunisia	-0.48	(0.08)	-1.59	(0.07)	-0.71	(0.02)	-0.23	(0.02)	0.60	(0.07)	0.86	(0.05)
	Uruguay	-0.53	(0.06)	-1.66	(0.04)	-0.99	(0.02)	-0.40	(0.03)	0.93	(0.10)	1.03	(0.05)

Note: Values that are statistically significant are indicated in bold (see Annex A3).
StatLink http://dx.doi.org/10.1787/888932343285

[Part 2/2]

Table IV.4.5 **Index of teacher-related factors affecting school climate and reading performance, by national quarters of this index**
Results based on school principals' reports

		Performance on the reading scale by national quarters of this index								Change in the reading score per unit of this index		Increased likelihood of students in the bottom quarter of this index scoring in the bottom quarter of the national reading performance distribution		Explained variance in student performance (r-squared x 100)	
		Bottom quarter		Second quarter		Third quarter		Top quarter							
		Mean score	S.E.	Mean score	S.E.	Mean score	S.E.	Mean score	S.E.	Effect	S.E.	Ratio	S.E.	%	S.E.
OECD	Australia	**481**	(5.3)	518	(6.6)	524	(4.7)	**536**	(3.9)	**20.7**	(2.56)	**1.7**	(0.15)	3.7	(0.92)
	Austria	477	(8.3)	468	(8.7)	467	(8.7)	469	(9.7)	-3.5	(6.64)	0.8	(0.14)	0.1	(0.44)
	Belgium	**480**	(8.6)	502	(7.3)	520	(6.3)	**524**	(7.3)	**20.3**	(5.28)	**1.6**	(0.21)	2.9	(1.48)
	Canada	**512**	(3.9)	525	(3.5)	525	(3.7)	**534**	(3.2)	**10.2**	(2.62)	**1.2**	(0.07)	0.8	(0.46)
	Chile	**427**	(7.7)	445	(8.6)	448	(7.0)	**478**	(6.1)	**16.4**	(3.44)	**1.5**	(0.21)	4.0	(1.55)
	Czech Republic	**465**	(6.3)	486	(9.2)	477	(5.8)	**482**	(7.8)	6.3	(5.27)	1.1	(0.15)	0.2	(0.42)
	Denmark	**481**	(4.0)	489	(5.0)	506	(3.6)	**504**	(4.2)	**12.5**	(2.53)	**1.3**	(0.11)	1.5	(0.62)
	Estonia	501	(5.2)	493	(5.1)	497	(5.3)	513	(6.4)	5.0	(3.34)	1.0	(0.11)	0.2	(0.33)
	Finland	533	(4.7)	535	(3.9)	533	(3.7)	543	(5.1)	6.2	(3.48)	1.0	(0.11)	0.2	(0.28)
	France	w	w	w	w	w	w	w	w	w	w	w	w	w	w
	Germany	483	(8.8)	497	(8.2)	510	(6.6)	500	(9.3)	7.7	(6.41)	1.4	(0.20)	0.4	(0.56)
	Greece	**468**	(11.5)	495	(7.0)	477	(12.1)	**492**	(7.8)	3.3	(3.82)	1.4	(0.25)	0.1	(0.34)
	Hungary	473	(10.4)	488	(8.1)	504	(7.9)	511	(10.5)	**17.1**	(6.50)	**1.6**	(0.29)	2.7	(1.99)
	Iceland	**491**	(2.9)	503	(3.5)	500	(3.1)	**500**	(3.1)	1.9	(1.74)	**1.2**	(0.07)	0.0	(0.05)
	Ireland	**483**	(8.0)	488	(10.3)	490	(7.2)	**514**	(5.7)	**14.1**	(3.89)	1.2	(0.18)	1.6	(0.94)
	Israel	**441**	(10.7)	480	(9.1)	495	(7.8)	**480**	(12.1)	**15.5**	(6.99)	**1.7**	(0.25)	1.4	(1.34)
	Italy	483	(4.9)	489	(5.2)	491	(4.8)	482	(5.8)	-1.1	(3.84)	1.0	(0.10)	0.0	(0.13)
	Japan	**492**	(7.9)	504	(8.6)	545	(8.1)	**538**	(7.7)	**20.3**	(4.89)	**1.6**	(0.19)	3.1	(1.40)
	Korea	**533**	(7.4)	536	(8.1)	542	(6.5)	**546**	(7.2)	8.8	(5.96)	1.1	(0.22)	0.8	(1.03)
	Luxembourg	**467**	(2.8)	461	(2.9)	483	(2.6)	**477**	(2.1)	**4.2**	(1.51)	1.0	(0.07)	0.1	(0.06)
	Mexico	**412**	(5.2)	424	(3.9)	429	(4.0)	**436**	(4.2)	**8.9**	(2.16)	**1.3**	(0.12)	1.1	(0.58)
	Netherlands	**500**	(12.2)	496	(9.4)	496	(7.6)	**541**	(9.2)	**19.4**	(8.20)	1.2	(0.24)	2.2	(1.79)
	New Zealand	**504**	(6.4)	519	(4.5)	530	(5.4)	**533**	(8.4)	**18.0**	(4.13)	**1.4**	(0.16)	2.0	(0.94)
	Norway	**495**	(4.6)	503	(4.5)	501	(5.3)	**513**	(4.1)	**9.8**	(3.02)	1.2	(0.10)	0.6	(0.35)
	Poland	501	(4.5)	500	(5.1)	499	(5.3)	502	(5.9)	-0.7	(2.84)	1.0	(0.10)	0.0	(0.08)
	Portugal	478	(7.7)	499	(6.6)	489	(7.7)	490	(7.6)	4.7	(4.54)	1.2	(0.17)	0.2	(0.49)
	Slovak Republic	478	(7.9)	499	(8.4)	468	(9.6)	465	(9.2)	-6.6	(5.94)	0.9	(0.14)	0.3	(0.69)
	Slovenia	**461**	(2.6)	479	(2.6)	499	(2.2)	**494**	(2.2)	**17.4**	(1.19)	**1.6**	(0.08)	2.6	(0.35)
	Spain	**465**	(3.2)	483	(4.2)	488	(4.6)	**488**	(5.3)	**9.7**	(2.11)	**1.4**	(0.09)	1.0	(0.48)
	Sweden	**485**	(6.6)	494	(6.2)	501	(5.8)	**510**	(5.1)	**11.4**	(3.68)	1.2	(0.13)	0.9	(0.58)
	Switzerland	489	(5.0)	503	(6.3)	506	(7.3)	503	(6.7)	**10.3**	(4.71)	1.2	(0.11)	0.7	(0.61)
	Turkey	470	(8.2)	472	(8.6)	455	(6.0)	459	(8.6)	-0.8	(4.10)	0.9	(0.14)	0.0	(0.39)
	United Kingdom	**485**	(5.9)	489	(6.9)	502	(6.4)	**507**	(6.9)	**11.4**	(3.68)	**1.2**	(0.12)	0.9	(0.58)
	United States	**478**	(7.3)	504	(8.8)	503	(5.4)	**514**	(6.7)	**17.5**	(5.23)	**1.5**	(0.17)	2.0	(1.21)
	OECD average	**481**	(1.2)	493	(1.2)	497	(1.1)	**502**	(1.2)	**9.6**	(0.78)	**1.3**	(0.03)	1.2	(0.15)
Partners	Albania	387	(6.0)	390	(10.5)	381	(8.2)	382	(10.0)	-3.7	(5.37)	1.0	(0.11)	0.1	(0.28)
	Argentina	**366**	(10.3)	397	(7.3)	400	(10.6)	**434**	(13.9)	**22.5**	(5.09)	**1.5**	(0.22)	5.1	(2.24)
	Azerbaijan	368	(6.8)	354	(8.5)	360	(9.0)	366	(4.9)	0.8	(3.23)	0.9	(0.14)	0.0	(0.18)
	Brazil	**401**	(4.4)	398	(4.8)	412	(7.3)	**439**	(6.9)	**19.9**	(4.03)	1.1	(0.09)	4.1	(1.50)
	Bulgaria	423	(15.2)	446	(10.2)	425	(15.3)	425	(9.9)	0.6	(5.71)	1.1	(0.21)	0.0	(0.28)
	Colombia	**396**	(6.9)	404	(8.4)	418	(9.6)	**435**	(6.8)	**12.8**	(3.24)	**1.4**	(0.19)	2.6	(1.27)
	Croatia	465	(6.3)	473	(8.1)	484	(7.2)	482	(8.5)	6.9	(5.80)	1.2	(0.16)	0.4	(0.71)
	Dubai (UAE)	**434**	(2.4)	448	(2.3)	459	(3.6)	**496**	(3.3)	**18.0**	(0.92)	**1.4**	(0.07)	4.3	(0.43)
	Hong Kong-China	**503**	(6.8)	540	(8.5)	542	(7.6)	**547**	(8.9)	**18.1**	(5.11)	**1.7**	(0.24)	3.1	(1.73)
	Indonesia	395	(8.8)	399	(6.2)	401	(6.6)	412	(8.1)	8.4	(5.86)	1.3	(0.25)	1.2	(1.88)
	Jordan	**397**	(6.1)	405	(9.2)	399	(7.9)	**419**	(8.5)	**6.8**	(3.40)	1.1	(0.15)	0.7	(0.71)
	Kazakhstan	**372**	(6.8)	390	(8.2)	402	(9.8)	**397**	(9.3)	5.9	(3.07)	1.3	(0.16)	0.8	(0.70)
	Kyrgyzstan	**287**	(6.9)	308	(6.9)	323	(8.1)	**337**	(10.8)	**12.4**	(3.48)	**1.4**	(0.16)	3.0	(1.52)
	Latvia	483	(6.1)	492	(4.7)	479	(6.2)	483	(7.4)	2.9	(4.74)	1.0	(0.14)	0.1	(0.34)
	Liechtenstein	487	(5.8)	503	(8.2)	535	(9.2)	472	(8.7)	4.1	(7.34)	1.0	(0.27)	0.1	(0.25)
	Lithuania	460	(6.6)	477	(8.1)	469	(7.7)	467	(6.3)	-0.5	(4.96)	1.1	(0.16)	0.0	(0.13)
	Macao-China	**471**	(1.4)	491	(1.7)	482	(2.3)	**502**	(1.5)	**9.5**	(0.51)	**1.3**	(0.06)	3.0	(0.32)
	Montenegro	405	(2.4)	396	(4.3)	435	(5.5)	400	(2.4)	1.0	(1.62)	1.0	(0.10)	0.0	(0.02)
	Panama	**350**	(7.7)	354	(12.6)	355	(12.1)	**423**	(17.2)	**25.7**	(6.45)	1.1	(0.21)	7.0	(3.70)
	Peru	**350**	(5.8)	360	(7.5)	373	(9.9)	**392**	(9.9)	**15.6**	(5.18)	1.2	(0.15)	2.3	(1.48)
	Qatar	**344**	(1.7)	382	(1.7)	394	(2.3)	**366**	(2.2)	**7.3**	(0.67)	**1.3**	(0.05)	0.5	(0.08)
	Romania	423	(10.6)	431	(7.9)	434	(9.4)	409	(11.2)	-4.7	(7.23)	1.0	(0.21)	0.2	(0.66)
	Russian Federation	**449**	(8.1)	458	(6.6)	462	(5.3)	**469**	(7.1)	5.4	(3.97)	1.2	(0.18)	0.4	(0.64)
	Serbia	**429**	(7.5)	441	(5.7)	444	(5.3)	**453**	(7.1)	10.1	(5.94)	1.3	(0.17)	0.9	(0.94)
	Shanghai-China	551	(7.2)	545	(7.8)	563	(7.0)	564	(9.6)	4.8	(3.55)	1.1	(0.17)	0.6	(0.91)
	Singapore	**504**	(2.3)	518	(2.4)	529	(2.7)	**552**	(3.0)	**18.5**	(1.29)	**1.4**	(0.07)	3.1	(0.42)
	Chinese Taipei	**481**	(6.1)	487	(7.0)	509	(7.7)	**504**	(9.2)	**8.8**	(2.79)	**1.3**	(0.17)	2.1	(1.35)
	Thailand	419	(4.9)	428	(6.3)	414	(5.8)	424	(6.7)	6.1	(3.83)	1.0	(0.12)	0.5	(0.69)
	Trinidad and Tobago	**383**	(2.8)	398	(3.4)	446	(3.7)	**458**	(2.7)	**31.6**	(1.32)	**1.7**	(0.10)	7.1	(0.55)
	Tunisia	403	(8.0)	399	(7.1)	404	(8.4)	408	(10.6)	2.3	(6.45)	1.0	(0.19)	0.1	(0.38)
	Uruguay	**409**	(4.7)	426	(7.1)	430	(6.9)	**438**	(7.4)	**10.3**	(3.63)	1.2	(0.11)	1.1	(0.79)

Note: Values that are statistically significant are indicated in bold (see Annex A3).
StatLink http://dx.doi.org/10.1787/888932343285

[Part 1/1]

Parents' involvement in schools

Table IV.4.6 ***Results based on reports from students' parents***

		Percentage of students whose parents reported that they participated in the following school-related actives in the last academic year																	
		Discussing their child's behaviour or progress with a teacher on their own initiative		Discussing their child's behaviour or progress on the initiative of one of their child's teachers		Discussing their child's behaviour or progress with a teacher on their own initiative or the initiative of one of their child's teachers		Volunteering in physical activities		Volunteering in extra-curricular activities		Volunteering in the school library or media center		Assisting a teacher in the school		Appearing as a guest speaker		Participating in local school government	
		%	S.E.	%	S.E.	%	S.E.	%	S.E.	%	S.E.	%	S.E.	%	S.E.	%	S.E.	%	S.E.
OECD	Chile	67.5	(0.8)	62.7	(1.0)	80.3	(0.7)	9.5	(0.6)	16.5	(0.7)	3.7	(0.2)	10.4	(0.5)	6.6	(0.4)	17.3	(0.7)
	Denmark	44.5	(1.1)	78.2	(0.9)	87.2	(0.7)	6.0	(0.9)	16.7	(0.9)	0.2	(0.1)	8.7	(0.5)	1.9	(0.3)	20.9	(0.9)
	Germany	68.1	(1.1)	36.8	(1.2)	74.4	(1.0)	6.3	(0.6)	18.7	(0.8)	1.9	(0.2)	12.7	(0.7)	1.6	(0.2)	17.0	(0.7)
	Hungary	52.5	(1.1)	38.2	(1.2)	63.6	(1.1)	5.5	(0.5)	13.1	(0.6)	2.3	(0.3)	12.9	(0.8)	1.6	(0.2)	4.7	(0.3)
	Italy	66.2	(0.5)	44.8	(0.5)	76.9	(0.5)	5.4	(0.3)	18.8	(0.4)	6.9	(0.2)	a	a	6.6	(0.3)	15.9	(0.3)
	Korea	34.6	(0.9)	77.7	(0.9)	80.8	(0.8)	24.9	(1.0)	17.5	(0.7)	10.4	(0.5)	9.2	(0.7)	2.8	(0.3)	17.2	(0.7)
	New Zealand	62.0	(1.0)	53.6	(1.0)	77.0	(0.9)	7.5	(0.6)	33.1	(1.0)	1.8	(0.2)	9.2	(0.6)	1.7	(0.3)	7.9	(0.5)
	Portugal	74.4	(0.9)	62.0	(1.3)	87.7	(0.6)	3.4	(0.4)	7.2	(0.5)	2.2	(0.3)	7.7	(0.4)	4.3	(0.4)	18.7	(0.6)
	8 OECD countries average	58.7	(0.3)	56.8	(0.4)	78.5	(0.3)	8.6	(0.2)	17.7	(0.3)	3.7	(0.1)	10.1	(0.2)	3.4	(0.1)	14.9	(0.2)
Partners	Croatia	82.3	(0.6)	32.0	(0.9)	85.2	(0.5)	7.4	(0.3)	15.1	(0.6)	2.4	(0.2)	a	a	2.2	(0.3)	10.7	(0.4)
	Hong Kong-China	43.3	(0.9)	52.2	(0.8)	62.0	(0.8)	4.5	(0.3)	8.0	(0.4)	3.1	(0.2)	7.2	(0.4)	3.1	(0.3)	5.5	(0.4)
	Lithuania	58.0	(0.8)	53.1	(0.9)	73.2	(0.7)	6.8	(0.4)	14.9	(0.6)	1.1	(0.2)	a	a	4.1	(0.3)	15.9	(0.8)
	Macao-China	29.1	(0.6)	58.5	(0.6)	64.6	(0.6)	9.3	(0.4)	20.3	(0.5)	5.3	(0.3)	16.5	(0.5)	3.1	(0.2)	20.9	(0.5)
	Panama	68.8	(1.0)	54.6	(1.7)	77.3	(1.0)	20.5	(1.8)	22.4	(1.0)	10.3	(0.9)	23.6	(1.4)	9.6	(0.7)	29.7	(1.4)
	Qatar	65.0	(0.6)	51.3	(0.6)	71.8	(0.5)	9.7	(0.4)	20.1	(0.5)	10.6	(0.4)	29.0	(0.5)	11.9	(0.4)	13.6	(0.4)

Note: Average missing rates on these parent questionnaire items are 2% in Macao-China, 3% in Korea, Hong Kong-China and Lithuania, 6% in Hungary, 11% in Croatia, 12% in Chile, 13% in Italy, 22% in Panama, 24% in Portugal, 26% in New Zealand, 34% in Denmark, 35% in Qatar and 38% in Germany.

StatLink http://dx.doi.org/10.1787/888932343285

[Part 1/1]
Parents' expectations for higher academic standards
Table IV.4.7 *Results based on school principals' reports*

		Parental expectations are characterised by pressure on the school to achieve high academic standards among students from:					
		Many parents		A minority of parents		Very few parents	
		%	S.E.	%	S.E.	%	S.E.
OECD	Australia	28.9	(2.9)	62.0	(3.0)	9.1	(1.9)
	Austria	3.5	(1.4)	24.6	(3.5)	71.9	(3.7)
	Belgium	12.7	(2.1)	29.9	(3.0)	57.4	(3.2)
	Canada	28.2	(2.0)	54.1	(2.3)	17.6	(1.6)
	Chile	21.4	(3.5)	51.4	(3.9)	27.1	(3.2)
	Czech Republic	24.5	(2.8)	67.4	(3.0)	8.1	(1.7)
	Denmark	22.7	(2.1)	41.0	(3.0)	36.3	(3.2)
	Estonia	13.9	(2.0)	52.7	(3.1)	33.4	(2.9)
	Finland	2.9	(1.1)	24.9	(3.4)	72.3	(3.5)
	France	w	w	w	w	w	w
	Germany	3.6	(1.4)	48.6	(3.9)	47.8	(3.9)
	Greece	15.0	(3.1)	38.6	(3.9)	46.4	(4.2)
	Hungary	18.2	(3.1)	46.3	(4.4)	35.6	(4.1)
	Iceland	13.6	(0.2)	49.2	(0.2)	37.1	(0.3)
	Ireland	37.1	(4.0)	47.6	(4.4)	15.3	(3.0)
	Israel	23.8	(3.4)	52.0	(4.0)	24.2	(3.6)
	Italy	14.4	(1.3)	59.9	(2.0)	25.6	(1.6)
	Japan	29.3	(2.8)	49.9	(3.0)	20.7	(2.3)
	Korea	12.1	(2.8)	66.9	(4.0)	20.9	(3.3)
	Luxembourg	8.7	(0.0)	23.4	(0.1)	67.9	(0.1)
	Mexico	22.9	(1.6)	41.4	(1.6)	35.7	(1.6)
	Netherlands	6.8	(2.0)	49.0	(5.0)	44.2	(4.9)
	New Zealand	48.2	(3.0)	42.6	(3.2)	9.1	(2.0)
	Norway	16.0	(3.0)	50.5	(3.7)	33.4	(3.3)
	Poland	11.4	(2.4)	55.9	(3.6)	32.7	(3.7)
	Portugal	13.3	(2.9)	57.2	(3.9)	29.5	(3.2)
	Slovak Republic	11.3	(2.4)	61.9	(3.6)	26.8	(3.6)
	Slovenia	27.5	(0.4)	38.2	(0.4)	34.4	(0.4)
	Spain	10.1	(1.8)	36.3	(2.7)	53.6	(2.9)
	Sweden	33.5	(3.8)	62.7	(3.9)	3.7	(1.5)
	Switzerland	6.6	(1.8)	50.6	(3.7)	42.8	(3.3)
	Turkey	10.7	(2.5)	49.9	(4.0)	39.4	(3.7)
	United Kingdom	33.7	(3.3)	54.4	(3.4)	11.9	(2.1)
	United States	34.1	(4.4)	45.6	(4.6)	20.3	(2.9)
	OECD average	18.8	(0.4)	48.1	(0.6)	33.1	(0.5)
Partners	Albania	25.6	(3.8)	63.2	(4.3)	11.3	(2.4)
	Argentina	9.1	(2.4)	40.1	(4.1)	50.7	(4.1)
	Azerbaijan	23.4	(3.8)	38.0	(4.8)	38.6	(4.4)
	Brazil	16.9	(2.1)	46.1	(2.7)	37.0	(2.7)
	Bulgaria	15.2	(2.8)	50.6	(4.3)	34.2	(4.2)
	Colombia	13.2	(3.1)	32.3	(4.1)	54.5	(4.2)
	Croatia	6.8	(1.7)	29.4	(3.4)	63.7	(3.5)
	Dubai (UAE)	40.9	(0.2)	43.5	(0.1)	15.6	(0.1)
	Hong Kong-China	2.4	(1.1)	64.7	(3.7)	32.9	(3.8)
	Indonesia	29.4	(4.3)	57.1	(4.4)	13.5	(3.2)
	Jordan	27.0	(3.4)	41.2	(4.1)	31.8	(3.8)
	Kazakhstan	13.2	(2.7)	67.5	(3.5)	19.3	(3.0)
	Kyrgyzstan	24.3	(3.3)	62.4	(3.7)	13.2	(2.3)
	Latvia	10.0	(2.0)	28.2	(3.8)	61.8	(3.9)
	Liechtenstein	0.0	c	38.1	(0.5)	61.9	(0.5)
	Lithuania	7.6	(1.7)	55.8	(3.6)	36.5	(3.6)
	Macao-China	1.2	(0.0)	43.6	(0.0)	55.2	(0.0)
	Montenegro	3.0	(0.1)	40.8	(1.1)	56.2	(1.0)
	Panama	22.1	(3.9)	39.1	(5.3)	38.8	(5.3)
	Peru	36.1	(3.4)	41.0	(3.5)	22.9	(3.2)
	Qatar	42.3	(0.1)	36.6	(0.1)	21.1	(0.1)
	Romania	16.7	(2.7)	30.8	(3.5)	52.5	(3.8)
	Russian Federation	22.5	(3.2)	56.2	(3.1)	21.3	(2.9)
	Serbia	5.8	(2.1)	41.8	(4.2)	52.4	(4.2)
	Shanghai-China	18.4	(3.1)	71.6	(3.4)	10.1	(2.3)
	Singapore	48.0	(0.5)	47.7	(0.8)	4.2	(0.3)
	Chinese Taipei	26.1	(3.7)	62.8	(4.4)	11.1	(2.8)
	Thailand	24.3	(3.3)	48.8	(3.7)	26.9	(3.0)
	Trinidad and Tobago	28.2	(0.2)	46.4	(0.3)	25.4	(0.3)
	Tunisia	16.2	(3.1)	41.3	(4.6)	42.5	(4.5)
	Uruguay	4.9	(1.7)	32.8	(3.1)	62.3	(3.0)

StatLink http://dx.doi.org/10.1787/888932343285

[Part 1/3]

Table IV.4.8 Index of school principal's leadership and reading performance, by national quarters of this index

Results based on school principals' reports

	Index of school principal's leadership															
	All students		Bottom quarter		Second quarter		Third quarter		Top quarter		In lower secondary education (ISCED 2)		In upper secondary education (ISCED 3)		Difference between lower and upper secondary education	
	Mean index	S.E.	Mean index	S.E.	Mean index	S.E.	Mean index	S.E.	Mean index	S.E.	Mean index	S.E.	Mean index	S.E.	Dif.	S.E.
OECD																
Australia	0.42	(0.06)	-0.64	(0.05)	0.04	(0.01)	0.60	(0.02)	1.70	(0.11)	0.43	(0.07)	0.33	(0.08)	0.10	(0.10)
Austria	-0.15	(0.07)	-1.12	(0.05)	-0.47	(0.02)	0.05	(0.02)	0.93	(0.10)	-0.24	(0.13)	-0.15	(0.08)	-0.09	(0.14)
Belgium	-0.34	(0.05)	-1.27	(0.04)	-0.60	(0.01)	-0.17	(0.02)	0.68	(0.06)	-0.22	(0.14)	-0.35	(0.05)	0.13	(0.15)
Canada	0.42	(0.04)	-0.66	(0.04)	0.05	(0.01)	0.63	(0.01)	1.68	(0.08)	0.25	(0.05)	0.45	(0.04)	**-0.20**	(0.06)
Chile	0.67	(0.09)	-0.61	(0.06)	0.23	(0.02)	0.89	(0.03)	2.16	(0.14)	0.81	(0.16)	0.66	(0.09)	0.15	(0.19)
Czech Republic	0.19	(0.06)	-0.71	(0.03)	-0.20	(0.02)	0.32	(0.02)	1.33	(0.10)	0.21	(0.08)	0.16	(0.09)	0.06	(0.12)
Denmark	-0.45	(0.04)	-1.20	(0.04)	-0.71	(0.01)	-0.30	(0.02)	0.41	(0.04)	-0.45	(0.04)	-0.56	(0.59)	0.11	(0.59)
Estonia	-0.15	(0.07)	-1.12	(0.05)	-0.51	(0.02)	0.01	(0.02)	1.02	(0.11)	-0.15	(0.07)	-0.11	(0.11)	-0.04	(0.12)
Finland	-0.61	(0.05)	-1.50	(0.05)	-0.82	(0.02)	-0.41	(0.02)	0.30	(0.08)	-0.61	(0.05)	c	c	c	c
France	w	w	w	w	w	w	w	w	w	w	w	w	w	w	w	w
Germany	-0.44	(0.05)	-1.18	(0.03)	-0.72	(0.01)	-0.32	(0.02)	0.47	(0.07)	-0.43	(0.05)	-0.62	(0.19)	0.19	(0.19)
Greece	-0.48	(0.07)	-1.67	(0.06)	-0.85	(0.03)	-0.16	(0.03)	0.77	(0.09)	-0.30	(0.21)	-0.49	(0.07)	0.20	(0.22)
Hungary	-0.05	(0.07)	-0.93	(0.05)	-0.34	(0.02)	0.13	(0.02)	0.94	(0.10)	0.04	(0.12)	-0.06	(0.08)	0.10	(0.14)
Iceland	-0.25	(0.00)	-1.13	(0.00)	-0.46	(0.00)	-0.09	(0.00)	0.66	(0.01)	-0.25	(0.00)	c	c	c	c
Ireland	-0.20	(0.08)	-1.31	(0.06)	-0.53	(0.03)	0.08	(0.03)	0.95	(0.07)	-0.21	(0.08)	-0.19	(0.08)	-0.02	(0.03)
Israel	0.41	(0.06)	-0.57	(0.05)	0.05	(0.02)	0.51	(0.03)	1.63	(0.11)	0.53	(0.11)	0.38	(0.07)	0.14	(0.12)
Italy	0.41	(0.03)	-0.65	(0.03)	0.14	(0.01)	0.64	(0.01)	1.49	(0.04)	0.58	(0.16)	0.40	(0.03)	0.18	(0.16)
Japan	-1.29	(0.06)	-2.20	(0.03)	-1.68	(0.02)	-1.15	(0.02)	-0.14	(0.10)	c	c	-1.29	(0.06)	c	c
Korea	-0.60	(0.11)	-1.92	(0.09)	-1.01	(0.02)	-0.43	(0.03)	0.97	(0.17)	-0.86	(0.25)	-0.59	(0.12)	-0.28	(0.28)
Luxembourg	-0.27	(0.00)	-1.41	(0.00)	-0.88	(0.00)	0.00	(0.00)	1.18	(0.00)	-0.35	(0.00)	-0.14	(0.01)	**-0.21**	(0.01)
Mexico	0.39	(0.04)	-0.73	(0.04)	-0.04	(0.01)	0.56	(0.02)	1.77	(0.07)	0.33	(0.06)	0.43	(0.05)	-0.11	(0.08)
Netherlands	-0.44	(0.06)	-1.26	(0.04)	-0.68	(0.02)	-0.26	(0.02)	0.46	(0.05)	-0.44	(0.06)	-0.41	(0.08)	-0.04	(0.09)
New Zealand	0.20	(0.06)	-0.91	(0.06)	-0.14	(0.02)	0.42	(0.02)	1.43	(0.12)	0.12	(0.09)	0.20	(0.06)	-0.08	(0.08)
Norway	-0.48	(0.05)	-1.21	(0.06)	-0.68	(0.01)	-0.35	(0.01)	0.33	(0.06)	-0.48	(0.05)	c	c	c	c
Poland	0.58	(0.07)	-0.45	(0.06)	0.31	(0.02)	0.80	(0.02)	1.64	(0.07)	0.57	(0.07)	c	c	c	c
Portugal	-0.15	(0.05)	-1.08	(0.05)	-0.34	(0.01)	0.05	(0.02)	0.78	(0.06)	-0.11	(0.07)	-0.17	(0.06)	0.06	(0.08)
Slovak Republic	0.37	(0.07)	-0.55	(0.06)	0.14	(0.02)	0.59	(0.01)	1.29	(0.07)	0.44	(0.09)	0.32	(0.09)	0.11	(0.13)
Slovenia	0.31	(0.01)	-0.60	(0.00)	0.00	(0.00)	0.50	(0.00)	1.36	(0.01)	0.15	(0.15)	0.32	(0.00)	-0.17	(0.15)
Spain	0.02	(0.05)	-1.04	(0.05)	-0.28	(0.01)	0.22	(0.01)	1.16	(0.06)	0.02	(0.05)	c	c	c	c
Sweden	-0.27	(0.06)	-1.17	(0.05)	-0.58	(0.02)	-0.12	(0.02)	0.79	(0.08)	-0.27	(0.06)	-0.20	(0.25)	-0.06	(0.27)
Switzerland	-0.55	(0.05)	-1.57	(0.04)	-0.85	(0.01)	-0.31	(0.02)	0.53	(0.10)	-0.66	(0.05)	-0.11	(0.17)	**-0.55**	(0.18)
Turkey	0.31	(0.07)	-0.73	(0.07)	-0.02	(0.02)	0.47	(0.02)	1.51	(0.08)	c	c	0.31	(0.07)	c	c
United Kingdom	1.03	(0.06)	0.01	(0.03)	0.62	(0.02)	1.17	(0.03)	2.32	(0.08)	0.67	(0.24)	1.04	(0.06)	-0.36	(0.24)
United States	0.88	(0.08)	-0.36	(0.14)	0.56	(0.02)	1.18	(0.02)	2.15	(0.07)	1.01	(0.10)	0.86	(0.09)	0.15	(0.08)
OECD average	-0.02	(0.01)	-1.01	(0.01)	-0.34	(0.00)	0.17	(0.00)	1.11	(0.01)	0.00	(0.02)	0.02	(0.03)	-0.02	(0.04)
Partners																
Albania	0.71	(0.06)	-0.27	(0.04)	0.45	(0.02)	0.93	(0.02)	1.74	(0.10)	0.74	(0.08)	0.68	(0.08)	0.05	(0.11)
Argentina	0.61	(0.07)	-0.52	(0.07)	0.30	(0.02)	0.83	(0.03)	1.81	(0.09)	0.54	(0.10)	0.65	(0.08)	-0.10	(0.11)
Azerbaijan	0.87	(0.09)	-0.16	(0.13)	0.54	(0.02)	1.07	(0.03)	2.02	(0.12)	0.88	(0.10)	0.85	(0.08)	0.03	(0.05)
Brazil	1.21	(0.05)	-0.08	(0.06)	0.86	(0.02)	1.48	(0.02)	2.57	(0.08)	1.15	(0.07)	1.22	(0.06)	-0.07	(0.08)
Bulgaria	0.65	(0.08)	-0.34	(0.09)	0.38	(0.02)	0.82	(0.02)	1.75	(0.10)	0.70	(0.12)	0.65	(0.09)	0.05	(0.15)
Colombia	0.56	(0.10)	-0.72	(0.07)	0.06	(0.03)	0.81	(0.03)	2.08	(0.17)	0.55	(0.12)	0.56	(0.10)	-0.02	(0.08)
Croatia	0.45	(0.06)	-0.49	(0.04)	0.17	(0.03)	0.70	(0.02)	1.44	(0.10)	c	c	0.45	(0.06)	c	c
Dubai (UAE)	1.47	(0.00)	0.08	(0.00)	1.02	(0.00)	1.67	(0.00)	3.08	(0.00)	1.36	(0.02)	1.49	(0.01)	**-0.13**	(0.03)
Hong Kong-China	1.13	(0.08)	0.03	(0.07)	0.72	(0.02)	1.42	(0.03)	2.33	(0.11)	1.19	(0.09)	1.09	(0.08)	0.09	(0.06)
Indonesia	0.38	(0.09)	-0.59	(0.05)	-0.05	(0.02)	0.45	(0.02)	1.70	(0.20)	0.40	(0.11)	0.35	(0.14)	0.05	(0.17)
Jordan	1.96	(0.08)	0.68	(0.07)	1.54	(0.02)	2.18	(0.03)	3.43	(0.08)	1.96	(0.08)	c	c	c	c
Kazakhstan	0.41	(0.06)	-0.55	(0.04)	0.08	(0.02)	0.67	(0.02)	1.42	(0.07)	0.40	(0.06)	0.43	(0.10)	-0.03	(0.10)
Kyrgyzstan	0.33	(0.07)	-0.60	(0.05)	-0.08	(0.02)	0.42	(0.02)	1.56	(0.12)	0.36	(0.08)	0.19	(0.10)	**0.18**	(0.09)
Latvia	0.33	(0.08)	-0.70	(0.10)	0.01	(0.02)	0.67	(0.03)	1.36	(0.05)	0.33	(0.08)	0.47	(0.17)	-0.14	(0.16)
Liechtenstein	-1.75	(0.01)	-2.51	(0.01)	-2.08	(0.00)	-1.60	(0.02)	-0.80	(0.01)	-1.72	(0.01)	c	c	c	c
Lithuania	-0.04	(0.06)	-0.97	(0.04)	-0.35	(0.02)	0.14	(0.02)	1.03	(0.06)	-0.04	(0.06)	1.05	(0.00)	**-1.09**	(0.06)
Macao-China	0.17	(0.00)	-0.86	(0.00)	-0.26	(0.00)	0.45	(0.00)	1.35	(0.00)	0.16	(0.00)	0.18	(0.00)	**-0.02**	(0.00)
Montenegro	0.98	(0.01)	0.15	(0.01)	0.73	(0.01)	1.25	(0.00)	1.79	(0.00)	c	c	0.99	(0.00)	c	c
Panama	0.49	(0.10)	-0.81	(0.11)	0.10	(0.03)	0.76	(0.05)	1.93	(0.08)	0.37	(0.12)	0.59	(0.14)	-0.22	(0.15)
Peru	0.48	(0.09)	-0.68	(0.05)	0.00	(0.01)	0.59	(0.03)	2.01	(0.11)	0.26	(0.10)	0.57	(0.09)	**-0.31**	(0.08)
Qatar	1.18	(0.00)	-0.10	(0.00)	0.74	(0.00)	1.38	(0.00)	2.71	(0.00)	1.29	(0.01)	1.16	(0.00)	**0.13**	(0.01)
Romania	1.00	(0.06)	0.04	(0.04)	0.72	(0.02)	1.22	(0.03)	2.01	(0.05)	1.00	(0.06)	c	c	c	c
Russian Federation	0.50	(0.08)	-0.50	(0.04)	0.10	(0.02)	0.70	(0.03)	1.71	(0.11)	0.46	(0.00)	0.60	(0.00)	-0.13	(0.09)
Serbia	0.54	(0.05)	-0.40	(0.05)	0.22	(0.02)	0.74	(0.02)	1.59	(0.10)	0.43	(0.23)	0.54	(0.06)	-0.11	(0.24)
Shanghai-China	0.02	(0.06)	-0.82	(0.05)	-0.23	(0.01)	0.13	(0.01)	1.01	(0.15)	0.16	(0.10)	-0.08	(0.06)	**0.24**	(0.11)
Singapore	0.71	(0.01)	-0.31	(0.00)	0.30	(0.00)	0.92	(0.01)	1.94	(0.00)	0.69	(0.07)	0.72	(0.01)	-0.02	(0.07)
Chinese Taipei	0.36	(0.07)	-0.58	(0.05)	-0.04	(0.01)	0.52	(0.03)	1.54	(0.10)	0.40	(0.11)	0.34	(0.09)	0.06	(0.13)
Thailand	0.68	(0.07)	-0.33	(0.05)	0.25	(0.02)	0.89	(0.03)	1.90	(0.08)	0.68	(0.08)	0.67	(0.08)	0.01	(0.09)
Trinidad and Tobago	0.45	(0.01)	-0.72	(0.01)	0.02	(0.00)	0.70	(0.00)	1.82	(0.01)	0.40	(0.01)	0.48	(0.01)	**-0.07**	(0.02)
Tunisia	0.42	(0.09)	-0.92	(0.11)	0.03	(0.03)	0.80	(0.04)	1.77	(0.10)	0.52	(0.11)	0.35	(0.13)	0.17	(0.16)
Uruguay	0.33	(0.06)	-0.89	(0.06)	-0.02	(0.02)	0.54	(0.02)	1.70	(0.08)	0.37	(0.10)	0.31	(0.06)	0.06	(0.11)

Note: Values that are statistically significant are indicated in bold (see Annex A3).

StatLink http://dx.doi.org/10.1787/888932343285

[Part 2/3]

Table IV.4.8 Index of school principal's leadership and reading performance, by national quarters of this index

Results based on school principals' reports

		Index of school principal's leadership												Variability in this index	
		In general programmes		In vocational programmes		Difference between general and vocational programmes		In public schools		In private schools		Difference between public and private schools			
		Mean index	S.E.	Mean index	S.E.	Dif.	S.E.	Mean index	S.E.	Mean index	S.E.	Dif.	S.E.	Standard deviation	S.E.
OECD	Australia	0.41	(0.06)	0.49	(0.21)	-0.09	(0.21)	0.58	(0.09)	0.17	(0.08)	**0.41**	(0.12)	1.0	(0.1)
	Austria	-0.45	(0.12)	-0.07	(0.10)	**-0.39**	(0.15)	-0.17	(0.07)	-0.18	(0.23)	0.01	(0.24)	0.8	(0.1)
	Belgium	-0.22	(0.07)	-0.48	(0.05)	**0.26**	(0.08)	-0.19	(0.11)	-0.41	(0.05)	0.21	(0.12)	0.8	(0.0)
	Canada	a	a	a	a	a	a	0.41	(0.04)	0.57	(0.12)	-0.16	(0.12)	1.0	(0.1)
	Chile	0.67	(0.09)	0.62	(0.13)	0.05	(0.12)	0.06	(0.09)	1.10	(0.13)	**-1.05**	(0.16)	1.1	(0.1)
	Czech Republic	0.20	(0.08)	0.16	(0.11)	0.04	(0.14)	0.20	(0.07)	-0.09	(0.20)	0.29	(0.21)	0.8	(0.1)
	Denmark	-0.45	(0.04)	c	c	c	c	-0.44	(0.05)	-0.49	(0.08)	0.05	(0.10)	0.6	(0.0)
	Estonia	-0.15	(0.07)	c	c	c	c	-0.17	(0.07)	0.43	(0.50)	-0.60	(0.51)	0.9	(0.1)
	Finland	-0.61	(0.05)	c	c	c	c	-0.59	(0.05)	-1.00	(0.22)	0.41	(0.22)	0.7	(0.1)
	France	w	w	w	w	w	w	w	w	w	w	w	w	w	w
	Germany	-0.44	(0.05)	-0.57	(0.22)	0.14	(0.23)	-0.44	(0.05)	-0.29	(0.18)	-0.15	(0.19)	0.7	(0.0)
	Greece	-0.50	(0.08)	-0.32	(0.18)	-0.18	(0.21)	-0.50	(0.07)	-0.08	(0.43)	-0.43	(0.45)	1.0	(0.1)
	Hungary	-0.06	(0.07)	0.03	(0.24)	-0.09	(0.25)	-0.07	(0.07)	0.07	(0.20)	-0.13	(0.21)	0.8	(0.1)
	Iceland	-0.25	(0.00)	c	c	c	c	-0.25	(0.00)	c	c	c	c	0.7	(0.0)
	Ireland	-0.20	(0.08)	c	c	c	c	-0.21	(0.10)	-0.20	(0.11)	-0.01	(0.15)	0.9	(0.0)
	Israel	0.41	(0.06)	c	c	c	c	0.43	(0.07)	0.33	(0.16)	0.09	(0.17)	0.9	(0.1)
	Italy	0.48	(0.04)	0.34	(0.05)	**0.14**	(0.06)	0.40	(0.03)	0.50	(0.14)	-0.10	(0.14)	0.9	(0.0)
	Japan	-1.26	(0.07)	-1.37	(0.14)	0.11	(0.16)	-1.26	(0.00)	-1.37	(0.00)	0.11	(0.16)	0.9	(0.1)
	Korea	-0.61	(0.13)	-0.55	(0.25)	-0.06	(0.28)	-0.63	(0.13)	-0.53	(0.19)	-0.10	(0.21)	1.2	(0.1)
	Luxembourg	-0.19	(0.00)	-0.57	(0.01)	**0.38**	(0.01)	-0.36	(0.00)	0.29	(0.01)	**-0.65**	(0.01)	1.0	(0.0)
	Mexico	0.39	(0.05)	0.37	(0.06)	0.02	(0.08)	0.31	(0.04)	0.98	(0.14)	**-0.67**	(0.15)	1.0	(0.0)
	Netherlands	-0.45	(0.06)	0.13	(0.24)	**-0.58**	(0.25)	-0.30	(0.07)	-0.50	(0.08)	0.20	(0.11)	0.7	(0.0)
	New Zealand	0.20	(0.06)	c	c	c	c	0.17	(0.06)	0.80	(0.29)	**-0.63**	(0.30)	1.0	(0.1)
	Norway	-0.48	(0.05)	c	c	c	c	-0.48	(0.05)	c	c	c	c	0.6	(0.1)
	Poland	0.57	(0.07)	c	c	c	c	0.58	(0.07)	0.51	(0.16)	0.07	(0.18)	0.8	(0.0)
	Portugal	-0.17	(0.05)	-0.08	(0.13)	-0.09	(0.11)	-0.23	(0.06)	0.35	(0.14)	**-0.58**	(0.15)	0.7	(0.0)
	Slovak Republic	0.38	(0.07)	0.41	(0.21)	-0.02	(0.22)	0.37	(0.07)	0.35	(0.21)	0.02	(0.22)	0.7	(0.0)
	Slovenia	0.16	(0.01)	0.45	(0.01)	**-0.28**	(0.01)	0.33	(0.01)	-0.10	(0.01)	**0.42**	(0.01)	0.8	(0.0)
	Spain	0.02	(0.05)	c	c	c	c	-0.18	(0.06)	0.39	(0.07)	**-0.57**	(0.08)	0.9	(0.0)
	Sweden	-0.27	(0.06)	c	c	c	c	-0.35	(0.06)	0.48	(0.24)	**-0.83**	(0.25)	0.8	(0.1)
	Switzerland	-0.56	(0.06)	-0.40	(0.18)	-0.16	(0.19)	-0.57	(0.05)	0.04	(0.37)	-0.61	(0.37)	0.8	(0.1)
	Turkey	0.36	(0.09)	0.24	(0.11)	0.12	(0.15)	0.30	(0.07)	c	c	c	c	0.9	(0.1)
	United Kingdom	1.04	(0.06)	c	c	c	c	1.08	(0.06)	0.49	(0.23)	**0.59**	(0.23)	0.9	(0.0)
	United States	0.88	(0.08)	c	c	c	c	0.90	(0.09)	0.67	(0.41)	0.23	(0.43)	1.1	(0.1)
	OECD average	-0.04	(0.01)	-0.06	(0.04)	-0.04	(0.04)	-0.04	(0.01)	0.11	(0.04)	**-0.14**	(0.04)	0.9	(0.0)
Partners	Albania	0.72	(0.06)	0.55	(0.10)	0.17	(0.12)	0.72	(0.06)	0.65	(0.15)	0.07	(0.17)	0.8	(0.1)
	Argentina	0.62	(0.08)	0.48	(0.15)	0.14	(0.17)	0.56	(0.08)	0.69	(0.12)	-0.12	(0.14)	0.9	(0.1)
	Azerbaijan	0.87	(0.09)	0.28	(0.51)	0.59	(0.50)	0.87	(0.09)	c	c	c	c	1.0	(0.1)
	Brazil	1.21	(0.05)	c	c	c	c	1.13	(0.06)	1.79	(0.13)	**-0.67**	(0.14)	1.1	(0.0)
	Bulgaria	0.62	(0.08)	0.70	(0.19)	-0.08	(0.20)	0.65	(0.09)	c	c	c	c	0.8	(0.1)
	Colombia	0.59	(0.12)	0.44	(0.14)	0.15	(0.17)	0.40	(0.11)	1.27	(0.26)	**-0.87**	(0.28)	1.2	(0.1)
	Croatia	0.60	(0.10)	0.39	(0.07)	0.21	(0.12)	0.43	(0.06)	c	c	c	c	0.8	(0.1)
	Dubai (UAE)	1.47	(0.00)	c	c	c	c	1.01	(0.00)	1.59	(0.00)	**-0.59**	(0.00)	1.2	(0.0)
	Hong Kong-China	1.13	(0.08)	c	c	c	c	1.59	(0.25)	1.09	(0.08)	0.50	(0.26)	0.9	(0.1)
	Indonesia	0.37	(0.08)	0.41	(0.37)	-0.04	(0.37)	0.53	(0.15)	0.18	(0.09)	0.35	(0.18)	1.0	(0.1)
	Jordan	1.96	(0.08)	c	c	c	c	1.92	(0.09)	2.12	(0.19)	-0.19	(0.21)	1.1	(0.0)
	Kazakhstan	0.40	(0.06)	0.44	(0.19)	-0.04	(0.19)	0.41	(0.06)	0.17	(0.32)	0.25	(0.31)	0.8	(0.0)
	Kyrgyzstan	0.33	(0.08)	0.04	(0.20)	0.30	(0.22)	0.29	(0.07)	1.52	(0.49)	**-1.23**	(0.48)	0.9	(0.1)
	Latvia	0.34	(0.08)	c	c	c	c	0.34	(0.08)	c	c	c	c	0.8	(0.1)
	Liechtenstein	-1.75	(0.01)	c	c	c	c	-1.83	(0.01)	c	c	c	c	0.7	(0.0)
	Lithuania	-0.04	(0.06)	c	c	c	c	-0.04	(0.06)	c	c	c	c	0.8	(0.0)
	Macao-China	0.17	(0.00)	c	c	c	c	c	c	0.18	(0.00)	c	c	0.9	(0.0)
	Montenegro	0.95	(0.02)	0.99	(0.00)	-0.04	(0.02)	0.98	(0.01)	c	c	c	c	0.7	(0.0)
	Panama	0.49	(0.10)	c	c	c	c	0.24	(0.11)	1.44	(0.18)	**-1.20**	(0.21)	1.1	(0.1)
	Peru	0.48	(0.09)	c	c	c	c	0.33	(0.08)	1.01	(0.19)	**-0.69**	(0.19)	1.1	(0.1)
	Qatar	1.18	(0.00)	c	c	c	c	1.20	(0.00)	1.19	(0.01)	0.02	(0.01)	1.1	(0.0)
	Romania	1.00	(0.07)	1.00	(0.12)	-0.01	(0.14)	1.00	(0.06)	c	c	c	c	0.8	(0.0)
	Russian Federation	0.51	(0.00)	0.38	(0.00)	0.13	(0.23)	0.50	(0.08)	c	c	c	c	0.9	(0.1)
	Serbia	0.56	(0.10)	0.46	(0.10)	0.09	(0.14)	0.55	(0.06)	c	c	c	c	0.8	(0.1)
	Shanghai-China	0.08	(0.07)	-0.17	(0.12)	0.25	(0.14)	-0.01	(0.05)	0.30	(0.39)	-0.31	(0.39)	0.8	(0.1)
	Singapore	0.71	(0.01)	c	c	c	c	0.72	(0.00)	c	c	c	c	0.9	(0.0)
	Chinese Taipei	0.39	(0.09)	0.32	(0.10)	0.07	(0.13)	0.32	(0.09)	0.43	(0.11)	-0.11	(0.15)	0.9	(0.1)
	Thailand	0.71	(0.08)	0.54	(0.15)	0.18	(0.17)	0.64	(0.08)	0.86	(0.16)	-0.23	(0.18)	0.9	(0.1)
	Trinidad and Tobago	0.44	(0.01)	0.53	(0.01)	**-0.09**	(0.01)	0.43	(0.01)	0.65	(0.01)	**-0.23**	(0.01)	1.0	(0.0)
	Tunisia	0.42	(0.09)	c	c	c	c	0.41	(0.09)	1.12	(0.67)	-0.71	(0.68)	1.1	(0.1)
	Uruguay	0.34	(0.06)	0.07	(0.20)	0.27	(0.20)	0.27	(0.07)	0.61	(0.12)	**-0.33**	(0.14)	1.0	(0.1)

Note: Values that are statistically significant are indicated in bold (see Annex A3).
StatLink http://dx.doi.org/10.1787/888932343285

[Part 3/3]
Table IV.4.8 Index of school principal's leadership and reading performance, by national quarters of this index
Results based on school principals' reports

		Performance on the reading scale by national quarters of this index								Change in the reading score per unit of this index		Increased likelihood of students in the bottom quarter of this index scoring in the bottom quarter of the national reading performance distribution		Explained variance in student performance (r-squared x 100)	
		Bottom quarter		Second quarter		Third quarter		Top quarter							
		Mean score	S.E.	Mean score	S.E.	Mean score	S.E.	Mean score	S.E.	Effect	S.E.	Ratio	S.E.	%	S.E.
OECD	Australia	**523**	(4.1)	514	(5.2)	517	(7.6)	**507**	(4.2)	-2.5	(2.59)	**0.8**	(0.07)	0.1	(0.17)
	Austria	480	(8.1)	481	(10.6)	461	(11.1)	456	(12.0)	-12.9	(7.05)	**0.7**	(0.14)	1.1	(1.24)
	Belgium	491	(7.7)	519	(8.5)	506	(7.5)	508	(10.1)	8.5	(6.39)	1.2	(0.17)	0.4	(0.69)
	Canada	**517**	(3.6)	526	(3.3)	525	(3.4)	**528**	(3.4)	4.1	(2.08)	1.1	(0.08)	0.2	(0.20)
	Chile	**433**	(8.8)	444	(7.6)	457	(7.3)	**464**	(6.2)	**9.6**	(3.54)	1.4	(0.20)	1.7	(1.27)
	Czech Republic	479	(8.0)	478	(6.6)	481	(8.4)	473	(9.3)	0.1	(5.47)	1.0	(0.15)	0.0	(0.19)
	Denmark	497	(4.1)	493	(4.7)	496	(4.4)	495	(4.8)	-0.7	(4.03)	1.0	(0.09)	0.0	(0.08)
	Estonia	**507**	(6.3)	498	(5.4)	511	(4.8)	**490**	(4.7)	-5.4	(3.50)	0.9	(0.12)	0.3	(0.41)
	Finland	533	(4.7)	544	(4.3)	537	(3.9)	530	(4.6)	-3.6	(2.71)	1.1	(0.11)	0.1	(0.13)
	France	w	w	w	w	w	w	w	w	w	w	w	w	w	w
	Germany	**518**	(7.7)	501	(9.3)	491	(8.0)	**480**	(10.1)	**-16.9**	(8.09)	**0.6**	(0.12)	1.4	(1.39)
	Greece	481	(12.0)	490	(7.7)	486	(8.0)	476	(9.9)	-2.2	(4.94)	1.0	(0.23)	0.1	(0.35)
	Hungary	510	(9.4)	483	(11.7)	491	(9.9)	493	(10.3)	-11.0	(6.08)	**0.7**	(0.16)	0.9	(1.02)
	Iceland	503	(3.4)	497	(3.3)	492	(3.4)	501	(3.5)	-1.1	(2.35)	1.0	(0.06)	0.0	(0.04)
	Ireland	499	(7.6)	488	(8.9)	488	(7.9)	501	(8.8)	-1.2	(5.36)	0.8	(0.13)	0.0	(0.20)
	Israel	**489**	(9.9)	481	(9.4)	478	(8.1)	**448**	(13.4)	-16.7	(8.54)	0.7	(0.15)	1.8	(1.81)
	Italy	488	(5.2)	488	(4.9)	489	(5.0)	480	(5.3)	-4.6	(2.99)	1.0	(0.09)	0.2	(0.24)
	Japan	515	(10.7)	520	(8.4)	519	(10.2)	526	(9.6)	4.5	(6.36)	1.1	(0.19)	0.1	(0.46)
	Korea	539	(6.0)	545	(6.6)	538	(9.5)	535	(9.1)	-0.1	(3.72)	1.0	(0.18)	0.0	(0.23)
	Luxembourg	**447**	(2.4)	459	(2.5)	489	(2.3)	**488**	(2.8)	**22.3**	(1.03)	**1.4**	(0.10)	5.0	(0.45)
	Mexico	**417**	(4.1)	415	(4.2)	430	(5.1)	**440**	(3.4)	**9.2**	(1.99)	1.2	(0.10)	1.3	(0.58)
	Netherlands	498	(10.7)	526	(14.7)	501	(9.6)	507	(12.0)	-1.0	(8.04)	1.1	(0.23)	0.0	(0.36)
	New Zealand	524	(5.9)	515	(5.1)	526	(5.3)	524	(5.5)	2.9	(2.80)	1.0	(0.11)	0.1	(0.16)
	Norway	499	(4.3)	508	(6.2)	506	(4.4)	498	(4.7)	1.8	(4.62)	1.1	(0.09)	0.0	(0.12)
	Poland	507	(5.3)	491	(5.8)	504	(5.9)	500	(4.2)	-2.9	(2.98)	0.9	(0.09)	0.1	(0.13)
	Portugal	488	(6.2)	491	(5.8)	483	(8.4)	495	(8.3)	2.1	(4.99)	1.0	(0.13)	0.0	(0.19)
	Slovak Republic	**490**	(10.6)	481	(8.9)	471	(8.1)	**467**	(8.3)	-13.5	(8.25)	0.8	(0.16)	1.2	(1.54)
	Slovenia	**488**	(3.4)	489	(2.3)	478	(2.0)	**477**	(2.2)	**-5.9**	(1.55)	1.0	(0.07)	0.3	(0.14)
	Spain	**470**	(4.0)	475	(4.0)	485	(4.5)	**494**	(5.7)	**10.7**	(2.67)	**1.3**	(0.10)	1.2	(0.62)
	Sweden	498	(5.6)	490	(4.5)	506	(4.4)	495	(8.4)	1.0	(4.45)	1.0	(0.10)	0.0	(0.13)
	Switzerland	**489**	(6.3)	496	(8.3)	503	(7.8)	**511**	(8.6)	**11.5**	(5.79)	1.2	(0.12)	1.1	(1.13)
	Turkey	463	(7.4)	458	(8.2)	462	(8.2)	475	(8.3)	6.1	(4.43)	1.0	(0.15)	0.5	(0.64)
	United Kingdom	**500**	(5.2)	505	(6.6)	496	(5.4)	**481**	(5.4)	**-7.0**	(2.95)	0.9	(0.09)	0.5	(0.38)
	United States	**517**	(10.1)	482	(6.4)	499	(7.6)	**502**	(7.2)	-4.1	(3.95)	0.7	(0.13)	0.2	(0.46)
	OECD average	494	(1.2)	493	(1.3)	494	(1.2)	492	(1.3)	-0.6	(0.85)	1.0	(0.02)	0.6	(0.12)
Partners	Albania	382	(7.8)	380	(9.9)	391	(9.8)	387	(8.6)	2.5	(4.55)	1.0	(0.14)	0.0	(0.20)
	Argentina	377	(10.7)	397	(10.1)	428	(11.1)	389	(10.8)	7.8	(6.21)	1.4	(0.19)	0.4	(0.73)
	Azerbaijan	**358**	(8.2)	377	(6.7)	353	(9.0)	**360**	(7.6)	0.8	(3.40)	1.1	(0.20)	0.0	(0.16)
	Brazil	**388**	(4.7)	423	(8.9)	415	(6.4)	**423**	(5.6)	**11.0**	(2.58)	**1.4**	(0.12)	1.6	(0.72)
	Bulgaria	438	(16.3)	432	(13.2)	413	(11.3)	434	(13.5)	1.9	(9.22)	0.8	(0.20)	0.0	(0.37)
	Colombia	403	(7.7)	411	(7.0)	419	(6.8)	418	(10.3)	2.3	(5.38)	1.2	(0.18)	0.1	(0.57)
	Croatia	**456**	(7.6)	477	(9.0)	486	(8.1)	**486**	(7.7)	11.7	(6.67)	**1.5**	(0.19)	1.1	(1.20)
	Dubai (UAE)	**466**	(2.2)	428	(2.3)	462	(2.5)	**481**	(2.3)	**7.7**	(0.86)	**1.1**	(0.06)	0.7	(0.16)
	Hong Kong-China	**542**	(8.5)	543	(7.2)	529	(8.2)	**522**	(7.5)	**-10.2**	(4.56)	0.8	(0.18)	1.3	(1.21)
	Indonesia	402	(7.3)	404	(8.6)	402	(6.6)	399	(6.7)	-3.4	(3.29)	1.0	(0.16)	0.3	(0.56)
	Jordan	**384**	(7.8)	402	(7.3)	419	(7.4)	**415**	(7.1)	**11.6**	(3.74)	**1.5**	(0.19)	1.9	(1.25)
	Kazakhstan	397	(7.8)	378	(8.7)	397	(7.7)	390	(9.4)	-2.0	(5.90)	0.9	(0.13)	0.0	(0.25)
	Kyrgyzstan	**295**	(6.7)	304	(6.6)	317	(8.1)	**340**	(11.1)	**19.5**	(6.43)	1.2	(0.15)	3.3	(2.06)
	Latvia	481	(6.4)	489	(5.3)	486	(4.7)	480	(7.8)	-2.8	(4.11)	0.9	(0.14)	0.1	(0.33)
	Liechtenstein	491	(11.3)	546	(14.0)	489	(8.5)	472	(7.8)	**-12.6**	(5.72)	1.0	(0.25)	1.1	(0.99)
	Lithuania	476	(7.1)	453	(6.0)	468	(6.4)	476	(5.6)	-1.5	(4.61)	0.9	(0.13)	0.0	(0.17)
	Macao-China	496	(1.4)	473	(2.1)	482	(2.2)	495	(2.0)	**2.7**	(0.92)	**0.7**	(0.04)	0.1	(0.06)
	Montenegro	**393**	(2.9)	409	(4.8)	412	(2.6)	**416**	(2.7)	**10.1**	(2.05)	**1.3**	(0.08)	0.5	(0.21)
	Panama	**345**	(12.1)	365	(9.1)	361	(18.3)	**412**	(16.3)	**20.6**	(6.18)	1.3	(0.33)	5.3	(3.12)
	Peru	**338**	(6.9)	379	(9.7)	368	(8.4)	**390**	(8.1)	**15.4**	(3.50)	**1.6**	(0.20)	3.1	(1.47)
	Qatar	367	(2.0)	387	(1.7)	371	(1.9)	363	(1.6)	-0.6	(0.72)	1.1	(0.05)	0.0	(0.01)
	Romania	431	(9.1)	398	(10.6)	442	(7.7)	426	(10.0)	3.1	(7.14)	0.9	(0.17)	0.1	(0.46)
	Russian Federation	465	(7.2)	455	(5.8)	451	(6.2)	467	(7.1)	2.2	(4.01)	1.0	(0.11)	0.0	(0.23)
	Serbia	445	(5.9)	425	(7.7)	450	(8.1)	448	(8.2)	1.6	(4.60)	0.9	(0.13)	0.0	(0.24)
	Shanghai-China	543	(7.0)	563	(8.1)	559	(7.6)	559	(7.0)	5.1	(5.64)	1.3	(0.21)	0.3	(0.58)
	Singapore	532	(2.8)	524	(2.3)	513	(3.1)	535	(2.5)	**-3.8**	(1.52)	1.0	(0.08)	0.1	(0.10)
	Chinese Taipei	**502**	(7.3)	498	(7.6)	491	(7.2)	**489**	(7.6)	-7.8	(4.85)	0.9	(0.15)	0.6	(0.76)
	Thailand	**407**	(6.3)	428	(5.6)	414	(6.7)	**436**	(5.8)	**10.0**	(3.41)	**1.3**	(0.16)	1.6	(1.09)
	Trinidad and Tobago	**392**	(2.9)	422	(2.9)	427	(3.0)	**444**	(2.6)	**15.9**	(1.33)	**1.5**	(0.09)	2.1	(0.33)
	Tunisia	**428**	(6.0)	391	(7.9)	403	(9.6)	**393**	(8.2)	-6.2	(3.82)	**0.5**	(0.09)	0.6	(0.80)
	Uruguay	**420**	(6.8)	440	(8.1)	405	(6.6)	**440**	(8.2)	0.5	(3.65)	1.1	(0.13)	0.0	(0.13)

Note: Values that are statistically significant are indicated in bold (see Annex A3).
StatLink http://dx.doi.org/10.1787/888932343285

[Part 1/2]

Table IV.4.9 **Correlations among six learning environment indices**

		Correlation between																	
		Teacher-student relations and:										Disciplinary climate and:							
		Disciplinary climate		Teachers' stimulation of students' reading engagement and reading skills		Student-related factors affecting school climate		Teacher-related factors affecting school climate		School principals' leadership		Teachers' stimulation of students' reading engagement and reading skills		Student-related factors affecting school climate		Teacher-related factors affecting school climate		School principals' leadership	
		Corr.	S.E.	Corr.	S.E.	Corr.	S.E.	Corr.	S.E.	Corr.	S.E.	Corr.	S.E.	Corr.	S.E.	Corr.	S.E.	Corr.	S.E.
OECD	Australia	**0.24**	(0.01)	**0.33**	(0.01)	**0.12**	(0.01)	**0.09**	(0.01)	-0.02	(0.02)	**0.26**	(0.01)	**0.15**	(0.02)	**0.10**	(0.02)	-0.03	(0.02)
	Austria	**0.20**	(0.02)	**0.29**	(0.02)	0.04	(0.02)	0.03	(0.02)	0.02	(0.02)	**0.12**	(0.02)	**0.15**	(0.03)	0.03	(0.03)	-0.05	(0.04)
	Belgium	**0.18**	(0.01)	**0.26**	(0.01)	-0.02	(0.02)	**-0.04**	(0.02)	0.00	(0.01)	**0.14**	(0.01)	0.04	(0.02)	0.00	(0.02)	0.02	(0.02)
	Canada	**0.18**	(0.01)	**0.28**	(0.01)	**0.04**	(0.01)	**0.03**	(0.01)	0.02	(0.01)	**0.21**	(0.01)	**0.08**	(0.02)	**0.06**	(0.02)	0.02	(0.02)
	Chile	**0.15**	(0.01)	**0.31**	(0.02)	0.04	(0.02)	0.04	(0.02)	**0.06**	(0.02)	**0.13**	(0.02)	**0.08**	(0.03)	0.05	(0.03)	**0.08**	(0.03)
	Czech Republic	**0.20**	(0.02)	**0.21**	(0.02)	**0.07**	(0.02)	**0.05**	(0.02)	**-0.04**	(0.02)	**0.14**	(0.02)	**0.13**	(0.04)	0.07	(0.04)	-0.07	(0.04)
	Denmark	**0.20**	(0.01)	**0.30**	(0.02)	**0.09**	(0.02)	**0.07**	(0.02)	-0.03	(0.02)	**0.19**	(0.02)	**0.11**	(0.03)	**0.09**	(0.02)	0.01	(0.03)
	Estonia	**0.14**	(0.02)	**0.27**	(0.02)	0.05	(0.03)	0.04	(0.02)	-0.02	(0.03)	**0.20**	(0.02)	**0.06**	(0.03)	-0.02	(0.04)	-0.05	(0.03)
	Finland	**0.20**	(0.02)	**0.25**	(0.02)	**0.06**	(0.02)	0.04	(0.02)	0.02	(0.02)	**0.13**	(0.02)	0.06	(0.03)	-0.02	(0.03)	0.01	(0.02)
	France	**0.17**	(0.02)	**0.23**	(0.02)	w	w	w	w	w	w	**0.12**	(0.02)	w	w	w	w	w	w
	Germany	**0.21**	(0.02)	**0.28**	(0.02)	0.00	(0.02)	0.03	(0.02)	0.03	(0.02)	**0.18**	(0.02)	**0.11**	(0.03)	**0.05**	(0.02)	0.00	(0.03)
	Greece	**0.15**	(0.02)	**0.35**	(0.02)	0.04	(0.02)	0.00	(0.02)	**0.08**	(0.03)	**0.09**	(0.02)	**0.06**	(0.03)	0.01	(0.03)	0.03	(0.03)
	Hungary	**0.24**	(0.02)	**0.32**	(0.02)	**0.10**	(0.02)	**0.08**	(0.03)	-0.03	(0.02)	**0.25**	(0.02)	**0.16**	(0.03)	**0.08**	(0.03)	-0.03	(0.03)
	Iceland	**0.21**	(0.02)	**0.29**	(0.02)	**0.06**	(0.01)	0.03	(0.02)	**0.06**	(0.02)	**0.18**	(0.02)	**0.07**	(0.01)	0.03	(0.02)	**0.08**	(0.02)
	Ireland	**0.22**	(0.02)	**0.30**	(0.02)	**0.07**	(0.03)	0.02	(0.02)	-0.03	(0.02)	**0.25**	(0.02)	0.02	(0.03)	0.06	(0.03)	0.03	(0.03)
	Israel	**0.24**	(0.02)	**0.40**	(0.01)	0.06	(0.03)	**0.07**	(0.03)	0.02	(0.03)	**0.17**	(0.02)	**0.09**	(0.03)	**0.13**	(0.03)	-0.01	(0.02)
	Italy	**0.21**	(0.01)	**0.30**	(0.01)	**0.05**	(0.01)	**0.05**	(0.01)	**0.04**	(0.01)	**0.22**	(0.01)	**0.19**	(0.02)	0.01	(0.02)	**0.04**	(0.02)
	Japan	**0.19**	(0.02)	**0.33**	(0.01)	**0.11**	(0.02)	**0.04**	(0.02)	0.03	(0.03)	**0.13**	(0.02)	**0.26**	(0.03)	**0.11**	(0.03)	0.06	(0.04)
	Korea	**0.14**	(0.02)	**0.33**	(0.02)	**0.06**	(0.03)	0.03	(0.03)	0.00	(0.02)	**0.14**	(0.02)	**0.11**	(0.04)	0.03	(0.04)	0.04	(0.04)
	Luxembourg	**0.18**	(0.02)	**0.24**	(0.02)	**0.07**	(0.01)	**0.09**	(0.01)	**0.04**	(0.01)	**0.11**	(0.02)	**0.07**	(0.02)	**0.07**	(0.01)	**0.06**	(0.01)
	Mexico	**0.14**	(0.01)	**0.31**	(0.01)	**0.05**	(0.01)	**0.05**	(0.01)	0.01	(0.01)	**0.08**	(0.01)	**0.08**	(0.01)	**0.04**	(0.01)	-0.01	(0.01)
	Netherlands	**0.21**	(0.02)	**0.24**	(0.02)	**0.05**	(0.02)	**0.05**	(0.02)	0.00	(0.02)	**0.16**	(0.02)	**0.05**	(0.02)	0.03	(0.02)	0.02	(0.03)
	New Zealand	**0.22**	(0.02)	**0.31**	(0.01)	**0.05**	(0.02)	**0.04**	(0.02)	0.02	(0.02)	**0.27**	(0.02)	**0.12**	(0.02)	**0.07**	(0.02)	**0.05**	(0.02)
	Norway	**0.24**	(0.02)	**0.33**	(0.02)	**0.06**	(0.02)	0.04	(0.02)	0.02	(0.02)	**0.20**	(0.02)	**0.11**	(0.03)	**0.06**	(0.02)	**0.06**	(0.03)
	Poland	**0.18**	(0.02)	**0.32**	(0.02)	**0.06**	(0.02)	0.01	(0.02)	0.00	(0.02)	**0.23**	(0.02)	**0.07**	(0.03)	0.05	(0.03)	0.00	(0.03)
	Portugal	**0.18**	(0.02)	**0.30**	(0.02)	**0.08**	(0.03)	**0.05**	(0.02)	**0.05**	(0.02)	**0.15**	(0.02)	**0.09**	(0.04)	**0.09**	(0.03)	0.03	(0.03)
	Slovak Republic	**0.20**	(0.02)	**0.26**	(0.02)	0.04	(0.03)	0.05	(0.03)	0.01	(0.03)	**0.14**	(0.02)	**0.08**	(0.03)	**0.06**	(0.03)	-0.02	(0.04)
	Slovenia	**0.16**	(0.02)	**0.23**	(0.02)	**0.06**	(0.01)	0.01	(0.02)	**0.03**	(0.02)	**0.14**	(0.02)	**0.19**	(0.01)	**0.10**	(0.01)	0.02	(0.01)
	Spain	**0.16**	(0.01)	**0.29**	(0.01)	**0.04**	(0.02)	**0.04**	(0.01)	**0.04**	(0.02)	**0.14**	(0.02)	**0.06**	(0.02)	**0.06**	(0.02)	0.03	(0.02)
	Sweden	**0.19**	(0.02)	**0.35**	(0.01)	0.04	(0.02)	**0.05**	(0.02)	0.04	(0.02)	**0.18**	(0.02)	**0.10**	(0.03)	**0.08**	(0.03)	0.03	(0.02)
	Switzerland	**0.26**	(0.02)	**0.24**	(0.02)	**0.04**	(0.02)	0.04	(0.02)	**-0.06**	(0.02)	**0.14**	(0.02)	**0.07**	(0.02)	0.02	(0.02)	-0.01	(0.03)
	Turkey	**0.15**	(0.02)	**0.37**	(0.01)	0.02	(0.02)	0.00	(0.02)	-0.01	(0.02)	**0.12**	(0.02)	0.03	(0.02)	0.03	(0.03)	0.01	(0.03)
	United Kingdom	**0.23**	(0.01)	**0.28**	(0.02)	**0.03**	(0.02)	**0.04**	(0.02)	0.02	(0.02)	**0.24**	(0.02)	**0.11**	(0.02)	**0.06**	(0.03)	-0.03	(0.02)
	United States	**0.20**	(0.02)	**0.35**	(0.02)	**0.10**	(0.02)	**0.09**	(0.02)	0.01	(0.02)	**0.16**	(0.02)	**0.11**	(0.02)	**0.11**	(0.02)	0.00	(0.03)
	OECD average	**0.19**	(0.00)	**0.29**	(0.00)	**0.05**	(0.00)	**0.04**	(0.00)	**0.01**	(0.00)	**0.17**	(0.00)	**0.10**	(0.00)	**0.05**	(0.00)	**0.01**	(0.00)
Partners	Albania	**0.18**	(0.02)	**0.36**	(0.02)	**0.11**	(0.03)	**0.12**	(0.03)	0.02	(0.02)	**0.10**	(0.02)	**0.14**	(0.04)	**0.13**	(0.03)	0.03	(0.03)
	Argentina	**0.14**	(0.02)	**0.32**	(0.02)	-0.02	(0.02)	-0.03	(0.03)	-0.01	(0.03)	**0.09**	(0.03)	0.02	(0.03)	-0.01	(0.03)	-0.02	(0.04)
	Azerbaijan	**0.16**	(0.02)	**0.34**	(0.02)	0.00	(0.03)	0.02	(0.02)	0.01	(0.02)	**0.10**	(0.03)	0.04	(0.03)	0.03	(0.03)	0.02	(0.04)
	Brazil	**0.10**	(0.01)	**0.33**	(0.01)	**0.10**	(0.01)	**0.06**	(0.02)	0.01	(0.02)	0.01	(0.01)	**0.12**	(0.02)	**0.09**	(0.02)	0.03	(0.02)
	Bulgaria	**0.08**	(0.02)	**0.33**	(0.02)	-0.03	(0.03)	0.02	(0.03)	-0.05	(0.03)	0.05	(0.03)	**0.12**	(0.03)	0.03	(0.03)	-0.06	(0.04)
	Colombia	**0.09**	(0.02)	**0.29**	(0.02)	0.00	(0.02)	0.03	(0.02)	0.02	(0.02)	**0.05**	(0.02)	**0.08**	(0.03)	0.07	(0.03)	0.00	(0.03)
	Croatia	**0.17**	(0.02)	**0.29**	(0.02)	**0.06**	(0.02)	0.03	(0.02)	-0.01	(0.03)	**0.19**	(0.02)	**0.15**	(0.03)	0.04	(0.03)	0.01	(0.04)
	Dubai (UAE)	**0.19**	(0.02)	**0.35**	(0.02)	-0.02	(0.02)	-0.02	(0.02)	**-0.03**	(0.02)	**0.20**	(0.02)	**0.16**	(0.01)	**0.12**	(0.01)	**0.04**	(0.01)
	Hong Kong-China	**0.17**	(0.01)	**0.29**	(0.02)	0.01	(0.02)	0.00	(0.02)	**-0.04**	(0.02)	**0.19**	(0.02)	**0.08**	(0.02)	**0.05**	(0.02)	-0.01	(0.02)
	Indonesia	**0.08**	(0.02)	**0.28**	(0.02)	-0.01	(0.02)	-0.02	(0.02)	0.03	(0.03)	0.03	(0.02)	**0.12**	(0.02)	**0.06**	(0.03)	0.01	(0.03)
	Jordan	**0.20**	(0.02)	**0.36**	(0.02)	0.00	(0.02)	0.00	(0.02)	-0.02	(0.02)	**0.17**	(0.02)	0.04	(0.03)	0.04	(0.03)	0.03	(0.03)
	Kazakhstan	**0.23**	(0.02)	**0.32**	(0.02)	0.01	(0.03)	0.02	(0.03)	**0.06**	(0.03)	**0.20**	(0.02)	**0.08**	(0.03)	0.06	(0.03)	0.00	(0.03)
	Kyrgyzstan	**0.05**	(0.02)	**0.35**	(0.02)	0.02	(0.03)	0.00	(0.02)	-0.03	(0.03)	**0.07**	(0.02)	0.03	(0.02)	0.03	(0.02)	0.04	(0.03)
	Latvia	**0.17**	(0.02)	**0.24**	(0.02)	0.05	(0.03)	**0.08**	(0.03)	0.02	(0.02)	**0.17**	(0.03)	**0.13**	(0.04)	**0.16**	(0.04)	0.04	(0.04)
	Liechtenstein	**0.33**	(0.05)	**0.41**	(0.04)	0.07	(0.05)	**0.10**	(0.05)	0.02	(0.05)	**0.20**	(0.06)	0.05	(0.07)	**0.20**	(0.05)	**0.14**	(0.05)
	Lithuania	**0.14**	(0.02)	**0.29**	(0.02)	0.00	(0.02)	-0.01	(0.02)	**-0.07**	(0.02)	**0.15**	(0.02)	**0.07**	(0.03)	0.00	(0.03)	-0.02	(0.03)
	Macao-China	**0.17**	(0.02)	**0.30**	(0.01)	0.00	(0.01)	0.00	(0.01)	0.02	(0.01)	**0.12**	(0.02)	**0.10**	(0.01)	**0.07**	(0.01)	-0.01	(0.01)
	Montenegro	**0.16**	(0.02)	**0.33**	(0.02)	**0.06**	(0.02)	0.01	(0.02)	-0.02	(0.02)	**0.15**	(0.02)	0.01	(0.01)	0.00	(0.01)	**0.04**	(0.01)
	Panama	-0.01	(0.04)	**0.32**	(0.03)	**-0.08**	(0.03)	0.01	(0.03)	**-0.04**	(0.02)	**-0.12**	(0.03)	0.04	(0.03)	-0.01	(0.03)	-0.02	(0.03)
	Peru	**0.11**	(0.02)	**0.34**	(0.02)	0.03	(0.02)	0.03	(0.02)	**0.05**	(0.02)	**0.06**	(0.02)	**0.07**	(0.02)	0.03	(0.02)	0.01	(0.02)
	Qatar	**0.12**	(0.01)	**0.39**	(0.01)	0.02	(0.01)	-0.01	(0.01)	0.01	(0.01)	**0.14**	(0.01)	**0.06**	(0.01)	**0.05**	(0.01)	**0.02**	(0.01)
	Romania	**0.13**	(0.02)	**0.29**	(0.02)	**0.04**	(0.02)	**0.05**	(0.02)	0.02	(0.02)	**0.09**	(0.02)	**0.11**	(0.04)	0.03	(0.03)	0.03	(0.04)
	Russian Federation	**0.18**	(0.02)	**0.28**	(0.02)	-0.02	(0.03)	-0.03	(0.04)	0.02	(0.03)	**0.16**	(0.02)	0.01	(0.02)	-0.01	(0.02)	0.02	(0.03)
	Serbia	**0.13**	(0.02)	**0.25**	(0.02)	0.02	(0.02)	0.03	(0.02)	0.00	(0.02)	**0.15**	(0.02)	**0.14**	(0.02)	0.07	(0.03)	0.00	(0.02)
	Shanghai-China	**0.27**	(0.02)	**0.30**	(0.02)	**0.05**	(0.02)	0.04	(0.03)	0.03	(0.02)	**0.24**	(0.02)	**0.09**	(0.03)	0.02	(0.04)	0.04	(0.03)
	Singapore	**0.14**	(0.01)	**0.30**	(0.01)	**0.05**	(0.02)	**0.03**	(0.01)	**0.05**	(0.02)	**0.19**	(0.02)	**0.13**	(0.01)	**0.04**	(0.01)	-0.01	(0.01)
	Chinese Taipei	**0.16**	(0.02)	**0.27**	(0.02)	0.00	(0.01)	0.01	(0.02)	-0.03	(0.02)	**0.15**	(0.02)	0.04	(0.02)	0.03	(0.03)	-0.03	(0.02)
	Thailand	**0.15**	(0.02)	**0.32**	(0.02)	0.01	(0.01)	**0.04**	(0.02)	0.03	(0.02)	**0.09**	(0.02)	0.04	(0.02)	0.04	(0.02)	0.01	(0.02)
	Trinidad and Tobago	**0.15**	(0.02)	**0.30**	(0.02)	**0.05**	(0.02)	**0.04**	(0.02)	0.03	(0.02)	**0.13**	(0.02)	**0.12**	(0.01)	**0.05**	(0.01)	**0.05**	(0.02)
	Tunisia	**0.12**	(0.02)	**0.38**	(0.01)	0.01	(0.02)	0.04	(0.03)	0.04	(0.02)	**0.17**	(0.02)	**0.04**	(0.02)	0.04	(0.02)	**0.07**	(0.02)
	Uruguay	**0.10**	(0.02)	**0.27**	(0.02)	-0.02	(0.02)	-0.03	(0.02)	0.01	(0.02)	0.02	(0.02)	**0.09**	(0.02)	0.03	(0.02)	-0.03	(0.02)

Note: Values that are statistically significant are indicated in bold (see Annex A3).
StatLink http://dx.doi.org/10.1787/888932343285

[Part 2/2]

Table IV. 4.9 Correlations among six learning environment indices

		Correlation between											
		Teachers' stimulation of students' reading engagement and reading skills and:						Student-related factors affecting school climate and:				Teacher-related factors affecting school climate and:	
		Student-related factors affecting school climate		Teacher-related factors affecting school climate		School principals' leadership		Teacher-related factors affecting school climate		School principals' leadership		School principals' leadership	
		Corr.	S.E.	Corr.	S.E.	Corr.	S.E.	Corr.	S.E.	Corr.	S.E.	Corr.	S.E.
OECD	Australia	**0.11**	(0.01)	**0.07**	(0.02)	-0.01	(0.02)	**0.72**	(0.03)	-0.04	(0.06)	**0.13**	(0.07)
	Austria	0.02	(0.02)	0.02	(0.02)	-0.03	(0.02)	**0.41**	(0.08)	0.02	(0.07)	0.15	(0.11)
	Belgium	0.02	(0.02)	**-0.04**	(0.02)	**0.06**	(0.02)	**0.60**	(0.03)	**0.16**	(0.07)	0.01	(0.06)
	Canada	0.01	(0.02)	**0.05**	(0.02)	**0.06**	(0.02)	**0.59**	(0.04)	**0.18**	(0.06)	**0.20**	(0.05)
	Chile	**0.08**	(0.02)	**0.09**	(0.03)	**0.11**	(0.03)	**0.67**	(0.05)	**0.38**	(0.06)	**0.49**	(0.06)
	Czech Republic	**0.05**	(0.02)	**0.05**	(0.02)	-0.03	(0.03)	**0.47**	(0.05)	**0.13**	(0.06)	**0.30**	(0.08)
	Denmark	**0.04**	(0.02)	**0.04**	(0.02)	0.02	(0.02)	**0.67**	(0.04)	-0.05	(0.07)	0.13	(0.07)
	Estonia	-0.01	(0.03)	-0.04	(0.02)	-0.01	(0.03)	**0.62**	(0.05)	-0.12	(0.08)	0.05	(0.07)
	Finland	0.01	(0.02)	0.01	(0.02)	-0.01	(0.02)	**0.55**	(0.06)	0.11	(0.08)	0.02	(0.08)
	France	w	w	w	w	w	w	w	w	w	w	w	w
	Germany	0.03	(0.02)	**0.04**	(0.02)	0.03	(0.02)	**0.50**	(0.05)	-0.11	(0.07)	0.08	(0.07)
	Greece	0.02	(0.03)	0.00	(0.02)	0.05	(0.03)	**0.69**	(0.05)	0.06	(0.10)	0.07	(0.09)
	Hungary	**0.08**	(0.03)	0.03	(0.03)	-0.03	(0.02)	**0.66**	(0.04)	0.05	(0.09)	**0.26**	(0.07)
	Iceland	0.01	(0.02)	**0.04**	(0.02)	0.03	(0.02)	**0.60**	(0.00)	**0.16**	(0.00)	**0.15**	(0.00)
	Ireland	-0.02	(0.02)	-0.01	(0.02)	0.00	(0.02)	**0.60**	(0.08)	**0.21**	(0.09)	**0.32**	(0.09)
	Israel	0.01	(0.04)	0.01	(0.03)	0.04	(0.04)	**0.64**	(0.05)	**0.25**	(0.09)	**0.18**	(0.08)
	Italy	**0.05**	(0.02)	0.03	(0.01)	0.03	(0.02)	**0.38**	(0.04)	0.08	(0.05)	**0.16**	(0.04)
	Japan	**0.09**	(0.02)	**0.04**	(0.02)	**0.07**	(0.02)	**0.74**	(0.04)	0.14	(0.08)	**0.15**	(0.07)
	Korea	0.04	(0.03)	0.02	(0.02)	-0.01	(0.03)	**0.67**	(0.07)	0.15	(0.10)	**0.33**	(0.10)
	Luxembourg	0.02	(0.01)	**0.05**	(0.01)	**0.03**	(0.01)	**0.73**	(0.00)	**0.49**	(0.00)	**0.47**	(0.00)
	Mexico	**0.05**	(0.01)	**0.04**	(0.01)	0.02	(0.01)	**0.67**	(0.02)	**0.20**	(0.04)	**0.30**	(0.04)
	Netherlands	**0.06**	(0.02)	0.04	(0.02)	0.04	(0.02)	**0.66**	(0.05)	0.08	(0.07)	**0.19**	(0.07)
	New Zealand	**0.07**	(0.02)	**0.06**	(0.02)	0.03	(0.02)	**0.69**	(0.04)	0.09	(0.07)	**0.15**	(0.06)
	Norway	**0.06**	(0.02)	**0.05**	(0.02)	-0.02	(0.02)	**0.56**	(0.05)	0.15	(0.08)	0.15	(0.09)
	Poland	**0.06**	(0.02)	0.02	(0.03)	-0.01	(0.02)	**0.39**	(0.08)	-0.03	(0.09)	**0.28**	(0.07)
	Portugal	0.02	(0.02)	**0.04**	(0.02)	0.03	(0.02)	**0.65**	(0.07)	0.11	(0.08)	**0.19**	(0.07)
	Slovak Republic	0.04	(0.03)	0.04	(0.03)	0.01	(0.03)	**0.54**	(0.07)	0.02	(0.10)	**0.24**	(0.09)
	Slovenia	0.03	(0.02)	0.00	(0.02)	0.00	(0.01)	**0.63**	(0.00)	**-0.07**	(0.01)	**0.08**	(0.01)
	Spain	-0.01	(0.02)	-0.02	(0.02)	0.00	(0.02)	**0.61**	(0.03)	**0.19**	(0.05)	**0.19**	(0.05)
	Sweden	**0.06**	(0.02)	0.04	(0.02)	0.04	(0.02)	**0.58**	(0.05)	**0.15**	(0.07)	**0.16**	(0.08)
	Switzerland	0.03	(0.02)	0.00	(0.02)	0.01	(0.03)	**0.54**	(0.04)	0.16	(0.08)	**0.21**	(0.06)
	Turkey	0.00	(0.03)	-0.02	(0.03)	-0.01	(0.02)	**0.88**	(0.02)	-0.12	(0.07)	-0.12	(0.07)
	United Kingdom	0.01	(0.02)	0.02	(0.02)	-0.01	(0.02)	**0.63**	(0.05)	0.01	(0.07)	**0.18**	(0.07)
	United States	0.04	(0.02)	**0.06**	(0.02)	0.01	(0.02)	**0.60**	(0.05)	0.11	(0.08)	**0.24**	(0.06)
	OECD average	**0.03**	(0.00)	**0.03**	(0.00)	**0.02**	(0.00)	**0.61**	(0.01)	**0.10**	(0.01)	**0.18**	(0.01)
Partners	Albania	**0.06**	(0.03)	**0.05**	(0.02)	0.02	(0.03)	**0.71**	(0.04)	0.10	(0.07)	**0.24**	(0.07)
	Argentina	0.01	(0.03)	-0.01	(0.02)	-0.02	(0.02)	**0.68**	(0.04)	0.11	(0.10)	**0.20**	(0.09)
	Azerbaijan	0.03	(0.03)	0.04	(0.04)	-0.04	(0.02)	**0.76**	(0.03)	0.00	(0.09)	0.00	(0.08)
	Brazil	**0.07**	(0.02)	**0.05**	(0.02)	0.02	(0.01)	**0.57**	(0.04)	**0.13**	(0.04)	**0.31**	(0.04)
	Bulgaria	0.03	(0.02)	0.01	(0.02)	**-0.05**	(0.02)	**0.70**	(0.05)	-0.02	(0.10)	0.02	(0.12)
	Colombia	0.01	(0.03)	0.03	(0.03)	0.03	(0.02)	**0.67**	(0.05)	**0.32**	(0.08)	**0.39**	(0.08)
	Croatia	**0.06**	(0.02)	0.04	(0.02)	0.00	(0.02)	**0.60**	(0.05)	**0.22**	(0.08)	**0.36**	(0.08)
	Dubai (UAE)	0.01	(0.02)	-0.02	(0.02)	-0.01	(0.01)	**0.78**	(0.00)	**0.26**	(0.00)	**0.44**	(0.00)
	Hong Kong-China	**0.07**	(0.03)	**0.08**	(0.03)	-0.02	(0.02)	**0.72**	(0.05)	0.01	(0.09)	0.12	(0.08)
	Indonesia	0.02	(0.03)	0.02	(0.02)	**0.05**	(0.03)	**0.59**	(0.06)	0.14	(0.09)	**0.27**	(0.09)
	Jordan	**0.05**	(0.02)	**0.05**	(0.02)	0.00	(0.02)	**0.79**	(0.03)	0.14	(0.08)	**0.19**	(0.08)
	Kazakhstan	-0.01	(0.03)	-0.02	(0.03)	0.05	(0.03)	**0.86**	(0.02)	-0.01	(0.08)	0.06	(0.08)
	Kyrgyzstan	0.03	(0.03)	0.01	(0.03)	-0.04	(0.03)	**0.87**	(0.02)	**0.17**	(0.08)	**0.20**	(0.08)
	Latvia	**0.08**	(0.03)	**0.09**	(0.03)	**0.05**	(0.03)	**0.53**	(0.06)	0.03	(0.09)	**0.31**	(0.07)
	Liechtenstein	**0.25**	(0.05)	0.04	(0.04)	-0.09	(0.06)	**0.59**	(0.00)	**-0.11**	(0.01)	**0.03**	(0.01)
	Lithuania	0.00	(0.02)	-0.02	(0.02)	-0.04	(0.02)	**0.55**	(0.07)	0.11	(0.07)	**0.24**	(0.08)
	Macao-China	0.00	(0.01)	**-0.02**	(0.01)	0.00	(0.01)	**0.89**	(0.00)	**0.21**	(0.00)	**0.21**	(0.00)
	Montenegro	**0.03**	(0.02)	0.00	(0.02)	0.00	(0.02)	**0.59**	(0.00)	**0.21**	(0.01)	**0.31**	(0.00)
	Panama	-0.04	(0.02)	-0.01	(0.03)	0.03	(0.03)	**0.66**	(0.06)	**0.31**	(0.08)	**0.34**	(0.09)
	Peru	0.00	(0.02)	0.00	(0.02)	0.01	(0.02)	**0.70**	(0.04)	0.13	(0.07)	**0.16**	(0.08)
	Qatar	**0.03**	(0.01)	0.01	(0.01)	0.02	(0.01)	**0.86**	(0.00)	**0.06**	(0.00)	**0.16**	(0.00)
	Romania	**0.05**	(0.02)	0.04	(0.03)	0.04	(0.03)	**0.52**	(0.06)	0.13	(0.09)	**0.31**	(0.08)
	Russian Federation	-0.04	(0.02)	-0.04	(0.03)	0.02	(0.02)	**0.77**	(0.03)	0.04	(0.06)	0.14	(0.09)
	Serbia	**0.06**	(0.02)	**0.05**	(0.02)	-0.01	(0.02)	**0.62**	(0.05)	0.10	(0.06)	**0.19**	(0.06)
	Shanghai-China	0.04	(0.02)	0.03	(0.02)	0.02	(0.02)	**0.81**	(0.03)	-0.02	(0.08)	0.00	(0.08)
	Singapore	**0.05**	(0.01)	0.02	(0.01)	**0.05**	(0.01)	**0.72**	(0.00)	**0.09**	(0.01)	**0.14**	(0.01)
	Chinese Taipei	0.00	(0.02)	0.01	(0.02)	0.00	(0.02)	**0.87**	(0.02)	-0.07	(0.09)	-0.04	(0.10)
	Thailand	0.00	(0.02)	0.01	(0.02)	0.02	(0.02)	**0.65**	(0.05)	**0.18**	(0.07)	**0.34**	(0.06)
	Trinidad and Tobago	**0.09**	(0.02)	**0.05**	(0.02)	**0.05**	(0.01)	**0.64**	(0.01)	**0.37**	(0.01)	**0.35**	(0.00)
	Tunisia	0.03	(0.02)	0.05	(0.03)	0.03	(0.02)	**0.68**	(0.05)	0.10	(0.08)	**0.19**	(0.09)
	Uruguay	**0.04**	(0.02)	0.02	(0.02)	0.02	(0.02)	**0.66**	(0.03)	**0.13**	(0.05)	0.10	(0.06)

Note: Values that are statistically significant are indicated in bold (see Annex A3).

StatLink http://dx.doi.org/10.1787/888932343285

ANNEX B2
RESULTS FOR REGIONS WITHIN COUNTRIES

[Part 1/3]
School admittance policies
Table S.IV.a *Results based on school principals' reports*

	Percentage of students in schools where the principal reported the following factors considered to be "never", "sometimes" or "always" for admittance at school																	
	Residence in a particular area						Students' records of academic performance						Recommendations of feeder schools					
	Never		Sometimes		Always		Never		Sometimes		Always		Never		Sometimes		Always	
	%	S.E.	%	S.E.	%	S.E.	%	S.E.	%	S.E.	%	S.E.	%	S.E.	%	S.E.	%	S.E.
Adjudicated																		
Belgium (Flemish Community)	92.0	(1.9)	6.7	(1.9)	1.3	(0.7)	37.7	(4.0)	41.6	(3.8)	20.8	(3.3)	51.2	(4.5)	44.2	(4.2)	4.7	(1.7)
Spain (Andalusia)	25.0	(4.9)	8.2	(3.4)	66.7	(5.0)	88.0	(3.9)	12.0	(3.9)	0.0	c	92.7	(3.7)	7.3	(3.7)	0.0	c
Spain (Aragon)	27.4	(5.8)	9.0	(4.0)	63.6	(5.6)	95.1	(3.6)	4.9	(3.6)	0.0	c	94.8	(3.0)	5.2	(3.0)	0.0	c
Spain (Asturias)	22.8	(5.6)	12.7	(4.9)	64.4	(5.5)	94.1	(3.3)	5.9	(3.3)	0.0	c	81.5	(6.0)	10.1	(4.5)	8.4	(4.1)
Spain (Balearic Islands)	18.5	(5.5)	18.2	(6.9)	63.3	(8.8)	87.7	(4.2)	12.3	(4.2)	0.0	c	73.6	(7.2)	26.4	(7.2)	0.0	c
Spain (Basque Country)	25.4	(2.9)	19.1	(2.9)	55.5	(3.7)	90.6	(2.1)	7.8	(2.1)	1.6	(1.0)	62.4	(3.4)	28.8	(3.4)	8.7	(2.2)
Spain (Canary Islands)	9.5	(3.3)	10.5	(4.3)	80.1	(5.4)	85.2	(5.3)	12.6	(4.7)	2.2	(2.3)	79.4	(6.5)	20.6	(6.5)	0.0	c
Spain (Cantabria)	28.7	(6.6)	12.8	(4.7)	58.5	(6.9)	92.0	(4.1)	8.0	(4.1)	0.0	c	80.7	(5.4)	14.5	(5.3)	4.9	(3.4)
Spain (Castile and Leon)	38.3	(5.8)	21.5	(5.3)	40.1	(7.5)	96.8	(2.6)	2.1	(2.1)	1.1	(1.6)	83.5	(5.1)	12.5	(4.3)	4.0	(2.7)
Spain (Catalonia)	4.8	(3.2)	9.9	(4.8)	85.3	(5.7)	91.0	(4.5)	9.0	(4.5)	0.0	c	86.2	(5.1)	11.9	(4.9)	1.9	(2.0)
Spain (Ceuta and Melilla)	16.5	(0.4)	0.0	c	83.5	(0.4)	82.7	(0.4)	14.3	(0.4)	3.0	(0.1)	93.4	(0.3)	6.6	(0.3)	0.0	c
Spain (Galicia)	31.4	(6.7)	15.8	(5.4)	52.8	(6.7)	85.7	(4.1)	14.3	(4.1)	0.0	c	92.7	(2.0)	7.3	(2.0)	0.0	c
Spain (La Rioja)	37.3	(0.6)	11.1	(0.5)	51.7	(0.6)	90.5	(0.5)	9.5	(0.5)	0.0	c	83.2	(0.4)	16.8	(0.4)	0.0	c
Spain (Madrid)	23.7	(7.4)	6.2	(3.8)	70.0	(5.9)	84.6	(6.7)	12.8	(6.3)	2.6	(2.6)	72.0	(7.5)	25.9	(8.0)	2.1	(2.1)
Spain (Murcia)	21.4	(5.5)	5.6	(3.3)	73.0	(5.6)	87.7	(5.1)	10.1	(4.6)	2.3	(2.3)	89.5	(4.3)	10.5	(4.3)	0.0	c
Spain (Navarre)	52.1	(3.8)	10.6	(3.7)	37.4	(4.1)	91.5	(2.5)	6.2	(1.1)	2.3	(2.3)	84.7	(3.9)	9.1	(3.3)	6.2	(2.3)
United Kingdom (Scotland)	21.4	(4.3)	7.7	(2.8)	70.9	(4.8)	90.4	(2.6)	3.1	(1.7)	6.5	(2.6)	65.4	(4.8)	20.0	(4.0)	14.6	(3.8)
Non-adjudicated																		
Belgium (French Community)	79.4	(3.9)	17.1	(3.8)	3.5	(1.8)	61.4	(4.9)	30.8	(4.0)	7.9	(2.7)	67.0	(5.3)	31.7	(5.2)	1.3	(1.2)
Belgium (German-Speaking Community)	53.3	(0.3)	45.7	(0.3)	1.0	(0.1)	34.9	(0.2)	52.6	(0.3)	12.5	(0.2)	34.9	(0.2)	49.5	(0.3)	15.6	(0.3)
Finland (Finnish Speaking)	17.0	(2.9)	6.6	(2.2)	76.4	(3.7)	82.2	(3.4)	16.8	(3.4)	1.0	(0.8)	72.7	(3.9)	24.5	(3.6)	2.8	(1.4)
Finland (Swedish Speaking)	54.0	(0.3)	4.6	(0.2)	41.3	(0.3)	82.6	(0.3)	17.1	(0.2)	0.3	(0.2)	78.7	(0.2)	15.2	(0.2)	6.2	(0.1)
Italy (Provincia Abruzzo)	47.6	(5.6)	32.3	(6.9)	20.0	(5.1)	44.6	(5.7)	20.8	(5.3)	34.6	(6.5)	41.1	(6.5)	39.8	(7.1)	19.1	(5.9)
Italy (Provincia Autonoma di Bolzano)	69.3	(1.2)	18.9	(0.4)	11.8	(1.5)	64.2	(0.6)	24.3	(0.4)	11.6	(0.3)	80.8	(1.6)	13.5	(1.6)	5.6	(0.2)
Italy (Provincia Basilicata)	45.0	(5.0)	18.7	(4.9)	36.2	(5.3)	43.2	(5.4)	28.0	(5.7)	28.8	(4.7)	38.4	(5.0)	32.6	(6.3)	29.0	(5.3)
Italy (Provincia Calabria)	37.4	(6.0)	25.0	(5.4)	37.7	(5.7)	37.8	(6.8)	25.4	(7.4)	36.8	(7.2)	40.5	(8.3)	28.0	(6.7)	31.4	(7.6)
Italy (Provincia Campania)	48.5	(7.5)	9.8	(4.9)	41.6	(7.5)	47.5	(6.4)	17.4	(6.2)	35.1	(6.3)	30.2	(6.3)	40.1	(7.2)	29.7	(6.1)
Italy (Provincia Emilia Romagna)	50.9	(7.5)	26.5	(6.9)	22.6	(5.7)	50.0	(5.9)	15.5	(4.9)	34.4	(5.9)	34.6	(6.0)	20.2	(5.9)	45.2	(6.5)
Italy (Provincia Friuli Venezia Giulia)	48.2	(5.6)	13.8	(3.0)	38.0	(5.2)	37.3	(5.8)	18.6	(5.0)	44.0	(4.7)	25.1	(4.1)	33.2	(4.7)	41.7	(5.3)
Italy (Provincia Lazio)	39.8	(7.2)	20.3	(5.4)	39.9	(7.0)	46.7	(7.3)	20.6	(6.5)	32.7	(7.3)	39.0	(6.7)	44.3	(7.3)	16.7	(5.5)
Italy (Provincia Liguria)	56.5	(6.6)	30.1	(5.7)	13.5	(3.4)	41.1	(6.7)	36.7	(7.7)	22.2	(6.0)	34.4	(7.7)	54.8	(7.4)	10.7	(3.5)
Italy (Provincia Lombardia)	64.4	(6.5)	13.5	(5.0)	22.1	(6.9)	36.3	(7.7)	31.3	(6.3)	32.4	(7.5)	30.3	(7.3)	37.2	(6.7)	32.5	(6.3)
Italy (Provincia Marche)	44.6	(7.9)	18.6	(6.0)	36.7	(7.6)	39.1	(7.6)	7.7	(4.2)	53.2	(7.3)	35.6	(8.1)	16.4	(4.2)	47.9	(8.2)
Italy (Provincia Molise)	52.7	(1.2)	17.3	(1.0)	30.0	(1.7)	35.2	(0.6)	25.0	(1.3)	39.8	(1.6)	28.0	(1.4)	43.8	(1.3)	28.3	(0.9)
Italy (Provincia Piemonte)	52.3	(8.6)	20.5	(7.7)	27.2	(6.1)	58.4	(6.2)	18.2	(5.8)	23.4	(5.1)	43.0	(6.8)	24.2	(6.0)	32.7	(6.2)
Italy (Provincia Puglia)	43.5	(5.6)	29.3	(7.0)	27.2	(6.6)	39.4	(5.7)	29.1	(6.3)	31.6	(6.2)	42.7	(6.4)	40.6	(6.2)	16.7	(4.8)
Italy (Provincia Sardegna)	50.4	(7.4)	22.6	(6.2)	27.0	(5.4)	44.6	(5.5)	24.8	(6.9)	30.6	(7.5)	45.0	(6.3)	32.8	(7.3)	22.3	(4.5)
Italy (Provincia Sicilia)	47.3	(7.6)	20.8	(6.2)	31.9	(6.3)	52.3	(8.3)	26.2	(7.0)	21.5	(6.7)	52.1	(8.0)	36.0	(7.4)	11.9	(4.4)
Italy (Provincia Toscana)	40.2	(7.1)	29.2	(6.1)	30.6	(6.6)	31.6	(6.7)	28.5	(6.4)	39.9	(6.1)	25.2	(6.4)	28.3	(6.0)	46.5	(6.8)
Italy (Provincia Trento)	57.8	(3.4)	16.8	(2.9)	25.4	(3.2)	64.9	(2.7)	6.1	(2.8)	29.1	(2.5)	41.6	(3.4)	44.9	(2.9)	13.5	(1.7)
Italy (Provincia Umbria)	44.8	(5.3)	18.5	(4.2)	36.7	(5.0)	33.2	(4.4)	25.5	(6.0)	41.3	(5.8)	27.1	(4.0)	36.5	(5.4)	36.4	(4.8)
Italy (Provincia Valle d'Aosta)	52.1	(0.5)	20.3	(0.2)	27.6	(0.4)	40.5	(0.4)	8.3	(0.2)	51.2	(0.5)	28.2	(0.4)	24.3	(0.4)	47.5	(0.4)
Italy (Provincia Veneto)	49.7	(7.2)	32.4	(7.9)	17.9	(5.6)	45.3	(6.2)	24.2	(6.2)	30.5	(7.0)	35.9	(7.5)	46.3	(8.2)	17.7	(6.3)
United Kingdom (England)	19.8	(3.0)	26.0	(3.6)	54.2	(3.3)	80.5	(2.8)	8.3	(2.4)	11.2	(2.1)	69.4	(3.6)	20.9	(3.5)	9.7	(2.3)
United Kingdom (Northern Ireland)	43.4	(5.5)	27.9	(5.2)	28.7	(3.8)	47.7	(3.0)	7.6	(2.9)	44.7	(3.0)	46.3	(5.1)	36.5	(5.2)	17.2	(3.8)
United Kingdom (Wales)	30.9	(3.6)	11.2	(2.7)	58.0	(3.9)	84.2	(2.9)	6.9	(1.9)	8.9	(2.5)	58.9	(4.2)	22.1	(3.5)	19.1	(3.2)

Note: See original Table IV.3.2b for national data.
StatLink http://dx.doi.org/10.1787/888932343304

[Part 2/3]
Table S.IV.a School admittance policies
Results based on school principals' reports

	Percentage of students in schools where the principal reported the following factors considered to be "never", "sometimes" or "always" for admittance at school											
	Parents' endorsement of the instructional or religious philosophy of the school						Whether the student requires or is interested in a special programe					
	Never		Sometimes		Always		Never		Sometimes		Always	
	%	S.E.	%	S.E.	%	S.E.	%	S.E.	%	S.E.	%	S.E.
Adjudicated												
Belgium (Flemish Community)	52.3	(3.9)	21.0	(3.0)	26.8	(3.8)	64.0	(4.1)	34.2	(4.1)	1.8	(0.8)
Spain (Andalusia)	83.2	(4.9)	14.8	(5.4)	2.1	(2.2)	51.4	(7.9)	31.8	(7.6)	16.8	(5.6)
Spain (Aragon)	87.2	(4.9)	9.4	(4.2)	3.4	(2.6)	68.7	(7.3)	22.7	(5.7)	8.6	(4.2)
Spain (Asturias)	73.7	(5.0)	8.8	(4.0)	17.5	(5.2)	56.7	(6.4)	29.8	(6.0)	13.4	(3.6)
Spain (Balearic Islands)	68.1	(7.0)	11.6	(4.8)	20.3	(7.3)	51.3	(8.4)	39.8	(8.7)	8.9	(5.8)
Spain (Basque Country)	66.3	(3.4)	17.7	(2.8)	16.0	(2.7)	50.2	(3.7)	40.9	(3.7)	9.0	(2.0)
Spain (Canary Islands)	78.5	(4.9)	7.8	(4.0)	13.6	(2.8)	43.9	(4.9)	33.3	(6.1)	22.8	(5.8)
Spain (Cantabria)	71.6	(5.4)	21.0	(6.0)	7.4	(2.7)	46.9	(5.9)	42.9	(6.3)	10.2	(4.0)
Spain (Castile and Leon)	69.1	(6.0)	20.8	(6.1)	10.2	(4.6)	54.9	(7.0)	39.7	(6.8)	5.4	(3.2)
Spain (Catalonia)	70.3	(7.0)	18.9	(6.3)	10.8	(4.8)	62.8	(8.0)	35.1	(7.9)	2.1	(2.2)
Spain (Ceuta and Melilla)	78.5	(0.4)	12.0	(0.3)	9.5	(0.2)	51.0	(0.5)	32.6	(0.5)	16.4	(0.4)
Spain (Galicia)	68.8	(2.7)	3.8	(2.7)	27.4	(3.8)	70.2	(6.8)	22.7	(6.8)	7.2	(3.3)
Spain (La Rioja)	80.7	(0.3)	7.9	(0.3)	11.4	(0.2)	49.1	(0.6)	44.7	(0.6)	6.2	(0.2)
Spain (Madrid)	66.5	(7.0)	15.3	(4.8)	18.1	(7.3)	36.8	(6.3)	41.1	(7.1)	22.1	(5.5)
Spain (Murcia)	78.9	(5.8)	10.7	(4.7)	10.4	(3.8)	45.0	(5.8)	34.6	(5.9)	20.3	(5.0)
Spain (Navarre)	79.2	(3.1)	5.4	(3.3)	15.4	(4.1)	46.7	(5.3)	45.0	(5.3)	8.3	(1.1)
United Kingdom (Scotland)	74.2	(4.6)	11.7	(3.6)	14.1	(3.3)	65.3	(4.1)	29.9	(4.0)	4.8	(2.2)
Non-adjudicated												
Belgium (French Community)	35.1	(4.9)	19.6	(4.1)	45.3	(5.5)	28.0	(5.3)	41.3	(4.9)	30.7	(4.5)
Belgium (German-Speaking Community)	41.1	(0.3)	12.9	(0.2)	45.9	(0.3)	0.0	c	65.5	(0.2)	34.5	(0.2)
Finland (Finnish Speaking)	81.9	(3.0)	16.7	(3.0)	1.4	(0.9)	46.6	(3.4)	45.8	(3.8)	7.6	(2.1)
Finland (Swedish Speaking)	84.0	(0.2)	15.4	(0.2)	0.6	(0.1)	64.7	(0.3)	29.6	(0.3)	5.7	(0.1)
Italy (Provincia Abruzzo)	60.0	(7.0)	12.9	(5.4)	27.1	(6.7)	15.2	(5.7)	30.3	(6.7)	54.5	(8.0)
Italy (Provincia Autonoma di Bolzano)	84.6	(1.6)	5.5	(0.1)	9.9	(1.7)	32.4	(1.1)	33.5	(1.5)	34.1	(1.0)
Italy (Provincia Basilicata)	45.1	(5.1)	19.7	(5.3)	35.1	(5.1)	28.5	(4.7)	31.1	(3.0)	40.4	(5.1)
Italy (Provincia Calabria)	31.0	(6.4)	18.0	(5.4)	51.0	(6.0)	17.6	(5.6)	18.4	(5.2)	64.0	(6.3)
Italy (Provincia Campania)	22.5	(5.5)	20.6	(3.9)	56.9	(5.8)	7.5	(3.8)	29.2	(6.2)	63.3	(7.4)
Italy (Provincia Emilia Romagna)	64.5	(5.0)	14.7	(3.8)	20.9	(4.4)	19.5	(5.2)	39.6	(5.1)	40.9	(6.4)
Italy (Provincia Friuli Venezia Giulia)	48.9	(5.7)	20.8	(5.3)	30.4	(3.4)	12.6	(3.4)	38.6	(5.2)	48.8	(6.0)
Italy (Provincia Lazio)	32.5	(5.4)	22.9	(5.8)	44.6	(6.1)	19.9	(4.8)	36.3	(6.5)	43.9	(5.5)
Italy (Provincia Liguria)	62.1	(5.6)	10.4	(3.6)	27.6	(6.3)	13.6	(5.9)	33.5	(6.9)	52.9	(8.7)
Italy (Provincia Lombardia)	60.0	(7.1)	14.1	(5.2)	25.9	(5.6)	16.3	(6.0)	31.7	(5.6)	52.0	(6.4)
Italy (Provincia Marche)	56.1	(7.4)	12.9	(5.1)	31.0	(7.6)	26.7	(5.9)	26.0	(7.0)	47.3	(7.8)
Italy (Provincia Molise)	37.6	(1.6)	9.1	(0.9)	53.3	(1.0)	17.9	(1.5)	17.7	(1.2)	64.4	(1.0)
Italy (Provincia Piemonte)	53.5	(6.6)	14.5	(4.2)	32.0	(5.3)	19.1	(5.8)	38.5	(6.5)	42.4	(6.3)
Italy (Provincia Puglia)	37.9	(7.4)	27.6	(6.5)	34.5	(7.8)	12.4	(5.2)	35.1	(6.6)	52.5	(7.4)
Italy (Provincia Sardegna)	40.3	(7.1)	33.3	(8.0)	26.4	(5.9)	25.4	(6.6)	29.1	(7.8)	45.5	(7.0)
Italy (Provincia Sicilia)	35.3	(7.3)	22.9	(5.5)	41.8	(7.6)	26.7	(7.8)	22.5	(6.2)	50.7	(6.6)
Italy (Provincia Toscana)	65.5	(6.3)	8.8	(2.7)	25.7	(5.6)	25.4	(6.5)	40.9	(7.6)	33.7	(6.5)
Italy (Provincia Trento)	72.0	(4.0)	13.3	(4.0)	14.8	(3.3)	21.0	(1.9)	34.4	(4.8)	44.7	(5.4)
Italy (Provincia Umbria)	39.6	(3.9)	27.0	(4.7)	33.4	(5.4)	17.5	(4.1)	35.4	(6.9)	47.1	(6.9)
Italy (Provincia Valle d'Aosta)	70.8	(0.4)	0.0	c	29.2	(0.4)	22.8	(0.4)	43.1	(0.4)	34.1	(0.4)
Italy (Provincia Veneto)	50.8	(7.7)	17.9	(6.0)	31.3	(6.5)	15.5	(4.6)	25.6	(6.8)	58.8	(7.3)
United Kingdom (England)	78.2	(3.3)	9.3	(2.2)	12.5	(2.7)	65.2	(4.1)	32.1	(4.0)	2.7	(1.4)
United Kingdom (Northern Ireland)	63.6	(5.7)	23.4	(4.8)	13.0	(3.7)	51.1	(5.6)	47.0	(5.5)	2.0	(1.4)
United Kingdom (Wales)	74.9	(3.7)	13.3	(2.8)	11.8	(3.0)	56.5	(3.8)	37.1	(3.7)	6.4	(2.1)

Note: See original Table IV.3.2b for national data.
StatLink http://dx.doi.org/10.1787/888932343304

[Part 3/3]
School admittance policies
Table S.IV.a *Results based on school principals' reports*

	Percentage of students in schools where the principal reported the following factors considered to be "never", "sometimes" or "always" for admittance at school											
	Preference given to family members of curred or former students						Other					
	Never		Sometimes		Always		Never		Sometimes		Always	
	%	S.E.	%	S.E.	%	S.E.	%	S.E.	%	S.E.	%	S.E.
Adjudicated												
Belgium (Flemish Community)	61.7	(4.1)	33.6	(3.9)	4.7	(1.9)	55.4	(5.2)	41.9	(5.1)	2.7	(1.4)
Spain (Andalusia)	43.1	(7.1)	30.2	(5.4)	26.7	(6.4)	63.1	(7.7)	25.4	(6.8)	11.5	(6.3)
Spain (Aragon)	40.9	(6.6)	29.4	(6.4)	29.7	(6.5)	62.3	(7.5)	13.9	(6.0)	23.8	(6.5)
Spain (Asturias)	35.6	(5.7)	28.1	(5.2)	36.3	(6.3)	41.4	(8.8)	41.8	(8.2)	16.8	(5.7)
Spain (Balearic Islands)	35.9	(5.2)	30.4	(7.5)	33.7	(6.1)	63.3	(9.5)	24.2	(7.3)	12.5	(5.5)
Spain (Basque Country)	30.9	(2.9)	27.0	(3.1)	42.2	(3.4)	37.5	(3.9)	38.0	(4.3)	24.5	(4.5)
Spain (Canary Islands)	27.6	(7.3)	29.3	(5.4)	43.2	(7.4)	51.8	(9.3)	31.0	(8.3)	17.2	(8.0)
Spain (Cantabria)	35.9	(7.5)	28.9	(6.7)	35.2	(6.3)	41.7	(8.0)	36.1	(9.3)	22.2	(5.4)
Spain (Castile and Leon)	36.0	(6.3)	24.8	(6.1)	39.2	(6.6)	58.8	(7.6)	18.2	(5.8)	23.0	(5.1)
Spain (Catalonia)	63.5	(7.7)	20.3	(6.5)	16.1	(6.2)	42.8	(8.4)	37.6	(9.0)	19.6	(7.5)
Spain (Ceuta and Melilla)	21.7	(0.4)	39.4	(0.5)	38.8	(0.5)	25.1	(0.5)	46.6	(0.5)	28.3	(0.4)
Spain (Galicia)	53.9	(5.2)	21.5	(5.2)	24.5	(5.4)	69.9	(7.2)	19.2	(5.7)	10.9	(5.0)
Spain (La Rioja)	29.3	(0.6)	25.2	(0.6)	45.4	(0.6)	42.8	(0.7)	31.8	(0.7)	25.4	(0.8)
Spain (Madrid)	11.2	(5.4)	34.5	(7.4)	54.3	(8.9)	21.9	(7.6)	40.2	(9.7)	37.9	(10.2)
Spain (Murcia)	32.4	(6.7)	24.8	(5.5)	42.9	(6.6)	40.1	(8.5)	20.9	(6.6)	39.0	(7.2)
Spain (Navarre)	44.8	(3.3)	15.6	(3.8)	39.6	(4.5)	54.8	(5.9)	28.5	(6.4)	16.7	(5.6)
United Kingdom (Scotland)	55.1	(5.8)	33.8	(4.9)	11.1	(3.3)	64.0	(6.1)	31.0	(6.2)	5.0	(3.0)
Non-adjudicated												
Belgium (French Community)	41.0	(5.1)	28.4	(5.0)	30.5	(4.2)	48.7	(7.1)	38.4	(6.1)	12.8	(4.9)
Belgium (German-Speaking Community)	100.0	(0.0)	0.0	c	0.0	c	76.3	(0.2)	23.7	(0.2)	0.0	c
Finland (Finnish Speaking)	73.2	(3.2)	24.7	(3.3)	2.1	(1.2)	50.4	(4.6)	48.8	(4.6)	0.8	(0.7)
Finland (Swedish Speaking)	68.9	(0.3)	19.4	(0.3)	11.7	(0.2)	64.7	(0.4)	33.2	(0.4)	2.1	(0.1)
Italy (Provincia Abruzzo)	17.2	(5.9)	45.8	(7.5)	37.0	(7.0)	42.1	(9.2)	43.6	(10.2)	14.3	(5.5)
Italy (Provincia Autonoma di Bolzano)	78.3	(1.7)	15.8	(0.4)	5.9	(1.9)	58.6	(1.2)	40.9	(1.2)	0.5	(0.1)
Italy (Provincia Basilicata)	31.2	(3.9)	44.5	(5.0)	24.3	(3.7)	55.9	(7.0)	33.4	(8.1)	10.7	(2.9)
Italy (Provincia Calabria)	23.2	(5.6)	42.9	(7.2)	33.8	(6.8)	41.2	(7.5)	49.7	(7.8)	9.1	(2.9)
Italy (Provincia Campania)	14.6	(5.5)	34.5	(4.7)	50.9	(6.8)	38.2	(10.2)	55.2	(11.0)	6.6	(4.9)
Italy (Provincia Emilia Romagna)	41.1	(5.1)	45.5	(6.8)	13.4	(4.5)	44.8	(7.9)	47.0	(8.0)	8.3	(4.8)
Italy (Provincia Friuli Venezia Giulia)	49.7	(5.7)	41.4	(5.2)	8.9	(1.8)	43.8	(6.0)	44.4	(6.0)	11.8	(3.1)
Italy (Provincia Lazio)	15.7	(5.5)	39.2	(6.6)	45.1	(5.1)	37.2	(9.3)	46.1	(9.8)	16.7	(6.9)
Italy (Provincia Liguria)	40.5	(7.6)	43.8	(7.4)	15.7	(4.7)	55.1	(8.4)	34.4	(6.2)	10.5	(6.7)
Italy (Provincia Lombardia)	47.6	(7.3)	33.3	(6.5)	19.1	(5.0)	36.3	(8.8)	50.3	(8.8)	13.4	(6.1)
Italy (Provincia Marche)	44.5	(7.9)	31.3	(8.2)	24.2	(6.9)	60.3	(8.4)	28.1	(7.9)	11.6	(3.9)
Italy (Provincia Molise)	21.0	(0.4)	36.3	(1.2)	42.7	(1.4)	64.3	(0.5)	24.4	(0.4)	11.3	(0.4)
Italy (Provincia Piemonte)	41.4	(7.8)	45.6	(7.5)	13.0	(4.3)	50.7	(10.2)	30.8	(8.2)	18.5	(10.3)
Italy (Provincia Puglia)	15.2	(5.7)	51.2	(7.2)	33.6	(7.1)	27.6	(7.3)	59.4	(8.6)	13.0	(5.0)
Italy (Provincia Sardegna)	37.7	(8.2)	34.0	(7.7)	28.3	(6.9)	26.7	(8.9)	64.4	(9.4)	8.9	(5.5)
Italy (Provincia Sicilia)	24.6	(4.8)	40.8	(6.6)	34.6	(5.9)	46.4	(8.8)	40.9	(8.3)	12.7	(5.0)
Italy (Provincia Toscana)	51.0	(6.8)	34.6	(7.1)	14.4	(5.6)	72.2	(6.0)	17.7	(5.5)	10.1	(3.0)
Italy (Provincia Trento)	59.2	(2.6)	20.5	(3.7)	20.3	(2.9)	67.5	(3.0)	18.3	(5.0)	14.1	(4.0)
Italy (Provincia Umbria)	32.9	(4.4)	43.0	(5.4)	24.1	(4.9)	40.4	(7.3)	42.4	(6.3)	17.3	(6.4)
Italy (Provincia Valle d'Aosta)	46.5	(0.4)	49.7	(0.4)	3.8	(0.2)	75.4	(0.4)	24.6	(0.4)	0.0	c
Italy (Provincia Veneto)	29.5	(6.4)	55.9	(8.1)	14.6	(5.4)	39.0	(9.1)	52.2	(9.6)	8.9	(4.9)
United Kingdom (England)	20.2	(3.5)	36.4	(4.0)	43.4	(4.3)	47.2	(5.4)	38.3	(4.9)	14.5	(3.3)
United Kingdom (Northern Ireland)	17.4	(3.2)	45.2	(5.3)	37.4	(5.5)	32.5	(6.7)	50.1	(6.1)	17.4	(4.7)
United Kingdom (Wales)	49.9	(3.7)	34.5	(4.2)	15.6	(3.1)	47.3	(5.3)	40.4	(5.4)	12.3	(3.9)

Note: See original Table IV.3.2b for national data.
StatLink http://dx.doi.org/10.1787/888932343304

[Part 1/1]
Table S.IV.b Horizontal differentiation at the school level: school transfer policies
Results based on school principals' reports

	Percentage of students in schools where the principal reported that a student in national modal grade for 15-year-olds in the school would be "likely" or "very likely" transferred to another school because of the following reasons:												Percentage of students in schools where the principal reported that a student in national modal grade for 15-year-olds in the school would be "very likely" transferred to another school because of one of the following reasons: "low academic achievement", "behavioural problems" or "special learning needs"	
	Low academic achievement		High academic achievement		Behavioural problems		Special learning needs		Parents' or guardians' request		Other			
	%	S.E.	%	S.E.	%	S.E.	%	S.E.	%	S.E.	%	S.E.	%	S.E.
Adjudicated														
Belgium (Flemish Community)	67.5	(3.2)	4.9	(1.8)	65.9	(3.5)	52.4	(4.1)	53.3	(4.0)	18.9	(3.9)	42.9	(4.0)
Spain (Andalusia)	2.8	(2.7)	2.8	(2.7)	32.6	(6.7)	22.6	(6.6)	47.3	(7.3)	23.2	(8.5)	2.8	(2.7)
Spain (Aragon)	5.2	(0.6)	0.0	c	14.3	(3.2)	41.2	(8.3)	47.0	(8.3)	18.0	(8.3)	8.9	(5.1)
Spain (Asturias)	5.3	(3.8)	0.0	c	34.6	(7.1)	11.9	(4.2)	53.8	(8.6)	30.7	(9.7)	2.7	(2.7)
Spain (Balearic Islands)	8.1	(4.2)	7.1	(5.0)	16.1	(6.4)	12.3	(5.5)	53.9	(8.4)	25.4	(8.6)	0.0	(0.0)
Spain (Basque Country)	11.6	(3.0)	4.7	(1.6)	26.5	(3.9)	39.0	(4.1)	50.9	(4.5)	27.1	(4.9)	6.9	(1.9)
Spain (Canary Islands)	2.6	(2.0)	0.0	c	56.9	(6.7)	24.4	(6.8)	61.1	(7.8)	25.4	(8.3)	0.0	(0.0)
Spain (Cantabria)	6.1	(3.5)	3.8	(2.7)	40.0	(7.5)	24.7	(6.3)	69.5	(6.7)	24.1	(6.9)	8.7	(4.4)
Spain (Castile and Leon)	6.4	(4.1)	0.0	c	34.6	(7.5)	27.6	(7.5)	69.3	(6.8)	25.5	(8.3)	9.7	(5.2)
Spain (Catalonia)	9.9	(5.1)	5.0	(3.6)	43.6	(8.3)	58.6	(9.5)	70.8	(8.0)	49.3	(9.6)	7.2	(4.3)
Spain (Ceuta and Melilla)	11.5	(0.3)	0.0	c	65.2	(0.5)	40.8	(0.5)	72.1	(0.5)	44.3	(0.9)	7.3	(0.3)
Spain (Galicia)	16.5	(5.7)	3.8	(2.2)	43.7	(7.5)	29.9	(7.0)	49.3	(6.6)	46.8	(9.0)	4.0	(2.8)
Spain (La Rioja)	1.8	(0.1)	0.0	c	31.1	(0.5)	27.5	(0.6)	71.3	(0.6)	11.7	(0.3)	0.0	(0.0)
Spain (Madrid)	8.7	(4.9)	5.3	(3.4)	49.9	(7.9)	51.0	(8.7)	60.9	(7.5)	32.8	(10.5)	20.6	(5.9)
Spain (Murcia)	2.7	(2.7)	0.0	c	44.4	(7.2)	24.8	(7.2)	66.5	(8.3)	39.2	(8.7)	7.8	(3.9)
Spain (Navarre)	12.9	(3.9)	6.1	(0.4)	24.2	(6.7)	25.2	(7.3)	46.9	(5.4)	36.1	(7.1)	3.4	(2.4)
United Kingdom (Scotland)	0.8	(0.9)	1.1	(1.1)	21.1	(4.2)	10.2	(3.3)	35.2	(5.1)	8.2	(3.8)	3.0	(1.8)
Non-adjudicated														
Belgium (French Community)	58.4	(5.3)	7.3	(2.8)	84.5	(3.8)	82.8	(4.6)	81.3	(4.6)	51.9	(7.8)	55.8	(5.4)
Belgium (German-Speaking Community)	83.4	(0.3)	21.2	(0.2)	80.3	(0.2)	58.5	(0.3)	46.3	(0.3)	42.4	(0.3)	34.6	(0.3)
Finland (Finnish Speaking)	6.0	(2.1)	1.4	(1.0)	19.6	(3.5)	19.5	(3.6)	54.1	(4.1)	23.3	(3.9)	1.7	(1.2)
Finland (Swedish Speaking)	9.5	(0.3)	0.0	c	38.5	(0.4)	55.7	(0.4)	56.9	(0.3)	16.5	(0.4)	3.1	(0.1)
Italy (Provincia Abruzzo)	64.5	(6.6)	2.2	(2.3)	54.5	(8.4)	24.0	(6.2)	86.0	(5.2)	47.5	(10.6)	25.6	(5.8)
Italy (Provincia Autonoma di Bolzano)	69.4	(0.3)	2.4	(0.1)	34.7	(0.3)	29.0	(0.4)	61.1	(0.4)	48.4	(0.4)	17.8	(0.2)
Italy (Provincia Basilicata)	68.4	(4.9)	0.0	c	40.5	(4.0)	20.9	(5.5)	89.3	(1.8)	46.1	(6.1)	21.9	(4.7)
Italy (Provincia Calabria)	61.6	(5.5)	0.0	c	48.7	(8.1)	31.9	(7.9)	94.4	(3.3)	45.0	(8.4)	20.7	(6.3)
Italy (Provincia Campania)	68.1	(7.1)	6.0	(4.3)	31.3	(5.8)	30.0	(7.1)	90.6	(3.1)	55.0	(9.0)	13.2	(5.5)
Italy (Provincia Emilia Romagna)	75.5	(5.8)	14.5	(4.1)	33.9	(6.3)	37.0	(6.2)	93.7	(3.2)	30.6	(9.2)	18.4	(5.9)
Italy (Provincia Friuli Venezia Giulia)	83.4	(4.4)	4.5	(1.8)	39.2	(6.0)	35.8	(4.4)	87.2	(4.6)	49.4	(8.8)	19.7	(4.4)
Italy (Provincia Lazio)	78.7	(5.7)	0.0	c	50.4	(7.1)	31.7	(5.9)	97.3	(2.7)	45.9	(9.9)	29.6	(5.4)
Italy (Provincia Liguria)	81.9	(7.1)	0.0	c	64.1	(8.0)	41.3	(8.0)	93.4	(2.7)	19.7	(9.9)	25.8	(5.6)
Italy (Provincia Lombardia)	65.8	(6.1)	5.3	(3.8)	40.8	(7.7)	32.3	(7.3)	87.4	(5.2)	39.1	(9.1)	20.6	(6.4)
Italy (Provincia Marche)	73.5	(5.7)	7.0	(6.5)	34.9	(7.4)	42.3	(7.5)	79.4	(6.8)	27.6	(7.6)	36.3	(7.7)
Italy (Provincia Molise)	63.5	(1.1)	0.1	(0.0)	34.3	(0.8)	22.8	(0.4)	88.6	(1.5)	40.1	(0.9)	16.0	(0.3)
Italy (Provincia Piemonte)	75.7	(4.9)	5.9	(1.9)	51.0	(7.9)	37.5	(8.4)	92.2	(3.9)	32.2	(8.0)	11.7	(4.8)
Italy (Provincia Puglia)	49.5	(7.3)	8.3	(4.3)	35.1	(9.3)	25.5	(8.2)	88.6	(3.8)	50.3	(10.2)	10.3	(4.5)
Italy (Provincia Sardegna)	60.9	(7.2)	2.0	(2.0)	47.7	(6.8)	41.8	(8.4)	90.7	(4.8)	53.0	(10.5)	17.6	(6.7)
Italy (Provincia Sicilia)	65.1	(7.6)	3.7	(2.7)	34.6	(7.0)	27.8	(6.8)	87.1	(5.6)	46.8	(9.8)	24.4	(6.5)
Italy (Provincia Toscana)	73.0	(5.6)	5.2	(0.8)	38.5	(7.4)	27.4	(7.4)	81.8	(6.2)	21.7	(6.3)	14.4	(5.3)
Italy (Provincia Trento)	75.9	(2.5)	7.1	(3.6)	26.0	(2.2)	41.1	(3.1)	82.5	(2.9)	14.6	(3.5)	19.8	(2.1)
Italy (Provincia Umbria)	74.4	(2.6)	4.2	(2.5)	34.3	(4.0)	31.8	(5.7)	90.2	(0.6)	31.7	(7.0)	22.0	(5.3)
Italy (Provincia Valle d'Aosta)	88.3	(0.3)	41.2	(0.4)	79.5	(0.4)	35.5	(0.4)	74.4	(0.3)	39.8	(0.4)	30.4	(0.4)
Italy (Provincia Veneto)	73.9	(7.6)	8.4	(4.3)	44.5	(7.7)	31.7	(7.3)	79.9	(5.4)	38.8	(8.5)	27.1	(6.7)
United Kingdom (England)	4.5	(1.5)	5.2	(2.1)	33.6	(4.1)	17.0	(3.4)	44.8	(3.6)	11.3	(3.4)	2.0	(1.1)
United Kingdom (Northern Ireland)	10.2	(3.5)	13.0	(3.8)	18.0	(4.8)	12.7	(3.1)	38.1	(5.3)	16.9	(5.2)	3.6	(2.1)
United Kingdom (Wales)	0.3	(0.3)	0.0	c	21.1	(3.7)	11.8	(3.0)	33.9	(3.8)	11.1	(3.6)	3.6	(1.7)

Note: See original Table IV.3.3a for national data.
StatLink http://dx.doi.org/10.1787/888932343304

[Part 1/1]
Table S.IV.c Horizontal differentiation at the school level: ability grouping and reading performance
Results based on school principals' reports

	Percentage of students in schools where the principal reported within school (between and/or within classes)						Performance on the reading scale							
	No ability grouping		Ability grouping for some subjects		Ability grouping for all subjects		No ability grouping or ability grouping for some subjects		Ability grouping for all subjects		Observed difference (Ability grouping for all subjects – no ability grouping or ability grouping for some subjects)		After accounting for the students' ESCS	
	%	S.E.	%	S.E.	%	S.E.	Mean score	S.E.	Mean score	S.E.	Score dif.	S.E.	Score dif.	S.E.
Adjudicated														
Belgium (Flemish Community)	35.4	(3.5)	35.0	(3.7)	29.6	(3.5)	525	(4.0)	508	(9.2)	-17.4	(12.1)	-13.9	(9.1)
Spain (Andalusia)	37.6	(6.5)	62.4	(6.5)	0.0	c	461	(5.5)	c	c	c	c	c	
Spain (Aragon)	50.9	(7.6)	47.3	(7.4)	1.8	(1.9)	494	(4.3)	511	(6.5)	**17.0**	(7.5)	**22.4**	(7.1)
Spain (Asturias)	50.5	(7.3)	49.5	(7.3)	0.0	c	491	(4.6)	c	c	c	c	c	c
Spain (Balearic Islands)	30.5	(7.8)	60.9	(8.3)	8.7	(3.0)	457	(6.3)	461	(8.3)	4.0	(10.3)	14.8	(8.4)
Spain (Basque Country)	51.3	(3.9)	43.3	(3.6)	5.3	(1.8)	496	(3.0)	481	(13.5)	-14.9	(13.6)	-13.4	(15.2)
Spain (Canary Islands)	44.0	(7.2)	50.2	(7.6)	5.8	(3.1)	446	(5.2)	478	(20.9)	31.4	(23.1)	22.7	(19.0)
Spain (Cantabria)	29.7	(5.2)	62.0	(6.2)	8.4	(4.3)	488	(4.5)	482	(31.9)	-5.8	(33.3)	-11.5	(32.5)
Spain (Castile and Leon)	68.9	(4.7)	23.3	(3.7)	7.9	(3.9)	501	(5.3)	517	(14.7)	15.9	(15.2)	0.6	(15.8)
Spain (Catalonia)	11.0	(5.0)	71.6	(6.6)	17.4	(6.4)	500	(6.5)	504	(11.1)	4.1	(12.5)	1.5	(9.6)
Spain (Ceuta and Melilla)	49.9	(0.5)	47.2	(0.5)	2.9	(0.3)	413	(2.5)	365	(13.8)	**-48.5**	(14.3)	**-32.9**	(15.0)
Spain (Galicia)	50.2	(6.4)	43.3	(7.0)	6.6	(3.7)	487	(4.7)	483	(8.7)	-4.0	(9.6)	0.9	(9.8)
Spain (La Rioja)	70.5	(0.6)	24.4	(0.5)	5.1	(0.3)	499	(2.5)	489	(10.3)	-10.0	(10.7)	-17.0	(10.8)
Spain (Madrid)	37.5	(8.3)	59.4	(8.6)	3.1	(2.4)	504	(4.5)	510	(29.3)	6.4	(30.3)	-13.7	(11.5)
Spain (Murcia)	57.3	(7.8)	36.1	(8.1)	6.7	(3.7)	481	(5.5)	491	(19.6)	9.9	(21.5)	8.0	(14.9)
Spain (Navarre)	36.2	(5.0)	53.3	(5.5)	10.5	(2.7)	496	(3.5)	504	(9.8)	8.0	(11.0)	5.4	(7.3)
United Kingdom (Scotland)	0.9	(0.9)	94.3	(2.2)	4.8	(2.0)	500	(3.2)	498	(13.8)	-2.2	(13.4)	5.4	(9.5)
Non-adjudicated														
Belgium (French Community)	78.5	(4.2)	17.0	(3.8)	4.4	(2.0)	490	(5.0)	515	(21.2)	25.9	(22.6)	21.9	(13.5)
Belgium (German-Speaking Community)	52.1	(0.2)	19.4	(0.2)	28.5	(0.3)	513	(2.9)	462	(5.3)	**-50.8**	(5.5)	**-41.8**	(5.7)
Finland (Finnish Speaking)	43.7	(4.3)	54.9	(4.4)	1.3	(1.0)	537	(2.4)	539	(37.6)	1.2	(37.7)	2.5	(36.0)
Finland (Swedish Speaking)	23.7	(0.3)	74.6	(0.3)	1.7	(0.1)	511	(2.7)	539	(12.8)	**28.5**	(13.2)	14.8	(14.8)
Italy (Provincia Abruzzo)	63.8	(8.1)	19.0	(5.3)	17.3	(6.9)	489	(7.4)	477	(29.5)	-11.4	(33.1)	-12.8	(28.0)
Italy (Provincia Autonoma di Bolzano)	27.5	(0.4)	65.9	(0.3)	6.6	(0.1)	494	(1.6)	541	(6.3)	**46.7**	(6.4)	**38.8**	(6.8)
Italy (Provincia Basilicata)	31.0	(3.8)	39.4	(5.4)	29.6	(4.7)	466	(6.9)	488	(7.7)	**22.7**	(11.4)	18.9	(9.9)
Italy (Provincia Calabria)	50.4	(8.0)	35.5	(7.0)	14.1	(4.9)	453	(6.4)	429	(13.3)	-24.6	(15.8)	-10.0	(13.3)
Italy (Provincia Campania)	38.8	(7.2)	42.1	(6.9)	19.2	(5.9)	449	(8.8)	463	(20.1)	13.6	(24.6)	17.2	(22.0)
Italy (Provincia Emilia Romagna)	33.0	(5.9)	56.4	(7.4)	10.6	(4.6)	507	(4.4)	478	(33.5)	-29.1	(35.7)	-30.8	(29.1)
Italy (Provincia Friuli Venezia Giulia)	48.7	(5.1)	35.9	(5.1)	15.4	(3.8)	507	(5.3)	583	(11.5)	**76.0**	(12.5)	**62.0**	(11.3)
Italy (Provincia Lazio)	49.6	(7.1)	33.5	(5.6)	16.9	(6.3)	485	(6.9)	464	(20.6)	-21.3	(25.9)	-15.2	(20.7)
Italy (Provincia Liguria)	32.5	(6.3)	61.4	(7.2)	6.2	(3.5)	491	(10.1)	513	(21.7)	21.9	(24.5)	27.8	(23.3)
Italy (Provincia Lombardia)	48.3	(6.8)	37.5	(5.7)	14.2	(5.0)	522	(5.9)	545	(19.5)	22.9	(21.8)	25.8	(16.1)
Italy (Provincia Marche)	57.5	(6.9)	34.7	(6.9)	7.8	(4.1)	497	(9.0)	507	(39.5)	10.3	(42.3)	15.8	(35.3)
Italy (Provincia Molise)	55.7	(0.9)	35.7	(1.4)	8.6	(0.8)	473	(3.4)	457	(9.2)	-15.9	(11.2)	-10.6	(10.7)
Italy (Provincia Piemonte)	48.5	(7.6)	44.8	(7.3)	6.6	(3.3)	502	(7.0)	477	(43.0)	-25.3	(45.8)	-17.6	(37.0)
Italy (Provincia Puglia)	34.3	(6.2)	45.2	(7.7)	20.5	(5.8)	489	(5.4)	490	(19.4)	0.8	(21.0)	1.0	(17.9)
Italy (Provincia Sardegna)	47.9	(7.9)	36.1	(7.1)	16.0	(4.9)	471	(7.0)	472	(22.3)	1.8	(27.5)	2.7	(25.0)
Italy (Provincia Sicilia)	56.5	(7.7)	33.0	(7.2)	10.5	(4.8)	465	(7.9)	429	(37.8)	-35.5	(40.5)	-23.9	(33.9)
Italy (Provincia Toscana)	27.9	(6.0)	54.5	(7.0)	17.6	(5.6)	496	(6.7)	482	(23.0)	-14.0	(27.1)	-15.8	(24.4)
Italy (Provincia Trento)	47.0	(4.2)	44.4	(4.2)	8.6	(0.3)	509	(3.0)	489	(6.8)	**-20.5**	(7.8)	-13.1	(8.4)
Italy (Provincia Umbria)	56.7	(6.4)	36.0	(6.0)	7.4	(3.5)	498	(4.5)	449	(28.4)	-48.7	(29.8)	-46.2	(25.4)
Italy (Provincia Valle d'Aosta)	47.0	(0.4)	53.0	(0.4)	0.0	c	516	(2.2)	c	c	c	c	c	c
Italy (Provincia Veneto)	40.8	(6.7)	49.6	(6.6)	9.7	(3.9)	503	(7.0)	528	(26.3)	24.9	(30.7)	19.6	(27.1)
United Kingdom (England)	0.8	(1.1)	91.6	(2.2)	7.6	(2.3)	496	(3.3)	497	(10.9)	0.3	(11.9)	-1.5	(10.2)
United Kingdom (Northern Ireland)	4.9	(2.3)	81.7	(3.9)	13.3	(3.6)	504	(5.7)	492	(16.6)	-12.3	(19.1)	-10.3	(14.4)
United Kingdom (Wales)	0.0	c	91.0	(2.8)	9.0	(2.8)	478	(3.5)	461	(11.8)	-17.0	(12.2)	-12.1	(10.3)

Notes: Values that are statistically significant are indicated in bold (see Annex A3). See original Table IV.3.4 for national data.
StatLink http://dx.doi.org/10.1787/888932343304

[Part 1/2]
Index of school responsibility for curriculum and assessment and reading performance, by national quarters of this index
Table S.IV.d *Results based on students' self-reports*

	Index of school responsibility for curriculum and assessment									
	All students		Bottom quarter		Second quarter		Third quarter		Top quarter	
	Mean index	S.E.	Mean index	S.E.	Mean index	S.E.	Mean index	S.E.	Mean index	S.E.
Adjudicated										
Belgium (Flemish Community)	0.18	(0.07)	-0.65	(0.02)	-0.35	(0.02)	0.37	(0.06)	1.36	(0.00)
Spain (Andalusia)	-0.52	(0.07)	-1.15	(0.03)	-0.87	(0.02)	-0.54	(0.03)	0.47	(0.15)
Spain (Aragon)	-0.65	(0.09)	-1.16	(0.02)	-0.91	(0.00)	-0.66	(0.03)	0.13	(0.21)
Spain (Asturias)	-0.68	(0.08)	-1.20	(0.01)	-0.95	(0.02)	-0.78	(0.03)	0.20	(0.24)
Spain (Balearic Islands)	-0.10	(0.14)	-0.97	(0.04)	-0.62	(0.03)	-0.17	(0.06)	1.36	(0.00)
Spain (Basque Country)	-0.05	(0.07)	-0.92	(0.02)	-0.68	(0.01)	0.04	(0.04)	1.36	(0.00)
Spain (Canary Islands)	-0.55	(0.09)	-1.17	(0.02)	-0.91	(0.00)	-0.55	(0.03)	0.43	(0.18)
Spain (Cantabria)	-0.56	(0.07)	-1.02	(0.02)	-0.87	(0.01)	-0.65	(0.02)	0.31	(0.18)
Spain (Castile and Leon)	-0.61	(0.08)	-1.13	(0.02)	-0.90	(0.01)	-0.65	(0.03)	0.22	(0.21)
Spain (Catalonia)	-0.24	(0.12)	-0.90	(0.00)	-0.71	(0.02)	-0.43	(0.05)	1.10	(0.12)
Spain (Ceuta and Melilla)	-0.62	(0.01)	-1.05	(0.00)	-0.87	(0.00)	-0.61	(0.00)	0.06	(0.01)
Spain (Galicia)	-0.46	(0.11)	-1.03	(0.03)	-0.83	(0.02)	-0.61	(0.02)	0.65	(0.22)
Spain (La Rioja)	-0.53	(0.01)	-1.09	(0.00)	-0.91	(0.00)	-0.64	(0.00)	0.53	(0.01)
Spain (Madrid)	-0.52	(0.09)	-1.07	(0.03)	-0.91	(0.00)	-0.65	(0.03)	0.56	(0.17)
Spain (Murcia)	-0.76	(0.06)	-1.21	(0.02)	-0.97	(0.02)	-0.81	(0.03)	-0.04	(0.14)
Spain (Navarre)	-0.53	(0.07)	-1.10	(0.01)	-0.87	(0.01)	-0.54	(0.02)	0.41	(0.15)
United Kingdom (Scotland)	0.07	(0.09)	-0.79	(0.01)	-0.52	(0.01)	0.21	(0.07)	1.36	(0.00)
Non-adjudicated										
Belgium (French Community)	-0.61	(0.05)	-1.04	(0.02)	-0.82	(0.01)	-0.62	(0.02)	0.04	(0.13)
Belgium (German-Speaking Community)	-0.72	(0.00)	c	c	-0.72	(0.00)	-0.72	(0.00)	-0.53	(0.00)
Finland (Finnish Speaking)	-0.14	(0.07)	-0.86	(0.02)	-0.61	(0.01)	-0.27	(0.03)	1.18	(0.05)
Finland (Swedish Speaking)	-0.32	(0.01)	-0.90	(0.00)	-0.76	(0.00)	-0.44	(0.00)	0.82	(0.01)
Italy (Provincia Abruzzo)	0.09	(0.14)	-0.78	(0.04)	-0.49	(0.02)	0.26	(0.13)	1.36	(0.00)
Italy (Provincia Autonoma di Bolzano)	-0.34	(0.03)	-0.91	(0.00)	-0.69	(0.00)	-0.44	(0.00)	0.68	(0.05)
Italy (Provincia Basilicata)	0.21	(0.11)	-0.76	(0.02)	-0.42	(0.02)	0.67	(0.12)	1.36	(0.00)
Italy (Provincia Calabria)	0.45	(0.13)	-0.66	(0.04)	-0.05	(0.07)	1.16	(0.05)	1.36	(0.00)
Italy (Provincia Campania)	0.65	(0.12)	-0.42	(0.07)	0.29	(0.11)	1.36	(0.00)	1.36	(0.00)
Italy (Provincia Emilia Romagna)	-0.02	(0.12)	-0.80	(0.02)	-0.54	(0.01)	-0.05	(0.09)	1.28	(0.05)
Italy (Provincia Friuli Venezia Giulia)	-0.19	(0.09)	-0.90	(0.01)	-0.62	(0.01)	-0.25	(0.03)	0.99	(0.09)
Italy (Provincia Lazio)	0.21	(0.12)	-0.85	(0.03)	-0.46	(0.03)	0.77	(0.10)	1.36	(0.00)
Italy (Provincia Liguria)	0.15	(0.13)	-0.76	(0.03)	-0.47	(0.03)	0.47	(0.07)	1.36	(0.00)
Italy (Provincia Lombardia)	0.07	(0.12)	-0.78	(0.04)	-0.35	(0.02)	0.12	(0.10)	1.27	(0.05)
Italy (Provincia Marche)	0.13	(0.13)	-0.78	(0.05)	-0.38	(0.03)	0.33	(0.13)	1.34	(0.02)
Italy (Provincia Molise)	0.44	(0.02)	-0.75	(0.01)	0.00	(0.02)	1.14	(0.01)	1.36	(0.00)
Italy (Provincia Piemonte)	0.07	(0.10)	-0.73	(0.03)	-0.47	(0.02)	0.11	(0.10)	1.36	(0.00)
Italy (Provincia Puglia)	0.24	(0.14)	-0.89	(0.04)	-0.23	(0.05)	0.72	(0.13)	1.36	(0.00)
Italy (Provincia Sardegna)	0.02	(0.13)	-0.82	(0.04)	-0.47	(0.02)	0.02	(0.07)	1.36	(0.01)
Italy (Provincia Sicilia)	0.39	(0.14)	-0.83	(0.04)	-0.18	(0.10)	1.19	(0.07)	1.36	(0.00)
Italy (Provincia Toscana)	0.16	(0.14)	-0.87	(0.06)	-0.43	(0.02)	0.59	(0.14)	1.36	(0.00)
Italy (Provincia Trento)	-0.28	(0.03)	-0.96	(0.02)	-0.61	(0.02)	-0.22	(0.02)	0.65	(0.06)
Italy (Provincia Umbria)	0.00	(0.10)	-0.79	(0.03)	-0.47	(0.01)	0.00	(0.06)	1.27	(0.03)
Italy (Provincia Valle d'Aosta)	-0.03	(0.01)	-0.74	(0.00)	-0.54	(0.00)	-0.13	(0.01)	1.29	(0.00)
Italy (Provincia Veneto)	0.03	(0.09)	-0.81	(0.03)	-0.52	(0.02)	0.10	(0.10)	1.36	(0.00)
United Kingdom (England)	0.92	(0.06)	-0.30	(0.05)	1.26	(0.02)	1.36	(0.00)	1.36	(0.00)
United Kingdom (Northern Ireland)	0.57	(0.10)	-0.60	(0.04)	0.15	(0.06)	1.36	(0.00)	1.36	(0.00)
United Kingdom (Wales)	0.79	(0.07)	-0.38	(0.05)	0.83	(0.06)	1.36	(0.00)	1.36	(0.00)

Notes: Values that are statistically significant are indicated in bold (see Annex A3). See original Table IV.3.6 for national data.
StatLink http://dx.doi.org/10.1787/888932343304

[Part 2/2]

Index of school responsibility for curriculum and assessment and reading performance, by national quarters of this index

Table S.IV.d *Results based on students' self-reports*

	Performance on the reading scale by quarters of this index								Change in the reading score per unit of this index		Increased likelihood of students in the bottom quarter of this index scoring in the bottom quarter of the reading performance distribution		Explained variance in student performance (r-squared X 100)	
	Bottom quarter		Second quarter		Third quarter		Top quarter							
	Mean index	S.E.	Mean index	S.E.	Mean index	S.E.	Mean index	S.E.	Effect	S.E.	Ratio	S.E.	%	S.E.
Adjudicated														
Belgium (Flemish Community)	518	(7.9)	522	(7.2)	512	(7.2)	522	(7.9)	0.9	(6.05)	0.9	(0.14)	0.0	(0.34)
Spain (Andalusia)	**443**	(10.7)	454	(13.9)	470	(9.0)	**475**	(10.6)	13.2	(8.64)	1.4	(0.27)	1.1	(1.53)
Spain (Aragon)	**477**	(10.1)	493	(7.8)	496	(8.5)	**515**	(6.9)	**15.2**	(6.01)	1.5	(0.29)	1.2	(0.86)
Spain (Asturias)	**478**	(9.8)	484	(9.9)	482	(8.3)	**516**	(11.3)	**17.1**	(5.08)	1.3	(0.20)	1.5	(0.98)
Spain (Balearic Islands)	456	(10.2)	462	(9.3)	462	(8.6)	449	(13.1)	-4.6	(6.89)	1.0	(0.22)	0.2	(0.58)
Spain (Basque Country)	**488**	(4.6)	494	(6.9)	494	(6.7)	**505**	(5.4)	6.1	(3.25)	1.1	(0.13)	0.5	(0.46)
Spain (Canary Islands)	437	(10.3)	434	(13.9)	464	(11.1)	457	(11.2)	9.8	(10.79)	1.2	(0.23)	0.6	(1.40)
Spain (Cantabria)	481	(5.9)	486	(7.4)	504	(8.2)	480	(10.4)	-1.4	(3.70)	1.1	(0.18)	0.0	(0.07)
Spain (Castile and Leon)	494	(8.8)	501	(9.1)	513	(9.5)	504	(9.0)	0.6	(7.85)	1.4	(0.24)	0.0	(0.29)
Spain (Catalonia)	502	(12.3)	496	(11.2)	511	(7.8)	493	(10.5)	-5.3	(6.85)	1.1	(0.28)	0.3	(0.86)
Spain (Ceuta and Melilla)	**398**	(4.8)	413	(5.1)	412	(4.8)	**426**	(5.3)	**-12.4**	(5.03)	1.1	(0.20)	0.3	(0.27)
Spain (Galicia)	484	(9.1)	479	(7.2)	484	(11.2)	500	(8.7)	11.7	(6.09)	1.1	(0.17)	1.1	(1.13)
Spain (La Rioja)	487	(6.7)	504	(8.1)	502	(4.7)	499	(4.8)	-1.6	(3.26)	1.3	(0.17)	0.0	(0.08)
Spain (Madrid)	**481**	(13.8)	498	(7.7)	511	(12.8)	**523**	(11.5)	**22.8**	(8.35)	1.5	(0.35)	4.1	(3.36)
Spain (Murcia)	468	(8.4)	478	(8.8)	486	(7.8)	490	(12.0)	11.8	(7.35)	1.3	(0.27)	0.7	(0.86)
Spain (Navarre)	**477**	(6.5)	491	(4.4)	506	(6.4)	**514**	(8.1)	**15.9**	(6.92)	**1.5**	(0.19)	1.7	(1.41)
United Kingdom (Scotland)	489	(5.6)	502	(7.1)	505	(6.5)	504	(8.4)	4.4	(5.14)	1.1	(0.12)	0.2	(0.43)
Non-adjudicated														
Belgium (French Community)	**452**	(10.3)	494	(11.4)	488	(11.9)	**527**	(10.1)	**48.2**	(10.01)	**1.7**	(0.26)	5.4	(2.10)
Belgium (German-Speaking Community)	c	c	519	(6.9)	511	(7.0)	511	(5.9)	**87.1**	(14.44)	**2.2**	(0.27)	2.6	(0.84)
Finland (Finnish Speaking)	539	(4.2)	541	(4.9)	529	(5.3)	540	(4.2)	1.4	(2.56)	1.0	(0.09)	0.0	(0.10)
Finland (Swedish Speaking)	509	(7.0)	510	(5.7)	513	(5.1)	514	(5.5)	2.5	(3.64)	1.1	(0.16)	0.1	(0.18)
Italy (Provincia Abruzzo)	496	(19.5)	483	(13.0)	478	(17.5)	469	(18.5)	-11.0	(10.91)	0.8	(0.34)	1.1	(2.24)
Italy (Provincia Autonoma di Bolzano)	476	(5.6)	474	(5.6)	520	(5.0)	490	(9.5)	**-1.6**	(8.11)	**1.4**	(0.17)	0.0	(0.28)
Italy (Provincia Basilicata)	488	(14.5)	493	(15.9)	448	(9.4)	462	(12.1)	-15.1	(8.46)	0.6	(0.21)	2.5	(2.85)
Italy (Provincia Calabria)	444	(16.2)	467	(14.7)	444	(13.5)	438	(12.1)	-6.0	(11.26)	1.0	(0.33)	0.3	(1.59)
Italy (Provincia Campania)	459	(13.4)	457	(19.6)	446	(13.6)	442	(13.9)	-11.3	(12.50)	0.8	(0.25)	0.9	(2.07)
Italy (Provincia Emilia Romagna)	504	(7.2)	507	(17.2)	483	(15.6)	516	(20.2)	6.7	(12.41)	0.7	(0.17)	0.3	(1.50)
Italy (Provincia Friuli Venezia Giulia)	492	(18.3)	535	(9.7)	519	(19.2)	506	(9.2)	**-1.8**	(9.33)	1.8	(0.60)	0.0	(0.58)
Italy (Provincia Lazio)	483	(18.1)	483	(12.7)	465	(8.6)	494	(12.3)	2.8	(8.82)	1.0	(0.36)	0.1	(0.49)
Italy (Provincia Liguria)	490	(14.6)	493	(12.7)	499	(15.4)	484	(23.2)	-4.3	(11.06)	1.0	(0.33)	0.2	(1.10)
Italy (Provincia Lombardia)	524	(15.1)	511	(15.5)	504	(12.5)	547	(15.2)	14.7	(10.85)	1.0	(0.33)	1.7	(2.68)
Italy (Provincia Marche)	528	(16.6)	473	(19.3)	470	(28.5)	519	(16.9)	-2.3	(15.96)	**0.5**	(0.22)	0.0	(1.68)
Italy (Provincia Molise)	**442**	(8.0)	471	(8.8)	479	(5.7)	**490**	(5.1)	**17.1**	(3.58)	**1.7**	(0.25)	3.5	(1.41)
Italy (Provincia Piemonte)	504	(15.6)	482	(12.1)	488	(17.3)	511	(13.8)	4.9	(9.94)	0.9	(0.28)	0.2	(0.87)
Italy (Provincia Puglia)	486	(19.1)	497	(14.6)	479	(11.6)	497	(14.5)	0.9	(10.63)	1.1	(0.53)	0.0	(1.29)
Italy (Provincia Sardegna)	446	(19.8)	450	(15.5)	486	(16.7)	491	(12.7)	**21.3**	(8.63)	1.4	(0.49)	3.7	(3.00)
Italy (Provincia Sicilia)	442	(15.2)	463	(23.2)	441	(15.7)	466	(15.5)	1.7	(9.90)	0.9	(0.32)	0.0	(0.86)
Italy (Provincia Toscana)	503	(17.0)	476	(21.6)	503	(21.4)	485	(14.7)	-0.8	(8.55)	0.8	(0.30)	0.0	(0.68)
Italy (Provincia Trento)	503	(11.2)	524	(12.6)	487	(11.5)	517	(14.8)	**16.9**	(7.04)	1.1	(0.29)	1.5	(1.25)
Italy (Provincia Umbria)	469	(14.6)	512	(12.5)	499	(13.3)	492	(14.6)	2.7	(10.28)	1.4	(0.39)	0.1	(0.72)
Italy (Provincia Valle d'Aosta)	512	(5.3)	526	(6.0)	515	(5.2)	507	(5.1)	**-6.9**	(2.87)	**1.5**	(0.17)	0.4	(0.36)
Italy (Provincia Veneto)	513	(11.7)	491	(14.6)	502	(18.8)	515	(13.2)	5.8	(7.57)	0.9	(0.27)	0.3	(1.02)
United Kingdom (England)	488	(6.7)	498	(6.3)	500	(4.8)	498	(5.4)	6.2	(4.98)	1.2	(0.15)	0.2	(0.38)
United Kingdom (Northern Ireland)	502	(12.9)	500	(16.9)	505	(10.6)	505	(10.0)	1.2	(9.44)	1.1	(0.29)	0.0	(0.67)
United Kingdom (Wales)	476	(7.7)	475	(5.1)	477	(5.0)	478	(5.9)	0.1	(4.68)	1.0	(0.12)	0.0	(0.13)

Notes: Values that are statistically significant are indicated in bold (see Annex A3). See original Table IV.3.6 for national data.

StatLink http://dx.doi.org/10.1787/888932343304

[Part 1/1]
Table S.IV.e School choice: school level
Results based on school principals' reports

	Percentage of students in schools where the principal reported that the number of schools competing for students in the same area are:					
	Two or more other schools		One other school		No other schools	
	%	S.E.	%	S.E.	%	S.E.
Adjudicated						
Belgium (Flemish Community)	83.0	(3.3)	11.5	(2.9)	5.5	(1.9)
Spain (Andalusia)	56.1	(6.6)	15.3	(5.6)	28.6	(5.6)
Spain (Aragon)	65.7	(6.1)	18.2	(5.6)	16.1	(2.9)
Spain (Asturias)	69.6	(5.1)	14.7	(5.2)	15.7	(4.8)
Spain (Balearic Islands)	60.3	(5.7)	20.8	(5.2)	18.9	(5.5)
Spain (Basque Country)	74.0	(3.5)	17.8	(3.2)	8.2	(1.8)
Spain (Canary Islands)	57.2	(6.2)	19.4	(6.1)	23.5	(6.0)
Spain (Cantabria)	65.1	(5.1)	24.0	(4.5)	11.0	(4.1)
Spain (Castile and Leon)	74.8	(5.4)	10.1	(4.2)	15.1	(5.3)
Spain (Catalonia)	83.1	(5.4)	7.1	(3.9)	9.8	(3.9)
Spain (Ceuta and Melilla)	62.6	(0.5)	27.9	(0.4)	9.5	(0.3)
Spain (Galicia)	64.8	(5.5)	10.7	(4.6)	24.6	(5.9)
Spain (La Rioja)	84.3	(0.3)	10.1	(0.2)	5.6	(0.2)
Spain (Madrid)	85.0	(4.5)	10.9	(3.9)	4.1	(3.4)
Spain (Murcia)	68.8	(6.0)	20.2	(5.4)	11.1	(3.8)
Spain (Navarre)	71.8	(4.6)	12.4	(3.1)	15.8	(4.3)
United Kingdom (Scotland)	53.2	(4.3)	16.5	(3.8)	30.3	(3.7)
Non-adjudicated						
Belgium (French Community)	81.1	(3.5)	14.0	(3.0)	5.0	(2.2)
Belgium (German-Speaking Community)	50.9	(0.3)	32.5	(0.2)	16.6	(0.3)
Finland (Finnish Speaking)	45.8	(3.5)	14.0	(3.2)	40.2	(3.4)
Finland (Swedish Speaking)	15.4	(0.3)	7.9	(0.1)	76.7	(0.3)
Italy (Provincia Abruzzo)	87.8	(4.8)	5.0	(3.7)	7.2	(3.4)
Italy (Provincia Autonoma di Bolzano)	31.0	(1.0)	25.5	(1.0)	43.5	(0.9)
Italy (Provincia Basilicata)	84.5	(3.6)	9.9	(3.3)	5.7	(1.0)
Italy (Provincia Calabria)	76.0	(4.4)	13.9	(3.4)	10.1	(3.8)
Italy (Provincia Campania)	83.7	(5.7)	6.8	(3.9)	9.5	(4.2)
Italy (Provincia Emilia Romagna)	69.9	(5.8)	12.5	(4.7)	17.5	(6.1)
Italy (Provincia Friuli Venezia Giulia)	78.6	(5.2)	7.2	(1.4)	14.2	(5.2)
Italy (Provincia Lazio)	77.6	(5.9)	10.9	(4.5)	11.5	(4.8)
Italy (Provincia Liguria)	79.5	(5.4)	8.3	(3.3)	12.2	(4.9)
Italy (Provincia Lombardia)	73.0	(5.9)	10.4	(4.6)	16.6	(4.2)
Italy (Provincia Marche)	76.7	(6.2)	4.6	(3.1)	18.8	(5.6)
Italy (Provincia Molise)	81.2	(0.4)	11.0	(0.2)	7.8	(0.2)
Italy (Provincia Piemonte)	75.5	(6.7)	17.3	(6.2)	7.2	(3.3)
Italy (Provincia Puglia)	86.9	(4.9)	10.3	(4.6)	2.8	(1.9)
Italy (Provincia Sardegna)	80.6	(6.0)	11.1	(4.4)	8.4	(5.4)
Italy (Provincia Sicilia)	91.4	(3.5)	1.8	(1.8)	6.8	(2.9)
Italy (Provincia Toscana)	65.0	(6.0)	17.8	(4.3)	17.3	(4.9)
Italy (Provincia Trento)	76.2	(3.8)	8.8	(2.4)	15.0	(3.4)
Italy (Provincia Umbria)	70.8	(5.2)	11.8	(4.4)	17.4	(2.9)
Italy (Provincia Valle d'Aosta)	62.1	(0.5)	14.4	(0.4)	23.5	(0.4)
Italy (Provincia Veneto)	75.7	(6.2)	7.9	(3.9)	16.3	(5.5)
United Kingdom (England)	80.8	(2.9)	10.4	(2.3)	8.8	(2.1)
United Kingdom (Northern Ireland)	88.5	(3.9)	5.9	(3.0)	5.6	(2.6)
United Kingdom (Wales)	67.3	(3.6)	12.4	(2.6)	20.3	(3.5)

Note: See original Table IV.3.8a for national data.
StatLink http://dx.doi.org/10.1787/888932343304

[Part 1/3]

Table S.IV.f **Percentage of students and performance in reading, mathematics and science, by type of school**

Results based on school principals' reports

	Government or public schools[1]								Government-dependent private schools[2]							
	Percentage of students		Performance on the reading scale		Performance on the mathematics scale		Performance on the science scale		Percentage of students		Performance on the reading scale		Performance on the mathematics scale		Performance on the science scale	
		S.E.	Mean score	S.E.	Mean score	S.E.	Mean score	S.E.		S.E.	Mean score	S.E.	Mean score	S.E.	Mean score	S.E.
Adjudicated																
Belgium (Flemish Community)	w	w	w	w	w	w	w	w	w	w	w	w	w	w	w	w
Spain (Andalusia)	74.5	(1.1)	451	(6.7)	455	(5.7)	460	(6.5)	24.1	(1.8)	494	(5.5)	484	(9.3)	498	(7.4)
Spain (Aragon)	69.6	(3.1)	485	(5.2)	493	(6.6)	498	(4.7)	26.4	(4.2)	508	(6.6)	527	(10.3)	510	(7.4)
Spain (Asturias)	67.4	(2.7)	478	(5.2)	483	(4.9)	490	(5.4)	30.6	(2.9)	511	(9.2)	511	(7.2)	520	(8.4)
Spain (Balearic Islands)	65.6	(5.7)	441	(7.4)	450	(6.0)	448	(8.9)	29.8	(6.6)	481	(11.0)	481	(10.1)	477	(7.6)
Spain (Basque Country)	42.3	(1.6)	480	(4.0)	499	(3.7)	481	(3.4)	57.7	(1.6)	506	(4.1)	519	(4.1)	505	(3.6)
Spain (Canary Islands)	81.8	(3.4)	434	(5.0)	424	(5.4)	439	(5.0)	18.2	(3.4)	493	(6.9)	468	(6.1)	496	(7.3)
Spain (Cantabria)	61.1	(1.5)	474	(5.6)	485	(5.8)	489	(6.0)	35.3	(2.9)	508	(6.1)	508	(9.9)	515	(8.7)
Spain (Castile and Leon)	67.1	(3.5)	499	(6.3)	516	(7.9)	511	(6.8)	23.7	(4.8)	509	(11.6)	509	(8.7)	522	(10.5)
Spain (Catalonia)	60.7	(3.5)	491	(7.6)	486	(8.7)	493	(9.5)	24.1	(5.5)	502	(14.3)	494	(13.0)	503	(12.2)
Spain (Ceuta and Melilla)	79.5	(0.3)	390	(3.0)	398	(2.9)	395	(3.1)	17.6	(0.2)	491	(4.4)	486	(4.3)	498	(4.7)
Spain (Galicia)	68.3	(1.2)	479	(5.8)	483	(5.5)	501	(6.5)	25.5	(3.5)	504	(8.5)	505	(7.6)	521	(9.4)
Spain (La Rioja)	67.3	(0.3)	494	(3.4)	498	(3.9)	505	(3.7)	32.7	(0.3)	506	(4.0)	515	(5.0)	517	(4.5)
Spain (Madrid)	60.6	(4.9)	490	(7.5)	482	(6.6)	496	(6.6)	32.1	(5.4)	517	(6.8)	511	(7.7)	518	(6.2)
Spain (Murcia)	74.8	(2.6)	476	(4.3)	479	(4.2)	482	(4.4)	22.7	(1.8)	488	(15.5)	476	(15.7)	486	(12.7)
Spain (Navarre)	62.8	(2.1)	480	(3.3)	499	(3.0)	493	(3.8)	34.7	(3.4)	525	(5.7)	534	(7.3)	536	(5.7)
United Kingdom (Scotland)	95.7	(1.9)	496	(3.3)	495	(3.3)	510	(3.5)	0.0	c	c	c	c	c	c	c
Non-adjudicated																
Belgium (French Community)	41.5	(1.6)	469	(5.4)	470	(6.0)	460	(5.4)	57.4	(1.6)	502	(7.8)	498	(7.1)	495	(7.6)
Belgium (German-Speaking Community)	w	w	w	w	w	w	w	w	w	w	w	w	w	w	w	w
Finland (Finnish Speaking)	96.0	(1.2)	537	(2.4)	542	(2.3)	555	(2.5)	4.0	(1.2)	544	(19.6)	535	(14.8)	566	(17.8)
Finland (Swedish Speaking)	97.2	(0.1)	511	(2.7)	527	(3.0)	529	(3.1)	2.8	(0.1)	510	(9.3)	524	(9.3)	508	(10.3)
Italy (Provincia Abruzzo)	97.8	(1.7)	482	(6.2)	478	(7.4)	482	(6.7)	0.0	c	c	c	c	c	c	c
Italy (Provincia Autonoma di Bolzano)	97.0	(0.1)	490	(3.3)	507	(3.4)	513	(2.6)	3.0	(0.1)	511	(7.6)	519	(7.1)	532	(6.8)
Italy (Provincia Basilicata)	100.0	(0.0)	472	(4.7)	473	(4.8)	465	(4.1)	0.0	c	c	c	c	c	c	c
Italy (Provincia Calabria)	98.8	(0.9)	448	(5.2)	443	(4.9)	443	(5.5)	0.0	c	c	c	c	c	c	c
Italy (Provincia Campania)	97.1	(2.0)	451	(7.0)	447	(8.4)	446	(7.3)	0.0	c	c	c	c	c	c	c
Italy (Provincia Emilia Romagna)	95.7	(1.8)	509	(3.8)	510	(4.4)	515	(4.4)	2.3	(1.1)	c	c	c	c	c	c
Italy (Provincia Friuli Venezia Giulia)	98.2	(0.1)	519	(4.4)	515	(4.5)	530	(4.5)	1.8	(0.1)	c	c	c	c	c	c
Italy (Provincia Lazio)	94.9	(1.2)	484	(4.3)	476	(5.9)	485	(5.4)	0.7	(0.7)	c	c	c	c	c	c
Italy (Provincia Liguria)	94.4	(2.5)	494	(9.8)	495	(9.8)	500	(10.4)	2.8	(2.3)	c	c	c	c	c	c
Italy (Provincia Lombardia)	87.4	(3.2)	532	(7.1)	527	(6.5)	535	(7.1)	4.3	(2.2)	c	c	c	c	c	c
Italy (Provincia Marche)	94.4	(5.6)	504	(5.2)	501	(4.7)	509	(5.5)	0.0	c	c	c	c	c	c	c
Italy (Provincia Molise)	100.0	(0.0)	471	(2.8)	467	(2.7)	469	(2.8)	0.0	c	c	c	c	c	c	c
Italy (Provincia Piemonte)	93.3	(2.1)	500	(6.1)	495	(5.8)	505	(4.9)	1.3	(0.2)	c	c	c	c	c	c
Italy (Provincia Puglia)	100.0	(0.0)	489	(5.0)	488	(6.9)	490	(6.3)	0.0	c	c	c	c	c	c	c
Italy (Provincia Sardegna)	98.1	(1.5)	467	(4.9)	456	(5.6)	473	(4.8)	0.0	c	c	c	c	c	c	c
Italy (Provincia Sicilia)	96.9	(1.6)	454	(7.8)	452	(8.2)	453	(7.8)	0.2	(0.2)	c	c	c	c	c	c
Italy (Provincia Toscana)	98.6	(1.0)	492	(5.0)	494	(5.7)	499	(6.2)	0.0	c	c	c	c	c	c	c
Italy (Provincia Trento)	79.1	(1.5)	527	(3.1)	528	(3.2)	540	(4.1)	19.8	(1.8)	455	(8.7)	475	(7.1)	473	(10.9)
Italy (Provincia Umbria)	98.2	(1.1)	495	(5.2)	491	(4.6)	502	(4.9)	0.8	(0.5)	c	c	c	c	c	c
Italy (Provincia Valle d'Aosta)	84.6	(0.4)	520	(2.5)	507	(2.3)	525	(2.8)	15.4	(0.4)	491	(5.6)	481	(5.9)	507	(6.5)
Italy (Provincia Veneto)	89.3	(4.0)	520	(5.5)	517	(6.3)	529	(5.9)	8.5	(3.3)	c	c	c	c	c	c
United Kingdom (England)	92.9	(1.3)	492	(3.2)	491	(3.4)	511	(3.5)	0.0	c	c	c	c	c	c	c
United Kingdom (Northern Ireland)	100.0	(0.0)	503	(4.7)	496	(3.6)	514	(5.1)	0.0	c	c	c	c	c	c	c
United Kingdom (Wales)	98.2	(1.2)	475	(3.4)	471	(2.8)	495	(3.5)	0.0	c	c	c	c	c	c	c

Note: Values that are statistically significant are indicated in bold (see Annex A3).

1. Schools which are directly controlled or managed by: *i)* a public education authority or agency or *ii)* by a government agency directly or by a governing body, most of whose members are either appointed by a public authority or elected by public franchise.

2. Schools which receive 50% or more of their core funding (*i.e.* funding that supports the basic educational services of the institution) from government agencies. See original Table IV.3.9 for national data.

3. Schools which receive less than 50% of their core funding (*i.e.* funding that supports the basic educational services of the institution) from government agencies. See original Table IV.3.9 for national data.

StatLink http://dx.doi.org/10.1787/888932343304

[Part 2/3]
Percentage of students and performance in reading, mathematics and science, by type of school
Table S.IV.f *Results based on school principals' reports*

	Government-independent private schools[3]								Difference in performance on the reading scale between public and private schools (government-dependent and government-independent schools combined)	
			Performance on the reading scale		Performance on the mathematics scale		Performance on the science scale			
	Percentage of students	S.E.	Mean score	S.E.	Mean score	S.E.	Mean score	S.E.	Dif. (Pub. – Priv.)	S.E.
Adjudicated										
Belgium (Flemish Community)	w	w	w	w	w	w	w	w	w	w
Spain (Andalusia)	1.4	(1.5)	c	c	c	c	c	c	**-37**	(11.0)
Spain (Aragon)	4.0	(2.8)	c	c	c	c	c	c	**-28**	(8.2)
Spain (Asturias)	2.1	(2.1)	c	c	c	c	c	c	**-38**	(11.9)
Spain (Balearic Islands)	4.5	(3.9)	c	c	c	c	c	c	**-35**	(11.8)
Spain (Basque Country)	0.0	c	c	c	c	c	c	c	**-26**	(5.7)
Spain (Canary Islands)	0.0	c	c	c	c	c	c	c	**-59**	(8.6)
Spain (Cantabria)	3.5	(2.5)	c	c	c	c	c	c	**-35**	(8.2)
Spain (Castile and Leon)	9.2	(4.4)	527	(9.1)	532	(6.9)	541	(13.0)	-15	(11.1)
Spain (Catalonia)	15.1	(4.2)	532	(7.3)	524	(7.7)	523	(8.0)	**-23**	(11.3)
Spain (Ceuta and Melilla)	2.9	(0.2)	c	c	c	c	c	c	**-103**	(5.3)
Spain (Galicia)	6.3	(3.6)	c	c	c	c	c	c	**-24**	(8.2)
Spain (La Rioja)	0.0	c	c	c	c	c	c	c	**-12**	(5.4)
Spain (Madrid)	7.3	(2.7)	c	c	c	c	c	c	**-30**	(10.9)
Spain (Murcia)	2.4	(2.4)	c	c	c	c	c	c	-17	(15.3)
Spain (Navarre)	2.6	(2.6)	c	c	c	c	c	c	**-46**	(6.3)
United Kingdom (Scotland)	4.3	(1.9)	c	c	c	c	c	c	c	c
Non-adjudicated										
Belgium (French Community)	1.2	(0.2)	c	c	c	c	c	c	**-35**	(9.4)
Belgium (German-Speaking Community)	w	w	w	w	w	w	w	w	w	w
Finland (Finnish Speaking)	0.0	c	c	c	c	c	c	c	-7	(19.7)
Finland (Swedish Speaking)	0.0	c	c	c	c	c	c	c	2	(9.4)
Italy (Provincia Abruzzo)	2.2	(1.7)	c	c	c	c	c	c	c	c
Italy (Provincia Autonoma di Bolzano)	0.0	c	c	c	c	c	c	c	**-22**	(8.1)
Italy (Provincia Basilicata)	0.0	c	c	c	c	c	c	c	c	c
Italy (Provincia Calabria)	1.2	(0.9)	c	c	c	c	c	c	c	c
Italy (Provincia Campania)	2.9	(2.0)	c	c	c	c	c	c	c	c
Italy (Provincia Emilia Romagna)	2.0	(1.4)	c	c	c	c	c	c	c	c
Italy (Provincia Friuli Venezia Giulia)	0.0	c	c	c	c	c	c	c	c	c
Italy (Provincia Lazio)	4.4	(1.0)	c	c	c	c	c	c	c	c
Italy (Provincia Liguria)	2.8	(1.1)	c	c	c	c	c	c	c	c
Italy (Provincia Lombardia)	8.3	(2.5)	501	(18.2)	472	(14.9)	506	(12.7)	**68**	(16.8)
Italy (Provincia Marche)	5.6	(5.6)	c	c	c	c	c	c	c	c
Italy (Provincia Molise)	0.0	c	c	c	c	c	c	c	c	c
Italy (Provincia Piemonte)	5.4	(2.1)	c	c	c	c	c	c	c	c
Italy (Provincia Puglia)	0.0	c	c	c	c	c	c	c	c	c
Italy (Provincia Sardegna)	1.9	(1.5)	c	c	c	c	c	c	c	c
Italy (Provincia Sicilia)	2.8	(1.6)	c	c	c	c	c	c	c	c
Italy (Provincia Toscana)	1.4	(1.0)	c	c	c	c	c	c	c	c
Italy (Provincia Trento)	1.1	(0.7)	c	c	c	c	c	c	**67**	(7.4)
Italy (Provincia Umbria)	1.0	(1.0)	c	c	c	c	c	c	c	c
Italy (Provincia Valle d'Aosta)	0.0	c	c	c	c	c	c	c	**29**	(6.3)
Italy (Provincia Veneto)	2.2	(2.6)	c	c	c	c	c	c	c	c
United Kingdom (England)	7.1	(1.3)	551	(5.5)	543	(5.8)	581	(7.2)	**-59**	(6.4)
United Kingdom (Northern Ireland)	0.0	c	c	c	c	c	c	c	c	c
United Kingdom (Wales)	1.8	(1.2)	c	c	c	c	c	c	c	c

Note: Values that are statistically significant are indicated in bold (see Annex A3).
1. Schools which are directly controlled or managed by: *i)* a public education authority or agency or *ii)* by a government agency directly or by a governing body, most of whose members are either appointed by a public authority or elected by public franchise.
2. Schools which receive 50% or more of their core funding (*i.e.* funding that supports the basic educational services of the institution) from government agencies. See original Table IV.3.9 for national data.
3. Schools which receive less than 50% of their core funding (*i.e.* funding that supports the basic educational services of the institution) from government agencies. See original Table IV.3.9 for national data.
StatLink http://dx.doi.org/10.1787/888932343304

[Part 3/3]

Table S.IV.f Percentage of students and performance in reading, mathematics and science, by type of school

Results based on school principals' reports

	PISA index of economic, social and cultural status						Difference in performance on the reading scale between public and private schools after accounting for the PISA index of economic, social and cultural status of:			
	Public schools		Private schools (Government-dependent and government-independent)		Difference		Students		Students and schools	
	Mean index	S.E.	Mean index	S.E.	Dif. (Pub. – Priv.)	S.E.	Dif. (Pub. – Priv.)	S.E.	Dif. (Pub. – Priv.)	S.E.
Adjudicated										
Belgium (Flemish Community)	w	w	w	w	w	w	w	w	w	w
Spain (Andalusia)	-0.76	(0.07)	-0.04	(0.20)	-0.72	(0.21)	16	(10.7)	7	(12.5)
Spain (Aragon)	-0.44	(0.06)	0.20	(0.15)	-0.64	(0.16)	**13**	(6.2)	0	(7.4)
Spain (Asturias)	-0.42	(0.06)	0.19	(0.12)	-0.61	(0.13)	**20**	(9.8)	11	(12.5)
Spain (Balearic Islands)	-0.60	(0.06)	0.07	(0.19)	-0.66	(0.20)	**20**	(8.8)	1	(7.3)
Spain (Basque Country)	-0.31	(0.04)	0.08	(0.05)	-0.39	(0.06)	**18**	(5.4)	7	(6.3)
Spain (Canary Islands)	-0.80	(0.06)	-0.30	(0.16)	-0.50	(0.17)	**46**	(7.9)	**32**	(12.2)
Spain (Cantabria)	-0.41	(0.08)	0.15	(0.11)	-0.57	(0.13)	**20**	(7.9)	**21**	(10.2)
Spain (Castile and Leon)	-0.35	(0.09)	0.16	(0.13)	-0.51	(0.16)	-1	(8.4)	-11	(7.9)
Spain (Catalonia)	-0.45	(0.10)	-0.04	(0.15)	-0.41	(0.18)	11	(10.2)	4	(10.8)
Spain (Ceuta and Melilla)	-0.76	(0.03)	0.22	(0.05)	-0.98	(0.06)	**73**	(6.0)	**28**	(7.3)
Spain (Galicia)	-0.52	(0.07)	-0.06	(0.11)	-0.46	(0.13)	14	(7.8)	2	(8.0)
Spain (La Rioja)	-0.46	(0.03)	0.07	(0.04)	-0.53	(0.05)	-8	(5.7)	**-28**	(6.0)
Spain (Madrid)	-0.20	(0.14)	0.01	(0.15)	-0.21	(0.18)	**23**	(7.2)	**19**	(5.7)
Spain (Murcia)	-0.53	(0.07)	-0.24	(0.27)	-0.29	(0.28)	8	(9.0)	4	(7.2)
Spain (Navarre)	-0.41	(0.04)	0.21	(0.10)	-0.62	(0.10)	**28**	(6.1)	**20**	(8.5)
United Kingdom (Scotland)	0.15	(0.03)	c	c	c	c	c	c	c	c
Non-adjudicated										
Belgium (French Community)	-0.01	(0.05)	0.31	(0.06)	-0.32	(0.08)	**18**	(6.4)	-2	(6.4)
Belgium (German-Speaking Community)	w	w	w	w	w	w	w	w	w	w
Finland (Finnish Speaking)	0.35	(0.02)	0.51	(0.17)	-0.15	(0.17)	1	(15.4)	-2	(13.8)
Finland (Swedish Speaking)	0.57	(0.02)	0.86	(0.09)	-0.30	(0.09)	-12	(8.6)	-14	(8.6)
Italy (Provincia Abruzzo)	-0.03	(0.06)	c	c	c	c	c	c	c	c
Italy (Provincia Autonoma di Bolzano)	-0.24	(0.02)	0.33	(0.07)	-0.56	(0.08)	6	(8.9)	**-46**	(11.3)
Italy (Provincia Basilicata)	-0.29	(0.03)	c	c	c	c	c	c	c	c
Italy (Provincia Calabria)	-0.26	(0.06)	c	c	c	c	c	c	c	c
Italy (Provincia Campania)	-0.36	(0.06)	c	c	c	c	c	c	c	c
Italy (Provincia Emilia Romagna)	0.08	(0.04)	c	c	c	c	c	c	c	c
Italy (Provincia Friuli Venezia Giulia)	-0.02	(0.03)	c	c	c	c	c	c	c	c
Italy (Provincia Lazio)	0.11	(0.05)	c	c	c	c	c	c	c	c
Italy (Provincia Liguria)	0.01	(0.05)	c	c	c	c	c	c	c	c
Italy (Provincia Lombardia)	-0.02	(0.04)	-0.05	(0.20)	0.03	(0.21)	**-67**	(12.2)	**-65**	(12.9)
Italy (Provincia Marche)	-0.12	(0.03)	c	c	c	c	c	c	c	c
Italy (Provincia Molise)	-0.12	(0.03)	c	c	c	c	c	c	c	c
Italy (Provincia Piemonte)	-0.14	(0.04)	c	c	c	c	c	c	c	c
Italy (Provincia Puglia)	-0.42	(0.05)	c	c	c	c	c	c	c	c
Italy (Provincia Sardegna)	-0.26	(0.06)	c	c	c	c	c	c	c	c
Italy (Provincia Sicilia)	-0.28	(0.07)	c	c	c	c	c	c	c	c
Italy (Provincia Toscana)	0.05	(0.04)	c	c	c	c	c	c	c	c
Italy (Provincia Trento)	-0.03	(0.03)	-0.39	(0.07)	0.36	(0.07)	**-57**	(6.6)	**-24**	(6.6)
Italy (Provincia Umbria)	0.08	(0.03)	c	c	c	c	c	c	c	c
Italy (Provincia Valle d'Aosta)	-0.07	(0.03)	-0.35	(0.06)	0.28	(0.07)	**-23**	(6.6)	4	(6.8)
Italy (Provincia Veneto)	-0.01	(0.04)	c	c	c	c	c	c	c	c
United Kingdom (England)	0.16	(0.03)	0.91	(0.05)	-0.74	(0.06)	**25**	(6.5)	**-22**	(7.8)
United Kingdom (Northern Ireland)	0.13	(0.02)	c	c	c	c	c	c	c	c
United Kingdom (Wales)	0.15	(0.03)	c	c	c	c	c	c	c	c

Note: Values that are statistically significant are indicated in bold (see Annex A3).

1. Schools which are directly controlled or managed by: *i)* a public education authority or agency or *ii)* by a government agency directly or by a governing body, most of whose members are either appointed by a public authority or elected by public franchise.

2. Schools which receive 50% or more of their core funding (*i.e.* funding that supports the basic educational services of the institution) from government agencies. See original Table IV.3.9 for national data.

3. Schools which receive less than 50% of their core funding (*i.e.* funding that supports the basic educational services of the institution) from government agencies. See original Table IV.3.9 for national data.

StatLink http://dx.doi.org/10.1787/888932343304

[Part 1/2]
Assessment practices
Table S.IV.g *Results based on school principals' reports*

	Percentage of students in schools with the following assessment practices:																	
	Standardised tests						Teacher-developed tests						Teachers' judgmental ratings					
	Never		1 to 5 times a year		At least once a month		Never		1 to 5 times a year		At least once a month		Never		1 to 5 times a year		At least once a month	
	%	S.E.	%	S.E.	%	S.E.	%	S.E.	%	S.E.	%	S.E.	%	S.E.	%	S.E.	%	S.E.
Adjudicated																		
Belgium (Flemish Community)	73.8	(3.6)	20.0	(3.4)	6.3	(2.1)	0.0	c	16.6	(2.9)	83.4	(2.9)	0.6	(0.6)	19.2	(2.9)	80.2	(3.0)
Spain (Andalusia)	73.7	(6.6)	24.6	(6.4)	1.7	(1.8)	0.0	c	20.9	(6.1)	79.1	(6.1)	2.4	(2.3)	22.2	(6.6)	75.3	(6.9)
Spain (Aragon)	79.1	(5.7)	20.9	(5.7)	0.0	c	0.0	c	17.6	(5.9)	82.4	(5.9)	3.9	(2.8)	36.5	(7.4)	59.7	(7.4)
Spain (Asturias)	64.2	(8.1)	34.1	(7.9)	1.7	(1.7)	0.0	c	7.9	(4.0)	92.1	(4.0)	7.4	(3.9)	15.6	(5.5)	76.9	(6.8)
Spain (Balearic Islands)	60.6	(8.3)	39.4	(8.3)	0.0	c	0.0	c	5.8	(3.0)	94.2	(3.0)	2.0	(2.0)	15.3	(4.7)	82.6	(5.0)
Spain (Basque Country)	52.5	(3.9)	45.7	(3.8)	1.8	(1.1)	0.0	c	18.3	(3.1)	81.7	(3.1)	2.8	(1.3)	37.8	(4.0)	59.5	(4.1)
Spain (Canary Islands)	73.5	(7.4)	26.5	(7.4)	0.0	c	0.0	c	8.5	(4.8)	91.5	(4.8)	8.2	(4.2)	18.1	(5.4)	73.7	(5.6)
Spain (Cantabria)	82.1	(5.5)	17.9	(5.5)	0.0	c	0.0	c	12.3	(4.3)	87.7	(4.3)	0.0	c	25.4	(5.8)	74.6	(5.8)
Spain (Castile and Leon)	94.3	(3.3)	5.7	(3.3)	0.0	c	0.0	c	18.4	(4.7)	81.6	(4.7)	8.3	(4.2)	16.4	(3.9)	75.3	(5.7)
Spain (Catalonia)	82.1	(5.2)	17.9	(5.2)	0.0	c	0.0	c	9.1	(4.3)	90.9	(4.3)	0.0	c	28.9	(5.3)	71.1	(5.3)
Spain (Ceuta and Melilla)	71.5	(0.4)	28.5	(0.4)	0.0	c	0.0	c	6.4	(0.3)	93.6	(0.3)	10.1	(0.3)	19.2	(0.4)	70.7	(0.5)
Spain (Galicia)	44.4	(7.9)	46.3	(8.4)	9.2	(3.7)	0.0	c	28.9	(6.3)	71.1	(6.3)	1.4	(1.5)	15.0	(4.6)	83.5	(4.9)
Spain (La Rioja)	49.5	(0.5)	50.5	(0.5)	0.0	c	0.0	c	21.6	(0.5)	78.4	(0.5)	3.8	(0.2)	24.4	(0.5)	71.8	(0.6)
Spain (Madrid)	67.4	(6.7)	29.1	(6.2)	3.5	(2.5)	0.0	c	8.5	(3.8)	91.5	(3.8)	0.0	c	18.9	(6.2)	81.1	(6.2)
Spain (Murcia)	72.7	(6.2)	27.3	(6.2)	0.0	c	2.3	(2.2)	10.2	(4.7)	87.5	(5.2)	6.3	(3.6)	15.7	(5.7)	78.0	(6.7)
Spain (Navarre)	44.6	(4.0)	52.8	(4.1)	2.6	(0.2)	0.0	c	25.2	(4.4)	74.8	(4.4)	2.4	(2.3)	31.2	(4.6)	66.5	(4.8)
United Kingdom (Scotland)	16.0	(3.9)	83.0	(4.0)	1.0	(1.0)	0.0	c	58.6	(4.8)	41.4	(4.8)	2.2	(1.6)	53.3	(5.2)	44.4	(5.0)
Non-adjudicated																		
Belgium (French Community)	72.2	(4.8)	25.8	(4.6)	2.0	(1.4)	0.0	c	29.4	(4.3)	70.6	(4.3)	7.8	(2.5)	37.6	(5.2)	54.5	(5.5)
Belgium (German-Speaking Community)	94.1	(0.1)	5.9	(0.1)	0.0	c	0.0	c	16.6	(0.3)	83.4	(0.3)	12.9	(0.2)	38.8	(0.3)	48.3	(0.3)
Finland (Finnish Speaking)	1.5	(0.9)	96.2	(1.6)	2.3	(1.3)	0.0	c	52.8	(3.9)	47.2	(3.9)	0.0	c	15.5	(3.3)	84.5	(3.3)
Finland (Swedish Speaking)	1.9	(0.1)	97.9	(0.2)	0.2	(0.2)	0.0	c	30.1	(0.4)	69.9	(0.4)	0.0	c	51.9	(0.4)	48.1	(0.4)
Italy (Provincia Abruzzo)	40.8	(7.8)	47.0	(7.1)	12.2	(5.1)	0.0	c	40.7	(7.4)	59.3	(7.4)	8.3	(5.4)	15.5	(4.8)	76.2	(6.0)
Italy (Provincia Autonoma di Bolzano)	55.5	(0.4)	41.5	(0.4)	3.0	(0.2)	0.0	c	17.4	(0.2)	82.6	(0.2)	0.0	c	27.2	(0.4)	72.8	(0.4)
Italy (Provincia Basilicata)	21.2	(3.0)	56.9	(5.7)	21.8	(5.6)	0.0	c	47.9	(5.6)	52.1	(5.6)	2.9	(0.1)	27.4	(4.5)	69.7	(4.5)
Italy (Provincia Calabria)	28.7	(5.1)	43.8	(7.2)	27.4	(5.8)	0.0	c	30.2	(6.0)	69.8	(6.0)	2.8	(2.2)	26.2	(7.1)	71.0	(7.2)
Italy (Provincia Campania)	26.6	(7.3)	42.7	(7.6)	30.6	(6.5)	0.0	c	19.1	(6.5)	80.9	(6.5)	2.2	(2.1)	12.2	(5.1)	85.7	(5.5)
Italy (Provincia Emilia Romagna)	35.8	(7.2)	56.8	(7.9)	7.4	(3.8)	0.0	c	20.3	(6.2)	79.7	(6.2)	13.4	(5.2)	15.7	(5.6)	70.9	(7.1)
Italy (Provincia Friuli Venezia Giulia)	24.6	(4.2)	63.0	(5.2)	12.4	(4.1)	0.0	c	30.1	(4.9)	69.9	(4.9)	2.1	(2.0)	20.5	(5.5)	77.5	(5.7)
Italy (Provincia Lazio)	20.0	(3.9)	62.1	(6.4)	17.8	(5.6)	0.0	c	17.3	(6.2)	82.7	(6.2)	5.8	(2.9)	27.5	(8.2)	66.7	(8.2)
Italy (Provincia Liguria)	21.3	(5.5)	60.1	(5.9)	18.6	(5.5)	0.0	c	29.8	(6.4)	70.2	(6.4)	4.7	(1.8)	37.1	(6.4)	58.2	(6.7)
Italy (Provincia Lombardia)	31.1	(6.7)	61.9	(6.9)	7.0	(3.4)	0.0	c	29.1	(6.5)	70.9	(6.5)	8.7	(4.3)	24.4	(7.3)	67.0	(8.5)
Italy (Provincia Marche)	26.5	(7.0)	61.8	(7.9)	11.7	(4.8)	2.6	(2.5)	30.7	(6.2)	66.8	(6.7)	8.3	(1.5)	35.3	(8.7)	56.4	(8.2)
Italy (Provincia Molise)	20.4	(0.5)	40.1	(0.7)	39.4	(0.6)	0.0	c	24.3	(0.4)	75.7	(0.4)	0.0	c	27.5	(1.4)	72.5	(1.4)
Italy (Provincia Piemonte)	28.3	(7.5)	52.9	(8.1)	18.8	(4.4)	2.1	(2.1)	24.8	(6.2)	73.1	(6.7)	3.6	(2.5)	43.6	(7.9)	52.8	(8.3)
Italy (Provincia Puglia)	26.2	(7.8)	61.3	(7.6)	12.5	(5.3)	2.3	(2.3)	30.1	(7.3)	67.6	(7.6)	2.4	(2.4)	24.2	(5.4)	73.4	(5.9)
Italy (Provincia Sardegna)	38.5	(7.4)	44.3	(7.0)	17.2	(5.4)	0.0	c	38.6	(6.9)	61.4	(6.9)	3.9	(2.8)	21.1	(6.1)	75.0	(6.7)
Italy (Provincia Sicilia)	27.2	(6.3)	58.5	(6.6)	14.2	(4.7)	0.0	c	30.8	(7.0)	69.2	(7.0)	11.2	(5.0)	8.7	(4.2)	80.1	(6.6)
Italy (Provincia Toscana)	33.1	(6.4)	52.1	(6.8)	14.8	(4.3)	1.5	(1.6)	28.8	(7.4)	69.7	(7.6)	7.7	(4.1)	12.3	(4.8)	80.0	(5.6)
Italy (Provincia Trento)	24.0	(4.1)	63.1	(5.2)	13.0	(3.2)	0.0	c	26.6	(3.7)	73.4	(3.7)	0.0	c	28.5	(4.6)	71.5	(4.6)
Italy (Provincia Umbria)	22.4	(5.0)	68.2	(5.7)	9.4	(3.1)	1.9	(2.0)	29.5	(6.0)	68.6	(6.3)	8.2	(2.4)	18.3	(4.7)	73.6	(5.3)
Italy (Provincia Valle d'Aosta)	48.4	(0.3)	30.9	(0.4)	20.7	(0.3)	0.0	c	13.2	(0.3)	86.8	(0.3)	39.2	(0.3)	16.4	(0.4)	44.4	(0.4)
Italy (Provincia Veneto)	36.0	(5.7)	53.6	(6.7)	10.4	(3.9)	0.0	c	28.1	(7.4)	71.9	(7.4)	8.9	(4.2)	21.5	(5.9)	69.6	(7.4)
United Kingdom (England)	34.0	(3.7)	65.2	(3.8)	0.7	(0.7)	0.0	c	70.7	(3.3)	29.3	(3.3)	0.6	(0.5)	63.1	(3.6)	36.3	(3.6)
United Kingdom (Northern Ireland)	26.2	(4.4)	68.6	(4.9)	5.2	(3.0)	1.5	(1.5)	42.8	(5.5)	55.6	(5.4)	7.9	(3.0)	61.6	(5.5)	30.5	(5.6)
United Kingdom (Wales)	38.4	(4.2)	60.6	(4.2)	1.1	(1.1)	0.0	c	78.6	(3.2)	21.4	(3.2)	3.9	(1.6)	66.9	(4.2)	29.2	(4.0)

Note: See original Table IV.3.10 for national data.
StatLink http://dx.doi.org/10.1787/888932343304

[Part 2/2]
Table S.IV.g Assessment practices
Results based on school principals' reports

	Percentage of students in schools with the following assessment practices:											
	Student portfolios						Student assignments/projects/homework					
	Never		1 to 5 times a year		At least once a month		Never		1 to 5 times a year		At least once a month	
	%	S.E.	%	S.E.	%	S.E.	%	S.E.	%	S.E.	%	S.E.
Adjudicated												
Belgium (Flemish Community)	14.8	(3.0)	74.6	(3.5)	10.6	(2.2)	0.1	(0.1)	13.6	(2.8)	86.3	(2.8)
Spain (Andalusia)	0.0	c	15.4	(5.6)	84.6	(5.6)	0.0	c	16.8	(5.2)	83.2	(5.2)
Spain (Aragon)	0.0	c	28.6	(6.4)	71.4	(6.4)	0.0	c	27.3	(7.5)	72.7	(7.5)
Spain (Asturias)	0.0	c	23.1	(5.4)	76.9	(5.4)	2.1	(2.1)	10.1	(3.5)	87.7	(4.1)
Spain (Balearic Islands)	23.5	(6.3)	16.6	(5.4)	59.9	(8.4)	5.8	(5.5)	8.2	(3.0)	86.0	(6.0)
Spain (Basque Country)	0.0	c	32.2	(3.3)	67.8	(3.3)	0.8	(0.0)	20.8	(3.3)	78.4	(3.3)
Spain (Canary Islands)	0.0	c	8.5	(4.3)	91.5	(4.3)	2.1	(2.1)	4.2	(3.0)	93.7	(3.7)
Spain (Cantabria)	0.0	c	13.1	(3.2)	86.9	(3.2)	0.0	c	4.6	(2.0)	95.4	(2.0)
Spain (Castile and Leon)	0.0	c	16.5	(5.7)	83.5	(5.7)	0.0	c	8.3	(4.0)	91.7	(4.0)
Spain (Catalonia)	5.4	(3.6)	35.5	(6.9)	59.1	(6.6)	0.0	c	9.6	(4.8)	90.4	(4.8)
Spain (Ceuta and Melilla)	0.0	c	0.0	c	100.0	(0.0)	0.0	c	5.4	(0.2)	94.6	(0.2)
Spain (Galicia)	2.1	(2.1)	25.3	(5.8)	72.6	(5.5)	0.0	c	14.9	(5.4)	85.1	(5.4)
Spain (La Rioja)	0.0	c	21.4	(0.5)	78.6	(0.5)	0.0	c	7.4	(0.2)	92.6	(0.2)
Spain (Madrid)	0.0	c	26.8	(7.9)	73.2	(7.9)	0.0	c	18.2	(6.7)	81.8	(6.7)
Spain (Murcia)	2.3	(2.2)	14.7	(6.0)	83.1	(6.4)	2.3	(2.2)	6.7	(3.9)	91.1	(4.5)
Spain (Navarre)	0.0	c	32.5	(3.7)	67.5	(3.7)	1.3	(1.3)	12.7	(3.5)	86.0	(3.7)
United Kingdom (Scotland)	6.7	(2.3)	78.6	(4.3)	14.7	(4.2)	0.0	c	32.9	(4.9)	67.1	(4.9)
Non-adjudicated												
Belgium (French Community)	39.4	(5.5)	50.4	(5.4)	10.2	(3.4)	0.0	(0.0)	18.6	(3.9)	81.4	(3.9)
Belgium (German-Speaking Community)	93.1	(0.2)	6.9	(0.2)	0.0	c	0.0	c	21.0	(0.1)	79.0	(0.1)
Finland (Finnish Speaking)	16.7	(3.4)	79.8	(3.8)	3.5	(1.5)	0.0	c	24.6	(3.7)	75.4	(3.7)
Finland (Swedish Speaking)	20.3	(0.2)	77.5	(0.2)	2.2	(0.1)	0.0	c	34.6	(0.3)	65.4	(0.3)
Italy (Provincia Abruzzo)	4.0	(2.9)	45.4	(7.2)	50.6	(7.9)	4.3	(3.0)	35.3	(6.7)	60.5	(7.5)
Italy (Provincia Autonoma di Bolzano)	3.3	(0.1)	29.6	(0.3)	67.1	(0.3)	4.0	(0.1)	24.4	(0.3)	71.6	(0.3)
Italy (Provincia Basilicata)	5.6	(0.2)	46.5	(6.0)	47.9	(6.0)	7.3	(1.9)	37.7	(6.3)	54.9	(6.0)
Italy (Provincia Calabria)	4.2	(2.9)	32.7	(7.8)	63.1	(7.7)	4.2	(2.9)	24.7	(7.0)	71.0	(7.5)
Italy (Provincia Campania)	4.2	(2.6)	29.5	(6.2)	66.2	(6.9)	0.0	c	20.8	(5.8)	79.2	(5.8)
Italy (Provincia Emilia Romagna)	7.8	(2.7)	34.8	(7.6)	57.4	(7.5)	10.6	(3.4)	31.4	(7.4)	58.0	(7.5)
Italy (Provincia Friuli Venezia Giulia)	16.7	(4.1)	45.2	(5.8)	38.1	(5.7)	12.6	(3.0)	35.7	(6.5)	51.8	(5.4)
Italy (Provincia Lazio)	6.6	(3.8)	39.3	(7.3)	54.0	(8.1)	7.3	(4.1)	35.9	(7.3)	56.7	(8.1)
Italy (Provincia Liguria)	2.9	(3.0)	61.3	(6.9)	35.8	(7.2)	0.0	c	53.3	(5.9)	46.7	(5.9)
Italy (Provincia Lombardia)	7.2	(4.1)	51.1	(8.3)	41.8	(7.3)	2.7	(2.3)	48.0	(8.4)	49.3	(8.5)
Italy (Provincia Marche)	2.8	(2.7)	57.4	(8.4)	39.8	(8.0)	2.5	(0.2)	50.0	(7.9)	47.5	(7.9)
Italy (Provincia Molise)	2.5	(0.0)	40.2	(1.3)	57.3	(1.3)	0.3	(0.2)	29.3	(1.7)	70.4	(1.5)
Italy (Provincia Piemonte)	6.2	(3.2)	53.7	(5.6)	40.2	(5.8)	6.8	(3.1)	37.9	(6.2)	55.3	(6.8)
Italy (Provincia Puglia)	5.1	(3.5)	39.0	(7.2)	55.9	(7.6)	2.3	(2.3)	30.1	(5.8)	67.6	(6.1)
Italy (Provincia Sardegna)	2.4	(2.4)	41.0	(8.2)	56.6	(7.9)	3.3	(2.5)	26.8	(7.1)	69.9	(7.2)
Italy (Provincia Sicilia)	5.1	(3.5)	24.8	(6.4)	70.1	(7.4)	2.5	(2.4)	16.1	(5.0)	81.3	(5.6)
Italy (Provincia Toscana)	11.3	(5.5)	38.6	(7.0)	50.2	(7.1)	16.3	(5.6)	23.4	(5.4)	60.4	(6.5)
Italy (Provincia Trento)	2.8	(3.0)	36.6	(4.6)	60.6	(3.9)	2.8	(3.0)	25.1	(4.0)	72.0	(3.3)
Italy (Provincia Umbria)	8.6	(3.4)	39.0	(5.9)	52.5	(5.6)	3.4	(2.4)	44.7	(5.7)	51.9	(6.2)
Italy (Provincia Valle d'Aosta)	22.1	(0.3)	35.2	(0.4)	42.6	(0.4)	0.0	c	55.7	(0.5)	44.3	(0.5)
Italy (Provincia Veneto)	6.3	(3.7)	40.5	(7.2)	53.2	(7.5)	2.4	(2.5)	30.4	(7.3)	67.1	(7.7)
United Kingdom (England)	14.8	(2.9)	62.6	(4.1)	22.6	(3.5)	0.0	c	36.4	(4.0)	63.6	(4.0)
United Kingdom (Northern Ireland)	28.8	(4.3)	61.6	(5.3)	9.6	(3.5)	0.0	c	25.0	(5.2)	75.0	(5.2)
United Kingdom (Wales)	13.7	(2.4)	68.8	(3.8)	17.5	(3.0)	0.0	c	39.6	(4.0)	60.4	(4.0)

Note: See original Table IV.3.10 for national data.
StatLink http://dx.doi.org/10.1787/888932343304

[Part 1/1]
Table S.IV.h Use of achievement data for accountability purposes
Results based on school principals' reports

	Percentage of students in schools with the following uses of achievement data:									
	Posted publicly		Used in evaluation of the principal's performance		Used in evaluation of teachers' performance		Used in decisions about instructional resource allocation to the school		Tracked over time by an administrative authority	
	%	S.E.	%	S.E.	%	S.E.	%	S.E.	%	S.E.
Adjudicated										
Belgium (Flemish Community)	0.9	(0.9)	5.4	(2.0)	23.6	(3.9)	3.7	(1.6)	54.6	(3.9)
Spain (Andalusia)	6.1	(3.4)	15.2	(5.5)	24.2	(6.7)	35.1	(7.1)	72.0	(6.6)
Spain (Aragon)	4.5	(3.1)	1.1	(1.1)	15.3	(4.1)	21.2	(5.6)	74.4	(5.7)
Spain (Asturias)	12.2	(4.9)	15.9	(5.5)	31.0	(6.4)	33.7	(7.9)	68.7	(7.2)
Spain (Balearic Islands)	11.2	(5.0)	32.2	(7.7)	49.1	(7.0)	50.3	(5.4)	54.1	(6.9)
Spain (Basque Country)	5.4	(1.9)	11.1	(2.3)	32.8	(3.5)	53.3	(3.6)	73.9	(3.5)
Spain (Canary Islands)	15.9	(5.7)	20.5	(6.7)	40.3	(7.0)	46.8	(6.9)	91.8	(4.7)
Spain (Cantabria)	1.6	(1.7)	12.8	(5.2)	41.6	(6.9)	48.7	(6.6)	89.0	(4.4)
Spain (Castile and Leon)	5.9	(3.5)	16.5	(4.0)	45.3	(7.2)	34.7	(6.9)	74.9	(5.5)
Spain (Catalonia)	4.3	(3.1)	26.7	(7.2)	31.1	(7.0)	50.6	(7.2)	61.8	(7.7)
Spain (Ceuta and Melilla)	3.0	(0.3)	29.9	(0.4)	35.9	(0.4)	41.6	(0.6)	85.8	(0.3)
Spain (Galicia)	2.9	(2.1)	30.4	(6.8)	37.7	(6.8)	39.4	(6.8)	35.4	(7.8)
Spain (La Rioja)	7.2	(0.2)	9.5	(0.3)	23.5	(0.4)	36.3	(0.4)	63.5	(0.6)
Spain (Madrid)	14.5	(5.3)	19.7	(7.7)	53.3	(8.4)	57.3	(7.2)	69.2	(6.5)
Spain (Murcia)	10.2	(3.7)	9.1	(4.5)	43.8	(6.9)	40.5	(6.6)	73.9	(6.8)
Spain (Navarre)	17.1	(4.6)	15.6	(3.0)	38.2	(5.7)	44.2	(3.5)	78.8	(4.8)
United Kingdom (Scotland)	78.7	(3.9)	66.8	(5.2)	66.5	(5.2)	27.6	(4.6)	97.7	(1.4)
Non-adjudicated										
Belgium (French Community)	3.3	(1.7)	18.2	(3.3)	13.6	(3.6)	45.7	(4.8)	33.6	(4.6)
Belgium (German-Speaking Community)	0.0	c	0.0	c	0.0	(0.2)	0.0	c	31.2	(0.3)
Finland (Finnish Speaking)	2.3	(1.5)	5.2	(1.9)	10.7	(2.7)	4.6	(2.1)	44.2	(4.4)
Finland (Swedish Speaking)	5.3	(0.2)	6.0	(0.1)	14.4	(0.3)	15.4	(0.3)	30.5	(0.3)
Italy (Provincia Abruzzo)	14.1	(5.0)	7.2	(3.4)	18.0	(4.6)	34.0	(6.1)	19.6	(6.3)
Italy (Provincia Autonoma di Bolzano)	4.8	(0.1)	21.7	(1.5)	14.5	(0.4)	30.1	(1.2)	49.1	(1.3)
Italy (Provincia Basilicata)	20.7	(4.1)	17.2	(3.4)	27.4	(5.7)	35.2	(4.8)	18.7	(4.3)
Italy (Provincia Calabria)	17.2	(5.9)	16.9	(5.8)	29.2	(6.6)	54.2	(7.4)	19.2	(5.4)
Italy (Provincia Campania)	18.6	(6.2)	33.7	(7.3)	38.3	(4.8)	48.3	(6.8)	16.5	(6.0)
Italy (Provincia Emilia Romagna)	53.2	(7.2)	11.2	(4.6)	22.3	(5.3)	28.6	(6.4)	36.1	(7.2)
Italy (Provincia Friuli Venezia Giulia)	52.0	(4.4)	6.5	(3.2)	19.7	(4.7)	35.1	(5.8)	27.0	(4.0)
Italy (Provincia Lazio)	29.9	(7.1)	4.8	(2.5)	22.7	(5.9)	36.3	(7.1)	39.5	(7.6)
Italy (Provincia Liguria)	60.8	(7.5)	10.7	(5.2)	24.9	(7.3)	24.2	(6.6)	11.1	(4.5)
Italy (Provincia Lombardia)	36.3	(7.2)	15.5	(6.0)	21.0	(6.1)	27.5	(7.5)	34.8	(7.0)
Italy (Provincia Marche)	25.0	(5.9)	6.8	(3.9)	27.4	(7.1)	38.0	(7.6)	25.6	(7.0)
Italy (Provincia Molise)	12.3	(1.5)	14.6	(1.1)	19.2	(1.8)	21.7	(1.1)	7.4	(0.7)
Italy (Provincia Piemonte)	51.3	(7.1)	18.1	(5.8)	18.3	(5.6)	52.1	(7.0)	24.8	(5.9)
Italy (Provincia Puglia)	13.6	(4.7)	26.0	(6.5)	31.9	(7.0)	55.6	(5.5)	26.8	(6.3)
Italy (Provincia Sardegna)	26.6	(7.3)	18.1	(5.8)	9.5	(4.0)	37.5	(7.5)	17.8	(4.7)
Italy (Provincia Sicilia)	17.2	(6.3)	15.4	(4.1)	16.6	(5.8)	43.9	(8.2)	23.6	(6.7)
Italy (Provincia Toscana)	27.9	(5.7)	1.3	(0.8)	10.5	(4.4)	33.1	(6.6)	6.4	(3.4)
Italy (Provincia Trento)	46.8	(3.5)	23.7	(1.5)	14.5	(2.5)	26.6	(3.9)	38.7	(3.6)
Italy (Provincia Umbria)	46.0	(5.3)	7.8	(2.0)	16.1	(4.3)	34.4	(5.9)	7.4	(3.6)
Italy (Provincia Valle d'Aosta)	35.6	(0.4)	11.5	(0.3)	3.2	(0.3)	15.7	(0.4)	26.8	(0.4)
Italy (Provincia Veneto)	36.9	(6.8)	15.5	(4.6)	34.0	(6.6)	29.0	(6.6)	25.5	(7.0)
United Kingdom (England)	82.2	(3.2)	96.4	(1.8)	97.8	(1.2)	61.3	(4.0)	93.2	(2.1)
United Kingdom (Northern Ireland)	68.0	(5.1)	78.1	(4.1)	79.2	(4.3)	50.9	(5.6)	91.1	(3.6)
United Kingdom (Wales)	59.2	(4.4)	93.3	(2.5)	93.3	(2.1)	54.8	(3.8)	95.9	(1.8)

Note: See original Table IV.3.13 for national data.
StatLink http://dx.doi.org/10.1787/888932343304

[Part 1/1]
School accountability to parents
Table S.IV.i *Results based on school principals' reports*

	Percentage of students in schools where the principal reported that the school provided information to parents on student performance:					
	Relative to other students in the same school		Relative to national or regional benchmarks		Relative to other students in other schools	
	%	S.E.	%	S.E.	%	S.E.
Adjudicated						
Belgium (Flemish Community)	58.9	(4.0)	1.9	(1.1)	1.4	(1.0)
Spain (Andalusia)	41.7	(6.2)	19.8	(6.1)	9.8	(4.4)
Spain (Aragon)	37.1	(7.1)	8.7	(4.5)	4.8	(3.2)
Spain (Asturias)	30.1	(7.1)	22.4	(5.3)	8.0	(4.0)
Spain (Balearic Islands)	35.4	(8.2)	8.8	(5.5)	16.0	(6.3)
Spain (Basque Country)	25.9	(3.5)	14.5	(2.7)	10.0	(2.4)
Spain (Canary Islands)	51.0	(7.0)	16.8	(5.2)	12.3	(5.3)
Spain (Cantabria)	35.9	(6.8)	19.2	(6.0)	13.5	(5.3)
Spain (Castile and Leon)	43.5	(6.8)	13.0	(5.2)	8.3	(4.2)
Spain (Catalonia)	25.4	(5.8)	4.6	(3.3)	9.4	(4.7)
Spain (Ceuta and Melilla)	17.5	(0.5)	0.0	c	0.0	c
Spain (Galicia)	41.7	(7.2)	10.6	(4.2)	4.3	(2.6)
Spain (La Rioja)	44.7	(0.6)	19.3	(0.4)	12.6	(0.4)
Spain (Madrid)	52.2	(8.1)	39.3	(8.4)	21.7	(7.1)
Spain (Murcia)	42.2	(7.7)	19.9	(6.2)	8.0	(3.9)
Spain (Navarre)	31.8	(5.0)	29.2	(5.5)	13.3	(2.6)
United Kingdom (Scotland)	23.2	(4.3)	63.6	(4.4)	31.5	(4.3)
Non-adjudicated						
Belgium (French Community)	8.2	(2.8)	77.5	(4.2)	1.1	(1.1)
Belgium (German-Speaking Community)	28.0	(0.3)	0.0	c	0.0	c
Finland (Finnish Speaking)	12.5	(2.7)	28.6	(3.6)	17.4	(3.3)
Finland (Swedish Speaking)	14.1	(0.3)	38.4	(0.3)	23.8	(0.3)
Italy (Provincia Abruzzo)	8.9	(4.5)	5.9	(2.5)	1.9	(1.9)
Italy (Provincia Autonoma di Bolzano)	10.9	(0.2)	11.3	(0.2)	8.0	(0.2)
Italy (Provincia Basilicata)	22.6	(4.1)	17.0	(4.2)	11.0	(3.5)
Italy (Provincia Calabria)	20.4	(4.4)	17.1	(6.1)	3.9	(2.9)
Italy (Provincia Campania)	27.3	(7.1)	23.4	(6.5)	7.1	(2.7)
Italy (Provincia Emilia Romagna)	10.6	(3.2)	19.8	(5.0)	5.9	(3.1)
Italy (Provincia Friuli Venezia Giulia)	10.3	(3.8)	13.6	(3.6)	6.1	(3.0)
Italy (Provincia Lazio)	14.5	(5.4)	9.0	(4.3)	7.5	(3.7)
Italy (Provincia Liguria)	8.7	(4.4)	16.1	(6.5)	1.7	(1.7)
Italy (Provincia Lombardia)	7.6	(4.0)	10.5	(4.5)	2.9	(2.2)
Italy (Provincia Marche)	5.0	(2.9)	19.0	(6.2)	0.9	(0.6)
Italy (Provincia Molise)	19.0	(1.5)	16.4	(0.3)	0.0	c
Italy (Provincia Piemonte)	20.4	(5.0)	15.5	(5.5)	2.1	(2.1)
Italy (Provincia Puglia)	10.1	(4.4)	15.0	(5.2)	5.6	(3.3)
Italy (Provincia Sardegna)	12.5	(5.1)	3.5	(2.8)	2.4	(1.8)
Italy (Provincia Sicilia)	9.2	(4.0)	10.6	(4.4)	3.5	(2.5)
Italy (Provincia Toscana)	11.8	(4.8)	6.2	(3.7)	0.0	c
Italy (Provincia Trento)	1.4	(1.0)	15.3	(2.7)	4.8	(1.9)
Italy (Provincia Umbria)	5.5	(1.8)	13.4	(3.9)	1.5	(1.0)
Italy (Provincia Valle d'Aosta)	0.0	c	9.0	(0.2)	0.0	c
Italy (Provincia Veneto)	11.8	(4.5)	20.3	(5.4)	3.7	(2.6)
United Kingdom (England)	34.0	(4.1)	68.8	(3.7)	28.6	(3.5)
United Kingdom (Northern Ireland)	71.9	(5.3)	35.9	(4.8)	32.1	(5.8)
United Kingdom (Wales)	39.4	(4.2)	62.7	(3.6)	27.4	(3.7)

Note: See original Table IV.3.14 for national data.
StatLink http://dx.doi.org/10.1787/888932343304

[Part 1/1]

Table S.IV.j Students' learning time at school and percentage of students attending after-school lessons, by remedial or enrichment lessons

Results based on students' self-reports

	Students' time spent per week in regular lessons at schools (minutes)						Percentage of students attending after-school lessons, by type (enrichment or remedial lessons)											
							Language of instruction				Mathematics				Science			
	Regular lessons at school in language of instruction		Regular lessons at school in mathematics		Regular lessons at school in science		Enrichment lessons		Remedial lessons		Enrichment lessons		Remedial lessons		Enrichment lessons		Remedial lessons	
	Mean	S.E.	Mean	S.E.	Mean	S.E.	%	S.E.	%	S.E.	%	S.E.	%	S.E.	%	S.E.	%	S.E.
Adjudicated																		
Belgium (Flemish Community)	195.8	(1.9)	206.2	(2.0)	194.0	(4.4)	3.4	(0.3)	1.4	(0.2)	6.6	(0.4)	9.3	(0.6)	3.6	(0.3)	3.2	(0.3)
Spain (Andalusia)	208.3	(2.9)	232.6	(2.3)	248.2	(7.6)	14.4	(1.0)	15.7	(1.2)	26.4	(1.4)	25.7	(1.4)	13.5	(1.0)	10.0	(0.7)
Spain (Aragon)	212.2	(1.8)	204.0	(1.8)	215.7	(8.2)	10.6	(1.0)	12.8	(1.4)	23.9	(1.0)	33.5	(1.8)	10.2	(0.9)	14.6	(1.6)
Spain (Asturias)	221.5	(1.6)	187.9	(1.8)	201.6	(5.5)	14.7	(1.2)	15.7	(1.1)	34.6	(1.3)	38.4	(1.2)	17.1	(1.2)	17.3	(1.1)
Spain (Balearic Islands)	176.4	(2.4)	207.2	(1.5)	231.7	(9.6)	8.2	(0.7)	12.2	(1.1)	19.4	(1.1)	31.0	(1.4)	11.3	(0.9)	15.0	(1.1)
Spain (Basque Country)	197.5	(1.5)	209.6	(1.6)	204.5	(2.5)	7.7	(0.6)	5.9	(0.5)	25.7	(0.9)	18.3	(0.7)	14.1	(0.6)	9.4	(0.5)
Spain (Canary Islands)	223.3	(1.9)	223.8	(1.7)	200.4	(4.8)	14.7	(1.2)	16.4	(1.5)	24.7	(1.6)	26.9	(1.4)	13.7	(1.4)	11.8	(1.0)
Spain (Cantabria)	212.4	(1.8)	203.7	(2.0)	207.7	(6.3)	14.4	(0.9)	16.6	(1.1)	34.1	(1.4)	37.7	(1.6)	16.2	(1.4)	18.8	(1.6)
Spain (Castile and Leon)	217.2	(2.2)	210.5	(1.5)	225.0	(5.8)	10.3	(0.9)	13.0	(1.0)	24.1	(1.6)	30.7	(1.8)	14.2	(1.3)	12.3	(1.3)
Spain (Catalonia)	175.9	(1.1)	185.1	(3.1)	217.9	(8.2)	6.0	(0.8)	9.5	(1.0)	14.3	(1.2)	23.2	(1.8)	6.4	(0.7)	10.4	(0.8)
Spain (Ceuta and Melilla)	206.9	(1.1)	210.4	(1.0)	175.5	(2.0)	21.4	(1.2)	17.1	(1.2)	33.4	(1.1)	28.2	(1.3)	20.0	(1.1)	13.4	(1.0)
Spain (Galicia)	156.9	(1.7)	173.8	(1.3)	182.8	(6.2)	9.4	(0.9)	11.3	(1.1)	28.4	(1.1)	35.9	(1.4)	14.9	(1.1)	17.5	(1.5)
Spain (La Rioja)	209.3	(0.9)	209.9	(0.7)	211.0	(3.0)	9.3	(1.1)	13.4	(1.1)	29.1	(1.2)	35.2	(1.5)	11.4	(1.0)	13.6	(1.2)
Spain (Madrid)	220.5	(1.8)	192.9	(3.3)	219.9	(4.9)	9.0	(0.6)	13.6	(1.1)	22.6	(1.8)	27.3	(1.6)	10.3	(1.0)	10.6	(0.9)
Spain (Murcia)	221.2	(1.1)	209.7	(1.2)	217.4	(6.0)	11.7	(1.2)	15.8	(1.2)	24.2	(1.2)	33.1	(1.1)	10.9	(0.9)	12.1	(1.2)
Spain (Navarre)	215.3	(1.2)	215.2	(2.1)	216.6	(3.9)	7.7	(0.8)	9.7	(0.9)	21.3	(1.2)	24.8	(1.4)	8.4	(0.7)	10.8	(1.0)
United Kingdom (Scotland)	230.5	(2.3)	224.8	(2.3)	240.1	(4.7)	11.5	(0.8)	18.5	(0.7)	20.4	(1.2)	26.4	(1.2)	14.0	(0.9)	20.9	(1.0)
Non-adjudicated																		
Belgium (French Community)	233.8	(2.1)	213.7	(3.1)	174.6	(3.4)	4.4	(0.5)	3.6	(0.4)	12.4	(0.6)	13.8	(1.0)	3.7	(0.5)	3.5	(0.4)
Belgium (German-Speaking Community)	216.1	(1.1)	207.6	(2.1)	137.6	(2.5)	2.8	(0.6)	3.0	(0.7)	8.3	(0.9)	7.2	(1.0)	3.1	(0.5)	4.0	(0.7)
Finland (Finnish Speaking)	150.5	(2.1)	172.0	(2.2)	193.9	(3.4)	1.2	(0.1)	1.8	(0.2)	2.3	(0.2)	8.7	(0.6)	1.7	(0.2)	1.7	(0.2)
Finland (Swedish Speaking)	146.8	(0.6)	166.6	(0.8)	201.6	(2.0)	3.0	(0.4)	8.3	(0.8)	5.1	(0.5)	15.4	(0.9)	3.2	(0.5)	6.4	(0.6)
Italy (Provincia Abruzzo)	288.6	(6.3)	231.9	(4.4)	162.8	(8.2)	4.0	(0.7)	6.6	(0.7)	14.0	(1.3)	17.6	(1.6)	2.8	(0.6)	3.8	(0.8)
Italy (Provincia Autonoma di Bolzano)	220.3	(1.7)	192.1	(1.4)	168.4	(2.1)	5.4	(1.3)	8.2	(1.5)	11.6	(1.1)	18.4	(1.5)	4.3	(0.6)	6.8	(0.8)
Italy (Provincia Basilicata)	285.8	(4.7)	241.7	(3.3)	185.5	(6.5)	8.2	(1.1)	8.4	(1.1)	17.0	(1.4)	21.5	(1.9)	3.5	(0.6)	4.3	(0.9)
Italy (Provincia Calabria)	291.8	(4.7)	232.0	(5.4)	172.7	(6.4)	8.1	(1.0)	8.1	(1.5)	18.0	(1.1)	21.7	(1.5)	5.2	(0.6)	6.4	(1.1)
Italy (Provincia Campania)	302.0	(6.3)	239.2	(5.3)	155.0	(5.2)	8.0	(1.1)	9.8	(1.1)	19.3	(1.5)	20.6	(1.9)	5.2	(0.7)	6.0	(0.8)
Italy (Provincia Emilia Romagna)	271.4	(3.8)	226.6	(4.1)	157.1	(8.1)	4.4	(0.7)	6.4	(1.0)	19.1	(1.7)	21.4	(2.0)	2.2	(0.4)	3.4	(0.5)
Italy (Provincia Friuli Venezia Giulia)	279.0	(4.5)	228.5	(3.1)	148.8	(6.6)	3.2	(0.4)	4.3	(0.6)	16.3	(1.1)	17.4	(1.5)	2.4	(0.4)	2.7	(0.6)
Italy (Provincia Lazio)	289.9	(5.2)	219.7	(4.7)	133.3	(5.7)	4.3	(0.7)	7.3	(1.0)	16.4	(0.8)	17.8	(1.2)	2.8	(0.5)	4.2	(1.0)
Italy (Provincia Liguria)	278.9	(5.3)	221.6	(4.9)	152.7	(6.4)	3.1	(0.5)	6.8	(0.7)	17.4	(2.0)	22.1	(1.8)	2.5	(0.5)	3.8	(0.7)
Italy (Provincia Lombardia)	278.9	(4.9)	229.1	(5.9)	167.3	(11.2)	3.3	(0.6)	5.4	(0.7)	16.1	(1.3)	21.6	(1.6)	2.0	(0.3)	3.8	(0.6)
Italy (Provincia Marche)	277.5	(4.7)	235.5	(2.9)	150.9	(6.5)	3.7	(0.7)	6.2	(1.2)	16.5	(1.1)	22.1	(1.5)	3.5	(0.8)	4.6	(1.0)
Italy (Provincia Molise)	291.7	(2.5)	241.1	(1.4)	162.6	(2.8)	3.8	(0.5)	7.7	(0.8)	13.4	(1.1)	18.2	(1.1)	4.3	(0.7)	8.1	(0.8)
Italy (Provincia Piemonte)	268.8	(6.0)	218.9	(3.5)	144.6	(6.4)	4.0	(0.4)	6.3	(1.0)	13.2	(1.1)	19.5	(1.3)	2.1	(0.5)	3.8	(0.7)
Italy (Provincia Puglia)	289.5	(4.0)	239.5	(3.9)	179.1	(6.9)	5.2	(0.8)	6.6	(1.0)	17.0	(1.6)	19.2	(1.2)	5.6	(0.8)	5.7	(1.0)
Italy (Provincia Sardegna)	281.7	(4.0)	231.8	(3.7)	156.4	(9.2)	6.1	(0.8)	8.0	(1.0)	15.4	(1.6)	21.6	(1.4)	3.9	(0.7)	4.1	(0.7)
Italy (Provincia Sicilia)	307.5	(8.4)	227.0	(5.9)	163.3	(7.1)	8.9	(1.1)	9.9	(1.3)	14.7	(1.4)	18.8	(1.6)	5.3	(0.9)	5.0	(0.7)
Italy (Provincia Toscana)	288.0	(5.5)	233.3	(4.5)	161.2	(8.0)	4.1	(0.7)	6.2	(1.1)	19.5	(1.3)	21.4	(1.3)	4.0	(0.7)	5.2	(0.8)
Italy (Provincia Trento)	249.6	(2.0)	209.0	(1.7)	159.4	(5.0)	4.1	(0.5)	6.0	(0.6)	12.4	(1.1)	15.6	(1.0)	2.0	(0.4)	4.3	(0.6)
Italy (Provincia Umbria)	281.1	(3.5)	225.8	(2.9)	150.3	(3.7)	4.5	(0.9)	6.4	(0.8)	16.8	(1.0)	17.9	(1.4)	2.5	(0.4)	3.7	(0.8)
Italy (Provincia Valle d'Aosta)	244.6	(1.7)	201.9	(1.0)	148.9	(1.7)	5.3	(0.7)	13.9	(1.1)	14.8	(1.2)	25.6	(1.4)	1.7	(0.4)	5.0	(0.7)
Italy (Provincia Veneto)	262.6	(4.8)	218.8	(3.5)	154.7	(12.1)	2.8	(0.4)	3.9	(0.6)	15.6	(1.3)	17.3	(1.3)	1.8	(0.4)	3.0	(0.4)
United Kingdom (England)	218.6	(2.7)	211.2	(2.8)	284.0	(2.8)	8.5	(0.5)	17.3	(0.9)	17.0	(1.0)	23.7	(1.1)	11.7	(0.7)	19.2	(1.1)
United Kingdom (Northern Ireland)	231.7	(4.8)	226.2	(4.9)	291.3	(7.0)	6.4	(0.8)	9.7	(1.1)	16.1	(1.0)	19.1	(1.1)	9.5	(0.9)	12.7	(1.1)
United Kingdom (Wales)	206.9	(1.9)	205.0	(1.8)	278.8	(2.6)	6.1	(0.5)	13.7	(0.9)	17.7	(1.0)	20.8	(1.1)	9.9	(0.6)	16.4	(0.9)

Note: See original Tables IV.3.16a and IV.3.17a for national data.

StatLink http://dx.doi.org/10.1787/888932343304

[Part 1/1]
Table S.IV.k Percentage of students attending pre-primary education
Results based on students' self-reports

	Not attended		For one year or less		For more than one year	
	%	S.E.	%	S.E.	%	S.E.
Adjudicated						
Belgium (Flemish Community)	2.1	(0.2)	2.6	(0.3)	95.3	(0.4)
Spain (Andalusia)	3.9	(0.5)	9.7	(1.3)	86.4	(1.5)
Spain (Aragon)	4.3	(0.5)	5.8	(0.8)	89.9	(1.0)
Spain (Asturias)	2.9	(0.5)	5.0	(0.6)	92.1	(0.9)
Spain (Balearic Islands)	5.0	(0.7)	8.0	(0.8)	87.0	(1.1)
Spain (Basque Country)	13.2	(0.8)	11.2	(0.7)	75.6	(1.2)
Spain (Canary Islands)	5.4	(0.9)	11.1	(1.0)	83.4	(1.4)
Spain (Cantabria)	3.2	(0.5)	5.4	(0.5)	91.4	(0.7)
Spain (Castile and Leon)	3.0	(0.5)	5.4	(0.7)	91.6	(0.9)
Spain (Catalonia)	4.3	(0.8)	4.7	(0.6)	91.1	(1.1)
Spain (Ceuta and Melilla)	6.9	(0.7)	9.0	(0.6)	84.2	(0.9)
Spain (Galicia)	2.1	(0.4)	14.8	(1.5)	83.2	(1.6)
Spain (La Rioja)	4.2	(0.6)	7.6	(0.7)	88.2	(1.0)
Spain (Madrid)	4.8	(0.6)	10.6	(0.9)	84.6	(1.0)
Spain (Murcia)	4.3	(0.5)	10.0	(0.6)	85.7	(0.9)
Spain (Navarre)	8.9	(1.0)	7.9	(1.0)	83.3	(1.4)
United Kingdom (Scotland)	3.6	(0.5)	32.1	(0.9)	64.2	(0.9)
Non-adjudicated						
Belgium (French Community)	3.1	(0.4)	5.4	(0.5)	91.5	(0.7)
Belgium (German-Speaking Community)	2.2	(0.6)	4.0	(0.7)	93.8	(0.9)
Finland (Finnish Speaking)	5.2	(0.6)	29.5	(1.0)	65.3	(1.1)
Finland (Swedish Speaking)	2.5	(0.5)	20.2	(1.0)	77.3	(1.0)
Italy (Provincia Abruzzo)	5.4	(0.6)	6.5	(0.6)	88.1	(0.9)
Italy (Provincia Autonoma di Bolzano)	5.3	(1.1)	10.8	(0.8)	83.9	(1.3)
Italy (Provincia Basilicata)	2.4	(0.5)	4.2	(0.5)	93.4	(0.6)
Italy (Provincia Calabria)	4.7	(0.7)	8.2	(1.1)	87.1	(1.4)
Italy (Provincia Campania)	4.5	(0.5)	11.7	(1.4)	83.8	(1.4)
Italy (Provincia Emilia Romagna)	7.3	(0.8)	8.9	(0.9)	83.8	(1.2)
Italy (Provincia Friuli Venezia Giulia)	5.6	(0.7)	6.6	(0.6)	87.8	(0.8)
Italy (Provincia Lazio)	4.3	(0.6)	8.0	(0.8)	87.8	(1.0)
Italy (Provincia Liguria)	6.8	(1.1)	10.9	(0.8)	82.3	(1.5)
Italy (Provincia Lombardia)	4.7	(0.6)	6.2	(0.5)	89.1	(0.8)
Italy (Provincia Marche)	5.3	(0.6)	8.2	(0.7)	86.5	(1.0)
Italy (Provincia Molise)	3.8	(0.7)	4.7	(0.7)	91.4	(0.9)
Italy (Provincia Piemonte)	6.4	(0.9)	10.3	(1.2)	83.3	(2.0)
Italy (Provincia Puglia)	3.8	(0.5)	5.3	(0.7)	90.8	(1.0)
Italy (Provincia Sardegna)	3.7	(0.5)	7.8	(1.0)	88.5	(1.1)
Italy (Provincia Sicilia)	6.6	(1.0)	14.4	(1.5)	79.0	(1.8)
Italy (Provincia Toscana)	6.6	(0.7)	8.9	(0.9)	84.5	(1.3)
Italy (Provincia Trento)	5.9	(0.9)	6.4	(0.9)	87.8	(1.1)
Italy (Provincia Umbria)	7.4	(0.7)	9.1	(1.0)	83.6	(1.3)
Italy (Provincia Valle d'Aosta)	3.9	(0.7)	5.0	(0.7)	91.1	(1.0)
Italy (Provincia Veneto)	4.9	(0.5)	6.0	(0.7)	89.1	(0.9)
United Kingdom (England)	5.9	(0.5)	26.9	(0.8)	67.2	(0.9)
United Kingdom (Northern Ireland)	9.1	(0.8)	51.8	(1.3)	39.1	(1.4)
United Kingdom (Wales)	6.3	(0.5)	27.7	(0.8)	66.0	(0.9)

Note: See original Table IV.3.18 for national data.
StatLink http://dx.doi.org/10.1787/888932343304

[Part 1/2]

Index of schools' extra-curricular activities and reading performance, by national quarters of this index

Table S.IV.l *Results based on school principals' reports*

	Index of schools' extra-curricular activities									
	All students		Bottom quarter		Second quarter		Third quarter		Top quarter	
	Mean index	S.E.	Mean index	S.E.	Mean index	S.E.	Mean index	S.E.	Mean index	S.E.
Adjudicated										
Belgium (Flemish Community)	-0.27	(0.07)	-1.46	(0.13)	-0.40	(0.02)	0.08	(0.02)	0.71	(0.08)
Spain (Andalusia)	-0.11	(0.11)	-1.11	(0.12)	-0.36	(0.05)	0.11	(0.02)	0.91	(0.14)
Spain (Aragon)	0.00	(0.11)	-0.93	(0.08)	-0.39	(0.03)	0.19	(0.04)	1.12	(0.14)
Spain (Asturias)	-0.19	(0.14)	-1.27	(0.17)	-0.58	(0.03)	-0.08	(0.05)	1.15	(0.16)
Spain (Balearic Islands)	-0.59	(0.14)	-1.52	(0.08)	-0.95	(0.06)	-0.43	(0.03)	0.54	(0.22)
Spain (Basque Country)	-0.62	(0.06)	-1.60	(0.07)	-0.88	(0.02)	-0.42	(0.02)	0.41	(0.09)
Spain (Canary Islands)	-0.84	(0.12)	-2.19	(0.15)	-0.91	(0.06)	-0.37	(0.03)	0.10	(0.06)
Spain (Cantabria)	-0.21	(0.10)	-1.16	(0.08)	-0.47	(0.03)	-0.01	(0.03)	0.79	(0.17)
Spain (Castile and Leon)	0.07	(0.08)	-0.68	(0.09)	-0.11	(0.00)	0.20	(0.03)	0.89	(0.08)
Spain (Catalonia)	-0.21	(0.10)	-1.04	(0.08)	-0.46	(0.04)	-0.09	(0.02)	0.75	(0.18)
Spain (Ceuta and Melilla)	-0.41	(0.01)	-1.12	(0.01)	-0.68	(0.01)	-0.15	(0.00)	0.32	(0.01)
Spain (Galicia)	-0.20	(0.17)	-1.47	(0.11)	-0.58	(0.03)	-0.11	(0.04)	1.35	(0.25)
Spain (La Rioja)	-0.14	(0.01)	-1.03	(0.01)	-0.32	(0.01)	-0.01	(0.00)	0.78	(0.01)
Spain (Madrid)	-0.17	(0.12)	-1.26	(0.11)	-0.41	(0.07)	0.09	(0.04)	0.90	(0.18)
Spain (Murcia)	0.08	(0.10)	-0.73	(0.13)	-0.07	(0.02)	0.32	(0.02)	0.80	(0.09)
Spain (Navarre)	-0.34	(0.09)	-1.44	(0.15)	-0.59	(0.03)	-0.01	(0.01)	0.68	(0.17)
United Kingdom (Scotland)	0.87	(0.09)	-0.10	(0.05)	0.51	(0.02)	0.93	(0.04)	2.13	(0.13)
Non-adjudicated										
Belgium (French Community)	-0.39	(0.08)	-1.29	(0.06)	-0.69	(0.02)	-0.16	(0.04)	0.58	(0.10)
Belgium (German-Speaking Community)	-0.68	(0.00)	-1.46	(0.01)	-0.91	(0.00)	-0.52	(0.01)	0.17	(0.01)
Finland (Finnish Speaking)	-0.30	(0.06)	-1.25	(0.06)	-0.53	(0.03)	-0.05	(0.01)	0.64	(0.06)
Finland (Swedish Speaking)	0.01	(0.00)	-0.78	(0.01)	-0.18	(0.00)	0.27	(0.00)	0.72	(0.01)
Italy (Provincia Abruzzo)	-0.10	(0.11)	-1.07	(0.06)	-0.44	(0.03)	-0.01	(0.02)	1.12	(0.17)
Italy (Provincia Autonoma di Bolzano)	0.13	(0.01)	-0.80	(0.01)	-0.13	(0.00)	0.25	(0.00)	1.21	(0.01)
Italy (Provincia Basilicata)	-0.25	(0.10)	-1.19	(0.12)	-0.55	(0.02)	0.04	(0.02)	0.69	(0.06)
Italy (Provincia Calabria)	-0.06	(0.06)	-0.90	(0.06)	-0.30	(0.03)	0.06	(0.04)	0.92	(0.09)
Italy (Provincia Campania)	0.17	(0.15)	-0.93	(0.09)	-0.15	(0.04)	0.37	(0.05)	1.38	(0.15)
Italy (Provincia Emilia Romagna)	0.34	(0.09)	-0.72	(0.08)	0.23	(0.03)	0.52	(0.04)	1.33	(0.11)
Italy (Provincia Friuli Venezia Giulia)	0.69	(0.09)	-0.41	(0.10)	0.28	(0.02)	0.79	(0.02)	2.11	(0.07)
Italy (Provincia Lazio)	0.01	(0.08)	-0.82	(0.12)	-0.19	(0.04)	0.22	(0.04)	0.84	(0.07)
Italy (Provincia Liguria)	0.09	(0.09)	-0.83	(0.07)	-0.14	(0.04)	0.32	(0.02)	1.03	(0.11)
Italy (Provincia Lombardia)	-0.04	(0.09)	-1.03	(0.11)	-0.34	(0.02)	0.21	(0.06)	1.00	(0.11)
Italy (Provincia Marche)	0.22	(0.12)	-0.82	(0.13)	-0.04	(0.03)	0.46	(0.06)	1.28	(0.08)
Italy (Provincia Molise)	0.01	(0.01)	-1.15	(0.04)	-0.21	(0.01)	0.44	(0.00)	0.94	(0.01)
Italy (Provincia Piemonte)	0.37	(0.11)	-0.66	(0.12)	0.01	(0.03)	0.57	(0.05)	1.55	(0.13)
Italy (Provincia Puglia)	0.22	(0.14)	-0.77	(0.06)	-0.09	(0.08)	0.39	(0.03)	1.35	(0.14)
Italy (Provincia Sardegna)	0.10	(0.12)	-0.90	(0.12)	-0.24	(0.04)	0.23	(0.06)	1.29	(0.16)
Italy (Provincia Sicilia)	0.19	(0.15)	-0.83	(0.13)	-0.15	(0.04)	0.40	(0.04)	1.33	(0.16)
Italy (Provincia Toscana)	0.17	(0.11)	-1.10	(0.08)	-0.02	(0.06)	0.42	(0.04)	1.37	(0.16)
Italy (Provincia Trento)	0.17	(0.06)	-0.85	(0.15)	-0.18	(0.02)	0.43	(0.02)	1.28	(0.02)
Italy (Provincia Umbria)	0.43	(0.09)	-0.59	(0.09)	0.03	(0.02)	0.46	(0.05)	1.82	(0.06)
Italy (Provincia Valle d'Aosta)	-0.38	(0.01)	-0.88	(0.00)	-0.68	(0.00)	-0.34	(0.00)	0.39	(0.01)
Italy (Provincia Veneto)	0.00	(0.12)	-1.13	(0.14)	-0.25	(0.04)	0.26	(0.05)	1.13	(0.07)
United Kingdom (England)	1.02	(0.07)	0.17	(0.05)	0.61	(0.02)	1.18	(0.03)	2.13	(0.10)
United Kingdom (Northern Ireland)	0.88	(0.09)	-0.03	(0.05)	0.60	(0.03)	0.98	(0.02)	1.97	(0.16)
United Kingdom (Wales)	1.05	(0.07)	0.09	(0.05)	0.69	(0.02)	1.21	(0.02)	2.20	(0.08)

Note: See original Tables IV.3.19 for national data.

StatLink http://dx.doi.org/10.1787/888932343304

[Part 2/2]

Table S.IV.l Index of schools' extra-curricular activities and reading performance, by national quarters of this index

Results based on school principals' reports

	Performance on the reading scale by quarters of this index								Change in the reading score per unit of this index		Increased likelihood of students in the bottom quarter of this index scoring in the bottom quarter of the reading performance distribution		Explained variance in student performance (r-squared x 100)	
	Bottom quarter		Second quarter		Third quarter		Top quarter							
	Mean index	S.E.	Mean index	S.E.	Mean index	S.E.	Mean index	S.E.	Effect	S.E.	Ratio	S.E.	%	S.E.
Adjudicated														
Belgium (Flemish Community)	**473**	(6.5)	513	(8.8)	543	(8.3)	**542**	(9.1)	28.2	(3.81)	2.0	(0.25)	7.8	(1.91)
Spain (Andalusia)	461	(9.7)	451	(10.8)	457	(7.6)	473	(16.4)	3.1	(9.02)	1.0	(0.22)	0.1	(0.75)
Spain (Aragon)	**495**	(9.5)	489	(7.7)	483	(6.3)	**515**	(5.7)	9.4	(4.99)	1.0	(0.21)	0.8	(0.89)
Spain (Asturias)	491	(9.4)	497	(10.6)	490	(9.5)	482	(9.8)	-0.3	(5.15)	1.0	(0.18)	0.0	(0.23)
Spain (Balearic Islands)	**449**	(7.9)	439	(11.8)	467	(6.2)	474	(14.1)	7.4	(10.27)	1.1	(0.19)	0.5	(0.78)
Spain (Basque Country)	**485**	(7.5)	491	(5.9)	501	(4.9)	**505**	(4.8)	10.8	(3.83)	1.3	(0.17)	1.2	(0.77)
Spain (Canary Islands)	448	(7.6)	425	(10.9)	464	(11.1)	456	(8.4)	3.7	(5.18)	1.0	(0.14)	0.2	(0.44)
Spain (Cantabria)	490	(6.5)	481	(7.8)	490	(9.2)	490	(13.8)	-5.2	(9.37)	0.9	(0.16)	0.2	(0.93)
Spain (Castile and Leon)	507	(7.2)	474	(11.3)	520	(7.8)	510	(6.4)	3.5	(7.17)	0.9	(0.16)	0.1	(0.38)
Spain (Catalonia)	**488**	(9.1)	495	(13.0)	500	(12.9)	**518**	(6.4)	15.2	(5.03)	1.3	(0.24)	1.9	(1.32)
Spain (Ceuta and Melilla)	**428**	(4.9)	423	(5.5)	398	(7.0)	**399**	(7.9)	-10.6	(3.21)	0.6	(0.10)	0.4	(0.24)
Spain (Galicia)	482	(9.7)	484	(7.4)	479	(9.6)	502	(10.5)	9.5	(4.23)	1.1	(0.20)	1.6	(1.51)
Spain (La Rioja)	498	(5.2)	495	(6.0)	493	(6.4)	508	(5.4)	5.0	(3.36)	1.0	(0.12)	0.2	(0.25)
Spain (Madrid)	**495**	(12.7)	494	(9.1)	501	(9.1)	**527**	(9.5)	11.7	(5.80)	1.0	(0.24)	1.5	(1.30)
Spain (Murcia)	480	(7.4)	474	(8.6)	484	(8.9)	488	(11.4)	5.4	(8.05)	1.1	(0.18)	0.2	(0.59)
Spain (Navarre)	**482**	(8.6)	504	(6.1)	493	(6.2)	**509**	(9.0)	10.1	(4.39)	1.3	(0.21)	1.1	(1.11)
United Kingdom (Scotland)	498	(6.7)	494	(6.3)	499	(6.6)	509	(6.5)	7.2	(3.80)	1.1	(0.15)	0.5	(0.53)
Non-adjudicated														
Belgium (French Community)	**441**	(12.1)	499	(12.9)	519	(9.2)	**506**	(12.4)	28.2	(11.60)	2.1	(0.35)	4.0	(2.91)
Belgium (German-Speaking Community)	**499**	(5.7)	453	(7.3)	510	(7.2)	**532**	(5.6)	17.0	(3.54)	0.8	(0.18)	1.7	(0.70)
Finland (Finnish Speaking)	535	(4.5)	535	(4.8)	539	(4.0)	541	(4.7)	2.4	(2.72)	1.0	(0.09)	0.0	(0.13)
Finland (Swedish Speaking)	507	(4.6)	519	(5.0)	508	(5.9)	512	(6.4)	5.4	(3.50)	1.1	(0.12)	0.2	(0.21)
Italy (Provincia Abruzzo)	**459**	(11.8)	488	(14.8)	497	(17.6)	**502**	(11.8)	19.9	(5.58)	1.9	(0.42)	4.3	(2.58)
Italy (Provincia Autonoma di Bolzano)	**474**	(3.4)	489	(4.7)	488	(5.0)	**531**	(3.9)	23.4	(1.97)	1.4	(0.14)	4.7	(0.79)
Italy (Provincia Basilicata)	455	(20.4)	483	(6.6)	464	(12.4)	488	(11.7)	18.0	(11.38)	1.6	(0.58)	2.5	(3.70)
Italy (Provincia Calabria)	**419**	(15.9)	441	(15.9)	452	(11.7)	**486**	(12.3)	35.9	(10.36)	1.8	(0.49)	8.3	(4.16)
Italy (Provincia Campania)	**427**	(21.2)	427	(16.5)	460	(13.4)	**493**	(11.9)	29.6	(9.93)	1.6	(0.51)	8.6	(5.12)
Italy (Provincia Emilia Romagna)	**444**	(12.6)	498	(11.3)	513	(12.3)	**555**	(10.8)	49.9	(7.00)	2.6	(0.45)	16.7	(4.60)
Italy (Provincia Friuli Venezia Giulia)	**505**	(10.4)	498	(7.2)	525	(17.9)	**556**	(12.9)	24.9	(5.92)	1.2	(0.26)	7.8	(3.64)
Italy (Provincia Lazio)	**428**	(9.2)	484	(10.3)	503	(14.1)	**515**	(15.3)	46.8	(9.87)	2.4	(0.58)	12.6	(5.32)
Italy (Provincia Liguria)	**452**	(23.3)	504	(10.0)	507	(16.8)	**505**	(17.0)	25.7	(13.96)	1.8	(0.58)	3.9	(4.12)
Italy (Provincia Lombardia)	**470**	(14.2)	517	(15.4)	537	(15.2)	**570**	(9.4)	45.3	(7.52)	2.7	(0.77)	17.2	(5.08)
Italy (Provincia Marche)	**463**	(23.3)	500	(16.8)	495	(16.7)	**533**	(14.4)	29.6	(12.49)	2.1	(0.69)	6.6	(5.40)
Italy (Provincia Molise)	**424**	(4.3)	458	(8.0)	510	(5.3)	**493**	(5.6)	30.8	(2.66)	2.6	(0.41)	9.4	(1.63)
Italy (Provincia Piemonte)	**448**	(17.9)	473	(13.1)	524	(9.9)	**555**	(10.5)	45.7	(8.15)	2.6	(0.68)	18.9	(4.48)
Italy (Provincia Puglia)	462	(13.5)	500	(12.2)	512	(13.4)	483	(13.8)	9.8	(8.14)	1.8	(0.43)	0.9	(1.48)
Italy (Provincia Sardegna)	**446**	(13.8)	455	(17.5)	478	(15.1)	**504**	(13.5)	27.5	(7.14)	1.5	(0.44)	7.0	(3.61)
Italy (Provincia Sicilia)	449	(18.5)	435	(15.1)	467	(19.6)	**492**	(20.1)	23.5	(10.64)	1.1	(0.42)	4.9	(4.73)
Italy (Provincia Toscana)	**412**	(13.1)	504	(7.6)	523	(12.1)	**534**	(14.1)	46.6	(9.24)	4.3	(0.85)	21.8	(6.44)
Italy (Provincia Trento)	**453**	(10.6)	508	(9.5)	545	(10.7)	**529**	(7.8)	37.6	(4.66)	2.9	(0.60)	12.6	(4.15)
Italy (Provincia Umbria)	**482**	(14.6)	480	(11.5)	479	(12.6)	**539**	(10.5)	26.1	(5.09)	1.1	(0.33)	6.7	(2.76)
Italy (Provincia Valle d'Aosta)	**507**	(6.1)	511	(6.1)	520	(5.4)	**529**	(4.3)	18.2	(4.20)	1.3	(0.19)	1.3	(0.59)
Italy (Provincia Veneto)	**465**	(15.7)	501	(9.3)	524	(14.4)	**540**	(10.6)	36.2	(6.34)	2.2	(0.56)	13.6	(5.07)
United Kingdom (England)	491	(6.1)	495	(6.7)	496	(8.1)	502	(6.3)	7.1	(3.94)	1.0	(0.12)	0.4	(0.41)
United Kingdom (Northern Ireland)	**464**	(15.1)	506	(12.3)	511	(12.8)	**530**	(7.9)	28.5	(7.68)	1.7	(0.39)	6.1	(3.08)
United Kingdom (Wales)	474	(7.0)	478	(5.8)	482	(6.5)	472	(6.7)	-1.2	(4.54)	1.1	(0.13)	0.0	(0.20)

Note: See original Tables IV.3.19 for national data.

StatLink http://dx.doi.org/10.1787/888932343304

[Part 1/2]
Index of quality of schools' educational resources and reading performance, by national quarters of this index
Table S.IV.m *Results based on school principals' reports*

	Index of the quality of the schools' educational resources									
	All students		Bottom quarter		Second quarter		Third quarter		Top quarter	
	Mean index	S.E.	Mean index	S.E.	Mean index	S.E.	Mean index	S.E.	Mean index	S.E.
Adjudicated										
Belgium (Flemish Community)	0.47	(0.08)	-0.63	(0.05)	0.06	(0.02)	0.72	(0.04)	1.72	(0.04)
Spain (Andalusia)	0.03	(0.12)	-0.88	(0.13)	-0.19	(0.02)	0.17	(0.04)	1.03	(0.18)
Spain (Aragon)	0.29	(0.13)	-0.71	(0.09)	-0.01	(0.04)	0.50	(0.04)	1.40	(0.12)
Spain (Asturias)	0.18	(0.12)	-0.83	(0.07)	-0.28	(0.04)	0.43	(0.06)	1.39	(0.12)
Spain (Balearic Islands)	-0.01	(0.10)	-0.79	(0.09)	-0.22	(0.02)	0.16	(0.04)	0.80	(0.14)
Spain (Basque Country)	0.11	(0.06)	-0.69	(0.04)	-0.20	(0.01)	0.16	(0.02)	1.15	(0.08)
Spain (Canary Islands)	-0.20	(0.14)	-1.41	(0.11)	-0.45	(0.04)	-0.03	(0.04)	1.08	(0.16)
Spain (Cantabria)	-0.02	(0.10)	-0.98	(0.09)	-0.32	(0.04)	0.17	(0.04)	1.02	(0.12)
Spain (Castile and Leon)	0.17	(0.14)	-0.97	(0.10)	-0.13	(0.05)	0.29	(0.03)	1.49	(0.19)
Spain (Catalonia)	0.17	(0.12)	-0.68	(0.07)	-0.12	(0.03)	0.32	(0.03)	1.18	(0.14)
Spain (Ceuta and Melilla)	0.02	(0.01)	-0.94	(0.01)	-0.27	(0.00)	0.25	(0.01)	1.06	(0.01)
Spain (Galicia)	-0.44	(0.11)	-1.33	(0.16)	-0.64	(0.03)	-0.27	(0.02)	0.47	(0.16)
Spain (La Rioja)	0.24	(0.01)	-0.70	(0.01)	-0.15	(0.00)	0.31	(0.01)	1.51	(0.01)
Spain (Madrid)	-0.14	(0.13)	-1.31	(0.14)	-0.51	(0.05)	-0.01	(0.04)	1.29	(0.20)
Spain (Murcia)	-0.01	(0.14)	-1.05	(0.13)	-0.37	(0.04)	0.21	(0.05)	1.16	(0.15)
Spain (Navarre)	-0.22	(0.07)	-1.21	(0.05)	-0.46	(0.02)	-0.05	(0.03)	0.82	(0.09)
United Kingdom (Scotland)	0.59	(0.11)	-0.75	(0.08)	0.07	(0.05)	1.09	(0.05)	1.93	(0.00)
Non-adjudicated										
Belgium (French Community)	-0.35	(0.10)	-1.45	(0.10)	-0.61	(0.03)	-0.19	(0.03)	0.86	(0.11)
Belgium (German-Speaking Community)	-0.17	(0.00)	-0.71	(0.00)	-0.26	(0.00)	-0.05	(0.00)	0.34	(0.00)
Finland (Finnish Speaking)	-0.18	(0.07)	-1.08	(0.05)	-0.47	(0.02)	-0.05	(0.02)	0.90	(0.11)
Finland (Swedish Speaking)	-0.30	(0.00)	-1.02	(0.00)	-0.57	(0.00)	-0.20	(0.00)	0.60	(0.01)
Italy (Provincia Abruzzo)	-0.15	(0.11)	-0.98	(0.08)	-0.46	(0.03)	-0.04	(0.03)	0.86	(0.22)
Italy (Provincia Autonoma di Bolzano)	0.67	(0.01)	-0.48	(0.00)	0.31	(0.00)	0.92	(0.03)	1.93	(0.00)
Italy (Provincia Basilicata)	-0.28	(0.08)	-1.60	(0.13)	-0.75	(0.06)	0.12	(0.02)	1.10	(0.05)
Italy (Provincia Calabria)	-0.41	(0.12)	-1.48	(0.17)	-0.78	(0.02)	-0.33	(0.04)	0.92	(0.14)
Italy (Provincia Campania)	-0.30	(0.10)	-1.19	(0.07)	-0.51	(0.03)	-0.06	(0.02)	0.54	(0.17)
Italy (Provincia Emilia Romagna)	0.04	(0.10)	-0.80	(0.09)	-0.26	(0.02)	0.16	(0.04)	1.03	(0.15)
Italy (Provincia Friuli Venezia Giulia)	-0.13	(0.11)	-0.97	(0.06)	-0.39	(0.03)	0.02	(0.02)	0.81	(0.15)
Italy (Provincia Lazio)	-0.27	(0.09)	-1.17	(0.13)	-0.50	(0.02)	-0.13	(0.03)	0.72	(0.21)
Italy (Provincia Liguria)	-0.09	(0.12)	-0.87	(0.11)	-0.35	(0.02)	0.03	(0.04)	0.85	(0.12)
Italy (Provincia Lombardia)	0.26	(0.13)	-0.87	(0.13)	-0.01	(0.05)	0.43	(0.04)	1.49	(0.15)
Italy (Provincia Marche)	-0.06	(0.15)	-1.29	(0.21)	-0.37	(0.04)	0.18	(0.06)	1.26	(0.15)
Italy (Provincia Molise)	0.17	(0.03)	-1.02	(0.06)	-0.30	(0.01)	0.51	(0.01)	1.48	(0.01)
Italy (Provincia Piemonte)	-0.24	(0.13)	-1.31	(0.07)	-0.67	(0.06)	-0.06	(0.04)	1.07	(0.14)
Italy (Provincia Puglia)	-0.21	(0.13)	-1.33	(0.08)	-0.52	(0.06)	0.12	(0.02)	0.90	(0.18)
Italy (Provincia Sardegna)	-0.31	(0.10)	-1.17	(0.12)	-0.64	(0.03)	-0.07	(0.03)	0.66	(0.05)
Italy (Provincia Sicilia)	-0.19	(0.11)	-1.15	(0.13)	-0.52	(0.02)	-0.05	(0.05)	0.97	(0.20)
Italy (Provincia Toscana)	-0.12	(0.12)	-1.00	(0.10)	-0.46	(0.02)	0.00	(0.05)	0.97	(0.18)
Italy (Provincia Trento)	0.69	(0.07)	-0.32	(0.05)	0.35	(0.01)	0.95	(0.03)	1.77	(0.03)
Italy (Provincia Umbria)	0.02	(0.11)	-0.76	(0.04)	-0.33	(0.02)	0.12	(0.03)	1.06	(0.14)
Italy (Provincia Valle d'Aosta)	-0.21	(0.00)	-0.56	(0.01)	-0.36	(0.00)	-0.22	(0.00)	0.32	(0.01)
Italy (Provincia Veneto)	0.11	(0.13)	-1.15	(0.09)	-0.20	(0.03)	0.36	(0.03)	1.44	(0.13)
United Kingdom (England)	0.47	(0.08)	-0.58	(0.05)	-0.01	(0.02)	0.62	(0.04)	1.85	(0.03)
United Kingdom (Northern Ireland)	0.44	(0.12)	-0.69	(0.06)	-0.16	(0.02)	0.68	(0.08)	1.92	(0.00)
United Kingdom (Wales)	0.00	(0.07)	-1.11	(0.05)	-0.44	(0.02)	0.20	(0.03)	1.32	(0.07)

Notes: Values that are statistically significant are indicated in bold (see Annex A3). See original Table IV.3.23 for national data.
StatLink http://dx.doi.org/10.1787/888932343304

[Part 2/2]

Table S.IV.m Index of quality of schools' educational resources and reading performance, by national quarters of this index

Results based on school principals' reports

	Performance on the reading scale by quarters of this index								Change in the reading score per unit of this index		Increased likelihood of students in the bottom quarter of this index scoring in the bottom quarter of the reading performance distribution		Explained variance in student performance (r-squared x 100)	
	Bottom quarter		Second quarter		Third quarter		Top quarter							
	Mean index	S.E.	Mean index	S.E.	Mean index	S.E.	Mean index	S.E.	Effect	S.E.	Ratio	S.E.	%	S.E.
Adjudicated														
Belgium (Flemish Community)	507	(9.2)	527	(8.5)	530	(8.9)	513	(11.0)	3.8	(6.60)	1.3	(0.20)	0.1	(0.58)
Spain (Andalusia)	446	(10.6)	464	(11.7)	469	(11.2)	463	(8.6)	6.1	(8.12)	1.2	(0.22)	0.3	(0.89)
Spain (Aragon)	494	(6.4)	484	(11.0)	502	(6.0)	501	(10.2)	3.4	(5.14)	1.0	(0.15)	0.1	(0.40)
Spain (Asturias)	487	(9.8)	483	(10.8)	489	(9.2)	502	(13.7)	8.5	(8.10)	1.1	(0.21)	0.7	(1.30)
Spain (Balearic Islands)	436	(9.2)	475	(12.8)	460	(11.6)	457	(14.3)	5.3	(9.10)	1.5	(0.31)	0.2	(0.73)
Spain (Basque Country)	488	(5.8)	504	(4.5)	499	(5.5)	491	(8.7)	0.3	(4.86)	1.2	(0.15)	0.0	(0.16)
Spain (Canary Islands)	447	(11.7)	456	(11.0)	441	(7.9)	449	(14.6)	-1.5	(7.30)	1.0	(0.23)	0.0	(0.49)
Spain (Cantabria)	498	(9.1)	492	(7.6)	470	(11.4)	491	(9.2)	-2.9	(6.12)	0.8	(0.18)	0.1	(0.39)
Spain (Castile and Leon)	509	(7.3)	502	(7.0)	501	(12.2)	499	(12.0)	-2.9	(5.63)	0.9	(0.17)	0.1	(0.61)
Spain (Catalonia)	502	(8.8)	507	(11.8)	490	(12.1)	501	(8.7)	-3.8	(4.77)	0.9	(0.20)	0.1	(0.31)
Spain (Ceuta and Melilla)	**454**	(5.5)	378	(5.3)	415	(5.2)	**402**	(4.8)	**-14.7**	(2.70)	**0.4**	(0.09)	1.3	(0.47)
Spain (Galicia)	475	(8.7)	498	(8.7)	485	(10.2)	489	(10.5)	-0.4	(6.18)	1.2	(0.22)	0.0	(0.25)
Spain (La Rioja)	**507**	(5.3)	492	(5.5)	503	(5.2)	**490**	(5.2)	**-9.1**	(3.17)	0.9	(0.12)	0.8	(0.49)
Spain (Madrid)	**479**	(10.5)	500	(7.9)	512	(10.4)	**522**	(13.2)	**18.9**	(5.17)	**1.6**	(0.29)	5.3	(2.92)
Spain (Murcia)	483	(10.6)	486	(10.0)	464	(7.8)	488	(10.8)	-2.9	(8.29)	0.9	(0.24)	0.1	(0.87)
Spain (Navarre)	**489**	(8.2)	484	(6.5)	495	(6.3)	**512**	(9.9)	10.4	(5.69)	1.2	(0.19)	1.0	(1.05)
United Kingdom (Scotland)	508	(6.7)	499	(7.5)	497	(8.1)	496	(7.5)	-2.8	(3.94)	0.9	(0.12)	0.1	(0.33)
Non-adjudicated														
Belgium (French Community)	480	(15.8)	517	(12.1)	473	(13.8)	494	(11.6)	4.1	(9.27)	1.2	(0.30)	0.1	(0.70)
Belgium (German-Speaking Community)	**469**	(5.8)	494	(7.2)	546	(5.9)	**486**	(5.6)	**31.5**	(6.82)	**1.9**	(0.23)	2.2	(0.92)
Finland (Finnish Speaking)	533	(4.2)	535	(4.0)	540	(4.9)	542	(4.5)	**5.4**	(2.70)	1.1	(0.10)	0.3	(0.27)
Finland (Swedish Speaking)	510	(4.5)	511	(5.8)	512	(5.6)	513	(4.0)	2.0	(2.89)	1.0	(0.10)	0.0	(0.07)
Italy (Provincia Abruzzo)	446	(19.0)	495	(15.5)	507	(11.8)	479	(14.9)	16.0	(10.54)	1.9	(0.53)	1.8	(2.49)
Italy (Provincia Autonoma di Bolzano)	**480**	(3.6)	477	(4.3)	473	(11.6)	**529**	(3.4)	**19.6**	(2.84)	1.2	(0.14)	3.7	(1.20)
Italy (Provincia Basilicata)	**463**	(16.3)	442	(7.5)	473	(10.4)	**511**	(5.9)	**19.0**	(4.36)	1.2	(0.32)	5.9	(2.54)
Italy (Provincia Calabria)	456	(16.7)	459	(13.8)	412	(18.5)	465	(11.6)	-0.5	(7.32)	0.9	(0.34)	0.0	(0.53)
Italy (Provincia Campania)	469	(16.6)	432	(13.7)	446	(21.7)	457	(15.8)	-0.6	(12.75)	0.8	(0.29)	0.0	(0.77)
Italy (Provincia Emilia Romagna)	469	(17.9)	513	(17.8)	542	(12.7)	493	(20.0)	12.4	(12.26)	1.9	(0.51)	0.9	(1.53)
Italy (Provincia Friuli Venezia Giulia)	503	(15.4)	511	(17.8)	536	(11.3)	502	(19.2)	1.2	(13.37)	1.1	(0.38)	0.0	(0.92)
Italy (Provincia Lazio)	**461**	(14.2)	492	(12.5)	463	(15.9)	**504**	(8.4)	14.5	(8.71)	1.5	(0.40)	1.7	(1.92)
Italy (Provincia Liguria)	495	(16.7)	508	(17.2)	491	(12.5)	497	(13.5)	-3.4	(12.14)	1.0	(0.42)	0.1	(0.96)
Italy (Provincia Lombardia)	503	(21.4)	542	(18.1)	521	(11.7)	526	(14.0)	9.3	(11.50)	1.7	(0.59)	0.9	(2.55)
Italy (Provincia Marche)	507	(22.0)	505	(16.8)	480	(29.8)	498	(15.2)	-7.6	(9.80)	0.7	(0.40)	0.7	(1.51)
Italy (Provincia Molise)	**430**	(7.6)	460	(4.5)	481	(6.9)	**511**	(5.1)	**29.9**	(2.88)	**2.4**	(0.36)	12.7	(2.69)
Italy (Provincia Piemonte)	471	(19.4)	495	(17.8)	514	(16.0)	505	(16.5)	14.9	(9.23)	1.7	(0.56)	2.3	(2.80)
Italy (Provincia Puglia)	480	(17.6)	477	(15.9)	501	(21.4)	500	(13.1)	11.1	(9.78)	1.3	(0.56)	1.3	(2.48)
Italy (Provincia Sardegna)	**439**	(12.3)	486	(15.6)	470	(22.6)	**478**	(11.0)	14.0	(9.48)	1.8	(0.48)	1.3	(1.47)
Italy (Provincia Sicilia)	424	(19.9)	465	(13.5)	466	(16.5)	459	(26.4)	19.0	(13.33)	1.8	(0.59)	2.8	(4.34)
Italy (Provincia Toscana)	**441**	(18.8)	503	(11.9)	534	(12.1)	**495**	(10.8)	20.2	(10.68)	**2.9**	(0.70)	3.0	(2.75)
Italy (Provincia Trento)	**460**	(8.7)	545	(6.9)	506	(5.7)	**520**	(11.8)	**21.7**	(10.10)	**3.0**	(0.54)	3.5	(3.23)
Italy (Provincia Umbria)	514	(14.3)	486	(15.2)	486	(13.2)	486	(13.8)	-12.5	(9.76)	0.7	(0.22)	1.0	(1.49)
Italy (Provincia Valle d'Aosta)	**497**	(5.5)	513	(7.2)	515	(7.7)	**537**	(4.7)	**24.5**	(6.14)	1.2	(0.17)	1.2	(0.61)
Italy (Provincia Veneto)	517	(12.8)	494	(11.9)	510	(19.4)	500	(18.8)	2.1	(7.74)	0.7	(0.23)	0.1	(0.94)
United Kingdom (England)	497	(6.3)	498	(7.4)	489	(7.6)	501	(6.8)	1.0	(4.18)	1.0	(0.12)	0.0	(0.15)
United Kingdom (Northern Ireland)	500	(12.1)	501	(12.1)	503	(20.1)	507	(15.9)	2.3	(8.79)	1.0	(0.26)	0.1	(0.86)
United Kingdom (Wales)	477	(6.9)	478	(7.0)	470	(6.4)	480	(4.6)	0.7	(2.82)	1.0	(0.12)	0.0	(0.07)

Notes: Values that are statistically significant are indicated in bold (see Annex A3). See original Table IV.3.23 for national data.

StatLink http://dx.doi.org/10.1787/888932343304

[Part 1/2]

Index of teacher-student relations and reading performance, by national quarters of this index

Table S.IV.n *Results based on students' self-reports*

	Index of teacher-student relations									
	All students		Bottom quarter		Second quarter		Third quarter		Top quarter	
	Mean index	S.E.	Mean index	S.E.	Mean index	S.E.	Mean index	S.E.	Mean index	S.E.
Adjudicated										
Belgium (Flemish Community)	-0.10	(0.02)	-1.06	(0.02)	-0.37	(0.01)	0.17	(0.00)	0.88	(0.02)
Spain (Andalusia)	0.13	(0.04)	-1.17	(0.03)	-0.24	(0.01)	0.34	(0.01)	1.57	(0.04)
Spain (Aragon)	-0.15	(0.04)	-1.37	(0.03)	-0.52	(0.01)	0.08	(0.01)	1.19	(0.04)
Spain (Asturias)	-0.07	(0.04)	-1.31	(0.03)	-0.49	(0.01)	0.17	(0.00)	1.35	(0.03)
Spain (Balearic Islands)	-0.03	(0.04)	-1.18	(0.03)	-0.40	(0.01)	0.19	(0.00)	1.27	(0.03)
Spain (Basque Country)	-0.06	(0.02)	-1.22	(0.02)	-0.36	(0.01)	0.17	(0.00)	1.17	(0.02)
Spain (Canary Islands)	0.13	(0.04)	-1.14	(0.02)	-0.27	(0.01)	0.38	(0.01)	1.56	(0.03)
Spain (Cantabria)	-0.04	(0.03)	-1.31	(0.03)	-0.43	(0.01)	0.22	(0.00)	1.33	(0.03)
Spain (Castile and Leon)	-0.11	(0.04)	-1.35	(0.03)	-0.50	(0.01)	0.12	(0.00)	1.30	(0.04)
Spain (Catalonia)	-0.07	(0.04)	-1.19	(0.03)	-0.42	(0.01)	0.18	(0.00)	1.15	(0.03)
Spain (Ceuta and Melilla)	0.23	(0.03)	-1.22	(0.03)	-0.19	(0.01)	0.57	(0.01)	1.74	(0.03)
Spain (Galicia)	-0.19	(0.04)	-1.43	(0.03)	-0.57	(0.01)	0.07	(0.01)	1.16	(0.03)
Spain (La Rioja)	-0.17	(0.03)	-1.33	(0.03)	-0.51	(0.01)	0.08	(0.01)	1.08	(0.04)
Spain (Madrid)	-0.09	(0.05)	-1.28	(0.04)	-0.47	(0.01)	0.13	(0.01)	1.26	(0.05)
Spain (Murcia)	0.04	(0.04)	-1.18	(0.03)	-0.33	(0.01)	0.27	(0.01)	1.39	(0.03)
Spain (Navarre)	-0.20	(0.04)	-1.32	(0.04)	-0.54	(0.01)	0.06	(0.01)	0.99	(0.03)
United Kingdom (Scotland)	0.15	(0.03)	-1.02	(0.02)	-0.08	(0.01)	0.25	(0.01)	1.43	(0.03)
Non-adjudicated										
Belgium (French Community)	0.02	(0.02)	-1.06	(0.02)	-0.31	(0.01)	0.23	(0.00)	1.24	(0.02)
Belgium (German-Speaking Community)	-0.01	(0.04)	-1.25	(0.03)	-0.40	(0.01)	0.30	(0.01)	1.30	(0.04)
Finland (Finnish Speaking)	-0.17	(0.02)	-1.19	(0.01)	-0.46	(0.00)	0.07	(0.00)	0.93	(0.02)
Finland (Swedish Speaking)	-0.04	(0.02)	-1.07	(0.02)	-0.29	(0.01)	0.17	(0.00)	1.05	(0.04)
Italy (Provincia Abruzzo)	-0.17	(0.03)	-1.30	(0.02)	-0.49	(0.01)	0.09	(0.01)	1.03	(0.03)
Italy (Provincia Autonoma di Bolzano)	0.09	(0.03)	-1.13	(0.02)	-0.29	(0.01)	0.35	(0.01)	1.43	(0.03)
Italy (Provincia Basilicata)	-0.09	(0.04)	-1.25	(0.03)	-0.43	(0.01)	0.15	(0.00)	1.16	(0.03)
Italy (Provincia Calabria)	0.10	(0.03)	-1.04	(0.02)	-0.18	(0.01)	0.29	(0.01)	1.34	(0.04)
Italy (Provincia Campania)	0.09	(0.04)	-1.04	(0.03)	-0.19	(0.01)	0.28	(0.01)	1.29	(0.04)
Italy (Provincia Emilia Romagna)	-0.17	(0.04)	-1.32	(0.04)	-0.45	(0.01)	0.07	(0.01)	1.02	(0.03)
Italy (Provincia Friuli Venezia Giulia)	-0.23	(0.03)	-1.34	(0.03)	-0.55	(0.01)	0.03	(0.01)	0.95	(0.03)
Italy (Provincia Lazio)	-0.17	(0.04)	-1.36	(0.04)	-0.49	(0.01)	0.12	(0.00)	1.03	(0.04)
Italy (Provincia Liguria)	-0.18	(0.03)	-1.36	(0.03)	-0.46	(0.01)	0.12	(0.01)	0.96	(0.04)
Italy (Provincia Lombardia)	-0.08	(0.04)	-1.23	(0.04)	-0.40	(0.01)	0.17	(0.00)	1.15	(0.03)
Italy (Provincia Marche)	-0.18	(0.03)	-1.31	(0.03)	-0.49	(0.01)	0.09	(0.01)	1.00	(0.03)
Italy (Provincia Molise)	-0.14	(0.03)	-1.28	(0.03)	-0.47	(0.01)	0.13	(0.01)	1.06	(0.04)
Italy (Provincia Piemonte)	-0.16	(0.05)	-1.31	(0.04)	-0.47	(0.01)	0.11	(0.01)	1.01	(0.04)
Italy (Provincia Puglia)	0.04	(0.04)	-1.15	(0.03)	-0.24	(0.01)	0.26	(0.01)	1.28	(0.04)
Italy (Provincia Sardegna)	-0.10	(0.03)	-1.32	(0.04)	-0.42	(0.01)	0.17	(0.00)	1.15	(0.04)
Italy (Provincia Sicilia)	0.14	(0.04)	-1.06	(0.03)	-0.10	(0.01)	0.31	(0.01)	1.41	(0.03)
Italy (Provincia Toscana)	-0.13	(0.04)	-1.30	(0.03)	-0.45	(0.01)	0.10	(0.01)	1.13	(0.04)
Italy (Provincia Trento)	-0.26	(0.03)	-1.36	(0.03)	-0.56	(0.01)	0.03	(0.01)	0.87	(0.04)
Italy (Provincia Umbria)	-0.08	(0.04)	-1.21	(0.02)	-0.44	(0.01)	0.16	(0.00)	1.18	(0.06)
Italy (Provincia Valle d'Aosta)	-0.15	(0.03)	-1.28	(0.03)	-0.50	(0.01)	0.08	(0.01)	1.07	(0.04)
Italy (Provincia Veneto)	-0.20	(0.03)	-1.34	(0.03)	-0.48	(0.01)	0.10	(0.00)	0.91	(0.03)
United Kingdom (England)	0.12	(0.02)	-0.99	(0.02)	-0.10	(0.01)	0.24	(0.00)	1.34	(0.02)
United Kingdom (Northern Ireland)	0.17	(0.02)	-0.98	(0.03)	-0.03	(0.01)	0.23	(0.00)	1.44	(0.03)
United Kingdom (Wales)	0.11	(0.02)	-0.99	(0.02)	-0.14	(0.01)	0.23	(0.00)	1.36	(0.02)

Notes: Values that are statistically significant are indicated in bold (see Annex A3). See original Table IV.4.1 for national data.

StatLink http://dx.doi.org/10.1787/888932343304

[Part 2/2]
Index of teacher-student relations and reading performance, by national quarters of this index

Table S.IV.n *Results based on students' self-reports*

	Performance on the reading scale by quarters of this index								Change in the reading score per unit of this index		Increased likelihood of students in the bottom quarter of this index scoring in the bottom quarter of the reading performance distribution		Explained variance in student performance (r-squared x 100)	
	Bottom quarter		Second quarter		Third quarter		Top quarter							
	Mean index	S.E.	Mean index	S.E.	Mean index	S.E.	Mean index	S.E.	Effect	S.E.	Ratio	S.E.	%	S.E.
Adjudicated														
Belgium (Flemish Community)	**506**	(3.6)	529	(3.5)	538	(3.9)	**527**	(4.5)	**8.1**	(2.54)	**1.4**	(0.10)	0.5	(0.35)
Spain (Andalusia)	**442**	(7.7)	469	(7.0)	468	(7.5)	**466**	(6.9)	**9.1**	(2.23)	**1.5**	(0.15)	1.2	(0.62)
Spain (Aragon)	**481**	(6.4)	498	(6.9)	508	(5.9)	**499**	(5.4)	**7.5**	(3.29)	**1.4**	(0.16)	0.9	(0.75)
Spain (Asturias)	483	(6.8)	497	(5.1)	501	(5.3)	484	(9.0)	0.8	(2.83)	1.1	(0.16)	0.0	(0.11)
Spain (Balearic Islands)	**443**	(10.4)	456	(6.1)	471	(6.6)	**467**	(6.3)	**8.7**	(3.92)	**1.5**	(0.19)	0.9	(0.88)
Spain (Basque Country)	**474**	(4.1)	497	(3.6)	504	(3.6)	**505**	(4.8)	**12.3**	(2.06)	**1.6**	(0.11)	2.1	(0.71)
Spain (Canary Islands)	**430**	(7.9)	450	(5.1)	464	(5.2)	**456**	(6.7)	**10.1**	(3.04)	**1.3**	(0.16)	1.4	(0.85)
Spain (Cantabria)	**466**	(9.1)	487	(5.8)	501	(5.6)	**497**	(5.8)	**13.4**	(2.64)	**1.5**	(0.22)	2.6	(0.96)
Spain (Castile and Leon)	**488**	(5.9)	506	(6.9)	514	(5.9)	**506**	(7.5)	**5.7**	(2.90)	**1.3**	(0.15)	0.5	(0.49)
Spain (Catalonia)	**477**	(6.2)	495	(6.6)	514	(6.7)	**510**	(7.3)	**14.0**	(2.82)	**1.5**	(0.23)	2.6	(1.10)
Spain (Ceuta and Melilla)	400	(6.1)	422	(6.7)	427	(5.8)	414	(6.3)	**5.7**	(2.71)	1.2	(0.15)	0.4	(0.43)
Spain (Galicia)	**467**	(6.8)	491	(6.7)	494	(6.5)	**495**	(5.5)	**10.3**	(2.60)	**1.5**	(0.17)	1.6	(0.78)
Spain (La Rioja)	**480**	(6.3)	509	(5.6)	507	(5.7)	**502**	(6.1)	5.3	(3.25)	**1.4**	(0.17)	0.3	(0.41)
Spain (Madrid)	491	(8.6)	509	(7.1)	513	(5.4)	505	(5.7)	3.4	(4.49)	1.3	(0.15)	0.2	(0.42)
Spain (Murcia)	476	(5.9)	487	(6.0)	486	(6.9)	475	(7.6)	0.1	(2.34)	1.1	(0.12)	0.0	(0.09)
Spain (Navarre)	487	(5.7)	497	(5.2)	509	(5.4)	500	(5.7)	**6.8**	(3.07)	1.2	(0.15)	0.6	(0.60)
United Kingdom (Scotland)	**468**	(4.0)	498	(5.3)	511	(5.0)	**530**	(4.2)	**23.1**	(2.44)	**1.8**	(0.15)	6.0	(1.15)
Non-adjudicated														
Belgium (French Community)	489	(5.6)	501	(6.1)	503	(5.1)	497	(5.9)	2.6	(2.70)	1.1	(0.09)	0.1	(0.12)
Belgium (German-Speaking Community)	**476**	(6.1)	500	(6.3)	513	(6.5)	**515**	(7.3)	**12.4**	(3.28)	1.4	(0.24)	2.1	(1.09)
Finland (Finnish Speaking)	**513**	(3.5)	533	(3.7)	547	(3.9)	**558**	(3.8)	**20.5**	(1.51)	**1.5**	(0.12)	4.3	(0.63)
Finland (Swedish Speaking)	**484**	(4.7)	507	(5.9)	526	(4.5)	**530**	(5.6)	**18.4**	(3.09)	**1.7**	(0.18)	3.5	(1.09)
Italy (Provincia Abruzzo)	**462**	(6.0)	481	(8.1)	497	(6.5)	**490**	(7.2)	**13.5**	(2.76)	**1.4**	(0.19)	2.1	(0.87)
Italy (Provincia Autonoma di Bolzano)	483	(6.2)	500	(6.0)	501	(4.2)	478	(4.9)	-0.8	(2.34)	1.0	(0.11)	0.0	(0.07)
Italy (Provincia Basilicata)	461	(7.9)	470	(5.8)	485	(4.4)	476	(6.5)	5.8	(3.34)	1.2	(0.17)	0.4	(0.46)
Italy (Provincia Calabria)	446	(7.3)	452	(6.9)	449	(6.7)	448	(6.6)	0.5	(2.71)	1.1	(0.13)	0.0	(0.08)
Italy (Provincia Campania)	444	(10.5)	450	(11.0)	457	(8.7)	455	(7.5)	4.8	(4.44)	1.2	(0.17)	0.2	(0.46)
Italy (Provincia Emilia Romagna)	**486**	(5.8)	499	(7.2)	517	(6.4)	**513**	(5.4)	**10.9**	(3.72)	1.2	(0.12)	1.1	(0.70)
Italy (Provincia Friuli Venezia Giulia)	**499**	(7.3)	509	(6.3)	528	(7.7)	**518**	(7.8)	**8.2**	(2.67)	1.2	(0.14)	0.7	(0.47)
Italy (Provincia Lazio)	469	(6.4)	486	(5.7)	491	(7.0)	481	(9.1)	6.3	(3.74)	1.2	(0.17)	0.5	(0.48)
Italy (Provincia Liguria)	475	(10.2)	494	(9.4)	501	(10.5)	496	(10.5)	**8.5**	(2.60)	**1.3**	(0.14)	0.7	(0.50)
Italy (Provincia Lombardia)	512	(8.0)	528	(6.9)	533	(7.4)	514	(8.4)	2.5	(4.28)	1.2	(0.15)	0.1	(0.31)
Italy (Provincia Marche)	484	(13.1)	503	(8.4)	509	(8.7)	499	(7.0)	5.8	(4.27)	1.3	(0.19)	0.3	(0.50)
Italy (Provincia Molise)	464	(6.5)	471	(5.1)	481	(6.3)	467	(6.3)	1.1	(3.32)	1.1	(0.16)	0.0	(0.18)
Italy (Provincia Piemonte)	**477**	(9.5)	502	(5.7)	508	(9.1)	**500**	(9.1)	8.4	(5.02)	1.4	(0.24)	0.7	(0.89)
Italy (Provincia Puglia)	**475**	(6.4)	493	(7.4)	497	(7.5)	**493**	(6.0)	**8.5**	(2.80)	**1.4**	(0.19)	0.9	(0.63)
Italy (Provincia Sardegna)	**450**	(6.6)	465	(5.9)	484	(6.7)	**484**	(5.7)	**13.8**	(2.60)	**1.4**	(0.13)	2.3	(0.80)
Italy (Provincia Sicilia)	446	(12.7)	454	(9.1)	460	(8.6)	457	(11.6)	2.6	(3.13)	1.1	(0.18)	0.1	(0.21)
Italy (Provincia Toscana)	**474**	(7.6)	494	(7.2)	510	(5.9)	**498**	(5.1)	**10.5**	(2.97)	**1.5**	(0.18)	1.2	(0.65)
Italy (Provincia Trento)	**494**	(5.0)	513	(6.6)	520	(5.4)	**508**	(5.6)	5.8	(3.08)	1.3	(0.17)	0.3	(0.37)
Italy (Provincia Umbria)	481	(7.6)	496	(6.5)	501	(6.7)	488	(7.7)	3.6	(4.13)	1.2	(0.14)	0.1	(0.31)
Italy (Provincia Valle d'Aosta)	**502**	(6.3)	511	(6.3)	526	(6.3)	**517**	(5.5)	**7.5**	(3.38)	1.2	(0.17)	0.7	(0.63)
Italy (Provincia Veneto)	494	(8.1)	507	(6.6)	517	(6.7)	508	(7.5)	**7.3**	(2.65)	1.2	(0.18)	0.6	(0.38)
United Kingdom (England)	**467**	(4.0)	496	(3.9)	509	(3.5)	**513**	(4.4)	**17.0**	(2.00)	**1.5**	(0.11)	2.8	(0.67)
United Kingdom (Northern Ireland)	**476**	(5.0)	499	(6.5)	506	(7.4)	**520**	(5.5)	**17.9**	(2.28)	**1.5**	(0.15)	3.3	(0.83)
United Kingdom (Wales)	**449**	(3.9)	476	(4.9)	485	(5.3)	**498**	(4.8)	**20.1**	(2.01)	**1.6**	(0.12)	4.2	(0.81)

Notes: Values that are statistically significant are indicated in bold (see Annex A3). See original Table IV.4.1 for national data.
StatLink http://dx.doi.org/10.1787/888932343304

[Part 1/2]

Table S.IV.o **Index of disciplinary climate and reading performance, by national quarters of this index**
Results based on students' self-reports

	Index of disciplinary climate									
	All students		Bottom quarter		Second quarter		Third quarter		Top quarter	
	Mean index	S.E.	Mean index	S.E.	Mean index	S.E.	Mean index	S.E.	Mean index	S.E.
Adjudicated										
Belgium (Flemish Community)	-0.11	(0.03)	-1.40	(0.02)	-0.33	(0.01)	0.23	(0.01)	1.06	(0.01)
Spain (Andalusia)	0.12	(0.05)	-1.26	(0.03)	-0.16	(0.01)	0.56	(0.01)	1.36	(0.03)
Spain (Aragon)	0.06	(0.05)	-1.33	(0.04)	-0.21	(0.01)	0.52	(0.01)	1.26	(0.02)
Spain (Asturias)	0.12	(0.07)	-1.36	(0.05)	-0.14	(0.01)	0.59	(0.01)	1.40	(0.03)
Spain (Balearic Islands)	-0.05	(0.06)	-1.37	(0.04)	-0.24	(0.01)	0.31	(0.01)	1.11	(0.02)
Spain (Basque Country)	0.02	(0.03)	-1.32	(0.02)	-0.22	(0.01)	0.41	(0.01)	1.22	(0.01)
Spain (Canary Islands)	0.11	(0.05)	-1.25	(0.04)	-0.17	(0.01)	0.52	(0.01)	1.32	(0.02)
Spain (Cantabria)	0.07	(0.04)	-1.27	(0.04)	-0.19	(0.01)	0.46	(0.01)	1.27	(0.01)
Spain (Castile and Leon)	0.18	(0.06)	-1.21	(0.05)	-0.06	(0.01)	0.59	(0.01)	1.39	(0.03)
Spain (Catalonia)	0.00	(0.06)	-1.33	(0.04)	-0.20	(0.01)	0.36	(0.01)	1.19	(0.02)
Spain (Ceuta and Melilla)	-0.02	(0.02)	-1.40	(0.03)	-0.26	(0.01)	0.36	(0.01)	1.23	(0.02)
Spain (Galicia)	-0.03	(0.07)	-1.45	(0.04)	-0.31	(0.02)	0.38	(0.01)	1.26	(0.03)
Spain (La Rioja)	-0.05	(0.03)	-1.64	(0.05)	-0.28	(0.02)	0.44	(0.01)	1.26	(0.02)
Spain (Madrid)	0.12	(0.04)	-1.20	(0.03)	-0.13	(0.01)	0.54	(0.01)	1.29	(0.02)
Spain (Murcia)	0.11	(0.07)	-1.35	(0.06)	-0.19	(0.01)	0.61	(0.01)	1.36	(0.02)
Spain (Navarre)	0.08	(0.05)	-1.30	(0.03)	-0.18	(0.01)	0.50	(0.01)	1.29	(0.02)
United Kingdom (Scotland)	0.03	(0.03)	-1.32	(0.03)	-0.18	(0.01)	0.42	(0.01)	1.20	(0.02)
Non-adjudicated										
Belgium (French Community)	-0.01	(0.04)	-1.38	(0.03)	-0.29	(0.01)	0.38	(0.01)	1.23	(0.02)
Belgium (German-Speaking Community)	0.19	(0.03)	-1.24	(0.05)	-0.07	(0.02)	0.63	(0.01)	1.46	(0.03)
Finland (Finnish Speaking)	-0.30	(0.02)	-1.52	(0.02)	-0.58	(0.01)	0.05	(0.01)	0.85	(0.02)
Finland (Swedish Speaking)	-0.17	(0.03)	-1.33	(0.02)	-0.42	(0.01)	0.13	(0.01)	0.94	(0.02)
Italy (Provincia Abruzzo)	-0.03	(0.06)	-1.53	(0.04)	-0.37	(0.02)	0.51	(0.01)	1.29	(0.02)
Italy (Provincia Autonoma di Bolzano)	0.13	(0.02)	-1.31	(0.03)	-0.16	(0.01)	0.60	(0.01)	1.40	(0.02)
Italy (Provincia Basilicata)	0.09	(0.04)	-1.31	(0.04)	-0.18	(0.01)	0.57	(0.01)	1.28	(0.02)
Italy (Provincia Calabria)	0.16	(0.04)	-1.25	(0.03)	-0.10	(0.02)	0.64	(0.01)	1.36	(0.02)
Italy (Provincia Campania)	0.24	(0.04)	-1.09	(0.06)	0.02	(0.02)	0.68	(0.01)	1.34	(0.02)
Italy (Provincia Emilia Romagna)	-0.03	(0.04)	-1.47	(0.03)	-0.33	(0.01)	0.46	(0.01)	1.21	(0.03)
Italy (Provincia Friuli Venezia Giulia)	-0.13	(0.05)	-1.55	(0.03)	-0.42	(0.01)	0.34	(0.01)	1.12	(0.02)
Italy (Provincia Lazio)	-0.08	(0.05)	-1.58	(0.04)	-0.39	(0.02)	0.39	(0.01)	1.25	(0.02)
Italy (Provincia Liguria)	-0.18	(0.06)	-1.68	(0.05)	-0.53	(0.02)	0.34	(0.01)	1.17	(0.03)
Italy (Provincia Lombardia)	0.05	(0.06)	-1.37	(0.03)	-0.21	(0.01)	0.57	(0.01)	1.23	(0.02)
Italy (Provincia Marche)	-0.05	(0.08)	-1.50	(0.06)	-0.35	(0.01)	0.44	(0.01)	1.22	(0.02)
Italy (Provincia Molise)	0.02	(0.03)	-1.29	(0.03)	-0.28	(0.02)	0.46	(0.01)	1.18	(0.02)
Italy (Provincia Piemonte)	-0.16	(0.07)	-1.64	(0.04)	-0.51	(0.01)	0.33	(0.02)	1.20	(0.02)
Italy (Provincia Puglia)	0.08	(0.06)	-1.32	(0.05)	-0.17	(0.01)	0.57	(0.01)	1.26	(0.02)
Italy (Provincia Sardegna)	-0.12	(0.05)	-1.54	(0.03)	-0.45	(0.02)	0.36	(0.02)	1.14	(0.02)
Italy (Provincia Sicilia)	0.18	(0.05)	-1.18	(0.04)	-0.05	(0.02)	0.64	(0.01)	1.31	(0.02)
Italy (Provincia Toscana)	-0.06	(0.05)	-1.48	(0.03)	-0.37	(0.01)	0.42	(0.01)	1.21	(0.03)
Italy (Provincia Trento)	-0.14	(0.03)	-1.60	(0.03)	-0.44	(0.01)	0.33	(0.02)	1.17	(0.03)
Italy (Provincia Umbria)	-0.02	(0.05)	-1.42	(0.03)	-0.33	(0.02)	0.43	(0.01)	1.25	(0.02)
Italy (Provincia Valle d'Aosta)	0.07	(0.03)	-1.39	(0.04)	-0.24	(0.02)	0.59	(0.01)	1.32	(0.02)
Italy (Provincia Veneto)	-0.02	(0.05)	-1.41	(0.03)	-0.27	(0.01)	0.42	(0.01)	1.18	(0.02)
United Kingdom (England)	0.12	(0.03)	-1.24	(0.02)	-0.12	(0.01)	0.55	(0.01)	1.32	(0.02)
United Kingdom (Northern Ireland)	0.15	(0.03)	-1.16	(0.03)	-0.09	(0.01)	0.56	(0.01)	1.29	(0.01)
United Kingdom (Wales)	-0.01	(0.03)	-1.40	(0.02)	-0.24	(0.01)	0.40	(0.01)	1.22	(0.02)

Notes: Values that are statistically significant are indicated in bold (see Annex A3). See original Table IV.4.2 for national data.
StatLink http://dx.doi.org/10.1787/888932343304

[Part 2/2]

Table S.IV.o Index of disciplinary climate and reading performance, by national quarters of this index
Results based on students' self-reports

	Performance on the reading scale by quarters of this index								Change in the reading score per unit of this index		Increased likelihood of students in the bottom quarter of this index scoring in the bottom quarter of the reading performance distribution		Explained variance in student performance (r-squared x 100)	
	Bottom quarter		Second quarter		Third quarter		Top quarter							
	Mean index	S.E.	Mean index	S.E.	Mean index	S.E.	Mean index	S.E.	Effect	S.E.	Ratio	S.E.	%	S.E.
Adjudicated														
Belgium (Flemish Community)	**511**	(4.9)	523	(3.5)	528	(4.2)	**539**	(3.8)	**10.7**	(2.49)	**1.4**	(0.13)	1.4	(0.61)
Spain (Andalusia)	**444**	(6.8)	450	(8.2)	482	(7.0)	**471**	(6.3)	**10.6**	(2.28)	**1.4**	(0.14)	1.6	(0.67)
Spain (Aragon)	**482**	(5.4)	498	(6.5)	509	(5.9)	**497**	(6.3)	**6.2**	(2.74)	**1.4**	(0.17)	0.6	(0.54)
Spain (Asturias)	481	(8.2)	487	(7.7)	501	(7.1)	497	(6.5)	**7.3**	(3.72)	1.3	(0.20)	0.8	(0.76)
Spain (Balearic Islands)	**447**	(8.0)	455	(6.6)	462	(7.4)	**482**	(6.6)	**13.4**	(4.62)	**1.5**	(0.22)	2.3	(1.48)
Spain (Basque Country)	**480**	(5.2)	493	(3.8)	496	(3.4)	**511**	(3.5)	**9.9**	(2.21)	**1.3**	(0.10)	1.4	(0.62)
Spain (Canary Islands)	**436**	(7.4)	437	(7.3)	456	(6.1)	**472**	(5.0)	**13.3**	(3.13)	**1.4**	(0.16)	2.2	(1.06)
Spain (Cantabria)	483	(5.6)	485	(6.2)	498	(6.1)	487	(6.0)	3.3	(2.89)	1.0	(0.11)	0.1	(0.27)
Spain (Castile and Leon)	**482**	(5.8)	496	(6.0)	512	(5.9)	**525**	(8.5)	**15.2**	(3.53)	**1.6**	(0.23)	3.5	(1.61)
Spain (Catalonia)	**481**	(8.0)	493	(6.8)	505	(5.9)	**519**	(6.7)	**14.6**	(3.15)	**1.5**	(0.20)	3.3	(1.37)
Spain (Ceuta and Melilla)	**393**	(6.0)	401	(5.4)	422	(5.6)	**445**	(5.3)	**15.4**	(2.37)	**1.5**	(0.16)	2.4	(0.71)
Spain (Galicia)	**479**	(6.8)	477	(5.8)	492	(6.7)	**500**	(5.9)	**6.9**	(3.03)	**1.3**	(0.15)	0.7	(0.66)
Spain (La Rioja)	**493**	(5.2)	491	(4.9)	501	(5.9)	**511**	(5.2)	4.6	(2.38)	1.1	(0.15)	0.3	(0.35)
Spain (Madrid)	**493**	(6.9)	499	(7.3)	509	(5.7)	**517**	(5.3)	**9.4**	(2.85)	**1.4**	(0.20)	1.2	(0.73)
Spain (Murcia)	**471**	(7.3)	474	(6.7)	486	(4.4)	**493**	(6.9)	**7.7**	(2.68)	**1.4**	(0.18)	1.1	(0.76)
Spain (Navarre)	**493**	(5.8)	492	(5.4)	498	(5.9)	**509**	(4.8)	4.8	(2.96)	1.1	(0.15)	0.4	(0.47)
United Kingdom (Scotland)	**471**	(4.6)	491	(6.2)	511	(5.0)	**534**	(5.1)	**24.9**	(2.38)	**1.8**	(0.14)	7.3	(1.38)
Non-adjudicated														
Belgium (French Community)	**484**	(7.1)	488	(7.0)	506	(5.7)	**514**	(5.3)	**10.9**	(3.04)	1.3	(0.14)	1.2	(0.65)
Belgium (German-Speaking Community)	**468**	(6.0)	497	(6.5)	514	(6.8)	**524**	(7.4)	**21.1**	(2.73)	**2.0**	(0.31)	6.8	(1.73)
Finland (Finnish Speaking)	**534**	(3.0)	536	(3.4)	533	(4.3)	**548**	(4.0)	**4.2**	(1.72)	1.1	(0.06)	0.2	(0.17)
Finland (Swedish Speaking)	**501**	(5.0)	515	(5.7)	515	(4.8)	**517**	(5.6)	**5.8**	(2.88)	1.3	(0.16)	0.4	(0.39)
Italy (Provincia Abruzzo)	**454**	(5.7)	461	(7.2)	504	(6.3)	**510**	(6.7)	**21.3**	(2.70)	**1.6**	(0.22)	7.3	(1.67)
Italy (Provincia Autonoma di Bolzano)	**467**	(6.9)	477	(7.0)	507	(5.3)	**509**	(4.8)	**14.0**	(3.01)	**1.6**	(0.21)	2.6	(1.02)
Italy (Provincia Basilicata)	**443**	(6.4)	462	(5.6)	482	(6.3)	**505**	(5.9)	**21.4**	(2.51)	**1.9**	(0.20)	6.6	(1.40)
Italy (Provincia Calabria)	**413**	(8.4)	443	(6.2)	463	(5.9)	**477**	(7.2)	**23.8**	(3.18)	**2.3**	(0.21)	7.7	(1.72)
Italy (Provincia Campania)	**414**	(8.7)	442	(9.9)	468	(7.2)	**482**	(7.8)	**27.9**	(3.77)	**2.0**	(0.25)	8.5	(1.94)
Italy (Provincia Emilia Romagna)	**473**	(6.2)	487	(6.4)	519	(5.0)	**536**	(6.2)	**23.1**	(2.37)	**1.7**	(0.22)	6.3	(1.28)
Italy (Provincia Friuli Venezia Giulia)	**477**	(7.3)	501	(6.5)	524	(6.5)	**550**	(6.9)	**27.3**	(2.64)	**1.9**	(0.27)	9.8	(1.76)
Italy (Provincia Lazio)	**449**	(6.8)	471	(5.1)	495	(7.1)	**511**	(7.1)	**20.1**	(3.54)	**1.8**	(0.24)	6.0	(2.06)
Italy (Provincia Liguria)	**460**	(14.5)	479	(10.9)	508	(8.8)	**522**	(5.8)	**22.5**	(4.80)	**1.8**	(0.20)	7.4	(2.35)
Italy (Provincia Lombardia)	**478**	(4.4)	512	(7.3)	545	(5.9)	**551**	(8.0)	**28.7**	(3.09)	**2.3**	(0.27)	11.0	(2.29)
Italy (Provincia Marche)	**459**	(15.7)	491	(9.3)	510	(5.9)	**535**	(5.4)	**27.1**	(6.41)	**2.2**	(0.35)	9.9	(4.39)
Italy (Provincia Molise)	**444**	(5.2)	455	(6.0)	483	(6.5)	**501**	(4.6)	**22.8**	(2.77)	**1.7**	(0.30)	7.0	(1.56)
Italy (Provincia Piemonte)	**455**	(6.5)	483	(6.5)	510	(10.5)	**536**	(6.2)	**27.8**	(3.26)	**2.1**	(0.28)	10.8	(2.32)
Italy (Provincia Puglia)	**456**	(7.1)	479	(6.2)	504	(6.4)	**520**	(7.3)	**24.5**	(3.53)	**2.0**	(0.25)	8.5	(2.25)
Italy (Provincia Sardegna)	**440**	(7.5)	460	(5.5)	482	(5.7)	**500**	(6.4)	**21.5**	(3.48)	**1.6**	(0.23)	6.3	(1.93)
Italy (Provincia Sicilia)	**416**	(11.7)	433	(12.8)	476	(9.8)	**493**	(8.0)	**29.8**	(4.90)	**2.0**	(0.31)	8.8	(2.19)
Italy (Provincia Toscana)	**466**	(7.8)	480	(8.8)	499	(8.2)	**532**	(5.5)	**22.3**	(3.41)	**1.6**	(0.23)	6.3	(1.87)
Italy (Provincia Trento)	**475**	(6.3)	495	(5.9)	514	(5.9)	**549**	(5.4)	**23.9**	(2.87)	**1.8**	(0.20)	8.0	(1.80)
Italy (Provincia Umbria)	**462**	(9.0)	483	(7.8)	497	(7.6)	**526**	(5.2)	**23.4**	(3.66)	**1.7**	(0.19)	6.5	(1.86)
Italy (Provincia Valle d'Aosta)	**479**	(5.4)	497	(6.4)	536	(5.3)	**546**	(6.2)	**25.7**	(2.21)	**1.7**	(0.23)	10.2	(1.61)
Italy (Provincia Veneto)	**468**	(9.2)	492	(7.1)	522	(5.9)	**542**	(6.4)	**28.2**	(4.10)	**2.1**	(0.25)	10.4	(2.66)
United Kingdom (England)	**464**	(4.2)	490	(3.8)	512	(3.7)	**519**	(3.6)	**20.9**	(1.95)	**1.8**	(0.12)	5.1	(0.93)
United Kingdom (Northern Ireland)	**472**	(6.4)	493	(5.9)	511	(5.2)	**527**	(4.3)	**21.0**	(2.39)	**1.8**	(0.14)	4.6	(0.94)
United Kingdom (Wales)	**452**	(4.5)	469	(5.2)	488	(5.6)	**500**	(4.3)	**18.1**	(2.05)	**1.6**	(0.12)	4.1	(0.88)

Notes: Values that are statistically significant are indicated in bold (see Annex A3). See original Table IV.4.2 for national data.
StatLink http://dx.doi.org/10.1787/888932343304

[Part 1/2]
Index of student-related factors affecting school climate and reading performance, by national quarters of this index
Table S.IV.p *Results based on school principals' reports*

	Index of student-related factors affecting school climate									
	All students		Bottom quarter		Second quarter		Third quarter		Top quarter	
	Mean index	S.E.	Mean index	S.E.	Mean index	S.E.	Mean index	S.E.	Mean index	S.E.
Adjudicated										
Belgium (Flemish Community)	0.55	(0.07)	-0.62	(0.07)	0.25	(0.03)	0.83	(0.03)	1.75	(0.08)
Spain (Andalusia)	-0.12	(0.11)	-1.14	(0.10)	-0.41	(0.04)	0.14	(0.04)	0.92	(0.12)
Spain (Aragon)	-0.05	(0.11)	-1.25	(0.15)	-0.36	(0.05)	0.25	(0.05)	1.15	(0.18)
Spain (Asturias)	0.30	(0.14)	-0.97	(0.14)	0.07	(0.04)	0.55	(0.04)	1.54	(0.14)
Spain (Balearic Islands)	0.31	(0.10)	-0.60	(0.14)	0.09	(0.02)	0.42	(0.04)	1.33	(0.10)
Spain (Basque Country)	0.55	(0.06)	-0.49	(0.09)	0.24	(0.02)	0.81	(0.02)	1.64	(0.06)
Spain (Canary Islands)	-0.21	(0.12)	-1.31	(0.09)	-0.56	(0.04)	0.02	(0.07)	1.02	(0.13)
Spain (Cantabria)	0.07	(0.11)	-1.01	(0.13)	-0.30	(0.03)	0.38	(0.05)	1.23	(0.17)
Spain (Castile and Leon)	0.29	(0.15)	-1.13	(0.14)	0.21	(0.06)	0.58	(0.04)	1.50	(0.14)
Spain (Catalonia)	0.70	(0.12)	-0.28	(0.09)	0.33	(0.04)	0.99	(0.06)	1.76	(0.11)
Spain (Ceuta and Melilla)	-0.51	(0.01)	-1.97	(0.01)	-1.11	(0.02)	0.23	(0.01)	0.82	(0.01)
Spain (Galicia)	0.20	(0.10)	-0.73	(0.07)	-0.10	(0.04)	0.47	(0.04)	1.17	(0.13)
Spain (La Rioja)	0.33	(0.01)	-0.57	(0.02)	0.11	(0.00)	0.65	(0.01)	1.13	(0.01)
Spain (Madrid)	-0.12	(0.12)	-1.24	(0.07)	-0.37	(0.07)	0.24	(0.04)	0.91	(0.11)
Spain (Murcia)	-0.17	(0.15)	-1.37	(0.19)	-0.43	(0.03)	0.06	(0.04)	1.09	(0.15)
Spain (Navarre)	0.16	(0.08)	-1.07	(0.04)	-0.20	(0.02)	0.44	(0.05)	1.49	(0.14)
United Kingdom (Scotland)	0.03	(0.06)	-0.90	(0.07)	-0.07	(0.03)	0.20	(0.03)	0.89	(0.09)
Non-adjudicated										
Belgium (French Community)	-0.08	(0.06)	-1.21	(0.05)	-0.38	(0.03)	0.20	(0.03)	1.07	(0.12)
Belgium (German-Speaking Community)	-0.01	(0.01)	-1.24	(0.02)	-0.12	(0.00)	0.51	(0.01)	0.82	(0.01)
Finland (Finnish Speaking)	-0.45	(0.07)	-1.35	(0.05)	-0.69	(0.03)	-0.18	(0.02)	0.43	(0.06)
Finland (Swedish Speaking)	-0.10	(0.00)	-0.79	(0.01)	-0.40	(0.00)	0.07	(0.01)	0.74	(0.01)
Italy (Provincia Abruzzo)	-0.04	(0.11)	-1.09	(0.11)	-0.29	(0.05)	0.29	(0.02)	0.92	(0.11)
Italy (Provincia Autonoma di Bolzano)	-0.27	(0.01)	-1.28	(0.00)	-0.61	(0.01)	0.02	(0.02)	0.79	(0.02)
Italy (Provincia Basilicata)	0.11	(0.10)	-0.96	(0.08)	-0.11	(0.03)	0.31	(0.02)	1.21	(0.11)
Italy (Provincia Calabria)	0.02	(0.08)	-0.84	(0.04)	-0.35	(0.05)	0.25	(0.06)	1.04	(0.14)
Italy (Provincia Campania)	-0.11	(0.10)	-1.24	(0.09)	-0.41	(0.05)	0.22	(0.05)	1.01	(0.11)
Italy (Provincia Emilia Romagna)	0.03	(0.08)	-1.00	(0.08)	-0.21	(0.04)	0.32	(0.04)	1.03	(0.13)
Italy (Provincia Friuli Venezia Giulia)	0.20	(0.07)	-0.94	(0.06)	-0.09	(0.07)	0.64	(0.03)	1.20	(0.02)
Italy (Provincia Lazio)	-0.08	(0.10)	-1.20	(0.06)	-0.52	(0.07)	0.33	(0.06)	1.06	(0.07)
Italy (Provincia Liguria)	-0.07	(0.11)	-0.93	(0.10)	-0.38	(0.04)	0.18	(0.04)	0.84	(0.09)
Italy (Provincia Lombardia)	-0.04	(0.12)	-1.36	(0.12)	-0.43	(0.05)	0.29	(0.06)	1.33	(0.18)
Italy (Provincia Marche)	-0.10	(0.10)	-1.23	(0.16)	-0.27	(0.04)	0.20	(0.04)	0.90	(0.09)
Italy (Provincia Molise)	0.24	(0.01)	-1.16	(0.02)	-0.08	(0.01)	0.73	(0.01)	1.47	(0.01)
Italy (Provincia Piemonte)	0.03	(0.12)	-1.14	(0.08)	-0.36	(0.04)	0.42	(0.07)	1.22	(0.08)
Italy (Provincia Puglia)	0.21	(0.09)	-0.88	(0.12)	-0.07	(0.05)	0.55	(0.03)	1.23	(0.12)
Italy (Provincia Sardegna)	-0.33	(0.09)	-1.38	(0.12)	-0.66	(0.05)	-0.09	(0.04)	0.81	(0.10)
Italy (Provincia Sicilia)	-0.19	(0.11)	-1.31	(0.06)	-0.60	(0.07)	0.03	(0.05)	1.14	(0.19)
Italy (Provincia Toscana)	0.02	(0.09)	-1.00	(0.06)	-0.31	(0.07)	0.25	(0.05)	1.12	(0.11)
Italy (Provincia Trento)	0.07	(0.07)	-0.92	(0.09)	-0.24	(0.00)	0.23	(0.02)	1.19	(0.04)
Italy (Provincia Umbria)	0.04	(0.08)	-0.97	(0.05)	-0.21	(0.04)	0.31	(0.02)	1.05	(0.15)
Italy (Provincia Valle d'Aosta)	-0.17	(0.01)	-0.84	(0.00)	-0.60	(0.01)	-0.10	(0.02)	0.88	(0.01)
Italy (Provincia Veneto)	0.12	(0.10)	-1.09	(0.09)	-0.11	(0.04)	0.48	(0.04)	1.21	(0.15)
United Kingdom (England)	0.20	(0.05)	-0.58	(0.05)	0.01	(0.01)	0.24	(0.02)	1.12	(0.07)
United Kingdom (Northern Ireland)	0.44	(0.09)	-0.61	(0.07)	0.09	(0.04)	0.65	(0.05)	1.63	(0.09)
United Kingdom (Wales)	0.17	(0.06)	-0.60	(0.04)	-0.06	(0.02)	0.27	(0.01)	1.04	(0.07)

Notes: Values that are statistically significant are indicated in bold (see Annex A3). See original Table IV.4.4 for national data.
StatLink http://dx.doi.org/10.1787/888932343304

[Part 2/2]

Index of student-related factors affecting school climate and reading performance, by national quarters of this index

Table S.IV.p *Results based on school principals' reports*

	Performance on the reading scale by quarters of this index													
	Bottom quarter		Second quarter		Third quarter		Top quarter		Change in the reading score per unit of this index		Increased likelihood of students in the bottom quarter of this index scoring in the bottom quarter of the reading performance distribution		Explained variance in student performance (r-squared x 100)	
	Mean index	S.E.	Mean index	S.E.	Mean index	S.E.	Mean index	S.E.	Effect	S.E.	Ratio	S.E.	%	S.E.
Adjudicated														
Belgium (Flemish Community)	**479**	(10.1)	519	(8.3)	520	(8.4)	**563**	(7.6)	**36.2**	(4.19)	**2.2**	(0.31)	13.5	(3.26)
Spain (Andalusia)	456	(9.3)	456	(8.9)	466	(8.8)	464	(12.7)	8.5	(5.07)	1.0	(0.17)	0.6	(0.82)
Spain (Aragon)	**497**	(5.6)	487	(11.0)	486	(7.6)	**512**	(5.6)	5.8	(3.32)	1.0	(0.18)	0.4	(0.49)
Spain (Asturias)	**477**	(10.1)	481	(9.5)	495	(9.3)	**509**	(13.1)	**14.0**	(6.88)	1.3	(0.23)	2.2	(2.27)
Spain (Balearic Islands)	**424**	(11.4)	447	(9.8)	480	(11.4)	**478**	(8.1)	**26.0**	(7.18)	**1.8**	(0.36)	4.8	(2.81)
Spain (Basque Country)	**476**	(7.3)	494	(5.2)	498	(4.8)	**514**	(5.7)	**16.5**	(4.34)	**1.5**	(0.17)	3.0	(1.53)
Spain (Canary Islands)	**425**	(9.1)	419	(10.2)	464	(10.5)	**486**	(9.6)	**30.6**	(4.87)	1.5	(0.29)	9.3	(2.99)
Spain (Cantabria)	483	(6.7)	481	(8.2)	499	(8.1)	488	(12.5)	4.6	(4.18)	1.2	(0.19)	0.2	(0.47)
Spain (Castile and Leon)	497	(11.4)	501	(8.4)	510	(6.8)	505	(10.2)	2.9	(5.88)	1.2	(0.22)	0.1	(0.65)
Spain (Catalonia)	**481**	(9.5)	502	(9.5)	503	(10.2)	**516**	(8.9)	**13.9**	(6.65)	1.6	(0.32)	2.0	(1.83)
Spain (Ceuta and Melilla)	**378**	(5.8)	419	(4.7)	397	(4.8)	**454**	(4.7)	**20.9**	(2.10)	**1.7**	(0.20)	5.3	(1.03)
Spain (Galicia)	**465**	(6.6)	483	(8.9)	483	(9.2)	**516**	(5.8)	**23.5**	(4.46)	**1.6**	(0.19)	4.2	(1.70)
Spain (La Rioja)	497	(5.7)	484	(7.0)	508	(6.2)	502	(4.3)	2.3	(3.45)	1.1	(0.14)	0.0	(0.12)
Spain (Madrid)	**482**	(7.5)	481	(11.1)	523	(7.7)	**526**	(11.4)	**22.5**	(6.18)	1.5	(0.30)	5.0	(2.69)
Spain (Murcia)	**467**	(10.0)	481	(7.6)	476	(8.9)	**497**	(10.9)	10.1	(5.48)	1.4	(0.32)	1.6	(1.94)
Spain (Navarre)	**483**	(4.5)	484	(4.7)	504	(8.4)	**518**	(8.2)	**14.1**	(2.72)	1.3	(0.19)	2.8	(1.21)
United Kingdom (Scotland)	**484**	(7.4)	501	(5.8)	500	(6.3)	**515**	(6.4)	**20.7**	(5.78)	**1.4**	(0.17)	2.4	(1.40)
Non-adjudicated														
Belgium (French Community)	**423**	(12.7)	480	(10.1)	514	(13.4)	**547**	(9.1)	**55.2**	(5.07)	**2.8**	(0.43)	21.2	(3.43)
Belgium (German-Speaking Community)	**450**	(5.7)	473	(6.0)	536	(5.8)	**535**	(6.6)	**46.9**	(2.81)	**2.6**	(0.34)	20.3	(2.12)
Finland (Finnish Speaking)	**532**	(4.4)	541	(4.2)	534	(5.4)	**543**	(4.9)	**6.5**	(3.12)	1.1	(0.11)	0.3	(0.27)
Finland (Swedish Speaking)	513	(6.0)	502	(5.1)	516	(5.4)	514	(4.6)	5.0	(3.61)	0.9	(0.14)	0.1	(0.19)
Italy (Provincia Abruzzo)	**430**	(8.8)	501	(12.7)	459	(13.6)	**537**	(8.9)	**38.1**	(6.60)	**2.6**	(0.49)	11.1	(4.89)
Italy (Provincia Autonoma di Bolzano)	**475**	(4.1)	475	(4.7)	495	(7.8)	**515**	(8.0)	**19.2**	(3.39)	1.2	(0.16)	2.9	(1.09)
Italy (Provincia Basilicata)	**431**	(12.1)	456	(11.1)	483	(8.2)	**519**	(15.5)	**37.3**	(9.82)	**2.0**	(0.42)	13.1	(5.88)
Italy (Provincia Calabria)	**390**	(13.7)	435	(21.2)	469	(9.9)	**497**	(8.7)	**46.6**	(10.72)	**2.9**	(0.63)	15.9	(5.63)
Italy (Provincia Campania)	**409**	(10.8)	447	(11.4)	465	(22.9)	**483**	(11.4)	**33.1**	(6.45)	**1.8**	(0.38)	10.0	(3.69)
Italy (Provincia Emilia Romagna)	**448**	(9.1)	495	(13.3)	507	(14.4)	**560**	(11.9)	**50.1**	(7.26)	**2.5**	(0.46)	17.0	(4.81)
Italy (Provincia Friuli Venezia Giulia)	**447**	(9.3)	521	(10.0)	553	(8.3)	**547**	(10.0)	**50.0**	(5.37)	**3.7**	(0.90)	22.3	(5.30)
Italy (Provincia Lazio)	**424**	(11.8)	481	(12.7)	504	(15.0)	**517**	(16.4)	**39.7**	(8.61)	**2.8**	(0.79)	15.2	(6.69)
Italy (Provincia Liguria)	**466**	(12.7)	487	(14.3)	491	(23.3)	**522**	(13.8)	**29.1**	(8.16)	1.5	(0.43)	4.9	(3.27)
Italy (Provincia Lombardia)	**492**	(17.1)	519	(13.2)	514	(15.5)	**561**	(9.6)	**22.9**	(6.49)	1.8	(0.54)	7.8	(4.25)
Italy (Provincia Marche)	**454**	(11.4)	501	(15.4)	490	(28.7)	**546**	(11.5)	**40.2**	(6.72)	1.8	(0.69)	12.8	(5.51)
Italy (Provincia Molise)	**416**	(5.4)	461	(5.6)	489	(4.5)	**517**	(5.2)	**38.5**	(2.48)	**2.8**	(0.33)	21.4	(2.00)
Italy (Provincia Piemonte)	**447**	(12.9)	466	(15.5)	533	(14.7)	**539**	(17.4)	**43.0**	(8.34)	2.2	(0.65)	17.6	(6.09)
Italy (Provincia Puglia)	**419**	(13.8)	493	(15.1)	526	(9.1)	**520**	(8.6)	**43.2**	(8.84)	**4.2**	(1.00)	18.9	(6.20)
Italy (Provincia Sardegna)	**415**	(8.6)	449	(15.9)	494	(13.4)	**514**	(12.0)	**46.3**	(6.26)	**2.5**	(0.39)	17.6	(4.57)
Italy (Provincia Sicilia)	**391**	(20.7)	465	(12.0)	474	(18.3)	**483**	(21.7)	**36.7**	(8.27)	**2.7**	(0.73)	12.5	(4.83)
Italy (Provincia Toscana)	**434**	(13.6)	469	(14.4)	523	(11.2)	**541**	(9.1)	**51.8**	(7.90)	**2.7**	(0.63)	20.3	(4.04)
Italy (Provincia Trento)	**489**	(13.7)	488	(13.2)	508	(16.3)	**546**	(5.3)	**30.1**	(5.67)	1.4	(0.41)	7.0	(3.16)
Italy (Provincia Umbria)	**438**	(13.0)	480	(9.1)	519	(11.9)	**535**	(11.8)	**44.4**	(7.49)	**2.8**	(0.64)	14.8	(4.47)
Italy (Provincia Valle d'Aosta)	**492**	(5.1)	493	(5.0)	510	(4.9)	**567**	(4.4)	**38.2**	(3.01)	**1.4**	(0.21)	10.1	(1.50)
Italy (Provincia Veneto)	**470**	(11.8)	491	(15.3)	510	(16.1)	**551**	(13.8)	**34.9**	(6.67)	1.8	(0.44)	12.3	(3.95)
United Kingdom (England)	**477**	(6.8)	491	(6.5)	497	(8.3)	**519**	(7.6)	**25.4**	(5.50)	**1.4**	(0.16)	3.4	(1.38)
United Kingdom (Northern Ireland)	**460**	(7.9)	485	(12.4)	517	(16.1)	**549**	(10.4)	**38.6**	(6.18)	**1.9**	(0.37)	12.1	(4.39)
United Kingdom (Wales)	**468**	(6.9)	479	(6.3)	475	(6.6)	**484**	(5.8)	**11.1**	(4.81)	1.2	(0.15)	0.6	(0.55)

Notes: Values that are statistically significant are indicated in bold (see Annex A3). See original Table IV.4.4 for national data.
StatLink http://dx.doi.org/10.1787/888932343304

[Part 1/2]
Index of teacher-related factors affecting school climate and reading performance, by national quarters of this index
Table S.IV.q *Results based on school principals' reports*

	Index of teacher-related factors affecting school climate									
	All students		Bottom quarter		Second quarter		Third quarter		Top quarter	
	Mean index	S.E.	Mean index	S.E.	Mean index	S.E.	Mean index	S.E.	Mean index	S.E.
Adjudicated										
Belgium (Flemish Community)	0.47	(0.07)	-0.54	(0.08)	0.24	(0.01)	0.70	(0.02)	1.48	(0.07)
Spain (Andalusia)	0.22	(0.11)	-0.78	(0.11)	-0.20	(0.03)	0.46	(0.05)	1.39	(0.13)
Spain (Aragon)	0.01	(0.13)	-1.30	(0.09)	-0.20	(0.04)	0.21	(0.03)	1.31	(0.20)
Spain (Asturias)	0.25	(0.14)	-0.97	(0.13)	-0.10	(0.03)	0.53	(0.09)	1.54	(0.09)
Spain (Balearic Islands)	-0.20	(0.08)	-0.88	(0.05)	-0.45	(0.03)	-0.07	(0.02)	0.61	(0.09)
Spain (Basque Country)	0.17	(0.06)	-0.77	(0.05)	-0.16	(0.02)	0.32	(0.02)	1.30	(0.08)
Spain (Canary Islands)	-0.31	(0.14)	-1.39	(0.12)	-0.78	(0.02)	-0.17	(0.05)	1.12	(0.14)
Spain (Cantabria)	-0.10	(0.13)	-1.32	(0.11)	-0.49	(0.06)	0.13	(0.04)	1.29	(0.12)
Spain (Castile and Leon)	0.22	(0.12)	-0.83	(0.21)	-0.09	(0.02)	0.44	(0.04)	1.36	(0.14)
Spain (Catalonia)	0.22	(0.13)	-0.75	(0.14)	0.00	(0.04)	0.50	(0.04)	1.13	(0.09)
Spain (Ceuta and Melilla)	-0.09	(0.01)	-1.48	(0.01)	-0.58	(0.01)	0.27	(0.01)	1.43	(0.01)
Spain (Galicia)	-0.09	(0.11)	-1.08	(0.09)	-0.35	(0.04)	0.16	(0.03)	0.90	(0.14)
Spain (La Rioja)	0.04	(0.01)	-0.88	(0.01)	-0.19	(0.00)	0.27	(0.01)	0.97	(0.01)
Spain (Madrid)	-0.26	(0.10)	-1.43	(0.11)	-0.50	(0.05)	-0.04	(0.03)	0.92	(0.17)
Spain (Murcia)	0.14	(0.12)	-0.97	(0.08)	-0.27	(0.05)	0.27	(0.06)	1.51	(0.14)
Spain (Navarre)	-0.09	(0.08)	-1.02	(0.07)	-0.33	(0.01)	0.07	(0.02)	0.91	(0.22)
United Kingdom (Scotland)	0.01	(0.09)	-1.03	(0.06)	-0.35	(0.02)	0.17	(0.04)	1.23	(0.11)
Non-adjudicated										
Belgium (French Community)	-0.36	(0.06)	-1.17	(0.05)	-0.61	(0.02)	-0.14	(0.03)	0.47	(0.05)
Belgium (German-Speaking Community)	-0.60	(0.01)	-1.72	(0.01)	-0.88	(0.00)	-0.17	(0.01)	0.34	(0.00)
Finland (Finnish Speaking)	-0.06	(0.06)	-0.92	(0.06)	-0.27	(0.02)	0.18	(0.01)	0.78	(0.07)
Finland (Swedish Speaking)	-0.07	(0.01)	-0.97	(0.01)	-0.33	(0.00)	0.23	(0.00)	0.80	(0.00)
Italy (Provincia Abruzzo)	-0.39	(0.11)	-1.35	(0.09)	-0.61	(0.03)	-0.18	(0.03)	0.59	(0.10)
Italy (Provincia Autonoma di Bolzano)	-0.41	(0.02)	-1.47	(0.01)	-0.64	(0.01)	-0.04	(0.01)	0.51	(0.01)
Italy (Provincia Basilicata)	-0.46	(0.10)	-1.52	(0.10)	-0.68	(0.04)	-0.14	(0.03)	0.51	(0.12)
Italy (Provincia Calabria)	-0.35	(0.10)	-1.56	(0.12)	-0.62	(0.06)	-0.04	(0.03)	0.82	(0.17)
Italy (Provincia Campania)	-0.22	(0.12)	-1.18	(0.05)	-0.59	(0.03)	-0.04	(0.07)	0.92	(0.20)
Italy (Provincia Emilia Romagna)	-0.22	(0.09)	-0.95	(0.07)	-0.54	(0.03)	-0.02	(0.03)	0.64	(0.07)
Italy (Provincia Friuli Venezia Giulia)	-0.36	(0.07)	-1.28	(0.12)	-0.61	(0.02)	-0.17	(0.02)	0.60	(0.06)
Italy (Provincia Lazio)	-0.32	(0.12)	-1.17	(0.07)	-0.59	(0.03)	-0.24	(0.01)	0.72	(0.15)
Italy (Provincia Liguria)	-0.32	(0.14)	-1.11	(0.05)	-0.70	(0.01)	-0.24	(0.05)	0.79	(0.21)
Italy (Provincia Lombardia)	-0.22	(0.12)	-1.25	(0.11)	-0.60	(0.05)	-0.04	(0.04)	1.01	(0.15)
Italy (Provincia Marche)	-0.49	(0.17)	-1.40	(0.05)	-1.06	(0.03)	-0.45	(0.12)	0.96	(0.24)
Italy (Provincia Molise)	0.09	(0.02)	-1.24	(0.01)	-0.44	(0.01)	0.55	(0.01)	1.47	(0.01)
Italy (Provincia Piemonte)	-0.27	(0.11)	-1.15	(0.12)	-0.56	(0.05)	-0.05	(0.04)	0.68	(0.13)
Italy (Provincia Puglia)	-0.20	(0.14)	-1.38	(0.10)	-0.47	(0.04)	-0.04	(0.03)	1.08	(0.14)
Italy (Provincia Sardegna)	-0.70	(0.12)	-1.61	(0.05)	-1.04	(0.07)	-0.58	(0.05)	0.44	(0.13)
Italy (Provincia Sicilia)	-0.33	(0.11)	-1.30	(0.08)	-0.64	(0.04)	-0.07	(0.04)	0.69	(0.13)
Italy (Provincia Toscana)	-0.50	(0.09)	-1.34	(0.06)	-0.79	(0.05)	-0.32	(0.03)	0.44	(0.11)
Italy (Provincia Trento)	-0.31	(0.06)	-1.12	(0.01)	-0.61	(0.02)	-0.19	(0.01)	0.68	(0.07)
Italy (Provincia Umbria)	-0.22	(0.11)	-1.27	(0.07)	-0.51	(0.01)	-0.09	(0.02)	1.00	(0.14)
Italy (Provincia Valle d'Aosta)	-0.22	(0.01)	-0.94	(0.00)	-0.46	(0.01)	-0.14	(0.00)	0.66	(0.01)
Italy (Provincia Veneto)	-0.36	(0.12)	-1.43	(0.11)	-0.59	(0.03)	-0.14	(0.04)	0.74	(0.11)
United Kingdom (England)	0.05	(0.06)	-0.90	(0.06)	-0.20	(0.02)	0.27	(0.02)	1.03	(0.08)
United Kingdom (Northern Ireland)	0.40	(0.09)	-0.67	(0.06)	0.10	(0.03)	0.63	(0.03)	1.55	(0.12)
United Kingdom (Wales)	0.26	(0.07)	-0.61	(0.06)	-0.05	(0.02)	0.43	(0.03)	1.26	(0.08)

Notes: Values that are statistically significant are indicated in bold (see Annex A3). See original Table IV.4.5 for national data.
StatLink http://dx.doi.org/10.1787/888932343304

[Part 2/2]

Table S.IV.q **Index of teacher-related factors affecting school climate and reading performance, by national quarters of this index**

Results based on school principals' reports

	Performance on the reading scale by quarters of this index								Change in the reading score per unit of this index		Increased likelihood of students in the bottom quarter of this index scoring in the bottom quarter of the reading performance distribution		Explained variance in student performance (r-squared x 100)	
	Bottom quarter		Second quarter		Third quarter		Top quarter							
	Mean index	S.E.	Mean index	S.E.	Mean index	S.E.	Mean index	S.E.	Effect	S.E.	Ratio	S.E.	%	S.E.
Adjudicated														
Belgium (Flemish Community)	508	(9.1)	519	(8.8)	521	(8.1)	527	(10.9)	10.1	(8.12)	1.3	(0.21)	0.8	(1.30)
Spain (Andalusia)	445	(7.9)	469	(11.9)	473	(7.7)	455	(13.8)	4.1	(7.60)	1.3	(0.21)	0.2	(0.62)
Spain (Aragon)	494	(10.4)	490	(7.8)	489	(8.7)	509	(6.0)	5.0	(3.21)	1.0	(0.22)	0.4	(0.48)
Spain (Asturias)	488	(10.8)	488	(10.4)	500	(8.9)	486	(13.0)	-0.9	(7.09)	1.1	(0.20)	0.0	(0.46)
Spain (Balearic Islands)	**435**	(12.0)	445	(9.9)	473	(10.1)	**476**	(7.8)	**29.7**	(7.32)	1.5	(0.29)	3.8	(1.92)
Spain (Basque Country)	499	(6.5)	486	(6.1)	496	(5.4)	501	(6.7)	3.0	(3.99)	1.0	(0.13)	0.1	(0.24)
Spain (Canary Islands)	**411**	(10.0)	436	(8.8)	454	(8.2)	**493**	(9.1)	**27.5**	(6.33)	**1.8**	(0.33)	9.2	(3.48)
Spain (Cantabria)	484	(6.2)	494	(13.5)	485	(9.2)	488	(10.6)	1.5	(4.19)	1.1	(0.15)	0.0	(0.25)
Spain (Castile and Leon)	509	(7.2)	496	(8.6)	499	(8.9)	508	(12.1)	-0.4	(6.76)	0.9	(0.17)	0.0	(0.41)
Spain (Catalonia)	485	(10.1)	504	(9.2)	510	(12.2)	503	(11.0)	13.2	(7.50)	1.5	(0.34)	1.5	(1.87)
Spain (Ceuta and Melilla)	**363**	(6.5)	429	(6.2)	403	(5.9)	**453**	(4.8)	**25.3**	(2.05)	**2.0**	(0.18)	7.5	(1.15)
Spain (Galicia)	472	(7.8)	488	(8.9)	499	(9.4)	488	(8.2)	9.5	(5.26)	**1.4**	(0.21)	0.8	(0.86)
Spain (La Rioja)	497	(6.0)	502	(5.9)	497	(5.9)	495	(4.3)	-1.2	(3.53)	1.0	(0.20)	0.0	(0.10)
Spain (Madrid)	**493**	(5.7)	495	(9.3)	503	(11.5)	**521**	(13.3)	**13.3**	(3.77)	1.3	(0.20)	2.3	(1.35)
Spain (Murcia)	476	(8.7)	489	(7.8)	471	(10.0)	486	(12.6)	2.8	(5.01)	1.2	(0.21)	0.1	(0.50)
Spain (Navarre)	**488**	(5.5)	490	(6.4)	502	(8.4)	**508**	(6.6)	**9.8**	(3.84)	1.1	(0.15)	0.9	(0.75)
United Kingdom (Scotland)	**497**	(6.4)	497	(8.2)	491	(7.6)	**515**	(6.4)	6.7	(4.27)	1.1	(0.13)	0.4	(0.45)
Non-adjudicated														
Belgium (French Community)	**459**	(13.1)	493	(11.6)	495	(14.5)	**516**	(11.9)	**27.6**	(11.30)	**1.7**	(0.27)	2.8	(2.33)
Belgium (German-Speaking Community)	**438**	(5.4)	496	(5.9)	509	(5.6)	**551**	(5.5)	**48.8**	(2.96)	**3.5**	(0.54)	20.0	(2.11)
Finland (Finnish Speaking)	534	(5.1)	537	(4.0)	534	(4.0)	545	(5.5)	6.1	(3.74)	1.0	(0.11)	0.2	(0.29)
Finland (Swedish Speaking)	**501**	(5.6)	511	(5.6)	516	(5.1)	**518**	(4.6)	**7.4**	(3.43)	1.2	(0.16)	0.4	(0.37)
Italy (Provincia Abruzzo)	496	(15.0)	479	(18.3)	479	(16.5)	473	(18.0)	-8.4	(12.44)	0.7	(0.27)	0.5	(1.62)
Italy (Provincia Autonoma di Bolzano)	475	(6.0)	484	(4.6)	511	(8.0)	490	(10.6)	9.6	(5.08)	1.2	(0.17)	0.7	(0.74)
Italy (Provincia Basilicata)	**470**	(14.5)	477	(12.7)	507	(10.1)	**436**	(9.7)	-11.6	(8.26)	1.1	(0.34)	1.2	(1.81)
Italy (Provincia Calabria)	444	(18.7)	444	(17.1)	443	(14.9)	461	(11.6)	4.9	(8.37)	1.1	(0.41)	0.3	(1.14)
Italy (Provincia Campania)	459	(14.1)	442	(20.1)	447	(18.0)	457	(20.5)	-0.2	(11.81)	0.7	(0.28)	0.0	(0.86)
Italy (Provincia Emilia Romagna)	489	(11.4)	508	(14.8)	518	(16.0)	494	(19.8)	-0.1	(16.72)	1.2	(0.28)	0.0	(0.94)
Italy (Provincia Friuli Venezia Giulia)	**487**	(8.4)	525	(6.9)	529	(12.0)	**526**	(12.4)	**22.4**	(6.71)	**1.8**	(0.36)	3.5	(2.27)
Italy (Provincia Lazio)	489	(18.1)	469	(15.7)	485	(15.1)	482	(20.4)	-0.5	(14.89)	0.9	(0.33)	0.0	(1.50)
Italy (Provincia Liguria)	**493**	(16.3)	508	(11.5)	527	(10.2)	**438**	(22.8)	**-35.0**	(16.76)	1.2	(0.39)	8.8	(9.39)
Italy (Provincia Lombardia)	520	(17.1)	525	(12.9)	521	(16.9)	522	(17.9)	-3.2	(10.71)	1.0	(0.35)	0.1	(1.10)
Italy (Provincia Marche)	514	(16.0)	484	(20.4)	492	(28.4)	501	(15.1)	-2.6	(10.88)	0.7	(0.31)	0.1	(1.08)
Italy (Provincia Molise)	**449**	(4.4)	460	(8.8)	467	(6.0)	**508**	(4.7)	**18.1**	(2.35)	**1.7**	(0.17)	5.4	(1.22)
Italy (Provincia Piemonte)	513	(14.2)	477	(17.1)	514	(20.5)	482	(18.4)	-13.0	(12.81)	**0.6**	(0.20)	1.0	(1.99)
Italy (Provincia Puglia)	480	(14.7)	504	(16.7)	491	(9.3)	483	(13.0)	2.7	(7.24)	1.4	(0.42)	0.1	(0.51)
Italy (Provincia Sardegna)	450	(12.6)	489	(12.1)	476	(15.4)	457	(22.3)	6.2	(11.50)	1.4	(0.42)	0.3	(1.56)
Italy (Provincia Sicilia)	456	(14.3)	462	(12.5)	455	(20.4)	439	(22.1)	-10.3	(12.88)	0.8	(0.29)	0.7	(1.86)
Italy (Provincia Toscana)	**464**	(15.1)	494	(13.8)	506	(20.0)	**503**	(14.6)	18.7	(12.35)	1.4	(0.42)	1.8	(2.49)
Italy (Provincia Trento)	**539**	(15.3)	505	(10.6)	513	(7.2)	**474**	(10.6)	**-34.7**	(10.65)	0.7	(0.29)	7.2	(4.51)
Italy (Provincia Umbria)	505	(14.3)	491	(9.1)	485	(11.9)	492	(16.0)	-3.0	(8.54)	0.7	(0.24)	0.1	(0.67)
Italy (Provincia Valle d'Aosta)	**505**	(5.8)	520	(7.6)	507	(5.6)	**531**	(4.9)	**22.5**	(3.09)	1.0	(0.12)	3.1	(0.83)
Italy (Provincia Veneto)	493	(12.3)	518	(10.6)	505	(15.6)	505	(18.3)	1.7	(11.90)	1.1	(0.33)	0.0	(0.70)
United Kingdom (England)	**483**	(7.1)	490	(7.9)	504	(7.0)	**507**	(8.2)	**12.9**	(4.67)	**1.3**	(0.15)	1.1	(0.78)
United Kingdom (Northern Ireland)	481	(10.3)	465	(16.8)	553	(9.0)	513	(15.0)	17.1	(9.55)	1.4	(0.25)	2.4	(2.80)
United Kingdom (Wales)	482	(6.1)	467	(5.9)	485	(6.4)	473	(6.4)	-0.3	(4.32)	0.9	(0.12)	0.0	(0.10)

Notes: Values that are statistically significant are indicated in bold (see Annex A3). See original Table IV.4.5 for national data.

StatLink http://dx.doi.org/10.1787/888932343304

[Part 1/1]
Table S.IV.r Parental expectations for higher academic standards
Results based on school principals' reports

	Parental expectations are characterised, by pressure on the school to achieve high academic standards among students from:					
	Many parents		A minority of parents		Very few parents	
	%	S.E.	%	S.E.	%	S.E.
Adjudicated						
Belgium (Flemish Community)	9.6	(2.6)	30.4	(3.8)	59.9	(3.9)
Spain (Andalusia)	5.9	(3.5)	31.5	(7.0)	62.5	(6.7)
Spain (Aragon)	3.0	(2.1)	24.4	(4.8)	72.6	(5.3)
Spain (Asturias)	4.3	(3.0)	26.4	(4.8)	69.3	(4.7)
Spain (Balearic Islands)	19.5	(6.5)	48.6	(7.4)	31.9	(6.5)
Spain (Basque Country)	8.0	(2.2)	43.9	(3.6)	48.1	(3.6)
Spain (Canary Islands)	5.2	(3.0)	37.0	(7.0)	57.8	(6.7)
Spain (Cantabria)	1.8	(1.9)	30.5	(6.3)	67.6	(6.6)
Spain (Castile and Leon)	7.5	(4.1)	48.4	(8.1)	44.1	(7.2)
Spain (Catalonia)	18.9	(5.9)	65.6	(5.7)	15.5	(4.7)
Spain (Ceuta and Melilla)	4.6	(0.2)	19.0	(0.3)	76.4	(0.4)
Spain (Galicia)	8.1	(3.1)	21.2	(5.9)	70.7	(6.1)
Spain (La Rioja)	6.3	(0.2)	20.6	(0.3)	73.1	(0.3)
Spain (Madrid)	9.2	(4.2)	47.0	(8.6)	43.8	(8.3)
Spain (Murcia)	2.5	(2.4)	26.9	(7.3)	70.6	(7.1)
Spain (Navarre)	11.1	(2.3)	34.7	(5.4)	54.2	(5.6)
United Kingdom (Scotland)	35.1	(3.8)	54.2	(4.4)	10.6	(3.0)
Non-adjudicated						
Belgium (French Community)	16.7	(3.6)	28.9	(4.1)	54.4	(4.4)
Belgium (German-Speaking Community)	0.0	c	51.9	(0.3)	48.1	(0.3)
Finland (Finnish Speaking)	2.1	(1.1)	21.6	(3.7)	76.3	(3.8)
Finland (Swedish Speaking)	15.0	(0.2)	73.1	(0.3)	11.9	(0.2)
Italy (Provincia Abruzzo)	24.0	(7.2)	54.9	(7.9)	21.0	(5.4)
Italy (Provincia Autonoma di Bolzano)	4.2	(1.7)	45.7	(1.3)	50.1	(1.1)
Italy (Provincia Basilicata)	20.9	(5.4)	47.1	(5.7)	32.0	(5.6)
Italy (Provincia Calabria)	11.7	(5.3)	57.6	(7.7)	30.8	(6.2)
Italy (Provincia Campania)	8.7	(3.1)	66.6	(6.8)	24.7	(6.1)
Italy (Provincia Emilia Romagna)	19.7	(5.1)	52.3	(8.4)	28.0	(6.5)
Italy (Provincia Friuli Venezia Giulia)	15.4	(3.6)	63.5	(4.9)	21.1	(3.6)
Italy (Provincia Lazio)	20.8	(5.5)	58.1	(8.8)	21.1	(7.0)
Italy (Provincia Liguria)	14.3	(4.4)	50.5	(7.1)	35.2	(5.9)
Italy (Provincia Lombardia)	11.8	(4.7)	68.8	(6.8)	19.5	(4.9)
Italy (Provincia Marche)	10.0	(4.1)	62.9	(7.6)	27.1	(6.1)
Italy (Provincia Molise)	26.1	(0.9)	37.0	(1.5)	36.9	(1.4)
Italy (Provincia Piemonte)	23.9	(5.0)	54.1	(7.9)	22.0	(7.0)
Italy (Provincia Puglia)	20.8	(6.4)	67.0	(8.0)	12.2	(5.1)
Italy (Provincia Sardegna)	13.9	(5.3)	62.5	(7.7)	23.6	(6.2)
Italy (Provincia Sicilia)	9.2	(4.2)	59.2	(6.5)	31.6	(6.4)
Italy (Provincia Toscana)	4.3	(0.9)	57.1	(7.1)	38.7	(7.1)
Italy (Provincia Trento)	9.8	(1.6)	57.3	(3.9)	33.0	(3.5)
Italy (Provincia Umbria)	11.1	(2.3)	61.5	(5.0)	27.4	(5.1)
Italy (Provincia Valle d'Aosta)	0.0	c	42.4	(0.4)	57.6	(0.4)
Italy (Provincia Veneto)	15.8	(4.8)	51.9	(7.9)	32.3	(6.6)
United Kingdom (England)	33.2	(3.9)	54.9	(4.0)	11.9	(2.5)
United Kingdom (Northern Ireland)	43.3	(4.5)	45.8	(5.3)	10.9	(3.8)
United Kingdom (Wales)	33.2	(4.2)	52.5	(4.1)	14.4	(3.0)

Note: See original Table IV.4.7 for national data.
StatLink http://dx.doi.org/10.1787/888932343304

Annex C

THE DEVELOPMENT AND IMPLEMENTATION OF PISA – A COLLABORATIVE EFFORT

INTRODUCTION

PISA is a collaborative effort, bringing together scientific expertise from the participating countries, steered jointly by their governments on the basis of shared, policy-driven interests.

A PISA Governing Board on which each country is represented determines, in the context of OECD objectives, the policy priorities for PISA and oversees adherence to these priorities during the implementation of the programme. This includes the setting of priorities for the development of indicators, for the establishment of the assessment instruments and for the reporting of the results.

Experts from participating countries also serve on working groups that are charged with linking policy objectives with the best internationally available technical expertise. By participating in these expert groups, countries ensure that the instruments are internationally valid and take into account the cultural and educational contexts in OECD Member countries, the assessment materials have strong measurement properties, and the instruments place an emphasis on authenticity and educational validity.

Through National Project Managers, participating countries implement PISA at the national level subject to the agreed administration procedures. National Project Managers play a vital role in ensuring that the implementation of the survey is of high quality, and verify and evaluate the survey results, analyses, reports and publications.

The design and implementation of the surveys, within the framework established by the PISA Governing Board, is the responsibility of external contractors. For PISA 2009, the questionnaire development was carried out by a consortium led by Cito International in partnership with the University of Twente. The development and implementation of the cognitive assessment and of the international options was carried out by a consortium led by the Australian Council for Educational Research (ACER). Other partners in this consortium include cApStAn Linguistic Quality Control in Belgium, the *Deutsches Institut für Internationale Pädagogische Forschung* (DIPF) in Germany, the National Institute for Educational Policy Research in Japan (NIER), the *Unité d'analyse des systèmes et des pratiques d'enseignement* (aSPe) in Belgium and WESTAT in the United States.

The OECD Secretariat has overall managerial responsibility for the programme, monitors its implementation on a day-to-day basis, acts as the secretariat for the PISA Governing Board, builds consensus among countries and serves as the interlocutor between the PISA Governing Board and the international consortium charged with the implementation of the activities. The OECD Secretariat also produces the indicators and analyses and prepares the international reports and publications in co-operation with the PISA consortium and in close consultation with Member countries both at the policy level (PISA Governing Board) and at the level of implementation (National Project Managers).

The following lists the members of the various PISA bodies and the individual experts and consultants who have contributed to PISA.

Members of the PISA Governing Board

Chair: Lorna Bertrand

OECD countries

Australia: Tony Zanderigo

Austria: Mark Német

Belgium: Christiane Blondin, Isabelle Erauw and Micheline Scheys

Canada: Pierre Brochu, Patrick Bussière and Tomasz Gluszynski

Chile: Leonor Cariola

Czech Republic: Jana Strakova

Denmark: Tine Bak

Estonia: Maie Kitsing

Finland: Jari Rajanen

France: Bruno Trosseille

Germany: Annemarie Klemm, Maximilian Müller-Härlin and Elfriede Ohrnberger

Greece: Panagiotis Kazantzis (1/7/05 – 31/03/10) Vassilia Hatzinikita (from 31/03/10)

Hungary: Benő Csapó

Iceland: Júlíus K. Björnsson

Ireland: Jude Cosgrove

Israel: Michal Beller

Italy: Piero Cipollone

Japan: Ryo Watanabe

Korea: Whan Sik Kim

Luxembourg: Michel Lanners

Mexico: Francisco Ciscomani

Netherlands: Paul van Oijen

New Zealand: Lynne Whitney

Norway: Anne-Berit Kavli

Poland: Stanislaw Drzazdzewski

Portugal: Carlos Pinto Ferreira

Slovak Republic: Julius Hauser, Romana Kanovska and Paulina Korsnakova

Slovenia: Andreja Barle Lakota

Spain: Carme Amorós Basté and Enrique Roca Cobo

Sweden: Anita Wester

Switzerland: Ariane Baechler Söderström and Heinz Rhyn

Turkey: Meral Alkan

United Kingdom: Lorna Bertrand and Mal Cooke

United States: Daniel McGrath and Eugene Owen

Observers

Albania: Ndricim Mehmeti

Argentina: Liliana Pascual

Azerbaijan: Talib Sharifov

Brazil: Joaquim José Soares Neto
Bulgaria: Neda Kristanova
Colombia: Margarita Peña
Croatia: Michelle Braš-Roth
Dubai (United Arab Emirates): Mariam Al Ali
Hong Kong-China: Esther Sui-chu Ho
Indonesia: Mansyur Ramli
Jordan: Khattab Mohammad Abulibdeh
Kazakhstan: Yermekov Nurmukhammed Turlynovich
Kyrgyz Republic: Inna Valkova
Latvia: Andris Kangro
Liechtenstein: Christian Nidegger
Lithuania: Rita Dukynaitė
Macao-China: Kwok-cheung Cheung
Montengegro: Zeljko Jacimovic
Panama: Arturo Rivera
Peru: Liliana Miranda Molina
Qatar: Adel Sayed
Romania: Roxana Mihail
Russian Federation: Galina Kovalyova
Serbia: Dragica Pavlovic Babic
Shanghai-China: Minxuan Zhang
Singapore: Low Khah Gek
Chinese Taipei: Chih-Wei Hue and Fou-Lai Lin
Thailand: Precharn Dechsri
Trinidad and Tobago: Harrilal Seecharan
Tunisia: Kameleddine Gaha
Uruguay: Andrés Peri

PISA 2009 National Project Managers

Albania: Alfonso Harizaj
Argentina: Antonio Gutiérrez
Australia: Sue Thomson
Austria: Ursula Schwantner
Azerbaijan: Emin Meherremov
Belgium: Ariane Baye and Inge De Meyer
Brazil: Sheyla Carvalho Lira
Bulgaria: Svetla Petrova
Canada: Pierre Brochu and Tamara Knighton
Chile: Ema Lagos
Chinese Taipei: Pi-Hsia Hung
Colombia: Francisco Ernesto Reyes
Croatia: Michelle Braš Roth
Czech Republic: Jana Paleckova
Denmark: Niels Egelund
Dubai (United Arab Emirates): Mariam Al Ali
Estonia: Gunda Tire
Finland: Jouni Välijärvi
France: Sylvie Fumel
Germany: Nina Jude and Eckhard Klieme
Greece: Panagiotis Kazantzis (from 1/7/05 to 18/11/08) Chryssa Sofianopoulou (from 18/11/08)
Hong Kong-China: Esther Sui-chu Ho
Hungary: Ildikó Balázsi
Iceland: Almar Midvik Halldorsson
Indonesia: Burhanuddin Tola
Ireland: Rachel Perkins
Israel: Inbal Ron Kaplan and Joel Rapp
Italy: Laura Palmerio
Japan: Ryo Watanabe
Jordan: Khattab Mohammad Abulibdeh
Kazakhstan: Damitov Bazar Kabdoshevich
Korea: Kyung-Hee Kim
Kyrgyz Republic: Inna Valkova
Latvia: Andris Kangro
Liechtenstein: Christian Nidegger
Lithuania: Jolita Dudaitė
Luxembourg: Bettina Boehm
Macao-China: Kwok-cheung Cheung
Mexico: María-Antonieta Díaz-Gutiérrez
Montenegro: Verica Ivanovic
Netherlands: Erna Gille
New Zealand: Maree Telford
Norway: Marit Kjaernsli
Panama: Zoila Castillo
Peru: Liliana Miranda Molina
Poland: Michal Federowicz
Portugal: Anabela Serrão
Qatar: Asaad Tounakti
Romania: Silviu Cristian Mirescu
Russian Federation: Galina Kovalyova
Serbia: Dragica Pavlovic Babic
Shanghai-China: Jing Lu and MinXuan Zhang
Singapore: Chia Siang Hwa and Poon Chew Leng
Slovak Republic: Paulina Korsnakova
Slovenia: Mojca Straus
Spain: Lis Cercadillo
Sweden: Karl-Göran Karlsson
Switzerland: Christian Nidegger
Thailand: Sunee Klainin
Trinidad and Tobago: Harrilal Seecharan
Tunisia: Kameleddine Gaha
Turkey: Müfide Çaliskan
United Kingdom: Jenny Bradshaw and Mal Cooke
United States: Dana Kelly and Holly Xie
Uruguay: María Sánchez

OECD Secretariat

Andreas Schleicher (Overall co-ordination of PISA and partner country/economy relations)

Marilyn Achiron (Editorial support)

Marika Boiron (Editorial support)

Simone Bloem (Analytic services)

Francesca Borgonovi (Analytic services)

Niccolina Clements (Editorial support)

Michael Davidson (Project management and analytic services)

Juliet Evans (Administration and partner country/economy relations)

Miyako Ikeda (Analytic services)

Maciej Jakubowski (Analytic services)

Guillermo Montt (Analytic services)

Diana Morales (Administrative support)

Soojin Park (Analytic services)

Mebrak Tareke (Editorial support)

Sophie Vayssettes (Analytic services)

Elisabeth Villoutreix (Editorial support)

Karin Zimmer (Project management)

Pablo Zoido (Analytic services)

PISA Expert Groups for PISA 2009

Reading Expert Group

Irwin Kirsch (Education Testing Service, New Jersey, USA)

Sachiko Adachi (Nigata University, Japan)

Charles Alderson (Lancaster University, UK)

John de Jong (Language Testing Services, Netherlands)

John Guthrie (University of Maryland, USA)

Dominique Lafontaine (University of Liège, Belgium)

Minwoo Nam (Korea Institute of Curriculum and Evaluation)

Jean-François Rouet (University of Poitiers, France)

Wolfgang Schnotz (University of Koblenz-Landau, Germany)

Eduardo Vidal-Abarca (University of Valencia, Spain

Mathematics Expert Group

Jan de Lange (Chair) (Utrecht University, Netherlands)

Werner Blum (University of Kassel, Germany)

John Dossey (Illinois State University, USA)

Zbigniew Marciniak (University of Warsaw, Poland)

Mogens Niss (University of Roskilde, Denmark)

Yoshinori Shimizu (University of Tsukuba, Japan)

Science Expert Group

Rodger Bybee (Chair) (BSCS, Colorado Springs, USA)

Peter Fensham (Queensland University of Technology, Australia)

Svein Lie (University of Oslo, Norway)

Yasushi Ogura (National Institute for Educational Policy Research, Japan)

Manfred Prenzel (University of Kiel, Germany)

Andrée Tiberghien (University of Lyon, France)

Questionnaire Expert Group

Jaap Scheerens (Chair) (University of Twente, Netherlands

Pascal Bressoux (Pierre Mendès University, France)

Yin Cheong Cheng (Hong Kong Institute of Education, Hong Kong-China)

David Kaplan (University of Wisconsin – Madison, USA)

Eckhard Klieme (DIPF, Germany)

Henry Levin (Columbia University, USA)

Pirjo Linnakylä (University of Jyväskylä, Finland)

Ludger Wößmann (University of Munich, Germany)

PISA Technical Advisory Group

Keith Rust (Chair) (Westat, USA)

Ray Adams (ACER)

John de Jong (Language Testing Services, Netherlands)

Cees Glas (University of Twente, Netherlands)

Aletta Grisay (Consultant, Saint-Maurice, France)

David Kaplan (University of Wisconsin – Madison, USA)

Christian Monseur (University of Liège, Belgium)

Sophia Rabe-Hesketh (University of California – Berkeley, USA)

Thierry Rocher (Ministry of Education, France)

Norman Verhelst (CITO, Netherlands)

Kentaro Yamamoto (ETS, New Jersey, USA)

Rebecca Zwick (University of California – Santa Barbara, USA)

PISA 2009 Consortium for questionnaire development

Cito International

Johanna Kordes

Hans Kuhlemeier

Astrid Mols

Henk Moelands

José Noijons

University of Twente

Cees Glas

Khurrem Jehangir

Jaap Scheerens

PISA 2009 Consortium for the development and implementation of the cognitive assessment and international options

Australian Council for Educational Research

Ray Adams (Director of the PISA 2009 Consortium)

Susan Bates (Project administration)

Alla Berezner (Data management and analysis)

Yan Bibby (Data processing and analysis)

Esther Brakey (Administrative support)

Wei Buttress (Project administration and quality monitoring)

Renee Chow (Data processing and analysis)

Judith Cosgrove (Data processing and analysis and national centre support)

John Cresswell (Reporting and dissemination)

Alex Daraganov (Data processing and analysis)

Daniel Duckworth (Reading instruments and test development)

Kate Fitzgerald (Data processing and sampling)

Daniel Fullarton (IT services)

Eveline Gebhardt (Data processing and analysis)

Mee-Young Handayani (Data processing and analysis)

Elizabeth Hersbach (Quality assurance)

Sam Haldane (IT services and computer-based assessment)

Karin Hohlfield (Reading instruments and test development)

Jennifer Hong (Data processing and sampling)

Tony Huang (Project administration and IT services)

Madelaine Imber (Reading instruments and administrative support)

Nora Kovarcikova (Survey operations)

Winson Lam (IT services)

Tom Lumley (Print and electronic reading instruments and test development)

Greg Macaskill (Data management and processing and sampling)

Ron Martin (Science instruments and test development)

Barry McCrae (Electronic Reading Assessment manager, science instruments and test development)

Juliette Mendelovits (Print and electronic reading instruments and test development)

Martin Murphy (Field operations and sampling)

Thoa Nguyen (Data processing and analysis)

Penny Pearson (Administrative support)

Anna Plotka (Graphic design)

Alla Routitsky (Data management and processing)

Wolfram Schulz (Management and data analysis)

Dara Searle (Print and electronic reading instruments and test development)

Naoko Tabata (Survey operations)

Ross Turner (Management, mathematics instruments and test development)

Daniel Urbach (Data processing and analysis)

Eva Van de gaer (Data analysis)

Charlotte Waters (Project administration, data processing and analysis)

Maurice Walker (Electronic Reading Assessment and sampling)

Wahyu Wardono (Project administration and IT services)

Louise Wenn (Data processing and analysis)

Yan Wiwecka (IT services)

Westat

Eugene Brown (Weighting)

Fran Cohen (Weighting)

Susan Fuss (Sampling and weighting)

Amita Gopinath (Weighting)

Sheila Krawchuk (Sampling, weighting and quality monitoring)

Thanh Le (Sampling, weighting, and quality monitoring)

Jane Li (Sampling and weighting)

John Lopdell (Sampling and weighting)

Shawn Lu (Weighting)

Keith Rust (Director of the PISA Consortium for sampling and weighting)

William Wall (Weighting)

Erin Wilson (Sampling and weighting)

Marianne Winglee (Weighting)

Sergey Yagodin (Weighting)

The National Institute for Educational Research in Japan

Hidefumi Arimoto (Reading instruments and test development)

Hisashi Kawai (Reading instruments and test development)

cApStAn Linguistic Quality Control

Steve Dept (Translation and verification operations)

Andrea Ferrari (Translation and verification methodology)

Laura Wäyrynen (Verification management)

Unité d'analyse des systèmes et des pratiques d'enseignement (aSPe)

Ariane Baye (Print reading and electronic reading instruments and test development)

Casto Grana-Monteirin (Translation and verification)

Dominique Lafontaine (Member of the Reading Expert Group)

Christian Monseur (Data analysis and member of the TAG)

Anne Matoul (Translation and verification)

Patricia Schillings (Print reading and electronic reading instruments and test development)

Deutsches Institut für Internationale Pädagogische Forschung (DIPF)

Cordula Artelt (University of Bamberg) (Reading instruments and framework development)

Michel Dorochevsky (Softcon) (Software Development)

Frank Goldhammer (Electronic reading instruments and test development)

Dieter Heyer (Softcon) (Software Development)

Nina Jude (Electronic reading instruments and test development)

Eckhard Klieme (Project Co-Director at DIPF)

Holger Martin (Softcon) (Software Development)

Johannes Naumann (Electronic reading instruments and test development)

Jean-Paul Reeff (International Consultant)

Heiko Roelke (Project Co-Director at DIPF)

Wolfgang Schneider (University of Würzburg) (Reading instruments and framework development)

Petra Stanat (Humboldt University, Berlin) (Reading instruments and test development)

Britta Upsing (Electronic reading instruments and test development)

Other experts

Tobias Dörfler, (University of Bamberg) (Reading instrument development)

Tove Stjern Frønes (ILS, University of Oslo) (Reading instrument development)

Béatrice Halleux (Consultant, HallStat SPRL) (Translation/verification referee and French source development)

Øystein Jetne (ILS, University of Oslo) (Print reading and electronic reading instruments and test development)

Kees Lagerwaard (Institute for Educational Measurement of Netherlands) (Math instrument development)

Pirjo Linnakylä (University of Jyväskylä) (Reading instrument development)

Anne-Laure Monnier (Consultant, France) (French source development)

Jan Mejding (Danish Schoool of Education, University of Aarhus) (Print reading and electronic reading development)

Eva Kristin Narvhus (ILS, University of Oslo) (Print reading and electronic reading instruments, test instruments and test development)

Rolf V. Olsen (ILS, University of Oslo) (Science instrument development)

Robert Laurie (New Brunswick Department of Education, Canada) (Science instrument development)

Astrid Roe (ILS, University of Oslo) (Print reading and electronic reading instruments and test development)

Hanako Senuma (University of Tamagawa, Japan) (Math instrument development)

Other contributors to this publication

Fung-Kwan Tam (Layout)

ORGANISATION FOR ECONOMIC CO-OPERATION AND DEVELOPMENT

The OECD is a unique forum where governments work together to address the economic, social and environmental challenges of globalisation. The OECD is also at the forefront of efforts to understand and to help governments respond to new developments and concerns, such as corporate governance, the information economy and the challenges of an ageing population. The Organisation provides a setting where governments can compare policy experiences, seek answers to common problems, identify good practice and work to co-ordinate domestic and international policies.

The OECD member countries are: Australia, Austria, Belgium, Canada, Chile, the Czech Republic, Denmark, Finland, France, Germany, Greece, Hungary, Iceland, Ireland, Israel, Italy, Japan, Korea, Luxembourg, Mexico, the Netherlands, New Zealand, Norway, Poland, Portugal, the Slovak Republic, Slovenia, Spain, Sweden, Switzerland, Turkey, the United Kingdom and the United States. The European Commission takes part in the work of the OECD.

OECD Publishing disseminates widely the results of the Organisation's statistics gathering and research on economic, social and environmental issues, as well as the conventions, guidelines and standards agreed by its members.

OECD PUBLISHING, 2, rue André-Pascal, 75775 PARIS CEDEX 16
(98 2010 10 1 P) ISBN 978-92-64-09148-1 – No. 57731 2010